The Folklore of World Holidays

First Edition

The Folklore of World Holidays

Margaret Read MacDonald, Editor

First Edition

Gale Research Inc. • DETROIT • LONDON

Margaret Read MacDonald, *Editor*

Gale Research Inc. Staff

Mary Beth Trimper, *Production Manager*
Evi Seoud, *Assistant Production Manager*
Mary Winterhalter, *Production Assistant*

Arthur Chartow, *Art Director*
Bonnie Gornie, *Graphic Designer*

Cover photo of Carnival Masqueraders in Venice by Dieter Strauss

The paper used in this publication meets the minimum requirements of American National Standard for Information Sciences—Permanence Paper for Printed Library Materials, ANSI Z39.48-1984. ™

Library of Congress Cataloging-in-Publication Data

Folklore of World Holidays / edited by Margaret Read MacDonald.
p. cm.
Includes bibliographical references and index.
ISBN 0-8103-7577-X : $80.00
1. Holidays. 2. Festivals. 3. Folklore. I. MacDonald, Margaret Read, 1940- .
GT3930.F65 1991
394.2'6—dc20 91-38032

A CIP catalogue record for this book is available from the British Library.

ISBN 0-8103-7577-X
Printed in the United States of America
Published simultaneously in the United Kingdom
by Gale Research International Limited
(An affiliated company of Gale Research Inc.)

Contents

February

March

April

May

June

July

August

September

December

Introduction

The Folklore of World Holidays hopes to give an insider's look at holiday celebrations in many cultures. Wherever possible, the information is given in quotations from people who actually celebrate those holidays in their own homes. Reports from anthropologists, folklorists, and foreign residents of the country were consulted for additional information.

Scope

To allow space for adequate treatment of those holidays selected, the parameters of *The Folklore of World Holidays* had to be drawn fairly narrowly. This book does not include political holidays (with a few exceptions such as Bastille Day and Cinco de Mayo). Holidays celebrated in only one city or village were generally excluded, though exceptions were made for small countries in which a celebration in the capital affects nearly everyone. For the most part, holiday celebrations of small tribal groups were omitted. The treatment of these many tribal groups would require another volume at least as voluminous as this one. As it is, this volume includes entries for over 340 holidays and festivals from over 150 countries.

The Folklore of World Holidays includes an abundance of information never before gathered together in one source. It is especially strong in its treatment of non-European countries, whose holidays have suffered scant representation on our reference shelves in the past.

Arrangement

This book is arranged according to the Gregorian Calendar, January 1 to December 31. Those Christian, Jewish, and Islamic holidays which vary in their Gregorian Calendar dates have been placed in the Gregorian time frame during which they fell in 1991. Easter, for example, is placed near the end of March, which is when that holiday occurred in 1991.

Buddhist, Chinese, and Indian lunar calendars are treated between each pair of Gregorian months. Because Southeast Asian and Indian holidays may occur on different dates in different areas, they are arranged here alphabetically within their approximate month. Keep in mind that this is an approximation only. Local scholars set holidays based on complicated astronomical calculations.

Agricultural holidays, whose placements are seasonal, are treated under ''Planting Festivals,'' placed arbitrarily at the beginning of April, and ''Harvest Festivals,'' placed between August and September.

Within each holiday section, the entries are arranged by country. When the spelling or name of a holiday varies, this name is found in italics below the country header. (Variant spellings occur frequently; the spelling found in the original source is what is used here.) Source information follows the corresponding passage or passages. In some cases, additional sources are cited for further reading.

Because of the great variation in calendar observances even within one country, it is recommended that you consult the embassy or consulate of a country to verify the actual date of a holiday in any given year. In today's westernized five-day work week, you may expect some holidays to be moved to create an extended weekend.

Subject Index

A detailed subject index, found in the book's rear, should enhance the book's usefulness for both scholars and the public. Geographic and ethnic entries are interfiled within the general subject listings. As a librarian, I find separate indexes cumbersome; thus you will find the two interfiled here for one-stop browsing.

About the Calendrical System

Julian Calendar

The Julian calendar was established by Julius Caesar in B.C. 44 and is the basis for our present calendrical system. Minor inaccuracies, however, cause the calendar to retrograde gradually away from its seasonal orientation. Thus by 1582 the vernal equinox was occurring on March 11. Since agriculture depended on calendrical dates for advice, this caused problems.

Gregorian Calendar

To correct these faults, Pope Gregory XII adopted a new calendar in 1582. October 6 of that year became October 15, resulting in ten dropped days. This brought the calendar of festivals back in line with their seasons. A system of leap years ensured that the calendar would keep its seasonal orientation. Every four years is a leap year and every century divisible by 400 is a leap year as well. Eastern Orthodox countries resisted the new calendar. Bulgaria finally adopted it in 1915, Russia and Finland in 1918, Rumania in 1919, and Greece in 1923. Vestiges of this resistance remain in festival customs. ''Old Christmas'' is still celebrated by some on January 6. Sources may refer to the Julian calendar as ''Old Style'' or ''O.S.'' and the Gregorian as ''New Style'' or ''N.S.'' Since 1900, the variation between the two calendars has been thirteen days.

Jewish Calendar

The Jewish calendar is a lunar calendar of twelve months. Months consist of 29 and 30 days alternatively. The calendar is modified in such a way that Yom Kippur (Tishri 10) should not fall on a Saturday or Sunday, and that Rosh Hashanah (Tishri 1) should fall on Sunday. Because seven years out of every nineteen contain an extra month, festivals fall within the same general season through the years. The year begins in September or October.

The months are: Tishri (circa October); Heshvan (circa November); Kislev (circa December); Tebet (circa January); Shebat (circa February); Adar (circa March); Nissan (circa April); Iyar (circa May); Sivan (circa June); Tammuz (circa July); Ab (circa August); and Elul (circa September).

Hindu Calendar

The Hindu religious calendar is a twelve-month lunar calendar. An intercalary month is added to every month having two new moons; thus this occurs once every two-and-a-half to three years. The New Year begins in the month of Chaitra in Northern India, in the month of Baisakha elsewhere.

In the south of India the month begins with the New Moon. Elsewhere the month begins with the Full Moon. Each month is divided into two halves. The Dark Fortnight (waning) ends on the New Moon. The Bright Fortnight (waxing) ends on the Full Moon.

The solar months of the Indian Calendar are:

Baisakha	April-May	Begins April 21
Jaistha	May-June	Begins May 22
Asadha	June-July	Begins June 22
Sravana	July-August	Begins July 23
Bhadra	August-September	Begins August 23
Asvina	September-October	Begins September 23
Kartika	October-November	Begins October 23
Aghrana	November-December	Begins November 22
Pausha	December-January	Begins December 22
Magha	January-February	Begins January 22
Phalguna	February-March	Begins February 22
Chaitra	March-April	Begins March 22 (21 in leap year)

The names for these months, and for all holidays, vary throughout the country, depending on linguistic area. These months follow a solar calendar. Holidays may be set by an intersection of the lunar and solar calendars.

Chinese Calendar

The North Asian countries follow a lunar calendar of twelve months. The fifteenth of the month falls on the full moon. Months may have 28, 29, or 30 days. Approximately every three years an intercalary month is inserted.

Buddhist Calendar

The Buddhist calendar is used in Cambodia, Laos, Myanmar (formerly Burma), Sri Lanka, and Thailand. The year begins on the Full Moon in Taurus (May). This is a lunar calendar, but varies slightly from country to country.

The Burmese calendar consists of twelve months: Tagu, Kason, Nayon, Wazo, Agaung, Tawthalin, Thadingyut, Tazaungmon, Nadaw, Pyatho, Tabodwe, and Tabaung. The months consist of 29 and 30 days alternately, except in leap years, when Wazo is followed by a Second Wazo (intercalary month). The Burmese month is divided into two halves, numbered from 1 to 14 or 15. The waxing half has 15 days, the fifteenth being the full moon. The waning half may have 14 or 15 days, the last day being the dark of the moon.

Islamic Calendar

The Islamic calendar consists of twelve lunar months. Months do not begin until the new moon is officially sighted. The Islamic calendar retrogrades in relation to the Gregorian calendar approximately seven days every year. Because of this, the Islamic holidays are not associated with a given season, but over a thirty-two-year period will gradually shift through the entire year.

The Islamic months are: Muharram (30 days); Rabi Awwal (29); Rabi Thani (30); Jumadah-l-Oula (30); Jumadah-l-Akhira (29); Rajab (30); Sha-ban (29); Ramadan (30); Shawwal (29); Dhu-l-Ku-'Dah (30); and Dhu-l-Hijjah (29/30 in intercalary years).

Agricultural Calendars

In many cultures celebrations occur at the time of spring planting or at harvest time. These festivals are set according to local conditions each year, rather than being fixed. Some African festivals, for example, are set by local leaders after observing the state of the crops. Pertinent spirits may also be consulted when setting festival dates. In this book, planting ceremonies are placed in April and harvest festivals in the fall. The reader should be aware, however, that in the Southern hemisphere these seasons are reversed, and in tropical areas the growing season is related to local rain patterns.

Acknowledgements

My thanks to the publishers and authors who granted permission for selections included in this volume. While the permissions and compensation requirements of some publishers proved a serious handicap to the production of a reference work of this nature, those individual scholars who maintained their own copyright were delighted to have their work quoted without fee.

Since several publishers suggested that the usage of 500-750 words was considered fair use, I have limited my use of materials to that range in many cases. This proved functional also in allowing me room to cite more sources than would have been possible had I quoted more extensively.

I wish to thank in particular certain copyright owners who allowed me to use generous citations from their works free of charge. Thanks to: The American Folklore Society; Arni Bjornsson, National Museum of Iceland; The Trapp Family Lodge, Inc.; Gene Sawyer, East-West Center; National Geographic Society; Charles E. Tuttle, Inc.; The Smithsonian Institution; and The University of California.

For sharing information on holiday customs thanks to: Carlton Appelo, Aliamma Cherian, Chee Keuk Fong, Myrna Hecht, Keiko Hirai, Winifred Jaegger, Ken Jackson, Peter Johnson, Jens Lund, Mariko Martin, Paulette Nelson, Rosemarie Peterson, Josh Rice, Emely Sather, Martha Smith, Bigi Unger, Su Vathanaprida, and the Islamic School of Seattle.

I owe an immense debt of gratitude to the reference staff of the King County Library System and in particular to Dorothy Zaleski and her interlibrary loan crew. Without their hard work in locating materials from across the country, this book would not have been possible. Thanks also to University of Washington librarian Bartley Dobb for assistance with the collection of Suzzallo Library, and to James T. Callow for reading the manuscript and offering useful comment.

And an enormous thank you to Jennifer Skye MacDonald for hours of typing in the final throes of this manuscript.

Margaret Read MacDonald

Permissions

Permission to reprint copyrighted material has been kindly granted by the following publications, organizations, and individuals.

BOOKS

Aguilera, Francisco Enrique. From *Santa Eulalia's People*. West Publishing, 1978. © Francisco Enrique Aguilera 1978. Reprinted by permission of the author. 2nd edition forthcoming from Waveland Press, fall 1990.

Allen, Catherine. *The Hold Life: Coca and Cultural Identity in the Andean Community*. Smithsonian Institution, 1988. Copyright © 1988 by Smithsonian Institution. Reproduced by permission of the Smithsonian Institution Press from *The Hold Life Has: Coca and Cultural Identity in the Andean Community* by Catherine Allen. © Smithsonian Institution, Washington, D.C. 1988, pp. 164, 166-67, 180-189.

Arasartnam, S. From *Indian Festivals in Malaya*. Department of Indian Studies, University of Malaya, 1966. Reprinted by permission of the publisher.

Archaimbault, Charles. From *The New Year Ceremony at Basak (South Laos)*. Cornell University Southeast Asia Program, 1971. © Cornell University Southeast Asia Program, 1971. Reprinted by permission of Cornell University Southeast Asia Program.

Bisignano, J.O. From *Japan Handbook*. Moon Publications, 1983. © Moon Publications, 1983. Reprinted by permission of the publisher.

Björnsson, Arni. From *Icelandic Feasts and Holidays*. National Museum of Iceland, 1980. Copyright © 1980. National Museum of Iceland. Reprinted by permission of the publisher and Arni Björnsson.

Burkhardt, V. R. From *Chinese Creeds and Customs*. South China Morning Post, 1982. Copyright © 1982 South China Morning Post. Reprinted by permission of the publisher.

Casal, U. A. From *The Five Sacred Festivals of Ancient Japan*. Charles E. Tuttle Co., Inc., 1967. © Charles E. Tuttle Co., Inc., 1967. Reprinted by permission of the publisher.

Casey, Daniel J., and Robert E. Rhodes. From *Views of the Irish Peasantry, 1800-1916*. Archon Books, 1977. © 1977 Daniel J. Casey and Robert E. Rhodes. Reprinted from *Views of the Irish Peasantry, 1800-1916* by permission of Archon Books, Hamden, Conn.

Crawford, Ann Caddell. From *Customs and Culture of Vietnam*. Charles E. Tuttle Co., Inc., 1966. © Charles E. Tuttle Co., Inc., 1966. Reprinted by permission of the publisher.

Dalton, Bill. From *Indonesia Handbook*. Moon Publications, 1988. © 1988 Moon Publications. Reprinted by permission of the publisher.

Deep, Dhurba K. From *Nepal Festivals*. Ratna Pustak Bhandar, 1978. Copyright © 1978 Ratna Pustak Bhandar. Reprinted by permission of the publisher.

deYoung, John E. From *Village Life in Modern Thailand*. University of California Press, 1955. Copyright © 1955 by the University of California Press. Reprinted with permission of the publisher.

Diqs, Isaak. From *A Bedouin Boyhood*. Unwin Hyman Limited, 1969. Copyright © 1969. Unwin Hyman Limited. Reprinted by permission of the publisher.

Eberhard, Wolfram. "The Dragon-Boat Festival" from *Time Out of Time* by Alessandro Falassi. University of New Mexico, 1987. Copyright © 1987 University of New Mexico. Used by permission of Irene Eberhard.

Fraser, Thomas M. Jr. From *Rusembilan: A Malay Fishing Village in Southern Thailand*, 1960. Copyright © 1960 by Cornell University. Used by permission of the publisher, Cornell University Press.

Hall, D. T. From *Romanian Furrow*. Peter Fraser & Dunlop Group Ltd., 1933. Copyright © 1933 Peter Fraser & Dunlop Group Ltd. Reprinted by permission of the publisher.

Harvey, Andrew. From *Journey in Ladakh*, Houghton Mifflin, 1983. Copyright © 1983 by Andrew Harvey. Reprinted by permission of Houghton Mifflin Co.

Hatsumi, Reiko. From *Rain and the Feast of Stars*. John Murray (Publishers) Ltd., 1960. Copyright © 1960 John Murray. Reprinted by permission of the publisher.

Hill, Errol. From *The Trinidad Carnival: Mandate for a National Theatre*. University of Texas Press, 1972. Copyright © 1972. University of texas Press. Reprinted by permission of the author.

Ihekweazu, Edith. From *Readings in African Humanities: Traditional and Modern Culture*. Fourth Dimension Publishing Co. Ltd., 1985. Reprinted by permission of the publisher.

Jay, Robert R. From *Javense Villagers: Social Relations in Rural Modjokuto.* MIT Press 1969. Copyright © 1969 MIT Press. Reprinted by permission of the publisher.

Kaufman, Howard Keva. From *Bangkhuad*. J. J. Augustin, 1960. Copyright © 1960 J.J. Augustin. Reprinted by permission of the publisher.

Kherdian, David. *The Road from Home*. William Morrow, 1979. © William Morrow & Co., 1979. Reprinted by permission of the publisher.

Leith-Ross, Sylvia. From *African Women: A Study of the Ibo of Nigeria*. Faber & Faber, 1939. Copyright © 1939 Faber and Faber Ltd. Reprinted by permission of the publisher.

Levine, Irving R. From *Main Street, Italy*. Doubleday, 1959. © Irving R. Levine, 1959. Reprinted by permission of Doubleday, a division of Bantam, Doubleday, Dell Publishing Group, Inc.

Lewis, Oscar. *Life in a Mexican Village*. University of Illinois Press, 1951. Copyright © 1951 University of Illinois Press. Reprinted by permission of Ruth M. Lewis.

Li, Mirok. *The Yalu Flows*. Michigan State University Press, 1956. Copyright © 1956 Michigan State University Press. Reprinted by permission of the publisher.

Martin, Pat. From *Czechoslovak Culture: Recipes, History, and Folk Arts*. Penfield Press, 1989. Copyright © 1989, Penfield Press. Reprinted by permission of Penfield Press, 215 Brown Street, Iowa City, Iowa 52245.

Myrdal, Jan. From *Report from a Chinese Village*. Pantheon, 1965. Copyright © 1965 Pantheon. Reprinted by permission of the publisher.

Orel, Harold. From *Irish History and Culture*. University Press of Kansas, 1976. Copyright © 1976. University Press of Kansas. Reprinted by permission of the publisher.

Osgood, Cornelius. From *Village Life in Old China*. Ronald Press, 1963. Copyright © 1963 Ronald Press. Reprinted by permission by Sui-ling Osgood.

Pasternak, Burton. From *Kinship and Community in Two Chinese Villages*. Stanford University Press, 1972. Copyright © 1972 by Stanford University Press. Reprinted by permission of the publisher.

Perl, Lila. From *Ethiopia*. William Morrow, 1972. © William Morrow & Co., 1972. Reprinted by permission of the publisher.

Robson, E. I. From *A Guide to French Fêtes*. Methuen, 1930. Copyright © 1930. Reprinted by permission of the publisher.

Rowen, Shirley, and David Rowen. From *Carnival in Venice*. Abrams, 1989. Copyright © 1989 Abrams. Reprinted by permission of the publisher.

Rutt, Richard. From *Korean Works and Days*. Charles E. Tuttle Co., Inc. 1963. © Charles E. Tuttle Co., Inc. 1963. Reprinted by permission of the publisher.

Salvador, Mary Lyn. From "Food for the Holy Ghost: Ritual Exchange in Azorean Festivals" in *Time Out of Time* by Alessandro Falassi. University of New Mexico, 1987. Copyright © 1987 University of New Mexico. Reprinted by permission of Mary Lyn Salvador.

Sawyer, Gene. From *Celebrations: Asia and the Pacific*. Friends of the East-West Center, 1978. Copyright © 1978. Reprinted by permission of the author.

Scanlon, Phil Jr. From *Southeast Asia: A Cultural Study Through Celebration*. Center for Southeast Asian Studies Special Report Series no. 23. DeKalb: Center for Southeast Asian Studies, Northern Illinois University, 1985.

Sharma, Brijendra Nath. From *The Festivals of India*. Abhinav Publications, 1978. Copyright © 1978 Abhinav Publications. Reprinted by permission of the publisher.

Stanley, David. From *Micronesia Handbook*. Moon Publications, 1985. Copyright © 1985 Moon Publications. Reprinted by permission of the publisher.

Sugimoto, Etsu Inagaki. From *The Daughter of the Samurai*. Charles E. Tuttle Co., Inc., 1966. © Charles E. Tuttle Co., Inc., 1966. Reprinted by permission of the publisher.

Trapp, Maria Augusta. From *Around the Year with the Trapp Family*. Pantheon, 1955. Copyright © 1955 Pantheon. Reprinted by permission of Trapp Family Lodge, Inc.

Turner, Victor. From *Celebration: Studies in Festivity and Ritual*. Smithsonian Institution, 1982. Copyright © Smithsonian Institution, 1982. Reproduced by permission of the Smithsonian Institution Press from *Celebration: Studies in Festivity and Ritual* by Victor Turner. © Smithsonian Institution, Washington, D.C., 1982, pp. 190-198.

Turney-High, Harry Holbert. From *Chateau-Gerard*. University of South Carolina Press, 1953. Copyright © 1953 University of South Carolina Press. Reprinted by permission of Lucille R. Turney-High.

Wenner, Kate. From *Shamba Letu*. Houghton Mifflin, 1959. Copyright © 1959 Houghton Mifflin. Reprinted by permission of Kate Wenner.

Whitten, Norman E., Jr., and John F. Szwed, editors. From *Afro-American Anthropology: Contemporary Perspectives*. The Free Press, 1970. © The Free Press, 1970. Reprinted by permission of the Free Press, a Division of Macmillan Inc.

Williams, Maslyn. From *Five Journeys from Jakarta*. William Morrow, 1965. © William Morrow & Co. 1965. Reprinted by permission of the publisher.

JOURNALS

African Arts, v. XVI, #3, May 1983 for "Street Nativities of Ouagadougou," by Priscilla B. Hinckley. Copyright 1983 by African Arts. Reprinted by permission of Priscilla B. Hinckley.

Anthropos, v. 78, 1983 for "Seged Celebration in Ethiopia and Israel," by J. Abbink. Copyright 1983 by *Anthropos*. Reprinted by permission of the publisher.

Asian Folklore Studies, v. 47, 1988 for "The Monsoon Festival Teej in Rajasthan," by Manju Bhatnagar. Copyright 1988 by Asian Folklore Studies. Reprinted by permission of the publisher.

Folklore, v. 81, Autumn 1970 for "Firewalking at San Pedro Manrique," by Lucille Armstrong. Copyright 1970 by *Folklore*. Reprinted by permission of the publisher.

Folklore, v. 83, Autumn 1972 for "Punkies," by K. Palmer. Copyright 1972 by *Folklore*. Reprinted by permission of the publisher.

Folklore, v. 93, 1983 for "Some Notes on Italian Folk Customs," by Stanley Gee. Copyright 1983 by *Folklore*. Reprinted by permission of the publisher.

Folklore, v. 95, 1984 for "The Carnival at Basle," by Lucille Armstrong. Copyright 1984 by *Folklore*. Reprinted by permission of the publisher.

Journal of American Folklore, v. 61, no. 242, October-December 1948 for ''Mother's Day in Ethiopia,'' by Wolf Leslau. Copyright 1948, American Folklore Society. Reproduced by permission of the American Folklore Society from *Journal of American Folklore* 61: 242, 1948. Not for further reproduction.

Journal of American Folklore, v. 63, no. 250, 1950 for ''The Chinese Feast of Lanterns,'' by Henry Winfred Splitter. Copyright 1950, American Folklore Society. Reproduced by permission of the American Folklore Society from *Journal of American Folklore* 63: 250, 1950. Not for sale or further reproduction.

Journal of American Folklore, v. 76, no. 302, 1963 for ''The Japanese Popular Christmas: Coping with Modernity,'' by David W. Plath. Copyright 1963, American Folklore Society. Reproduced by permission of the American Folklore Society from *Journal of American Folklore* 76: 302, 1963. Not for further reproduction.

Journal of Latin American Lore, v. 7, no. 2, 1981 for ''Fireworks and Fiestas,'' by Stanley H. Brandes. Copyright 1981, *Journal of Latin American Lore*. By permission of The Regents of the University of California.

Journal of Latin American Lore, v. 8, no. 1, 1982 for ''Ritual de la Fiesta del Agua en San Pedro de Casta, Peru,'' by Oliverio Llanos and Jorge P. Osterling. Copyright 1982 *Journal of Latin American Lore*. By permission of The Regents of the University of California.

Journal of Latin American Lore, v. 12, no. 1, 1986 for ''Calendrical Cycles and Their Projections in Pacariqtambo, Peru,'' by Gary Upton, ''The Holy Family of the Festival of Life,'' by Suzel Ana Reily, and ''Judas Burning: A Venesuelan Community Ritual,'' by Maria Elinor Medina de Callarotti. Copyright 1986, *Journal of Latin American Lore*. By permission of The Regents of the University of California.

Journal of Popular Culture, v. 16, no. 1, Summer 1982 for ''Festivals of Tibet,'' by Thubten Norbu. Copyright 1982, *Journal of Popular Culture*. Reprinted by permission of the publisher.

Journal of Popular Culture, v. 19, no. 1, Summer 1985 for ''Festive Customs and Ritual Games on St. Lazarus' Day,'' by Nikolai Ivanov Kolve and for ''Bulgarian Folk Feasts and Rites,'' by Sofia Press Agency. Copyright 1985, *Journal of Popular Culture*. Reprinted by permission of the publisher.

Journal of Popular Culture, v. 20, no. 2, Fall 1986 for ''The Carnival in Goa,'' by Isaac Sequeira. Copyright 1986 *Journal of Popular Culture*. Reprinted by permission of the publisher.

Journal of Popular Culture, v. 21, no. 1, Summer 1987 for ''Firewalking: From Sacred to Secular,'' by Marie L. Ahearn. Copyright 1986 *Journal of Popular Culture*. Reprinted by permission of the publisher.

Journal of Popular Culture, v. 21, no. 4, Spring 1988 for ''The Trinidad Carnival: Ritual, Performance, Spectacle, and Symbol,'' by Renu Juneja. Copyright 1988 *Journal of Popular Culture*. Reprinted by permission of the publisher.

National Geographic, v. 106, no. 4, October 1954 for ''Spearing Lions with Africa's Masia,'' by Edgar Monsanto Queeny. Copyright 1954 National Geographic Society. Reprinted by permission of the publisher.

National Geographic, v. 108, no. 1, July 1955 for ''My Life in Forbidden Lhasa,'' by Heinrich Harrer. Copyright 1955 National Geographic Society. Reprinted by permission of the publisher.

National Geographic, v. 126, no. 4, October 1964 for ''Cambodia, Indochina's Neutral Corner,'' by Thomas J. Abercrombie. Copyright 1964 National Geographic Society. Reprinted by permission of the publisher.

National Geographic, v. 157, no. 3, March 1980 for ''Bali Celebrates a Festival of Faith,'' by Peter Miller. Copyright 1980 National Geographic Society. Reprinted by permission of the publisher.

National Geographic, v. 160, no. 4, October 1981 for ''Crosscurrents Sweep the Indian Ocean,'' by Bart McDowell. Copyright 1981 National Geographic Society. Reprinted by permission of the publisher.

National Geographic, v. 162, no. 1, July 1982 for ''The Ivory Coast—African Success Story,'' by Michael and Aubine Kirtley. Copyright 1982 National Geographic Society. Reprinted by permission of the publisher.

The Folklore of World Holidays

First Edition

January 1

New Year's Day

The first day of the year is an auspicious day, a time to foretell the future and to take ritual precautions to preserve good luck in the coming year. A thorough housecleaning, the payment of old debts, and a literal sweeping out of the old precede the New Year in many cultures. Though the European New Year is celebrated on January 1, the Asian New Year begins on the first new moon after the sun enters Aquarius. This could occur between January 21 and February 19. Agriculturally based cultures sometimes begin the New Year with the beginning of the harvest cycle. The Celtic year began on the first of November with the Winter Kalends.

Austria

New Year's dinner

New Year's dinner is a big occasion. This is the day of the suckling pig, the little pig being one of the good luck symbols. The family table is decorated with little pigs made of marzipan, chocolate, maple sugar, fudge, or cookie dough. Besides the pig, there is also the four-leaf clover, and, in Austria, the chimney sweep. As the recipe for the roast suckling pig might not be generally known, here it is:

> *Roast Suckling Pig*
>
> Clean the pig carefully. Insert a piece of wood into its mouth to keep it open while roasting.
>
> You may use sage and onion dressing, which would taste more American, but we always use the old Austrian apple stuffing. (We have heard of people there who used to stuff their pigs with sausages, but that is awfully rich.)
>
> Now stuff the pig, truss and skewer it. Make four parallel incisions about four inches long on each side of the backbone. Place it on a rack, sprinkle it with salt and some pepper, brush thoroughly with melted butter, and dust with flour.
>
> Roast for 15 minutes at 480 degrees. Then reduce to 350. Continue roasting, allowing 30 minutes to the pound. If you wish to have the skin soft, baste every 15 minutes with hot stock. If you want it crisp (we think it is much better that way), baste with melted butter. When the roast is ready, remove to a hot serving platter. Now remove the piece of wood from the mouth, replace with a bright red apple, and insert cranberries for eyes. Finally crown with a wreath of bay leaves. Be careful to wrap the ears and the tail during the roasting in buttered paper, which you remove only the last half hour. Otherwise they easily burn.

The dessert, after the roast pig, is green peppermint ice cream in the shape of a four-leaf clover.

Source: *Around The Year with the Trapp Family* by Maria Augusta Trapp. New York: Pantheon, 1955, pp. 76-77. See pp. 74-75 for New Year's games in this family.

Belgium

New Year's letters

Another big day for us was New Year's day. For this day we made no end of preparations. A month before we had to tell the schoolmaster how many New Year's letters we had to write: we wrote them to our parents, to our grandfather and grandmother, to aunts and uncles, and often even to some special family friend. We wrote these letters at school with the utmost care on fine, big, white sheets of paper adorned with colored flowers and other illustrations in the left-hand corner. We had to practise reading these letters aloud, and often one letter was rewritten five or six times before the master would find it good enough to be given and read at New Year's.

The day before Christmas, when the holiday began, we took the letters home and carefully hid them. Then on New Year's morning at the breakfast-table I had to stand up and formally wish Father and Mother a "happy and blessed New Year," at the same time handing them my New Year's letter.

After Father had looked it over, he would ask me to read it. I can still see myself standing there with the letter held fast by both hands, saluting first Mother then Father, and starting, "Dear Father and Dear Mother," and finishing with the date. After I had read my letter, the New Year's cake was brought in and put on the table,—a big, square currant-cake with circular flat decorations in the middle of the crust. Then Father gave me a double-franc-piece, and Mother also a franc, which were to be put to my account at the post-office bank. (A postal bank-book is given each school-child, and each Monday he has to bring to school at least one cent, which is put to his savings account.)

But this was only the beginning of the day, and many visits were to be made. I had to go to my grandparents', to my uncles' and aunts', and everywhere I had to read my New Year's letters, drink chocolate, and eat New Year's cake, and receive one franc or double-francs for the bank. My rich Uncle Camille would even sometimes give me a big five-franc-piece, but that was the exception.

Source: *When I Was a Boy in Belgium* by Robert Jonckheere. Boston: Lothrop, Lee & Shepard Co., 1915, pp. 40-42.

France

The Peille fête

New Year's Day has always been a great day in France, and has no doubt gained, as in Scotland, from the lessening observance, as a religious feast, of Christmas. Presents are made then (these belonged originally to the Roman Saturnalia, some of whose festive nature passed into Christmas). Visiting cards are exchanged, in greater numbers than our Christmas cards (themselves not a very early institution). It is interesting to know that for six years New Year's Day was 'suppressed' (1791-1796). All sorts of customs go on in the country; familiar songs of greeting are sung at people's doors; particular cakes or gifts in baskets are made; various divinations are practised; girls are supposed to dream of their sweethearts (as on various other occasions) and so on.

The Peille fête of January 1st is a curious one; the master of the festival and the curé present to the young men an orange in which some flower is set, called a 'flowering apple'; they in turn give it to their sweethearts, and there is much merry-making and dancing. On September 8 the young women, by a just exchange, give the young men ribbons.

Source: *A Guide to French Fêtes* by E. I. Robson. London: Methuen, 1930, p. 63.

New Year's letters and gifts in Besançon

Oh, those New Year's letters! Mother could judge so many things through them. They were to be perfect, presenting our good wishes, showing our repentance for our faults of the past year and giving promises for the next, assuring our deep devotion, reverence and filial love. All that had to be written in a fluent and good style, without any faults of spelling, and never the same as the year preceding. We polished and repolished them, two evenings long.

On New Year's Day, we were already awake at half-past five, all my sisters and I. Wrapped in warm morning gowns, a lighted candle in one hand, parcels and letter in the other, we went on tiptoe to the door of our parents' room.

Goby, the smallest knocks gently, first: Tap! Tap!

A sleepy voice from within: "Who is there?"

Goby's timid voice: "It is I, the New Year!"

Father's voice: "I'm still sleeping!"

Subdued laughter.

I knock next: Tap! Tap! Tap!

"Who is there?"

It is I, Health!"

Mother's voice: "Wait a bit, the door is locked."

Renewed laughter.

Fanny knocks louder: Tap—Tap! Tap—Tap!

"Who is there?"

"It is I, Prosperity!"

Father's voice, quite loud: "Oh! I'm getting up, then!"

Adèle raps vigorously: Rap-a-tat-tat! Rap-a-tat-tat! Tat!

"Who is there, again?"

"It is I, Happiness!"

"Oh, come in; come in quick!"

And we burst the door open! All four rush to the bed.

"Oh, my children, my little ones, what a surprise! It was you, and you, and you and you!"

Kisses and kisses and kisses!

We light the candles on the mantelpiece and carefully place our parcels on the table. Then the reading of our letters begins. We all four stand at the foot of the bed, like respectful courtiers, while Mother and Father, like a Queen and King at their *Petite Lever,* listen gravely. A smile betrays their contentment.

"*C'est très, très bien, mes enfants. N'oubliez jamais vos bonnes promesses!* And now call Nou-nou to light the fire in the chimney."

This meant that we could at last present our gifts, and following the old, old custom of the province—not to be found elsewhere in France—we climbed into the big, large bed beside Father and Mother, yes, all four of us.

Breakfast is a treat—les gaudes—and each of us children receives a beautiful book, generally poetry by Lamartine, Victor Hugo, Musset, le Comte de Lisle, Prudhomme, or some other great poet. Mother did not believe in spoiling us with presents; did we not have all we needed?

"Furnish your brain and your heart," she would say, "and Life will be full of presents for you!" And it is true.

The rest of the day goes on with visits and visiting. This is a little tedious for us, even the dinner with guests, for we must be so good, so quiet!

Source: *When I Was a Girl in France* by Georgette Beuret. Boston: Lothrop, Lee & Shepard Co., 1916, pp. 166-167.

Great Britain

Giftgiving

On New Year's morn, children in Scotland, Wales, and the English border countries may rise early and make the rounds of their neighbors singing. They are treated with coins, mince pies, apples, or other sweets. The giftgiving must be ended by noon or the singers will be called fools and refused any gift.

A typical song is

I wish you a merry Christmas
A Happy New Year.
A pocket full of money
And a cellar full of beer.
A good fat pig
To last you all the year.
Please to give a New Year's Gift
For this New Year.

Source: *Lore and Language of Schoolchildren* by Peter and Iona Opie. Oxford: Oxford Univ. Press, 1959, p. 233.

First footers, or the first person to enter the door

The first person to cross the threshold in the New Year portends good or ill for the coming year. The caller should be male, preferably of dark coloring. In eastern Scotland, East Yorkshire, and Lincolnshire, however, fair men bring best luck, and in Bradford in West Yorkshire red heads are preferred. The luckiest qualities vary from area to area. In Scotland a high instep is required, as flat-footed folk are unlucky. Nor should the visitor arrive empty-handed. A piece of coal for the fire, a loaf for the table, and a glass of whisky for the head of the house are traditional gifts. The first footer enters by the front door and leaves by the back door. In Wales and the Marches, the back door is opened to release the Old Year at the first stroke of midnight, then locked to keep luck in while the front door is opened at the last stroke to welcome the New Year.

Source: *Customs and Ceremonies of Britain* by Charles Kightly. London: Thames and Hudson, 1986, p. 175. (See this source for historical information on this holiday.)

"Burning the Bush"

A nineteenth century custom which carried into the early years of this century was "Burning the Bush". In Radnorshire and Herefordshire farmhands would get up before dawn on New Year's Day and carry a hawthorn 'bush' (a branch whose twigs had been bent to form a globe) into the fields. This was burnt in a straw fire on the wheatfield, sometimes being carried burning over twelve ridges. If it went out before crossing the twelfth, this was bad luck for the crops. A new hawthorn 'bush' was prepared and its ends [were] singed in the fire. The bush might also be doused with cider. This bush might hang in the kitchen until the next year, to bring luck. The men ended the ceremony by "halloa-ing the cider" and drinking.

> The men stand in a ring round the fire and 'holloa old cider'. They sing, on a very deep note, very slowly, holding each note as long as possible, 'Auld Ci—der'. The 'der' becomes a sort of growl at the end, and is an octave below the first two notes; it has a weird dirge-like effect. This is repeated thrice, bowing as low as possible as each note is sung, nine bows altogether. Then follows cheering and drinking, cider and cake being provided for the purpose.

Source: *The Folklore of the Welsh Border* by Jacqueline Simpson. Totowa, New Jersey: Rowman and Littlefield, 1976, p. 134.

Hobby horse performance in Sheffield in 1971, a nearly defunct custom

Of the two animal-disguise customs documented in the Sheffield area, "the Old Tap" and "the Old Horse", the latter appears to have been far less commonly reported. It was all the more pleasing therefore to discover in 1970 an example still being performed in the area. The custom takes the form of a house-visit: a song, 'Poor Old Horse" is sung by two men, Chris and Billy, whilst the third member of the team, Reg, operates the horse-figure, following the text of the song and miming appropriate actions.

> POOR OLD HORSE
> W Palmer and C Ralphs, Dore, Jan. 1st 1971.
> We have a Poor Old Horse, and he's standing at your door,
> and if you wish to let him in, he'll please you all I'm sure,
> Poor Old Horse, Poor Old Horse.

According to the performers, the Old Horse custom is in decline. In the past the team has included up to ten men and boys and the number of calling places was considerably larger, including casual door-to-door visits and street performances in a wide area including Coal Aston, Norton, Holmesfield, Dore and Totley as well as in the performers' home town, Dronfield. In recent years the number of performers has dwindled to the present three, and the number of calling places to the present two private and two public houses in Dore on New Year's Day.

The only disguise is the horse itself; it consists of a pony's skull about eighteen inches long, painted a shiny black, with convex glass bottle ends for eyes, painted white with red centres. The skull is mounted on a pole by means of a U-shaped iron bracket. A black cloth of heavy cotton is fastened to the back of the skull and covers both the operator and the wooden handle which raises and lowers the hinged upper jaw. The handle is connected to an iron rod in the skull and when it is pulled downwards the upper jaw is raised. The top of the skull is decorated with small multicoloured woollen balls and plaits, and has two "ears" consisting of stuffed cone-shapes made from white cotton.

Source: "We have a poor old horse" by Rory Greig in *Lore and Language* 9, (July 1973), 7-10.

For more information on hobby horse visits see: *Ritual Animal Disguise* by E. C. Cawte. Cambridge: Folklore Society, 1978.

Haiti

New Year's Day combined with Independence Day

January 1 is an important holiday in Haiti, because it combines New Year's Day with Independence Day, the day when the Haitians finally revolted from the French. On this day, fireworks are set off in the cities. Even the poorest people make a big effort to have a new dress or shirt or suit to wear on that day. They believe that whatever happens to them on January 1 is a sign of what will happen during the year. Therefore, they like to wear new clothes, give and receive gifts (especially money), and visit their friends, in the hope that these pleasures may be enjoyed throughout the year. The day is spent in feasting, visiting, and making merry in general.

Source: *Children's Festivals in Many Lands* by Nina Mullen. New York: Friendship Press, 1964, p. 129.

Japan

Though New Year's Day is now celebrated on January 1, it is placed in this book with the lunar new year under Moon 1, Day 1.

Nigeria (Ibibio)

The Ndok season

There was also a cultural society into which men only were initiated. It was known as 'Ndok'. Masquerade display marked the arrival of the season which came every other year. The masquerader applied some pipe covered at one end with the soft membranous wing of a bat to his lips. This changed the voice to something hoarse. Moonlight was the most favourable time for them. Women could only listen to the singing and funny stories produced by the masqueraders from behind their yards. On the last day of the year when the season was to be ended, certain traditional rites were observed in every family. On the last day, the initiated men would go to sacrifice for the dead men on their graves. The requirements included a cock, a yam, and some herbs. A small tent was built near the grave with mats. The head of the cock was cut and the blood sprinkled around the small tent and the yam cut in pieces and left there around the grave. The body of the fowl was taken home and eaten by all members of the family.

At midnight on December 31st, both the end of the year and the termination of 'Ndok' season were marked by gun shots, throwing of smouldering wood all over the place and shooting of arrows carrying fire. These were accompanied by indiscriminate shouting from all houses asking the old year to disappear with all its attendant evils and ill luck. The new year was heralded in the following day with many plays and dances. Around the village the 'Ekpe' masquerade would dance picking from street to street all the pieces of wood thrown away the previous night.

Source: *Old Wives' Tales: Life-Stories from Ibibioland* by Irish Andreski. New York: Schocken, 1970, p. 139.

Paraguay

"Niño del Año Nuevo"

New Year's Day is spent in much the same way as Christmas. It is said that a family should celebrate this holiday as a group in order to insure being together all through the year. Crèches are also used for the New Year observances. An entirely new one may be made, or the reclining Child may be removed and replaced by a standing or sitting representation with the world in his hand. All the toys now face away from the figure of the Child, which is called "Niño del Año Nuevo" instead of "Niño de la Navidad."

Source: *Tobati: Paraguayan Town* by Elman R. Service and Helen S. Service. Chicago: Univ. of Chicago Press, 1954, p. 198.

Poland

Vagabonds New Year's

The Vagabonds perform on New Year's Eve day from early morning until after midnight and again on New Year's Day from mid-afternoon until late evening. Their performance consists of a random conglomerate of scenes of ritual origin—mostly through pantomime—and improvised actions and pranks. Each experience of this tradition varies considerably. The following sketch of a Vagabond "run" is based on taped conversations with players from the villages of Cieçina and Pietrzykowice on articles and books, and on observations of performances at the festival in Bedzin.

In the early morning on New Year's Eve day about thirty Vagabonds assemble at the village brewery. The players come in their costumes which they have prepared weeks in advance, using sheepskin coats turned inside out, sleighbells, fur, papier mâché, ears of corn, beads, strips of colored blotting paper, cardboard, rags, and sheets. Their masks are made by the village mask-maker.

When the whole group has assembled, they begin their run into the hills. The gypsy leads the way, followed by the two horses who wear large Napoleonic headdresses and move inside rectangular wooden frames covered with patterned blankets. Others in the entourage follow at random. Death swings her cudgel to the right and left while the Devil slides down a hill. As the Vagabonds lash through the hills and valleys, they separate and then meet periodically at the homes of their acquaintances, which in these mountain villages are often far apart. Thus, their run is similar to a cross-country run. As they run, the jangling of sleighbells fuses with the music of accordions and the cracking of whips. . . .

Gathering bystanders become spectators to the performance as the Gypsy and the Jew squat down in the snow, and the Gypsy reads the Jew's fortune for the New Year. Just a few feet away, the Devil stands threateningly behind the chimney sweep ready to poke him with his stick, while two horses whirl about in a trance-like dance. A bear chases a woman into a barn.

In another section of the village, the Devil and the Plowman engage in a duel in the snow. As a sleigh full of villagers passes by, their play becomes performance.

Gradually, the group reassembles at a village cottage where the door stands open in expectation of their arrival. As the sounds of bells and whips become more and more audible, the family gathers excitedly and waits for the motley entourage to tumble into the vestibule. The priest leads the way, sprinkling drops of "holy water" as he enters. The horses, soldiers, shepherds, old man, chimney sweep, and Death follow him. Gradually, two gypsies and two devils elbow their way through the door. The accordian player takes his place in a corner of the room and begins to play, while the family of spectators mills about freely with the players.

As short scenes emerge out of the romping and chaos, the room becomes noisy and crowded. Several actions take place at the same time or freely overlap with one another. The horses jump about at a dizzying pace, whinnying and jangling the bells attached to their wooden frames. One of them falls to the floor, initiating a scene of probable magic origin. The shepherds and the soldiers stand on either side of him and, holding their whips to the floor, jerk the horse's reins in an effort to make him stand up. He remains immobile. One of the shepherds asks the gypsy woman to invoke a magic spell, whereupon she stands over the horse and showers him with incense from her magic lamp. While she does this, her husband, the gypsy, squats down on his knees and shoes the horse, using pantomime gesture. Once again the soldiers and shepherds jerk his reins. This time, he rises. They help him to his feet, and he begins to dance about the room again.

Meanwhile, two other gypsies have settled on the floor in a corner of the room where they squabble and tell fortunes with their playing cards. Suddenly, they rise to their feet and sing short songs. They walk about the cottage, "stealing" books, plates, and pictures, and asking the host to "buy" the items back—with vodka.

The Devil and the bear are still outside and can be seen frolicking in the snow under the window. Suddenly, the bear rushes into the room, bumps into one of the gypsies, and rolls around on the cottage floor. He grabs one of the girls, drags her out the door, and tosses her into the snow. Next the Jew enters, carrying a goose "stolen" from the host's barn in a cloth sack slung over his back. When some space clears, he hops about the room and engages the family in dancing and singing.

The chimney sweep plugs up the chimney shaft, while an "old woman" wearing rags and a stocking mask over her face squats in the center of the room and feeds her rubber baby doll with a bottle. An "old man" recites humorous prayers on his chestnut rosary. He leads a goat by a chain. As the goat scampers around the room, the spectators spontaneously become a chorus, chanting, "Where the goat goes, the rye will grow." Death weaves in and out of the spectators, poking them with her cudgel and forcing them to dance with her.

For awhile this lively commotion distracts the householders from the pranks being played outside and in the barn. Suddenly, some Vagabonds enter the house, bringing the spoils of their pranks. A soldier brings rabbits and chickens into the house in a sack and lets them loose on the floor. The Devil and the Gypsy undo sheaves of hay and toss bits of it onto the Christmas tree. The clowns braid husks of corn into a huge tail and drag it into the cottage, while the chimney sweep drags chairs and benches from the living room out into the fields. The doctor and the shepherds take apart the host's wagon and reassemble it on the cottage roof.

Gradually, the commotion of performing, dancing, and playing pranks comes to a halt. After sharing in vodka and cakes with the family, the Vagabonds stampede off into the hills and go on to the next cottage. Several gangs of Vagabonds weaving in and out of the valleys transform the whole village into pandemonium. When two gangs of Vagabonds meet, it is the custom that they fight. In the late evening, they appear at New Year's Eve balls. The orchestra strikes up a polka, the Vagabonds choose partners, and for a few minutes the party becomes a masked ball. When the dance has ended, the Vagabonds quench their thirst and speed out again into the night. In the early afternoon of the following day—New Year's Day—they begin their run again, and continue through the evening.

Source: "Performance in Polish Villages" by Marjorie Young. *The Drama Review* 18:4 (T-64) Dec. 74, 17-19.

Scotland

First footing

The first person to put his foot over the threshold of the door was called the "first-footer," and the custom "first-fittin."

It was considered very unlucky to enter a house empty-handed on the first day of January.

Indeed some of the older people would "keek," Scotch for peep, to see the first-footer. If they were empty-handed, or not in high favor, they were not admitted.

When very young, my brother Jack and I were official first-footers to my maternal grandmother. We held our positions by her favor. She was a rigid old dame, with a sharp tongue and sharper manners, which she used to cover a kindly heart. Beggars and small boys left her house with their hands full of cake and their hearts full of gratitude. Aye! and sometimes a "make" (halfpenny) in their pockets.

On New Year's morning she opened the door cautiously. Her head, with her "mutch" (white cap) still on, would appear. Behind the door her foot was jammed ready for an emergency. Her keen eyes searched us. When satisfied that we were alone and our hands full, we were admitted.

What rare currant buns, short bread, scones, and yellow puddings she could make!

Her whole assortment was prepared for New Year's morning. I stood ready to challenge the world's grandmothers to beat mine at making a New Year's feast. To satisfy some unbelieving boys I made a sacrifice and shared some samples of her skill with them. They were speechless with delight. . . .

Groups of young men would go around to their friends first-footing. Generally they sang a common ballad:

> "A guid New Year to yin an' a',
> An' mony may ye see,
> An' durin' a' the years to come,
> Oh, happy may ye be!"

Once my father's apprentices came to our house about one o'clock on a New Year's morning. They sang and danced in the kitchen to our amazement and delight.

In nearly all the cities crowds gather at the Cross. At Glasgow Cross people assembled and waited until the town steeple clock chimed twelve, cheers and greetings rang out, then they dispersed on first-footing expeditions.

Source: *When I Was a Boy in Scotland* by George McPherson Hunter. Boston: Lothrop, Lee & Shepard Co., 1920, pp. 54-57.

Sicily

New Year's lasagne cacate

Writing in 1897, Salvatore Salomone-Marino told of a dish known as "lasagne cacate" or "shitty noodles". They are made of a wide, wavy lasagne, which is cooked full length, unbroken. The ricotta and sauce are added at the table. To eat any other form of pasta on this day brings ill luck. "Whoever eats macaroni on New Year's Day, will have a hard time the whole year," goes the saying.

Source: *Customs and Habits of the Sicilian Peasants* by Salvatore Salomone-Marino. Translated by Rosalie N. Norris. London: Associated University Presses, 1981. (First published 1897, see "Happy New Year!", pp. 147-151).

Spain

Gifts and grapes in Madrid, c. 1940

Between Christmas and New Year I spent a good part of the day on grandmother's balcony, which was filled with plants and singing birds. From there I had a splendid view of the endless trays of cakes, flowers and plants being carried swiftly from house to house, almost airborne they seemed to be, by armies of laughing errand boys: New Year gifts for teachers, patrons of various kinds (always so important in Spain) and family doctors and dentists. Even the policemen on traffic duty had mounds of presents piled round them.

Five minutes before the magic hour of midnight, grandmother had distributed little bags containing twelve grapes to every member of the family. As the clock began to strike we stood round the dining-room table and ate one grape for every stroke. This meant that we would have good luck in every month of the coming year—so the ceremony was taken very seriously. Then, to wash down the so-hurriedly eaten grapes, we toasted each other in Moscatel wine. (The custom of eating twelve grapes for luck at the stroke of midnight is so firmly entrenched that in theatres and cinemas—where the last performance ends about 1 a.m.—programmes are interrupted so that the spectators may consume the grapes which they have religiously brought with them, together with a bottle of wine, for the traditional celebration.)

Source: *Spanish Fiestas* by Nina Epton. New York: A. S. Barnes, 1968, pp. 217-218.

Surinam

Firecrackers and parties bring in New Year

New Year's Eve and New Year's Day start on the 31st of December with lots of fireworks. Firecrackers and the liveliest festivities and grand parties are very common in Surinam. These parties last till the next day.

Source: Embassy of the Republic of Surinam.

Thailand

Celebrating at the Pra Mane Grounds in Bangkok

The evening of December 31 is one round of merry-making in the fairy-like capital city of Bangkok with its golden temples and palaces.

Children on that night go with their parents or their older brothers and sisters to join the gay throngs of people on the downtown streets. Many of them carry along musical instruments or some kind of noisemaker and take part in the fun everyone seems bent on having.

Shouting, laughing, singing, the crowds move toward the Pra Mane Grounds in the center of the city. This is the Royal Plaza in front of the Grand Palace in Bangkok where a gala show is put on by the government on New Year's Eve. Children and grown-ups alike enjoy every minute of the entertainment.

As midnight approaches, the crowds become more hilarious and more excited. At the stroke of twelve their excitement seems to explode. The crowds go wild as they hear the *bong bong bong* of the great temple bells being struck with a wooden bar to announce the arrival of the New Year. Everyone shouts "Happy New Year, Happy New Year" (in the Thai language—*Kwam Suk Pee Mai*). Noises from the whistles, the horns, and the instruments they brought with them all add to one long deafening din. Everyone is gay and happy.

Early on New Year's morning, children present their parents with the New Year gifts they have for them—candy, small articles, and greeting cards. Their brothers and sisters, their other relatives, their teachers and friends are all remembered, too, for gift-giving to Thai children is a very important part of New Year. In return they receive gifts. For many days before New Year, children have been saving their *bahts* (money) in order to buy their gifts and cards.

Soon after this gift exchange at home, boys and girls go with their parents back to the Pra Mane Grounds where they welcomed the New Year the night before.

There saffron-robed monks from the four hundred *wats* (temples) in Bangkok gather to receive their New Year gifts of rice and other foods which the children and their elders bring to fill the monks' alms bowls.

Source: *Happy New Year Round the World* by Lois S. Johnson. Chicago: Rand McNally, 1966, pp. 141-142.

Tonga

Ta'u Fo'ou

Perhaps because New Year, *Ta'u Fo'ou,* as it is called here in Tonga, comes to these "Down Under" islands during midsummer when the schools have their long holidays, it is a particularly happy time for children. On New Year's Day itself and for all the rest of the warm days of the first week of the year, the boys and girls form themselves into groups and go about from house to house serenading their families and friends. Some of them play harmonicas; others strum ukuleles or guitars; still others beat drums; and everybody sings.

As befits a new year, the songs they sing are all new, made up by the children themselves for the occasion. Some of them are hymns, thanking God for helping them through the problems of the past year, and some are songs of hope for the new year, and some are gay rounds.

When they have finished all the numbers in their little concert, the children move on to another house, but not before the householder who has enjoyed their music shows his appreciation by giving them fruit or cool drinks. Sometimes a particularly generous listener will give each performer a little woven mat or piece of tapa, the bark cloth that is made in the islands.

Source: *Children's Festivals from Many Lands* by Nina Millen. New York: Friendship Press, 1964, p. 170.

Trinidad

Feeding the dead

An account of "feeding" the dead—which shows how intimate is the relationship between a person and his dead forebears, and how human these beings are conceived to be—may be given here. "What I does, now, every good day, Christmas, Easter, New Year, I always throw. I go down the steps, say, 'Look, I don' make it a promise. Also, you mus' take whatever I give you.' I don' make it a promise for no special place, either. Give beef, a little cooked apart without salt, rice, ginger beer, rum, cake. When I go down the steps I call everybody I can remember to come. I say, 'My ol' daddy like to smoke. I go len' you a pipe and tobacco.' Leave it, stop there the whole night and the morning, then say, 'Well, you finish with the pipe. Well, I take it.' In the night, I leave the table set, food on the table, drinks, the pipe in one corner of the table. Put that pretty cotton on the table, too. When you get up, you smell tobacco strong. Say, 'He enjoyin' it fine.' "

Source: *Trinidad Village* by Melville J. Herskovits and Frances S. Herskovits. New York: Alfred A. Knopf, 1947, pp. 155-156.

U.S.S.R.

Grandfather Frost

Santa Claus is replaced with "Grandfather Frost," or *D'yed Moroz*. Clad in a red, fur-trimmed costume, with boots and a long white beard, he looks very much like his counterpart but arrives with his bag of toys on New Year's Eve. For a fee you can engage a Grandfather Frost to drop by your home and deliver your presents to the children. Over a thousand Grandfather Frosts are in service for Moscow's door-to-door service on New Year's Eve. *Snegourka,* the Snow Maiden, usually accompanies him on his rounds.

The winter tree

Gigantic decorated trees still grace the city centers of the U.S.S.R. They are erected to celebrate the New Year. Over 50,000 decorated trees are put up in the Moscow area in public places, and over 700,000 are sold for home use.

Children's party at the Kremlin

Of all the official New Year's celebrations in the USSR, none is staged with greater panache and style than the party given within the walls of Moscow's Kremlin in the modern Palace of Congresses. As many as 50,000 attendance tickets are sold in the weeks before the annual event, and parents go to great lengths to snap them up before they're gone.

For the occasion, the huge hall is transformed into a fairyland. A towering New Year's Tree, as high as 75 feet, stands in the center of the hall. As on Christmas trees of European tradition, garlands of glittering balls, tinsel, and colored lights festoon its spreading branches.

As each child presents a ticket to the clown at the door, he or she is handed a gaily wrapped gift. Then everyone jostles for a place to stand and watch the entertainment. First comes *D'yed Moroz,* or Grandfather Frost, with white beard and a brilliant red robe and hat rimmed in white fur. His arrival, aboard a Sputnik-drawn sleigh or some other fantastical conveyance, is staged with great fanfare. He is followed by a dozen or more attendants, including the Snow Maiden, snow bunnies, and a clown, and costumed youngsters—boys in old time peasant tunics, baggy pants, and boots, girls in pinafores and blouses.

Then on the stage at one end of the hall troops of folk dancers glide into sight, their feet flying across the floor to the sound of *balalaikas* and *gusli*. Choruses from far-off provinces present their wonderful melodies; magicians, clowns, and tumblers all perform, to the great delight of the children and their parents.

The Kremlin party is geared mostly to younger Muscovites. Older children and young adults have dances to go to—at schools, clubs, theaters, and union halls. Intermissions feature wonderful food and a variety of entertainments, and everyone stays up very late. Far beyond Moscow, at farm collectives, at factories, and in mining communities, the story is much the same but on a more modest scale, as young and old alike gather to mark the start of the New Year. Everywhere, holiday decorations—lights, paper lanterns, evergreen boughs, and New Year's trees—brighten public buildings.

Source: *Joy Through the World* by the United States Committee for *UNICEF*. New York: Dodd, Mead, 1985, pp. 144-145.

Yugoslavia

Children's parties

Father Christmas, *Deda Mraz,* appears the week before Christmas to hear children's gift requests and to invite them to a party on January 1. A New Year's tree is decorated for January 1 and on New Year's Day the candles on the tree are lit and presents opened. Children's parties are given on January first with singing and dancing around the New Year's tree.

Source: *Hi Neighbor. Book 6* by the United States Committee for UNICEF. New York: Hasting House, 1963, p. 58.

For more on New Year's see: "New Year's Day" in *Folklore of American Holidays* edited by Tristram Potter Coffin and Hennig Cohen. 2nd ed. Detroit: Gale Research, 1991.

January 1

The Feast of the Circumcision

January 1 is in some places celebrated as a religious day in commemoration of Christ's submission to Jewish law.

Costa Rica

Carnivals and other festivities

New Year's and the Feast of the Circumcision are celebrated with bullfights, carnivals, and a parade, the "Tope."

Source: *Fiesta Time in Latin America* by Jean Milne. Los Angeles: The Ward Ritchie Press, 1965, p. 17.

Syria

Visitors and visiting

On January 1 Syrians exchange presents, as this is a day of rejoicing, the Day of Circumcision. Children go from house to house for sweets. Guests visit to enjoy coffee and pastries. January 2 is the day for women to go visiting, as they stayed home to serve their guests on January 1.

Source: *Christmas Customs Around the World* by Herbert H. Wernecke. Philadelphia: The Westminster Press, 1959, p. 122.

January 2

Second New Year

South Africa

Annual Minstrels' Carnival

A well-known festival in South Africa, particularly in Cape Town, is the Annual Minstrels' Carnival, with whose music and song the streets resound at New Year, and who give expression to the zest for life by their animated dancing and prancing.

The carnival is an old institution in Cape Town and originated under the influence of the black singers of America, who dressed and disported themselves in a similar fashion. Every year bands are organized, each with its own leader, name and meeting-place. During the year members pay dues out of which costume material is purchased. The design and colours of the costume are a closely guarded secret, and competition between the groups is keen. On New Year's Day, on Second New Year (2 January) and during the week or so following there is a period of joyous festivity during which the carnival participants ''take over'' the city.

Another important feature in Cape Town during the Christmas and New Year season is the string bands which parade the streets. Unlike the Annual Minstrels' Carnival, these minstrels are dressed neatly and with great dignity, and their bright rendering of sacred and other songs is a source of delight to all who hear them.

Source: Embassy of South Africa, Washington, D.C.

January 1 or 2

St. Basil's Day

St. Basil was born at Caesarea in Cappadocia. As metropolitan of Caesarea he fought Byzantium and saved Cappadocia for the Catholic faith. His work on the Holy Ghost is still respected in Catholic theology. He is known as one of the Three Holy Heirarchs in the East and as one of the Four Greek Doctors in the West. St. Basil lived from 329 to 379 A.D. Some cultures celebrate St. Basil's Day on January 1, combining his day with New Year's festivities.

Greece

Kalanda singing

On New Year's Eve children and grown-ups go from house to house singing kalanda. They carry an apple, an orange, a paper ship, a paper star, and a green rod cut from a cornel-tree. They tap the master of the house and his family on the back with this rod while they sing their good wishes. The housewife gives the children sweets, nuts, or coins. On New Year's Day this singing continues but may be accompanied by symbolic acts to insure prosperity, such as poking the fire or sprinkling wheat in the backyard.

First visitor on New Year's Day

The first person to enter the house on New Year's Day must be auspicious. In some parts of Greece it should be the master of the house or a "lucky child" (one whose parents are both alive). In some areas rituals accompany the entry. On the Island of Amorgos the person must be a member of the family returning from church, carrying an icon. He takes two steps into the house and says "Come in good luck!" and takes two steps backwards and says "Out bad luck!" He repeats this three times, then throws a pomegranate to the floor smashing it. All family members then dip their fingers in honey and eat this, so the coming year will be as sweet as honey. Boiled wheat is then eaten in St. Basil's name. On the Island of Carpathos a white dog is brought into the house and fed baklava on New Year's morning to give the household strength of body and spirit during the coming year.

Vassilopitta

Vassilopitta, a round cake made of milk, eggs, butter, and sugar is eaten on New Year's Day. This "St. Basil's Cake" is cut by the head of the house. The first slice is for St. Basil, the second for the house, then one for each family member in order of seniority. Lastly, a slice for the cattle and a slice for the poor are cut. A gold coin is hidden in the cake, and the one who finds it will have a lucky year.

St. Basil's visit

St. Basil, one of the four Fathers of the Church, visits every house on his feast day, January 1. As he is particularly interested in the farm's work animals, these are tended well on New Year's Eve, so that St. Basil will find them brushed and groomed when he inspects the stables. Each animal gets a share of the *Vassilopitta* and receives wheat with their fodder on New Year's Day instead of oats.

On the Island of Skyros a tray is prepared with a bowl of water, two dishes of pancakes or sweets, a pomegranate, and a pestle so that St. Basil may refresh himself and sweeten his tongue; thus will the house remain fresh and sweet all year long. At Aghiassos in Lesbos a table is laid and left all night for St. Basil. A log is placed upright in the grate to enable St. Basil to step down the chimney easily. At Kydoniae (Aivali) in Asia Minor a tray with jellied pork pie, fish, sweets, a slice of *Vassilopitta,* and a glass of water are left.

Source: *Greek Calendar Customs* by George A. Megas. Athens: B. & M. Rhodis, 1963, pp. 37-45.

Saint Basil carol

New Year's day is another holiday, when boys go singing from house to house the song of Saint Basil, which is very old:

> "Saint Basil has come from Caesarea.
> He holds a book and paper, and carries an ink-stand.
> He writes in the book, and he reads from the paper.
> 'Basil, do you know how to read? Basil, do you know any songs?'
> 'I have learned how to read, but I don't know any songs.'
> And he leaned upon his staff to say his alpha, beta.
> The staff was of dry wood, and it put forth green branches."

The boys wish a happy new year at all the houses where they call, and they receive in return candy or little presents, and for the elder people it is a day for making and receiving visits.

Source: *When I Was a Boy in Greece* by George Demetrios. Boston: Lothrop, Lee & Shepard Co., 1913, pp. 60-62.

January 5 and 6

Epiphany Eve and Epiphany

Christ was baptized by St. John on January 6. This day, Epiphany (or "manifestation"), celebrates three epiphanies: the adoration of the baby Jesus by the magi; the baptism of Jesus; and the transformation of water into wine, Jesus' first miracle.

Austria

Burning incense on the Vigil of Epiphany

In earlier times there were twelve holy nights between Christmas and Epiphany—called "Smoke Nights," because the people went through their houses and barns burning incense, blessing their homestead. Only one such night is left, but this is celebrated with great solemnity: the Vigil of Epiphany, January 5th. After the supper dishes are done, the whole family, dressed in Sunday clothes, follow the father, who goes ahead with a shovel of charcoal on which he burns incense, while the oldest son has a bowl with holy water—Epiphany water, blessed with a much longer formula than the ordinary holy water, a formula that contains a prolonged exorcism, which makes it efficacious against all demoniacal influence—which he sprinkles freely all over house and grounds and barns, while the rest of the family follow behind, saying the rosary and singing hymns. While the father and the oldest son are incensing and blessing the house, the youngest child carries on a plate a piece of chalk. This has been blessed with a special blessing from the Rituale after the morning Mass. In the old country every household would be most careful to send somebody into church for the blessing of the chalk. At the very end, when the whole homestead had been blessed, room by room, the father took the blessed chalk and wrote over every room that led from the house into the open:

AD 19 C M B 55

which stands for "Anno Domini 1955—Caspar, Melchior, Balthasar" and means that the three Holy Kings, Caspar, Melchior, and Balthasar, in this year of Our Lord, 1955 (or whatever the year may be), are protecting this house against all evil spirits.

Epiphany is also known as "Little Christmas." As a feast it is even much older than our Christmas. On the Vigil, the eve before the feast, there comes to the table a special Epiphany cake, in which three beans are hidden—two white ones, one black one. Whoever gets a bean in his piece has to dress up next day as a Holy King. The one who got the dark bean will be the black King. (Soot from the fireplace or black shoe polish are recommended.) On Epiphany Day the three Holy Kings, with golden crowns and richly dressed in oriental splendor, are the guests of honor at the table. Afterwards the whole family tries to entertain them and they have the say of the evening. This is always an evening much looked forward to by the whole house. We have had the most fantastic-looking magi at our table. Before the three majesties leave the house again, they hand over their gifts—equivalents for gold, incense, and myrrh.

Source: *Around the Year with the Trapp Family* by Maria Augusta Trapp. New York: Pantheon, 1955, pp. 80-81.

Canada (Labrador)

Naluyuks visit on January 6 in Makkovik

The 'naluyuks' are widely discussed on the days before their arrival. Adults wonder who the 'naluyuks' will be this year, and parents reiterate to the children the "rules of the game." Throughout the excitement adults are cautious not to let the children hear that real persons play the role of the 'naluyuks. . . .'

. . . This physical transformation is achieved by the use of a three-piece costume: a cover for the body, for example, bearskin, coarse sacking, or an over-sized coat; a paper, cloth, or commercial mask to cover the face; and a stick. One or more of the 'naluyuks' are equipped with bags. During the turmoil which accompanies this dressing up, Eskimo parents come with wrapped packages containing gifts, mostly sweets, for their children. Some parents are overtly reluctant to come, but if so they sent their gifts by others. Those who deliver the packages stay only long enough for the name of the child to be written on the package and then are quick to depart. With the costumes completed and the gifts stowed in the bags, the 'naluyuks' are ready to start their rounds.

The procedures in each house are similar. The members of any household are well aware that the 'naluyuks' are approaching. The commotion which accompanies the short walk from house to house and the streaming into the house of visitors in advance of the 'naluyuks,' tell the children that their nerve-wracking anticipation is nearing its climax. For days they have practised for this moment and from the beginning of the evening have not deserted their lookouts at the windows. Now they take their seats on the chairs or benches usually placed for this purpose. In some homes, other seats, facing the children, are prepared for the 'naluyuks.' The parents sit by the children and invariably embrace them in a protective manner. The suspense and fear which lead to this protective gesture are understandable if we remember that the 'naluyuks' are the most prominent of the Eskimo bogey-figures. The 'naluyuks' are regularly used to discipline young children and are said to take bad children away. The annual visit of the 'naluyuks' reinforces the image.

The 'naluyuks' enter the house and face the children. At this point the children are expected to sing a hymn or a Christmas carol to which the 'naluyuks' respond noisily by pounding their sticks on the floor. The observer might think that the 'naluyuks' are demanding more, but the explanation given by the Eskimos is that they are expressing their satisfaction in this way. The pounding, however, seems to increase the children's anxiety. Often a child becomes choked with fright and cannot utter a word; others bury their faces in their parents' laps; and some seem on the verge of tears. But all usually complete the carefully rehearsed hymns. The parents share the anxiety of their children and the audience too exhibits signs of concern. Often, an older person in the crowd interrupts the proceedings with a loud 'taymak' (enough), which sometimes ends the performance.

As soon as the singing part ends, the 'naluyuks' proceed with a series of questions. These questions are asked in a disguised voice and are usually answerable with the simple 'ah' or 'auk' (yes and no respectively). The questions are not crystallized formally but left to the individual 'naluyuk.' Yet the range of inquiry is limited by the one topic of interest—the behaviour of the interrogated child. "Are you a good boy?" "Are you lazy?" "Do you help your mother?" The youngsters whisper their answers. The questions and answers constitute the second part of the visit. To the relief of the children the 'naluyuks' now proceed to the final stage. They browse in the gift bag, locate the right package, and hand it to the child.

Source: "The 'Naluyuks' of Northern Labrador, a Mechanism of Social Control" by Shmuel Ben-Dor in *Christmas Mumming in Newfoundland* edited by Herbert Halpert and G. M. Story. Toronto: Univ. of Toronto Press for Memorial University of Newfoundland, 1969, pp. 122-124.

Cyprus

Kalanta

A rousting of the Kalikandjari on Epiphany Eve

On Christmas Eve God sets loose a crowd of evil spirits, the Kalikandjari, who roam the world until Epiphany. On Epiphany Eve the priest goes from house to house after the morning church service, blessing each home with holy water, singing hymns in memory of the family's dead, and blessing the traditional table of food spread by the housewife. After this blessing, the Kalikandjari cannot enter the house, stable, or yard but must perch on the roof until their departure on Epiphany Day. On Epiphany Eve, after dark, pastry balls (*Xerotighna,* made especially for this eve) are thrown onto the roof to appease the spirits on this, their last eve in the world for the year.

Source: *International What's What When & Where* by Ardith Nehrt. Columbus, Ohio: Shawnee International Publishing Co., 1965, p. 69.

France

Les Rois

Les Rois! Readers of Mistral will know something of what that means, for Provence understands this festival better than most parts of France; and no little child can forget the Epiphany 'cribs'.

There is the Epiphany cake (with its bean, or some other counter-part of our sixpenny-bit), there are *galettes,* there are popular hymns and songs. All the mystery of the East is in 'Les Rois'; they come from far; all the mystery of the skies is in 'Les Rois'; they followed a wonderful star unknown to their astronomy. There are the Santons, those little Nativity and Epiphany figures which go back to the fifteenth, perhaps fourteenth, century. There is alms-giving to the poor. There are lightings of candles. There is everything that speaks of the strange mystic charm of childhood, for those wise kings came many weary miles to see a little child. There used to be odd processions; poor folk had the right of collecting alms; at St. Pol-de-Léon was a remarkable ceremony called the 'Inguinane'. But it is to Provence and Mistral (in his Memoirs) that we must go to find the full meaning to the devout mind of 'Les Rois'.

Source: *A Guide to French Fêtes* by E. I. Robson. London: Methuen, 1930, p. 64.

Germany

Sternsinger (Starsingers)

Sternsinger are usually three boys who dress in royal gowns with crowns of gold paper, one with blackened face, to represent the Three Kings. They carry a star on a pole through the streets while singing carols and are given treats. In some places men may perform the star carols house to house and be treated with drinks. One starsinger verse runs

> Die heiligen Drei Kȯnig' mit
> ihrm Stern
> Sie essen, sie trinken und
> bezahlen nicht gern.

The Bean King and Queen

Whoever receives the black bean in his piece of *Dreikonigskuchen* becomes *Bohnenkonigswahl* (Bean King) for the day and rules the party. In the Rhineland two beans may be baked into two New Year's doughnuts. If found by an unmarried boy and girl, they are destined to come together.

Source: *German Festivals and Customs* by Jennifer M. Russe. London: Oswald Wolff, 1982, p. 77.

Greece

Epiphany Eve blessings

The heavens open at dawn on Epiphany Eve. Young girls may sit up all night around a pot of sweet basil to see it flower when the heavens open. Wishes made on Epiphany can be heard more easily because the heavens open. Even the winds are baptized at Epiphany, and stable animals break into speech on this night and talk together.

A ''Blessing of the Waters'' takes place on Epiphany Eve. The priest passes through the village after mass blessing homes and sprinkling them with a sprig of basil dipped in holy water. Thus the *Kallikantzaroi* may be kept away.

In Western Macedonia new clothes should be first worn at Epiphany to be blessed.

Blessing of the waters on Epiphany Day

On this day a procession from the church carries the Cross to the waters and it is thrown in. Young men dive for the cross. Recovering it is a great honor, and the young man who brings it up bears it around the town and receives gifts from the townsfolk.

Sea water has special purifying qualities after the Cross is dipped into it; thus farm implements and household icons may be washed in the sea for benefit. On Epiphany Eve sea water becomes potable.

Godchildren

Since Jesus was baptized by St. John on Epiphany, this is a day for godparents to send gifts to godchildren. In Thrace a special *photiki* is made for the godchild. A string of fruits and candies with a small candle at its end is attached to a stick and presented to the godchild.

Source: *Greek Calendar Customs* by George A. Megas. Athens: B. & M. Rhodis, 1963, pp. 50-52.

Ireland

Epiphany, known as ''Women's Christmas'' in early Ireland

Epiphany [was] known in [early] Ireland as 'Little Christmas' or *Nollaig na mBa* ('Women's Christmas').

Source: *Life & Tradition in Rural Ireland* by Timothy P. O'Neill. London: J. M. Dent & Sons Ltd., 1977, p. 98.

Italy

Befana's visit in Levigliani, Italy c. 1979

Early in the evening an indeterminate number of people gather together dressed in the scruffiest and oldest clothing possible. They black their faces with carbon and use unwound pieces of rope to make imitation hair. La Befana and her husband Befano are dressed similarly, except that both sport humped backs and carry long sticks. It does not matter who plays what, but it is important that the dress of the two characters is quite obviously male and female. Thus it is that two girls or two men may play the principal roles, or a man and a girl. The Befano does not seem to be very important and acts only as a companion to La Befana.

Meanwhile the children wait at home and are busy writing their Wishes on bits of paper which are then allowed to float up the chimney, a custom that I remember well, as a child in Manchester. As they do this they chant the following rhyme:

Befana Befana	Befana Befana
sei la mi dama	you are my lady
sei la mi sposa	you are my wife
tirimi gia qualcosa	Throw something down to me
Un arancino un pefanino	A little orange or a *pefanino*
Unpitoro di pecorino	or a small piece of *pecorino*

Pefanino is a small biscuit made in the shape of Befana, and *pecorino* is a special type of cheese.

La Befana takes to the streets with her husband Befano and her entourage. She is accompanied by a makeshift band of three or four musicians and a live horse.

The completed procession now tours the village, calling at each house where children live. Her they sing the Befana song, and the Befana dances with Befano.

The following translation is given without any attempt to make the words rhyme.

Upon the mountain the snow is falling
And is blown on the wind before
And with a light step she descends to us
A fairy that is dear to you all
A fairy that many here love
Who comes every year to find you
She has arrived with us 'la Befana'
Every heart is full of joy
From among the valleys, villages and countryside
Our Befana has arrived here
She has brought a great sackfull of presents
That she wants to give to your dear children
That promise to be good for their mothers and fathers

Tempo change and repeat twice.

And now friends you that are here
We want to sing and dance
And a ballet we want to do
With the Befana and the Befano
And we want to salute you all
Friends we shall always remain

> And the Befana before she goes
> Wishes you all happiness and prosperity.

Having done this, the Befana and her company receive a glass of wine or a bite to eat or a little money from the householder, and then continue to the next house.

Hanging of stockings in Val d'Aosta

Further to the North in the region of Val d'Aosta the same custom occurs, but there presents are given on the 25th December, and on the eve of 5th January bright coloured or multicoloured stockings are hung up by the fireplace to receive the gifts from La Befana which usually comprise sweets, nuts, fruit and a few trinkets. Unfortunately in this area the custom of playing the Befana on the streets has died out.

Source: "Some Notes on Italian Folk Customs" by Stanley Gee in *Folklore,* 93 (1982), 93-97.

Befana arrives and policemen receive presents

The traditional Italian time for exchanging gifts comes 12 days after Christmas, on January 6. This is Epiphany, the day on which the Magi—the Three Wise Men or the Kings of the Orient—arrived in Bethlehem with gifts. Italian children have been taught that Epiphany gifts are brought by the Befana, a benevolent old witch who rides a broomstick. Children who do not behave are warned that the Befana will leave them a piece of coal.

On Epiphany a memorable sight in Italian communities is that of policemen directing traffic with gifts piled around their feet. Passing motorists slow down to hand their presents out the window.

The Christmas season in Italy is 32 days long, starting on December 6, St. Nicholas Day, and ending on Epiphany, when every well-tended Christmas crèche has the three figures of the Magi added; then the *presepio* is dismantled until the next year.

Source: *Main Street Italy* by Irving R. Levine. Garden City, N.Y.: Doubleday, 1963, pp. 489-491.

Sweden

The Star Boys make their rounds

The most typical Swedish aspect of the celebration of Epiphany, or the Night of the Three Holy Kings, in old times, was the play of the Star Boys. In some ways, it serves the same purpose as the Staffan ride. The two have their most important moments in common: the costumes, the practice of treating, the songs, and the collection of food for the party, and so on. In other respects, other and entirely different elements are involved.

In contrast to the Staffan procession, the Star Boys walked their rounds. The three kings were motifs for the costumes, one of which must always be a negro, inasmuch as the kings represented the three known divisions of the ancient world: Europe, Asia, and Africa. The retinue of the kings included various strange figures, the most well known of which was Judas with a purse.

Source: *Swedish Christmas.* Gottenburg: Tre Tryckare, 1955, p. 77.

Syria

Bowing trees and a camel bearing gifts

Among the many beliefs related to Epiphany Eve, . . .the most universally accepted one relates that just at midnight every tree bends its trunk and inclines its branches in homage to the Christchild.

In southern Syria the gentle camel of Jesus travels over the desert and brings presents to the children, supposedly the youngest camel of those which brought the Wise Men to the manger! Which makes it how old? In their childhood faith they leave bowls of water and bowls of wheat outside their door. In the morning the good children find gifts, the others a black mark on the wrist!

Source: *Christmas Customs Around the World* by Herbert H. Wernecke. Philadelphia: The Westminster Press, 1959, p. 132.

January 5-6

Día de los Tres Reyes (Day of the Three Kings)

On the evening of January 5 (the eve of January 6, Epiphany), The Three Magi visit homes bringing gifts for the children. Special masses or festivals for Los Tres Reyes may occur on January 6.

Belgium

Children celebrate Three Kings' Day

On such days as Three Kings' Day in January we would feast at Grandmother's home together with my cousins, and other girls and boys of the neighborhood were assembled.

You remember the story of three kings who came to Bethlehem, bringing gold, incense, and myrrh to Jesus. In Belgium that day is still a kind of a holiday for the children; the evening before and the whole Day of the Three Kings children march through the streets, each one carrying a stick tipped with a star. The star is adorned with all kinds of colored paper, and can be turned round by drawing a cord. The boys and girls go singing from door to door, making their stars turn round quickly as they sing. They receive small presents from many kindhearted people.

The song which the children sing is as follows:

"Mÿn sterre, mÿn sterre niet stille meer staan
Wÿ moeten te samen naar Betlehem gaan
Naar Betlehem die schoone stad
Waar kindje Jesus geboren lag."

"My star, my star, do not stand still;
To Bethlehem we must now be hieing,
To Bethlehem, that wonderful town
Where Child Jesus is in his manger lying."

Source: *When I Was a Boy in Belgium* by Robert Jonckheere. Boston: Lothrop, Lee & Shepard Co., 1915, p. 64-65.

Mexico

Gifts and parties for the little ones

Presents are given on New Year's Day to the grown-up persons and toys and other gifts to the children on Kings' Day, January sixth. The Kings are the Mexican Santa Claus and are supposed to bring toys to the little ones. On that day a party is given for children, a large cake being placed on the table, in the center of all the other sweetmeats. This special cake contains a bean, and if a girl gets it she is the queen and selects a king from among the boys present, while if, on the other hand, the bean falls to a boy, he chooses the queen, and I was that lucky person at one of these parties that I attended. The king is supposed to give a few days later a party or picnic to all those who had attended, so of course we children loved this party, as in reality it meant two parties.

Source: *When I Was a Girl in Mexico* by Mercedes Godoy. Boston: Lothrop, Lee & Shepard Co., 1919, p. 59.

Paraguay

The Fiesta of the Three Kings in Tobatí

The fiesta of the Three Kings is primarily a secualar one, organized for amusement, particularly for the children, although it is celebrated with a Mass and procession of the saints' images on the morning of January 6. Ordinarily, *santos* are brought into the church on the evening of January 5 and are left there overnight and then carried back to the homes the next day after the Mass and procession. The games are traditional ones: climbing a greased pole, blindfold games, bow-and-arrow shooting contests, and the usual horse races and games played on horseback. Prizes may consist of *chipa* bread, money, chickens, or fruit. The Society of the Three Kings is a very old and strong one, both in town and in the *compañías*. At times the celebrations and games have been sponsored by society members in the town of Tobatí, but in recent years the games have been held in the *compañías*.

In 1949, when we witnessed the fiesta, the first small groups of families from the country began to come into Tobatí early in the morning, carrying the images of the kings, Baltasar, Gaspar, and Melchior. After a number of families had arrived, they formed a procession with men on horseback carrying the flag of Paraguay in advance and the women and children following on foot, carrying the images. They were escorted by a small band of drums, flutes, and cymbals, and the masked clowns, the *cambá ra'angá,* cavorted on all sides.

The *cambá* seem to be especially associated with this fiesta. Their masks are made occasionally of leather but more often of the carved root of the *sammuú,* a large tree with a light, cork-like root. They should be made by the individuals who wear them, since no one should know who is wearing the mask.

The clowns dance, play flutes and drums, sing and talk in falsetto voices, and tell obscene jokes. They are not permitted to follow the procession into the church plaza, because they are considered exceptionally profane.

Source: *Tobatí: A Paraguayan Town* by Elman R. Service and Helen S. Service. Chicago: Univ. of Chicago Press, 1954, pp. 190-191.

Spain

The Three Kings visit Madrid, c. 1940

Grandmother allowed me to help her lay out the crib on a special table and to decorate it with tiny candles and miniature censers. In the evening I was permitted to light the candles and throw a few grains of lavender into the minute censers. The Three Kings, who were still far from Bethlehem, were placed behind a mountain. 'We shall move them a little closer to Bethlehem every day,' said grandmother, 'about half an inch at a time, so that they reach the manger at midnight on Christmas Eve.'

From then until Epiphany the whole family gathered round the brightly lit manger every evening to sing *villancicos*. I especially liked one about a blind man who gave the Virgin a drink of water while she and Joseph were on their way to Bethlethem, and how he immediately recovered his sight—the unborn Christ-Child had performed His first miracle.

These *villancicos* brought a new kind of Christmas to me, centred less on myself and more on the happenings round the Crib, which were made to sound so thrilling. The tambourines made me feel like dancing, even in church—because they were played by the nuns in the convent where I was taken to hear Midnight Mass on Christmas Eve as a special treat. If it had not been for the tambourines and the *zambombas,* I might have fallen asleep.

On Christmas day the traditional dishes were bream, *gachas* or fried semolina balls dipped in hot treacle and a marzipan serpent with its tail in its mouth which, as I have realized since, is a symbol which suitably marks the end of the year's cycle.

By the time 5 January came round I was almost exhausted by the long-drawn-out pleasure of anticipation. The Three Kings were at last approaching Madrid. 'Can I write to them?' I asked grandmother. She said I could and that I should put my letter in an empty box near the balcony. The Kings' camels would presumably be left in the street while the Kings climbed up and through the balcony between the plants in Jack-and-the-Beanstalk fashion.

Source: *Spanish Fiestas* by Nina Epton. New York: A. S. Barnes, 1968, pp. 216-218.

January 5-6

Twelfth Night

The twelfth night after Christmas Eve is January 5. January 6 is the twelfth day after Christmas Day. The Magi arrived on this day to adore the Baby Jesus. The Christmas season extends from Christmas to January 6 in many European and Latin American cultures.

Denmark

Twelfth night dream of future husband

With Twelfth Night our Yule came to an end. In that night, if a girl would know her fate, she must go to bed walking backward and throw a shoe over her left shoulder, or hide it under her pillow, I forget which, perhaps both, and say aloud a verse that prayed the Three Holy Kings to show her the man

> Whose table I must set,
> Whose bed I must spread,
> Whose name I must bear,
> Whose bride I must be.

The man who appeared to her in her sleep was to be her husband. There was no escape from it, and consequently she did not try. He was her Christmas gift, and she took him for better or for worse.

Source: *The Old Town* by Jacob A. Riis. New York: Macmillan, 1909, p. 103.

Great Britain

Twelfth Night in Shakespeare's Day

Twelfth Night was once a time of masking, plays, games of forfeit, and other revelries, as seen in Shakespeare's comedy *Twelfth Night*. A "Lord of Misrule" or "King of the Bean" (the guest served the slice of Twelfth Cake containing the lucky bean) presided over the party. These customs declined in the 18th century, though elaborately iced Twelfth Cakes remained popular until late Victorian times. At London's Theatre Royal, Drury Lane, a Twelfth Cake is cut with ritual by the performing company each January 6.

Source: *The Customs and Ceremonies of Britain* by Charles Kightly. London: Thames and Hudson, 1986, p. 222.

Pastries and pranks

Scenes outside the pastrycooks at Twelfth tide were highly amusing. The windows were filled with cakes, some simple, some very elaborate, ornamented with stars, castles, cottages, kings, dragons, trees, fishes, cats, dogs, lions, churches, knights, serpents, or, in fact, almost any device. People crowded round, looking in to see which they would choose or what other people were buying. This gave the little street urchins a real chance to get into mischief and their regular trick was to pin together as many coat tails and mantles as they could. As many as eight people might be seen all pinned together. They had an almost more embarrassing one, too. They carried a hammer and tacks and when opportunity occurred with a quick, smart tap they nailed luckless creatures to the window ledge by coat or dress. How the little wretches yah-ed and boo-ed and cried,

> "Huzza! *More* people pinned and *plenty* nailed up!"

However, those who stayed to laugh ran the risk of being caught by the constables, who did their best to keep "free ingress, egress and regress" to the shops, though they were not very successful.

The spirit of Twelfth tide spread even to the gingerbread makers, who frosted over a few plum buns and adorned their gingerbread with untarnished Dutch gilt to brighten their windows. Their big glass lollipop jars were polished up and filled with a fresh store of peppermint drops, brandy balls, hardbake, bullseyes, sugar sticks and elecampane. Their very candlesticks were decorated with strips of white paper.

Twelfth Night Feasts

Twelfth Day Feasts took place not so long ago in country places. They were mostly paid for by the people themselves and consisted in the north largely of a dish called "Lobscouse," which was made of beef, potatoes and onions fried together, and a drink called "Ponsondie," which was very like the "lambs wool" of the Wassaillers at Christmas.

At these Twelfth Night suppers the company indulged in what was called a Twelfth Night Gambol. One of these was a grinning match, another a whistling match, and a third was a yawning match.

The yawning match took place at midnight so that the whole company might be as drowsy as possible. The prize offered was a Cheshire cheese and it went to the man who yawned the widest yawn so naturally that he produced the greatest number of yawns among the spectators.

In Devonshire it was a day to think of the orchards and their crops. They had feasts of cyder and cakes but a portion of each had to be taken down to the trees. A piece of cake was put on a bough and hot cyder was poured over the roots of the tree. The men fired a salute and the girls sang one of the Devonshire Twelfth Night Songs.

Source: *Happy Holidays* by Eleanor Graham. New York: E. P. Dutton, 1933, pp. 34-35.

Iceland

The dream of the Magi

Hallgrimur Petursson, an Icelandic hymnist of the 17th century, wrote:

> Twelfth Night is the manifestation feast,
> the day the Three Wise Men came from the East.

Twelfth Night was also called the *Great Night of Dreams,* because that was when the Eastern Kings were supposed to have dreamt of the birth of Jesus. Moreover, in some places of the country Twelfth Night was demonstrably called *The Old Christmas* or *The Old Christmas Eve.*

Source: *Icelandic Feasts and Holidays* by Arni Bjornsson. Trans. by May and Hallberg Hallmundson. Reykjavik: Iceland Review History Series, 1980, p. 101.

Twelfth Day in Iceland c. 1910

Among the amusements are the fairy-dances. They are especially danced on New Year's Eve or on Twelfth Day's evening. A fairy king and a fairy queen are the leaders in the dancing. They are dressed in white robes with golden crowns on their heads. The dresses of the other fairies are like those of a masquerade.

Some are white fairies, others are black fairies, with all kinds of head-dresses. The fairy folk generally start from among rocks or high cliffs, carrying burning torches. They parade singing to a place where there is a big bonfire. They dance in a circle around the fire, singing fairy songs and reciting poems made for that purpose. A crowd of people are surrounding them all the time. When the bonfire has burned out, all parade to a dancing-hall, where the general dance begins.

Source: *When I Was a Girl in Iceland* by Hólmfrídur Árnadóttir. Boston: Lothrop, Lee & Shepard Books, 1919.

First Monday after Twelfth Day

Plough Monday

Great Britain

Back-to-work day

This is the day for men to get back to work after Christmas. It is for them what St. Distaff is for women. To celebrate it they used to drag the plough through the streets and sing and collect money. The hands from several farms would often join together for this outing. Thirty or forty of them in clean white smocks decorated with gay ribands went out with the plough. One was dressed as an old woman. He was called "The Bessy." Another was dressed in skins with a tail hanging down the back, more ribands about him. He was called the "Fool Plow." The Bessy carried the money box. They trooped from village to village and sometimes ploughed up the land before the door of any house where alms were refused them.

A Plough Monday Supper was usually given by the farmer for his men at which there was much good ale and beef. The Lord Mayor of London still gives a Plough Monday Dinner on that night, but its old significance is forgotten.

Gender rivalry

This was a time of friendly rivalry between girls and men. It was a time-honoured custom for them to race to be first at work next morning. If a man managed to bring his whip or his plough staff or any other of his outdoor tools and dash it down on the hearth before the girl could get her kettle on for breakfast then the man could claim a cock from his master on Shrove Tuesday. If the maid won, she had the cock.

Sometimes work actually began on the Monday and then the men raced back at night to the farm kitchen. If one of them got there and cried "Cock in the pot" before the maids within doors had time to cry, "Cock on the dung-hill," then again the man could claim his cock at Shrove-tide.

Source: *Happy Holidays* by Eleanor Graham. New York: E. P. Dutton, 1933, pp. 28-29.

January 7

St. Distaff's Day

On this day, women go back to their spinning work.

Great Britain

St. Distaff's day tricks

On St. Distaff's Day there was plenty of mischief afoot.

The farmers themselves had not gone back to work and it was a time-honoured game for them to try to burn the flax from their womenfolk's distaffs. If they succeeded, then they ran the risk of being soused with water from the women's water pails that night.

> Partly work and partly play,
> Must ye on St. Distaff's Day.
>
> From the plough soon free your team
> Then come home and tether them.
> If the maids a-spinning goe
> Burne their flax and fire their tow.
> Bring the pailes of water then
> Let the maides bewash the men.
> Give St. Distaff all the right
> Then bid Christmas sport good night.
> And next morrow everyone
> To his own vocation.

Robert Herrick.

Source: *Happy Holidays* by Eleanor Graham. New York: E. P. Dutton, 1933, p. 26.

January 7

Gannā

Christmas in Ethiopia is celebrated on January 7, as in Eastern Orthodox religions. The holiday is called *Gannā* (*Genna*), which is also the name of the stick and wooden puck game played by boys on *Genna*. Special church services are held on this religious holiday.

Ethiopia (Amhara)

Aggressive games are played

Christmas, celebrated in early January, is marked chiefly by the playing of secular games. The common word for Christmas, *gannā,* is actually the name of an outdoors game played with sticks and a wooden puck. Played by boys, young men, and occasionally elders on the afternoon of Christmas Day, *gannā* is marked by a spirit of aggressive license. Accustomed norms of deference are held in abeyance. The game is played in so rough and disorderly a manner that it often results in broken limbs and scarred faces. Staged by two teams made up on the spot, *gannā* is concluded at dusk by volleys of abusive limericks with which the victors revile their adversaries.

Source: *Wax & Gold: Tradition and Innovation in Ethiopian Culture* by Donald N. Levine. Chicago: Univ. of Chicago, 1965, p. 77.

Genna customs

The Ethiopian Christmas, like that of the Eastern Orthodox Church, falls on January 7. It is called Genna and, while not among the most important of Ethiopia's religious holidays, church services are held, with ceremonial dances accompanied by sounds of sistra and prayer sticks. The sistrum, or *tsenatsel,* is a rattlelike percussion instrument with rows of metal rods set crosswise within a spade- or pear-shaped frame. The rods are strung with small metal discs that make a jingling sound when the sistrum is shaken.

The prayer stick, or *makamiya,* is a long pole with a T-shaped, crutchlike top. It is used to tap the beat of the dance and also serves as an underarm support for the clergy during the lengthy services. A tapering drum with skin stretched over both ends, called a *kabaro,* is another percussion instrument used to accompany religious dances. Melody-producing instruments are not used in religious ceremonies.

Late in the afternoon on Genna day, the hockeylike game known as *genna* is played. Using curved wooden sticks, two teams composed of older boys and young men attempt to drive a wooden or hard leather ball over a goal line. *Genna* is a rough game, the excitement runs high at this once-a-year event, and the playing often continues until darkness falls. The competition may be between villages, with the game played on an open field, or it may be played on a village main street as a local contest.

Small children may receive simple presents from their parents on Genna but Christmas gift giving, as practiced in other parts of the Christian world, is not traditional in Ethiopia.

Source: *Ethiopia: Land of the Lion* by Lila Perl. New York: William Morrow, 1972, p. 74.

January 6 or 7

Old Christmas

In 1582 Pope Gregory XII introduced the Gregorian calendar. However, the Eastern Church continued to celebrate Christmas according to the Julian calendar. In 1923 the Church of Greece and the Ecumenical Patriarchate of Constantinople adopted the Gregorian calendar. However, some ethnic groups continue to celebrate Christmas according to the ''old-style'' calendar on January 6 or 7. There is a 13-day difference between the calendars.

Canada

Ukrainian traditions

Canadian Ukrainians celebrate Old Christmas on January 7. On Christmas Eve, January 6, the family displays a candle in the window to guide the Holy Family. A sheaf of wheat, didukh, is stood in a corner of the room to symbolize the family. Hay is placed under the tablecloth and on the floor and a goat, dog, or other animal may be brought into the house. Twelve meatless and milkless dishes are eaten.

Source: *Let's Celebrate!* by Caroline Parry. Toronto: Kids Can Press, 1987, pp. 58-60.

Great Britain

The blossoming of the Glastonbury Thorn at midnight

Throughout Herefordshire specimens grown from cuttings of the famous Glastonbury Thorn still thrive. This plant was believed to bloom precisely at midnight, the hour when Christ was born. The blooms would drop an hour later. This occurs on January 6, Old Christmas. [T]he calendar change in 1752, which altered the date of Christmas to December 25, ha[d] no effect on the plants and animals, who continue to celebrate the ''real'' Christmas. Both in Herefordshire and in Monmouthshire, for example, bees are said to leave their hives and hum at midnight on this night. Cattle kneel in their stalls and weep, and rosemary blossoms.

Source: *The Folklore of the Welsh Border* by Jacqueline Simpson. Totowa, New Jersey: Rowman and Littlefield, 1976, p. 137.

A bloom as proof for old Christmas

In England, too, the legend of the flowering tree of Yuletide is known. Until the year 1753 the old reckoning according to the Julian calendar had been used, by which the New Year commenced on the 25th of March. As all other civilised states had already adopted the Gregorian calendar, the alteration of the New Year, and the change from the old to the new calendar, was accomplished without opposition on the part of the people in England. It was only in Buckinghamshire that a rebel rising threatened, and the cause of this was an old belief which was threatened by the new calendar.

In the old English legend Joseph of Arimathaea plays a part. His figure is also connected with the story of the Holy Grail, which was widespread all through the Middle Ages. Of Joseph of Arimathaea it is told, that he once planted a staff on Christmas Eve which he had cut years ago from a hawthorn. It immediately took root and put forth leaves, and the next day was covered with blossoms. For many years this bush used to be in full bloom on Christmas night, and any cutting taken from it had the same miraculous power. Many of the bushes had withered and died in the course of centuries. Only one had survived, which stood on a mound in the churchyard of the Abbey of Glastonbury. In the reign of Charles I, it was still the custom to have a stately procession on Christmas Day, and to bring a branch of Glastonbury thorn, plucked the preceding night and always in full bloom, to the King and Queen. At the time of the civil war between the King and Parliament this wonderful bush was burned during an attack on the abbey. But not even then was the miraculous plant quite exterminated: a cutting had been planted some time before in Quainton in Buckinghamshire, and it also blossomed every Christmas night, although it was covered with blossoms in early summer like every other hawthorn-bush. During the night of the 24th to 25th December, in the year 1753, New S., a large crowd had gathered with torches, candles, and lanthorns around the wonderful bush, anxious to behold the development of the white blossoms. Midnight struck, but the bush remained bleak and dead: no sign of life could be detected. After waiting in vain till dawn, the people dispersed, but the excitement still continued.

There was no doubting possible: the new Christmas Day was not the right one. The authorities had already decided to exterminate the bush, when lo and behold, on the 5th of January, the old Christmas Day, it stood in full bloom.

Source: ''German Christmas and the Christmas Tree'' by Alexander Tille in *Folklore* III (December 1892), 180-181.

January 7

St. John the Baptist's Day

This is a day of honor for St. John the Baptist, who baptized Jesus.

Greece

Sprinkling in honor of St. John the Baptist

Since St. John baptized Jesus, his day recalls the act of baptism. In Thrace, villagers carry bowls of water and dip boughs in these to sprinkle each other.

Source: *Greek Calendar Customs* by George A. Megas. Athens: B. & M. Rhodis, 1963, p. 52.

January 11
St. Brictiva's Day

Norway

End of the Christmas season

On St. Brictiva's Day all leftovers from the Christmas season were mixed together and eaten up. All of the Christmas ale had to be finished off. In the old days, neighbors went from home to home, helping finish off the Christmas treats.

Source: *Notes from a Scandinavian Parlor* by Florence Ekstrand. Seattle: Welcome Press, 1984, p. 90.

January 12

Old New Year's Day

The vestige of an ancient Welsh holiday, January 12 is still celebrated in some Sunday Schools.

Wales

Calan Hen Pwnc

A remnant of the ancient Eisteddfod held at Christmas in King Arthur's time remains in the Calan Hen, held by Sunday Schools on January twelfth. They go through a Pwnc, a public recital and catchecism on a portion of the Scripture. This is held in a church and accompanied by choral competitions.

Source: *Holidays in Wales* by William H. Crawford, Jr. New York: Oxford Univ. Press, 1950, pp. 18-19.

January 12-15

Festival of Our Lord Bonfim

This Bahian festival honors Our Lord Bonfim. Voodoo elements combine with Catholic.

Brazil

Waters of Oxala

The women of Bahia dance through the streets bearing pitchers of water and flowers. They chant voodoo hymns as they dance, but carry the water to cleanse the steps of the Bonfim church and worship Our Lord Bonfim. This rite is known as the ''waters of Oxala.''

Source: *International What's What When and Where* by Ardith Nehrt. Columbus, Ohio: Shawnee Publishing, 1965, p. 58.

January 13

St. Knut's Day

The final day of Christmas in Sweden is known as Tivgondag Knut or ''Knut.'' Canute the Great decreed circa 1036 that fasting between Christmas and the Epiphany Octave should be eliminated. In addition, this is the day to toss out the Christmas tree. In Norway January 13 is also called Tyvendedagen (Twentieth Day) since it is the twentieth day after Christmas. According to Norwegian legend, trolls led by the troll woman Kari-Tretten raced over the countryside on this night. Christmas races were once held on this day.

Sweden

Knut parties and masquerades

This is the day people finally part with their Christmas trees—if they haven't already done so. All the decorations are first removed, and the act is often the occasion for a final party—this one especially for the children. Friends and classmates are invited over to eat cakes and candies, play games and ''plunder'' the tree. All the small trinkets are carefully removed and stored away, while edible ornaments—ginger biscuits, caramels, and the like—are gobbled up. Finally, the group pick up the tree and literally toss it out of the house or flat, singing a song that, in translation, goes something like this:

Christmas has come to an end,
And the tree must go.
But next year once again
We shall see our dear old friend,
For he has promised us so.

In the past Knut was also an occasion for masquerading. Men and boys dressed up as ''Old Knut'' would prowl about, playing practical jokes and doing mischief. In some parts of the country—particularly where immigrant Walloons settled in the seventeenth century—Knut is the occasion for regular carnivals, especially in the province of Uppland just north of Stockholm.

Source: *Traditional Festivities of Sweden* by Ingemar Liman. Stockholm: The Swedish Institute, 1985.

The twentieth day of Christmas

By the ''twentieth day of Christmas'', January 13th, the festivities should be over. For now the Christmas tree is danced out. Shorn of its decorations and plundered of its small presents and bags of sweets, specially put there for the occasion, it's cast out into the snow.

This is the time of children's parties. Day after day they dance out each other's trees and return home clutching their prize package of homemade sweets. How they survive is a mystery. But they do. And turn up next day at the next party ready to dance the old dances and join in the games, willing and even eager to fill themselves once more with cake and fruit juice. And to-morrow, they'll begin again, in another home.

The floor above you sways, and thumps reverberate from the noisy and energetic throng in the flat over yours. You hardly need go through the anxieties of a party of your own. But of course you do, some day towards the middle of January.

Source: *Round the Swedish Year* by Lorna Downman, Paul Britten Austin, Anthony Baird. Stockholm: The Swedish Institute/Bokförlaget Fabel, 1967, pp. 110-111.

January 13

Old Silvester

Old Silvester is a New Year holiday remnant from earlier times. In Urnäsch, Switzerland, masked singers tour the town on both January 13, Old Silvester, and on December 31, New Silvester.

Switzerland

The Silvesterklausen in Urnäsch, Switzerland, c. 1980

Twice a year, the male inhabitants of the small village of Urnäsch in eastern Switzerland disguise themselves in various costumes. Thus decorated and supporting harnesses with heavy bells, they walk in groups from house to house, and at each house where they are received, they sing three wordless yodels. This custom is called *Silvesterklausen* (or just *Chlause*), and the men themselves—bearers of this custom—*Silvesterchläus* (or just *Chläus*). They perform on New Year's Eve (*Silvester* in German-speaking Switzerland) and on January 13, but to connect the name *Chläus* to St. Nicholas would be doing the custom and the men who perform it an injustice.

I had my first opportunity to witness Silvesterklausen in Urnäsch, located in the canton of Appenzell, during a brief field excursion with a folklore seminar on January 13, 1980. An hour before dawn we were guided to a farmhouse where nine men were in the process of getting dressed for a strenuous day as active participants in this winter custom. Intense excitement emanated from them as they put on their heavy costumes and even heavier bells and headdresses. At the crack of dawn they marched off in single file to another farmhouse a quarter of a mile away. Shaking their bells rhythmically, they announced their arrival. The inhabitants seemed to be expecting them; a man stepped out of the door, followed by his wife carrying a tray with a bottle and glasses. The group of disguised men gathered in a circle and sang several wordless, polyphonic yodels, which was received with great favor by the couple. Each visitor was offered a drink; then each disguised man shook hands with their hosts and marched off, heading for the next house.

Groups perform in the village streets and inside restaurants but their favorite scenes are the countryside visits

The reasons for preferring the nebedosse (''outside'') routes varied, but one was mentioned by everyone: ''It is much more rewarding to go chlause at an individual farmhouse. There you can really see the people's joy. The farmer might even sing along with you, the children marvel at your Huet and Huube, and you end up singing more Zäuerli than usual because it just feels so right,'' said a schöne Chlaus. An older Chlaus, himself a farmer, said: ''Good chlause is always nebedosse. We once visited a farmer who usually doesn't get Chläus, and his hands were shaking hard when he poured the wine because he was so moved.'' Others mentioned the romantic aspects of walking along in the midst of snowy hills, far from the road, and seeing the farmhouses nestled among them. Avoiding the crowds also makes nebedosse routes attractive: ''On the Old Silvester, there are sometimes so many people that you barely have room to chlause if you stay in the Tal.''

Source: *Progress and Nostalgia: Silvesterklausen in Urnäsch, Switzerland* by Regina Bendix. Berkeley: Univ. of California Press, 1985, pp. 1, 2, 43. See this source for detail of costume, bells, yodels, events, and function of Silvesterklausen.

January 15

Seijin-No-Hi (Adult's Day)

Seijin no Hi is a day of shrine visits and parties for all who reached age 20 during this year. Traditional kimonos are worn.

Japan

Seijin-No-Hi in Miyamoto-cho, Tokyo c. 1980

Until the middle 1970's the chōkai put on a coming-of-age party for all young people in Miyamoto-chō who were celebrating their twentieth birthday (the age of legal majority) during the year. That event was discontinued owing to the apparent lack of interest on the part of the young people themselves. Most clearly preferred to mark the milestone with friends on the national holiday in their honor (Adult's Day, or Seijin no Hi, January 15), attending one of the many large public ceremonies sponsored by the ward government and showing off their adult finery (especially the young women, dressed in gorgeous kimono) at a major shrine or temple.

Source: *Neighborhood Tokyo* by Theodore C. Bestor. Stanford, California: Stanford Univ. Press, 1989, p. 158.

January 16

St. Honoratus' Day

January 15 honors St. Honoratus of Arles, who died in 429. He was born in Lorraine, probably of a Roman consular family. He converted in his youth and studied monasticism in the East, then returned to found the abbey of Lerins on the Mediterranean isle of Lerins. He became archbishop of Arles in 426.

France

The legend of St. Honoré

St. Honorat (or Honoré), January 16, was a hermit saint who introduced into the islands off Cannes the Egyptian type of monastic life; there was no fixed order, but hermits lived in their cells about the island, where were various chapels. The pretty legend is worth repeating that he promised to come and see his sister St. Marguerite, on her neighbouring island whenever the almond trees blossomed; and by her prayer they blossomed all the year round.

Source: *A Guide to French Fêtes* by E. I. Robson. London: Methuen, 1930, p. 64.

January 19 and 20

Timqat (Epiphany) and St. Michael's Feast

As Genna, the Ethiopian Christmas, falls on January 7, the Ethiopian Epiphany, called Timqat or Timkat, falls two weeks later on January 19. Epiphany celebrates the baptism of Jesus. Celebrations continue into January 20, St. Michael's Feast.

Ethiopia (Amhara)

Timqat rituals

But the giant of holidays in this season is Epiphany, about a fortnight after Christmas. The holiday commemorates the baptism of Jesus; the name of the holiday, *Timqat,* means "baptism." In preparation for Timqat new clothes are given to children and the adults' *shammā,* grown very gray over the months, are washed in every household.

The program for Timqat is long and complicated. At sunset on the eve of the holiday, the people don their white clothes and repair to the local church, from whence they escort the *tābot* to a place where it will spend the night—near some stream or pool. They go home for supper, and return to that site for singing and dancing until late at night. About two o'clock in the morning Mass is performed, after which quantities of *dābo* and *tallā* are consumed. Toward dawn, or shortly after, the clergy bless the water and sprinkle it on those assembled. Many like to bathe in the sanctified water at this time. It is the occasion for baptizing the children of syphilitic mothers and those who want to be rebaptized.

By noon on Timqat Day a large crowd has assembled at the ritual site, those who went home for a little sleep having returned, and the holy ark is escorted back to its church in colorful procession. The clergy, bearing robes and umbrellas of many hues, perform rollicking dances and songs; the elders march solemnly with their weapons, attended by middle-aged men singing a long-drawn, low-pitched *haaa hooo;* and the children run about with sticks and games. Dressed up in their finest, the women chatter excitedly on their one real day of freedom in the year. The young braves leap up and down in spirited dances, tirelessly repeating rhythmic songs. When the holy ark has been safely restored to its dwelling-place, everyone goes home for feasting. In the meantime, the eyes of gamesome men and women have met and secret rendezvous have been arranged.

Source: *Wax & Gold: Tradition and Innovation in Ethiopian Culture* by Donald N. Levine. Chicago: Univ. of Chicago Press, 1965, p. 63.

Timkat and St. Michael's Feast on January 20

Timkat, or Epiphany, falls on January 19 and is, along with Maskal, a colorful and uniquely Ethiopian festival. Timkat celebrates the baptism of Christ in the River Jordan. On January 18, the eve of the holy day, the *tabot* is carried from the church in a glorious procession and taken to a nearby lake, stream, or pond of sanctified water. White-turbanned priests, deacons, and *dabtaras,* with prayer sticks, drums, and sistra, hold aloft the intricately designed processional crosses. Brilliant flashes of color are provided by the rich ceremonial robes and by the gorgeous fringed and embroidered umbrellas that are a part of all Ethiopian religious processions. The *tabot* is set down beside the baptismal stream or pond, where it rests throughout the night in a tent guarded by the clergy and by the villagers, who light campfires and eat, drink, sing, and dance until it is time for the early-morning baptismal ceremony. The priests light candles and sprinkle the holy water from the pool or stream on the heads of all those who wish to renew their Christian vows. Some people bathe in the pool, immersing themselves completely in the sanctified water. The procession, bearing the *tabot,* then starts back to the church.

The festivities continue into the next day, January 20, which is a second occasion (in addition to November 22) for celebrating the feast of St. Michael. Timkat is therefore a three-day holiday that happily blends a deeply religious occasion with a joyous public festival.

Often the exciting national sport of *yeferas guks* is played at Timkat. *Guks* is an exhibition of wildly brilliant horsemanship played on a large meadow by teams of warriors clad in white and wearing lion-mane capes and headdresses. The warriors, on gorgeously decked steeds, wield bamboo lances and are armed with shields of hippopotamus or other tough animal hide. The play consists of pursuit of one horseman by another and the throwing of the lance. *Guks* derives from the mounted-warrior battles of former days, when sharp-tipped javelins were used against the foe, no armor was worn, and the speed and skill of one's horsemanship were the only protection against injury or death. When *guks* is performed nowadays it is usually at Timkat, Maskal, or on some special state occasion.

Source: *Ethiopia: Land of the Lion* by Lila Perl. New York: William Morrow, 1972, pp. 74-75.

January 20

Día de San Sebastián

January 20 is a day to honor St. Sebastian. St. Sebastian died circa 288. He was an officer in the Roman army and a favorite of Diocletian. When it was discovered that he was a Christian, he was tied to a tree and used as a target for Roman archers. A basilica stands over his tomb on the Appian Way.

Mexico

Día de San Sebastián in Zinacantan

San Sebastián's day in the Catholic calendar is January 20, but this ceremony lasts nine days, from January 17, when the Mayordomos renew the flowers on their house altars until January 25 when the Big Alcalde transfers sacred symbols of his authority to his successor. It is, by all odds, the most complex ceremony performed in Zinacantan, and it has some unusual features, perhaps the most remarkable being that the major costumed performers are the cargoholders who have "officially" finished their year of service but who must perform throughout this ceremony before they finish their duties. Thus, for example, the Alcaldes of the previous year become "Spanish Gentlemen" dressed in gold embroidered red coats and knickers; the two most senior Alféreces become "Spanish Ladies" wearing white embroidered blouses and carrying combs in small bowls; the Regidores become "White Heads" with white hats, shirts, capes, and breeches and "Twins" (probable translation) dressed in purple dress coats and breeches; two other Alféreces become "Jaguars" dressed in jaguar suits with tails; others become "Crows," "Spanish Moss Wearers," and "Blackmen." All in all, a most extraordinary collection of "celebrators" of the fiesta.

Sacred objects are brought into the Center from various hamlets: a small sacred drum that is played for some of the dances, a jousting target and a lance used for a jousting pantomime, and so on. The sequence of events includes the arrival of the Spanish Gentlemen and Ladies on horseback for the jousting pantomime and dancing; the "Blackmen" dancing with stuffed squirrels with which they engage in comic play, including simulating intercourse between the squirrels; the climbing of a "Jaguar Tree" and the ritual burning of a "Jaguar House"; two enormous ritual meals during which the entire hierarchy of cargoholders sits down to servings of whole chickens, the "Jaguars" performing a caricature of a curing ceremony with one Jaguar impersonating a shaman, the other playing the role of his patient.

The ceremony finally ends on January 25 when the past year's cargoholders escort the outgoing Big Alcalde with his articles of office to the house of the incoming Big Alcalde. An elaborate ritual follows in which he hands over the sacred picture of San Sebastián, two candleholders, a box containing a stamp, a seal, and some papers, and the branding iron for Zinacantan.

This ceremony appears to have a vague connection with the myth of the slaying of San Sebastián as told in Catholic theology, but it has obviously developed an accretion of many additional complex elements, the total symbolism of which still escapes us even after a decade of field work in Zinacantan.

Source: *The Zinacantecos of Mexico: A Modern Maya Way of Life* by Evan Z. Vogt. New York: Holt, Rinehart and Winston, 1970, p. 86.

January 21

St. Sarkis's Day

January 21 honors St. Sarkis, an Armenian saint who fought against the Georgians.

Armenia

Folk customs herald future spouses

Folk customs of romantic youth cluster about this Armenian saint. On this day young lovers eat salty bread before retiring. They may dream that their future spouse comes to bring them water. Crumbs for birds are put out and the birds are observed. They will fly off in the direction from which the future spouse will come. A Saint Sarkis Day dish called *pokhint* is made of flour, butter, and honey. When Saint Sarkis was fighting the Georgians, the roasted wheat in his pocket turned into *pokhint* magically. A bit of *pokhint* is put outside the door as an offering to this saint. Saint Sarkis also protects from storms while traveling. Once he kidnapped a Byzantine girl and rushed away on horseback from west to east, raising a snow and dust storm behind him on a road without snow.

Source: *Armenian Village Life Before 1914* by Susie Hoogasian Villa and Mary Kilbourne Matossian. Detroit: Wayne State Univ., 1982, pp. 133-134.

January 22

St. Dominique's Day (Midwife's Day)

January 22 is St. Dominique's day. In some areas of Greece the day honors the village midwife. This is a women's festival, in which all women of childbearing age participate.

Greece

Women visit the midwife

Although a minor feast, there are several very interesting customs attached to this day; they survived particularly in the villages of Eastern Rumelia, but are more common today in Macedonia, the new home of the Greek refugees from Bulgaria.

St. Dominique's is best known as the Midwife's Day. It is essentially a woman's feast, but only women who are still of age to bear children are allowed to take part in it. The honoured person on this day is not the Saint herself, but one of the most important members of the village community: the midwife.

On St. Dominique's Day all the village-women who are still able to bear children visit the midwife and bring her gifts: articles useful to her profession (soap, towels, etc.), food and wine. Each woman pours out some water for the midwife to wash her hands, thus anticipating the day when the midwife will assist her in childbirth. Then she must kiss the '*schema*' offered to her by the old women who attend the midwife; this '*schema*' is a phallic-shaped object made from a large leek, or a sausage. The women kiss the phallus fervently and weep over it. Meanwhile the midwife, adorned with gilded flowers, onion and garlic tresses, necklaces of dried figs, currants and carob-beans, and one large onion instead of a watch, sits proudly upon a makeshift throne, watching the scene with satisfaction. The village-women surround her with great veneration—as if she were a reincarnation of Genetyllis, the ancient Greek goddess of childbirth.

There follows a banquet, during which the womenfolk indulge in continuous and potent libations. It is not considered improper for women to get drunk on this occasion. After much eating and drinking, the midwife, still heavily bedecked, is led on a carriage through the streets of the village, as if she were a bride; she is taken to the public fountain, where she is sprinkled with water. The womenfolk escort her all the way, singing and dancing. Some of them are in fancy dress. Their songs and jokes are often extremely lewd. Needless to say, all the menfolk stay indoors on St. Dominique's Day. Woe to the man who dares go out into the street and falls into the hands of the frantic women.

Source: *Greek Calendar Customs* by George A. Megas. Athens: B. & M. Rhodis, 1963.

January 22
St. Vincent's Day

January 22 is celebrated as St. Vincent's Day. He is especially honored by vintners.

France

Celebrating in Champlitte, France

This festival commences the winter labors of the vintners. The progress of the vineyards is predicted by the weather on this day: ''Saint-Vincent au pied sec; La vigne a la serpette'' or ''A la Saint-Vincent; Le vin monte au sarment; Ou s'il gele, il en descend.'' On this day a statue of Saint Vincent is borne in procession through the town.

Source: *Fêtes en France* by Michele Boudignon-Hamon and Jacqueline Demoinet. Paris: Chênes, 1977, pp. 30-31.

January 24
Alasitas

Bolivia

Alasitas in an Aymara community, Compi, Bolivia

A miniature market takes place in altiplano communities on this day. Cattle are modeled of quinoa dough and bargained for by the men as if they were real. Women sell small quantities of bread and other foods in similar ''play'' bargaining. The market lasts three or four days. The miniature bargaining takes only a few minutes. Then everyone eats the treats they have purchased, boiled tarwi (lupine seeds), roasted broad beans, cheese, and bread.

Source: *The Masked Media: Aymara Fiestas and Social Interaction in the Bolivian Highlands* by Hans C. Buechler. The Hague: Mouton, 1980, p. 60.

January 25

Burns Night

The birthday of Robert Burns has become a folk holiday among Scots. It is celebrated by groups of expatriates and those with Scottish ancestry throughout the world.

Scotland

A Burns Night supper

This day has become a patriotic festival wherever Scots live and now surpasses the St. Andrew's Day events. A supper may include "Powsowdie" (sheep's head broth), "Cabbie-claw" (wind-dried cod with horseradish and egg sauce), "Finnan Toasties" (smoked haddock), and, of course, will feature the "haggis" (a sheep's stomach stuffed with minced mutton, oatmeal, and spices and boiled). The haggis is piped in and addressed in Burns's words

> "Fair fa' your honest sonsie face
> Great chieftain o' the pudden race. . .".

Source: *The Customs and Ceremonies of Britain* by Charles Kightly. London: Thames and Hudson, 1986, pp. 62-63.

Last Tuesday in January

Up Helly Aa

Shetland Islands

Celebrating the end of winter

More than a thousand years ago Norsemen pillaged and colonized the Shetland Islands, Scotland's most northern domain. The spirit of those adventurers lives today in the festival of Up Helly Aa, held each year at Lerwick, the island's capital. On the last Tuesday of January bands of costumed guizers, or mummers, celebrating the approaching end of winter, march in a torchlight parade, fire a Viking ship and revel in the manner of their Nordic forebears.

Tradition requires that guizers attending parties remain masked until their identity is disclosed. While still unknown they indulge in the "aff-lay," a humorous commentary on public events and Lerwick people, not sparing themselves. Costumes may be fashioned to suggest any event in history or even an item in Shetland gossip. Once used, they may never be worn again for Up Helly Aa. These masks create intake problems for hungry, thirsty mummers.

Guizer squads are honor bound to visit all open halls and restaurants hired for the occasion. Each group presents a skit; indulges in the aff-lay; dances Highland reels, schottisches, and waltzes; and partakes of the feast.

With many a laugh the revelers recall the jokes in the Bill, a posted proclamation that pries good-humoredly into Lerwick's private lives. Having eaten and danced its fill, each squad cheers its hosts and passes on to another establishment. In 1953, fifty squads made the rounds.

By 5 or 6 in the morning even the sturdiest feet are weary and the brightest eyes are bleary. As the final squad concludes its show, everyone sings "Auld Lang Syne."

Then the old folks climb into bed while the young troop out to watch the sun come up over the sea. Soon they, too, will be asleep, and Up Helly Aa, the strange festival recalling the lusty days of the Norsemen, will be gone for another year. Happily, the day following Up Helly Aa is always a holiday in Lerwick.

Torching the Viking galley

When the galley reaches its anchorage on Clickimin Loch, hundreds of torches trace paths across the night to the ship's side. Soon the flaming galley silhouettes the figures of guizers moving townward for a night of merrymaking.

The Up Helly Aa festival and its ceremonial use of fire evolved from the old Norse midwinter feast. The tradition of burning a ship echoes a Viking funeral rite of consigning to flames a long ship, together with its master and many of his possessions.

Originally the Shetlanders confined themselves to dragging burning tar barrels through Lerwick's streets. By 1874 public opinion and the courts had forbidden this practice, and the festival gradually achieved its present form.

Old rowboats once served as galleys. Now master carpenters build the 28-foot dragon ship and launch her on a billowy sea of canvas waves supported by a wheeled chassis.

The timbered vessel is often painted red, black, and gold. Shields of the galley's warrior-rowers add touches of heraldic splendor. The ram used to shatter enemy hulls projects from the bow. Mast, crow's-nest, and raven banner complete the picture.

A crimson hand mounted on a pole forward of the mast memorializes a fearless Viking leader.

Norse tradition gave to the jarl who first touched a new land all rights of loot, conquest, and colonization. Legend tells of two Viking ships that made landfall simultaneously. Rowing furiously, the crews neared shore in a dead heat.

Finally, with land only a few feet away and the galleys matching each other stroke for stroke, one jarl laid his left arm on the deck and cut off his hand with his sword. Seizing the severed hand, he hurled it ashore and claimed the land as his right. Thus the blood-red hand became a symbol of reckless valor.

Source: "Viking Festival in the Shetlands" by Karl W. Gullers in *The National Geographic Magazine*. December 1954. v. CVI, no. 6, pp. 853-859.

15th day, Shevat (January-February)

Tu Bi-Shevat

Tu Bi-Shevat developed in the 17th century. Ashkenazim ate fruits of the Land of Israel on this day. Sephardim created a ritual Seder in which 15 fruits and four glasses of wine were accompanied by readings from the Zohar and the Talmud. Known as the "New Year for Trees," this has become a day for planting trees in Israel. It was celebrated on January 30, 1991, and, in future years, on January 20 in 1992, and on February 6 in 1993.

Israel

The Jewish National Fund sponsors tree planting

In the Holy Land, trees are very important as they give shade in the hot climate, they provide food in the form of fruit, and they provide timber for building purposes. For over eighty years, Jews from all over the world have given small contributions to the Jewish National Fund, making it possible to plant millions of trees in Israel—to provide picnic areas and to develop land in the desert and on mountain tops. During the festival, schoolchildren, who are given saplings by this organization to plant, recite a special blessing as they place the roots of the saplings into the soil.

By observing this minor festival, Jews show their faith in the future and in the day when, as the Bible says, everyone will be able to sit under his own fig tree and be unafraid. Various types of fruit are eaten on this day. Some people try to eat as many as fifteen different kinds of fruit—equal in number to the date of the month—especially those fruits that they have not eaten before. A prayer is recited when a fruit is eaten for the first time in the season.

Source: *Holidays & Festivals: Jewish Festivals* by Reuben Turner. Vero Beach, Florida: Rourke, 1987, pp. 36-37.

For more on Tu Bi-Shevat see: "Tu Bi-Shevat" in *The Jewish Party Book* by Mae Shafter Rockland. New York: Schocken, 1978, pp. 153-159.

Month of Tagu, Days 1-4

Thingyan

Myanmar (formerly Burma)

Water-throwing and acts of merit

The word "*Thingyan*" is derived from Pali and Sanskrit words meaning to change and to transfer. The period of transition of the Sun from the asterism Revati in Meen to the Asterism Aswini in Mesh is designated "Thingyan."

This special Burmese festival falls in the Burmese month of Tagu. During this festival people throw clear or fragrant water on each other. This act is full of meaning. Since this is the height of summer, water is thrown in sport to cool the heat and also to cleanse away the grime of the old year.

During the Thingyan Buddhists perform such acts of merit as observing the precepts, cleansing pagodas and icons, washing the hair of elders with sap[on]aceous barks and pods and perfumed water, and cutting their nails. Charities are held for both fun and merit where people from the four quarters of the compass are offered traditional Burmese delicacies. Cattle and fish are also set free in the act of granting life.

Source: Embassy of the Union of Myanmar.

Thingyan festivities

. . . In Lord Buddha's time the royal Sakya family visited a beautiful lake during this season where they frolicked and splashed each other with water. Also, it is recorded in the *Glass Palace Chronicles* (Luce & Pe Maung Tin 1960) that a Pagan king, Narasihapte, the last of the Pagan dynasty in the eleventh century A.D., engaged in water throwing by enclosing the royal route from his palace to the bathing site while he and his maids of honor indulged in water frolics.

This lighthearted spirit characterizes the Thingyan Festival. The first day of the festival, a *kyo nay,* is primarily for children. Buddhists in Rangoon inaugurate the festival with a visit to the great Shwe Dagon Pagoda, glimmering gold with the early morning sun reflecting off its brilliant gold-leafed and diamond-studded spire. There they make offerings of jasmine, flowers, incense, fruit and rice to the many Buddha images within the Shwe Dagon complex. Then the first splashes occur as devotees ceremoniously bathe the images with scented water.

While devotees may remain in the pagoda reading Buddhist scriptures and praying, children outside begin spraying or pouring water on passersby and unfortunate vehicles. Vehicles mounted with floats for the main festivities are spared to be enjoyed later.

Early the next day, everyone joins in the water-throwing festivities. This is the day Tha-gya min (the King of the Nats) is believed to arrive, and the water throwing begins in earnest. Fire hydrants are opened and barrels of water line the streets. Groups of celebrants, usually boys against girls, alternate their attacks on one another while all receive a thorough drenching.

During these festivities, vehicles carrying dance and music troupes traverse the streets. These vehicles are not sprayed, nor are monks or those devotees who are fasting, distinguishable by their clothing and prayer beads.

Young people at the monasteries join the festivities on the third day. The games continue and some boys, captured by a girls' team, must suffer the humiliation of being bound and led around with soot smeared on their faces.

Another activity of the festival is a verbal contest known as *Thingyat,* in which one group hurls a one-line politically satirical or critical slogan at another group. That group then responds in kind. Some older Burmese find this practice a bit too invective, but the contest ends good-naturedly as one group concedes victory to the other.

The merrymaking concludes on the third night. Final water throwing takes place as drum orchestras beat a tempo, and prizes are awarded for the best float, best dancing, and best *Thingyat* rhymes. Some people do not sleep during this night, as the fourth day of the festival, *a tet nay,* marks the traditional Burmese New Year.

New Year's day is observed quietly by families. By this fourth day Tha-gya min has returned to his heavenly abode. Buddhists visit the pagoda to bathe the Buddha images again and offer new gold leaf to decorate the inside and outside of the pagoda. Then they return home and await the monks' visit to collect rice and supplies for the monastery. The festival closes with one final washing ceremony, the family hair washing. Burmese Buddhists believe that the noblest part of the body, the head, should be clean for the new year.

Source: *Southeast Asia: A Cultural Study Through Celebration* by Phil Scanlon, Jr. De Kalb, Ill.: Northern Illinois University, 1985, pp. 113-115.

Last Month, Last Day of Lunar Year

Ōmisoka

Japan

Preparing for the New Year

Now celebrated December 31, on this last day of the year, all preparation for New Year's celebrations must be completed and all debts of the old year paid. A special noodle dish is eaten by those who have settled all accounts and is followed by a hot bath and well-earned rest.

Ōmisoka, c. 1933

Ōmisoka, is the great accounting day of the year. There used to be three; the first at the time of the Boys' Festival, the second at the time of the Chrysanthemum Festival, (the fifth [day] of the fifth month and the ninth [day] of the ninth month,) but this December settlement day was the greatest of the year.

A popular feast on this night is the "*okake*" or the hot soup "thrown over" noodles, for the man who has settled all his "*kake*" or accounts. Many will borrow in order to settle (and there is a good deal of robbing Peter to pay Paul) but it does help many to save face and to approach the New Year with hope and a little sense of self-respect.

The housewife who has made all the preparations for the next three days can also enjoy this feast of "*kake.*" She has enough vegetables, for her family for three days as the stores will be closed. The *mochi* has been prepared in many forms. She has decorated the alcove with the two layers of *mochi* cakes, pink and white. Her flower arrangement is in place and is as handsome as she can afford, or she has prepared a set piece of the three congratulatory plants growing in one bowl, the *shōchikubai,* or pine, bamboo and plum. The front entrance has been prepared for the reception of the cards of the callers who do not come in. The side entrance is thoroughly cleansed to welcome the guests who are more intimate—those who come in to exchange greetings over *sake* cups.

The philanthropic minded have prepared many bowls of hot *zōni,* or *mochi,* soup to give to the beggars and the suffering ones of the city. . . .

Then the long night's work is ended and each person takes the final hot bath of the year, pays his or her respects to the rising sun and goes to bed, some to sleep until noon, others until the evening.

Source: *Japanese Festival And Calendar Lore* by William Hugh Erskine. Tokyo: Kyo Bun Kwan, 1933, pp. 148-149.

Moon 1, Days 1-15

The New Year

The New Year was traditionally celebrated on the first day of the first lunar moon. This moon officially begins with the first new moon after the sun enters Aquarius, which can occur between January 21 and February 9. In China this festival has been called the Spring Festival since 1911. Owing to the influence of the western calendar, some countries, such as Japan, now celebrate the New Year on January 1.

China (Pre-Revolutionary)

A New Year's feast in a wealthy Peking family, c. 1930

The dishes on this special occasion were well qualified to offset the cold: a pork shoulder, "red-cooked" in soy and wine to the quintessence of its flavor, of a succulence and aroma to whet the appetite; a whole chicken, baked in clay, to retain all its tenderness and delicacy; and a firepot, typical of northern China, in which all kinds of foods, specially prepared in the same shapes and sizes, are put into a broth. The pot has a central cone through which the heat rises from glowing charcoal underneath, and as the liquid simmers, everyone seated around the table, which is circular, puts his choice of ingredients into the pot. The food looks delicious even before it is cooked, for the chef lays out the plates as an artist composes a picture. Everything possible is round; shrimp balls, all kinds of meat and fish balls—as we say, "round for togetherness." Dried mushrooms, as subtle as truffles, steamed and seasoned, join transparent noodles (*fan-tzu*) and a variety of vegetables to add an infinite range to the aromas rising from the soup. Lotus seeds, steamed with dragon eye and dates, and simmered with dried *kuei-hua* flowers, from the Chinese wild olive, were traditional ingredients of the desserts.

As we drank the steaming broth, or tasted the textures and flavors of meats, mushrooms, the slippery transparency of the noodles contrasted with crisp winter cabbage or lotus root, we could turn our heads from time to time to see through the windows the snowflakes softly falling, which gave an added zest to the feast before us.

A large fish, cooked whole, glistening with sauce, and lying on its belly as though still swimming, now made its appearance; someone, doubtless, had had to break the ice to get it from the river. Of all the dishes, this was my particular favorite. The fish was first fried a little, then simmered with wine, soy sauce, a hint of garlic, ginger, scallions, and just enough water to make a sauce. The result was a dish of ambrosial delicacy. It also signaled that dinner was coming to an end.

After the feast we would sit up until midnight, watching with sleepy eyes the flickering of tall, splendid candles, *shousui*, for at the stroke of twelve we knew we would be one year older (the Chinese, like racehorses, are one year older at the first of the year, whatever the birth date may be). This custom is called *shou-sui* or "watching the year steal away." Firecrackers rent the air, for a happy New Year, or as some believed, to chase away evil spirits, as we were firmly and finally carried off to bed—some of us still awake in anticipation of the excitement of the coming morning.

My father, like all Chinese parents, used to hide money, wrapped up in red paper (*ya-sui ch'ien*) for the children to find on New Year's Day: inside each package; we found he had written a lucky adage and had put in a sprig of evergreen as well, as a good omen.

Source: *The Mandarin Way* by Cecilia Sun Yun Ching. Boston: Little, Brown & Co., 1974, pp. 9-10.

A silver dollar under the pillow

Each of us had a bowl of sweets from Mother and a silver dollar wrapped in red paper. We used to put the dollars under our pillows until the eighteenth day of the next month. When the New Year celebrations were over we gave the dollars to our nurse.

Red paper wishes, first day of the New Year

On the first day of the New Year we had to write a kindly wish on red paper so that the first words we wrote in the year were good ones. After that we had many good things to eat, and exhanged good wishes all round.

Source: *The Lotus Pool* by Chow Chung-cheng. New York: Appleton-Century Crofts, 1961, p. 46.

For more on New Year in Pre-Revolutionary China see: "The New Year's Festival" in *Chinese Festivals* by Wolfram Eberhard. New York: Henry Schuman, 1952, pp. 3-68. "Guardians of the Gate" in *Tales of a Chinese Grandmother* by Frances Carpenter. Garden City, New York: Doubleday, 1937, pp. 47-55. (Pasting up red papers and Guardian of the Gate pictures for New Year's.)

Hmong

Hmong New Year celebrations

The New Year Festival officially began on the first day of the waxing moon of the twelfth month of the year. More precisely, it began at the first cock's crowing of that day, which is about three in the morning. Unofficially, it commenced as close to that date as the demands of the harvest permitted.

The New Year Festival was the only Hmong religious ceremony shared by the entire community. As often as not, it included members of neighboring communities. It was the time for courting, a time when eligible bachelors and young Hmong maidens dressed in their finest clothes and when ball games were organized to bring couples together. It was a time for feasting and visiting friends, and in the better-off communities, for bull fights.

The fights were not between man and beast but between bulls. It was a sport the Hmong brought with them from China or, more properly, from Kweichow where buffalo rather than bulls are still used in the ceremonial combats. The fights were not to the death.

Usually the match ended when one bull turned tail and ran. If one bull was in danger of being seriously injured or even killed by the other, referees jumped in with long poles to separate the two beasts. In Kweichow, buffalo were specially raised for the sport and were larger and stronger than those yoked to the plow. There the fights were also a matter of considerable ceremony. Before the contest, the combatants, draped in red cloth and some with silver tips slipped onto their horns, were led around the arena, usually a cleared field, followed by a shaman beating a gong.

In addition to courting and bullfights, ritual sacrifices were performed to placate the spirits of the forest and field, to honor the house spirits, dead ancestors, and the souls of the living members of the family as well as the souls of the family's livestock. Shamans burned the jaws of the pigs that were given in payment for their services during the year so that the souls of the sacrificed animals could be reincarnated. It was a time to honor all beings living and dead, to show gratitude for whatever help they had given the family during the year or, if times had not been so good, to placate them in hopes that the new year would bring better fortune.

The festival lasted three days. And except for the time reserved for ritual sacrifices, during those three days Hmong, young and old, visited friends and relatives, ate and drank, and played games from dawn to dusk. It was a celebration looked forward to and warmly remembered.

Source: *Hmong: History of a People* by Keith Quincy. Cheney, Washington: Eastern Washington University, 1989, pp. 92-99.

Hong Kong

New Year's traditions observed, c. 1982

On this day everyone becomes a year older, as age is calculated by the year in which one was born, rather than from the actual date of birth. A special family dinner is held to celebrate the New Year. Parents give children red packets with "lucky money" inside. They may be tucked under the sleeping child's pillow at night. Children greet their parents formally on New Year's morning.

Traditionally the head of the family offered incense and paid respect to the family ancestors and their guardian spirits on New Year's Eve, then locked and sealed the doors of the house before midnight to keep out the evil spirits which roamed on this night. The thousands of firecrackers exploded were also effective in frightening away those spirits. At dawn the doors were reopened and the ancestors and guardians paid honor once more. On this morning The Kitchen God returned from his visit in Heaven.

New Year's prohibitions

No meat was eaten on New Year's Day, a symbolic act of renewal. No work, especially sweeping could be done for two days and no knives or scissors could be used. Hence all such work must be prepared ahead of time. Breaking or tearing things, or stumbling or falling were bad omens. Even words with bad meanings should not be spoken. And words which "sound like" the bad words must also be avoided!

Visiting

Families visit friends and relatives on this occasion. Children receive red packets of "lucky money" at the homes they visit. Any married person is expected to give a red packet to unmarried relatives or friends who greet them on this day.

The God of Wealth

Like the Kitchen God, the God of Wealth has a place in the traditional home. His presence is represented by a picture or a strip of red paper with his name scribed on it. On New Year's Eve children sell Wealth God pictures. On Day 2 of the New Year the new God of Wealth pictures replace the old.

The Lantern Festival in Hong Kong and the New Territories

In North China the New Year was celebrated with lantern processions, masked parades, and dragon dances. An annual children's lantern parade has been started recently in Hong Kong. In the New Territories lanterns are decorated and hung in the Ancestral Halls on this time. Any family bearing a son during the year brings a lantern to the Ancestral Hall. The clan men eat a special meal in the Ancestral Hall on this occasion.

Source: *Chinese Festivals in Hong Kong* by Joan Law and Barbara E. Ward. Hong Kong: A South China Morning Post Production, 1982, p. 8.

Japan

Oshōgatsu

Homes are decorated

Now celebrated January 1-15, Oshōgatsu extends for the first fifteen days of the New Year. Businesses are closed for the first three days. The home is thoroughly cleaned and all debts are paid before the New Year begins. Homes may be decorated with sacred straw ropes and pine boughs. Pyramids of *kagami mochi* are displayed on a mirror. Visitors are received and visits are made to friends and relatives. Gifts are given to servants and sent to friends. A special bonfire at the end of the fifteen days may burn the straw or pine decorations of the season.

Preparations, *mochi* making

During the last few days of the old year, then, the *mochi*-makers went from house to house, as they still do in country districts, carrying with them a wooden mortar, pestles, a portable fire-box, and a square wooden container in which the rice is steamed over a large kettle. The *mochi* rice is a specially glutinous kind, and when thoroughly steamed can be pounded into a stiff, rubbery dough which is then shaped into the large *kagami mochi* or into the various sweetened dumplings, *dango*. Two men do the pounding with the long-headed mallets; a third one shifts the sticky paste with strong, deft snatches. Occasionally he nurses his hands in a pail of water; the dough is extremely hot and has to be worked before it cools off, to get an evenly consistent *mochi*. A special chanty accompanies the cadenced movements of the trio, who are clad in clean if simple garb of white "shirt" and shorts, and with a cotton towel tied around the perspiring brow. The finished cakes are placed on a board liberally sprinkled with rice-flour.

Foremost among the New Year's decorations is the *sambō*, or raised tray of plain wood, with its *mochi* . . . cakes made of steamed and pounded glutinous rice. For New Year, an unusually large size is made; thick, perfectly circular disks with a rounded edge, flat underneath and only slightly convex on top. Because of their size, shape and white colour, these cakes are sometimes compared with the Moon, but on New Year more generally with a (round) Mirror, whence they are known as *kagami mochi*. . . .

Two *kagami mochi*, a larger one surmounted by a smaller one, "like parent and child," are placed on a clean white paper in the center of the *sambō* stand. After having been consecratingly "offered" to the *kami*, the arrangement is then exhibited in the *tokonoma* (alcove) of the main room, flanked by a vase containing the *shōchikubai* and backed by a *kakemono* with a lucky design.

Preparations, cleaning

It is quite logical that in view of the solemnity of the New Year, preparations for a proper celebration should be taken in hand long before. The 8th of December is still called Needle Day; it is time to go ahead with unfinished dresses, which simply must be ready by New Year; and sewing always needs looking ahead. . . . But it would be equally unfortunate to carry over into the new life-period any other kind of work not terminated, and worse still the dirt and breakage of the old life.

It was usual to renew or recover the home's *tatami* (mats) during the last part of the twelfth month, and to repaper sliding-doors and screens, so that the callers might be received in spotless surroundings. Where poverty prevailed, scrubbings and patches did the best they could to make the house more presentable.

For similar reasons of propriety all the paper charms and amulets which are pasted up in kitchen and sleeping quarters, byre and shed, should be removed and respectfully burned at the end of the year, and replaced by freshly obtained ones early in the new year. Various extra charms are also made use of during the festivities, to invigorate utensils and furniture, farming implements and fishermen's boats, and what not.

At last, when everything is spick and span and settled, a hot bath should be taken, and then one may go to bed, although, since the first rituals begin so early, most adults do not sleep at all during this "night of change." It is imperative to be up long before the first day breaks, so as to "welcome Luck." The wise men of old laid down that "one should rise at the hour of the Tiger, wash one's feet and hands, and don new clothes to meet the auspicious morn." Scrupulous cleanliness of home, dress and body, more than even of the spirit, was insisted upon by Shintoism as the base of all moral thought. While old dresses, to which so much "evil" may adhere, cannot entirely be discarded, the first day of the year should be welcomed in a *kimono* never worn before, or at least carefully taken apart, washed and sewn together again for the occasion. Also, "if one drinks *toso* at the hour of the Tiger on that day, he will be untouched by fevers through the year." We have already noted that the drinking of this *sake* is not only ceremonial but a recognized prophylactic, and it was advisable to have the first sip as early as possible. The hour of the Tiger was from 3 to 5 a.m., and was obviously particularly propitious because of the strength and courage of the animal whose emanation governed it.

New Year's Day activities

The New Year's day should be opened with propitiating prayers to the gods and the spirits of one's forefathers, before the domestic shrine. . . . The New Year being a fresh start in life, the people give thanks for past and pray for future boons, that their life may be blessed with greater prosperity and greater happiness than ever. Then, having done one's best to enlist the help of the supernatural beings, the rest of the day should be given over to amusements. Not even cooking should be done, there being enough cold dishes prepared beforehand. The very first day of the year must not be profaned by toil or drudgery, this is the "standard day" of the "standard month" that sets the pace for the rest of the year. It is a sacred day.

Many an hour will be spent by the girls and young women in playing battledore and shuttlecock, the New Year's game *par excellence*. The graceful, willowy movements of this youth, in their colourful, long-sleeved *kimono*, playing in groups and singing a ditty asking the wind not to interfere with the light, feathery thing, are a frequent theme with painters and wood-engravers, and the highly decorated *hagoita* alone—a stemmed quadrangle of light wood—is as recurrent a subject symbolical of this day. . . .

Small girls also bounce a ball to the accompaniment of a verselet, and a *temari* of compressed cotton, wound with coloured silks to form rainbow stripes, in turn covered with stitched patterns, is another emblem of the festival.

Not only the boys but also grown men flew kites, some of enormous size, all with the colourful imprint of some valiant figure or with an ideogram expressing luck. The kite, of variegated outlines in Japan, straining at its string is a symbol of ascendency which should further the boy's future. The spring wind which raises it is an auspicious wind. *Tako,* kite, also means "great happiness." Spinning-tops, of which there were a great variety, took the place of balls with the boys, teaching them that being active would keep them on their legs.

Both kites and tops are thus found in art. Of course many other games were indulged in; the festival was one of pure enjoyment, all thoughts of work and trouble being laid aside. But these four: battledore and ball, kite and spinning-top, are typical of the holiday.

New Year's visits

Friends will visit friends, and inferiors pay their respects to superiors; the calls are seldom long, because everyone has so many of them to make. To somewhat lessen the strain, visits to one's relatives and one's chiefs are spread over the first three days, divided according to precedence dictated by etiquette, while those to persons of less immediate concern may be made at any time within the first fortnight.

New Year's bells

The actual arrival of the new year is announced by the ringing of the Buddhist temple-bells, those enormous thimbles which are one of the wonders of bronze-casting. Struck by a horizontally suspended beam, their vibrations will travel over many miles, and the effect on the hearer is both powerful and weirdly compelling. Few sounds are more solemn than the mellow, booming tone of a Japanese temple-bell. Each of the one hundred and eight long-drawn peals of the *joya no kane,* the "year-end bell," of which the last one is struck on the point of midnight, subdues one of the thirty-six celestial and the seventy-two terrestrial Evil Influences, or the hundred and eight *klésa,* the Earthly Lusts.

New Year's cards

Those not so intimate with a family are allowed to leave their card at the entrance, without the formality of a personal interview. A fine tray or bowl is set in a conspicuous place in the *genkan,* the "hall," left wide open on these days—on a red mat, backed by a golden or painted screen, with the pine vase near it. The written greetings dispatched to friends and patrons at greater distance—the *nengajō*—are equally a very ancient custom, and during the later Tokugawa era developed into those most effectful *surimono* which now form the delight of the collector. These "printed (or "rubbed") things," smaller than the regular *ukiyoe* and on thicker paper, apart from gorgeous colour combinations made lavish use of all the technical *raffinements* of the block-printer, such as relief impressions and the sprinkling of gold and silver powder. Unlike the common prints, *surimono* were made to order and for private circulation alone. They generally served for only one New Year, whose features (cyclical animal and so forth) were usually embodied in its auspicious design, accompanied by a congratulatory inscription.

Second day of the first month, Shigoto Hajime

. . . Principally the second day of the first month was dedicated to a ritual commencement of one's arts or crafts or favourite pursuit. Craftsmen used their tools for a few moments to ensure that their hand and eye be strong and true during the ensuing twelve months, and the women sewed a little—just enough not to make it appear as "work." Artists and *littérateurs* took in hand their brushes "for the first time"; dancers and musicians had their *hatsugeiko,* "first accomplishment." It is still important that the children write a few lucky characters or some famous verses with a new brush on clean white or coloured papers, in the very best style they know. This *kakizome,* the first writing, will ensure learning, especially also a beautiful calligraphy, which in this country is even more highly appreciated than painting. Practicing anything on the second day is presumed to help in attaining perfection, and the success in any enterprise was popularly believed to depend on how well it was begun on this day.

First dream, second night of the year

A most momentous omen was therefore the *hatsuyume,* the first dream, dreamt on the night of the second day. It is said that this night was chosen in preference to the very first one because the slumbers of the New Year's day might be unpleasantly affected by the conviviality enjoyed all day long. . . . In fact, most people on that evening are so "full of spirit" that they will hardly be able to dream—or to remember what they have dreamt. On the evening of the second day the streets were enlivened by shouting sellers of "*Otakara! otakara!*," pictures of the Boat of Luck, the *takarabune,* which is expected to come into port on New Year's day. The dragon- or phoenix-headed vessel is heavily laden with *takaramono,* "treasure things" like the Seven Precious Jewels (*shippō*), bags of rice, gold coins and vermillion coral, or the *shichifukujin* themselves, the Seven Gods of Luck, may sit in it. To dream of this boat will make one happy and wealthy "beyond all dreams"; the paper talisman, placed in the pillow, will exert its good influence. When in the morning each one recounts his or her dream, some old crone is able to give the "correct" interpretation, which will rarely be a disagreeable one on this important advent.

Source: *The Five Sacred Festivals of Ancient Japan* by U.A. Casal. Rutland, Vermont: Charles E. Tuttle in cooperation with Sophia University, Tokyo, 1967, pp. 13-14, 20, 24-25, 27-29.

New Year's celebrations in a nineteenth century Nagaoka home

The first seven days of the first month were the important holidays of the Japanese year. Men in pleated skirts and crest coats made greeting calls on the families of their friends, where they were received by hostesses in ceremonious garments who entertained them with most elaborate and especial New Year dishes; little boys held exciting battles in the sky with wonderful painted kites having knives fastened to their pulling cords; girls in new sashes tossed gay, feathery shuttlecocks back and forth or played poem cards with their brothers and brothers' friends, in the only social gatherings of the year where boys and girls met together. Even babies had a part in this holiday time, for each wee one had another birthday on New Year's Day—thus suddenly being ushered into its second year before the first had scarcely begun.

***Mochi* making**

With the hot smell of steaming rice and the "Ton-g—click! Ton-g—click!" of *mochi*-pounding were mingled the voices of Jiya and Ishi in the old song, "The Mouse in the House of Plenty," which always accompanies the making of the oldest food of Japan—the rice-dough called *mochi*.

"We are the messengers of the Good-luck god,
The merry messengers.
We're a hundred years old, yet never have heard
The fearful cry of cat;
For we're the messengers of the Good-luck god,
The merry messengers."

Bean tossing to chase off demons

About two days before New Year, Ishi came into the kitchen looking for me. I was sitting on a mat with Taki, who was here to help for New Year time, and we were picking out round beans from a pile in a low, flat basket. They were the "stones of health" with which the demons of evil were to be pelted and chased away on New Year's Eve. Jiya, in ceremonious dress, would scatter them through the house, closely followed by Taki, Ishi, and Toshi, with Sister and Etsu-bo running after, all vigorously sweeping, pushing, tossing, and throwing; and while the rolling beans went flying across the porches into the garden or on to the walks, our high-pitched voices would merrily sing, over and over:

"Good luck within!
Evil, go out! Out!"

New Year's market

The sidewalk panels were down in some places, just like summer time, and the shops seemed very light with the sky showing. On each side of every doorway stood a pine tree, and stretched above was a Shinto rope with its ragged tufts and dangling zig-zag papers. Most of the shops on that street were small, with open fronts, and we could plainly see the sloping tiers of shelves laden with all the bright attractions of the season. . . . a display of large kites painted with dragons and actors' masks that would look truly fearful gazing down from the sky. In some places young girls were gathered about shops whose shelves held rows of wooden clogs with bright-coloured toe-thongs; or where, beneath low eaves, swung long straw cones struck full of New Year hairpins, gay with pine leaves and plum blossoms. There were, or course, many shops which sold painted battledores and long split sticks holding rows of five or ten feathery shuttlecocks of all colours. The biggest crowds of all were in front of these shops, for nobody was too poor or too busy to play *hane* on New Year days.

New Year's visits

Notwithstanding our quiet house, the first three days of the New Year Mother was pretty busy receiving calls from our men kinsfolk and family friends. They were entertained with every-vegetable soup, with *miso*-stuffed salmon, fried bean-curd, seaweed of a certain kind, and frozen gelatin. *Mochi,* as a matter of course, was in everything, for mochi meant "happy congratulations" and was indispensable to every house during New Year holidays. With the food was served a rice-wine called *toso-sake,* which was rarely used except on certain natal occasions and at New Year time. Toso means "fountain of youth," and its significance is that with the new year, a new life begins.

The following days were more informal. Old retainers and old servants called to pay respect, and always on one day during the season Mother entertained all the servants of the house. They would gather in the large living room, dressed in their best clothes. Then little lacquer tables with our dishes laden with New Year dainties were brought in and the rice served by Sister and myself. Even Mother helped. There were Taki, Ishi, Toshi, and Kin, with Jiya and two menservants, and all behaved with great ceremony.

Removing pines on the eighth day

The pleasant days of New Year barely lasted through the holidays. We usually left the *mochi* cakes on the *tokonoma* until the fifteenth, but it was everywhere the custom to remove the pines from the gateways on the morning of the eighth day. There was a tradition (which nobody believed, however) that during the seventh night the trees sink into the earth, leaving only the tips visible above the ground.

Source: *A Daughter of the Samurai* by Etsu Inagaki Sugimoto. Rutland, Vt.: Charles E. Tuttle, 1924, c.1966, pp. 47-52.

Children's games at New Year

Breakfast over and the sun really up, still there was no time to waste. Callers would soon begin to arrive, as the earlier the call the greater the honor. Aunt Sui daintily held up her ceremonial kimono and went into the kitchen to direct the maids. Ryoko polished with silk napkins the lacquer trays, cups, bowls, and plates, while Mother folded sheets of white paper into the good-luck "flying goose" shape and placed one on each little plate. Then she artistically arranged on each a few sugar cakes shaped like sprays of pine, bamboo, and plum.

Kimiko and I, being the "children" of the home, ran out into the garden with battledores, and soon our voices were keeping time to the "tap-tap" of flying shuttlecocks as we sang the merry little counting song:

> "Single One! Double Two!
> And Three!
> Four is my—"

We suddenly stopped, for there was a great commotion of children's voices on the other side of the tall hedge, interspersed with laughing and the clatter of wooden shoes with their hidden bells. Then came a sing-song of many voices:

> "Let's begin! sa-sa SA!"
> "Let's begin! sa-sa SA!"

"They are bouncing balls. Come!" said Kimiko, running to the hedge. We found peep holes and through mine I saw eight or ten little girls standing in an irregular circle, all bouncing bright silk-wound balls. All wore big-flowered kimonos and gay sashes, and all black heads were bobbed and banged.

Up-down—up-down—went swiftly moving hands in the midst of gay flying sleeves. Thump! thump! went the balls as they flew between hands and ground. I never saw a prettier sight! And the song was one I had not heard for over ten years! My feet danced as my hands struck at imaginary balls and I could scarcely keep my voice quiet.

> "One! Two! Three! Four!
> Three sparrows chased by a pigeon.
> The sparrows cried, 'chiu-chiu! chiu-chiu!'
> The pigeons replied, 'po-po! po-po!'
> And the ball counts a hundred."

New Year's time called "Within the Pine"

"Tell me the meaning of 'Within the Pine.' "

"Yes. That is a good plan," Mother replied. "Well you know that at New Year's time all the houses, whether rich or humble, have pine trees standing like sentinels on either side of the gate, and stretched above is a ragged straw rope with strips of zigzag papers hanging from it here and there. These represent certain incidents in the lives of our long-ago ancestors, and since ancient times we have placed them at our gates as an expression of gratitude and loyalty."

"I thought they were just symbols of good luck," I said.

"People usually speak of them in that careless way," said Mother. "Ideals are often lost in superstition, so gradually the decorations themselves have come to be looked upon as being a protection from evil. But we Japanese are a trusting people, and I think no one ever plants a pine tree at the gate or stretches a straw rope between the posts with fear of anything. It is only to remind us of our duty to be loyal to our ancestors and the country which they founded for us."

Source: *Chiyo's Return* by Chiyono Sugimoto Kiyooka. Garden City, N.Y.: Doubleday, Doran & Co., 1936, pp. 239-240.

Temple visits (New Year's c. 1933)

The *EHO-HAI* is the first duty of the New Year and while it is by some attended to at dawn, by others it becomes the duty of first importance after getting dressed for the day. It consists of visiting that shrine or temple which stands in the lucky direction for the year. The directions change yearly, but one can always find one of his denomination, either shrine or temple, in the lucky direction. The National Shrines are mostly used but the Temples of *Fudō,* the Seven Gods of Fortune, the *Hachiman* and *Inari* have their devotees.

There are three New Year Holidays of national importance; the *Shihōhai,* the *Genshisai,* and the *Shinnen Enkai.* It used to be the custom to have a week of holidays, but since the banking world could not stand the strain of such long inactivity in the money market, the days offically set apart as New Year Holidays are the first, third and fifth, named respectively as above. Banks are closed on these three days but not on the second and fourth unless they should fall on Sundays.

The *SHIHOO-HAI* is the worship of the Four Directions and is connected with Ancestor Worship and "*Amaterasu Omikami.*" This consists of an impressive ceremony very early in the morning of the first day of the year, wherein the Emperor, as the High Priest of the Nation, performs, first, his purification known as the "*Hatsu-mizu*" or "first cleansing," in which he throws dippers of cold water over his naked body. Then follows his obeisance before the three sacred and holy places in the worship hall of the Palace.

In every home a similar ceremony takes place before the Shintoist's God-shelf and the ancestral tablets, or before the altar or *Butsudan* of the Buddhist. The offerings of pink and white rice-*mochi,* known as "looking-glass *mochi,*" and fruits are offered to the ancestors, also many other things their dead enjoyed, at the New Year's feasts, such as "*ozōni*" or "*Azuki-zōni.*"

Home decoration

The flower arrangement for the New Year Season is the one known as *Sho-chiku-bai;* pine, bamboo, and plum. These three are arranged on a tray as miniature plants and not as cut flowers. One of the most acceptable New Year gifts is a tray arranged with its "*sho-chiku-bai*" and all the happy and and congratulatory meaning which it carries with it.

Every home in the street has been cleaned throughout and at the gate there stands a decoration of bamboo (signifying adjustability), pine branches (signifying unchangebleness), and, artfully twisted and festooned over the gateway, the *shimenawa* (strong ties), which is a straw rope stuck with white paper, and with an orange in the center (signifying pure and round). The entrance has been scrubbed and strewn with salt to purify, and all this adds to the beauty and significance of the occasion.

Source: *Japanese Festival and Calendar Lore* by William Hugh Erskine. Tokyo: Kyo Bun Kwan, 1933, pp. 23, 26.

Daruma Ichi, January 2-6

Daruma Ichi. Stalls are set up at temples all over the country selling good luck *daruma* dolls. An especially good stall area is at Hajima Daishi Temple in Tokyo. The *daruma* dolls have no eyes painted in. The custom is to paint in one eye and make a wish. If it comes true, then the other eye is painted in.

Source: *Japan Handbook* by J. D. Bisignani. Chico, Calif.: Moon Publications, 1983, p. 72.

The New Year's fish, early twentieth century

. . .[A]t New Year most families bought one salted salmon, though only after an awful fuss. Toward the end of December fish sellers used to come up to the village with large baskets on their backs (if they were women) or buckets hanging from a yoke (if they were men). They knew roughly which families bought from them each year, so they'd go along and show the whole household what they had to offer. "This salmon's nice and big," they'd say, "but it's a bit on the pricey side. Here's a smaller one—I can let you have that fairly cheap," and so on. The whole family would crowd around to have a look, and together they'd eventually decide which one they wanted.

The salmon was then hung from a lintel in the kitchen till the first of January. And every day till then, when I walked past and saw the thing hanging there, I'd get more and more impatient. When the fish was finally served up, not a thing was wasted: the head was boiled with soybeans for several hours and eaten, and even the bones were edible if you cooked them long enough in the same way. In the end we ate the whole fish—tail, bones, and all. We used to say that even the fish must've felt its life had meant something, it being polished off so thoroughly.

Source: "Country Food" by Mr. Orinosuke Ihara in *Memories of Silk and Straw: A Self-Portrait of Small-Town Japan* by Dr. Junichi Saga. Tokyo: Kodansha, 1987, p. 189.

O-Sechi dishes to celebrate the New Year

New Year is one of the most important celebrations of the year for the Japanese family and a whole range of special dishes including o-sechi, rice cakes and o-toso (sweet rice wine) have become associated with the festivities. Cooked beans and tangle, grilled salmon and sea bream have become indispensable parts of the New Year menu.

Since entertaining guests is part of the New Year tradition, it has become the custom for housewives to prepare O-sechi dishes in advance so they can be used over the first few days of the New Year. In this way, the lady of the house can be free to enjoy the company of her guests away from the kitchen.

DEEP-FRIED RICE CAKE SOUP

Ingredients (to serve 4)

4 blocks pounded rice cake (mochi)
4 Japanese mushrooms
3 cups broth
150 grams chicken
Yuzu peel
8 sprigs watercress
Salad oil

Directions

1 Cut the watercress, chicken and mushrooms into 4cm lengths.

2 Boil the chicken and mushrooms in the broth. Add seasoning to taste.

3 Deep-fry the rice cakes over medium heat until they are brown.

4 Place the watercress in the broth, bring to boil again and turn off the heat. Place 1 rice cake in each bowl and pour soup over it. Garnish with the yuzu peel.

JAPANESE STYLE ROAST BEEF

Ingredients (to serve 4)

600 grams of beef loin of fillet
1 onion
1 small piece of garlic
1/2 cup soy sauce
2 tablespoons sake
2 tablespoons mirin

Directions

1 Select a piece of beef that is thin and long; about 10cms in diameter is best.

2 Grate the onion and garlic and mix with the soy sauce, mirin and sake. Place the beef in the mixture and allow to stand for about an hour.

3 Place in a high temperature oven to brown for about 20-25 minutes. Remove the beef from the oven and turn off the heat. Then replace the beef and leave for another 20 minutes. The same can be done in a pan or griller by wrapping the meat in foil after it has been browned and then returning to the warm pan or grill. Slice and serve.

Source: *A Taste of Japan* edited by Itsuko Hamada. Japan Air Lines Co., Ltd., 1986, p. 89.

January 2 sale, an early twentieth-century memory

On January 2 each year we held a grand sale—I can remember it as clearly as if it was only yesterday. My brothers and sisters and I all went to bed early on the evening of the first, and at midnight we'd be woken up by one of the shop boys running around the house shouting at the top of his voice, "The sale's starting, the sale's starting. Wake up, wake up." I'd rub the sleep out my eyes and force myself to get up. When I went downstairs the place would already be buzzing with excitement and the boys putting the final touch to things. Outside in the dark there'd be a bonfire burning; I could see the flames dance and spit in the freezing wind, and dozens of people around the fire, pushing and shoving, impatient with waiting for us to open.

Inside the shop were five or six hundred "lucky bags" stacked in piles reaching almost to the ceiling. Customers came from miles away to buy them. They only cost fifty sen each and were full of all sorts of odds and ends like scraps of belt material, slightly damaged underwear, hems for slips, waistcloths, smocks, aprons, and loose bits of cloth. The contents of the bags were worth anything between three and five yen at normal prices, so people would begin queuing outside from early in the evening on New Year's Day to make sure they didn't miss out on such a bargain. Many of them walked, or came by horse and cart, from villages up to ten or fifteen miles away.

Right through the morning the number of customers milling around gradually built up. The shop boys shouted and greeted them from every corner; it was like a fairground. It made our department stores today look very drab and boring.

Upstairs we'd put on sideshows to entertain the customers. In one of these a maid, dressed up in a sumptuous costume as the goddess Amaterasu, would suddenly emerge from behind a large rock. The audience loved it. . . .

Source: "The General Store" by Mrs. Iku Sato in *Memories of Silk and Straw: A Self-Portrait of Small-Town Japan* by Dr. Junichi Saga. Tokyo: Kodansha, 1987, pp. 106-107.

The Namahage (masked visitors) in Northeastern Japan

Animal-like sounds echo in the late snowy evening. It is New Year's Eve, the night the people in Oga Peninsula are visited by the Namahage. Young men disguised in masks and straw coats rush into a house. They search every room for new brides and children, whom they catch and pinch on the legs and thighs while roaring like animals. The masked visitors are received courteously by the household head and his wife, and are served sake and several dishes on wooden trays. After a short conversation with the host, the Namahage dash on to the next house, while one of the group stays behind long enough to receive either money or rice cakes from the wife of the household head.

The Namahage at Iinomori village, 1966

With shouts the Namahage rush to the house. The rest of the young men follow them, shouting and continuously banging on the entrance door. The Namahage remove their straw shoes and enter, their straw skirts making rustling noises as they move. Shouting constantly, they search for children, girls, and brides. "Are there naughty boys and girls in this house?" "Do they listen to their parents?" "Is there a cry-baby?" "Does the new bride (or new bridegroom) get up early in the morning or not?" (meaning is she or he diligent or not). "If she (or he) sleeps late in the morning, we'll do magic to her (him)" (meaning the Namahage will pinch the skin of idle persons). "Where is Yukiko (a single girl in the household)? Where did you hide her?" The Namahage know from their childhood experiences where the hiding places will be, but the children and others still try to outguess them. On the earth floor of the outer room of the house the followers shout and make other noises to encourage the Namahage inside the main part of the house to act violently.

The adults of the hamlet know who are going to be Namahage each year and may ask these young men ahead of time to teach a particular lesson to their children. The naughty boy may be forced by his parents to sit in front of the Namahage, or the parents may let the Namahage know his hiding place. The conversation is not always the same. There are no prescribed words to be said, only impromptu words instructing the children not to be idle and to behave well. The young men are familiar with the household gossip and refer to it in their conversations. If the head of the household is elderly, he will recover some of the composure he lost in the tumult and excitement of the Namahage's entrance and will ask rational questions. It is the role of the Namahage to answer these questions with as great a wit and rapidity as possible, taking time to think while shouting. A spontaneous conversation such as the following might occur:

> "What is your name, Mr. Namahage?"
> "My name is *Nabe no futa to te no suke*. Wa-aw."
> "I understand that the ice on Hachiro Lagoon is thinner this year. You must have had trouble crossing it."
> "Wa-aw, wa-aw. Yes. It was so difficult that we had to come by helicopter."

Hiding behind the large masks, but lifting them quickly to get a clear view, the Namahage search the entire house. As they go through the house, the wife of the head of the household tries to calm and distract the visitors so they will not find her children or grandchildren or break anything. She follows them carrying sake bottles and a cup in her hands and pleads, "Have a drink, first."

Until they become three or four years old, children are cuddled by grandparents and safely watch the masqueraders. Some boys after that age are told to stay with their parents to greet the visitors.

If the children and brides are found, they are pinched by the Namahage. Once all are out of their hiding places, the Namahage go to the room where the head of the household sits. The wife brings in a tray for each visitor. Although they are treated politely by the host, the masqueraders continue to shout in front of the trays. The host humbles himself and asks them to drink sake. The Namahage rarely touch the food they are offered, but drink the sake by quickly lifting their masks. It is said that the Namahage should always move and make noise. With a last burst of noise and a final search, they leave the house, repeating the lessons so that the children and brides will not fail to hear them. As they leave for another house, the bag carrier receives either money or rice cakes, wrapped in a sheet of paper with decoration. He places the gift in his bag and leaves immediately for the next house. The Namahage stay less than ten minutes, but their visit is accompanied by such tension that members of the household feel great relief when they leave.

The Namahage adjust their costumes on the street before the next visit, talk about the household they are approaching, and check the names of the children. Because of the festival, no other pedestrians walk about.

Source: *The Namahage: A Festival in the Northeast of Japan* by Yoshiko Yamamoto. Philadelphia: Institute for the Study of Human Issues, 1978, p. 9. See this study for a detailed discussion of the Namahage observance of 1966 and its social ramifications. The author also discusses the history of the Namahage tradition, which has died out in many places since World War II, and includes brief information on New Year's masked visitor traditions, Koshogatsu, from these regions: Kapakapa, Shinwa Village, Aomori; Chasengo, Miyagi; Suneka, Yoshihama Village, Iwate; Amamehagi, Murakami City, Niigata; Okatabuchi, Akemi Hamlet, Yamanashi; Hotohoto, Tottori; Kotokoto, Tokushima, Shikoku; Fukiyoshi, Kumamoto, Kyushu; Kayutsuri, Tosa Kami-gun, Kochi, Shikoku; Akamata-Kuromata, Yaeyama Islands, the Ryukyus.

Fortune-telling dreams on the night of January 2

For the 2[n]d of January Plum-blossom bought some pictures of the treasure-ship or ship of riches in which were seated the seven Gods of Wealth. It has been sung thus about this Ship of Luck:—

"Nagaki yo no,	It is a long night.
To no numuri no.	The gods of luck sleep.
Mina mé samé.	They all open their eyes.
Nami nori funé no.	They ride in a boat on the waves.
Oto no yoki kana."	The sound is pleasing!

These pictures they each tied on their pillow to bring lucky dreams. Great was the laughter in the morning when they related their dreams. Yoshi-san said he had dreamt he had a beautiful portmanteau full of nice foreign things, such as comforters, note-books, pencils, india-rubber, condensed milk, lama, wide-awakes, boots, and brass jewelry. Just as he opened it, everything vanished and he found only a torn fan, an odd chopstick, a horse's cast straw shoe, and a live crow.

New Year's games

. . .They spent most of the day playing with their pretty new battledores, striking with its plain side the airy little shuttlecock whose head is made of a black seed. All the while they sang a rhyme on the numbers up to ten:—

"Hitogo ni futa-go—mi-watashi yo me-go,
Itsu yoni musashi nan no yakushi,
Kokono-ya ja—to yo."

When tired of this fun, they would play with a ball made of paper and wadding evenly wound about with thread of silk of various colors. They sang to the throws a song which seems abrupt because some portions have probably fallen into disuse; it runs thus:—

"See opposite—see Shin-kawa! A very beautiful lady who is one of the daughters of a chief magistrate of Odawara-cho. She was married to a salt merchant. He was a man fond of display, and he thought how he would dress her this year. He said to the dyer, 'Please dye this brocade and the brocade for the middle dress into seven- or eight-fold dresses;' and the dyer said, 'I am a dyer, and therefore I will dye and stretch it. What pattern do you wish?' The merchant replied, 'The pattern of falling snow and broken twigs, and in the centre the curved bridge of Gojo.' "

Then to fill up the rhyme come the words, "Chokin, chokera, kokin, kokera," and the tale goes on: "Crossing this bridge the girl was struck here and there, and the tea-house girls laughed. Put out of countenance by this ridicule, she drowned herself in the river Karas, the body sunk, the hair floated. How full of grief the husband's heart—now the ball counts a hundred."

This they varied with another song:—

"One, two, three, four,
Grate hard charcoal, shave kiri wood;
Put in the pocket, the pocket is wet,
Kiyomadzu, on three yenoki trees
Were three sparrows, chased by a pigeon.
The sparrows said, 'Chiu, chiu,'
The pigeon said, 'po, po,'—now the
Ball counts a hundred."

The pocket referred to means the bottom of the long sleeve which is apt to trail and get wet when a child stoops at play. Kiyomadzu may mean a famous temple that bears that name. Sometimes they would simply count the turns and make a sort of game of forteiting and returning the number of rebounds kept up by each.

Yoshi-san had begun to think battledore and balls too girlish an amusement. He preferred flying his eagle or mask-like kite or playing at cards, verses, or lotteries. Sometimes he played a lively game with his father, in which the board is divided into squares and diagonals. On these move sixteen men held by one player and one large piece held by the second player. The point of the game is either that the holder of the sixteen pieces hedges the large piece so it . . . can make no move, or that the big piece takes all its adversaries. A take can only be made by the large piece when it finds a piece immediately on each side of it and a blank point beyond. Or he watched a party of several, with the pictured sheet of Japanese backgammon before them, write their names on slips of paper or wood, and throw in turn a die. The slips are placed on the pictures whose numbers correspond with the throw. At the next round, if the number thrown by the particular player is written on the picture, he finds directions as to which picture to move his slip backward or forward to. He may, however, find his throw a blank and have to remain at his place. The winning consists in reaching a certain picture. When tired of these quieter games, the strolling woman player on a guitar-like instrument, would be called in. Or, a party of Kangura boy performers afforded pastime by the quaint animal-like movements of the draped figure. He wears a huge grotesque scarlet mask on his head, and at times makes this monster appear to stretch out and draw in its neck by an unseen change in position of the mask from the head to the gradually extended and draped hand of the actor. The beat of a drum and the whistle of a bamboo flute formed the accompaniment to the dumb-show acting.

The fire-brigade performs

Yoshi-san thought the 4th and 5th days of January great fun, because loud shoutings were heard. Running in the direction of the sound, he found the men of a fire-brigade who had formed a procession to carry their new paper standard, bamboo ladders, paper lanterns, etc. This procession paused at intervals. Then the men steadied the ladder with their long fire-hooks, whilst an agile member of the bank mounted the erect ladder and performed gymnastics at the top. His performance concluded, he dismounted, and the march continued, the men as before yelling joyously, at the highest pitch of their voices.

Source: *Child-Life in Japan and Japanese Child Stories* by Mrs. M. Chaplin Ayrton. Boston: D. C. Heath, 1901, pp. 26-29.

For more information on the Japanese New Year see: "The Eighth Day Festival on Miyakejima" by William P. Malm, *Journal of American Folklore,* 76, no. 301, (1963), 195-205. Descriptions of the New Year's festival on a rural island. The Shinto festival is meant to ensure an abundant harvest in the coming year. Malm is particularly interested in the dance and music; some musical notation and a few black and white photographs are included. *The Five Sacred Festivals of Ancient Japan* by U. A. Casal. Rutland, Vermont: Charles E. Tuttle in cooperation with Sophia University, Tokyo, 1967. A 50-year resident of Japan, U. A. Casals offers detailed discussion of history and symbolism of Oshōgatsu, the New Year Festival. "Japanese New Year" in *Folklore of American Holidays* edited by Hennig Cohen and Tristram Potter Coffin. 2nd ed. Detroit: Gale Research, 1991.

Korea

Je-sok (Je-ya)

Defending the New Year

The most symbolic of all is Je-ya or Je-sok "New Year's Eve," the last day of the twelfth month by the lunar calendar. As the word suggests, the evening hours, dark with the moon hidden seem to contain some covert meaning. Hence, we may come to a conclusion that Koreans grope for meaning more in the dark than in the broad daylight of the sun.

At night people light torches [in] every corner of the house—the rooms, the yard, the kitchen, the barn, and the privy and so on—and sit up all night. We call this Su-se, meaning "defending the New Year." Lighting the torches is meant to keep away devils from man. A torch behind a pot on the cooking fireplace is for a god Jo-wang-shin. It is said that if you fall asleep on this particular day your eyebrows become grey. To prevent a misfortune like this, people try hard not to fall asleep killing time telling stories, playing yut or other interesting games. In case one fails to stay awake, others apply some flour on his eyebrows and, when he wakes up, tease him that he became old overnight. Nowadays citizens in Seoul stay up until midnight to listen to the Bells which ring thirty-three times on the New Year's Eve, and some attend mass on the day. This is modern Su-se.

Source: *Customs and Manners in Korea* by Chun Shin-yong. Seoul, Korea: Si-sa-yong-o-sa, Inc., 1982, pp. 37-38.

New Year's Day at home

New Year's Day is the greatest of all days in the Land of the Morning Calm. Adults wear newly ironed, snow-white clothes, and the children, many-colored garments. All get up very early and the women have already been busy preparing the dishes for the annual offering to the family ancestors.

With these dishes set on the table—fish on the east, meat on the west, fruits in front, rice and soup behind, drink on the foremost table and other dishes in their appropriate places, the annual ceremony begins. In well-to-do families this is performed in the family shrine, but in families where no such shrines are maintained, it is conducted in the living room or in the hall.

The male members of the house line up in front of the tables in order of seniority, and the head of the family conducts the ceremony in a most solemn manner. He is, indeed, this day, the chief priest, robed in a long snow-white "Dooroomagi" or overcoat (the Korean equivalent of a frock coat) and, if an old fashioned man, wearing a horsehair-net band around his forehead, and over it a horsehair hat (equivalent of a silk hat).

First he pours wine in the cups and then lays chopsticks on the meat and vegetables and spoons on the soup plates; the candles burn and flicker on each side of the table, and fumes curl up from the incense burner.

The whole company prostrate themselves, striking their heads three times against the floor. The candles flicker more furiously and cold winds sweep over the table and it seems as if the spirits really stoop down to the table and partake of the food.

When this ceremony is over, they remove the viands and have a merry breakfast themselves.

The women eat in a separate room. During the New Year's festivals from the first to the 15th of the First Moon, men and women, boys and girls wear new clothes. The elders remain at home and receive the younger generations and other visitors who bow before them (called "sebae"—the New Year prostrate bow in which the forehead touches the floor).

The younger people and children, after having finished the honors to their parents at home, call on elders, kinsmen and friends to perform the same ceremony, sometimes walking as far as 10 or 12 miles.

Mourners, however, do not make such visits until after the 15th of the moon, as they would be unwelcome and are not supposed to leave their own homes during the period of mourning.

The host usually entertains the adults with rice wine (sool), soup and meat, while rewarding the children with candy and fruits.

Ladies do not make New Year calls, but, in the middle and upper classes, dress up their maidservants and send them round between the third and 15th days of the First Moon as their representatives.

The New Year's food at each home varies according to its economic and social conditions, but New Year's soup (duggook) is universal, from prince to peasant. Its preparation is a complicated process.

First, the glutinous rice is steamed and placed on a large board where it is pounded with wooden hammers till it is like dough.

This doughy paste is kneaded and cut into pieces in the shape of small coins. The paste pieces are mixed with water, pheasant, chicken, meat, pinenuts, and chestnuts, and the whole stewed together till soft.

When the soup is ready, it is seasoned with soy and pepper before serving. This soup is a favorite dish of Koreans at all seasons, but that served on the New Year's Day is considered the best.

It is interesting to know that the Koreans drink cold ''sool'' (rice wine) on New Year's Day. It is warmed at other times.

Origin of the girls' seesawing

The Korean Lunar New Year comes in the season when the plum flowers bloom in the garden and snow flakes whirl in the air. When Koreans celebrate their New Year, the rosy-cheeked young girls play at see-saw.

Now low and now high, but in great glee, the fair players dressed in gay costumes, their hair in long plaits, throw their winning smiles above the garden walls, balancing with lithesome grace and swaying to the rhythm of their flying feet stamping on the wooden board, for in Korean see-saw the girls stand on the planks and are thrown into the air as a companion descends on the opposite end.

With the rising influence of Confucianism during the early Yi Dynasty men forsook most of the sterner kinds of sports and women were forbidden to have any outdoor exercises. Partly in sadness and partly in curiosity the girls adopted see-saw to gain a fleeting glimpse of their swains over the garden walls.

Thus see-saw became a sport of love instead of physical exercise. So deeply rooted in the hearts of young Korean women in this time-honored game that it is highly popular even today.

Playing yoot

New Year's Day is joyfully spent in banquets and rounds of visits. From the next day, holidays begin with different kinds of amusements, of which there are quite a number, and one of the most popular is ''yoot.''

''Yoot' is a game utilizing four wooden blocks, one side of each flat, and one side round, each measuring about six inches long and one inch in diameter. Smaller yoot, .6 of an inch long and .4 of an inch in diameter are used among farmers.

The players are divided into the home and visiting teams; each player throws the yoot two or three feet in the air letting the four pieces fall on a mat, with one of the five following results: One flat, three round; two flat two round; three flat one round; four flat or four round.

The first counts like a one-base hit in baseball, the second a two-bagger, the third a three-bagger, the fourth and fifth home runs. A diagram of a circle with diameters drawn on a mat is the game board, and, as each member of the two teams throws the yoot with a yell, his results advance a marble round the circle in a race to reach ''home'' first. Yoot is great fun. It is one of the special indoor games in Korea.

Lucky baskets

On New Year's Eve the basket peddlers cry all night long—'Jori sa! Bok jori sa!'' (meaning, Buy baskets! Buy lucky baskets!). No one sleeps during the night, for the superstition is: if one does not keep awake, the eyebrows will grow white.

The next morning housewives are busy hanging out these queer little bamboo baskets over the door or on the walls. In south Korea they hang up rakes in addition to baskets, as a sign for the good luck that will bring plenty of kindling wood to gather with the rake and plenty of grain to scoop with the baskets.

The actual use of these implements begins from the last day of the First Moon.

The ghost who tries on shoes

GHOST WARNING

Superstition reports that on the first night of the New Year, a ghost comes down from heaven, and tries every shoe in every house and goes away with the shoe best fitting him—now bad luck all the year will follow the person whose shoe is thus stolen. Therefore they stretch a straw rope across the gate to keep out the evil spirit, and hide all the shoes indoors. Everybody goes early to bed with lights out that night.

Source: *Customs and Manners in Korea* by Chun Shin-yong. Seoul, Korea: Si-sa-yong-o-sa, Inc., 1982, pp. 3-5.

Battles among the boys in 1910

At the turn of the year we celebrated the biggest family feast of my homeland. It began around midnight, when sacrifices were offered at the altars of our ancestors. Then we children were called into my mother's big room and regaled with the finest dishes and fruit; we could stay up as long as we pleased. Next morning, dressed in our best, we were sent out to pay New Year visits to all relatives and friends. The cold was severe, the roads were ice-bound and very slippery, a biting wind stung our faces, but, full of excitement and joy, we ran from house to house to give messages which we had learned by heart. Everywhere our hosts received us with words of kindness and offers of sweets and fruit. What a happy feast-day that was, when one heard only friendly and flattering words and was offered nothing but sweets to eat! At home, everybody, from grandmother down to Kuori, was in his best garments, all wore smiles throughout the day, and no one spoke an unpleasant word. Even rough Sunok, who lived with us as bailiff and always called me a good-for-nothing, proved cheerful and gentle that day and remarked that perhaps I might become a proper man one day after all. Everybody joked with us and gave us presents, and as we went to sleep late at night—for some time now Suam and I had shared a room—my mind became blissfully aware that there were still a whole fifteen days without lessons ahead. ''How beautiful the world is!'' I said to myself. But Suam was already snoring.

After the children, it was the turn of the adults to pay their calls. Numberless visitors—girls and women, young and old men—came to our house, which was filled with gaiety and laughter. In this way feast day followed feast day in unending succession.

While I lost count of time in this festive mood, Suam would quietly disappear in the evenings and return home very late. Among the boys New Year battles had begun, and he could not resist the temptation of taking part. His beautiful clothes bore traces of kicks and nose-bleeding which he attempted with great care to remove. One evening he returned in a terrible state. The two sleeves were half torn off and his head was bruised and swollen in many places. He told me that, when they had taken him prisoner, three hostile boys had beaten him until he was freed by a comrade. This experience seems to have cooled somewhat his ardor for battle; during the next few evenings he remained quietly at home, although the fighting became more violent than ever and the decision of the whole war was but a few days off.

Source: *The Yalu Flows: A Korean Childhood* by Mirok Li, Translated by H.A. Hammelmann, East Lansing, Michigan: The Michigan State University Press, 1956, 27-28.

Celebrations c. 1910

The third holiday is the greatest of all days throughout the Orient. The pulse of the nation automatically stops for fifteen days. During the entire twelfth month the housewives are busy laundering, making new clothing, and changing the paper in their houses. The men are busy clearing up all business transactions, paying all debts, and putting their house in order.

New Year's day is started bright and early with a very delicious soup in which is a particular delicacy called "mandoo." This is made of a thin wheat flour dough, with a highly seasoned meat and vegetable filling.

This time of the year is especially precious to the women of the land, for at no other time do they exchange dinner calls and perform other social duties. With an abundance of clean clothes and new clothes, with her house well in order, with the delicacies prepared as far as possible, she seems a new individual. She has put aside the burden of every-day routine and goes from house to house paying her calls, tasting of the sweetmeats of her friends, drinking in the freedom of each one of the fifteen days.

As one goes out into the streets, the only mass of color discernible during the year greets the eyes. Everywhere children are resplendent in bright silk padded coats with sleeves rivaling Joseph's, being fashioned of narrow strips of various colors. As the wind blows the coat back, the brilliant cerise vest peeps out and sometimes even the bright blue short-coat may be seen. On their heads are little helmet-shaped hoods with fur ear-laps and tail-pieces to protect their necks from the bitter winds of this season. This head-dress is embellished with much gay embroidery and with tiny round looking-glasses for the younger ones, and many gold ornaments for the wealthier class. Soft shades are unknown, so the colors are all very vivid and, at the time of year at which they are predominant, give a warmth to the general festivity. The hearts of the mothers are always glad when there is no snow at this time, for the colors are not fast and, after a hard storm, the costume is apt to take on the appearance of an artist's palette. The idea that the child should remain at home in bad weather, instead of calling, is one that would never enter the mind, the custom is so old.

Every household, during the week preceding New Year's day, has been busy wrapping money and pieces of jewelry, such as a chain, a charm, or an ornament for the head-dress, in colored paper. These packages are heaped in the outer waiting-room, the abundance depending upon the master's business status and the number of his friends. A man in moderate circumstances would have prepared at least a hundred such gifts. A similar heap fills a corner of the inner waiting-room which is used only by the women members of the family. These packages contain candies, fruits, and cakes, however. Now it is the custom for the children of the family, always accompanied by their fathers, to pay New Year greetings to every friend and business acquaintance. This visit is made at any time during the fifteen days. After arriving at a friend's house the son makes deep bows to the master, wishing him much joy and longevity. The master graciously acknowledges this and claps for a servant who presents the child with one of the packages from the corner. The little guest shows his gratitude by more deep bows. He is then led to the inner reception-room to greet the mistress of the house, while his father settles himself for a smoke and a short chat with his friend, for men may not enter the inner court with the exception of the immediate members of the family. The same deep bows are given and, again, a servant presents a gift. The presents are stuffed into one of the very large pockets of the vest, and the youngster is ready to go on to the next establishment. The circumference of children with the cotton-wadded clothes is already impressive, but with the four large pockets of the vest filled to overflowing, one can imagine the peculiar shapes seen upon the streets at this time of year.

This is the only time at which gifts are made especially to the children, and every one prides himself upon his generosity. The money and jewelry received by some little guests whose fathers have extensive business operations may reach a total of several hundred yen, a fact that is readily understood when it is remembered that Korean gold is always a pure twenty-four-carat metal without any alloy. Since the children always have some spending money at this time, energetic money-makers are apt to bring to the village such amusements as a side-show consisting of a monkey and a tiger, or acrobats whose chief feat consists of balancing themselves upon one another's shoulders, a marvel only to be seen at this time.

Throughout the Orient firecrackers and fireworks furnish a great deal of the excitement at this time. In very olden days, it was believed that the noise and bright flashes frightened away the evil spirits. This superstition no longer prevails, but the custom is one that adds gaiety and brightness, and so has withstood the test of centuries. The fund for the amusement is provided by the municipality or a benevolent person in the village who, you may be certain, becomes the beloved patriarch in the years following.

To this day, China is known the world over for her firecrackers and fireworks. The crackers are suspended in a string of from ten to fifty thousand in number and fired from the bottom. A bomb tops the string and its report terminates the fusillade. I remember particularly that, with the explosion of the bomb, a ball of fire would shoot into the sky and be transformed into the lighted shape of a man, a fish, or sometimes a lantern.

The boys amuse themselves on the ice with small sleds about eighteen inches square. They squat upon these singly, and, with a sharpened ice-pick in each hand to push themselves, go sailing down the rivers for miles with incredible speed. No top-driving impedes their progress, for Korea is one of the most seasonal countries known. The season for tops is before the holiday, and no boy would think of playing with them at any other time.

Just so, the girls jump on their seesaws at this time. The seesaws are like those in the States, but instead of sitting on the ends of the planks the girls stand on them. As one end goes down with the sudden weight of a youngster, the girl on the other end is tossed high into the air. The exercise is invigorating but daring, and it is hard to believe that these are the same quiet girls of the rest of the year.

New Year's foods

The food eaten at this time is of the best. The rice in every home is of flaky whiteness. At all other times, in the majority of homes, the rice is mixed with small red beans, green peas, millet, or larger beans, both for variation of taste and economy, but on the holidays the rice reigns alone in its glory of unbroken whiteness for every one. When one mentions rice in this country he simultaneously thinks of "kim-chee," a national dish without which no meal, however meager, is complete. The dish is a type of highly seasoned pickle which is made in every household just before the first frost. The side-dishes include delicious preparations of venison, pheasant, and wild boar, as well as the usual pork and beef.

Mounds of dainty little cakes which are made of rice or bean flour and covered with green or pink puffed rice, sesame seed, or peanuts, appear on every small table. On other brass stands is a candy made of barley flour and malt. The syrup is not pulled, but is cooked to the consistency at which it will hold its shape on being poured. A pulverized bean flour is made and round patties of the syrup poured into it; then nuts are pressed into the candies as they are lifted from the flour.

These sweets are accompanied by a delicious pale-amber drink, in which are floating several blanched pine-nuts. Pine-nuts of Korea are at least the dignified ancestors of those in the West; they are two to three times as large, with their shells as thick in comparison. The Diamond Mountains are famous the Orient over for scenery and for pine-nuts, and, in autumn, huge pine-cones can be purchased with the nuts in their original habitat. The pale-amber fluid is made of wild honey combined with a fruit juice. Bees have not been cultivated to any extent in the country and the universal sweetening agent in the household is wild honey, gathered from the hives found in the rocks. In a mountainous country covered with the greatest variety of wild flowers from early spring to very late autumn, it is possible to believe the flavor most delicious.

The fifteenth day of the New Year's celebration

And so the time passes quickly in feasting and visiting, and the fifteenth day, which marks the close of the festivities, comes all too soon. On this day each housewife prepares twelve kinds of dishes of vegetables, for it is said that one should eat nine different times. The moon is usually full and, as evening approaches, each family can be seen carrying its mats to the top of the nearest hill to watch it rise. Those who are farmers wish at this time for an abundant crop; those whose households have not yet been blessed by the advent of children wish for a son; those in poor health ask for good health. All these favors are asked of the moon whose beneficent powers cannot be sought after at any other time. As the moon rides higher, the worshippers turn towards their homes with a sigh; the holiday is over and, on the morrow, life must resume its ordinary tenor.

Source: *When I Was A Boy in Korea* by Ilhan New. Boston: Lothrop, Lee & Shepard Co., 1928, p. 85-94.

Mauritius

Spring festival

The Chinese New Year's Day, which every year falls on a different day because of the adjustment of lunar days to solar days, is preceded by a thorough spring-cleaning of the home. No scissors or knives are used on the day. Red, symbolic of happiness, is the dominant colour. Food is piled up to ensure abundance during the year, and the traditional wax cake is distributed to relatives and friends. Crackers are fired to ward off evil spirits.

Source: Embassy of Mauritius.

Okinawa

Shōgatsu

Preparing for the New Year

As in Japan, the New Year is preceded by house cleaning, bathing, and debt paying. A New Year's pig is killed. Visits are made on New Year's Day and the celebration continues for two days. On the third day, "Hachibaru" (Begin Farming), some token work is performed.

Shimenawa (rice straw ropes)

Before the war, these preparations were more elaborate than they are now. In Minatogawa, bamboo and pine poles with a rice straw rope (*shimenawa*) hanging across the top were placed at the compound entrance. The purpose was to scare off evil spirits and devils. A piece of charcoal wrapped in sea weed and an orange hung from the rice rope. This custom now is also rare in Matsuda.

Young water

In all the villages, the custom of new or young water (*wakamizu*) has survived. In Minatogawa, at 5 or 6 o'clock in the morning of the New Year, young children take fresh water in a tea pot to the homes of relatives. The new water is poured into a cup, placed on the Buddhist god shelf, or on the shelf of the fire god in the kitchen. The children are given Y5 or Y10 by the relatives, who are then supposed to stay young themselves. In Matsuda, new water is taken from a well early in the morning, and some is put on the god shelf. The first tea of the New Year is made with "young water".

A parent may also give a piece of pork with salt on it to his child announcing that he is now one year older. This custom is still observed, even though ages officially are now reckoned in the western manner.

In all the villages, the morning observances are family affairs; the public nature of the holiday is evident later. Tea and *sake* are placed in front of the ancestral tablets on the god shelf. A fresh kimono is put on and the offering is made before breakfast. Then the father takes the *sake* from the god shelf, offering sips first to his wife and then to the children.

Later there are visits to the place of the patron deity or first ancestor of the village (*ujigami*).

Source: *Studies of Okinawan Village Life* by Clarence J. Glacken. Scientific Investigations in the Ryukyu Islands (SIRI) Report #4. Washington D.C. Pacific Science Board. National Research Council, 1953, p. 322.

People's Republic of China

Spring festival in the city

Housewives begin to prepare food dishes two or three days ahead of time. Dumplings are a "must" in north China, of course. When all is prepared, one begins to decorate. Red, yellow-tasselled palace lanterns and streamers with couplets are hung on public buildings. Multi-colored displays and show windows attract the eye. Today the streamers generally carry only a few words, such as "Spring Festival" or "New Year". In the home people prefer flowers or lanterns. In 1981 Shanghai did an excellent business in narcissi and other flowers as well as silk lanterns, a symbol of good luck, according to a newspaper article on January 31.

On New Year's Eve everyone tries to be at home. When all the family is together, they usually exchange small presents. For the children there may be some new clothes, toys, sweets or a small sum of money. In old-fashioned families, there are presents for the older people as well, mostly gifts of food for the grandparents and the in-laws. Then comes the feast. In many families a big fish is set on the table, whole, to symbolize the unity of the family. People try to put the best of everything on the table for this occasion, depending on their means. I have noticed that many families then watch television programs until midnight, this having become a favored pastime. A variety of programs are shown, including athletic events and films for children. Or else one might see a play, an opera or some other stage performance. During the 1981 Spring Festival 166 performances of operas, plays, concerts, and ballets were given in Beijing, including 20 performances specifically for children.

The first day of the New Year is devoted to feasting and visiting relatives. On the second or third day friends and acquaintances visit and exchange good wishes.

In recent years stores do business even on holidays. Many people prefer to do their shopping then, for the stores are less crowded. The main occupation of the children is as always, setting off firecrackers.

In contrast to the old times the Spring Festival is now a true festival of joy. Debts, usurious rates of interests, and exorbitant rents need no longer be feared. There was a time when the peasants in Shandong considered it a good year when they could buy enough cloth to patch their old garments. Today every family in the countryside of Anhui Province slaughters a pig for the Spring Festival.

Source: *Chinese Traditional Festivals* by Marie-luise Latsch. Beijing, China: New World Press, 1984, pp. 34-35.

Spring Festival in Upper Felicity village, Honan Province

For several weeks before the three-day Spring Festival the propaganda workers of the commune were urging us to celebrate it in revolutionary style. All agreed that its good features should be retained, but any features linked with feudal superstition, bad customs, and habits, such as wastefulness, drunkenness, gambling, and laziness, must be resolutely rejected.

. . . "Don't give wasteful feasts and presents. Don't drink or play cards or mah-jongg [once the most notorious gambling game in China and the ruin of many families]. Don't let off firecrackers or fireworks late at night. Don't laze around and go visiting after the third day of the three-day holiday, but get back promptly to work. Don't visit the ancestral graves to pray and offer sacrifices even of paper tokens or incense and don't let the children kowtow to the elders."

On the eve of the festival, every house in the hamlet was cleaned up. Many put up new portraits of Chairman Mao and new New Year pictures (*nien hwa*), and all pasted new red slogans on and around their doors. I was one of a group of cadres that went to all the households with menfolk in the People's Liberation Army or who had fought in the war to aid Korea repel the invading U.S. forces led by MacArthur. We brought them festival greetings and Chairman Mao badges and portraits and pasted up new red slogans on their doors: two long strips on either doorpost and one over the lintel. Some of these read: "Long live the Chinese Communist Party!" "Long live Chairman Mao!" and "Long live the People's Commune!" Some carried the current popular slogans, quotations from Chairman Mao: "Be self-reliant" and "Serve the people"; "Concern yourself with state affairs; carry the Great Proletarian Revolution through to the end!" On the two door panels we pasted larger rectangular pieces of red paper with longer quotations from Chairman Mao printed on them: "The basic task in political work is constantly to imbue the peasant masses with socialist ideology and to criticize the tendency towards capitalism." Or one short slogan in larger letters, like "Never forget the class struggle!"

On the first day of the festival everyone in the hamlet ate *chiaotze*. Until late the previous night we had heard the tap, tap, tap of the choppers cutting up the meat and vegetables. Upper Felicity ate *chiaotze* at every festival. After the meal there was general visiting. Our cottage was rarely empty. It was open house, and the children swarmed in to see my drawings and be treated to sweets. Their elders came to offer greetings and could usually be prevailed upon to stay for a smoke and a chat.

In the afternoon a performance was put on at the big threshing floor near the tractor repair workshop. Hundreds of members came in from all over the commune. A temporary stage had been built, and the commune's concert troupe gave a performance of songs, dances, and sketches. Many of the songs were quotations from Chairman Mao's works set to music. Practically everybody blossomed out in new clothes. Some wore new things from top to toe, especially the children. Nearly everyone wore a badge with the Chairman's portrait on it and the children sported large red plastic rosettes. The little girls had rouged faces, a round smudge of cochineal on each cheek and four dots placed in a square on their foreheads. The older girls were a pretty sight in bright-colored hair ribbons. Many dropped in to see us on their way to the show. It was quite in order to offer cigarettes to the men and sweets to the women and children, but that was as far as hospitality should go. In Peking we would have served wine.

The second day of the festival was family visiting day. The married women took their children to see their maternal grandmothers. Sometimes their menfolk accompanied them. Quite a number of family parties went out from our hamlet. Often the mother sat with the wee ones in a handcart pulled by the father or the older boys. Ren Ming-fan, a pretty young mother who lived four courtyards away from us, was excited to be able to introduce her husband, a railway worker who lived in the provincial capital and had got Spring Festival leave to pay a visit home. This was a time when, as for ages past, every Chinese household tried to renew the ties of family.

Many other young men working elsewhere came home for the festival. Not a few came from hundreds of miles away. They all brought gifts for the folks at home and made the festival full of gaiety with interesting talk of other places. Most had a holiday leave of a week or a fortnight, and some who had saved up their leave were able to stay longer.

On this second day of the festival several activists were already back at work in the fields, and on the third day they were joined by more enthusiasts and the boys and girls from the school.

Only a few of the older people went to tend their ancestral graves. Though held down at first by the stones or clods of earth they placed on them, the squares of white votive paper they had put on the grave mounds were soon torn away by the wind, or fading, became an indistinguishable part of the brown-yellow earth around them.

Source: *A Year in Upper Felicity: Life in a Chinese Village During the Cultural Revolution* by Jack Chen. New York: Macmillan, 1973, pp. 146-151. (British citizen Jack Chen lived for a year in this commune.)

Recipes from a Liu Ling village peasant woman

For the New Year I make salt patties of 'sticky millet'. I leave the 'sticky millet' soaking overnight, pound and steam it. Then I make a filling of potato and salt or grated carrots and salt; this filling is given a quick fry, stirring strongly. I roll out the dough and make it into patties with the salty mass as filling. Then I fry the patties in oil. If you want to make sweet patties, you do just the same, but fill them with pumpkin and sugar or beans and sugar. This filling is fried just the same as the salt filling, and the patties are made in the same way. Children like them. If you want to make 'sticky millet' cakes, the recipe is basically the same, but you don't use any filling and the dough is fried in oil as square cakes. They can be eaten with sugar or with gruel or how you like.

Bean curd is made for the New Year. I take some black beans and let them stand in water overnight. Then I peel them and grind them. I put the pulp in a piece of cloth and squeeze out the water. Then I boil them up in a pot, then I put in a little soda, which makes it like jelly. Then I put in a cloth again and press it till it becomes quite hard. Then I cut it into bits and fry or boil them and serve.

You can also divide the year by the festivals. I'm still speaking of the moon year. We haven't anything to do with the sun year. We butcher our pig and goats for the New Year festival. Then we make millet cakes and 'Chinese bean pudding'. We eat dumplings filled with pork and lots of other things. Then we go visiting, and our neighbours come to see us, and, on New Year's Day, everyone eats until you can't squeeze another bit of food down. We drink home-made wine and spirits from the shop. We paste paper cut-outs on the paper windows of the cave. My sister does that. She is clever at that sort of thing. We fix up verses beside the door, but I can't read those, because I can't read.

On these feast days the men go to work as usual and the women stay at home in the caves to prepare the food. Otherwise, we eat the same things the whole year round. Millet is our main food; we cook it in various ways. Mostly, though, we eat it as porridge. We have meat at the New Year. We have a proper meat meal then; afterwards we salt down the rest of the pig and use a bit for each of the festivals when one eats meat. Sometimes, if we have guests, we will buy meat in the market and make something. This year we must have had meat three or four times in addition to the festivals. Vegetables we have according to the season. We don't grow tobacco. My husband does not smoke.

Source: *Report from a Chinese Village* by Jan Myrdal. New York: Pantheon, 1965, p. 234.

Taiwan

Sang-Sin

"Seeing off the gods"

Celebrations begin with "Seeing Off the Gods" on the twenty-fourth day of the twelfth lunar month and continue through the Feast of Lanterns on the fifteenth day of the first month. At the close of the year the household deities are required to go to heaven and report to the Jade Emperor on the activities of the mortals.

Legend of the first New Year's feast

. . . [A] popular Taiwan folk story, which can be bought on the street, and is retold by many a temple story-teller, recounts how once long ago a household deity was offended and reported to heaven that all mankind should be destroyed. But before the Jade Emperor could issue an imperial edict to destroy the world, the other gods went up to heaven and memorialized the throne that men were after all[,] quite filial, and the Jade Emperor should hold off the edict until in an imperial progress down to earth, he could see for himself the virtue of men and the reverence they paid to the spirits and heaven.

Informed of impending disaster, the men on earth decreed, along with a general cessation of all work, an especially great "Bai-bai," to appease spirits, ancestors, and heaven.

Firecrackers and paper houses to burn

The sending off of the household spirits is then the first in a series of sacrifices to insure prosperity and peace for the coming year. Firecrackers, the burning of paper money, and a banquet are used to see them off. Some families also burn small paper horses and palanquins, cut from yellow paper, as a means of conveyance for the spirit to ride to heaven on. These are called *sin-be* or "spirit horses."

Steamed rice pudding (*chhe-ti-ke*)

On Taiwan, however, all the household gods are seen off on the 24th, and the steamed rice-pudding is given as a gift to relatives and friends. Families in which there is a funeral in progress are not allowed to make the pudding, and must be offered some by neighbors. There is a special exorcism performed before making this pudding, as well as the other special New Year dishes, to insure that nothing but blessings will be accrued from the making and eating of them.

Housecleaning

Custom demands that the Taiwanese wash all the pots and pans[,] furniture, and the entire house, after the gods have departed. . . . It is not until after the gods of the cupboard and the hidden corners have left that the whole house can be turned upside down for a cleaning. The spirits, when present, can cause sickness or loss of fortune if disturbed. Not until after their departure can the position of furniture and other articles be changed from their customary places.

The family altar and the metal incense pot hanging from the ceiling are the first things to be cleaned. The incense burner is called the "Thi-Kong" or "god's" incense pot. It is scrubbed with a special oil mixed with charcoal ashes, called "Ki-yû." Then all the pots and pans, and the whole house is scrubbed from top to bottom.

Source: *Taiwan Feasts and Customs* by Michael R. Saso. Hsinchu, Taiwan: Chabanel Language Institute, pp. 5-8.

New Year's feast

The feast is usually prepared in the afternoon of the 29th, or the 30th, should it be an intercalary lunar month, the last day of the old year. The banquet is laid out before the ancestor shrine at about 5 in the afternoon, with the burning of paper money, and incense. Then towards seven in the evening, after the ancestors have eaten their fill, the dishes are taken away, re-heated, and the family gathers around the table for its New Year banquet. The food is supposed to be less tasty after the ancestors have partaken of it. Probably the re-heating adds to the diminishing delectability as well. Though Thi-Kong and other celestial figures are honored in uneven numbers, 3 or 5 kinds of dishes being prepared for them, human beings are feted with even numbers, and 16 or 20 dishes are liable to turn up at a New Year banquet.

There are special dishes prepared for the New Year ancestor sacrifice, to which quite a ritual is attached. These are sweet fruits, the New Year or sweet rice-pudding cake, the vegetable rice-pudding cake, the baking powder cake (hoat-ké) and an over-flowing bowl of steamed rice. Before making the above dishes, the stove is first exorcised with salt and ashes, sprinkled in the four directions above the stove. . . . Great care must be payed lest the "hoat-ké" or baking powder cake does not rise properly, since a fully risen and abundant "hoat-ké" is one of the signs of a prosperous new year.

As the new year cakes are finished, they are put on the ancestor altar with a stick of incense to burn in the center of them. On the afternoon of the new year eve celebration, the "hoat-ké" and the overflowing bowl of steamed rice are put in front of the ancestor shrine with a red paper streamer inserted in the middle. On the red streamer is printed in golden letters the word chhun, or "Spring." But since the word "chhun" has the same pronunciation as [another word romanized as "chhun," meaning] add to one's wealth, the streamer is in reality a prayer for abundance during the coming year, as well as a welcome of the new spring. This paper streamer is called "pn̄g chhun hoe" and is seen for sale on the streets during the New Year season.

Before the new year banquet, all the members of the family are supposed to bathe, and put on new clothes, especially the children. Paper money and incense are burned before the ancestor shrine, and then one by one the dishes are cooked and layed out on a special table before the ancestors. Seven small cups of wine and seven sets of chop-sticks are laid before the ancestor tablet. In families with two sets of ancestors, that is, where an adopted son has brought his ancestors, or a family with no male offspring have allied themselves with another family that the sacrifices may be carried out, fourteen cups and fourteen pairs of chopsticks are layed out. The greater the abundance of food, the greater will be the reward for the coming year. This concept of limited good dispensed by a jealous heaven is a typically Eastern one, and not to be confused with a Greco-roman or Hebraic idea of sacrifice. The family goods and blessings, have been given by heaven. The family now must share these goods with ancestor and with neighbor, lest heaven be offended and not dispense the same good things for the coming year. Heaven rewards those who have and give of their plenty.

While the ancestors are being feted at the ancestor shrine and family altar, another sacrifice is being prepared in the small room between the kitchen and the main hall where the altar and ancestor tablets are kept. This sacrifice is to the god or spirit of the house foundations. A much smaller kind of paper money is burned for this spirit, and only some of the dishes layed out for his banquet.

Meanwhile the matriarch of the family casts the wooden moon-cakes before the ancestor shrine to determine when the ancestors have eaten their fill. A continued clack of the wooden disks on the floor assure[s] the family that the ancestors have been satisfied, and as the dishes are carried out to be warmed once more, the family assembles around the table, and the banquet begins. But if a new stove (firepot) has been bought that year, it is first wrapped with red ribbons, and a fire with fresh coals lit in it. The stove is then placed beneath the main table, so that the partakers of the banquet seem to warm their feet by it, while dining. Only the most fortuitous talk is allowed during and after the meal. A pleasant peace reigns as the family gathers and enjoys the new year meal.

Children are given red envelopes with money inside, and a little extra money is sometimes left on the table to thank the gods, a kind of tip after a great banquet. In years when the lotus blossom is plentiful, some of these are placed on the table too, a sign of an abundance of luck for the coming year.

After the banquet, while the family is sitting around the main hall and talking, oranges are stacked in fives before the ancestor tablets and the household gods. A red cloth with a dragon on it is then hung before the altar. The dragon is the spirit of rain and abundance, the oranges an invitation to the gods to share in the family's feasting. The bowl of rice and the ''hoat-ké'' remain on the altar until the gods come back on the fourth of the new year. The oranges remain until after the lantern festival on the 15th. Older ladies still preserve the custom of putting red paper flowers in their hair, with the character ''chhun'' written on it, again, asking for abundance for the coming year.

Midnight activities

At midnight, after the arrival of the New Year and the firing of firecrackers, or if the family went to bed early, at the first possible moment in the New Year, the children and younger members of the family must come and bow to their elders. They say ''Sin-nî Kiong-hí'', ''new year felicitations''; ''Hō lí chíah kàu pah jī hè,'' that is, ''may you eat (live) until 120 years old,'' and other such fortuitous language. The daughter-in-law must offer a cup of sweet tea to her mother and father-in-law to drink. To the boys fall[s] the duty of shooting off firecrackers.

New Year's Day

At daybreak guests begin to arrive, to bring new year's greetings. Sweet candies are prepared for them, called the ''five sweet things'': red dates, rock candy, candied nuts, rice-powder candy, and deep fried cookies dipped in sugar. If the lady of the house offers the candies to the guest, the proper reply is, ''Hō lí si hāu si'', that is, ''may you give birth to a boy.'' When leaving the house, the guest should give a red envelope to the children; the red envelope contains a gift of money.

Fourth day of the New Year

The fourth day of the new year is called ''Ngîa-sîn'' or ''Chhía-sîn'', the ''Welcome back the family spirits'' feast. The usual three meats are laid on the family altar, incense and paper money are burned, and the house is more or less back to normal.

Source: *Taiwan Feasts and Customs* by Michael R. Saso. Hsinchu, Taiwan: Chabanel Language Institute, pp. 16-20.

Vietnam

Tet celebrations

All over Vietnam streets become crowded and take on a festive air just before *Tet*. Not only does everyone have to buy material and clothes and decorations but fireworks and special cakes with meat and beans, candied fruits and sweets, and certain kinds of flowers and plants. All are necessary to celebrate *Tet* properly. Many new stalls pop up in market places to sell special items associated with *Tet,* doing a brisk business for a week or two and then closing until the same time next year.

The first day of *Tet* sets the tone for the entire year, so it must be the very best day possible. Everyone tries to be cheerful, polite, optimistic, careful not to break anything or become annoyed or angry. All are well dressed and houses are beautifully decorated as people visit back and forth.

The feeling of celebration lasts for several days or a week. But the ancestors are believed to depart on the fourth day, and by then most people today have to go back to work.

One of the outstanding features of *Tet* is the great effort everyone makes to be with the family. The warmth and security of close ties to family and relatives, are why *Tet* is such a good and important time.

Source: *Celebrations: Asia and the Pacific* by Gene Sawyer. Honolulu: Friends of the East-West Center, 1978, p. 12.

Tet customs

On the afternoon before Tet of "Tat Nien" (New Year ceremony) a special ceremony takes place at which a sacrifice is offered to the deceased relatives and they are invited to come back for a few days and share the festivities with the living members of the family.

At midnight on New Year's Eve, a ceremony called "Giao Thua" is held in which a sacrifice for the spirits and the ancestors is made on a lovely candle-lit altar in the open air near the home. Fire-crackers which heralded in the new year may still be heard. After this, the family may break off some new buds from the special new plants and trees recently purchased for Tet and go to the Pagoda. There, they place incense before the altar and pray for the prosperity of the new year. When they leave the pagoda, another new bud is picked from a plant or tree and placed on the top of a column at their home on returning. This symbolizes good luck.

The next morning, the family arises early and [they] dress in their new clothes. Dishes of special foods are prepared to be placed on the family altar for the ancestors who are back in the home during Tet. This will be repeated twice daily until Tet is over.

Everyone offers each other New Year wishes, and the children are given lucky red envelopes containing money. Tradition attaches great importance to the first visitor from outside the home on the New Year. He is believed to influence the happiness or well-being of the family during the rest of the year. If a rich man visits first, the family's fortune will increase. A man with a good name such as Phuoc which means "happiness" is preferable to one named Cho, "dog." Some families do not trust anything to luck. They invite their first guests and discourage those they consider unlucky not to come early. Generally, the visitors receive some form of refreshment at each home they visit.

On the fourth day of Tet, the Vietnamese believe that their ancestors return to their heavenly abode. The stores begin to reopen and life regains its normalcy. People visit graves on this day acting as an escort for their departing ancestors.

On the seventh day of Tet, the "Cay Neu" is removed from in front of the home. It is a high bamboo pole that is set up on the last day of the old lunar year. Various items are placed on the top, including red paper with an inscription written on it; a small basket containing betel and areca nuts; wind chimes; and a small square of woven bamboo representing a barrier to stop the evil spirits. A few colorful cock feathers may also decorate the pole. The offerings in the basket are intended for the good spirits.

The Vietnamese believe that the good spirits of the household must report to heaven during Tet, so they take many precautionary measures to scare off the bad spirits who know the good ones are away. They do not rely completely on the Cay Neu because legend tells them that it cannot stop a certain bad spirit. It is necessary for lime powder to be scattered around the house and to draw, with lime also, a bow and an arrow in front of the threshold.

Source: *Customs and Culture of Vietnam* by Ann Caddell Crawford. Rutland, Vt.: Charles E. Tuttle, 1966, pp. 191-192.

The peach tree branch for Tet

One of the most characteristic customs of the Tet consists in buying a flowering branch of the peach tree which is placed in a vase for the whole duration of the Tet.

Certain villages of Hanoi specialize in the cultivation of peach trees for this purpose, specially on the Great Lake, near the village of Chem. There are firms in Hanoi, however, that have a reputation for manufacturing artificial peachtree branches that exactly resemble real flowers and have the advantage of being much cheaper and lasting the whole year!

Source: *We the Vietnamese: Voices from Vietnam* edited by Francois Sully. New York: Praeger, 1971, p. 59.

Moon 1, Day 1

Losar, The Tibetan New Year

Bhutan

New Year dances

The New Year, which falls at either the beginning or the end of February, is the biggest celebration. Dances then are performed usually by specially trained monks. . . . [T]he dances were a way of teaching religion to a people who could not read or write. However, the dances have an even deeper function in that they are believed to be a way of controlling and influencing the spirits. The dance steps and patterns are very complicated, and they have been handed down over the generations without changes. Some of the dances are believed to have originated in the dreams and visions of the lamas where the gods and spirits danced in a heavenly kingdom. Beautiful robes, elaborate masks, and the sound of cymbals and long brass horns combine to fix the attention of the watchers.

The Drum Dance of Dramitse represents a vision of heavenly beings at the palace of the Guru Rimpoche. The dancers wear masks representing different animals—deer, tigers, elephants, crocodiles—and carry decorated drums. Their costumes are of multicolored silk with skirts of various colored scarves. The drum symbolized the essence of religion that defeats the demons. The ''Black Hat'' dancer is magnificently costumed in brocade robes and an elaborate black hat. The dance has two meanings: a portrayal of the assassination of a Tibetan king in A.D. 842, who persecuted Buddhists; and a conquering of and offering to the earth deities. In some of the dances, skulls and death are emphasized as a reminder that the good and bad deeds of a person will influence destiny on rebirth. A lighter note is introduced by the clowns who joke with the audience and mimic the serious dancers.

Source: *Enchantment of the World: Bhutan* by Leila Merrell Foster. Chicago: Children's Press, 1989, p. 90.

Ladakh

Festivities among Tibetan refugees in India

Losar is New Year's Day by their calendar. In order to transit smoothly from the old year to the new, the Ladakhis as well as the refugee Tibetans perform an elaborate ritual, covering five days. It begins on the second last day of the Tibetan year. According to their faith they believe that an account of each man's good and evil deeds is kept in the shape of white and black pebbles, respectively, and that on the Day of Judgement the two lots are weighed against each other, to decide his fate. So the devotees worship *Jigeje* (one with six arms) a responsible deity of the pantheon, repent for the sins, that they have committed during that year, and pray for a remission so as to secure a favourable balance, promising good conduct for the coming year. Small balls made of *sattu* (oat-flour) called *torma*, are cast away at the end of the ceremony. The *torma,* supposed to be a scapegoat, is believed to take evil away with itself. It is to be thrown in a particular direction determined by the *lama* (monk) who consults his calendar and charts for the purpose.

Over the year evil forces may have entered the *gompha* (temple). They are driven away by a ritual of masked dances, the *chham*. The blowing of long horns is accompanied by the clash of huge cymbals. Fingers work the steps of the *gya'ling* (flute) while a hooked drumstick beats out a rhythm on the *gna'chung* (drum). A hush of expectancy descends upon the crowd. A colourful figure, elaborately dressed, wearing an ogre-like mask rises inside the encircling crowd and makes swift movements to the quick music. Wisps of smoke of incense rise from the swinging censers and waft and curl with the dancer. Soon the number of these ritual dancers goes up.

The protracted dance goes on, covering many sequences, each one ending with the casting of *torma*. Often this ritual has been wrongly referred to as the 'Devil's Dance', for these figures represent the *gompos* (demi-gods) and their *khor* (assistants). The dance enacts a ritual combat of the good against the evil. The ceremony ends with the burning of an esoteric model—a fretworked mount shaped like a pyramid, bearing a skull-like head at the apex. This sacrifice is taken to be a mark that the temple has been rid of evil.

The last day of the year is devoted to white-washing the house, repainting lucky signs on it, decorating the rooms and preparing ritual and festive foods for New Year's Day. As the New Year dawns, people hasten to the source of water—a river, lake, stream, pond or spring—and take a drink of water. This ritual drinking of water at the crack of dawn on this day is regarded to be auspicious, as it is believed to ensure that the year will pass smoothly, without obstacles. Soon after returning home, they drink hot *chhang* (a native beer usually consumed cold), again considered auspicious. This day the monks also revel, for it is a day of merriment. The *Dakar,* a mendicant beggar well versed in acrobatics, goes from door to door, singing and dancing, setting the tone of frolic for the festival. He makes lucky, auspicious and favourable utterances to the inmates. For the happy tidings he is welcomed and given snacks or money in return. Rice cooked with butter and garnished with a number of things is invariably eaten on Losar, for nothing else is as auspicious. Greetings are exchanged cheerily as people visit one another. Spontaneous merriment is the order of the day.

Celebrations carry over to the following day. It is a day of worship too. *Lamas* are called home by the laiety for conducting worship. Prayers are also held in the temple. Within the *gompha* the *lamas* chant *mantras* (formulae) in a grave tone, not ranging over more than four notes of a low octave. At most irregular intervals a prayer bell tinkles in sharp contrast to the bass refrain of the chant. The prayer flags are to be changed for the new year. This, however, is done on the second or third day, as the calendars and charts may help the *lama* decide. The day passes in song and dance, meeting one another, and in watching operas. In case the prayer flag changing ceremony does not fall on the second day, it is held on the third day of the new year.

Source: *Festive India* by Gurmeet Thukral, New Delhi: Frank Bros., 1987, p. 6-7.

Tibet

Losar celebrations

I remember I always had a hard time falling asleep on the night before *Losar*. I was very anxious to wear my new clothes in the morning and to see everything all brightened up. Even the yaks' and sheep's horns are oiled and shined. The animals wear fancy collars and new bells are put on their necks. The men and women all wash their hair and braid it. They put on their jewelry and their very best clothes.

Early on *Losar* morning, the first day of the first month of the year, even before it gets light enough for anyone to see the lines on their palms, the adult men and women walk silently to the stream or lake where the villagers normally get their daily water. Along with their large water buckets, they carry bells, and cymbals. They fill up the buckets and carry them on their backs. As they walk home they ring the bells and play cymbals. The sound is like a big herd of animals coming home. When they arrive at the house, the grandmother and grandfather of the house bring out frest butter in a large bowl, and take a pinch of it, and stick some on, right above the forehead of each member of the family.

Then everyone else gets dressed and goes into the house and sits down in a row. The oldest person in the family sits in the place of honor, at the top of the row of seats, next to the altar. The mother or grandmother of the family brings in the *chemar (tsampa* mixed with butter and sugar) and passes it around. Each member of the family takes a pinchful and throws it into the air along with prayers. They do this three times and eat the fourth pinch. This is to symbolize plenty for the grain harvest in the year to come. Next each member of the family is served with a bowl of yoghurt. This symbolizes a plentiful supply of products from the animals in the year to come. Since most Tibetans are either farmers or nomads, these prayers are very important.

Each person next receives a *derka,* a plate of *kapse* along with other treats. Everyone gets exactly the same amount of *derka,* even the unborn baby in its mother's womb is given a *derka,* which is saved.

Then the *cha* (butter tea) is served to everyone. The mother and daughter of the house are usually the servers. For this occasion the tea is made as thick as possible and is churned with lots of fresh butter and cream. There are old stories about how the tea is judged to be thick enough and best quality for serving. After the tea is poured into the cup, a coin is set carefully over the tea. If the coin floats without sinking, then the tea is proved to be good.

Before noon every family goes to the monasteries and nunneries and temples and offers *katas* (white greeting scarves), and makes donations to the monks and nuns of food and all kinds of different gifts. A large crowd of villagers get together in the courtyard of the monastery or nunnery where the juniper and other leaves are piled. The abbot of the monastery comes out, and one of the monks starts a fire. As it burns, clouds of sweet smelling smoke will rise into the air. Now the abbot starts chanting and the rest of the monks play religious musical instruments such as drums, conchshells, large oboes, large trumpets, cymbals and bells. The villagers all circumambulate the pile of burning incense by walking around it in a clockwise circle.

One of the monks comes out with a large plate of *tsampa* and passes it around to the people. Each person takes a good handful and slowly continues to walk around the pile. The abbot chants a traditional chant of victory over misfortune. Everyone joins his chanting. As they chant they raise their right hands into the air holding the *tsampa.* They will chant with the abbot three times; at the fourth, with great shouts, everyone throws the *tsampa* into the air. And it comes down like snow on everyone. Then the prayer flags are put up on tall poles, and everyone goes home and puts up their home prayer flags. Some people put them on the roofs, some on the poles in the yard.

In the afternoon, everyone starts drinking the *chang* that has been fermenting for the last few months. People visit each other, relatives come over. Men start playing with their *mah jong* or *sho* (a dice game) or card games. Tibetans love to gamble especially eastern Tibetans and people from Lhasa. The women dance and sing and dring *chang* too. Children play with other children and show off to each other the new sets of clothes that they have received.

Losar lasts for six or seven days. . . .

Source: *Food in Tibetan Life* by Rinjing Dorje. London: Prospect Books, 1985, pp. 12-13.

Gutuk soup

On the twenty-ninth day of the twelfth month a soup called *gutuk,* a dumpling soup similar to *boctuk* is served. This is the day before the thirtieth, the last day of the year, and a special celebration is held to get ready for *Losar,* New Year's Day. The celebration is held on the twenty-ninth because the thirtieth, like the fifteenth, is a holy day in Tibet.

The dumplings for *gutuk* include big ones with surprises inside, such as the objects listed below. When the soup is served in bowls, each member of the family gets one dumpling with one of these objects inside, along with other dumplings to be eaten in the normal way. Each member first opens the special large dumpling with the object inside. Whatever one finds indicates that person's personality. For instance, if a person gets:

salt	- good sign, you are all right
wool	- very lazy
coal	- malicious
chili	- rough spoken
white stone	- long life
sheep pellets	- good sign, very clever
butter	- you are very sweet and easy-going

These are the traditional objects put into the dumplings. Nowadays written messages are also included, much like fortune cookies. Everyone reads these out loud and has a good laugh.

Gutuk means ninth soup. According to custom everything has to be not less than nine. There must be at least nine ingredients in the soup, and each person must eat at least nine bowls. Everyone will insist on this, and so some clever guests bring their own small bowls along. Everyone saves a little at the end and then dumps this into a large wok. They each cut off a piece of hair, a piece of fingernail, and a piece of old clothing. These are put into the wok too. Then they clean the chimney and put the dirt in the wok. Finally they make an effigy of a person out of dough and set it in the center of the pile in the wok.

The youngsters take this out late at night and set it in the middle of a trail junction. While doing this they make as much noise as they can by shouting, ringing bells, booming guns, even beating pots and pans. This traditional ceremony is called *lue*. This is done to get rid of all the negative forces at the end of the year and get ready for a new year.

Peasant celebrations

On this occasion the people present offering gifts to the monasteries. Namgyal[, a peasant,] went to Tingmogang on the day before the beginning of the festival in order to donate a few brass offering lamps, as well as butter used for fuel in these lamps, barley, rice, and beer in brass bowls, at the monastery located there. The gifts were placed before the images of the gods. Outside on the door posts of his house and on the inside along the beams of the ceiling he fastened twigs of juniper just as everybody else did. By this, the evil spirits of the old year were to be exorcized so that they would leave the house peacefully to those of the new year. In his own household temple Namgyal placed bowls with fresh offerings before the statues and images of the Buddhas and gods, in order to maintain their favor; he decorated the house altar with dried flowers, placed burning offering lamps on it.

King's procession

Thus, shortly before the beginning of the celebrations Namgyal rode to Leh in two days. In Leh he moved in with a distant relative. On the evening of the first holiday, the 28th of the tenth month, he saw, for the first time, the illumination of the town; the houses at the foot of the mountain on which the castle was situated, and along the southern slope of the same, the castle, and the monasteries gleamed in the shine of thousands of little lamps lit to celebrate this lamaistic ''ascension festival,'' something which made a great impression upon Namgyal.

Escorted by about thirty horsemen, the king now rode to Leh, crossing the Indus by a bridge. He rode across the bazaar and was greeted everywhere by the people of Ladakh in a most respectful manner. The people had come together in great numbers from all the neighboring villages, in part from very great distances. Today they were for once allowed to dream of ancient, long-past royal splendor. The procession rode up the steep mountain on which the castle stood, accompanied by crowds of the populace. In front of the lions' gate the riders dismounted. At their approach the lion who was roughly carved out of wood, and who peered out over the gate from a niche, had begun to growl violently, and at the same time there resounded the furious barking of dogs. A mighty Tibetan mastiff which was lying on the inside of the gate on a chain was connected by means of a string with the wooden lion up above. When the barking dog jumped around and tugged at the string, the wooden lion above the gate, through whose belly went an axle, began to skip about, and the populace gaped at this wonder of technology.

Source: *Progpa Namgyal: Ein Tibeterleben (Progpa Namgyal: The Life of a Tibetan)* by Samuel Heinrich Ribbach. München-Planegg: Otto Wilhelm Barth-Verlag GMBH, 1940 (in Human Relations Area Files), p. 134.

Fireworks and jump rope in Lhasa

The children and grownups continually shoot off rockets, with the most attention being evidently accorded the sound rather than to the color. Matches are lit in the darkness giving off a rosy light. Group dancing and singing is held in the streets; children, adults, and especially the women play *shuttle-cock* and jump rope in the following manner: two women hold a not especially long rope by the ends and turn it; a third woman, usually a girl of from ten to fifteen, taking a place in the middle, jumps over the rope, alternating legs. This is done either moving forward or remaining in the same place, while a short colloquy takes place between the two women on one hand and the girl on the other, which I did not record exactly, but only learned that first the women holding the rope ask the jumping girl: ''Where are you going?'' ''I'm going there.'' ''Why are you going?'' ''To celebrate the New Year'', and so forth.

Source: *Buddhist Palomnik U Sviatyn. Tibeta. Po Dnevnikam, Redennym. (1899-1902). A Bhuddist Pilgrim to the Holy Places of Tibet: From Diaries Kept from 1899-1902.* Petrograd: Russian Geographical Society, 1919 (HRAF).

Moon 1, 1st two weeks (circa February)
Mon Lam Chen Mo

This is a commemoration of the two weeks in which Skakyamuni Buddha exhibited miraculous powers. Monks came from throughout the country for prayers and public examinations. Thousands of pilgrims came from all parts of Tibet.

Tibet

Religious devotions and socializing

The *Mon Lam Chen Mo* was a time of great pageantry. People would parade through the streets of Lhasa wearing antique armour and traditional costumes. But for the majority of the people, this was a time for performing religious devotions, such as making offerings to the assembled monks and lighting innumerable butter lamps. It was a fine opportunity to attend the examinations of the monks and especially for socializing, doing business and enjoying such diversions as archery, horse-racing and wrestling contests. In addition, with people from many regions gathered in one place, news and stories circulated freely.

Source: ''Festivals of Tibet'' by Thubten Norbu in *Journal of Popular Culture*, 16, no. 1 (Summer, 1982), 126-135.

Mönlam in Lhasa

Prior to 1959 the most jubilant and colourful events in Tibetan life were the different festivals that occured throughout the year. These were soon banned by the Chinese and denounced as wasteful and indulgent. Only since 1985 have moves been made to reinstate them. In the early spring of 1986, the greatest festival of all, the 'Mönlam' or Prayer festival, took place again for the first time in nearly thirty years. This festival follows the Tibetan New Year ('Losar') celebrations and begins on the fourth day of the first lunar month. Huge butter sculptures are erected outside the Jokhang cathedral in Lhasa, monks and pilgrims pour into the city, and there is a long procession around the Barkor carrying a famous statue of Maitreya, the future Buddha. The Mönlam festival was started by Tsongkhapa in the early years of the fifteenth century and continued unbroken until the Chinese occupation. What takes place now is apparently only a poor imitation of what it was like before.

Source: *The Tibet Guide* by Stephen Batchelor. London: Wisdom, 1987, p. 67.

Moon 1, Day 7

Nanakusa, Festival of the Seven Grasses

On this day seven young herbs are mixed with rice in a special dish. The gathering of the young herbs is a sign of spring to come.

Japan

Sampling a soup of seven herbs

The NANAKUSA or Festival of the Seven Grasses comes on the seventh and is the first of the five seasonal services (*go-sekku*) of old Japan. Another name is *Wakana-setsu*, or Festival of Young Herbs, because of the custom of eating rice with a stew made of herbs. Still another name is *Jin-jitsu* or "Man Day," given to it because it falls on the zodical day for "man." The *Nenchukoreiki* or Accounts of Annual Festivities says that it was proclaimed a national holiday during the Feudal Days. Because of its proximity to New Years, it was declared by the *Tokugawa* Shogunate to be the most important holiday of the five.

The day was soon named *Nanakusa* or Seven Grasses in preference to Young Herb Day, because it fell on the seventh, for we see the new name in the old song which is sung as the herbs were prepared for the feast:

> The seven young herbs are delicious,
> Of all these the Shepherd's Purse the best!
> Let us pound it! Let's enjoy it!
> Ere we welcome the birds from the south!
> Or the winter birds leave for the north!

One version of the song has it speaking of the Mongols from the south and the Russians from the north.

After the young herbs are mixed with the rice gruel, an offering of the feast is made to the clan deity (*Ujigami*) and then to the Three Treasures (*Sanbo*), and partaken of by the family. Superstitions growing up around the feast are mostly connected with warding off sickness caused by evil spirits, depressing spirits like our spring fever, and warding off summer complaint, dysentery in autumn, and jaundice in winter.

The origin of the feast goes back to China where the Chinese celebrated the first Rat day by gathering seven young spring herbs. An ancient record shows that in the reign of Emperor *Saga* (809-823 A.D.), the baby Prince was served with the soup of the seven young herbs. The name of the seven herbs was not a matter of importance at first, it was merely collecting herbs between the end of winter and the beginning of spring to be served on the seventh of the first month. The list of the seven herbs as finally worked out is; Parsley, Shepherd's Purse, Cudweed, Chickweed, Buddha's Throne, Chinese-rape, and Radish.

To get the best effects of the ceremony, it was advisable to pound the grasses on a willow block with a branch of the privet, being sure to pound the parsley at the hour of the Cock, the Shepherd's Purse at the hour of the Dog, the cudweed at the hour of the Boar, the chickweed at the hour of the Rat, the radish at the hour of the Hare, and then to compound them at the hour of the Dragon. The mixing must be done by water drawn from a well to the east, getting what is supposed to be "Water of Youth."

Another story has it that the grasses are to be beaten seven times seven, i.e. forty-nine times in all, and thus they get a connection with the forty-nine luminaries. Star worship is used to ward off danger and evil spirits on this day by the warrior class, especially was this so during the *Kamakura* period of 1192-1219 A.D.

A few years after the Restoration, in 1874, the official observance of this and the other four of the "*gosekku*" was abolished, and with that order much of the pomp and ceremony of these days ha[ve] been dropped. Yet in many places in the homes where reverence for the ancient ways still prevails, the *Nanakusa* is still observed as a very alive and meaningful festival.

Source: *Japanese Festival and Calendar Lore* by William Hugh Erskine. Tokyo: Kyo Bun Kwan, 1933, pp. 29-30.

Seven vegetables in rice gruel

After the over-indulgence in rice cakes and sake that has become part of the New Year's celebration, the digestion deserves a rest. This appears to be the origin of [the] custom of eating rice gruel in which are mixed many kinds of vegetables on the seventh day of the new year. Apart from the idea that the vegetables are the harbingers of the eagerly-awaited spring, this dish also gives us a chance to savor the gentle flavor of each kind of vegetable.

Ingredients (to serve 4)

2 cups rice
2 bunches watercress
2-3 spring onions
1 pack mustard cress
15 cms dried tangle
3 cups water

2 tablespoons sake
2 tablespoons soy sauce
2 tablespoons salt

Directions

1 Wash the rice well and allow to drain.

2 Wash the watercress and mustard cress and cut into 1cm long pieces.

3 Wash and chop up the spring onions.

4 Using a thick saucepan, place the washed tangle in the bottom, cover with the rice and pour in the water and seasoning.

5 Simmer for 30-40 minutes until the rice is soft and the consistency of porridge.

6 Mix in the cut up vegetables before serving.

Source: *A Taste of Japan,* edited by Itsuko Hamada. Japan Air Lines Co., Ltd., 1986, p. 89.

Moon 1, Day 9

Tso-Fu (Making Happiness Festival)

Tso-Fu is a day to pay respect to the gods. Mothers of newborn sons pay their respects by presenting "new-male cakes" at the temple.

Taiwan

Villagers celebrate

Tso-fu, or "Making Happiness," follows closely upon New Year. The various activities involved in the Making Happiness Festival are coordinated by the Happiness Master. On the afternoon of the ninth day of the first month, the Happiness Master, the headman, the chief medium, and a number of other villagers "invite the gods." Accompanied by banners, gongs, a hired band, and a multitude of children, these representatives collect several gods that dwell in various shrines and private homes and carry them to the temple. Women who have given birth to sons during the year are then invited to present their *hsin-ting ping,* or "new-male cakes," in the temple. In the evening, all households provide sacrifices in the temple and a community sacrifice is offered to the Heaven God and his host in the temple plaza.

The next morning, village ceremonial leaders conduct an elaborate sacrificial rite in the temple, and most villagers come to offer incense and worship the gods. At noon, all villagers 60 years of age and over, all women who have given birth to sons during the year, all neighborhood chiefs, the headman, and a miscellany of important outside guests are feasted at community expense. In the afternoon, the new mothers distribute their "new-male cakes," one to every village household except those of other new mothers. With suitable pomp and ceremony, the gods that have been brought to the temple are returned to their respective shrines.

Source: *Kinship & Community in Two Chinese Villages* by Burton Pasternak. Stanford, Calif.: Stanford Univ. Press, 1972, p. 72.

Moon 1, Days 14-19 (circa February)

Butter Sculpture Offering Festival

Tibet

Colored Butter Sculptures

Monks of the five religious colleges of Kumbum monastery prepare elaborate sculptures made of colored butter. Pilgrims arrive from all over Tibet. On the afternoon of the 14th day of the 1st Moon, the College of Religious Dance performs the Cham masked dance. On the 15th the butter sculptures are viewed. The College of Tantra conducts a *torma*-throwing ceremony at the festival's end. On the 19th the *torma* and the *zur* are burnt in ceremony, thus burning the evil that has been attracted to them.

Classes plan butter sculpture themes

In the College of Philosophy there were two Prajnaparamita Classes, each following the tradition of a different famous Tibetan philosophical scholar. One studied the tradition of Je Tsunpa and the other the tradition of Jamyang Shaypa. These two Prajnaparamita classes were always given the largest assignment. Their sculptures would be hung on frames and would often fill an area twenty feet high by forty feet wide. These displays involved fairly complex themes with a variety of characters and scenes.

The other classes from the College of Philosophy offered smaller displays, which might have as a theme the four harmonious brothers or the six long life symbols. The themes differed from year to year. The classes decided on a theme which was kept secret until the unveiling of the sculptures on the evening of the 15th day of the first month.

Making the butter sculptures

Each sculpter used a bucket of cold water to keep the butter cool and a bucket of hot water to keep his hands clean. If the hands were not clean, the butter would stick. The proper method of handling butter was to first put the fingers in hot water then into dry flour, then to rub the fingers together in order to remove any dirt. Next, fingers were rinsed in hot water, dipped into cold water, and only then would the butter be picked up to be shaped as needed.

The sculptor sat on a cushion behind a small table. On the table was a board about six inches wide and three to four feet long, which served as a painter's palette. It held rows of colored butter stick having variable degrees of shading; dark to light for each color. Next to the table was a small brazier of charcoal on which was kept the pot of hot water and on the floor next to it sat the pot of cold water.

The scupture being shaped was hung by a large iron nail. This nail eventually was used to fasten the completed figure to the frame erected to display the sculptures. If the sculpture was handled directly the temperature of the hand would be sufficient to melt it. Layer by layer, piece by piece, the sculptures were completed over a period of many months.

Viewing the butter sculptures

On the morning of the fifteenth, the three sides of the viewing enclosure, made of embroidered panels, were put into place. It was not until approximately four in the afternoon that the sculptures were finally brought out. Still covered with paper, they were nailed to the frames and then bits of appropriately colored butter were put over the nail heads to complete the installation.

The butter lamps were arranged and the papers removed when the monks came to consecrate the display. It was not until after dark that they were ready for public viewing. People walked back and forth around the displays. As they viewed them, they related to one another the stories therein depicted, and either praised or criticized the skill of the rendition. Nomads and city dwellers, farmers and merchants, monks and officials, indeed all the visitors came together in a very festive mood. This lasted until about three in the morning when all the monks performed the *Shag Sol* ceremony.

Earlier, during the consecration they had invited the Buddhas to come into the display and now they invited them to leave the display. As soon as this ceremony was completed, the sculptures started to come down. They were removed without care and stacked together in piles for storage in the warehouse until the next year. At that time the old color was scraped off and mixed with ash to make the first coat of the new sculptures. After the sculptures were dismantled the embroidered panels were removed for storage with the canopies. The umbrellas and poles were taken down and the area cleaned up. By the afternoon of the sixteenth there was hardly a trace of the sculpture display left. Between the 16th and the 19th the market areas were quite active with people preparing to return home. By the end of the 19th day the entire place was back to normal.

Throwing the *torma*

At the end of the festival the College of Tantra had a *torma*-throwing ceremony. The actual throwing of the *torma* was on the afternoon of the 19th day and this happened outside the monastery. It was called a *torma* festival but the actual object to be thrown was called *zur*. This was an eight or nine-foot high tripod of sticks connected with very stiff paper and decorated with butter sculptures of flames, clouds, gems and other symbols. On the top was a big skull, from the mouth of which issued large flames. There were also many ribbons or strings tied to the top of the tripod. These steadied the tripod as it was carried. Inside the legs of the tripod was a *torma,* and depending on the purpose, its size and color varied.

Source: ''Festivals of Tibet'' by Thubten Norbu in *Journal of Popular Culture,* 16, no. 1 (Summer, 1982), 126-134. (See this article for details of the sculpture making and description of the Cham dance. Written by a monk, brother of the Dalai Lama.)

The butter sculpture festival in Lhasa, c. 1950

Tibet's New Year started with a roar. An avalanche of 20,000 red-robed monks streamed into the holy city, doubling its population. The cacophony of prayers, drums, and cymbals echoed night and day.

I dragged myself to the roof of Tsarong's mansion and watched the city whip itself into a religious frenzy. Work stopped. Offices were closed. Men and women appeared in their newest silks and brocades.

The celebration reached its climax at the Butter Festival on the New Year's 15th day. Tsarong warned us not to venture into the unruly hustling crowds. He stationed us with Mrs. Tsarong in one of his houses on the Barkhor.

After sundown, monks towed towering sculptures of yak butter, pigmented with dark and vibrant dyes, into the Barkhor. Throngs gathered to admire the grinning caricatures of gods, the elaborate flower patterns, and intricate filigree work, fixed to pyramidal wooden stands 30 feet high.

Mrs. Tsarong explained that months of work go into the displays. Each monastery maintains a workshop where its own artists shape the cold-hardened butter. The Government awards a prize to the best entry.

The gallery of art stood ready. As we watched, hundreds of butter lamps and gas lanterns flickered in the darkness, conjuring a semblance of life into the effigies. Suddenly we heard trumpet blasts and the deep rumble of drums.

The Dalai Lama stepped from the cathedral. He looked straight ahead, his almond-shaped face inscrutable beneath a peaked yellow-silk cap. For the first time I looked upon the god-king, the 14th incarnation of Tibet's patron god, Chenrezi. The 11-year-old boy gazed down upon thousands of bowed heads. To them he was a living god.

The grave little King paced slowly along the array of grotesque images. Abbots supported him, their hands beneath his arms. The highest officials of the State followed.

It was an electrifying tableau. The Dalai Lama withdrew into the cathedral. At once a religious madness seemed to seize the throngs. All night long we heard cries, weeping, and laughter, punctuated by the hoarse shouts of Dob-Dobs.

Source: ''My Life in Forbidden Lhasa'' by Heinrich Harrer in *National Geographic Magazine,* CVIII, no. 1, (July, 1955), 16-17.

Moon 1, Day 15

Great Fifteenth

The "Great Fifteenth" ends the New Year holiday season. Celebrations on this day may include kite flying, kite fighting, and straw rope tug-of-war games. In earlier times straw figures with coins and paper prayers hidden inside were dressed in discarded clothing to represent the men of the house and tossed into the streets. There waiting boys tore them apart to get the coins. Thus the evil spirits are fooled and good luck insured for the coming year. On this day also the number nine is lucky and everything must be done nine times for luck.

Korea

Lucky nines

I washed my face nine times, Yong Tu, and I cleaned my teeth with salt nine times, too," Ok Cha said to her brother on the morning of the Fifteenth Day of the First Month.

"I combed my hair nine times, and I shall eat nine kinds of nuts today," the Korean boy replied.

It was the Great Fifteenth Day, the day which ended the New Year holiday season, and it was the last chance to make sure of the New Year good luck. Each child raced with the others to see how many "lucky nines" he could collect during the day.

The women also believed the number nine would bring them good luck. They gladly prepared the nine meals for the family; they swept the floors nine times; and nine times they stuffed fuel into the stove. The Master of the House himself bowed nine times before the tablets in the Ancestors' House.

Straw men

This dignified father of Ok Cha and Yong Tu was careful to omit none of the usual doing of this day. Under his watchful eyes his younger brothers and the boys made the three straw figures which should represent each of the three men of the household. To hide amid the straw, he gave them pieces of cash, Korean copper coins with big holes cut in their centers. He decided which old coats should be put upon the straw manikins. Together, all the men and boys of the household went to the gate to see the straw men tossed into the street.

"You should have seen the street boys fall on our straw men, Halmoni," Yong Tu reported to his grandmother. "They pulled off the old garments, and they tore at the straw to get the cash out."

"That is well, my grandson." The old woman nodded her head in great satisfaction. "The more they kick the straw figures, the luckier our men will be. The bad spirits will be well fooled. They will think those are truly your father and uncles. The good spirits will read the paper prayers you tucked inside them. They will then help keep away ill luck from our house."

Yong Tu himself wrote the prayers on the strips of paper hidden inside the straw figures. With careful brush strokes he had written this sentence on each, "For the coming twelve months, from sickness and bad luck protect me." The boy had kept watch through the bamboo gate until he could be sure that the straw figures were well kicked apart.

"All the bad luck of the past year has gone with those straw men," the Korean grandmother told the children. "Your fathers can now make a fresh start. They have cast out their old, unlucky selves. Today they are new men, beginning a new year."

Source: *Tales of a Korean Grandmother* by Frances Carpenter. Garden City, New York: Doubleday, 1951, pp. 107-112.

Kite flying

On this Great Fifteenth Day the sky above the Kim courts was dotted with kites. Those that were lowest showed their red, green, and purple colorings. Those higher up were like a flock of dark birds, flying across the blue sky.

Yong Tu and his cousins had finished the kites they were making for the contest to be held on this day. With strong silken thread they had carefully tied two splints of bamboo across each other to form a giant letter X. They had run other silk threads from end to end on these rods, to form the outside frame of the kite. Then they had covered the frame well with fine Korean paper, made from the bark of the mulberry tree. They took care to leave the center crossing uncovered, cutting out a small disc of the paper, so that the silken kite string could be tied to the bamboo splints. The reels for the kite strings were as carefully made as were the kites themselves.

Halmoni had provided bits of old pottery which the boys pounded into tiny sharp bits for coating their kite strings. Running the strings first through sticky glue, then through the powdered pottery, they gave them a good cutting edge. For in kite fighting it was the string that could cut in two any other string crossing it, which won the day. Yong Tu was proud because he managed to keep his kite longest up in the air. Of all the kitefliers of his age, he thus became the champion.

More kite flying

Flying kites is another favorite pastime of the young folks in Korea. During the whole of the First Moon the children in towns and villages spend their holidays at this amusement and, on the last day of the moon, they write "Away Evils, Come Blessings" on the kite and attach a lighted thread to the string.

Higher and higher the kite soars in the air as they lengthen the string by turning the four-horned reel, and nearer and nearer the sparks fly toward the string till at last it bursts apart and frees the kite to float far, far away. It is a picturesque scene in which so many kites, floating together, and thus many fired, flutter in the sky at the mercy of the wind.

Sometimes the boys have a contest between two kites by crossing the strings partly covered with glass dust. After some minutes of pulling and releasing these little paper airplanes by the pilots on land, the better-maneuvered kite cuts the string of the weaker, with the vanquished plane tottering to a crash and the winner soaring high up in the sky.

Tradition maintains that An Lu Shan used to fly a kite to carry messages between himself and his lady love, Yang Kuei Fay, the beautiful queen of Tang Ming Wang. The history of kites is a long and romantic one.

Source: *Customs and Manners in Korea* by Chun Shin-yong. Seoul, Korea: Si-sa-yong-o-sa, Inc., 1982, pp. 18-19.

Tug-of-war

One of the greatest sports of the First Moon, tug-of-war has been practiced since olden times with enthusiasm in all places, especially in the south on the 15th or the 16th day.

The villagers are divided into two opposing teams, east and west; rice-straw is collected from each home and made into a big rope. Men and women, boys and girls all join in the contest, pulling at the rope with all their might, trying hard to win.

The eastern side of the rope is called the male line and western side the female line, but this is in name only and the contestants facing each other, striving for victory, cry, "Come on, let's see who shall be cock or hen! Heave ho! Heave ho!"

They believe that the winning side shall suffer from no cholera or any other plague and shall have a good harvest. Plenty or famine depends on this single action, and every one strives his hardest with yells and shouts—"Victory or Death."

In some localities a whole township or a county is divided into east and west to show its strength at this tug-of-war. Sometimes there are even wounded warriors.

Moon 1, Day 15

Dal-jip-tae-u-gee/Dal-ma-ji

In Kyungsang Province of Korea the moon is celebrated on the 15th day of the 1st Month by viewing it through a cavern made in a burning pile. The pine trees that form the fuel are laid in such a way that the rising moon can be viewed through them. This is called the Dal-mun or ''moon-gate'' and the festival Dal-jip-tae-u-gee means ''burning of the moon house.'' In other parts of Korea the festival is termed Dal-ma-Ji; here too people climb a hill to build a bonfire to greet the year's first full moon, but without the ''gate'' element. Various signs are observed for auspiciousness on this night.

Korea

Burning the moon-gate in Kyungsang Province

Another moon festival called Dal-jip-tae-u-gee, ''burning of the moon house'' is widely observed in Kyungsang Provinces. According to Prof. Chung, this event refers to a folk tradition in which the boys in town gather sticks and burn them when the moon rises. They usually choose for the occasion the top of a hill, near the stream, a threshing ground, or the seashore, then with the twigs of pine trees, lean them against one another in such a way that the boys can see through this pile the moon rise. The hollow thus made is termed Dal-mun meaning ''moon-gate.'' Sometimes they pile dirt and put twigs on it and thrust a stick in the middle of it. They put in some bamboo sticks among the pile so that they would make much noise burning. When the moon is seen through this gate, they set the fire on it and circle around it shouting ''Fire, fire on the moon-gate!'' beating cymbals and drums. Sometimes they tie a kite on the moon-gate so that when the string is on fire they let the kite fly away or burn down. When this happens, they bow down on the ground and pray for wish-fulfillment and for domestic peace. They believe jumping over the moon-gate while burning exorcises evils. They also think that the direction toward which the moon-gate collapses will bring good luck. Some say that if it falls toward the east or the south it means good luck; if toward the north or the west, bad luck. And again if it collapses towards oneself, one has bad luck.

Source: *Customs and Manners in Korea* by Chun Shin-yong. Seoul, Korea: Si-sa-yong-a-sa, Inc., 1982, p. 36.

Climbing a hill to view the year's first full moon

Though there are quite a few moon festivals, Dal-ma-ji, ''viewing the first full moon,'' is more significant in its primitiveness. On the eve of the First Full Moon, people climb up the hill to greet the moon. Despite the biting-cold weather, they hurry to be the first one to welcome the moon, which they believe will bring them luck. When, against the flaming sky, the biggest full moon of the year rises, they put down the torch on the ground, clasp their hands together and make their wishes: the farmer for an abundant crop, a young man for success in the official examination, an unmarried boy for his sweetheart and a maiden for a bridegroom. They firmly believe that the wishes are to be fulfilled. Judging from the color and the light of the moon, one can foretell the fortunes of the year: the bright color of the moon brings rain; its red tint, lack of rain; the bright light assures a rich harvest; the blurry light, a year of famine; if the moon slants toward the south, the seaside area will have a good harvest; if toward the north, the mountainside will.

Source: *Customs and Manners in Korea* by Chun Shin-yong. Seoul, Korea: Si-sa-yong-o-sa, Inc., 1982, pp. 35-36.

Moon 1, Day 15

Lantern Festival

The last day of the New Year Festival is celebrated in Chinese communities with elaborate decorated paper lanterns. Processions are held, often with children taking a major role. Firecrackers and dragon dances may round out the festivities. This is basically a secular festival, though the 15th is, of course, an auspicious day.

China (Pre-Revolutionary)

Celebrations in pre-1949 China

In the old days those who were well-off would decorate their houses as brilliantly as possible with lanterns and also set off many firecrackers. There was every variety of fireworks manufactured, such as small boxes, flower pots, fire and smoke rockets poles, "peonies strung on a thread", "lotus sprinkled with water", "falling moons", "grape arbors", "flags of fire", and many others. "Silver flowers" and "fire trees" were perhaps the most popular. Wealthy and prominent households competed with one another in buying fireworks of all types. The usual practice on the evening of the 15th was for a family to offer prayers to certain deities and then to hold a great feast amid revelry and much imbibing. Furthermore, respectable married women were granted greater license that evening than perhaps any other time. Normally they were confined strictly to their homes; because of Lantern Festival they could go out in the evening to view the display of lanterns.

Many of the customs associated with Lantern Festival have to do with eating, as is true with most of China's traditional festivals. One such custom was known "eating taro under the lanterns". First a quantity of taro would be boiled till soft. Close to midnight all the members of the family, young and old, male and female, assembled beneath the brightest light suspended high overhead and proceeded to eat the taro provided. Some people said that in this way they could become clear-sighted. Others held that this custom was observed so as to avoid the transmigration of the soul which Buddhists believe follows one's death.

In some cotton-growing regions people used to mold cotton bolls out of wheat flour and stick them in the fields. Then, with burning incense sticks held in their hands, they walked through the fields, hoping by this means to induce a good cotton harvest. Following the completion of the ceremony, the false cotton bolls would be shared among the children in the belief that they would thus be protected from danger.

Yet another food-related custom common both past and present is the eating of *tang yuan*, or *yuan xiao* as it is called in the north, glutinous rice-flour balls with many types of sweet filling in a soup.

In Fujian and other provinces families would light up as many lanterns as the number of family members. To express their desire for more children, they would display many extra lanterns.

Lantern Festival did not of course only mean eating to the Chinese. There were also many types of colorful and exciting performances for people to enjoy, for example, stilt dance, *yao gu* (waist drum), boat dance and the donkey dance. Most widespread of all are the dragon dance and lion dance, though the stilt dancers with their carnival spirit were very popular. These groups of men, some with false beards and painted faces, and others masquerading as women, varying and cavorting about with an amusing gait.

In the Chaozhou and Shantou (Swatow) regions of Guangdong Province swings and merry-go-rounds were common forms of amusements. Said to have originated during the Tang dynasty, these were later introduced to Korea, where young women still follow the custom of playing on swings at the time of Lantern Festival.

Lantern riddles

A literary game that was once very popular among the old educated classes on the evening of the 15th day was called Guessing the Lantern's Riddle (*Cai Deng Mi*). A number of riddles would first be written on slips of paper which were then pasted lightly onto lanterns suspended either in front of the house or inside. If required by particular riddles, certain objects could sometimes be hung from the lanterns. These were called *Mi Mian* (the riddle's face) and had written upon them a hint pointing to the correct solution of the riddle, such as given a Chinese character, a line of verse, the name of a well-known person, or a place name. Anyone who guessed correctly was rewarded on the spot.

Source: *Chinese Traditional Festivals* by Marie-Luise Latsch. Beijing, China: New World Press, 1984, pp. 41-44.

Giant ferris wheel

An ancient story tells of the great ferris wheel, two hundred feet high, which was erected for this night, in the capital of China, A.D. 713. The wheel glittered with gold and silver flowers and was lighted by fifty thousand lamps. Beautiful maidens adorned with flowers and jewels danced and sang below the wheel for three days and nights.

The Lantern Festival in 1845

An early missionary to China records his impressions of this feast as seen at Amoy in the year 1845. There were, he observed, continuous discharge of fireworks, noise of gambling tables, play-actors blocking the streets with their impromptu stages, and everywhere, lanterns of infinitely varied pattern and design. Some were made of glass, others of gauze, but mostly of paper; their shape was that of birds, beasts, fishes, and dragons. Many of them were kept in constant motion by the rarefied air produced by their lights, and were bobbing and tossing about like a vast zoo in fairyland. In the principal temples and in the houses of rich men glowed huge candles, some of which were two feet in circumference. Here and there marched bands of pipers, to the sound of gongs and cymbals. Geysers of light spurted up, subsided, and renewed themselves in great streams of colored fire, as the pieces purchased for the public delight by rich men were set off. Within the temples he could glimpse, on the principal tables, large cakes made in the form of a tortoise, the sacred symbol of Buddhist mythology. And, finally, there were occasional bonfires, over which daring individuals were, for future good luck, leaping like deer, amid the sound of gongs and the plaudits of the people.

Source: "The Chinese Feast of Lanterns" by Henry Winfred Splitter in *Journal of American Folklore,* 63, no. 250, Oct.-Dec. 1950, pp. 438-439.

People's Republic of China

Paper lanterns, c. 1985

It was late February, nearly the fifteenth of the first lunar month, and all Guiyang was dressed up with strings of paper lanterns. Some were as small and simple as a baby pumpkin, some as large and complex, literally, as a cow, for it was now the year of the ox. There were hundreds of variations on that theme, from pairs of solitary horns to full-blown bovines suspended plumply in the air, udders and all. There were airplanes, too, and rocket ships for the Four Modernizations, and every conceivable living thing, from fish, frogs, dragonflies, and birds to tigers and horses and the gods and goddesses of legend. By night they were all lit from within by electric lights, and the inhabitants of the city came out and strolled the length of them, reading the signature tags and commenting critically. This ancient event seemed a celebration of variety, creativity, and bounty, coming as it did, for the first time on this scale, after so many years of cultural barrenness.

Source: *After the Nightmare* by Liang Heng and Judith Shapiro. New York: Alfred Knopf, 1986, p. 99.

Hong Kong

Lantern Festival in Hong Kong and the New Territories

In North China the Lantern Festival which marked the end of the New Year period really was a public occasion for lantern processions, masked parades and dragon dances. In Hong Kong more lanterns are seen at the Mid-Autumn Festival in Moon Eight than now, though a rather recent attempt to start an annual children's lantern parade has caught on successfully in the city.

In the villages of the New Territories, however, lanterns are dressed and hung in the *Ancestral Halls* at this time, and any local family to whom a son has been born during the past year brings a lantern to the *Ancestral Hall.* Later, the male members of the clan sit together in the *Ancestral Hall* to eat a special meal.

Source: *Chinese Festivals in Hong Kong* by Joan Law and Barbara E. Ward. Hong Kong: A South China Morning Post Production, 1982, p. 7.

1981 Lantern Festival in Beijing

In 1981 Lantern Festival came on February 19. The snowfall that morning was taken as an auspicious omen of a coming bumper harvest.

Many different programs were scheduled. At the Children's Palace in Beijing some children stood with lanterns in their hands, others danced around them, while still others set off firecrackers. One could also enjoy Peking Opera, *qu yi* (a category of folk art forms including ballad singing, story telling, comic dialogues, clapper talks, and cross talks), puppet shows, calligraphy and painting exhibitions, including New Year pictures, and ship and plane model displays. All of these activities were organized by young people.

Source: *Chinese Traditional Festivals* by Marie-Luise Latch. Beijing, China: New World Press, 1984, pp. 44-45.

Taiwan

Lanterns in many shapes

Some of the most popular kinds of lanterns are those made in the shape of Kuan Kung's great sword, the Lotus Blossom, or the animal who's horary character is patron protector for that year. Thus in the year of the rabbit, rabbits will be in great abundance; and so with dragons, tigers, monkeys, horse, or snake. A candle is usually burned inside the children's lanterns, whereas electric lightbulbs burn in the temple exhibits. The larger temples compete with each other in the size and beauty of lanterns. Sometimes complete historical scenes are depicted, such as the visit of Wen Wang at the beginning of the Chou Dynasty (1050 B.C.) to the famous minister Chiang T'ai-kung, who is seen fishing with a pole but no hook.

The origin of the lanterns was supposed to be from an ancient ceremony welcoming back the Spring light. Willow branches and lanterns were used, the willow being used to welcome spring rains. Another tradition says that the lanterns are used to ward off evil spirits which roam about on this night, the first full moon of the new year. Evil spirits can be seen in the eerie light made by the lanterns, and thus avoided. But as long ago as T'ang Dynasty it had become a purely secular feast, the Emperor decreeing that all of Ch'ang An, the ancient capitol, be decked out in great splendor for the entertainment of the court and foreign visitors. A Ming Emperor was supposed to have set out so many lanterns that even Buddha came down from heaven to see it.

Historical background of the Lantern Festival

The Lantern Festival in the evening of the 15th, is mainly a children's feast day. There is no longer any religious significance given to the lanterns which the children carry about. Originally the lanterns hung in the temples were supposed to be given in Thi-kong's honor; others say in honor of "T'ai Chi" or the Eternal Principle from which all things flow. But in reality the lanterns carried about in the evening are simply for everyone's enjoyment. They are made in every shape and size, and show great ingenuity on the part of the artisans who make them.

Dragon dance

Also the dragon dance is performed in the streets, consisting of 8 young men carrying about a huge dragon made of cloth and strung along bamboo poles. The dragon is eternally chasing a large red pearl, carried by the leader of the group. Bystanders throw firecrackers, often of alarming size, at the performers, and scream with delight as the dragon-dancers try to get out from under the exploding fireworks. The dragon dance is more popular in Hakka territories, Miao Li being most famous for the size and number of its dragons.

Source: *Taiwan Feasts and Customs* by Michael R. Saso. Hsinchu, Taiwan: Chabanel Language Institute, pp. 30-31.

For more information on the Lantern Festival, see: "The Chinese Feast of Lanterns" by Henry Winfred Splitter in *Journal of American Folklore,* 63, no. 250 (Oct.-Dec. 1950), pp. 438-443. "The Lantern Festival" in *Chinese Traditional Festivals* by Marie-Luise Latsch. Beijing, China: New World Press, 1984. pp. 37-45.

Moon 1, Day 15

Síong Goan

This is the birthday of Thian-koan Tai-te, the Great Emperor-official of the Heavens. The year is divided into three parts: heaven, earth, and water. The first lunar moon marks the ''upper principle'' (i.e., heaven).

Taiwan

Síong Goan and the Lantern Festival

Two different feasts are celebrated on the 15th of the first month. The first is the birthday of ''Thian-koan Tai-tè'', The Great Emperor-official of the Heavens. He is one of the Taoist Trinity, who rule the heaven, the earth, and the Sea. The second is the Lantern Festival, observed in the evening of the same day. The Lantern Festival is more of a children's holiday, while the birthday of ''Thian-koan'' centers more around the popular temples.

Source: *Taiwan Feasts and Customs* by Michael R. Saso. Hsinchu, Taiwan: Chabanel Language Institute, p. 26.

Moon 1, Day 16

Jurokunichi (16th day)

On the sixteenth day of the first moon, Okinawans visit family graves. The graves are cleaned on this day and food and prayers are offered.

Okinawa

Food offerings in Hanashiro c. 1953

In Hanashiro, food is taken in two lacquer boxes (*jūbako*) the first of which contains rice cakes, the second, fritters, meat, bean curd, and other food depending on the resources of the family. For the first observance after death, two boxes are taken on this holiday. On succeeding anniversaries only the box containing the fritters, meat, bean curd and other foods is taken. The purpose of this offering is to comfort the dead. The food, usually with tea and *sake,* is left before the tomb for about two hours and taken home, where it is eaten.

Source: *Studies of Okinawan Village Life* by Clarence J. Glacken. Scientific Investigations in the Ryukyu Islands (SIRI) Report no. 4. Wash. D.C., Pacific Science Board Council, 1953, p. 323.

Moon 1, Day 19

The Rat's Wedding Day

On the nineteenth day of the first moon, the ''Rat's Wedding Day'' is observed in some Chinese households. Household rats may be feted on this day, especially the ''Money Rat,'' whose auspicious presence is desired.

China

A day to propitiate household rats

The celebration of the Rats' Wedding Day is annually observed on the 19th of the First Moon. Everyone goes to bed early, so as not to disturb the revels of their four-footed tenants. As a wedding without a banquet would be a Barmecide's Feast, at which the rats would be certain to take umbrage, a collation is spread, and placed within the reach of these exalted visitors. The offering is made to induce the more benevolent rodents to exercise restraint over the more unruly of their tribe, to moderate their appetites during the year or, at any rate, divert their depredations from the household of their benefactor.

If a very large rat, with a paunch of aldermanic proportions, takes up its residence in a house, it is treated as an honoured guest, for this is the Money Rat whose arrival indicates the advent of affluence, more than compensating for his board and lodging.

Source: *Chinese Creeds and Customs* by V.R. Burkhardt. Hong Kong: South China Morning Post, 1982, p. 197.

Mid-January

Magh Sankranti

This is a solar holiday, celebrating the day on which the sun heads back toward the northern hemisphere.

Nepal

Bathing and sunning on Magh Sankranti

Though this day is usually very cold, the Nepalese visit holy bathing spots on this day. Musicians and singers perform on open porches at the river's edge. The more interpid worshippers strip to their loincloths to bathe in the shallow water. Others merely splash the water on their hands and face, and flick drops over their heads. The temple of the Red Machhendranath at Patan is visited by crowds of worshippers on this day. Especially auspicious foods are sesame seeds, sweet potatoes, spinach, a mixture of rice and lentils called *khichari,* meat, and home-brewed wine and beer. Married daughters return to their parental homes and the mother blesses all her children by patting mustard oil on their heads and placing a few drops in the ear for a long life of good fortune. People sit in the sun on this day, using mustard-oil massage. Priests sit on meeting platforms reading aloud from holy books and receive alms and gifts of the season's auspicious foods. A clay fire pot and a small bundle of wood are traditional gifts for Brahman priests on this day.

Source: ''The Holy Month of Magh'' by Mary K. Anderson, in *The Festivals of Nepal.* London: Allen and Unwin, 1971, pp. 223-224.

Pausa/Thai, Days 1-4

Pongal/Sankranti

A harvest festival lasting three days, it is called Pongal in Tamil and Sankranti in Karnataka.

India

Pongal-Sankranti in South India

The Hindus in South India celebrate the Pongal-Sankranti festival every year in the month of Pausa (January-February)—mainly in the State of Tamil Nadu, Andhra Pradesh and Karnataka. It is the gayest and the biggest harvest festival spread over three days. In Tamil Nadu, it is named Pongal and in Karnataka as Sankranti. Pongal denotes a sweet preparation of rice. A *Ratha-Yatra* procession is taken out from the Kandaswamy temple in Madras on Pongal day.

Bhogi Pongal is the first of the three-day festival and is observed as a family festival. The second day's festival is celebrated for the worship of Surya, the Sun god. Thus, it is named Surya Pongal. Rice boiled in milk and jaggery is offered to the sun. Friends greet one another and ask each other ''Is it boiled?'' and the reply is ''Yes, it is''. Great rejoicing prevails during the festival days. On the third day, *Mattu-Pongal* is observed for the worship of cattle (*mattu*). The cattle are given bath [*sic*] and their horns nicely cleaned and polished. Beautiful flower garlands are hung round their necks. The Pongal that has been offered to the local deities is also given to the cattle and birds to eat.

In Madurai, Tiruchirapalli and Tanjore (Tamil Nadu) the festival known as *Jellikattu,* is observed on this occasion. Bundles containing money are tied to the horns of ferocious bulls, and unarmed villagers try to wrest the bundles from them. Community meals are prepared from the freshly gathered harvest. The rich, the poor and even the passers-by are invited to join the feast.

Source: *Festivals of India* by Brijendra Nath Sharma. New Delhi: Abhinav, 1978, p. 56.

A period of thanksgiving for harvests

As has already been stated, Pongal in its present form is celebrated as a four-day festival but the fourth day is slowly ceasing to be observed. The first day of Pongal, called ''Bogi'', falls on the first day of the month, ''Thi'', the day of Sankranti and the Ganga Sagar Mela, ''Bogi'' can be compared to Dante's ''Purgatario'' because it is the day of cleansing. As the Bengalis do on their New Year's Day, on ''Bogi'' every cobweb is swept off by a broom, every speck of dirt is mopped off by a duster, every moth-eaten volume is taken out, dusted, and restored with a fresh quota of napthalene balls, and every inch of the walls and ceilings is colour-washed. Houses, shops, offices, factories, all are cleaned and renovated thoroughly; lock, stock, and barrel in the manner of the Dutch scrubbing their houses. When pilgrims wash away their spiritual sins in the Ganga on Sankranti, the Tamils wash away their material sins on ''Bogi''.

The second day is the actual day of Pongal. On that day the new and freshly harvested rice is cooked in a new pitcher on a new ''chula'' out in the open. Once the rice gets cooked, directly an offering is made to the Sun-God with a part of the cooked rice, plantains, sugar-cane and betel-nuts. It is an expression of thanksgiving to the originator and preserver of all life on earth, the Sun, for the bounty of the harvest. Freshly cooked rice is the main offering because rice is the staple food of the Tamils. The offering of sugar-cane beside is, of course, sweetness symbolised. Importance is also attached to the rich foaming of milk while boiling, without spilling over, on this day. That is considered an auspicious sign. As already mentioned, the foaming of milk is one of the literal implications of the word ''Pongal''. Apart from this offering and worship to the sun, the second day is one of social get-togethers and feasting, an expression of joy and triumphant delight in the abundance of the harvest.

The third day is the ''Festival of the Cow'' or ''Mattuppongal''. On this day the main event is bull-chasing. The horns of a rough bull are sharpened and painted. A network of tamarind fibres soaked in paints and dried, coconut husk, and bananas, loaded with silver coins, gold rings, and other such valuables, is fastened to the neck of the bull, and the bull is worshipped for a while. After the worship a host of trumpets is sounded to induce the bull to wildly run about helter-skelter. The young men who participate in the event would each try to literally catch the bull by the horns and untie the network of valuables from its neck. To him who succeeds belong all the valuables untied. The victor is also acclaimed as the bravest of the lot.

The fourth day is the day of meeting people, of re-establishing old and forgotten connections and relationships. As said before, this has lost its importance because the second day itself is observed as a day of social feasting, of playing hosts and guests. This has reduced Pongal from a four-day festival to a three-day one.

Source: ''Pongal of Tamil Nadu'' by S.H. Venkatramani in

Popular Festivals of India ed. by Sunil Kumar Nag. Calcutta, Golden Books of India, 1983, p. 45.

Malaya

Pongal in Tamil families

The first day of *Thai* is, of course, the most important day of this festival. A couple of days earlier the entire house and compound is meticulously cleaned up and all things necessary for celebrations are assembled. As it is a festival of thanksgiving for the new harvest that is collected at this time, the chief item is the cooking of some of the newly harvested rice. The place where the rice is to be cooked is washed with cow dung mixed with water and decorated by a lotus pattern drawn out of powdered rice by the housewife. In the centre is the design of the Sun God. This art of decoration (*kolam*) is a speciality of the Indian housewife. They sometimes weave some delightful patterns and a beautifully executed decoration is a compliment to the womenfolk in the house. The householders are up before sunrise and bathe their whole bodies in water. They wear new clothes. The pot is decorated with saffron. Sometimes fresh produce from the gardens such as sugar cane, pumpkins, *valli* yam is ceremoniously spread out. Then a new pot is put on a fire built up in the courtyard of the house and filled with milk and water. As the milk boils up, a male in the household puts into it some of the rice from the year's harvest. The rice is now allowed to boil in the pot for some time and when the rice is cooked, diverse other items are added to it for taste. While the pot is boiling crackers are fired profusely with intermittent cries of *pongalo-pongal* (Hail! Pongal). The cooked rice, called *pukkai* (in Tamil), is then served on three banana leaves and offered to the Sun-God. Camphor is lighted and the God is invoked. Thereafter the householders partake of the rice. No non-vegetarian food may be cooked in the house on that day. It is this boiling over—*pongal*—that has given this name to the festival. People would greet each other with the phrase: 'has it boiled-over'. The *pooja* (worship) thus performed is in the way of offering the first fruits to the Sun-God on the day the Sun begins the northward course. Later in the evening people visit the temple where special *poojas* are carried on and the ceremonial boiled rice is served. Sometimes bullocks are tied to the cart and taken in procession to shouts of *pongalo-pongal*.

The day following *pongal* is a day of reverence and homage to cattle—*mattu* (cow) *pongal*. This is in recognition of the importance of cattle to an agrarian community. This is observed in the rural settlements of Malaya where most Tamil workers rear cattle as a bye-employment. On this day the cattle are given a good scrub and bath and decorated with garlands and red saffron (*kunkumam*) on the horns. They are not burdened in any way on that day but are the centre of all attention. The ceremonial boiled rice is offered to them together with other sweetmeats and sugar cane. Then they are allowed to roam the countryside in all their finery. On the following day there is general merry-making and visiting of friend's houses to exchange *pongal* greetings. Labourers and domestic workers visit the houses of their employers to receive gifts.

Source: *Indian Festivals in Malaya* by S. Arasaratnam. Kuala Lumpur: Department of Indian Studies, University of Malaya, 1966, pp. 7-8.

Thai/Tai

Thai Poosam

This is the day when the asterism Poosam is in the ascendant in the month of Thai. This is the birthday of Lord Subramaniam and is the occasion for temple visits and processions. Kavadee-carrying is popular at this festival in several places.

India

Tai Pusam

Observances in South India

The festival known as Tai Pusam is observed every year in South India in the Tamil month of Tai (January-February). People believe that kings like Indra, Hamsa-Dvajan and Varaguna Pandyan were liberated from sins on the Tai Pusam day. This day is all the more important, because on this day Parvati had given to her second son Subrahmanyam, a weapon called lance or *Vel* at Vathiswarankoil. Besides other places, the festival is observed with great fervour at Tiruvidaimarudur in Tanjore district and also at Palni, all in Tamil Nadu.

Source: *The Festivals of India* by Brijendra Nath Sharma. New Delhi: Abhinav, 1978, p. 59.

Malaya

Thai Poosam

Celebrations in Kuala Lumpur

The festival generally lasts for three days. Nationally the most famous venue for celebrations is Batu Caves situated about 8 miles away from Kuala Lumpur. The starting point is the Maha Mariamman Temple at High Street. On the day previous to *Thai Poosam,* the first day of celebrations, the statue of Subramanya is decorated with expensive jewels and finery and, together with his two consorts, *Valli* and *Theivanai,* on either side, is set on a tall chariot (*ratham*) drawn by bullocks. The chariot is a work of art made out of carved wood, plated over with silver and decorated with statues of gods, goddesses and animals. Each large temple has its own chariot expensively made and taken out on festive occasions to carry the deity in procession. The chariot is decked with flags, tinsel and streamers, and on the whole presents a magnificent spectacle. Early in the morning after *poojas* the chariot with the deity is drawn in procession along a pre-planned route, taking it through the main streets of the city to Ipoh Road and to Batu Caves. The procession is joined by many devotees singing hymns in praise of Subramanya and frequently chanting the slogan "*vel-vel, vetri-vel,*" in honour of the invincible weapon of this deity. Some devotees throw coins into the chariot but this is now discouraged by the organizers. When the procession reaches the foot of Batu Caves, the statue is lifted out of the chariot and carried up the steep steps into the Cave. It is placed in the shrine beside the statue that is permanently there.

The scene at Batu Caves

The following day, the *Poosam* festival proper begins. Batu Caves, situated so close to the city and yet offering wide open spaces for extensive lay-out of the festivities, is an ideal place for such an occasion. It is the Malayan equivalent of the historical Palani hill shrine in India. Hill-top shrines have been traditionally considered suitable for dedication to Subramanya. On this occasion, the whole area takes on the aspect of a religiously inspired carnival. In recent years the numbers that throng to participate in and witness the festival keep increasing and now the organizers cater for a crowd of about 200,000. Elaborate traffic arrangements are made in co-operation with the Police authorities. The whole place is electrically illuminated from funds contributed voluntarily. Temporary sheds and stalls are erected to house devotees who come from distant parts and spend three to four days at this place. Youth volunteer organizations are at hand to look after the diverse needs and problems created by such a vast assemblage. Baby-sitters, for example, are available to look after babies of people while they climb the steps into the Caves. Film shows, merry-go-rounds and similar entertainment are provided in the extensive grounds to keep the people amused. From early morning of *Poosam* day, devotees of Subramanya will pour into the Caves to pay homage to him and perform the rituals of this homage.

Carrying the kavadi

The modes of devotion on this day are many and varied. They differ according to the intensity of religious fervour of the worshiper. The most extreme form of devotion is the carrying of *kavadi* for the deity. Carrying a *kavadi* is a popular form of penance for Subramanya and the practice will be found in all parts where Hinduism is practised. It is usually in fufilment of a vow that the devotee has taken in furtherance of some desired objective in his life or as recompense for the avoidance of some calamity. The recovery from some serious illness or the realization of a great desire such as the birth of a child would be the occasion for a vow to bear *kavadi* for Subramanya on *Thai Poosam* day. The prospective *kavadi* bearer must prepare himself spiritually for the event by a life of abstinence for a period before the date of the ceremony. He must live on a fully vegetarian diet and must not indulge in physical pleasures. The *kavadi* is a wooden arch on a wooden base decorated with peacock feathers and paper, carried by the devotee on his shoulders. It supports on this base ritual objects like a pot of milk, jaggery or different kinds of fruits. All these objects are offered to the deity at the end of the journey, the milk being used for libations. Before the *kavadi* bearer begins his journey he and other bearers assemble at a shrine where a ceremony is performed and he is put in the proper spiritual mood. The bearers subject themselves to varying degrees of torture. Sharp skewers are thrust through the middle of their tongues and through both cheeks. Their bodies are pierced with hooks or spear-like needles. Some times these hooks are attached with strings to the kavadi and sometimes they are held on a rope by a person who guides the devotee. Some penitents dance their way through the entire route in spiritual frenzy. In a state of utter exhaustion they begin the painful ascent to the Caves where the *kavadi* is deposited at the feet of the deity and their penitence accepted.

Non-Hindus and Thai Poosam

The growing popularity of *Thai Poosam* as the festival of the Hindus in Malaya has attracted many non-Hindus who now begin to participate in these ceremonies. Many of them visit the various shrines at which the festivals are held and take part in the rituals. One occasionally hears of a few Chinese carrying the *kavadi*. In Singapore, before independence, Colonial Governors used to visit the temple on this day. This tradition is now carried on by the Prime Minister of the state who is officially received by the priests at the temple.

Source: *Indian Festivals in Malaya* by S. Arasaratnam. Kuala Lumpur: Department of Indian Studies, Univ. of Malaya, 1966, pp. 17-19.

Mauritius

Cavadee observance

Mind over pain is put to the test by a man of the Tamil people in Mauritius, who has been pierced with pins and skewers for the religious observances of Cavadee. Indians were brought to Mauritius by the British in the 19th century as indentured laborers and are now the largest group on an overpopulated, cyclone-wracked island dependent on sugar as its main crop.

Source: "Crosscurrents Sweep the Indian Ocean" by Bart McDowell in *National Geographic*, (October, 1981), 422-457.

Singapore

Thaipusam

Thaipusam in Singapore

A major local Hindu temple, the Perumal Temple, located in the Serangoon Road precincts is the centre from which Hindu celebrations radiate. The most vibrant and colourful of these is perhaps the *Thaipusam* ceremony. In Serangoon Road, Thaipuṣam starts some days before the actual event. The elaborate paraphernalia, from the simplest kavadi to the ritual offerings, can be obtained here. The astonishing array of items includes banana leaves on which offerings are made—coconut, turmeric, *sambrani*—peacock feathers; plastic-moulded images of central deities especially the boy-god Muruga with his peacock carrier; flowers for the gods and flowers for the women-folk; tinsel decorations and the various embellishments that make up at least the basic frame of a kavadi.

As dawn breaks in Serangoon Road on Thaipusam day, the trickle of Indians into the area gradually becomes a vibrant flood. Gaily decorated *pandals* set up the day before, front temples and shops along the route of the procession; these stalls provide free drinks for the devotees—a welcome thirst-quencher as the day grows hotter. Financed by devotees as another form of obeisance to the day, the drinks popularly offered at the pandals usually include lime juice and lassi. Some devotees converge on the grounds of the Perumal Temple itself where there is a bustle of activity. Here prayers are made by kavadi-carriers, their offerings including the paraphernalia which is to be blessed before it is worn. Their family and friends gather round to help set up the kavadis, most of which are very elaborately constucted. And as the kavadi-carrier finally walks out from the temple, he is followed by his faithful supporters whose loud prayers (sometimes accompanied by sounds from tin cans and plastic containers, as the government has now banned music from these processions) filling the environs of Serangoon Road are essential to help the kavadi-carrier concentrate and so ease his load. Other devotees, having completed their *pujas* at the various Serangoon Road temples, crowd along the roads at vantage points to await the passing-by of an acquaintance kavadi-carrier, finally joining him in the procession as it winds its way along the set route, eventually to disperse at the Chettiar Temple in Tank Road.

Source: *Singapore's Little India: Past, Present and Future* by Sharon Siooique and Nirmala Puru Shotam. Singapore: Institute of Southeast Asian Studies, 1982, pp. 113-115.

South Africa

Kavady during Thai Poosam

Kavady, a Hindu rite, is carried out by devotees at several Durban Temples during Thai Poosam and also during Chitray Massum (April-May). Devotees carry ritual shrines on their head and shoulders. These and other ornaments are often fastened to the body by hooks and skewers. Kavady is usually carried in fulfillment of a vow. The Kavady period lasts 12 days, the climax being the procession on day 10.

The opening of kavady

Each devotee takes a vow of abstinence from all ''flesh'' and contamination with things ''unclean'' during the period of *kavady*. To signify the vow, the priest ties round the wrist of each, beginning with the *koval kavady* carrier, a bangle of *dharbar* grass (a grass used in many Hindu rituals) or a bangle with a special seed. The ceremony is known as *kaapu katoorangu*—bangle tying.

The people gather in front of the temple again and pray in an atmosphere of gathering excitement. The musicians play loudly on their varied instruments, the priest leads in the chanting of prayers, and the audience gives periodic cries of '*Arogora*'. The night air is heavy with the scent of flowers and the burning of incense. Everything is set for the god to manifest himself.

It is usual for a few of the devotees, particularly the *koval kavady* carrier, to get the trance.

The 10th-day procession

The next stage of the ritual takes place at the nearest river or stream. Before picking up their burdens, each carrier lights a camphor and prays, and the priest performs *devrathnum*—the ritual circling with holy substances and prayers to remove evil for the *kavady* and the chariots. Music is again essential and a public address system is installed in most of the temples in addition to the temple musicians, and plays both secular and religious records.

Towards noon, the procession led by the musicians and followed by the priest, devotees and temple officials, circle the temple and make a prayer before leaving for the river. Though at this stage some begin to go into trance, it is not encouraged and soon ''passes''. The chariots, laden with ritual ingredients, are pulled by devotees not yet in trance.

The procession must cross the river and put the *kavady* in a cleared space on the opposite bank. (If the river is too far, a hose pipe has been substituted; people must go through the ritual cleansing of running water.) After a ritual wash, the devotees return to the final preparation of their burdens. The carriers put on special clothing—the women wear saris usually of yellow, the men, most of whom are exposed to the waist, usually wear the *soremum* over shorts or trunks. All have the bangle, and many wear a traditional rosary with a single bead; the *koval kovady* is distinguished by a rosary of six-faced beads.

The *kavady* are arranged in an outer square with the chariots; within the square, in positions laid down by the priest, are the *polkodum* and various purifying substances, leaving a special place for an essential preliminary rite—the *egium* (*jagnam*), sacred fire ritual. The *kavady* and *polkodum* are all anointed with sacred unguents—turmeric water, rose water, sandalwood paste, milk, sweet oil or sometimes honey. Each ointment is washed off with fresh water before the next is put on, and eventually sacred ash is placed on the sides in the sign of Siva and marked with red dots. Additional garlands are woven round the *kavady*, banana leaves and *dharbar* grass are tied to the frame.

Once the *egium* is over, the devotees return to their burdens, put the final garlands round their necks and wait for the priest to tell the musicians when they must begin. The first piercing sound on the wind instruments (*nagasurum* and *thothee*) usually has an immediate and startling effect. Many devotees begin to show the symptoms of the oncoming trance, and those who will carry their burdens without the trance share in the tension and excitement of the crowd.

A man in a blue shirt and dark trousers sings hymns for a young man in a pale yellow *dhoti* who takes three or four minutes to go into a trance. When he does, they stick needles into his forehead. At 1.59 another man (yellow *dhoti*) puts out his tongue and a tongue pin is stuck through. The one in lemon *dhoti* now has hooks in his chest and a spike through both cheeks over the ends of which is fixed a U-shaped piece of silver wire with eyes in its ends to slip over the spike.

''There are now four or five young men with tongue pin in and hooks in various parts of the body. On some of these are hung limes and carnations and limes and marigolds. One has pendants symmetrically arranged on back and front of arms and in his back. A boy of twelve to fourteen has tongue pin and hooks in his back. Women prostrate themselves before those in trance. We see tongue pins and hooks being inserted. There is no sign of pain in expression on face which give a feeling of serenity. . . . The only woman who appears to be in trance (at this stage) sways and dances—difficult to say which—quietly with a blank expression on her face. The woman has a tongue pin (gold) and five pins in the forehead. There are two young men (probably under 20) who have not gone into a trance. They stand quietly with rather strained expressions on their faces. A woman (''probably his mother'' according to our assistant) stands next to one of them with her palms together. . . . The man with pendants now has seven brass bowls (with milk) suspended in a row from upper arms and chest''.

All possible means are invoked to spread the trance. The musicians blow loudly on any wind instruments they possess and beat *woodika* (drums). Devotees who have the trance wander among the crowd trying to communicate their power and bestow blessings. Those not yet affected often stand deep in concentration and meditation while their assistants pray from the sacred books.

When the worshippers are at their highest pitch of identification, the priest directs the return to the temple. Each devotee raises his or her *kavady* on to a shoulder, or balances the *polkodum* on the head. Generally the left side is considered the man's and the right the woman's, and the left hand is ''unclean'' and the right ''clean''. In *kavady* ''man or woman doesn't matter''. In the front of the procession comes the *koval kavady* carrier and the child devotees, and the chariot puller brings up the rear. Assistants sprinkle rose water or milk on the tongues of devotees in trance and drop water and light camphor at their feet. Bystanders prostrate themselves and supplicate blessings, and some devotees pour milk from their bowls into eagerly outstretched hands, and the recipients drink it or rub it over their persons.

The procession circles the temple three times, then the devotees place their *kavady* in front of the flag post and go inside to the priest who is waiting to remove the instruments. When he has done so, assistants rub holy ash on the bodies. After having bowed low before the image, the devotees who show no signs of exhaustion, go outside to join the crowd. They partake of their first cooked meal—again vegetarian—since the previous evening.

Source: ''An Ethnographic Description of Kavady, a Hindu Ceremony in South Africa'' by Hilda Kuper in *African Studies* 18, no. 3 (1959), 118-132.

February

Clean Tent Ceremony

This is a Nganasan ceremony that took place when the sun first appeared after the polar winter.

U.S.S.R. (Nganasan)

The clean tent and stone gate rituals

The most important religious rites of the Nganasans were the celebration of the ''clean tent'' (madusya) and the custom of passing through ''stone gates'' (fala-futu). The ceremony of the ''clean tent'' took place in February, when the sun was beginning to appear after the polar night. A special tent was erected, and from morn till night for 3 to 9 days the shaman sat in it, invoking the beneficence of the deities for the whole of the people in the coming year.

During the ceremony, the young people danced and played near the ''clean tent.'' Sometimes this festival was replaced by the ritual of passage through the stone gates. For this purpose something like a tunnel was made from stone slabs. For 3 days the spells were cast, after which the shaman and all those present passed three times through the gates.

Source: *The Peoples of Siberia,* Ed. by M. G. Levine and L. P. Potapov. Chicago: Univ. of Chicago Press, 1964, p. 579.

Circa February

Tsagan Sara (New Year)

A Mongolian New Year observance, Tsagan Sara, the White Moon celebration, has been altered into an agricultural event under the communist regime.

Mongolia

White Moon celebration

Originally the New Year celebration, Tsagan Sara, this festival is now an agricultural celebration of the collective farmers. The "Three Manly Games," *Eryn Gurvan Nadom,* are enjoyed. They are wrestling, horse racing, and archery.

Source: *International What's What When & Where* by Ardith Nehrt. Columbus, Ohio: Shawnee International Publishing, 1965, p. 72.

February
Winterlude

This is a civic midwinter festival held in Ottawa. Winterlude is a 10-day extravaganza of sports, entertainment, fun and games.

Canada (Ottawa)

A celebration of winter sports

Focal point for most activities is the frozen surface of the Rideau Canal, billed as the world's longest skating rink. Granted, most other Canadian cities provide outdoor skating facilities. But none can match the length (eight kilometres) and prime location of the one in Canada's capital.

But Winterlude is more than just a frozen canal. It celebrates virtually all winter sports. In addition to pleasure skating, there's everything from snowshoeing, skiing, speedskating, curling, tobogganing and sleigh rides, to ice sculpting, dogsled racing, lumberjack contests, barrel jumping and harness racing.

Participation and enjoyment are the main ingredients—and some 450,000 people took part last year.

That people can choose between participating or watching is the beauty of Winterlude—although some argue otherwise. As one critic commented after last year's festival: ''The rink was designed to get people out on skates; (but) the main focus of Winterlude seems to be a series of events which people are invited to come and watch.''

True, it's better to wear warm boots than skates to some events, particularly Ice Dream, a wonderland of snow sculptures which requires an hour-long stroll to appreciate fully. But on the whole, Winterlude happily accommodates both skaters and non-skaters; the canal is big enough for both. Everyone can play. In fact, everyone does play, one way or another, if only to keep warm.

Source: ''Winterlude: The Nation's Capital Pauses to Revel in the Cold'' by Eric Harris in *Canadian Geographic* 104 (6) (December 84/January 85), 45-46.

February 1
St. Brigid's Day

Saint Brigid was the fifth-century nun who founded the first convent in Ireland. She was known for her generosity. Saint Brigid is the patron Saint of Ireland.

Ireland

The legend of Saint Brigid

After New Year's, the first noteworthy festival day is February first, the feast of St. Brigid. This good woman, with Patrick and Columeille (Columba) one of the three great saints of Ireland, was born in bondage. Sold by her father, she was later freed and then returned voluntarily to him as a serving girl. As a cowherd, she milked the cows and made the butter. Extremely warmhearted, she gave things away with a prodigality that was often the despair of her associates. She wove the first piece of cloth in Ireland, and so became the patron of weavers and spinners. Even when she became the head of a monastery, she remained devoted to rural occupations—reaping, and making butter and ale. Wild ducks came to her when she called; she was also able to tame a wild boar. A common woman, then, and an Irish woman, she was warm, compassionate, generous, and with a delightful vision of paradise: "A great lake of ale for the King of Kings;. . .the family of heaven to be drinking it through all time;. . .cheerfulness to be in their drinking;. . .Jesus to be here among them;. . .vessels full of alms to be giving away."

St. Brigid is closely linked with the Virgin Mary, whose festival of Candlemas falls on February second. It is said that when Mary was giving birth to Jesus, Brigid averted the eyes of the onlookers, so a grateful Mary let Brigid have her festival first.

St. Brigid's Day superstitions

Brigid has become associated with fire, and the fire that is blessed at Candlemas is thought to be hers. Indeed, St. Brigid has a number of attributes that may be carried over from pre-Christian times: On her day, people can do no work that involves spinning, digging, or turning a wheel: "St. Brigid's Day is free from twistings." St. Brigid's crosses are made from rushes on this day, then stuck in the roof thatching to protect the house. The first good weather comes with her day, because (variant 1) she placed her foot in water on her feast day or because (variant 2) she dipped her finger in the brook, and off went the hen that hatches the cold.

Source: *Irish History and Culture* by Harold Orel. Lawrence: Univ. Press of Kansas, 1976, pp. 131-132.

Saint Brigid's Day crosses

In Ballymenone crosses were woven of rushes and hung over the door for luck on Saint Brigid's Eve. They would hang there during the coming year. They might be hung over byre doors, as well as at the entrance, or over the bedroom doors.

Source: *Passing the Time in Ballymenone* by Henry Glassie. Philadelphia: Univ. of Pennsylvania, 1982, p. 355.

St. Brigid's customs in early Ireland

St. Brighid's Day, 1st February, was not only the feast-day of the national female patron saint but also the beginning of the new agricultural year. In a less sophisticated society it marked the end of the privations of winter and the beginnings of growth and renewal. In pre-Christian times it was undoubtedly also a folk festival, and the early missionaries probably turned the old pagan feast into one of religious significance. St. Brighid became the symbol of the season, and the year's agricultural prospects were regarded as depending on her intercession and consequently her feast-day was celebrated with due reverence. The omens observed on that day were carefully noted, but the ritual was of prime importance and this varied from district to district. The most common custom was that of making St. Brighid's Crosses. These took different forms in different districts and were usually made either on the eve of the feast-day or on the day itself. In the midlands only a small number of crosses were made, but in the north crosses were made in large numbers and placed in different places. In some areas a small folk play was enacted when a girl playing the part of the saint sought admission to the house, was allowed in, blessed the family, joined them for supper and helped make the crosses. In some areas a doll, sometimes made of straw and called a *Brideóg* represented the saint and was carried from house to house by a group in disguise who collected money or gifts. The rhymes used by the groups were handed down from generation to generation and probably are faint reminders of a medieval religious ceremony.

Festive meals

By St. Brighid's Day half the winter stock of food and fuel was supposed to be used up. In the O'Neill land of Co. Armagh apples were saved for St. Brighid's Eve to make griddle apple cakes for a festive meal following the making of the St.

Brighid's Crosses. Shellfish were eaten around Galway on the same day to bring luck to the fishermen for the following year.

Source: *Life and Tradition in Rural Ireland* by Timothy P. O'Neill. London: J.M. Dent and Sons, Ltd., 1977, p. 62, 64, 101.

February 1-3 (Circa)

Setsubun

During this last-day-of-winter festival, dried beans are tossed to drive out devils and bring in good luck.

Japan

Mame-maki (bean throwing)

Commenorating the last day of winter according to the lunar calendar, this festival is held at all major temples throughout the country. The main attraction is *mame-maki* (bean throwing) when the temple priests or luminaries such as actors and sumo wrestlers throw handfuls of beans to the crowd who chant in unison, ''*Fuku wa uchi, oni wa soto*'' (in with good luck, out with the devils). Some people go home and eat the number of beans that correspond with their age to insure their good luck. During this time, the *Mandoro* Festival also takes place where thousands of stone and bronze lanterns are lit at Kasuga Shrine in Nara.

Source: *Japan Handbook* by J. D. Bisignani. Chico, Calif.: Moon Publications, 1983, p. 73.

Setsubun at Miyaamoto-cho, Tokyo, c. 1980

The Setsubun holiday in February (at the end of winter, according to the old calendar) is a time for assuring good luck for the coming year by scattering dried beans to the chant of ''*Oni ga soto, fuku ga uchi!*'' (''Out with the devils, and in with good fortune!''). Members of the ujiko sōdai and other prominent local leaders (especially those born in the current year of the 12-year zodiacal cycle) toss dried beans—loose and in packets—from the shrine veranda as children, housewives, and grandmothers clamber to catch the scattered beans in hands, purses, or shopping bags; beans caught at the shrine are taken home for household exorcisms.

Source: *Neighborhood Tokyo* by Theodore C. Bestor. Stanford, Calif.: Stanford Univ. Press, 1989, p. 157.

February 2

Candlemas/Candelaria

Candlemas is a Celebration of the presentation of Jesus at the temple. Simeon took the Babe in his arms and said Jesus would be the "Light to lighten the Gentiles." Thus the day is celebrated with candles. It is also called the purification of Mary, as Mary underwent the ritual purification forty days after childbirth on this day. Candlemas is thus forty days after Christmas.

Austria

Candlemas in an Austrian family

All through the month of January the crèche is standing in the living room, even if the Christmas tree has been removed, and every night the family prayers will be said beside the crib, followed by at least one Christmas song.

When Holy Mother Church came to Rome, in the time of the Apostles, she found that the Roman women went around town with torches and other lights on February 1st in honor of the goddess Ceres. The Church continued the same custom but "baptized" it: Forty days after the birth of a child the Jewish mother had to be purified in the temple, and so we celebrate on February 2nd the Purification of Mary and the Presentation of her little Son in the Temple; this should be celebrated in the light of many candles, in honor of Him of Whom the old Simeon said on that day, "He shall illumine the Gentiles with His light and shall be the glory of the people of Israel." There was a special blessing for the water on Epiphany Day, and there is a special solemn blessing for the candles on this Candlemas Day. Besides having beautiful prayers, the Church helps us to understand the symbolism of the light blessed on this day, so that we may make the right use of it by the bed of the dying, during storms, and in all perils to which may be exposed "our bodies and souls on land and on the waters." The five special prayers of Candlemas Day are so beautiful and so full of meaning that they should be read aloud as evening prayer the night before and explained by parents to their children.

On Candlemas Day every family should carry home a blessed candle, which will have a special place on the home altar and will be lit in all moments of danger, during thunderstorms, during sickness, in time of tribulation.

Candlemas Day is a bitter-sweet feast. While in the morning the church is bathed in the light of hundreds of candles in the hands of the faithful, afterwards the crèche is stored again. It marks the end of the Christmas season; and the sheep and shepherds, the Gloria angel, the ox and the ass, Mary and Joseph with the Infant, and the whole little town of Bethlehem are hidden away for another year. There is always a tinge of sadness in the air, because, during these long nine weeks, the Holy Family has become so much a part of our household that it is hard to see them go.

Source: *Around the Year with the Trapp Family* by Maria Augusta Trapp. New York: Pantheon, pp. 81-82.

Canada

La Chandeleur

Celebration in Newfoundland and the Maritimes

In Newfoundland and the Maritimes a type of mumming occurred on February 2. The leader bore a staff with a rooster image on top decorated with ribbons. People gave food to La Chandeleur visitors and tied a ribbon onto their staff. The custom died out but is being revived in some areas.

Source: *Let's Celebrate* by Caroline Perry. Toronto: Kids Can Press, 1987, pp. 72-73.

Colombia

Virgen de la Candelaria

Honoring patron of Cartagena, Colombia

The Virgin of Candelaria is patron of Cartagena, Colombia. For nine days before this date pilgrims carrying lighted candles climb La Popa, a 500-foot mount, highest point of the city, to visit her church. Dancing and fairs continue into the night. In the *cumbia* musicians sit in the middle of a circle of dancers. Each woman holds three or four lighted candles in a bunch at shoulder height. Her partner dances around her. The dance continues without pause; when a dance couple or musician wears out, another simply slips into their place, allowing the dance to continue without break for hours.

Source: *Fiesta Time in Latin America* by Jean Milne. Los Angeles: The Ward Ritchie Press, 1965, pp. 26-27.

France

La Chandeleur

The Candlemas Bear Hunt

Now very slyly a head appears above the aqueduct bank, dark and shaggy, with great, bloody teeth. A shambling body rears up, then climbs out cautiously. Shots ring out, children scream, men with poles aid the handsome orator of the morning, and after ten minutes excitement the beast is caught alive, chained and led back into the town. The *Cobla* repeats the bear tune a hundred times until it becomes a musical incantation, and as it approaches the cry goes up "*L'ous ! l'ous !*" It takes all the vigilance of the trainer to save Rosetta from the knitted brown paws, but presently the mountain bear ignominiously becomes a dancing bear, tries to climb his master's pole and turns aside to take a proffered drink. But in spite of this education he still desires Rosetta.

"A la caverne" they cry, and there on the square is a "cave" composed of a henhouse and sacking. Almost immediately the beast breaks loose in earnest, seizes a *minyuneta* out of the crowd, who amid shrieks is dragged into the lair. The bear enters too, and the old red barretina'd guardian closes the door and there they are, shut up in a dark space measuring about two yards square. Happily all passes off peacefully, the bear offers his lady sausages, cake and white wine, but there is surely confusion here. The captive should always be and sometimes is Rosetta, the accompanying priestess, who to judge from a hundred analogous rites once served the dying chief as spouse. Things move to their appointed end, the barrel-heads are beaten in by the bear (I do not see any reason for this, neither do the people of Arles, but they must be "finished off" they say) till their sawdust brains pour out on the pavement. They seat the beast in a chair, his trainer, facing him, begins to dance, catching without interrupting his steps a cloth, a basin, an apple, a hatchet, all of which come hurtling out of the crowd in alarming fashion. He proceeds now to shave his beast with the hatchet, using the apple for soap, pinning the cloth round his shaggy neck. Yet even now nature will out. In a final impulse the creature leaps once again upon Rosetta, a single shot rings out, he staggers, and every breath is held until his great body falls helpless to the stones. A moment's silence, a dance round the carcass, and the ritualists bear away their Candlemas bear to the sound of dirge-like music.

Source: *Pyrenean Festivals* by Violet Alford. London: Chatto and Windus, 1937, pp. 18-19.

La Chandeleur customs

On February 2, La Chandeleur candles were carried in procession and drops of candle-grease let fall in the form of a cross by way of benediction—this, at least, in Franche Comté. Candles were held also to have some mysterious charm against storms. In Touraine, special Candlemas *crêpes* are made (at Chinon, Preuilly, Reignac and elsewhere).

Source: *A Guide to French Fêtes* by E. I. Robson. London: Methuen, 1930, p. 65.

Germany

German Catholic Candlemas customs

Candlemas processions are held in which everyone carries a lighted candle to be blessed. In earlier days the father might pour three drops of the blessed wax onto a piece of bread and give it to his children and cattle. This wax was protection against death and storms. Superstitions about childbirth are found on this day because it is also the Purification of Mary.

Source: *German Festivals and Customs* by Jennifer M. Russ. London: Oswald Wolff, 1982, p. 40.

Great Britain

British Candlemas tradition

Candle lighting processions at Candlemas were condemned by Protestant reformers but never died out in Wales and northern England and are today being revived.

Candlemas weather forecasts

> If Candlemas Day is fair and clear
> There'll be two winters in one year
> (Scotland)
>
> If Candlemass Day be wind and rain
> Winter is gone, and won't come again.
> (Warwickshire)

Source: *Customs and Ceremonies of Britain* by Charles Kightly. London: Thames and Hudson, 1986, p. 66.

Badgers and flowers

> "If Candlemas Day be dry and fair,
> The half of winter's to come and mair.
> If Candlemass Day be wet and foul,
> The half of winter's gone at Yule."

Everyone remembers the old rhyme and looks at the weather on Candlemas Day. Even badgers, it is said, creep out of their holes on Candlemas to see what it is like. If they see snow on the ground they come out and walk abroad, but if the sun is shining they slip back into their holes and sleep again.

Snowdrops are the special Candlemas flowers. They are always out ready to take the place of the holly and ivy which has to be taken down and thrown out of the house before the day dawns. The emblem for the day is a hand holding a lighted torch, a sign to encourage the earth through the rest of the winter, for it hails the coming of spring.

Wives' Feast Day

A name for this day in the north country was "Wives' Feast Day." There it was the custom for the women of the household to take a sheaf of oats overnight and to dress it up in a woman's clothes. Then they got out a great basket and laid the sheaf in it. Alongside they laid a wooden club. The club was called "Brüd," the basket was "Brüd's Bed," and when all was ready the mistress and her maids would cry three times over,

"Brüd is come ! Brüd is come ! Brüd is come ! Brüd is welcome! Brüd is welcome ! Brüd is welcome !"

The next morning as soon as they were up they went to the hearth and looked among the ashes to see if they could find the imprint of Brüd's club there. If they did, all would be well with the family for the following year; in particular, the crops would flourish.

If the wind is in the west at noon on Candlemas Day, fruit trees will bear well!

Source: *Happy Holidays* by Eleanor Graham. New York: E. P. Dutton, 1933, pp. 57-58.

Greece

Superstitions

Whatever the weather at Candlemas, it will remain the same for forty days. However Cretans believe that if the weather is fine at Candlemas a long winter lies ahead. On Crete it is said that if a miller attempts to turn his mill on Candlemas the boards will refuse to turn.

"Candlemas drives away all festivals with the distaff" runs the proverb. Only two feasts remain during February, the minor feasts of St. Charalambos and St. Vlasios. It is time to return to work after the Christmas festivities.

Source: *Greek Calendar Customs* by George A. Megas. Athens: B. & M. Rhodis, 1963, pp. 56-67.

Feast of the Purification of the Virgin; weather traditions

On Feb. 2nd is celebrated the feast of the Purification of the Virgin, our Candlemas Day. The weather which prevails on that day is expected to last forty days—a period which occurs constantly in modern Greek prognostications concerning the weather and is also familiar in the folklore of most European countries.

The superstition attached to this day is also common. Sir Thomas Browne, in his *Vulgar Errors,* quotes a Latin distich expressive of a parallel belief:

> Si sol splendescat Maria purificante,
> Major erit glacies post festum quam fuit ante;

which is well reproduced in the homely Scottish rhyme:

> If Candlemass day be dry and fair,
> The half o' winter's to come and mair.
> If Candlemass day be wet and foul,
> The half o' winter's gane at Yule.

Source: *Macedonian Folklore* by G. F. Abbott. Cambridge: Cambridge Univ. Press, 1903, p. 14.

Guatemala

A novelist describes Candlemas

The torrent of people coming down that way on the pilgrimage of Our Lady of Candlemas had run dry. Crosses wreathed with faded paper flowers, names written on rocks in charcoal with pitchpine tips, the ashes of fires extinguished beneath the shade of the amates, stakes to which animals had been tethered, shoals of corn shucks and dried maize leaves, nothing more remained of the pilgrims who passed by year after year, as the yucca fences bloomed like a procession of white candlesticks.

The most macho of the Machojones had come down that way in February, on the rising swell of pilgrim folk, eve of Candlemas, when the stream of faithful come from afar meets the rivulets of local folk joining the highway from other roads. Morning stars, rockets, chants. Hymns, lemon sellers, wet nurses, dogs, squalling children and men and women with their hats decked out in yellow chichita berries and swathes of long moss round their palm-leaf hatbands, staff in hand, the day's victuals on their backs, and their bedding stored away in cane baskets with their candlesticks.

Thronging crowds. Shawls. Candlemas flowers. Candy "rosaries" like sugared cartridge belts around young bosoms. Little figures dressed in huipiles sculpted in colored icing sugar in boxes of candy delights. Sweet loaves with sesame seeds.

Source: *Men of Maize* by Miguel Angel Asturias. Translated by Gerald Martin. New York: Delacorte Press/Seymour Lawrence, 1949, pp. 124-126.

Spain

Live doves

The candles used on Candlemas are elaborately decorated and are displayed in the home all year. In northern and central Spain children carry a special bread, *torta,* and a pair of live doves to Mass. The Virgin Mary brought two doves when she presented herself at the temple for purification.

A village celebration

Horche, a small village ten kilometers south of Guadalajara, has a Candlemas celebration which, although more elaborate than most, illustrates traditional patterns. We visited the village on this day in 1950. About 9:30 the priest, accompanied by acolytes, several white-garbed girls of ten years of age or so, the youths of Catholic Action, and most of the children in town, went to the bakery, from which they emerged shortly thereafter with the torta. This turned out to be a three-layer cake with pink frosting decorated with chicken feathers dyed green, carried on a small litter by several girls. A procession quickly formed, which included another young girl carrying a pair of doves in a small basket. This procession entered the church where it was joined by an altar boy with a processional cross, the image of the Virgin of Dolores, standards, and cantors. Thus enlarged, the procession emerged through the main doors of the church, especially opened for this occasion, and made the circuit of the building to re-enter through the smaller porch entrance on the right side. The cake and the doves were placed below the altar, to be picked up for a second procession during Mass which, however, went only as far as the rear of the nave before returning to the altar. After the Mass the cake was carried to the municipal building, where it was raffled off later in the afternoon. The proceeds from the chances, sold at fifteen céntimos by young girls, went to the church.

Source: *Culture and Conquest* by George M. Foster. Chicago: Quadrangle Books, 1960, p. 171.

For more information on Candelaria see: ''Candelaria'' in *Fiesta Time in Latin America* by Jean Milne. Los Angeles: Ward Ritchie, 1965, pp. 21-29. This article discusses Candelaria at Copacabana, Bolivia; Puno, Peru; Cartagena, Colombia; Chiantla, Guatemala; and Tiacotalpan, San Juan de los Lagos, and Tzintzuntzan, Mexico.

February 3, 5

St. Blaise's Day, St. Agatha's Day

St. Blaise was Bishop of Sebastea. When the Governor of Armenia persecuted Christians, St. Blaise hid in a cave where he and the wild animals cared for each other. He cures sore throats and is patron of sick cattle. St. Agatha was a virgin martyr of the third century. This Sicilian girl was taken by a consul named Quintian, who tried to force her to become his wife. To punish her for refusing, he put her in a brothel, and then had her tortured to death as a Christian.

France

A boy's festival for St. Blaise; a girl's festival for St. Agatha

On St. Blaise's Day, February 3, there were great doings in Savoie. His name got confused with Blé, and he became a saint interested in agriculture. In several districts (Mâconnais, Chalonnais, Bresse) he is, like St. Christopher, patron of labourers. His day at Seyssel is the Boys' Festival; and two days later there is St. Agatha's Day—the Girls' Festival; a ribboned tree was carried in procession, and bread was blessed. At St. Desiré (Allier) herdsmen had their sticks blessed on one or other day (probably St. Blaise's). St. Agatha was thought to protect against fires; her veil was supposed to have once extinguished a fire. Bread is blessed, and the blessed bread kept on the chimneypiece, and at Queige this bread was (I believe still is) in shape of a *mamelle,* in memory of St. Agatha's torture; these cakes are called 'Agathas' (in Peisey, Bozel, and Val d'Isère). One commune in Savoie is called by her name.

Source: *A Guide to French Fêtes* by E. I. Robson. London: Methuen, 1930, p. 65.

St. Blas's Day in Pays de Luchon

Candlemas provides nothing for our attention, its celebration being probably retarded till next day, that of St. Blas. On this day people take apples, garlic, salt and chocolate—a drink as usual as tea in England—to be blessed in church. These are then divided between the children and the pigs, and in return for the benediction every household gives the priest a pig's trotter.

Source: *Pyrenean Festivals* by Violet Alford. London: Chatto and Windus, 1937, p. 97.

Spain

Tortas de San Blas

Small loaves known as *panecillos del santo, Panes benditos,* or *tortas de San Blas* are baked on this day. They are blessed at Mass and each child eats a bit. This should protect from choking during the year. If someone does choke, a friend will thump him on the back, saying, "San Blas, adelante o atras" ("Saint Blaise, forward or backward") to stop the choking.

Source: *Culture and Conquest* by George M. Foster. Chicago: Quadrangle Books, 1960, p. 171.

February 5

Igbi

Igbi is a celebration of the day marking the middle of winter. The sun shines for the first time on Khora, a community situated opposite Shaitli on February 5. The event is celebrated both in Shaitli and in neighboring Kituri. The Tsezy (Didoitsy) are members of the Avar ethnic group. They live in the Tsuntin and Tsumadyn regions of Dagestan.

U.S.S.R. (Tsezy)

The Igbi celebrations in Shaitli, Dagestan, in 1982

How was the Shaitli *igbi* observed in 1982? Before we describe the feast itself, we should say a few words about its preparation and about the meaning of the word *igbi*. *Ig* in the Tsezian language means a ring-shaped bread, like a bagel, 20-30 cm in diameter, and *igbi* is the plural of *ig;* that is, *igbi* are bagels. They are baked not only for the *igbi* feast, but also at other Tsezian festivals, in particular the day of the first plowing. On this day, the *igbis* are hung on the horns of oxen during the plowing. The custom of baking ritual rolls for a feast is known among other peoples of Dagestan as well. The Shaitli people count the fifth of February, i.e. the middle of winter, as the day of *igbi*. Boys and young men, usually between the ages of 14 and 25, take part in the feast. Recently, because it is mainly schoolchildren who participate in it, and the fifth of February is usually a school day, the holiday has been shifted to the nearest Sunday in the traditional calendar. In 1982, *igbi* was observed on February 7.

Preparations for the festival begin long before its date. Throughout the year, young people organizing the *igbi* note down various positive and negative deeds of the villagers. The holiday is the day of reckoning for all those who have distinguished themselves or transgressed. One-and-a-half to two months before the *igbi* day, the direct preparations for it begin: costumes are made, and duties are assigned to the *igbi* participants. The personages in the feast are wolves (*botsi,* singular), forest people (*tsikes zheklu,* singular), a devil, a skeleton, a doctor, speculators, a hiker, a policeman, a soldier, and the *kvidili* (*kh'vidili*)—a central figure of the festival. Cone-shaped wolf masks are made out of calf, cow, sheep, and goat skins with the fur on the outside, and slits for the eyes, nose and mouth. Short motley ribbons may be hung from the pointed end of the mask. In addition to the mask, the wolf costume consists of a fur coat with the fur turned outward and cinched with a leather belt, traditional knitted shoes (*gedobi*), and manufactured gloves. Overalls with moss and pine branches sewed on them are made for the forest people; their masks are made in the same way. For the devil costume, rags, pieces of fur, and empty jars are used. The masks for the other participants (doctor, speculator, hiker, policeman) were made of papier-mâché, or cloth. Manufactured goods corresponding to the functions of the personages served as costumes. The skeleton costume was overalls with strips of white fabric imitating bones sewn to it.

The figure of the *kvidili* is an enigma even to the inhabitants of Shaitli. In their conception it corresponds to no existing animal: neither a bear nor a wolf nor a deer nor a horse. Nor is it a fabulous snake or dragon. "We don't know what kind of an animal this is," say the people of Shaitli, "but it has a big mouth, like a crocodile." "*Kvidili*" cannot be translated either from the Tsezian or the Avar language. The *kvidili* mask as it has been made in the past few years was the head of a horned animal, in some respects resembling the head of a horse. The making of this mask is quite complicated. First a wood base is made in the form of a head, and the skin of a cow or goat is stretched over it with the fur outward. The *kvidili* mask does indeed have a big mouth which moves by means of a string attached to the lower jaw. The mask is attached to the end of a two-meter pole carried by the person playing the role of *kvidili*. The costume of this figure of the festival is made out of sewn furs and resembles a loose overall.

A week before the *igbi,* three to four "wolves" accompanied by boys appear in the center of the settlement; these wolves announce to the inhabitants, in the name of the *botsi,* the need to prepare for the feast, to make the *igbi* breads; those who do not make the breads will be punished by the Botsi. On the eve of the feast, Saturday evening, the *botsi* again appear in the center of the village accompanied by boys, and again proclaim the same warning. The night of the eve of the holiday is hard for the women of Shaitli. They must bake several dozen small *igbi* and a few large ones. The dough used for them is the ordinary dough.

Then comes the morning of the feast. On the fifth of February the sun should for the first time shine on the locality of Khora situated opposite Shaitli. The people of Shaitli say that when this happens it means that half of the winter is passed and a turn toward the spring has taken place in nature; spring will soon arrive. On this day the children get up earlier than usual. There are already many children carrying bags on the streets by seven in the morning, collecting in groups. They begin to walk about the village and collect the small *igbi* especially made for them from each house. Soon their little bags are filled with *igbi* and they carry them off to their houses.

About ten o'clock in the morning, six *botsi*—''wolves'' disguised in costumes, with wooden swords in their hands—come to the *godekan* from the different ends of the village. Among these wolves is a senior wolf who carries a stick with a fur belt tied to it as a sign of seniority; horns are attached to his mask. About thirty boys gather around the wolves to accompany them as they walk about the village. The botsi choose two adult men from among the spectators and force them to carry the *gari,* a five-meter-long pole on which the *igbi* will be strung. No one can refuse this order by the *botsi.* They can punish all those who refuse in various ways: striking them with wooden swords, or throwing them in a hole in the ice. After the duties are assigned, collection of the *igbi* begins. *Botsi,* accompanied by a group of boys and two men, bearing the *giri,* begin to walk about the village. All the while the *igbi* are being collected, the boys shout loud and long: make *igbi!* He who does not give *igbi* will be punished! (The punishment they threaten is that they will fill the traditional knitted shoe [*gedobi*] of a housewife who did not give them an *ig* with wet snow and ice—*khatamu*). This processing moves from the edge of the village to the center. If they are not greeted by the owner at some house, one of the *botsi* tries to get into the house and punish (by beating with a sword) the housewife. Usually, however, when they go up to a house where they are already expected, one of the wolves extends the sword and the housewife or man of the house puts an *ig* on it. After this, the *botsi* himself begins to string the *ig* on the *giri.* Thus they gradually get around to all the houses. As the processing with its collection of *igbi* moves around the village, some women try to break off one or several of the *igbi* hanging on the *giri;* the wolves in turn try with all their might not to permit this, and chase the women off with their swords. After finishing the collection in the eastern part of the village, the procession goes off to the west. During this time, a doctor in a white robe, white hat, and cloth mask on his face appears on the *godekan.* He begins to offer his services in gestures to the villagers gathered there. The forest people, one in the moss costume, the other in a costume of pine branches, and the *shaitan,* whose function it is to frighten people, follow the doctor to the *godekan.* Then the skeleton appears, speaking for the edification of those who observe the *uraz.* At this same time, female and male figures appear and disappear immediately several times on the roof of one of the houses above the *godekan.* Soon they appear on the *godekan;* these are the speculators—two women and two men in bright costumes and as many bright masks accompanied by a donkey loaded with various wares. They stop here and begin trading. A policeman appears and chases them from the *godekan.* The last to come up are the tourists, a man and a woman with provocative appearance, and a soldier. All these personages amuse the spectators with their actions.

By this time all the *igbi* are collected, and the *botsi,* accompanied by the small boys, return to the center of the village. The *igbi* are put on the roof of a makeshift constuction situated on the *godekan.* The boys stay to guard them, and the *botsi* go over to the *godekan* where they enter into the performance. At eleven o'clock, the *kvidili* appears from the direction of Khora. He gathers all the participants in the feast and the spectators together. The ''official'' part begins. The *kvidili* steps up on a platform constructed of snow and ice especially for this occasion and, in Tsezian, wishes the villagers good weather and a good harvest in the new year, and urges all of them to participate actively in all civic work. Then a teacher from the local school goes up on the platform and, in the name of the *kvidili,* reads out a list of villagers who have committed some transgression with regard to the village or the young people. On the order of the *kvidili* the *botsi* drag the transgressors to the river and immerse them through a hole in the ice up to their knees (in the past, instead of this their knitted shoes were filled with wet snow). Thus, in 1982 one villager was punished for drunkenness; they wanted also to punish one of the teachers, but let him go half way to the river. After these punishments, another person speaking in the name of the *kvidili* congratulated those Shaitli inhabitants who distinguished themselves with good works in 1982. This year they were: an old collective farm worker who was still doing his share in everything, a party worker of the local forestry farm, and a shepherd. The teacher thanked them for their good work, and expressed the wish that they would continue to work as well in the future, and handed each of them an *ig.*

By mid-day, the feast had entered into its final phase. All the participants gathered on the *godekan* around the *kvidili* and dragged him to the bridge over the river passing through the middle of the settlement. The *kvidili* was placed on the bridge and the elder *botsi* symbolically cut his throat with a wooden sword. In past years, so the Shaitli inhabitants related, a small vessel with red paint was hidden under the *kvidili*'s costume; as he was being ''murdered'' the *kvidili* would open the container unnoticed and the paint, looking just like blood, would flow out into the river. This year, there was no blood. The body of the *kvidili* was placed on a bier and the *botsi* carried him off behind the buildings. Outsiders and country folk were not allowed into the procession; the *botsi* would chase them away with their swords.

Source: ''The Communal Winter Festival among the Tsezy'' by Iu. Iu. Karpov in *Soviet Anthropology and Archeology,* XXII, no. 2, (Fall 1983), 39-45.

February 10

Feast of St. Paul's Shipwreck

This feast day is a Maltese holiday celebrating the origin of Christianity in Malta.

Malta

Origin of holiday

This feast commemorates the shipwreck of St. Paul in Malta in 60 A.D., an event registered in the Acts of the Apostles. St. Paul was on his way to Rome, where he was to stand trial, when a violent storm brought the ship he was travelling on crashing on to the rocks. This was the beginning of Christianity in Malta.

Source: ''Malta & Gozo: Events Calendar, 1990.'' National Tourism Organization, 1990.

February 11

St. Vlasios's Day

February 11 honors the Greek saint Vlasios.

Greece

St. Vlasios's Day customs

On this day the congregation eat and drink together after church. Wheat, cooked in butter and honey, and mutton or goat are eaten. The sheep or goats to be cooked are sacrificed in front of the church earlier. In Corfu, watermelon is also a traditional food on this day.

No work should be done on Saint Vlasios's Day. In Anatolia oxen, mules, or horses should not be loaded, for St. Vlasios is the ''cattle-strangler'' and will cause them to drown. St. Vlasios protects against wolves and other wild animals. If you absolutely must work on his day, you must sew a cloth bag behind your back. While you are sewing, a neighbor must ask, ''What are you sewing?'' You reply, ''I am sewing stone and whetstone. I am sewing up the wolf's jaw,'' repeating this three times.

Source: *Greek Calendar Customs* by George A. Megas. Athens: B. & M. Rhodis, 1963, pp. 57-58.

27th Day of Rajab (February 12 in 1991)

Lélé-I-Mirach

Lélé-I-Mirach is the night on which the Prophet Mohammed flew from Mecca to Jerusalem on a winged horse and ascended into heaven.

Turkey

Night of ascension

On the fifth day of Resheb, which is the seventh month, is the Lélé-I-Mirach (night of ascension). It was on this night that Mohammed is supposed to have ascended into heaven and prayed before Allah, whose face was hidden by a cloud. It is recorded in the Koran that on this occasion Mohammed saw Jesus sitting at the right hand of Allah and Moses at the left. This night there are extra prayers and the minarets are again illuminated.

Source: *When I Was a Boy in Turkey* by Ahmed Sabri Bey. Boston: Lothrop, Lee & Shepard Co., 1924, p. 82.

Miraç Kandili in Turkey

The 26th of the month of Recep, Miraç Kandili celebrates Muhammad's miraculous nocturnal journey from Mecca to Jerusalem and to heaven astride a winged horse named Burak. Mosques are illuminated and special foods eaten.

Source: *Turkey: A Travel Survival Kit* by Tom Broshahan. Lonely Planet, 1988, p. 28.

Moveable: February-March (Sunday before Lent)

Cheese Sunday

Macedonia

Cheese Sunday in Macedonia c. 1900

The boys of each village rise early in the morning and, divided into several parties, go forth collecting bundles of firewood, which they pile up on the tops of the heights and hills in the neighbourhood. These preparations completed, they amuse themselves during the rest of the day by throwing stones with a sling, each shot accompanied with these mysterious words: "Whithersoever this arrow hies, may the flea follow in its track." In some districts of Macedonia these slings are replaced by actual cross-bows generally constucted of a fragment of a barrel-hoop, which is passed through a hole at the end of a stock. The missile,—a long nail as a rule—laid in the groove of the stock, is propelled by a string drawn tight across the bow and held fast by a catch, which is nailed to the stock, acting as a sort of trigger. At nightfall the bonfires built up in the morning are kindled, and the boys jump over them.

In the evening of Cheese-Sunday it is the custom for the younger members of the community to call on their elder relatives, godfathers and godmothers, in order to beg forgiveness for their trespasses and beseech their blessing. Women for some reason or other, take with them a cake, an orange or a lemon as a propitiatory offering to those on whom they call. The symbolic meaning of these gifts, if they ever had one, has long since gone the way of all tradition.

At supper-time a tripod is set near the hearth, or in the middle of the room, and upon it is placed a wooden or copper tray. Round the table thus extemporized sit the members of the family cross-legged, with the chief of the household at the head. The repast is as sumptuous as befits the eve of a long fast, and a cake forms one of the most conspicuous items on the menu. Before they commence eating the younger members of the family kneel to their elders and obtain absolution, after which performance the banquet begins.

When the plates are removed there follows an amusing game called 'Gaping' and corresponding to our Christmas game of Bob-cherry or Bobbing Apple. A long thread is tied to the end of a stick, and from it is suspended a bit of confectionery, or a boiled egg. The person that holds it bobs it towards the others who sit in a ring, with their mouths wide open, trying to catch the morsel by turns. Their struggles and failures naturally cause much jollity and the game soon gets exciting. This amusement is succeeded by songs sung round the table and sometimes by dancing.

A quaint superstition attached to the proceedings of this evening deserves mention. If anyone of those present happens to sneeze, it is imperative that he should tear a bit off the front of his shirt in order to ward off evil influences.

Source: *Macedonian Folklore* by G. F. Abbott. Cambridge: Cambridge Univ. Press, 1903, pp. 27-130.

Moveable: February-March

Shrove Monday

Shrove Monday is the Monday before Ash Wednesday. (It fell on February 11 in 1991.) It is a day for pastry treats in many countries, as the remaining butter and eggs must be used up before the beginning of Lent. In Greece this is a fast day, "Clean Monday."

Bulgaria

Sirna Sedmitza (Cheese Week)

Food presents

In Bulgaria the entire week preceding Lent is "Cheese Week." All cheese, milk, lard, and fish must be eaten up before the six-week Lenten fast begins. Young people visit their elders at this time and present male relatives and godparents with a lemon, females with an orange, wishing them a "light fast, and a happy fast night." The night before Lent may be a festive occasion with games for the young, such as trying to catch in the mouth a piece of candy or cheese hung from the ceiling on a string, while holding the hands behind the back. In some areas bonfires are built and boys try jumping through them.

Source: *The Book of Festivals* by Dorothy Gladys Spicer. Detroit: Gale Research Company, 1969, p. 67.

Greece

Clean Monday

Picnics

Clean Monday is the first day of Lent. It is celebrated by picnics of Lenten foods. A few areas continue the carnival masquerades on this last day. Housewives clean their pots and pans with hot water mixed with ashes on this day.

Clean Monday picnics are popular throughout Greece, and kite flying by the children is a featured activity. The Lenten picnic foods may include fish-roe salad, green onions, lettuce, and seafoods. *Lagana,* flat, oval loaves of unleavened bread, are traditional on this day. As soon as the church bells toll the evening service, the partying comes to an end and the Lenten fast begins.

Source: *Greek Calendar Customs* by George A. Megas. Athens: B. & M. Rhodis, 1963, pp. 72-73.

Fasting meal in Kalamata

Sheelagh Kanelli reports that Clean Monday always promises fair weather for the outdoor picnic on this day. On this day her family visited an outdoor restaurant in the country and ordered a fasting meal consisting of *taramasalata* (a creamy roe paste seasoned with sea-salt), pickles and salad without oil, Clean Monday bread, crabs and shrimp (allowed during fast), halva, and fruit.

Source: *Earth and Water: A Marriage into Greece* by Sheelagh Kanelli. New York: Coward-McCann, 1965, pp. 137-138.

Iceland

Bun Day

Bun treats

This is what Monday before Lent is presently called. The name is fairly recent, although the custom of the day certainly has about a century-old history in Iceland. In all likelihood it was brought to the country by Danish or Norwegian bakers who immigrated in the second half of the 19th century. In Iceland, however, the day acquired some indigenous peculiarities.

The main feature is two-fold: to rap someone on the buttocks with a stick before he (or she) gets out of bed and to be rewarded with some kind of delicacy, in this case buns with whip-cream.

Source: *Icelandic Feasts and Holidays: Celebrations, Past and Present* by Arni Bjornsson. Translated by May and Hallberg Hallmundsson. Reykjavik: Iceland Review History Series, 1980, pp. 24-25.

Moveable: February-March

Shrove Tuesday/Mardi Gras

Shrove Tuesday is the Tuesday before Ash Wednesday. (It fell on February 12 in 1991.) Its activities are similar to those of Shrove Monday.

Great Britain

The Olney, Buckinghamshire Pancake Race

The Shrove Tuesday Pancake Race at Olney is thought to have a history of over five hundred years. According to the legend, in 1445 a woman heard the shriving bell while she was making pancakes. She ran to church in her apron, still holding her frying pan with the pancake in it. Nowadays women compete in racing, carrying a still cooking pancake. The pancake must be tossed three times during the race from market square to church door. The first woman to reach the church and serve her pancake to the bellringer receives a kiss from him and wins the race. All participants must wear a skirt, an apron, and a hat or scarf. Bodiam in Sussex and North Somercote in Lincolnshire also have pancake racing events.

Football matches

Football games on Shrove Tuesday date from the Middle Ages. That of Chester is recorded as early as 1553. At Ashton, Derbyshire, the custom continues. The game has very few rules. The Up'ards, men born north of the River Henmore, play the Down'ards. The mill-wheels at Clifton and Sturston, three miles apart, are the goals. In between, anything goes.

Source: *A Year of Festivals* by Geoffrey Palmer and Noel Lloyd. London: Frederick Warne, 1972, pp. 125-127.

Mexico

Fiesta de Febrero

Painting of Christ

This is a festival on the Tuesday before Ash Wednesday. It is held in honor of a miraculous painting of Christ, the Señor del Rescate.

Fireworks displays in Tzintzuntzan

There are two main categories of fireworks: ''La Obra,'' which is presented by El Ojo de Agua, and *los castillos,* which are gifts of La Vuelta and the people of Tzintzuntzan.

La Obra is a term of uncertain origin which refers collectively to a gift package of fireworks presented by El Ojo de Agua to Tzintzuntzan each year. It consists of two basic kinds of fireworks: (1) *enchorizados,* or long strings of firecrackers, so named because of their resemblance to strings of sausage (*chorizo*); and (2) *cohetes,* or skyrockets, some of them relatively small, others of the massive type known as *cohetones,* and yet others (the *cohetes de luces*) designed to produce a shower of nighttime stars. In 1977 the Obra consisted of a substantial quantity of items, measured locally by *gruesa,* or unit of twelve dozen. On that occasion, six gruesas of enchorizados and one and one-half gruesas of cohetes made up the Obra.

Los castillos in 1977

[Castillos are described as] cubic skeletons of cane, raised in three, four, or five sections, up to twenty feet in the air. [In Tzintzuntzan, a dozen meters would be more like it.] Each section is wired with explosives, pinwheels, flares, and skyrockets, all connected to a single serpentine fuse, which winds upward from the bottom of the castle to the top. The higher the fuse burns, the more spectacular become the effects, and the thicker grows the cloud of acrid powder-smoke, until the fuse reaches the top, and a large pinwheel is sent into the air, discharging, at the greatest height of its trajectory, a shower of sparks, colored flares, and explosions.

In 1977, the castillo of La Vuelta went first at about 10:00 P.M., followed by that of La Comunidad, making for a total hour-long event. Large crowds of men, women, and children from all over the municipio gathered around the periphery of the churchyard. In fact, the burning of each castillo was preceded by the running of a *toro,* a wooden structure in the form of a bull, laced with fireworks and carried on the back of a young man who dispersed the crowds by rushing into them and forcing them into the background. The same dispersal occurred through the crackling of *buscapiés,* strings of flaring rockets that hover at the ground for a total of five or ten seconds and scoot around in unpredictable directions. Both the toro and the buscapiés, say informants, are meant to scatter the audience to clear the way for the castillo display, but, as might be imagined, a few spectators are usually injured in the process.

Source: ''Fireworks and Fiestas: The Case from Tzintzuntzan'' by Stanley H. Brandes in *Journal of Latin American Lore* 7:2 (1981), 171-190.

Sweden

Meat stew and buns

In the north of Sweden people eat a meat stew on this day. In southern Sweden folks eat "Shrove Tuesday buns" called "semlor." These are cardamom buns, filled with almond paste and whipped cream. They may be eaten in a dish of warm milk with cinnamon.

Source: *Traditional Festivities of Sweden* by Ingemar Liman. Stockholm: The Swedish Institute, 1985, p. 6.

Moveable: February-March

Carnival/Carnaval

Carnival derives from the Latin phrase *carnem levare,* meaning "to take meat away." It is a final midwinter fling before the 40 days of Lenten fasting preceding Easter. Carnival is especially popular in the Latin countries—Italy, France, Spain, and Portugal—and in their former territories in Latin America, the Caribbean, and even Goa. The Germans carried the tradition north as *Fastnacht* (*Faschung, Fassennacht, Fasnet, Karneval*). In Switzerland some Protestant towns hold their carnival on the Monday after Ash Wednesday rather than the Monday before.

Armenia

Pareegentahn in Armenia

In addition to the masquerades and parties, this was a time for swinging, with boys pushing the young girls. In the Van basin a woman would take her daughter in her arms and be pushed on a swing in order to get the same weight in butter during the new year.

An onion or orange with feathers stuck into it would count the weeks of Lent. Each week one more feather was removed. In some areas the onion was considered the foot of an old man called Aklatiz. On the last day of Lent he turned into a bird and flew off.

In the Hark area housewives made stars of dough and stuck them to their blackened ceilings to make a map of the sky during Lent.

Source: *Armenian Village Life Before 1914* by Susie Hoogasian Villa and Mary Kilbourne Matossian. Detroit: Wayne State Univ., 1982, pp. 138-139.

Aruba

Tumba music

Steel band contests, Tumba contests, and Carnival queens highlight this festival. The Main Parade in Oranjestad takes eight hours as it winds through the city, ending at sundown. Musicians compete in performing Tumba compositions, each hoping to have composed the piece chosen as that year's official Carnival song. Tumba is a special musical form of the Netherlands Antilles. On the Tuesday before Ash Wednesday the three days of celebration come to a close with the Old Mask Parade and the burning of "King Momo."

Source: *A Guide to World Fairs and Festivals* by Frances Shemanski. Westport, Ct.: Greenwood, 1985, pp. 4-5.

Belgium

La Carnaval De Binche

Colorful costumes

Here are the Gilles in their towering, frothing plumes of white ostrich feathers, with flowing ribbons, the jackets and trousers decorated with black and orange lions, white lace flounces at the wrists and above the sabots. And here are the *Paysans,* with *cloche* hats of the same ostrich feathers, decorated with a *dizaine* of flowers, the turned-up brims studded with three golden stars. They wear blue smock-like jackets with white trousers and glazed black shoes, and, like the Gilles, each carries the *ramon* of white osier, and over the left shoulder is slung a game-bag filled with oranges. There are other groups—the pierrots and clowns in yellow, red and blue, Castilians in scarlet shirts, bolero hats and black trousers, Calabrian brigands in dark clothes of felt (all these Spanish elements would seem to confirm the popularly accepted origins). The culminating feature of all the traditional rites is the *rondeau* in the Grand Place, which now resembles the arena of a tattoo, the *Paysans,* clowns, pierrots, sailors and the rest massed in the centre and ringed by the Gilles, who weave round and round beneath the belfry of the little Hôtel de Ville. Meanwhile the fun has begun and there are volleys of oranges, literally a rain of gold—and at night it goes on, the dancing, the music, the torchlight processions, the fairy-lights, the fountains of fire and cascades of magnesium.

Source: *Belgium and Luxembourg* by Tudor Edwards. London: B.T. Batsford, 1951, p. 101.

Bolivia

Celebrations in Oruro

First come the cargamentos, a motorcade of vehicles laden with fine embroideries, jewels, gold and silverware, old coins and banknotes, which recall the treasures once offered up in the worship of Inti (the sun) on the Incan Inti Raymi feast day, or the wealth of the Tío (Uncle) who dwells in the mineshafts.

Behind this motorcade comes the company of the Diablos, led by Lucifer and two Satans among a clattering din of reports from rockets and small cannon, and surrounded by five dancing she-devils. The masks of these Diablos sport plaster-of-paris horns, painted light bulbs for eyes, little mirrors for teeth, and hair from the tails of oxen or horses, and are adorned with toads, snakes and lizards. They are followed by the angel guarding the Virgen del Socavón, who is carried by the standard bearer. A band brings up the rear of this section, and condors and bears, survivals from ancient totemic rites, walk in and out among the dancers.

Next comes the company of the Incas, representing historical personages from the time of the conquest: the Inca Huáscar, the Spaniards Francisco Pizarro and Diego de Almagro, and the priest Vicente de Valverde (who, failing to convert Atahualpa, the last of the Incas, to Christianity, allowed him to be sentenced to death). Just as the Diablos, who on Socavón Square stage the relato (story) of the Seven Deadly Sins in which the Archangel Michael is victorious, the Incas put on a fine theatrical piece. La Conquista de los Españoles (The Conquest of the Spaniards), by an anonymous colonial author.

The Tobas with large tropical feathers on their heads and lances in their hands, present war dances that remind spectators of the jungle tribes conquered by the Inca Yupanqui when he extended his empire eastward.

The Llameros (llama drivers) with their slings call to mind the long llama caravans from the different lands of the Tahuantinsuyo (the lands of the ports of Lima and Buenos Aires) for shipment to Europe.

The Callahuallas (witch doctors) dance with their bags of herbs and the other materials they use to fight diseases and preserve the heat of the body. There are also the Cullahuas, who spin and weave as well as a host of other companies with intriguing titles: the Chutas, the Cambas, Antahuaras, Potolos, Tincus, Corimaitas, Tollcas, Caporales.

The Morenada, led by the Rey Moreno (Black King) and the Caporal (Chief), advance slowly with their heavy costumes, whirling their rattles. According to tradition, they represent for some the black slaves brought over from Africa to stomp grapes for juice, while for others they are the blacks led off in chains to work the mines of Potosi in colonial times. Their richly decorated costumes represent the wealth of the slave owners, the protruding eyes and tongue of their masks convey the black's fatigue and the soroche (altitude sickness) from which he suffered.

The Entrada ends with the entry of all the masked companies into the church to hear mass in honor of the Virgen del Socavón.

Carnival and its music, dances, eating and drinking, and challas (offerings) to Pachamama (Mother Earth) continue for a week. At the Despedida (Farewell) on Temptation Sunday, challas are held for the Condor, the Toad, the Viper and other rock formations that are part of the town's myths. The celebration ends with an outing to the country-side for participants and spectators in the Agua de Castilla district, where the Carnival is "buried" until next year.

The challa consists of sprinkling drinks on all things, both fixed and movable, and in adorning them with confetti and streamers so that abundance will come, or that it will continue or increase. This is how the protection of the gods of increase and abundance is invoked, and respect shown to them.

Source: "The Carnival of Oruro" by Manuel Vargas in *An Insider's Guide to Bolivia* compiled by Peter McFarren. La Paz: Fundacion Cultural Quipus, 1990, pp. 241-242.

Men and women sing and dance

In February the rains peak and the Sun passes its zenith; the first early potatoes, *ullucus,* and *tarwi* (small beans) are ready to harvest. Peaches, maize, and wheat appear in the Sunday market. The soil is wet and warm, and men can be seen with their foot plows opening the fields for next year's planting. This is the season of *Puqllay,* Carnival. Women dance with bundles of maize, grain, and fruit in their shawls. Young mothers bundle in their infants as well, who bounce wide-eyed above the maternal twirling and stamping. Sometimes, women and men form two choirs to sing back and forth:

Kay kanmi lliklIay!	Here I have my shawl!
—Puqllay!—	*—Puqllay!—*
Puqliay lloqsimushán!	*Puqllay*'s starting up!
—Puqllay!—	*—Puqllay!—*
Durasnus q'epintín!	Bringing peaches!
—Puqllay!—	*—Puqllay!—*
Irampu q'epintín!	Bringing wheat!
—Puqllay!—	*—Puqllay!—*
Muyurikusunchís!	We'll go twirling around!
—Puqllay!—	*—Puqllay!—*
Kantarikusunchís!	We'll all start singing!
—Puqllay!—	*—Puqllay!—*
Muyurikusunmí!	Let's really twirl around!
—Noqapas!—	—Me too!—
Kirilla yachará!	And taste the battle!

Of Sonqo's community festivals, *Puqllay* contains the least Christian imagery and is still a time for boisterous sexual play and ritual fighting. Although the ancestral mummies are long gone, Carnival is still an occasion for surveying community boundaries and for making offerings to Sacred Places. The Thursday before Carnival, on *Comadres P'unchay* (*Comadres'* Day, Feast of the *Comadres*), many *Runakuna* climb beyond the upper boundaries of their community to a high plain below a pass called Panapunku. There an ancient footpath crosses the boundary between the provinces of Paucartambo and Calca.

Although three districts meet on Chiwchillani, Sonqueños view the *tinkuy* as an encounter between the two provinces, in which Paucartambo *ayllus* compete with *ayllus* from Calca. "We're on the border of Paucartambo," Luis explained, "so we have to defend its boundaries. The border *ayllus* meet (*topanku*) at the provincial boundaries on *Comadres P'unchay.*"

With fighting banned, *tinkuy* survives as a competitive dance. Contingents from the various *ayllus* arrive with the men dressed in *sargento* costumes and the women clad in their best clothes, decked with ribbons and tassels. The dance groups meet and mingle, each trying to out-dance the others. Although musicians from each community play *sargento* music, they make no attempt at coordination. The whole point is to drown each other out.

Sargento is danced in pairs: two men bob and sidle back and forth facing each other, occasionally switching the other's calves. When male and female dancers pair up, the whipping gets more ferocious. Men were expected to seek out partners from other communities; the *tinkuy* must have originally been "fought" with sex as well as slings and stones.

A rainy and moonless night set in, but that did not stop us from setting off on *paseo* to visit the houses of community authorities beginning with the *mayordomo,* and then going on to the *alcalde,* the *segundo,* and the four *regidores*. Don Luis, as President, was included as the last stop. In each house, sleepy hosts hauled themselves out of bed to serve us hot soup, *trago,* and coca, after which we danced the *sargento,* doing our best not to trip in the fireplace or step on the crockery.

The *paseos* had been held every Sunday for five weeks and would culminate the following Sunday to usher in Carnival week. Ideally, young unmarried people should make these rainy nocturnal rounds, but in 1976 most of the dancers were young married couples, for most of the local bachelors were off working in Cuzco or serving in the army.

On Monday, each family turned to its own ritual obligations to the sheep. Communal festivities did not start up again until Tuesday, *Puqllay P'unchay,* Carnival itself, when the *ayllu Runakuna purinku* (go around) to their authorities' houses in a mass *paseo*. On Wednesday the *alcalde* himself passes through the community, visiting his fellow staff bearers with an entourage of any *ayllu Runakuna* who want to join him.

Eustaquio . . . made an admirable *alcalde*. On Tuesday he presided behind the ritual table with the *vara* (staff of office) held firmly in his right hand. Arriving in groups of five to ten, the *Runakuna* showered him with tiny blossoms of the red and yellow *waqankilla* plant, which blooms in the very high *puna* during Carnival season.

I too was showered with this natural confetti by my new *compadres* on the morning of *Comadres P'unchay;* and at about the same time, the *ayllu*'s staff bearers were sprinkling the petals over the little mothers in the church as well. As the sun set on Monday, each family sprinkled *waqankilla* over its courtyard and herds—a *ch'uyay* not of *chicha,* but of flowers.

Sunday was the last and final day of Carnival, *Puqllay Kachaypari* (Carnival Send-Off).

Qhawayachiwaspá	Now that it's got us looking
—Puqllay!—	*—Puqllay!—*
Puqllayqa ripushán!	*Puqllay*'s going away!
—Puqllay!—	*—Puqllay!—*
Sapa runachawán	Now that it's tossed its *sami*
—Puqllay!—	*—Puqllay!—*
Saminman churaspá!	To each little man!
—Puqllay!—	*—Puqllay!—*
Llapa sultiratán	Now that it's made us notice
—Puqllay!—	*—Puqllay!—*
Qhawachiwaspá!	All the unmarried girls!
—Puqllay!—	*—Puqllay!—*

Source: *The Hold Life Has: Coca and Cultural Identity in an Andean Community* by Catherine J. Allen. Washington: Smithsonian Institution Press, 1988, pp. 180-189.

Brazil

Costume balls

Carnival events begin the Saturday before Ash Wednesday with a parade along Rio's eight-mile beachfront. Costume balls are held each night, with various clubs each holding their own ball. The dances begin at 11 p.m. and continue to daybreak or longer. On Sunday the Escola de Samba parade takes place at 7 p.m. Each Samba Club develops its own theme and choreography for the parade. The special samba numbers used are written by members of the group and may be recorded and sold weeks before the festival. Each of the top ten samba schools has around 3,000 performers, though some may accumulate up to 30,000, all costumed. Judging of the samba schools is based on nine categories.

Source: *A Guide to World Fairs and Festivals* by Frances Shemanski. Westport, Conn.: Greenwood, 1985, pp. 24-25.

Judging of the samba schools

The samba schools are organized into three leagues with demotion of the last two schools in the first and second leagues and promotion of two schools from the second and third to replace them. To judge them there is an awards committee. Although their numbers fluctuate, my best information suggests that there are now nine jurors. The first evaluates the guild's flag since each "school" is officially a guild (*gremio*) and the line of its officials known as the *comissão de frente,* usually fifteen, who march at the head of the parade, often in frock coats and top hats. The second juror evaluates the performance of the flag bearer, the *porta-bandeira,* and the major-domo, or *mestresala;* usually the *porta-bandeira* is the most beautiful woman of the *escola* and the best dancer—always she appears in the dress of an eighteenth-century lady. At every carnival the *escola* presents a different, beautifully embroidered flag, showing on one side the emblem of the guild and on the other some design allusive of the plot which is presented in that particular pageant.

The third evaluates the *escola*'s current plot (*enredo*) and the lyrics of the samba, which always refers to the plot and indeed creates its emotional tone. The fourth evaluates the appearance of the *escola* as a whole and the choreography of the ensemble: the main components are the *alas* (wings), consisting of about ten to thirty persons, often of the same sex, who are organized around a subplot, which must conform to the school's main plot.

In addition to the *alas,* there are the *destaques* or *figuras de destaque* (the stand-outs or individual items), persons wearing sumptuous and magnificent costumes and plumes, who strut down the avenue in solitary, solar, lunar, or rainbow splendor. . . . Floats are also a carnival component, limited by regulation to four per school, including the float which spearheads the pageant—known as the *Abre-alas* (literally "Wings opener or usher"). Its purpose is to proclaim the name of the Escola and the title of its plot for the year. An *Abre-alas* may represent an open book, a large portal, or a baroque cartouche (like those which appear in old maps and charts—"heere be mermaids, theer be gryphons," and so on).

The fifth judge evaluates the tunefulness and musical texture of the samba and the performance of the *bateria* (percussion battery). An *escola* without a *bateria* would be unthinkable. The number of bandsmen—or *ritmistas*—may vary greatly. A small *bateria* may make great music.

The sixth juror evaluates the masquerades and the individual floats. . . . The jurors are drawn from the ranks of professional artists or art critics, dress designers, newspaper persons or television professionals, professional ballet dancers and choreographers, professional musicians and composers.

Source: "Carnival, Ritual, and Play in Rio de Janeiro" by Victor Turner in *Time Out of Time* by Alessandro Falassi. Albuquerque: Univ. of New Mexico, 1987, pp. 217-218.

More on the Samba schools

But the Carnaval that Brazil is renowned for—the opulent street parades of Rio de Janeiro—did not become a tradition until the 1930s. That's when neighborhoods started adding choreography, elaborate costumes and theme songs to their street forays. By 1932 the neighborhood groups had begun to compete and became known as *escolas de samba* or samba schools. Samba in the south of Brazil has become the signature music of Carnaval—a derivation of west African rhythms best recognized by the thump-thump undercurrent of the bass drum.

Today the competition between samba schools is akin to the rivalry between top sports teams. Almost all the major schools are from around Rio, and Carnaval there is charged with suspense over which school will be champion. Months of preparation now go into brief moments of glory before thousands of live spectators and millions of television viewers. Some of the funding comes from ticket sales and television rights, and much comes from the minimum wage. And most members of the samba schools come from the humblest of Rio's neighborhoods, including the hovels known as *favelas* clinging to steep hillsides. Many of the schools are also underwritten by the kingpins of the local numbers game, who acquire royalty status among the poor for this philanthropy.

Samba schools hold practice sessions for months before Carnaval, to which the public is often invited for a small admission. A theme is chosen for each year's Carnaval, and sambas are composed and costumes designed reflecting that motif. The moment of glory comes at the gates of Rio's one-of-a-kind samba stadium, the Sambadrome, which was designed by the leading architect of Brasilia, Oscar Niemeyer, and erected in 1984. Eighty five thousand spectators can be seated along this kilometer-long parade strip to watch the samba schools dance by.

The 'moving opera': To the untrained eye, the samba schools may first all appear to be similar frenetic waves of skin and glitter. But each one has a different story to tell, and the distinct groups, or wings (*asas*), that dance within each school are all chapters of these epics. "The samba school must be seen as a moving opera," says Brazilian anthropologist Maria Julia Goldwasser. Unlike opera, though, the spectators are expected to join in the singing, which is led by the *puxador*, who belts out his samba through a rolling sound system to the chorussed response of the school and the crowd.

A night at the Sambadrome can begin at eight and end well after sunrise. For some, it becomes an endurance test to sit (or dance) through it all; many others feel as if they've died and gone to samba heaven. Excess is the essence of Carnaval, and the Sambadrome is no exception.

Throughout Brazil, Carnaval is an affair of both streets and clubs. The best street dancing is in Salvador, where musicians called *trio eletricos* play atop deafening soundtracks as the hordes leap around behind them through the city. As in the case everywhere during Carnaval, it's best to dress minimally (shorts or bathing suits) to blend into the crowds and not attract thieves. A less frenetic street Carnaval can be found in the two historic cities of Olinda and Ouro Preto as well as in the outlying suburbs of Rio. In Rio itself, there's dancing both in Copacabana and Ipanema led by traditional neighborhood *blocos.* Class lines seem to dissolve as elated revelers hop together down the streets in camaraderie fueled by generous amounts of beer and *cachaca,* the sugarcane brandy that's ubiquitous during Carnaval.

But Carnaval has increasingly moved off the streets and into the clubs in recent years. People go to the clubs both to see and to show themselves—the clubs are where Carnaval's most intense debauchery and exhibitionism goes on. Club Monte Libano's "Night in Baghdad" on Tuesday, the last soirée of Carnaval, undoubtedly has the hottest reputation.

The most unusual balls are those held in Rio by the city's large transvestite community. They're a showcase for the amazingly deceptive transformations these men have made—the Marilyn Monroe look-alike contest at Sugarloaf Mountain is a must.

Source: *Insight Guides: South America.* APA Productions, 1990, p. 191.

Canada (Quebec)

Carnaval in Quebec City

This festival was started in 1954 as a civic event and has captured the hearts of the area.

Snow castle and ice sculptures

A large snow castle is built each year. Over 40,000 tons of snow are trucked in to construct the castle. It is illuminated at night and serves as a mock jail for those who fail to remain smiling throughout Carnaval. A seven-foot-high snowman mascot, Bonhomme Carnaval, roams the streets locking up nonsmilers. A snow sculpture contest nearby creates a display of fascinating snow-art pieces.

Boat races

An unusual boat race takes place over the semifrozen St. Lawrence River. Steel-bottomed boats that can slide easily over ice are used. The boats must be manipulated around the floating ice or dragged over especially large patches of ice. Five-member teams race against each other.

"Caribou"

The festival spirit is enlivened by a stiff drink called "caribou," a mixture of white alcohol and red wine.

Source: "Carnaval: Quebec City's Delightful Solution to Our Midwinter Blues" by Lewis Harris in *Canadian Geographic* 102, no. 6 (December 1982/January 1983), 10-19.

France

A half-day school holiday in Besançon circa 1900

We really could be mischievous on that day, and nobody had the right to scold us. Right after lunch, Fanny and Adèle helped us to put on our carnival costumes, on which all four of us had been busy the day before. I loved to be a little white Pierrot, with the face thickly powdered with flour, the huge frill-collarette, and over-long sleeves. Goby made a delightful little pink-and-black Columbine.

Once in the street, with my sisters and mother, the spirit of prankishness and fun would get hold of me, and I would hop and run and pirouette and laugh and sing and talk with a parrot voice, and say and do all kinds of nonsense. But I was not the only one! The streets, the whole city was alive with bands of boys and girls—the only time they dared go together—all masked and in amusing costumes of every color, laughing, jesting, dancing in whirling rounds, and throwing millions of confetti in every one's faces. 'Ware those who are in their path; the whirlwind of masks may carry them off!

The streets grow fuller and fuller of masks and curious onlookers. Suddenly every one runs to the next corner, whence come discordant music and screams of fun.

"*La cavalcade! Les chars! La reine!*"

And a fantastic procession of floats, big and small, drawn by magnificent horses—also dressed up, passes slowly on, offering to the wild crowd the most unexpected and grotesque spectacle imaginable. On the last float, higher than the first story of the houses, among her ladies of honor rides enthroned the Queen of Carnival, elected by her work-companions as the prettiest laundress in the city.

She goes thus, with her court, to the Town Hall, where the Mayor and Aldermen offer her a banquet and a jewel. She is Queen, absolutely, for the whole day. In past times she had the right to save three prisoners, from death by burning, by hanging, and by drowning; the three old punishments of the fire, the rope, and the sack.

Then comes King Carnival, himself, an absurd man of straw which the crowd burns cheerfully on the bridge and throws in the river while still burning, at the end of the mad day. So, with him, go down all our folly and badness—such is the symbol.

Back again home, most exhilarated, we ate invariably the traditional pancakes, and received, until late in the night, visits from masked friends. You must guess who they are, but it is very difficult, for they change their voices, tell you funny things, make faces at you, and disappear suddenly, all in a few minutes.

Source: *When I Was a Girl in France* by Georgette Beuret. Boston: Lothrop, Lee & Shepard, 1916, pp. 173-174.

Germany

Karneval (Rhineland); Fassenacht (Mainz); Fasching (Bavaria); Fastnacht or Fasnet (South West Germany)

Regional celebrations

In theory the Lenten season starts on November 11 at 11:11 am; however, the actual Kolner Carnival celebrations climax on Shrove Tuesday. Parades, masquerades, and a special Kaschingskrapfen doughnut are part of the festivities.

In Cologne around forty carnival clubs organize Sitzungen (sessions) at the beginning of the carnival season and hold balls. The Sitzungen feature silly speeches from an upturned half barrel, clowning, and group singing.

In Southwest Germany Fastnacht is celebrated with curiously dressed fools who roust through town. Schuddig Fools, for example, wear red-fringed clothes, wooden masks, and huge hats decorated with snail shells, and carry a blown-up hog's bladder to beat every one they meet. In Überlingen and Villingen the fools wear foxes' tails and smiling wooden masks and crack whips as they race through town, tossing fruit or nuts to the children. Fasching in Munich features a royal court and elegant balls. Carnival ends with Kehraus (sweeping out). At midnight the Court Fool is put into a mock coffin and carried out amid farewells and a dousing of beer. A sweeper follows the crowd out of the hall, literally sweeping out the trash.

Source: *German Festivals and Customs* by Jennifer M. Russ.

London: Oswald Wolff, 1982, pp. 78-90. See this article for much more on the German carnival customs.

Goa

Carnival in Goa, India, formerly a Portuguese territory

In Goa it is known as ''carnival'' or *Intruz* in Konkani, the mother tongue of the fun-loving Goans, indicating entry into the Lenten period. The festivities start on *sabado gordo,* ''fat Saturday,'' before Ash Wednesday. In all the villages and towns of Goa, plays called *khell* or *fell* are performed. As in Europe, the carnival has played a significant role in the development of popular theatre, vernacular song and folk dance in Goa.

During the carnival there is a general relaxation of rules and regulations. People in all kinds of masks go about throwing small paper packets containing flour and saw dust called *cocotes* and *cartuchos* at one another. Some people take the trouble to prepare perfumed colored water and using syringes called *bisnagas* sprinkle passers by with it. This aspect of the carnival fits right into the traditional practice of throwing colored powder and water at one another during the Hindu festival of *Holi* in other states in India. The Goan Hindu counterpart of *Holi* is called *Xigmo.*

The carnival is to be seen in its most spectacular form at Panaji (Panjim), the capital of Goa. ''See Naples and die, but first, see the carnival at Panjim'' goes a line from an old travelogue. Since Goa became independent and a part of the Indian Union in 1961, the State Department of Tourism has got into the act in a big way. A massive procession in honor of King *Momo,* the Lord of the Revels, is organized with gigantic floats complete with dance troupes and swing bands from various towns and organizations. The procession is held on Shrove Tuesday or *mardi gras,* and the floats are entered as in a competition. Thousands line the streets of Panaji through which the procession moves. Bearded and sometimes bare-chested motorcyclists form the vanguard of the procession. There is revving of motor cycle machines; there are fire crackers; and there is fanfare, at the starting of the procession. There is dancing in the streets. The procession may take three to four hours to pass by any given point but it usually ends at the magnificent Church of Our Lady of Immaculate Conception. In addition to the floats there are groups of dancers dressed in spectacular costumes; there are tableaux and stilt-walkers who are dressed up as famous Walt Disney figures, Goofy, Donald Duck, Mickey Mouse etc. Included are strange grotesque figures in African masks which may have been imported from Angola and Mozambique where the Portuguese ruled for many years.

After the procession has passed there is dancing in the Squares, piazzas, large halls and even on the beaches. The older people tend to congregate in the halls and it is not uncommon to see waltzes and tangos executed *a la* Rudolph Valentino. Where the dancers are younger, the scene is more like ''Saturday Night Fever'' *a la* Travolta. The dancing continues till the wee hours of the morning.

A few decades ago the assalto (assault) was very common. People used to move in masked groups in the late evening in gaily decorated bullock carts or motor cars, going from house to house assaulting the inmates with *cocotes* and *bisnagas.* Sometimes a ''trick or treat'' situation would emerge and this would be followed by impromptu parties with the local brew, *feni* (made from the caju fruit or the coconut), flowing freely. The *assalto* however is slowly being discontinued. One reason may be the influx of tourists during the carnival season, who understandably cannot take part in an activity that was originally meant for a friendly neighborhood where every one knew every one else.

The carnival festivities come to a close with most of the revellers going to an early morning mass on Ash Wednesday. Having gone into the church in a festive mood they come out considerably chastened with the holy ash smeared on their foreheads and the injection, ''Remember Man that thou art dust and to dust thou shalt return,'' ringing in their ears.

Source: ''The Carnival in Goa'' by Isaac Sequeira in *Journal of Popular Culture,* 20, no. 2 (Fall, 1986), 167-173.

Greece

Three-week festival

The Carnival season lasts three weeks. During the first week fattened pigs are killed, during the second, ''Meat-Eating Week,'' the pigs are eaten. During the third, ''Cheese-Eating Week,'' only dairy products and eggs may be eaten. On Tsiknopefti, Thursday of the second week, the Lenten revelry begins with masquerading and dancing. The masqueraders may perform plays, such as a carnival courtroom scene or the funeral of a miser.

Source: ''Carnival (Apokreos)'' in *Greek Calendar Customs* by George A. Megas. Athens: B. & M. Rhodis, 1963, pp. 59-75.

Haiti

Rara

Rara bands

In Haiti the carnaval tradition continues through Lent and into Easter Week with loud processions each weekend. Rara bands include flag bearers; a band chief; two or more major joncs, who twirl the ''jonc''; a queen with attendants; a musical group; a women's choir; women vendors selling food; and a rear guard. Near Holy Week a banner with the group's emblem will be carried. Rara has deep ties with vodoun and is imbedded with ritual, unlike the looser carnival, which it resembles only superficially. On Shrove Tuesday night, Rara bands perform a ''Bruler Carnival,'' burning carnival objects ritually, pouring rum libations to the four cardinal directions, and ending by each drawing a cross in ash on the forehead. Rara begins with the invocation of Legba, who appears as Carrefour, guardian of crossroads and thresholds. The association chief placates Carrefour with libations of water and the cracking of a long sisal whip.

Source: ''Rara in Haiti'' by Dolores Yonker in *Caribbean Festival Arts* by John W. Nunley and Judith Bettelheim. Seattle: Univ. of Washington Press, 1988, pp. 147-155. For more information see: *Dances of Haiti* by Katharine Dunham. Los Angeles: Center for African-American Studies, Univ. of California at Los Angeles, 1983.

Hungary

Carnival masks in Hungary

In southern Hungary, the preservation of masks presents no problem as, here, they are made of carved wood painted with ox blood. From the animal skins which cover the top emerge impressive, curving ram's horns. These masks are passed on from father to son and are said to be so terrifying that they frightened the Turkish hordes. Every year, in February, the inhabitants of Mohacs, near Pecs on the banks of the Danube, commemorate this ancient victory during Mardi Gras. In former times, only an adult, married male could wear these masks, known as *buso*. Now, young unmarried men take part in the activities—they whirl giant wooden rattles, set off cannons which shower everyone with all kinds of rubbish, and tease the women. Except in very rare cases, women do not wear masks. The younger women are chased by the pomets of the Kukeris (long sticks with a sheepskin gourd attached at one end—a phallic substitute). In the region of Ptluj (Slovenia), the big *kurent* masks, which have dangling red tongues, race around in bands carrying clubs covered at one end with the skin of a hedgehog.

Source: ''Winter Customs in Eastern European Countries'' by Jean Marie Steinlen in *The Drama Review,* T96, pp. 21-22.

Italy

Sophisticated Carnival in Venice

At Carnival time in Venice today, the city literally crackles with excitement and spontaneous gaiety. But the atmosphere is quite unlike the gaudy Mardi Gras celebrations of Rio de Janeiro and New Orleans. Venetians are not necessarily more restrained than New World revelers, but their Carnival breathes a sophistication born of the long tradition—even with its interruptions.

The people of Venice, of course, have a strong sense of their city's history, and, thus, unlike the Carnival of other cities, where costumes are designed mainly to dazzle and delight, the Venetian insists that a costume do all this and more. It must also cling closely to the historic tradition of past costume characterizations, of which there are a number of basic personages. By far the most popular of these is *La Bautta* (the domino), for which the wearer dons a black cape, a jaunty three-cornered black hat, and a ghostly white mask. One can also become a count or countess of Renaissance times. Another favorite costume is *Il Dottore,* which consists of a black gown and a black mask that satirizes the stern visage of the professor or doctor of law.

Most common of all, however, are those costumes derived from the Italian popular theater of the sixteenth and eighteenth centuries—the commedia dell'arte. Here is the clown Harlequin, the dizzy acrobat with his suit of many colors; here is Punchinello—the hunchback—with his tall, white, cylindrical hat and black mask featuring a hooked nose of considerable size. (It is he who became the aggressive character Punch in the puppet-show world of Punch and Judy.) Equally familiar is Pierrot, a character the French adapted from the commedia dell'arte, the sad white-faced clown in the oversized white jacket with big buttons.

These characters and many others mingle with such present-day creations as a Kabuki dancer, an extraterrestrial visitor, and dozens of imaginative creations of the wearer's own invention. Oftentimes, of course, dozens of celebrants will be found wearing the same costumes, for the old tradition of the young men's clubs has found a modern counterpart in groups of men and women today (often students) who costume themselves identically and roam the city as a band.

. . . Trainload upon trainload of Italian university students arrive in improvised costumes; they are virtually everywhere, dancing in the streets and performing in the cafés. Meanwhile, on another level of society, masked balls are under way throughout the city, the most spectacular parties coming near the end of Carnival. One of the most important of these costume parties is the annual charity ball at Teatro La Fenice. It draws a splashy international crowd, including movie stars and European aristocrats. During the final five days before Ash Wednesday the pace of the festivities is stepped up, and Venice becomes a whirling frenzy of parties and dances. Finally, as the Carnival ends on Shrove Thursday, its thousands of participants have already begun discussing with each other the preparation of their costumes for next year's celebration.

Source: Introduction to *Carnival in Venice* by Shirley and David Rowen. New York: Harry N. Abrams, 1989. See this book for its photographs of costumes in the 1980s.

Giovedi grasso (Thursday Fat)

In the middle of Lent—we call it *Giovedi grasso* (Thursday Fat)—we ''burn the old woman,'' and we do it in this way: Almost every house in Brescia has a courtyard surrounded with balconies; we tie a rope to each of these balconies, and in the middle we hang the ''old woman'' (sometimes she is accompanied by her old man).

To make up the ''old woman,'' we take an old undershirt, drawers and stockings; we stuff these up with rags, paper and straw, and with this stuffing we put lots of fire-crackers. We put on, for her head, a grotesque mask, a good wig made of fine paper or shavings.

Then we dress her up with some old clothes, and paper skirts. Her hands are made up with a pair of old gloves, and on her feet she wears real boots. She has a parasol in one hand; in the other she holds a nice paper lace handkerchief, and a good poke bonnet is on her head. Then we place all the rest of the fireworks on her parasol and around her petticoats. We let her hang there all day for the children to come to see her, and meantime we go around to the courtyards to see the others.

We all arrange the time to fire each ''old woman'' off, so that we all can manage to go and see every one. That night we are free to go into any courtyards. As we meet around the fence, a big fellow puts a match to her skirts, and up she goes; first in a little flame then a fire-cracker explodes, now her hand that was holding the paper handkerchief goes off with a bang; pretty soon one of her legs begins to tremble, and as you watch it it flies off with a kick; her parasol was tied very well on her other arm, so it holds the longest, and from that you see the fireworks start up.

After that we children start for the other places. It is about midnight when we go home.

After that hour every kind of enjoyment must stop, as Lent begins again.

Source: *When I Was a Girl in Italy* by Marietta Ambrosi. Boston: Lothrop, Lee & Shepard Co., 1906, pp. 26-27.

Malta

Carnival overview

The short season of colour and general jollification, traditionally preceding Lent, is characterised by the defilé of grotesque masks and decorated floats, and open-air dancing competitions.

The festivities are held in various villages but the main events take place in Valletta.

Many people take active participation in the celebrations, not only by taking part in the official events but also by joining in the fun during King Carnival's reign.

In Malta, the Carnival festivities have strong historical roots dating far back into the centuries. Their great popularity has withstood the various changes which this event has experienced throughout the years. With its unique combination of traditional and modern elements, today's carnival in Malta is still as popular as ever before.

Source: ''Malta & Gozo: Event's Calendar 1990.'' National Tourism Organization, 1990.

Martinique

Carnival celebration

On Martinique and neighboring Guadeloupe the carnival celebrations continue through the first day of Lent rather than end on Shrove Tuesday as elsewhere. On Sunday before Lent the streets are filled with costumed parades. Monday is an official holiday, with all offices closed and masked balls into the night. Shrove Tuesday is the children's day, during which they parade dressed in red-devil costumes and carrying tridents. Ash Wednesday is the day for she-devils. La Fere des Diablesses, over 10,000 masked and costumed lady devils, parade. Many are men in drag. Only the colors black and white are allowed on this day and faces are smeared with ash. King Vaval and his alter ego, Bois-Bois (Wood-Wood) lead the festivities. That night Vaval's effigy is burnt and his coffin lowered into the ground. The crowds sing, ''Carnival, don't leave us.'' But the celebration is over.

Source: *A Guide to World Fairs and Festivals* by Frances Shemanski. Westport, Conn.: Greenwood, 1985, p. 133.

Mexico

Carnival in Chamula, the five lost days

In Chamula, the five lost days of the Maya calendar fall at the time of Carnival. The Mayan calendar is adjusted each year so that Carnival occurs during Ch'ay K'in. At this time evil spirits walk on the earth and the world is turned upside down. The festival begins with an animal sacrifice and ends with a sign of new life.

Turkeys and the dead

In Chenalho, Carnaval begins at noon on Sunday. Two turkeys are strung up on a rope over the street, hung to represent the heart of Saint Sebastian. Men gallop by on horseback, pulling out feathers. Three passes are made, and then the turkeys are taken down and decapitated by men painted black who represent the Dead. The Dead carry the plucked turkeys over their backs to the house of a religious official where they call, ''Woop. Woop. Woop. We are the DEAD!'' Everyone in the house pretends to be afraid and hides, but The Dead enter and fling their dead turkeys down on the table. They refer to the turkeys as their ''Dead Uncle,'' make the sign of the cross backwards, and pour ''posh'' into the beaks of the turkeys, or put cigarettes into their beaks. The Dead thus shame those who go to offer food to the ancestors at the grave but only smoke and drink.

Men in drag and mock intercourse

Sunday night transvestites appear in borrowed skirts and *huipiles*.

They sing ''I am half a woman, half a girl.'' The men sing in feminine style, but there is little ribaldry. On Monday, however, Lacandons take over. The men have white circles and crosses painted on their bodies. The female impersonators wear striped shawls and ceremonial one-piece smocks, or *huipiles*. They wander the streets pretending to cure people by stroking them with leafy branches. After dark the Lacandon women rush into a religious official's home and ask for refuge. They are hidden under a mat until men playing a Ladino hunter and his three dogs enter. They leap on the "women" and pretend to copulate with them. The "women" protest and throw the men down and do the same to them. Then all rise and tell the children, "This is how it's done. Watch carefully." Tradition has it that at the beginning of the world people did not know how to have sex. God was too embarrassed to show them, so the Devil told the first man to watch, while he made love to the man's wife. This skit makes sure that the Devil need not do that again.

Source: *Living Maya* by Walter E. Morris, Jr. New York: Harry N. Abrams, 1987, pp. 172-173.

The Chamula: a Tzotzil-speaking Mayan group

The Chamula call carnival *Tahimoltik,* or "The Festival of the Games," with the name bearing connotations of competition and play.

As a religious event, carnival celebrates the young warriorlike Christ of Chamula myth, who fled in a deadly game from pursuit by evil demons. They finally captured and killed him on a cross by thrusting a lance into his side. In Chamula myth and in Catholic teaching, Christ died to rise up again later. . . .

A large cast of characters participates in a complex series of rituals which must be logistically coordinated and arranged. The men sponsoring this (and all other festivals) in English are called "cargo holders," a name deriving from the Spanish word *cargo,* meaning burden. Among many indigenous groups in Mexico and Guatemala—not only in Chamula—cargo holders bear the burden of a year's service to their village, either in a religious or a political office. Cargo holders gain prestige from these offices according to the political power of their office or the amount of money they spend, especially when celebrating festivals. The major cargo holders of carnival, called "Passions" and "Flowers" in Tzotzil must use up a vast amount of their savings, the equivalent of thousands of dollars, hence they gain the greatest prestige among religious cargo holders of Chamula.

Passions and Flowers, though never called divine in themselves, serve as Christ's guardians and corporal representatives. A female impersonator, acting as Nana Marina Corcorina, Cortés's mistress, and the Ladina in the Town Crier's proclamation, wearing a specially woven blouse over traditional male ceremonial attire, accompanies one of the Passions. Passions and onlookers joke with "her," emphasizing "her" shameless ways. The Passions run with "her" in the plaza of the ceremonial center, not haphazardly, however, but in a set path whenever the proclamation triggers their flight. Since the Chamula almost never run in everyday life, this in itself is an unusual act, a reversal of normal movement. It is balanced, however, by its performance in a context of order and sequence which the Passions with their sexually disorderly Ladina mistress do not disrupt if possible. . . .

Two other dramatically warlike events occur in carnival and merit special attention here. The first, a staged fight with dried horse dung, recalls the war between Mexico and Guatemala, and the second is a rite of purification by running through fire—a rite that is presented in the *Celebration* exhibit. Both take place on the second-to-the-last day of the Festival of Games, while the run through fire is a climax of the gamelike testing which occurs throughout carnival. The horse-dung fight takes place shortly before the run through fire, as youths form two opposing lines, one representing Mexican Carrancistas, the other, Guatemalan Pinedistas. The youths pelt each other vigorously with the dried horse dung, but the "war" ends in a draw after three forays, with each side winning once by overtaking the other. It is significant to note that the battle does not end in a free-for-all but follows prescribed rules.

Likewise, the run through fire follows its own ceremonial order. Shortly after noontime, the Passions and Monkeys, bearing flags both with and without sacred lance tips on their staffs, run through burning thatch which young boys strew on the plaza in front of the church. If a runner has gravely sinned, he will be punished by falling into the flames which lick his sandaled feet. This happened to a Monkey in 1972, who luckily emerged unscathed from his tumble, while the others continued to lope past him. A fall can be caused by Passions and Monkeys carelessly jostling one another but may only be blamed on a runner's own lack of coordination. Runners must follow each other in a set sequence, finishing the course even if they momentarily stumble.

. . . Perhaps the most striking military object is found in the Chamula presentation of Christ. Instead of a plaster, wood, and cloth image which cargo holders and their ritual specialists tend in other saints'-day celebrations, in carnival, Christ and the Virgin Mary take the form of weapons. These deities appear as sacred silver lance tips, the same kind of lances which killed Christ in Chamula myth. They fit by means of a socket at their base to the end of wooden flagpoles about 2 1/2 meters long. The attached flag becomes "clothes" for the lance tip, with its floral pattern signifying divinity. Sacred as well are the red, green, and sometimes yellow ribbons attached to the base of the lance tip when fastened to the pole. The Passion, when running and dancing with the flags and lance tips, enables Christ to reenact the games played shortly before His death. Thus the Chamula, in their struggle to overcome violence, transform a destructive implement into an object of extreme divinity. . . .

The Passions and Flowers, especially, must uphold the highest standards of generosity, etiquette, purity, foresight, and self-control, while at the same time enacting the ritual which is linked to the traumatic disruptions of war, rebellion, and conquest. During the five days of carnival, as incoming and outgoing office holders, they must cheerfully and without reserve provide three costly ritual meals of beef, salt, chili, tamales, tortillas, coffee, sweet rolls, sweet water, and cane liquor to all their male and female helpers, as well as to assembled onlookers. The outgoing Passions must sacrifice a bull, entailing great financial outlay, and offer its meat during these ritual meals. (It is the penis of this bull which usually forms one of the bull penis rods for a Monkey.) They must feed and provide cane liquor for their helpers so that no complaints of stinginess arise. They must not fight with other religious cargo holders or any other person while they are celebrating, no matter what grievances arise. They, their wives, and their helpers must remain sexually pure, keep their appearance clean (shown in the cleanliness of the costumes displayed in the *Celebration* exhibit), and provide copious, pure offerings of candles and incense to the images of the deities entrusted to their care.

The gods put not only the cargo holder's virtue to a test, but also his stamina. Beginning weeks before the actual festival, activity continues day and night with hardly a rest. Cargo holders groggily fulfill their ceremonial requirements, exhausted and seemingly asleep, keeping up this pace until each returns to his house in an outlying hamlet and a more normal life.

Source: "Chamula Carnival: The 'Soul' of the Celebration" by Priscilla Rachun Linn in *Celebration: Studies in Festivity and Ritual* edited by Victor Turner. Washington, D.C.: Smithsonian Institution Press, 1982, pp. 190-198.

For more on Chamula Carnival see: *Chamulas in the World of the Sun* by Gary H. Gossen. Cambridge, Mass.: Harvard Univ. Press, 1974; *Crazy February: Death and Life in the Mayan Highlands of Mexico* by George Carter. Berkeley: Univ. of California Press, 1966, 1974 reprint; *Juan the Chamula: An Ethnological Re-creation of the Life of a Mexican Indian* by Ricardo A. Pozas. Berkeley: Univ. of California Press, 1948, 1962 reprint; and *Ritual Humor in Highland Chiapas* by Victoria Reifler Bricker. Austin: Univ. of Texas Press, 1973.

Carnaval in Zinacantan

The ritual for this period is focused around one saint, *Santo Entierro,* who is called "The Buyer" in Tzotzil. This is a very large image of a crucified Christ kept in the church of San Lorenzo. The theme for the season is the pursuit of "The Buyer" by demons and the death of "The Buyer" by crucifixion on Good Friday.

Carnaval is called "the fiesta of games" and it lasts a week, ending on the eve of Ash Wednesday. The most important performers are two *Pasioneros* who offer candles, dance, say prayers at cross shrines, and provide food and drink for other participants. Their ritual service continues through Holy Week when they portray two Jews and have the duty of guarding the bier of the crucified Christ and of stroking the image with flowers from the other cargo-holders. Also active for Carnaval are an indefinite number of "Blackmen," impersonated by young Zinacantecos dressed as Ladinos, and the "Father Blackman" who blackens his face, wears an old black hat, shirt, breeches, an army coat, an old patched blanket and carries a bull's horn full of *chicha.* (This corn "beer" is especially fermented for Carnaval by the Zinacantecos.) These "Blackmen" drink *chicha,* make the rounds of all the cargoholders' houses where they are given liquor, and dance and recite *bombas,* short comical songs. The "Blackmen" represent the demons who later pursue "The Buyer."

Source: *The Zinacantecos of Mexico: A Modern Maya Way of Life* by Evon Z. Vogt. New York: Holt, Rinehart and Winston, 1970, p. 87.

Panama

Burial of the Sardine

Carnival in Panama City lasts for four days and nights before Ash Wednesday. King Momus and his queen preside. Floats and beauty pageants abound. The Carnival ends at dawn on Ash Wednesday with the "Burial of the Sardine." A mock funeral is carried out for a dead fish and it is dumped with ceremony into the ocean or a swimming pool.

Source: *Fiesta Time in Latin America* by Jean Milne. Los Angeles: The Ward Ritchie Press, 1965, pp. 42-44.

St. Vincent

Maskers, characters, and singers

. . . [T]he central organization is the touring musical band, but the center of attraction is the one or two maskers who lead the group. Characteristically, the masker organizes the activity and enlists the services of the band. Others in the community will decide to follow along with this group, "jumping up" to the music; and the band will costume themselves, sometimes using the same theme as the lead-figure, but more often, simply by putting lantern-blacking on their faces and painting "rude" words and phrases on newly-purchased white pants and T-shirt, wearing *washikongs* (tennis shoes), and fashioning an unusual hat.

The most common traditional characters portrayed are the Devil, "Wild Indian," "Bold Robber," the humpbacked "Bruise-ee-Back," a two-headed donkey, a monkey, or a bull. As leader, they commonly are at the head of the dancers, but there are also performances in which one dances alone, is chastised by some other masker and attacks members of the audience (especially children) to frighten them.

The group will commonly have one song, written for the occasion by the leader, which it performs wherever it goes. In some cases, the song may be advertisement for the group, as in the following which was fashioned by the late Isaac Glasgow of Mesopatamia to be sung as an accompaniment to the high antics of his Monkey Band.

> Only come, Glasgow, come,
> Only come, Glasgow, come,
> Only come, Glasgow, come,
> He favor a monkey more than a man.
>
> How long he come in this land,
> How long he come in this land,
> How long he come in this land,
> He favor a monkey more than a man.

His costume was only broadly interpreted as a monkey; it had a coxcomb on the head, his suit was of red velvet, his mask had a long snout, and he wore a long tail which he would pick up and try to lash the onlookers. He always organized a group that dressed up in the same red cloth and he was followed by a string band.

All such groups have, as their primary motive, the objective of making money, as opposed to the equivalent Christmas players. Consequently, the scaring of members of the crowd is generally accompanied by a demand for money. The group will have, as part of its performance, some kind of violent argument. This both amuses and scares the audience, attracting onlookers but preparing them to be coerced out of some coins. In the case of the Monkey, Donkey, or Bruise-ee-back groups, the conflict is central to the performances, but with the "old mas' " calypso groups, the focus is on the song used to road-march; this has resulted in the addition of players who will enact an argument of some sort, such as one between a cowboy and a gambler.

The songs composed by the "washover," or calypso singers, are usually concerned with some individual from a locale about whom the song is made. As opposed to the "hangings" (effigy burnings connected with an extreme occasion of scandal) in which the social offense dramatized is extreme, for Carnival slander songs almost anything can be singled out as a basis for a joke. For instance, one year a song was made by a Richland Park man and performed by a group from there which discussed the social faux pas made by a woman of having a cooking failure in her first encounter with a special kind of fish, the kitty; her mistake was not the disastrous fish-tea, but in telling anyone about it. The *tree-tree* mentioned is a fish caught in the rivers which turns soap-like when boiled (and therefore is commonly eaten fried).

> Nanna go to town and she buy some Bequia kitty;
> Nanna go to town and she buy some Bequia kitty;
> And she put de kit' in de pot to cook
> And it turn tree-tree soup.
> "What I doing do fo' me man' dinner tonight
> In dis colony!"
> "You better run in de shop and buy penny saltfish,
> In dis colony."

Source: "Christmas and Carnival on Saint Vincent" by Roger D. Abrahams in *Western Folklore,* XXI (4) (October, 1972), 275-289.

Switzerland

Celebrations, c. 1936, as seen by a British folkdance collector

. . . I next learned that Switzerland indulges in Carnival twice over; first in the Catholic Cantons which follow the Gregorian Calendar, and all over again in the Protestant Cantons which do not 'hold' with Pope Gregory and his Calendar, but celebrate their Carnival according to the Old Style a week later—this is also, I was told, to demonstrate to the unreformed that the reformed are not obliged to fast in Lent.

Blätzli Narren and the Ship of Fools at Schwyz

Then on to the quiet old town of Schwyz, higher and colder than Zug by its sheltered lake, and immediately we came upon the *Nüssler,* dozens of them, all masked and belled. Here we first saw the famous *Blätzli Narren,* the Leafy Fools, whose habitat stretches from Germany and Switzerland to the other end of the Austrian Alps.

. . . As the Guilds grew rich a ship appeared, the famous *Narrenschiff,* the Ship of Fools. It would carry a crew of winter demons armed with squirts and more dangerous weapons, and was drawn by a dozen men and attacked by scores. The Leafy Fools, up to one hundred or more, would scale the ship on ladders and of course always routed winter in the end. . . . It still goes out, shrunken now to a children's ship. . . .

Bread and fools at Einsiedeln

It was dusk when we arrived at the enormous chalet inn, *Der Schwann,* so we rushed straight out into the snowy street and plunged into a stream of guisers. Some were vulgar, many were ordinary; hundreds wore homemade masks of paper pulp shaped on moulds, and we learned of a mask competition that morning. Some of these youths, wearing their handmade masks and great cowbells resting on small pillows tied to their backs, ran to greet the strangers. They danced round us in a circle, making their bells clang, bending forward to whisper gibberish in falsetto voices.

Sharp pistol shots came to our ears. Peering cautiously round the corner of a chalet we saw a street deserted save for one solitary figure. This was a masked guiser indulging in the most wonderful whip-cracking display. He had no audience and needed none. Alone he drove out Winter with his magical whip; the lash, some eight feet long, swirling from side to side, occupied the entire breadth of the street, biting the snow into miniature dust storms with every swirl.

After supper—we were the only guests, for the pilgrimage season was far off yet—the clanging in the street swelled to carillon volume, and the innkeeper rushed up to say 'they' had come to see us, that if we did not want them he could not stop them—in fact here they were! Up the stairs and into the great dining-room came the belled and masked line of men, whether our attentive friends in the street or others we could not tell. I noticed how the little waiting maids, and even the daughters of the inn, got together and flattened themselves apprehensively against the walls. Spring magic had got inside.

Our uninvited guests ranged themselves in rows in front of us, each bent forward on account of the great bell on his back, each dancing, that is to say throwing up each foot behind in turn in a lumbering fashion. *Clang, clang, clang!* It was deafening. When at last they straightened up each man pulled off his mask and there under the goggling, simpering false faces were the red, grinning real ones of honest Einsiedeln youth. Then they had to be entertained, beers all round. . . . They run, these men and boys, from the Sunday till Ash Wednesday morning, day and night, night and day, only going home to eat and sleep when they can run no more. Then up and run again.

Source: "Swiss Fools and Festivals." In *The Singing of the Travels* by Violet Alford. London: Max Parrish, 1956, pp. 167-183.

Protestant celebration

Because of a special extension of Carnival given to Swiss Protestants during the second Reformation, Carnival is held the Monday after Ash Wednesday in Swiss Protestant areas.

Basel parades

On the stroke of 4 a.m. all the street lights went out, and the procession was set in motion. As the whole district was in pitch darkness, you could only see the lanterns carried high, at the head of each group, but not the people themselves. Some had smallish round lanterns shaped like biscuit tins painted in bright colours representing some special theme, with an electric battery to keep the light inside the lantern. Some groups carried from two to 24 lanterns as they filed past us, depending on the size of the group. These carriers were followed by bands of pipes, and these in turn by ear-splitting drummers. One team had 44 drummers. An enormous lantern brought up the rear of each group, and that showed the theme of the group. Some large lanterns (up to 14 feet high) had peculiar shapes, like cubes miraculously balanced at various angles. Others were plain square ones, but all were brilliantly painted in intricate designs, according to the theme of the group of that year.

Some groups wore pig masks, as a protest against pigs being bred in battery farms. Some wore calves' masks, protesting against the injection of hormones to fatten the animals quickly. Some had plastic wigs in bright reds, yellow, blue, purple, green or white 'hair' under their various headdresses. Some headgear were the traditional peaked hat of 'wizards,' or special grotesque caps, or gigantic leering heads, or crowns, or even electric candles over their wigs, nestling in what looked like a bird's nest.

The music played by all these bands was martial. . . . They had practised their bands the whole year round to learn to march in time, and this they achieved remarkably well.

After watching in the cold early morning for over two hours, we decided to go home to bed as we were frozen. On reaching home we drank the traditional *Mahl suppe* (flour soup), which is really meat broth with flour, eggs and other tasty ingredients added. We then retired to bed. For breakfast we had the usual 'onion cake,' which was really a meat pie in which quantities of onions had been added together with eggs and flavouring of various kinds.

The daytime parade

It seems that anyone who has a complaint, a grudge or an axe to grind, can let off steam and display his reasons for dissatisfaction by writing verses in Swiss-German, printing them and distributing these strips of paper along the path of the procession.

What I particularly liked to see was the 'Wild Man'—our Green Man—who dressed in twigs, ivy, pine branches, and looked wild indeed! He towered above the crowd who hailed him enthusiastically. Actually he belongs to the Small Basel, for three weeks before Lent he navigates a raft on two boats, halfway across the Rhein, and dances in midstream some 'very special steps with queer movements'—to bring forth new life. He will not land on Big Basel.

In the evening strange masks appeared, like bull's heads with horns; grotesque faces with elaborate comic characters; huge dogs' heads that looked despairingly at the crowd; enormous birds of prey with colossal beaks, or gigantic cats with heads towering above the shoulders of their wearers, who were playing flutes and beating drums. Others looked like ghosts with frightening eyes and gaping mouths. I wonder the children were not terrified.

There were also Fire-Waggons, made of iron, on which hot coals burned. They were dragged through the streets, while 'Devils' lit garden brooms from the coals and used them as lanterns to show the way. Flames rose high to the roof tops. This was presumably to purify the community before the new year.

Source: "The Carnival at Basel, Switzerland, Spring 1981" by Lucille Armstrong in *Folklore* 95 (1984), 55-56.

Turn-of-the-century Fasnacht

The one full holiday was that known as Fasnacht, and it fell on February 14th. On that day children dressed in fantastic attire and formed processions. Boys would try to imitate their fathers; for instance, a boy whose father was a chimney-sweep would black his face and carry a small ladder and broom and brush. A boy whose father was an officer in the army would dress as a soldier. Girls and women would dress as fairies. In the evening would be bonfires and singing.

What appealed most to us children on Fasnacht Day was the Fasnacht cake, a sort of shortcake liberally sprinkled with caraway seeds. My godfather always supplied me plentifully with this delicacy.

Source: *When I Was a Girl in Switzerland* by S. Louise Patteson. Boston: Lothrop, Lee & Shepard Co., 1921, pp. 141-142.

Tobago

The Carnival mas

In these Carnival *mas'es* the stylistic traits of the man-of-words performance pattern are harmonized with certain Carnival characteristics. Most of the groups found on Trinidad and Tobago during Carnival exhibit the following traits: (1) they represent a community, or in the cities, a neighborhood; (2) traditional roles are played, and the roles are designated by traditional costumes and masks, and by a certain type of performance consonant with the role; (3) the roles (and costumes) usually portray power figures, either characters from the underworld (criminals, devils) or impersonations of hero-types (military figures, warriors); (4) individual performers usually take on stage names which are appropriate to the character being played; (5) they usually accumulate groups of followers who dress in similar style; and (6) the performer, while he may perform simply by interacting with the audience, nevertheless finds opportunity for the fullest statement of his abilities in competition with another performer playing the same type of role. The man-of-words pattern fits easily into this type of Carnival performance.

A *mas'* usually is organized around a virtuoso performer; a singer, a dancer, a stickfighter, or a speechmaker. He often performs alone, and especially in those roles in which money-making is the primary motivation. More often, he performs alone one day of Carnival and with his group the next. When he performs with his group, it is generally recognized that they represent the honor of their community, and they may use this factor in building up the dramatic interest in contests with other groups.

Most of these contests call for the performance of certain set pieces prepared by each virtuoso ahead of time, and then an improvised battle. This is true, for instance, in the *Caiso Mas'*, the ancestor of the modern calypso competitions, found on both Trinidad and Tobago. The various "chant-wells" or mastersingers would compose a song for the season and each would try to have it widely sung. Then when he met another calypsonian, he and his group would trade songs and the two chantwells would then generally engage in a "war," or contest of invective. As with most of these conflicts, they were for the amusement of the crowd; seldom was a winner declared.

Source: "Patterns of Performance in the British West Indies" by Roger Abrahams in *Afro-American Anthropology: Contemporary Perspectives* edited by Norman E. Whitten, Jr. and John F. Szwed. New York: The Free Press, 1970, p. 166.

Trinidad

Pre-carnival fetes

Here almost the whole nation limes [relaxes and plays] for two days, as a grand climax to weeks of pre-carnival fetes, the mounting fever of calypso tents and panyards (practising and performing locations for calypsonians and steelbands), and of the various competitions which will lead to the winning of the Panorama championships for the panists, and the crowning of the Carnival King and Queen and of the Calypso Monarch.

While the Monday and Tuesday before Ash Wednesday are not public holidays, work virtually comes to a halt as thousands of masqueraders take to the streets to *jump up* (dance) with mas (masquerade) bands. The population of the island is swollen by an influx of tourists, many of them Trinidadians settled abroad and making this annual pilgrimage to play mas.

Source: "The Trinidad Carnival: Ritual, Performance, Spectacle, and Symbol" by Renu Juneja in *Journal of Popular Culture* 21 (4) (Spring, 1988), 87-92.

Celebration in the air

The night of Dimanche Gras is not for sleep. Frenzied activity goes on in countless houses and backyards, last touches are put on thousands of costumes and other paraphernalia. A new Calypso King has been crowned, but the people's choice of the Roadmarch King is still to be made. Private coronation ceremonies take place in masquerade tents, and new sovereigns prepare to lead their bands into battle. To take to the streets disguised on carnival day is to join battle with a host of rival masqueraders whose every word and action is a challenge that must be met. Contest, competition, the desire to excel all others in perfection of representation is the keynote of the Trinidad carnival. Here, two maskers, meeting in the middle of the road, stand facing each other, displaying their costumes with peacock spread, rocking on their heels, arms outstretched, pivoting to the music, each confident he has outshone the other in fidelity and magnificence. "The Field of the Cloth of Gold" is repeated in every encounter between bands. There are physical combats too. Walking the dimly lit streets of the city, that Dimanche Gras night of 1912, a famous stick fighter, veteran of many battles, "held his stick up in the air, looked up at it, and with a gesture of appeal to heaven shouted out the following little verse in one of the familiar tunes:

> 'O Gad, O Gad
> Gad have mercy pan dem deme-matin.' "

The air is charged with expectancy on that night before carnival. Yet there is no hectic scamper to be first on the road, as the dawn breaks to usher in the masquerade. The maskers observe an order of appearance befitting the characters they portray. There are five acts to the Carnival Monday performance; and the Tuesday parade elaborates the highlights of Monday's spectacle. First is the jouvay turnout from daybreak to 9:00 A.M. Characters from folklore, satiric "old masks" including Dame Lorraine types, and nondisguised revelers from all-night festivities flood the streets dancing and singing calypso choruses. Next come the traditional maskers and mummers who rule the road until midday. After them, the military bands, sailors, and small "original" bands appear. By 2:00 P.M. in the high afternoon, when the sun is sharpest, the big historical and fantastical bands take to the road in dazzling array. This spectacle is the climax to the day's presentation. The last act begins at dusk, when once again the streets are packed with revelers in and out of costume, celebrating the triumph of the day's magnificence.

In 1965 bands registered in Port-of-Spain numbered 171, to which should be added diverse numbers of individual maskers. It is roughly estimated that nowadays over 100,000 people are in costume during the two-day festival.

Source: *The Trinidad Carnival: Mandate for a National Theatre* by Errol Hill. Austin and London: Univ. of Texas Press, 1972, pp. 84-85. (See this source for history, costume, and dance.)

For more on Carnival see: "Carnival," in *Customs and Habits of the Sicilian Peasant* by Salvatore Salomone-Marino. London: Associated University Presses, 1981 (originally published 1897) pp. 152-165; "Carnival in Multiple Planes" by Roberto da Matta in *Rite, Drama, Festival, Spectacle* edited by John J. MacAloon. Philadelphia: ISHI Press, 1984; "Carnival, Ritual, and Play in Rio de Janeiro" by Victor Turner in *Time Out of Time* by Alesandro Falassi. Albuquerque: Univ. of New Mexico Press, 1987; "Shrove Tuesday or Mardi Gras" in *Folklore of American Holidays* edited by Tristram Potter Coffin and Hennig Cohen. 2nd ed. Gale Research, 1991.

Moveable: February-March

Ash Wednesday

Ashes made from palms consecrated the previous Palm Sunday are applied to the forehead of each member of the congregation by the priest, who reminds them, "Remember you are dust, and to dust you shall return." This is the first day of the forty-day Lenten fast.

England

Foods

On this first day of the Lenten fast special dishes may be served such as "hasty pudding" (English Midlands); fried dough fritters (Northern England); grey peas cooked in bacon fat (Warwickshire); or minced meat (Somerset). The day is sometimes known as "Hash Wednesday."

Source: *The Customs and Ceremonies of Britain* by Charles Kightly. London: Thames and Hudson, 1986, p. 47.

Iceland

Ash bag teasing

. . . But an innocent-looking game with the symbol of repentance, the ashes, survived. This is the amusing custom of furtively hanging a small bag of ashes on a person's back and making him carry it a certain distance, such as three steps, or across three thresholds.

This trick was especially tried by girls on boys. In return, the boys would attempt to make the girls carry small pebbles for a similar distance. Stones were probably selected because of the old punishment of drowning adulterous women with stones tied around their necks. In Reykjavik and other towns, however, it became a great sport among children to hang ash bags on the backs of respectable citizens, some of whom would react quite angrily. A still younger variation is to leave the bag empty, but to sew some symbol of love on it. Then it is the recipient's to wonder who might be the sender.

Cat-batting

Mention should be made here of the custom of "batting the cat from the barrel," which has been mainly observed in Akureyri. Originally, it was not necessarily tied to Ash Wednesday, but rather a specific *Cat-Batting Day* or *Cask-Batting Day* at a similar time of winter. Common in Denmark, where it had been introduced by Dutchmen, the custom is believed to have been brought to Iceland by Danes in the 19th century.

This game was probably played in various ways over the years. Suffice it to print here a description by an old citizen of Akureyri, pertaining to the early years of this century:

"In Akureyri, we tried to catch an alley cat and shoot it, but if that proved difficult, a raven would be killed, of which there were plenty. But a raven, we felt, was less sport, probably because of the name of this exciting game. Sometimes, we would be offered a house cat due to be destroyed, for which we were always grateful.

"Another thing needed in the preparation of the game was an empty barrel. A rope would be strung through it, to which the cat or the raven was fastened. The cask was decorated with mulitcolored paper.

"We would don fancy costumes with hats of colored paper, arm ourselves with clubs resembling baseball bats and swords of sundry make and quality. These would range from straightened barrel hoops to steel swords, depending upon finances and other circumstances.

"Then we would march in an orderly fashion, singing some lively songs, and bat the cask with differing force and enthusiasm. There was often great excitement among the boys, and no less among the spectators who were usually many, when only one small stave remained of the cask, for the lightness of it would make it difficult to beat off the rope. Who would be the lucky one to strike the last blow and become king of the cask, with a crown on his head instead of a paltry hat? He would be admired by the other boys, the little girls would look at him adoringly, and the grown-ups would congratulate him with proper respect.

"Even more prestige, however, came with the title of cat king. I think the swords were mainly responsible for the fact that everybody, young and old alike, would esteem him more who was fortunate enough to cut the last strand of the rope, so that the cat or the raven fell to the ground. Whoever had the stroke of luck to get the cat-king crown on his head did not have to complain—at least, not for the rest of the day—that he was not admired and respected in every way.

"When we had thus acquired two great and powerful kings, we would march in a phalanx through town, enter all the stores, and sing for clerks and customers. The rewards were usually a big bag of sweets and frequently money, too.

"Adults would also bat the cat from the cask. They would be mounted on horses for the occasion and dressed in colorful costumes, while the heads of their mounts were adorned with feathers."

• There is a source for a similar march about town in Reykjavik during the 1880s, though on Bun Day. The custom apparently did not last. In Akureyri it has in recent years been restricted to Ash Wednesday, which is a school holiday.

Source: *Icelandic Feasts and Holidays: Celebrations, Past and Present* by Arni Bjornsson. Translated by May and Hallberg Hallmundsson. Reykjavik: Iceland Review History Series, 1980, pp. 24-25.

Moveable: February-April

Lent

The six-week period before Easter Sunday is a period of fasting and self-denial for much of the Christian world. After the riotous last-chance celebration of the carnival season, the religious settle down to a period of denial and contemplation, marked by religious ceremonies to note the approach of the Holy Week and its culmination on Easter Sunday.

Denmark

Barrel-beating

The next great holiday after Christmas is Lent, when all the boys carry masks and go around shaking a bank begging for money and afterwards have a meeting in the backyard where they beat the cat in the barrel, an old custom, which, however, of late has been somewhat modified. The barrel is now filled with buns and is swinging freely, suspended from a rope. The boys now approach the barrel hitting it as hard as possible with their clubs till the staves are broken and contents come out.

Source: *When I Was a Boy in Denmark* by H. Trolle-Steenstrup. Boston: Lothrop, Lee & Shepard Co., 1923, p. 207.

Great Britain

The Sundays of Lent

THE SUNDAYS OF LENT ARE SIX

They are:—

The First Sunday in Lent.

The Second, called "Tid."

The Third, called "Mid."

The Fourth, called "Misers" or Mid-Lent or *Mothering Sunday*. This is the day when children bring presents to their parents, particularly to their mothers.

The Fifth, called "Carling" or Passion Sunday. On this day people eat a dish of grey peas fried in butter. Some say it is in memory of the ears of corn plucked by the disciples as they passed through the corn fields with Jesus on the Sabbath day.

The Sixth, called "Palm" Sunday, and the next is Easter Day, called "Paste-egg Day."

You can always remember them by the rhyme:

After the first Sunday in Lent,
Tid, Mid, Misera,
Carling, Palm and Paste-egg Day.

Source: *Happy Holidays* by Eleanor Graham. New York: E. P. Dutton, 1933, p. 77.

Greece

Megali Sarakosti

Fasting during Lent

The fast requires no animal products, meat, eggs, fish, or dairy. In addition wine and olive oil are not permitted on Wednesdays and Fridays and during Holy Week. A special fast of no water or bread for the first three days of Lent may be observed by the most religious. A nun figure drawn on paper may be used to count the days of Lent. She has seven feet representing the seven weeks of fasting. She is made with no mouth, representing the fast, and with her hands crossed in prayer. One of her feet is folded off each week to count the passing weeks. In Pontus a potato or onion is stuck with seven chicken feathers and hung from the ceiling. One is pulled off each week. This is called a "Kukaras" and was used to threaten the children if they misbehaved by some parents.

Source: *Greek Calendar Customs* by George A. Megas. Athens: B. & M. Rhodis, 1963, pp. 75-76.

Iceland

Lenten customs, c. 1910

From an old tradition several festivities were bound to the first three days of Lent. Monday is always called *Bolludagur* or *Flengingardagur* (The day of muffins, or the day of whipping). The children provide small whips or wands, often made of colored paper. They get up early Monday morning, before anybody else, to whip those who are in bed. They beat with their wands a few times upon the bed where the person lies. Some people start out of bed when they hear somebody coming, but others stay in it longer than usual, in order to please the children. They who are whipped have to give the whipper a *bollu* (muffin) or a few cents to buy one with. Children in towns go from house to house to whip their friends; both old and young are whipped but it is done mostly by children. Sometimes young people like that fun, too. Wherever you pay a visit that day, at least in towns, muffins are served with the coffee. That Monday is a holiday in many schools.

The Tuesday was a great meat-eating day, which is a tradition from the Catholic times. In connection with that was the game *að sitja i fästunni* (To sit in the fast). That meant never to mention any common words for meat, dripping, or gravy during Lent. To be able to speak of these things, they were given other names instead of the proper ones. Some failed the first or second day, others kept it all through Lent. They tried to tempt each other to errors, especially those who had themselves failed. At my home this game was only practised by the servants.

On the third day of Lent, Ash Wednesday, or as we call it, *Öskudagur,* the fun came to its height. Many days before, the children began to make preparations for that, which consisted of sewing small bags. They had all imaginable colors and were of all sorts of cloth or fabric, even embroidered stuff. The boys had as a rule to have their bags made by mother or one of the girls. In these bags were either put ashes from the stove or small stones; in those intended for men or boys to carry were ashes, but in those for girls or women, were small stones. At the edge of them were drawing-strings, at the ends of which were fastened bent pins, for hooking them into people's clothing. Naturally boys and girls opposed each other. If one walked a few steps with a stone or ashes, he or she had "carried it," and he or she who "put it on," endeavored to be near to prove that the attempt had been successful.

The grown-up often joined the children in that game. On one such occasion no less than thirty bags were hooked in my dress. I did not avoid it at all, but was only pleased if it added to the boys' fun. I suppose if something like that had happened to me when a young girl I would not have stopped crying that day. It sometimes looks droll to see ladies and gentlemen walking in the streets with red or green bags dangling on their backs, of which they have no idea.

Source: *When I Was a Girl in Iceland* by Hólmfrídur Árnadóttir. Boston: Lothrop, Lee & Shepard Co., 1919, pp. 146-148.

Italy

Playing Al Verdo (the Green) in Brescia, c. 1900

We have a game that we children play during Lent. We call it playing *Al Verdo* (the green), and it is this:

Lots of girls and boys meet in a yard or house, each one holding a piece of cauliflower leaf, and we take an oath to play fair. After that day whenever we meet, two at a time, or several together, we shout, "*Verdo!*" and we must show a piece of cauliflower leaf; if it looks suspiciously dry we require that it should be tried on some wall; if it doesn't leave any green mark the party holding it has to pay the forfeit; that is, at Easter, she or he has to bring to the other a *Colombina* (a dove), made by our bakers, with a dyed egg in the middle of it. I had to pay several of these forfeits because I shouted many times "*Verdo!*" and when it came time to produce the cauliflower leaf I had left it in my other dress pocket.

Source: *When I Was a Girl in Italy* by Marietta Ambrosi. Boston: Lothrop, Lee & Shepard Co., 1906, p. 33.

Lebanon

Springtime festival

Of all the festivities in the year, the spring festival is the outstanding ceremony. In it the peasants' sense of piety finds greatest expression, and in it are combined the basic sentiments of peasant life. The festival is set outside the Muslim lunar calendrical count, since otherwise it would not fall annually in the spring of the year. It is in fact computed in terms of the Christian calendar, its series of increasingly important feast days falling on successive Thursdays preceding Eastern Orthodox Easter Sunday. The festival is a regional celebration participated in by all peasants of the general area, irrespective of religious faith.

First comes the Thursday-of-the-Animals. On this day it is said all animals meet and mate, reproducing their kind. Household working animals are given a rest on this day, while henna, as a sign of blood and life, is dabbed upon their foreheads. Next comes the Thursday-of-the-Plants when unmarried girls, in anticipation of the day that they will become brides, wash themselves in sweet-scented water in which blossoms and wild flowers have been crushed. Young children, as well, are washed in the scented water to ensure their growth and well-being during the year. Next falls the Thursday-of-the-Dead when family graves are visited in commemoration of the departed. Colored hard-boiled eggs are distributed and special wheat cakes baked. Lastly comes the Thursday or Day-of-the-Jumping, when the inhabitants of Buarij leave the mountain side and troop downward to the plain, where all peasants of the region unite in festival.

On the final Thursday the tomb of Noah situated in a foothill settlement is visited first. It lies in a separate room off a mosque, the raised tomb fit for the proportions of a giant, which peasants say is appropriate since men were larger in ancient days. Here peasants, by touching the tomb or leaving upon it cast-off clothing, receive therapeutic blessing. Near the tomb is a cylinder of limestone, of phallic shape, which persons roll on one another's bodies as a cure and prevention of bodily ills.

Following this, the villagers cross the plain to a place near which the Beirut-Damascus highway enters the Anti-Lebanon mountains. Here on a raised hill is the domed shrine of the Wali Zaur, a legendary local Muslim saint; near the tomb is a well. Peasants and townsfolk within a radius of fifteen miles congregate at this place, coming by overloaded automobiles, trucks, camels, donkeys, horses, horse and cart, on bicycle and on foot. The animals are decked in blue beads and colored garlands for the occasion and the tails of the horses are dyed in henna. Bicycles are wreathed in paper flowers. All persons are dressed in their best garments, varying from out-moded embroidered costumes to smart sailor suits for children. The crowd consisting of some two thousand persons moves group by group into the shrine to receive its blessing of health and well-being. Barren women and those desiring further children seek out the well.

This springtime festival is celebrated in varying manifestations throughout the Beqaa Valley, which extends from Syria through Lebanon into former Palestine.

On returning to the village at the end of the day the festival atmosphere continues. Dancing is held in the street to the playing of pipes and drums. Even the outdoor court of the mosque, the place of ablutions and prayers, is trod by dancing feet. What is more, men and women break line, members of the opposite sex dancing shoulder to shoulder.

Source: *Buarij: Portrait of a Lebanese Muslim Village* by Anne H. Fuller. Cambridge, Mass.: Center for Middle Eastern Studies of Harvard Univ., 1961, pp. 84-86.

Palestine

Special Thursdays

Special celebrations occur on six Thursdays near Easter. The special day begins Thursday evening and lasts until Friday evening. They are *djum 'et el-mnadat* (hamîs or *djum 'et en-nabât* to Bedouins), 14 days before Good Friday; *djum 'et el-bêraq (hamîs el-amwât hamîs* or *djum 'et el-bêd* to Bedouins), 8 days before Good Friday; *djum 'et el-elêmat (djum 'et el-maghri* or *djum 'et el-haiwânât* to Bedouins), Good Friday; *djum 'et er-raghâib* or *djum 'et el-halâwi* or *ed-djum 'et et-tâîuli,* 8 days after Good Friday; *djum 'et el-ghurabâ,* 14 days after Good Friday; and *djum 'et el-hazânâ,* 21 days after Good Friday.

Many say that the three Fridays following *djum'et el-elêmât* are known collectively as *djuma' er-reghâyb* (the Fridays of desires), the first bearing this designation *par excellence,* while the last is known as *el-hazânâ* (the Friday of the sorrowful). According to the people of Jerusalem only the first Friday bears the name of *djum'et er-ragháyb* (also *djum'et el-halâwî,* the Friday of the sweets). In all three the peasants buy sweets to be distributed to members of their families and to others. On the first Friday the members of the family enjoy the sweets, on the second *djum'et el-ghurabâ* (the Friday of the strangers) strangers, and on the third the "sorrowful" are presented with them. By "sorrowful" are meant widows and orphans, since they have no male support. It is to be noted here that this exact division, although known, is not preserved everywhere. The last week used to be called in Jerusalem *djum'et en-náwar* (the Friday of the gypsies), but this expression is no longer known. The gypsies used to go in a body, dressed in their best clothes, to the mosque of Omar on this day.

Poor women or those having no male support are said to express their grief on such a day by the saying:

fi djum'et er-raghâyb yâwêl illî djôzhâ ghâyb

"On the Friday of the desires woe to the woman whose husband is absent."

In *djum'et* (also called *hamîs) en-nabât* the young unmarried girls go out Thursday afternoon to the fields and gather flowers and sweet-smelling herbs. In cutting the herbs they ask the plants:

taqš u-natš šû dáwâ er-râs yâ šdjêrah

"Crack and pull out—what is the remedy for the head, O little tree." These flowers are placed in water and left all night under the open sky; in order to be acted upon by the stars. This practice is known as *tandjîm.* With this water they wash their hair on the following day (Friday) believing that it will grow thicker and longer. Some mix the water with their bath. They dress themselves afterwards in their best clothes and go out into the fields. Many think that performing these acts will hasten their chances of marriage.

A corruption of a well known proverb points indirectly to this day: *talâti bitâwilû el-'umr mašyak 'ala nabât urukbak 'alâ es-sâfinât u ahdak el-banât*

Three (things) will prolong thy life: walking on grass, riding on good horses and taking girls (in marriage).

In *djum'et el-amwât,* better known as *hamîs el-amwât,* the women of Jerusalem go on Thursday afternoon to the cemeteries to visit their dead. They take with them dyed eggs, sweets and even cooked food and meat. The greater part is distributed to the poor—who gather on such a day—as an *adjr* (recompence). The meaning is that, since some help is given to the needy in the name of the deceased, God will reckon such an act in his favour. In some villages the women go before sunrise to the cemetery, believing that a visit after this time is not so good. Soon after sunrise they go home. The children of the peasants go on Thursday afternoon to the houses of their neighbours and beg: *a'tûnî bêda 'an amwâtkum,* "give me an egg in the name of your dead". Those in the house give an egg, dried figs, raisins or a piece of bread. The children express their thanks with the words *allah yirhamhum,* God be merciful to them. This day, therefore, bears also the name *hamîs el-bêd* (Thursday of eggs).

Source: "Folklore of the Seasons in Palestine" by T. Canaan in *Journal of the Palestine Oriental Society,* 1923, pp. 21-35.

Russia (U.S.S.R.)

Butter Week in Petersburg, c. 1910

. . . [I]t takes place before Easter. All the peasants try to get strong after the long fast. The festival lasts a week, one meal is taken after another, and people go here and there, and everywhere food is on the table. An ice-hill is made in the village; the young people play games and act. Masked figures run through the village, and are treated as their costumes find favour or not in the sight of the lookers-on. On the last day of the feast Prince Carnival says good-bye. Ten horses, harnessed in single file, draw an especially high cart; a drunken man with a pitcher of beer and bottle of wine, sits on it holding a huge goblet in one hand. In front of him is a table covered with food which he seems to enjoy; in spite of entreaties to remain a little longer he leaves the village and hospitality is at an end. The young men burn the *Maslenitza.* Great bundles of straw and barrels rubbed with tar are set on fire, and there is a display of primitive fireworks.

Fasting begins at midnight, and oil takes the place of butter. In St Petersburg the festival has been cut down to its narrowest limits in order not to interfere with the work of a great city, but the noise is just as great. The Admiralty Square was set apart for the people a few years ago. Booths stood everywhere, but these have already been ordered elsewhere, to the Field of Mars near the summer garden which, because of its extent, is better fitted for the people's pleasure.

The Field of Mars is changed into a city of booths. Shows of all sorts, swings, panoramas, giants and giantesses, animals, and so on, and the criers who stand in the galleries describe their shows in even more varied language. The panorama of the burning of Paris has wandered to the banks of the Neva in its long pilgrimage, and the crier says, "Here you see the city of Paris burning; who wishes can be burnt at the same time. Come in, come in, the fire is at its height just now!" And while he is recovering his breath, a voice calls from somewhere else, "The great General Skobeleff stands in the thickest of the battle; around him lie mountains of slain, among whom our soldier-heroes. A cannon ball takes off a head, two feet, two hands—but what does our hero mind, he smokes on!"

. . . Swings and switchbacks are the great attraction. The man of the people loves a swing, he can swing himself for hours together without tiring of the motion. The ice mountains are arranged with a wooden staircase leading to the summit, about 50 feet, and there the journey begins. Moujiks stand at the foot of the staircase and offer their services and a little sledge; the passenger sits behind the moujik, then the man in charge at the top gives the sledge a push and down it rushes along the smooth surface. The habitués do not require the moujik, who steers the sledge and prevents it from running into others. Many a red beard can guide his lady, amid cries of pleasure, to the finish where tea or vodka is hurriedly swallowed, and the whole affair begins over again.

The air makes them want food, so they go to the booth where food is sold, and buy *bliny* and cream cakes made of butter and flour, and nuts which every one old and young cracks with glee. The day has to be finished with drink. It would not be according to tradition if it did not finish in that way.

Source: *Home Life in Russia* by A. S. Rappoport. New York: Macmillan, 1913, pp. 55-57.

Sweden

Birch branches for Fastlag Och Fasta (Lent and the Fast)

During the Lenten season bare birch branches are decorated with bright feathers. They are placed in a vase of water to bud.

Good Friday thrashings

In some families, the head of the household may give the family and servants a playful birch switch thrashing on Good Friday morning.

Source: *Traditional Festivities of Sweden* by Ingemar Liman. Stockholm: The Swedish Institute, 1985, p. 7.

Moveable: February-March (First Sunday in Lent)

Chalk Sunday

Ireland

Chalking the church doors to mark the unmarried

. . . The ban on marriage ceremonies for Catholics during Lent meant that unmarried Catholics remained in that state until the following Easter at least and probably longer. In the past when people were encouraged to marry, this Lenten ban led to the custom on the first Sunday of Lent of marking the unmarried with chalk as they went to church—giving that day the name 'Chalk Sunday'. The custom was mainly one of fun, but rural society was never reluctant to show genuine disapproval. . . .

Source: *Life & Tradition in Rural Ireland* by Timothy P. O'Neill. London: J. M. Dent & Sons Ltd., 1977, p. 64.

Moveable: March-April (Fourth Sunday in Lent)

Mothering Sunday

A custom of visiting the family home on this day and bringing a small gift for mother died out early in this century but was revived after W.W. II under the influence of the American Mother's Day. A popular gift is the simnel cake. A mythic couple named Simon and Nell argued over whether to bake or boil their cake, so did both. The simnel cake recipes used in Great Britain vary from area to area. Most contain fruits and are glazed.

Great Britain

Simnel cake and violets

On Mothering Sunday a traditional gift is a bunch of violets.

In some areas the flowers are blessed in an afternoon family church service, and the flowers may be distributed to the younger members of the congregation.

Simnel Cake is the treat of the day. This is a rich saffron-flavored fruit cake with almond icing. It is popular in the countries adjoining the Welsh border.

Source: *Lore and Language of Schoolchildren* by Peter and Iona Opie. Oxford: Oxford Univ. Press, 1959, p. 243.

Moveable: March-April (Fifth Sunday in Lent)

Carlings Sunday

On this day, Passion Sunday, Christ's sufferings are contemplated. In Northern England and Scotland carlings (a type of grey pea) are eaten.

Great Britain

Grey peas

They may be boiled with bacon fat and eaten with salt and vinegar, dried and fried in butter, soaked in beer before cooking, or eaten with rum and sugar, depending on local custom. This is called "Carling Sunday," perhaps from the word "caring."

Source: *The Customs and Ceremonies of Britain* by Charles Kightly. London: Thames and Hudson, 1986, p. 67.

March-April (Saturday before Palm Sunday)

St. Lazarus' Day (Lazarovden)

This is a ritual day to remember Lazarus, whom Jesus raised from the dead.

Bulgaria

Original meaning is no longer intact

An important holiday in Bulgaria up until the early twentieth century, some of the holiday songs and dances are still popular as folk revivals, although their original meaning is no longer intact.

Rituals in Old Bulgaria

The chief performers of the songs sung on St. Lazarus' Day and the chief participants in the ritual games played on the same day were girls, whose ages varied from 5 or 6 to 10 or 12. They started preparing for the holiday in Lent. Their preparation consisted in learning characteristic songs and ritual games. They were usually helped and instructed by an elderly woman familiar with the songs and games in question. The preparation included making special costumes and various ritual objects. The girls were dressed in bridal costumes, which had been worn by recently married women, and they were provided with ornaments that had a ritual significance.

On the morning of St. Lazarus' Day, the youngest girls were the first to start their tour of the village. They went round the houses singing and dancing for which they were given eggs and, more seldom, small coins. Their activities went on till midday.

On the following day, Palm Sunday, the older girls started their tour. Unlike the younger girls they performed special ritual games accompanied by a rich repertoire of songs. Their choice of songs depended on the house they happened to be visiting at the moment, on the members of the family living in it, and on their hosts' wishes. Their subjects varied: some songs were meant to ensure the health and good fortune of very young children; others dealt with love and the dreams of unmarried young men and women; still others were dedicated to the merits of newly married couples and especially to the beauty of the young wife, to her joy in her husband and her children; and still others treated of the happiness enjoyed by a big and united family, of the prosperity and hospitality of their hosts:

> Boyo, Boyo, handsome Boyo,
> Are you within?
> Let us enter your yard!
> Do not shut your boxwood gates to our faces,
> For we are singers on St. Lazarus' Day.

The system of festive customs and ritual games associated with St. Lazarus' Day includes also the Kumitchene and the Buenets. On Palm Sunday girls made small wreaths of willow twigs, went to the river or to the village fountain, placed the wreaths on a beetle, and then they dipped the beetle into the water and the wreaths floated on the surface. The girl whose wreath was the first to start floating was given the "title" of "kumitsa." She received special treatment from the rest of the girls till next Easter.

Immediately after the election of the "kumitsa" she was escorted to her home by her friends who sang ritual songs. The singing continued at the "kumitsa's" home where the girls were given a ritual meal. At this stage their songs usually contained allusions to some young man and young woman that were known to be sweet on each other:

> A snowdrop grows in Zlatka's garden,
> The fairest flower to be seen.
> She waters it at sundown,
> Stamen picks it at sunup.

From Palm Sunday to Easter Day a special penance was imposed on the girls; they were not to speak to their "kumitsa." On Easter Day they went to see her with presents of Easter eggs and a special kind of ritual bread. As a result the "kumitsa" granted her "forgiveness." Fasting is over. The wide cycle of St. Lazarus' Day customs and rites ends with visiting one's godfather and mother and the usual visiting at Easter.

St. Lazar's Day customs, rites and songs and their influence in particular varied with one's age. Little girls who most often follow the example of bigger ones in their songs and dances consider their participation in them a child's game which is the first step to their future maidenhood.

Unmarried young girls experience their most cherished expectations and hopes in connection with their marriage and future family life. St. Lazar's Day is a red letter day for them which they remember all their life.

Everybody else in the village, who is either a spectator or a participant, has trepidations of his own. Men, having admired the beautiful ring dance and having recalled to mind their youth, would listen seriously to the song addressed to them singing of honor, health and wealth. On St. Lazar's Day everybody from the village eyed the young unmarried girls all dressed up and dancing in a ring; on such an occasion mothers and unmarried men would choose their future daughters-in-law and wives.

Source: "Festive Customs and Ritual Games on St. Lazarus' Day" by Nikolai Ivanov Kolev in *Journal of Popular Culture,* 19:1 (Summer 1985), 143-148. (Contains good bibliographical references.)

Greece

Saturday of Lazarus

Children go from house to house singing "Lazarakia," songs about the resurrection of Lazarus. They carry a small picture depicting the story. In Central Greece, Macedonia, and Thrace this performance is carried out only by girls aged 10 to 12 years who carry a washing pestle wrapped in bright cloth. In other areas Lazarus is represented by a doll or a staff decorated with flowers, cloth, and ribbons. In Crete a cross of reeds decorated with lemon blossom and wild red blossoms is carried. In Cyprus a boy is covered with yellow flowers to impersonate Lazarus. Boys lead this young "Lazarus" from house to house and he lies on the ground feigning death as they sing, then rises when they call, "Lazarus, Come Out!" Custom has it that the resurrection of Lazarus is the "First Easter."

Source: *Greek Calendar Customs* by George A. Megas. Athens: B. & M. Rhodis, 1963, p. 88.

Roumania

Lazarus Saturday

This, the day before Palm Sunday, is Lazarus Saturday. In the poor quarters of the towns, as well as in the country, the ancient custom survives of celebrating in songs three persons of that name: Lazarus of Bethany, who was restored to life; Lazarus the ill-fated one, who perished on his wedding-eve; and Lazarel, or Little Lazarus, a mysterious character who died from a longing to eat cake.

Three little girls, all under eight years old, go round singing a ballad from door to door, the youngest decked out in bridal array, with the silver thread, and veil, and citron blossom. Naive players of a threefold drama, they make pretence of grief, and are called the Lazarines.

They first sang the story of *Lazar din Vitania,* Lazarus of Bethany, the brother of Martha and Mary whom Our Lord loved:

> Thy name is blessed, Bethany,—the boasted birthplace, thou,—of three rays of light—God looked upon with love!
>
> From Bethany village—three children went forth—born of two parents,—with names sweet to hear,—Lazarus, Martha and Mary. . . .

"That's done," said Outza to the children. "Now sing 'Little Lazarus,' so as you'll get some cakes, my chicks, and not be like him and die of impatience to be eating them!"

And when they had told how Lazarel had asked his mother to bake him a cake, and she'd refused, and how the boy, in the fury of his thwarted wish, had pierced his own heart with a spindle which his mother had let fall,—then, it was all over. I had no more to learn about the three Lazaruses.

The eyes of the three tearful ones were sparkling, when I gave them the cakes which Outza had been hiding in her apron.

Source: *Isvor: The Country of Willows* by Princess Bibesco. New York: Frederick A. Stokes, 1924, pp. 33-34, 37-38.

March-April (Sunday before Easter)

Palm Sunday

Palm Sunday commemorates Christ's entry into Jerusalem, and is marked by the waving of palm branches.

France

Rameaux

Blessing of palms

Palm Sunday or Rameaux is naturally a great day. Many ceremonies (most of a similar kind) take place at the blessing and distribution of palms. The old palms are usually burned the evening before. In some places people bring their own *buis* to be blessed, and either take these home, or plant them on graves. At some places (e.g. Toulon, Avignon, I think Hyères) children carry wooden 'thyrses' with oranges fixed on the top; elsewhere branches, with crystallized fruits hung on them.

Source: *A Guide to French Fêtes* by E. I. Robson. London: Methuen, 1930, p. 76.

Italy

Palm Sunday in Brescia, Italy, c. 1900

Palm Sunday is a very gay Sunday with us. Early in the morning our cathedral is surrounded with olive branches, some as large as a Christmas-tree in America. The small branches are sold gilded, with little wax doves stuck on them.

The air is full of the fragrance and the noise of them, because we children each take a leaf of the branch, and splitting it as a quill pen is split, we bend it, and putting it between our lips, we get a pleasant sound from it; and as almost everybody does it on that day the music is great.

Source: *When I Was a Girl in Italy* by Marietta Ambrosi. Boston: Lothrop, Lee & Shepard Co., 1906, p. 34-35.

The Netherlands

Bearing the Palmpass

Children go from farm to farm on Palm Sunday carrying a Palmpass, or "Easter Palm." This is actually a decorated staff, covered with Easter emblems. It is made of a hoop attached to a stick. The hoop is twined with boxwood and decorated with eggshells, paper flags, sugar rings, oranges, raisins, figs, small cakes, and chocolate eggs. At the top, little dough figures of cocks or swans are placed. Awards may be given for the finest Palmpass in some areas. The children carry their Palmpass and tour the area singing:

"One more Sunday
And we'll get an egg.
And we'll get an egg.
One egg is no egg.
Two eggs are half an egg.
Three eggs are an Easter egg.

They are given eggs.

Source: *Easter the World Over* by Priscilla Lord Sawyer and Daniel J. Foley. Philadelphia: Chilton, 1967.

Peru

La Fiesta de Ramos in Moche

The town arises very early, and with the arising, begins Palm Sunday. The earliest risers have already visited the altar of the image. Amid rustic aromas and surrounded by flowers, the happy image of Christ Triumphant distributes his benedictions to his adorers. Again the bells sound forth their merry tones and groups of people fill the streets. The temple is filled with Christian people from town and *campiña,* from port and city, from hacienda and *chacra.* The mass begins with the rituals of the cult. The padre, from the sacred pulpit, begins the sermon, turns his eyes to heaven, and blesses in the name of God the crowd in the temple. A few minutes later the music stops with the distribution of palms and olive branches. Shortly afterward begins the renactment of the entrance of Jesus into Jerusalem. For this the padre, followed by the faithful, goes forth from the temple, and they proceed to cover the streets to the image with palms and olive branches.

After this the people begin to look for a place to eat lunch, some searching among the booths for those with the best dishes and music, while others go to visit the houses of their *comadres.* In many cases these visits are occasions for household fiestas for hair cutting or ear opening of the small children.

In the afternoon begin the kormes and the dance. There near the booth where they are selling cabrito, yuca, and sweetpotatoes, the people are indulging in *criollismo* without equal. Here others are eating *sopa teóloga* and other typical dishes. Over there is a merry party quaffing *chicha*. In other booths lively maidens offer, in addition to food and drink, the temptation of ruby lips. The orchestra and the band animate the dance and there is no place to sit quietly. Everywhere is movement, agitation, and music. The minutes slip away, the hours. The moment of the procession draws near. The merry throng thins out as people go to the place of the image.

The tradition is displayed in this procession. A white female ass is present in front of the altar. [This white donkey roams the town freely during the rest of the year and is fed and watered by whomever she visits.] The *mayor-domos* divide into committees, one to direct the band of music and the other to put the saddle on the ''little donkey of Our Lord.'' Here is the band of the Maestro Antonio Sachún with his justly famous musicians. The image of The Señor is placed on the ass, and then begins the majestic procession of Palm Sunday to the temple.

The view which this transcendental procession affords is magnificent. Palms and candles, music and faith, confounded together in the most remarkable act of the year in the town of Santa Lucia de Moche. Along the line of this procession have been erected various altars, and the people along the streets have been stirred by the explosions of numerous rockets. The bystanders carpet the pathway of God with flowers they throw from their hands. In front of the temple, the image of Christ Triumphant is lowered from the saddle and carried in the arms of the *mayordomos* to the main altar of the church. After a few words by the priest, the religious fiesta is terminated.

It is 7 o'clock in the evening and almost the entire crowd which took part in the procession begins to dance again.

Source: *Moche: A Peruvian Coastal Community* by John Gillin. Westport, Conn.: Greenwood Press, 1973. Smithsonian Institution. Institute of Social Anthropology. Pub. no. 3, 1947, pp. 147-148.

Spain

Palm Sunday, c. 1938

Children bore full-sized palm branches to church to be blessed on this day. Each was decorated with tinsel, colored glass ornaments, wrapped candies, and spring flowers.

Source: *My Spain* by Ruth Sawyer. New York: Viking, 1941, p. 133.

February 14

St. Valentine's Day

According to some historians, two Christian martyrs named Valentine were buried on the Flaminian Way outside the Porta del Popolo of Rome. Other historians believe they were the same man. Since the middle ages, the day has been associated with romantic love.

General Information

The real St. Valentine

Valentine, Bishop of Terni, a small town 80 miles from Rome was martyred sometime between *A.D.* 270 and *A.D.* 273. A second Valentine, a Roman priest, was also martyred in the same spot at about the same time. Since Terni was under Roman jurisdiction at the time of the executions, it is possible that the two priests are the same person, though some scholars have identified them as two separate martyred priests, both named Valentine. A small basilica in honor of Valentine, Bishop of Terni is located at Terni, and an altar there contains his relics. The church of St. Praxedes in Rome also contains a glass-fronted box with bones of St. Valentine.

Denmark

Valentine exchanges

Young people exchanged pressed snowdrops and original poems. A humorous message called a *Gaekkebrev* can be sent. It is signed with a line of dots, one for each letter in the sender's name. If the recipient guesses who the sender is, the friend should be sent a candy egg at Easter.

Source: *The Book of Festivals* by Dorothy Gladys Spicer. Detroit: Gale Research, 1969, p. 94.

Germany, Austria, and Spain

Valentine customs

American servicemen in European countries spread the custom of sending valentines on February 14. Giving flowers to the sweetheart on Valentine's Day became popular in some German cities and in Vienna and other parts of Austria. In Spain sweethearts exchange gifts and husbands send flowers to their wives.

Source: *Lore and Language of Schoolchildren* by Peter and Iona Opie. Oxford: Oxford Univ. Press, 1959, pp. 235-236.

Great Britain

Divination of lovers

In earlier times girls forecast their future on Valentine's Eve by pinning five bay leaves to the pillow, one at each corner and one in the middle. The girl then ate a specially prepared hard-boiled egg. This egg had had the yolk removed and replaced with salt. After eating this, one would dream of one's future husband.

Names of lovers were sometimes rolled in balls of wet clay and soaked in a bowl of water. The paper that floated to the surface first held the name of the husband-to-be.

Birds choose their mates

According to English tradition, birds choose their mates on Valentine's Day. The seventeenth-century poet Robert Herrick writes:

> 'Oft have I heard both youths and virgins say,
> Birds chuse their mates, and couple too, this day,
> But by their flight I never can divine
> When I shall couple with my Valentine.'

Insulting caricatures

In my youth the stationers' shops were full of gross caricatures of the most offensively personal character, known as Valentines. These criminal libels consisted of a most insulting portrait of some individual together with a quatrain of feeble verse calling attention to some physical or moral characteristic of the person, so worded as to be likely to lead to murder if he found out who sent it. These lampoons were forwarded under a cloak of the discreetest anonymity, and were regarded in certain social circles as delightfully humorous. The milkman had the grossest references to the alleged malpractices of his trade with the pump, the grocer was reminded of his fondness for sanding sugar, while the old maid was assured of the utter hopelessness of her unending quest. Happily the spread of education and the improved manners of the people have almost extinguished these gross pleasantries, and such Valentines as survive to-day are usually sugary effusions of the 'hearts and love knots' variety.

Source: *The Folklore Calendar* by George Long. London: Philip Allan, 1930. Reprint. Detroit: Gale Research, 1970, p. 25.

East Anglian children "catch" valentines

Until recently, moreover, East Anglian children expected presents of sweets or pennies from *all* the adult 'valentines' they could 'catch' by repeating (before they themselves could be spoken to) some such rhyme as:

> Good morning to you, Valentine
> Curl your locks as I do mine
> Two in front and two behind
> Good morning to you, Valentine.

Source: *The Customs and Ceremonies of Britain* by Charles Kightly. London: Thames and Hudson, 1986, p. 226.

Children's customs

Girls may believe that the first boy seen on St. Valentine's Day will be their future spouse. Some may even go so far as to have their friends lead them to school on that morning with closed eyes, in order to open them on just the right boy.

In Birmingham a custom of running through the streets shouting "I'll be yours if you'll be mine, please to give at Valentine" is reported. Sweets, coins, or shuttles (oval Valentine buns) are given. At Tuttington, near Aylsham they chant "Good morning, Father Valentine. Trim your hair as I do mine. Two to the fore and two behind. Good morning Father Valentine." Then the children run and hide and oranges or candies are tossed out for them. April Fool's types of pranks are sometimes played on this day as well, such as setting a bucket of water against a door so that it will fall when someone opens it.

In villages such as Heydon, Stalham, and Loddon young children play "Jack Valentine" by knocking on doors and leaving small gifts on the doorsteps.

Source: *Lore and Language of Schoolchildren* by Peter and Iona Opie. Oxford: Oxford Univ. Press, 1959, pp. 235-236.

19th century British valentine customs

In Hertfordshire children would go to the houses of wealthy folks and chant. They would be thrown wreaths of flowers and true-lovers' knots. The girls would decorate one of the youngest boys in the group with these garlands and set him at the head of their procession. They might also be thrown halfpennies. In Upwick, children chanted, "Tomorrow is come, Tomorrow is come" and received halfpennies.

In Derbyshire, girls would peep through the keyholes of their doors before opening them on St. Valentine's Day morn. If a cock and hen were seen together, the girl would be married within the year.

Source: *The Valentine & its Origins* by Frank Staff. New York: Frederick A. Praeger, 1969, p. 12.

St. Valentine chants

In some places children have always been given presents on St. Valentine's Day but they can only "catch" a grown-up by getting hold of them before sunrise and saying,

> Good morrow to you Valentine,
> First it's yours, then it's mine,
> So please give me a Valentine.

But if the sun gets up first the children are "sunburnt" and the charm does not work.

There was a rhyme village children used to sing as they went from door to door.

> Knock the kettle against the pan!
> Give us a penny, if you can.
> We be ragged and you be fine
> Please to give us a Valentine.
> Up with the kettle and down with the spout!
> Give us a penny and we'll go out.

St. Valentine spells

Girls used to try certain spells on Valentine's Day to find out whom they might marry. This was one of them. She had to pick five bay leaves and pin one to each corner of her pillow and one to the middle. Then as she went to bed she had to take a hard boiled egg and remove the yolk. The hole that was left in the egg had to be filled with salt. She had to eat the egg, salt, shell and all sitting up in bed, in silence and without a drink of any sort. She must not speak to anyone nor drink till the morning. Then as she lay on her back she would dream of the man who would marry her—but, of course, she must not mention her dream to anyone for full ten days after or the charm would be broken.

St. Valentine can grant a wish for you but he does not do so for everyone. If you want to try it write your wish very small on a thin, thin piece of paper and roll it in a little piece of clay. Throw this into a bowl of water. If the paper escapes and comes to the surface—without any help from you—you will get your wish.

Source: *Happy Holidays* by Eleanor Graham. New York: E. P. Dutton, 1933, p. 63.

Italy

Italian valentine customs

In Turin, it has become popular to announce engagements on February 14. Confiserie shops sell little china baskets and cups filled with candies and tied with ribbons for valentine gifts.

Source: *The Valentine & Its Origins* by Frank Staff. New York: Frederick A. Praeger, 1969, pp. 13, 122.

Japan

Consolation candies

In Japan girls give special candies to the boys in their classes who have no sweetheart to send them a gift.

Source: Keiko Hirai (teacher), Kirkland, Washington.

For more on Saint Valentine's Day see: ''St. Valentine's Day, February 14'' in *The Folklore of American Holidays* by Hennig Cohen and Tristram Potter Coffin. 2nd ed. Gale Research, 1991; *The Valentine and Its Origins* by Frank Staff. New York: Frederick A. Praeger, 1969; ''St. Valentine's Day'' in *The Folklore Calendar*, p. 22-26; *A History of Valentines* by Ruth Webb Lee. Wellesley Hills, Mass.: Lee Publications, 1952.

Circa February 15-17

Kamakura Matsuri

Children in Akita prefecture, Japan, build igloos and serve sake to passing neighbors. They are given coins or fruit in return.

Japan

The Suijin Altar

In the snowy districts of Tohoku in N. Japan, especially in Akita Pref., children build *kamakura* (igloos) in which they sit and receive guests. In the rear is a snowy alcove dedicated to *Suijin,* the god of water, whom they honor to insure good crops in the coming year.

Source: *Japan Handbook* by J. D. Bisignani. Chico, California: Moon Publications, 1983, pp. 73-74. (For a photo of children entertaining in their igloos see: Japanese Festivals by Helen Bauer and Sherwin Carlquist. Garden City, N.Y.: Doubleday, 1965, p. 127.

February 22
Boys' Day

U.S.S.R.

Parades and gifts

Parades honor Army Day on February 22. Little boys are also honored with presents at home to begin the day, a small functional gift usually. Close friends and their girl classmates also give small gifts to the boys at school.

February 25

St. George's Day

This day is celebrated as the national day of the Georgian Republic. The Catholic Church celebrates St. George's Day on April 23.

U.S.S.R. (Georgia)

Celebrations in Mtskheta

Many Georgian families give parties in their homes on this day. There is also a festival at the cathedral of Mtskheta, the old capital of the country and still its active religious center.

Busloads of Georgians crowd the town, beside the River Kura, at festival time. The cathedral is easy to find, for it is still largely surrounded by the high protective wall, with watchtowers, that made it a kind of fortress in early days. Of course there are souvenir stands near the cathedral's main gate to supply the festival crowd with mementoes of the holiday. But the sound of music soon draws them into the church.

There, the lofty stone walls shimmer with the soft jewel tones of 800-year-old paintings of saints and holy scenes. Down the center aisle a solemn processional makes its slow way toward the great golden cross before the altar. Priests and choir chant in harmony, and swinging censers release their smoky fragrance. To the worshipers bowing their heads over folded hands, the Christian religion is very much alive in Georgia.

Source: *A Parade of Soviet Holidays* by Jane Werner Watson. Champaign, Ill.: Garrard, 1974, p. 56.

Moveable: February-March (14th day of Adar)

Purim

Purim celebrates the rescue of the Jews from the plot of Haman by Queen Esther. The day of Haman's massacre was chosen by lots (purim). The synagogue reading of the Megillah (telling the story of Esther) is drowned out by the congregation's noisemakers every time the name of "Haman" is mentioned. Plays and masquerades representing the story are popular. Children in costume may go door to door begging for goodies. Hamantash, a triangular pastry shaped like Haman's hat, is served. Dates for Purim are: Feb. 28 in 1991; March 19, 1992; March 7, 1993; February 25, 1994; and March 16, 1995.

Iran

Festival in Persia

As the festival of Purim had its origins in Persia, this was a most important holiday. Reading of the Book of Esther took place in particular at the tombs of Mordecai and Esther in Hamadan.

The spirit of the festival moved into high gear on the Sabbath of *Zachor—remember* what Amalek did to thee on thy way from Egypt'. The *Mula* delivered the gist of the Book of Esther, as the congregation shook its collective fist against the enemies of Israel. The Fast of Esther was observed most scrupulously, and the reading of the *megillah* was punctuated with noise-makers and the stamping of feet at each mention of Haman. On the following day the streets of the Jewish Quarter were filled with children in masquerade, *mishloach manot* in hand. The poor were also given silver coins. The festivities culminated with the burning, in effigy, of a towering Haman fashioned by the youngsters.

Source: *One People: The Story of the Eastern Jews* by Devora and Menachem Hacohen. New York: Sabra, 1969, pp. 35-36.

Yemen

Elaborate celebrations

Purim, . . . received elaborate attention. Children began studying the Book of Esther two months before the festival. Haman was fashioned in the form of a scarecrow in Arab dress and was mounted on wheels so as to parade the effigy throughout the Jewish Quarter. The youngsters gathered with their creations and formed a caravan which wound its way to the "gallows." In contrast with custom elsewhere, the effigies were not burned but put away in a hiding place until the following year.

Purim dress, worn to the synagogue for the reading of the *megillah,* consisted of a blue shirt striped with white and a black hat. Draped in their prayer shawls, the men and boys read the Book of Esther through. When they were done, the cantor cried out: "Cursed be Haman!" to which the congregation replied: "Blessed be Mordecai!" This was said thrice, and thrice again with the phrases reversed. All the characters of the Book of Esther plus the oppressors of the Jews of that particular year, were mentioned by name, one way or another. There was no noise-making or stamping of feet at the mention of Haman's name, out of respect for the synagogue. On their return home, the males would read the *megillah* to the womenfolk, at the conclusion of which all would say: "Thus shall all Thy enemies perish, O Lord, and those that love Thee be as the sun, setting out in its might."

The Purim feast was the chief gastronomic event of the year. Between courses, the housewife would set aside a portion for the poor. Couples married that year received special gifts from their parents and, at the home of the young husband's parents, they received a copper tray laden with sweets and a bag of silver coins. The sweets were distributed on the following day among neighbors and relatives.

Source: *One People: The Story of the Eastern Jews* by Devora and Menachem Hacohen. New York: Sabra, 1969, p. 146.

For more on Purim see: "The Purim Players" in *Burning Lights* by Bell Chagall. New York: Shocken, 1946, p. 184-191; "Purim," in *Folklore of American Holidays* by Hennig Cohen and Tristram Potter Coffin. 2nd ed. Detroit: Gale Research, 1991. 103-111.

February 29

Leap Year Day/Saint Oswald's Day

An intercalary day added every four years to regulate the solar calendar, since the earth takes five hours and forty-eight minutes longer than 365 days to circle the sun. This is also Saint Oswald's Day. Saint Oswald was a tenth-century archbishop of York who died on February 29, 992.

For more on Leap Year see: ''Leap Year Day, February 29'' in Folklore of American Holidays by Tristram Potter Coffin and Hennig Cohen. 2nd ed. Detroit: Gale Research, 1991.

Full Moon (February-March)

Kason

This is a celebration of the birth and enlightenment of Buddha.

Myanmar

Kason Festival of Watering the Banyan Tree

Of the twelve Burmese festivals of the months, Kason Fullmoon Day is the noblest for Buddhists. On this day, the Bodhisatta, the hermit Thumedha, received the dispensation from Dipankara Buddha; on this day Gautama, the Buddha-to-be was born; on this day, Gautama became enlightened; and on this day, Buddha passed into Parinirvana. Since this day is fraught with special significance for Buddha it is named Buddha Day.

On this noble Buddha Day, Buddhists perform various acts of merit. They gather at monasteries, Dhamma pavilions and precept halls to observe the precepts, practise meditation, and give in charity for both mundane and supramundane benefit.

Furthermore, celebration of Gautama Buddha's attainment of enlightment and Buddhahood at the foot of the Banyan tree on Kason Fullmoon Day, the Kason Festival of Watering the Banyan Tree has been celebrated since ancient times for the preservation of the banyan tree.

In accordance with the saying "Dry in Tagu, parched in Kason," the streams, ponds, wells, and tanks dry up in Kason. Because of the heat of the sun and drying up in Kason the fish are transferred to places where there is more water thus performing the meritorious act of granting life.

Just as the pouring of water at the Kason Festival is done individually old people and youth, men and women get together and collectively pour water to the music of drums and gongs and dancing.

Source: Embassy of the Union of Myanmar.

Full Moon (February)

Maka Buja

On a full moon night when the moon entered the sign of the Maakha asterism, 1,250 *arahantas* (saintly monks, who had been ordained by the Buddha himself, convened at Veluvan Monastery in Rajagriha, then capital of the Magadhan Empire of India. Each had traveled there unaware of the others' journeys.

Laos

Makha Bouxa

Calling together of Buddha's disciples

Makha Bouxa, in the third month (February), originates in the Buddhist texts. It commemorates the calling together of Buddha's disciples before his death and his entrance into a state of nirvana. Prayers, processions, offerings, and masques mark the ceremonies.

Source: *Laos: A Country Study* by Donald P. Whitaker et al. Foreign Area Studies: The American University, 1971, p. 122.

Thailand

A commemoration of miracles

An important Buddhist holy day commemorating a series of miracles just three months before Buddha's death, this is a national holiday in Thailand. It commemorates the miraculous occasion when 1,250 of the Buddha's disciples gathered without prior arrangement to hear him preach. On this day Thai temples are crowded, and the faithful gain merit by such acts as releasing caged birds. The day's ceremonies culminate in a candlelight procession around the *bot,* the main temple building.

Source: *Thailand.* Insight Guides. Hong Kong: A. P. A., 1980, p. 296.

The sermon

The observance of the Maakhá Buuchaa is a one-night festival, and the performance is done in the same spirit and manner as the Wísaakhaa Buuchaa, the anniversary of Buddha's birth, enlightenment, and entering the final Nirvana, save that the sermons preached in the chapel have as their subject the Buddhist Code of Discipline for monks. It was on this day that this Code of Discipline of the Vinaya was promulgated or preached by the Lord. No decorated candles and lights are hung on this occasion as is done during the Wísaakhaa Day.

Source: *Life and Ritual in Old Siam* by Phya Anuman Rajadhon. New Haven: HRAF Press, 1961, p. 97.

Moon 2, Day 1 (February-March)

Wind Festival

In certain provinces of Korea a grandmother called "Yungdeung Mama" comes down to earth every year on the first day of the second moon. She returns on the twentieth day. When her daughter-in-law accompanies her, stormy winds ensue. Propitious papers are tied to bamboo branches on the first and left until the twentieth, and other propitious rituals may be performed on the first day.

Korea

Propitious actions and a dangerous daughter-in-law

This ceremony is conducted on the first day of the Second Moon in the country districts of Kyongsang-namdo and Kyongsang-pukto Provinces. At each home people get up early and spread tempting foods together with boiled rice in the kitchen or garden, then offer prayers to heaven. White paper is cut—a piece for each member of the family—and on each piece the date of his birth is written.

A prayer for good luck is offered as these papers are burned one by one, and the higher fly the ashes of the burnt paper, the better luck it is sure to bring.

In the coastal districts they set up the branches and leaves of bamboo trees in kitchens or gardens, tying colored cloths and papers to them. Thus, an altar is made, and under it sacrifices are laid and prayers offered. When the ceremony is finished they leave the bamboos until the 20th day of the moon; and in the early morning each day water fresh from the well is served in a new gourd placed under them.

According to tradition, a grandmother, called "Yungdeung Mama," from heaven, comes down to the earth every year on the first day of the Second Moon and returns on the 20th. When she comes she is sure to bring either her daughter or her daughter-in-law. When the daughter accompanies the mother there is no trouble, but the daughter-in-law coming as the companion falls into an epileptic fit and brings a stormy wind which devastates the harvest and wrecks ships.

People call this wind "Yungdeung Baram," and in order that no damage be done to their crops and their boats, the farmers, fishermen and sailors offer sacrifices and prayers to " Yungdeung Mama" and her daughter-in-law. Stormy winds come to Korea in the Second Moon when shipwrecks are frequent, taken to be acts of the God of Winds in his displeasure.

Source: *Folk Customs and Family Life* by Tae Hung Ha. Seoul, Korean: Yonsei, 1958, p. 22-23.

Full Moon, Phalguna (February-March)

Dol Purnima

This is an Indian celebration of the Lord Krishna. His image is garlanded and carried in procession on this day. As the day is also the birthday of Gauranga (Chaitanya Mahaprabbhu), a sixteenth-century Bengali saint and Vaishnavite poet, the day is also important for Vishnu's followers.

India

Dol Purnima celebrations

The Dol Purnima festival is celebrated throughout the country in the month of Phalguna (February-March) by the followers of Krishna. An image of Lord Krishna, smeared with coloured powder, is placed in a swinging cradle decorated with flowers and garlands and is carried in a procession by the devotees, who sing different types of songs composed specially for this auspicious occasion. A large number of people accompanying the procession offer flowers to the Lord.

Being also the birthday of Gauranga or Chaitanya Mahaprabhu, a sixteenth century Vaishnavite poet and saint of Bengal, the festival assumes special significance for the followers of Vishnu.

Source: *The Festivals of India* by Brijendra Nath Sharma. New Delhi: Abhinav, 1978, p. 61.

Full Moon, Phalguna (February-March)

Holi

This festival is held in honor of the Goddess Holika. Holi is celebrated in a variety of ways throughout India. It begins with a bonfire. An effigy of the demoness Holika may be burnt. The next day the streets are filled with holiday revelers tossing colored water or colored powder on each other. In some areas the festival lasts several days.

The Holi tradition is very ancient. Lord Krishna himself is said to have celebrated with a Festival of Colours, playing at red powder tossing with 16,000 milkmaids of Brindaban!

Bangladesh

Dol-Jatra

Swing Festival

A Holi festival of Bangladesh is the Dol-Jatra (Swing Festival). Vishnu is placed on a throne in a pavilion facing south. An image of the child Krishna is kept in a small dol or swinging cradle. Images of Lord Krishna and Radha are also placed in special swings. All are adorned with flowers and colored powder as the center of worship.

The Holiki legend

. . . There are many legends concerning the origin of this gay spring festival. The most popular among these concerns Prince Prahlad, the god-fearing son of the evil King Hiranyakasipu. Prahlad did not give up worshipping the god Vishnu in spite of fearful persecution by his father and his demon aunt Holika. Ultimately, when Holika, who was immune to death by fire, took Prahlad and entered a blazing furnace built for his destruction, it was the wicked Holika who was burnt to ashes by divine intervention, while Prahlad came out unscathed.

Source: *Festivals of India*. Publication Division. Ministry of Information and Broadcasting. Government of India, 1956, p. 12.

India

Festival of Colours

In Northern India Holi is now celebrated as the 'Festival of Colours' because of its distinguishing feature of throwing coloured water and powder at people. Children throw coloured water with their syringes. People march through the streets in a jubilant, clapping, singing, dancing and playing on the tabors. So great indeed is the quantity of the coloured water that the ground all round looks dyed and the water getting mixed with coloured powder (*gulal*) turns into a big mass of coloured paste. Throwing mud, refuse, etc. is also not uncommon in the rural areas. In certain sections wine and many other intoxicants, particularly, the hemp is consumed freely, especially by the servant class. The Holi carnival reaches its climax on the morning following the burning of Holi fire, the day reckoned as *Dhurahandi*. At sunset people repair to a garden or some other public place wearing ceremonial costumes. They greet each other, dine in groups, enjoy gossiping and feel free even to use vulgar language. Ladies enjoy swinging to the accompaniment of dancing, singing and instrumental music. Children play, buy toys, eat sweets and make merry in many other ways. Friends and relatives exchange gifts.

The Holi bonfire

. . . The lighting of bonfires at the time fixed as auspicious by the astronomers is a common Holi ritual observed in almost every region of India. The ceremony also known as *Hutashni* (consuming fire) symbolizes the burning of all evils or the end of winter. There is a legend that Holi or Holika was the sister of *Samvat* or Hindu year. Once at the beginning *Samvat* died and Holika who had excessive love for her brother insisted on burning herself on her brother's pyre and by this unique act of devotion she was restored to life. Sometimes the lighting of bonfire is also associated with other mythological events such as the burning of demoness Holika, the sister of Hiranyakashyapu or the death of demoness Putana at the hands of cowherd boy Krishna or the burning of Kamadeva, the god of passion, by Lord Shiva. The last tradition seems to be much in vogue in the south where the ladies sing the lamentations of Rati, Kamas consort over her husband's death.

Source: *Our Cultural Fabric: Festivals of India.* Ministry of Education and Social Welfare, Government of India, 1977, pp. 23-24.

The ambiance of Holi

The grand and colourful festival of Holi is celebrated every year in all parts of India in the month of Phalguna (February-March). It falls when the season is neither cold nor hot and the fields and trees bloom with different types of enchanting flowers. People feel themselves happy, gay and healthy. . . . A thing most important about this festival is that the people on Holi day embrace each other forgetting all their personal differences and no distinction between high and low or rich and poor is observed. Our top-most national leaders also participate with all and sundry in playing Holi. The festival, thus embodies not only rejoicing and fun but also the principles of secularism and equality of all.

More bonfires

The festival takes two days for its observance. On the first day, a bonfire is lit either in the evening or in the night. Before this is done, another bonfire is lit on a place previously prepared, and an effigy of Holika, made of bamboos and straw, is formally carried to the spot by the Brahmanas, in regular procession attended by local singers and musicians. The figure is placed in the centre of the pile, and the ministering Brahmana circumambulates it seven times and recites verses in worship of Holi, before setting it on fire.

Tossing colored water

On the second day, from early morning till noon, people irrespective of caste and creed amuse themselves by throwing handfuls of coloured powder on their friends and relatives. Or they spray coloured water with sprayers. Boys and persons of the lower castes come out in the streets and throw coloured water through syringes, using at the same time, abusive and obscene language. But the elderly people gently put red powder on the faces of each other. The damage to one's clothes is taken in good spirit. In the same evening, people exchange sweetmeats and the friends embrace each other three times and wish a good luck. The children and the young touch the feet of their elders to express their reverence.

Source: *Festivals of India* by Brijendra Nath Sharma. New Delhi: Abhinav Publications, 1978, pp. 66-67.

Mauritius

A festival of revelry

This Hindu festival is as colourful as the numerous legends which inspire it. Essentially, it is a festival of revelry when men and women enjoy themselves by squirting coloured water and powder on one another. It is time for rejoicing and exchanging greetings.

Source: Embassy of Mauritius.

Nepal

Rung Khelna

In Nepal the onset of Rung Khelna, playing with colour, is marked by erection of a 25-foot, three-tiered umbrella at Basantpur. People light joss and strew flowers and red powder at its base throughout Holi week. During Holi the water tossing in Nepal may take the form of water balloons of red water tossed from upstairs windows in addition to red powder tossing.

For more on Holi in Nepal see: "Holi: Red Powder, Romance and Hunting Demons," in *Festivals of Nepal* by Mary K. Anderson, London: Allen and Unwin, 1971, pp. 250-257.

Pakistan

Day for horseplay

Another Hindu spring festival, Holi, is observed in some communities around the vernal equinox when the sun begins to climb higher in the sky. Holi is a day for good-natured horseplay. If one goes out in the streets where Holi is celebrated, he should not wear his best clothes, because crowds of young people will be squirting colored water or throwing red and yellow powder at passersby. Soon everybody's skin and clothing are dyed in mad colors like a carnival. In villages Holi is an occasion for teasing between the sexes. Girls throw water at boys; wives drench their husband's younger brothers and beat the men with sticks.

Source: *The Land and People of Pakistan* by Robert Lang. New York: J. B. Lippincott, 1974, p. 137.

Surinam

Holi Phagwa

Celebrations of Spring and the New Year

This is not only a Spring Festival (Vasant-Utsav) but also the New Year's festival of the Hindus, which is celebrated with great enthusiasm, while non-hindus also participate in this happening. The day before Holi Phagwa the Hindu community sets a stack on fire, personifying the witch named Holika, after which the festival becomes universal.

Special Holi-songs (Chautals) can be heard, while the custom is to throw colored, scented water to each other . . . to protect against evil spirits. . . .

Source: Embassy of the Republic of Surinam.

See also: "Holi" in *Our Cultural Fabric: Festivals of India.* Ministry of Education and Social Welfare, Government of India, 1977.

Full Moon, Masi (February-March)

Masi Magham

This is the day when the asterism Magha (Leonis) is on the ascendant. It usually falls on the full moon of Masi.

Malaya

Festival in Malacca

In Malaya this festival is very elaborately celebrated at Malacca. It goes on for two days. The celebrations are organized and conducted by the Malacca Chetties in co-operation with the Chettiyar community there. On the day previous to *Masi Magham,* the image of Subramanya is taken in procession on a silver chariot from Poyyatha Vinayagar Kovil to Sannasi Malai Kovil. This latter is a temple situated on a hill which tradition relates was the abode of a famous ascetic many years ago with miraculous powers of healing. This place is the venue of the main festivities on *Magham* day. *Kavadis* are carried by devotees to the temple. It is a very important festival for the Malacca Chetty community. They hold oratorical contests and stage dramas on this day. Crowds gather there from all parts of Malaya to witness these. At the end of the day the statue is taken back in procession through the streets of Malacca. Formerly there used to be massive fireworks displays but now these have been stopped.

The festival is also celebrated at Mariamman temple in Kuala Lumpur and at Thandayuthapani Kovil in Alor Star. In both these places chariot processions of Subramanya are an important feature.

Source: *Indian Festivals in Malaya* by S. Arasaratnam. Luala Lumpur: Dept. of Indian Studies, Univ. of Malaya, 1966, pp. 21-22.

Phalguna (February-March)

Sivaratri

A festival in honor of Lord Siva. His emblem, the Shiva Lingam, is revered on this day, and gatherings take place at Shiva's temples.

India

The worship of Siva

The festival of Sivaratri is cerebrated by the Hindus of all castes throughout India in the month of Phalguna (February-March). It is the main festival in honour of Siva, the Great God Mahadeva and the destroyer of the Universe. On this occasion, people spend the whole night in the *japa* and *dhyana* of Siva, without any thought of food and sleep and offer *bilwa* leaves to the *Siva-linga.*

According to the ancient scriptures, Siva manifests himself in the form of a huge flaming *linga* (*Jyotirlinga*) on Sivaratri to shower his grace on his devotees. It is the sacred duty of every worshipper that he keeps vigil and worships him at midnight at least with one leaf of the *bilwa* tree. There is an old adage that even an intelligent dog will not touch its food on the Sivaratri day.

The worship of Siva at Sivaratri is permitted to all castes and even to the Chandalas. The poor people have to satisfy themselves by pouring water on the Siva-*linga,* while the rich perform their elaborate rites with costly offerings to the deity and substantial gifts to the poor. But in any case the offerings must consist of *bilwa* leaves, *dhatura,* rice and water.

On Sivaratri, tremendous gatherings take place in the temples situated in all parts of the country and even in the rural areas, where besides singing of songs in praise of Siva, the ringing of bell is continued through the night. The festival has a special significance in Kashmir and there it lasts for 15 days. The 13th day known as *Heratha* is observed as a day of fast, followed by a family feast.

Sivaratri legends

According to legends, on the night of Sivaratri, Lord Siva performs the heavenly dance of Creation, Preservation and Destruction. So the devotees spend the night in reading the Siva Purana and chanting Siva *bhajanas.*

The following story is also narrated on this occasion. A hunter whose name was Suswar had to live without food on the night of Sivaratri perched on a *bilwa* tree. He wept on the tree and his tears, accompanied by withered leaves of the *bilwa* tree, dropped on the ground. Siva thought that some pious votary was worshipping him and so he blessed the hunter, who was born as a king in his next birth. At the time of worship this tale is narrated and just hearing it is believed to be a form of blessing.

Source: *Festivals of India* by Brijendra Nath Sharma. New Delhi: Abhinav, 1978, pp. 64-65.

Mauritius

Maha Shivaratree

Pilgrimage to collect holy water

Maha Shivaratree is celebrated in honour of God Siva (February or mid-March). Following an all-night vigil, Hindu devotees, clad in spotless white, carry the Kanwar, wooden arches smothered in flowers, in pilgrimage to Grand Bassin to fetch holy water from the lake. The whole scene is reminiscent of the great rituals on the banks of the Holy Ganges.

Source: Embassy of Mauritius.

Nepal

Worshiping with Shiva lingams

The Shiva lingam is a popular object of worship in Nepal. The stone lingams are found in temples and set beside roads and paths throughout the country. Holy water is poured over the lingam and they are sprinkled with flower petals and vermillion. The lingam represents Lord Shiva himself.

For more on Shiva Ratri in Nepal see: "Shiva Ratri: The Sacred Night of Lord Shiva" in *Festivals of Nepal,* London: Allen and Unwin, 1971, by Mary K. Anderson, pp. 242-250.

February or March

Ku-omboko

This is a floodtime festival of the Lozi people of Zambia. It is held when the Zambezi River begins its annual flooding of the Barotze flood plains.

Zambia (Lozi)

Festival at Lealul Knoll, Mongu

This festival occurs when the Zambezi River in the Barotse flood plains begins its annual flooding. Ku-omboko means "getting out of the water." A regatta of thousands of boats and canoes, led by the paramount chief on his royal barge rowed by sixty chanting paddlers, makes its way to higher land. At the time of this ritual moving-to-higher-ground, the people who live on the flood plain must actually move to higher ground to escape the coming flood. On the arrival of the celebrants at the new headquarters of the chief at Limulunga, they dance and make music well into the night. In July the group return to their lowland homes, but with less ceremony.

Source: *Fielding's Africa South of the Sahara* by Sherry A. Suttles and Billy Suttles-Graham. New York: Fielding Travel Books/William Morrow, 1986, p. 197.

Circa mid-March, 1½ Moons after Dosmoche

Storlog

This is a Tibetan spring festival during which demons are exorcised.

Tibet

Exorcising demons

One to one and a half months after the dosmocho festival (from the middle to the end of March) the storlog (gtor-log) is celebrated in all the large and small villages. This is a spring festival at which the exorcism of the threatening demons is again in the foreground. This exorcism is carried out by means of a storma (gtor-ma), a scattered offering with the exorcising formulas belonging to it. Here too there are numerous amusements. The men shoot with arrows at targets that have been set up.

Source: *Progpa Namgyal: Ein Tibeterleben (Progpa Namgyal: The Life of a Tibetan)* by Samuel Heinrich Ribbach. München-Planegg: Otto Wilhelm Barth-Verlag GMBH, 1940 (HRAF), p. 148.

March 1

First of March / Priv Mart

An auspicious day in some cultures, it is considered the beginning of spring in Bulgaria, and the first month of the year and the beginning of summer in Greece.

Bulgaria

A First of March legend

People wear a red and white pin on this day, symbolizing good health and happiness. A legend associated with the day tells of a mythic girl with eleven brothers. Whenever the brothers drink, then rain and unhappiness descend.

Wearing *martenitsa* (red and white tassels)

March 1 is considered the beginning of spring. By tradition, on this day everyone pins tassels of red and white threads (*martenitsa*) on his or her dress. The custom is of Slav origin. It is also common in South Romania, Albania and North Greece. Yet it is most widespread in Bulgaria. People believe that the red color can drive away evil. It is the color of life. The white symbolizes the sun and purity. The *martenitsa* goes with a wishing for good health, vigor, buoyancy and happiness throughout the year.

Source: ''Bulgarian Folk Feasts and Rites'' by Sofia Press Agency in *Journal of Popular Culture,* 19:1 (Summer, 1985), 156.

Canada

Priv Mart

Exchanging *marteniki*

In Canada Macedonian-Bulgarians continue the custom of exchanging *marteniki* on March 1. *Marteniki* are twists of red and white threads. They are tossed down for the first robins seen on this day to use in nest building. Pins, cards, and ornaments of *marteniki* threads are made and may bear the greeting ''Chestito Baba Marta,'' ''Happy March First.''

Source: *Let's Celebrate* by Caroline Parry. Toronto: Kids Can Press, 1984, pp. 83-84.

Greece

Master March laughs and weeps

Legends suggest why March laughs one day and weeps the next. An Athenian legend says that March has two wives, one pretty and poor, the other ugly and rich. When March turns toward his ugly wife, he is glum and it rains. When he turns over in bed and cuddles his lovely wife, the sun shines.

Out with February

Children may march around banging tins and singing ''Out with you, lame February, and let March come to us with joy and flowers.'' February is seen as a lame man on a donkey. Housewives give everything a thorough sweeping and break old jugs against their doors, saying ''Bad year out! Good year in! Out with lame February, out with fleas and mice, in comes March and Joy and the good housewife.''

Tying on a March

A ''March,'' twined threads of white and red or gold and red are tied to the wrist or big toe of children to protect them from the rays of the March sun. The threads are tied first to a rosebush all night, receiving blessing from the stars. Children may wear their ''March'' until they see the first swallow and stork of the year. It is then hid under a stone. After forty days the stone is lifted. If ants are there, wealth and happiness will come; if worms, bad luck.

Drimes, evil fairies

Drimes, who have an evil influence on water, are active during the first three days, the three middle days, and the last three days of March. Clothing washed on these days will be worn to shreds, wood hewn will rot. An iron horse shoe in the washbasin can counteract their evil, however. Washing hair is also not advised during these times.

Tapping the oxen and the cat

Touching humans or animals with a sprig of wild hyacinth or asphodel can bring health, prosperity, or fertility. In Crete Cretans touch oxen with asphodel on March 1 saying, ''March has come today, change your hair, put on pounds of lard and ounces of fat.'' People on the island of Cos also tap the house cat, saying, ''March has come, keep your tail up.'' They believe this keeps the cat healthy.

Procession of the swallow

In Thrace two children fill a basket with ivy and hang it from a rod with a ''swallow'' (wooden bird) at the end. Little bells hang from the bird's neck. The children go from house to house singing, ''A swallow came to us . . . she sat on a bough and sweetly sang . . . March, good March . . . and ugly February. . .'' The housewife takes ivy leaves from the basket and puts them in the nest of her hen so that she will lay well. The children are given eggs as a treat.

Source: *Greek Calendar Customs* by George A. Megas. Athens: B. & M. Rhodis, 1963, pp. 79-83.

Greeting the first swallow

Our spring is earlier than in Northern Europe and our March may be compared to a fine May here in New England. On the first of March the boys celebrate the return of spring, and we have songs about the swallows dating back to ancient times which we boys sing as we go from house to house, we carry a carved wooden swallow at the end of a stick and we are welcomed everywhere. Here is a verse of a swallow song translated by an English friend of Greece, Lewis Sergeant:

> ''She is here, she is here!
> The swallow that brings us the beautiful year;
> Wide open the door!
> We are children again, we are old no more.''

And how the old people would receive us, listening to our songs with moist eyes and patting us on the head and giving us little presents of candy, thinking of ''Springtime, youth of the year, and Youth, springtime of life.''

Our mothers used to tie a red and white string round our wrists, which we wore till we had seen the first swallow, which would sometimes arrive late, even a few days after the first of March, and then we would throw the strings on the rose-bush in our garden. In our village there was no school on the first of March, and it was always a happy holiday for the children. ''The swallow has arrived, she has crossed the white seas.''

Source: *When I Was a Boy in Greece* by George Demetrios. Boston: Lothrop, Lee & Shepard Co., 1913, pp. 60-61.

Macedonia

The reception of the Spring

. . . The first of March is by tradition set apart for the reception of the Spring. Morning excursions into the fields are in great vogue. The wooden image of the swallow finds a parallel in their clay image of the lark, and the swallow-song in similar compositions sung in honour of Vesna, the vernal season, or of Lada, the vernal goddess of love and fertility.

On the same day the Macedonian mothers tie round their children's wrists a skein consisting of red and white yarn, twisted together and called after the month. The children at the sight of a swallow throw this thread to the bird, as an offering, or place it under a stone. A few days after they lift the stone and, if they find beneath it a swarm of ants, they anticipate a healthy and prosperous year; the reverse, should the thread lie deserted. The explanation of this custom must perhaps be sought in some forgotten notion of a sympathetic relation between the skein and the child which wore it.

Source: *Macedonian Folklore* by G. F. Abbott. Cambridge: Cambridge Univ. Press, 1903, p. 19.

Drymiais

Drymiais prohibitions

The first three days of March are known by the name of Drymiais. During those days the peasants refrain from washing clothes and from bathing. They do not prune their trees nor do they plant; for they believe that the trees will at once wither. The same belief holds with regard to the last three days and all Wednesdays and Fridays of the month. As a proof that those days are unlucky, especially for gardening purposes, they advise you to try the following experiement: Take seven twigs, strip them of their leaves, mark them each with the name of a day of the week, and then put them in a jug filled with water. If you examine them a few days later, you will find that they have all put forth new leaves, except those marked with the names of the fatal days.

In some parts of Macedonia the superstition prevails that a priest should not divulge to his parishioners on which day of the week will be the first of March, or he will lose his wife.

Source: *Macedonian Folklore* by G. F. Abbott. Cambridge: Cambridge Univ. Press, 1903, p. 20.

March 1

St. David's Day

This day commemorates Wales's patron saint, St. David.

Wales

St. David's Day legend

St. David, patron saint of Wales, was born in the 5th century at Henfynyw, Cardigan. He founded a spartan order of monks at Mynyw. St. David is credited with winning a victory over the Saxons by telling the Welsh soldiers to wear leeks in their helmets so they could recognize each other on the battlefield. Leeks are worn on his day by the Welsh. New Welsh recruits must eat ritual leeks on this day.

For more on St. David's Day see: ''St. David's Day, March 1'' in *Folklore of American Holidays* by Hennig Cohen and Tristram Potter Coffin. 2nd ed. Detroit: Gale Research, 1991.

Moveable: March 2 (Month of Shaban)

Shaban

Shaban is a sacred night on which Allah ordains the actions of men for the coming year.

General history

This night, known in Persia, Pakistan and India as *Shab-i-barát,* is held by many to be occasion when God ordains all actions people are to perform during ensuing year. In some countries it is occasion for a festival; in others the night is spent in prayer and mosques are lit and well attended. In some countries the prayers are in commemoration of dead; elsewhere people believe that such attendance to prayer during night may result in good being ordained for them, failing to note inconsistency that they could not have spent night in prayer if it had not been ordained for them. On this night the waters of al-Kawthar are believed to flow into well Zamzam.

Source: *Dictionary of Comparative Religion* by S. G. F. Brandon. New York: Charles Scribner's Sons, 1970, p. 570.

India

The night men's destinies are ordained

Shaaban, every year throughout India. According to popular belief, the destinies of men are recorded for the coming year.

Prophet Mohammad had fixed this day for fasting and prayers, because on this night god is said to make a record of all the good and bad actions of men and women and dispenses their fate according to their actions. He also records the duties of the men for the ensuing year. Accordingly, Muslims observe a fast on 14th and 15th day of *Shaaban* and do not sleep the whole night. They also offer prayers for their well-being and recite the holy *Koran.*

It has now developed into a merry-making festival as there are illuminations and a display of fireworks and crackers. In some places, simply for the sake of enjoyment, two parties go to a vast ground outside their town and throw burning crackers upon each other. Then one party, either on account of running short of crackers or tiredness under the continuous strong attacks by the other, finding itself unable to resist the attack any more has to acknowledge defeat and run away from there. Thousands of spectators enjoy this unique game. But this game is now gradually going out of fashion.

Sweetmeats including *halwa* and bread are specially prepared and *fatihah* is read for the welfare of deceased relatives.

Source: *Festivals of India* by Brijenora Nath Sharma. New Delhi: Abhinav, 1978, p. 99.

Iran

Shaban in Azerbaijan, c. 1910

Shaban comes on the fifteenth day of the eighth month of Shaban, and it is to the Persians as the Fourth of July is to Americans. It is celebrated in honor of Imam Mehdah, the last descendant of Caliph Ali and of Ali's marriage anniversary to Fatima, the famous daughter of the Prophet Mohammed. Fatima, besides being beautiful, was a descendant of one of the noblest tribes of Arabia, called Karoush. On account of her noble birth she had many suitors. Her father wanted her to marry Ali, a blood relative, but, not wanting to create any friction and ill feeling among her admirers, it is said that he decreed "no one, except he on whose house a shooting-star will fall, can have Fatima." Ali, being the favorite of the Prophet, naturally was lucky enough to have his house hit by the star.

On the evening of the Sahban festival practically the whole population of Persia can be seen in the streets and on the housetops watching the fireworks. No one is too poor to buy skyrockets on this occasion. Some people actually go without food to save money to take part in this event, and any one who is not participating in the evening's performances is considered to be a poor Mussulman and unbeloved of Allah. This festival, with the exception of those celebrated by the Christians, is the sanest of all Persian festivals.

Source: *When I Was a Boy in Persia* by Youel B. Mirza. Boston: Lothrop, Lee & Shepard Co., 1920, pp. 108-109.

Pakistan

Shab-i-Barat

The night man's deeds are accounted

Now approaches the most sacred month of Ramazan, the time of fasting. But about two weeks before Ramazan occurs the night of Shab-i-Barat, when God takes account of all human deeds and misdeeds and the destinies of men are shaped for the year ahead. For serious folk it is a night of reading the Koran and of prayer for the dead; for the frivolous and for children there are fireworks.

Source: *The Land and People of Pakistan* by Robert Lang. New York: J. B. Lippincott, 1974, p. 136.

Turkey

Berat Kandili

Sacred night

The 'sacred night' between the 14th and 15th of the month of Saban, this has various meanings in different Islamic countries, like Hallowe'en (All Saints, Day of the Dead). Mosque illuminations, special foods.

Source: *Turkey: A Travel Survival Kit* by Tom Brosnahan. Lonely Planet, 1988, p. 28.

Lélé-Beraet, the Night of Forgiveness

The next month is Shaban and on the fifth day comes Lélé-I-Beraet (night of forgiveness). On this night Allah is believed to review the sins of all and to make the decision as to their fate during the coming year. Many people pray all night. The minarets are again illuminated. This is the last festival before Ramazan.

Source: *When I Was a Boy in Turkey* by Ahmed Sabri Bey. Boston: Lothrop, Lee & Shepard Co., 1924, p. 82.

March 3

Hina Matsuri (Girls' Day)

On the 3rd day of the 3rd month, an elegant display of stylized court dolls is arranged in each girl's home. A special miniature feast may be served by the child to guests assembled to admire the doll display. The holiday, also called Dolls' Day, is now celebrated on March 3 rather than on the lunar date.

Japan

Elaborate doll set

There can be no hard and fast rule as to the *hina* exhibition, when so much will depend not only on money, but also on inheritances from mother, grandmothers, and even earlier forbears. . . . The dolls and paraphernalia, once on a stand, will hardly ever be touched; they are admired as if they were in a museum's showcase; they are the worshipful *ohinasama.*

A few days before the festival, the dolls and things are taken out of the boxes in which they had been stored, carefully unwrapped and dusted. Tiers of shelf-like steps are built up against a wall of the main room, and covered with cloth of scarlet, the colour of vigour and good fortune. There should be three steps at least; five are more common, and many girls have seven steps. While the arrangement of the exhibits is allowed considerable freedom, and much depends on their number and size, the Prince and Princess always sit in the middle of the top-shelf, in splendid isolation. The two together are still termed the *dairi* or Court. It is decidedly wrong to call these two personages the Emperor and Empress: such an idea is contrary to the Japanese spirit. The Japanese refer to them as *taishisama,* the Imperial Prince, or *tonosama,* the Feudal Lord, and *himesama,* his Lady.

According to the old Kyoto style, the lady should sit on the left of the beholder; the now generally fashionable Tokyo style, however, places her on the right. She will wear the *jūni hitoe,* twelve unlined silk-garments of different colours, one over the other, the uppermost generally of a glorious red. Her hair will fall down in a long cascade, only slightly bound towards the bottom, and at times she may wear a sort of diadem or crown, which in more modern dolls is often replaced by a tall *eboshi,* modern Court *coiffure* also being introduced. In her hands she will carry an open fan, the *hiōgi.* The prince is generally clad in a purplish or black robe with auspicious damask patterns, the *hō,* and wear the ceremonial *kammuri* or *eboshi* cap. He holds a flat sceptre, the *shaku,* and nowadays usually carries a long sword, the *tachi,* stuck in his belt; but this is again a later addition, due to feudalism in its last stages. It is generally presumed that, in accordance with Murasaki Shikibu's romance, the male figure is intended to represent *Hikaru Genji,* the Brilliant "Don Juan" of the Imperial Court, whom she made live around the year 800.

Both of these dolls sit on a multicoloured dais, in front of a beautiful screen, a small replica of those found in the noble homes; sometimes they are also protected by a sort of roof with curtained sides, the so-called *goten* or Palace. Further ceremonial curtains with phoenix and paulownia designs may be placed immediately behind the couple, and sometimes there is a stand with some auspicious object between the two seats. In some older arrangements two *chigo,* or pages, may sit on either side of the double dais, and usually two rather large stand-lanterns, *bombori,* will be seen at the ends of the top-shelf.

On the step immediately below are the three maids of honour, *kanjo,* in long-sleeved white damask *kimono* with wide, trailing trousers of crimson. They are supposed to represent youth, middle age, and old age, and serve the festive *sake,* the elixir of life. The one on the left holds a small ceremonial wine-kettle, the *sagechōshi;* the one on the right another, long-stemmed one, the *nagae chōshi.* The central figure is occupied with the *sakazuki,* with or without their respective ritual stand, or contemplates a *shimadai,* an "Island of the Blest" on which grow the pine, plum and bamboo of good augury, and where the cranes and tortoises of longevity disport themselves. Two of these dolls will stand, and the middle one kneel, or vice-versa.

On the next step are the five Court musicians, the *gonin bayashi* (orchestra). They are said to have been young men selected for their beauty and they are mostly represented looking like boys. They play the large and the small hand-drums (*tsutsumi*), the flat drum (*taiko*) on its stand, and the flute (*fue*), while the fifth one, wielding a closed fan, sings a congratulatory ballad. In a more recent evolution these court-musicians are sometimes replaced by *geisha,* in beautiful but banal modern *kimono!*

These ten dolls should be there; also a potted cherry-tree on the left and a kind of orange tree on the right of the *dairi.* These trees are respectively known as the *sakon no sakura* and the *ukon no tachibana,* and have sundry auspicious meanings. At Court they flanked the steps to the *shishinden,* which more or less corresponds to a Throne-hall, but has a more sacred character. There must furthermore be a ritual tray, the *sambō,* with two *omikidokkuri,* ritual *sake*-bottles, into which are stuck festooned branches of the holy *sakaki* tree.

The regulation dolls are commonly increased to fifteen, by adding two guarding noblemen and three servants. . . .

The three footmen, who will generally occupy the space between the two Ministers, on the penultimate step of five, incarnate the three human moods: one should laugh, one weep, one make an angry face. This, however, is not always clearly expressed. Instead of *jichō* they are often also called the *sannin jōgo,* the three tipplers. Dressed in plain white robes with wide trousers, the true (Kyoto) style gives them various attributes connected with a rustic picnic: a kettle hung on a stick-tripod, a broom to gather dry leaves for a fire, various utensils for food and drink. A memory, no doubt, of the original festive spring-outing, the herb-gathering. The Tokyo style, based rather on the *daimyō* ceremonial, makes them menials wearing straw-sandals (*waraji,* as worn on journeys), and carrying the lacquered shoes, the state-umbrella, and ceremonial spear of their feudal lord.

Gorgeous as all these dresses of days gone by are, stiff with gold threads, damasks and starched silks, they are not removable ones, not even completed where the parts become invisible. The dolls have no imitative body underneath, as have the *ningyō:* they are a core of sorts, over which the manifold dress-components are draped, glued or stitched, in permanent folds. The heads are carefully moulded in clay and usually coated with a kind of enamel, so that the faces are very white; the jet-black hair is made of floss-silk and elegantly arranged in the mode of former days. A short and strong skewer serves as kernel for the head, and is stuck into a doll's body. Hands and feet are similarly formed and applied, but in many cases are still left out, the dress covering them up, so to say. The *hina* may be from a few inches to a foot or more in height, and they need not match; in fact in many households the set represents a gradual assortment of the separate groups, heirlooms from several generations back. . . .

Two "animals of good augury" should be present, but are rarely seen nowadays. The principal is a very stylized "dog," the dog-box previously referred to, which of old was the girl's most intimate amulet. The oval base offers a container for both trinkets and other talismans or charms, and its cover has the outline of a dog with round, rather human face. The *inubariko,* of *papier-mâché,* was given to the infant at an early auspicious occasion, remained near her bed during adolescence, and accompanied the grown maid into her new home upon marriage. It was supposed to make the woman fertile, and to assist in an easy childbirth. The other one was the *musubizaru,* the "knotted monkey," sewn from two unequal oblong pieces of cloth which, when stuffed, looks like a bent body with four extremities, and receives a stuffed ball for a head. The monkey was again a fertility and progeny animal, and *musubu* is a very old expression having to do with the tying of the marriage knot and with fresh production, the continuance of life in one's descendants. . . .

Unavoidable are the food-trays on which offerings are made to the prince and princess, and indirectly to the spirits of the ancestors, as was the original custom. The black and gold lacquer *ozen* will bear all the little bowls that are needed for soups and the more solid foods, correct to the smallest detail. There will be two special lozenge-shaped stands on which green, white and red dumplings of identical outline, the *hishimochi,* are offered—very important on this day for reasons which have become somewhat misty. There will be taller stands with a single stem for the *kagami mochi,* the round rice-cakes. And there will be *sake* bottles and cups, nests of boxes for sweets and *sushi,* and anything else connected with a good and copious meal—*en miniature.*

But there may also be any number of articles otherwise used in the home: writing boxes and letter or document boxes of gold lacquer, an outfit for the tea-ceremony or the game of matching incense, and reproductions of musical instruments. There will be elegant furniture, with drawers and shelves that could actually be used: chests and travelling trunks (*nagamochi* and *hasamibako*) and toilet boxes with contents; bowls and trays and the tall, screen-like racks, *emonkake,* over which were draped the fine *kimono* for an airing. A description of the various *hina dōgu* would practically introduce us into the civil life of the former lords. There will even be tiny picnic boxes, complete with individual lacquer plates, the *sake* bottles, the *sakazuki.* There will be infinitesimal playing-cards, or oblong boxes containing the decorated slips used at poetry competitions, or illustrated books hardly over an inch big, and game-boards of all kinds.

And there will be a *norikago,* palanquin, or a *goshoguruma,* the princely travelling cart: because Prince and Princess on this day come as visitors, to be royally entertained by the little hostess, and bestow their favours in return. . . .

On the mats in front of the shelves, on a red blanket spread for the purpose, there will be miniature cooking utensils, and in these the little girl should herself prepare some fancy meal with which to treat her guests. Tiny dishes, hardly larger than those before the "Court," are loaded with small fish, diminutive vegetables and cakes, flanked by soups in fairy bowls and provided with the smallest chopsticks that can be found. Special dumplings are eaten at this festival as being of good portent to the child, and a special kind of wine, the *shiro-sake* which is sweetish and but slightly fermented, must be partaken by everybody, to wish the hostess good health. Hostess and friends are of course dressed in their very best garb, with flowing sleeves and bright sashes. The parents too, are invited to gravely eat of the make-believe meal. On this one day, the little daughter is the principal person, and even her overbearing brother has for once to be well-mannered. Everywhere in Japan, "even in the most forlorn places in the mountains," as the old chronicler says, all the girls, rich and poor, have their *hina* and *dōgu* out on the 3rd day of the 3rd moon, and feel as if they themselves were the doll-princess on the top-shelf—so important are they on this day.

Source: *The Five Sacred Festivals of Ancient Japan: Their Symbolism & Historical Development* by U. A. Casal. Tokyo: Sohia University and Charles E. Tuttle Co., 1967, pp. 52-57. (Casal includes much speculation regarding the origins of this festival.)

The *kamibina* dolls

Etsu inagaki Sugimoto, the daughter of a samurai family in 19th century Japan, saw her families' treasured doll display sold one by one to pay for the exigencies of daily living. Later, after marrying and moving to the United States, she receives a shipment containing the more modest doll set used in her own childhood and two remaining family treasures—the *kamibina* dolls.

When Matsuo returned from Japan, he brought an entire set of school readers, from kindergarten to high school; also the five steps of articles for the Doll Festival. This festival is ages old and educational in character. Any one who understands it thoroughly has a nearly complete knowledge of Japanese folklore, history, customs, and ideals. Every girl has a doll festival set, and when she marries, takes it with her to her new home. The set Matsuo brought to Hanano was mine—the one which Brother objected to my bringing with me to America.

When the set came we all went out to the big, light carriage house, and after William had opened the rough board box, Matsuo and he carefully lifted out the smooth, various-sized whitewood boxes, each holding a doll. My eyes fell on a long, flat package wrapped in purple crêpe bearing the Inagaki crest.

''Why, Mother has sent the Komoro *kamibina!*'' I cried in astonishment, lifting the package respectfully to my forehead.

''I thought all the Komoro dolls were gone except the two that you used to play with,''

''The *kamibina* are different,'' said Matsuo.

''Yes,'' I said slowly, ''the *kamibina* are different. They belong to the family. They can never be sold, or given away, or disposed of in any way. My mother must have had these put away for years—and now she has sent them to me.''

I was touched, for it brought forcibly before me the truth that I was the last of the ''honourable inside'' of the house of Inagaki. A doll festival set belonged to the daughter; the master of the house having no control over the home department.

No doll festival set, however elaborate, is complete without these two long, odd-shaped dolls. In olden time they were always of paper. Later, extravagant families sometimes made them of brocade or crêpe, but however rich the material, they were *called* paper dolls and were always folded in the same crude shape of the primitive originals. When the set is arranged for the celebration, these dolls have no fixed place, as all the others have, but may be put anywhere, except on the top shelf reserved for the Emperor and Empress.

. . . Five steps were put up in the parlour and covered with red cloth. On these we arranged the miniature Emperor and Empress with court ladies, musicians, and various attendants. There were also doll furniture and household implements. On the lowest steps were tiny tables with food prepared by Hanano herself, with some help from me, and served by her to the playmates who were always invited to join her. And so ''Third Day of Third Month'' came to be looked forward to by Hanano's little American friends just as it has been by little Japanese girls for almost a thousand years.

Source: *The Daughter of the Samurai* by Etsu Inagaki Sugimoto Rutland, Vt.: Charles E. Tuttle, 1926, c. 1966, pp. 236-238.

For more on Girls' Day see: *Dolls on Display: Japan in Miniature, Being an Illustrated Commentary on the Girls' Festival and the Boys' Festival* by G. Caiger. Nishikicho, Kanda, Tokyo: Hakuseido Press, 1933. (B & w photos of dolls with descriptions); ''Dolls' Day and Boys' Day'' in *Festivals in Asia*. Sponsored by the Asian Cultural Centre for Unesco. Tokyo: Kodansha, 1975, pp. 23-30; ''Girls' Day'' in *Folklore of American Holidays* by Tristram Potter Coffin and Hennig Cohen. 2nd ed. Detroit: Gale Research, 1991; *Suzu and the Bride Doll* by Patricia Miles Martin. Chicago: Rand McNally, 1960. (Children's story, several illus. of Dolls' Day celebration.)

Circa March 5

Feast of Excited Insects

This is when insects arouse from hibernation. This day falls around March 5.

Korea

Kyongchip

The beginning of Spring

There are twenty-four days that indicate a change of season in the lunar calendar year.

In Korea this is one of the days. It is supposed to be the time when insects stir themselves and awake from their long winter hibernation.

Thus *Kyongchip,* which may be translated "excited insects," indicates the beginning of spring. . . .

In the country, farmers go into the fields and sow rice and wheat with perennial faith that sun, wind and rain can be relied upon to produce a good harvest.

And, in a grateful and benevolent mood, families carry flower bouquets to the graves of their ancestors as an auspicious beginning of another spring.

Source: *Celebrations: Asia and the Pacific* by Gene Sawyer. Honolulu: Friends of the East-West Center, 1978, p. 19.

People's Republic of China

Ching Che

Dragon calls insects to life

This is the time when, as the Chinese say, "the dragon raises his head". The lordly Dragon goes into hibernation in September in the form of a tiny creature, and thus remains unobserved till he calls the insects to life. On the day of the "Excited Insects" certain fetishes are displayed to placate them. In North China, a block of ice is often laid on the dung heap in the farm-yard, possibly to delay their depredations, or a paper pennant is mounted on a reed. In Shantung, people awake before sunrise and cook a sort of dumpling guaranteed to assist Nature in her work of stirring the dormant vitality in the vegetable and animal kingdoms. Water-jars have to be scoured, and the clay sleeping platform must be fumigated before its torpid inhabitants wake up and get to work. Women are debarred from needlework lest their implement prick the Dragon, and he retaliate by afflicting them with boils.

In the South, women worship the White Tiger. They may be seen carrying paper images of the beast which, when introduced into the house, keep out rats and snakes and prevent quarrels.

Source: *Chinese Creeds and Customs* by V. R. Bunkhardt. Hong Kong: South China Morning Post, 1982, p. 13.

March 8

Women's Day

This is a day to honor all women in the U.S.S.R.

U.S.S.R.

Gifts for women workers and schoolmates

Outstanding women are honored on this day and all women receive a vacation from work. Male coworkers give them small gifts the day before Women's Day. A festive meal may conclude the day, with presents for the women of the house. At school, boys bring small presents to their seatmates.

Source: *A Parade of Soviet Holidays* by Jane Werner Watson. Champaign, Ill.: Garrard Publishing Co., 1974, p. 17.

March 9

Feast of the Forty Martyrs

This day commemorates the Forty Christian Martyrs who were put to death in Sevastia in A.D. 320.

Greece

Foods and customs

Forty Christian martyrs were put to death in A.D. 320 in Sevastia. Special dishes are prepared in their remembrance. The number forty is especially symbolic. There are pies with forty thin pastry sheets, forty pancakes, a dish with forty different herbs, and a stew with forty kinds of corn. A Greek motto says, "Eat forty, drink forty, and give forty to save your soul." In the old days in Eastern Rumelia the men had to drink forty glasses of wine, and everybody had to tell forty lies! In Laconia, if there is thunder on this day, the snakes bury themselves forty yards in the earth; if there is no thunder, they will crawl up forty yards.

Source: *Greek Calendar Customs* by George A. Megas. Athens: B. & M. Rhodis, 1963, p. 85.

Roumania

Forty Saints' Day

Preparing tools for work

The ninth day of March is called the Forty Saints' Day. On that day beautiful wheat cracknels or twisted bread made in a figure-8 shape with pounded walnut and with honey on top is eaten in honor of the Saints. These cakes, called *colaci,* also called *sfintisori,* or little saints, are given away to every passer-by. The giving and taking is universal. Then, too, there is the *coliva!* This is a soft cake made of broken corn with honey and walnut. On Forty Saints' Day it is a settled custom to take out the farm tools and prepare them for work. On that day, too, the ashes are taken from the hearth or ash-bin and spread around the cottage so that "the serpent" may not enter. Every home has its serpent or snake and it would be a great sin to kill it as it protects the home.

Source: *When I Was a Boy in Roumania* by Dr. J. S. Van Teslaar. Boston: Lothrop, Lee & Shepard Co., 1917, pp. 63-64.

Moveable: Circa February-March

Ramadan (The Month of Fasting)

This is a holy month of fasting. No food or water may be taken from sunrise to sunset. Only young children, nursing or pregnant women, and the ill or aged, are excused. The family rises for an early meal before dawn. This month is a time of prayer, reading of the Koran, and worship in the mosque. The festival Id-Al-Fitr celebrates breaking of the fast, which begins at the sighting of the new moon. Future dates for the beginning of Ramadan are as follows: March 5, 1992; February 23, 1993; February 12, 1994; and February 1, 1995.

Bahrain

Ramadan fasting, c. 1909

Fasting is the third Pillar [of Islam]. Ramadhan is the tenth month of the lunar year, and toward the end is the Night of Power, when the Koran came down entire to the lowest heaven, from whence it was revealed in portions by Gabriel, as the occasion required.

''How many Moslems really fast, Sudika?'' I asked her in my early days. I knew that young children and the mentally defective were exempt, and that sick people and those on a journey of more than three days were excused, but had to make it up eventually.

''Everyone!'' she said firmly. ''Of course you know that women who are pregnant are excused, and those who are nursing a child. One may not fast at her time of the month, and so we are always left with a debt to make up afterward.''

I happened to know that some of my husband's men friends did not fast, but I prudently did not argue the point with her.

If I had asked her the question thirty years later, she could not have answered it so categorically. It is impossible now to estimate how many do or don't fast, but certainly the prestige and importance of the principle has as firm a hold on the Moslem world as it ever did. I have heard broadcasts from Cairo on the spiritual benefits of the fast, the psychological benefits, and the physical benefits. Religion and nationalism are closely interwoven and it is a demonstration of loyalty as well as piety to observe this Pillar.

Eed el Fitur

The fast-breaking holiday, the Eed el Fitur, at the end of Ramadhan, is a three-day period after the new moon has been seen by reliable witnesses, and everyone rejoices at the completion of the fast. All who can afford it have new clothes; calls are paid; and swings, merry-go-rounds, and little Ferris wheels are erected in every vacant space. Donkeys are beautified with patterns of henna and fancy harness, and cheap rides are one of the great treats for children. Every sort of vehicle is brought out and gaily decorated and pressed into service. A general holiday spirit prevails, and the social side of the festival is emphasized rather than the religious one.

Source: *Fatima and Her Sisters* by Dorothy Van Ess. New York: The John Day Co., 1961, p. 127.

Bedouin

A Bedouin Ramadan feast

. . . Early in the morning I was awakened by the great loud sound of a huge crowd of people chanting 'God is great! God is great! Thanks be to Him! Thanks be to Him!' I washed my face, put on my new clothes and ran towards the nearby hill. I saw many horses and camels tethered near the *Shik.* A mass of people was repeating the prayers. I saw the men of our tribe with many strangers. It was a tradition that the people of the neighbouring tribes used to come to our tribe's land to pray on the two feasts.

Abu Tamaa had been leading the festal praying as long as I could remember. He was in the middle of the big human circle. The recitation stopped when Abu Tamaa turned his face towards the south—to Mecca—and began to call loudly to prayer. Quickly the people lined up in six long lines and the praying began. It lasted for about twenty minutes, then Abu Tamaa turned his face towards the people and began to preach to them and to tell them about happiness in heaven and torture in hell. The people were silent as if they were white and black stones.

When Abu Tamaa came to the end of his sermon, the people ran quickly to him to shake hands; then they turned to both my grandfathers, Sheikh Hussein who was the *sheikh* of the tribe, and his brother Haj Ibrahim, who was the recognized judge in the district and the eldest of his brothers. Many lambs were killed that day. The strangers were invited: some accepted, while others excused themselves, mounted their beasts and went off towards their tribes. At lunch time many big plates were brought to the *Shik,* where both guests and hosts ate. Then the guests left, hastily, for their tribes.

Source: *A Bedouin Boyhood* by Isaak Diqs. London: George Allen & Unwin, 1934, pp. 30-33.

Egypt

The tension of the Ramadan fast

. . . Ramadan is widely and vigorously observed in Egypt. Many sinners "cease to sin," drunkards and hashish smokers abstain, even many professional thieves curb their activities. Since the Moslem year consists of 12 lunar months and is shorter by 11 or 12 days than the astronomical year, Ramadan periodically falls during the midsummer heat, its observance then becoming a test of the utmost severity. The psychological effect of the fast is marked; as the month progresses the tempers of the people become shorter, personal violence and divorce statistics usually rise sharply, and riots are plentiful. The firing of a cannon at nightfall is the signal for all to repair home to break their fast, and, with hunger pangs increasing daily, it is not unusual for the evening meal to become a banquet which extends far into the night. Business in many instances comes almost to a standstill; household servants refuse to work. The tension is even harder to bear for the uneducated (who are likely to keep the fast more rigidly), and they tend to dramatize their sufferings to find favor before Allah. A somewhat more skeptical attitude toward full observance is to be found among the Westernized elements of the population.

Source: *United Arab Republic: Egypt* by Donald N. Wilber. New Haven: HRAF Press, 1969, p. 65.

Activities in Kafr el-Elow village, Egypt

In late afternoon men purchase food for the *iftar,* the first meal after sunset. At one time male members of each clan convened to take this meal together, but now it is more often taken with the family in one's own home. After the meal, the men crowd into the mosque for the *isha,* the fifth prayer of the day, and *il-tarawish,* a special prayer for Ramadan. Male members of each clan may meet at their guest house to read the Koran later. A *mujid* (one who reads the Koran) may read aloud until 2 or 3 a.m. At that time the muezzin announces on the radio or from the minaret that it is time for *sahur,* the meal before dawn breaks and the fast resumes. A *musahir* (village crier) goes through the streets rapping on doors with a stick, beating a drum, and crying for all to wake up and take their sahur and offer morning prayers.

The most important religious event during the month is Laylat il-Qader, the "Night of Power." This commemorates God's revelation to the prophet Muhammad and is celebrated on the 27th of the month. At this time the heavens are believed to open and the favor of Allah descends onto the devout.

Source: *Kafr el-Elow: An Egyptian Village in Transition* by Hani Fakhouri. New York: Holt, Rinehart and Winston, 1973, pp. 78-79.

Indonesia

Lebaran

A young boy's Ramadan fast

The next morning the ring of the alarm wakes me up. It is two o'clock and time for our dawn meal. After washing my face and brushing my teeth, I join my family around the dining table. There is fish, soup and rice that Mother has prepared.

Father asks me if I know the meaning of this meal. I shake my head.

"This meal, my son, is a gift from God, so be thankful to God for it and obey Him always," says Father seriously. Yes, the meal given by God is very tasty indeed.

After dinner Father took me with him to the mosque. . . . We prayed and recited the Holy Book and then we had some fruit. When it was time to leave, Yaman went out without saying a single word to me. And day after day, for nearly a whole month, Yaman did not speak to me.

One day, while I was fasting, Father asked me if I felt hungry. "Yes, Father, I am very hungry," I replied. "So remember, son, what it is like for the poor to be always hungry. That's why we try to help the poor by giving them food and money just before the Lebaran festival."

Lebaran at Grandfather's house

Three days before Lebaran Father showed us the train tickets he had bought. "Oh! we're going by train to visit Granddad!" I exclaimed. When we got to the station the day before Lebaran there was such a large crowd there. The capital city of Jakarta was empty because so many people were going to the country. The stationmaster blew his whistle and the train pulled out of the station.

At Granddad's house the gates and fences were all decorated with lamps for Lebaran. Uncles, aunts and little cousins came to the door and embraced us. Every room in the house was brightly lit with lamps. In the evening the big drum of the mosque sounded, followed by the chanting, "God is great!" We joined in the chanting and even on the streets we heard men and children saying "God is great! God is great!"

At the mosque Father offered a sack of rice and some money to the poor. Grandma, Mother and my aunts were at home cooking the *ketupat* rice, which we eat for our Lebaran meal.

The next day was Lebaran. We all put on our best clothes and went to a field for special prayers. The field was full of people lined up in long rows chanting "God is great!" After the prayers we greeted one another and asked for forgiveness. When we got home we ate the delicious Lebaran meal and then we all exchanged greetings and asked for forgiveness for our faults.

Source: *More Festivals in Asia* sponsored by The Asian Cultural for UNESCO. New York: Kodansha, 1975, pp. 24-25, 27.

Indonesia (Java)

Pasa

Megengan, the week before Ramadan in Java

Megengan in the Javanese Islamic calendar is the period immediately preceding the beginning of *Pasa* (*Ramadan*), the Islamic month of fasting. It is the period when each family sends prayers to the spirits (*arwa*) of deceased kinsmen. During this period, which lasts a week in rural Modjokuto, each nuclear family holds a *slametan* and sends its male head to visit the graves of these kinsmen and invoke the blessing of *slamet* from the kinsmen for the nuclear family. The graves are then visited again, in rural Modjokuto at the end of *Pasa*.

Source: *Javanese Villagers: Social Relations in Rural Modjokuto* by Robert R. Jay. Cambridge, Mass.: MIT, 1969, p. 179.

Ramadan and Padusan in Java

A month-long fast in the 97th month of the Javanese calendar. It's preceded on Java by *Padusan,* a cleansing ceremony to prepare the spirit for the coming fast. Islamic fasting is less drastic than the Hindu custom of total abstinence from all food and drink, Gandhi-style. Muslims are more into a moon cycle. The whole family rises at 0300 or 0400, gorges themselves, then eats nothing during the daylight hours. Many visit family graves and royal cemeteries (Kota Gede and Imogiri in C. Java) where they recite prayers, strew flowers and holy water, burn incense. Special prayers are said at mosques and at home. Brand new velvet *peci* are sold everywhere on the street. The fasting month ends when you can properly sight the crescent of the new moon with the naked eye.

Source: *Indonesia Handbook* by Bill Dalton. Chico, California: Moon Pub., 1988, p. 27.

Wewehan exchange in Java in 1953

. . . The last ten days of Ramadan, the Moslem month of fast, has much mystical significance for syncretist as well as orthodox Javanese, though in Modjokuto the former do not keep the fast. During this ten-day period a large-scale exchange of food gifts, termed *wèwèhan* (from "*wèwèh,*" the act of giving such food gifts) takes place among a wide circle of kin and neighbors. Each hearthhold selects one day of the ten and sends trays of cooked food around to a number of kinsmen and neighbors. The more well-to-do and socially active the hearthhold, the more widely it is expected to exchange food.

In 1953 the numbers of hearthholds with whom a single hearthhold in the Kradjan exchanged trays of cooked food ranged from seventeen to sixty.

Source: *Javanese Villagers: Social Relations in Rural Modjokuto* by Robert R. Jay. Cambridge, Mass: MIT, 1969, p. 228.

Indonesia (Sumatra)

Puasa

Puasa in Atjehn, Indonesia (northern tip of Sumatra), c. 1967

At the beginning of the month, men rise shortly after their wives in order to eat before sunrise. As the month draws on, however, many of them sleep later, getting up only just in time for the sunrise prayer and then going back to bed. They rise again for the mid-morning prayer, stay awake usually until after the midday prayer, and then return to bed for a long afternoon nap.

In the evening, men break their fast at home with a snack and then go to the *meunasah* where they eat rice porridge cooked by someone selected by the chairman of the *meunasah* and paid for by the men of the *meunasah* as a whole. After their porridge, men pray the sunset prayer together and then return home to eat a substantial meal and rest. Occasionally during the month a family will cook for all the men of the *meunasah,* bringing the food there where it is eaten after the sunset prayer. No one is obliged to do this, but it is considered a good deed. There were five such meals provided during *puasa* of 1964 in our *meunasah.*

After they have rested at home and digested their evening meal, men return to the *meunasah* where they pray *teraweh. Teraweh* is the ordinary evening prayer with extra *raka'at;* it is recommended in Islamic law but is not obligatory. When they have finished, they read the Koran. On most occasions when the Koran is read in the village, only the first two *surah* are recited. During *puasa,* however, men try to read the whole book during the course of the month. Very few men can do this—only three in the *meunasah* in which we lived—but others sit and listen. The Koran recitation continues until 1:00 A.M. or later, but not all of the men stay to listen to the end: many return home to sleep.

Urou Raja Puasa (Idulfitri)

. . . People put on their new clothes and go to ask forgiveness from their neighbors. The men and women go separately, the women often taking cakes. This marks the beginning of the ceremonial visiting in which the young are expected to visit the old, after which the old will return the visits. Men visit neighbors first, then relatives, especially those in other villages.

These visits are carried out over two days. Visiting someone outside the village always means drinking tea and eating cakes. But visits to neighbors and other villagers, except for the *teungku ineong* and the *teungku tjihk,* are usually limited to the asking of pardon. (The first says, "*maaf lahe baten*" [forgive me in all ways], and the second responds, ''*lahe baten*'' [in all ways].)

Urou Raja Puasa sermon extract

By fasting, we make *hawa nafsu* [man's physical nature] an instrument. It is for this reason that God gave us *hawa nafsu*. *Akal* is the head, the chief. *Hawa nafsu* is the instrument. *Hawa nafsu* is channeled thus into the simple path, the right way. This way we are not used by other men or other creatures.

The fast is over, but God remains. So do not tell lies, do not disobey God's word. In this way, we profit from the fast. Our deeds will appear again when we confront God. Those who do not so profit will go to Hell. If we do evil acts, acts forbidden by God, all of the good of the fast disappears.

Source: *The Rope of God* by James T. Siegel. Berkeley: Univ. of California, 1969, pp. 184-185, 188-189, 192. (An anthropologist's report.)

Iran

Ramazan

A Teheran social worker's observations

On the twenty-sixth of Ramazan my mother came to Sarbandan. The end of the month of fasting is the time in my country for visiting people you love. With her came my nephew Ali. All day Mother and I cooked. With butter, flour, sugar and zafaran spice we made halva, a kind of sweet that Persians like better than any other, for the twenty-seventh of Ramazan marks the closing of the fast and in the mosque it is a time for feasting. The halva we baked in a long covered baker of clay in a charcoal fire out of doors behind my house. We would bake again on the twenty-seventh, for I planned to take enough halva to the mosque for everybody.

At sunset Ali climbed to the roof of my house. With one of the most beautiful voices in all of Persia he began to sing the song that my heart had hungered for:

Praise be to God, Lord of the worlds,
The compassionate, the merciful,
King on the day of reckoning.
Thee only do we worship and to Thee we cry for help.
Guide Thou us on the straight path,
The path of those to whom Thou hast been gracious;
With whom Thou art not angry, and who go not astray.

At that moment the deep meaning of the words, the man-voice of Ali singing for all the young men in Islam, the simplicity of the way of life that I had adopted, my mother with her hair whiter than silver and the serene face of an angel, all combined to produce in me the strangest of emotions. The tears flooded my eyes, tears of happiness and sadness. All this that was so deeply ours we must not lose for a sewerage system, for electric lights to replace our kerosene lanterns, not even for food for the always-hungry body of man.

At eftar, sunset, Mother and I and Ali took the great copper trays to the mosque. On them we had placed small plates of halva, and fruit, and slices of cucumbers which Mother had brought from Teheran, available there because they had been trucked in from the warm southern countries.

Ali took his tray to the men's side of the mosque; Mother and I took ours to the side where the women and children were waiting.

This was the first time I had been in the mosque at Sarbandan and now I saw it by the light of hundreds of lanterns. It was a very large room with a red brick floor and a flat ceiling supported by wooden pillars which had once been covered with stone and brickwork. Now some of the bricks had crumbled and the wood was visible. We knelt upon straw mats on the floor, the men on one side of a tattered curtain, the women and children on the other.

Many times I have knelt in a mosque at the closing of the month of Ramazan; but never in a simple mosque like this. Yet the flickering light and shadow that cross the faces of those who kneel is as beautiful to me as the light from a thousand electric bulbs in the ornate chandeliers of the mosque in Teheran where I had most often prayed. We are kneeling in long lines, our faces toward Mecca. From the pulpit come the words of the young mullah, but it is not his voice alone, but his voice amplified by the concentration of a multitude of hearts.

''God is great,'' the mullah reads.

''God is great,'' we repeat, and again we put our foreheads to the red brick earth, the earth from which the body of man is made.

Source: *Reveille for a Persian Village* by Najmeh Najafi and Helen Hinckley. New York: Harper, 1958, pp. 38-39, 44-46.

Ramazan, c. 1910

It is observed in commemoration of the death of Ali and his two sons, Hassan and Hosein. The Persian boys who bear these names are particularly proud of them during this fast. The fasting begins with the sight of the new moon. I have seen people climbing tall trees and on the housetops looking for it. The first person who sees it considers himself quite fortunate. When it is cloudy the Government informs the population by firing a cannon or by special messenger, that the moon has risen. As soon as the appearance of the new moon is established, the people all over the country become at once more religious than they were before. The poor, the Jews, and the Christians, if they show a sober face during the fast are treated better than usual.

To observe the fast, no one except infants, sick people, and the sons of the road, i.e., travelers, are supposed to eat, drink, swear, smoke, or enjoy any social pleasures from sunrise to sunset. In the cities those who fast are summoned by the firing of a cannon to fast and later to feast. As soon as the Muezzin call, or the firing of the cannon is heard by the people in the evening the daily meal begins. They rush from housetops and the streets or wherever they happen to be, and they continue eating until the next morning, when they are again informed by a Muezzin call or gun-fire to stop eating. There are more deaths from overeating during this month of fasting than from all other causes put together.

When this fast falls in the summer season when the days are long and hot, it becomes unbearable. But, "What of it?" they say, "even if one should die from heat and thirst while fasting, what is that compared to everlasting life, or to the final reward with which one could obtain the password to heaven?"

The Mohammedans continue this fast until the new moon is seen again. The last ten days of the fast of Ramazan are full of excitement. In the evenings I used to see companies of men, women, and boys in the streets of our village carrying banners, clubs, emblems and metallic bands. They cried, beating their heads and breasts with their fists, pulling their hair, and, like lunatics, shouted aloud the names of Ali, Hassan and Hosein, their martyred prophets.

On the last three days of the fast all the shops and bazars are closed. The mosques all over Persia are draped with black, prayers are conducted and everybody is gloomy, as the saints are about to be executed by their enemies.

The most agonizing of all fast days is the last day of Ramazan. It may be properly termed the Mohammedan slashing day. In the morning all the Mohammedans, young and old, form processions. They march through the streets and graveyards, shouting as usual the names of Ali, Hassan, and Hosein, in such a manner that the names can be heard at a great distance. At first the name of Ali is shouted three times, then they continue with all the famous names and repeat them successively, saying, "Hassan, Hosein ya Ali," until they are hoarse from shouting and can hardly whisper.

In the morning each young man reports to the village priest or to a barber who inflicts with a razor a wound in his forehead. The blood then streams on the white apron which he wears for the occasion to show the public how much blood he has shed. Then the young men go into the streets with swords and sabers in their hands and form a line. Suddenly the leader will shout, "Ya, Ali!" Immediately each follower begins inflicting deeper wounds on his scalp. In order to keep them from slashing themselves, friends and relatives hold sticks on the foreheads of the frenzied young men.

The procession continues all day long. They go into the hills and into the graveyards, and visit different villages, shouting the names of Ali and his comrades. Each village has its band. If the band of one village can show more blood than the others it is considered that the more pious men are in that village.

Source: *When I Was a Boy in Persia* by Youel B. Mirza. Boston: Lothrop, Lee & Shepard, 1920, p. 112-113.

Iraq

A Ramadan kraya in El Nahra, Iraq

Almost every evening during Ramadan I went to krayas—at the shiek's house, at Laila's house, at Abdulla's and Mohammed's. The tone of each kraya depended on the personality of the mullah, but the basic ritual remained the same: The *latmya* invocation with preliminary chant and breast-beating; the sermon, different for each day of Ramadan, but followed by the telling of Hussein's betrayal (*hadith*); the latmya again, at a faster pace, with the circles of women moving together in strict tempo, the spontaneous cries and wails, the profession of inspired penitence by the few women who join the mullah in the inner circle and finally the *da-a,* or moment of silence and prayer at the end. This final moment is considered to be the climax of the kraya, I was told, for then, in a state of purification, the women may ask great favors from Allah and expect to have them granted. Often these favors are requested conditionally. A woman may pray for a son, and vow that if her prayer is granted, she will hold krayas in her house during Ramadan for a stipulated number of years. Such vows are sacred, and if for some reason the woman cannot fulfill them, she may be released only by a gift to the mosque or to the mullah.

. . . The krayas . . . provide religious fulfillment for both men and women, and they also seem important as social occasions in the lives of the women, who seldom congregate in large groups. Women gather for two hours before a kraya is scheduled to begin, and stay long after the mullah has departed, talking and smoking. No refreshments other than cigarettes are ever offered.

Source: *Guests of the Sheik* by Elizabeth Warnock Fernea. Garden City, N.Y.: Doubleday, 1965, p. 118.

Jordan

Jordanian customs during Ramadan

No Muslim may eat, drink, or smoke until the gun signals the official end of day. Many wait with a bowl of the "Soup of Ramadan" in their hands, ready to partake as soon as the signal sounds. Wealthy families can sleep during the day and stay up all night feasting, thus hardly suffering during Ramadan. But poor workers must get their sleep during the night and work all day without nourishment. To ease this hardship the Jordanian government sets shorter working hours during Ramadan . . . 9:30 am to 1:30 pm.

Around one thirty every morning, a man roams the streets beating a bass drum, clashing cymbals and singing to wake everyone so they can eat before dawn.

The three-day celebration at the end of the month, Id-el-Fitr, is a time of rejoicing. Everyone wears new clothes and visits friends. Gifts are exchanged, drums are beaten, and men dance the debke. Special services are held at the mosque, and women visit the cemeteries.

Source: *The Land and People of Jordan* by Paul W. Copeland. Philadelphia: J. B. Lippincott, 1965, 1972, p. 51.

Lebanon

Buarij villagers, c. 1960

Previous to the commencement of Ramadan, families go on foot to the district center of Zahle to buy new clothes for the occasion and to lay in special supplies for the meal before dawn and for the evening meal, when the daytime fast is broken. On the day before the beginning of the fast, villagers wash both themselves and their clothing, the men indulging in haircuts. Ramadan to the peasants is a time of spiritual cleansing, symbolized by attention to outward cleanliness, while the fast itself is a means of obtaining spiritual purity by handing the body over to God. On the first day of Ramadan a service is held in the mosque, the men attending. Throughout the month the prescribed five daily calls to prayer echo from the turret of the mosque, though during the remaining portion of the year no more than the evening call is rendered, despite religious injunction.

The month of Ramadan is especially propitious for the answering of prayers, thereby renewing the life of man. The twenty-seventh night of the month, or the ''night of power'' (*lailat alqadr*), is the most propitious date of all. Then the doors of heaven are said to open, the angel Gabriel asking grace for every person. Old persons in particular pray for the forgiveness of sins on this night, knowing their lives are advancing towards the realm of God, whose presence is particularly near as the gates of heaven swing wide. Even the trees are said to kneel in reverence on this night lest they look into the face of the Almighty. In Muslim thought there is always the close identification of the secular and the sacred. On the Night of Power it is the sacred itself that suffuses the world, all creation being subject to its rule.

Source: *Buarij: Portrait of a Lebanese Muslim Village* by Anne H. Fuller. Cambridge, Mass.: Center for Middle Eastern Studies of Harvard Univ., 1961, pp. 80-81.

Malaya

Hari Raya

Ethnic Festival and Open Houses

Ethnic festivals are prominent among the recurring special events of life in Malaysia, and the holding of ''at homes'' or open houses to accommodate the exchange of goodwill visits is a central feature of festival celebrations. The intra-ethnic exchange of visits is a tradition of long standing but, since independence in 1957, interethnic visiting has been officially encouraged as part of social planning to increase contact and communication across ethnic lines.

The exchange of visits at festival times has been identified as a way for Malaysians of different ethnicities to take the preliminary steps of more interaction with each other and more understanding of each other. The festivals chiefly involved are the annual ones of Hari Raya, celebrated by Malays at the end of the Muslim fasting month. Chinese New Year, Deepavali, the main festival for Malaysia's Hindu Indians, and Christmas which is observed by the country's multi-ethnic community of Christians.

Under the established pattern of visits on an intra-ethnic basis, Malays make goodwill visits to other Malays during the celebration of Hari Raya, Chinese visit other Chinese for Chinese New Year, and so on. A lot of this ''old'' kind of festival visiting still occurs. Interethnic visiting is a ''new'' or modern extension of the old behavior. It represents additional, not alternative, festival visiting. If I were a Malaysian Malay, I should now plan, for example, to also visit my Chinese friends during their open house at Chinese New Year, my Hindu Indian workmates at Deepavali, my business contacts in the Christian community at Christmas, and expect them to reciprocate with a visit during the open house I shall stage when Hari Raya comes around.

Source: ''Festival Open Houses: Settings for Interethnic Communication in Urban Malaysia'' by M. Jocelyn Armstrong in *Human Organization* 47 (2) (1988), pp. 127-128.

Morocco

Iid el Sageer in Marrakech, as seen by an American family; the sheep market

The streets were full of people on this, the final day of Ramadan, for at sundown the horns would blow and the drums would sound and the season of fasting would come to an end. A new season would begin, the season of feasts: Iid el Sageer would be followed by Iid el Kabeer, Ashura, the Fête du Trone, the moussems of the saints. Everyone was out doing last-minute shopping, and many people seemed bound in the same direction as we.

We passed under the high double-stone arch of the gate at Bab el Robb to find the *mechouar,* the stretch of land between the city walls and the mountain highway, transformed from an empty plain into an enormous sheep market. As far as we could see, the plain was alive with moving, milling flocks of sheep, and the noise was deafening.

At the gate, rows of small peddlers were ranged together in an impromptu market, offering items that would be needed for the ceremonial slaughtering: long knives, knife sharpeners, metal skewers for brochettes; rope to tie the sheep; blocks of wood in various sizes to be used as cutting boards; piles of straw and fresh-cut fodder to fatten the sheep already sold, to keep alive and well those that were still for sale.

A professional butcher stood there, too, who would, his son was shouting, for only a small fee, slaughter a sheep for a family without a male head or anyone able to perform the ritual.

Iid el Sageer feasting

Early on the morning of Thursday, January 27, we heard the blaring of radios and television sets. King Hassan II had returned from prayers at the royal mosque in Rabat. The Iid had officially begun, marked in Marrakech by a long siren sounding across the city. A great stillness settled over Rue Trésor.

. . . On the roof, we looked over the edge of the dividing wall to see Hajja Kenza and Naima, with the help of a hired butcher, still at work on their twenty-dollar sheep. They nodded and kept on with their task. The butcher was chopping the meat into appropriate-sized pieces while Kenza laid out the liver and lights, tidily, on a clean slab of wood. Naima was scrubbing the roof, and while we watched, she stood up and helped her mother turn the sheepskin inside out to dry before slitting it to be cured and sheared of its wool.

''The first day we eat the soup from the bones, and the liver,'' Kenza said, after shaking hands with Pansy. ''Then the chops in brochette the second day, and the third day the rest of the meat in tajeen stew.''

. . . There were no really public aspects to the Iid in Marrakech, except in the mosques. One went to the mosque, one prayed and gave thanks to God that one had enough of this world's goods to be able to buy a sheep and give a portion of it to one less fortunate; one went home and ate with one's family. Abdul Lateef deplored the fact that people spent more than they could afford on the feast. ''Everyone feels he must have a sheep or he's not respectable or self-sufficient.''

''We all take some food to the mosque,'' Aisha was saying, ''and we eat together and give a meal to the poor.''

Source: *A Street in Marrakech* by Elizabeth Warnock Fernea. Garden City, N.Y.: Anchor, 1980, pp. 170, 172-173.

Nigeria

Azumi

Fasting in Katsina, Nigeria, a Hausa community

The fast was strictly observed by everyone. Anyone seen eating or drinking during the day would be questioned and censored. The fine for unintentional eating, like waking up and taking a drink before remembering that this was Ramadan, could be simply adding another day to the fast period after everyone else was through. But intentional eating or drinking could draw a large fine, such as feeding sixty poor people.

Source: *Katsina: Profile of a Nigerian City* by Gretchen Dihoff. New York: Praeger, 1970, pp. 54-55, 62-63.

Pakistan

Ramazan

The rule during Ramazan is that one cannot eat after there is enough daylight to distinguish a white thread from a black one. In country villages people wake and watch the stars to tell when it is time to eat so they can finish an early meal before dawn. Then they nap in the afternoon. In modern cities, work goes on until sunset. When the *iftar* (sundown) siren blows, traffic screeches to a halt, passengers and rickshaw drivers jump from their vehicles and rush to the tea stalls. People crave a drink first, tea or sweet lemonade. There is also a thriving business in dates and in sugarcane, preserved (along with sundry insects) in huge blocks of ice.

Some upper-class, Westernized people do not strictly observe Ramazan, merely giving up some favorite foods or pleasures, as many Christians do in Lent. There are also exceptions for the ill and infirm. A few modern Muslim theologians assert that the Koran offers alternatives to fasting. Many people agree that the rigors of the month-long fast, which may have been tolerable in the days when one could retire to a desert cave, are unrealistic today.

Source: *The Land and People of Pakistan* by Robert Lang. New York: J. B. Lippincott, 1974, p. 133.

Saudi Arabia

Ramadan in Mecca in 1926

. . . Every night at about the hour of half-past eight by Arabic time [the Arabic day begins at 6 P.M.-2:30 A.M. our time], in the darkness before dawn, a gun was fired from the Fort of Jiyâd. This gave notice of the arrival of the hour of the *sabûr*, the meal before dawn. Two hours later, the gun was fired a second time, giving notice of the *imsâk*, the abstention.

. . . At this early hour the Meccans commonly ate the cold rice and meat left at the evening meal, followed by dates and *finjâns* [cups] of tea. The moment the second gunshot is heard, those who have not finished eating, quickly swallow the last mouthfuls. They then mentally declare their 'intention' of fasting during the ensuing daylight hours. . . .

Those who have eaten their *sahûr* meal soon after the first gunshot will either lie down to sleep again until the hour of the dawn-prayer (about 4:45 A.M.) or sit to read the Koran aloud. After praying the dawn-prayer in the Haram, the Meccans return to their houses, and enter their private apartments to sleep. The more religious among them read aloud a thirtieth part of the Koran every morning during Ramadân, and thus go completely through the Book during the month. Some read as much as a quarter of the volume (of some three hundred pages) every day—reading the whole some seven times during the month.

As the hour of sunset approaches, the Mosque becomes ever

more crowded, until the pavement beneath the cloisters is almost completely covered with turbaned figures sitting cross-legged on their prayer-mats. Many chant the Koran in an undertone, swaying their bodies from side to side, others sit talking among themselves, or staring at the Ka'ba. Most of them have a small bundle of dates and bread, tied in a handkerchief. Here the famished multitude sits, patiently waiting for sunset. At last the gun booms out from the hill-top of Jiyâd. Instantly a buzzing murmur is heard all over the great quadrangle, of many voices giving praise to God. The handkerchiefs of food, the knots of which have already been loosened, are now spread open; and repeating the brief Muslim word of grace, the ravenous fasters eat a few dates or a piece of bread. Those who have food, gently invite others who sit near them to partake of their fragmentary repast. . . .

While the members of the assembled multitude are thus relieving their hunger, the *mu'adhdhins* in the minarets are already chanting forth the *adhân* for the sunset prayer. Now all rise, wiping their lips, to perform their devotions. Prayers being over, they quickly disperse to their houses.

Returning to his house after prayers, the Meccan eats plentifully of a white soup, of wheat boiled in meat broth. This is followed, after an interval of half-an-hour, by the usual dinner-dishes of meat, rice, and vegetables. At this meal, the principal one in the Ramadân day, the Meccan sits for perhaps an hour—eating, drinking tea, and smoking. Later on, he will sit with his cronies until midnight, with an interval for the purpose of performing the '*ishâ*' prayer (between the end of dusk and the passing of one third of the night) in the Haram. Those of a more religious order say long supererogatory prayers during the nights of the second half of this month. Many of the Meccans remain awake, praying or amusing themselves, until the *sahûr* gun is fired.

Source: *Muhammadem Festivals* by G. E. Von Gruenbaum. New York: Henry Schuman, 1951, pp. 60-61.

Senegal

Korité feast in Dakar c. 1932

On this end-of-Ramadan feast day, women prepare special dishes their husbands and their husband's relatives. Braised mutton leg, roast chicken, beans with meat sauce, couscous, ices, and custard tarts are typical dishes. The children carry these foods to the homes of relatives and receive small tips or treats in return.

Source: *A Dakar Childhood* by Nafissatou Diallo. Trans. by Dorothy S. Blair. London: Longman, 1933, p. 27.

Sierra Leone

Lantern festival in Freetown

The festival in Freetown, Sierra Leone, known as Lanterns occurs during the Muslim holy month of Ramadan. It is characterized by elaborate float-like stuctures illuminated from within—"lanterns"—employing a variety of iconographic elements whose origin remains obscure.

Lanterns were introduced to Freetown during the 1930s by the trader Daddy Maggay, who witnessed the celebrations while on business in Banjul (Bathurst), the Gambia. According to his account, the Catholic fathers of that city paraded with hand-held lighted objects at Easter. At the time, lanterns were presented at Ramadan as well. Daddy Maggay build Freetown lanterns solely for the celebration of the twenty-sixth day of Ramadan, the day of light, Lai-Lai-Tu-Gadri, when the Koran was sent to earth by Allah. His followers first used lighted hand-held paper-box enclosures mounted on sticks.

The early celebrations were small and peaceful. Later, however, Maggay's wife's reputation for home-cooked corn *kpa* and *ogi* (couscous) spread, and more people joined in. Occasionally the crowds became unruly, prompting Maggay and his followers to wear heavy boots for protection. Some Muslims discourage the use of drums, but Lanterns participants soon discovered that the sound of the boots on the paved streets could be coordinated in effective drum-like rhythmical patterns. Unexpectedly, this drew larger and more unruly crowds. Maggay's followers introduced a particular beat called *bobo,* the name by which the group was later known. Afterwards, professional musicians and a bugler were hired to complement the marching.

Attracted by the shipping industry during World War II, many ethnic groups moved to the city and established new neighborhoods. The economic boom created by wartime industry allowed lantern builders to stage large and expensive celebrations, and as a result neighborhood rivalries developed, based on lantern competition. For example, in the central part of Freetown, where the Lanterns tradition first spread from the Fourah Bay Muslim community, the Temne (who are renowned for lantern building) and Manding at first combined their efforts in Lanterns and in the ancestral Egungun masquerades introduced by Yoruba slaves repatriated to the Sierra Leone colony in the early nineteenth century, even building a mosque to celebrate their solidarity. The Egungun society was called Obasai Ojeh (meaning "other side branch" of the Egungun). One year, however, this ethnic alliance in the Egungun society was disrupted, and each group built its own lantern. The competition led to violence. Subsequently the Temne faction, under Pa Musa Koroma, established its own Egungun cult, Navy Ojeh, named for the economic prosperity brought to Freetown by the British Navy. Naval motifs, including the cult's masked costumes converge with similar lantern motifs.

In the 1950s, to reduce the violence and to organize the festival further, the Young Men's Muslim Association (YMMA) took control of Lanterns and organized the entries by iconographical type. Group A was for ships, group B for animals and people, and group C for miscellaneous subjects covering such secular themes as amusement parks with merry-go-rounds and ferris wheels. Prizes were awarded to the first three winners in each group based on building technique and creative imagery. The YMMA raised funds for the festival and distributed them among the qualified entrants, thus bringing about a new age in lantern-building competition.

Freetown lanterns have evolved from the simple hand-carried objects of the 1930s to large floats comprising bamboo platforms with wire images and bamboo substructures covered with layers of fine fabric and paper. Today these constructions are pulled by eight-man teams or by motor vehicle. The turbulence surrounding Lanterns after the war prompted the elders of the Fourah Bay Muslim community to change the date of the procession from the twenty-sixth to the thirtieth day of Ramadan in deference to those who wished to observe Lai-Lai-Tu-Gadri in peace.

Source: "The Lantern Festival in Sierra Leone" by John W. Nunley in *African Arts* XVII (2) (February 1985), 45-49.

Syria

Blessed month in Tell Toqaan village, Syria, in 1954

Ramadaan, the Muslim fast month, began in 1954 at sunset May 3. Ramadaan was described as a shahr baarakii, "blessed month." During this time one who fasts should not smoke, eat or drink from "halfway through the night" (about 2:00 A. M.) until the following sunset, although a light snack may be eaten just before daybreak. If one breaks the fast one day, this day must be made up later. Those who are working need not fast, but they ought to do so. Shayx MaHmuud did not fast because, he said, he could not talk and teach all day unless he could eat and drink. A number of others, including a few women, began the month with fasting according to rule but within a week or ten days had stopped. The heads of several peasant households were maintaining their fast up to the time the field session closed about May 20 and remained in seclusion most of the day; the other members of their households went about their daily activities as usual. In 1954 Ramadaan coincided with the beginning of harvest season and the increase in work in the fields, and fasting during a period of heavy work was commented upon as a physical hardship which only the most pious could endure.

A number of other features of Ramadaan were described; the first of the month there should be a special meal or feast, Hasanii, "alms," "charity," but none was known to be held in Tell Toqaan households. During the last ten days of Ramadaan a man should spend much time in the mosque. The last two days before ciid l akal or ciid iz zghiir, the feast which ends Ramadaan, are know as waqfaat. The first is called waqfit l gharaba on which there is another Hasanii. Some say, explained my host, that this feast is for those whose fathers have died from their own home; some say that at this time one should turn to one's home if one is away.

Source: *Tell Toqaan: A Syrian Village* by Louise E. Sweet. Ann Arbor, Mich.: Univ. of Michigan, 1960, p. 272.

Thailand

Ramadan in a Malay village in Southern Thailand c. 1956

. . . Two days before the beginning of the month of Ramadan, most families prepare *ketupat*, a triangular packet, wrapped in a banana leaf, of cooked glutinous rice with coconut. They distribute *ketupat* to all their friends, relatives, and neighbors. The fasting of Ramadan is not started in the Pattani area until the day after the first night that the new moon is actually seen, and in case of cloudy weather this may not be until several days after the official start of the month.

At Rusembilan during Ramadan, many people sleep during the day and remain awake at night, when they may eat and smoke. The usual waking time is about one in the afternoon, in time for the *sembayang lohor* or midday prayer. Later in the afternoon, some light work may be done by the men, but if it can be put off for the rest of the month, it usually is. Men will often prepare the sweets for the evening meal while the women make ready other food before the *sembayang asar*. At sunset, after prayers, the main meal is served, consisting of sweets and a sweet drink first and then rice and curry. Following the *menamat* which is the point when one entire Koran has been read during the evening recitations of this month, a fast-breaking feast is customarily held in the mosque instead of the evening meal at home. In 1956, this feast was given for the people of Kampong Pata by the residents of Kampong Surau; it was reciprocated at the *balaisa* in Kampong Pata two nights later. Later in the month, fast-breaking parties are often held in the coffee shops.

Source: *Rusembilan: A Malay Fishing Village in Southern Thailand* by Thomas M. Fraser, Jr. Ithaca, N.Y.: Cornell, 1960, pp. 157-158.

Turkey

Cannon fire

At the firing of a cannon the families of Dermirciler would rise and quickly eat their predawn meal. At dawn a second cannon was fired and the fast began. At sunset a third cannon would signal breaking of the fast. During the day people went about their usual activities. As soon as the cannon signaled the break of fast, the women would serve a huge meal.

Seker Bayram

At the end of Ramadan came the feast of Seker Bayram. After breakfast the children would visit their grandparents, kissing the backs of their hands and touching the spot that had been kissed to their foreheads. The grandparents would give the children candy and small gifts. For the entire three days of feasting visits to various relatives would continue. Special prayers were offered at the mosque on Seker Bayram, and the Hoca presented a sermon.

Source: *Life in a Turkish Village* by Joe E. Pierce. New York: Holt, Rinehart and Winston, 1964, p. 177.

Kara-geuz show, c. 1910

On the last day of Shaban towards sunset some inhabitants go off into the mountains to look for the moon. Others climb to the tops of trees or to the roofs of houses for the same purpose. The reason for this is that as soon as the moon is seen the month of Ramazan begins. As soon as any one sees the moon he hurries to the mufti and says, "I am a good Moslem and I have seen the moon this night," whereupon the mufti tells the muezzin who then calls from the minaret, "To-morrow is Ramazan! To-morrow is Ramazan!" The town criers go about the city repeating the same words. Drums are sounded and cannons are exploded to tell the faithful that the holy month has begun.

We have been ordered in the Koran to fast during the month of Ramazan from sunrise to sunset. This does not merely mean that we cannot take food while the sun is above the horizon but also that we cannot drink, smoke, or even smell of a flower.

With the setting of the sun the fast turns into a feast. Every house has its visitors. Great meals are prepared. Everybody eats more than is good for him. There are many special Ramazan dishes, and it is during this month that a Turkish housewife is called upon to demonstrate her skill as a cook.

The eating is accompanied by music and dancing and what for me was always more enjoyable, a Kara-geuz show. This resembles somewhat your Punch and Judy, but instead of dolls we have cardboard figrues which throw their shadows on a white screen behind which is a brilliant light. Kara-geuz is our national buffoon and the leading character in these shadow plays. Many are the hours of laughter he has given me.

The evening's entertainment usually comes to an end towards midnight, when everybody steals a few hours of sleep. In the early hours of the morning it begins again. However, with the coming of dawn the revelry stops entirely. The drums and cannons are sounded and everybody prepares himself for the first prayer of the day.

Lélé-I-Kadir prayers

On the twenty-seventh of Ramazan is the Lélé-I-Kadir (night of power). This is the most important religious date in the Moslem year. On this night Moslems believe that Allah sent down the Koran to the lowest of the seven heavens from where it was given to Mohammed in revelations as he needed it, that Moses received the ten commandments from Allah, that Christ rose from the dead and that Allah finished the creation of the world and made Adam and Eve. The mosques are crowded as on no other occasion in the entire year. The prayers continue late into the night and the feasting this night is broken by no sleep but continues uninterrupted right up till the moment when the sun shows its edge on the horizon.

Source: *When I Was a Boy in Turkey* by Ahmed Sabri Bey. Boston: Lothrop, Lee & Shepard Co., 1924, pp. 83-88.

Upper Volta (Burkina Faso)

Boys' Dodo masquerade

The present form of Dodo has undergone significant changes from the traditional Ramadan children's entertainment. Informants in Ouagadougou recount that the masquerade was introduced by Hausa traders in the mid-nineteenth century. During the full moon of the Moslem lenten month, older boys would secretly wrap themselves in white cloth with a hump on their backs and a rope tail, whiten their bodies with kaolin, and don a calabash headpiece sprouting two horns. They went from compound to compound performing a slow dance, accompanied by clapping and singing in Hausa, in return for gifts of food.

According to informants, about the time of the Second World War, Dodo changed dramatically. The masquerade began to reflect local Mossi culture. Instead of singing in Hausa, the boys sang in More, the local language. Drums and tin cans replaced hand clapping. Mossi dance steps were incorporated, and movements were more varied and dynamic. Each dancer began carrying long sticks, permitting more sweeping movement patterns. Rhythms quickened. Pantomimed animals emerged from local folklore to delight and frighten viewers. In addition, younger boys between the ages of 7 and 12 began to form their own groups, called Petit Dodo, which paralleled the Grand Dodo of the boys aged 12 to about 16. By the mid-fifties, little boys were dancing Dodo in many Mossi villages and towns around Ouagadougou and as far north as the city of Ouahigouya. It continued to be a secret affair whose preparations were hidden from girls and women.

Today Dodo remains a child-initiated, child-guided play activity. As the Ramadan season approaches, boys form groups in their neighborhood, or *quartier,* consisting of a principal singer and a chorus, five or more dancers, a drummer, sometimes a few costumed wild animals, and a leader who tells the group when and where to perform and who bargains for gratuities. He may be dressed in military style with a Sam Browne belt. Informally boys make a drum and decide on roles and dance steps, usually elaborating on a dozen commonly accepted patterns. Each dancer decorates two sticks about a meter in length by peeling away the bark in stripes or other patterns or by applying paint or kaolin. Knee bells are created out of can tops with metal rings around the edges. All the members of the group help to make the masks and costumes, scrounging many of the materials. Fathers and older brothers contribute to the purchase of supplies if they are able, but, to their pride, the boys organize the rest themselves.

On the night of the full moon during Ramadan, wearing masks they have made and with bodies decorated, the troupe goes from compound to compound, singing and dancing in return for gifts of money. The performance lasts about fifteen minutes and is composed of five parts: the greeting and entrance; vigorous dancing in a circle; the pairs competition known as the "two by two"; the entrance of animal masquerades, such as a lion, monkey, or elephant, sometimes accompanied by a hunter, and the exit.

Standing outside the compound gate, the chorus sings the greeting to the head of the house, asking to perform for everyone. One neighborhood Dodo troupe's song was recorded as follows: "We greet the Naba [chief] Saaga./ We greet the Naba Kugri, a rock we can depend on which will be difficult to ever remove./ Peace be with you./ Is the owner of the house in?/ If he is away, God protect him./ Our grandfather Adam will give him health./ Our grandmother Eve will give him health./ Peace be with you./ Is the head of the house sleeping?/ We want to bring you good news./ Brother! Don't you hear?/ Bring out your twenty-five francs, / And give it to the Ouidi [*a quartier*] boys, / Give it to the Larle boys./ Peace be with you./ Our ancestor Adam will give you health./ Our ancestor Eve will give you health./ God will give you health."

A Dodo origin legend

An elder told me in 1982 that the origin of the masquerade can be traced to a Hausa story. A hunter had promised his good friend, the Emir, not to kill anything on the Moslem holy day, Friday. One day, responding to a plea for help from some shepherd boys whose cattle were being threatened by a monster, the hunter fired his gun without thinking. He killed the monster and was immediately transformed into a creature half-man and half-beast. In his shame, he ran off into the bush. The Emir, mourning his friend, sent an army to find him, and they subsequently returned with the "beast." The chief was happy to have his friend restored, and when the village children asked if the creature could dance with them in their Ramadan celebrations, he consented. Everyone was pleased by this, and many years later, when the beast died, the chief suggested to the children that they make animal masks in memory of the hunter who had saved the boys. The calabash headpiece with horns made from the borassus palm became the symbol of Dodo.

Source: "The Dodo Masquerade of Burkina Faso" by Priscilla Baird Hinckley in *African Arts* XIX (2) (February 1986), 74-77.

West Africa

West African Ramadan traditions

Ramadān is preceded by two days of festival (cf. Shrove Tuesday). The fast is observed fairly strictly, for African life is so open that it is difficult to conceal the fact that one is not fasting. The daily prayers, neglected throughout most of the year, are more strictly observed. Hausa have a saying (*azumin jemage*) for those who observe the fast but neglect the devotions, which has acquired proverbial significance for half-doing something. Many are assiduous about both because they believe that thereby sins committed during the year are remitted. The 27th day, Lailat al-Qadr, generally confused with the Night of Power, is observed by clergy who say that God spends this night regulating the affairs of the world. Since it is the night the Qur'ān descended, many spend it reading the Qur'ān in relays. In the evening ablutions are performed and incense burned to speed the *jinn* on their way to prison. A Mande feast of the virgins has been attached to this date. In western Guinea children sing for presents, young men and maidens parade the streets, singing and dancing all night. They carry around "floats" with representations of animals, boats, and the like. In Hausaland during Ramadān the commentary of Jalālain is read and translated by two *mālams,* disposing of two *hizbs* each day, and during the last night the whole Qur'ān is recited (called *tukuri*). In the entrance hut of the chief cleric a group of from five to ten read a *hizb* in turn until the sixty are completed. People drop in and leave alms in a calabash placed in the centre of the circle.

Source: *Islam in West Africa* by J. Spencer Trimingham. Oxford: Clarendon Press, 1959, pp. 77-78.

First Day of the Tenth Month, at End of Ramadan

Id Al-Fitr (The Little Feast)

The month-long Ramadan fast is broken with this feast. The feasting cannot begin, however, until the new moon is officially cited. If it is overcast, the fast may have to continue another day. Humorous tales are told of religious officials who ascend in a jet to "officially sight" the new moon.

Egypt

Eid il-Fitr

Cemetery activities in Kafr el-Elow village, c. 1970

On the first day of the festival the men go to the mosque early, while the women go to the cemetery taking cookies (fatir) and fruits to give to the beggars who assemble there. The men join the women at the cemetery after prayers. When the men arrive the women cease the wailing in which they have been engaged. A *mukre* (one who recites the Koran) may be called to the cemetery during this time to recite the Fatiha over the tombs. After rites at the cemetery, the men exchange holiday greetings, "Kul am wa inta tayib" (hope to see you healthy and happy at all times) and retire to their clan guest houses to exchange greetings with relatives. The children kiss the hands of the elderly, hoping to be given money for candy or for the amusement rides set up by itinerant companies at this time.

Source: *Kafr el-Elow: An Egyptian Village in Transition* by Hani Fakhouri. New York: Holt, Rinehart and Winston, 1973, p. 84.

Hausa

Courting at Salla festivals, c. 1907

When a young girl was going to be married for the first time, this is what happened. If both the man and the girl were free people, he gave her these presents while he was courting her: at each of the two *Salla* festivals he gave her 20,000 cowries, a short petticoat, a blouse and a head-scarf. Then on market-days he gave her her market-gift, he gave this to her once weekly, although markets were held more often. When he saw her in the market-place he called her *kawa* and gave her a thousand or two thousand or even three thousand cowries. At Zarewa the market was held every other day, and at Karo there was a little market under the tree every day.

Source: *Baba of Karo: A Woman of the Moslem Hausa* by Mary Smith. New York: Frederick A. Praeger, 1964, pp. 85, 242.

Indonesia

Lebaran/Hari Raya/Idul Fitri

Lebaran celebrations in Indonesia

Also called *Hari Raya* (or in Arabic, *Idul Fitri*). The first day of the 10th month of the Arabic calendar, this marks the end of the Muslim fast, an outburst of celebrations climaxing a month of pent-up tension and austerity. After tom-toms and firecrackers all night long, the festivities usually begin at 0700 when everyone turns out for an open-air service in the village *alun-alun*. Mass prayers are held the first morning followed by 2 days of continuous feasting and public holidays. Women dress in white, like nuns. A house holder buys new clothing for his children and servants, verses are sung from the holy *Koran,* and sometimes there are religious processions. This is a joyous time for mutual forgiveness when pardon is asked for all wrongs of the past year. *Leberan* is like Christmas, Valentine's Day, and the New Year's resolutions all rolled into one! With everyone dressed in their finery, Muslim Indonesians all day long visit and revisit neighbors and relatives, bringing gifts of specially prepared food, the best the family can afford. At each house a cup of tea is served with helping after helping of sweet doughy cake and bright cookies until you burst. *Lebaran* continues until all the visits to relatives are ended. A large extended family could celebrate *Lebaran* for as long as a week.

Source: *Indonesia Handbook* by Bill Dalton. Chico, Calif.: Moon Pub., 1988, p. 75.

Iraq

Eed-al-Fittur

Breaking of the Fast

The Breaking of the Fast, *Eed-al-Fittir,* is celebrated by Muslims everywhere, including Syria, Jordan, Iraq, and Morocco. It marks the end of the fifth lunar month, called Ramadan, the time of fasting that is followed by all true Muslims, who do not eat or drink between sunrise and sundown for each day of that month. During Ramadan all eating by the faithful Muslim is done before sunrise or after sunset.

Then comes *Eed-al-Fittir,* a time of joy and feasting. The beginning of the festival may be announced by the booming of cannon or the beating of drums. For three days everyone stops work and celebrates.

A great deal of attention is paid to the children. For days before, mothers shop for or sew new clothes, so that the boys may have bright new sateen blouses and the girls gay silk dresses. All the young people go to the village or town square where they find swings, merry-go-rounds, and perhaps a ferris wheel. There may also be puppet shows. Hot roasted chestnuts, salted peanuts, and watermelon seeds are on sale.

When the sun has set, everyone goes home to eat the special foods that have been prepared. Particular favorites are a kind of wheat-and-meat ball, fried in deep fat, called *kibbie,* and a sweet made of many layers of pastry, soaked in honey, called *baklava.* Family gatherings take place on the following evenings, and the children receive gifts from their parents and relatives. On the third day the mother finds time to go visiting, too. The festival is a time of rejoicing for the whole family.

Source: *Children's Festivals from Many Lands* by Nina Millen. New York: Friendship Press, 1964, pp. 61-62.

Jordan

Al-zid al-Saghir

Jordanian villagers, c. 1965

On the day before and the morning of al-zid al-Saghir *zakat* (tithes) are given. Zakat are given by the more wealthy villagers to those in need. Zakat may be given in cash or "in kind," in services or commodities. All who can do so sacrifice a sheep or goat on this day in memory of Abraham's willingness to sacrifice his son. This meat is consumed in feasting by the family, and little is given to poor relatives. Poorer families may join together to purchase an animal for their sacrifice and feast.

Source: *Baytin: A Jordanian Village* by Abdulla M. Lutfiyya. The Hague: Mouton, 1966, pp. 58-59.

Libya

Eid al Fitr

Libyan customs

The feast following Ramadan lasts three days, during which families receive guests and make calls on relatives. Children are given presents of coins or sweets wherever they go. All dress in their finest for this festive occasion.

Source: *Hi Neighbor. Book 8.* New York: Hastings House/ U.S. Committee for UNICEF, 1965, p. 17.

Morocco

Celebration in the city of Sale, c. 1930

Every male in the city attended morning prayer at the cemetery on this day, wearing new clothes and new shoes. The poor lined the streets leading to the cemetery as this was a day for giving alms.

The celebration continued for seven days, with visiting among friends and a rest from work. Many marriages took place at this time.

Source: *People of Salé: Tradition and Change in a Moroccan City 1830-1930* by Kenneth Li Brown. Manchester: Manchester Univ., 1976, p. 92.

Pakistan

Id-ul-Fitr/Eid

A day of community rejoicing

Everyone longs for the new moon that marks the end of Ramazan. "Did you see it last night?" people hopefully ask. If the weather is cloudy, astronomers must be consulted. Finally comes the dawn of Id-ul-Fitr, the feast that ushers in the new month. Much as Christians feel joyful at Easter, Muslims are thankful and happy at Id; it is a day of community rejoicing. Men and boys go to the mosque to pray: city mosque courtyards are crammed with tens of thousands of worshippers. The great Bad-shahi Mosque in Lahore is said to have attracted three hundred thousand faithful at one Id ceremony: more than half of these were obliged to worship in the square outside. After prayer and a sermon, throngs of people stroll through the streets, wearing new clothes if they can afford them. Some of the women are enveloped in burqas of black or fashionable pale hues, but little girls in pigtails are dressed in vivid purples, pink or blue satin trimmed with silver or gold. Everywhere the greeting is "*Id mu-barak*" (happy Id). Everyone is in a friendly mood. Sweetmeat sellers do a thriving business and press gifts on strangers. Relatives visit one another or send presents; servants are given new clothes. Boys get a new ball or a flute and children's swings are hung in trees.

Source: *The Land and People of Pakistan* by Robert Lang. New York: J. B. Lippincott, 1974, p. 134.

Eid Festival

Eid marks the end of Ramadan, the Moslem month of fasting, when devout Moslems do not touch food or drink from sunrise to sundown. Special prayers are offered during Ramadan, and the mood is solemn and quiet, but when the new moon appears, quiet is forgotten and merrymaking begins, after a brief thanksgiving prayer. Mothers rush to market for last-minute shopping and children eagerly discuss plans for the next day.

Children get up very early on Eid day, and put on their new clothes. Boys are particularly proud of their lambskin hats and gold-and-silk-embroidered shoes with upturned, pointed toes. Little girls show off their gauzy, bright-colored stoles and wiggle their wrists to make their glass bangles jingle. First comes a trip to the mosque, which is surrounded by booths selling candy, spicy meatballs, and inexpensive clay and paper toys. There are merry-go-rounds, too, and hand-operated Ferris wheels.

Eid is a little like Christmas for Pakistani children since they receive presents from everyone. Visitors come to call, rustling in their new clothes, and are given the traditional sweet of the season, *saiwiyan*. This is noodles cooked in milk and sugar and sprinkled with coconut and dried fruit.

The highlight of the second day of the festival is the fair, where children are offered elephant and camel rides, fireworks, magicians' and jugglers' shows, as well as an endless variety of spicy tidbits to eat. There are motorcycle shows and miniature circuses, target shooting and other games of skill, all to the constant sound of music, played very loud.

Source: *Hi Neighbor. Book 6.* New York: Hastings House/ U.S. Committee for UNICEF, 1963, p. 30.

Philippines

Hari-Raya Poasa

Muslim Philippine communities celebrate

. . . On this day, a Muslim wears his best clothes and calls on his elders and relatives to kiss their hands and beg forgiveness for offenses he may have committed in the past. The elders give the younger ones and children money or gifts. It is occasion for Muslims to exchange greeting cards, and they go about greeting each other "Salamat Hari-Raya", which is equivalent to the Christian "Merry Christmas".

On this occasion, every Muslim house and premises get a general clean-up and face-lifting. Muslim delicacies are prepared in every home and the *pagduwaa,* special prayers and blessing for the food, is recited.

The festival day is ushered by groups of men who beat gongs around the streets in the morning, calling on the people to assemble in their mosques or in any place designated for worship to give prayers of thanksgiving. Prayers are held at 4 a.m., 1 p.m. and 6 p.m.

The wealthy go to the town plaza to shower coins on the children. The Muslim priests, called *imams,* or religious leaders, are particularly called upon to do this, to show generosity and to ask blessings from God.

The day is devoted to sports, like horse-racing, carabao fighting, boat-racing, and games of strength and skill, called *pagsilat*.

In the evening, a *madrasa,* or musical and literary program, is held. Verses from the Koran are chanted, and contests in Koran reading are held by participants representing various groups.

The feast of Hari-Raya Poasa is also called "Boka" or "Idilpitri" in Maranaw.

Source: *The Galleon Guide to Philippine Festivals* by Alfonso J. Aluit. Manila: Galleon, 1969, pp. 106-107.

South Africa (Cape Malay)

Lebaran

Traditional Lebaran foods

Malays settled in South Africa over 300 years ago and still maintain their traditions. On Lebaran, the feast at the end of Ramadan, special dishes are prepared such as *sosaties, bobotie, bredie, koesisters, kerries, blatjang, atjar,* and *sambal*. Cooking may be done out-of-doors over wood fires, since the quantities required are too large for the average kitchen.

For more on Lebaran in South Africa see: *African Cooking* by Laurens van der Post and the Editors of Time-Life Books. New York: Time-Life, 1970, p. 133.

Sudan

Eid Saghir

Children's festivities

Children have new clothing on Eid Saghir to celebrate the end of the Ramadan fast. Red candy dolls holding paper fans are given to children, along with other special sweets. Hand-operated Ferris wheels and merry-go-rounds appear in public squares for the children's enjoyment on this occasion. Visits to friends and relatives occur too at this time.

Source: *Hi Neighbour. Book 5.* New York: U.S. Committee for UNICEF/Hastings House, 1962, p. 49.

Surinam

Idul Fitre in Surinam

Idul Fitre is the Moslems' name and "Lebaran" or "Bodo" is the same in the Indonesian language. Indonesians and Moslems celebrate the end of the 40-day fast. Everyone celebrates this festival by eating with Moslem families and the Moslems are dressed in new clothing, while presents are being exchanged [among] the family members.

This is the most important Moslem holiday. Moslems extend invitations to non-Moslems and for this special occasion a dish called ''senvai'', made of noodles, will be served to the guests.

Source: Embassy of the Republic of Surinam.

Thailand

Hari Raya Puasa

Festivities in a Malay village

The first day of Shawwal, the month following Ramadan, is *Hari Raya Puasa* (great day [after] fasting). Of the three *hari raya* observed in Malay communities, this is by far the most important at Rusembilan, as it is a day of feasting and festivities following the month-long fast. All villagers dress in their newest and finest clothes and greet each other with the *salam.* Many of the village households prepare large quantities of food to serve to friends who may drop in, as visiting is common this day. A complete service is held in the mosque during the morning, an the daily prayers are said more assiduously on this day than perhaps on any other in the year. On most *Hari Raya Puasa,* a carnival opens in Pattani, and large groups of young men from the village spend much of the afternoon and evening watching the Malay dancing, Thai boxing, and bullfighting as well as enjoying the side shows and ''rides'' to be found there. During the evening, or the previous evening if the village has been notified by then of the end of the fasting month, children and adults alike set fire to great ''candles'' of coconut shells, which are placed one on top of the other on sticks, and set off firecrackers made in the village either from gunpowder or from water-filled bamboo sections which are heated until they explode.

On the eighth day of Shawwal, *Hari Raya Enam* (great day [after] six [days of fasting]) is celebrated. This feast after the six-day fasting period following Ramadan is never as elaborately observed as *Hari Raya Puasa,* and most of the village pays little heed to it.

Source: *Rusembilian: A Malay Fishing Village in Southern Thailand* by Thomas M. Fraser, Jr. Ithaca, N.Y.: Cornell, 1960, pp. 157-158.

Turkey

Sheker Bairam

1910 festivities

Ramazan ended, the first three days of Sheval, the succeeding month, are given over to general merry-making. This period is known as Sheker (sugar) Bairam, or as Ramazan Bairam to distinguish it from Kourban (sacrifice) Bairam, of which we will speak a little later. These two festivals are the great merrymaking occasions in our life. During Sheker Bairam visits are made from one village to another. There is a great deal of dancing and wrestling and all present their friends with candy and sweets. It is at this time that children receive gifts from their parents and relatives. As a children's festival, Sheker Bairam is the most similar to Christmas of any festival in the Moslem year.

Source: *When I Was a Boy in Turkey* by Ahmed Sabri Bey. Boston: Lothrop, Lee & Shepard Co., 1924, p. 90.

The Night of Power in Turkey

The 27th day of the Holy Month of Ramazan is the 'Night of Power,' when the Koran was revealed and Muhammad was appointed to be the Messenger of God. His duty was to communicate the Word of God to the world. Mosque illuminations, special prayers and foods celebrate the day.

Source: *Turkey: A Travel Survival Kit* by Tom Brosnahan. Lonely Planet, 1988, p. 29.

West Africa

West African Id-al-Fitr traditions

This festival (Ar. *al-īd as-saghīr* or *al-fitr*), like the Great Feast, is known as *salla;* particular terms are: Tamahaqq *tisendar, amūd (Air);* Tokolor *korka;* Wolof *kori;* Soninke *suñkaso n'tyale;* Western Mandingo *suñkaro sali;* Dyula *miñgare tulu,* 'feast of the moon of drinking'; Fuloe *julde sumave;* Songhay *ferme dyinger,* '(mouth-) opening festival'; Hausa *karamar salla* or *sallar azumi;* Nupe *sálagi,* 'little feast'; Yoruba *irun awe,* 'prayer of the fast'.

The new moon is anxiously awaited for if it is not seen the clerics will insist on another day of fasting. Its appearance is greeted with bursts of firing, beating of drums, and general rejoicing. About eight o'clock in the morning the festival prayer (*salāt al-'īd,* Songhay *sarty-ille*) is held at a special praying-place outside the town (Hausa *masallachi yīdi*) where the men assemble by quarters. The *imām* leads a prayer of two *rak'as* in a low voice which is shrilled out by another cleric, then mounts the pulpit-block which has been carried from the mosque and recites a two-part *khutba.* In Nupeland this is translated from Arabic into Hausa and then into Nupe, for having studied through the medium of Hausa they seem unable to translate directly. In western Guinea they have an unusual practice at both *'īds.* The *almāmi* standing on the block is covered with a white cloth (or a number of cloaks) like a canopy, under which he remains for half an hour reading sermons aloud and interpreting. Temne said he was communing with Muhammad, Gabriel and the spirits of the dead. When the cloth is removed the people press upon him to rub their hands in his sweat and wipe it over their heads and bodies. Mende said there was power (*kpaya*) in the sweat, and when they rubbed it on themselves they got *ngauwanda* ('grace'). Many return home from the prayer by a different route from the one taken when going. This, they say, is in accordance with a tradition that the Prophet ordered the first believers to perform the prayer outside the mosque in order not to be surprised by the infidels, and to return by different routes in order not to seem too large a group of people. Strict clergy disapprove of the drumming and dancing that goes on throughout the night.

Source: *Islam in West Africa* by J. Spencer Trimingham. Oxford: Clarendon Press, 1959, pp. 78-79.

March 17

St. Patrick's Day

St. Patrick was born in Britain of Roman stock around A.D. 389. As a youth he was kidnapped by Irish raiders and carried off to Ireland. He escaped six years later and fled to Gaul. After fifteen years or so in a monastic life, he returned to Ireland to Christianize the land of his captors. He confronted King Laoghaire at Tara, confounded the druids, and converted the king's daughters. He is said to have driven all snakes from Ireland. The shamrock, which he used to explain the Trinity because of its three leaves, is associated with his day.

Canada

Customs and festivities

Canadians wear a shamrock or something green on St. Patrick's Day, even if they are not Irish. Irish clubs hold special St. Patrick's Day parties, and in Montreal there is a St. Patrick's Day parade.

Source: *Let's Celebrate* by Caroline Parry. Toronto: Kids Can Press, 1984, p. 87.

Ireland

St. Patrick turns the stone and alters the weather

The months of February and March are the most menacing to the health of man and animal: "February kills the sheep," they say, "March the people." Of a man whose health is failing, it may be said that "he'll never go up the March hill." Halfway up that hill, on the seventeenth, comes St. Patrick's day. On that day, St. Patrick removed the cold stone from the stream (or turned the worn side of the stone up), so, while every other day after St. Brigid's Day has been fine, *every* day is fine after his own day. This is the end of the cold weather, and farmers can start to work in the fields. They should begin planting their potatoes and sowing their grain.

Turning the snakes to stone

Most of the legends about Patrick deal with the time that he spent in Ireland after his return. The most persistent one, of course, is the one that represents him as having driven the snakes out of Ireland. "Yet in Ierland is stupendyous thynges," says Dr. Andrew Boorde in his *The Fyrst Boke of the Introduction of Knowledge,* written in the first half of the sixteenth century (by which time it was already an old story); "for there is neyther Pyes [magpies] nor venymus wormes. There is no Adder, nor Snake, no Toode, nor Lyzerd, nor no Euyt, nor none such lyke. I haue sene stones the whiche haue had the forme and shap of a snake and other venimous wormes. And the people of the countre sayth that suche stones were wormes, and they were turned into stones by the power of God and the prayers of saynt Patryk. And Englysh marchauntes of England do fetch of the erth of Irlonde to caste in their gardens, to kepe out and to kyll venimous wormes."

Wearing the green in honor of a deed

In another contest, Patrick's followers were put in a house made of dry wood, while a Protestant's (*sic*) followers were put in a house of green wood, and both houses were then put to the torch. The protestants were burned to a crisp, while Patrick's followers emerged unscathed (and ever since, goes one version, people have worn green on St. Patrick's Day).

St. Patrick's Day celebrated with more ado in the United States than in Ireland

Given Ireland's strong identification with the saint, it is perhaps surprising that local observances of his day are not more pronounced. An important pilgrimage to his mountain comes later in the year, but his day is celebrated much more in New York than in Ireland. Nevertheless, however fragile the connection between myth and ritual in this case, the image of Patrick is a major one, localizing and concretizing the attributes of God—powerful, stern, subject to rage, dangerous, though also protective of those who obey him—and identifying these attributes with Ireland itself.

Source: *Irish History and Culture* by Harold Orel. Lawrence: Univ. Press of Kansas, 1976, pp. 131-132.

Holiday bands in the old days

Once or twice a week and on certain Great Days too—Patrick's, the Twelfth of July, the Twelfth of August, and the Fifteenth—bands swung along the country lanes. If they met on the road, they beat competitively against each other for hours. "Man dear!" Joe Flanagan said. "It was *great.*

"They had big flutes, wee flutes, and piccolos. They had the big drum and the wee drum. They were great bands, too, great.

"Oh man, you wouldn't be tired listenin to them. The Wearin of the Green. Old Folks at Home. The Harp Without the Crown. O'Donnell Abu. Napoleon's March. Oh man, they could play.

"But this old Troubles ruined that. Bigotry. It takes unity and peace in a country to do that. If a Catholic band went out now, they'd have to get a permit. And that left the people careless. They had no heart for goin out, you know. And now, surely, with the Trouble, it's worse.

"The old generation had a better interest in a band, you know; the young don't take an interest. And it's a bad thing in a way because a good band in a country is a great thing.

"If a good day comes on, boys-a-dear, it's a great thing to have a band turn out."

Source: *Passing the Time in Ballymenone* by Henry Glassie. Philadelphia: Univ. of Pennsylvania Press, 1982, p. 279.

For more information on St. Patrick's Day see: "St. Patrick's Day, March 17" in *Folklore of American Holidays* by Hennig Cohen and Tristram Potter Coffin. 2nd ed. Detroit: Gale Research, 1991.

Drowning the shamrock

. . . St. Patrick's Day was the only day during Lent when people were free to eat and drink their fill, and drowning the shamrock is a tradition established for at least a hundred years.

OED, s.v. "Shamrock," 1b: "*To drown the shamrock:* to drink, or go drinking, in honour of the shamrock, on St. Patrick's day." The earliest quotation cited is 1888.

Source: *Life & Tradition in Rural Ireland* by Timothy P. O'Neill. London: J. M. Dent & Sons Ltd., 1977, p. 64.

March 19

St. Joseph's Day

St. Joseph, father of Jesus, is honored on this day.

Sicily

Holy Family actors

On this day, a respected elderly carpenter is chosen to act the part of San Giuseppe, a poor girl plays the part of Mary, and a young orphan boy becomes the Bambino. For months, these three, dressed in robes and crowns, are feted at the homes of rich and poor and showered with gifts. The gifts are divided among them, the church, and the poor. Household articles given are kept by the girl for her dowry.

In Palermo, on the eve of March 19, bonfires are lit in the streets in honor of San Giuseppe. Boys keep them going, adding whatever old wooden objects they can find to the fire and dancing round the flames.

After the midday mass on the 19th, the banchetto de San Giuseppe is held outdoors, with a priest and town fathers waiting on the Holy Family. In Agrigento, nineteen people are invited to this banquet, corresponding to the date. *Crespoli di riso* (rice made into sausages and fried in honey) and *sfinci* cakes are eaten on this day. In Catania a minestra of beans and vegetables called *maccu* is eaten. After the banchetto, the Holy Family mounts mules covered with rich cloths and lead a procession to receive gifts and acclamation.

Source: *Festivals and Folkways of Italy* by Frances Toor. New York: Crown, 1953, pp. 30-32.

Spain

The *Fallas* of San Jose in Valencia

Fallas are intricate scenes made of wood and papier-mâché that satirize local and international events. They are set afire on the night of March 19. *Falleros* from all over the city compete for the best falla, and the best Ninot (doll) from each of the fallas is carried in procession by the falleros. At the Stock Exchange spectators with ballots vote on the one Ninot to be spared from the flames. These Ninots are preserved in a special museum. At midnight the church bells ring and the falleros torch their fallas to the cry of "Fire . . . Fire . . ." from the waiting crowd.

Source: *Spanish Fiestas* by Nina Epton. New York: A. S. Barnes, 1968, pp. 238-239.

For more information on St. Joseph's Day see: "St. Joseph's Day, March 19" in *Folklore of American Holdays* by Hennig Cohen and Tristram Potter Coffin. 2nd ed. Detroit: Gale Research, 1991.

Circa March 20

Ibū Afo Festival

This is an Igbo end-of-year rite, whose exact date is determined by a council of elders. The old year is sent off with a wailing cacophony; the new, greeted with applause.

Nigeria (Igbo)

A noisy goodbye to the old year and a welcome to the new

About the night of the 20th of March the Igbo celebrate the Ibū Afo Festival. This is a solemn rite which is not marked by any feasting. In Ihitenansa, for example, the council of Nze Elders that fix the annual calendar (igu afo) compute the day and hour of the celebration of the Ibū Afo rite, a rite that marks the end of the year and heralds the new. At the appointed hour weird noises, symbolising the wailing noise of the departing year, rent the air. At this noise every child is expected to rush inside the house, bolt the door and start banging at it to add to the general lament. The children are told that those who dare to come out of their houses may be carried away by the departing year. As soon as the wailing dies down, all doors are thrown open and people rush out of their hiding places to welcome the new year with spontaneous applause.

Source: ''Standardizing Igbo Festivals'' by Nnabuenyi Ugonna in *Nigeria Magazine,* 136 (1981), 25.

Circa March 20

Emume Ala

This is an Igbo festival to offer sacrifice at the Ala Shrine and join in communal feasting.

Nigeria (Igbo)

Celebrating the Ala Festival

It is also around this time that the Ala Festival (Emume Ala) is celebrated. It is a major festival which involves the whole community. On the festival day the priest of Ala who is always the oldest man in the community goes to offer sacrifice at the Ala shrine (ihu ala). Members of the community would have invited their friends and relations from other communities to come to the feast. In every household, animals will be slaughtered and meals prepared in readiness for entertaining both the members of the household and their guests. About 2 o'clock in the afternoon guests begin to arrive and feasting will commence. At about 5 p.m. hosts with their guests will take food and drinks to the Ala shrine where there will be communal feasting.

Source: ''Standardizing Igbo Festivals'' by Nnabuenyi Ugonna in *Nigeria Magazine,* 136 (1981), 25-26.

Circa March 21

Vernal Equinox

An equinox is one of two days each year on which the sun shines directly onto the equator. The length of the day is the same as the length of the night on this day.

Assam

Bohag Bihu

Garu Bihu, a day for cattle

Bihu starts on the last day of Chot, but begins with a sort of cattle worship. The first day is called *Garu* Bihu or the day for cattle, the second is *Manuh* Bihu or the day for men, the third is sometimes called *Gosain* Bihu or the day for God. Another important aspect of Bihu is the *Huchari* carol singing, and this starts from the Manuh Bihu day.

As in Magh Bihu in this Bihu also there is Uruka or Bihu eve. This is a day for house cleaning, washing of clothes old and new, preparation of various kinds of eatables, like *chira* or parched rice, *pitha* or cakes and *laru* or balls of cocoanut scraping and fried sesame, etc. After dinner is over, the cooking pans are cleaned. Next day is Garu Bihu or day meant for cattle. This is also the Samkranti day, Vernal Equinox.

Early in the morning children prepare pieces of bottle-gourd, brinjal, turmeric and bitter-gourd and keep them fixed on three-pronged bamboo sticks. They rub paste of mati-kalai and turmeric on the foreheads and horns of the cattle. They also rub mustard oil on the horns and what remains of it they rub on their own bodies. The cattle are then taken to a neighbouring lake or river for a wash. On the way the pieces of gourd, brinjal, etc. are thrown on the cattle. The boys also strike the animals with sprigs of *dighlati* and *makhiyati* plants and recite:

> Eat gourd, eat brinjal,
> grow from year to year,
> your mother is small, your father is small,
> may you be a large one.

. . . The plough and harrow are also washed in the morning of the Garu Bihu day and given cakes as an offering. This morning it is customary for men to take a little of green mango and jute leaves mixed with mustard oil and salt. Eating of tender mango on the New Year day was also an old Indian custom, known as *Navamrakhadika*.

Manuh Bihu

The day after Garu Bihu is Manuh Bihu, the first of Bohag, and meant for men. This day people show respects to their elders, are given new clothes, especially, the *bihuwan* or Bihu present, in the shape of a *hachati* or kerchief, *gamocha* or towel, *dhuti* or dhoti, and *cheleng* or chaddar. Nowadays only a gamocha is given; in towns children may be given pants and frocks. *Huchari* carol singing starts on this day, it being first sung at the communal Namghar. Huchari may sometimes start on the Garu Bihu day as well, for it is considered beneficial to secure the blessings of the carol singers on this day:

> On the Garu Bihu day take the blessings,
> only then can you find a place in Heaven.

The cloth presents are family affairs, but near relatives and close friends are likely to get them. A cloth present is often a love token. The borders of a gamocha are usually red; at one end or both ends there are usually some designs of flower motifs or wavy lines. Women may even weave names into them.

A magical practice observed on this day is the writing of a Sanskrit mantra on leaves of the nahar (ironwood) tree and keeping them under the rafters. The mantra is a prayer to Mahadeva (Rudra, the howling terrible god of the Vedas), and meant as a protection against storms, lightning and fire. It is usually written by a Brahman. In rural areas the Brahman or some astrologer consults an almanac and tells the members of a family how they are going to fare in the coming year. Visiting of friends and relatives may start on the Manuh Bihu day. . . .

Gosain Bihu

The third day is Gosain Bihu and meant for God. The chief feature of the day is congregational prayer held at the Namghar. There is no caste restriction within the Namghar, though the eatables offered to God are not distributed to persons of higher castes by one one of the fisherman caste. The Vaishnavite character of the land is observed in these prayers, sung vigorously to the accompaniment of large cymbals and kettle-drums. Even Adivasis like Kacharis and Rabbas take part in these communal nam-prasangas.

The other days till *Satbihu* or the seventh Bihu day have no special functions assigned to them, but Huchari singing goes on all these days and, in the fields, go on dance and music characterizing the spirit of the season. On the seventh day it is customary to eat seven kinds of herbs which normally grow after the first showers have fallen. These are not vegetables which may be grown in the garden. The herbs together are known as *sat-saki* or the seven sags.

At Barpeta elderly ladies go to some open wasteland, dance a little, sing cheerful songs, and in a merry mood pick the seven kinds of herbs. They do not allow malefolk to go near them and do not allow others to know what songs they sing. As I have been informed, some of them also put on male clothes for the occasion.

In upper Assam, when Huchari singing is over, Bihu is given a ceremonial parting.

Source: *The Springtime Bihu of Assam* by Praphulladatta Goswami. Gauhati, Assam: Lawyer's Bookstall, 1966, pp. 1-23. (Goswami discusses various Bihu customs and dwells particularly on Bihu dance and song. Some historical information on Bihu included.)

Bali

Nyepí

A purification at the start of a new year

Once a year, at the spring equinox, every community holds a general cleaning-out of devils, driving them out of the village with magical curses and rioting by the entire population. This is followed by a day of absolute stillness, the suspension of all activity, from which the ceremony takes its name. *Nyepí* marks the New Year and the arrival of spring, the end of the troublesome rainy season, when even the earth is said to be sick and feverish (*panas*). It is believed that then the Lord of Hell, Yama, sweeps Hades of devils, which fall on Bali, making it imperative that the whole of the island be purified.

There is great excitement all over Bali at this time, and in the days before *nyepí* everybody is busy erecting altars for the offerings and scaffolds for the priests at the village crossroads. Since no cooking is allowed on *nyepí* day, the food for the next day is prepared and there are *melis* processions all over Bali to take the gods to the sea for their symbolical bath. The celebration proper extends over a period of two days: the metjaru, the great purification offering, and *nyepí,* the day of silence. On the first day the Government allows unrestricted gambling and cockfighting, an essential part of the ceremony, because the land is cured by spilling blood over impure earth.

In Den Pasar round after round was fought all morning; crowds of men gathered in the meeting hall of every *bandjar,* each bringing his favourite fighting cock in a curious satchel of fresh coconut leaves, handle and all, woven over the cock's body, its tail left sticking out so as not to damage the feathers.

[After the cocks die in their fight, they] are taken home and cooked for the *nyepí* meal. After the cockfights, in Den Pasar it is customary to give a banquet for the children of each *bandjar,* a double row of beautifully decorated trays filled with sweets and cakes served to them by the *bandjar* officials.

Before sunset the evil spirits had to be lured and concentrated at the great offering, the *metjaru,* then cast out by the powerful spells of the priests of the village. Facing towards *kangin,* the East of Den Pasar, were tall altars filled with offerings: one for the Sun and for the Trinity (*sanggah agung*), one for the ancestors, and a third for the great *kalas,* the evil gods. In the centre of the ground an elaborate conglomeration of objects was arranged: food of all sorts, every kind of strong drink, money and house utensils, hundreds of containers of banana leaf with a sample of every seed and fruit that grew on the island, and a piece of the flesh of every wild and domestic animal in Bali (a small piece of dried tiger flesh was pointed out); all arranged in the shape of an eight-pointed star representing the Rose of the Winds, the whole surrounded by a low fence of woven palm-leaf.

The demons were thus lured to the great offering and then expelled from the village by the curses of the priests. The Regent of Badung joined in the prayers with his entire family, kneeling in front of the Sun-altar and making reverences while the nine priests rang bells and chanted formulas. When they finished, "new fire" and holy water were given by the priests to the heads of each *bandjar,* and the poor were allowed to loot the offerings for money and other useful objects. Firecrackers exploded in every direction and all the *kulkuls* in Den Pasar were beaten furiously, the populace ran all over town in groups, often with their faces and bodies painted, carrying torches on the end of long poles, beating drums, gongs, tin cans or anything that made a noise, yelling at the top of their lungs: "*Megedí, megedí!* Get out! Get out!"—beating the trees and the ground, to scare away the unsuspecting *butas* who had assembled to partake of the offerings.

The following day, *nyepí,* was supposed to be one of absolute stillness, a day when no fires, no sexual intercourse, and no work of any sort were permitted.

Source: *Island of Bali* by Miguel Covarrubias. New York: Alfred A. Knopf, 1956, pp. 277-282.

Egypt

Shem al Nessim

First day of spring in Egypt

Although all the Moslem holidays are observed in Egypt, one day is celebrated by everyone of every religion. This is Shem al Nessim, March 21, the first day of spring. On this day every family goes on a picnic—perhaps a trip to a beach on the Mediterranean Sea or the Red Sea, or an excursion up the Nile. Traditional foods for the picnic are dried fish and kidney beans. In the villages the storyteller comes with tales for the children. This is a day for everyone to have fun, the grownups talking and dancing, the children playing games and singing.

Source: *Hi Neighbor. Book 5.* New York: Hastings House, 1962, p. 62.

Japan

Higan/Shumbum-No-Hi

A day to honor ancestors

This is one of two Higan, celebrated at the spring and fall equinoxes. Ancestors are honored on these days, graves are visited and cleaned, and food offerings are made. *O-hagi,* rice balls covered with sweet bean paste, and sushi are offered. *Higan* means "other shore," and the entire week during the vernal equinox is called *higan.*

Okinawa

Offerings at the spring equinox

Buddhist holiday, *higan,* celebrating the spring equinox. Here it is a home festival of thanksgiving. Barley (*ōmugi*) or barley cakes with brown sugar are offered with prayers for continued good fortune. Other grains, such as rice, millet (*awa*) may be offered, though the cakes (*mugimochi*) are of barley. In Matsuda, this is not a home ceremony. An offering of white rice cakes is made by the village head man, with the assistance of lower orders of the former priestess system, at the site of the village patron deity.

Source: *Studies of Okinawan Village Life* by Clarence J. Clacken. Scientific Investigations in the Ryukyu Islands (SIRI). Report no. 4. Washington, D.C.: Pacific Science Board Council, 1953, p. 323. (Source says the celebration is held on the 15th day of the 2nd moon.)

Circa March 21 and Thirteen Days Thereafter

Navrouz

A pre-Islamic holiday whose founding is attributed to the mythical King Djemchid, Navrouz is a thirteen-day celebration beginning March 21, the day when the sun enters Aries.

Afghanistan

Nauroz

New Year or Farmer's Day

The New Year celebrations include animal shows and agricultural fairs throughout the country. The day, an official state holiday, is sometimes called "Farmer's Day."

New Year's Day in Afghanistan

In Afghanistan this is New Year's Day, the first day of the Afghan calendar. It is also the first day of spring and Farmers Day. Farm fairs are held throughout the country as a celebration of life.

In the provinces, farmers decorate their cows with paper flowers and garlands and sometimes paint their hides in bright designs.

In village homes the women prepare special food. Because there is no fresh fruit at this time of year, a favorite dessert is made of dried fruits, soaked to softness, and nuts and almonds. They also make a kind of fancy cookie which they share with friends and villagers.

In the Kabul area, farmers come into the city from the surrounding countryside for the annual agricultural fair. Wearing turbans, long shirts, vests, flowing trousers, and shawls slung over their shoulders, they bring their sheep, cattle and horses to be exhibited.

The minister of agriculture and government officials give opening speeches at the fairgrounds and announce the program for the day. Excitement runs high and competition is keen as the exhibits are judged and prizes are awarded.

Then the crowds break up to celebrate. Some go to the bazaars. Others fly kites they have made—gay kites of colored paper, geometric patterns with cut-outs of birds and butterflies. As the kites go aloft, they are cleverly maneuvered to fight one another, and people watching make bets on the winners.

Source: *Celebrations: Asia and the Pacific* by Gene Sawyer. Honolulu: Friends of the East-West Center, 1978, p. 21.

India (Parsi)

Jamshed Navroz

A festival observed by the Parsis in India.

Iran

No Ruz in Teheran

The sabzeh is a plate of wheat or barley seeds that germinate in water. Already each green shoot was about three inches tall. Mother had tied a pink ribbon around the growing grain to make it specially festive. It is an old tradition that as these grains germinate and grow they absorb all of the tensions, the troubles, the unhappiness of the family in the home. "We do not need a sabzeh; there is no unhappiness here," I told her, but she knew from the shine in my eyes that I was happy to follow every tradition.

"We will even have bonfires in the courtyard. That's my secret," Sina said. I grabbed him up and kissed him. It seemed that in the few months I had been away he had changed from a baby to a little boy with all of the words that he needed for grown-up conversation.

The Wednesday before No Ruz, Mohsen's boy brought the faggots for the three small bonfires, and as soon as it was dark the fires were lighted in the courtyard. It is traditional to jump over these fires—every member of the family should jump—and as we jump we say a verse which does not translate into a verse at all.

> "My yellowness [sickness] to you,
> Your redness [health] to me."

With much laughter and romping I put Nassim and Sina to bed, then rejoined the family for the booming of the cannon that would announce the vernal equinox at the exact second. Here were all the members of my family who lived in Teheran. But Shapoor was still in America. If only Shapoor were here the circle would be complete.

Directly after the roar of the cannon Mother, in the traditional way, took the Koran out of the house and brought it in again.

The Koran must come into the house before any guest in the New Year. This is a symbol of the place of God in the home. Many go to the mosque to pray when the cannon sounds; others, like my mother, find a quiet spot in the home.

An so it was No Ruz, a time for gift giving like Christmas in the West. For everyone there is some gift. First the servants must be remembered. In Iran we employ servants for small wages, but we are responsible for all of their needs—every piece of clothing, every pair of shoes, every haircut. No Ruz is a good time for giving a new suit and a pair of two-toned shoes to Ramazan, a dress of figured rayon and a new black chadar to Nannie. These they had taken in a package to Sarbandan. For Nassim and Sina and Mohsen's children there were toys, and for the grownups perhaps a piece of jewelry, some delicate soap, some perfume, a potted plant or cut flowers. All day long there will be guests and for each of these guests there should be a gift.

On the carpet in Mohsen's salon a beautiful banquet cloth was spread. On the cloth were seven foods beginning with S: vinegar, garlic, sumac, apple, jujube fruit, smoked fish and olives; a sweet pudding made of wheat, and the sabzeh. There must be a bowl of goldfish—not to be eaten—silver, a mirror, a jar of rosewater, a lamp, a Koran, a bowl of hard-boiled eggs, yogurt and cheese.

On the eighth day after No Ruz the men always return to their work. . . . The thirteenth day after No Ruz is Sizdah-Bedar (thirteenth day out) and everybody including the Shah goes on a picnic.

Source: *A Wall and Three Willows* by Najmeh Najafi and Helen Hinckley. New York: Harper & Row, 1967, pp. 85-88.

Door-to-door visiting and a bonfire at New Year

. . . The children, even the older boys and girls in Persia, go out at New Year's as American children do at Halloween, asking from door to door for gifts. We would not turn any of these away.

On the last Wednesday of the year a big outdoor fire is built. It is an ancient custom to burn the old willow roofs at this time and to weave new roofs for the houses. Perhaps this is a tradition from the time of Zoroaster, who taught that fire is the symbol of all good.

Sprouting the No Ruz wheat cake

In each home the mother has been making a strange cake. This is not an ordinary cake for eating. It is uncooked and in it are many whole grains of wheat. The cake is kept moist and the wheat sprouts and soon the cake becomes a beautiful green thing. In many homes there is a layer of the cake for each member of the family and the children watch this sprouting of wheat on their own layer. On the thirteenth day of the New Year the family takes the cake out into the fields and throws it away. With it go all the bad feelings, all the fussing and fighting and quarreling.

Everybody is in the fields on this day; it is bad luck to stay in the home, so the village is empty. The girls swing in rope swings hung from the old cherry trees. They play singing games—"Uncle, Who keeps the Bread?"—hop tag, and a dozen others. The boys, from five to fifty, play the rowdy game of alak-do-lak.

Source: *Reveille for a Persian Village* by Najmeh Najafi and Helen Hinckley. New York: Harper, 1958, p. 197-198.

Iraq

No Ruz

This is a national holiday in Iraq.

Kashmir

Nav Roz

Kashmiri New Year's festivities

The Nav Roz enjoined with water festival is celebrated in the months of Chaitra-Vaisakha (March-April) in the happy valley of Kashmir. It continues from March to May, but it remains in full swing in April and the middle of May. It starts when the first almond blooms appear. People gather in the almond orchards near the picturesque Dal Lake and enjoy themselves in various ways. Singing and merry-making continues all through. The Vaisakhi day is observed in the famous Mughal Gardens on April 15. It is the New Year's Day for the Kashmiris.

Source: *The Festivals of India* by Brijendra Nath Sharma. New Delhi: Abhinav, 1978, p. 77.

For more on Navrouz see: *Persian Beliefs and Customs* by Henri Masse. New Haven: Human Relations Area Files. Translated by Charles A. Messner from *Croyances et coutumes persanes*. Paris: Librarie orientale et americaine, 1938, pp. 138-155.

March 25

Day of the Annunciation

This is the day, nine months before Christmas, on which the Archangel Gabriel revealed to Mary that she would bear the Christ.

Great Britain

Lady Day

Lady Day as the first day of the year

Around the 12th century Lady Day became regarded as the first day of the year, replacing the Roman January 1. By the 17th century most of Europe reverted to the January New Year's Day, but England did not officially change to January until 1752. This day, however, remained an important Quarter Day, a day on which rents were paid and employees hired and fired.

Source: *The Customs and Ceremonies of Britain* by Charles Kightly. London: Thames & Hudson, 1986, p. 150.

Greece

An independence day and a spring festival

On March 25 the swallows return from the South and children take off their ''March-thread,'' which has been worn on the wrist, and hang it on a tree for the swallows. In Crete shepherds take their sheep to the mountain pastures on this day.

This is also a national celebration of independence. March 25, 1821 was the date on which Germanos, Bishop of Patras, raised the flag of the Greek Revolution against Turkish rule.

Source: *Greek Calendar Customs* by George A. Megas. Athens: B. & M. Rhodis, 1963, p. 86.

Sweden

Varfrudagen

Waffles on Lady's Day

Feast of the Annunciation, March 25, was called ''*Varfrudagen*'' in Sweden, literally ''Our Lady's Day.'' The common pronunciation became ''*vafferdagen.*'' Along the way it turned into ''*vaffeldagen*'' (''waffle day'') and it became customary to eat waffles on that day! This explains the origin of the heart-shaped waffle irons you see in Scandinavian gift stores; the waffles were to commemorate the heart of the Virgin Mary.

Source: *Notes from a Scandinavian Parlor* by Florence Ekstrand. Seattle: Welcome Press, 1984, p. 82.

Moveable: March 22-April 25

Easter and Holy Week

Easter falls on the Sunday after the first full moon on or following the vernal equinox. It commemorates the Resurrection of Jesus. On Maundy Thursday, the Thursday before Easter, Christ's last supper with his disciples is remembered. On Good Friday, the Friday before Easter, his crucifixion is mourned. Easter Sunday dawn is greeted with joy, as this day celebrates Christ's resurrection from the tomb. In some countries the holiday continues on the Monday after Easter and into the following week.

Albania

Egg cracking among Albanian Orthodox Christians and Moslems

In egg-cracking games it was customary for the younger friend or relative to offer his egg with the pointed end up. The older person struck the egg with his own egg, saying, "Christ is risen." The reply: "He is risen indeed." In prerevolutionary Albania both Moslems and Christians played at the egg-tapping game.

Source: *An Egg at Easter: A Folklore Study* by Venetia Newell. Bloomington: Indiana Univ. Press, 1971, p. 346.

Armenia

Easter Monday in pre-1914 Armenia

Villagers took food to the cemetery on Easter Monday. There they offered prayers and partook of the food or left some for the poor.

Source: *Armenian Village Life before 1914* by Susie Hoogasian Villa and Mary Kilbourne Matossian. Detroit: Wayne State Univ., 1982, p. 139.

Easter greetings and egg fighting

In the spring, we fast for forty days before Easter, during which time we strictly abstain from meat and fish.

On the evening preceding Easter morning, we break our fasts. It is a great day of feasting, and on this occasion we prepare elaborate meals. On Easter morning we go to church and following an Easter dinner, greetings are exchanged after the fashion of Christmas celebration. The visitor greets the host saying, "Christ has risen from the dead!" To which the host replies, "Blessed be the resurrection of Christ!" After the greetings are over, the people gather in an open place where wrestling and *djirit* games are held.

The great pastime on Easter day is "egg-fighting." There are hard-boiled-egg sellers in the amusement place. Two young men buy a dozen or more of these vari-colored eggs, place them in a row, squat on the ground, then each takes an egg from one end, with which they begin the fight. That one who holds in his hand the last unbroken egg wins and collects the entire dozen. I have seen men carry home a whole basketful of eggs in triumph.

Source: *When I Was a Boy in Armenia* by Manoog Der Alexanian. Boston: Lothrop, Lee & Shepard Co., 1926, pp. 119-120.

Austria

The Easter breakfast in an Austrian family

Following a custom going back to the tenth century, all the kinds of food that were forbidden during the weeks of Lent are arranged in baskets and the Church has a special blessing to be pronounced on this food on Easter morning by the priest—the meat and eggs and butter, salt and Easter bread. We remember how in small country churches these baskets would be placed on the Communion rail, and how in larger communities the people would hold them in their arms while the priest, after pronouncing the blessing, would go down the aisle sprinkling holy water over the food.

This is what singles out the Easter breakfast from among all other meals of the year—that we partake of this solemnly blessed food. Ham and Easter bread and colored eggs and many, many flowers and pussy willows and silken ribbons give the table a festive look. Artistically painted eggs are usually kept by the owners throughout the year, but the simply colored eggs are now used for "*Eierpecken.*" Around the table everyone takes an egg in hand, and now, by two's, they try to "peck" the other one's egg first. The one who indents the other's egg, while his own remains uncracked, harvests the cracked egg. The one who finally has the most is hailed as victor.

Boellerschiessen

In the old country all the big feasts, but especially Easter, are accompanied by "*Boellerschiessen.*" The young men use old fashioned heavy rifles, and particularly in mountainous parts of the country where the echo takes up those cannon-like detonations, they add tremendously to the festive character of the day.

Easter bonfires

And there's still another thing—the Easter fire. On all the heights and summits innumerable bonfires are lit in honor of the Risen Lord.

Visiting the sick on Easter Monday

For Easter Monday there is an old custom, still very much alive in the old country, which might well be duplicated here, even though Easter Monday is not generally a holiday, as it is in Europe. In honor of the Gospel of the day, which tells of the two disciples who went to Emmaus and met Our Lord on the way, Easter Monday became a visiting day. Wherever there are old or sick people, they are visited by young and old.

Source: *Around the Year with the Trapp Family* by Maria Augusta Trapp. New York: Pantheon, 1955, pp. 141-142.

Belgium

Zaterdag Voor Paschen

Holy Saturday egg-hunting and holy-water-for-eggs exchange

Holy Saturday is especially a children's day in Condroz. Although the restrictions of Lent lie lightly on them, they are the ones who celebrate relaxation of the restrictions. This, and not Easter, is the day for hunting eggs, colored or otherwise. The boys parade the village chanting:

Walloon	*English*
Taratata	Taratata
Cwèrème è va	Lent goes away
Tcharnal rivint	Meat-eating returns
Voci l'bon timps	Here are good times
Cakans les ous	Let's thump eggs
Cwèrème èst foû	Lent is dead

Tcharnal or *charnal* is an old word which has disappeared from standard French, but which in Old French refers to a piece of meat. A near-by village has corrupted this chant to *Tchalmange* which in itself is a corruption of *Challemaine,* indicating that it is Charlemagne who has returned. It is difficult for an American to appreciate the living reality of this first citizen of Liege in Walloon folklore.

The boys proceed from house to house demanding a fee for chasing Lent away, usually in the form of eggs, preferably a quarter-dozen from each housewife. Much to the disgust of the clergy, this egg fee is being replaced by a payment in money, sometimes as much as twenty francs. Thus, the simplicity of a medieval tension-release festival is being altered into the "trick or treat" highwaymanship of juvenile American Halloween.

When the priest begins the *Gloria in Excelsis* for Mass on Holy Saturday, the beadle of the church rings the great bell, and the choir men chime the smaller one to welcome the return from Rome. This is a signal for the small children to rush to the yards and gardens to hunt eggs. The older ones play a game called *cakan* (cocogne) wherein the players each grasp an egg firmly in their closed hands and knock each other's eggs. The one who cracks his opponent's egg without spoiling his own wins.

The choir and altar boys are permitted to form teams of four or more to carry holy water to the households. The priest blesses a great deal of water on Saturday morning as he will hold public baptism that afternoon. One boy carries a milk can of holy water, a second a measuring vessel, a third two large baskets swing from his shoulders by a yoke for the receipt of gifts, and a fourth a dinner bell which he rings from house to house. The housewives greet them at the door, receive a gift of holy water for the family stoops and, in return, make a present of eggs to the boys. In some parishes this present has likewise degenerated into a cash payment, but the curé of Château-Gérard so modern in many ways, will have none of this. He insists that there is no payment due for holy water and that cash destroys the original idea, the exchange of blessings. The rounds of the parish being accomplished, the boys bring their gifts to the curé, or some other trusted person, who divides the gifts among the boys, the older boys receiving more than the younger. Some curés risk their juvenile popularity by making this a disciplinary occasion, keeping out an egg otherwise due to a chorister or altar boy for each time he has been inexcusably absent or tardy for Sunday Mass.

Source: *Chateau-Gerard: The Life and Times of a Walloon Village* by Harry Hulbert Turney-High. Columbia: Univ. of South Carolina Press, 1953, pp. 254-255.

Easter in Belgium, c. 1910

During the Easter holdays the weather was better, and we could play outside. On Good Friday the church-bells and the chimes were never rung, and we were told that the bells had gone to Rome and would return next morning with the Easter eggs. We were up early Saturday morning, making little nests of hay, which we hid about the garden between bushes and in the flower-beds.

Then while we had breakfast, Father or Mother would go into the garden and put the colored eggs and also chocolate and sugar eggs in the nests. And when at eight o'clock the church-bells rang, we would all cry out: "The church-bells have returned from Rome! The church-bells have come back!"

And I would rush to the garden and look for my little nest, and find the eggs, and shout for joy! Everywhere the children were on the street with their nests of Easter eggs, showing and comparing their treasures. The richer people gave their children big chocolate eggs filled with smaller sugar eggs; the poorer people gave hen's eggs which the mothers had colored gold and red and blue, but all the children were equally happy and glad that day.

Source: *When I Was a Boy in Belgium* by Robert Jonckheere. Boston: Lothrop, Lee & Shepard Co., 1915, pp. 42-43.

Belgium (Wallonia)

Church bells and rattles

Throughout the Roman Catholic world the church bells cease to ring on Holy, or Maundy, Thursday. In Château-Gérard and neighboring villages the faithful are summoned to church by young boys, usually the altar servers, creating a fearful din with wooden rattles or, in the American term, "rackets." These are the machines with thin and resonant strips of wood sounded by wooden rachets over their tongues—the origin of the identical instruments distributed to American night club patrons in order that they may make noise on New Year's Eve. These noisemakers may vary in Wallonia from a half-foot in length to more than two, and are either private property of the boys' families and kept in the attic during the rest of the year, or belong to the parish.

At one time the altar boys played their rattles through the village, but today they stand on the porch of the Templar church rattling and chanting the following at the time the bells would normally be rung:

Walloon	*French*	*English*
A messe, a messe	A la messe, à la messe	To mass, to mass
Po l' prumi coûp	Pour le premier coup	For the first stroke

And a quarter of an hour later:

Au salut, au salut	Au salut, au salut	Hail, hail
Po l' dérin coûp	Pour le dernier coup	For the last stroke

The young children are told that the bells cannot ring because on Holy Thursday they fly to Rome to be blessed by the Pope, to fly back to their own parishes on Holy Saturday. The youngsters strain their eyes on that day, trying to see the bells in flight, and many a distant bird is mistaken for the bells of the neighboring parish. One faraway swallow caused a child to cry out, "Man! dj'a vèyu passer ine clôtche!" The children are never told the truth about the bells until they discover the gentle deception for themselves.

Selling holy bread

A very general practice throughout Wallonia, including Château-Gérard, is for the clergy to give young children a certain amount of the round, thin wafers used as the priest's host at Mass, to sell at the church doors on Maundy, or Holy Thursday, the anniversary of the institution of the Holy Communion. Whatever money the children collect is given to the clergy to distribute to the parish's most needy families. The lay folk who buy these wafers take them home and nail them over their front doors to ward off evil.

Source: *Chateau-Gerard: The Life and Times of a Walloon Village* by Harry Holbert Turney-High. Columbia: Univ. of South Carolina Press, 1953, pp. 254-259.

Bermuda

Good Friday kite-flying

Children compete in kite-flying on Good Friday. According to tradition, a teacher once explained Christ's Ascension to Heaven by flying a kite and cutting the string. Children still fly kites on Good Friday to remember this.

The "Codfish and Banana Breakfast"

Easter Breakfast is known as the "Codfish and Banana Breakfast." Salted cod is soaked overnight, then strained on Easter Morning and boiled with small, whole potatoes. It is served with olive oil and mayonnaise topping. Sliced bananas complement the meal.

Source: *Easter the World Over* by Priscilla Sawyer Lord and Daniel J. Foley. Philadelphia: Chilton, 1971, pp. 197-198.

Bohemia

Easter in Bohemia, c. 1913

Not too long after the same routine was on schedule for spring house-cleaning, painting and getting ready for Easter in general. Large drawers were filled to capacity with all kinds of homemade cookies and cakes.

Baskets with hardboiled hand-painted eggs stood ready in a cool pantry for the big celebrations on Easter Sunday and Monday. Everything was ready for the two big days, including new clothes and shoes. But this was only Green Thursday and the time moved much too slowly for us young people. We went to the ancient St. Peter's Cathedral in the afternoon and watched the ceremony of the feet washing.

On Friday, we again went to church to see the tomb of our Saviour. In a large cavelike niche made of rocks, lay the body of Christ, so real to life. The grave was illuminated, but there was a boulder in front of the entrance. Two soldiers stood on each side of the famous grave, like stone statues and were relieved every hour.

Stuffed goose or pigeons or both, baked ham and pork roast were the types of meat selected for Easter. A fifteen-inch-long spongecake lamb graced our dinner table, and it looked so sweet that it was too bad to cut into it.

After the lamb had been baked to a medium brown, Mother used coffee beans for the lamb's eyes, then frosted the whole cake-animal and strew shredded coconut onto the still wet frosting. Next, she fastened a tiny silver bell onto a pink ribbon and tied it about the lamb's neck and then stuck the stem of a daisy through its mouth to give the impression that it was eating the flower.

Breakfast had to be eaten on the jump in the forenoon, because of the old tradition of the willow whip. The willow whip is made of several thin switches braided together and tied at intervals with different colored ribbons.

It was on this day of the year that the boys jumped out of their beds early in the morning without being called several times. Taking their fancy switches, they called on all the girls in the neighborhood to wish them a ''Happy Easter''. The switch was used to persuade the girls to give the boys some of their Easter eggs and sweets. Then everyone went to church to enjoy Easter services. We exchanged gifts in the afternoon and then came the elaborately prepared dinner. On Easter Monday it was turnabout and the girls could spank the boys, but there were hardly any of these creatures to be found! We got even with them anyway, when their stomachs told them to come out from their hiding places.

Source: *Echoing Memories* by Anna J. F. Humula. Boston: Christopher Publishing House, 1963, pp. 89-91. (Childhood in Jinec Czenkov, Czechoslovakia.)

Costa Rica

A living procession

As the image of Christ is carried through the streets, living participants perform acts for the Christ. A girl representing the Samaritan woman at the well offers water to the statue. Mary Magdalene anoints the statue's feet with oil, and Veronica wipes His brow with a white cloth. In the afternoon another procession takes place. This time little angels, depicted by girls from 2 to 7 years of age, are carried aloft on a platform. The vacant cross, Veronica, Mary Magdalene, and the Samaritan woman are also carried on platforms.

Source: *Fiesta Time in Latin America* by Jean Milne. Los Angeles: The Ward Ritchie Press, 1965, p. 77.

Czechoslovakia

Egg trees, burning Judas, and drowning Smrt

In Czechoslovakia, Easter is the most joyous holiday of the year. Friends exchange eggs with the greeting ''Christ is risen'' and the reply, ''He is risen indeed.'' Flowers and eggs abound in the markets, homes and churches.

In times past, the most beautiful egg painted by the boy or girl was saved for the special best-loved person. It was very often a pre-engagement symbol. Young people on the farm carried their eggs in a basket, delivering them from farm house to farm house.

One story tells of a young man who decorated an egg tree below the window of his loved one. On Easter morning there it was, to her surprise. Trees in the yard or garden were sometimes decorated.

Another old Christian practice occurred on Easter Saturday afternoon when the village boys collected and stacked wood and placed a straw-covered cross in the center of that stack. After an evening church service, the boys would light lanterns at the Paschal Candle, hurry to the stack of wood, and set fire to the cross. They would chant, ''We are burning Judas.'' The ashes were guarded throughout the night, and in the morning were thrown into a flowing stream. Church ladies would then give decorated eggs to the one boy lucky enough to have lighted the fire in this annual observance.

Villages had egg artists, usually older people who utilized many designs and then taught them to others. Moravians placed pebbles or beads inside dried eggshells to make rattles for children. Long ago such rattles were believed to drive away evil spirits, and only recently have rattles become simply toys for children.

Inscribed eggs, a rarity in egg decorating, were fashioned by Moravians and Slovakians. Moravians threaded eggs with ribbon and displayed them on the traditional Easter Egg Tree. One custom was to adorn the tree with colored eggshells and flowers, and then young girls would parade house to house in their village. In another Moravian technique, cut-out straw pieces were glued to the eggshells to make beautiful designs or patterns. The straw pieces were either dyed or of natural color.

An old Bohemian custom involved ''Smrt,'' an effigy of ''Death.'' Numerous variations of this custom are recorded. One featured the doll burned or thrown into a running stream or river on Palm Sunday. The figure, symbolizing ''Old Woman Winter,'' might be fashioned of straw and dressed in old clothes or decorated with rags. She might have had a necklace of eggs. As she was tossed into the river, the children would sing a welcome to the arrival of spring.

Another old custom involved making willow switches to ''dust away the dreariness of winter when spring arrived.'' Then decorated eggs were presented to an individual's favorites following the ''switching.'' These customs are as numerous as the villages in Czechoslovakia.

Source: *Czechoslovak Culture: Recipes, History, and Folk Arts* by Pat Martin. Iowa City, Iowa: Penfield Press, 1989, p. 107.

Estonia

Colored eggs

In Estonia colored eggs are prepared at Whitsun also, although the lack of wild birds' eggs is not a problem here as in Finland. Domestic poultry were known here as early as the middle ages.

Source: *An Egg at Easter: A Folklore Study* by Venetia Newell. Bloomington: Indiana Univ. Press, 1971, p. 191.

Ethiopia

Fasika

Ethiopian Easter customs

Easter, or Fasika, is the last of the major feast days of the Ethiopian year and takes place about two weeks later than the Roman Catholic and Protestant Easter of the West.

Fasika is preceded by the eight-week Lenten fast, and the clergy, along with their devout parishioners, practice total abstinence from food for the last forty-eight hours, beginning with Good Friday. By early Saturday evening the churches are thronged. The special Easter service begins at midnight and ends at dawn on Sunday with the lighting of the Resurrection candles. Ethiopians do not consider that the new day begins at one stroke past midnight, but rather at daybreak. In Addis Ababa, a twenty-one gun salute announces the dawn of Easter Day.

Feasting begins with an early-morning breakfast after church and continues throughout the day, into Easter Monday, and even longer, with sheep slaughtered and many special *wats* prepared for the occasion.

Easter Sunday is rather quietly spent. Many families read from the Bible on this day and play such games as *gebeta*, a chesslike game in which stones or large beans are moved about on a wooden board with sunken cups.

Source: *Ethiopia: Land of the Lion* by Lila Perl. New York: William Morrow, 1972, pp. 75-76.

Finland

Palm Sunday switching

In East Finland, Palm Sunday is known as Virposunnuntai, Willowswitch Sunday, and Palm Saturday is known as Willowswitch Saturday. Children used to go from house to house early on Saturday morning with freshly cut willow switches, decorated with cloth streamers. They would spank the woman of the house lightly and recite, "*Virpoi, varpoi, vitsat kayvat. Tulevaks vueks tuoreeks, terveeks*" or, "Switching, switching, switches, wishing freshness and health this year." The woman of the house used a switch on her livestock in the same way, and the switches were saved, stuck in the barn ceiling, to be used the first time the cattle were driven to pasture in the new year. On Easter Sunday the children returned to collect a treat for their switching service. Eligible young girls were also switched in some areas to wish them a good marriage.

Foretelling the spring with budded branches

Willow or birch branches brought inside on this day were watched. The forest trees would bud in as many weeks as the days it took these branches to open.

Easter swings and teeter-totters

In southwest Finland, children constucted teeter-totters on Easter Morning or set up Easter swings.

Source: *Easter the World Over* by Priscilla Sawyer Lord and Daniel J. Foley. Philadelphia: Chilton, 1971, pp. 86-88.

France

Maundy Thursday hammering and Good Friday customs

On Maundy Thursday, Jeudi Saint, or Jeudi Vert (Alsace), a curious custom, differing in details, prevails in many parts of France; little wooden hammers are taken to church and benches, chairs, etc., are beaten with them; sometimes the exterior of the church; in some places this is called "tuer les Juifs"; in others it is on Good Friday that the hammering is done, and this has been skilfully diverted so as to announce the services in the absence of the bells.

In Alsace different bitter herbs used to be eaten (in remembrance perhaps of the Charoseth or Jewish dish of bitter herbs); and hence apparently the name Jeudi Vert. In Abbeville *martelets*, or little planchettes with three or four hammers attached—sometimes also "crécelles" or castaquettes—were used to announce the services. This hammering, other than for the above purpose, seems very difficult to explain. The "tuer les Juifs" explanation seems unlikely. In Picardy children chant the hours of services and are rewarded with eggs. In Anjou on Good Friday at three o'clock millers stopped their mills, leaving the sails up, in a sort of mourning. No animal must be killed on Good Friday, and no washing is done in some parts (Franche-Comté, e.g.) in the latter half of the week. Holy-water stoups will be found empty early on Easter Eve. The water is blessed in the morning.

Source: *A Guide to French Fetes* by E. I. Robson. London: Methuen, 1930, p. 77.

Easter Sunday in Besançon, c. 1900

Following the legend, the bells of all the churches come back on Easter Day from Rome where they have gone on Good Friday to be blessed by the Pope. All children fancy that they have seen them flying back to their beloved home belfry.

"Oh, I saw the bells of St. Maurice, all dressed up in a thin blue veil; the last one caught her train in the weathercock, as it came flying by the steeple," the little peasants tell each other as they listen, face upwards, to the vibrant calling of the bells, filling up the whole blue sky.

Everywhere the mountain-springs and the birds sing together, and flowers by the million embroider the old roads and young hedges. All the country churches are in flower; the fields, full of promising young wheat, seem to await the Easter benediction.

The solemn procession walks slowly out of the little portico, banners float in the spring breeze, litanies—sung by the villagers—rise in the soft air, and the flame of the long candles borne by them flicker in the sunlight. Little choir-boys in lace and red robes swing incense-burners in front of the old priest carrying the Host, walking under a canopy. His hieratic gestures of benediction bless the fields, the trees, the houses, the flocks, the people. Young girls, carrying baskets full of spring flowers, strew them gracefully along the road as the Host passes, as so many promises for a good harvest. Nature is so young, so generous, that all hopes are renewed afresh.

Source: *When I Was a Girl in France* by Georgette Beuret. Boston: Lothrop, Lee & Shepard Co., 1916, pp. 170-172.

Germany

The Easter Hare

The Easter Hare (Osterhase) leaves eggs and a life-size chocolate version of himself on Easter Morning. Children may make nests of grass or straw for him to leave his eggs in.

Who brings the eggs?

In Upper Bavaria it is the cockerel who brings the eggs. In Franconia and Thuringia the fox brings them; in Hanover it is the cuckoo; and in Bad Salzungen in Hess, the crane.

Color of first egg found brings good or bad luck

If the first egg found is blue, this is unlucky; if it is red, three days of good luck will follow.

Egg presents

Blown eggs with messages inside promising to do some task, such as polishing the father's shoes or doing the dishes, may be given to parents. Small presents may also be given to friends inside manufactured cardboard Easter Eggs that open to reveal the gift.

Egg decorations

Blown eggs are decorated and hung on forsythia branches or a small "Easter Tree." They may be stuck on sticks, decorated with ribbons, and arranged in a vase with an Easter bird made of an eggshell and paper as the centerpiece, or they may be strung in chains and hung from branches.

Well dressing

In the Franconian mountains wells are dressed at Easter, decorated with pine and bunting, and cleaned for the occasion. Water taken from the well before dawn on Easter Sunday may be sprinkled over the field for a good harvest.

Source: *German Festivals and Customs* by Jennifer M. Russ. London: Oswald Wolff, 1982, p. 45-55.

German egg tree customs

A branch hung with blown egg shells, or tiny wooden eggs is popular in many German homes. At Bastei, children hang coloured shells or roots on a fruit tree in the garden. In Schandau people plant a birch trunk in the ground near the house and decorate it. In Rathmannsdorf, young boys and girls walked round the Easter tree on Easter night. They presented the tree to the Easter Virgin, who gave them cake and coffee.

Source: *An Egg at Easter: A Folklore Study* by Venetia Newell. Bloomington: Indiana Univ. Press, 1971, pp. 308-309.

Good Friday superstitions

Seeds sown on Good Friday will thrive. Hair cut on Good Friday will grow thick and luxuriant. The water in which a hot iron has been cooled on Good Friday will cure warts. If it rains on Good Friday the whole year is blessed.

Source: *German Festivals and Customs* by Jennifer M. Russ. London: Oswald Wolff, 1982, p. 48.

Great Britain

Egg rolling

Egg rolling is most popular in northern Britain. Hard-boiled eggs are rolled down a hill. Customs differ; the winner's egg may be the one that rolls the farthest, survives the most rolls, or is rolled between two pegs. In several places egg rolling is an Easter Monday sport. Popular egg rollings take place at Arthur's Seat in Edinburgh, at the castle moat at Penrith, Cumbria, Bunker's Hill, Derby, and Avenham Park in Preston, Lancashire.

Natural dyes

Eggs may be dyed with onion skins (golden brown), furze-blossom (yellow), pasqueflower (bright green), cochineal (red), or with a colored cloth.

Pace egging

Paste (Pasche = Easter) or Pace Egging was once popular in northern England and Scotland. As late as World War II the customs survived in parts of Cheshire. Young men would tour, chanting and performing a Pace = Egg Play, a variation of a mumming play. They would be given money and drinks. Children would tour for eggs. A Cheshire chant follows: Here come three jovie lads all in a row. We've come a pace eggin', we hope you'll prove kind. Prove kind, prove kind, with your eggs and small beer. We hope you'll remember it's pace eggin' time.

Source: *Customs and Ceremonies of Great Britain* by Charles Kightly. London: Thames and Hudson, 1986, pp. 106-107.

Hot cross buns on Good Friday

Good Friday. Called in the early Church *The Pasch of the Cross.* On this day all penitents were absolved, and it was kept throughout Europe as a day of fasting and mourning, "the day that the Bridegroom is taken from them," for this is the anniversary of the Crucifixion. It was originally called "Good" to distinguish it from other Fridays, whose luck would be notoriously bad; but this idea has been much obscured, and most people regard Good Friday as a day of very ill-omen.

So the bread baked on Good Friday would be marked by cautious housewives with a cross, "to keep away the Devil," and there is a lingering superstition that a hot-cross bun hung up in a house will ensure against ill-luck till Good Friday comes again.

In an old tavern in Chelsea until lately, there was quite a collection of old Good Friday buns kept in a wire basket hanging from the ceiling. One had been added every Good Friday for many years running, to bring good luck to the house. They were black and hard with age and dust.

In some farmhouses the Good Friday cake hung on the rack till next Good Friday, and a little was supposed to be beneficial to sick cows. To preserve friendship, two friends broke a bun within the church doors, and if they kept the halves they could preserve their friendship.

On Good Friday, herb pudding was eaten formerly, in which leaves of the Passion dock appear as an essential element. It was the day for the annual meeting of the witches.

Innumerable other curious customs connect themselves with Good Friday.

Village lads hunted the squirrel, on account of the legend that Judas Iscariot was changed into that animal!

Source: *Festivals, Holy Days, and Saints' Days* by Ethel L. Urlin. London: Simpkin, Marshall, Hamilton, Kent. Reprint. Detroit: Gale Research, 1979, pp. 62-63.

Matching the sun dance on Easter morning

Another custom inspired by religion was that of rising before dawn on Easter Day and climbing a hill to see the rising sun dance in the sky in joy at the Resurrection; this was quite commonly done in Shropshire and Herefordshire in the nineteenth century, but has now died out. In other districts, for instance round Clyro in Kilvert's time, it was held that one must look at the sun reflected in a pool, in order 'to see the sun dance and play in the water, and the angels who were at the Resurrection playing backwards and forwards before the sun.' This method is certainly to be preferred; the quivering surface of the water would favour one's chances of observing an effect of 'dancing' in the reflexion, and furthermore there is no risk of damage to the eyes.

Washing and baking on Good Friday

As our Blessed Lord was carrying His Cross on the way to His Crucifixion, a woman who had been washing came out of her house and threw her dirty water over the Saviour; another woman who was standing near with some freshly baked bread said to her "Why do you treat that poor man like that, one who never did you any harm?" And she gave Our Blessed Lord a loaf, which He ate, and said 'From henceforth blessed be the baker, and cursed be the washer.'

Hot Cross Buns in particular were baked on Good Friday and each marked with a cross. Some would be kept all year for good luck. They could also serve as medicine when crumbled and mixed with water. They cured intestinal disorders in men and in animals. Good Friday bread would never mold.

Pace egging and egg rolling on Easter Monday

A later generation of Cheshire children, in the Wirral between the two wars, used to go round on Easter Monday collecting pennies, but their verse still alluded to eggs:

> Please, Mrs Whiteleg.
> Please to give us an Easter egg.
> If you won't give us an Easter egg,
> Your hens will lay all addled eggs,
> And your cocks lay all stones.

Egg rolling could also take place on Easter Monday instead of on Easter Sunday. Sometimes pegs were placed at the foot of the hill and the colored hard-boiled eggs had to pass between them without smashing.

Source: *The Folklore of the Welsh Border* by Jacqueline Simpson. Totowa, New Jersey, 1976, pp. 144-146.

Hunting the Easter Hare

The custom of eating the Easter hare is classed by Mr. Elton among those ceremonies which bear most openly the marks of their original paganism. It is best known in Pomerania, where hares are caught at Easter-tide to provide a public meal. In other parts of Germany there are traces of a similar tradition. Thus, the children in South Germany are told that a hare lays the Pasche eggs, and a nest is made for the hare to lay them in; and it is customary in many parts of the country "to place a figure of the hare among the Easter eggs, when given as a present, either a hare in a basket of eggs, or a small figure of a hare in one of the fancy eggs". The same object is common on Easter cards.

In England there are a few indications of the same kind. "It would appear", writes Mr. James Britten, "that the hare was at one time in some way associated with Easter observance in this country"; and he quotes an entry from the Calendar of State Papers (Domestic Series), which is as follows:

"1620, April 2. Thos Fulnety solicits the permission of Lord Zouch, Lord Warden of the Cinque Ports, to kill a hare on Good Friday, as huntsmen say that those who have not a hare against Easter must eat a red herring."

At Coleshill, in Warwickshire, if the young men of the parish can catch a hare, and bring it to the parson before 10 o'clock on Easter Monday, the parson is bound to give them a calf's head and a hundred of eggs for their breakfast, and a groat in money.

But the most complete instances of Easter-hare ritual surviving in this country are furnished by two striking customs, both of which were once observed on Easter Monday in the county of Leicester, and one of which is still celebrated.

The custom of Hunting the Easter Hare at Leicester is thus described in Throsby's History of the town:

"It had long been customary on Easter Monday for the Mayor and his brethren, in their scarlet gowns, attended by their proper officers, in form, to go to a certain close, called Black-Annis' Bower Close, parcel of, or bordering upon, Leicester Forest, to see the diversion of hunting, or rather the trailing of a cat before a pack of hounds; a custom perhaps originating out of a claim to the royalty of the forest. Hither, on a fair day, resorted the young and old, and those of all denominations. In the greatest harmony the Spring was welcomed. The morning was spent in various amusements and athletic exercises, till a dead cat, about noon, was prepared by aniseed water for commencing the mock-hunting of the hare. In about half-an-hour, after the cat had been trailed at the tail of a horse over the grounds in zig-zag directions, the hounds were directed to the spot where the cat had been trailed from. Here the hounds gave tongue in glorious concert. The people from the various eminences who had placed themselves to behold the sight, with shouts of rapture, gave applause; the horsemen dashing after the hounds through foul passages and over fences, were emulous for taking the lead of their fellows. . . . As the cat had been trailed to the Mayor's door, through some of the principal streets, consequently the dogs and horsemen followed. After the hunt was over, the Mayor gave a handsome treat to his friends; in this manner the day ended."

This description is by an eye-witness of this old municipal custom, which began to fall into disuse about the year 1767, although traces of it lingered within recent years in an annual holiday or fair held on the Danes' Hills and the Fosse Road, on Easter Monday.

Source: "The Easter Hare" by Charles J. Billson in *Folk-Lore* III (no. IV) (Dec. 1892), pp. 441-442.

Greece

Tossing dynamite from the mountains at Easter in Kalymnos

. . . Throwing dynamite off the mountain tops announces and honors the Kalymnian who perishes tragically at sea; it is also thought the only seemly tribute to the old sponge-diver who disembarks the Athens steamer in a coffin. It is also thrown on a dare. Very much in the tradition of noise-makers everywhere else in Greece, the thunder and crack of dynamite marks the beginning of Easter. On Easter day several years ago, an accidental explosion, with the power to shatter windows of the harbor shops, killed four young men, but though local businessmen and politicians circulated pleas to stop the madness, the mourners were among the most adamant that the Easter "tradition" must continue. It still goes on.

Source: *Insight Guides: Greece*. Edited by Karen Van Dyck. Hong Kong: APA Productions, 1988, p. 77.

Easter Sunday in Castellorizo, Greece, c. 1985

On Easter Sunday, . . . services are held at the monastery, high above the town. Children carry fat candles, at the base of which they have fashioned paper ornamental cutouts to catch the drippings. The men sit on one side, the women on the other. Chants are given while the congregation chats with one another and the children run in endless circles. After the ceremony, everyone moves to the mosaicked courtyard where trays of Easter liquors are distributed while you watch the folkdancing.

Source: *The Eye and the Eyebrow: A History of Kas, Turkey and Castellorizo, Greece* by Gail Chase. Seattle: Writer's Publishing House, 1986, p. 40.

Guatemala

Holy Week enactment of Judas

In Cantel, Guatemala, where I spent the year 1953-54, Judas, or San Simón, is the patron of a cult organization sponsored by the traditional religious figures. He is permanently ensconced in the house of the brotherhood of San Buenaventura. The caricature of a Ladino in a black wool suit, felt hat, and Ladino shoes, is embellished with a wooden mask equipped with a pair of sunglasses. A rubber stomach is attached to a tube at his mouth to receive contributions of liquor. He visits all of the shops and is given donations of $5 by the owners to ensure luck in their commercial operations throughout the year. After the round of the shops, he is put in the local jail on the premise that his stay will attract many drunks and result in fines for the town. On the following day, he is ceremonially seated on the bandstand in the plaza in a chair with a table set before him. Donations of cooked food are placed before him by people who wish to succeed in their negotiations throughout the year.

In their icon of Judas, the Canteleños have symbolized the transaction in which Judas deceived Christ for the payment of thirty pieces of silver. In San Simón, they recognize the commercial superiority of Ladinos and cultivate his patronage in order to secure luck in business.

Source: "The Passion Play in Maya Indian Communities" by June Nash in *Comparative Studies in Society and History,* 10 (3) (1968), 318-327.

Iran

Easter in Azerbaijan

Easter comes in the spring when the land is a vast carpet of wild flowers. The festival is celebrated in the home, the orchards, and the hayfields. Joy and happiness reign supreme for a whole week. The people dress up in their best attire and pay visits. They greet each other by saying, "May your Easter be a blessing." Each day is given over to a different program. The first day of the festival is a visiting day, the second day is for running and ball-playing. The third and fourth days they match colored eggs and play games. The final day the fun reaches its climax, as all these various pleasures are enjoyed together. They play, run, dance, and the boys have wrestling matches. The young people enjoy themselves to such an extent that, for a week after they are heartbroken because the festival is over.

Source: *When I Was a Boy in Persia* by Yovel B. Mirza. Boston: Lothrop, Lee & Shepard, 1920, p. 107.

Ireland

Easter foods

. . . Easter was the occasion of yet another ceremonial meal, when veal or young lamb was eaten. In certain areas a young kid was cooked on this day, and the eating of gaily decorated Easter eggs is an old tradition which may be of pagan origin.

Source: *Life & Tradition in Rural Ireland* by Timothy P. O'Neill. London: J.M. Dent & Sons Ltd., 1977, p. 64.

Egg rolling on the Isle of Man and in Ulster

Egg rolling is traditional on the Isle of Man, and is reported from many places in Ulster, such as Lisburn, Dundrum, and Kilkeel. The Ulster eggs are colored by boiling them with whin blossom and have faces painted on them.

Source: *Lore and Language of Schoolchildren* by Peter and Iona Opie. Oxford, 1959, p. 253.

Italy

Blessing the house in Tuscany

. . . Before the Monday of Holy Week Silvana prepares for a very ancient ceremony, pre-Christian in origin. She cleans her large house from attic to kitchen, sweeping away old cobwebs from the high raftered ceilings, polishing the red-tiled floors and washing the small-paned windows to an unaccustomed glitter. The shutters are flung wide open in all the rooms on the middle floor of the house which are filled with cumbersome country wardrobes and oversized beds with bedsteads of curved decorative metal, painted with panels of violets and pansies, or carved slats of stylised roses. The mattresses of firm horsehair are turned and covered with fresh sheets of heavy cream linen scented with the fields where each week they are hung to dry. Fresh coverlets crocheted in bright wools are laid on each bed.

Next the dining-room table is laid with the best tablecloth and on it Silvana places a large bowl full of new-laid eggs, covered with a white napkin. Fresh lilac is stuffed into the glass pot under the plaster image of Jesus and the house is ready, with Silvana neat in a new headscarf and apron, to receive the visit of the parish priest, Don Franco. He starts his round with the Cerotti house and arrives early in the morning. . . .

When the priest is robed, accompanied by a young server who is also begowned, he walks through the house and sprinkles holy water in each room, blessing the house and the family as he goes. Finally the priest blesses the eggs. The small ceremony pleases Silvana and initiates a fertile new season. The official Roman Catholic attitude to this very old custom is that it reminds the individual of his own baptism and is a renewal of old vows. Years ago the priests went to all houses with their blessing but today they only visit those people who request their presence.

Source: *The Tuscan Year: Life and Food in an Italian Valley* by Elizabeth Romer. New York: Atheneum, 1985, pp. 53-54.

Jordan

Khamīs al-Amwāt (Dead Remembrance Thursday)

The Thursday after Easter is a day to visit cemeteries and give colored eggs to the children. Before World War II, a visit to the shrine of the Prophet Moses extended this into a three-day major holiday. Ziyārit al-Nabi Mūsi (Visit to the Shrine of the Prophet Moses) or al-Ziyāra (The Visit). The holiday was instituted by the Muslim warrior Saladin to counteract the huge gatherings of Christians and Jews in Jerusalem at this time of year.

Source: *Baytin: A Jordanian Village* by Abdulla M. Lutfiyya. The Hague: Mouton, 1966, pp. 61-62.

Macedonia

Holy Week in Macedonia, c. 1900

Holy Thursday. In some districts on this day, as well as on Lady Day, March 25th, the people are in the habit of hanging from the balconies and the windows of their houses red kerchiefs or sashes. On this day also the Paschal eggs are dyed. The peasant mother takes the first coloured egg and with it crosses her child's face and neck saying: "Mayest thou grow red as is this egg and strong as a stone." This egg is then placed near the icon of the Panaghia and is left there until the following year, when a new one takes its place. The red colour of the Easter eggs and of the kerchiefs mentioned above is explained by folklorists as referring to the brightness of spring. On this day they also make a kind of cakes, called from their shape ''turtle-doves'', with a clove or a grain of pepper doing duty as an eye.

Good Friday. On this day the peasants eschew all kinds of food prepared with vinegar, because, they say, it was on this day that the Jews moistened our Lord's lips with vinegar.

Holy Saturday. They are careful not to wash their heads, lest their hair should turn grey.

Easter Sunday (''Bright''). This last name corresponds to the Russian *Svyetlaya* and may be compared with our own Easter, both of which appellations suggest brightness. The Resurrection is celebrated twice. First at a midnight mass on the eve, and again about mid-day on Easter Day. The first is also called the ''Good Word.'' The gospel for the day is read out in the churchyard beneath the star-bespangled sky and is immediately followed by the hymn beginning with the words ''Christ is risen'', in which the whole congregation joins. The announcement of the ''good word'' is greeted with loud peals of fire-arms and with the sound of bells or the wood gongs still in use in some parts of the country. In the midst of this uproar the priest holds up a lighted candle and calls on the congregation to ''Come and receive light''. The faithful obey the summons with great alacrity. There is an onrush at the priest, and those who get near him first kindle their candles at the very fountain-head of light; the less fortunate, or less muscular, ones have to be content with illumination at second hand. But the result from a purely aesthetic point of view is the same. The dark night is suddenly lighted up with hundreds of small flickering flames, trembling in the hands of people anxious to escape from the fire-arms, squibs, and crackers, which boom and hiss in dangerous proximity all round them.

On the tapers secured at the cost of so much exertion, not unattended by some risk to life and limb, is set a proportionally high value. The miraculous powers attributed to these Easter tapers may be compared to those which were ascribed to the Candlemas candles in Catholic times in England. The women, on their return from church, use these tapers for the purpose of burning the bugs, in the pious hope that they will thus get rid of them for ever—a custom which agrees well with the extermination of fleas: the avowed object of the Macedonian bonfires.

The congregation having lighted their tapers turn towards the church and find the doors closed. They knock upon them chanting in chorus: ''Lift the gates, O ye rulers of ours, and ye eternal gates be lifted; for there will enter Christ, the King of glory!'' Those without reply: ''He is a Lord strong and powerful. He is a Lord mighty in war!'' Thereupon the doors are thrown open, and the congregation troop into the building, where the service is resumed.

The words ''Christ is risen'' are the signal for breaking the long fast of Lent, and many take to church a red egg and a bun which, as soon as the words are uttered, they devour with pardonable eagerness. After service the peasant mothers secretly place under their children's pillows red eggs, and when the little ones wake in the morning, they are told that this is a present brought in the dead of night by *Paschalia*, a female personification of Easter.

To the second service, which takes place in the day-time, the people go with lighted tapers, and when it is over, the congregation embrace, forgiving and forgetting mutual offences, and salute each other with the formula: ''Christ is risen,'' to which the answer is ''He is risen indeed!'', and this continues to be the regular form of greeting until Ascension day. The Easter feast lasts three days, during which visits are exchanged, the visitors being presented with a red egg. The *pièce de résistance* of the Easter banquet is a lamb roasted whole. Indeed so indispensable is this item, that it has given rise to a proverb, ''Easter without a lamb is a thing that cannot be,'' applied to those whose ambition exceeds their means.

Easter Tuesday sports

On Easter Tuesday the people resort to the open country, where the girls dance and the youths amuse themselves by shooting at the mark, wrestling, jumping, running, the throwing of heavy stones and similar sports, all possible successors to the old Greek games.

A favourite song at Easter is one beginning as follows:

''Holy Saturday is come and Holy Thursday too,
The Bright Sunday is also come with the Good Word.
A mother dresses her son and his sister girds him,
She girds him with a gold girdle, a girdle of pure gold.
They set out to participate in the sacrament, etc.''

Source: *Macedonian Folklore* by G. F. Abbott. Cambridge: Cambridge Univ. Press, 1903, pp. 36-38.

Malta

Good Friday (Public Holiday)

Processions commemorate Christ's Passion

Special church services are held in the afternoon starting at 3 p.m. Good Friday pageants are held in fourteen different towns and villages. During these pageants, a number of life-size statues depicting scenes from the passion and death of Jesus Christ are carried shoulder-high in procession along the main streets of the particular locality. Men and women personifying Biblical characters from the Old and New Testament all dressed in authentic costumes take part in the processions.

Easter Sunday

Early morning processions with the Statue of the Risen Christ are held in various towns and villages. Particularly interesting are the ones held at Vittoriosa and Cospicua. It is still customary for children to have their 'figolla' blessed by the Risen Christ during these processions. The 'figolla' is a special sweet for Easter. Two identically cut pieces of pastry are filled with marzipan and baked. The top pastry is then decorated with coloured icing sugar. The 'figolla' can take various shapes, the most popular being a lamb, a basket or a fish.

Source: "Malta & Gozo: Events Calendar '90." National Tourism Organization, 1990.

Mexico

Holy Week in Tepoztlan

Fiesta of Holy Monday and Holy Tuesday, celebrated in the parish church: These are days of great devotion. The religious associations are very active, visiting the church and barrio chapels. Many Tepoztecans choose these days for their annual confession.

Fiesta of Holy Wednesday: Rigorous fasting begins. Meat is not eaten until the Saturday of Glory. Substitute foods are beans, *huauzontle, tortas,* stuffed peppers, fish, *revoltijo,* and lentils. All work must stop through the Sunday of Resurrection. Women prepare tortillas for the rest of the week. In the evening is the vigil of the Lord, the men taking turns all through the night. Women customarily go to church in the late afternoon to pray the thirty-three Credos, one for each year of Jesus' life. It is believed that those who do this will triple their earnings during the year.

Holy Thursday: The church is full on this day. The priest dramatically describes the passion of Christ, and crying on the part of women is common. Not to do so is "to have a cold heart." In the afternoon is the ceremonial foot-washing of the apostles.

Holy Friday: This is the culminating day of Holy Week. Throughout the village there is profound quietude. No one must run or shout or use bad words, so as not to offend the Lord. The men silently drink their *ponche* together while the women, dressed in black, go to church. On this day, children are not to be struck, for "it would be striking the Lord."

Holy Saturday: At 7:00 A.M. the faithful of the village and the municipio go to the church where the priest pronounces the "Gloria in Excelsis Deo." With this all the bells, which have been silent since Wednesday, are rung, and joy spreads through the village. While the bells ring, old men trim their plants so that they will produce more, mothers snip the ends of their daughter's hair to make it grow longer, and children are struck on the legs to make them grow taller. Two or three *comparsas* are organized to dance on this day.

Easter Sunday: Everyone dresses well and goes to Mass. Sometimes the *chinelos* leap in the afternoon. People stand in little groups in the plaza, and men drink a great deal.

Source: *Life in a Mexican Village: Tepoztlan Restudied* by Oscar Lewis. Urbana: Univ. of Illinois Press, 1963, p. 460.

Holy Week in Santa Cruz Etla

Holy Week is for them a much more important celebration than Christmas. There is no work for four days. In the back alcove of the church at San Pablo there is a glass-covered coffin with a plaster model of the corpse of Jesus inside. He lies asleep, a crown of thorns on His head, blood staining His bare trunk. He seems pitiful, but the people love Him. On Good Friday, the people of both towns used to carry Him in a long parade with candles, up from the church to the Santa Cruz *municipio* and back; the bells of both schools were kept ringing for thirty-six hours, little boys tugging in shifts at the bell ropes. I am prone to wonder what has happened to this joint effort, with the one Holy Coffin, now that Santa Cruz Etla has its own church. A statue like that in a coffin must be very expensive, and Santa Cruz, taxed so hard for the completion of the church, could not hope to buy one for years. But its church is actually dedicated to the Holy Cross (the Santa Cruz) and not to a mere saint like San Pablo, and by rights the Easter parade should center in the Santa Cruz church. On Holy Saturday, the men play cards and *pelota* all day, but the women grind *mole* and chocolate, make tortillas, butcher hogs, and cook turkeys. A priest always comes to San Pablo for the five o'clock mass on Easter morning, and the rest of the day, Doña Patrocina said, is spent in eating all the good things prepared.

Source: *Santa Cruz of the Etla Hills* by Helen Miller Bailey. Gainesville: Univ. of Florida Press, 1958, pp. 124-125. (Bailey is an American teacher who spent two terms teaching in Santa Cruz Etla and made several visits over a 20-year period.)

Holy Week Judas passion play in Amatenango del Valle, Chiapas, Mexico, c. 1965

In the role of the anti-Christ in the Passion Play in Amatenango, Judas is unequivocally identified with Ladinos. His figure, made of hay stuffed into a pair of Ladino style pants, shirt and boots, with a mask tied to his head and a felt hat such as that worn only by non-Indians, is a caricature of the Ladino.

On Thursday of Holy Week, Judas is hauled up by ropes and hung from the bell tower "to show the world that he killed Christ." As he is raised aloft the mayordomos on the ground, who are assisting those up in the bell tower, jab him with long poles. In this horseplay they symbolically castrate him: I heard one mayordomo say "Merčunun" (transvestite) as one well-directed blow struck Judas. On Saturday, he is let down and given a ride on horseback around town. Formerly, riding a horse was the prerogative only of Ladinos in the department of San Cristobal Las Casas. . . . Placing Judas on a horse has possibly a rhetorical value in identifying this man as one of the hated dominant group who asserted this privilege. As he rides around town, the mayordomos solicit gifts from the people. Everyone gives fruits except the curers who donate money. This transaction may indicate an obligation they feel toward Judas as one source of their power over witchcraft-derived illnesses. The money is used to buy liquor, called "the washing of the arms and legs of our Lord Esquipulas," a reference to an origin myth which indicates that liquor was derived from the water used to bathe Christ when he was lowered from the cross. The drinking is mandatory for all the religious officials who have participated in the hanging of Judas.

The Judas figure, which was the church's symbol of the hated semite, is subverted by the Indians to appear as their enemy, the Ladino. In the acts in which he figures he symbolizes the sexual license of Ladinos with Indian women, the oppression of Indians, and the killer of Christ. In retaliation, the Indians symbolically castrate and hang him, and finally burn his body, thus dramatically vanquishing the alien in their midst. The subversive implications of these acts are not recognized by the priest. However, he prevented the ride of Judas through town during his presence because of its pagan association. The Indians rescheduled the act after his departure.

Source: ''The Passion Play in Maya Indian Communities'' by June Nash in *Comparative Studies in Society and History* 10, no. 3, 1968, pp. 318-327.

Lenten processions and Holy Week in Zinzcantan

Every Friday during Lent a procession forms inside the church of San Lorenzo and the crucified Christ image is taken in a slow circuit around the church. On the Fourth Friday, the procession is larger and goes out into the churchyard. On Monday of Holy Week the Sacristans buy after-shave lotion in San Cristóbal which they will use on Wednesday to wash the image. The washing is done by the Alcaldes and the six Holy Elders, six old men who occupy these positions on a permanent basis and whose major duty occurs during Holy Week. At noon on Good Friday the Alcaldes and the Holy Elders place the image on a large cross inside the church while the Sacristans sound wooden clappers and a choir chants Lenten hymns. From noon until 2 P.M. the church is thronged with Zinacantecos who come to bring candles and flowers and pray. Then by sundown the image is lowered and placed back in its bier. On Saturday the Mayordomos come to take down the cross and clean up the church. Easter Sunday resembles the third day of any fiesta with the Alféreces drinking and dancing their ''dance of the drunks'' in front of the church and being joined by the Mayordomos who engage in reciprocal drinking and then all go off to the houses of outgoing Alféreces for *atole*.

Source: *The Zinacantecos of Mexico: A Modern Maya Way of Life* by Evan Z. Vogt. New York: Holt, Rinehart and Winston, 1970, p. 89.

Holy Week in Mexico City

. . . Thursday is the day to visit the altars at the different churches. These are beautifully ornamented with flowers and plants and lighted by hundreds of candles and electric lights. As flowers are so cheap and bountiful there, it is easy to secure great quantities of them. Thousands of people are seen going in and out of these churches all day long, and in reality some of the altars or temples are so artistically and prettily arranged that they are wondrously beautiful.

Good Friday is a solemn day; in former years no carriages or any kind of vehicles were allowed on the streets. This is not the case at present, still even now very few persons will play the piano or go to the theatre or to a party on this day.

On Holy Saturday in the morning at ten o'clock the burning of ''Judas'' takes place. This custom is observed a great deal, and more so in Mexico City than elsewhere. Toys made of card-board representing men and animals, and having firecrackers fastened to them, are sold in great quantities to children, who suspend these figures in the court-yards or corridors of their homes. At the stroke of ten, when the church-bells are heard, the children light and burn them. In some streets the laboring classes hang up large figures, sometimes even six or seven feet high, made of straw or rags and dressed to represent men. These also contain firecrackers and have fireworks attached to them. It is needless to say that there is a deafening noise when the burning of ''Judas'' occurs, something which we when children used so much to enjoy seeing and hearing. This well-known custom of burning Judas is supposed to be done as a reminder and condemnation of the betrayal of Our Lord the Saviour by Judas, an apostle and one of His companions.

Easter is gay, and all the drives and streets are crowded with pleasure-seekers, also all the theatres and places of amusements.

Source: *When I Was a Girl in Mexico* by Mercedes Godoy. Boston: Lothrop, Lee & Shepard Co., 1919, pp. 48-50.

Moravia

Slamenky (cut wheat goose eggs)

This technique, particularly popular in Hana, Moravia, is one of the most exacting of all methods of decorating eggs. It requires a great deal of skill and patience. This form of decoration is used on eggs dyed a dark color, most frequently dark red or brown.

Using good pieces of oat, barley, or wheat straw, first remove the joints. The stalks are soaked in hot water about one hour, and then they are split lengthwise and the pith scraped away with a sharp knife. The straw is then smoothed out with an iron and then cut into squares, triangles, diamonds, and narrow strips—in fact, all the elements from which decorations can be composed.

A good, colorless glue can be used to attach the individual pieces. A tweezer and toothpicks are used in the application of the glue (toothpicks) and cut wheat pieces (tweezers).

Source: ''Slamenky (Cut Wheat Goose Eggs)'' by Sidonka Wadina-Lee in *Czechoslovak Culture* compiled by Pat Martin. Iowa City, Iowa: Penfield Press, 1989, p. 110.

The Netherlands

Easter Eve bonfires

In rural areas Easter Eve bonfires may be built. The boys chase the girls around the fires and throw soot at them. This is supposed to bring good luck.

Easter Sunday preparations

Yards are cut and bushes trimmed in preparation for Easter. Houses are cleaned and vases of flowers arranged. On the dining table sits a basket of colored Easter eggs, including chocolate eggs, and nosegays of spring flowers. *Paasbrood,* Easter bread, with raisins and currants, is served to guests.

Easter lifting

Easter lifting consists of raising a woman into the air three times. This is done between nine a.m. and noon on Easter Monday. The payment is a kiss for every man in the group that lifted her. On the next day, the women lift a man. The "lifting" seems to refer to Christ's Resurrection.

Source: *Easter the World Over* by Priscilla Sawyer Lord and Daniel J. Foley. Philadelphia: Chilton, 1971, p. 141.

Pace egging in the 19th century

In Belgium, Denmark, and The Netherlands children went from house to house singing for eggs. In Denekemp, a boy, representing Judas, led the group on Palm Sunday. The eggs were sold to buy wood for an Easter fire and raisin bread. In the southern part of The Netherlands boys sang for eggs for several days before Easter, collecting as many as possible from each housewife. If eggs were not given, rude songs were sung and the doors and windows thumped. In the Isle of Sylt in Northern Friesland the children sang; "I have an egg decked on its shell with bunting. I have an egg that says 'Good Morning,' One paste egg is nothing, two are a bit, three are a whole paste egg."

Source: *An Egg at Easter: A Folklore Study* by Venetia Newell. Bloomington: Indiana Univ. Press, 1971, pp. 374-375.

Nigeria

Easter in Calabar

Easter is greeted with great joy, particularly after the period of Lenten fasting which several churches observe. On Good Friday, life-size effigies of Judas Iscariot are paraded around the town and then publicly flogged and denounced for the betrayal of Jesus Christ. The continuity between this popular ritual known as *mbre Judas* and the traditional ceremony for purifying the town of evil spirits (ndok) has been noted. . . . This annual ritual catharsis not only serves to reinforce Christian values and mythology but also functions as a form of social criticism for dramatizing and mocking disloyalty, dishonesty and the quest for personal gain.

Source: *Religion in Calabar: The Religious Life and History of A Nigerian Town* by Roasalind I. J. Hackett. Berlin/New York: Mouton de Gruyter, 1989, p. 275.

Norway

Seeing the sun dance on Easter morning

If you are the first—the very first—to see the sunrise on Easter morning, you will see the sun dance. And if you are lucky enough to see the sun dance on Easter morning, then you will have happiness for all the rest of your life.

But it is not easy. To begin with, you can try only once: you must be all alone, and above all, you must have been born on Sunday.

Source: *Sidsel Longskirt and Solve Suntrap: Two Children of Norway* by Hans Aanrud. New York: Junior Literary Guild and John C. Winston, 1935, p. 129. (A children's novel.)

Palestine

Easter Week

Easter is the chief festival in Palestine. It takes a week to celebrate it, and during that time the last week of Christ's life is rehearsed amidst brilliant ceremonies, not unlike the Passion-play of Oberammergau. An important ceremony takes place during Khmis il-Gusul ("Thursday of the Washing"), commemorating the washing of the disciples' feet by Christ. Upon this day, under the gaze of great crowds, the Patriarch of the Greeks himself washes the feet of some of his bishops.

On Saturday of Easter week as many as half a million people are in Jerusalem, for the Moslems provide a counter attraction in the feast of Nebi Mousa in order to bring the Moslem peasants into the city. They come in great numbers, and go to the mosque. Here they unfurl their old war banners of green, and form a parade, probably the most picturesque of its kind in the world. They march from the mosque to the shrine of Moses near the Dead Sea. The fact that this shrine is, undoubtedly, fictitous does not keep down the crowds. It takes several hours to watch the parade pass, and during that time one sees all one wants to of fanatic humanity. Some of the sights strike awe into the hearts of thousands of children.

The Christians are not inactive on Saturday, for upon that day "En-Nour" (the Light) must spring out of the old tomb of Christ in the Church of the Holy Sepulchre. The tomb is directly under the dome, in a small round building surrounded by the churches of all the sects. One enters the first room, and then, through a low door, the next one, in which to the right lies the supposed tomb. Most modern scholars agree that Gordon's tomb, described in the chapter on Jerusalem, is the genuine one, but the controversy is still undecided. This tomb is of gray marble, about a foot and a half in height. People that enter kiss the marble, and slip a coin into the hand of the polite and careful attendant. The marble top of the tomb has a crack that runs across it, and it is through this crack that the light must come on every Easter Saturday.

Many peasants believe that this light comes directly from God as an annual miracle. They also believe that the flame will not harm; it does not burn until it gets into the hands of sinners. Lanterns are lighted with it and sent post-haste through the country, and the peasants light candles from it, taking them to their houses. Just before a lantern of the sacred flame reaches a village, the men carrying it form a procession, and by lifting a few of their number on to their shoulders, they can escort the light in lofty triumph into the village. First they go to the church and then to the different houses. As they enter the village, they sing a simple chant with great enthusiasm.

Sabt in-noor wa ayyadua,
Zurna Kabir Seyyadua,
Seyyadua Easa l-Masseeh;
Ma Deen illa Deen In-Nasara.

We have made a feast of the Saturday of the Light,
We have visited the tombs of our Master, who is Easa, the Christ;
There is no other save the Nazarite's religion.

Source: *When I Was a Boy in Palestine* by Mousa J. Kaleel. Boston: Lothrop, Lee & Shepard Co., 1914, pp. 129-132.

Poland

Easter food and games

On Saturday night before Easter the families of the village take their bread, salt, sugar and decorated eggs to church to be blessed. The village priest visits families to bless the Easter table, decked with evergreens and heavy with food.

Easter Sunday, after the church service, the whole family gathers for the holiday meal. The blessed egg is sliced and shared among family and guests, with everyone exchanging good wishes. After this little ceremony everyone sits down to eat the wonderful meal of ham, sausages, salads, *babka*—the Polish national cake—and *mazurki,* which are sweet cakes filled with nuts, fruit and honey. Marysia loves Easter, with the bells ringing out joyously after the long weeks of silence during Lent. All day long friends and family come to visit.

On Easter Monday everyone puts on old clothes for *smigus* (SHMEE-goose), a water-throwing game which is fun. The children particularly love this game and the boys drench the girls with water. Their squeals and laughter fill the air. Easter has come and so has spring—two reasons for joy and happiness.

Source: *UNICEF'S Festival Book* by Judith Spiegelman. New York: United States Committee for UNICEF, 1966, n.p.

Scotland

Egg rolling

At Edinburgh egg rolling takes place on Arthur's Seat, at Glasgow, on the Glasgow green. It occurs also at Aberdeen, Golspie, Lairg, Newtonmore, Rothesay, Langholm, Eyemouth, Falkirk, Forfar, Dundee, and Perth. Some egg rollings are organized by communities: in other places children retire to grassy slopes to stage their own egg-rolling contests. Dyed eggs are rolled down the hill until they break. The last egg to break is the winner. Then the broken eggs are eaten.

Source: *Lore and Language of Schoolchildren* by Peter and Iona Opie. Oxford, 1959, p. 253.

Sicily

Holy week in Sicily

Every home is cleaned well before the priest visits to bestow the Easter blessing. In Agrigento, the housewives come to their doors when they hear the church bells sound after the Mass of Glory. They wave sticks and shout "Let the devil leave and Christ enter!"

The churches are all adorned with flowers and lights. Each person visits seven churches on Thursday afternoon and evening. On Good Friday a Crucifixion procession takes place in each area, with the marchers clothed in mourning black.

After the Mass of Glory, the mourning curtains are taken from the altar to reveal a triumphant Christ. In Novara he is raised to the ceiling by a pulley, amid clouds and angels. In some places the Incontro, the meeting of Christ with His Mother, is enacted on Easter Sunday. Easter Monday is a holiday, and visits to the country are popular.

Source: *Festivals and Folkways of Italy* by Frances Toor. New York: Crown, 1953, pp. 80-81.

Red Easter eggs tossed to Albanian congregation

In Piano degli Albanese, near Palermo, red Easter eggs are tossed to the congregation after the priest says "Christ is risen." The red eggs are also part of the celebrations at Contessa Entellina, Sicily. The Albanian colony at Piano degli Albanese has been in Sicily since the fifteenth century.

Source: *An Egg at Easter: A Folklore Study* by Venetia Newell. Bloomington: Indiana Univ. Press, 1971, p. 225.

Spain

Easter drumming

In Jumilla, Alcañiz, and other villages south of Valencia, a *tamborada* takes place. In this event, drumming continues without stop for three days before Good Friday. In Hellin, in Albacete province, between eight and ten thousand drums are beaten between Holy Wednesday and Easter Sunday. On Good Friday everyone rises at dawn to climb between the chapels of the Calvary. Flowers and candies are thrown at the Virgin as she passes in procession. Even the children beat small drums as they process.

Source: *Spanish Fiestas* by Nina Epton. New York: A. S. Barnes, 1968, p. 24.

Spain (Catalan)

Moxigana, tiers of men, parade

Holy Week *Pasos* (tableaux) are created by men forming tiers, standing on each other's shoulders. A small child may crown the tier. They process to the music of pipe and drum, and form special designs such as the "Descent from the Cross."

A dancing egg

At the Barcelona Cathedral an egg is set atop the jet of water in the decorated fountain in the cloisters. There it dances in the waters all day long.

Source: *Pyrenean Festivals* by Violet Alford. London: Chatto and Windus, 1937, pp. 40-41.

Sweden

Easter witches

On Maundy Thursday, Easter hags were thought to fly on their brooms to Blakulla to frolic with the Devil. To protect against this evil abroad, people built bonfires, shot off guns, painted crosses over their doors, and hung crossed scythes in their stables.

Today on Maundy Thursday or Easter Eve, children dress as witches and make housecalls. Some leave a decorated "Easter letter" and hope for a treat in return. Easter letters are a widespread custom in western Sweden. They are slipped under the door or into the mailbox, and the sender's identity is kept secret. In the western provinces Easter bonfires are also popular, with villages competing for the biggest blaze. Fireworks may be shot off.

Source: *Traditional Festivities of Sweden* by Ingemar Liman. Stockholm: The Swedish Institute, 1985, p. 9.

Dressing up like an Easter witch

To an Easter witch, a shining copper kettle is essential. She should have a broomstick and a black cat as well, but the throngs of little witches who suddenly appear about the streets on the Saturday before Easter usually content themselves with a copper kettle. And, of course, mother's old cotton summer skirt, reaching right down to the ground, a shawl, kerchief and apron.

"Ring!" goes the doorbell—and there are three small witches shaking their kettles at you. A coin, or some sweets? Either will do. The round, rouge-blobbed cheeks of the little girls burn even redder with pleasure. Then, with a Swedish little-girl curtsey, they're off to the next door.

These Easter witches, both the neighbour's young daughters and the small hand-made decorations on the dinner-table, are a survival of an old belief. For it was once thought that witches flew off to Blakulla—or the Brocken—in Germany in order to celebrate Easter there.

Source: *Round the Swedish Year* by Lorna Downman, Paul Britten Austin, and Anthony Baird. Stockholm: The Swedish Institute/Bokförlaget Fabel, 1967, pp. 19-20.

Ukraine

Easter celebrations

In the Ukraine, Easter celebration lasted until the Thursday after Easter, with visiting and festivities at which one might sing and dance the *hahilki*.

Pysanki

The intricate designs on *pysanki* eggs are created by applying beeswax designs to the egg with a hair brush. The eggs are then dipped in dye. After each dipping, wax is added to protect the dyed area from further dippings. Geometric designs and symbols of spring and good luck decorate the eggs. *Pysanki* may be blessed by the priest before being given away. They will be kept for years as works of folk art.

Source: *Easter the World Over* by Priscilla Sawyer Lord and Daniel J. Foley. Philadelphia: Chilton, 1971, p. 186.

Uruguay

Semana Criolla in Uruguay

In Uruguay Semana Criolla (Creole Week) coincides with Holy Week. It is a time to celebrate the Uruguayan gaucho heritage. Roping and riding shows and traditional gaucho music are featured.

Source: *Easter the World Over* by Priscilla Sawyer Lord and Daniel J. Foley. Philadelphia: Chilton, 1971, p. 234.

Venezuela

Judas burning

Every year, on the evening of Easter Sunday in Venezuela, Judas the apostle is burned in effigy in an event known as "la quema de Judas." In hundreds of communities throughout the land—from the Andes to Guayana, from the Caribbean to the vast inland plains—the ritual execution of Judas marks a joyous end to the Lenten period of penance and the mournful solemnities of Holy Week. In contrast to the complex and largely obligatory public devotionals directed by the Roman Catholic church during Holy Week, which culminate in multitudinous processionals on Good Friday and solemn high masses on Resurrection Sunday, Judas burning takes place at the village or urban neighborhood level, where it is organized and staged by volunteers in a highly participatory manner. Although the precise origins of the ritual are not clear, account of it appear in chronicles as far back as thirteenth-century Spain.

By Wednesday of Holy Week, often after much riotous, good-natured arguing, a consensus as to the nature of the year's Judas has been arrived at. For it is an essential element of the event that the effigy of Judas be made to resemble the person against whom the group has decided to stage a formal protest that year. Usually a public figure, the community's Judas can be a local government or church official, a prominent land-owner or merchant, a politician, a judge—anyone, even the president of the republic. (In fact, with the growth of mass media communications, isolated groups have lately elected to have Judases of state or national prominence.)

Thursday and Friday evenings, upon returning from the solemn rituals and processions of Holy Week, the group's preparations continue. Displaying much ingenuity, the women constuct a life-sized figure stuffed with rags or straw, with characteristics of face, body, and dress that make it instantly recognizable. Spontaneous contributions of suitable (and expendable) items of clothing, headgear, and footwear abound. The men and older boys have used the money collected to buy liquor and an assortment of fireworks, some of which are concealed in the effigy. By Saturday the men have constucted a wooden stand where the Judas figure will be placed, always in some central open area, a plaza, or the main street of the neighborhood. The community's grievances against the year's Judas, arrived at by noisy consensus, have been listed and either memorized by the leader or written down on paper. A sign of wood or cardboard, bearing the inscription "Judas" or "Judas Iscariot," is hung around the effigy's neck. Though some food is prepared, it does not appear to be as important to the event as is an ample supply of liquor.

The morning of Resurrection Sunday is spent attending official church solemnities. By mid-afternoon, about half of the group has convened and, led by the principal organizer, they proceed en masse to the house where the effigy has been stored for safekeeping. The beginning of the ritual is signaled by the leader, who asks in a loud voice that Judas Iscariot, traitor of Christ and of the people, be turned over for the punishment he rightly deserves. In some communities, the crowd actually enters the house and drags the effigy out into the open. More often, those in the house hand Judas over, declaring that giving him over to the people is a happy duty.

Judas is now borne high on the shoulders of the crowd and displayed through the village or neighborhood, amid much shouting and the detonation of fireworks. Depending on the group's possibilities, Judas might also be tied to a burro or a horse, or to a motor vehicle such as a jeep, a small truck, or a tractor. As the neighbors receive the "visit" of Judas, they are expected to come out, examine Judas very closely.

"The Judas"—as the effigy is called—is placed on the stand and for the next hour or so the drinking and fireworks continue; everyone approaches the Judas, many slap or punch it (particularly the children), and the few dogs who have not fled the din sniff it curiously. The mood is one of growing anticipation.

At dusk the leader stands in front of the Judas and commands everyone's attention, whereupon he formally pronounces words proclaiming that Judas Iscariot betrayed Christ and turned Him over to the Romans to be crucified and that on this day the people have decided to obtain retribution by trying Judas and sentencing him to death by burning. The leader then reads or recites the list of grievances previously agreed upon; in some communities the document is formally introduced as "The Testament of Judas," although the content is clearly accusatory, often quite humorous, and frequently written in verse. The name of the person represented by the effigy is never actually announced, but shouts of approval follow each accusation. The leader asks the group if the list of betrayals and broken promises warrants a guilty verdict. After the crowd has vociferously assented, the leader then asks what form the punishment shall take, to which the group cries that Judas be burned.

The Judas is doused with kerosene or gasoline; the leader lights a torch and, holding it aloft, dramatically sentences Judas to death by burning and sets the effigy on fire. To general applause and cheering, the fireworks concealed inside the effigy go off in every direction; individuals continue to shout insults and epithets at the burning Judas. In one of the communities observed, the group dances around the flames; in the others the crowd faces the pyre and much excited jumping and gesticulating take place. Fist-waving and indignant shouting is the norm, together with derisive laughter and loud rejoicing at having obtained revenge, during this, the climax of the ritual event.

The people mill about the charred remains, commenting on the spectacle and comparing it to those of past years. Children often kick the embers and set off any remaining fireworks. Drinking continues and dancing usually follows until quite late, when, with repetitive effusive commentary on the timeliness and correctness (*justicia*) of the year's Judas burning, the group gradually disperses and everyone goes home.

Source: "Judas Burning: A Venezuelan Community Ritual" by Maria Elinor Medina de Callarotti in *Journal of Latin American Lore* 12:1 (1986), 72-82.

Yugoslavia

Veliki Petak (Good Friday)

In Arandjelovac a livestock fair was held on Good Friday. Everyone dressed in their best and enjoyed the fair, even those who did not join in the religious celebrations of the season.

Easter egg dyes

Grandmother and grandchildren enjoyed dyeing the Easter eggs on Good Friday. Colors were made from huckleberry juice, boiled onion skins, and boiled walnut shells. Rubbing the eggs with a rag dipped in lard gave them a sheen.

Source: *A Serbian Village in Historical Perspective* by Joel M. Halpern and Barbara Kerewsky Halpern. New York: Holt, Rinehart and Winston, 1972, pp. 114-115.

For more information on Easter see: *An Egg at Easter: A Folklore Study* by Venetia Newell. Bloomington: Indiana Univ. Press, 1971; *Easter the World Over* by Priscilla Sawyer Lord and Daniel J. Foley. Philadelphia: Chilton, 1971; "Easter Week and Easter" in *Folklore of American Holidays* by Hennig Cohen and Tristram Potter Coffin, editors. Detroit: Gale, 1991; *Pysanka: Icon of the Universe* by Mary Tkachuk, Marie Kushchuk, and Alice Nicholaichuk. Saskatoon, Saskatchewan, Canada: Ukrainian Museum, 1977.

First Sunday after Easter

St. Thomas's Day

This is a day for young people's outings in Macedonia.

Greece (Macedonia)

This Sunday is also celebrated with great *éclat*. After morning service the villagers go out to an open space where the sports are to be held. At Nigrita the favourite spot is on the sloping banks of a watercourse. To that place may early in the forenoon be seen repairing a miscellaneous crowd of country folk in festive mood and attire. A group of some twenty or thirty maids, with snow-white kerchiefs over their heads, leads the procession; singing various songs, among which the following is perhaps the most popular:

> Maroudia, a maid of Achinos, set out on a Monday
> To go for silver-earth, flooring-earth.
> She took not a common spade, but took a silver spade.
> She strikes once, she strikes twice, she strikes three and four times,
> And there fell the silver-earth and covered up Maroudia.
> She sent forth a shrill cry: 'My voice, rend the mountains
> And carry to my mother a message to sweep the courts clean,
> To spread the carpet. . . .'

The song is not of a very high order as poetry, yet it is interesting as referring to an everyday occupation of the women of the district.

Having reached the rendezvous, the damsels disperse and pick from the stones in the torrent-bed a kind of moss . . . and with it they dye their finger-tips and palms. In this excursion they are usually escorted by a cavalcade of young men, and, while they are busy embellishing their hands, their cavaliers run races. In the meantime the sports are in full swing. The prizes given to the winners vary according to the different events. Thus, for instance, the winner at running gets a lamb or a kid. He slings it across his shoulders and, preceded by an ear-rending band of drums and pipes, leads the crowd away; the damsels follow dancing and singing. This event comes off in the morning. After lunch take place wrestling matches, the combatants being stripped to the waist. The prize for this event is likewise a lamb or kid, and the victor is greeted with loud rolling of drums, shrill screaming of pipes, firing of pistols and flint-locks, and promiscuous shouting and cheering from the crowd. These somewhat discordant noises gradually subside into song, and dancing ensues.

Source: *Macedonian Folklore* by G. F. Abbott. Cambridge: Cambridge Univ. Press, 1903, p. 39.

Day after St. Thomas's Day (Low Sunday)

Blajini Day

Roumania

Eggshells for the *blajini*

The day after St. Thomas (Low Sunday) is well remembered by Roumanian children because of a curious custom connected with a fanciful story. That day is consecrated to the *Blajini*, a race of meek, good-natured, innocent beings supposed to dwell in a distant fairy-land, "by the Sunday water." The *blajini* are favorites of the Lord because of their purity and innocence. They dwell so much apart that they do not know what is going on in the world at large. Therefore we children are taught to throw the red egg-shells into running brooks and streams so that the waters may carry the token to the *blajini* and they may also know that Easter has arrived and rejoice.

On that day women and children gather before the running brooks and rivers or on the little bridges and with appropriate ceremonials and conjurations the fragments of the colored egg-shells are thrown into the running stream as a message of good cheer to the *blajini*. The word *blajini* means "meek." This ceremony is undoubtedly of pagan origin.

Source: *When I Was a Boy in Roumania* by Dr. J. S. Van Teslaar. Boston: Lothrop, Lee & Shepard Co., 1917, pp. 67-68.

Second Monday and Tuesday after Easter
Hocktide

Hocktide is a British custom of the Middle Ages, in which men were put into mock imprisonment (in hock) by women. Hocktide was also one of the Quarter Days for rent collection and the hiring of farmhands.

Great Britain

Hocktide customs

During the Middle Ages this was a time of mock imprisonment of men by women. A ransom had to be paid to the church funds to escape. On Hock Tuesday the men imprisoned the women. Hocktide was also one of the Quarter Days for rent collection and hiring and firing of farmhands. Today only the Hungerford, Berkshire, Hocktide ceremonies remain. Men of Hungerford tour the town with a flowered ''tutti pole'' kissing every woman they meet and throwing fruit to the children. Women who lock their homes against the ''tutti men'' find that the men climb ladders to steal their kisses through the windows.

Source: *The Customs and Ceremonies of Britain* by Charles Kightly. London: Thames and Hudson, 1986, pp. 139-140.

Day 25 after Easter

Feast of Rousa

A day to perform rites to ward off scarlatina, or scarlet fever.

Greece

Preventing or curing scarlatina

On the feast of Mid-Pentecost, that is on the twenty-fifth day after Easter, occurs a ceremony which has for its object the warding off of scarlatina. At Melenik it is called Rousa or Rosa, a designation which some of the natives derive from the crimson colour of the eruption, accompanying the fever; but which may possibly be a remnant of the old Roman Rosalia or Feast of the Roses.

The children rise betimes and assemble in a place fixed upon the eve. Three girls are deputed to go round to three different houses and beg at each of them a small quantity of flour which they bring to the meeting-place. This flour is handed to a girl who must bear a name unique in the neighbourhood. She sifts it with a sieve which she holds behind her back, then kneads it and forms it into ring-shaped cakes, which are baked in a small toy oven built for the nonce. While this is doing, the rest of the girls and boys of the party run round to other houses in the neighbourhood and collect flour, butter, honey, sesame-oil, etc. Out of these materials the eldest among them make a number of little rolls, which are baked in an ordinary public oven, and cook other viands. When all is ready, boys and girls sit down to a banquet, followed by songs and dancing. Towards evening the party breaks up, and the children disperse to their several homes.

The ring-shaped cakes, which were made by the girl of the unique name and baked in the specially built little oven, are divided among them and are hung up to dry behind a door. Whenever anyone of the children who participated in the *fête* is attacked by scarlatina, or any kindred disease, a piece of these cakes is pounded and sprinkled over the skin, which is previously smeared with molten sugar, honey, or sesame-oil. This is supposed to be an infallible cure.

In certain other districts the rite has been simplified. The children go round begging flour, oil, etc., and out of these ingredients a pie is made in each house separately. The children partake of it singing.

Source: *Macedonian Folklore* by G. F. Abbott. Cambridge: Cambridge Univ. Press, 1903, pp. 41-42.

Day 28 after Easter

Ropotine / Repotini

On this Roumanian women's feast day, men are banned and treated harshly.

Roumania

A woman's day

''As great a feast as Easter,'' says Outza, lowering her voice as if it were a secret, ''only it's the day of rejoicing for the women, and the men don't take any part in *Repotine.*''

The women meet in couples in a garden, and with potter's clay they make a sort of baking dish in the shape of a reversed shield. This mould they dry in the sun upon walnut leaves, and then use it to bake rolls and flat cakes which they distribute to the children and poor people of the neighbourhood, in order, as they say, ''to keep away wars.''

And to-day, obeying some antique usage of long-lost origin, the women treat the men with harshness. They eat and drink and make merry without them, feigning to be angry, as if to punish them for some offence done to the women, and never forgotten.

Source: *Isvor: The Country of Willows* by Princess Bibesco. New York: Frederick A. Stokes, 1924, p. 137.

Repotini, a woman's holiday

Another curious spring ceremony which excites the curiosity of children and which antedates Christianity is called *Repotini.* It is undoubtedly a remnant of the old Roman *Repotia,* as the very name indicates. This holiday falls on the third Tuesday after Easter. It is celebrated exclusively by the women who, putting aside all other work, gather and build household utensils of clay and straw, particularly the *tzesturi,* a kind of vessel to bake bread in (from the Latin *testum*), and stopples for the stove. On this occasion women partake of wine with which they also besprinkle their work. It is the one day in the year when they are the masters and may be allowed to behave harshly towards their husbands.

Source: *When I Was a Boy in Roumania* by Dr. J. S. Van Teslar. Boston: Lothrop, Lee & Shepard Co., 1917, pp. 68-69.

Moon 3, Day 5

Thanh-Minh (Pure and Bright)

Thanh-Minh is a Vietnamese day for visiting graves with food, flowers, and incense.

Vietnam

Thanh Minh Day might be compared with the American Memorial Day. Families of deceased persons prepare offerings consisting of food, flowers, incense sticks, votive papers, etc., and pay a visit to the grave. A few days before the visit, family members clean the area surrounding the grave, paint the tombs and make preparation for the solemn visit on the special holiday.

Source: *Customs and Culture of Vietnam* by Ann Caddell Crawford. Rutland, Vt.: Charles E. Tuttle, 1966, p. 194.

For more information on Thanh-Minh, see also: *Ba-Nam* by Jeanne M. Lee. New York: Henry Holt, 1987. (A children's picture book about a visit to the graveyard on Thanh-Minh. The illustrations contain many ethnographic details. *Ba-Nam* is based on the author-illustrator's childhood.)

Moon 3, Day 23

Birthday of Matsu

Matsu was a pious young girl who studied Buddhist and Taoist scriptures and performed miracles during her life. She died (or was taken up to heaven) sometime between the ages of 18 and 28 years. She is a patron of fishermen because she appeared to her brother in a dream and saved him from a storm at sea.

Taiwan

Matsu's festival

Soon after the Festival of Graves, during the third month, comes the village's most important festival, that of the goddess Matsu, the main village deity. Preparations for the festival begin long in advance. The village council convenes several times to work out procedures, and a meeting of all household heads is called to solicit suggestions and opinions. The usual sequence of events is for Matsu and an assemblage of other gods to be carried on an inspection tour of her domain. Her parade through the village is marked by great excitement. Altars bearing sacrifices of food and incense are set up in front of compound gates. Watermelon stalls, sling-shot ranges, and cotton candy stalls line the roadside as the procession passes. A puppet show is given to mark the occasion. After the gods have returned to the temple, every household provides a sacrifice in the temple for their enjoyment.

The next morning, the village as a whole performs an elaborate sacrificial rite in the temple. At noon, every household feasts friends and relatives from other communities. Acquaintances are literally dragged off the streets as they pass and urged to eat and drink. No family spares expense or effort on this occasion.

Several days before the Matsu Festival during my stay in Tatieh, the three images of Matsu housed in the temple were transported to Peikang, a town in central Taiwan, by a large delegation of villagers. Peikang is reportedly the earliest center of Matsu worship on the island; it was from the temple there that the fire (i.e. incense) of the goddess was originally taken to Tatieh. The trip to Peikang entailed considerable negotiation, expense, and advance planning: a bus had to be hired and hotel accomodations arranged for two nights. The costs of this trip were borne in part by the ''Make Prosperous Corporation'' and in part by those villagers who made the pilgrimage.

Source: *Kinship & Community in Two Chinese Villages* by Burton Pasternak. Stanford, Calif.: Stanford Univ. Press, 1972, pp. 111-112.

For information on the festivals of other gods see: *Chinese Festivals in Hong Kong* by Joan Law and Barbara E. Ward. Hong Kong: A South China Morning Post Production, 1982. (Ch'e Kung; T'o Tei Kung; Hung Shing Kung; Koon Wam; Pak Tai; T'in Hau; T'am Kung; Kwan Tai; Hau Wom; Lu Pan; Sun Wu K'ung); *Chinese Temples in Singapore* by Leon Comber. Singapore: Eastern Univ. Press, 1958; *Taiwan Feasts and Customs* by Michael R. Saso. Hsinchu, Taiwan: Chabanel Language Institute, no date. (Thi-Kung Se; Kuan Kung; Ch'eng Huang; Wen Ch'ang.)

Chaitra (March-April)

Gājan of Siva

This is a rededication ritual and festival honoring Śiva.

Bengal

Caitra

Bhaktas receive sacred threads (paitā)

The festival takes place at the end of the Bengali year in the month of Caitra (March-April). The full gājan is performed over sixteen days, of which eight contain rituals of special, cumulative significance. The rituals of the festival as a whole are divided into daily prescribed actions and pūjās specific to the major days. Each of these is designated by a term for the nonrecurrent additional ritual of the day. A month later, at the end of Boiśakh (April-May) the *ābārgājans* are performed (gājan-again). These are on a smaller scale and somewhat different in detail. The following outline gives the framework shared by the two festivals. Paitāneyoā is the day when the leader of the bhaktas (*pātbhakta*) receives the sacred thread (*paitā*) that separates him from everyday life and confers on him certain status, powers, and duties. He has to fast and offer pūjās to and meditate on Śiva and the sun every day. These actions will continue until the end of the gājan sixteen days later. The pātbhakta, however, is not joined by other bhaktas till the second major day, Kamilatulā, eleven days later. The ābārgājans of the town are similar in this regard: the gājan of the Boltalā Śiva follows the lunar calendar, and that of Buro Śiva the solar calendar (lasting sixteen days). The Caitra gājan is an exception: there the initiation of the pātbhakta is followed by the journey of Bhairab on the twenty-second of Caitra, ten days before the end of the festival.

Kamilatulā is the second major day, when more bhaktas receive the sacred thread. In the evening the Goddess Kāmakkā (Durgā) is brought to the gājan (Sāreśvar, twenty-sixth lunar day of Caitra; Buro Śiva, twenty-seventh of Boiśakh; Boltalā, twelfth of Boiśakh).

Rājābheta is the day of paying a visit to the king. Most bhaktas receive the paitā, and the gājan begins in earnest on this day.

Rātgājan, the peak of intensity and excitement, is reached in the gājan of the night.

On Dingājan, gājan of the day, a number of special rites occur in the morning, and at midnight bhaktas eat cooked rice for the first time since assuming the sacred thread.

Paitābisarjan is the final day, when the sacred thread is immersed and bhaktas return to everyday life.

Source: *The Play of the Gods* by Akos Östör. Chicago: Univ. of Chicago Press, 1980, p 28-29.

For more info on the Gājan of Siva see: *The Play of the Gods: Locality, Ideology, Structure, and Time in the Festivals of a Bengali Town.* Chicago: Univ. of Chicago Press, 1980.

Chaitra (March-April)

Hanuman Jayanti

Hanuman Jayanti is an Indian festival honoring Hanuman, the Monkey God. Hanuman is associated with Rama, whom he assisted. His adventures are recounted in the Ramayana.

India

Day to honor Hanuman, the Monkey God

Hanuman Jayanti is celebrated all over the country in honour of the Monkey-God, Hanuman, in the month of Chaitra (March-April). It is observed as the birth anniversary of Hanuman, who is famous for his learning, power, celibacy, selflessness and devotion.

On the festival day, the *Ramayana* and *Hanuman-Chalisa* are recited in homes and people observe strict celibacy and fast. People visit his temples to offer prayers and also for giving new coatings of vermilion on the image. At some places, fairs are also held in the vicinity of a Hanuman temple.

Hanuman, being a great devotee of Rama, is always worshipped with his Lord, Lakshmana and Sita. At the time of his coronation, Rama blessed Hanuman that he will be always worshipped along with him by all his devotees. There are numerous temples of Hanuman all over India, where even now he is daily worshipped by all the Hindus.

Source: *The Festivals of India* by Brijendra Nath Sharma. New Delhi: Abhinav, 1978, pp. 74-75.

Thirteenth Day of the Bright Half of Chaitra (March-April)

Mahavira Jayanti

This is a celebration of the birthday of Lord Vardhamana Mahavira, who was a founder of Jainism.

India

Birthdate of Mahavira, founder of Jainism

The Jainas or the followers of the Jaina religion observe Mahavira Jayanti on the 13th day of the bright half of the month of Chaitra (March-April) to commemorate the birth anniversary of Lord Vardhamana Mahavira, the 24th Tirthankara, who flourished in the sixth century B.C., when Lord Buddha was also propagating his new religion, Buddhism.

On this auspicious Jayanti day, pilgrims from different parts of the country reach the ancient Jaina shrines at Girnar and Palitana in Gujarat to observe the religious festival. People of Eastern India attend the festival at Pawapuri in Bihar where Mahavira died centuries ago. It is also celebrated with great fervour at the Parasnatha temple at Calcutta.

Besides these, in every town and city, where there is a Jaina temple, attractive and costly ceremonies are held and the idol of the divinity is taken out in a procession in charming wooden cars in the streets. Local fairs are also held on this occasion. People fast on this day, which is broken on the following day in the morning. A continuous recitation of the *Samayák Sutra,* a Jaina scripture, is made by one and all.

Source: *The Festivals of India* by Brijendra Nath Sharma. New Delhi: Abhinav, 1978, p. 37.

Full Moon, Panguni (March-April)

Panguni Uttiram

Panguni Uttiram is a Hindu festival celebrating celestial marriages. Lord Shiva wed the goddess Meenakshi (a Parvati incarnation) on this date at Madura. Also celebrated is the marriage of Lord Subramanya to Theivanai, adopted daughter of Indra. The festival lasts for ten days.

Malaya

Panguni Uttiram in Malaya

This is a popular festival in Malaya because of the popularity of the worship of Subramanya. It is celebrated elaborately at Thandayuthapani Temple, Sentul, Marathandavar Koil, Maran, and at Subramanya Temple, Batu Gajah. The final day's festivities are very gay and noisy with fun fairs and fetes within the temple premises. Processions of the deities on decorated chariots are taken through the streets. In Kuala Lumpar, the deity of Subramanya and his consort are taken from the Sentul temple in their large and beautiful chariot through the streets of the city. The entire day meals are freely served in the temple precincts to all visitors and special *poojas* are offered.

Panguni Uttiram in Singapore

In Singapore the Sri Veeramakaliamman Temple is the most noted venue for these celebrations. It holds a two-day festival. On the first day is a procession of Subramanya and on the following day special *poojas* are held at the temple. The *kavadi* is carried by some devotees on this day.

Panguni Uttiram at Bukit Mertajam

At Bukit Mertajam, known to the Tamils as Sungurumbai, festivities are held on this occasion at the Sri Mariamman Temple. One feature is the fire-walking ceremony held on this day. A couple of days later a *Katagam* dancing ceremony is held. Here a devotee carries on his head a pot full of yellow-coloured water and decorated with flowers and leads a procession of followers along the streets. He dances all the way keeping the pot balanced on his head and is accompanied by a band of musicians.

Source: *Indian Festivals in Malaya* by S. Arasaratnam. Kuala Lumpar: Dept. of Indian Studies, Univ. of Malaya, 1966, pp. 23-24.

Day 9, Bright Fortnight, Chaitra (March-April)

Ramanavami

This festival commemorates the birth of Shri Rama.

India

Ramanavami religious ceremonies

The festival of Ramanavami is celebrated throughout India to commemorate the birth of Shri Rama, who was born to king Dasharatha of Ayodhya on the ninth lunar day in the bright fortnight of Chaitra (March-April) It is observed with sanctity and fasting. On this day temples are decorated, religious discourses held and the *Ramayana*, narrating the life story of Rama is recited in every Hindu home. People have sincere faith and deep devotion in him. Thousands of devotees throng in shrines to have *darshana* of the beautiful images of Rama enshrined in the temples. The worshippers rotate the rosary repeating his name to free themselves from the cycle of births. *Ratha-Yatra* processions carrying the idols of Rama, Sita, Lakshmana and Hanuman are taken out in cities and towns, so that people can also have their *darshana*.

Source: *The Festivals of India* by Brijendra Nath Sharma. New Delhi: Abhinav, 1978, pp. 73-74.

April (Biannual)

Awuru Odo

This is a biannual Igbo festival during which Odo masqueraders represent the Odo spirits themselves. The spirits have arrived sometime between September and November and are feted by their family groups as they arrive. A general feting of all Odo groups takes place in April before the Odo return to their land of the dead.

Nigeria (Igbo)

The Odo festival of the Igbo of Ukehe, Nsukka, Nigeria

Odo festival comes up once every two years. Elaborate preparations are made by family units and kindreds to receive their departed relations. Men make elaborate artistic and ritual preparations to receive the Odo. They fence the shrines where the returning Odo will worship and at the same time they renovate the masks used or prepare entirely new ones. The element of secrecy surrounds these preparations because women and non-initiates are not allowed to see the activities carried out or told what goes on in the sacred groves. Women on their part are responsible for enough food for the Odo and visitors who may come to watch the performance. The Odo, as a matter of rule, are received in the same way that very important visitors are received. Strict hygienic rules are kept and the entire community is spick and span.

The Odo arrive for their earthly sojourn between September and November every other year. Because of kindred considerations, the time of arrival of each group of Odo is determined by the family group to which it belongs. As each group of Odo arrives, the family group to which it belongs celebrate in their honour. Such celebrations take place between the time of arrival and April. In April there is a grand celebration, *Awuru Odo,* which features all Odo groups from all the family units. This celebration is the *grand finale* of Odo appearance because immediately after it Odo will climb the Ukehe hills in an atmosphere of great distress and disappointment, and descend once more into the land of the dead.

Odo makes great demands on the people. Their long stay between September and April or May means a great deal of expenditure of energy and income among their hosts. The demand is even more stringent since the *Awuru Odo* occurs in April, a time of farming, food scarcity, and perhaps inclement weather. The people provide enough food for the celebration, take time off their active farm work and insure against the marring of the occasion by rain. In addition, because the costumes brought back by the Odo from the land of the dead are worn and torn at this time, new costumes are provided for their return journey. But the people stand to gain from their kindness to their departed ones. They request several favours from the Odo. They ask Odo to protect them particularly during their absence from earth. They request Odo "to take their lives and keep for them in the spirit world where they believe they are safer." Being an agricultural people, the hosts ask Odo for intercession with the Earth deity, for abundance in the current farming season so that they may continue to fulfill their obligations to Odo and to themselves. Barren women offer gifts and prayers for fertility and those who have given birth present their children with gifts in thanksgiving to Odo.

The Stage: The *Awuru Odo* main stage is located in the Nwankwo market square. Prominent in this environment is the Odo shrine from where Odo music vibrates mysteriously. Odo music is believed to be supplied by the spirits themselves and as such women and non-initiates know nothing of it except the sound they hear. All Odo characters perform in this environment as they arrive from their different kindred quarters. Later, they will travel along a marked route crossing the Enugu-Nsukka road and disappear into the hills of Ukehe. The ritual stage is located at kindred Odo shrines where the characters worship their ancestors before appearing at the market square.

The Performers: Odo performers include Odo characters proper and the people themselves who accompany them. The characters are all masked but their legs are very often exposed. The following character types feature during the performance.

1. The elderly Odo who are usually accompanied by titled and middle-aged men who blow elephant tusks and horns respectively. There are also in this group men who praise the Odo with songs and chants.

2. There are the youthful Odo who move in the company of young men or go alone.

3. The children Odo characters like the youthful ones go alone or in groups.

4. The Odo of evil men, Ikenwankpankpa or Ike for short, who represent people who were criminals while they lived on earth. Its costume is jet-black colour and the body is covered with thorns. Because they have been rejected in the spirit world they wander about feared and dreaded by performers and spectators alike.

5. There are the "Ebule Uwele," rams from Uwenu village. Like rams which they represent, they are very obdurate and

pugnacious but they love women and women love them. They are costumed like rams with horns and the hands of the actors are completely hidden under the thick wool of the rams.

The men, women, and children who constitute the bulk of the performers are the villagers themselves. They are the chorus of the production and as we have noted earlier, they are ultimately the subject of the performance, that is, the performance is about them. The men are armed with long sticks, dane guns and matchets. Women wear expensive clothing and jewelry provided by their husbands or relations and among the different kindred units there is silent but eloquent competition in terms of the costumes worn and properties featured.

The Story: The story *Awuru Odo,* performance re-enacts concerns the end of Odo sojourn on earth and how they return to the spirit world. Before their appearance at Nwankwo market square, each Odo worships its particular *Ndihi,* the ancestral father, to ask for blessings for a successful performance. At the Nwankwo market the story re-enacted is the role played by each character to portray its cultural significance, that is, the sum total of its relationship with the people.

The major story concerning the characters is, of course, the story behind the existence of the festival itself. The dead have been staying with the living and on this last day, they are communally escorted, part of the way, on their agonizing journey. It will be seen that some of them do not, in fact, wish to go back. The people know it already and as such systematic dramatic representation of it would be unnecessary. The cultural, artistic and aesthetic conventions are satisfied by the presentation of a series of symbolic characters who interact with the people.

On this grand day of *Awuru Odo,* the spirits in the spirit-world are already anxious that the Odo should return. They are angry that these dead returnees are enjoying themselves too much here on earth and as such they place lots of obstacles on their part to make them fall and be shamed. The Odo are therefore very careful not to fall because it would bring bad luck on the living. This is why when the circling of the market has been successfully completed there is great rejoicing and exuberant dancing.

Source: ''Festival Theatre in Traditional African Societies: An Igbo Case Study'' by Dr. J. N. Amankulor. *Readings in African Humanities: Traditional and Modern Culture* edited by Edith Ihekweazu. Enugu, Nigeria: Fourth Dimension Publishers, 1985, pp. 83-96.

April

Cherry Blossom Festival

During the time of the blossoming cherry trees a festive viewing of the cherry blossoms occurs at many sites throughout Japan. It is not a single festival, but a month of celebrations.

Japan

Cherry blossom viewing and the Cherry Dance

During this month, some place in Japan is having its cherry season, as there is two to three weeks difference in the climate of southwest Japan and northeast Japan. The people are resting from one day to seven in order to visit the parks, shrines, and hillsides. The most visited places are *Arashiyama* and *Kiyomizudera* in Kyoto, and *Yoshino* near *Nara*. Under the cherry trees, the crowds eat, drink, and are merry.

The most commonly quoted poems used by the vulgar at the flower-viewing parties are

> "*Hana yori dango*" or "Better than the flowers is the food."
> "*Sake nakute, nanno, onorega sakura kana!*" or
> "Without the wine, the flowers have no attraction."

The most quoted poem about the cherry is *Moto-ori's* which has been translated by *Saito* as follows:

> The Spirit of *Yamato's* isles
> Perchance the stranger may inquire,
> Go show the morning sun that rises
> Upon the mountain-cherry.

Another is the one that says "the *Samurai* of Japan is like the cherry, which blossoms and dies so suddenly and so beautifully."

There is a proverb about the changeable man who is said to be like "the three days of the *Sakura*," "*mikka minu ma no sakura,*" because within three days such marvelous changes take place in the *Sakura*.

The Cherry Dance comes during the season when the blossoms are at their best, but the famous cherry dance in Kyoto is set for the month of April each year. In Japan it is known as the *Miyako Odori*, or the dance of the capital, but because it has been lucky enough to be in the season of the Cherry, it has become known abroad as the Cherry Dance. In Tokyo, in Osaka, and in all the places where there are *geisha*, there is a cherry dance at this season of the year.

Source: *Japanese Festival and Calendar Lore* by William Hugh Erskine. Tokyo: Kyo Bun Kwan, 1933, pp. 59-60.

Neighborhood cherry blossom viewing

The annual O-hanami (cherry-blossom-viewing party) sponsored each spring by the women's auxiliary provides a much more rollicking time. Sixty or 70 local residents travel to a park several stations away on the private train line, where—along with several thousand other people, most of whom are there with similar-sized groups from their companies, their schools, or their neighborhoods—they spread out mats and eat, drink, dance, and sing for several hours.

Source: *Neighborhood Tokyo* by Theodore C. Bestor. Stanford, Calif.: Stanford Univ. Press, 1989, p. 158.

For more information on the Cherry Blossom Festival, see: *Japanese Festival and Calendar Lore* by William Hugh Erskine. Tokyo: Kyo Bun Kwan, 1933, pp. 59-60. (Erskine describes the nine scenes of the cherry blossom festival dance performed in Kyoto in 1932.)

Circa April

Emume Ibo Uzo (Road Building)

This is an Igbo community gathering to maintain the main routes through communities. This was especially important in the days before government-sponsored road building.

Nigeria (Igbo)

In some parts of Igbo land especially in Mbaise area this festival for road reconstruction is celebrated. Important routes in the community are cleared and levelled by community effort and a festival day is declared. People from neighbouring communities are invited.

Source: ''Standardizing Igbo Festivals'' by Nnabuenyi Ugonna in *Nigeria Magazine* 136 (1981), p. 26.

April

New Year

The Micronesian New Year on Satawal is signaled by the position of the star Na and the new moon.

Micronesia

The New Year begins in Satawal, Micronesia

It was now the month of Ceuta, our April. Na, the storm star forming the dorsal fin of Cu, the Dolphin, had finished storming as the new moon appeared in the evening sky. The end of the fighting of Na heralded the beginning of *leraak,* ''the year.'' The strong winds of winter were diminishing and the voyaging season would soon begin. Skipjack tuna were still running on Wuligee, and two canoes went to West Fayu, returning with turtles, fish, and a multitude of sooty terns.

Source: *The Last Navigator* by Stephen D. Thomas. New York: Henry Holt, 1987, p. 92.

April 1
April Fools' Day

This is a day, beloved by children, for tricking people. April 1 is celebrated in several European countries. The customs may have originated in 1582 when the change to the Gregorian calendar moved New Year from March 25 to January 1. Those who forgot were April fools.

France
Poisson D'Avril

Paper fish pranks

On this day, schoolchildren stick paper cutouts of fish on their classmates' backs. Both the day and the dupes are called "Poisson d'avril," "April fish."

Fastening rabbit skin to clothing

You make each other April fish, not, perhaps, in our way, but I have never learned exactly how, and have never risked a *procès verbal* by experimenting;—and (this one could do) you attach little bits of rabbit-skin to people's clothes (at least you did in the Franche-Comté which, after all, was a free country).

Source: *A Guide to French Fetes* by E. I. Robson. London: Methuen, 1930, p. 79.

Germany

German April 1 customs

April Fools' Day jokes and pranks are popular. The pranksters cry "April, April!" when someone is caught. Newspapers print Zeitungsente (newspaper ducks), fake articles which hoax the public. This is an unlucky day, however, because Judas was born on this day (some say because Judas died on this day, or because Lucifer was cast out of Heaven on this day).

Source: *German Festivals and Customs* by Jennifer M. Russ. London: Oswald Wolff, 1982, p. 56.

Great Britain

April Fools' Day tricks in Great Britain

Pranks are played on this day. Dupes are sent for "left-handed screwdrivers" or "striped-paint." And the media get into the act with hoaxes. The *Guardian* printed an article on the Island of San Seriffe one year, and the BBC announced a bumper spaghetti harvest in Italy. The pranking can last only until noon, however, after that "April Fools' Day's past and gone, You're the fool for making one" is chanted at the prankster.

Source: *The Customs and Ceremonies of Britain* by Charles Kightly. London: Thames & Hudson, 1986, p. 45.

Macedonia

First of April practical jokes

The First of April is in some parts of Macedonia, as in most parts of Europe, believed to authorize harmless fibs, and many practical jokes are played on that day by the Macedonian wags.

Source: *Macedonian Folklore* by G. F. Abbott. Cambridge: Cambridge Univ. Press, 1903, p. 43.

New Zealand

April Fools' Day in New Zealand c. 1949

My observation of April Fool at a later day was that it completely interrupted the normal playground play, at least for the preschool period 8:30 A.M. until 9:00 A.M. At Forbury in 1949 I observed groups of children wandering around arm in arm as if fortifying each other by expressing their hostile tricks and jeers only against those outside the arm-linked group. At North East Valley School, Dunedin, if other children tried to trick you after twelve o'clock you said:

> April Fool's Day is past
> And you're the April Fool at last,
> Four farthings make a penny
> And you're a bigger fool than any.

Or simply "Ya Ha! You're the biggest April Fool." Sentiments could be expressed in terms of playground scribble: "A duck in the pond, a fish in the pool, whoever reads this is a big April Fool" (1941; North East Valley, Dunedin). Other tricks were:

We put books on the cupboard so that they would fall on the teacher (1935; Wadestown).

At one time I used to dread April Fools' Day, as my mother was so good at putting things across me. When we were small our main gags on the way to school were "Look at the monkey over there in the paddock," "So-and-so has a new duck pond. Look at it" (1945; Hawkes Bay).

April Fools' Day is a day on which you try to fool everyone without them knowing it, for example, pin paper on their backs, put a drawing pin on a chair, tell a person to look in his or her letterbox, and so on, everything being silly (1949; Devonport).

Source: *A History of Children's Play: New Zealand 1840-1950* by Brian Sutton-Smith. Philadelphia: Univ. of Pennsylvania Press, 1981, p. 117.

Scandinavia

An April fish verse

One of the non-church holidays Scandinavians enjoy is the same as one of ours—April Fools Day. There's a little verse:

> "*April, April, din dumma sil,*
> *Jag kan lura dig vart jag vill.*"

Or,

> "April, April, you silly fish,
> I can trick you however I wish."

Source: *Notes from a Scandinavian Parlor* by Florence Ekstrand. Seattle: Welcome Press, 1984, p. 85.

Scotland

Huntigowk Day

Hunting the gowk

In Scotland April 1 has been known as "Huntigowk Day." It is a day for playing pranks. The name comes from the familiar prank of sending someone to "hunt the gowk another mile." Someone is sent on an errand bearing a message that says, "Don't you laugh and don't you smile. Hunt the gowk another mile". The receiver, who is in on the joke, reads it and tells the bearer that this is the wrong place, sending him on. Thus the fool "hunts the gowk another mile" until he catches on.

Source: *Lore and Language of Schoolchildren* by Peter and Iona Opie. Oxford: Oxford Univ. Press, 1959, p. 245.

An April Fool extension in Fife

In Kirkcaldy, Fife the children add a second fooling day on April 2. They call this Taily Day. It is a day for pinning notes such as "Kick Me" on people's backs or pinning long tails onto a person when they are not aware.

Source: *Lore and Language of Schoolchildren* by Peter and Iona Opie. Oxford: Oxford Univ. Press, 1959, p. 247-248.

A March-April change-of-month rhyme

> March said to Aperill,
> "I see three hogges on a hill
> And if you'll lende me dayes three
> I'll find a way to make them dee."
>
> Oh, the first of them was wind and weet;
> The second of them was snaw and sleet,
> The third of them was sic a freeze,
> It froze the wee birds to the trees.
>
> When the three days were past and gane
> The three silly hogges came hirpling hame.

Source: *Happy Holidays* by Eleanor Graham. New York: E. P. Dutton, 1933, p. 80.

A March-April turn-of-the-month chant

> *The Borrowing Days.*
>
> March borrowed from Aperill
> Three days and they were ill.
> The first began wi' wind and weet,
> The next come in with snaw and sleet,
> The third was sic a bitter freeze,
> It froze the birds' claws to the trees.

Source: *Macedonian Folklore* by G. F. Abbott. Cambridge: Cambridge Univ. Press, 1903, p. 24.

Sweden

Practical Joking on Första April in Sweden

If you are in Sweden on the 1st of April, be prepared to be fooled by young and old alike. This is the one day when "anything goes" in the way of a joke—"practical" or otherwise. At home, children invent all kinds of ways of fooling grown-ups, and when their victims discover the ruse, they are apt to hear a verse which in English translates something like this:

> April, April, you silly fish,
> I can fool you as I wish.

Source: *Traditional Festivities of Sweden* by Ingemar Liman. Stockholm: The Swedish Institute, 1985, p. 71.

For more information on April Fools' Day see: "All Fools' Day, April 1" in *Folklore of American Holidays* by Hennig Cohen and Tristram Potter Coffin. 2nd ed. Detroit: Gale Research, 1991.

Various Dates
Planting Festivals

Angola
Kapesi

A Planting time feast in Angola

When the busy planting time in Angola is over and the work is light, little girls and older girls and even women name a day, and on that day they all go to some prearranged place near a stream. They take various kinds of food with them and spend the day there. The main feature of this feast is that the girls make baskets all day long from morning until evening when they return to the village. While the food is cooking in the pots, they work at their baskets until it is time to eat, and after they have eaten, they work again on their baskets. And as they work, the girls sing and tell stories. No boys are invited to this feast, but sometimes saucy little fellows go out to where the girls are in order to taste the food they have. When the sun has gone down and darkness begins to fall, the girls all go home, singing songs as they go to their houses in the village.

Source: *Children's Festivals from Many Lands* by Nina Millen. New York: Friendship Press, 1964, p. 19.

Ghana (Akan)
Apo

The Apo festival at Tanosu

During the annual *Apo* festival, at the season of sowing and planting, Nana Ameyaa Ampromfi's black stool, the shrine of her divine soul, or *kra*, is still carried to Takyiman; and when it reaches the outskirts of the town, a sword-bearer is sent to the Bono-Takyimanhene to inform them of its arrival. The Bono-Takyimanhene then comes in person to welcome the stool, which always has to arrive on Monday, the day of the moon before the *Apo*. It is housed in the sanctuary of Akane Asia and Mframa, the *abosom* which owe their lives to relatives of Ameyaa Ampromfi. On Wednesday, the stool is brought ceremoniously into the temple of Taa Kese, where the high priest welcomes and embraces its priestess; a sheep is then sacrificed over the stool. There it remains until the end of the *Apo* festival, and is carried back to Tanosu on Monday morning, New Year's Day, before sunrise, for Ameyaa's divine *kra* to receive offerings there later in the day.

The Death and Resurrection of the Mouse-god at Tanoboase

The *akyeneboa,* which incarnates the *obosom* Amii, is a mouse (*akura*). The rite differs greatly from that performed at Winneba, but can nevertheless be regarded as a variation on the same primitive pattern, since the festival is still exclusively concerned with the *akyeneboa*.

Centuries ago, the people of Mansu in the Nkoranza State formed an alliance with the Tanoboase worshippers of the Antelope-god Taa Kora (Tano). This alliance is still so close that the death and resurrection ritual of the Mouse-god is celebrated in conjunction with that of the Antelope-god. Moreover, the priest of Amii is permitted to carry the shrine of Taa Kora, and *vice versa,* should one or the other priest be prevented from doing so.

On *Fo-Dwoo* ('Fertile Monday', day of the moon) of the *Apo* festival, the priest of Amii, carrying the shrine of his god and a mummified mouse, walks with his people to meet the high priest of Taa Kora and his people after the completion of their rites in the sacred cave of Tanoboase. After forming a single procession they go to a near-by field and assemble around a hole in the ground in which the priest of Amii had just deposited the mummified mouse. A libation of palm wine is poured over it, while the priest of Amii offers a prayer for the well-being of the people of Mansu and Tanoboase in the year to come. Everyone present takes a sip from the calabash, and the last drop is also poured over the mouse. They sing:

Priest: Mouse, ee, this hole is not yours alone.
There are 30 entrances to the same chamber,
This hole is not yours alone at night.
We come from Amowi,* OO,
We come from Amowi, creator, EEE,
Red (i.e. life-giving) River** yield up,
Lion,** ee,
We are coming.
This is the song by which we invoke him.

*Amowi is the name of the cave where the Bono kingdom was founded.
**Appellation of the Mouse god.

Chorus: But we do not invoke him till we have passed.
Priest: To the King of Takyiman, to Ameyaw Kwaakye. To Mouse, kinsman.
Chorus: But we do not invoke him till we have passed.
Priest: To the King of Asante, to Tano kinsman.
Chorus: But we do not invoke him till we have passed.
Priest: To the King of the Thousand Brongs, Tano kinsman.
Chorus: But we do not invoke him till we have passed.
Priest: To the Asante nation, to Tano, kinsman.

Kinsman God, on the throne cushion of the Apo festival.
To Takyifiri, to Tano, kinsman.
etc.

Next, a shot is fired at the mouse, and if it misses the mark misfortune can be expected in the coming year. Finally, a grass fire is kindled around the hole and allowed to spread. On the following morning the people return to the field, and find a live mouse in the hole—the resurrected Mouse god. They shoot it, when found, and joyfully take the corpse home to Mansu, where the priests mummify it for the next year's ritual.

Source: *The Akan of Ghana: Their Ancient Beliefs* by Eva L. R. Meyerowitz. London: Faber and Faber, 1958, pp. 42-43.

Ghana (Effutu)

Aboakyer

The deer-hunting festival

On this day two Asafo companies, of 150 people each, stage a deer hunt. The companies are divided into ten divisions, and include males ages 8-68. All are in new costumes wearing the colors of their company. Drums call everyone to the hunt. Amid drumming, dancing, and bell ringing, the hunt begins. The first deer caught is brought to the paramount chief alive and carried back to town with dancing and drumming. It is important that the god Panche Otu be placated on this day and the hunt go well, to insure a bountiful year.

Source: *Hi Neighbor. Book 2*. United Nations, N.Y.: United States Committee for UNICEF, no copyright date, p. 22.

Mozambique

Blessing of Seeds and Tools

A Christian blessing

As the planting season starts, the Christian families at Kambine, Mozambique, come to the church for a short service of worship. They bring with them the seeds and the tools they will use in planting. The women and girls, who do the majority of the garden work, lay their baskets of seeds and their hoes on the altar, while the first line of the planting song is chanted by the leader, followed by the entire group singing the rest of the verses. The teacher then talks about planting the seeds in the right way and how all must work to make the gardens grow.

Seeds and tools are left on the altar of the church for the night. At sunrise, the workers return and sing the last verse. Then they pick up the seeds and hoes and go out to start work on their gardens, often singing as they go, "The man who is happy is the one who digs." In the song they cover the activities of planting, tending the crop, and getting a good harvest.

Source: *Children's Festivals of Many Lands* by Nina Millen. New York: Friendship Press, 1964, pp. 35-36.

Namibia (Kwangali)

Nyambinyambi

Annual rain-calling ceremony

The Kwangali also worship Kalunga whom they call Karunga, and to whom they pray for rain during the annual ceremony called Nyambinyambi. The purpose of this ceremony is to chase all the ill luck out of the country, for only when the land is cleansed can rain fall again.

The chief will order his grandson to go and cut a tree and bring it to the kraal where it is erected at the entrance gate. Hoes, seed, axes, hunting weapons and pumpkins are laid at its root as offerings. The chief and the people will then pray that the women may receive good crops and that the men may catch many animals. Food is cooked in great quantity, which the people all eat together. Fish and an antelope are offered to the god by the chief. Here is one of the prayers:

Oh Karunga!
Help us now with rain in plenty
let the rain fall on the branches
let there be fish in the river
may the fruits bend down the branches
may the cows bear many young ones
may the land receive your blessing
may misfortune not befall us
may we all be rich and happy. . . .

Source: *Namibia: Land and Peoples, Myths and Fables* by Jan Knappert. Leiden, E. J. Brill, 1981, pp. 136-137.

Niger (Songhay)

Genji Bi Hori: Black Spirit Festival

Three possession ceremonies are tied to farming activities. The first of these is called the Black Spirit festival (*genji bi hori*). The zimas organize this ceremony in April to pay homage to the spirits of the land, who control soil fertility and various forms of pestilence. If the ceremony is successful, said Adamu Jenitongo, the millet crop will be protected from rats, birds and insects. "When these rites were widespread," Adamu Jenitongo insisted, "our fields were filled with millet. Today, today, just look at the fields. Nothing. Look."

Source: *Fusion of the Worlds: An Ethnography of Possession among the Songhay of Niger* by Paul Stoller. Chicago: Univ. of Chicago Press, 1989, p. 131.

Yenaandi: Rain-bringing ceremony

The second farming ceremony is the *yenaandi* or rain dance, which is the reenactment of the first possession ceremony that took place in the ancestral past and is still staged in most Songhay villages. In the rain dance, priests call to the social world four principal Tooru deities: Dongo, deity of thunder; Cirey, deity of lightning; Moussa Nyori, deity of clouds and wind; and Hausakoy, deity of smithing. If the rain dance is well staged, the spirits are pleased and the community is assured of enough rain to produce a bountiful harvest. . . .

In Songhay, rainfall, which is controlled by invisible forces, is associated with the spirit world. When rain falls it comes as scattered thunderstorms, dropping torrents of water on one village, leaving an adjacent town untouched. The spirits control the path of rain—Dongo's path—and can prevent it from falling on non-observant villages.

To protect their fields from pestilence, some farmers make private offerings to the spirits. In most Songhay communities, Tillaberi included, the possession troupe stages elaborate rain ceremonies, *yenaandi,* which are human attempts to control the rain by making offerings to the spirits.

Yenaandi, which means "the act of cooling off," is organized at the end of the hot-dry season. It is a Tooru festival, for the Tooru, especially Dongo (thunder), Cirey (lightning), and Moussa Nyori (wind and clouds), control the natural forces that bring rain. Rain dances are generally held on a Thursday, the Tooru's sacred day, in an open space that is usually ancestral land. In Tillaberi, the yenaandi space is a sandy plaza that sits on a bluff overlooking the Niger River.

Source: *Fusion of the Worlds: An Ethnography of Possession among the Songhay of Niger* by Paul Stoller. Chicago: Univ. of Chicago, 1989, p. 131.

For more information see: *Fusion of the Worlds,* Chapter 6.

Russia (Buryat)

Sur-Kharban

The Buryat Sur-Kharban in prerevolutionary Russia

Among the most ancient folk festivals is sur-kharban (archery). It was commonest among the western Buryats (Kuda, Kapsal, Verkholensk, Lena and Ol'khon). This festival was usually held in the spring, and several thousand Buryats would gather together for it. All men, irrespective of age or status, were admitted to the festival, but only unmarried women and young girls were allowed to be present. The height of the festival was a set of three contests—archery, wrestling and horse trotting-racing.

The first was the archery contest, which gave the festival its name. A stick bound with leather straps (khur) was set up as the target in a semi-circle formed by the onlookers. In the old days every clan had its own khur. The arrows were brought by the archers from home, while the same bow was used by everyone, being passed on from one to the other.

Source: *The Peoples of Siberia* edited by M. G. Levine and L. P. Potapov. Chicago: Univ. of Chicago Press, 1964, p. 284.

Russia (Chuckchi)

Festival of the Baydar

Celebrating the *baydar* (boat)

In the early spring, every baydar party celebrated the festival of the baydar. In the morning the baydar was taken off the rack, and meat food was sacrificed to the sea. Afterwards, the baydar was brought to the yaranga, and another sacrifice was offered. All participants in the celebration walked around the yaranga. First came the eldest woman in the family, after her the owner of the baydar, the helmsman, the oarsmen, and the rest. On the following morning the baydar was carried to the sea and placed on special racks which had been set up there. After offering a sacrifice to the sea, the baydar was lowered into the water, and the men departed on their first hunting expedition.

Source: *The Peoples of Siberia* edited by M. G. Levin and L. P. Potapov. Chicago: Univ. of Chicago Press, 1964, p. 822.

Russia (Koryak)

Kil' vey

Festival of Horns

The reindeer-breeding and the sedentary Koryaks held various seasonal celebrations. The main holiday of the reindeer-breeders was the spring kil'vey—the festival of horns. It was celebrated after the calving, when the herd was brought to the encampment. The people brought out of their dwelling bowls with pieces of meat and the sacred wooden fire-making device which they proceeded to "feed." In autumn, they celebrated the festival of the autumn deer slaughter. This festival was also attended by shamanistic performances, sacrifices, and the "feeding" of the wooden fire-maker. The coastal hunters celebrated the festival of floating the baydar in the spring, at the beginning of the spring hunting season. At this time they sacrificed dogs. After the celebration, they opened the summer entrance to the semi-dugout.

Source: *The Peoples of Siberia* edited by M. G. Levin and L. P. Potapov. Chicago: Univ. of Chicago Press, 1964, p. 868.

Togo (Ewé)

Planting Ceremony

Planting ceremony in Agome-yo village, c. 1980

Most of the men are wearing Western dress. The elder conducting the ceremony is wearing a piece of bright-colored cotton wrapped around his waist, and the village chief is wearing a handwoven boubou (similar to a dashiki). All the women are wearing traditional West African dress; a long skirt that is not sewn but rather fashioned from a two-yard piece of cloth wrapped around the waist; a blouse, either of Western manufacture or tailored out of a matching piece of cloth; and a second piece of cloth holding a baby on the back or worn draped around the hips.

A drummer walks through the rocky dirt paths of the village beating a talking drum, calling everyone to the ceremony. People begin to gather in the courtyard of the chief's house. At first they wait on benches under a canopy of green plants. Then the men move to chairs and the women to the mud doorway stoops.

The chattering and laughing stops. The elder who is conducting the ritual raises his arms, invoking the gods and forefathers of the village. Pouring a thick white liquid from a calabash onto the ground, he prays to them for a successful planting season and an abundant harvest.

This liquid is the libation—always part of an Ewé ceremony. Here the liquid is made of maize and water. The elder pours the libation on the ground first as an offering to the ancestors. The ground represents the spirit of air, water and earth, and is considered the giver of life.

"Drink is for the enemy," says the elder, and pours another libation on the ground. This offering will appease any evil spirit who may be present.

In front of the elder sits an enamel basin filled with corn, symbolizing the desired harvest. The white goat that has been chosen for the sacrifice is tied up and lying on the ground next to the basin of corn. A goat—a large animal—is an important sacrifice. Its whiteness (thus purity) makes it worthy of being offered to the gods.

The elder pours some schnapps into a glass. Hard liquor is part of any ceremony with a sacrifice; it is considered special because it is imported rather than local.

Two villagers lift the goat and lower it three times, showing it to the forefathers.

"This is what we offer," says the elder. "This is the way you did it, so this is the way we do it."

The elder feeds the goat a glass of schnapps. Then he swiftly slits the goat's throat and holds its head over a pot to catch the blood.

The men throw the goat in front of them. It is not quite dead. It squirms and tries to get up. "Ahh!" the people gasp softly.

The men step on the goat's throat, twist its neck and cut it again. Again the goat tries to get up. "Ah!" sigh the villagers in unison.

The men twist the goat's neck again. At last it's dead. They cut off the head and hold it over the basin to catch the last drops of blood. This blood will go to the spirit and the ancestors.

They take the goat off to be butchered for tonight's feast. The villagers will consume the meat, sharing communion with the ancestors and within the community.

The music starts. There is an ensemble of two large drums, one medium-sized drum, one little drum and two tambourines. The musicians are men and boys.

The women and girls sing and dance a traditional Togolese dance. Moving their feet rhythmically to the drum beat, they rock forward and back pivoting at the waist: in one position the shoulder blades are thrust way back and the elbows almost meet at the shoulder blades, the waist is bowed forward and the hips and shoulders back; in the other position the shoulders, elbows and hips come forward and the waist is bowed back.

At first the women form a line and dance in a circle. Then they rotate and dance facing inward, still in a circle. One woman in the center leads a song, singing verses, swaying her hips and pointing with her right hand.

Afterwards we go to the fields to see the women prepare the ground for planting. It's a hot fifteen-minute walk to the nearest field; we have to race over a colony of biting driver ants and jump across a stream. The fields are being cleared by burning, an old procedure that is gradually giving way to better and more modern techniques.

Source: "Three Ceremonies in Togo" by Gene Reisner in *The Drama Review* 25 (4) (T 92) (Winter 1981), 51-58.

Upper Volta, Yatenga Region (Mossi)

Bega

Mossi Bega ceremonies

Bega occurs at the time of the annual cleaning and clearing in preparation for planting. The vegetation spirit Tido Wende must be propitiated at this time. The Earth priest sacrifices at the Earth shrine and then pays a visit to the Bega, the priest in charge of intercession with the deity regarding plant growth. The Bega then makes ritual rounds of the farmers within his area. For seven nights after the Bega rituals, the young single girls dance, singing joyful songs of the coming growing season. The farmers can now begin preparing their fields for planting.

Source: *Technology in the Culture of a West African Kingdom: Yatenga* by Peter B. Hammond. New York: The Free Press, 1966, pp. 189-191.

Volta

New Year Purification before Planting

Dudulsi, a Gurunsi village in Lela, celebrates

Dudulsi, a small Gurunsi village in Lela, offers one example of how different groups incorporate the masks into the life of their community. The village was first settled by the Bazie family. The patriarch of this group now heads the cult of the earth and also functions as the leading costume-maker. His authority, however, is only nominal, as the three family groups which make up the village community lead relatively autonomous lives. Each family inhabits its respective territory under the direction of an elder who is responsible for the family's ancestral cult.

Only the mask society is able to integrate and harmonize the centrifugal forces at the heart of this village community. The nine members of the mask society are elected from the elders of the three families. The masks are simple in form, zoomorphic, covered in multicolored geometric designs and completed by a black costume made of baobab fibers. They appear in the following order: antelope, cayman, snake, lion, hornbill, cock, ram, buffalo, and hyena. . . . The masks intervene in a man's life three times: during initiation when the adolescent enters the adult community; during the funeral ceremonies of those who, after a long and fruitful life, have been called to rejoin the ancestral spirits (here, at the great festivities which take place at the end of the mourning period, the masks dance for three days for a man and four days for a woman); and finally, at the important yearly purification which takes place just before planting at the beginning of the rainy season (April-May). This is the most important mask ceremony—"the time of the masks." For nine days (3 x 3) the masks take over, and carry out their mission to chase away evil spirits and to purify the hearts of men. Once regenerated, the community draws god's blessings upon itself as promised by the spirit-snake and as symbolized by abundant rains, the source of fertility for the land and for the women.

Source: "Voltaic Masks" by Michael Voltz in *The Drama Review* 26 (4) (T 96) (Winter 1982), 43-45.

April 2

13 Farvardin / Sizdeh Bedar

Iran

Spring outing marks end of New Year season

This is the end of the New Year season. To avoid bad luck on the first ''thirteen'' of the year, one goes on an outing to enjoy the spring countryside. The sprouts planted at No Ruz are thrown into a stream to toss away bad luck.

April 4

San Isidro

This is a day to commemorate St. Isidore (San Isidro). St. Isidore of Seville, c. 560-636, was a native of Cartagena, Spain. He was educated by St. Leander, his elder brother, and succeeded him in the see of Seville in 600. He reorganized the Spanish church and was responsible for the decree of the council of Toledo in 633. He founded schools throughout Spain, calling for the teaching of law, medicine, Hebrew, and Greek, as well as the classics. He compiled a twenty-volume encyclopedia of all knowledge available in seventh-century Europe. He continosly gave to the poor and at the end of his life his house in Seville was crowded with beggars and other unfortunate souls.

Colombia

San Isidro brings the rain in Río Frío, Colombia

In Río Frío, Colombia, St. Isidore is saddled with the very special obligation of bringing rain. The beginning of April is supposed to mark the end of the dry season, so on April 4 the image of the saint is carried through town with everyone following and chanting his praises. The need for rain is carefully explained, and he is expected to produce at least a shower before the observances are over. To give him plenty of time, the procession proceeds slowly, taking two steps forward and one backward each time. If there is still no shower after several turns through town, the chanting changes from praises to reproaches. After several more times around, this becomes hearty abuse interspersed with variegated profanity. If the skies remain unmoved, poor San Isidro is angrily shoved back into his niche and left there for another year.

Source: *Fiesta Time in Latin America* by Jean Milne. Los Angeles: The Ward Ritchie Press, 1965, p. 60.

April 5 or 6 (105 Days after the Winter Solstice)

Ch'ing Ming/Han Sik-il

Family graves are visited on this day. The grave site is tended, paper money, artifacts and incense sticks are burnt, and tribute is paid to the dead. The family shares a picnic on the grave site. The grave is then cleaned and new trees or flowers may be planted.

Hong Kong

Ch'ing Ming in Hong Kong circa 1984

The words 'Ch'ing Ming', which mean 'clear and bright', refer to the weather at the time of the year when most Chinese go to visit their family graves. The first activity of the visit is to clear away the weeds and repaint the inscriptions (the so-called 'sweeping of the graves'). Then incense sticks and red candles are lighted and rice, wine, tea, and many other foods set out. Paper clothing and *spirit money* are burned and the whole group kneels to pay respects; even the littlest children are gently pressed down and shown how to move their tiny hands up and down—palms together, fingers straight—in the proper gesture of respect to spirits.

The greetings over, the occasion turns into a family picnic which the living share on the hillsides with their dead. Before they leave they tuck several pieces of offering paper under a stone on top of the grave. They flap a little in the wind, a sign that the grave has been tended for another year.

Wearing willow catkins

. . . On the day of Ch'ing Ming, all Chinese women and children must wear the willow catkin. If they neglect this precaution, they risk being reborn as dogs in the transmigration of souls. The custom of sporting the willow dates from the Emperor Kao Tsung, of the T'ang Dynasty, who reigned from 650 to 683 A.D. On the third day of the third moon, after bathing in the waters of Wei Yang, he plucked some willow branches, and distributed them to his retinue, with orders to wear them in their caps. He explained that this was a sovereign remedy against the stings of scorpions.

Source: *Chinese Creeds and Customs* by V. R. Bunkhardt. Hong Kong: South China Morning Post, 1982, p. 16.

Korea

Han Sik-il/Cold Food Day

Every year when ''Hansik'' Day arrives, the graveyards in the suburbs are covered with people of all ages and both sexes in full dress. They weed and repair the graves, planting trees around them on this day.

While the mourners cry aloud ''Aigo! Aigo!'' before the graves, the sound echoing in the hills moves the hearts of the solitary woodsmen to melancholy folksongs:

> ''Second moon came and cold food I eat.
> Far over the mountain spring buds are out,
> Withered trees revive and faded flowers bloom.
> Yea, his memory reflects in my heart.
> But a man once gone comes back no more;
> My hot tears drop on this cold food,
> Even this cold food I offer on thy grave
> For you hungry soul to partake.
> Butterflies dance with heavy wings.
> With heavy heart I bathe in the icy water
> And sit by the stream to sing to thy memory.
> Lo, the mountains turn pink and azaleas laugh,
> Willow branches wave green in the breeze
> Like the hair of a maiden of sweet sixteen.
> The farmers take plough to the fields
> And the herd boys astride their pets
> Raise golden whips to catch the spring.''

On the Cold Food Day, in the olden times, people refrained from making a fire all day long, eating only cold food. The observance is said to have started thus:

Han Sik Legend

Long, long ago in China in the Kingdom of Chin there lived a loyal subject named Kai Ja Chu. The treacherous retainers hated him and drove him out of the King's presence.

Poor Kai Ja Chu then ran far away and hid himself in a mountain called Chinshan, courting full solitude if he was to be banished from the King's presence. The King heard this, and, as he admired the steadfast loyalty of Kai Ja Chu, searched for him throughout the kingdom, but without success. At last it was learned that he was hiding in a cave in the mountain and, in order to force him out, they set fire to the forest.

He did not come out, but remained hiding and was suffocated to death. Out of pity and admiration for his staunch fidelity, all the people throughout the country refrained from making any fire to cook their food and ate only cold things in memory of his sad end. In due course this custom was brought to Korea.

Source: *Folk Customs and Family Life* by Tae Hung Ha. Seoul, Korea: Yonsei, 1963, pp. 25-27.

Tree planting at Hansik time

In recent years another custom, Arbor Day, has been observed at this time. It is a program of beautification and reforestation.

Officials take part in tree-planting ceremonies in public parks and city centers. Social organizations, civic groups, office workers, plant trees on hillsides and along highways. School children plant young trees in their school yards and learn how to take care of them.

Source: *Celebrations: Asia and the Pacific* by Gene Sawyer. Honolulu: Friends of the East-West Center, 1978, p. 23.

Azalea cakes

There was a Korean custom of eating special dough cakes made with azalea flowers on this day, but it is more important as the day when family graves are visited and repaired after the winter frosts. I am told it is also the most appropriate day for moving graves in cases where that is considered desirable for geomantic reasons, and this is still sometimes done in our district.

The day is computed as being one hundred and five days after Tong-ji, the winter solstice.

Source: *Korean Works and Days: Notes from the Diary of a Country Priest* by Richard Rutt. Rutland, Vt.: Charles E. Tuttle, 1955, p. 225.

People's Republic of China

Qing Ming

Pre-1949 Fuzhou family

A passage from an old book describes how a well-to-do family in pre-1949 Fuzhou, the capital of Fujian Province, conducted the *Qing Ming* grave-sweeping ceremonies. "The festival arrives with all necessary preparations completed. The family arrives at the tomb site, which is dominated by a large semi-circular altar standing in the foreground. They place offerings of food, tea, and wine together with candles on each side of the altar or before the gravestone; an incense burner claims pride of place at the altar.

"The burning of incense and candles signals the beginning of the ceremony. Each male member of the household performs in turn the kowtow—the ritual of three-prostrations and three bows, accompanied by the explosions of firecrackers. A libation of wine is sprinkled over burning paper money, and then the cup is refilled and put back in place. Next follows a repetition of the kowtow. The offerings of food may either be consumed then and there or taken home. The ceremony comes to an end as more firecrackers are set off. Back at home they make offerings again before the family's ancestral tablet of food, candles, incense, and a few evergreen sprigs or heads of wheat, all arranged neatly on a platter."

Cold Food Day

Another name for *Qing Ming* Festival is "Cold Food Day". This appellation applied originally to the preceding day, when people could eat only cold food. Cooking on that day was considered to be taboo. Although this practice has long been neglected, the legend surrounding its origin, which dates back to the State of Jin (present day Shanxi Province together with parts of Henan and Shaanxi) during the Spring and Autumn Period (770-475 B.C.), is a well-known one among the Chinese.

Beijing, c. 1981

In China's cities traditional ancestor worship ceremonies are largely a thing of the past and are now confined mainly to a few state-run public graveyards and monuments. The modern *Qing Ming* Festival has been recast as a day of patriotism. During my stay in Beijing, for instance, I witnessed the presentation of memorial wreaths to heroes of the Chinese revolution by relatives and primary school children at the Babaoshan Cemetery and the Tian'anmen Square Monument of the People's Heroes.

In the vast countryside, however, tradition dies hard. Burial continues to be widely practiced. *Qing Ming* is still the time for families to visit their family gravesite, and in many places people burn paper money and make simple offerings. The major difference is that public graveyards are now the norm, and no land that can be used for productive purposes may be occupied by graves. The 1981 festival witnessed the revival of an extremely ancient memorial ceremony in honor of the Yellow Emperor, who is considered to be the foremost ancestor of the Chinese people. This ceremony occurred in Huangling County, Shaanxi Province, at the site which is reputed to be the gravesite of this legendary figure in Chinese history.

Source: *Chinese Traditional Festivals* by Marie-Luise Latsch. Beijing, China: New World Press, 1984, pp. 46-49.

Taiwan

The Cold Food Feast/Han Shih

Legend associated with the Cold Food day

The story is told of a certain Kài Chú-chhui, pronounced Chieh Tzu-t'ui in mandarin, who was one of the five loyal ministers of Duke Wen of Ch'in. Before being made Duke of Ch'in in 635 B.C., he had wandered in exile for several years, accompanied by his five loyal ministers. On one occasion, being quite weak and without food, the Duke was near death until Kài Chú-chhui cut a piece of flesh from his own leg, and cooking it, gave it to the Duke to eat, thus saving his life. But when the Duke came into his inheritance, he awarded the other four ministers with high office, while entirely forgetting about Kài Chú-chhui. This gentleman thereupon retired from public office, and went to live in a forest hut where he cared for his aged mother. The Duke Wen, remembering suddenly his erstwhile friend, went looking for him in the forest, seeking now at last to reward Kài Chú-chhui with high office. But Kai, still angry about the rebuff, or content with his hermitage, refused to come out. The Duke then set fire to the forest, hoping to scare him out and force the office upon him. Kài Chú-chhui chose to remain there and burn to death, thus becoming the patron of the "cold food" feast day, a day on which it is unthinkable to light fires in his memory.

Ch'ing Ming visit to graves

First the grave is cleaned, weeds and other undesirable elements being swept away. Then a special package of paper called "bō-chóa" is broken open, and prepared to be placed about the grave. The "Bō-chóa" consists of about twenty pieces of long yellow paper strips, about 3 inches wide and a foot long. On top of these are stapled several pieces of shorter red and blue paper. The package is broken open, and some of the red paper is put at the head of the gravestone, and held there with a rock. Then the remaining part is put in front of the small shrine to the god of the soil, usually to the right of the grave, and also held in place with a rock. Finally all of the yellow paper is stuck in the ground over the grave, as if one were re-shingling a house. This is called "Oā hīa," that is, literally, changing the roof tiles. It is a symbolic gesture of taking care of the residence of one's ancestors. These preparations having been made, the bai-bai then may take place: food is laid out, incense burned, and paper money set on fire in front of the grave. Finally firecrackers are exploded.

The prayers recited during this ceremony relate to the ancestors what is being done, and beg for life and health for the male offspring, that they may grow up and lead prosperous lives. Peace at home and good crops are also asked for. The ceremony is also called "siā-thó" or thanking the earth (god).

If it is the first or third year after the burial of a family head, a large banquet must be laid out at home, with at least 12 kinds of dishes, and a much more elaborate ceremony performed at the grave. This ceremony is called "chhīu-bō," meaning a sacrifice performed at the grave. It is used only on this occasion.

Source: *Taiwan Feasts and Customs* by Michael R. Saso. Hsinchu, Taiwan: Chabanel Language Institute, pp. 37-40.

For more on Ch'ing-Ming see: "Ch'ing-Ming, the Spring Festival" in *Chinese Festivals* by Wolfram Eberhard. New York: Henry Schuman, 1952, pp. 113-128; "The Pure Brightness Festival" in *Chinese Traditional Festivals* by Marie-Luise Latsch. Beijing, China: New World Press, 1984, pp. 46-54.

Eight Days Beginning on Day 15 of Nisan (Circa April)

Pesach/Passover

Passover celebrates the release of the Jews from Egypt after God's Plagues on the Egyptians. The Angel of Death slew every firstborn child in the country but spared God's chosen people, who marked their doors with the blood of a lamb. The bread they baked for their flight was unleavened; hence matzot (unleavened) are eaten to commemorate this. The home must be thoroughly cleaned and special Passover dishes used. The night before Passover the entire house is ritually searched for any crumb of unleavened bread. The ritual Seder dinner includes a ceremonial plate containing a roasted lamb shank bone (symbolizing the sacrificed lamb), a roasted egg (symbolizing the offering at the temple and mourning at the destruction of the temple), bitter herbs (a reminder of slavery), greens (representing spring and renewal), a mixture of ground spiced fruits and nuts (resembling the mortar used by the enslaved Jews), and three matzot representing Kohanim, Levites, and Israel. These items are sampled as the Haggadah is read. The reading climaxes with the opening of the door to let the Prophet Elijah enter and drink from his cup of wine. In a bit of levity during the meal that follows, one of the children will steal a piece of the *afikomen* (hard bread) and demand a prize of the father for its return. (In future years, this holiday season begins on April 18, 1992; April 6, 1993; March 27, 1994; and April 21, 1995.)

Bukhara

Preparation of Passover matza

Preparations for Passover began with the wheat harvest. The wheat to be used in matzos was picked up between Lag B'eomer and Shavuot and kept dry until milling. Each family milled and stored its own flour. When the month of Nisan arrived, the women began making the matza. They were constrained to keep their mouths covered while kneading the dough and talking was not allowed. If a woman spoke during this process, her matzos were unfit to use. On completing the matza making, the woman would prepare a feast for her family to celebrate the successful completion of this sacred task.

Each family slaughtered a sheep for the Seder. The men went to the bathhouse on this day, and then to the synagogue. The women prepared the meal. For the Seder everyone sat in a circle on the carpeted floor. The Seder plate and matzots were placed on a white silk cloth, embroidered colorfully. The meal was lit with oil lamps on metal stands. At the end of the Seder, the women retreated to their own quarters, while the men remained to chant the Songs of Songs.

During the intermediate days of Passover no work was done. Then at the festival's end, the oldest male in the family would bring forth a sheaf of green stalks. Each male in the family would kiss the elder's hand and be tapped lightly with the stalks.

Source: *One People: The Story of the Eastern Jews* by Devorah and Menachem Hacohen. New York: Sabra, 1969, pp. 102-103.

Israel

Pesach on a Kibbutz, c. 1958

First march the reapers, carrying their scythes over the shoulders. With them go their oldest sons and daughters. The sons help them reap, the daughters do the gleaning. Uri's father leads, and Uri's sister and brother follow close behind.

After the reapers comes an open wagon. The little children and the band ride in it. Behind the wagon walk the dancers in their long white dresses. And then come all the rest of us.

The music plays, and we sing:

> Shuru habitu uréu . . .
>
> See, and look, and behold
> How great is this day . . .

When we come to the fields, we sit on the ground around them. The reapers swing their scythes and cut the sheaves. The gleaners follow behind, gather the sheaves, and bind them into bundles.

The reapers work their way through the field with dashing strokes. It does not take long before the first field is harvested.

The reapers stand aside now, and the gleaners carry their bundles in their outstretched arms and put them down before the people. And now the dancers stand up. My cousin Loga is among them and so are five others from my group.

First they stand still and raise their arms solemnly toward the sky. Then they begin the round dance of Spring. They move to and fro, and some of them kneel while others dance around them with outstretched arms.

Michael accompanies the dancers on his shepherd's drum. Then two mouth organs take over and an accordion and a trumpet, and we all sing:

Artza Aleenu . . .

We came to our land
And we have ploughed
And we have sown
And now we'll reap the harvest . . .

A meal for seven hundred follows in the Kibbutz dining hall.

When everybody is seated the doors open, and ten girls walk through the rows of tables to the front. They carry the newly cut barley sheaves high above their heads, and lay them down on the stage. The choir sings:

Come to the fields and
Look at the vineyards,
See how everything blossoms and grows.

The rains are gone and
The dew is coming
See how everything blossoms and grows.

Everybody has a book with the Haggadah, the story of Pesach, in front of him. Ben Ami leads us in reading it aloud.

After the reading and the meal, entertainment is given, including dances and a pantomime of "The Song of the Kid."

And now Yigal sings the song again, from the last verse backwards. He sings it faster and faster, and everybody in the dining hall joins in the song:

"He smote the angel of death who slew the slaughterer who killed the ox that drank the water that quenched the fire that burned the stick that beat the dog that bit the cat that ate the kid my father bought for two farthings, for two farthings!"

Our Pesach celebration always ends with this song. After that we all move the tables and benches and chairs and orange crates to the walls. Two chaverim bring their accordions and the dancing begins. First, the hora is danced in big circles, and then come the polka and the krakoviak in fours and twos.

When we return to the Mosad it is long after midnight. The full moon shines in the clear sky between the cypress trees. I see the whole Emek in its gleam. A few lights glitter in the valley. All is quiet now in my village.

Source: *My Village in Israel* by Sonia and Tim Gidal. Pantheon, 1959, pp. 68-76.

Libya

Passover foods and traditions

At the Seder, a child took the afikoman, wrapped it in a napkin, and left the room. Everyone cried, "Thief! Thief!" When the child came back, the father asked, "Where were you?" "In Egypt." "And where are you going?" "To Jerusalem." Then all called out, "Next year in Jerusalem!" The woman of the house held the stack of matzos above the head of every person in the house before the Four Questions. The Seder plate contained an egg for each family member and slices of roast liver and lung along with the shankbone. In some areas, such as Maslatta, the juice of boiled raisins was used for the Four Cups rather than wine.

In the intermediate days of Passover picnics were held in the orange groves near town. The Moslem owners encouraged the Jews to picnic in the belief that their presence brought prosperity to the grove's owner.

On the last day of Passover young men roamed the streets calling, "Ha taruna, ha ahamaman," "Give natru, give kamun." These were ingredients of flour, signifying the last day of matza eating. Young women watched from their balconies and rooftops on this day, as young men paraded the streets.

The young man might throw a flower to his chosen love as he passed. In the evening homes were decorated with flowers and lettuce leaves, and brides and grooms exchanged baskets of these as symbols of frangrance and prosperity.

In port communities, men carried a bit of the afikoman and a few salt crystals given by the shamash in order to calm the stormy seas.

Source: *One People: The Story of the Eastern Jews* by Devorah and Menachem Hacohen. New York: Sabra, 1969, pp. 102-103.

Morocco

Passover storytelling

The leaven searched for on Passover eve contained slices of grilled liver in Morocco. The matzos were not baked until after the leaven had been burned on the morning of Passover eve. Thus the baking was hurried. It was accompanied by the chanting of Psalms.

The Seder plate was carried round, passing it over the heads of all present, before sitting down to the Seder. After the Four Questions, the leader of the Seder took up a staff and the afikoman and left the room by one door, returning by another. He was asked, "Whence comest thou?" and proceeded to tell the entire story of the exodus with embellishments. Everyone commented when he concluded, "He that tells of the exodus from Egypt at greater length is the more praiseworthy."

During the intermediate days a special Seder, served in small dishes, was held for the young children, who usually fell asleep during the Seder itself.

Source: *One People: The Story of the Eastern Jews* by Devora and Menachem Hacohen. New York: Sabra, 1969, p. 66.

Tunis

Passover customs in Tunis

On the eve of rosh hodesh Nisan each family dipped a coin or ornament into the oil of the kandil, making good wishes for the coming year. The following day a lamb was purchased, to be slaughtered on the thirteenth day of Nisan. A son touched the blood with his palm and made a print on the outside of the home's doorpost. The lamb was roasted and eaten on the eve of the fourteenth.

On the morning of Passover eve, the men studied the Talmud and partook of special food. Bits from the meal were taken home to the eldest daughter, and to the mother if she were also an eldest daughter.

The main Passover dish was masuki, cooked vegetables, lamb, and matza. Bits of the harosset were fastened to the outer doorpost to ward off evil spirits. Bits of the afikoman were carried by sailors to protect from storms.

On the seventh day of Passover, prayers were said near a body of water. The congregation returned to the synagogue to sing songs of the sea, taken from the bible, while dancing around two men dressed as Moses and Aaron. The women tossed flowers and perfume on the men as they returned from the waterside.

Counting the omer began on the second night of Passover. As they prayed they held bits of salt in their palms to ward off the demons which were abroad at this time.

At the end of Passover the head of the household put lettuce leaves and green vegetables in the corners of the house and on its furnishings. This symbolized a fresh and vigorous year.

Source: *One People: The Story of the Eastern Jews* by Devora and Manachem Hacohen. New York: Sabra, 1969, pp. 90-91.

Yemen

Passover food

Flour for the matzos was prepared by a special method. The wheat was placed on a wild plant (harmel), then covered with another layer of the plant. A mat covered the whole, and this was placed in the sun. The vapors given off by the plant loosened the outer hull of the wheat and made milling easier.

Matzos were baked daily during Passover. The dough was salted slightly. As many as thirteen kinds of harosset were also prepared.

The Seder table was piled with arrangements of vegetables, lettuce, radishes, parsley, and horseradish. The entire table was covered by vegetables. In the middle, several kinds of harosset were put out in small dishes and sprinkled with grains to represent "straw" on top of "clay."

The haggadah was read in Hebrew but explained in the vernacular. Elijah's Cup was not known in Yemen.

Source: *One People: The Story of the Eastern Jews* by Devorah and Menachem Hacohen. New York: Sabra, 1969, pp. 147-148.

For more on Passover see: *Burning Lights* by Bella Chagall. New York: Shocken, 1946, pp. 228-239; *My Life* by Marc Chagall. New York: The Orion Press, 1960, p. 39; "Passover," in *The Jewish Party Book: A Contemporary Guild to Customs, Crafts and Foods* by Mae Shafter Rockland. New York: Schocken, 1978, pp. 177-199. (The seder is described.); "Passover," in *Folklore of American Holidays* by Hennig Cohen and Tristram Potter Coffin. 2nd ed. Detroit: Gale Research, 1991, pp. 145-151.

Evening of Last Day of Passover and Day after Passover

Maimona

North African Jews honor Maimonides on this date. Pitchers of milk, heads of wheat, fig branches, garlands of flowers, and a bowl of live fish are displayed on the table. Dairy foods, especially a pancake, *muflita,* are eaten.

Libya

Commemorating the death of Maimonides

On the day after Passover the hametz is brought back with much ceremony. Each family member receives a small loaf of bread with a baked egg inside, the *maimona.* This is eaten with slices of lamb. This custom dates to the year 1204, when Maimonides passed away. Since the news of his death reached Tripoli during Passover, the Jewish people could not mourn for the sage in the traditional way of eating bread and an egg. This act was postponed until the following day and called Maimona.

Source: *One People: The Story of the Eastern Jews* by Devora and Menachem Hacohen. New York: Sabra, 1969, p. 104.

Morocco

Maimona customs

The last day of Passover was the beginning of the maimona festival. Women wore velvet dresses embroidered with gold and silver thread. Girls wore bridal white, or dressed up as Arab women. Young men dressed as Berbers or famous figures and roamed the streets, exchanging glances with the girls.

The table was set with a white cloth decorated with green wheat stalks and flowers, brought by the Arab villagers. In the center stood a pitcher of milk, and a bowl of flour with five eggs, five bean stalks, and five dates on top. Plates of honey, fruit, nuts, cookies, muflita, pancakes, lettuce, and wine surrounded the bowl.

Returning from the synagogue, worshippers stopped to bless their friends with "Alallah maimuna amarcha masauda," "Best wishes for a blessed maimuna." They tasted the refreshments at each stop, especially the lettuce, honey, and muflita.

In port cities, people went to the sea to dip their feet in the water. Elsewhere rivers or springs had to serve.

Source: *One People: The Story of the Eastern Jews* by Devora and Menachem Hacohen. New York: Sabra, 1969, pp. 66-67.

April 12 or 13

New Year

This is the day when the sun enters Aries. It is celebrated as the beginning of the New Year in Southeast Asia.

Burma

Thingyan

Playing with water

On Thingyan, Tha-gya Min, King of the Tha-gyas, descends from heaven. The holiday has its pious side, with visits to monasteries and temples. But it is especially noted for the playful squirting of water on all who pass. According to some sources, children alone get to toss water on the first day; for the remaining three days adults join the water play.

More water

This takes place some time around the middle of April, to celebrate the Burmese New Year. The old year must be washed away and the new one baptized with water. The exact date of Thingyan must be chosen by astrologers and marks the arrival each year of Thagyamin, the king of the *nats,* bringing peace and prosperity to Burma in the coming year, symbolized by a jar of water.

The whole country greets this visitation with an explosion of celebrations: *pwes,* fetes, parades and every sort of display. But what lives most in the memory is the deluge of water that makes every outing hazardous during the festival. This was once a symbolic ritual, gently performed for the benefit of the recipient; a grave and deferential pouring of the cleansing stream after permission to do so had been given. Now, it has evolved into a slapstick comedy—no one is immune and permission is seldom requested. Water is hurled from buckets, mugs, bowls, thrown in balloons, squirted from pumps, sprayed from hydrants, and cascaded from balconies and upper windows. Lasting officially for three or four days, it often goes on longer.

Source: *Thailand & Burma* by Frank Kusy and Frances Capel. Cadogan Guides, Chester Conn.: The Globe Pequot Press, 1958, p. 269.

A splashing festival

During the Water Festival people pour water on the images of Buddha and on one another as a sign of blessing. They also sprinkle the bodhi trees, in memory of the original tree under which Buddha sat to meditate.

The four-day festival starts with children pouring water on the first day. This has become such a popular custom that nowadays young people go out in trucks and jeeps and stop to have water fights with one another. Little children douse all the vehicles and passers-by in sight. During the remaining three days of the festival, the grownups join in the fun.

Source: *Hi Neighbor. Book 5.* New York: Hastings House in cooperation with the United States Committee for UNICEF, 1962, p. 17.

Thingyan in a traditional village

Traditionally, the New Year festival calls for visiting the pagodas and monasteries and washing the images of the Buddha, after which one calls upon his elders and sprinkles them gently with scented water from a silver bowl. The young men of the village go from house to house, dancing and singing to the accompaniment of an orchestra. At each house they sprinkle water on the elders and ask them to call out the young girls. The girls are likewise sprinkled with water by means of a flower carried in the bowls.

In Tadagale today, many of the traditional customs of the New Year are still observed. Preparatory to the holiday, houses are swept and compounds cleared of all refuse. Everything is made clean and orderly. The images of the Buddha are washed, elders are called upon, sprinkled with water, and wished well. But, as in many parts of the country, the New Year festival has tended to take on a rather secularized character in modern times. Water sprinkling has become water throwing; groups of people, especially youngsters, go into the towns in carts or trucks, armed with buckets of water which they throw at passers-by. . . . These activities are in contrast with the traditionally serious, sacred character of the New Year as conceived by older villagers. The schoolmaster of the community, a middle-aged man with many years of religious training, spoke of the New Year:

> Thingyan is the New Year festival, but the villagers do not know the significance of the festival. They know only that it is a feast day and a holiday and a day for having fun. In reality there should be no frivolity on New Year's day; it is a day on which one should fast and pray, for one is now one year older and therefore nearer death. One should meditate on the futility of frivolity as compared with the blessedness of deeds of merit.

Source: *Tadagale: A Burmese Village in 1950* by Charles

Brandt. Cornell, Southeast Asia Program. Data Paper no. 13, Ithaca, 1954, p. 39.

Children's names recorded in the King of the Gods' book

To children, this particular festival is of special interest, though they enjoy them all. According to legend, it is during *Thingyan* that each child has his name inscribed in one of two big volumes carried by the King of the Gods. Names of children who have been well behaved during the year and have performed acts of merit are recorded in the volume bound in gold. The others have their names recorded in the volume bound in dog skin.

Thingyan's quieter side

Yet with all this boisterous, roisterous, rowdy fun, somehow, at some time the revelers find themselves at a pagoda, offering flowers, lights, and pure sweet water. For one quiet moment in a noisome day, they will pray to the All-Enlightened One, the Calm One. Also they will visit the homes of their elders to pay homage with a bowl of lavender water and sprigs of victory flowers and to receive their blessings. They will participate in the setting free of bullocks and fish, for the Burmese are fond of saving those at the threshold of death and giving them a new lease on life. One of *Thingyan's* most moving sights is the procession led by dancers and drummers, which includes a bullock garlanded with *padauk* flowers with a silk carpet on its back and the words "Not to be harmed" painted on its sides, and women carrying pots of fish to be released in the streams and rivers.

Source: "The Burmese Water Festival" by U Win Pe in *We The Burmese: Voices from Burma* by Helen C. Trager. New York: Federick A. Praeger, 1968, pp. 263, 267.

An Arakan water festival

In Arakan, on the northwest coast of Burma on the Bay of Bengal, the Arakanese have a special custom. Boys and girls are not usually allowed to socialize, but on this holiday they have a way of romancing. . . .

Temporary thatch houses called *mandats* are built, one *mandat* in each quarter of the village. Then long boats are brought ashore from waterways and placed inside.

The boat is filled with water and shy, pretty village girls line up along one side of the boat. The boys, with eyes on the girl of their choice, wait in line on the other side. Each boy carries a bowl.

When his turn comes, a boy extends his bowl to his favorite girl. If she likes him she takes the bowl, fills it with water, and returns it to him. This gives him permission to throw water over her, which is what the Water Festival is all about.

She in turn, laughing and dripping, refills his bowl and throws water over him. Meanwhile they can talk briefly to each other, a rare treat in their sheltered lives.

This is their chance to arrange a secret meeting, and often the boy and girl fall in love.

Source: *Celebrations: Asia and the Pacific* by Gene Sawyer. Honolulu: Friends of the East-West Center, 1978, p. 28.

Meritorious hairwashing

. . . In the evening, too, we carried out Grandmother's good deed of inviting a number of people from the village to come and wash their hair. Hairwashing is part of the New Year's rituals because the noblest part of the body, the head, must be in a clean condition at this time. In the days of the Burmese kings, there was a ceremonial washing of the King's hair at the New Year, called the *tha-gyan daw gyi*.

Burmese people wash their hair with the alkaline juices of the bark of a tree known as *tha-yaw,* combined with the seeds of the *accacia concina*. The bark, which is stored in a dried condition, is soaked for a few hours before washing, the accacia seeds are boiled in their pods until they are soft and are then crushed into the tha-yaw water. The result is a slippery mixture which we still use in preference to modern shampoos on the market. The provision of this in basins, and of clear water in big jars on our bamboo platform, was considered a meritorious act on New Year's eve. About twenty people came, bringing towels and a change of clothing. They washed their hair and bathed on the bamboo platform over the creek. The ladies put thanakha thickly on their cheeks and gave children blobs where the "roses" of English children's cheeks are, and we all sat on the edge of the platform, hair floating free in the breeze, and watched the sun go down. At night we helped to put the ground bark into little cups and stuck tha-byay leaves in the pots and went to bed full of pleasant anticipations. Tha-gya Min usually arrived about midnight, when Uncle Pyant got out his revolver and fired a salute to announce his arrival to the village. My male cousins stayed up to pour the water pots away, but we slept right through this actual arrival.

Source: *My Burmese Family* by Mi Mi Khaing. Bloomington: Indiana Univ. Press, 1967, p. 99.

For more on Thingyan see: "Happy Thingyan" in *We the Burmese: Voices from Burma* by Helen C. Trager. New York: Frederick A. Praeger, 1967. (A newspaper article asking for moderation in the celebration and more attention to meritorious deeds.); "The New Year's Feast" in *The Burman: His Life and Notions* by Sir James George. London: Macmillan, 1910, pp. 347-355. (Description of Thi'gyan in Mandalay circa 1900.)

Khmer Republic/Cambodia/Kampuchea

Prewar Cambodia New Year games

This is another New Year's game where the players are divided into two teams, to see which team can throw more red beans into a basket. They are trying hard, stooping low, twisting their bodies, and taking aim carefully. But they are not as skillful as the older men and women who have their own game nearby. The older people, of course, have had more experience and know exactly how to toss the beans into the basket.

But the game I like to watch most is the New Year tug-of-war. It is a game that you probably know, except that in our country we play it with a snake. Not a real snake, of course, but several strands of rope plaited like a snake. The snake is one of our gods of mythology, and if you have ever visited our oldest city of Angkor Thom, you will find this snake carved in stone at all the entrances to the city.

Source: *Festivals in Asia* sponsored by the Asian Cultural Committee for UNESCO. Tokyo: Kodanshan, 1975, pp. 47-48.

New Year in Cambodia, c. 1964

A three-day celebration begins on April 13. On the last day of the old year, houses are cleaned and decorated for the New Year. An unprepared house would invite misfortune and evil spirits. On New Year's Day temples are visited and Buddha images are sprinkled with water. Prayers for health, wealth, and happiness in the New Year are offered. On the last day of the celebration small mounds of sand are made in the temple yard and bright paper banners are stuck in each. These banners carry the prayer for a happy and properous life, a life with as many days as the grains of sand in the mound.

Source: *Hi Neighbor. Book 8.* New York: U.S. Committee for UNICEF/Hastings House, 1965, p. 58.

For more on the Cambodian New Year see: "Nouvel-An," in *Ceremonies des douze mois: Fetes annuelles cambodgiennes.* Commision des moeurs et coutumes du Cambodge, pp. 19-25.

Laos

Pimai

New Year in Luang Prabang

The Laotian lunar year begins in December, but Lao prefer to think of the year as beginning with the fifth month (April), when the astrological signs point to light and prosperity and the hot season is about to be followed by the rains. The end of the old year is celebrated with a procession, with prayers, and with a long period of festivities. The houses are swept, symbolically indicating the expulsion of the evil and marauding spirits that might have taken up residence. On the first day of the year the bonzes and the people cleanse the statutes of the Buddha with holy water. It is a time for visiting, and all dress in their best clothing. Votive mounds (usually of sand or stones) are erected in the courts of the *wat* and along the banks of the Mekong. Streamers of colored paper bearing the signs of the zodiac decorate homes and buildings.

•

In Luang Prabang the festival is elaborately celebrated with the release of birds and animals, processions of royal elephants, and court gatherings. The king himself sprinkles the Buddha images with holy water. Dances and masques commemorate the legendary ancestors of the Lao, and offerings are made of fruits, flowers, new vegetables, and candles. (It is the growing season, and many spring rites have crept into new year celebrations.) The king gives a feast for the bonzes in Luang Prabang, and since 1941 there have been festivities expecially for the children—who are "exposed" to the good genie of the new year.

Source: *Laos: A Country Study* by Donald P. Whitaker et al. Foreign Area Studies, The American University, 1971, pp. 121-122.

Bathing Buddhas, splashing friends, a family ceremony, and prayer mounds

First everyone goes to pagodas carrying silver bowls filled with scented water. They anoint the statues of Buddha, offer flowers, and pray for blessings in the new year.

Walking to and from the pagodas, they toss water from their bowls on anyone they meet. Children blow up balloons, fill them with water and squirt whomever is in range. Young people fill large cans with water, put them in jeeps, drive to houses of friends and douse them. It's all part of the fun and no one seems to mind getting wet.

In every home the family prepares for the traditional *baci,* or ceremony. A low table is covered with a silk cloth or banana leaves and a bowl is placed in the center. In the bowl, banana leaves are arranged in the shape of a tree and flowers are pinned on the leaves. Finally, a long string is wound around the tree.

A few monks are invited to come and pray. After the little ceremony, they cut pieces of the string and tie them around the wrists of members of the family to bring them good luck in the coming year.

Another custom is to pile up small mounds of sand around a pagoda or on the banks of a river. These are topped with a scroll on which are drawn the animals of the zodiac. A person building a sand pile asks the grace of heaven for a life as rich in joys as there are grains of sand in the pile.

Source: *Asia and the Pacific* by Gene Sawyer. Honolulu: Friends of the East-West Center, 1978, p. 26.

The days of Pimai

. . . And even today, in the kingdom of Laos, people still consult an astrologer to fix the time for Pimai, the New Year, which usually falls in April.

And how do the people of Laos celebrate Pimai? First of all, schools and offices are closed so that everyone can enjoy the festivities, which last for two weeks in the royal capital of Luang Prabang, and three days elsewhere.

The people of Laos like to think that when the year ends, the goddess of the old year leaves and the goddess of the new year comes to take her place. In between these two days there is one day with no goddess at all, when everybody is waiting for the new goddess to arrive.

The first day of Pimai is called "the goddess leaves," and everyone goes to the temples, carrying silver bowls of scented water, to help the monks wash all the statues in honor of the new goddess. People in Laos also believe in the cleansing effect of water, like the people of Burma, so there is a water-throwing festival at this time, and all houses are washed and scrubbed from floor to ceiling.

And amid much laughter and gaiety people wash away their sins of the old year. Indeed, it is just as well for you to remain dripping wet all the time, otherwise someone is sure to sneak up from behind and tip a bowl of water over your head. If you happen to be outdoors at this time of year, arm yourself with a bucket or a squirt gun and splash as much water as you want. The people of Laos believe that the gayer you are at Pimai, the happier the year will be for you.

You can also join in the fun of carrying sand to the temples, for it counts as a good deed for you in the New Year, and sand is also useful for repair work and for laying on the ground. Most people will make sand mounds in the temple courtyard and stick decorations of flowers, flags and money on them. If you make a sand mound together with a good friend, it means that you will remain good friends for the rest of the year. Young men and women take this chance to make sand mounds together, especially if they wish to get married in the future.

The second day when there is no goddess is called "the day stops," and no one should do any hard work, for without a goddess, who will protect you from danger? In order to make the day pass quickly, parents take their children to the countryside where water-throwing still goes on.

On the third day of Pimai, "the goddess arrives," everyone in Laos breathes a sigh of relief and satisfaction. The goddess has brought the New Year with her and everyone flocks to the temples to offer her food and flowers and to say special prayers to her. And when they return home, families will tie white thread to their fingers to welcome the New Year.

At this time children promise their parents to be obedient and good for the rest of the year, and once this is over the children sprinkle perfumed water on their parents. The day is spent in eating, drinking and getting wetter and wetter.

Source: *Festivals in Asia* sponsored by the Asian Cultural Committee for UNESCO. Tokyo: Kodansha, 1975, pp. 50-54.

The New Year period

The New Year period includes

(1) the *sphutamahāsankranti* day, when the real sun crosses over to the vernal equinox; called in Lao *sangkhan pai,* "(the day when) the year goes away";

(2) an interval of one or two days, depending on the year of the Era; called in Lao *mü nao,* "day (or days) in between";

(3) the *madhyamamahāsankrānti* day, when the mean or theoretical sun crosses over to the vernal equinox; called in Lao *sangkhan khün,* "(the day when) the (new) year begins."

New Year legend of the sun

For the peasants of Campasak, who know nothing of astronomy, the New Year's festival celebrates the journey of the Sun, son of Nang Suvannā. One day, according to a legend recorded in the text called *Sangkhan,* an old beggar woman named Suvanna, having gone down to the river to bathe, saw a monk who hesitated to perform his ablutions because he had no bathing-cloth to cover his nakedness; so she gave him her only piece of cloth; and when he finished bathing she presented him the food she had received as alms. As a result of the merit she thus earned, she was reborn as a beautiful young girl. She had eighty husbands, and bore eight children. The eldest of them, who had a luminous body, was name the Sun. The others were named the Moon, the planets, and Rahu. The Sun became king; his sister the Moon became queen; Rahu stayed with his brother as preceptor; the others looked after the palace and the ministries. In the 5th or 6th month, the legend continues, rain falls and wets the trees; the year comes to an end; and the Sun says goodbye to his queen, who gives him a magical protective device called a "soul-tray." Then he goes forth from his palace, riding in a jeweled chariot—a mode of travel which is said to bring peace and happiness to the people. The day he leaves is called *sangkhan pai;* the day he returns, *sangkhan khün;* but before returning he stops to rest for one or two days, namely the intervening period called *mü nao.*

Preparing for the New Year

On the morning of *sangkhan pai* day, the people of Basak bathe at home or in the river. Houses are swept out and clothes washed, to rid them of the contagions accumulated during the year. In all the monasteries images of the Buddha and his disciples are set out in the preaching halls, or placed in the courtyard on tables decorated with greenery.

Prince's rituals, the *ba si* ceremony

At half-past eleven all the notables of the village gather in the state apartment of the Prince's residence, while the women go into a back parlor to offer their good wishes to the ladies of the household. Servants set out four "soul-trays" or *ba si* of seven tiers. The Prince sits in the middle, near one of them. Facing him is the Acan who is to recite Buddhist prayers in the afternoon in front of the palladium of the principality. He is now functioning as a *mò p'òn* or "expert in wishes." Beside him is a tray of presents containing a banana, a skein of cotton, a bottle of perfume, and some candles, an offering from the members of the Prince's family. The Acan, lighting two candles on one of the "soul-trays" and the tray of presents, lifts them to the height of his forehead.

In a quavering voice he chants a formula beginning with good wishes to "all nāgas, garudas, men, gandharvas, yaksas, and protective spirits, as well as Indra and the king of the underworld," declaring the day to be unusually auspicious, and adding: "May Your Highness thrust aside cupidity, anger and error! May Māra's armies and the five hundred sins draw away from you! May you live long! May you have a fresh and billiant complexion! May you have an immeasurable store of merits! May fortune favor you! May your wife be a faultless and devoted queen! May you be happy! May you possess elephants and horses (in abundance)! May the Kha and Khmer tribes who live (near) lakes and mountains bring you heaps of red gold and countless elephant-tusks as tribute! May the renown of your honors fill the world! May the hundred thousand *devata* dwelling on the Mountain of the Universe come to escort and protect you! May your stature be great! May your fame spread throughout Jambudvīpa! May your enemies leap (with fear) and run away! May you know the magical sciences! May the eighty-four thousand kings pay you tribute! May you be a king of kings, with a palace of gems which will last as long as you live! May you receive heaps of jewels and splendid striped cloth as tribute from many races, Chinese, Cham, N̄uon, Burmese, Hò, Vietnamese and Mòn! May you receive homage from the Hò, and from the T'ai of Chieng Sèn, Luong P'rabang and Lamp'un! May you be free of misfortune and disease! May you live to the age of 108! May your sons and daughters, your queen and your concubines, all live to the age of 108!"

Having finished his chanting, the Acan places the banana from the tray of presents in the Prince's right hand, then performs the wrist-tying rite on the Prince and his children, after which the others in the room approach the Prince on their knees and perform the same rite. One of the "soul-trays" is carried into an inner room, where the Prince's paternal aunt carries out the wrist-tying rite on the ladies of the family, at the same time wishing them happiness and prosperity. Meanwhile the two other "soul-trays" are carried out to the homes of the Prince's brothers, Cao Bun Om and Cao Silomé, where the same Acan repeats his chant and performs the wrist-tying rite.

When the *ba si* ceremony is over, the village notables meet at Cao Bun Um's house and then, led by the Prince carrying a ewer of water, they track down the young girls of the locality. Going into all the houses from north to south, they forcibly sprinkle the girls with water or rub them with soot (a prophylactic rite); on this day the girls cannot count on protection from their fathers. While on the *sangkhan pai* day the women contributed to the re-creation of the *Müang* by sprinkling the Prince and his followers, on *sangkhan khün* day a new order is established which restores the power of the men.

I suppose he was thinking of me mainly as a descendant of Queen Nang P'ao, King S'òi Si Samut, Cao K'am Suk and Cao Ras'adanai. As a stage setting, there was Basak, with its reliquary monuments of my ancestors. When I preside over the ceremonies there, especially the boat races—when I sit alone, all dressed up, on the veranda of the Hò S'ai in front of my ancestors' portraits, for days and days which seem like centuries—of course I can't help thinking about our family history. But the reader of this article may get the impression that I think about these things all the time, or that if I stop thinking about them I get a feeling of guilt.

Source: *The New Year Ceremony at Basak (South Laos)* by Charles Archaim Gault with and afterward by Prince Boun Om. No. 78, South East Asia Program. Ithaca, New York: Cornell Univ., January 1971, pp. 2-3, 10-11, 45-46. (See entire paper for details of this ceremony.)

Malaya (Hindu)

The Hindu New Year in Malaya

On the previous day the house and compound are given a thorough clean-up and purified by sprinkling water mixed with cowdung or with saffron. Brass vessels and brass oil lamps in the house are brought out and polished. On New Year day the householders get up very early in the morning and must set their eyes on auspicious objects. For this purpose the lady of the house would have got up before the others and laid out the shrine room for worship. A lamp is lit in front of a picture of the family-deity and a religious text is kept open near it. Fruits, cucumber, flowers and a split coconut are also laid there in offering. The members of the family, as soon as they are up, without opening their eyes, are led to this shrine before which they open their eyes for the first time and worship there. Some children make it a point to see their parents first on this day as they get up for this is also considered auspicious.

The 'oil bath' is the next important item on this day. Here the orthodox would smear the head and body a special medicament prepared from certain leaves, flowers, saffron and milk. After the bath, everyone gets into new clothes. The men wear white *veshtis* and the women sarees of the prescribed auspicious colour. There is a more elaborate worship at the shrine and then the first meal is taken at the auspicious time. Then many people visit the nearest temple where there will be special *poojas*. In some temples there is a procession where the deity is carried round the outer court.

The rest of the day is devoted to visiting friends and exchanging New Year greetings. A popular custom is the exchange of money. When one visits a friend's house, he is entertained and presented with money enclosed in betel leaves. This money is first placed before the deity and sanctified. Sometimes people honour their elders by presenting betel with money in it. The receiving of gifts of money on this day from a wealthy and influential person is held to bring good luck to the receiver. It is also a form of charity indulged in by wealthy people when all their servants, dependants and needy neighbours visit them and receive gifts of money. This gift is known as *kaivishesham*. Generally non-vegetarian food is prohibited on this day and only vegetarian meals are cooked and eaten, though this is not strictly followed by all people.

Source: *Indian Festivals in Malaya* by S. Arasaratnam. Kuala Lumpur: Dept. of Indian Studies, Univ. of Malaya, 1966, pp. 25-26.

April 13-15

New Year

The Thai New Year, celebrated at the beginning of the solar year, when the sun enters Aries, is a national holiday in Thailand (April 13). The days include ritual blessing of monks, bathing of Buddha images, and reverence to elders. The young celebrate by splashing water on everyone who passes!

Thailand

Songkran

Songkran in Bangkhuad village

Songkran: On New Year's Day (celebrated in the fifth lunar month, April) the laity bring the monks special glutinous rice cakes. A sermon is given in the morning. New Year's Day is actually a very small occasion, for the big festival comes at the time of the full moon (in urban areas at the vernal equinox) and lasts three days. On the first day, the people bring food to the *wat* and listen to a sermon, usually expounding merit. The urns holding the cremated fragments of the deceased are brought to the *wat* by each household. These are placed on a special table in the corner of the *wihan.* A holy string is placed around each urn and tied to the Buddha. The farmers congregate in the *wihan* and chat until noon, at which time they return home. In the evening they return to the *wihan.* The monks, holding a part of the holy string, recite the *Bangsakun* (the same text which is used at all pre-cremation services in the home, and which deals with the ephemerality of life and material possessions). There follows a three-fold recitation of the seven lessons, each lesson lasting about 25 minutes. The readings continue thus until dawn. Some male laymen play chess during the evening, other members talk, chew betel, and drink tea. After each lesson, money is put into the special bowl by the laity and the total amount is publicly announced by the monk.

Blessing the monks with water

The morning of the second day is similar to the first. At noon the urns are taken back to their respective households, however, and the laymen do not return to the *wat* until the third day. On this day, they again bring food to the monks. The morning ceremony is similar to that of any other holy day. At 2:00 p.m., as the monks, wearing only the *ciwaun* and *sabong,* sit in a row on the north side of the dais, the villagers walk behind the monks with bowls of water, pouring a little on each monk while offering him a blessing. The monks meanwhile continue to chant the *hajphaunhajsin* blessing, wishing the congregation well. After the ablutions, several wealthy members of the community may each present a monk with a set of clothing (excluding the *sangkhali*). Thus ends the ceremony insofar as the *wat* is involved.

Blessing the elders

On the last day, the younger members of the family visit the homes of the respected elders of the community as well as the elders of their own family. They *krab* before each elder and say, "The year is commencing, may you continue to have health and prosperity." The elder then takes some holy water mixed with perfume and daubs it over the donor's face and hands, while offering a short blessing. If the visiting household can afford it, a suit of clothing or a *phakhowma* is presented to the elder at this time.

The popular tradition of water-throwing is indulged in only by the children and young people of the community. During the entire three days, they run about drenching one another with water, but are careful not to wet the elders unduly.

New Year's games

Until twenty years ago, adults in mixed groups played a game at New Year's similar to drop-the-handkerchief. The players sat around in a circle, alternating men and women. A *phakhawma* was used with a large knot tied in one end. It was usually dropped behind a member of the opposite sex. The object of the game was to pick up the *phakhawma,* catch up with the opponent, and swat him (or her) as frequently and as hard as possible on the buttocks as he circled the ring twice before returning to his original place.

Source: *Bangkhuad: A Community Study in Thailand* by Howard Neva Kaufman. Locust Valley, N.Y.: J. J. Augustin, 1960, pp. 169, 195.

Songkran, c. 1950

. . . Preliminary arrangements for the festival may begin on the day of the full moon, which is known as *Wan Dar,* or "preparing day," but the festival proper begins the first day of the new lunar period, known in the north as *Sankranti,* and in central Thailand as *Maha Song-gram.* The New Year festival is called in the northern regions *Pi Mai,* and in the other areas *Songkran.*

On the morning of *Sankranti,* the opening day of the festival, the peasant family takes special food to the temple, and presents food to the old people of the village. In the north, special cakes of brown sugar and rice flour are presented, and peasants may send these to friends and neighbors. It was once the custom to put food and water in bamboo tubes tied to the trees so that roving spirits would also be fed, and to fire guns to frighten away evil spirits; a remnant of this custom is the exploding of firecrackers during the festival.

On the second day—*Wan Nao*—villagers bring sand to the *wat* compound, each family shaping its sand contribution in the form of a *chedi* (stupa) in the courtyard. Later this sand will be distributed throughout the compound.

On the third day—*Wan Phya* in the north, and *Wan Ta Loen Sok* in the central area—special food offerings are presented to the monks. Lustral water (*som poi*) is taken to the temple by the monks to wash or sprinkle the sacred images of Buddha, and a morning service is conducted there for the congregation.

The anointing of the Buddha with holy water has its counterpart in the custom of villagers sprinkling each other. For the young people, dousing each other has become largely a mirth-making occasion, but the older villagers retain remnants of the older religious character of the custom.

On the fourth day—*Pak Pi*—villagers pay their respects to the abbot, commune headman, village headman, and the old people of the village. They carry a silver bowl of lustral water, incense, flowers, puffed rice, and other offerings, and the person visited sprinkles the visitor with the holy water and gives a blessing. Services are held in the temple by the monks from eight to ten in the evenings.

Much the same sequence of events is followed on the next two days, *Wan Pak Pi* and *Wan Pak Tuan*. According to the lunar calendar, the festival ends on the fifth day, but in the northern areas, young people continue dousing each other and keep up other festive activities for several additional days.

During the five-day period of the festival a host of other ritual observances are carried out, the meanings of which have been forgotten. Some are survivals of animistic customs, others are Brahmanistic; the very festival of *Songkran*, for example, is Brahmanistic in origin. On the opening day of the New Year, villagers wash their hair and clothes, and clean the house compound of the dirt of the past year. On the second day, any caged pets in the household are freed. On the third day, in addition to presenting food at the temple, the villagers also place paper flags on poles in the temple compound. These paper flags are similar to the bamboo flags erected as spirit offerings in the rice fields.

Source: *Village Life in Modern Thailand* by John E. deYoung. Berkeley: Univ. of Calif., 1955, pp. 135-136.

Rituals and celebrations

Early in the morning of the first day of Sŏngkraan, the thirteenth of April, the people in their new clothes repair to the wat of their village to offer food to monks. A long bench, either temporary or permanent, is erected in the compound of the wat where monks' alms bowls stand in a row on either side of the bench. There is a special alms bowl bigger than the rest placed at the head of the row. This is meant as the alms bowl peculiar to the Buddha. Into the alms bowls, first into the so-called Buddha's alms bowl and then into the others, the gathering crowd in pious mood queues up to put boiled rice, and into the covers of the alms bowls lying upturned other food, fruits, and sweetmeats. Paradoxically there is more food than a monk can take in a day even though a monk by discipline cannot take food offered to him if any is left after his last day's meal. Economically it is really a waste, but it was not so in the old days when food, especially rice and fish, were in abundance and money to a people with simple needs was not a necessity. The people attached the highest value to their religion; and this is the only way for them to express their faith.

In the afternoon and on the next days there is a ceremonial bathing of the Buddha image and also of the abbot of the wat, followed by the well-known ''water throwing festival'' which in the old days was considered a magic means to cause abundance of water or rain but which has degenerated into a form of amusement pure and simple. On this day and also on the succeeding days there is a ceremonial bathing of elder relatives and respected persons carried out by the younger generation. A memorial service to the departed ones and the releasing of live fish and birds are also performed as deeds of merit. During the three days of Sŏngkraan young people of both sexes amuse themselves by throwing water at one or another, playing games, dancing, singing, or other such pastimes as they can devise.

Source: *Life and Rituals in Old Siam* by Phya Anuman Rajadhon. New Haven: HRAF Press, 1961, p. 93.

Releasing live birds and fish

On *Songkran* days it is the custom for young people to release live birds from a cage or to set fish free from their bowls to swim in the river or canal. In some districts and villages, young girls in gay, colorful costumes form a procession to the river. Each girl carries a bowl of fish. When the girls reach the bank of the river, they all stoop down together and very solemnly and carefully empty the bowls and let the fish swim free. This ritual is thought to bring good luck.

Source: *Happy Birthday Round the World* by Lois S. Johnson. New York: Rand McNally, 1066, p. 146.

April 19-25 (The Thursday in This Period)

First Day of Summer

A special Icelandic holiday, after the long northern winters it is greeted as the first day of summer. (It was on Thursday in 1991.)

Iceland

Nineteenth-century first-day-of-summer customs

The First Day of Summer was a great day of feasting all over the country, and it was in most places considered second only to Christmas and New Year in terms of celebration. There is mention of this as early as the mid-18th century. All the best foods and beverages would be served on this occasion, though in fact the larder would frequently be nearly bare at this time of spring. For that reason, people generally tried to put away some tidbits specifically for this day. There were even instances of storing food in a special barrel during the autumn, which was not to be touched until the First Day of Summer. But that seems to have been done mainly in the Western Fjords.

Special *summer-day cakes* were baked in many places of the Northwest. These were enormous rye "cakes" (actually, flat rye breads), up to one foot (30 cm) in diameter and three quarters of an inch (2 cm) thick. On top of these would be piled the day's share of food for each individual: butter, *hangiket,* flanks, *lundabaggar,* hard fish, halibut fins, etc., all according to means and circumstances.

In the South and West, skippers commonly made their crew a banquet on this day.

Summer presents were very peculiar to Iceland. They seem to antedate even Christmas presents as a custom among the common people. The oldest known example is from 1545 when Bishop Gissur Einarsson of Skalholt brought "summer gifts" for the members of his household. By the middle of the 19th century this seems to have become general practice, at least in the North and East.

Most often, the presents were home-made articles, though in some instances, they were bought in town. A special kind of present in the Southwest and the Westman Islands where the fishing season would still be on, was the so-called "summer-day share." This was the fisherman's share of the catch during the First Day of Summer, which he would bring to his wife for her own personal disposal and not directly for the household.

Since children were not expected to work on the First Day of Summer, those from neighboring farms would sometimes get together to play games, and at times even adults would participate. The elderly would also visit each other this day and exchange gifts. . . . After the turn of the century, however, the Youth Movement adopted the day as its own, with speeches, poetry readings, sports, singing, dancing, and even dramatic performances.

Source: *Icelandic Feasts and Holidays: Celebrations, Past and Present* by Arni Bjornsson. Translated by May and Hallberg Hallmundson. Rekjavik: Iceland Review History Series, 1980, pp. 41-42.

First day of summer, c. 1910

The ground had thrown off its white robe and was waiting for the green to be ready. The long, dark nights were gone. Lamps were becoming keepsakes, waiting for the next fall to be needed. The first birds of passage had arrived. The ptarmigan was changing clothing, taking off her white winter costume and making her brown summer suit. The brooks were flowing over their banks and hopped cheerfully down the meadow into the *Hjalta-dalsá,* which embraced them and carried them into the great ocean. *Sumarda-gurinn-fyrsti var kominn!* (The first summer day had arrived) the real national holiday in Iceland. It is fixed on Thursday and varied in date from the twenty-first to the twenty-fifth of April.

I had been up early that morning, I knew I should be surprised, as always on that day, with some presents. I was not mistaken. On my bed was a packet addressed to me. What was in it, I wondered. It did not take me long to untie the string. Well! A beautiful box and in it a thimble, thread and needles, and beside that a petticoat of the kind I always had admired so much. Such a beauty! That was a day of surprise not only for me but for everybody, as presents were exchanged from one to another. When the flood of admiration had settled a little, a domestic service followed with special hymns and sermon for that day. Coffee, cakes, pastry, and several kinds of delicate foods belonged to the festivity. Later on the whole youth joined in blindman's buff on the lawn behind the farmhouse, and it might happen that mother would favor us with her presence, but I cannot remember that we could move father to that.

Source: *When I Was a Girl in Iceland* by Hólmfrídur Árnadóttir. Boston: Lothrop, Lee & Shepard Co., 1919, pp. 150-152.

April 23

St. George's Day

This is a day to honor St. George, a Cappadocian knight who slew a dragon at Sylene in Libya after enlisting a promise from the townspeople to accept Christianity. Fifteen thousand persons were baptized. According to the legend, four ox-carts were needed to carry off the dead dragon's body. St. George is patron saint of England, Greece, Portugal, and Aragon.

England

St. George's Day in England

St. George is patron saint of England and also of soldiers and boy scouts. The red cross of St. George flies from every English church on April 23. Special services are sometimes held, and red roses may be worn in his honor.

Source: *The Customs and Ceremonies of Britain* by Charles Kightly. London: Thames & Hudson, 1986, p. 203.

Macedonia

Ballads of St. George

The song given below was dictated to the writer by a peasant girl of Sochos. From this composition it appears that St George is regarded as a kind of mediaeval knight on horse-back, armed in the orthodox fashion, and as the bearer of gifts to those who are fortunate enough to win his favour.

I. *Ballad of St George.*

"St George, knight of the sword and spear,
Give me thy little key that I may open thy little eye,
And see what thou carriest within."
"Wheat and barley, and grains of pearl."
"Give to the bride chestnuts and to the groom walnuts,
To our dear mother-in-law kerchiefs of pure gold,
And to the children pencils."

In another ballad sung, like the above, on the saint's feast, St George plays rather an unchivalrous *rôle*. I will give here only the translation, as the text, which I took down at Nigrita, is merely a variant of a song already published in Passow's collection.

II. *Ballad of St George.*

"A young Turk, the king's own grandson, falls in love with a Christian maid and wishes to make her his. He desires her; but she desires him not. She runs away, placing hills and mountains between her pursuer and herself. In the way which she goes, she finds St George sitting at a deserted little chapel.

'My lord St George, great be thy name! I beseech thee hide me this instant. Oh save me from the hands of the Turk!'

The marble walls were rent asunder, and the maid entered.

At that very moment, lo! the Turk arrived before St George. 'My lord St George, great be thy name! The maid whom thou keepest here, I beseech thee give her to me. I will bring thee cartloads of candles, cartloads of frankincense, and oil will I bring thee in big buffalo-skins. I will also be christened into thy faith, and my name shall be George.'

The marble walls were rent asunder, and the maid came forth. The Turk seized her and sped away."

The poet does not say whether the young Turk fulfilled his vow; but one would not be sorry to hear that he did not.

Source: *Macedonian Folklore* by G. F. Abbott. Cambridge: Cambridge Univ. Press, 1903, pp. 45-46.

Roumania

Vampires on St. George's Night

"The feast of the goodness of things. . . . St. George is master of the weather; he plays with weather as he pleases!"

Thus speaks Outza. She has a profound reverence for this fine knight, patron of the flocks, divinity of cowsheds. We are not talking here of the knight of Cappadocia, the Christian Theseus who delivered his princess from that monster inevitably associated with princesses; we talk rather of a certain cowherd on horseback, the good genius of horned beasts, and protector of the wells of milk: "Saint George of the Cows," they call him here.

Every year the thresholds of houses and cowsheds and sheepfolds are decked in his honour with green branches, and at the same time the thorny sprigs of the wild rose are nailed to door-frames and fixed beside the windows. These are efficacious for keeping evil spirits at a distance, and miraculously endowed with the property of hooking the raiment of theives.

To-night, St. George's Night, a watch is kept. The milk-vampires are prowling the countryside in search of the sustenance their fate compels them to seek.

The vampires, to bring about their monopoly of milk, resort to a magical stratagem. On this night they go out from their unholy houses, with an earthenware pot in one hand, and in the other a long strip of cloth, spun, woven and stitched "by moonlight and before the first cockcrow." They drag their enchanted sheet across the meadows, and when it is covered with dew they wring into their jug the precious water thus lifted from the grass.

Here is the prayer of the vampires, as Outza recites it:

> "I have dragged my cloth in the fields,—I have gathered the milk of my neighbours' kine,—it is not the dew that I caught in my cloth,—it is the manna of my neighbour that I caught.—For her, milk as clear as water,—for me, milk as sweet as honey,—as golden as bees' wax,—as rich as the broth of maize!"

By vigil and prayer, and by repeating other magical words to combat the effect of these, and above all by the blessed aid of St. George, they count on thwarting the designs of the vampires.

"But it's difficult," says Outza, "because the grass is robbed of its dew, wherever they've gone past dragging their cloths, and it goes bad."

And when our beasts graze there, they turn sickly, and their eyes grow dim and their coats bristle up; they get thin and languish and tire, as if it were winter. But the cows of the vampires! *They* get fatter every day, and more frisky too, and more lovely. O! may St. George confound them, and help *our* cows!

Source: *Isvor: The Country of Willows* by Princess Bibesco. New York: Frederick A. Stokes, 1924, pp. 113-115.

Protecting the cattle on St. George's eve

The twenty-third of April is a great red-letter day for children. That day is consecrated to St. George. It marks the real beginning of fine weather, for spring is late in Roumania.

The eve of St. George is always remembered by children as the occasion when doors and windows of stable and home are adorned with willow branches or ivy or honeysuckle which has been brought for the purpose from the neighboring forest. These green decorations preserve man and beast against the evil spirits who on that night are very active and may disturb the baby's sleep or do some other damage if they get in. If they break into the barn, the spirits are sure to dry the milk in the cow's udder.

The shepherds on the hills take special care on St. George's eve to prevent the milk of sheep and cows being taken away by witchcraft. They get up before dawn and blow their *bucium*, the Alp-horn (from Latin, *Bucina*).

This is supposed by the shepherds to save their ewes, as witchcraft cannot have any power within the sound of the *bucium*.

A St. George's Day omen

At about St. George's Day "the rook hides easily in the green corn," it is said, especially if the spring has been wet and warm.

A dawn waterfight

At dawn, on that day, the girls put on their finest clothes and, wooden pails in hand, flock to the well to fetch fresh water; the young men, the *flacai* of the village, meet them on their return and a contest is fought, each side throwing handfuls of water. The battle usually ends with the flight of the girls; each girl rushes home to prepare for the merry dance on the village green. The dance on that day is an important event and it lasts till late into the night.

Source: *When I Was a Boy in Roumania* by Dr. J. S. Van Teslaar. Boston: Lothrop, Lee & Shepard Co., 1917, pp. 56-57.

Russia

Jerjew Den

Blessing of the sheep in prerevolutionary Russia

Another great festival in Russia is St George's Day, *Jerjew Den*, which is celebrated twice in the year, in spring (April 23) and in autumn (November 26). The cattle are driven out into the meadows on April 23, when sowing begins, and every one prays to St George, the patron of flocks and agriculture.

St George, who lived at the end of the third century, is the patron of herds and flocks and of agriculture in nearly all Christian countries, but in Russia St George's Day is the feast day of the shepherds. Without his consent the wolf cannot steal a lamb, therefore if he take one, assuredly the shepherd must have displeased St George. So the peasants say: "The wolf carries in his teeth what St George has given him."

The customs on this day vary very much. When the priest has sprinkled the herds with holy water, they are driven to pasture with consecrated birch sticks. The shepherd has eggs and milk and prepares a pancake for himself. A procession round the herds is made in some places with the icon. In Olonetz, where the snow lies very deep, the flocks are not taken to pasture on the 23rd, but young people go from house to house with bells, ring them before windows, and make a collection. Young men and girls dance, and the dew on St George's Day gives them power and strength. The stables are sprinkled with holy water and incensed to keep away evil spirits who cannot endure the smell of it. The evil spirits are not idle on St George's Day. In the Ukraine, or Little Russia, the El Dorado of Russian witches, where there are more of them than in any other part of the world, the witches gather the dew in drops, and hang them on the horns of the cattle, who immediately get thin and give no milk.

Source: *Home Life in Russia* by A. S. Rappoport. New York: Macmillan, 1913, p. 50.

Spain

St. George and the Moors and Christians of Alcoy

This festival is held April 22 to 24 at Alicante, Spain. An elaborate enactment of the battle with the Moors and a procession in honor of St. George share this festival. St. George was the saint on whom the people of Alicante called during the Moorish siege of 1276. April 22 features entry processions of the Christians in the morning and the Moors in the afternoon. On April 23 St. George's relic is removed from his temple to the church of Santa Maria. On April 24 battle takes place.

For more on this festival see: "St. George and the Moors and Christians of Alcoy," in *Spanish Festivals* by Nina Epton. New York: A. S. Barnes, 1968, pp. 43-51.

Yugoslavia

Djurdjevdan

A traditional celebration

On the eve of Djurdjevdan, Saint George's Day, young people dance in the moonlight on some grassy meadow. The girls pick willow branches to weave into wreaths for their waists, and carry boughs home to decorate their houses later. Each type of branch has a certain significance, growth, fertility, health, etc. Girls wash their faces in the dew for a beautiful complexion. They weave wreaths of flowers and toss them over gateposts, onto roofs, and into wells for good health and good luck.

Source: *A Serbian Village* by Joel Martin Halpern. New York: Columbia, 1958, p. 242.

St. George's Day in Orasac, Yugoslavia, c. 1970

Today wreaths are still fashioned from spring boughs and fastened outside doors, hitched over gateposts, and tossed down wells. Dogwood is for health, white beech for fertility, and spiny hawthorne to ward off the evil eye. One even sees such a wreath occasionally over a door in a Belgrade apartment buiding.

This day signals the beginning of the swimming and out-of-doors season. Young people once rocked in the branches of the dogwood tree as a charm for virility and strength.

Source: *A Serbian Village in Historical Perspective* by Joel M. Halpern and Barbara Kerewsky Halpern. New York: Holt, Rinehart, and Winston, 1972, p. 117.

Shepherd's Day in Communist Bulgaria

A lamb was once offered on St. George's Day, a custom originating in pagan times. Today the holiday has evolved into Shepherd's Day in Communist Bulgaria.

Source: "Bulgarian Folk Feasts and Rites" by Sofia Press Agency in *Journal of Popular Culture,* 19:1 (Summer 1985), pp. 155-156.

April 25

St. Mark's Day

This day commemorates St. Mark. Mark is author of one of the four gospels. His work is said to be derived from St. Peter, who speaks of Mark in his First Letter as "my son Mark." Mark was a missionary companion of SS. Paul and Barnabas.

Hungary

The feast of the wheat

Hungarians celebrate two festivals in connection with the gathering of crops. In the spring, on St. Mark's Day (April 25), is held "the feast of the wheat." Led by their priest or minister the people go in procession to the wheat fields where the future bread is blessed. Each person takes home with him some ears of wheat from the fields thus blessed. In some districts these ears are supposed to have a healing, magic effect and they are everywhere greatly esteemed. The fields and crops are blessed again on Sts. Peter and Paul's Day, June 29th, the day when harvesting begins in Hungary.

Source: *Foreign Festival Customs* by Marian Schibsby and Hanny Cohrsen. New York: American Council for Nationalities Service, 1974, p. 91.

April 30

Walpurgis Night

This is the night on which witches ride through the air to Germany's Brocken Mountain. The festival probably originated in a heathen spring festival in which Wodan and Freya gave birth to Spring (Lenz). St. Walpurga's birthday is April 30. The daughter of King Richard of England, the became abbess of Heidenheim. She is the protectress against magic and May 1 is her Saint's Day.

Germany

Witches fly on Walpurgisnacht

Witches fly to the Brocken, North Germany's highest mountaintop, on this night to convene. To protect against these wandering witches farmers put three crosses and bunches of potent herbs over their stable doors. People hide their broomsticks, lest these be used by a witch in her flight. Stockings crossed on children's beds also offer protection. It is said that the witches take a bite out of each church bell they pass en route.

On this night fires may be kept burning to ensure a fruitful harvest in orchards. The smoke is said to protect the trees.

Source: *German Festivals and Customs* by Jennifer M. Russe. London: Oswald Wolff, 1982, p. 57.

Sweden

Valborgsmässoafton

Walpurgis Eve in university towns

On Walpurgis Eve, she's wooed in song in the five university towns, and particularly in the two oldest: Upsala and Lund.

The ceremony begins at three in the afternoon when students gather in huge flocks outside the grave university walls. On the stroke of the hour, the crowd breaks into a resounding cheer and thousands of white student caps, like a field of daisies bursting into flower, are waved or flung into the air. Then—silence. A speaker appears on a platform.

For, like so many other events in the Swedish year, this is an occasion for *högtidlighet,* rarest and queerest of purely Swedish moods. "Hightimeliness" they call it, this vein of moving solemnity, when all jokes are for a moment out of order and everyone seems to be thinking over his whole life.

A chilly wind, it is true, blows the speaker's words hither and thither, but fails to scatter his time-honoured conclusion: "Let us therefore all join in a four-fold cheer for our Nordic spring. Long may it live!" Four heartfelt hurrahs fill the cool spring air and then one more, for good measure.

The blue evening falls, bringing with it a dim reminder of pagan times. Huge bonfires are lit throughout the country, preferably on a hill or mound.

This is an evening for parties and for young love. Only the unimaginative go home to bed. The others, bewitched, press a little closer to the bonfires in the cold night air, awaiting the clear stillness of the early northern dawn.

Source: *Round the Swedish Year* by Lorna Downman, Paul Britten Austin, Anthony Baird. Stockholm: The Swedish Institute/Bokförlaget, 1967, p. 17.

April 31
May Eve

Ireland

May Eve, a holiday for the daoine sidhe (fairies)

May Eve, Mr. Griffith told us, is a day devoted by the fairy people to pugilistic combat, especially every seventh year when they fight among themselves for the crops, taking as their spoil the finest ears of wheat, barley and oats. With the barley and with dew gathered from a mountain top at midnight they make a potent liquor, one drink of which is sufficient to set them to dancing for twenty-four hours without pausing to catch breath.

You did not know the fairy people were such great dancers, did you? Oh, yes indeed they are! They keep the *lepracaun,* their cobbler and only one among them that ever does a stroke of work, busy making new shoes for them, because they wear them out so quickly at their dances.

Source: *When I Was a Boy in Ireland* by Alan M. Buck. New York: Lothrop, Lee & Shepard Co., 1936, p. 93.

Moon 4, Day 8

Birthday of the Buddha

This is a day to honor the birthday of Gautama Buddha.

China

Bathing the Buddha

There is also the great festival of the birthday of Buddha, the eighth day of the fourth month, an affair for only the true believers. It differs from the normal birthday party in that the statue of Buddha is taken out of his temple and given a bath, to clear away the dust and dirt of the year. Then he is given a new dress, the donation of a pious believer.

Source: *Chinese Festivals* by Wolfram Eberhard. New York: Henry Schuman, 1952, p. 143.

Korea

Buddha's Birthday in Korea

The eighth day of the Fourth Moon is Buddha's Birthday. Families visit Buddhist temples, and homes display colored paper lanterns in the evening. In some areas shops are decorated with artificial flowers, and children set off firecrackers.

In earlier days tall lantern posts were erected in front of homes in Seoul with pheasant feathers, pine branches, and colored silks atop them. They were hung with colored lanterns, one for each member of the family. Children hung firecrackers from these poles and lit them or made rice-straw dolls and hung them from the poles. Lanterns of that night were made in many shapes such as phoenix, fish, tortoise, and lotus. In ancient days the eight gates of Seoul were closed at curfew and people were forbidden to walk the streets, but on this night all could roam in the hills and streets until midnight to view the illuminations.

Source: *Folk Customs and Family Life* by Tae Hung Ha. Seoul, Korea: Yonsei, 1963, pp. 34-35.

A village celebration, c. 1910

. . . Only once a year, on the eighth of April—the day when the divine Buddha resumed his baths after his nineteenth meditation and began to preach—festive Buddhist celebrations took place in our town. High trees, often four times taller than the house themselves, were set up all along the main street. The trunks were swathed and decorated with multi-colored pieces of cloth, and from the branches countless gay ribbons were spread out to the roofs and to the ground. At night colored paper lanterns hung from the ropes and ribbons, and made you feel as if you were walking through a garden filled with iridescent flowers.

Source: *The Yalu Flows: A Korean Childhood* by Mirok Li. East Lansing, Mich.: The Michigan State Univ., 1956, p. 45.

Day 1, Vaisakh (April-May)

First of Baisakh / Vaisakh

The day on which Guru Gobind Singh founded the Khalsa (elect) and instituted the baptism of the sword. Asking five volunteers to offer their lives, he took them one at a time into a tent and emerged with a bloody sword. He in fact sacrificed a goat. The five were named The Panch Pyare, the Beloved Five.

India (Sikh)

First of Vaisakh

The first of Vaisakh or Baisakh (April-May) is the most important day of the year for the Sikhs, for it is on this day that Guru Gobind Singh instituted the baptism of the sword and founded the Khalsa. These events are celebrated by the Sikhs annually, and it is incumbent on every Sikh to visit on this day the largest and most important Gurudwara he can, and if possible the Golden Temple at Amritsar. The main religious function, as in all Sikh festivals, is the reading of the *Granth* from beginning to end, known as Akhand Path (continuous reading), and taking the holy book in procession, to the accompaniment of religious music. Five leaders of the congregation walk in front of the *Granth* with drawn swords in memory of the Panch Pyare of Guru Gobind Singh.

After the religious obligation is over, there is feasting. Village communities celebrate the occasion by many folk dances, of which the vigorous Bhangra is the most popular.

During the days of Moghul hostility, the approaches to the Golden Temple at Amritsar used to be guarded by Moghul soldiers on Baisakhi day, so that they could seize guerilla leaders, to whom, as the Moghuls knew, it was a religious obligation to visit the temple during the feast. And it was a point of honour with the more militant of the Sikhs to run the gauntlet of the Moghul cordon, have a dip in the sacred tank and cut their way back to safety. In those days, the Golden Temple during Baisakhi, was a scene of many a daring act and much bloodshed.

At present, however, a pilgrimage to the Golden Temple is a pleasure and not a hazard, and thousands of Sikhs visit the shrine during Baisakhi and take the bath in the Pool of Immortality.

Source: *Festivals and Holidays of India* by Paul Thomas. Bombay: D. B. Taraporevala Sons & Co., 1971, p. 62.

Malaya (Sikh)

Baisakh in the Malaya Sikh community

In Malaya this day is celebrated in all Sikh temples. The entire Sikh community in the neighbourhood assembles at the temple. One of the major items is the reading of the *Granth Sahib* (the Sikh Bible) which goes on continuously for forty-eight hours. Then there are prayers, religious lectures and singing of devotional hymns. Meals are served in the temple to all worshippers, everyone sitting and eating together, emphasizing the castelessness and equality of Sikh society. This institution of the common kitchen (*langar*), to which present day Sikhs give so much importance, was started by the third *Guru* to demolish the caste system among Sikhs and establish equality among the followers of Sikhism.

Source: *Indian Festivals in Malaya* by S. Arasaratnam. Kuala Lumpur: Dept. of Indian Studies, Univ. of Malaya, 1966, p. 45.

Day 1, Baisakh
Baisakhi

This is a harvest festival in North India and a New Year celebration.

India

Reaping of the harvest begins

Baisakhi, the first day of the month of *Baisakh* (April/May) is New Year's Day, going by the *Saka* calendar. It corresponds to April 13th of the Gregorian calendar.

Essentially it is a North Indian harvest festival, for it is the day when the reaping of the *rabi* (winter crop) begins. The jubilation at a bountiful harvest becomes the reason for celebration.

Though celebrated all over North India, it is nowhere as colourful as it is in Punjab, India's granary. The joy of the energetic Punjabis is manifest in the strenuous folk dance, the *bhangra*. This dance usually enacts the entire process of agriculture from the tilling of the soil through harvesting. As the beat of the *dholak* (drum) changes, the sequences progress. The dance movements express ploughing, sowing, weeding, reaping and winnowing. The final sequence shows the farmer celebrating the harvest.

Though in real life the farmer has to toil hard in order to win grain from the soil, this dance shows him performing his labours with grace and ease, a smile to his lips. Women too join the menfolk, both at reaping during the day, and in the many dances and folk songs at evening.

Baisakhi has a special significance for the Hindus. It is believed that the Ganga descended to the earth on this auspicious day. The Kumbha is held every twelve years at Hardwar on this occasion.

Source: *Festive India* by Arun Sanon. Photos by Gurmeet Thukral. New Delhi: Frank Bros., 1987, p. 30.

India (Bengal)

Baisakh in Bengal

Last year Minu and Montu had a glorious time in the country house of their grandparents. Minu still remembers the farmers' wives drawing colored patterns on their doorsteps as a sign of welcome to all the New Year guests. And she remembers the delicious rice cakes, too. Some were shaped like flowers, others like water chestnuts. Some had cream inside them and others had coconut fillings. And all of them had such beautiful names that Minu wrote them down in her diary in case she forgot them.

When all the children had gathered as many flowers as they could hold, Montu asked everyone to stand in a line behind him. Then he started to march and they all followed him singing, "May the New Year come again and again!" Up and down the streets they went and everyone who saw this little procession smiled and felt happy.

When the singing was over Minu and Montu returned home to make the garlands. As she was stringing the flowers together, the New Year guests began to arrive to wish them a Happy New Year and to bring them presents of cakes and sweets.

The children were longing to go outdoors and look at the shops. The first day of the New Year is a great day for the shopkeepers, for having settled all their accounts of the old year, they decorate their shops with flowers and streamers, and children who come to their shops are treated to sweets.

When the last guests had left Minu's mother changed into her new clothes to go out. She wore red and yellow because they are the colors of spring, and Minu pinned a yellow marigold in her mother's hair.

They were going to the auditorium to see a special New Year performance. Montu had wanted to go to the soccer match and Minu had wanted to go to the New Year music program, but in the end Minu's mother decided on the dance. The story of the dance is taken from the well-known collection of fairy tales called *Grandmother's Bag*. Minu's mother was sure that both the children would enjoy it.

Thier father was waiting for them at the auditorium. When they got there the building was ablaze with colored lights. Inside the hall there were flowers everywhere, even on the stage. Minu saw many of her friends, all wearing their garlands.

Her father was dressed in white trousers and a silk *kurta* shirt just like all the other fathers there. And all the other mothers were dressed in red and yellow. When the lights went out the dancing started. Both Montu and Minu were so dazzled by the bright lights, the colors and the dancers that the two hours went by in a flash.

And after the dance there was still something else to look forward to. The New Year fair, the biggest event of the day.

They pushed their way through the crowds and headed for the banks of the river where the fair is held every year. Even before they got near the river they could hear the cries and laughter of the crowds. . . .

When the children got to the merry-go-round, they wanted a ride. Up and down, round and round they went on their horses. . . . And when they passed the magician's stall they stopped to watch him.

Source: *Festivals in Asia.* Sponsored by the Asian Cultural Committee for UNESCO. Tokyo: Kodansha, 1975, pp. 32-35.

Full Moon (Purnima) of Vaisakha (April-May)

Buddha Jayanti

Buddha's birth, enlightenment, and salvation all fall on this day.

India

Fasting and processions

Buddhists celebrate with great devotion and fervour the Buddha Jayanti festival all over India on the full moon day of the month of Vaisakha (April-May). According to the popular belief of the Buddhists, Lord Buddha was born on the Vaisakha Purnima at Lumbini, in the Nepal Tarai; attained enlightenment at Uruvela near Bodh Gaya, in Bihar, and finally salvation at Kusinara in Uttar Pradesh, on the very same day. These three events have greatly enhanced the importance of Vaisakha Purnima for all the Buddhists the world over.

Buddhists observe a full day fast on this day and break it at night by taking only light food. They recite the sacred scriptures and worship the image of Buddha both at home and in the temples. They also take out processions carrying big photographs of Buddha. Special celebrations are observed at the Buddhist holy places like Bodh Gaya, Sarnath (near Varanasi), Sanchi (near Vidisha), Kusinagar (near Gorakhpur) and several other places.

Source: *Festivals of India* by Brijendra Nath Sharma. New Delhi: Abhinav Publications, 1978, p. 82.

May (throughout the Month)

Flores de Mayo

Celebrations in honor of the Virgin are held throughout May in El Salvador, called Flores de Mayo, "Flowers of May."

El Salvador

Flores de Mayo celebrations in San Vicente

Flores de Mayo celebrations in honor of the Virgin are held throughout El Salvador during May. At San Vicente the fiesta begins early in the morning with guitar and marimba bands. At noon a parade of masqueraders passes through town, and around 5:00 p.m. La Flor takes place. The fiesta organizers go through the streets throwing candy and anise seeds to the crowds. Men posted along their route toss back flowers and grain. At 6:00 p.m. the Virgin is carried from the house of the fiesta capitana (organizer for the year) to the church in procession. Each day throughout the month a different capitana hosts the processions.

Source: *Fiesta Time in Latin America* by Jean Milne. Los Angeles: The Ward Ritchie Press, 1965, pp. 85-86.

First Sunday in May
Faka Me

As Tonga is a Protestant (Methodist) country, it is only natural that the most important church holiday should be one which is shared with Protestant children of many lands. This is Sunday School Day, known in Tonga as *Faka Me,* and celebrated on the first Sunday in May.

Tonga

Sunday School Day

During the week preceding *Faka Me,* all the mothers have been busy sewing—for the girls new dresses, for the boys new *valas,* which are kiltlike skirts worn by boys instead of trousers. Bright and early on *Faka Me* morning, the children go down to the sea for their baths. Then they put on their new clothes and go to church. The sermon that day is preached especially for them, so they are all there.

As soon as the regular service is over, the *Faka Me* program begins. Even the little ones who have just learned to talk, stand up before the congregation and recite a verse or two of scripture or sing a hymn. The older boys and girls take part in Bible plays which they have made up or sing hymns to which they dance, using slow, solemn movements. Sometimes they even do a dance to the words of the Ten Commandments!

In Tonga, there is never a church service without a feast, and *Faka Me* is no exception. For the children, it is the most exciting feast of the year. Usually they have to wait until their parents and the older people have finished, but not on *Faka Me*. The children sit down first and the adults serve them. All the children of the Sunday school eat together. They do not sit at tables with knives and forks and spoons. Instead they sit on mats spread on the ground and eat with their fingers from long trays made of woven coconut fronds.

The trays, or *volas,* are piled high with all sorts of Polynesian foods—whole roast pigs, big lobsters in their red shells, chicken and fish steamed in coconut milk, yard-long potato-like vegetables called *ufi* and all sorts of delicious fruits. The parents stand behind the children and fan them to keep them cool as they eat; and no matter how much a girl or boy eats, those mothers and fathers never say a word! For *Faka Me* is children's day.

Source: *Children's Festivals from Many Lands* by Nina Millen. New York: Friendship Press, 1964, p. 172.

First Tuesday in May

Ffair Ffyliaid (Fool's Fair)

This is an annual fair held in Llanerfyl, Wales.

Wales

The Ffair Ffyliaid in Llanerfyl, Wales

The neighbouring hamlet of Llanerfyl has an annual event more reminiscent of the *gwylmabsant*. It is know as *Ffair Ffyliaid* (Fool's Fair), and is held on the first Tuesday in May. It differs from other fairs in that it is a pleasure fair which has had no economic function, at least within living memory. People, drawn from many miles around, begin to congregate at Llanerfyl about three o'clock in the afternoon, but the crowd is not at its densest until between ten and eleven o'clock and the last do not leave until three in the morning, or later.

In the war and blackout year of 1940 when I visited the fair there were fewer people present than in normal times, but even so they numbered something between six and eight hundred. Everyone at the fair agreed that there was nothing there "except people". Actually, there were two china-stalls at the roadside selling by auction, the auctioneer entertaining the crowd with jokes. There was a less frequented clothing stall and an ice-cream cart, while the local shop did a flourishing trade in refreshments. A yard, off the road, contained swings, a shooting-booth, a coconut-stall, a gaming table and slot machines, but none of these seemed to be popular. The main enjoyment was to be found in moving up and down and meeting in little groups in the thickly crowded highway. Young people formed the majority of the crowd, but there were many older people and some of these remained until after midnight. The crowded road had an atmosphere comparable with that of a dance or a large party. All were sociable and an introduction was unnecessary as a preliminary to a chat. Old acquaintances were renewed and coming across neighbours at the fair also held a certain novelty justifying the exchange of a few words.

For the young men the opportunity of meeting girls from other districts was a major attraction. They were specially groomed for the occasion, and the girls smartly dressed. Small parties of each sex moved about accosting one another and forming little conversational groups. Later at night there is usually a fight or two between young men from different districts. The pretexts for such battles vary, but most of them are fought over girls. It is the custom for the lads of Llanerfyl in particular to challenge anyone who ventures to escort a local girl to her home.

Source: *Life in a Welsh Countryside: A Social Study of Llanfihangel Yng Ngwynfa* by Alwyn D. Rees. Cardiff: Univ. of Wales Press, 1961, pp. 134-135.

May to July (Height of Rainy Season)

Okere Juju

This is a five-week festival of religious masquerades, healing rituals for children, and a carnavalesque atmosphere in which the women satirize the men and break into bawdy dance. The festival is held in honor of Itsekiri ancestors and the God Erimebo.

Nigeria (Itsekiri)

The festival

Pre-festival cleansing begins three months before the festival with Ajafifa, a procession of male elders to the compounds of certain ancestors, inviting them to the festival. Two months later Ibibi (Eriribiri) takes place, an attack on the filth and evil of the previous year. A group of men (who will be maskers later) roust about tearing up roofs, livestock, plantain, and banana trees in a symbolic fight against evil. These materials will make their costumes later. After the men have gone away, the postmenopausal women call each other out to make food offerings and invite the ancestors to the festival. A week later, Odegbigba begins, a month of ritual cleansing of the village by unwed girls. They reside in a group home during this time, leaving to sweep the streets while singing and clapping clappers. The final phase of purification is Awerewere. Awerewere leaves are gathered in the morning. All age and sex groups join in waving the leaves, dancing, and whipping their friends with them. Precisely as the tide begins to ebb, all rush to bathe in the river. The ebb tide carries away all ills and sicknesses.

Confessions and departure of the spirits

About 3.00 p.m. on the closing day of the festival, a large box is brought out to the arena, and stationed under *Ogungbaja-Okeredola.* As the festivities progress, people go up to the box and make donations. Indigenes and foreigners alike participate in these donations. As an indigene makes his contribution, he confesses all transgressions committed during the festival. These confessions are between the individual and the *juju,* no medium is used. Confessions take the following form:

> *Okere Juju,* during the dances, I was in my menses, and I called a certain masquerade[r] by name, and touched as well, forgive me.

Towards sundown, all the masquerade[r]s gather together at the river (at Esisi), where they pray to the deity to keep them all and the community till the next performances. Then they return to the arena.

. . . Then in single file, the masquerade[r]s drop their whips in a pile by the central shrine in the arena, to signify that the festival has ended.

. . . Then opening their faces for all to see, the masquerade[r]s race back to the shrine, and the people depart solemnly after shouting prayers to the effect that the fleeing masquerade[r]s should carry away all ills from the community.

Source: ''Okere Juju: Itsekiri Religious Ritual Festival'' by Stanley Amah in *Nigeria Magazine* 54 (4) (October-December 1980), 48-65.

May 1

May Day

May 1 is celebrated as a spring outing in Europe with maypoles, flower gathering, and the crowning of a May Queen. In Socialist countries May Day is now a political ''workers holiday.'' In Celtic Britain the first of May was ''Beltane,'' a time when herds were turned out to their summer grazing and gods were invoked. Bonfires were lit on hilltops and cattle were driven between fires for protection.

Canada

Collecting dew

The old custom of collecting dew on May morn to prevent aging and guarantee beauty is still followed by some Acadians and Quebecois who collect *l'eau de mai*.

Source: *Let's Celebrate* by Caroline Parry. Toronto: Kids Can Press, 1987, p. 124.

Finland

Vappu

A wild May Day Eve

Vappu comes on the eve of May Day, and there is no way to describe it. Anything goes, provided it isn't actually indecent or criminal. Young people find that it is an ideal time to let off steam, and the white caps worn by university students are much in evidence. (Be warned: that graybeard so rakishly white-capped may not be a student just now; has-been students sport theirs, too.) In Helsinki, the long-suffering statue of Havis Amanda is their traditional victim. Droves of students wade across the moat that surrounds her in order to climb up into her stony arms and crown her with their caps. All day long there are parades of students and workers, and by night there's singing, impromptu dancing in the streets, and all manner of revelry. Nobody goes to bed. We would put it down to spring fever—the giddy excitement that comes with the first flush of warm days—and that could certainly account for the high spirits.

Source: *Of Finnish Ways* by Ainu Rajanen. Minneapolis: Dillon, 1981, p. 164.

France

Various French May Day customs

On May 1 there were curious customs whereby it was sought to bring wife-beaters to a better sense. They were even paraded on donkeys, real or wooden, and treated with appropriate contumely. As for Queens of May (Mairiottes), they are everywhere; as for street decorations, they go on too; and still in happy Arcadian spots maid-servants at inns give travellers little bouquets, for which due recompense is customary. The French still twine ribbons round maypoles (this takes some doing), though they do not dance 'round the ale-stake' (a performance only to be accomplished by flies or beetles); and they plant 'mays' everywhere, especially before the cottage of young women. These 'mays' are usually trees; but 'mays' also mean a conventional tree, a sort of thyrsus, or stick twined with foliage; and it was this kind of 'may' which was used in King René's great Fête-Dieu procession at Aix-en-Provence. May (on the Somme, and in Brittany) is the month of pilgrimages to wells and fountains—e.g. to that of Hemencourt near Doullens: I do not know if it is in May that the Plougastel people go off to St. Fiacre en Crozon and sprinkle the children with the spring water (this custom in 1906 'tendait a disparaître').

Round about Paris one still drinks May milk, which is thought to be better than that of other months; you must drink it at dawn foaming and frothing (and before anyone has had time to put preservatives in it). You do not get married in May if you can help it. It is the month of the Virgin; and in Roman times it was Maia's month, and she did not, apparently, encourage marriages in her month.

In Lorraine girls dress in be-ribboned white, dance and sing, and ask alms (they are called *trimazos*, both the girls, that is, and their songs). All sorts of things happen on May Day!

May Day pilgrimages

Now for May Day. On this day, or soon after, the Fête of the Jeux Floraux at Toulouse is held. . . .

There are all sorts of pilgrimages; in the old days there was a very interesting one in the Jura (Archelangel) a pilgrimage to the Chapel of St. Marcoul, a saint who cured the King's Evil or Scrofula. But as in so many of these old pilgrimages and 'cures', there was a good deal of common sense mixed up in the business (like 'fearing God and keeping your powder dry'), since the pilgrim had to vow three years vegetarianism (whereby the correct anti-scrofula vitamines would be acquired).

Source: *A Guide to French Fetes* by E. I. Robson. London: Methuen, 1930, pp. 65-6.

Germany

Decorating the May Pole

Groups of youth (*Burschenschaften*) fell a spruce, strip all but the top branches, remove the bark, and decorate it with ribbons and a May wreath. This is set up as the May Pole (*der Maibaum, die Maie, der Maien*). Candies or sausages may be fastened to the wreath that crowns the pole. Young boys shinny to the top to claim them. The May Pole is the center of dancing, beer drinking, and games.

Source: *German Festivals and Customs* by Jennifer M. Russe. London: Oswald Wolff, 1982, p. 57.

Great Britain

May Day decorations

The main custom was "bringing in the May." May Eve and early morn were spent gathering blossoms and branches in the fields. In England, hawthorn is a favorite; in Cornwall, sycamore; and in Scotland and Wales, rowan (mountain ash) and birch. Marsh marigold (mayflower) was woven into garlands and still graces primary school May Day celebrations. Maypoles, presided over by a May Queen and May King, were popular in the Middle Ages. They were banned in 1644 by Parliament and reinstated in 1660. The May Pole was revived as a children's festivity in mid-nineteenth century.

Source: *The Customs and Ceremonies of Britain* by Charles Kightly. London: Thames & Hudson, 1986, p. 160.

May Goslings

In several areas of England children repeat their April Fool's Day jokes on May 1, making "May Goslings" of their friends. Notes reading "May Gosling" may be part of the prank. An umbrella may have a note tied inside so that it dangles in the person's face when opened, or a letter may be opened to find only this message inside. After noon, however, victims can respond, "May Gosling's dead and gone. You're the gosling for carrying one."

Source: *Lore and Language of Schoolchildren* by Peter and Iona Opie. Oxford: Oxford Univ. Press, 1959, pp. 256-257.

Children tour the streets with a maypole

An observor reported seeing four separate groups of children touring with a maypole in the building estates of Monkmoor in Shrewsbury between six and seven o'clock in the evening on May 1, 1952. They had constructed maypoles of pram wheels decorated with crepe paper streamers, fixed on the top of a pole so that it could turn. A Queen, seated on a stool, held the pole. From four to ten girls danced round the pole. They sang and acted out verses such as "Round and round the maypole, / Merrily we go, / Singing hip-a-cherry, / Dancing as we go. / All the happy children, / Upon the village green, / Sitting in the sunshine, / *Hurrah* for the queen!" After the dancers perform this, each kneels on one knee while the Queen, standing, sings: "I'm the Queen don't you see. / I have come from a far country. / If you wait a little while / I will dance the maypole style." The dancers are dressed in crepe paper. Attending children collect coins from the houses near which the performance is staged.

Source: *Lore and Language of Schoolchildren* by Peter and Iona Opie. Oxford: Oxford Univ. Press, 1959, pp. 257-259.

Nineteenth-century May Birchers

May Birchers would visit homes after dark to leave a certain branch on the doorstep to be discovered by the person who lived there in the morning. If a nut branch was left . . . the May Birchers were calling you a "slut." A pear meant you are "fair," a plum . . . you are "glum," an alder (pronounced 'owler') you are a "scowler." Thus the rhyming insult or compliment was clear. Gorse was for "whores." But hawthorn, which didn't rhyme with anything, was left as a compliment.

Source: *The Folklore of the Welsh Border* by Jacqueline Simpson. Totowa, New Jersey: Rowman and Littlefield, 1976, p. 149.

Ireland

No borrowing on May Day, lest the year's luck be stolen

A person who borrowed on May Day was thought to never repay it, and this meant that he had stolen the farm's luck for the year. Proper folk would neither borrow nor lend on this day. Even the ashes on the hearth were not thrown out on May 1.

Letting the fire die on May Day

In past times this was the only day of the year on which the hearth fire was allowed to die out. Eggs were hung on bushes, and flowers were strewn in the street, symbols of life to protect the home's life force.

Source: *Passing the Time in Ballymenone* by Henry Glassie. Philadelphia: Univ. of Pennsylvania Press, 1982, pp. 534, 355.

May day customs in early Ireland

. . . May Day was yet another folk festival which was closely connected with agriculture, and it was a day that represented the beginning of summer. In the high period of Irish landlordism it was also rent day. Folk custom dictated that may bushes should be decorated with ribbons, egg shells or flowers. In the midlands may pole dances were held and folk plays were performed in Wexford by mummers. The religious aspect of May Day was not great, though in that month many houses erected small altars with a statue and flowers in honour of Mary.

Source: *Life & Tradition in Rural Ireland* by Timothy P. O'Neill. London: J. M. Dent & Sons, Ltd., 1977, p. 67.

Moving to the summer pasture in early Irish tradition

. . . One aspect of this pastoral life was the removal of some of the herds to summer pastures in the hills. Though medieval records tell little of this a picture of how it operated can be reconstructed from oral accounts from areas where it survived into the present century. The best of these accounts was recorded by Seán O'hEochaidh of the Irish Folklore Commission from a Donegal man called Niall O'Dubhthaigh who was born on 9 April 1874. He recalled how his mother described the fun and pleasure she had in her youth when she and the daughters of three other families took the animals to the hill pastures from May to October. Significantly the terminal days are celebrated in two feast-days—May Day and All Hallows—which were festive days even before Christianity. The men went up first and built the huts which were to be the girls' homes. These were sometimes large enough to accommodate a sick animal and were usually made of sod in a dry spot near a stream. Sheepskins were used for the windows, and heather was strewn on the floors which were made of blue clay. The girls' time on the hills was fully occupied for besides tending the flocks they also made butter, grew potatoes, carded wool, knitted socks and generally worked hard. Yet the booley huts, as such huts were called, were regarded as places of pleasure, and occasional nights of singing and dancing took place, when boys from the home villages visited. Transhumance, as this custom was called, was well known in Europe and, although it died out in the last century, there is widespread evidence that it once was common in many parts of Ireland. There are remains of booley huts on many hills, and in the valley of the King's river in Co. Wicklow the remains of a cluster of six can be seen at a height of 1120 feet above sea level in the townland of Garryknock.

Source: *Life & Tradition in Rural Ireland* by Timothy P. O'Neill. London: J. M. Dent & Sons, Ltd., 1977, p. 101.

Removing to the mountains

"On the first of May the people would remove to the mountains, and make a bit of a house against a rock with sticks and scraws. They would carry their cattle, their milking cattle, with them, and milk them, and make butter and pack firkins, and send them to Cork by the carriers.

"When they were out of potatoes, they used to live on so many pints of blood out of the cow. First of all they would pull the rushes, and then pull the heart out of them and put it crosswise into a pot, and put the blood on to that. About halfways again they would put another crossing of rushes and then more blood, and then they would boil the blood until it was hard like a cake, and that was what they would have for food.

"They would make curds, too, of sour milk, and mix goats' milk through it. They would leave the whey run out of the door, and it would run out through the land. When November came, there would be a green stream of grass from the door, and they would measure this. By the length of this green stream the wealth of a man was measured. The man with the longest stream was the man who had the best times.

Source: *The Tailor and Ansty* by Eric Cross. Dublin and Cork: Mercier Press, 1900, p. 33.

Macedonia

May 1 flowers

The first of May is spent "in dance and song and game and jest." Parties are formed "to fetchen home May" and go to picnic in the plains and meadows. The youths weave wreaths of wild flowers and of sprays of the fragrant tree called after the day *Protomaia,* and hang them outside the doors of their sweethearts, according to the common European custom which is explained by folklorists as due to the belief in the fertilising power of the tree-spirit. Similar garlands adorn the lintels, beams, and windows of each cottage and are allowed to remain there until they are quite dry, when they are burnt.

One of the flowers gathered on this day is picked out by the girls for purposes of divination on the subject which is uppermost in maids' minds the world over. This privileged blossom is the humble daisy, in Macedonia called *pappas*. They pluck its white petals one by one, repeating the familiar "He loves me; he loves me not". Some of these blossoms are dried, to be used in winter as medicine against coughs.

Source: *Macedonian Folklore* by G. F. Abbott. Cambridge: Cambridge Univ. Press, 1903, p. 46.

Norway

Cuckoo Mass

The cuckoo's call as omen

A pre-Christian belief held that if the cuckoo's first call in spring was heard from the north one would become ill or die during the ensuing year. If heard from the south, the year would be good; if from the west, one would succeed; if from the east, one would be lucky in love. Traditional Norwegian calendar sticks show a bird perched in a tree at the May 1 mark, denoting this day.

Source: *Notes from a Scandinavian Parlor* by Florence Ekstrand. Seattle: Welcome Press, 1984, p. 82.

Scotland

Flittin' Day in Glasgow

May Day was sometimes called "term day" because leases on houses terminated on that day. In Glasgow it is usually known as "flittin' day." Householders moved into new houses then. It is also the first day in the Scottish summer.

Girls rose very early on May morn and went out to the fields to wash their faces in the dew on the grass. It kept their cheeks bright and rosy all the year round.

Source: *When I Was a Boy in Scotland* by George McPherson Hunter. Boston: Lothrop, Lee & Shepard Co., 1920, p. 58.

Spain

La Maya

La Maya festivities

Both the festival queen and the girls who take part in the festival are called *la maya*. The maypole and the King of the May are called *mayo*. On the night of April 30 the young men cut a tall tree, strip its branches, decorate it with flowers and ribbons, and set it in the village plaza. It remains there throughout the month. On this night a young lover may leave a tree branch decorated with flowers at the window of his sweetheart, and young men may serenade the girls.

A May Queen may be elected to reign over the festivities. While the young people dance and sing around the maypole, the queen sits enthroned and receives small donations from passersby, which are used for the day's party supplies.

In Galicia a May King dressed in leaves and flowers begs through the streets, collecting chestnuts and other treats.

Source: *Culture and Conquest* by George M. Foster. Chicago: Quadrangle Books, 1960, p. 189.

May Trees in San Pedro Manrique

Here in San Pedro Manrique, a spring rite is doubled, so to speak. The May tree (in this case a sycamore or a poplar), with all its branches and leaves still on, is planted in front of the *Móndidas'* house. It belongs to her individually, and repesents spring and new growth. Of course nowadays no one is likely to know this any longer and the explanation "it has always been done like this" is sufficient reason for its yearly performance. But having it there a metre away from her own doorstep, in the street where all can see it looking so gay and beautifully decorated with paper garlands and japanese lanterns, is a symbol of honour. At night the lanterns are lit up, this shows up the ribbons and other decorations to advantage. The fact that it is not any tree, but always a poplar or preferably a sycamore tree is no accident either. Sycamores were sacred and were worshipped in the form of a tree-Goddess in ancient Egyptian times. This custom may be a relic of Egyptian influence which may have come to Spain along with the worship of Isis, and then extended far inland along the great river Ebro. Egyptian beliefs have travelled along the northern Mediterranean coast, and scraps of traditions are to be found in unexpected forms. The poplar is a masculine symbol.

The Maypole, on the other hand, is quite a different looking tree. It is an enormous poplar, its bark removed and branches cut off, which stands some ten to twelve metres high above ground level. It is planted in the old square, its place marked by the cobbles having been put in concentric circles where the tree is to be erected. It is fetched from the riverside, where there is a grove, and brought in on St John's Eve, and planted early, at 6 a.m. When the faithful come out for Mass, it stands there, not decorated in any way.

Source: "Fire-Walking at San Pedro Manrique, Spain" by Lucile Armstrong in *Folklore,* 81 (Autumn, 1970), pp. 208-209.

Sweden

Valborgsmässoafton och Första Maj, the Feast of Valborg and May Day

University communities make much of this festival. In Uppsala, students wear their white student's caps and gather in a huge crowd to hear songs and speeches. The night is filled with parties. Huge community bonfires are popular in many areas in Sweden.

Source: *Traditional Festivities of Sweden* by Ingemar Liman. Stockholm: The Swedish Institute, 1985, p. 17.

Yugoslavia

Workers' holiday

The First of May is now a "workers' holiday." This replaces St. George's Day festivals of the past. The First of May is now an occasion for a Slava, since the traditional saints' day Slavas are no longer appropriate.

The Slava was formerly celebrated on the feast day of a group's patron saint. Now Slava is held on May 1st, at New Year, or as a birthday celebration. Slava customs include:

Guests at home

Homes are cleaned from top to bottom and walls freshly

whitewashed before the Slava. The guest room is readied and a long table with benches used especially for the Slava was prepared. A colored lithograph of the patron saint is hung in a place of honor in the home, with sprigs of sweet basil around it. Family photographs hang nearby, with a large portrait of a deceased elder, draped with a hand-loomed towel.

When guests arrive they are served *slatko,* sweet preserves, and hot or cold *rakija,* followed by Turkish coffee. When all are present the host, Domacin, lights a beeswax candle and crosses himself three times. He asks his patron saint for blessings on the household. Hot coals from the oven are brought in by the wife and the host places these in a pottery holder with incense. This incense burner is offered to the saint's picture and then carried around the room, letting the incense waft blessings to each guest.

A young girl carries in the Slava loaf. It is adorned with a candle (formed as a flat cross with the ends bent up and lit), a serpentine candle, an apple, a sugar lump, and a sprig of basil. The host ritually breaks the bread and the loaf is cut along the lines of a cross. A best neighbor assists in the cutting. Each turns the loaf and breaks it into quarters. Red wine is poured on the cut surfaces and the men kiss each other on the cheeks and lips, saying, "Christ is in our midst now and forever. Amen." The ritual is repeated three times, manifesting the presence of the Father, the Son, and the Holy Ghost. The loaf is sliced and distributed to all, and each man gets a sprig of basil to tuck behind his ear. The feast then commences, with the host moving around the table to make sure all are served. After the meal all stay at the table, reminiscing and telling stories. Guests who come from a distance spend the night on cornhusk mattresses on the floor.

The Birthday Slava

The celebration of a child's birthday now serves as occasion for Slava. The party is held at the home of the child; grandparents come to visit, which is a change from the traditional focus.

Source: *A Serbian Village in Historical Perspective* by Joel M. Halpern and Barbara Kerewsky Halpern. New York: Holt, Rinehart, and Winston, 1972, pp. 112-118.

U.S.S.R.

May Day/International Labor Day

Soviet May Day customs

This is a day of holidays and parades in the Soviet Union. The holiday includes a fine meal as well as small gifts for the children and perhaps a party. Fireworks may end the day.

May 1

St. Joseph's Day

In addition to his March 19 feast, St. Joseph has a second feast day, St. Joseph the Workman, on May 1.

Guam/Northern Marianas (Chamorros)

A typical saint's day celebration

Village fiestas take place in Guam and the Northern Marianas every month of the year, except during Lent, which offer an excellent opportunity to try typical Chamorro food and get to know the people in an informal atmosphere. Since most of the population is Catholic, each fiesta begins with a procession and Mass on the Sat. closest to the village patron saint's day, followed by feasting into the night. Sunday is the village open-house when the people open their homes one and all. . . . St. Joseph's Day (early May) is celebrated with great fervor at San Jose villages on both Saipan and Tinian. Other important fiestas include those dedicated to Our Lady of Lourdes (Feb.), San Vicente (April), San Isidro (at Chalan Kanoa in mid-May), San Antonio (June), Our Lady of Mt. Carmel (at Chalan Kanoa in mid-July), San Roque (Aug.), San Francisco de Borja (on Rota in Oct.), and Christ the King (at Garapan in mid-Nov.). . . .

A typical Chamorro feast consists of roast suckling pig cooked on a spit, red rice, a selection of fish, taro, coconut crabs, pastries, and *tuba*—a coconut wine fermented from sap drawn from a palm sprout. Another favorite is chicken *kelaguen* (prepared with lemon, onions, and shredded coconut meat and touch of that super-hot *finadene* sauce that goes well on everything). Also try *escabeche* (fried fish with cooked vegetables), *cadon guihan* (fish cooked in its own juices with coconut milk), *lumpia* (pork, shrimp, and vegetables in a pastry wrapping), *pancit* (fried noodles), *bonelos aga* (fried bananas), and *bonelos dago* (deep-fried grated yam served with syrup).

Source: *Micronesia Handbook: Guide to an American Lake* by David Stanley. Chico, Calif.: Moon Publications, 1985, p. 167.

Thirty-third Day of the Omer Period (Circa May)

Lag Ba-Omer

The seven-week period between Passover and Shavuot is known as the days of ''counting omer.'' Leviticus 23:15-17 commands that forty-nine days be counted from the offering of the first sheaf (omer) of barley until the spring harvest is celebrated. The counting begins on the second night of Passover and ends with Shavuot. This is a period of semi-mourning. New clothes are not worn, marriages are not held, and hair should not be cut. Lag Ba-Omer is a suspension of the semi-mourning held on the thirty-third day.

Lag Ba-Omer is called the scholars's holiday because during the Bar Kokhba rebellion against Rome (132-135 C.E.) the students of Rabbi Akiba went into the forests with bows and arrows, ostensibly to practice but actually to study the Torah. On this day also, Rabbi Simeon bar Yohai died. The Kabbalists attribute the Zohar to him and visit his grave on this day. Singing, dancing, and bonfires celebrate his death, since he died in joy. With their mood of mourning, the ''counting omer'' also recall days of plague-induced death of Rabbi Akiba's students.

Persia

Lag Ba-Omer in Persia

Jews in Persia held Rabbi Simon Bar-Yohai in special esteem. They invited friends to festive meals at Lag B'eomer, and a Mula went from house to house to recite from the Zohar. After the meal musicians played and the group sang special ''Bar-Yohai'' songs in Persian. Each person lit a candle in memory of Rabbi Simon Bar-Yohai, his son Rabbi Elazar, and Rabbi Meir Ba'al Haness at the synagogue. During the seven weeks of counting omer a piece of matza and a bit of salt were carried in the pocket.

Source: *One People: The Story of the Eastern Jews* by Devora and Menachem Hacohen. New York: Sabra Books/Funk and Wagnalls, 1969, p. 35.

May 3

Día de la Cruz / Day of the Holy Cross

This commemorates the discovery by St. Helena in 326 of the cross on which Jesus was crucified. Roadside and village crosses throughout Latin America are decorated with flowers on this day.

Argentina

La Rioja and Santiago del Estero provinces, Argentina

Large crosses are erected in the foothills of the Andes near their villages to protect the crops during the year. On La Día de la Cruz these crosses are brought into the town in procession, placed on a white cloth-covered table, and heaped with flowers. The crowds pray by the cross, and festivities follow. After the fiesta, the cross is again returned to its hillside in procession.

Source: *Fiesta Time in Latin America* by Jean Milne. Los Angeles: The Ward Ritchie Press, 1965, p. 87.

Chile

La Cruz de Mayo in Chile

The Fiesta of the Cross is celebrated in various ways throughout Chile. The Cross may be made of wood or of branches. It is decorated with flowers and taken in procession through the streets or stood in one spot. In many areas the cross is "dressed" on May 1 and "undressed" on May 31. A smaller cross may be erected at each home as well, but since May is a rainy month, many families keep the cross inside the home. Others stand them in their yards. Special ceremonies, including saying the rosary and the singing of litanies, are held to honor the cross. The last night of the month, especially, is a time for such worship. In Temuco the cross is carried in procession at night, taken from house to house. At each door the cross stops and a chant is recited. One example is

> Aqui anda la Santa Cruz
> Visitando sus devotos.
> Con un cabito de vela
> y un traguito de mosto.
>
> (Here comes the Holy Cross
> Visiting its devotees.
> With a stump of candle
> and a sip of grape-juice.)

When stopping by the home of the nondevout, the participants may chant harsh rhymes such as

> Esta es la casa de los tachos
> Donde viven los borrachos.
>
> (This is the house of the rejects
> Where the drunkards live.)

Source: *Folklore Chileno* by Oreste Plath. Santiago: Nascimento, 1969, pp. 316-317.

Dominican Republic

The Cross of May

This fiesta has been celebrated since the year 1606 in the Dominican Republic. In the capital a permanent cross base was constructed in each location that would erect a cross. The festival begins on May 2 after sunrise and includes dancing, music, bullfights, and games such as sack races and greased pole climbing.

Source: *Folklore Chileno* by Oreste Plath. Santiago: Nascimento, 1969, p. 319.

Paraguay

La Adoracion de la Cruz in Paraguay

In Paraguay the Holy Cross of May is associated with a commemoration of the dead. The crosses of the dead are taken from cemetery sepulchurs during Holy Week and carried in procession to homes. There they stay in a place of honor until the Día de la Cruz on May 2, when they are returned in solemn procession to the cemetery.

Source: *Folklore Chileno* by Oreste Plath. Santiago: Nascimento, 1969, p. 320.

Peru

Cruz Velakuy (May 3) in Pacarigtambo c. 1985

The next festival, Cruz Velakuy (May 3), is celebrated officially in alternate years by the lowest-ranking ayllus, the fifth of each moiety. During Cruz Velakuy, the crosses of the ayllus, which have been decorated with flowers for the occasion, are brought in from the mountain-tops; each cross is feted in an all-night celebration held at the house of the ayllu member who has the cargo for the cross that year. The agricultural year ends officially with the festival of San Juan (June 24), which is sponsored by ayllu Waychu, the next-to-lowest-ranking ayllu of the lower moiety. As with all the other ayllu-sponsored festivals, one event in the celebration of the day of San Juan is a procession in which the image of the saint is paraded through the two plazas of Pacariqtambo; during the procession, cornstalks are placed at the corners of the litter bearing the image of San Juan. The celebration of San Juan continues up to the beginning of the festival of San Pedro (June 29) which is the cargo of Quinhuara, Aqchakar, and Qarhuacalla ayllus (the second-, third-, and fourth-ranking ayllus of the upper moiety). With the festival of San Pedro, which is followed by the celebration of the day of the Virgin of the Assumption (August 15), we have completed one cycle of the ritual calendar of the ayllus and moieties in Pacariqtambo.

Source: "Calendrical Cycles and Their Projections" by Gary Upton in *Journal of Latin American Lore* 12:1 (1986), p. 55.

Philippines

The Santacruzan novena and procession

A Maytime festival, one may come upon a Santacruzan procession any mild jazmin-scented evening, on the streets of any Philippine town, big or small. . . . The Santacruzan is actually nine days of prayers, or a novena, in honor of the Holy Cross, during May. At the end of the novena, usually timed so it falls on a week-end, the Santacruzan procession is held.

The procession is featured by pretty girls lavishly costumed, personifying Biblical characters, although somehow secular characters have been included in the cast.

Thus, we have the Reina Abanderada, who carries the Philippine flag, supposedly symbolizing "the Christian Army"; the Reina Justicia, who is blind-folded and carries scales in her hands, representing justice, probably a personification of the Blessed Virgin as "Mirror of Justice"; the Queen of Liberty, who is dressed in white and carries a torch, like the Statue of Liberty in New York harbor.

Some Biblical characters are Methuselah, a bearded old man; Reina Judith, who carries a sword, obviously representing the one which the Biblical Judith used to hack off the head of Holofernes; Reina Esther, a Biblical queen whose presence in the line-up does not seem to have any explanation, except that she is said to be a precursor of the Virgin Mary.

Other girls represent the various incarnations of the Blessed Virgin Mary. Thus there is a Divina Pastora (Divine Shepherdess), who carries a shepherdess's crook; the Reina de las Estrellas (Queen of Stars), who carries a wand topped by a star; the Reina de las Flores (Queen of Flowers), who walks under a canopy of flowers; the Reina de las Rosas (Mystical Rose); the Sentenciada, who is a prisoner; and the Abogada, in a barrister's toga, probably a personification of the Blessed Virgin as "Seat of Wisdom."

Other girls represent the three Christian virtues, Faith, Hope and Charity. All the characters have a retinue of pretty girls, or sometimes little girls dressed as angels, called *sagalas,* who sing "Ave Maria" as they march in the procession.

But the principal character in the Santacruzan is the Reina Elena (Queen Helena), who is accompanied by a little boy representing King Constantine, usually dressed as little Lord Fauntleroy.

Source: *The Galleon Guide to Philippine Festivals* by Alfonso J. Alvit. Manila: Galleon, 1969, pp. 56-58.

Spain

May crosses in Western Andalucia c. 1968

In Cordoba, crosses covered in flowers and leaves are erected in the patios of homes. In Lebrija, near Cadiz, each of the fifteen barios of the city decorates a street cross, and dancing and singing take place around the cross in the evenings. In Seville boys form small processions with miniature floats carried by one or two boys. The float bears a crucifix surrounded by flowers and lit by candles. One of the boys collects coins from onlookers as they pass through the streets.

Source: *Spanish Fiestas* by Nina Epton. New York: A. S. Barnes, 1968, pp. 89-90.

Festival preparations

In Santa Eulalia, Andalucia, preparations for the Crosses of May festival begin immediately following Easter. The community is divided into two hermandads (brotherhoods) who each decorate a cross.

On April nights at about ten-thirty each hermandad fires its rockets and people begin to go to Las Flores. . . . While only a handful of children and young adults are present, they all sit together on the same bench and make paper flowers in assembly line fashion. One person cuts out petals, another makes the center of the flower by twisting paper around a slender wire. At the end of the bench are the people who combine the parts, tying the flower off with thread. One of the older girls oversees this process, since the flowers must be just right, but both boys and girls participate. They use the wide tamborines for containers while they make flowers. . . . While a small core of flower makers continue to work, the rest clamor for the tamborines to be given over to their rightful use as musical instruments.

Domingo de Churbarba

The pace quickens on the Sunday before the actual Cross of May ceremony. On this Sunday each hermandad holds a major preparatory ritual called the Sunday of *Chubarba* or The Bringing of the *Chubarba*. This ritual marks the beginning of the actual ceremony time. "*Desde la traida de la chubarba a la gira*" ("from the bringing of the chubarba to the picnic"), is a common phrase encompassing the entire festival. Chubarba is a green holly-like plant which is one of the indispensible ritual items used in decorating the Cross. It is a low shrub which grows along the creeks and in low damp places and has a sharp, thorny point at the end of each small laurel-shaped leaf.

Each brotherhood has its own traditional picnic spot and a traditional chubarba picking area located on the side of town associated with its cross. The Liano picnic area is about a mile to the east with their chubarba area in the wilder countryside to the south of the picnic spot. The Fuente picnic area is on the west about three-quarters of a mile from town. Their chubarba site is a short distance beyond to the southwest.

Walking in couples, singing songs of the cross, it takes about an hour to get to the chubarba area. The way leads along the gullies and creeks, and the members cut *chubarba* with pen knives as they go. The thorns prick and cut their hands as they collect the chubarba which gives rise, along with the wild asparagus, to many suggestive jokes. When each brotherhood arrives at its chubarba area, it throws down its bunches of the shrub and has a snack of bread and wine and tapas. After this snack, couples used to go off alone to "pick chubarba," but today so many younger children go along with the couples that this is difficult. Instead, while some continue to pick chubarba, "so that the Llano will be sure to bring in a bigger load than the Fuente," the rest dance and play at Corro. As the day wanes, each group loads its donkey with an impressive bundle of *chubarba* and then starts for home. At the edge of town the rest of the hermandad and the tamborilero meet and join their group.

Día de las Flores

At sunset on Saturday, the *Dia de Las Flores,* each hermandad returns from its picnic area where it has spent the late afternoon. As in the Chubarba ceremony of the Sunday before, the rest of the hermandad awaits them on the outskirts of town. This time each member has a long branch of poplar. The Llaneros are again the first into the town. They return from El Venero, their picnic spot in the campo, to the Era de la Cuesta, where the rest await them. The poplar branches are symbolic of the wild flowers that they are supposed to pick during the afternoon to decorate the cross. They don't pick any flowers; instead they adorn the cross with the paper ones they have been making throughout April. Spring and efflorescence are important elements of the entire ritual as the following Copla del Romero indicates:

En primavera florida adoramos a la Cruz y la cubrimos de flores de canciones y de luz.	In flowery spring we venerate the Cross and cover it with flowers, songs and with light.

This parade on the Dia de Las Flores is the first act in which ritual roles are recognized, in this case the Mayordoma. The hermandad comes down from the Era de la Cuesta in double file. The people in each file hold branches in such a way as to make an arch. Then the Mayordoma walks between two girls designated as *Diputadas*. These three are just behind the tamborilero and the leaders of the two lines who play the tamborines. Rockets are fired nonstop. When the Llano reaches their cross and end their parade, the Fuente enters town from the other side. Until quite recently both brotherhoods came into town simultaneously, but cases of pushing and shoving and hair-pulling, as well as firing of rockets into the crowd, forced the civil authorities to put them on a rigid time schedule.

After the parades each hermandad holds a traditional dance. These take place in rented halls where the secular festivities are held. Traditional dances have the tamborilero as music maker. Non-traditional dances are those which have modern electrified bands as replacements for the old pattern of guitar, mandolin and drum bands. As the dance breaks up at about one A.M., the Night of the Pines begins.

The following three coplas del Romero are sung by both groups and can be heard almost every night of the flowers:

Ya vienen las golondrinas con el vuelo muy sereno para quitarle las espinas a Jesús de Nazareno	Now comes the swallows with quiet flight to take out the thorns from Jesus of Nazareth
Bendita sea la Cruz Bendits sean las flores y también bendita sean todas las que se las ponen. (Copla del Romero)	Blessed by the Cross, blessed be the flowers and also blessed be all of those who place them (on the cross).
De las que están bailando la que lleva el delantal es la novia de mi hermano pronto tengo una cuñá (cuñada). (Fandango de la Cruz)	Of those who are dancing the one who is wearing the apron is the girlfriend of my brother, very soon I'll have a sister-in-law.

Noche de los Pínos

Each hermandad takes to the street behind its tamborilero and spends the night singing through the town. Partisan feeling is running high. Along with rockets, the night is punctuated with cries of "Viva la calle de la Fuente!" and "Viva el Llano!" Although every active member is supposed to stay up, by three o'clock, most have gone to bed. When most people have slipped off, the core of stalwart boys continues to go about town. By about three-thirty, when only a dozen or so remain on the streets, an odd bit of pragmatism creeps through. One of the tamborileros goes off to nap and the boys from both crosses go around together. At five they begin to bang on the shuttered windows of those who didn't stay up. Abruptly the group splits back into two parties and they each go about waking their members.

At this point the *Noche de los Pínos* has its climax. Each group goes out in the predawn darkness to the pine groves on their side of town. They cut down four pine trees, each about twenty feet high. These pine trees, like the chubarba, are indispensible ritual elements of the Cross ceremony. Just at daybreak the groups come into town carrying the trees. They are still singing fandangos of the cross, many of which are love songs. But on the morning of the pines, some are closer to the central feeling of the moment than others.

Toda la noche me llevo	All night I've spent
atravesando pinares	crossing through pine groves
por darle los Buenos Dias	to say good morning
al Divino Sol que sale.	to the divine sun that rises.

This is the moment at which the cross itself is fully decorated. The four pine trees, undecorated, are erected at the four corners of the cross. The chubarba arch is attached to the pillar to frame the cross. Paintings of Christ on the cross and tapestries are hung on the pillar itself, with more paper flowers and chubarba. Potted lilies and other real flowers are placed on the ground around the cross, within the pine tree boundaries. A red carpet is laid, leading to the front of the cross. A white silk scarf is draped over the cross itself, symbolic of a shroud.

Sunday of the Cross

This is the day of the Romerías, the parades called Romeros which are the major ritual on the Crosses festival. The ritual is called a romeria, "pilgrimage," because the parades go outside the town and into the countryside, symbolically, that is, since they go no farther than the Era de la Cuesta. Each parade is the mirror image of the other, and most of the songs are the same with only minor variations. Both the ritual's meaning and geography of the town fix the parade route. One group follows it clockwise; the other counter clockwise.

Starting at its own cross, each group takes a short loop which is the "search for the Mayordoma." Then it proceeds from the cross to the Era de la Cuesta where the Mayordomo waits. After reentering town, the group goes to the opposition's cross. Before returning to the home cross, each brotherhood visits the church and the ayuntamiento. Although the parades have always taken turns, first one hermandad's and then the other's, in the past one group often jumped the gun and thus their paths would cross. Civil authority has settled the question with its time table. First the Romero of the Fuente at midmorning; then the official mass for the Day of the Cross with its own nonsectarian procession; then the secular festivity of the Mayordomos of the Fuente, a lavish refresco; then in the afternoon, the Romero of the Llano; the secular contribution of the Llano mayordomos is held at midnight in the Llano, a spectacular fireworks display.

Romerito de los Ninos, the children's parades

On Monday the romerías of the Llano and the Fuente are repeated in their entirety. The only difference between the parades of Sunday and Monday are the paraders themselves.

Source: *Santa Eulalia's People: Ritual Structure and Process in an Andalucian Multi Community* by Francisco Enrique Aguilera. St. Paul: West Publishing, 1962, pp. 65-88.

May 5

Cinco de Mayo

Puebla Battle Day commemorates the defeat of the forces of Napoleon III in 1867.

Mexico

The Cinco de Mayo play at Peñón, Mexico City

At Peñón, near the great central airport of Mexico City, an elaborate folk play takes place; it not only depicts the historical battle but also some of the events leading up to it. The village plaza is the main stage, while the nearby peñón (big rock), from which the place derives its name, represents the Puebla forts. The act of treaties usually takes place in a nearby schoolyard.

The play begins at eleven o'clock in the morning with a parade of all the forces accompanied by bands and native musicians. General Zaragoza, the leader of the Mexican army, is dressed in an elegant *charro* suit and rides a magnificent horse. From the back of his hat hangs a cloth with "Viva Mexico!" embroidered on it. Porfirio Díaz, another famous general, wears a plumed hat and lavishly embroidered uniform hung with many medals. Also recognizable are General Negrete, General Berriozabal, General Doblado, and General Prim. On the back of the French leader, Marshal Lorencz, hangs a cloth embroidered with "Viva Francia!" The Zacapoaxtlas from the Sierra de Puebla are present with their Indian leader, Lucas. There are large numbers of Chinacos divided into cavalry and infantry. Groups of common soldiers wearing uniforms of all periods surge through the crowd. Not even the *soldaderas* have been left out. These are the women who follow their men to cook for them and often fight at their side. Each one carries on her back a doll, to represent a baby, and a small basket with food and water. The French Zouaves are dressed in red or blue trousers, a small blue sack coat, white canvas leggings, and a red or blue fez.

At the end of the parade the order to break ranks is given, and the soldiers go to eat in small groups. For the next hour they play their own little game of trying to steal food, ammunition, and arms from the enemy. Adding comedy to the situation is the clipping of the "wild" Zacapoaxtlas who have arrived from the sierra with long hair. They pretend to be afraid of the scissors and weep bitterly over the loss of their hair.

During the first scene of the actual drama the diplomats seat themselves around a table to present their claims before the Juárez government for injuries to persons and property during the Three Year War. Gesticulating expressively and trying to speak in the manner of the country they represent, the diplomats repeat verbatim long sections of the real treaties. The English and Spanish representatives, finally realizing the injustice of their claims, agree to withdraw and leave the country with their troops. Only France declares war.

When the envoy reaches Zaragoza with the declaration of war, the latter tears it up angrily and tells his soldiers to prepare for battle. The Mexican army takes possession of the hill, and the French rush up in a sweeping circle. Three times they attack the fort and are repulsed. At one point the Mexican army drives them down to the village. The fighting goes on for several hours. There is continuous noise from the rifles and cannons, loaded with powder only. There are shouted dialogues—some memorized, others extemporaneous. Over it all can be heard the bugles sounding orders. There is hand-to-hand fighting and at times the spectators, carried away by the reality of the scene, rush in to the aid of the Mexicans, beating the enemy with their fists or throwing dirt in their faces. When a soldier's powder gives out, he is "dead" and must leave the battlefield.

As night begins to fall, Zaragoza and Lorencez meet face to face, showing off their skill in fencing and riding. They both fight valiantly, but the Mexican leader wins. While the French flag is lowered, he reads aloud the report sent by the real Zaragoza to President Juárez: "The arms of the Republic have been covered with glory. The French soldiers behaved with courage and their generals blunderingly." But the play is not over yet, for the "dead" must be buried. Soldiers from both sides are placed on cots or stretchers or in coffins. Led by bands playing funeral marches, the procession leaves the plaza and is soon lost in the darkness.

Source: *Fiesta Time in Latin America* by Jean Milne. Los Angeles: The Ward Ritchie Press, 1965, pp. 91-93.

May 5 (Formerly Moon 5, Day 5)

Tango No Sekku (Boys' Day)

On this day a bamboo pole is set before the house with a carp kite flying for each boy in the household. The largest kite, for the oldest boy, flies from the top. His siblings' smaller kites hang in descending order below. The boys may also arrange a display of military dolls in the tokonoma or on a special stand. Friends may come to visit and taste iris-wine. The day also celebrates Iris Day. This day is now called Kodomo-no-hi (Children's Day).

Japan

Noborigoi, carp streamers

. . . This is the long bamboo-pole from whose apex floats an enormous carp, the *noborigoi,* which means "streamer-carp" but also "ascending carp." Made of cloth or tough paper, it is coloured red or black, with whitish lines to show the scales and the glittering streaks of the fish's agile body, out of whose head two aggressive round eyes stare. The mouth is held wide open by a bamboo hoop from which several cords combine to be knotted to the pole. The broad tail is simply left unstitched (or unglued), and when the wind is caught in the gaping mouth, to emerge by the tail, it inflates the body and imparts to it waving and floating movements of a very realistic aspect.

Before every home one such *noborigoi* is hoisted for each male child. For the eldest boy, a red one is usually chosen, of tremendous proportions—as much as twenty or more feet long. Younger sons, being less important, may have only a black one each, and they gradually decrease in size, just as the progeny does. However, no rule is set as to colours or dimensions. All the carp are affixed to the same stout bamboo, one beneath the other, and with a prolific family it is quite a sight to watch the many carp merrily swinging above the roof, breasting the elements at the slightest breeze. And when there is no wind whatsoever, they look like a gigantic catch at the end of a fishing-rod. . . . Probably older than the carp-*nobori* were those made of multicoloured, long and rather broad streamers gathered around a circlet, the *fuki-nagashi* pennons. The flutterings and crossings of these ribbons were intended to entangle or shoo away evil. The term really means "flowing-blown"; but *fuki* also stands for an unrestrained, free life, as one would like to have. The *fuki-nagashi* were very generally set up of old, and may have been identical with the streamers of the seventh birthday celebration, but are rare nowadays.

The bamboo-poles of both carp and pennons are often surmounted by a *kaza-guruma,* a double wind-wheel which automatically adjusts itself through an arrow-shaped rudder and merrily twirls in the breeze. More commonly they are topped by a pine-sapling or a bunch of greens and flowers—again the "May-bush" which we find with so many races, and which is but a symbol of nature and of spring.

Doll display

What strikes us most, when we compare the various "dolls" for sale in shops in time for the Boys' Festival, is that there is no unity in their character. The girls' dolls consist of ten or fifteen defined figures, a certain number of equally standardized pieces of furniture and other objects, to which may be added incidental dolls and paraphernalia of various types, which however are secondary and do not affect the main aspect of the display. The boys' exhibition can be expanded or reduced *ad libitum,* and actually only needs the few military implements—*bugu*—used by the old warrior, even if some of the puppets are more regularly found than others. There is no formula prescribed.

The arrangement of these figures and *bugu* may take place in the *tokonoma* or on a special stand, usually consisting of three or five steps, carpeted with a green cloth or, more orthodoxically, with a mat woven of green stalks. Green is the colour not only of all vegetation, but also to some extent of water, the source of all life: the cloth or mat once more connects the festival with fertility-lore.

At both ends of the topmost shelf may be two ancient oil-lamps—*andon*—which supposedly stand for vigilance; between them a toy-cuirass, complete with helmet and leggings, sits on its container, the *yoroi bitsu.* To its right and left should be miniature spears, bows and arrows, and a long sword, all duly erected in their respective stands. Martial flags and banners of various types, as well as paper-lanterns on long poles, may flank them, and behind it all may be a rather imposing miniature screen with the picture of an ancient camp-curtain, such as the generals used for an enclosure.

On the tier below will be a pair of ritual *sake*-bottles on their tray, rice-wine being always a congratulatory and prophylactic adjunct of festivities. From their gullets will emerge a few irises wrapped in ceremonial paper-cuffs, bound with gold and silver string. The *chimaki dango* and *kashiwa mochi* may also be devotionally placed on *sambō*-trays on the shelf, before being eaten by the boys. Another helmet, *kabuto,* or a war-hat, *jingasa,* may be shown, and such other paraphernalia as a large war-drum, the *gunsen* or leader's fan with the sun-disk, or the *saihai,* a short stick with a heavy tassel of white or gilt leather strips at the far end, serving as commander's baton. An old, eight-sided object, slightly elliptic and with truncated ends, usually on solid wheels, will also as a rule be found there. It is suggestive of a cannon, but originally was probably a fertility-amulet. Some of these are among the oldest exhibits used. Formerly more than at present, they were accompanied by various trunks and boxes such as the *samurai* employed for his armour and accoutrements.

On the lowest step there should be three figures, one human and two animal: a white horse, a striped tiger, and Shōki, the devil-expeller.

The *musha ningyō,* "military dolls," placed on the various steps agreeably to one's predilection, vary a good deal in their character, yet may all be considered as "ambassadors from history." They are not random puppets without personality: they all convey a distinct message. Remarkable also is their marvellous fidelity to details in dress and accoutrement as based on ancient traditions. Among the military dolls, however, we also find civilian personages, provided that they played some important part in the history of Japan.

According to U. A. Casal, the warrior figurines may include Kusunoki Masahige, Minamoto Yorimitsu, Toyotomi Hideyoshi, Tokugawa Ieyasu, Jimmu Tenno, and the warrior-empress Jingu Kogo. Most popular is Yoshitsune, often accompanied by Benkei. The exhibit may also include folktale heroes Kintaro and Momotaro.

On the sides of the exhibition shelves may be stood further, somewhat larger banners, with all sorts of auspicious inscriptions and drawings, as well as any real arms and cuirasses which the family might possess. . . .

The boy's friends are of course invited to admire his beautiful exhibits, and to partake of the beneficent and aromatic iris-wine. But much of his time will be spent out-of-doors, parading his own military accoutrements, or fighting sham-engagements with the neighbourhood boys, and having a good time in spending his pocket-money on the pleasurable things which hawkers of all kinds seem particularly willing to part with on this day of days.

In the evening he will rapturously listen to the father's or elder brother's tales of loyal devotion, to feats of inconceivable heroism of the people depicted on his shelves, or to the good fortune of Momotarō, with which he repaid his foster parents.

The Iris

. . . The iris is a spiritual weapon, like so many other flowers and herbs, and the victory of the professed leaf-sword was one over occult powers. These upright blades will defeat the goblins of darkness, and their pungent smell was believed to be evil-dispelling. Therefore dried iris-leaves were also stuffed into pillows, to protect the sleeper, and hung in bunches from the roof's eaves. And as, because of its plentiful sap—water—the iris will also protect a house against conflagration, flowers and leaves are, in the fifth month, scattered over the roof itself.

On the fifth day of the fifth moon, iris leaves should equally be soaked in one's bath, to prevent illness during the summer. The petals were macerated in *sake,* which not only renders the beverage prophylactic, but assures longevity. On this day *sake* so treated was drunk by the boys, their parents, and all the friends who came visiting.

The *kusudama*

The *kusudama* is hung up near the door to the room in which the exhibition is held, although no longer directly connected with it. The round *kusudama,* for a long time past made of stiff cloth-flowers (or now even of celluloid!), is in fact nothing but a bunch of grasses, a charm against disease, reinforced by the five-coloured threads which in China have always had an amuletic potency, both because threads can bind a child's soul to this earth—while the Five Colours (blue/green, white, red, yellow and purple/black) sway and benefit its destiny—and because thread-clusters will entangle the devils' feet.

Source: *The Five Sacred Festivals of Ancient Japan: Their Symbolism & Historical Development* by U. A. Casal. Tokyo: Sophia University and Charles E. Tuttle, 1966, pp. 66-68. (Casal discusses origins of this festival and gives details of the festival and its figurines.)

For More on Boys' Day see: "Boys' Day" in *Folklore of American Holidays* by Hennig Cohen and Tristram Potter Coffin. 2nd ed. Detroit: Gale Research, 1991; *Dolls on Display: Japan in Miniature, Being an Illustrated Commentary on the Girls' Festival and the Boys' Festival* by G. Caiger. Nishikicho, Kanda, Tokyo: Hokuseido Press, 1933. (Black and white photographs of dolls with descriptions); "Dolls' Day and Boys' Day" in *Festivals in Asia.* Sponsored by the Asian Cultural Centre for Unesco. Tokyo: Kodansha, 1975, pp. 23-30.

Easter to July

Altura Do Espírito Santo (Holy Ghost Season)

Celebrations honor the Holy Ghost, who is personified as powerful and vindictive. Azoreans have celebrated the Holy Ghost since the late fifteenth century and have carried the celebration to Brazil, Canada, Bermuda, and the United States, while the celebration seems to have nearly disappeared in continental Portugal.

Azores

Altura Do Espírito Santo in the Azores

. . . Two types of celebration are held in honor of the Holy Ghost, the *bodo* (banquet) and the *função* (function). The *bodo,* a large-scale public festival organized by a committee of Brotherhood members includes a Novena; Mass: a procession and coronation of young children; the distribution of meat, bread, and wine; an auction of gifts given to the Holy Ghost; and an array of secular activities including extemporaneous competitive singing and Azorean-style bullfights.

The *função,* a small-scale ritual performance sponsored by a voluntary Emperor as payment of a promise to the Holy Ghost, is held in a private home. It includes a Novena: Mass; procession and coronation of the Emperor; distribution of food to the poor: offering of gifts to the guests; and a communal meal.

The context for these ritual activities is the Império. These elaborately painted one-room buildings are divided into three parts by the placement of the door and two windows. Impérios, although they are permanent structures, are opened and used only once a year for the festival celebration.

During the celebration, an interior altar is decorated with crepe paper and fresh flowers. When the Coroa (crown) is placed on the altar, the space becomes sacred. People who have promises to pay bring offerings and place them at the altar. By the end of the day, the Império is filled with sugar and bread ex-votos, beeswax candles, olive oil, live chickens, bananas, cakes, and other gifts. These gifts are auctioned to the crowd during the afternoon. Profits from the auction which are used to support the celebrations are not given by the Brotherhood to the church.

The Altura Do Espírito Santo, Holy Ghost season, falls mainly between Easter and Trinity Sunday with the high point of ritual activities throughout the Azores on Pentecost and Trinity. In most rural communities on the island of Terceira the cycle begins at Easter and a *função* is held each week. The coronations of the *funções* coincide with the *bodos* on Pentecost and Trinity. Urban Impérios have now extended the season by staggering their celebrations from Pentecost through July which enable the Brotherhoods to share the crowns, brocade flags, and other expensive paraphernalia needed for the festival.

The week of the *bodo* is a sacred time marked by excitement and extraordinary events. Firecrackers and rockets announce the beginning and end of important activities and call people to the Império. Flags and elaborate strings of lights decorate the street in front of the Império, transforming it temporarily into a sacred space for religious and social activities.

Ritual activities begin during the week before the coronation. Brotherhood members gather at the Império to visit the Holy Ghost, recite the rosary led by a lay person, and pay their annual dues. After the novena they stroll under the colored lights, visit, listen to Azorean music, buy special foods from street vendors, or bid on bread, candy, and liqueurs at the auction.

Pezinho

The *pezinho,* a serenade with a parade of decorated cattle, begins the exchange events in those Impérios that distribute meat. During the previous year young animals donated or purchased by the Brotherhood are fattened throughout the year and the meat is distributed. At the end of the week before the coronation, the cattle, decorated with ribbons and flowers and accompanied by the *festa* committee, singers, musicians, and firecracker launchers, are paraded through the neighborhood. The group stops at the Império, the church, the homes of the *festa* committee and those people who have contributed to the *festa.* While the decorated animals pace, the singers, accompanied by the stringed instruments, create extemporaneous verses to honor the Holy Ghost and the person being serenaded. A committee member provides the initial singer with facts about the contributor, and subsequent singers compete to create more and more beautiful verses elaborating on the theme. These verses give details, often humorous, about the person's life and about his contributions, generally food or labor. The singers thank the family for helping, assure them that the Holy Ghost helps those who help the *festa,* and encourage them to give again next year with verses like the following.

A senhora diga ao seu marido
Que o ''pezinho'' por aqui passou
Que o Divino esta reconhecido
Da res bela que êle engordou

Lady, please tell your husband
That the ''pezinho'' passed here

And the Divine is grateful
For his beautiful fat steer.

After the *pezinho* (serenade), the person honored often provides food for the singers and spectators. In some cases wine, soft drinks, and sweet bread may be served outside the house, or the whole group may be invited into the house for elaborate snacks of codfish cakes, potatoes with hot peppers, clams, crab, soft drinks, beer, and wine. As the brass band plays, the group walks on to the next house to continue the serenade.

The presentation of the meat varies considerably. In most urban Impérios young boys deliver a share of raw meat and bread, and sometimes wine, to the houses of the Brotherhood members. The cut and size of the meat depends on the amount a person pays in annual dues or any additional contribution. In most rural areas the meat is laid out on tables in front of the Império for each Brotherhood member to pick up and take home.

Função

The *função* (function), a small-scale celebration sponsored by a voluntary Emperor, represents the payment of a personal promise to the Holy Ghost and involves a series of ritual exchange events. Just as Queen Isabela, through her act of charity, fulfilled her promise to the Holy Ghost, so the Emperor repeats her action, thereby fulfilling his own promise.

The symbolic crown, decorated staffs, and practical items such as pans, dishes, and benches used for the ritual, belong to the Holy Ghost and are administered by the lay Brotherhoods. All of the necessary ritual paraphernalia circulate from family to family in each community in an order established by lot on Pentecost of the prior year.

The event takes place in the home of the Emperor, which becomes the context for ritual activities. A banner of the Holy Ghost with fresh flowers placed in the front of the home marks it as a ritual space and signifies that the Holy Ghost is there. The crown is installed on an altar decorated with crepe-paper flowers, and olive oil and candles are burned at its base. The presence of the crown transforms the domestic, secular space of a private home into the public ritual space of a chapel. During this time anyone may enter the house to worship, and each day of the week people gather to recite the rosary that is led by a lay person.

The main participants in the *função* are: the Emperor, sponsor or host; the *criador,* cattle raiser; the *marchant,* butcher; the *mestra,* ritual specialist and supervisor; and those who help with the cooking. These are the performers, the active participants, and those who generate the gifts. The invited guests, the poor, and the general public are the audience—the passive participants and the recipients of the gifts.

The Coronation. On Sunday morning, the Emperor, accompanied by the guests, walks in a procession to the church. The procession generally is organized in two parallel lines. People designated as "special," such as the representatives of the *criador* or *mestra,* carry symbolic objects, crown, staffs, batons, banners, and flags and walk between the lines. They are further marked by a person on each side carrying decorated staffs. The procession reads from front to back with the Emperor, the most important person, at the very end. These processions provide a cogent visual delineation of one's personal network and not only make it clear who is and who is not present but also indicate prestige within the network by one's position in the procession and by the carrying of ritual objects. After the Mass, the priest crowns the Emperor with a silver crown. The procession of the crowned Emperor returns to the house in triumph.

Two types of gifts are then distributed by the crowned Emperor. *Pão dos inocentes,* bread of the innocents, is given to the children in the audiences, and *esmolas da mesa,* alms of the table, are given to the poor. First the Emperor kneels, kisses the head of each loaf of bread for the innocents and gives it to the children. He then moves to the tables where *esmolas* have been laid out and gives a bowl of bread covered with broth, cooked meat, cabbage, and cooked blood and two loaves of bread to a previously designated group of poor people.

After the distribution of gifts to the poor, the guests join the Emperor for a communal meal which often includes 200-300 people. All guests walk in the procession and return to the home to eat together. The meal consists of three courses. The first, *sopas,* bread with mint soaked with meat broth, is followed by boiled meat and cabbage served with *pão de leite. Alcatra,* meat with bacon, onion, and wine and *massa sovada* are served as a last course. The guests stay and eat together while the poor are given baskets of food to take home. Late in the afternoon the guests accompany the Emperor as he delivers the crown to the home of the Emperor for the following week and the cycle begins again.

The *bodo*

Bread and wine, a medium of gift exchanges, are central to Holy Ghost festivals. Pentecost and Trinity Sundays are days of great excitement. *Bodos* are held in rural Impérios throughout the Azores and in some of the urban Impérios as well. The word *bodo* (banquet) is not only used for the large-scale public Holy Ghost festivals but also specifically for one part of the festival—the distribution of bread and wine at the *festa.*

On *festa* Sunday in the urban Impérios sweet bread is distributed after the procession and coronation of young children. The bread, generally purchased at local bakeries, is given out to the children who have participated in the coronation and sometimes to the audience. Throughout the day, as people come to the Império to visit the Holy Ghost and to bring their offerings, they are given a slice of sweet bread. Friends and relatives of committee members also bring gifts of food, fancy cakes, alfinim, and decorated loaves of sweet bread to give in support of the *festa.* All of these gifts are auctioned off, and the money raised is used by the committee to pay for the expenses of the *festa.*

The distibution of gifts is more complex in the rural communities. In the cities the bread is purchased from bakeries but in the rural Impérios an elaborate system for the preparation, presentation, and distribution of bread continued to flourish. In Lages and Vila Nova, for example, several couples are chosen by the *festa* committee to be *mordomos* (stewards). Each couple is responsible for a designated number of loaves of bread—generally between 200 and 400. The *mordomo's* family and friends make about half the required loaves and the rest are produced, ten per family, by other Brotherhood members.

On Saturday all those who have made bread for a particular *mordomo* gather at his or her home for a communal meal of *sopa do espírito santo,* meat cooked with vegetables and broth poured over bread, *carne asada,* baked meat, bread, and wine. In the late afternoon the group loads baskets of bread onto elaborately decorated ox carts and walks in a procession through town, gathering the rest of the bread as they go. The *mordomo* carrying a decorated wooden staff with a silver head, the symbol of his authority, is followed by young girls carrying enormous loaves of decorated sweet bread. As the *mordomo* and his party enter the storehouse of the Império in triumph, the bread is given to the Holy Ghost, counted by the *festa* committee and stored along with barrels and barrels of wine. A table is set with glasses, a pitcher of wine, and the large loaves of sweet bread, and the *mordomo's* staff is installed on the wall behind the table. The *mordomo's* family sits at the table and offers bread and wine to visitors.

On Pentecost and Trinity Sunday the Emperors for the week preside over the ritual activities in the Império, and the *mordomos* interact within the sphere of the *despenca,* the ritual storehouse. On these Sundays the Coronation tends to be grander, often embellished with a larger guest list. . . .

The legend

The origin of the Holy Ghost celebrations is attributed to celebration sponsored by the Rainha Santa Isabela, Queen Isabela of Portugal, who reigned between 1295 and 1322. The charter, or rationale, for the event in which food is a central element, is part of Portuguese folk tradition and is illustrated in the following three narratives told over and over again in the Azores.

Queen Isabel, the wife of King Diniz of Portugal, loved the poor. One day in the middle of winter she was going with buns in her cape to give to some poor people. Her husband stopped her and asked what she had in her cape. She said, "Roses," and he asked, "In the middle of winter?" When she opened her cape, the buns had turned to red roses.

Dom Diniz and his son, Dom Pedro, after arguing for many years, decided to have a battle on the mainland of Portugal. Both sides brought their armies to a certain place, still marked in Portugal today, and prepared to fight. Queen Isabela prayed to the Holy Ghost that they wouldn't fight and made a promise that she would make a celebration each year. She would put a poor person on her throne and crown him with her own crown. On the eve of the battle, Dom Diniz gave in, they didn't fight, and the celebration began. Later other members of the court began to have a celebration to the Holy Ghost on Pentecost Sunday.

Queen Isabela pleaded with God for help with her starving people, even to the point of promising to sell all her jewels, including her crown. Sometime after this there suddenly appeared two ships in a Portuguese harbor. Neither of the ships had any living person upon it. The only contents were cattle on one ship and grain on the other. These ships were thought to be a miracle sent from God in answer to Queen Isabela's pleas for her starving people. With this supply of cattle and grain, a large meal of meat and bread was prepared and a banquet served to the poor. From this date forward, an annual banquet for the poor was given in the same manner as the first. Queen Isabela continued to offer this yearly ceremony as a thanksgiving to God for the peace bestowed within Portugal and for the health of the Portuguese people. Queen Isabela gathered twelve poor men around a banquet table who were served by royalty as an expression of equality.

Source: "Food for the Holy Ghost: Ritual Exchange in Azorean Festivals" by Marilyn Salvador, pp. 244-260, in *Time out of Time: Essays on the Festival* by Alessandro Falassi. Albuquerque: Univ. of New Mexico, 1987, pp. 247-253.

Monday, Tuesday, and Wednesday before Ascension

Rogation Days

Austria

Blessing the fields on St. Mark's Day and the Rogation Days

In the weeks between Easter and the Ascension there are four days set aside where the Church has her children go out into the fields and pastures chanting the litany of All Saints and asking God's blessing for a good harvest and as protection against hailstorms, floods, and droughts. One day is the feast of St. Mark, April 25th, and the other three days are called "Rogation Days" and are the Monday, Tuesday, and Wednesday preceding the Ascension, which always falls on a Thursday. We always make these outdoor processions up on our mountain. The very first hue of green is appearing in the meadows, the birds are singing in the woods again, and the whole atmosphere is one of spring and hope.

Source: *Around the Year with the Trapp Family* by Maria Augusta Trapp. New York: Pantheon, 1955, p. 142.

France

Rogation processions and blessing of the crops

Rogation-tide, apart from Rogation processions and blessings of crops, has certain special customs. The crops, including the vineyards, are the object of much solicitude, as well may be expected; on St. George's Day in Disatines (Allier) a clean little towel is offered to the statue of St. George and with this his feet are washed in wine, amid cries of Vive Monsieur St. Georges! But if frost has touched the vines, woe to St. George; unkind things are said even to his face, and though his feet are washed, it is with a rough and scarifying cloth.

In some places the *buis bénit* of Palm Sunday (*Rameaux*) is not planted in the churchyard but carried into the fields, to bring a blessing (so in Touraine, recently at Mareuil, Preuilly, Nouâtre, Céré, Chaumussay). In Touraine also you must bake in Rogation week (I am not sure about washing; you do not wash in the latter part of Holy Week, and in some places not on the Annunciation). In the same district, at Rogation-tide, there were (I hope are) processions for the three Rogation days; no doubt this held also elsewhere; but besides this, the sacristan went round the houses of the village (no doubt after gentle persuasion). Sometimes also this is the day for the blessing of springs and wells; but usually that comes earlier.

Source: *A Guide to French Fetes* by E. I. Robson. London: Methuen, 1930, pp. 82-83.

Moveable: Forty Days after Easter

Ascension Day

Ascension Thursday commemorates the Ascension of Christ to heaven after his brief time on earth following the Resurrection. It falls in May or June.

Germany

Himmelfahrtstag

Himmelfahrtstag (Ascension Day) customs in Germany

Herrenpartien, men's outings, were popular on this day in Protestant areas. The men wore straw boater hats and carried cane walking sticks. In earlier days they went to the countryside in horse carriages with a huge barrel of beer aboard. Ascension Day is sometimes called Father's Day, Vatertag, because it is a day for men's outings.

In some Alpine areas a figure of Christ and the angels is raised into the dome of the church, from whence a shower of flowers and tiny saint's images rain. In Catholic areas processions are held on this day.

Blood Friday

A Blutritt procession takes place across the fields on Blood Friday the day after Ascension Day. At Weingarten in Upper Swabia over two thousand horsemen in traditional costumes join in this ride each year.

Source: *German Festivals and Customs* by Jennifer M. Russ. London: Oswald Wolff, 1982, p. 62.

Great Britain

The holy water of Ascension day

Ascensiontide rain is a remedy for sore eyes, as it falls straight from the heaven opened for Christ's entry. Water drawn from "holy wells" on Ascension morning is also curative. Well dressings occur in several spots at this time of year. Well dressing is an ancient custom that has survived in several parts of Britain. On a certain day each year an auspicious community well is adorned with great festivity.

Source: *The Customs and Ceremonies of Britain* by Charles Kightly. London: Thames and Hudson, 1986, p. 46. (See this source for more information on well dressing.)

The Netherlands

Baking bread for the poor

In eastern Holland's rural areas, special Ascension loaves of raisin bread are distributed to hospitals and to the aged. Once farmers were allowed to dig peat as they chose provided they baked at least twenty-five pounds of bread for the poor on Ascension Day. They vied for baking the largest loaf, some weighing as much as one hundred pounds.

Source: *Holland* by Nina Nelson. New York: Hastings House, 1970, p. 27.

Roumania

Sending the *Caloyan* on the water before Ascension Day

A band of quite tiny girls carries down to the river a coffin made of wood-shavings containing a clay figure of a little man. He is called the *Caloyan*. They have shaped him themselves with their little fingers, and, making pretence of bitter weeping, they are carrying out his obsequies.

The tallest of the children represents the priest, and a smaller one the deacon; a third is a standard-bearer, holding the funeral banner, a cloth on the end of a stick. And then come the bearers in their skirts, and the choir, and then the hired mourners and then the crowd.

The procession winds down towards the river by the footpath skirting Anica's enclosure. Sharp, shrill little voices sing a funeral song which is extremely old. An exercise in sorrow, one might fancy, which these young souls are trying over in preparation for the full-grown griefs of life:

Yan!
Yan!
Caloyan!

Your mother seeks you
In the thick places of the woods,
Her heart afire,
And in the sparse places of the woods,
Her heart burnt up!

Yan!
Yan!
Caloyan!

Your mother weeps you
In the clearing,
With tears of blood!

They are bearing their well-beloved to the foot of a willow-tree. Tenderly they kiss him. And then they cast him into the river, beseeching the divinity of the waters, in return, to spread the tide of his blessings over the earth, thinking by this sacrifice to ensure the rich June rains for the year's crops.

Source: *Isvor: The Country of Willows* by Princess Bibesco. New York: Frederick A. Stokes, 1924, pp. 139-140.

Sweden

Kristi Himmelsfärds Dag

Ascension Day outings

An early morning outing may greet this day. Rising at 3:00 or 4:00 a.m. folks go to the forests to hear the birds sing at sunrise. If the cuckoo is heard from the east or west, good luck will come. But if it is heard first from the north or south, this portends ill. "Cuckoo in the west is the very best," goes the saying. After sunrise the group may hold a picnic breakfast and make music. These outings are called *gök-otta,* "early cuckoo morning."

Source: *Traditional Festivities of Sweden* by Ingemar Lima. Stockholm: The Swedish Institute, 1985, p. 12.

For more information see: "Ascension Day and Associated Days" in *Folklore of American Holidays* by Hennig Cohen and Tristram Potter Coffin. 2nd ed. Detroit: Gale Research, 1991.

Moveable: Fifty Days after Easter

Whitsun / Pentecost

This Sunday in May or June celebrates Pentecost, the occasion when the Holy Spirit descended in tongues of flame on the apostles. This is a traditional time for baptism; hence the English term White Sunday, for the white baptismal robes worn. Whitsunday is a popular spring outing day in Europe as well as a religious occasion. The week following continues as Whitsuntide and religious observances may extend over the week. Whitsunday is the seventh Sunday after Easter.

Brazil

Pentecost

A festival in Santa Rita

The celebration of Pentecost, the Festival of the Divine Holy Spirit, is, without the slightest doubt, the event of greatest importance in the calendar of Santa Rita. Its structure incorporates almost all the elements, both religious and secular, associated with religious festivals in Brazil. Numerous activities with a more or less religious character surround the event, including the novena, the masses, the processions, as well as the *cavalhada* (a simulated battle between the Christians and the Moors in which the participants perform on horseback) and the performances of the various "folk groups," which sing and dance in the streets to honor the saints. Clearly profane manifestations take place as well, such as the occasional appearances of the gigantic dolls known as João Paulino and Maria Angu who run up and down the streets to delight the children, the *forrós* (social dances), the auctions, the excessive drinking, and so on. But as far as popular opinion is concerned, the two most important events during the entire ten days of the Festival are the great public and free feasting of the typical dish for the occasion, the *afogado*, and the pompous final Procession.

The Festival of the Divine Holy Spirit in Santa Rita, as in many Brazilian towns, is synonymous with the Festival of Abundance. It is the moment in which the people of the region take pleasure in the fruits of their year's labor. They celebrate in thanksgiving to the Holy Spirit, the entity to whom they attribute the abundance of the regional production.

In order to give the reader an idea of the dimension of this celebration of abundance, in 1983, during the first communal repast served on the Sábado do Encontro, a ritual event to mark the beginning of the Festival, 12 bulls were slaughtered. The community members considered the amount insufficient, since they remember better days in which up to 60 animals were sacrificed for the feast. On the following Saturday, a new distribution of the afogado took place, for which 18 animals were killed. Besides the abundant afogado, during the week of the novena, both lunch and supper were served daily to the population at the Casa da Festa (a sort of headquarters for the Festival) and, on the principal festive days, sweets were distributed to all, along with the traditional coffee and *paçoca* (a dish of manioc flour base into which chunks of meat are mixed).

Like the afogado, the Procession also provides a space in which the members of the community are united, grouping themselves, this time, in a sort of public prayer. This event marks the climax of the Festival, as it is the only truly collective manifestation of devotion during the entire celebration.

In 1983 the Procession of the Divine Holy Spirit lasted almost two full hours, from the time of the organization of the ritual participants to the return of the train to the Cathedral. With eight highly elaborate *andores* (litters for conveying religious images) and a large number of "*destaques*" (term used in Santa Rita to designate persons in special attire to decorate the andores), the town band, and the amplified collective prayers and hymns, this tremendous bombardment of visual and auditory stimulus attracted approximately 15,000 people. The itinerary, the longest of the town processions, followed a route covering three kilometers. From the beginning of the Procession to the last of the faithful, the crowd occupied a total of more than six blocks.

Source: "The Holy Family of the Festival of Life: The Pentecost Festival in a Small Brazilian Town" by Suzel Ana Reily in *Journal of Latin American Lore* 11 (2) (1985), 177-193.

Finland/Estonia

"Easter" eggs in Finland

At Easter-time in Finland the birds of passage are still to come and local varieties have not yet begun to lay; so, as in parts of Norway, the egg feast is enjoyed at Whitsun, when eggs are more readily available. This is the case even today, when local conditions have altered.

Eggs in Estonia

Similar geographical influence on local folk-custom seems to be common to much of the Baltic—for example, in Estonia they prepare coloured eggs, and this too is at Whitsun, no doubt for like reasons. But here the problem cannot have been so acute, for we read of boys and girls collecting Easter eggs from the woodland and water birds. Sometimes girls performed this task and presented the findings to their sweethearts. In any case domestic poultry was not a modern innovation in Estonia; there are records of a medieval tithe of eggs and chickens, paid by the peasant to his feudal lord.

Source: *An Egg at Easter: A Folklore Study* by Venetia Newell. Bloomington: Indiana Univ. Press, 1971, p. 191.

Germany

Pfingsten

Whitsun customs

In most cases the may pole is taken down on Whitsun Eve, though in Silesia it is not put up until Whitsuntide. The birch tree and pink and red peonies, called Whitsun roses (*Pfingstrosen*), are symbols of Whitsuntide. Church services may include "swinging the Holy Ghost," lowering a carved dove from the ceiling into the congregation. Processions of cattle being driven to their summer pastures may occur at this time, or if they are already in pasture, they may be decorated with leaves, ribbons, and cowbells on this day. The Germans have a saying, "*Geputzt wie ein Pfingstochs*" (dressed like a Whitsun ox) for the overdressed person. In some areas a young man may camouflage himself with leaves and moss and hide while other children hunt him. This is known as "hunting the green man" (*Laubmannchen*). Many variations of this custom exist throughout Germany.

Source: *German Festivals and Customs* by Jennifer M. Russe. London: Oswald Wolff, 1982, p. 59.

Great Britain

Whitsun

Whitsun games

In England, Whitsun events include fairs, beating the bounds, well dressings, walking days, the Cooper Hill cheese rolling, and the Dunmor Flitch Trial, among others. Morris dancing is popular at Whitsun festivities. Today many secular Whitsuntide events have moved to the Spring Bank Holiday on the last weekend in May. It is called Whit, though the Whitsunday itself may fall on a different week.

Showing off new clothing

The house visitation which is associated with the buying of new clothes for children at Whitsuntide is common throughout the South Yorkshire area. The form of the visitation is extremely simple. Children, usually between about four and ten years old, go from door to door on Whit Sunday morning (mostly in family groups) knocking and telling the householder that they have come to show their Whit clothes. The clothes are then admired and the children given money.

The dresses which are bought and shown for Whitsuntide are normally "best" dresses, reserved for Sundays or parties, and in the north of Sheffield, where I lived, two Whitsun dressed were needed—one for Sunday itself and another for the Whit Sing on Monday.

Source: "Whitsuntide House Visitation" by Georgina Smith in *Lore and Language 3* (August 1970), 15.

Whitsun Ales, Walking Days

The Whitsun Church Ale was, at one time, a popular parish feast. All joined for a meal after Whitsun communion, the wealthy bringing enough for those less fortunate. In the nineteenth century this custom diminished into Club Feasts and Club Walks. Today the custom remains in the north of England, in Lancashire and Yorkshire, where Walking Days are organized by the Sunday Schools for the children. The girls wear veils and wreaths and carry flowers. All are in white. The older members of the parish follow. In Cornwall the custom continues accompanied by a brass band.

Source: *A Year of Festivals* by Geoffrey Palmer and Noel Lloyd. London: Frederick Warne, 1972, pp. 36-37.

Hungary

Whitmonday

The maypole and Whitmonday dances on a puszta near Ozora, Hungary, c. 1920

In May the maypole was danced out. It was a strong, slender poplar, with all the branches stripped from its long trunk except for a little foliage left at the very top, about the size of an umbrella. Once they used to set up a maypole outside each house where there was an unmarried girl; later one had to do for the whole puszta. Originally this was set up outside the farm manager's house, but after the wife of one of them had forbidden this owing to the appalling noise, another place was found for it. They rammed it into the ground outside the ox-stables, this being the next place of honour. Custom demanded that it should be set up during the night of the first of May.

For weeks the maypole stood in all its glory in front of the stables. It was brought down on Whit Saturday, when its real decoration began. Now every unmarried girl had to tie a ribbon to it. It was also the duty of every craftsman on the puszta to put something on it. The cooper made a little wooden tub about the size of one's hand, the smith a horse-shoe decorated with brass, the vinedresser a raffia garland, the shepherds each gave a piece of cheese. The farm officials would contribute a bottle of wine or two, if they happened to be in a good mood. Then the tree was set up again. We were burning with excitement. After lunch on Whit Monday the festival began. Those who possessed zithers and mouth-organs formed themselves into a band. They played just one overture, the latest hit-tune, and they had to play it really well. Then came the tree-climbing. Everybody except the children had the right to climb to the top of the tree and bring down whatever he wanted, but only one article, of course. It was a noble trial of strength for the young men, or rather for those who had a pair of top-boots, for these were compulsory. What an entertainment that was! The audience grew noisy. "Try harder, Sanyi!" they shouted, "Get down to it!" Here I quote only those cries of encouragement which can be quoted. Sanyi got half way up and slipped down again. "Poor old chap," they said, and their enthusiasm turned to mockery and then to witty improvisation, for this was also a contest of wit. In the end somebody reached the top of the tree and flopped down again with the bottle of wine—if it really was wine in the bottle, for in one or two of them the yellowish liquid resembled wine only in colour. This was the kind of trick played by the folk in the manor-house to increase the general amusement. Nor was it without effect. The farm servants, fleeing from the victim who tried to spray them with its contents, had a good laugh at the expense of their comrades. When all the objects had been brought down from the tree, the dance began. It lasted until they began to fight each other.

Whitsun queen

. . . The crowning of the Whitsun Queen was another custom which survived only among the children—it was still performed at Rácegres. Four older girls held a sheet over a younger one as they went singing from house to house. At the end of their song, the four girls ran to the middle, snatched up the little girl in the sheet and then they ate whatever they were given.

Whitsun beauty aid

. . . We awaited Whitsuntide not only with the Christian devotion appropriate to the great festivals, but with a bottle of rainwater caught on Trinity Sunday as well; to wash in it is a sure aid to beauty, particularly if one drinks red wine afterwards.

Source: *People of the Puszta* by Gyula Illyes. Translated by G. F. Cushing. New York: Corvina Press, 1967, pp. 154-155.

Iceland

Whitsunday confirmation

All children looked forward to the time of confirmation and so did I. That took place at fourteen years of age. Whit-Sunday was the general day for that in the parish church we belonged to. I had reached that age. We were about twenty who had been prepared for confirmation by Reverend Z. Halldórson. Hólar was the name of the farm, where the parish church was. It was an old cathedral from the days when Hólar in Hjaltadal was a see, which it had been for centuries. Now there was an agricultural school there. The church was built of red granite from a quarry in the mountain, Hólabyrda, at the foot of which the church had been placed, in the midst of a cemetery.

People from far-away districts made their way to Hólakirkja, that day, riding their ponies. That was the day for children to visit the church, to learn from the candidates for confirmation how to behave when their turn came.

Not one stayed at home in Kálfssadir that day. We had to go early, for mother and I brought to Hólar in boxes the dresses we were to wear in the church, and it always took some time to put them on. Mother's dress was of black cloth, the bodice embroidered, with silver thread, and the skirt adorned with appliqué of velvet.

It was called *Skautbúningur*. A little white cap with a golden coronet at the forehead and a white veil going down on the back, was the headgear of us both. But my dress was of white stuff, and after the style of it, it was called *Kyrtill*. That style of gown was mostly used for girls, the other kind of dress for older ladies. A belt belonged to both, mother's embroidered with silver thread with a buckle of filigree, while mine was altogether handmade filigree. How grand, that from that day I should be dressed as the grown-up women! Of course we only wore these dresses occasionally at festivities, but I got another costume for Sundays and travelling purposes.

The candidates had to answer several questions, asked by the minister, and recite from the catechism and the Bible, in order to prove to the parishioners their capacities and abilities. After the sermon was over, our friends congratulated us, and the relatives of ours who had come from a distance were invited to our home for dinner and coffee and so forth.

Source: *When I Was a Girl in Iceland* by Hólmforídur Árnadóttir. Boston: Lothrop, Lee & Shepard Co., 1919, pp. 153-155.

The Netherlands

Luiluk/Lazybones Day

On the Saturday before Whitsunday, teenagers ring doorbells early in the morning, banging on pots and pans and calling, "*Luilak!*" which means "Lazybones!"

Whitsun vacation in Holland

Easter and Whitsuntide—the latter falls on the seventh Sunday after Easter—were celebrated for two days; therefore, we had vacation on Easter Monday and on the Monday after Whitsunday, as also on Good Friday and on Ascension Day. On Whitsunday we dressed up in new clothes, and put on new spring hats, as you do on Easter. On Easter it is too cold in Holland for spring clothes. Even on Whitsunday it may hail or snow and be very disagreeable.

Source: *When I Was a Girl in Holland* by Cornelia de Groot. Boston: Lothrop, Lee & Shepard Co., 1917, p. 70.

Roumania

Rusalii

The Calisari

A week of elaborate rituals are performed beginning on the eve of Pentecost. A performing group known as the Calisari perform in the village. They carry a special wooden staff, wear garlic and wormwood in their belts, and are costumed in a variety of set roles. Their tasks include house-to-house visits and ritual dances and dramatic performances in the village.

Source: *Calus: Symbolic Transformation in Romanian Ritual* by Gail Klingman. Chicago: Univ. of Chicago, 1981.

For more on Whitsuntide see: *German Festivals and Customs* by Jennifer M. Russ. London: Oswald Wolff, 1982, pp. 62-66; ''Whitsun'' in *The Customs and Ceremonies of Britain* by Charles Kightly. London: Thames and Hudson, 1986, pp. 233-234; ''Whitsuntide'' in *A Year of Festivals: A Guide to British Calendar Customs* by Geoffrey Palmer and Noel Lloyd. London: Frederick Warne, 1972, pp. 36-44; and ''Whitsunday and Whitsuntide'' in *Folklore of American Holidays* edited by Hennig Cohen and Tristram Potter Coffin. 2nd ed. Detroit: Gale Research, 1991.

First Sunday after Whitsunday

Trinity

This holiday was instituted in the year 828 by Pope Gregory IX in honor of the Three Persons in One Godhead.

Roumania

Rusalii

Protection against the Rusalii

Trinity Day is a very respected and much-dreaded holiday. It is really not a Christian holiday, being devoted to the *Rusalii,* hostile divinities. In fact the holiday is better known among the peasants by the latter name. The *Rusalii,* according to tradition, are the three daughters of an emperor who are ill-disposed towards all mankind because they did not receive proper attention during their life on earth. Nothing will induce the Roumanian to do any work on Trinity Day. It is an evil day. The *Rusalii* are sure to cause mischief.

From Trinity to St. Peter's Day, which falls on the twenty-ninth of June, the *Rusalii* are said to roam over fields and woods raising winds and storms. If a man is caught unawares in the open he may be lifted by a whirlwind and carried to his destruction. This is the work of the *Rusalii.* They may snatch a child from the very arms of its mother and it is therefore a good precaution for children to keep indoors. On that day we seldom ventured out-of-doors or any distance from home.

Twigs of wormwood are placed under the pillow on the eve of *Rusalii;* otherwise you may find yourself carried off by them, roof and all! Throughout the day it is well to wear a bunch of wormwood in the belt. It helps ward off the *Rusalii.* For several weeks after *Rusalii* the medicinal herbs lose their virtue, and if they have been pinched by the *Rusalii,* they may even do mischief. Therefore we were told not to gather any medicinal herbs from the fields until at least nine weeks have passed after Trinity Day.

Source: *When I Was a Boy in Roumania* by Dr. J. S. Van Teslar. Boston: Lothrop, Lee & Shepard Co., 1917, pp. 60-62.

Russia/U.S.S.R.

Trinity in prerevolutionary Russia as recalled by a former Central Russian villager

Maurice Hindus writes that neither Christmas nor Easter vie with Trinity in its romantic appeal. Villagers clean the entire village for this summertime event. Streets were swept and yards cleaned and decked with fresh cut birch saplings and carpeted with newly mown grass. Leafy twigs were twined around windows, gates, and fences. Ikons and lamps in the house were garlanded with flowers, especially the cornflower, which was in season at that time.

The villagers brought flowers and freshly cut grasses to church and made wreaths as part of the service and then hung these on their home icons. Sometimes a young girl would toss a wreath into the stream. If it floated away, she would wed within the year; if it sunk, she would remain unwed.

Trinity in 1929 in a central Russian village

Here was Trinity, and as I sauntered up and down the village I saw but faint attempts at the customary decorations. Not a yard could boast of the boulevard-like double row of saplings nor of the layers of grass that clothed the village in loveliness. A lone stick of brush, a few handfuls of grass carelessly scattered, a stray twig over a window was all that remained of the ancient ornamentation. Still people did observe it. They did not work and they dressed up in their best clothes. Few of them went to church and fewer still carried flowers. Also Trinity had remained the wedding season that it always was.

Wrath towards holidays such as Trinity

. . . In *The Calendar of Religious Holidays,* the author, F. Covalef, inveighs wrathfully against their nature and purposes. Holidays, he argues, were an occasion and an excuse for drunkenness and gluttony and all their accompanying evils. "On holidays," he writes, "it was drummed into the heads of the people that they must fulfill the commands of Christ, which in reality were the commands of the exploiting classes. . . . On holidays, with the aid of services and ceremonies, the priest and the exploiting classes hovering back of them, sought to prevent the unification of the toiling masses for the struggle against their oppressors. . . . The customs and ceremonials that pertain to the purely nature basis of holidays resulted in colossal damage to the people . . . served to perpetuate backward and unproductive methods of tillage and prevented man from wrenching himself free from poverty. . . . Now these customs and ceremonials hamper the spread of the *kolhoz* movement."

. . . "The day of Elijah," he says in speaking of the work of certain Soviets, "was turned into a day of electrification; Trinity into an arbor day; Pokrov into a harvest day and, in 1929, into a day of electrification. Easter was made the day of the first furrow, and in the future it ought to be the day of collective ploughing and sowing."

Source: *Red Bread* by Maurice Hindus. New York: Jonathan Cape & Harrison Smith, 1931, pp. 186-187.

Moveable: Thursday after Trinity

Corpus Christi

Corpus Christi is celebrated on the Thursday after Trinity Sunday. Trinity falls one week after Whitsunday. Corpus Christi celebrates the Body of Christ as transformed in the Eucharist. It was officially instituted in 1246 and adopted throughout the Christian world in 1264.

France (Basque)

Celebration in a French Basque village

The French Basques celebrate Corpus Christi on the Sunday following the festival and on its octave. It is called Phesta Berria in Basque.

In a small tract of Basse Navarre lying between the Nive and the Joyeuse, *Phesta Berria* has a flavour all its own. The first procession I saw there was at St. Esteban, a village between Hasparren and St Palais. I see them still, the National Guard as they call themselves, coming up the sunken lane edged with sweet-smelling honeysuckle, the band leading, the Voltigeurs in the rear. The rank and file was composed of some twenty young men in white trousers and their Sunday jackets, white berets on their heads stuck all over with gold leaves standing straight upright, all armed with any sort of shot-gun or rifle, even to flintlock muskets. In front came four large Sappers, *Sapurak,* wearing some sort of uniform—the postman kindly lends his and even the gendarmes—with enormous busbies of black sheepskin topped with red feathers, decorated in front with small mirrors. They wore the old-fashioned Sappers' apron but decorated it with golden leaves, and they carried heavy axes on their right shoulders. The white-gloved left hand rested elegantly on the left hip. There was an imitation Beadle with beribboned halberd and cocked hat; there was a Drum Major who danced backwards before the band, hired from Bayonne, who bore patiently with his antic conducting. There were flagbearers with incessantly and beautifully twirling flags and there were the Voltigeurs, two boys who danced without ceasing to the church, into the church and out again to the porch, where their steps became grotesque and they turned into comic characters.

Source: *The Singing of the Travels* by Violet Alford. London: Max Parrish, 1956, pp. 186-187. See ''The New Feast'' in pp. 186-193.

Germany

Fron Leichnam

Fronleichnam processions in Germany

Towns are decorated with greenery and flowers on the route of the procession on this day. The Eucharist is carried from the church under a special canopy and makes the rounds of the village. The procession stops in four places for a blessing of the quarters of the town. Greenery from the altars will protect homes from lightning during the coming year.

Source: *German Festivals and Customs* by Jennifer M. Russ. London: Oswald Wolff, 1982, pp. 66-67.

Mexico

Corpus Christi at Tzintzuntzan

The festival at Tzintzuntzan features a procession with loaded mules, horses, and burros and with oxen dragging their plows. The oxen are adorned with dried corn tied in pairs by the husks, with paper ornaments, and with wheat cakes cut into animal shapes. The small children march with tiny crates on their backs filled with flowers, fans, toys, plants, and other ''merchandise.'' Each group is accompanied by its own band. When they reach the atrium, the yunteros begin to plow a piece of ground set aside for that purpose. A boy and a woman follow the plows and pretend to be planting. This is a joke, as women do not do that kind of work in Tzintzuntzan. Just before the afternoon Rosario, fruit, wheat cakes, and pots are tossed from the church porch to those who can catch them.

Source: *A Treasury of Mexican Folkways* by Frances Toor. New York: Crown, 1947, pp. 231-232.

Los Voladores in 1611 and 1933

Among other methods of diversion that these western Indians had was a kind of flying, taking turns through the air tied with ropes which hung from a tall stout tree; and for the reader's entertainment I shall tell of their doings.

When they were going to fly, they brought from the mountain a tree, very tall and thick, and stripped it and left it smooth. It was very straight, and tall enough to allow thirteen revolutions in the flight. The trick to this invention was a mortar on top, from which hung a square of wood like a frame, attached from its four corners to the mortar by strong ropes. Between the mortar and this square they tied four other ropes, strong enough to sustain those who hung from them, who might be three or four or more. These ropes went through holes in the middle of the braces which made the frame, and so that they should work, they wound them on the pole with much care and evenness, winding the four together as thread is put on the loom for weaving. At their lower ends these ropes finished in loops of about a yard, and were wound up to kiss the frame around the tree.

The Indians who flew were not just anybody, but those who were well trained for the service, which they practiced many days in order to do it with expertness and dash. The four principals were dressed as birds: red-tailed eagles, griffins, and others—all birds that represented magnificence and splendor. They all wore extended wings to simulate the natural flight of birds; and they climbed quickly and lightly to the top, while eight or ten others, all richly and gorgeously dressed with many armlets and feathered crests, increased the noise and embellished the brilliance of their flight. All seated themselves, orderly, and each in turn climbed to the top of the mortar and there balanced himself and danced to the sound of an instrument, each one trying to surpass the others.

After entertaining the by-standers who, gaping, watched what they did, the four who represented the four birds tied themselves around the middle, and letting themselves hang from the ropes, with the weight of their bodies they turned the frame and put themselves in flight; and as they came down, the turns were constantly enlarging in such a way that the second gained on the first, in speed and sweep, and the third on the second, and so they ended at last in the form of a large round bell, gaining also in speed and force, and so they reached the ground with great impetus and violence.

Others, who had stayed on top, when they saw the Voladores in mid-flight, grasped the ropes and came after them, shouting nonsense, so that when the Voladores reached the ground, the others came with them. This brought forth the amusement and delight of all, because if the flyer was not very adroit as he came down, he sometimes landed, instead of on his feet, on his hands or on his head and was rolled around on the ground until the rope lost the force it had.

This contraption, I think, was invented by the Devil to keep his false cult alive and to perpetuate his infernal and abominable service; because it was a recognition of the fifty-two years which they counted in their century, at the end of which they renewed with new fire the pact they had made with the Devil to serve him so many more years in the future.

These I have seen in the little plaza called *El Volador,* in a feast of excessive grandeur in the time of the Viceroy Don Martín Enriquez in a fiesta which the Mexicans made of the Conquest of Mexico. At the end of the day an Indian climbed to the mortar; and when it seemed to him time to come after those who flew, he hurled himself out to seize one of the ropes of the Voladores, and because he was holding a drum and a rattle, or because his head weighed much from taking wine, he did not catch it; and although he wore wings, they were like those of Icarus, fastened with wax and worthless, and he reached the ground ahead of his flying companions and made of himself a thousand pieces.

Many others were killed because they were heavy with wine when they went up; and on this account I was one in this said City of Mexico, with the honorable viceroys, to prohibit it. But since, as a wise one has said, "there are as many judgments and counsels in this world as there are heads," they have revived the game this last year, 1611, which is the second since an Indian fell from the top and died of the fall.

This is my own adaptation, done with liberty if not with absolute license; but anyone who questions it is free to consult Friar Juan de Torquemada's *Historia Indiana,* Book X, chapter xxxviii, and make a better one.

Almost as Torquemada describes it, the game of Los Voladores may be seen today: one of the few pre-Cortesian ceremonies which persist practically untouched by modern life. It is found only in La Sierra de Puebla, between the states of Vera Cruz and Puebla—a region so remote that the language is Olmeca or Totonaca instead of Spanish, that customs and costumes have changed very little since the Conquest, and where it is persistently whispered that the people worship idols instead of saints. Papantla, center of the vanilla region and notable for the beauty of its people and the richness of their dress, is supposed to have Los Voladores on Corpus Christi Day, in June, but did not in 1933. It was said, however, that there would certainly be flyers in Coxquihui during the fiesta of San Mateo, in the last week of September. In many Totonaca villages they celebrate autumn saints' days, carrying on, they say, the pre-Cortesian harvest ceremonies.

Source: *Fiestas in Mexico* by Erna Fergusson. New York: Alfred A. Knopf, 1934, pp. 157-160. (See "Los Voladores" in *Fiestas in Mexico,* pp. 157-177, for the 1933 festival of San Mateo in Coxquihui, Mexico.)

"Corpus Day" in Mexico City

"Corpus Day" is another festivity in which we young people used to take much interest. The religious ceremonies on that day are elaborate; the parks and drives, as on other holidays, are full of people, promenading and enjoying themselves, while everywhere toy-sellers are seen, and more than ever fruit-venders are plying their trade. On that day little "huacales" are sold. These are little boxes or crates made out of pieces of sticks, leaves, and greens, filled with fruits of the season. These "huacales" are sometimes quite expensive, when they contain choice fruits, but usually the majority are cheap and a child can with a few cents buy his "huacal."

Source: *When I Was a Girl in Mexico* by Mercedes Godoy. Boston: Lothrop, Lee & Shepard Co., 1919, pp. 50-51.

For more information on Corpus Christi see: "The Feast of

Corpus Christi'' in *Folklore of American Holidays* edited by Hennig Cohen and Tristram Potter Coffin. 2nd ed. Detroit: Gale Research, 1991.

Seventh Thursday after Easter

Semik

The festival name "Semik" comes from "*Semy,*" meaning "the seventh." Held on the seventh Thursday after Easter, the holiday may have had pagan origins. Young girls went into the forests to gather boughs and frolic, joined later, of course, by young men.

Russia (Prerevolutionary)

Wreath-making and fortune-telling among girls in prerevolutionary Russia

. . . The principal feast of this kind falls on the seventh Thursday after Easter and takes its name *Semik* from Semy, meaning the seventh. This is the feast of the village girls. They go to the woods, pick branches of birch, decorate them with wreaths and ribbons and drag them singing through the villages. In some districts they bend the branches to make frames, and through these frames they kiss each other and promise to be friends. This is the feast at which one can read the future! The young girls carry wreaths they have made and throw them into the brook. If the wreath swim quietly on the water, it means that the girl will be married in a year, but if it sink, she will surely not wear the "cap" that year, or if she does, she will soon be a widow. With beating hearts they go to throw their wreaths into the water, and with anxiety they watch them until they have disappeared. In some districts, if the wreath sinks it means that the girl will die in the year. In another district the wreath is not thrown into the water, but hung upon a tree, and the girl often comes to see if her wreath be still hanging. If it is not there, it is a very bad sign; the girl will not marry in the year, or, sometimes, will die. In old times the *Semik* was the feast of a wood-god. It is celebrated at the coming of the first leaves and it is celebrated by those who are most in the wood during the year, namely the girls. While men and women work in the fields the girls pass whole days in the woods, picking berries and mushrooms or making wreaths. The forest and its ruler, the wood-spirit, have quite a meaning for the villager, and the wreaths which they hang on the trees are offerings which at one time their heathen sisters brought to the wood-god. The *Semik* is celebrated throughout Russia even in the extreme north.

Semik dramas

The songs of the *semik,* which are sung about the seventh week after Easter, are almost plays, and may be considered the starting-point of Russian dramatic art. Young girls and youths go into the forest and open the performance by forming a ring round a birch tree, which they decorate with ribbons. Then they dance round it, singing:

> "The birch is not washed with rain, young girls are coming towards it; jump, dance, beautiful maidens, and you, young men, admire us. You shall not carry off the young girls from the feast; you shall not have them, without their full pleasure, without their father's leave, and their mother's blessing; and when the fiancés have finished their labours."

Another ring is then formed, and a girl and boy turn round in the middle, singing with the chorus:

> "Ah! there was a little lime tree growing in a field; under the lime a tent; within the tent a table; at the table a young girl. She was embroidering with gold a *cherinka* (waist-belt). She was decorating with pearls the bridle of a horse."

A young man passed.

Male voices:

> "Is not that *cherinka* for me? That bridle for my horse?"

Women's voices:

> "The *cherinka* is not for that young man; the bridle is not for his horse."

Suddenly all begin to dance, singing:

> "The Tsar is walking through the town, the Tsar seeks his Tsarevna.
> Where is my Tsarevna, where is the young princess?
> There is the Tsarevna, she is waving a silk handkerchief, she is lighting her way with her gold ring. Doors open wide."

At these words the ring opens, a young man and a girl holding on high a handkerchief which represents a door, under which the Tsarevna passes. The song begins again:

> "Close up your ranks, draw near to each other, embrace tenderly, even more tenderly."

Between the verses, singers of both sexes sit round tables and share nuts, sweetmeats, and beer. Before beginning their songs again, they uproot birch saplings, cut off the branches which they twine into crowns, and then return to the village, where the young trees are planted. A new ring is formed, while the young men holding hands pass under the uplifted arms, and the girls singing:

> "A youth was walking on the green grass round a large town."

At these words a young man, or more often a girl wearing a man's hat, darts from the ring and walks haughtily round the *khorovod*.

> "O Tour (a pagan goddess), the youth, the champion of the town, invites a young girl to come and pit herself against him."

At this invitation, another young girl leaves the ranks, and stands in the middle of the *khorovod*.

> "O Did Lado" (another pagan goddess).

The young girl comes forward.

> "She has vanquished the valiant youth, she has thrown him on the grass."

At these words the girl knocks off the man's (or the girl's) hat, and pulls his or her hair.

The chorus sings:

> "The youth arising hides his face in his hands; he wipes away his bitter tears. He dares not tell his friends of his misfortune. O Tour, Did Lado."

In many places these crowns are kept until Pentecost; in others, they are thrown into the river to see if they sink or swim, as a sign whether the thrower will have a long or short life. If any get ahead of the others, it is a sign of success; these are games for brothers and sisters.

Lovers also have their turn; they throw their crowns into the air, and if they meet it is a good sign. The ribbons with which the wreaths are tied, are preserved through life, and serve to decorate the marriage candles.

Source: *Home Life in Russia* by A. S. Rappoport. New York: Macmillan, 1913, pp. 40-43.

First Thursday after Corpus Christi
Lajkonik

Lajkonik is originally a festival sponsored by the ''*wloczkow,*'' the guild furnishing wood for Krakow and the adjacent salt mines. The festival has lost much of the meaning of its medieval roots, but still bears traces of themes stemming from the Tartar invasions of the thirteenth century.

Poland (Krakow)

The celebration in Krakow

. . . The name of this most popular of all Krakow fetes comes from the central character and actor of the pageant. He is a bearded rider in pseudo-oriental dress, mounted on a richly draped and disproportionately small wooden horse without legs, standing on the legs of the rider, which are visible from underneath the horse's cape. Originally known as the ''Horse'' or the ''Zwierzyniec Horse,'' towards the end of the 19th century, it is more and more often referred to as ''Lajkonik.'' Finally, the two former names fall into oblivion.

Lajkonik has become an unofficial symbol of Krakow. It appears in brand names of shops, cafes, coffee-bars, milk bars and even institutions. It is also used as a decorative motif in the headpieces of Krakow newspapers, commercials, postcards, etc. Its image is reflected in countless toys and souvenirs.

Before we turn to the discussion of the history of the custom, let us sketch the present shape of the ceremony. Traditionally, the pageant should take place on the first Thursday after Corpus Christi, that is the so-called Corpus Christi octave. Within the past few years the ceremony was twice shifted to some other days, which cause wide-spread protest of the people of Krakow, who are strongly attached to the tradition. This attachment is best to be seen on the day of the Lajkonik pageant, when annually throngs of thousands gather from the early hours of the noon along the Lajkonik route. People crowd in open windows and on balconies; those standing in the streets try to take the best positions; boys climb the trees, lamp-posts, car roofs, etc. All that creates the atmosphere of a true folk festival so rare in Krakow. At about 2 p.m. the actors of the show gather in the vicinity of the Norbertine Monastery, beautifully situated on the bank of the Vistula in the suburb of Zwierzyniec. In the past those actors were provided from among the members of the Boatman Congregation, so important for the economic life of the city. (Since the Middle Ages they had floated timber down the Vistula and supplied Krakow with it.) Today they came from among the workers of various Krakow factories who are interested in the Lajkonik tradition.

Around 2:30 p.m. a group of eighteen people, constituting the entourage of the standard-bearer, enters the courtyard of the Monastery. The standard-bearer carries a folded banner and is dressed in the traditional long gown of the Polish nobleman, while a few members of his entourage wear the folk costumes of the Krakow region. They carry white-and-blue flags, symbolizing the City of Krakow. The remaining members of the entourage are dressed in pseudo-oriental clothes and hold horse-tail ensigns and red-and-yellow flags. The group is accompanied by a band called ''mlaskoty'' dressed in the traditional long gowns and overcoats of the Polish nobility. The band consists of the drum, the trumpet, the fiddle, the flute, the clarinet and the double-bass. The entourage makes a big circle, with the standard-bearer in the middle of it. The band begins to play and Lajkonik rushes into the courtyard. He dances around the standard-bearer who unfolds the banner and lowers it parallel to the ground, turning around slowly three times. Lajkonik follows the banner. Then, they both make a bow in the direction of the Monastery, from the windows of which the nuns watch the ceremony, as well as in the direction of the vicarage where the vicar appears. The band quickens the tempo of the tune, and Lajkonik, basket in hand, collects money from the crowd, striking every contributor lightly with his baton. According to the tradition, this is supposed to ''bring good luck.'' Next, he enters the locutory where the nuns treat him to wine and offer him some money. He then goes to the vicarage where he receives a treat from the vicar. After Lajkonik's return to the courtyard, the standard-bearer makes with the banner a bow of thanks to the nuns and the vicar. A procession is formed to the sound of a lively tune. It leaves the courtyard and moves along Zwierzyniecka street in the direction of the City. It is accompanied by the crowds, excepting the children, who have stayed in the courtyard awaiting the customary shower of candies to fall from the windows of the vicarage. In the meantime, Lajkonik prances among the crowds, dealing out blows. The people disperse amid shouts and laughter. The procession moves along very slowly. Around 4 p.m. it reaches the restaurant called ''Lajkonik,'' half way up Zwierzyniecka street, where Lajkonik makes his first stop and takes a rest. After a few drinks, half an hour later, he moves further and, surrounded by denser and denser crowds, reaches the end of Zwierzyniecka street. Here, Lajkonik prances again by the building of the Philharmonic. Next, along Franciszkanska and Grodzka streets, he passes into the Market Square, where he makes his next stop at the student club ''Pod Jaszczurami.'' At 6 p.m. the whole procession appears in the Market Square. Here, the most important part of the ceremony takes place. The fathers of the City await Lajkonik on the steps of the Town Hall. He performs a dance with the banner for them, for which he is rewarded with a leather purse full of money, and a glass of wine, which he drinks to the prosperity of Krakow and the health of its inhabitants.

Lajkonik capers around the Market Square until late at night. Then the procession moves to the old Krakow restaurant nearby, called ''Hawelka,'' for an abundant supper. Amused crowds slowly leave the Market Square and the merry-making is over.

Source: ''Lajkonik: The Origin and Transformations of Krakow Folk Customs'' by Jan Bujak and Bogdana Pilichowska in *Urban Anthropology*, 12 (3-4) (1983), 288-289.

May 11-14

Eisheiligan / Ice Saints

This is a period when the weather is usually cooler than normal. The Eisheiligan, or Ice Saints, honored on these days are St. Pancras, who died May 12, 304 A.D.; St. Servatus, who died May 13, 384 A.D.; and St. Boniface, who died May 14, 307 A.D..

Germany

The days from May 11 to 14 are known as Eisheiligen (The Ice Saints) because they bring cooler weather than normal. Gardeners wait until after this season to plant seedlings. Green wood is burnt all night in the Austrian Alps to protect new growth from frost with the smoke.

Source: *German Festivals and Customs* by Jennifer M. Russe. London: Oswald Wolff, 1982, p. 59.

For more information see: "St. Sofia's Day," May 15; *Folklore of American Holidays* by Hennig Cohen and Tristram Potter Coffin. 2nd ed. Detroit: Gale Research, 1991, p. 210. (This source cites the Icemänner as Bonfatz, Pancratz, and Ignatz.)

May 14

Krossmessa (Crossmas)

This is moving day for servants.

Iceland

Domestics' moving day

The fourteenth of May was the date fixed for the domestics' moving-day. My parents were so fortunate that their people did not move frequently. Most of them stayed from four to ten years. They were not hired for less than one year at a time, and it was considered a great shame, if anybody moved before the next *Krossmessa* (Crossmas) which was the name of May 14th.

Source: *When I Was a Girl in Iceland* by Hólmfrídur Árnadóttir. Boston: Lothrop, Lee & Shepard Co., 1919, p. 152.

May 15

St. Sofia's Day (St. Zofie)

This is a day to commemorate St. Sofia (Zofie). May 12, 13, and 14 are known as the days of the ''three frost saints'' because farmers planting before this time run the risk of a late frost.

Czechoslovakia

Waiting for the ''three frost saints'' before planting

Gardeners watch their favorite signals to determine when to plant. A Czech legend warns not to plant before May 12, 13, and 14 because of the ''three frozen kings'' or ''three frost saints.''

Pangrac (also Pangras) died May 12, 304 A.D. Servac (also Servais or Servitus) died on a May 13 and Bonifac (or Tarsus) died on a May 14.

Then, on May 15, Sophia (Zofie) brought about a thaw with a kettle of boiling water. Sophia was undoubtedly brought into the legend because her feast day is May 15 and because she was known for her excellent cooking and baking. So, on May 15 or later it's safe to plant.

Source: *Czechoslovak Culture* by Pat Martin. Iowa City, Iowa: Penfield Press, 1989, p. 121.

May 15

St. Isidore's Day / San Isidro

A worker on the estate of Juan de Vergas, Isidore spent much time in prayer though his farmwork was always accomplished. He gave of his meager provisions to the poor. Once when he shared half of his sack of corn with the hungry winter birds, he found the sack magically replenished. He was born in 1070 to a poor family in Madrid. He is considered the patron saint of farmers.

Philippines

Carabaos honored on San Isidro's day

The feastday of San Isidro is also occasion for doing honor to the lowly carabao. In the towns of San Isidro, Nueva Ecija; Pulilan, Bulacan; and Angono, Rizal, this day is occasion for much celebration.

On May 15th, each farmer brings his carabao to town. Newly-bathed and well-scrubed, its toes manicured, its tail combed and plaited and be-ribboned, the otherwise ugly beast is decked with bunting and flowers. The carabaos are assembled at the churchyard and the priest comes out to bless them, sprinkle them with holy water, and say a prayer over them. Then the parade around town begins, with hundreds and thousands of carabaos in colorful regalia in the parade. Then the assembly gathers at the town's square or the community playground, where the carabaos participate in races, or they are made to perform special tricks that they have learned.

Source: *The Galleon Guide to Philippine Festivals* by Alfonso J. Aluit. Manila: Galleon, 1969, pp. 62-63.

Carabao festival

This old custom is still observed in towns and villages in the Philippines. In honor of Saint Isidore, patron of farmers, *carabao* ("water buffalo") are scrubbed and decorated with flowers and driven into town.

In the plaza they stop in front of the parish church. Trained by their owners, the *carabao* kneel and bow their heads. A priest then anoints them with holy water.

After the ceremony, the *carabao* are taken to a nearby field where their owners arrange racing events.

The whole town turns out.

On this same day, in Quezon Province, there is a harvest celebration to invoke the blessings of Saint Isidore.

Vegetables, fruits and sheaves of rice are piled by doorways in bright display. Ornaments called *kiping* are made from rice meal, pounded into thin sheets, dyed in different colors, and cut into the shapes of leaves and flowers to decorate the front of houses.

There are processions of townspeople and priests, and, when all is over, the *kiping* are taken down and eaten as a special treat of the day.

Source: *Asia and the Pacific* by Gene Sawyer. Honolulu: Friends of the East-West Center, 1978, p. 44.

Saipan

Honoring the patron saint of Saipan

. . . There is a particular fiesta of great importance, especially to the Carolinians of Saipan, that is celebrated each year. This is the feast in honor of San Isidro, the Patron Saint of Saipan, which takes place in May.

Before the fiesta, groups of Carolinians will practice traditional dances to perform for the occasion. Men will also get together to fish and hunt in order to provide food for the fiesta. The fiesta will be held at the community hall and sometimes the youth organization will have the responsibility of cleaning the area and preparing the hall. Nearly everyone contributes in goods, talent, money, or labor to a fiesta.

A novena is a period of prayers and services in the Catholic religion lasting for nine days. Following the novena, the fiesta in honor of the saint is held. At this time, traditional skills in games and dances will be shown. Events are held for children as well as for adults and prizes are awarded to the winners. In the past, these prizes consisted of such things as pigs, chickens, and goats. Today, however, prizes are usually material items. Food is the most important part of any fiesta, and a great variety of local and imported food is served.

Source: *Some Things of Value: Micronesian Customs as Seen by Micronesians* by the students of The Community College of Micronesia. Compiled and edited by Gene Ashby. Eugene, Oregon: Rainy Day Press, 1983, pp. 122-123.

Spain

San Isidro's cult in Spain

San Isidro is the patron saint of farmers and of Madrid. He was canonized in 1622. When the Empress Isabela, wife of Carlos I, cured the little Infante Felipe of a fever with water from San Isidro's fountain, the Empress ordered a shrine built to his honor. On his day processions pass through the streets, especially in Madrid. A special mass for San Isidro may be paid for by local farm workers, as he is their patron.

Source: *Culture and Conquest* by George M. Foster. Chicago: Quadrangle Books, 1960, p. 193.

May 17

Mūt l-ard

Mūt l-ard is considered the first day of summer in Morocco. Mūt l-ard literally means "death of the ground." This is a day of many taboos and inauspicious signs.

Morocco

Moroccan first-day-of-summer rites c. 1920

The 17th of May, which is regarded as the first day of summer, is called *mūt l-ard,* "the death of the ground" During that day the people must not sleep (Garbîya, etc.); should anybody do so he would be tired the next day (Ait Waráin) or afterwards as well (Bni 'Aros), or "his heart would die", that is, he would lose all his courage (Hiáina, Andjra). In Andjra it is also believed that a husband's affection for his wife may easily pass away on that day; hence she tries to make herself attractive by means of cosmetics. It is perhaps for fear of evil influences from *mūt l-ard* that among the Tsūl everybody gets up at daybreak and has a bath, the women in their houses and the men and boys at springs in the gardens. Such a bath is said to strengthen their bodies since the water this morning comes from the well Zemzem and consequently has *baraka* in it; but the original object of the practice may nevertheless have been to neutralise the dangers of the day by a ceremonial washing.

On the other hand, the magic force in the death of the earth is also utilised in various ways. The Arabs of the Hiáina on the day in question take some barley to the field, put it into the *késkas,* or steamer used for the making of *ta'âm* (*seksu*), leave it there for a while over the fire, then dry it in the sun, roast it in an earthenware pan, grind and sift it, and at last mix it with fresh milk or buttermilk together with the root of a plant called *bûzeffūr*. This is eaten to destroy the *bas.* It makes the people strong as there is much *baraka* in it—but only on the condition that the rainbow is seen on that day; otherwise the *baraka* in it is slight, and if it thunders then there is none.

Mūt l-ard, however, not only indicates the death of the ground, but is also the commencement of a new season—that of harvesting, threshing, and grinding. The women of the Ait Sádden on that day fill their handmills with wheat and cover them up; and among the At Ubáhti the men then buy new clothes for themselves and their women.

Source: *Ritual and Belief in Morocco* by Edward Westermarck. New Hyde Park, New York: University Books, 1968, pp. 180-181.

May 24

The Queen's Birthday (Victoria Day)

This day commemorates the birth of Victoria, Queen of the United Kingdom of Great Britain and Ireland from 1837 until 1901 and Empress of India from 1876.

Canada

Victoria Day customs

Celebrated on the Monday before May 24, the birthday of Queen Victoria, May 24, is still a holiday in Canada. Queen Elizabeth II is honored now on this day, though her actual birthday is April 21. In Quebec a holiday called Fête de Dollard des Ormeaux is held on May 24.

Canadian celebrations include sporting events, parades, and at Victoria, British Columbia, maypole dancing and a May Queen. In Southern Canada Victoria Day is the day to plant the garden as the danger of frost is past.

Source: *Let's Celebrate!* by Caroline Parry. Toronto: Kids Can Press, 1987, pp. 140-141.

New Zealand

Chants during Victoria's time

Until the death of Victoria, the Queen's Birthday was always a holiday. Subsequently, royal holidays appear to have been somewhat more commonplace. In Queen Victoria's day any holiday was a community holiday and a reason for joint celebration. Later a holiday was everyone's private concern and there was no peculiarly group lore arising out of it. But in Victoria's time—

Hip hip hooray!
For the Queen's Birthday
If you don't give us a holiday
We'll all run away.
(Dunedin 1870; 1890)

Hip hip hooray,
For the Queen's Birthday
On the twenty-fourth of May.
(Charleston, 1890)

Children's amusements c. 1880

Some Saturdays or a holiday, such as the Queen's Birthday, we would have a Paper Chase or Hares and Hounds in the bush. Generally the two hares would end up in a tree in the middle of the bush somewhere. Once in the bush there was plenty to eat, lawyer berry, fuchsia, blackberry, honey from the flax. There was a lot of honey in a big flax stick. We would suck the juice out of the toot (tutu) leaves through a cloth in order to get only the juice. The berries were poisonous.

Source: *A History of Children's Play: New Zealand 1840-1950* by Brian Sutton-Smith. Philadelphia: Univ. of Pennsylvania Press, 1981, pp. 141, 203.

May 24-25

Pilgrimage of Sainte Sara

This event is an annual pilgrimage held at Saintes-Marie-de-la-Mer, France. People of the Rom, Gypsies, arrive at this town, traveling from throughout Europe to join the Gypsies of Provence in the pilgrimage of Sainte Sara. The cult of the Two Marys, Marie Jacobé and Marie Salomé, is strong in this town. The Marys are believed to have landed here, arriving by boat after fleeing a persecution of the Jews. These are the two Marys who kept watch at the foot of the cross as Jesus died. Their black servant, Sara l'Égyptienne, arrived with them. Theories differ not only as to Sainte Sara's exact identity but also as to her antiquity and origins.

France

Feast for Gypsies

There are two Saras revered at this site. The first was servant of the three Marys, Mary Salomé, Mary Jacobé, and Mary Magdalene, who were supposed to have landed at the village of Saintes-Maries-de-la-Mer. This Sara was not canonized and remains in the crypt. This is a Catholic tradition. The Sara of the Gypsies was probably a Gitane who lived on the banks of the Rhone at the time and greeted the three Marys when they landed. Tradition says that she saw the Three Marys arriving and threw her dress on the waves, using it as a raft, to float toward them and guide them to land. At that time the Rom took the statue of Ishtari (Astarte) into the sea each year to receive a blessing.

The Gypsies come to this site every year and spend the night in the crypt with the statue. The women hang up bits of clothing, handkerchiefs, slips, and so on by the statue and touch the hems of her many dresses.

During the day, the statue is carried to the sea in procession and is symbolically dipped in the waters.

Source: *The Gypsies* by Jean-Paul Clebert. New York: E. P. Dutton, 1963, pp. 141-143.

The tradition of Les-Saintes-Marie-de-la-Mer, Bouches-du-Rhône

Tradition affirms that, shortly after the death of Christ, a boat came from Palestine, with neither sail nor oars, washing up on the Provence shore. It carried the "Two Maries" . . . those whom the evangelist Saint Mark showed at the foot of the Cross . . . Marie Jacobé and Marie Salomé, and their black servant, Sara. On board also were Madeleine, Martha, Lazare, Trophime, Maximin, and Sidoine, fleeing the persecutions of the Jews. They separated there to carry the Good Word throughout the country. Only the Two Maries and Sara were set onto the bench, where they finished their days, after having founded a Christian village to which they left their name.

Source: *Fêtes en france*. Textes de Michèle Boudignon-Hamon et Jacqueline Demoinent. Photographies de Jacques Verroust. Editiones du Chêne, 1977, p. 117. Translation by Margaret MacDonald.

The service for Sainte Sara c. 1951

At last the window opened and the battered reliquary appeared sustained by two cables, and as it began slowly to descend men in the window attached bouquets to the cables, transforming them into chains of flowers. Every now and then the roar of the multitude was punctuated by raucous cries from the Gypsies below, shouting out "Vive Sainte Sara!" in answer to "Vivent les Saintes Maries". A tremendous tussle followed, when the relics descended within touching distance, for every pilgrim in the milling crowd near the altar tried to stretch out his hands to touch them: children were lifted on high, sick people were pushed forward, even the wax candles in the heat seemed to bend over the relics. The music never stopped, for the congregation further away from the relics kept up their singing in support of the choir.

At last, when the relics rested on the trestles in front of the altar, peace and calm were restored. The pilgrims began to leave the church for the fair, which was now in full swing. In the distance I could hear the street music of the merry-go-rounds and the blaring loudspeakers. Many, however, lingered in the church to pray by the casket of relics and touch it to their heart's content. I followed the Gypsies in their procession round the village with Saint Sara. At their head went Titi, the so-called King of the Gypsies of the Camargue, whom I hardly recognized, for he was dressed in a long white surplice which looked like a nightshirt, and he marched at the head of the Romanichals, singing the hymns of the Saintes Maries. Beside him walked a swashbuckling old Gypsy with bushy moustaches—an uncle of Titi, from Saint Gilles.

The Gypsies carried the statue of Saint Sara through the village and along the shore and out into the sea. They were followed by the *gardians* and horsemen of Camargue on their white steeds, dressed in black velvet coats and check tight-fitting trousers. When the procession returned to the crypt, Titi in the presence of the *Curé-doyen* made a speech to the assembled Gypsies in which he appealed for unity among the Romanichals of the world, in spite of their varied nationalities and religious sects. "A year ago," said he, "four thousand Gitans came here as pilgrims, a greater number than any year since 1914; this year seven thousand have come and it seems as if the Gitans of the world are at last aware that here in this village of Les Saintes Maries and Saint Sara they will always find as cordial a welcome as in their own countries. We want you foreign *manouches* to realize how much we Gitans of south France desire your presence here; we feel that it is only by the continual co-operation of the foreign Tziganes with our Romanichals that the Gypsy cause in the world can flourish."

Source: *In Sara's Tents* by Walter Starkie. New York: Dutton, 1953, pp. 260-263. (See the entire chapter, "The Pilgrimage of Saint Sara," pp. 248-312.)

May 25

St. Urban's Day

A day to honor St. Urban, Urban I, a Roman, who succeeded Callistus to the papal chair. He was Pope from 222 to 230.

Germany

The patron of wine growers is feted

Saint Urban is the patron saint of wine growers. Some areas, such as South Tyrol, have a Saint Urban's Day procession. It is believed that if the sun shines on Saint Urban's Day the vines will grow well, but if it rains the vines will do poorly. In Franconia he is sprinkled with wine if he brings good weather but splashed with dirty water if he brings poor.

Source: *German Festivals and Customs* by Jennifer M. Russ. London: Oswald Wolff, 1982, pp. 61-62.

May 29

Oak-Apple Day (Royal Oak Day)

This is a celebration of Charles II's birthday, and the day he reentered Whitehall at his Restoration in 1660. For generations it has been an official holiday, and certain aspects of the day remained extant in children's games until the 1940s in some areas. In Fawnhope, Herefordshire, the Heart of Oak Friendly Society still parades on this day, carrying staves decorated with wooden oak-apples.

Great Britain

A nineteenth-century Oak Apple Day

The 29th was our real May Day in Bromyard; you'd see Maypoles all the way down Sheep Street, decorated with oak boughs and flowers, and people dancing round them, all wearing oak leaves.

Children gathered oak twigs, especially those with oak-apples on them and sold them, chanting a jeer at anyone who refused to buy:

> Shig-shag, penny-a-rag
> Bang his head with Cromwell's bag.
> All up in a bundle!

Source: *The Folklore of the Welsh Border* by Jacqueline Simpson. Totowa, N.J.: Rowman and Littlefield, 1976, p. 153.

Nettling those who don't wear oak-apples

On this day children in several parts of England must wear an oak-apple or risk being stung with nettles by their classmates. The custom has remained longest in the north in Cumberland, Westmorland, Furness, and North Riding, and in the north Midlands from Shrewsbury to the Wash. The custom is a historical remnant based on an episode in which King Charles II hid in an oak tree to escape pursuing soldiers.

Source: *Lore and Language of Schoolchildren* by Peter and Iona Opie. Oxford: Oxford Univ. Press, 1959, pp. 263-264.

May 31 (Culminating Date)

Flores de Mayo

The month of May is the occasion for Flores de Mayo festivals throughout the Philippines. The Christian festivals feature novenas, processions honoring local patron saints, parties, dances, and, in Manila, a May Queen.

Philippines

May 31: Culmination of a month-long floral festival

The last day of May is the climax of the month-long flower festival, *Flores de Mayo*. Principally a Christian festival, towns and villages from northern Luzon to southern Mindanao celebrate the birthday of their patron saints.

During the month, children make floral offerings and take them in the afternoons to the churches. Novenas are said, and processions are formed and wind through the streets. The prettiest girls are chosen to take part. They wear national dress and carry floral offerings that symbolize the virtues of Christian womanhood.

Page boys walk with the procession and little flower girls scatter rose petals along the way. Relatives and friends follow, singing Hail Marys. The processions are lovely to see, and when darkness falls they become even more beautiful by candlelight.

On the last night of May, the final night of the festival, there are fiestas with music, dancing and fabulous food. At homes there is a special treat for the children. A square bamboo frame arranged on a pulley hangs in the air; dangling from it on strings, like a mobile, are packets of candy, fruit, favors, toys. The children jump to reach them but, controlled by the pulley, the gifts are elusive and there is a great hubbub and excitement.

In metropolitan cities like Manila, *Flores de Mayo* is celebrated on May 31 as one of the biggest festivals of the year, with May Queens and fancy balls.

Source: *Celebrations: Asia and the Pacific* by Gene Sawyer. Honolulu: Friends of the East-West Center, 1978, p. 47.

May 31

Memorial Day (Day of the Dead)

This is a day of remembrance for the dead in Roumania.

Roumania

Gifts for the dead

The last day of May, on the eve of the Trinity, is "Memorial Day," or "Day of the Dead." On that day alms are given away for the repose of the souls of the dead. Besides small coins, earthen vessels, pitchers, wooden pails, all sorts of dishes adorned with flowers and herbs and filled with eatables and wine are given away right and left or sent to friends and acquaintances. Many give presents also for the repose of their own souls. "Whoever gives, gives to himself" and "whatever one gives away in this world one gets back tenfold in the next" are the rules of the day. These presents or gifts, *dari,* as they are called, are accepted with good grace even by the wealthier persons to whom they are offered, as it is never considered embarrassing or humiliating to receive a gift for the repose of one's soul. On the contrary it is a kindness to accept and eat and drink from the vessels and to use those vessels as long as they last, for the sake of the giver's soul or of that of any person mentioned with the gift. Moreover the peasant will feel hurt if you offer or even suggest pay for any kindness or hospitality. He, in turn, will accept an offering and make careful use of it with the feeling that he has done you a kindness in accepting if it was for the benefit of your soul. To give, a *darui,* is a duty in this world. Man distributes alms while still in this life for the repose of his soul in the next world. Whatever the peasant gives or receives for nothing he considers alms. But the giving is never a charity act for the sake of others, nor is the receiving of gifts considered in the light of anything less than a pleasant duty. Children have their hands full on the last day of May and they are busy counting up the gifts they have received.

Source: *When I Was a Boy in Roumania* by Dr. J. S. Van Teslaar. Boston: Lothrop, Lee & Shepard, 1917, p. 58-59.

Full Moon (May)

Wesak Day

Wesak Day is a commemoration of the anniversary of the birth, enlightenment, and entry to Nirvana (death) of the Buddha.

Burma

Kason Festival

Watering the Bodhi trees

The main attraction of the Kason Festival is the sacred Bodhi tree, a holy Buddhist relic. Prince Siddhartha attained his enlightenment (Buddhahood) under a Bo tree on the full-moon day of Kason more than twenty-five hundred years ago. The primary activity of the month is the Kason Water-Pouring Ceremony, an occasion for gaiety as well as solemnity. Throughout the country, people visit local pagodas and monasteries with banyan trees growing on their grounds.

For the ceremony, young women carry pots of scented water on their heads in procession to the banyan trees. There devotees chant prayers for the happiness and peace of mankind and pour the made-blessed water on the roots of the sacred Bo trees. The chant begins: "The Lord, the joy of the Royal Sakya tribe—on its noble Throne of Victory at the foot of the Great Bodhi tree, quelled the five Enemies of Mara"; the chant continues in adoration of the tree as a source of delight and inspiration.

Source: *Southeast Asia: A Cultural Study through Celebration* by Phil Scanlon, Jr. De Kalb, Ill.: Northern Illinois Univ., 1985, p. 116.

Laos

Vixakha Bouxa

Rockets and festivities

The festival of Vixakha Bouxa or Boun Bang-Fay occurs in the sixth month (at the full moon of May) and is popularly called the Festival of the Rockets. It commemorates the birth, enlightenment, and death of Buddha. Bonzes are shown more than usual deference at this time. There are dances, processions, puppet shows, and celebrations. Children, young people, and expectant mothers are blessed; there are offerings to the bonzes. The ideas of pilgrimage and merit making play major roles in the processions, decorations, and puppet shows.

Grafted onto this Buddhist festival are important Lao rites. The festival gets its name from one of these, a contest between *wat* communities as to which can build and launch the rocket that makes the longest flight. Monks are generally the best rocket makers. Also connected with this festival are erotic songs, dances, and rites celebrating life and fertility. The government has reported that such rites were on the wane in the 1960s.

Source: *Laos: A Country Study* by Donald P. Whitaker et al. Foreign Area Studies. Washington, D.C.: The American University, 1971, p. 123.

Boun Bang Fay

One part of the celebration is called *Boun Bang Fay,* the Rocket Festival. It invokes Buddha to send rain so that there will be good harvests and food for all.

Traditionally, monks made the rockets, and there was one for every pagoda. They used bamboo stalks, which are straight and hollow, and stuffed them with gunpowder. Then they sealed them and added bright paper streamers. On the morning of the fete, the monks walked in procession from their pagodas to Vientiane, wheeling their rockets in carts decorated with flowers.

In recent years there have been more participants and many more rockets. Competition is keen between civic and military groups and neighborhood teams. The launching pad is set up on a beach or, in Vientiane, on the banks of the Mekong River. People gather in long lines, waiting with their rockets. At dusk, one by one, the rockets are lighted and go off with a fiery blast. Shouts and cheers heighten the excitement of betting that goes on for rockets belonging to favorite teams and friends.

Officials watch from a grandstand above the river and give prizes for the most brilliant, fastest, and highest rockets. A prize, usually a silver bowl, also goes to the best procession from a pagoda.

And sometimes it really happens that rain begins to fall!

Source: *Celebrations: Asia and the Pacific* by Gene Sawyer. Honolulu: Friends of the East-West Center, 1978, p. 36.

Sri Lanka

Wesak meditation and carnival

Anuradhapura, ancient capital of Ceylon, is one of the sacred places of Buddhism where *Wesak* is devoutly observed. Today more than ninety percent of the people of Anuradhapura are Buddhists.

The day starts with an hour-long radio broadcast on the life of Buddha. Then with the sunrise come the barefoot monks walking along the streets in yellow robes and carrying brass begging bowls. People greet them with gifts of food and alms and receive merit for their good deed. Devotees then take baskets of food and flowers to the temple, where, in the misty fragrance of incense, they light candles and offer prayers.

Older people dress in white garments and go to meditate in the pagodas. They often spend the entire day in worship while others bring water and food to them.

Among younger people, especially in the cities, *Wesak* is celebrated in more of a carnival spirit. Archways are built over streets and decorated with huge paper lotus flowers of every color. At street junctions and along roads, big *pandals* that look like billboards are erected, twenty by thirty feet high. Painted on them are vivid pictures depicting the many phases of the life of Buddha. They are bordered with colored lights.

Sightseers jostle through the streets, gazing at the *pandals* and listening to recorded music and an occasional narration of the story each *pandal* represents.

Source: *Celebrations: Asia and the Pacific* by Gene Sawyer. Honolulu: Friends of the East-West Center, 1978, pp. 36, 37.

Thailand

Visakha

Countryside observations

. . . In rural areas the commemoration is observed for three days, commencing on the fourteenth of the waxing moon, and ending on the first of the waning moon (or the sixteenth of the month). On the first day there is an evening recitation of the sacred texts at the wat followed by sermons on the life of the Buddha. At dark the ceremony comes to an end for the first day. Next morning, that is, on the day of the full moon, there is an offering of food to the monks. There is also a circumambulation round the chapel three times in a clockwise direction with lighted tapers. In some places such a circumambulation is performed on the previous day also. Sermons as a continuation from the previous day are preached from morning until evening and further continued to the third and last day.

Visakha in Bangkok

In Bangkok Visakha (Wísǎakhǎa) Day is a one-day observance in the evening of the full moon. There is a circumambulation, after which there are sermons preached by monks in succession and continuing throughout the whole night. In some of the bigger wats there are huge crowds of people circumambulating the chapel. In the Royal Chapel of the Emerald Buddha the king and queen, followed by the royal family and officials, honor the Buddha by thrice circumambulating the sacred building with lighted tapers in the evening. Hung around the royal chapel are decorated candles and lights with which the royal family and officials honor the Buddha on this important occasion. These candles and lights are mostly decorated with fresh flowers in many beautiful designs. In some wats there may be exhibits along the corridor of the chapel of altars decorated with rare and beautiful pieces of brass or porcelain ware.

Source: *Life and Ritual in Old Siam* by Phya Anuman Rajadhon. New Haven: HRAF Press, 1961, pp. 93-94.

Moon 5, Day 5 (May-June)

Double Fifth

This is an inauspicious day in Chinese cultures. Precautions must be taken against five poisonous insects. Dragon boat festivals are held on this day at several locations. Large canoes with carved dragon heads and tails race in memory of a drowned third-century B.C. minister, Wat Yuen. Sticky rice dumplings, *zong ze,* are eaten. The races are held on the "double fifth," an inauspicious day in the Chinese year. Disease and other dangers abound at this hot and sultry time.

China

The "Evil Month" and the "five poisonous creatures"

Many of the other customs that have always been associated with Dragon Boat Festival have to do with the fact that the fifth month is held to be the "Evil Month", the time of hot, steamy weather which facilitates the growth of harmful insects and germs and contributes to the spread of infectious diseases. For the purpose of expelling the gods of plague, people pasted both inside and outside the house strips of yellow paper of varied lengths inscribed with incantations and printed with the images of certain animal-shaped deities. Many people also burned realgar, a reddish mineral which burns with a yellow smoke and a foul odor. It was considered to have the power to exterminate insects. In many places old women would cut red paper into the shapes of the "five poisonous creatures" (scorpion, viper, centipede, house lizard and spider) and place them, together with a cut-paper tiger, into a gourd, thus implying that all poisonous creatures and fierce beasts were confined within and so unable to harm human beings. During festival time girls wore a "fragrant pouch" made of bits of cloth wound round with colored silk threads. In some areas these became a highly developed form of local handicrafts.

Come Dragon Boat Festival time, some shops in Beijing used to sell foot-long strips of yellow paper embossed with a scarlet seal (the color scarlet was believed helpful in dispelling ghosts), pictures showing Zhong Kui gobbling up the "five ghosts", or the image of Zhong Kui alone. On sale also were cakes in the shape of the five poisonous creatures; people believed that symbolic poison could be employed as an antidote for the real thing and that the image of evil could be used to combat evil. Therefore eating cakes shaped like poisonous creatures could protect one from harm.

Zong zi, sticky rice dumplings

Of all the customs associated with the Dragon Boat Festival, possibly the most wide spread is the preparation and eating of *zong zi,* leaf-wrapped glutinous rice balls with various kinds of filling. The story behind *zong zi* also goes back to Qu Yuan's death. After the poet had killed himself, people cast sections of bamboo filled with rice into the river to honor his soul. His spirit, however, was not satisfied with this practice, according to a popular legend. During the reign of Jianwu (26-55 A.D.) of the Eastern Han dynasty a man from Changsha named Ou Hui was confronted by the spirit of Qu Yuan who told him that the rice-filled bamboo offerings were being devoured by the river dragon before he could get them. The proper method, said the spirit, was to wrap the bamboo sections in chinaberry leaves and to close the opening with silk threads in five colors, as the dragon would thus not dare to interfere (for unexplained reasons).

Ou Hui did as he was told and this in time became the accepted custom.

The earliest *zong zi,* I presume, did indeed take the form of a rice-filled bamboo section, but the term was not then used. The people of that region cooked rice in bamboo as a regular practice. Even today the Zhuang and Dai minorities in south China and the Vietnamese and Thai people continue to make use of bamboo sections in this way. The rice thus prepared is said to be particularly tasty. Later on palm leaves were used to wrap rice, green beans, peanuts and dates into pyramid-shaped dumplings. Only from that time on did the name *zong zi* appear, because *zong* is a homonym of the written character for palm. Though festival activities are much less than in the past, dragon boat races are still conducted on an extensive scale in the south; eating *zong zi* becomes evermore popular throughout the country. Food shops supply this festive favorite, but many families prefer to their own *zong zi.*

The usual custom was to place food platters together with realgar wine side by side on the altar and to burn incense before the images of the deities and the family's own ancestor tablets. The realgar wine, mixed with cinnabar, would then be spread over the ears, nose and forehead of a male child to exorcise any lurking evil spirits.

Realgar compounds have in fact a definite utility toward disinfection. Realgar wine is also said to be good for one's health, and this too has a certain scientific basis. Another example of a popular custom with a sound medical basis is that of hanging Chinese mugwort leaves, calamus, or garlic in the doorway in order to prevent plagues.

Superstitious activities are no longer much in evidence. Realgar wine is seldom drunk these days, but in some families, the display of mugwort and calamus leaves is continued. In 1981, I was able to buy a variety of cloth figures embroidered with threads in five colors and cloth tigers filled with fragrant herbs, but these are taken only as articles of decorative art.

Source: *Chinese Traditional Festivals* by Marie-Luise Latsch. Beijing, China: New World Press, 1984, pp. 60-68.

The Feast of Poisonous Insects in Peking c. 1930

Cecilia Sun Yun Chiang describes the customs of her home on this day. Her mother embroidered special shoes with tigers on them, and a yellow robe embroidered in black like tiger's stripes was worn to ward off evil at this time. A yellow spot of *hsiung-huang* (sulphur) was placed on foreheads and around noses and ears. Sulphur was burned all night to drive away the evil insects. In the daytime *ch'ang-p'u* grasses, shaped like sword blades, were waved about to chase off the evil insects. These "swords" represented Ch'ung-kueri, who kills all devils. *Ali,* wormwood, was also used as an insect repellent. Another protection was the shaving of the heads of young children at this time.

Source: *The Mandarin Way* by Cecilia Sun Yun Chiang. Boston: Little, Brown and Co., 1974, p. 101.

The legend of Zhong Kui

Emperor Ming Huang (reigned 712-756) of the Tang dynasty one day came down with a high temperature. In his dream he was confronted by a demon. Suddenly a tall but extremely ugly figure holding a wooden sword appeared before the emperor and proceeded to gouge out and swallow one of the demon's eyes. In response to the emperor's enquiry, this man revealed himself to be Zhong Kui, a scholar from the previous dynasty who, upon failing the imperial examination because of his ugly appearance, committed suicide. He had sworn to slay all demons in the other world so as to protect the emperor and decent people. Awaking from his dream, the emperor found that his high temperature had disappeared. He therefore ordered a court artisan to paint an image based on his descriptions of Zhong Kui and bestowed upon him the title of "Great Demon-Expelling General".

Source: *Chinese Traditional Festivals* by Marie-Luise Latsch. Beijing, China: New World Press, 1984, p. 65.

Dragon-boat races in Peking c. 1940

Brilliant streamers of silk and paper in cinnabar red and other bright colors dazzled in the sun; and the search for Ch'ü Yüan's body was re-enacted in Nanghai at a regatta, rowed on the middle reaches of the south lake in the Forbidden City, in which the beflagged boats, manned by young oarsmen, were enthusiastically cheered by the crowds watching them from the banks, to the sputtering and crackling of fireworks. Even if some overenthusiastic rower fell in, or an entire boatload was swamped, it only added to the excitement, and was certainly in keeping with the tragic event the festival set out to commemorate.

Source: *The Mandarin Way* by Cecilia Sun Yun Chiang. Boston: Little, Brown and Co., 1974, p. 103.

Watching the dragon-boat races

When the great day arrives, crowds in the coastal provinces of Central and South China hire boats or go to the shore of the nearest river or lake, dressed in their best holiday costumes. Sounds of folk songs or melodies from famous operas, sung or played on the Chinese flute, echo over the hazy surface of the romantic "West Lake" in Hangchow or the mouth of the West River in Canton. A barely perceptible breeze keeps the small boats in constant movement. They float around without aim or direction while the celebrants eat their dinner, talk, or admire the neighbor's boat or his daughter's new dress.

The crowds on the shore are perhaps still gayer. They move around from one shed of straw mats to another, or sit under one of the bamboo awnings and drink tea. They wait. A tension is in the air, comparable to that which we feel before a big race begins.

And suddenly the parade of the dragon boats has begun. These boats are different from all common boats; they are big—up to a hundred feet in length—and so narrow that two members of the crew have difficulty sitting side by side. The body of the boat is shaped like a dragon, and the high prow shows the beast's fierce mouth and its dangerous fangs . . . playing cymbals or beating gongs. . . . The parade of the dragon boats is accompanied by a deafening noise, exciting the crew and the onlookers alike.

The boats are manned by different guilds or clubs or any two crews from the same village with a hereditary or traditional enmity toward each other, such as exists between the crews of Oxford and Cambridge during the races on the Thames. What a tremendous increase in prestige for the crew that wins the contest this day! And what an exciting as well as aesthetic sight—the slim, shining boats shooting through the water! The motions of the crew are coordinated and rhythmic to the utmost; a single slip of one of the rowers will cause the boat to capsize, and this not only means losing the contest but may be fatal to the crew.

The evening following the race brings another highlight of the festival, as the boats, decorated with colorful lanterns, parade on the river. Slowly they pass the crowds, emerging from the still, lukewarm, dark waters like fairies, and disappearing again in the phosphorescent gleam of the summer night.

The legend of the Chü Yüan

The third century B.C. was the period of the "warring states," the age of incessant, heroic struggles among the great feudal lords for supremacy. Most of the feudal kingdoms had already disappeared; only seven were left, and Ch'u, in the South, in the modern provinces of Hupei and Hunan, was one of the mightiest of the seven. This was a somewhat barbarian kingdom, and the "true" Chinese despised it, but it had an elegant, luxurious court, the center of politics as well as of refinement. Ch'ü Yüan, member of one of the highest native families, was minister and councilor to the king of Ch'u. He was also a court poet of great fame. He was deeply concerned with the fate of his country and tried to influence the king to do his best for his country. His advice was not accepted; he had to leave. He departed, wandering restlessly about in deep despair and growing melancholy. Thus he reached the river. He saw the endless stream of water flowing toward the great Yangtse, to the ocean. Here he composed one of his most beautiful poems, a summary of his life and activity, ideals and achievements, a farewell to the world, his country, and his king. Then he threw himself into the water. People in his country pitied him and threw rice into the water as a sacrifice to the dead, because a soul which gets no offerings will suffer all the vexations of starvation. But the soul of Ch'ü Yüan appeared to a group of fishermen, telling them that he was still starving because a huge dragon had taken away the rice they had offered him. They should wrap the rice in small pieces of silk and bind the packages with silk threads of five different colors. This they did, and appeased the soul of the loyal minister of Ch'u. The rice cakes still exist today, wrapped not in silk but in leaves. Everyone likes these rice cakes, and the sacrifice to Ch'ü Yüan is now forgotten. But the fishermen's boats still start out to offer the sacrifice. Such is the origin of the Dragon-Boat festival.

Ch'ü Yüan is undoubtedly a historical figure, and the poem he wrote supposedly just before his suicide, one of the "Elegies of Ch'u," is one of the most beautiful of classical Chinese poetry.

Source: "The Dragon-Boat Festival" by Wolfram Eberhard in *Time Out of Time: Essays on the Festival* by Alessandro Falassi. Albuquerque: Univ. of New Mexico, 1987, pp. 286-299.

Celebrating in Wuchang, Hupeh province, c. 1920

Before the relentless heat of summer began, we celebrated as usual the feast of the fifth day of the fifth month. . . . On this day, tarragon was burned, the ashes mixed with sulphurated water and poured into every corner of the rooms. This symbolised the destruction of all insects at the beginning of summer. The smell was very strong, like a strong infusion of herbs, and quite suffocating; but I still love it because it reminds me of this feast day.

Some days before, the members of our family exchanged presents. One was supposed to eat two particular dishes at this time: boiled rice wrapped in leaves with bacon or dates (Tsung Tzu) and cakes made out of green bean flour (Lu Tou Kao). Usually we gave each other the ingredients for these dishes, or, alternatively, wine and fruit. It meant a lot of work and trouble for Mother, because our family was so big. Suitable parcels had to be made up for everyone, yet everyone could not have the same. Sometimes a flask of wine which Mother had given an aunt went from the aunt to Grandmother and from Grandmother to a cousin, and came, in the end, back to us. We always had a few flasks over every year, and these would be passed on to aunts and cousins the following year.

Source: *The Lotus Pool* by Chow Chung-cheng. New York: Appleton-Century Crofts, 1961, pp. 74-75.

Tuan Wu in Kao Yao, Yunnan, 1938

Tuan Wu was called the Dragon-Boat Festival. On this day people feasted on pork, chicken, and beans and drank a wine with a special antitoxin against poisonous bites. This feast was held at breakfast time and then everyone went to work as usual. Children from ages one to six years had a red or green string tied around their wrists as protection against snake bite and wore a dried water caltrop in the upper button loop of their coats for protection.

Source: *Village Life in Old China: A Community Study of Kao Yao Yunnan* by Cornelius Osgood. New York: Ronald Press, 1963, pp. 336-337.

Memories of dragon-boat races

In the fifth month are held the dragon-boat races. These boats are narrow and long, capable of holding about one hundred men sitting one behind the other. Each one carries a paddle, and the boat is so made that it can go just as well backwards as forwards. The direction devolves upon the men in the ends of the boat. In the centre the idol from whose ward or district the boat hails, sits enthroned with an immense umbrella of red silk to keep the sun from tanning his complexion. A band of music accompanies each boat. By its warlike clangor it encourages the racers, while its drum beats the time for the stroke. Banners are given after the race, as spoils of victory, to be placed in the temple of the patron deity. The scene on the rivers on such an occasion is very animated and the cheers of the spectators from the different districts attest their interest.

Source: *When I Was a Boy in China* by Yan Phou Lee. Boston: Lothrop, Lee & Shepard Co., 1887, pp. 79-80.

Hong Kong

The dragon boats

The Hong Kong Dragon Boats may cost between HK $80,000 and HK $100,000. They can be up to one hundred feet in length and are rowed by as many as fifty paddlers. A drummer keeps time and an oarsman steers. The head and tails of the boats can be removed and stored in local temples during the year. A ceremony called "opening the light" initiates new heads. Each eye is painted with a dot of vermilion paint mixed with blood from the comb of a brown chicken. The head now invested with spirit, must be treated with respect and presented with incense and candles.

The benevolent power of the dragon boats and the dangerous Double Fifth

The dragons are believed to bring rain, and indeed rain usually falls during or just after the Dragon Boat Festival in Hong Kong.

The dragon boats are also efficacious in preventing disease. Paddlers especially gain benefit from this. The dragon-boat races come at the time of the dangerous Double Fifth when dangers and disease abound; thus their preventative powers are needed. The boats are hung with pointed iris leaves to protect them; these signify demon-slaying swords. The doors of homes may be hung with bunches of mugwort, a bit of temple-offering pork, and an onion at this time as protection.

Source: *Chinese Festivals in Hong Kong* by Joan Law and Barbara E. Ward. Hong Kong: A South China Morning Post Production, 1982, p. 53.

Taiwan

Toan-Ngo Choeh

Five Taiwanese observances

Five observances occur on this day: (1) sweet rice dumplings are made in honor of Ch'ü Yüan; (2) dragon-boat races take place; (3) charms are made of incense to ward off the "five poisonous things"; (4) mugwort plants are stuck on the doorpost of the house; and (5) a noontime bath is taken.

The legend of Chü Yüan as the origin of Tseng-tzu dumplings and of dragon-boat races

The first person mentioned in connection with today's feast is the famous official of the Ch'u Kingdom during China's period of the warring states, Ch'ü Yüan. Ch'ü Yüan's personal name was P'ing, and he belonged to the royal house of Ch'u, serving as a high official under King Huai (328-299 B.C.). History says of him that he was an extremely upright and honest man, but due to intrigues at court he lost his high position, and was made a sort of minister-without-portfolio abroad. Refusing to compromise himself with the corruption at court, Ch'ü Yüan wandered around the southern Kingdom for several years, advising the court to change its ways, and unheeded, witnessing the gradual downfall of King Huai. Finally, in desperation, he threw himself into the Mi Lo river, on the fifth day of the fifth month, and so perished.

For this reason the people of China make a special rice dumpling wrapped in a wide bamboo leaf, and throw it into the water in Ch'ü Yüan's memory. Glutinous rice is used, and the package when finished is called "Tseng-tzu" in Mandarin or "chàng" in Taiwanese The bamboo leaf used to wrap the Tseng-tzu is called "môa-tek-hióh", and a special grass called "Kiâm-chháu", used to tie it. Originally the rice thrown into the river was stuffed into a bamboo tube, so that the "scaly dragon" could not eat it up before Ch'ü Yüan found it.

When the people who lived by the Mi Lo river heard that Ch'ü Yüan had thrown himself into the river, they were supposed to have jumped into their boats and paddled out furiously to save him. Failing in this, they then wrapped rice in bamboo leaves or bamboo tubes to give to his spirit for sustenance. If a package of rice floated upon the water, they would race to pick it up, thus symbolically representing their desire to save Ch'ü Yüan.

The "Five Poisonous Things"

The "Five Poisonous Things" vary in different parts of China, depending upon the climate and the kinds of small creatures which bother human beings. In Taiwan the five things specifically mentioned are the wall-lizards, toads, centipedes, spiders, and snakes. In North China the scorpion is sometimes substituted for the spider, and ordinary lizards for the famous "wall-tigers" or wall lizards of South China, the Philippines, and Taiwan. The wall-lizard is actually a helpful creature, who devours mosquitoes and other insects omnivorously, and can run up the walls and along ceilings to catch them. But much as with the toad in Western lands, folk-tradition has attached some sort of a harmful fluid to his skin, which causes warts, when touched. Perhaps it is but a protective agency to keep the small fellow from harm, as one or two wall lizards in a room can fulfill the roll of several flyswatters. At any rate they are classified as one of the five harmful creatures, along with other more terrifying things such as the many varieties of truly poisonous snakes, and so forth. To ward off any evil effects from them, chunks of incense called "hiu-phang" are made into the shapes of the five harmful creatures, and hung about the children's necks. In north China small cakes are made into the shape of the 5 bad insects, and eaten with the same end in view. In Taiwan sometimes little cloth figures are also sewn, stuffed with incense, and used as a sort of charm against evil. This is the third of the observances for the 5th day festival.

Mugwort

The fourth observance is called "chhah hia" or to "stick mugwort" plants into the doorposts of one s house. The people coming back from the rivers or streams where rice was thrown in Ch'ü Yüan's honor are supposed to bring with them branches of mugwort, banian tree leaves, and water grass, sometimes called sword grass. These branches terrify evil spirits, and are quite efficacious when stuck in cracks by the wooden doorposts, for preserving the house from summer illnesses.

When asked why the grass is so efficacious, one of the reasons given by the Taiwanese is the similarity between the names of the grasses and the good things desired. Thus the word for mugwort sounds like bodily strength, banian leaf "chheng" sounds like strong dragon "leng"; and water grass or sword grass "chhiong" sounds like good fortune "chhiong-seng."

Another custom is for children to use a branch of the calamus as a sword and the mugwort as a standrend to drive away demons. Also, "calamus soup" is rubbed on the chest and "Yellow hero wine" i.e. medicinal wine with sulfur in it, is drunk, to strengthen one against summer illness.

Noontime bath

Finally the fifth custom of the day is called the "noontime bath." If one takes a bath just at noon on the fifth day of the fifth month, all sickness will be avoided for one year. Likewise a bucket of water pulled up from the family well just at noon, can "cure the hundred ills."

Source: *Taiwan Feasts and Customs* by Michael R. Saso. Hsinchu, Taiwan. Chabanel Language Institute, pp. 48-51.

For more on the Dragon-Boat Festival see: "The Dragon-Boat Festival" by Wolfram Eberhard in *Time Out of Time* by Alejandro Falassi. Albuquerque: Univ. of New Mexico, 1987, pp. 286-299; "The Dragon-boat Festival" in *Chinese Festivals* by Wolfram Eberhard. New York: Henry Schuman, 1952, pp. 69-96; "The Dragon Boat Festival" in *Chinese Traditional Festivals* by Marie Luise Latsch. Beijing: New World Press, 1984, pp. 55-68; and "The Dragon Boat Festival" in *Chinese Creeds and Customs* by V. R. Burkhardt. Hong Kong: South China Morning Post, 1982, pp. 36-38.

Moon 5, Day 5

Tano

This is a day for summer celebrations featuring swinging contests for the girls.

Korea

Festivities in the 1970s

Years ago this was a time for making fans for the summer weather ahead, painting them delicately with scenic pictures. The most beautiful were presented to the king and officials at the court.

In modern Korea, the *Tano* festival is a national holiday.

For the girls there are swinging contests. Using old-fashioned rope and board swings, the girls compete to see who can swing the highest and kick a suspended bell. They wear Korean dresses, whose colors and billowing skirts make a pretty picture as the girls demonstrate their skill. Prizes are usually mirrors or chests or something for the home.

For boys and young men, there are amateur wrestling matches. Each town and village selects the biggest, strongest man to represent them in the contests and there is great rivalry. However it's all in fun, because only hands and feet can be used. The victor wins the biggest ox to be found in the countryside.

Festival crowds enjoy music, kite flying, games and food treats. Rice cakes are cut in the shape of Korean characters standing for happiness and long life. The specialty of the day is rainbow rice cakes, made with rice flour that has been dyed in bright colors.

Source: *Celebrations: Asia and the Pacific* by Gene Sawyer. Honolulu: Friends of the East-West Center, 1978, p. 35.

Swinging

It fell on Sunday this year. A huge swing was hung on pine poles in one of the schoolyards. Another was hung from a tall pine tree by the church door. Elsewhere they were suspended from bridges and other suitable points, but it was not only the girls in their bright Sunday best who risked their necks in the exhilarating exercise.

Singly or in pairs (paired swinging, two on one swing, is both more dangerous and more exciting because more momentum can be gained), boys and men, as well as women and girls, happily did the right thing on the right day, in spite of the commonly told story that swinging is a sport strictly reserved for the female sex.

Source: *Korean Works and Days: Notes from the Diary of a Country Priest* by Richard Rutt. Rutland, Vt.: Charles E. Tuttle, 1965, p. 72.

Swing Day (Geune)

The fifth day of the Fifth Moon is called "Dano-nal," one of the three great days of the year—New Year's Day, Swing Day and the Eighth Full Moon Night. On this day at each home the new summer food is offered at the family shrine and women and children in new clothes flock together for amusements as they do in the New Year holidays.

Boys and girls wash their hair in hot water boiled with iris and the girls make ornamental hairpins with iris roots, carving on them two Chinese characters "Long Life" and "Blessings" or painting them with rouge before arranging them in their hair (knotted as for a bride-to-be). . . .

Among the amusements of this day the greatest is swinging. Everywhere in Seoul and in the country people hang long ropes from the branches of tall trees, especially willow trees, and large numbers of men and women swing energetically.

Swinging is, however, primarily for women, many of whom had been secluded in their homes all the year round but came out this day to the village gardens or forests in beautiful colored dresses and flew to and fro like swallows or fairies on the high swings. An ancient poet described the sight in the following lines:

> "Not in heaven, not on earth,
> But you are in the mid-sky.
> Blue hills, and green waters
> Seem to swing to and fro.
> You come as falling flowers;
> You go as skimming swallows."

Swinging is especially popular in Pyongyang, where it is most picturesque. Crowds of women, some in blue skirts with white jackets and some in yellow jackets with red skirts, wearing jade rings on their fingers, come to enjoy the swinging. Here is one on a swing, there two on another, all gay, like butterflies in the summer breeze.

Source: *Folk Customs and Family Life* by Tae Hung Ha. Seoul, Korea: Yonsei, 1958, pp. 35-36.

Moon 5, Day 14

Gods of the Sea Festival (and Boat Race Day)

This is a festival in Okinawa. Boat races follow offerings to the gods.

Okinawa

The boat race in Minatogawa

The 14th day of the 5th month (June 18, 1951) is the festival of the Gods of the Sea and is observed only in Minatogawa. It is this village's greatest celebration. The boat race, held on this day, attracts many from the interior villages. In Hanashiro, most activity ceases while everyone goes to the boat races. Before the races, the villagers go to the religious sites to make small offerings and to pray. The races are held in the estuary of the river. In their excitement, children with infants on their back often wade out in the water to chear their favorite boat.

Source: *Studies of Okinawan Village Life* by Clarence J. Glacken. Scientific Investigations in the Ryukyu Islands (SIRI). Report no. 4. Washington, D.C.: Pacific Science Board. National Research Council, 1953, p. 322.

Boat Race Day in Taira

. . . An important religious event for the community is Boat Race Day in lunar June. On Boat Race Day Taira and the neighboring village of Kawata race fishing canoes against each other. Spectators at this event are enthusiastic supporters of their favorites. After the races this holiday ends like any other, in celebrations with dance and drinking.

Source: ''Taira: An Okinawan Village'' by Thomas W. Maretzki and Hatsumi Maretzki in *Six Cultures: Studies of Child Rearing* edited by Beatrice B. Whiting. New York: John Wiley & Sons, Inc., 1963, pp. 363-539.

Moon 5, Day 15

Gogatsumatsuri

This is a day of thanksgiving for the rice crop, held on the fifteenth day of the fifth month.

Okinawa

A day of thanksgiving

The Festival of the Fifth Month (*Gogatsumatsuri*) is held on the 15th day of the 5th lunar month (June 19, 1951). Like the festival of the spring equinox, it is a day of thanksgiving. Thanks are given for rice instead of for barley. In Matsuda, the ceremony is conducted by the village head men and former members of the priestess system.

According to a Hatsuda informant, women should not sew on this day. It is a rest day. If work is done, including gathering plants for fertiliser, the dreaded poisonous snake, the *habu,* will come. These customs were not encountered in the other villages.

Source: *Studies of Okinawan Village Life* by Clarence J. Glacken. Scientific Investigations in the Ryukyu Islands (SIRI). Report no. 4. Washington, D.C.: Pacific Science Board. National Research Council, 1953, p. 322.

Jaistha (May-June)

Ganga Dussehra

Ganga Dussehra is a bathing festival held on Sukla Dasami Day in the month of Jaistha. Every Hindu wishes to bathe in the Ganges River on this day, but if that is not possible, sacred water from the Ganges can be sprinkled for purification.

India

Ganga revives sixty thousand princes

. . . Queen Keshani gave birth to a son named Asmajas and the other queen Sumti bore 60,000 sons. King Sagara in his joy performed an *Ashvamedha Yajna* (the horse sacrifice, a ceremony performed by ancient kings of India) to declare his suzerainty over his neighbouring kingdoms.

The 60,000 sons of the king were protecting and watching the horse sent out in connection with *Ashvamedha Yajna*. The horse entered the place where the great sage Kapila was meditating. The sage begin disturbed, cursed the sons accompanying the horse, who were immediately burnt to ashes. King Sagara waited long for them and then deputed his grandson Anshuman to trace them, who was told how his uncles met their fate due to the curse of Kapila.

When Sagara came to know about it, he was overwhelmed with grief and in anguish he visited different sages, seeking consolation. During this sojourn, Sagara was told that if Ganga be brought anyhow on the earth and touched the ashes, his 60,000 sons could come to life again. On getting the required information and visiting the place himself, Sagara returned home with the horse.

Failure to propitiate Ganga through meditation

After Dilipa, his worthy son Bhagiratha reigned at Ayodhya and after sometime went to the holy place Gokarna, where he practised fervid penance to invite the Ganga. The gods were pleased by his untiring efforts. Brahma requested Ganga to go down to the earth for deliverance of Bhagiratha's ancestors. In consequence, Ganga left her celestial abode (heaven) with sharp and fast flow. When no other god dared to endure the torrential flow, Lord Siva, on being invoked by Bhagiratha, took the stream of the holy river on his matted locks. Thereafter, the Ganga left for the plains of Northern India following the chariot of Bhagiratha, touching the ashes of the 60,000 princes and liberating them for salvation and reached Bay of Bengal, fertilising the whole region on her way.

Bathing in the Ganga

On the Ganga Dussehra day, men, women and children reach the banks of the Ganga to take a dip in the river. People from the rural areas go walking or in the bullock carts singing songs in praise of the Ganges. The banks of the river are crowded at Hardwar, Garh Muktesvar, Prayaga, Varanasi and all such places, where it flows. Those who on account of being at far off places are unable to reach Ganga, take dip in some nearby river, tank, pond or sea, saying "*Hara Hara Gangey*". On this great festival, everywhere and specially at all the religious places great congregations are held to invoke Mata (Mother) Ganga. Local fairs are also organised on this occasion, for the enjoyment of the people.

Ganga is a sacred name on the lips of every Hindu and it is believed that its mere utterance purifies all the sins. Besides the fact that the water of the Ganges is clear like a crystal, it is never turbid and dirty. It is very holy, healthy and pure, and also has the qualities of saving a person from ailments. This is the reason why saints and other people meditate for her peace of mind and salvation and the sick utilise it for curing themselves from various diseases and also for their good health.

That is why the Hindus have always aspired for a bath in the Ganga and after death, their ashes are immersed in its holy water for the peace of their souls. Further, the water of Ganga with *tulsi* (*basil*) leaves is administered to the dying person to ease his agony and also the journey for the next world.

Source: *Festivals of India* by Brijendra Nath Sharma. New Delhi: Abhinav, 1978, pp. 83-84.

Sixth Day, Brightening Fortnight, Jestha (May)

Sithinakha / Kumar Sasthi

This is the birthday of the God Kumar, son of Shiva. Kumar has six heads, representing the six senses (including extrasensory perception). In addition to the procession to honor Kumar and worship at his temple, this is a day to clean wells and tanks. The snake gods are away performing their worship too, so it is safe to clean their habitats.

Lotus-shaped paper windmills are set on roofs on this day, and children play with them. The windmill symbolizes the end of evil times and the approach of holier days.

Nepal

Eight cakes

One of the main features of this festival is the preparation of a rich variety of cakes. If we are to follow the tantric injunction eight different kinds of cakes from eight different kinds of foodgrains, such as, black pulse, *masoor* dry peas, rice, corn, barely, millet, and arrowroot should be made and offered to Lord Kumar.

Cleansing and worship

Another interesting aspect of this festival is the cleanliness of one's body and house. Most of the people on this auspicious day get up early in the morning and go to the nearest river to take the purification-bath which is a big traditional 'must', and then they go to the temples to worship their favourite God Kumar with all the best dishes they have prepared for the occasion.

Source: ''Sithi: The Cake Festival'' in *The Nepal Festivals, Part 1* by Dhurba K. Deep. Bhotahity, Kathmandu: Ratna Rustak Bhandar, 1978, pp. 40, 43.

For more on Sithinakha see: *The Nepal Festivals, Part 1* by Dhurba K. Deep. Bhotahity, Kathmandu: Ratna Pustak Bhandar, 1978. (Deep is a prominent Nepali poet and scholar.); ''Sithinakha or Kumar Sasthi: The Birthday of Warrior-God Kumar'' in *The Festivals of Nepal* by Mary M. Anderson. London: Allen & Unwin, 1971, pp. 66-71.

Jaistha (May-June)

Vata Savitri

This is a festival of Hindu married women, held for the sake of the longevity of their husbands.

India

Worshipping the banyan tree

According to scriptures, Savitri, a deified woman, had rescued her husband from the clutches of Yama, the god of death, after worshipping the *Vata* (banyan) tree. Even now, the Hindu women wish to predecease their husbands and not die as widows.

On the festival day, after taking bath early in the morning, they wear their best clothes and ornaments and go out at mid-day in groups to worship the banyan tree. During worship, vermilion is sprinkled on it and raw cotton threads are wrapped round its trunk. Sugar and clarified butter are also offered to the fire. They make seven rounds of the tree and put various articles near the place where the tree stands. They also observe fast till the *puja* is over.

The women take some articles of the worship for breaking their fast and happily return to their respective homes. Some women, who are unable to go to the tree, worship a twig of it at home. Sweets are distributed to all the family members and neighbours.

Source: *Festivals of India* by Brijendra Nath Sharma. New Delhi: Abhinav, 1978, p. 37.

Sixth Day of Sivan (May-June)

Shavuot

Shavuot is the Feast of Weeks, the Feast of Harvest, or the Day of the First Fruits. The home and synagogue are decorated with green branches and flowers. Dairy foods are eaten. This celebrates the day on which God gave to Moses the Ten Commandments. Originally on this day farmers brought their first fruits (*bikkurim*) to the temple.

Libya

Celebrating the festival of the Torah

On Shavuot it was the custom in Libya for children to sprinkle water on people who passed by. Water represents the Torah and Shavuot is the festival of the Torah. Children were given cookies baked in the shape of the tablets of the Ten Commandments, in order that they might digest the Torah easily. Cookies in the form of a ladder, recalling Moses' ascent to Mount Sinai, were also baked.

Source: *One People: The Story of the Eastern Jews* by Devora and Menachem Hacohen. New York: Sabra, 1969, p. 104.

Kurdistan

Savuot pilgrimages

This festival was known as *zeira* or ''pilgrimage.'' Iraqi Jews visited the tomb of Ezekiel at Kiffil and the tomb of Ezra. Kurdish Jews visited the tomb of Jonah in Mossul. In Alkosh, the burial place of the prophet Nahum was visited. Pilgrims visited Elijah's Cave at Bet-Tanura and Daniel's tomb at Kirkuk. The Jewish communities at these places of pilgrimage catered to the pilgrims with food and shelter.

Another Shavuot custom was the spraying of water from roof tops onto the people passing below.

Source: *One People: The Story of the Eastern Jews* by Devora and Menachem Hacohen. New York: Sabra, 1969, p. 204.

Persia

A night of remembrance

Shavuot symbolized the marriage between the Torah and the people. Therefore, the preparations for this festival were like a wedding preparation. A ''sweet table'' covered with tidbits was arranged in every home. Shavuot night was a night for remembrance at the homes of those who had lost family members during the year. Friends and relatives gathered at these homes. Seated on mats and holding a vase of roses, each recited passages from the Bible. A reading of the Book of Ruth would end the event. Women served coffee to the men to help them stay awake for the long night's reading.

Source: *One People: The Story of the Eastern Jews* by Devora and Menachem Hacohen. New York: Sabra, 1969, p. 34.

Yemen

Shavout food and readings

Blintzes and other dairy delicacies were eaten on this night, as in the Ashkenazic diaspora. The *ketuba,* the marriage contract between God and the Community of Israel, was read aloud on this night, and the Book of Ruth was read both in the original and in the vernacular. Each man took a turn reading. On Shavuot night the gates of heaven open at some time between nightfall and dawn. It was customary to stay up all night to watch. A shooting star was said to be the key to the gates.

Source: *One People: The Story of the Eastern Jews* by Devora and Menachem Hacohen. New York: Sabra, 1969, p. 148.

For more on Shavout see: ''Shavout,'' in *Folklore of American Holidays* edited by Hennig Cohen and Tristram Potter Coffin. 2nd ed. Detroit: Gale Research, 1991, pp. 224-225.

June

Egungun Festival

This is a masked festival of the Egungun secret society. The masked dancers are possessed of the spirits of the ancestors they represent.

Nigeria (Ede)

The Egungun masks

Egungun is a secret society headed by a hereditary chief called the Alagba. An Egun mask usually represents the spirit of a particular person and it is always the priest of the Ifa oracle who will decide which spirit must thus receive special worship. A man who is ordered to worship his ancestor will be called the 'owner' of the mask. It is he who has the mask made, but he does not himself dance under it. Instead he takes it to the Alagba with appropriate presents, when the Alagba will secretly appoint a member of the Egungun society to wear it.

The masks are of different types. Many consist merely of coloured cloth and leather covering the whole body, the dancer looking out through a closely knitted net. Some actually have wooden masks in front of the face, while others may wear a carved head on top of their own head.

It is considered extremely dangerous to come too close to the spirits of the deceased when they are out. As a Yoruba proverb says: 'Even a Prince cannot go near an Egungun with impunity'. The masqueraders are therefore, always accompanied by men holding sticks who keep the crowd away. It is also considered dangerous to see the face of the man under the mask, or even part of his body. In olden days an offence of this sort would have meant death at the hands of the cult members. The Olubadan of Ibadan (Chief Akinyele) in his History published in 1946, says that the whole of Ibadan was once destroyed for such an offence.

In reality, however, every Yoruba is fully aware that there is a human being under the mask. After all, the 'owner' of the mask, who is *not* a cult member, knows quite well that he has had the mask made himself and that he asked the Alagba to find him a dancer. But it *is* believed that the spirit of the deceased may be evoked to enter into the masquerader during the dance. At the height of the dance every true Egungun will enter into a state of possession, when he will speak with a new voice.

The appearance of the Egungun masks underlines the feeling of oneness between the living and the dead and will fill the crowd with a feeling of love as well as of fear.

The Egungun Festival

The great Egungun festival takes place in June, when all the masks come to the market place to dance for the Timi. This is a magnificent occasion indeed. Some thirty-odd masqueraders, in colourful costumes, dance simultaneously. Each mask has his own orchestra of drums, is surrounded by young men wielding whips, and is followed by chanting women and girls.

There is a constant movement and cross movement on the market place. Some Egungun may dance on one spot for a while; others will suddenly burst forward in one direction, the drummers hastily backing away before them but still drumming and facing the dancer. When the masquerader leaps forward the young men will lash out wildly with their whips to prevent anybody from coming near the mask. The young girls following the masquerader are usually Abiku children, who have their own masked society. The women may be relatives of the owner of the mask, or they may be women who received children from the spirit.

The height of the festival comes with the appearance of Andu, the most powerful and important mask in Ede. Other masqueraders clear the way with their drummers and followers when Andu storms onto the market place. The air is electrified by his coming and the drums beat louder and faster.

This is undoubtedly one of the most exciting days of the year in Ede.

Source: *A Year of Sacred Festivals in One Yoruba Town* by Ulli Beier. Lagos, Nigeria: Nigeria Magazine, 1959, pp. 26-28.

For more information on Egungun see: *African Arts* XI (3) (April 1978), 18-76.

June 1-2

Gawai Dayak

A harvest festival of the Dayak of Sarawak.

Sarawak (Dayak)

Gawai Dayak, a harvest festival

Dayaks, who live in all five administrative districts of Sarawak, gather on the first of June to make offerings of foods and *tuak,* their rice wine. A bard recites a poem asking guidance and long life. He swings a sacrificial white cock to drive away evil spirits, and the blood of the cock is put onto the offerings. The celebrations include the recitation of pantuns and the performance of *ngajet,* a war dance. Blowpipe demonstrations and cockfights take place. This festival celebrates the end of the paddy season after harvest and asks for blessings on the coming season.

Source: *A Guide to World Fairs and Festivals* by Frances Shemanski. Westport, Conn.: Greenwood, 1985, p. 132.

June 11
Cataclysmos Day

A remnant of a much earlier rite, Cataclysmos Day on Cyprus remains a day for residents to visit the seaside to sprinkle water on each other and to engage in verse battles, *Chattismat.*

Cyprus

Sprinkling at Cataclysmos Day

Adonis was said to rise one day each year, after his death, to rejoin Aphrodite. Celebrants would gather at the temple on this day and the young girls would sing; then all would go to the sea, sprinkle each other with water, and conduct a poetry contest.

Today this sprinkling of water continues. It is bad luck not to be sprinkled on this day. After the seaside sprinkling, *Chattismat* (verse arguments) are held. Rhyming insults are exchanged between two contestants. The response must be quick, appropriate, and clever. A duel between two skilled contestants may last for hours.

Source: *International What's What When & Where* by Ardith Nehrt. Columbus, Ohio: Shawnee International Publishing Co., 1965, p. 26.

June 13

St. Anthony's Day

St. Anthony of Padua is the patron of people who lose things, children or animals; he is also the patron of animals. He is often depicted in statues holding the infant Jesus and a lily. Born in Portugal in 1195, he sailed to Morocco as a missionary but became ill and was blown off course en route home, landing in Sicily. He preached in France and Italy and was buried at Padua.

Chile

Día de San Antonio

Popular Chilean saint

San Antonio is one of the most popular Chilean saints. He is the shepherd of lost animals and also has the virtue of helping young girls find spouses. On this day they say to him, "San Antonio bendito, solo te pido, una bolsa con plata, y un buen marido," asking St. Anthony to give them a purse full of silver and a good husband.

Source: *Folklore Chilena* by Oreste Plath. Santiago: Nascimento, 1969, pp. 323-324.

Italy

St. Anthony's Day in Rome and Padua

St. Anthony is the patron of Padua. In the Franciscan church dedicated to him in Rome, horses, mules, and their harnesses are blessed on this day.

Source: *Festivals and Folkways of Italy* by Frances Toor. New York: Crown, 1953, p. 213.

Portugal

The patron of Lisbon

On his Eve young folks dance around bonfires. Children set up street altars in his honor by covering boxes or tables with a white cloth and decorating the altar with flowers, candles, images, and pictures of St. Anthony's life. Children also go through the streets begging for coins in his name.

Source: *The Book of Festivals* by Dorothy Gladys Spicer. Detroit: Gale Research Company, 1969, p. 269.

Spain

Giants and Big Heads (*Cabezudos*) parade in El Pinar village at the fiesta of San Antonio de Padua (St. Antony of Padua)

The fiesta begins on June 3rd with a novena in honor of San Antonio, and ends with vespers and a Rosary on the evening of the 12th. At 8:30 p.m., after the Rosary, the festivities begin. The band marches in the streets playing pasodobles, and the gigantes and cabezudos parade. These are huge papier mache heads of historical or imaginative characters set on frames ten feet tall and gowned in long robes. Small children run from them in terror, while older boys toss firecrackers at them. Fireworks are set off, dancing takes place, and a street of carnival booths is set up. This partying occurs every night during the festival. On the final day, the band and cabezudos and gigantes begin their parade at 9 a.m. and a high mass is held at noon. The statue of San Antonio is processed through the village after mass in a three-hour-long procession. The band plays lively jota music and the men dance the jota in front of San Antonio. The dance is done in two lines, each man with a male partner. As dancers wear out, others replace them. When the statue finally reaches the church again, the dancers block the church doors to prevent the Saint from entering, so the dancing can continue. Worshippers lay money silently at the statue's feet at this time, for church expenses during the coming year.

On the next day, the 14th, the bullfight is held. And on the 15th a bullfight for the youth is staged, with yearling bulls. This is a free-for-all with anyone who wants allowed to hop into the ring and have a go. A professional torero is in charge of the event, and of the actual killing of the bull.

Source: *Social Change in a Spanish Village* by Joseph Aceves. Cambridge, Mass.: Schenkman, 1971, pp. 49-51.

For more information on St. Anthony's Day see: "St. Anthony's Day, June 13" in *Folklore of American Holidays* edited by Hennig Cohen and Tristram Potter Coffin. 2nd ed. Detroit: Gale Research, 1991.

June 13-29

Festas Juninas

Brazil

The Bumba-meu-Boi folk drama

Typically, the scene of the Bumba-meu-Boi is a quiet provincial town with narrow streets and small, colored houses. The ordinary tranquil rhythm of life is interrupted by the invasion of a raucous colorful procession. Guitars, drums, flutes, tambourines, whistles, and other musical instruments play a special song announcing a remarkable happening. Children and adults run to their windows, applauding and screaming. "Eh! Bumba, Eh! Boi," greeting the group, recognizing its name embroidered on a flag that leads the procession. The performers ask the public to be their audience, to be "in" their procession.

First comes the Chorus, four or more persons, sometimes dressed like the colonial aristocracy, singing and dancing. Next come the rest of the characters, wearing improvised fantastic costumes, according to their role, and each dancing his particular character. People applaud them or jeer at those who are more aggressive or frightening. These characters commonly attack the audience, who either run from them or counterattack. This establishes a kind of game that is maintained throughout the procession, until the group arrives at a house (almost always that of important people of the village) where they enter and perform the play.

In some places this second part of the Bumba-meu-Boi is called *embaixada* (embassy). These embassies also can take place in front of a church or in the main square of the town. Many performances may be presented during the course of the procession, or there may be one complete procession throughout the whole village announcing the performance.

The play begins. The band is seated at one side of a large living room or kitchen. In the back two people hold tall sticks from which hangs a colored fabric, like a curtain, used by the performers to enter and leave the scene. Where there is room, some spectators enter, the rest remaining outside peering through the open windows at the scene.

The Chorus sings the "overture," usually songs specific to Bumba-meu-Boi, staying hidden behind the curtain to introduce the main characters. In the band are two important figures of the drama, the *Violeiro* and *Cantador,* who play guitars and improvise new songs referring to community life and to what is happening during the performance.

During the introduction, the *Cavalo Marinho* (sea horse) first appears—a man in a sea captain's costume. He wears a colored jacket with golden ornaments, pants with red stripes down the sides, a red satin ribbon across his chest, and a paper crown with mirrors and ribbons. He carries a sword and enters riding a horse. This is a skirt-like attachment that consists of a wicker structure covered by colored fabric, attached at the waist. The front of the structure is in the form of a horse's head. He dances. He is the "white one," the rich farmer who owns the Ox, all the other animals, the lands, and the cowboys.

Vaqueiros (cowboys) enter, among them the comic leads Mateus and Birico. Catarina, mistress of Mateus, being pregnant, desires an ox's tongue to eat. The heroes travel in search of an ox, meeting many comic characters en route.

The Ox is usually one or two men under a wicker structure, similar to that of Cavalo Marinho. This structure, which serves as the Ox's body, is covered either by colored fabric or embroidered velvet (similar to a bullfighter's costume). The head is an ox skull or mask, adorned with flowers, stars and ribbons.

The Ox enters dancing, while the spectators sing with the Chorus and applaud enthusiastically. This is the climax of the play. The Ox dances a *Lundu,* a traditional tap-dance; the music is a type of primitive samba. He attacks the cowboys, the Chorus, and the audience. Mateus shoots the Ox; it dies.

The Chorus and the audience mourn its death, singing a popular Brazilian song:

My Ox has died
What am I going to do?
I will have to search for another Ox
Far, in Piaui.

Mateus then cuts out the Ox's tongue and offers it to Catirina. The meat is distributed to the audience in a symbolic way—wine is offered, or handkerchiefs are given out, to be returned with money or gifts.

The Doctor arrives, making a comic entrance. He says that the Ox has not died and prescribes an enema, accomplished by inserting a boy into the Ox's behind. Mateus and Birico are pressed into this service. They hunt for a boy in the audience and then perform the enema.

The Ox stands up and starts dancing. The spectators become excited and begin to sing and dance. (Sometimes the resurrection occurs by touching the Ox's back with a sword or by offering presents and money to the Ox.)

The Capitão do Mato enters tied up with the rope he brought to secure the guilty ones. The audience jeers excitedly.

All the characters dance together while the Chorus sings the Farewell. This may be either polite, if the host and the audience have given the performers good money, food and drinks, or sarcastic and aggressive if their efforts have not been well rewarded.

Source: ''The Bumba-meu-Boi'' by Jose Possi Neto. *The Drama Review* 21 (3) (T 75) (September 1977), pp. 5-11.

Tenth of Dhu'l-hija

Id Al-Kabir (The Great Feast)

Id al-Kabir, The Great Feast, falls approximately sixty-nine days after the Id-al-Sagheer, Little Feast. The day commemorates Abraham's willingness to sacrifice his son. The yearly haj (pilgrimage to Mecca) occurs at this time. Those who have already made the pilgrimage, hajii, are prominent during this time. Pilgrims should arrive at Mecca by the sixth of Dhul-Hijjah (the month of the Hadj). This feast falls on June 23, 1991; June 12, 1992; June 1, 1993; May 21, 1994; and May 10, 1995.

Cameroun

Saving for the Hadj

Ask a farmer in northern Cameroun what he's going to do with any profits from a development assistance project and he's likely to tell you that he'll use it to finance a pilgrimage to Mecca. Many other Muslims would say the same. All Muslims who are of good health and have the means are supposed to make the pilgrimage at least once in their life.

Those who make the pilgrimage receive the honorific title of Hadj for men, and Hadjia for women. For some, this can involve a lifetime of savings, typically several thousand dollars. It's not unusual for families to save up and send one member. Before the invention of the aeroplane, it used to involve a journey overland of a year or more, sometimes requiring stops on the way to earn money.

Source: *Central Africa: A Travel Survival Kit* by Alex Newton. Hawthorne, Victoria, Australia: Lonely Planet, 1989, p. 23.

Chad

Tabaski

Tabaski in Central Africa, an official holiday in Chad and Cameroun

Also known as the Great Feast, Tabaski is the most important celebration throughout northern Central Africa. This is the day that Muslims kill a sheep to commemorate the moment when Abraham was about to sacrifice his son in obedience to God's command, only to have God intercede at the last moment and substitute a ram instead. It also coincides with the end of the pilgrimage (hadj) to Mecca. In the preceding two weeks, sheep prices can jump 50% or more.

One-third of the sacrificed animal is supposed to be given to the poor, one-third to friends, and one-third for the family. Those who cannot afford a sheep are really embarrassed; most will do anything to scrape up the money.

If you can manage to get an invitation, you'll be participating in what is for African Muslims the most important and festive day of the year. It's mainly lots of eating and visiting friends following several hours at the mosque. It's an official government holiday only in Chad and Cameroun, usually lasting two days.

Source: *Central Africa: A Travel Survival Kit* by Alex Newton. Hawthorne, Victoria, Australia: Lonely Planet, 1989, p. 22.

Hausa pilgrims as migrants

There is another category of migrant, however, which has contributed a great deal to the life of the estimated 1.5 million Hausa outside Hausaland. This is the Hausa pilgrim. Just as the expansion of long-distance trade in West Africa gradually led to the formation of Hausa commercial communities, the overland pilgrimage eastward to Mecca bred a string of pilgrim settlements along the changing routes. Stretching from Nigeria to Arabia, these enclaves represent a characteristic communal identity which has differentiated them simultaneously from those around them and from their compatriots in other parts of the Hausa diaspora. Pilgrims who have settled as close as Maiduguri or as far as Medina share a common purpose in migration and settlement which manifests itself in a multitude of forms. In size, the enclaves range from small groups of settled pilgrims in Tripoli in the nineteenth century (as opposed to the city's larger population of Hausa slaves to more than 100,000 migrants from Hausaland revealed in the 1964 Sudan census. The existing network of Hausa settlements in Chad owes its foundation and expansion in large measure to its close and continuing association with the hajj.

The Muslim Pilgrimage to Mecca

Although the hajj is a duty incumbent upon all Muslims who have the resources (the Arabic concept of *istita'a*) to make the voyage, it has had an uneven frequency among African Muslims. The economic and social class of a potential pilgrim has often affected his decision, if not his desire, to make what until recently was an arduous and often dangerous trip. The actual travel conditions—distance from Mecca, organization of travel, and security along the route—have also resulted in varying numbers of pilgrims from different regions. A third consideration, beyond economic and geographical realities, is that of ethnic group. Certain Muslim groups in Africa, West Africa in particular, have a longer tradition of pilgrimage, and the practice seems more pervasive among them. For centuries small numbers of Hausa have crossed the Sahara or Sudan to visit *Dakin Alla,* "the House of God." Although statistics are rare for all but the most recent years, the pilgrimage from Hausaland has undoubtedly increased in popularity over the past 100 years, giving the Hausa a leading popularity over the past 100 years, giving the Hausa a leading position among West African pilgrims. Figures from the hajj season of 1970 (A.H. 1389) underscore both the increasing importance of the pilgrimage for all African Muslims and the large Hausa contingent from Nigeria. These figures reflect the revolution which air travel and motor transport have effected in the past thirty years. In this period, however, the pilgrimage from Africa has lost many of its migratory aspects, becoming more a simple voyage—albeit a very important one—than a form of population movement.

AFRICAN PILGRIMS IN MECCA, 1970 (A.H. 1389)

Algeria	6,376	Morocco	6,935
Cameroon	1,244	Niger	2,801
Central African Rep.	262	Nigeria	24,185
Chad	4,271	Senegal	2,097
Dahomey	356	Sierra Leone	284
Egypt	13,547	Somali Republic	1,457
Ethiopia	2,399	South Africa	1,426
Ghana	518	Sudan	8,537
Guinea	786	Tanzania	309
Ivory Coast	683	Togo	94
Kenya	333	Tunisia	4,608
Liberia	126	Uganda	408
Libya	4,570	Upper Volta	630
Malagasy Republic	20	Zaire	7
Mali	999	Zambia	379
Mauritania	316	Other Places	137
Mauritius	59	TOTAL	90,109

Source: *Pilgrims in a Strange Land: Hausa Communities in Chad* by John A. Works, Jr. New York: Columbia Univ. Press, 1976, pp. 4-6.

Egypt

Aid al-Kabir

Departure for the Hajji in Egypt

Both urban dwellers and village folk observe the religious festivals and holidays. Aid al-Kabir (the Great Feast) is the most prominent. Lasting four days, it commemorates Abraham's willingness to sacrifice his son, and it is marked by the yearly pilgrimage to Mecca.

The departure for the pilgrimage is a great occasion in Egypt. The ceremony of Mahmal, at which gifts of carpets and shrouds for the Kaaba at Mecca and for the tomb of Muhammad at Medina are presented and made ready for dispatch to Mecca, draws great crowds. This ritual must be completed in order to give time for the presentation of the gifts at their destinations on the eighth day of Dhu'l-Hijja, the last month of the Moslem year. Those who make the pilgrimage may assume the title of Hajji (pilgrim), which carries prestige in both religious and social circles.

Source: *United Arab Republic: Egypt* by Donald N. Wilber. New Haven: HRAF Press, 1969, pp. 70, 72.

Eid-il-adha in Kafr el-Elow village

Each family who can afford it should sacrifice a sheep after morning prayer on this day. Butchers do much of the slaughtering, but some householders perform the rite themselves, dipping their hands in the blood and leaving a mark on the doors of their homes to show their sacrifice. Two thirds of the animal should be given to the poor. The third to be consumed by the family is cooked and served on a thin bread (*battawi*) soaked in the meat juice. The male members of the clan dine on this dish in their guest house after returning from the cemetery on the first day of the festival. More affluent villagers who have lost a relative recently will hire a mukre to recite the Koran in memory of their loved one, and may rent loud speaker equipment to set up in front of their home on the night when the mukre recites.

Source: *Kafr el-Elow: An Egyptian Village in Transition* by Hani Fakhouri. New York: Holt, Rinehart and Winston, 1972, pp. 84-85.

Korban Biram

. . . a friend remembered visiting Cairo during the holiday of Korban Biram, which commemorates the commitment that Abraham, the "first Moslem," made to God by sacrificing a ram, after first offering his own son. It is a sacred and yet cheerful family holiday. Many streets are strung with colored lights. The children wear new clothes and flourish toy drums or ride a street fair merry-go-round rotated by a donkey. What particularly sparked his memory was the sight of paddle-tailed sheep tethered for sale all around Cairo, and city men in suits and fellaheen in galabias carrying these home on their shoulders. . . . In Egypt government agricultural experts complain that because people insist on carrying away the very best livestock for Korban Biram feasts, the quality of the nation's herds is depleted.

Source: "Christmases Past" by Edward Hoagland in *The Nation* (Dec. 26, 1987/January 2, 1988, p. 776-777.

Iran

Arafa

Day of Arafa in pre-1938 Iran

On the eve of the Feast of Sacrifices (day of Arafa), women never sweep their rooms and do not do any needlework, for fear that bits of the broom or the needle may fall to the floor and stick in the foot of some hajji (this is the day when pilgrims from Mecca walk barefoot).

Sacrifice of the sheep in pre-1938 Iran

The sheep must be purchased the day before the holiday. The next day, henna is applied to its head and back. The edge of its eyelids must be rubbed with kohl (as Abraham rubbed some on Ismael and dressed him in his best clothes), and sugar is put into its mouth before the sacrifice. It is sometimes sent as a present (to one's betrothed, for example, between the contract and the wedding), and in this case the animal is decorated with a small mirror or bells on the neck, or even with jewels and sometimes with a Cashmir shawl. When it is slaughtered it must be turned towards Mecca, and it must be killed with a single gash in the neck, but without severing the head. The meat is distributed and the skin kept as a rug. The intestines have the power to ward off the evil eye, and are dried and kept. The right eye is likewise dried and preserved to be put on a child's bonnet (together with kodji shells) as a talisman against the evil eye. A piece of cotton is also dipped in the sheep's blood and allowed to dry; if a child has a pain in the throat a bit of this cotton is placed in water and the water fed to him with a spoon.

It is commonly believed that on the day of resurrection the faithful will spring from the plain of judgment to heaven, mounted on the animal which he has sacrificed on this holiday.

Source: *Persian Beliefs and Customs* by Henri Masse. New Haven: Human Relations Area Files, 1951. Trans. from Croyances et coutumes persanes, 1938, p. 127.

Iraq

The pilgrimage from Iraq in early twentieth century

The Pilgrimage to Mecca is the fifth and last Pillar. It is performed in Dhu el Hajj, the last month of the lunar year, and is completed on the tenth day of that month. How I used to enjoy hearing my Hajjia and her sister, and their venerable mother when she was alive, relate their experiences when the whole family went on the pilgrimage in an early year of the century. Those were the days when the entire journey from Basrah was made by ship and took a month or more. The pilgrim ship they traveled on must have been quite de luxe, for they had two cabins, and a good-sized space on deck, curtained off for privacy. They took all their own provisions with them, complete with several crates of live chickens, and a goat to provide them with fresh milk. They landed at Mother Eve's town, the seaport of Jidda, and from there traveled by camel up to Mecca.

"When we got there," related my friends, "we had to leave off our own clothes and put on pilgrims' garb. It was wonderful! Everyone equal with everyone else, before God! Then for ten days we went back and forth and round and round. We encircled the Kaaba, we kissed the Black Stone, we stoned the Devil, and we drank of the well Zem-zem. You know that is the well from which Abraham's wife Hagar and her son Ishmael drank in the wilderness."

"We made many prayers," continued her daughter, "and listened to many sermons. Then, on the tenth day, the great Day of the Sacrifice, my father had a sheep sacrificed for each one of us. After that he and my brothers had their heads shaved, everyone had his nails pared, and we put on our regular clothes again. Each of us was given a certificate to show that we had performed the Hajj."

The Feast of the Sacrifice, the tenth day of the month, is one of the two great festivals of Moslems the world over. The religious nature of this one is stressed much more than the Eed el Fitur at the end of Ramadhan, though it is celebrated in much the same way. Every family who can afford it sacrifices a sheep, and the tradition is said to go back to the days of Abraham. I have heard a legend that the Milky Way is the path in the sky of the Heavenly Ram which God sent to be sacrificed in the place of Isaac.

Boys and girls with the name Mekki or Mekkia have presumably been born or conceived at Mecca.

Source: *Fatima and Her Sisters* by Dorothy Van Ers. New York: The John Day Co., 1961, pp. 124-130.

Jordan

Al-Adha Al-zid al-Kabir

The Pilgrimage to Mecca

Pilgrims must plan so that they arrive at Mecca before the sixth day of Dhul-Hijjah. Specially charted pilgrim ships carry them. The pilgrims are housed just outside Mecca, and are turned away unless they have a return ticket home. After bathing, the pilgrims don special clothing, a black robe and veil for the women, two cotton towels for the men. In several days of ritual the pilgrims circle the Kaaba and run between the two holy hills at the site. They sacrifice sheep and camels, traveling to the hill of Arafat, 12 miles east of Mecca.

When the pilgrims arrive home, they are met by families who have hired a taxi to greet them at airport or dock. Their home has been decorated by friends with palm leaf arches, carpets, and colored lights. Feasting and thanksgiving follow the safe return from the pilgrimage.

Source: *The Land and People of Jordan* by Paul W. Copeland. Philadelphia: J. B. Lippincott, 1965, 1972, pp. 52-53.

Offering prayers for the dead

On this day, women prepare special foods and sweets and take some to the tombs of their deceased relatives. The men attend a morning service at the mosque and then process to the cemetery, where they read together the Fatiha (the first chapter of the Koran) and offer prayers for the dead. Each person then goes to the grave of his own relative, tastes the food left there, and recites the Fatiha for the benefit of that relative. The food is then distributed to the poor or others passing. As soon as the container is empty, it must be removed from the grave, lest an angel discover an empty container and curse the deceased. The rest of the day is spent in visiting and feasting.

Source: *Baytin: A Jordanian Village* by Abdulla M. Lutfiyya. The Hague: Mouton, 1966, pp. 71-72.

Kuwait

Id al Adha

Homage to the shaikh

H. R. P. Dickson describes the visit of over 2,000 persons to pay respects to the shaikh and wish him "Id mubdrak" on this day. The shaikh replies "ayyamkum sa' ida" ("May your days be happy").

Children's swinging

Dickson notes the brightly colored holiday finery of the children and their play on specially constructed swings, merry-go-rounds, and ferris wheels. The young men of the area construct and power these special devices for the delight of the children, who sit in shallow boxes in small groups of seven or eight to be swung about. Dickson mentions the "raucous singing" of the swing man and the happy choruses of the children.

Id Al Adha and Id Al Ramahdan dancing among Bedouin tribal girls

Dickson describes the dancing of the unmarried girls, which continues for seven days at festival time. They dance in seclusion within their tents, but related young men may watch from a proper distance. The girls dance three at a time, to the accompaniment of a chant by the older women, who clap to keep time. The dancers take off their 'abas and burqas and dance in their brilliantly colored clothing, which is usually hidden by the dark overgarments. The dance consists of short, straight-legged jerks, and a swinging movement of the head to make the hair fly. The girl may cover her lower face with her sleeve in modesty as she dances.

Source: *The Arab of the Desert: A Glimpse into Badawin Life in Kuwait and Sau'di Arabia* by H. R. P. Dickson. London: Barnes & Noble, 1949, pp. 218-224.

The pilgrimage from Kuwait

I was always pleased when my annual visit to Kuwait coincided with the preparations for people going from there on the pilgrimage. They usually went overland, by caravan, and the camel bazaars there and in Zobeir were hives of industry. Camel saddles, brightly colored harness and saddlebags, and litters for the women, called *kajawahs,* were all made ready for the great exodus across the desert. Tents, bedding, fodder for the animals as well as all the food supplies for the human beings, cooking pots and fuel, all had to be carefully organized.

The whole pilgrimage was a much more lengthy and complicated affair in those days than now, when most people go by plane; though there are still many contractors who arrange transportation for those who prefer cars and buses.

The pilgrimage to Mecca is incumbent on every Moslem, man or woman, who can pay his own expenses and provide for his dependents at home during his absence. A person who is incapacitated may pay the expenses of a substitute and get the credit himself. A woman must be accompanied by a husband or a male relative. I had one enterprising friend who lacked a male escort, so she married in order to have a lawful protector for the expedition, and after they returned home divorced him amicably by mutual consent.

Source: *Fatima and Her Sisters* by Dorothy Van Ers. New York: The John Day Co., 1961, p. 129.

Morocco

Prayers and sheep in Salé, c. 1930

The Slawis visited the musalla to perform ablutions and prayers at Id al-Kabir. Early in the morning straw mats were brought to the cemetery, and the crowd began arriving around 8 a.m. The group consisted mainly of men with their sons, though a small group of women gathered at the rear of the crowd.

The qadi led prayers and climbed the portable wooden stairs (minbar) to give his sermon (khutba). He then sacrificed a sheep in behind the prayer niche. This was the first sheep sacrificed that day.

Sacrificing sheep, c. 1930

As the men returned home, they bought sweets and gave alms to the poor. A sheep was sacrificed in each home, either by a man of the family or by a visiting butcher. Certain parts of the sheep were traditionally prepared and eaten at certain times during the festival and the week following. Some of the meat was preserved and put aside for other festivals later in the year. Nearly half of the sheep eaten during the entire year in Salé were slaughtered on this day.

Friends and relatives visited each other's homes on this day.

Source: *The People of Salé: Tradition and Change in a Moroccan City 1830-1930* by Kenneth L. Brown. Manchester: Manchester Univ., 1976, p. 93.

Nigeria (Hausa)

Sallah

A Sallah procession in Katsina, c. 1969

On the day before Sallah, the horse of each district head in the Emirate is brought into town with great pomp. The horse is riderless, its owner arriving by car; but it is surrounded by royally robed riders and accompanied by recorder and drum music. The recorder-like pipes have a bulb-shaped mouth tapering to the mouthpiece and require strong lungs.

On the morning of Sallah, the Emir, his entourage, and the district heads with their entourages ride from the palace to the prayer grounds. The Imama leads prayers there, and all remain seated on their horses during the service. There may be hundreds of mounted men at the event. The riders are garbed in velvet and brocade and the horses' saddles and bridles are richly ornamented with silver and gold.

Later the Emir arrives to sit in *durbar*. He rides a white horse and is robed in white, with a white turban. He carries a short silver sword, the Sword of Katsina. This is the sword with which Koray killed Sanau at Durbi in 1260. A huge umbrella is held over the Emir's head by a walking servant. Behind follow three camels bearing large drums, the ancient war drums of Katsina. After he is seated in state the *durbar* begins. Each group of men rides up and salutes the Emir. They arrive at a gallop, reining in at the last moment so that the horses rear up onto their hind legs. The men raise their right hands in a clench-fisted greeting to the Emir. He answers by raising the Sword of Katsina in his right hand.

Source: *Katsina: Profile of a Nigerian City* by Gretchen Dihoff. New York: Praeger, 1970, pp. 60-64.

Pakistan

Id-ul-Bakr

The Sacrifice of the Ram

During the last month of the Muslim year comes the Sacrifice of the Ram, Id-ul-Bakr. This is a great feast commemorating the Old Testament story of Abraham's willingness to sacrifice his son. Usually for this occasion a sheep is killed, prayers are said, and then the meat is cooked with saffron rice (pilao). Well-to-do farmers sacrifice a cow; this is a bone of contention between Muslims and Hindus, since Hindus maintain that cows are sacred and must never be killed, while Muslims insist that the sacrifice is obligatory for their religion.

Prosperous village families cook enough food for the Feast of the Ram so that everyone may share. The meat is divided into three portions: one-third for the household, one-third for relatives, and one-third for the poor. The food for relatives is sent on trays to their own houses; poor people come to the door and ask for food. It is thought to be wrong to turn anyone away empty-handed.

Id-ul-Bakr occurs during Haj, the month of pilgrimage and there is more feasting before a pilgrim departs for Mecca. Usually a man is elderly by the time he has saved enough or has leisure for the voyage—a long trip up the Red Sea by chartered pilgrimage ships, vessels sometimes of doubtful seaworthiness. Though long and arduous, the pilgrimage (*hajj*) is the culmination of a devout Muslim life. The returning pilgrim is greeted with respect as Hajji. He may dye his beard red with henna or wear a green turban which sets him apart.

Source: *The Land and People of Pakistan* by Robert Lang. New York: J. Q. Lippincott, 1974, p. 134-135.

Saudi Arabia

The pilgrims arrive at Mecca

Robert Lacey described the arrival of pilgrims in the 1980s as evoking a spirit of pageantry and celebration. He describes the flood of white-clothed pilgrims filling the roads and flowing past the long white buses filled with more pilgrims and flying their national flags. King Hussein, the Gulf sheiks, and the king and princes of the Al Sa'ud join the throngs, white-toweled and bareheaded like the other pilgrims.

Source: *The Kingdom* by Robet Lacey. New York: Harcourt Brace Jovanovich, 1981, p. 516.

Senegal

Tabaski

Tradition in Dakar c. 1952

Author Nafissatov Diallo tells of slaughtering a sheep and taking the meat to relatives and friends. A "sister-in-law" would get a leg of mutton and one thousand francs. A cousin or friend could be denoted as "sister-in-law" for the day, to receive the honour for her parents-in-law. Traditionally every home must have meat on this day, given to those who need.

Source: *A Dakar Childhood* by Nafissatov Diallo. Translated by Dorothy S. Blair. Longman, 1952.

Syria

Returning from the Haj

During the days following the ritual in Mecca, the pilgrims begin to return to their homes. Families are notified of their arrival time. Together with friends, they hire taxis and decorate them with palm branches and the families' best rugs. They then go to the edge of the city to await the pilgrim's arrival.

He is now greeted as *al Hajji* and may wear the distinctive green scarf around his head. The family and friends noisily embrace and kiss the returned traveler and escort him to his home.

The doorway has been decorated with palm-leaf arches and, if possible, the house has been outlined with lights. In the Kurdish villages and in Egypt, the doorways will be decorated in colored designs suggesting the journey: gay drawings of camels, boats, donkeys, and airplanes. A sheep is killed before the threshold, and then the whole party goes inside to a feast that has been in preparation for days.

Source: *The Land and People of Syria* by Paul W. Copeland. Philadelphia: J. B. Lippincott, 1972, pp. 50-51.

Turkey

Kurban Bayram/Kourban Bairam

Sacrificial sheep

. . . Mahmud held the rope as his father took a knife from his belt and straddled the tethered animal. The sharp blade was carefully placed over a ritually sanctioned spot on the sheep's throat, and Mahmud's father said a short prayer and severed the great arteries with a single quick stroke. For an instant life seemed to flicker in the animal's eyes, and then it was all over. Thus they had rendered unto God the sacrifice, as Abraham had done so long ago as a substitute for his son, that was now required annually of all good Moslems.

The animal jerked a few times and then lay still. It was allowed to bleed freely for a long while before Mahmud's father opened the abdomen, removed the entrails, piled them high on a piece of heavy canvas, and began to carve up the carcass. Some of the meat was carried by Mahmud to relatives who were in need, but most of it was taken home where his mother and the new *gelin* were already preparing a huge feast for the evening meal.

Evening feast

Later the men go to the mosque where the hoca delivers a sermon. During the afternoon the men rest while the women prepare the feast for the evening. The men are served first with delicacies such as *etli fasulye* (a thin broth with beans and lamb), *ic pilav* (seasoned rice with pine nuts), *labmacun dolmasi* (stuffed cabbage leaves), and *borek* (ground meat or cheese in a pastry, fried). The dishes are served one at a time. A dish of tomatoes and cucumbers in olive oil and vinegar is served last, while the women prepare the *kadayif* dessert (a pastry saturated with sugar water). A fruit tray rounds off the feast. The women eat in another room while the men debate religion and politics.

Source: "The Kurban Bayram" in *Life in a Turkish Village* by Joe E. Pierce. New York: Holt, Rinehart and Winston, 1964, pp. 54-56.

The pilgrims arrive at Mecca

Shortly after Sheker Bairam, the Delil would come to our town. He is a representative of the Koraiish tribe of Arabia which governs Mecca and to which Mohammed belonged. His duty is to enlist Moslems for the pilgrimage. Our Delil was an old man and a Sheik. His name was Mohammed Salih Brindji. On his arrival all the people of the town would turn out to bid him welcome. He was highly respected, as he was a member of the same tribe as the Prophet. All the rich men vied with one another in entertaining him and he would stay a few days at each of their houses.

The beginning of Zilkadeh, the eleventh month, the pilgrims would leave for Mecca. On the day of their departure they would gather together at the mosque. There were usually about twenty from Kemer and the surrounding villages. They were all men, with occasionally an old woman among them. Young women are not allowed to take the pilgrimage. All the town and countryside was out to see them off. In the courtyard of the mosque a great feast was prepared and everybody ate to their heart's content. Afterwards there was special prayer for the pilgrims in which Allah was asked to watch over them in their long and perilous voyage. As they left the town on donkeys, in carts, or on foot for Smyrna and the sea, they were accompanied the first part of the way by the singing populace.

On the tenth day of the next month, Zilhidcha, the final month of the year, is Kourban (sacrifice) Bairam. It is on this day that Abraham prepared to sacrifice his son Ismail to Allah. This is according to the Koran. The Old Testament gives the name of his son as Isaac. In honor of this event every Moslem family kills a lamb and on the following four days there is music, dancing, and general merry-making. All visitors are asked to partake of the sacrificial animal. It is also on this day that the pilgrims must be in the Valley of Arafat outside of Mecca in order to qualify for the title of hadji.

This ends the festivals except for that on the occasion of the return of the pilgrims, which is liable to take place at any time during the next two months. It is seldom that they return in numbers the same as they left. Usually some succumb to the rigors of the voyage or to epidemics that break out continually in the pilgrim camps. Their return is celebrated by practically the same ceremony as their going. There are prayers of thanks, songs and feasting. Many are the objects which the pilgrims bring back with them, perfume, holy soil from the Valley of Arafat, books of songs, strings of holy beads, bottles of Zem-zem water, and the *kefin* or pilgrim's dress in which they are buried when they die. The Zem-zem water comes from the spring, which tradition says is the one Allah caused to come forth when Hagar, wife of Abraham, was wandering in the desert with her son Ismail. This water is believed to have great powers in the curing of disease and the returned pilgrims jealously guard it, sipping of it on rare occasions.

Source: *When I Was a Boy in Turkey* by Ahmed Sabri Bey. Boston: Lothrop, Lee & Shepard Co., 1924, pp. 94-97.

West Africa

Id al-Kabir traditions

Before the most important feast of the year, *al-'īd al-kabīr* on 12th of Dhū'l-hijja, towns are thronged with sheep. They are particular to ensure that the ram fulfils the legal specifications otherwise the benefit may be lost. Hausa say the best animal is a ram with black rings around the eyes, and when it has not been blessed with these characteristics they anoint its head and feet with henna and put kohl round the eyes. On the festival morning the men process to the *'id* plot outside the town for prayer and homily as at the previous festival. When this is finished the drum sounds and they bring a ram to the *imām* who, citing 'In the name of God, God is great, O God accept this offering' cuts its throat and the drum sounds again. Then everyone returns home, slaughters his ram before his house, and distributes it among relatives, clerics, and poor. The bones are carefully buried, but head and feet are kept for the *'Ashūrā*. The skin is often tanned and dressed for use as a prayer-rug. North African beliefs regarding the utility of the sacrificial ram on the Last Day have spread throughout the Sudan. Songhay say they support the bridge Sirāt on their backs, but the majority believe that all the rams turn into a large horse which carries you over the Sirāt. Unlike other feasts there is little drumming and dancing, and the three days are spent resting and visiting friends.

Source: *Islam in West Africa* by J. Spencer Trimingham. Oxford: Clarendon Press, 1959, p. 80.

June 24

St. John's Day / Midsummer Day

The Feast of St. John the Baptist falls on June 24 and it is on the eve of this day, June 23, that the European summer solstice celebrations occur as Midsummer's Eve. St. John, born to Mary's cousin Elizabeth, prophesied the coming of Jesus and prepared the way for his coming, baptizing people in the River Jordan.

Finland

Juhannus Day

Sauna and birches

The sauna is always part of the celebration of midsummer, which has been conveniently fixed on a Saturday so that everyone can spend it in the country. Now birch takes the place of the Christmas fir, and great branches are cut to decorate houses, cars, and even railway engines. After the sauna, there is outdoor dancing, and bonfires are lit on lake and sea shores. Midsummer is a simpler festival than Christmas, but for the Finns it has a greater, if pagan appeal, relating them more closely to the life of the countryside and celebrating the precious gift of twenty to twenty-four hours of daylight, compared with none to six, according to latitude, at Christmas.

Source: *The Finns and Their Country* by Wendy Hall. New York: Paul S. Eriksson, 1967, p. 61.

Bonfires and nightlong dancing

Then comes Midsummer, or Juhannus Day, which celebrates the longest day of the year and the feast of Saint John. It's another marathon festival, and the practical Finns celebrate it on a weekend, regardless of the actual day which is longest. The Saturday closest to June 24 is almost like a medieval holiday. All who are able to go to their favorite lake shore, where they build a huge bonfire to be fired at midnight, and dance, and dance, and dance. . . .

Since it was grafted onto a pagan celebration, a number of superstitions cling to the observance of Midsummer. You must be sure to have birch in the house to insure future happiness. You should also hang a birch wreath on your cow's horns to protect it, and woe betide the cow whose wreath falls off. When the animal brings it home in the evening, it becomes part of her meal for a special invigorating effect.

Source: *Of Finnish Ways* by Ainu Rajanen. Minneapolis: Oillon, 1981, pp. 164-165.

St. John's Day, c. 1910

St John's Day is more gaily kept. The previous day is called the black day, and the evening is spent in superstitious practices. Little flames proclaim where treasure is hidden, but only that man can see these flames who is on the roof of a house which has been moved three times. This is the reason why so many of the smaller buildings are moved. Great care must be taken not to swear when digging for treasure, for nothing offends the powers of the underworld as much as swearing. Once upon a time a man had dug up part of a treasure; it was getting very heavy, so he swore just a little oath, then the treasure disappeared and was never seen again. Great fires are made, and casks smeared with tar are lit and sent rolling down the hills, and all the people come along singing down the hills behind them. They keep awake all night, and tell stories and sing and dance and play. The next day is also a feast day, and sometimes the house is made clean and the table laid and the family go out of doors, so that the *domowoi* (house spirit) may be unhindered in his movements. Strangers are recommended to go to the clergy house on these occasions, especially in villages, because every one is out making merry.

Source: *Home Life in Russia* by A. S. Rappoport. New York: Macmillan, 1913, p. 57.

A turn-of-the-century midsummernight

Half an hour after midnight the sun began to rise from the red clouds in the east. On Koko Hill, which long had borne the name of a family of Finnish wizards, the blazing tar barrel, lording it on top of a fresh pine pole in the center of the midsummernight bonfire, staggered and fell crashing into the remains of logs and sticks below. The fire ceased to roar. The dance must end.

Olli, head of the fiddlers, his faithful, curved back hot with fire and hard work, finished the wolf-trot with a waggish swing of his bow. He and his three helpers cased their fiddles, while wearily grinning at the two bearded balalaika men whose gaudy instruments, uncovered, lay on the dry grass. It had been a strenuous, though a jolly jubilee.

Girls in red, blue and green blouses, and men in blue coats and white breeches stepped and jumped helter-skelter from the roofless pavilion, the walls of which consisted of a few slender birch trunks, decorated with women's scarves, and wreaths of fern and spring violets. Children, skipping about the fire and reluctant to leave, howled and shrieked; dogs barked; girls tittered; young men laughed in a rolling baritone.

The musicians, too proud and important to walk, piled into a cart drawn by two small horses, with deeply concave backs and sumptuous bellies. All older people, with the children, were off to the village that lay a verst eastward; but for young folk the night was still young, so these sauntered down the slope in all directions, the boys temporarily separated from the girls, in keeping with midsummernight usage. By and by boys would meet girls to play at flirting in the net huts and the groves and the sandy nooks along the Kaara Lake near by, not to mention the more dignified milk houses scattered here and there on the wide meadows.

Presently the window was rapped three times with the birch rod. Aino giggled to herself, drawing the quilt closer to her throat. There were three more taps, a little louder, and she did not answer. Then a voice asked:

''Do you hear anything at all?''

She remained silent, as was the custom. The birch rod played its tap-tap on the window, while a slow sing-song sounded from below:

> ''Kick your covers to the feet,
> Kick up to the ceiling your sleep,
> Lay your foot on the floor,
> Put your hand on the door,
> And let us meet.''

Source: *Midsummernight* by Carl Wilhelmson. New York: Farrar & Rinehart, 1930, pp. 3-11. (A fictionalized account.)

France

St. Jean's Day

The flames of St. Jean

On the Ile d'Ouessant there was recently (still is, I hope) much ceremonial on St. Jean's Day. There was leaping on and over the bonfire, in which many rushes (*joncs*) were consumed; and torches (called *bispouns*) were carried on poles and waved hither and thither all over the island. Mariners give a wide berth to Ushant on the eve of St. Jean! not to say on the eve of St. Peter also, when these insatiable bonfires did, and perhaps do, blaze again.

At Saint-Jean-du-Doigt no mere curé sufficed to light the bonfire (called a *tantad*). An Angel with a lighted wand fixed to its arm was slid down a wire. The *tantad* is built near the church, and it is odd that the wind always blows from the church on that evening. One day the church may catch, and a wave of rationalism sweep over these villagers.

Vendée and Provence are great places for fires of St. Jean. Bombs are exploded; torches thrown; the amazing custom in Poitou of a cart with a flaming wheel seems to suggest the Celtic origin of the performance, namely, the summer solstice. Paris used to keep St. Jean in open spaces, and Louis XIV once lighted the bonfire. The Druids used (it is said) to hold a review of all the local babies on this day, and in Brittany you may see infants surreptitiously held towards the flames.

Here is a vivid description of St. Jean in Périgord, from *Jacquou le Croquant,* by Eugène le Roy:

'In our country we light fires at the cross-roads, and near the villages. In the towns there are fine bonfires, with a bunch of lilies, roses, and St. John's herbs' (a vervain, still gathered specially on this date) 'which you try to get hold of afterwards. As in old times the Druid kept his festival of the solstice at nightfall, so the curé comes now to bless the fire; you take some of the ashes home to keep your house safe from lightning' (and ordinary fires also. In the story, these fires suggest to the hero, then a little boy, the idea of burning the great wood belonging to the persecutor of his parents, a local count.) This vervain is so much connected with St. Jean (or the solstice) that it has in Spain given its name to the festival (or its eve). *Verbena* (though not our modern vervain) was the regular name for herbs used by the Romans in their sacrifices.

No doubt the flames of St. Jean exhaust all the inflammable material in the peasant mind, so that St. Peter's Day, though sometimes forming a milder repetition of St. Jean, is not usually a great popular fête. But there are many *fêtes patronales*.

Source: *A Guide to French Fetes* by E. I. Robson. London: Methuen, 1930, pp. 68-69.

France/Spain (Pyrénées)

Midsummer Eve in the Pyrénées

Fires are lit on Midsummer Eve by families, neighborhood groups, and villagers, each on their own peak, or in their village plaza or field. A visitor to Barcelona recalls counting thirty-seven fires from one rooftop on a Midsummer Eve.

The fire may be over seven meters high, a pyramid topped with a wreath. The priest may bless the fire and light it. Jumpers may leap the fire, and brands may be pulled from the fire and carried in dance. The charred remains are protection from thunderstorms. Lucky twigs are sold at market the next day, and cinders from the fire can be mixed with the first corn-sowing or put into the garden to ensure rapid growth. Seed sown at midnight on this eve comes up with magic speed. In Urgell it is believed that cabbages will come up within twenty-four hours. Beans sown then will be ready by St. Peter's Day, six days later. At Aux-les-Thermes, adders are thrown onto the fire and burnt. In Guipuzko, villagers drag the burning sticks to their fields chanting that they have burnt up ''wild beasts, toads, vipers, and all evil pests.'' In the Baztan valley children jump every fire in the street down and back again, reciting a charm against the itch: ''St. John Baptist,

Good in, Evil out, Itch out too.'' This protects against an itch endemic to Basque children.

Source: *Pyrenean Festivals* by Violet Alford. London: Chatto and Windus, 1937, pp. 235-238.

Germany

Sommersonenwende (Summer Solstice)/Johannisnacht (St. John's Night)

Customs

In Thurningia wreaths were hung on the door because John the Baptist was thought to walk through the streets on this night, and he would bow to any door with a wreath on it.

A wreath made of cornflowers outside a young girl's door meant that her answer to her sweetheart was ''yes.'' But a thistle wreath meant ''no.''

Larch trees were decorated with colored eggs and flowers on this day.

Jumping over a fire on this eve brought good luck. Cattle driven over the fire's ashes would be safe during the coming year. Couples who jumped the fire hand in hand would wed. The fires could become rowdy, with empty tar barrels set alight and swung round and round, or flaming wheels rolled down hills.

Couching the printer apprentice

This day was dedicated to Gutenberg, inventor of the printing press. Printer apprentices were soaked in barrels of water as if they were being made into paper on this day. They would then treat their master to drinks and be given a certificate saying they had been ''couched.''

Source: *German Festivals and Customs* by Jennifer M. Russ. London: Oswald Wolf, 1982, pp. 67-70.

Ireland

A holiday for the *daoine sidhe* (fairies)

Midsummer Eve finds the *daoine sidhe* at their merriest. Mr. Griffith warned us that if we ever grew up to have a beautiful daughter, we were to be sure and keep her indoors on Midsummer Eve because that is when the *daoine sidhe* steal, for themselves, beautiful mortal brides.

He knew of a girl who had been so treated. She disappeared for seven years and when she came back, her feet were worn off from dancing, she was as ugly as an ugly duckling and she roamed about the countryside on crutches the rest of her mortal days, muttering. ''At your service M'lord. At your service!''

Source: *When I Was a Boy in Ireland* by Alan M. Buck. New York: Lothrop, Lee & Shepard Co., 1936, p. 94.

Italy

The flowers of St. John's Eve

The eve of St. John we don't go to bed at all.

At sunset, the little square where St. John's church stands is beginning to be filled up with flowers in all styles, cut, in pots and dried; all the gardeners, amateurs and professionals, male and female, come to the little piazza of St. John to sell their wares, for with the flowers they also sell fancy baskets and picture frames, all made with some dried plants and flowers.

We citizens after supper don our best clothes and go to see this fair, and for that night we hardly recognize that thoroughfare, as from the four different streets by which we can approach it, there hang hundreds of Venetian lanterns, around and on top of the porticoes, made from fresh flowers.

Good music comes through the open church door, as this large door opens facing the principal street. On that night when the church is all illuminated inside, the sight is grand.

We walk up and down the square until midnight, when we go into the church to hear some good organ music and an appropriate talk on St. John. After 1 A. M. we go out into the square again, and there we wait for the *Rugiada,* the dew of St. John. When we get that we proceed to buy the flowers we want. It is customary to buy fresh lavender in branches or *altea* (marshmallow) root, strung up to put in our bureaus.

We children would buy little flower-pots with a sprig of some sort in it. The man that sold it to us would say that the sprig had a root to it; but very often there is no root at all, and we are minus two cents.

Source: *When I Was a Girl in Italy* by Marietta Ambrosi. Boston: Lothrop, Lee & Shepard Co., 1906, p. 111.

Latvia

Līgo Festival

The Līgo festival c. 1930

The Līgo festival—still the greatest feast of the year in Latvia, being now celebrated annually in every town and village on June 24.

The bonfire was burning, the religious ceremonies were progressing in the oaken forest grove, the young men and maidens had begun the preliminaries of their midnight frolic. . . .

Source: *Latvia: Country and People* by R. O. Urch. Riga: Walter and Rapa, 1935, pp. 32-34.

Macedonia

Telling omens on St. John's Eve

In Macedonia the ceremony, or pastime—for, like most of these rites, it has long been shorn of its serious character—is performed as follows.

On the eve of the day young people of both sexes,—for this is a social spell,—and not unfrequently married men and women also, fix upon a certain spot where the performance is to be held. Then a child is sent round to collect from the members of the party different tokens, consisting of rings, beads, buttons, or anything that the participators in the ceremony are in the habit of wearing about their persons. To each of these tokens is attached a flower, or a sprig of basil, and then they are all cast into a jug or pitcher, which is also crowned with flowers, especially with basil and the blossom of a creeping plant, resembling the honeysuckle and from its association with the rite called St. John's Flower. In some districts a gigantic cucumber, or an onion, is cast in along with the tokens. The vessel is then carried to the fountain, the spout of which is likewise decorated in a manner recalling the well-flowering and tap-dressing customs once popular in England. The maid who bears the vessel must not utter a single word, and if spoken to she must not answer. Having filled the pitcher, she carries it back in silence. A red kerchief is spread over its mouth and fastened round the edges with a ribbon, or a string, and a padlock. The last mentioned article seems to be due partly to the mistaken etymology of the name (unless, indeed, the etymology has been suggested by the article), and partly no doubt to the mystic significance attributed by popular superstition to a lock. This part of the ceremony is known as the 'locking' and in some places, as Nigrita, for example, where the silence rule is not observed, the action is accompanied by the following song, sung by a chorus of maidens both on the way to the fountain and round it, while the pitcher is filling. . . .

The locking of the vessel

Come together, oh be ye gathered together,
That we may lock the pitcher
With St. John's flower.
"Who planted thee? Who watered thee,
And thy blossoms are faded!"
"An old woman planted me, an old woman watered me,
Therefore my blossoms are faded."
"O Thomaë, dear Thomaë, thy daughter
Give her not to another youth."
"O Doukena, dear Doukena, I have betrothed her
To a Bulgarian gentleman,
To the one who owns a thousand sheep,
And three hundred heifers!"

The pitcher thus prepared, is exposed "to the light of the stars", or is placed under a rose-tree, where it remains during the night. Early next morning it is taken indoors and set in the corner of a room. In the afternoon of the festal day the young people assemble once more round the pitcher and proceed to 'unlock' it, accompanying the action with a variation of the same song. . . .

The unlocking of the vessel

Come together, oh be ye gathered together,
That we may unlock the pitcher, etc.

A little boy, the most guileless-looking that can be found, is appointed to lift off the kerchief, which is then thrown over his face, and thus blindfolded he dips his right hand into the pitcher. While the boy is doing this, one of the bystanders cries out: "We open the vessel. May good luck issue forth!" Then the boy draws out the first token, singing

"Whose token comes forth,
May they go to Serres and enjoy all manner of happiness."

The owner of this first token is cheered by the others and congratulated on his or her good luck. Then each of the company by turns or some one, generally an old woman well versed in Luck-lore, recites or improvises a couplet as each token is being drawn. In some districts, in lieu of couplets, they propound riddles. In either case the saying is considered as foreshadowing the future of the person to whom the token belongs. As may be imagined, all the predictions are not equally pleasing. Some of them are grotesque and sometimes even such as a more cultured audience would pronounce coarse. These give rise to many sallies of rustic wit at one another's expense.

The cucumber is drawn out last and eaten. Then the real broad farce begins. The tokens are flung back into the pitcher, and the company give free play to their sense of fun in the way of sayings which, when the circle is exclusively confined to married women, are neither meant nor meet for male ears. The festival generally ends with dancing and singing.

Source: *Macedonian Folklore* by G. F. Abbott. Cambridge: Cambridge Univ. Press, 1903, pp. 54-56.

Mexico

Midnight swims in Mexico City

In Mexico City and other cities, swimming parties are arranged by the teenagers on this night. Flowers are tossed into the pool, and musical groups play. Coffee and tamales are served afterward. In some areas the parties are outdoors near a stream; elsewhere they are near a swimming pool.

Cutting the hair on La Día de San Juan

Hair cut on this day will grow well; it will grow best if the cutting is done on the threshold.

San Juan weeps when it rains

It often rains on this day, and folks say that "*San Juan llora*" or St. John weeps. "But they are good tears," people add.

Source: *A Treasury of Mexican Folkways* by Frances Toor. New York: Crown, 1947, p. 233.

Norway

A turn-of-the-century midsummernight

One of the last summers before my emigration from Norway, I lived on an island in the Christiania fjord. At this place a group of us prepared a St. John's festival. We built an immense fire of logs and many old tar-barrels. The light was reflected far over the water, and could be seen both from the city and from hundreds of summer resorts on the surrounding islands. Beautiful was the sight of the many and different kinds of boats, which, from all directions, swiftly skimmed over the water to join our celebration. From the boats floated the strains of different musical instruments and the air being perfectly calm, the music on the water sounded charmingly. All the boats carried young men and maidens, and many of the latter were dressed in national costume. Below our great bonfire was a large level meadow. In the centre of this we built a smaller fire, and the dancing around it was continued all night.

The nights in Norway, at this season of the year, are so light that one may read until two o'clock in the morning without the use of arificial light.

On the many islands surrounding us were built hundreds of fires on the highest promontories and from afar one could observe shadow-like figures dancing as fairies around the fires. The spectator at such a festival enjoys the frolics, sports, and pastimes, and the various beautiful folk dances, as well as the spectacular sport by the boys and young men of leaping through the flame.

Source: *When I Was a Boy in Norway* by Dr. J. O. Hall. Boston: Lothrop, Lee & Shepard Co., 1921, pp. 167-168.

Paraguay

Fiesta de San Juan

Fortelling the future on San Juan's Eve

Many young girls believe thqt they may find out something about the man they will marry, a young man or an old one, blond or brunette, or may even find out the initials or occupation of a future husband by following certain rituals. Most of these rituals are carried out on the eve of San Juan's Day.

A cross of laurel leaves placed under the pillow will bring a dream of a future sweetheart.

Corn and beans may be planted on the eve of the Saint's day. If the corn grows, the girls who planted it will marry a foreigner, since corn is blond. If beans grow, it will be a Paraguayan, for beans are dark.

If a shoe thrown over the house lands upside down, the thrower will not marry within the year.

A green lime plucked from a tree by a blindfolded girl means marriage to a young husband; a ripe lime indicates marriage to an old man.

One old custom still common in the country, is telling fortunes from the forms taken by molten lead or candle dripppings dropped into a pan of water.

Source: *Hi Neighbor. Book 1.* United Nations. New York: United States Committee for UNICEF, p. 42.

Firewalking, c. 1980

It was June in Asuncion, Paraguay where I was spending a term as a Fulbright lecturer. My students had insisted that I attend a "special" festival on the edge of town. So there we all were making our way slowly through the attractions of a rather run-of-the-mill carnival, a common enough sight anywhere in the world. When the attractions began to pall, I was told to be patient, for around midnight I would see something I would not forget.

As the evening lengthened, groups began to congregate around fires in what seemed a spontaneous response to the chill and damp of a Paraguayan winter's night. Yet in moving closer to the warmth I noticed the fires were set in narrow, shallow barbeque-like pits around 10 feet long. Soon the flames died down and the bed of coals glowed fiercely; radiant heat flushed the faces of the encircling congregation. My students pushed me close to the fire and told me to wait and watch. The group stood silently, not stirring, illumined by the glow cast by the long bed of red hot coals. After a prolonged period of quiet and patient waiting, a young man slowly moved out of the crowd, took off his shoes, and carefully rolled up his trouser legs as though for wading; amid profound silence he walked barefoot and stood at the head of the bed of coals. After making several signs of the cross and intense silent prayer, the young man proceeded to walk across the length of the burning coals. He did not run, but walked briskly, barefoot, on top of the four to five inch deep bed of red-hot coals covering the length of the open pit. Once safe on the other side he fell into the arms of cheering friends, and so far as I or anyone could tell seemed none the worse for his ordeal. His feet did not appear to be burned. Soon others came forward one by one to walk barefoot across the bed of hot coals. Again, so far as I could tell, there seemed to be no immediate harmful effects, even though their bare feet made contact with burning embers.

Source: "Firewalking: From Sacred to Secular" by Marie L. Ahearn in *Journal of Popular Culture* 21:1 (Summer 1987), 11.

Peru

Inti Raymi in San Antonio de Pinchincha, Cuzco, Andahuaylas, and Apurimac valleys

This Incan festival of the Sun God coincides now with the Feast Day of St. John the Baptist, falling on June 24, South America's winter solstice. Bonfires are lit as the sun is reborn on this day, and old clothes are burnt, a sign of destroying poverty and ending the harvest cycle. In Cuzco there is a procession and mock sacrifice to the sun at Sacsayhuaman Fortress, a folkloric revival.

Source: *A Guide to World Fairs and Festivals* by Frances Shemanski. Westport, Conn.: Greenwood, 1985, pp. 149-150.

Sardinia

San Giovanni

The festival of San Giovanni in Fonni, Sardinia

On the day of the festival of S. Giovanni the whole village of Fonni assembled in its best costumes for the mass in the church: even the children, for the most part, wore the national and not the modern costume. After it was over the confraternity of the Madonna, all mounted on white horses, rode round the village with their banner, which was carried by one of their number, while the rest held the strings. The leader of the confraternity of S. John, also on horseback, carried a 'torta', or cake, on a small circular platter of wood with a handle below, which was concealed by festoons. Into the cake were stuck a number of sugar doves fixed on long spits of wood, which were afterwards distributed: we as honoured guests received one each. In the afternoon the horse-races took place up the main street of the village, and the whole crowd was there to see.

Source: *Some Italian Scenes and Festivals* by Thomas Ashby. New York: E. P. Dutton, p. 170.

Spain

Firewalking at San Pedro Manrique

At 9 p.m. the logs were only half consumed but the 'tower' of the fire started to sag and spread under the eye of the warden. The attraction for the young was the moment when the tower would topple over and the red embers scatter around. Crowds started to come up from the town and fill the seats of stone tiers, built around the grassy terrace where the fire-walking takes place. No grass can grow on the fire space, it is bare earth.

At 10.30 the tower of fire, now only about a metre and a half high, suddenly heaved over, to wild cries of joy from the onlookers. The fire wardens still watched it but didn't touch it until about eleven o'clock, when they brought out their long poles, the *hogueneros* or *foguеneros,*—oven poles some four to five metres long—which are still used in bakeries to put loaves in and out from the ovens in San Pedro Manrique. The wardens started then to sift through the red hot coals, or embers, for unburnt parts, sticks still smoking, stones, bits of brick, etc. These were jerked out of the fire, now spread to a blazing mass some 3-4 metres long by 1 1/2 metres wide and 12 cm deep. The heat was so fierce that a paper put a metre away from the hot embers would have burnt up. Sitting some six metres away, if someone stood between the fire and any onlooker, they felt the cold wind and were glad to feel the warmth once more when the person moved away.

Suddenly, at midnight, the band stopped playing and a trumpet sounded. The fire wardens retired a little from the burning mass, someone fanned the redhot embers with his jacket to remove the ash, and the glowing embers were ready. (Fanning the embers with a jacket was an act often repeated during the evening's fire-walking.)

The fire-walkers placed themselves with their back to the church, facing the cliff-wall (overlooking the town) with the back to the wind, and walked over the embers towards the cliff. The first to go across was a girl of eighteen, Irene Garcia, short, fair-haired, laughing incessantly. She hoisted one of the *móndidas* onto her back, and started stamping steadily towards the embers, from about a metre and a half away, and continued unhesitatingly walking to the other side of the embers, never stopping or altering her walk. Once over, she dropped her burden, with a cry the two girls embraced lustily while cries of joy and approbation rose from the crowd and the band struck up a tune while talking and shouting resumed. Blasita Espuelas, was the next girl to cross the embers, also carrying a woman, and they too embraced after crossing. A young man rushed and kissed them too, while another roar of approbation rose from the crowd. Blasita trod firmly and resolutely across the fire; she too was eighteen. Next followed a man, Vicente García, cousin of Irene, carrying a man on his back. He also trod the ground firmly and resolutely, never stopping until he reached the other side, and embraced his passenger after crossing.

All the walkers started their regular tread some distance before reaching the embers and walked about one step a second, or a little faster, treading firmly while some seemed to stamp across nearly two steps per second. Only one man changed to a jota-type step. He danced a bas-de-basque across, raising his arms as if dancing, and considered crossing the embers the one occasion a year when everyone made a fuss of him. He carried no one on his back. He had been crossing the embers for thirty-five years on end, and he was single. His name was Cirilo Garcia.

The last to cross was the seventeen-year-old baker's apprentice, Narciso, who had started walking the fire, 'la pasa del fuego', at the age of fourteen. He said he had never been burnt, except for the first time, and had crossed the fire for the last four years consecutively. When asked how it came about, he said (as they all do) that he had faith in the Virgin of *La Peña,* who would not let them get burnt. That year, 1969, Narciso carried the mayor across the embers, a hefty middle-aged man. One man carried his wife across, another crossed with a man on his back, and a boy on the back of that man. Some children get the urge to cross the fire, but they are not allowed to until they are fourteen unless they have the father's express consent.

Altogether some twelve men as well as the two girls, crossed the embers on 23 June 1969, at San Pedro Manrique. . . . Quico repeated that if you had faith in the Virgin of *La Peña,* she did not let you get burnt. He added 'tread firmly and with faith and no fear. Don't ever hesitate, nor go slowly, nor too quickly, just two steps per second and tread firmly and nothing can happen. If you are too slow or hesitate you do get burnt.'

Source: "Fire Walking at San Pedro Manrique, Spain" by Lucille Armstrong in *Folklore* 81 (Autumn 1970), pp. 198-214.

Midsummer's Eve in a Barcelona women students' hostel, c. 1940

From the flat roof of the Palacio on Midsummer Eve thirty-two Midsummer fires were visible, many actually in the streets of the city. One was enriched by a bomb—a not unusual occurrence there—which wrecked a near-by school and injured a few fire-leapers. The students spent most of the night on the roof, dancing and playing elaborate Singing Games which must have descended from mediaeval romances. It is significant that the words were in Castilian. One I remember built up a beautiful pattern of girls to represent a lady imprisoned in a Moorish castle. A lovely girl, whose name was Montserrat after the Black Virgin of the Mountain, stood on a chair placed against the wall; two joined her kneeling, one on either side, to represent her pages. The next verse introduced two Moors whose raised arms made a window through which the captive gazed towards her home. Each verse brought in other characters up to ten or twelve, everyone assuming their correct position and attitude, so that a symmetrical group grew before one's eyes rather like a *Château d'Amour* carved in ivory. Finally several Christian Knights rode up on imaginary horses, attacked the castle and delivered the lady. It was too dark even on that Midsummer night to write, but the whole is photographed in my memory.

Source: *The Singing of the Travels* by Violet Alford. London: Max Parrish, 1956, pp. 60-61.

Love omens

St. John's Day or Midsummer's Eve is supposedly a night of magic and soothsaying, celebrated in rural areas by fig-eating expeditions; groups of young people go out to gather and eat fresh figs after dark, making special wishes. On this evening, too, girls may make love tests: tear a fig leaf and, if the break heals overnight, one's true love will be found. Gather two shoots of wild artichokes and put them outside a window. If they have flowered by morning, true love will be serene. Spin a needle on the surface of a saucer of water. If it stays afloat, the boy to whom it points will be a love for life.

Obviously, young Spaniards—like most lovers in the world—find a touch of trouble stimulating to affection, since none of the tests can possibly bring positive results!

Source: *Spanish Roundabout* by Maureen Daly. New York: Dodd, Mead, 1961, p. 63.

Sweden

Midsommar

Midsummer Eve festivities

Midsommar is now celebrated on the Friday night nearest to June 24 in Sweden.

Cars, homes, pavilions, and churches are decorated with flower garlands and greenery on the morning of Midsummer Eve. In the afternoon crowds gather at the maypole, a tall pole with a circlet of leaves and flowers atop. Dancing takes place around the maypole, and continues into the evening, perhaps at an outdoor pavilion.

To forecast your true love on this night, pick seven or nine different wildflowers from as many different meadows and sleep with them under your pillow. You will dream of your future spouse. Or try eating "dream herring" or "dream porridge" with plenty of salt in it. On this night also the ferns bloom. And the dew of this night can cure illness.

Source: *Traditional Festivities of Sweden* by Ingemar Liman. Stockholm: The Swedish Institute, 1985, p. 27.

Midsummer pole

Out in a field, a tall pole lies outstretched while the women twine leafy branches round it and hang two circlets of flowers from its cross-bar. Then, in the afternoon, the entire village arrives: men in shirt sleeves, women and girls in soft gay frocks or the colourful dress traditional in the parish. The fiddler and accordionist are ready and strike up a lively Swedish air. With a shout from the on-lookers and a heave and push from the men, up goes the gigantic midsummer pole against the blue sky. Strong arms balance its swaying weight until it is firmly wedged upright.

Circle upon circle of boys and girls, men and women, join hands and dance round the bedecked pole, led by the fiddlers through the old tunes and the beloved children's songs. The youngsters laugh, and skirts ripple in the summer breeze.

There's magic abroad at Midsummer. The young girl who goes out into the fields and, in the covenant of unbroken silence, picks seven different kinds of flowers and tucks them under her pillow, will dream of her loved one to be.

Source: *Round the Swedish Year* by Lorna Downman, Paul Britten Austin, Anthony Baird. Stockholm: The Swedish Institute, Bokförlaget, 1967, pp. 41-42.

St. John's Day, c. 1910

Midsummer Eve! A happy warm glow of summer warmth and golden sunshine had transformed all Nature. The towns and the country alike seemed to be throbbing and tingling with life-joy. We decorated our houses, inside and out, and hung posies and wreaths and green garlands around the windows. The fireplaces were filled with huge branches of maple, and the corners of the living-rooms banked with green things and sheaves of wild flowers. Over our doorways and gates we erected arches of birch and maple, interlaced with chains of daisies and wild phlox.

But the most fascinating features of this Midsummer celebration were the ''magic ceremonies'' in which the young people liked to take part. These ceremonies usually took place after sundown on the night of June twenty-third. Pagan spells were woven. Fairies and all the unseen forces in Nature were about and eager to help those who had faith in their power to aid mortals in attaining their wishes.

Usually one chose a faithful chum to take part in those magic functions which had previously been decided on as being most potent. Because every normal Swedish girl, as soon as she put up her hair and lengthened her frock, begins to dream of a home of her own, of a husband and babies (a spinster is almost a disgrace in this country), most of the Midsummer Night spells were supposed to enable one to look into the future and see one's mate.

Blenda, my adored pal and leader, and I went through some of those mysterious rites during my last Midsummer Night spent in Sweden. I was fifteen at the time and had been confirmed the previous year, so I felt myself to be a full-fledged *Fröken.*

We had decided on a ''silence-round'' as being the most interesting, dangerous, and romantic. I had taken Mother into my confidence, for the family had to be warned not to speak to me after the sun was no longer visible that evening. But my sister Constance impishly tried every trick she could think of to make me break silence. At last, with Mother's sympathetic coöperation, I managed to get away from the house without having uttered a word.

I met Blenda at the appointed place, a little way out of town. Each one carried with her an empty water tumbler carefully wrapped in paper. Our first task was to climb nine rail-fences and to pick a different herb or flower near each fence. These growing things were to be woven into a magic wreath to be put under our pillows to dream on, and our respective future husbands would appear before us in a vision. We were also to walk sun-wise nine times around a vacant building, while reciting a magic formula. For an empty building, we chose the tiny Gospel Chapel used by the Baptists. So far all had gone well; we wove our spell around this humble place of worship.

Next we had to find a well or a spring where our water tumblers could be filled. The Baptist pump was pressed into service. Dire misfortune would befall us if one single drop of water were spilled on the ground before we reached the crossroad where we were to sit and wait for *things to happen.* A crossroad a little way farther out in the country had previously been selected. After we had carefully filled our tumblers at the Baptist pump, we made high collars from the paper in which our tumblers were wrapped and, with these collars fortifying the rims to prevent splashing, we set off for the crossroad. Of course we did not speak to each other, but how we did giggle as we tried to convey ideas to one another! We met a few youthful couples seemingly bent on some ''magic'' errand of their own, because they pretended not to see us, and for this we were grateful.

Finally we arrived at the crossroad, where we sat down with our precious water. If our hearts beat twice as fast as is normal, it must be known that this most potent ''magic'' would, on the stroke of midnight, cause our future husbands to appear before us, drain our tumblers, and rush off. It was our task to follow, and try to get a good look at the man who appeared—so that we would be sure to refuse all other suitors.

At last, on the balmy air we heard the distant town-clock boom out twelve midnight strokes. Scarcely had the last note stopped vibrating when, from down the hillside in front of us two white-robed, masked shapes came tearing, as if chased by mad bulls. They fairly flew towards us, and their footfalls hardly seemed like those of flesh-and-blood beings. I was shivering with fear, and my scalp tingled.

Automatically Blenda and I sprang to our feet. Each one of the uncanny creatures grabbed a tumbler and seemed to dispose of the contents in great gulps. The face masks, decorated in the weirdest manner and fringed at the lower edges, were only slightly raised when the water was disposed of.

They turned about swiftly and then ran with incredible speed down the road towards town, Blenda and I following. But apparently in a few moments they realized that they would soon be overtaken, and so stopped and faced us.

Blenda, brave Blenda, reached out and snatched away the masks. And since this is to be in all respects a true account, I am forced to state that those two white-draped figures were only two of our girl friends; Constance had mischievously told Hilma and Edla that we were to try some magic ''stunts.'' We all laughed. Then Edla gave us a note from Fru Nyholm, Blenda's mother, inviting us to come to the Nyholm home to spend the night and try some more ''magic.''

Still in silence but with happy chuckles we returned to town. Fru Nyholm received us and invited us out to the kitchen where she conveyed by signs and nods the idea that we were to make ''dream-pancakes.'' Blenda and I also had our bunches of growing things to dispose of first of all, so we went to my chum's room and hurriedly made our wreaths in the dark, laying them carefully under our pillows. Then we returned to the kitchen.

''Dream-pancakes'' are said to contain wonderful potencies. The recipe is: Three tablespoonfuls of flour, three tablespoonfuls of salt, and water enough to make a batter that will spread on the griddle. All who are to eat these cakes must hold the spoon when the ingredients are measured; they must all help to stir the batter, grease the griddle, pour the batter, and turn the pancakes. But above all, not a word must be uttered during the whole performance. Each participant must eat three of these very salty little cakes and go to sleep without taking a drink of water. Then in the dream the future mate will come with a glassful of water. Eagerly we carried out the program. Then, just as we were about to slip between the sheets, into the room came Fru Nyholm carrying a tray on which stood four tumblers half full of water, and a blue bowl with four eggs. She made signs to us to break the eggs, drop the whites into the water and the yolks into the blue bowl. This we did. Surely we had done enough "magic stunts" to feel that our fortunes, or rather our futures, would be revealed during this Midsummer season.

Fru Nyholm made some queer signs above each one of the water tumblers as she placed it by our bedsides. Then she kissed us all good-night and left us.

Next morning at the breakfast table our hostess interpreted for each one of us the meaning of the strangely pretty figures formed by the whites of each egg dropped in the water. Edla was to marry a doctor and travel for pleasure now and then; we all saw the delicate surgical instruments, also a railroad train at the very bottom of the tumbler. Poor Hilma would become an old maid—from choice, Fru Nyholm added. Blenda would marry a jeweler and silversmith; we all saw strings of pearls and fanciful shapes of delicate design and fine tools such as jewelers work with. For me there would be a long voyage and an early marriage to a bookish man. Plainly I could see the man in my own tumbler, and naturally, that was the important thing.

But alas for my carefully gathered posies of nine kinds on which I slept during the night! They caused me to shed many tears when, after breakfast, I helped Blenda make our bed. For an evil chance had caused me to put among my collection a stalk of a plant which was literally covered with the squashiest kind of green and full-grown caterpillars. Blenda laughed until her mother thought she would become hysterical, and I wept from vexation and shame, for the pillow-case and undersheet were fearsome to see, what with that sickly green smear of crushed insects.

Out in the country, Midsummer is celebrated with the raising of the May-pole—although May-day is past. The most popular and pretty girl in the village was always crowned "Midsummer bride." The May-pole was usually erected by the most prominent farmer, who also gave an all-night dance accompanied with abundant food and strong drink. The music consisted of accordion, flute, and violin. This night in the country was wholly given over to the frolic of the young people, many engagements were the result. Also not a few bloody encounters between rivals, "scraps," which occurred as a rule between sailors and the country lads. The latter rightfully resented having these smart sailors carry off their girls merely to amuse themselves with for a little while, for they seldom married the country girls, and of course the sailors were quick to draw their knives in defense of their temporary sweethearts.

Source: *When I Was a Girl in Sweden* by Anna-Mia Hertzman. Boston: Lothrop, Lee & Shepard Co., 1926, pp. 106-112.

For more on St. John's Day/Eve or Midsummer's Day/Eve see: "Día de San Juan," in *Fiesta Time in Latin America* by Jean Milne. Los Angeles: Ward Ritchie Press, 1965, pp. 98-103; "Midsummer," in *The Customs and Ceremonies of Britain* by Charles Kightly. London: Thames and Hudson, 1986, pp. 163-165; "Midsummer Festivities," in *Of Swedish Ways* by Lilly Lorenzen. Minneapolis: Dillon Press, 1964, pp. 255-259; "St. John's or Midsummer's Day, June 24" in *Folklore of American Holidays* edited by Hennig Cohen and Tristram Potter Coffin. 2nd ed. Detroit: Gale Research, 1991.

June 25

Saban Tuy (Festival of the Plow)

This is a Mongolian spring farming celebration held on the anniversary of when the Tatar Republic was established. The festival is held in Kazan on the Volga River.

U.S.S.R. (Tatar Autonomous Soviet Socialist Republic)

The greased pole climb

A cock is set in a cage atop a tall pole. Young men attempt to climb the greased pole and fetch down the cock.

Smashing the crocks

A blindfolded player is given a stick and whirled until he is dizzy. He then tries to smash a set of earthenware crocks set out on the ground. Each crock contains a prize inside. The prizes might be a pair of socks, a shirt, or a small radio.

Horse racing

The highlight of the festival is the horse race. Riders are blindfolded ''to keep the wind out'' as they race across the plains.

Source: *A Parade of Soviet Holidays* by Jane Werner Watson. Champaign, Ill.: Garrard, 1974, pp. 59-60.

June 29

Day of St. Peter and St. Paul

St. Peter and St. Paul were both martyred on this day. Peter, originally named Simon, was named Kephas by Jesus. This Aramaic word means "rock"; hence the English translation Peter. Peter was a disciple of Jesus and a founder of the church. St. Paul, originally a persecuter of Christians, was converted on the road to Damascus and became a founder of the early Christian church.

Chile

San Pedro in Valparaiso, Chile

This procession has been celebrated since 1682. A parade of fishermen and others who make their living on the water, military bands, and various civil and religious organizations takes place. The procession begins on the land, reaches the bay, and goes aboard a barge to tour in a water procession, followed by boats decorated with flowers and flags, some carrying musical groups.

Source: *Folklore Chileno* by Oreste Plath. Santiago: Nascimento, 1969, pp. 341-342. (See this source for San Pedro customs from several Chilean towns.)

Malta

Mnarja

Feat of St. Peter and St. Paul

The feast is traditionally a harvest festival, the origins of which are lost in the mist of Time. It is still held at Buskett, a wooded park not far from Mdina, Malta's mediaeval capital.

Mnarja used to be one of the most important and popular feasts in the annual calendar of events, so much so that on the wedding day, the husband had to promise his new bride to take her to Buskett on Mnarja-day every year.

The festivities open on the eve, when open air folk singing and folk music competitions are held at Buskett Gardens. Maltese dishes are served for the occasion but fried rabbit is the traditional speciality of the evening.

An agrarian show is held on the eve (between 1600 hrs.-2400 hrs.) and during the morning (0700 hrs.-12 noon) on the 29th June. Horse and donkey races, ridden bareback, are held in the afternoon near Mdina. The races bring the festivities to an end.

Mnarja is derived from "Luminaria", meaning illumination, because in times goneby, the bastions around Mdina used to be illuminated by bonfires to mark the event.

Source: "Malta & Gozo: Events Calendar '90" National Tourism Organization, 1990.

Imnarja, a Harvest festival

Besides the local parochial 'festas', there are others which are celebrated on a national scale. The 'Imnarja' (a corruption of Italian 'luminaria' (illumination), a Harvest festival which is celebrated on June 29, is characterized by a night-long picnic at Buskett Gardens, Rabat on the eve of which the native dish, stewed rabbit, is consumed in large quantities, accompanied by equally large volumes of wine. Exhibits of local agricultural produce, band marches, decorated carts and folklore singing competitions enliven the night-long proceedings. The following day, the festivities reach a climax when bare-back donkey and horse races are held in the street leading to Rabat. The prizes awarded for these races are paljj (brocaded banners) which the winners traditionally donate to their village church.

Source: "Malta: Where the Sun Shines from the Heart." Malta National Tourist Office.

Paraguay

San Pedro and San Juán

Games and church celebrations

Two other large festivals are those of San Juán and San Pedro, which fall on June 24 and June 29. The religious part of the celebrations involves the usual Masses and, in the case of San Pedro, a procession, but the games played on these two days are special because of the association of San Juán with the fire miracle. In former times one of the features of the profane fiesta was walking barefoot over live coals, but this has been discontinued in recent years. Children do build a great many bonfires and run about with burning torches as a preliminary to the regular games held in the street before the home of the *mayordomo*.

The more traditional, almost ritual games include most typically the *cambá* in a simulated bullfight with the *toro candil*. The bull is made of a light frame covered with hide with a bull's skull fixed in front; the horns are covered with rags which are soaked in kerosene and lighted. When the man in the *toro candil* dashes around in the night chasing the crowds, the flaming horns make a fearsome sight. Some of the *cambá* taunt the bull, while others stand around playing their flutes and drums. On this occasion, the *cambá* are called "San Juán."

Two other apparitions usually appear at these games, a *ñandú guazú* (rhea) and a man representing a Guaycurú Indian. The *ñandú* consists of a small cage of wood covered with leaves to represent feathers and surmounted by a long stick for a neck. Another small piece of wood simulates the small head and beak of the bird. A child inside the cage walks around inside the circle of spectators and bobs the neck and head down to peck at the *toro* from behind, harassing him while he chases the San Juáns. The Guaycurú, in outlandish rag costume and blackened face, meanwhile dashes around, pretending to kidnap women. Some of the *cambá* chase women with blazing torches; the total effect is one of great activity in the huge crowd, and there is much screaming and laughter.

These games have become part of the celebrations of both San Juán and San Pedro, but they are supposed to be more appropriate to San Juán. San Pedro is the patron of Tobatí and supposedly has attributes different from those of San Juán.

The church celebration for San Pedro is more formal. By long-standing local custom the procession of the Corpus Christi (which should be on June 16) is held on the morning of the day of San Pedro. Each of the four corners of the church plaza is decorated with leaves of palm, laurel, and flowers. The procession stops for prayers at each of these four *sitiales*, after which the people take the leaves home for medicines and the flowers as offerings to their household saints. In some towns the *sitiales* are made of manioc, banana, and sugar-cane plants, and tables are heaped with garden products; it is believed that the blessings will insure good crops in the coming year. In the afternoon the procession of San Pedro is held.

Source: *Tobatí: Paraguayan Town* by Elman R. Service and Helen S. Service. Chicago: The Univ. of Chicago Press, 1954, pp. 191-192.

Peru

Día de San Pedro Y San Pablo

The fishermen's festival in Callao

Saints Peter and Paul were martyred on the same day; thus they share the same feast day. Fishing villages throughout Latin America celebrate especially in honor of Saint Peter, because he was a fisherman and is a popular patron saint of fishermen. Processions of decorated boats carry an image of Saint Peter. Often a special altar is arranged on a float or on shore with shell and seaweed decorations. In Callao, Peru the mayordomos of the fiesta fish during the fluvial procession and donate their catch to adorn the saint's litter.

Source: *Fiesta Time in Latin America* by Jean Milne. Los Angeles: The Ward Ritchie Press, 1965, p. 104.

Trinidad

Fishermen celebrate

For the fishermen, of whatever faith, and the villagers, St. Peter's day is a festive occasion. The boats first go out to the fishing ground, if weather permits, to obtain fish to be given the poor. When they return to the jetty, the Anglican minister awaits them. It is a gay sight, the boats flying red, white, and blue flags, and people in their best clothes. As the boats are slowly rowed out to sea and back to shore, the minister prays and blesses the sea, and hymns are sung. "People cook, have rum. All kind of thing." They eat at the cove, and all who come are fed, while rum and food are "thrown away" in "all corners" and in the bay, also. "After they eat done, they take people for rides in the boats. Go out an' come back." If the fishermen are able to provide a "band," social dances are held. But after the minister leaves, "Then dance the bongo and bele dances," to honor the saint.

Source: *Trinidad Village* by Melville J. Herskovits and Frances S. Herskovits. New York: Alfred A. Knopf, 1947, p. 177.

June 30

Fandroana

This is a ritual celebrated in Madagascar. The feast originated in the sixteenth century under the realm of King Ralambo.

Madagascar

A ritual bath and feast

This feast has been celebrated since at least the sixteenth century and is said to have been started by King Ralambo, who wished to celebrate the fine meat of his herd. In early days a prince would eat the meat of an unborn calf, taken from the womb of its mother. This gave the eater the possibilities of the new life inherent in the unborn animal. As soon as the words ''The King is taking a bath'' were heard, the celebration could begin. Today the feast features beef, the fully grown variety.

Source: *International What's What When & Where* by Ardith Nehrt. Columbus, Ohio: Shawnee International Publishing, 1965, p. 108.

Moon 8, Waning Day–Moon 11, Full Moon (June/July to September/October)

Vossa / Khao Vatsa / Waso

This is a three-month period of religious retreat for Buddhist monks, and lay novitiates. It is also a Lenten season of devotions, sermons, and daily temple visits. Abstinence from liquors and frivolous delights is required of the religious. This period coincides with the rainy season.

On this day, Prince Siddhartha was conceived, renounced his life of luxury, and preached his First Sermon, the Dhammacakka Sutra.

Burma/Myanmar

Waso

Offerings to monks

What could be more meritorious than to make it possible for the *Bhikkus* to devote themselves to study and meditation with the minimum of hindrance and inconvenience? The offering of *Waso* candles and *Waso* robes to the *Bhikkus* for use during the retreat is indeed regarded as possessing particular merit. Though there is no specific day for the offerings to be made, the Full Moon Day of *Waso* is considered by some to be an auspicious or at least convenient occasion particularly with regard to venerable *Sayadaws*. For, today we commemorate the First Sermon of the Enlightened One, the Dhammacakka Sutta, and the most profoundly auspicious way of commemorating it has been to invite learned *Bhikkus,* the venerable *sayadaws,* to give the sermon again. This is therefore the traditional time for the offerings to be made to the *sayadaws*.

Lay persons' activities on Waso

The Full Moon Day of *Waso* is once again with us today. Thousands and thousands of Buddhists all over the country will go about their self-imposed religious tasks, getting up before dawn to take the Sabbath, to make offerings, to feed the *Sangha,* to listen to sermons, or to spend the day in quiet contemplation. It is a day imbued with an atmosphere of piety and religiousness, a fitting remembrance for the day when the *Dhamma* was for the first time revealed to humanity.

Source: "The Full Moon of Waso" editorial from The Woring People's Diary in *We the Burmese: Voices from Burma* by Helen G. Traeger. New York: Frederick A. Praeger, 1965, p. 275.

Wazo Festival

Wazo Fullmoon Day is a big day for Buddhists. Gautama Buddha, after realising the Four Noble Truths in the year 103 preached the First Sermon, the Dhammasakka Suta, to the five mendicants in the Migadawon Forest near Benares on Wazo Fullmoon day. The gist of the Sermon is that suffering takes root in life due to attachment. The attachment can be cut off by means of the Eightfold Path of the Middle Way.

On Wazo Fullmoon Day, Gautama Buddha departed for Tavatimsa, where in repaying the debt of gratitude owed to the Santussita nat who was once his mother, he preached the Abhidhamma to the nat and brahma till Fullmoon Day of Thadingyut.

From Wazo Fullmoon Day till Thadingyut Fullmoon Day monks have to go into retreat in their monasteries. So for being the day on which Buddha preached the first Sermon on the Turning of the Wheel of the Law, for being the day on which Buddha initiated the teaching of the Abhidhamma and for being the day on which monks begin the Retreat, the people revere the Buddha and offer Wazo flowers and Wazo robes, observe the precepts and meditate in keeping with tradition.

Source: Embassy of the Union of Myanmar.

Cambodia

Vossa

Candle ceremony

The ceremony of the *tien vossa* (candle of the *vossa*) took place at different times of day at the different monasteries. At Kdaing Ngea, where I had witnessed the ordination ceremony, the villagers appointed one of themselves to make the candle. The idea was that the candle should remain alight throughout the three-month period of the Vossa.

Village celebration

When I arrived in the village of Kdaing Ngea, another nearby monastery was already celebrating the festival. A procession was making its way downstream—three canoe-like craft pulling a larger boat to the accompaniment of tinkling xylophones and ringing gongs. The larger boat was decorated with coloured paper, and I could just see the candle, a comical object about the height of a long-handled cricket bat, and gaily decorated like a *baysei*.

Now the villagers assembled for the procession. . . . Many of them carried presents for the Buddhist monks. The traditional present at the Entry into the Vossa is a piece of yellow stuff, called a *sadok*. This is for the monk to wear when washing himself. By the end of the rainy season much of the colour has usually faded from these garments. But now they were bright yellow, folded in picturesque shapes by the villagers, some like the flower of a lotus, others like the uneven surface of a pineapple. Each monk would receive a kind of Vossa-hamper—without the hamper—which included ink, paper, medicine and several bottles of aerated water. These presents were arranged on trays and looked very attractive. . . . There was a volley of gunfire, and we moved clockwise round the temple. Monks were visible in the buildings beyond. Some were busy robing, and I saw the newly ordained novice of the previous day watching the procession with interest. There were five drums carried by vagabondish-looking boys. When we had completed three circuits round the temple, the litter bearing the candle was set down carefully and the white tapes removed. The trays of presents were taken inside together with nine four-gallon cans, seven of which contained paraffin and two-oil. These would be offered at the same time as the candle. The monks entered and sat down in six rows facing the candle. The scene was colourful—two splashes of yellow, the shiny yellow paint on the huge image of Buddha, and the more opaque yellow of the monks' robes. The Khmer villagers sat round in a horse-shoe, venerating these wearers of the yellow toga and praying earnestly that their actions would bring great merit. In return for the gifts, the monks faced the people and prayed loud and clear for a few minutes. . . .

Source: *Mistapim in Cambodia* by Christopher Pim. London: Hodder & Stoughton, 1960, pp. 86, 88-89.

For more information on Vossa in Cambodia see: ''Entering the Vossa'' in *Mistapim in Cambodia* by Christopher Pim. London: Hodder & Stoughton, 1960, pp. 81-90.

Laos

Khao Vatsa

Khao Vatsa in Laos

Khao Vatsa, the beginning of a period of *sangha* retreat in the eighth Laotian month (the full moon of July), coincides with the height of the rainy season. During Khao Vatsa, processions are held by the clergy and the laity. There is little rejoicing because the bonzes, so important in the life of the village, are about to go into retreat for three months.

Source: *Laos: A Country Study* by Donald P. Whitaker et al. Foreign Area Studies. Washington, D.C.: The American University, 1971, p. 122.

Thailand

Waso

Buddhist Lent among the villagers

The three-and-a-half month period of Buddhist Lent opens ordinarily about the middle of June, when the moon begins to wane. The most important days are *Khao Wasa* and *Ok-Barnsa,* respectively the first and last days of the lenten period. Many religious observances are celebrated by the monks, but among the laity only older villagers attend special ceremonies. On the morning of the days when regular lenten services are held in the *vihara,* villagers come bearing gifts of food, money, incense, and flowers to the *wat.* After presenting food to the monks, they retire to the temple. The old people, who spend each lenten *Wan Pra* in the *wat,* sit in the front of the congregation. All Buddhists are expected to display unusual devotion during Lent—to sleep in the *wat* on the eve of each *Wan Pra* and to pass the holy day in the *wat* in attendance at the services. White garments are supposed to be worn on *Wan Pra* throughout the year but particularly during Lent. However, it is only old people who observe the regulations about sleeping in the *wat* and wearing white clothing (which even this devout group wears usually only during Lent), and usually only old people, women, and girls attend the *Wan Pra* services, for the lenten season falls at the time when villagers are busiest in the fields. Old people who sleep in the *wat* on the vigil of the twelve *Wan Pra* days of Lent also sleep there on New Year's Night (*Wan Paya Wan*) and on the eves of the festivals of *Visaka Buja, Loi Katong, Makka Buja,* and the offering for new rice.

The lenten *Wan Pra* begins with an early morning service in the *vihara* conducted by old men who were once monks. After this service, the younger women and girls return home, leaving the old men and women in the *wat.* After lunch people gather in the *vihara* for another service conducted by the monks. The first and last days of Lent are national holidays, on which special services are conducted by the monks, and on the evening of the last day the devout light many candles and tiny lamps in their homes and in the *wat.*

Previously, the important ceremony known officially as *Tot Kathin* (literally ''laying down of the holy cloth'') began at the second half of the lunar month of October and continued for one lunar month. During this time robes and other gifts were presented to the *wat.*

Source: *Village Life in Modern Thailand* by John E. deYoung. Berkeley: Univ. of California, 1955, p. 137.

The Lenten candle

Before the lenten days begin the people cast a big candle of molten beeswax. The ceremony may take place at a village or, as is usually the case at the present time, in the compound of a wat. This candle, called the lenten candle, is lighted and kept burning continuously throughout the three months of the lenten period. If the lenten candle is cast in the village, it is borne in a decorated cart or other conveyance with a procession to a wat, where there is a celebration. People also present articles to the monks as befits the occasion. These things are decorated with artificial flowers and leaves of varied colors and designs.

Source: *Life and Ritual in Old Siam* by Phya Anuman Rajadhon. New Haven: HRAF Press, 1961, p. 95.

Moon 6, Day 6

Airing the Classics

This Buddhist day is for tending to monastic library collections. In tropical climates, books are particularly susceptible to mold and vermin.

China

Airing the library books

The "Double Sixth" is purely a Buddhist observance known as Airing the Classics, in commemoration of a disaster which overtook the scriptures on their journey from India. The boat carrying the pilgrims upset at a river crossing, and the books had to be spread out to dry after their immersion. In all monasteries the library books are taken from their shelves and examined, to prevent mould and the ravages of noxious insects. In the days of the Empire this day was also chosen for going through the Imperial archives. Women wash their hair, and give baths to their pets.

Source: *Chinese Creeds and Customs* by V. R. Burkhardt. Hong Kong: South China Morning Post, 1982, p. 39.

Moon 6, Day 15

Yoodoonal (Shampoo Day)

On this day all should repair to the countryside to bathe and to wash hair in the cool streams and waterfalls.

Korea

Cold Water Shampoo Day

The fifteenth day of the sixth moon is Yoodoonal or Shampoo Day. Villagers go out to streams and waterfalls to spend the day bathing in the cool water and shampooing their hair. Whoever cools his head and body on this day will not suffer from heat or fever during the coming year.

Since the Silla Dynasty, scholars have gone on Yoodoonal outings to picnic, drink wine, and compose poems.

Macaroni and wheat flour cakes are made on this day. They are offered at family shrines along with melons and other fruits of the season.

Source: *Folk Customs and Family Life* by Tai Hung Ha. Seoul, Korea: Yonsei, 1963, p. 77.

Moon 6, Day 24

Birthday of the Lotus

Buddha envisioned man as rising like the lotus from mud to blossom at the lake's surface. Buddha himself appears seated on a lotus throne. The lotus is one of the Eight Treasures depicted on the sole of the Buddha's foot. This is a day to honor the lotus.

China

Viewing the Lotus in Peking

The birthday of flowers in general is celebrated on the twelfth, or in some provinces the fifteenth, of the Second Moon, and their protectress, Wei Shen, is honoured on the 19th of the Fourth, the day being known as the ''washing of the blossoms''. The Lotus, however, having a special sanctity, on account of its connection with Buddhism, enjoys an anniversary of its own on the 24th of the Sixth Moon when the summer rains are expected to break in the North. Its blooming in the ponds and moats around Peking, particularly in the once Royal enclosures, is a sign that the prayers to the Dragon Prince have borne fruit, and that the moisture necessary for an abundant harvest has been showered on the parched earth. Viewing the lotus is to the inhabitants of the capital what the cherry blossom is to the Japanese, and crowds invade the lakes of the Winter Palace to enjoy the pink blossom through which lanes are cut to facilitate the passage of rowing boats.

Source: *Chinese Creeds and Customs* by V. R. Burkhardt. Hong Kong: South China Morning Post, 1982, p. 40.

July (May to October, peaking in July)

Festa Season

Malta

Five-day festivities

Each town and village parish church in the Maltese Islands is dedicated to a patron saint. The 'festa' (feast) commemorating the saint is celebrated by the village every year. The five-day festivities include the "triduum," the eve of the feast and the feast-day itself. Apart from the church services, the celebrations are highlighted by outdoor festivities, marked by band marches and spectacular fireworks displays. Some sea-side towns also organise the 'greasy-pole'. Streets and even homes are specially decorated and the Parish Church embellished with damask, chandeliers and silverware, is a 'must' to see. The climax of the 'festa' is reached on the feast-day (normally falling on a Sunday) when the artistic life-size statue of the Saint is carried shoulder high along the village streets.

Source: "Malta & Gozo: Events Calendar '90." National Tourism Organization, 1990.

Decorations, processions, and fireworks

Between May and October every town and village in Malta and Gozo celebrates the feast day or 'festa' of its patron saint. The festa is the most important event in each village's annual calendar and the villagers eagerly look forward to this very special day.

Considerable preparation goes into these celebrations. The village church, which is the pride of every villager, is draped with red damask and decorated with beautiful flowers. All its gold and silver treasures, as well as the crystal chandeliers are put on display thus creating a fitting setting for the statue of the patron saint which is placed in a prominent position in the Church. The church facade is illuminated with hundreds of multicolored bulbs, as also are the streets, across which are suspended massive and colourful drapes. Hundreds of flags are flown on roof tops whilst drapes and light bulbs are hung across the width of the covered balconies which are typical of Maltese traditional houses. The houses on the main streets, through which the religious procession passes, are generally given a fresh coat of paint for the occasion, and on festa day are lit up and adorned so that they look their best.

There is a three-day build-up to the feast and the atmosphere throughout is one of gaiety and merriment. On the festa day, as the statue of the saint is carried shoulder-high along the streets of the village the church bells ring and several massed bands play marches. Children throw confetti from balconies on to the passing procession. The nougat and candy-floss stands make excellent business whilst the crowds walk up and down the village streets stopping every now and then for a drink or to greet an old friend. The noise becomes quite deafening as the statue is about to re-enter the church; at this stage noisy but colourful fireworks are let off in abundant quantities. The Maltese specialise in the manufacture of fireworks and, in Maltese inter-village rivalry, fireworks often constitute the bench mark for comparing the success of the various festas. During the summer season there is a festa practically every weekend and no holidaymaker to Malta should leave the Island without experiencing one.

Source: "Malta: Where the Sun Shines from the Heart." Malta National Tourist Office.

Late June to Early September

Powwow

Saskatchewan, Canada (Native American)

Singing and dancing groups compete

Powwows are held today in many areas of Canada and the United States. Each is sponsored by a local Indian association and draws participants from a wide area. Many individuals camp on the powwow grounds during the event. Singing and dancing groups from several areas may compete in these secular festivals.

A Saskatchewan powwow

While each celebration is unique in at least some respects, a powwow held by the local urban Indian association in the Prarie city of Parklund [a fictitious name] can be used to illustrate the chain of events that constitutes a more or less typical Western Canadian powwow. On Friday afternoon and evening carloads of Indians from various locations in Western Canada and the United States began arriving at the powwow site, which was situated at the Parklund Exhibition Ground on the outskirts of the city. At the site a large canvas fly had been erected upon posts over the dancing area. Piles of firewood were stacked some distance away. As the cars from different reserves and cities arrived, these were directed by members of the Powwow Committee to the campgrounds where the visitors pitched their tents and teepees and parked their campers. By 6.00 p.m. some thirty tents had been set up including some from Arizona, Montana and North Dakota. The arrival of cars, trucks and buses and the camp-making continued through Friday evening into Saturday.

The morning comes early at powwow. Just before sunrise a group of men went from tent to tent, singing people awake. By this time there were forty-eight tents and truck-campers and seventeen teepees set up on the grounds. Shortly after eight o'clock the Powwow Committee brought in a truck load of rations and sorted them into hampers, each of which contained a day's supply of food for one family. The rations were piled into a pickup truck which was driven from tent to tent as the president and vicepresident of the Committee personally delivered a hamper of food to each family. . . .

Shortly before 10.30 a.m. it was announced over the public address system that all veterans of the armed services should assemble at the head of the dancing area for the flag raising ceremony. About twenty American and Canadian Indian veterans formed a circle around the three flagpoles which had been erected behind the sound booth. Prior to the raising of the three flags, the Union Jack, flanked by the Stars and Stripes and the Red Maple Leaf flag—the announcer explained that this ceremony was very important to Indians because these were the flags under which their people had signed treaties and served their countries. A small crowd of campers stood quietly by as the Mosquito Singers sang the Canadian Indian Honorary Song, the veterans stood to attention and the flags were slowly raised. With this done, the announcer welcomed the guests to the Parklund Urban Indian Association's Fourth Annual Powwow. He also mentioned that the hand game would soon be starting under the big top, and that dancers and groups of singers should register at the sound booth. . . .

Shortly after supper, dancers and singers once again assembled at the dancing area and the dancing and singing recommenced. By 10.00 p.m. the tempo of the music and action had been greatly intensified, and there were few people on the site who were not either performing or watching the action under the big top. All twelve groups of singers, each group numbering from four to ten singers, where arranged along the side of the area. Including children, there were around two hundred and fifty dancers under the big top, although only for certain warmups were all the performers on the floor at the same time. Interspersed with the warmups were war dances, which allowed the male dancers to demonstrate their skills, and a number of slow and fast grass dances in which both men and women took part. As the evening drew on, many of the children were put to bed and the dancing came to a peak. The highlight of the evening came when the Red Eagle Brothers of the Crow Agency, Montana, gave an exhibition of 'fancy' synchronized dancing—a style which is not often seen in Canada. Just before midnight it was announced that the official proceedings would come to an end in a few minutes, and a circle dance was initiated in which dancers and the remaining singers joined hands and danced in a circle around the area. Following an extended encore, when some of the spectators joined in the circle dance, most of the performers and the members of the audience headed towards their tents or back into the town to turn in.

But the lights remained on at the big top, and a small crowd of teenagers and young people clustered around a makeshift group of singers to sing "forty-niners" or fun songs. One of the most popular of the forty-niners was:

> "Oh, yes, I love you honey dear
> "I don't care if you're married sixteen times
> "I'll get you yet
> "I love you honey dear."

After a while the session broke up and small groups and couples filtered off into the bushes to do some drinking and courting.

The pattern of events on Sunday morning was similar to that of the previous day. Rations were issued, the flag ceremony was repeated and the hand game was played again. At 1.00 p.m., however, an appeal was made from the sound booth asking people to come to the big top as the ''give away'' would be held in a short time. In a few minutes virtually every person on the grounds headed toward the dancing area to watch the proceedings.

The nine leading members of the Powwow Committee and their wives were seated on a line of benches located at the head of the dancing area, just in front of the sound booth. Behind the benches, the Committee members had stacked piles of blankets, sleeping bags, household items, folding camp chairs and cloth. A microphone had been set up just in front of the benches. During the hour and a half that the ''give away'' lasted, the announcer—a well-known singer and dancer from another part of the province—handled all of the speaking duties. One after another, visitors to the powwow were called forth to receive gifts or money from the seated Committee members. As the various visitors were called to come forward, the Committee member giving the gift handed it to the announcer who then gave it to the recipient, shook his hand, and explained to the audience why the gift had been given. Then the recipient, holding his gift, went down the line of Powwow Committee members, shaking hands with each member. This process was repeated twenty-three times. Immediately after the last gift was given, the Frog Lake Singers sang an honorary song and the Committee members slowly shuffled around the dancing area. As they danced, they were identified to the large audience by the announcer as being ''the people who made this powwow possible.''

Source: ''Powwow and the Expression of Community in Western Canada'' by Noel Dyck. Ethnos, 1979: 1-2, pp. 78-79.

July

Nazareth Baptist Church Festival

This is one of the three annual festivals of the Nazareth Baptist Church, founded in 1911 by Isaiah Shembe. Shembe, who grew up as a farmhand in the Harrismith district of the Orange Free State, received directions for the songs and dances of these festivals through "voices" he heard. The sect has over five hundred thousand members.

South Africa

July festival at Ematabetulu village near Inanda in 1980

Central to the church's calendar are the three annual festivals: the October festival at Judia near Ginginglovu, the January festival at the mountain Inhlangakazi, and the July festival in the new village at Ematabetulu near Inanda. All aspects of worship, including details of dress and the number of annual festivals, were established by Isaiah Shembe. They are still rigorously adhered to and are supported by Bible references. The three annual festivals are referred to in Deuteronomy Chapter 16 verse 16: "Three times in a year shall all thy males appear before the Lord thy God in the place which he shall choose; in the feast of the unleavened bread, and in the feast of the weeks, and in the feast of the tabernacles; and they shall not appear before the Lord empty." The present membership of the church is estimated at 500,000, and church members come from all over South Africa and from neighboring states to attend the festivals. Temporary encampments are built to house the visitors who may remain for as long as a month. . . . For the duration of the festivals, an encampment, containing as many as four hundred temporary huts, is set out according to traditional divisions: an area for chiefs; an area for married men and their sons, who live apart from their wives and mothers for the duration of the festival; and areas for married and unmarried women. This is mirrored during the days of dancing, each group dancing separately in its alloted place. . . .

The July festival, the most popular of the three festivals, continues over three or four weeks. It begins on the first of July and culminates in a day of sacred dance on the last Sunday of the month. Activities during this period include sermons by a variety of preachers, testimonies by church members, and prayer for the sick by the church leader. The festival is characterized by alternate days of dancing and rest. Saturday, as in the Old Testament, is a day of rest and prayer. On this day no fires may be lit, no food cooked. Many church members, who are unable to attend the festivals during the week because of work commitments, arrive for the church service and the mass dancing and singing over the weekend. On Sundays, and especially the last Sunday of the festival, attendance by both dancers and spectators increases considerably. Approximately 20,000 participants were present on the final day of the July 1980 festival, arriving by bus and car throughout the day.

Iscotch and Njobo

As in all traditional rituals and ceremonies, men and women dance separately. The two male group divisions are the "Iscotch"and the "Njobo." The "Iscotch" are younger, while the "Njobo" group has a majority of older men. Unlike the women, men—whether young, old, married, or unmarried—may elect to dance with whichever group they choose. The dancing of the "Iscotch" is energetic and demanding. As a result, younger men tend to align themselves with this group. The "Njobo," wearing more traditional costumes and dancing a slower, less energetic dance, attracts the elders of the church.

—Members of the "Njobo" group wear a costume that closely resembles traditional Zulu dress. . . . The costume of the "Iscotch" is strikingly different from that of the "Njobo" and the female groups in its sharp deviation from traditional dress. The basic garment consists of a long-sleeved, hip-length white smock over a black knee-length, pleated, cotton kilt. The smock has a white tasseled border at its hem. Other characteristic features include a white pith helmet, a long thin light-green tie onto which icons of the prophet Isaiah Shembe and subsequent church leaders are fastened, and black army boots worn with black and white football socks. The only similarity with the "Njobo" group is the switch and shield carried by all members of this group.

Dancers

Each group of dancers is arranged in the same manner. Rows of dancers, fifty or more in each row, line up one behind the other, facing the spectators. Each row takes its turn at the front, as the row closest to the spectators. The change over is effected through a formal movement, the back row moving out from behind in single file in a large semi-circle and finally joining the group again, this time positioned as the new front row.

In this way, dancers, when at the rear, are given the opportunity to rest and refresh themselves. If dancers join or leave the group during the performance, they do so unobtrusively from the back of the group. Through this method of exchange, each group can remain dancing for the entire day with little perceptible change in the structure, energy or concentration of the group.

Another traditional feature retained at the festivals during the days of dancing is the presence of a number of male elders who can be seen striding up and down in front of the dancing groups reciting ''izibongi,'' or ''praise poems.'' A ''praise poem'' in honor of Isaiah Shembe, delivered at the July festival 1980 by a male church member, follows. This ''praise poem'' spontaneously delivered amongst a crowd of spectators was, in turn, quite spontaneously interspersed with a chorus of cries of support and agreement by a group of elderly women seated nearby.

Source: ''Festivals of the Nazareth Baptist Church'' by Peter Larlham in *The Drama Review* 25 (4) (T 92) (Winter 1981), pp. 59-74.

Circa July

Olojo Festival (Ogun Festival)

The Olojo Festival commemorates the age when the god Ogun was a warrior and he abdicated from the throne of Ile-Ife. The festival also commemorates the birth of King Oranmiyan.

Nigeria, Oyo State (Ife, Yoruba)

Olojo celebration

''Indisputably, Ogun is popularly styled''.

''*Lalere Edan*
Olu Irin
Alaso Ina
Elewu Eje
Alagbede Ode Orun. . .
ti o ni omi nile ti o nfi eje we.''

Literarily translates:

''Lalere Edan
The god of Iron
Clad in fiery
Soaked in blood
The blacksmith of heaven who
has water home but
prefers to bathe in bloods''

Ogun was one of the Yoruba deities who descended from the Ark with our ancestor—the Oduduwa—to this sacred city of Ile-Ife. Ogun ranks very high in status among Yoruba deities. He was acknowledged in the indigenous belief of the Yorubes as the most indispensable deity because he was the god of iron and war. He is the patron—god of the blacksmiths and the hunters. The sacred and sacrificial animal of Ogun is ''Dog'' and the image of worship is a piece of iron rod. Ogun was the god who possessed the implement strong and adequate for making the way for all other deities to descend to the earth, by means of chain, hence the people of Ile-Ife used to say as follows:

''*Ewon Amuro Oduduwa*''
Ogun also, as a master—artist, gave finishing touches to the creative work of the Supreme Being traditionally allocated to Orisa-Nla. Whenever Orisa-Nla finished the moulding of the physical man or woman, it was left to Ogun to work on the body-marks, that may be necessary to keep man in good shape. Ogun, when he abdicated the throne of Ile-Ife, finally settled at the present site of Oke Mogun where the Ifes used to worship him from time immemorial. During the annual festival of Olojo or the Ogun festival the following paramount chiefs have roles to play. *The Chief Obaware* - to represent Elefon Erekoseju.

The Oba Osegun, who is the high priest to the Ogun shrine *Obadio,* represents the Oduduwa. The Olorin Akogun, the Onilebe, the flag bearer. *Gbonkaa,* the peace flag bearer is decorated in three colours of white, red and green, and *Chief Obalufe* as the Prime-Minister of Ooni Ode.

The Olojo festival is held for three days with series of ceremonies. The vigil, known as ''Ilagun'' or ''Asoro'' festival which takes place annually at the midnight. On this night, the ''Oba Ojugbede'' on behalf of all the blacksmiths in the city donates two new hoes and a number of iron bell-gons necessary for the ritual. The ''Olorin'' decorates the ''Ogun'' shrine with palm fronds and two dogs to be sacrificed will be tied up in readiness for the sacrifice. At the ceremony, Chief ''Osogun'' and ''Obaware'' in company of Chiefs ''Obadio'' and ''Obajio'' will pour libation to the Ogun and pray for the people. The ''Oba 'Ogun' leads the ritual dance round the Ogun shrine seven times together with Chiefs ''Obadio'', ''Obawara'', ''Obajio'' and the ''Ooni''. The Oba Ooni returns to his palace while other chiefs go back to their homes in jubilation.

On the second day, the whole city is in a festive mood. The traditional chiefs in their full regalia or complete traditional attire, dance to the tune of their ''Ibembe'' drums, while Chiefs Osogun, Obawara and Ojugbede will dance to the tune of iron bell-gongs called ''Laalo'' with various traditional Ogun songs. The Oba Ooni has to be fully dressed in his traditional paraphernalia with the beaded Ife Royal crown called ''ARE''. This crown is estimated to be as heavy as an average man's load. The procession of the Oba Ooni from the palace to ''Oke Mogun'' is in company of priest and priestesses of these gods and goddesses Oya, Sango, Osanyin, Soponna, Osun and others. The booming of guns announce the arrival of the Oba Ooni at the Oke Mogun. Rituals are performed at the shrine. At the end of the ritual ceremony, the Oba Ooni proceeds to ''Oja 'fe'' where he will donate one ram to Chief Eredumi to be sacrificed to all the past Oonis (ancestors).

There is need to briefly narrate the history of king Oranmiyan here, because of the colour decorations of the palace courtiers during this annual festival. Oranmiyan was said to be a son of two fathers, namely Ogun and Oduduwa. Ogun was dark skinned, while Oduduwa was yellow complexioned. Anihunka was the mother of Oranmiyan, she was a female prisoner captured by Ogun. Ogun being in possession of this lady put her in the family way on their way back to Ife from war front. When Ogun got back to Ile-Ife, he, Ogun, handed all the war captives to his father, ''Oduduwa''. Oduduwa too, so much admired the beauty of Anihunka, slept with her. Both Ogun and Oduduwa laid claim to the pregnancy of Anihunka. When she delivered the baby, it was a peculiar baby-boy having white and dark skin. So in commemoration of the two colours, all the Ilaris-Emeses from Ogun house have to be spotted with chalk (white) and comwood powder (coloured).

As previously stated, the Ooni wears a type of crown called 'Are' on Ogun festival. The 'Are' crown is a symbol of Ooni as a rare living divinity of Ile-Ife and therefore, attracts itself many invisible spirits the day it comes out once a year. It is the common belief of the people of Ife that the power of the ''Are'' usually causes rain to fall on the ''Olojo'' day. Another important aspect of the Olojo festival in ancient days was the high regard to the war chiefs of Ile-Ife, in honour of the great warrior and King Oranmiyan. All the Elegbe chiefs otherwise known as ''War Chiefs'' used to wear their full paraphernalia of office made up of leopard, and tiger skins.

Source: ''Ife Traditional Festivals: A Dialectical Hermeneutics'' by Ola Olapade in *Nigeria Magazine* 55 (3) (July-September 1987), 42-48.

For more on Olojo see: ''The Olojo Festival at Ife'' by William Bascom in *Time Out of Time* by Alessadro Falassi. Albuquerque: Univ. of New Mexico, 1987, pp. 62-73.

Early July

Schrulblha (Festival of the Ears of Grain)

This is a Tibetan first-fruits festival to celebrate the first ears of grain appearing on wheat and barley.

Tibet

Celebrating grain

So they all celebrated a merky *"festival of the ears of grain,"* the Schrulblha (srub-lha). That took place in the beginning of July when the first ears appeared on the barley and wheat stalks. On the eve of this festival, Namgyal, like all his neighbors, brought in a bundle of green ears from the field, which he attached to the door posts, the beams, and the wooden columns of the house: an offering for the earth deities (sa-bdag) and for the household and local divinities. On the afternoon of the festival the villagers all gathered in the open place of the village where they ate, drank, and danced. They sang songs about the origin of the world and about the gods who brought the first grain kernels down to earth.

Source: *Progpa Namgyal: Ein Tibeterleben (Progpa Namgyal: The Life of a Tibetan)* by Samuel Heinrich Ribbach. München-Planegg: Otto Wilhelm Barth-Verlag GMBH, 1940 (Human Relations Area Files).

July 1-2

Canada Day / Dominion Day

This day commemorates the confederation of Canada in 1867 and the Constitution Act of 1982. Since that date Canada has severed the last of her ties with Great Britain.

July 8

Fiesta De Santa Isabel

The celebration of St. Elizabeth's feast day takes place in Huyalas, Peru, on July 8 rather than on July 2, her traditional feast day in that area. St. Elizabeth was the mother of John the Baptist and a cousin of Mary, Mother of Jesus. This festival celebrates the visitation of Mary to her cousin, Elizabeth.

Peru

Celebration in Huaylas, Peru, an Andean community, c. 1960

This festival lasts from July 6 to 9 and celebrates the visitation of Our Blessed Lady to her cousin Elizabeth. Saint Elizabeth's feast day is actually July 2, but at one time the brawls between indios and "mistis" were so horrendous that the indios were ordered to celebrate on July 8. Their fiesta was so much more exciting that the whites' July 2 celebration gradually died out. Bullwhip fights were still popular until an alcade of the 1930s started musical contests and dancing instead. Today several bands may be playing at once in the plaza as dancers whirl, raising handkerchiefs and bottles high. A Huyalino writes: This night I am disguising myself. . . . Thou wilt wear a pollera down to thy ankles and a mantle that will cover thy face and a hat of *jipe* or however thou may wish . . . let's go with the band from Yacup, it's better . . . but hurry-up, a drink, thou must be thirsty. . . . There's the "boat" from Shuyo, let's go. . . . How sweet it is to live, knowing how to enjoy . . . thy health!. . .

I danced so much at the *alba gané* [dawn dance] that my feet can't continue. . . . Saint Elizabeth will make them better. . . . Those from Delicados thought they would beat us to the plaza by going quietly . . . but we were at the atrium, already dancing. . . . Commerce Street is like a blanket of products for sale. . . . So many people have come this year. . . . What beautiful girls from Lima showing off their figures and dresses and good humor. . . . Won't many return saying that "Our Patroness Saint Elizabeth was at fault. . . .

It is now time for the procession . . . the contrite *pashas* whispering their prayers, cease to snap their "thunderers" [bull whips] the *toros,* with deep genuflections seem as souls in pain, purging themselves of their errors . . . the smiling *pallas* dressed like flowers and singing their songs finishing with the classic chorus, "qu-yaya," waving their kerchiefs in the air . . . the *chapetones,* white and elegant, dance together, swelling with pride, remembering the arrogance and nobility—mark of the intrepid Spaniard. . . . One after another *caballudanza* goes meandering about. . . .

> Today is the last day. . . . Let's go dance. . . . It is the *shillca* [last night]. Perhaps we won't be here next year . . . perhaps our bones will rest in a coffin.
>
> Long live the Fiesta of Saint Elizabeth!. . . Long live my *barrio!* Long live Huaylas!

Source: *Huaylas: An Andean District in Search of Progress* by Paul L. Doughty. Ithaca, New York: Cornell, 1968, p. 77.

July 11

Naadam Festival

This national festival is a celebration of the 1921 Mongolian Revolution.

Mongolia

The "three manly games": horse racing, archery, and wrestling

. . . Winners of local club contests compete at these meets for titles and places on a national ranking system; national champions win admiration and fame.

Mongolian horseracing is similar to Western steeplechase racing, because the races are conducted overland rather than on closed-circuit tracks. Races are held for riders of all ages, but at the National Naadam, the featured race is in the children's division. Children from seven to twelve years of age, dressed in traditional costumes, race over a 20-mile cross-country course, displaying a skill in horsemanship possible only in a country where many people learn to ride in infancy.

Archery contests feature the ancient Mongolian compound bow, short but powerful enough to propel a heavy arrow for several hundred yards. Contestants, in both men's and women's divisions, compete both from horseback and from a standing position, aiming at a leather target of traditional design. Champions are awarded such poetic titles as Supermarksman and Miraculous Archer.

Mongolian wrestling is the most distinctive of the three manly games. Contestants wear a colorful traditional costume consisting of tight-fitting briefs; a tight vest that covers the back, shoulders, and upper arms, but leaves the chest bare; and heavy leather boots. The distinctive wrestling vest is said to be a way of making it obvious that neither of the contestants is a woman. Legend has it that hundreds of years ago a champion wrestler was discovered to be a woman in disguise, which greatly embarrassed the many men she had defeated.

The wrestlers enter the ring with slow, exaggerated steps, arms extended at their sides, dipping and swooping in imitation of the magical Garuda bird of Buddhist legend. When the referee starts a match, the wrestlers grab each others' vests, and each tries, with a variety of throws, tripping kicks, and other maneuvers, to topple the other. The first wrestler to touch the ground with anything other than the soles of his feet loses. When the match is over, the loser kneels and the winner passes his hand over the loser's head in a sign of victory. Champion wrestlers, like archers, receive colorful titles, such as Titan, Lion, Elephant, and Falcon.

Source: *The Land and People of Mongolia* by John S. Major. New York: J. B. Lippincott, 1990, pp. 147-148.

Circa May-July

First to Tenth Days of the Mohammaden Month of Muharram

This period is one of the most important religious occasions for the Shi'ite followers of Muhammad. The Shi'ites believe that the leadership of Islam should follow the bloodlines of the prophet Muhammed. The Sunnites disagree and thus has arisen a fundamental split within Islam. The fourth caliph (after Mohammed) was Mohammed's cousin Ali. He was assassinated and his eldest son, Hasan, poisoned. His second son, Hussein, became champion of the Shi'ite cause. On the first of Muharram, A.H. 61/A.D. 680, Hussein was attacked on the desert of Kerbela. Cut off from water, he and his group suffered for ten days. Hussein refused to pledge allegiance to the enemy. Yazid, who had usurped the caliphate and installed it in Damascus. On the tenth of Muharram, known as Ashura, a battle ensued in which Hussein and all male members of his party were slain (except for one boy who was ill in the women's tents). The women and girls were taken as trophies to Yazid in Damascus, as were the heads of the slain men. The martyrs of this massacre are mourned every year during the first ten days of Muharram. The events of this tragedy are re-enacted through processions and through a passion play, the ta'ziya. Future dates of this Muharram observance are July 2-11, 1992; June 21-30, 1993; June 10-19, 1994; and May 31-June 9, 1995.

Multiple countries

The ta'ziya

[T]he *ta'ziya,* or Passion play, became the real climax of the Shi'ite Tenth of Muharram celebrations. The stage requires few properties besides a large *tâbût* (coffin), "receptacles in front to hold lights," and Husain's arms and banner. The poet speaks the introduction and, supported by a choir of boys, chants a *khutba*-like lamentation. Another male choir, dressed as mourning women, utters the wailing of the women and mothers. The spectators are given cakes of earth from Kerbela, steeped in musk, "on which they press their foreheads in abject grief." To defray the expense for a *ta'ziya* is a meritorious work, with which the donor "builds himself the palace in Paradise."

The play consists of a loose sequence of some forty to fifty scenes. Dramatic suspense would be absent even if the events were not known to the audience, for they are foretold by Gabriel to the prophets, foreseen in dreams, and frequently narrated at length before being acted on the stage. The performance is highly realistic, especially in the portrayal of Husain's sufferings from thirst and in the battle and death episodes. Old Testament figures are introduced to typify the events of Husain's Passion. National animosity against the Arabs expresses itself on occasion, but the true villains are Caliph Yazid, who gives the order to kill Husain, and Shammar, or Shimr, who is believed to have struck the fatal blow.

The excitement of the audience reaches such a pitch that the spectators not infrequently try to lynch the actors representing the murderers of Husain. Anti-Sunnite feeling is said to be such that no Sunni would be knowingly tolerated among the spectators. The final scenes usually depict the progress of the martyr's severed head to the Court of the Caliph. On the way, the cortège halts at a Christian monastery whose abbot, upon the sight of the head, swears off his faith and professes Islam. The sight of the head produces the same effect on some Christian ambassadors who happen to be at the Court of Yazid when it arrives. Not only Christians, but Jews and pagans are affected in the same way; even a lion is seen to bow low before Husain's head.

Source: "Shi'a" by R. Strothman in *EI IV,* p. 712.

Sample ending of a ta'ziya

Gabriel reappears and, taking the verdict out of the Prophet's hands, delivers to him this message from the Lord: "None has suffered the pain and afflictions which Husain has undergone. None has, like him, been obedient in My service. As he has taken no steps save in sincerity in all that he has done, thou must put the key of Paradise in his hand. The privilege of making intercession is exclusively his. Husain is, by My peculiar grace, the mediator for all.

"*The Prophet,* handing over the key: Go thou and deliver from the flames every one who has in his life-time shed but a single tear for thee, every one who has in any way helped thee, every one who has performed a pilgrimage to they shrine, or mourned for thee, and every one who has written tragic verse for thee. Bear each and all with thee to Paradise.

"*Husain:* O my friends, be ye relieved from grief, and come along with me to the mansions of the blest. Sorrow has past away, it is now time for joy and rest; trouble has gone by, it is the hour to be at ease and tranquillity.

"*The Sinners* (entering Paradise): God be praised! By Husain's grace we are made happy, and by his favor we are delivered from destruction. By Husain's loving-kindness is our path decked with roses and flowers. We were thorns and thistles, but are now made cedars owing to his merciful intercession."

Source: *The Miracle Play of Hasan and Husain* by Sir L. Pelly. London, (2) (1879), 348.

Symbolic objects of the procession

Certain important smybolic objects must be carried. The *Alams* are the most important and sacred of these. They symbolize the ensign of Hussein at Kerbela and signify courage, truth, right and fighting uncompromisingly for a cause. The *Alams* generate the feeling of fighting for Hussein in the present. Flexible steel blades form the upright part of an *Alam* and are often engraved. Many symbolic objects are attached to the outstretched arms of the *Alam*. The *Alam* is further decorated by plumes and fine embroidered silks and brocades and may be as tall as 15 feet. Procession participants carry green banners representing the color of the Islam prophet, red flags representing blood and injustice, black flags for mourning, and white flags, signifying readiness for sacrifice and martyrdom. A *Kotal* is a structure built around a lance. At the top is a metal hand symbolizing the severed hand of Abbas, as well as the five sacred personalities of the Shia Islam: Muhammad, Fatima, Ali, Hassan and Hussein. Green, red, black and white banners are attached to the lance from top to bottom. Each district or guild has its own black banner inscribed with its name.

The Muharram procession in Iran

The beating follows the rhythm of the accompanying drums and cymbals. The sub-group's leader, singing dirges, follows the same beat. They all stop before a religious edifice, the tomb of a local saint or in an open space. There, one group beats itself rhythmically while the others join in the singing. The tempo quickens until the excitement reaches an uncontrollable pitch, and then the leader resumes the march. While marching, the self-mortification continues at a slower pace regulated by the tempo of the march. The cries of participants are mingled with mournful songs:

> *"Kerbela this day has been despoiled*
> *Hussein with his own blood is soiled*
> *(Chorus) Murder! By the hand of Shimr*
> *Cry out! By the hand of Shimr.*
> *"O shameless Shimr! not at all abashed*
> *Ruthless against Hussein you dashed. (Chorus)*
> *"Surely the stones shall weep today!*
> *Seventy and two were slain today! (Chorus)*
> *"Hassan, Hussein, are like a flower.*
> *Yazid fell in the filth of a sewer. (Chorus)"*

Canetti describes these processions as "an orchestra of grief; and their effect is that of a crowd crystal. The pain they inflict on themselves is the pain of Hussein, which by being exhibited, becomes the pain of the whole community. Their beating on their chests, which is taken up by the spectators, gives rise to a rhythmic crowd sustained by the emotion of the lament. Hussein has been torn away from all of them and belongs to all of them together."

Although Hussein and his band were unable to get water, the processional routes are lined by water containers to revive the marchers, some of whom faint from exhaustion or loss of blood. In so far as the performers identify with Hussein and his forlorn group at Kerbela, the bystanders in the huge crowd beside the parade identify with the participants, until such a stage of breast-beating and wailing is attained they they begin to join the procession themselves—resulting in a total merging of all three phases. There is, nevertheless, an astonishing degree of crowd discipline, which derives from the mosque and *Husseiniyeh* organizations that maintain the order of the day.

The Muharram procession in Iraq, Lebanon, Turkey, and Eastern Anatolia

The processions in Iraq do not differ greatly from those in Iran. In Iran the procession is called *dasta,* while in Iraq it is called *mawkib*. As in Iran the processions are organized by town districts and guilds. There are local differences in timing and manner of execution. In the city of Kazmain, for example, the chain-beaters advance along both sides of the road in single file, wearing black shirts with cut-outs on the back. The band music provides the rhythm for the feet and hands. There are, however, fewer costumed people representing various characters. When a procession stops in an open space to perform a scene from the Kerbela tragedy such as the wedding of Qasim, it is not acted but rather sung about in elegies and dirges. The surrounding crowd acts as a chorus, picking up a refrain or striking their breasts.

In Lebanon, where one of the oldest Shia communities lives, Muharram rituals were restrained until the second half of the 19th century. A great deal of the Iranian influence can be noticed. Proportional to the role that the Shiites of Lebanon play in the affairs of the country, more and more ritual processions may be seen now in Southern Lebanon and the Bekaa Valley. In Bahrain, where more than 50% of the population are Shiites, the processions follow the Iranian pattern with local modifications.

Among the Turkish people the processions in the Caucasus were seen by many Europeans and were recorded before the 1917 Soviet revolution. Most notable was the involvement and fervor of the marchers and bystanders. Night processions ended in a large public square lit by torches and large petroleum burners, where staged battles re-enacted Kerbela. They even dug ditches and erected tents that were subsequently destroyed by fire. Hussein's handcuffed women and children were placed in processions as if going into Syrian captivity.

In Eastern Anatolia, processions take place on a limited scale. On the Indo-Pakistani sub-continent the visual qualities and size of the processions are prominent. Non-Shiites frequently participate in processions. The main centers of processions are Lucknow, Hyderabad and Delhi. Characteristic of the Indian processions are large and small replicas of Hussein's tomb carried by marchers. These so-called *Ta'ziyehs* (not to be confused with the Ta'ziyeh passion play, the term is derived from an Arabic word, *aza,* meaning mourning) are the local versions of the Imam's tomb in terms of Indian architecture.

Ta'ziyehs are made of bamboo, sticks, colorful papers and papier-maché. At the end of the procession some of the tombs are buried in local ''Kerbela'' grounds. Because of the great distance of the sub-continent from the Shia holy places, the Indian Shiites consecrated local lands and call them ''Kerbela'' grounds, where solid replicas of the Hussein tomb were built on a small scale. The people of the community are buried in these grounds.

Source: ''Shia Muslim Processional Performances'' by Peter Chelkowski in *The Drama Review,* 29, (3) (Fall 1985), 18-30.

Caribbean

Muharram / Hosay / Tadja

Multiethnic celebration

This Muslim festival, imported to the Caribbean by East Indian Muslims, finds Hindus and in some cases Afro-Americans joining in its celebration. In Jamaica Hosay is celebrated as a symbol of East Indian unity by both Muslims and Hindus. In Guyana, Afro-Guyanese have joined the Indo-Guyanese in their celebration of Tadja. In Trinidad, Hosay is also multi-ethnic.

Basic paraphernalia of the procession, the ta'ziya and the alam

A symbolic replica of the domed tomb of Imam Husain at Karbala is contructed as the *ta'ziya.* This can be built in layers, resembling a multistoried house with a domed roof. These replicas are constructed of bamboo, cardboard, or even spun sugar and are elaborately decorated. Paper filigree may be applied as well as cut glass or plastic, mica, and tinsel. In coastal areas the *ta'ziya* may be set afloat on the sea after the festival; in other areas it may be buried to recall the burial of Husain at Karbala. *Ta'ziya* are decorated in red, for Husain, and green, for Hasan. The *alam,* a standard with a crest and an embroidered banner, is also carried. This represents the banner carried by Husain. Other symbols associated with this festival are the *Panjtan,* an open hand symbolizing the five pure members of the Prophet's family; twelve hands, recalling the twelve Imams; a footprint of the Prophet, Qadam-i-rasu; or the horseshoe from Ali's horse, Nal Sahib, a large, crescent shape.

Source: ''The Hosay Festival'' by Judith Bettelheim and John Nunley, in *Caribbean Festival Arts* by John W. Nunley and Judith Bettelheim. Seattle: Univ. of Washington Press, 1988, pp. 119-123.

Egypt

'Ashûrâ

'Ashûrâ at the Hasanain Mosque in Cairo

While the Tenth of Muharram procession remained confined to the Shi'ite world, the veneration of Husain has spread into Sunnism. The Fâtimids (969-1171) had Husain's head transferred to Cairo and the Mosque of the Hasanain (literally: of the two Hasan—that is, Hasan and his brother Husain) was erected over the relic and still preserves a reputation of especial sanctity. While the mourners in the Shi'a procession are all men, the crowd that assembles in the Hasanain Mosque on the occasion of *'Ashûrâ* is composed almost exclusively of women who gather apparently in order to witness a *dhikr* meeting.

Source: *Muhammadan Festivals* by G.E. Von Grunebaum. New York: Henry Schuman, 1951, p. 89.

Guyana

Tadja

Tadja in Guyana prior to 1930

Tadja was once a vital tradition in Guyana. In the excitement of the festival, groups from different estates would clash in the streets over the right of way, and Muslims would clash with Hindus when the celebration happened to coincide with Dasserah or Durga Pujah. Because of these street troubles, the government outlawed Tadja in the 1930s.

Source: ''The Hosay Festival'' by Judith Bettelheim and John Nunley in *Caribbean Festival Arts* by John W. Nunley and Judith Bettleheim. Seattle: Univ. of Washington Press, 1988, pp. 125-126.

India

Moharrum

Moharrum in Hyderabad; the Shia sect

It is well known fact that Muslim conquerors of South India were all Sunnis, as also the emperors who rule at Delhi and Agra. Nevertheless, Shia influence from Persia was at times very strong and many Shias found their way into India especially South India, and established their say on the land. . . .

They are found concentrated in the South at Hyderabad. Cities like Bombay, Surat, Punjab and Lucknow are also important centres of Shia faith.

Sultan Quli Qutub Shah V, the founder of Hyderabad City, adopted the Shia faith in 1001 A.H. when he observed ''I have left my faith and have adopted this faith. Otherwise I would have been so far a Hindu.

He adopted this faith when he came in contact with Mir Momin, a saint, who came from Persia, and later on was appointed as Prime Minister of his kingdom.

Moharrum in Hyderabad, compared with Irani and Iraqi versions

''We had been to Iraq and Iran several times for the purpose of visit to holy places located in these countries, and keenly observed the Moharrum performance there by the Iraqi and Irani people. There is much similarity with a little difference in the performance of Moharrum compared to our Hyderabad Moharrum. Keeping Alams, Tazias and doing Matam from 1st day to 10th day of Moharrum are main features in Iraq and Iran. The same we find in Hyderabad also. Procession of Alams and Tazias with the performance of Matam are taken out in both these countries on specific dates fixed for this purpose just as we do here. Religious scholars deliver theological lectures by narrating the events of Kerbala at Kerbala, Moalla and Najf Ashraf just as our religious heads do here. At the end of majlises coffee is served among the audience whereas in Hyderabad we distribute sweets and sherbat etc. Making Faqir (beggar) of children with green clothes, preparing sweets in different shapes and sharbat in different earthen pots with certain colours, giving tiger disguise to human body, making fire in Alawa in front of Ashurkhanas and going round it with slogans 'Ya Ali' Dhosla 'Hasan and Hussain', all these are not performed there. This has been adopted mostly from Hindus in our country.

Source: *A Monograph on Muharram in Hyderabad City* by Khaja Moinudoin. Census of India 1971. Series 2, Andra Pradesh, pp. 8, 22.

Iran

Muharram in Teheran in 1816

Toward the end of the Muslim year, black tents are pitched in the streets. These tents are adorned with draperies, arms and candelabra. Here and there wooden pulpits are erected. On the first of Muharram, when the festival proper begins, mourning clothes are donned; people refrain from shaving and bathing, and a simple diet is adopted. From the pulpit the beginning of Husain's story is narrated with as much detail and elaboration of episodes as possible. The listeners are deeply affected. Their cries of ''O, Husain, O, Husain!'' are accompanied by groans and tears. This kind of recitation continues throughout the day, the mullahs taking turns on the several pulpits. At one time the notables of a quarter would fit out a tent and pay a mullah to recite in it, while the listeners were served food and drink. During the first nine days of Muharram groups of men, with their half-naked bodies dyed black or red, tour the streets. They pull out their hair, inflict sword wounds upon themselves or drag chains behind them, or perform wild dances. Not infrequently fights with Sunnites or other adversaries will develop, resulting in casualties and even deaths.

The celebration culminates on the Tenth of Muharram in a big procession originally designed as a funerary parade to reenact the burial of Husain. The center of this procession is formed by the coffin of Husain, carried by eight men and accompanied on each side by a banner-bearer. Four horses and some sixty blood-smeared men march behind the coffin and sing a martial tune. They are followed by a horse, representing Duldul, the war-horse of Husain. In the rear there is usually a group of perhaps fifty men rhythmically beating two wooden staves, one against the other.

Source: *Muhammaden Festivals* by G.E. Von Grunebaum. New York: Henry Schuman, 1951, pp. 86-87. (Based on reports of J. Morier in Teheran in 1816.)

Iraq

Hussein martyred in Karbala

The tomb of Hussein is in Karbala, Iraq. He was martyred here during the Battle of Karbala betwen Sunni and Sh'ite Moslems. Karbala and its sister city Majaf are a center of Shi'ite pilgrimage during Muharram.

Source: *International What's What When & Where* by Ardith Nehrt. Columbus, Ohio: Shawnee, 1967, p. 95.

Jamaica

Hosay

Hosay in Jamaica, c. 1984

On the first day of Muharram a *chauk* is built. This is a sacred square of earth where prayers are offered. The soil square is cut and consecrated with a sacred paste, and a clay representation of Husain and Hasan is set on the *chauk*. Banana leaves are placed on the four corners of the *chauk,* and the *chauk* is circled five times. Men must refrain from meat, alcohol, and sexual relations during preparations for Hosay.

On Friday night a community Hosay procession is held, with large *taziyah* carried. Sometime six to ten men are required to bear them. The *dhol* and *jhanj* (drum and cymbals) accompany the procession. Before the procession, participants are offered *malida,* a fried specialty of burnt sugar, flour, and molasses. At the end of the Taziyah on Friday night the *taziyah* are pushed out to sea or destroyed. On Thursday a procession of smaller, individual *taziyah* takes place. Participants carry *taziyah* that are small enough to fit on a turbaned head, or to set atop a stick.

Source: ''The Hosay Festival'' by Judith Bettelheim and John Nunley in *Caribbean Festival Arts* by John W. Nunley and Judith Bettelheim. Seattle: Univ. of Washington Press, 1988, pp. 119-122.

For more information see: *The Hussay Festival in Jamaica* by

Martha Warren Beckwith. Poughkeepsie, N.Y.: Vassar College Folk-Lore Foundation, no. 4, 1924.

Morocco

First Muharram and Ashura, a Sunni celebration as observed by an American family

[T]he seriousness of the butchers' strike, which had begun in Marrakech and was sweeping the country, was blunted by the holiday on the first day of the month of Muharram, the beginning of the Islamic New Year. Schools and offices and food markets were closed, and people thronged through Djemaa el Fna, eating and drinking, watching the entertainments, and buying drums for their children.

Drums, it seemed, were a sure sign that Muharram had begun. Bob had counted more than seventy shops that had been set up overnight in the square to sell nothing but drums, filling this special annual demand.

Along rue Trésor, as on all the streets in Marrakech during these days, the human percussion of hand-clapping was being replaced by the drums. Every child seemed to have one or two; Shadeeya and Ali and even little Kamal sat in the entrance to the sibha all day, drumming, drumming, drumming. Hind and Naima organized drumming among the groups of girls, and the rhythmic patterns of beats punctuated all the daily activities on the street. In the square by the clinic, the teen-aged boys had switched temporarily from soccer to percussion, and the group finished each evening with a walking drumming procession through Rue Trésor.

"Oh, Mama, why can't we get drums, too?" asked Laila.

Why not? I took them to Djemaa el Fna to choose from the hundreds of drums for sale: the big cylindrical glazed pottery drums that the women had beaten so skillfully at the wedding party; the wide wooden skin-covered drums, open on one side, used by the Gnaoua dancers; drums in the shape of a rough hourglass, used for more private festivities. But the majority were children's drums, manufactured especially for the Ashura holiday, cheap clay overlaid with shiny paper; the paper, pasted on in shades of hot pink, blue, green, and gold, cleverly simulated the famous pottery of the Safi drums.

"Oh, look, Mama!" Laura Ann had discovered a collection of tiny drums suitable for a dollhouse. We bought several, plus three medium-sized children's drums (at twenty cents each), and wandered through the other temporary stalls where walnuts, almonds, raisins, and ropes of figs were for sale. These, Aisha told us, were the ingredients for *kooreeshaat,* special sweets to be made and given to children on Ashura.

Abdul Lateef and Moulay Mustapha explained that Ashura was like Christmas, when children received presents, new clothes, and sweets.

"Just as the Prophet's birthday is a special holiday for men, so Ashura is special for women and children," they said.

But no one seemed to know the religious origins of Ashura, which commemorates a famous battle between the forces of two clans of early Islam, a battle that split Islam into the two major sects that still exist today: Shi'a and Sunna. In the village in Shi'a Iraq where we had lived, the first ten days of Muharram had been days of penitence, and Ashura, the day of the battle, was a day of sorrow and mourning. Here, in Sunna North Africa, Ashura was a day of triumph and success, transformed over the centuries into a cheerful holiday for children.

Source: *A Street in Marrakech, A Personal Encounter with the Lives of Moroccan Women* by Elizabeth Warnock Fernea. Garden City, N.Y.: Anchor/Doubleday, 1980, pp. 217-219.

Pakistan

Charity in Mohla, West Pakistan, c. 1955

On the tenth day of Muharram, well-to-do *zamindars* and *kammis* cook plenty of rice and sweet syrup for distribution. Everybody in the village knows which houses have cooked food for the occasion. The wives of poor *kammis* of the village go there and are given rice and syrup in small cups and saucers which have been made to order by the potter. Children of the rich and poor alike flock to those houses and are given rice and syrup. The custom is never to refuse food to children.

Source: *A Punjabi Village in Pakistan* by Zekiye Eglar. New York: Columbia Univ. Press, 1960, p. 69.

Muharram in Pakistan

The Islamic calendar begins with the month of Muharram. Properly this is a month of general mourning: boys repair the graves and strew marigolds or rose petals over them in memory of the departed. But the tenth day of the month commemorates the murder of Husain, the grandson of Mohammed—a special day of sorrow for the Shi'as. Traditionally, they "take out a procession," which consists of elaborately decorated paper and bamboo towers, called *tazias,* representing the tomb of Husain. The tazias are followed by mourners who cry, "Ya Husain," and strike themselves with sticks and knives.

Before Partition, Muharram processions were frequent occasions for riots in narrow city streets when Muslims collided with Hindus. Nowadays there may be tension between Shi'as and the dominant Sunnis, but otherwise the processions are relatively peaceful affairs, and the self-inflicted wounds of mourners are less common. At the end of the day the tazias are dropped into a river, if there is one handy, or buried.

Source: *The Land and People of Pakistan* by Robert Lang. New York: J. B. Lippincott, 1974, p. 132.

Trinidad

Hosay

Hosay in Port of Spain in 1986

In the St. James neighborhood of Port of Spain four *tadjah* are built each year. The building takes place in a private enclosure erected for the purpose, and only the building crews are allowed inside. Prayers and ritual food are shared by the builders and their guests each night. The work is carried on in a quiet and hushed atmosphere.

On Friday evening the large tadjah process through the streets. On Saturday the Husain and Hasan moons are carried in a procession.

The moons were brought out Saturday evening in what is called Small Hosay to celebrate the death of the younger brother. This performance ended at 3 a.m. the next day. That evening, the Hasan Moon was carried out of the enclosure and attached to bamboo tubing. The crew who would carry it prayed on the *chauk* with an Imam from a neighborhood mosque. Then Joey Muller lifted the moon onto his shoulders, placed the shaft in a holster at his waist and spun the object in perfect balance. Others followed Muller to the street to take their turn in the ancient dance. Members of the moon camp threw coins and rice for good luck. Shouts of Hosay! Hosay! filled the air.

To the beat of the *tassa* drums participants pushed their *tadjah* into the streets. At about 1 a.m. on Monday, the two moons, symbols of Husain and Hasan met, touching in a symbolic kiss, thereby joining together in the holy mission. The two moons then led the way to music heard in the far reaches of the city.

On the morning of September 15th, the four *tadjah* appeared one by one on the main route. Ahead waited the Hasan Moon, its supporters dressed in white pants and blue-green shirts. Rain fell, each drop adding to the moon's weight. When the *tadjah* lined the western Main Road, the Husain Moon made its triumphal appearance at the back of the procession. Before passing the waiting *tadjah,* this gleaming white and red object stopped parallel to each tomb and touched it in a symbolic kiss, releasing the spirits of Husain and Hasan into unbounded space. In this fashion, the brothers met and kissed for the last time. The crescendos of the *tassa* drums urged the procession onward and called forth the followers.

Source: "The Hosay Festival" by Judith Bettelheim and John W. Nunley in *Caribbean Festival Arts* by John W. Nunley and Judith Bettelheim. Seattle: Univ. of Washington Press, 1988, pp. 119-135.

Turkey

Yevmi Ashurer

The Day of Sweet Soup

New Year's is known to us as Yil Basher (year head) and is not an important festival. The first really important festival is Yevmi Ashurer (day of sweet soup) which comes ten days later. On this day Noah is supposed to have left the ark and, more important for Moslems, it is the day that Houssein, the son of Ali and Mohammed's grandson by his daughter Fatima, was killed. On this day and succeeding days until the end of the second month of the year we are ordered to share Allah's gifts with others, therefore every family makes *ashurer* (sweet soup) of sugar, barley, corn, and chick-peas and invites its neighbors to come and partake of it with them. Every person has a different day assigned to him by custom. As our family were descendants of the original governor of the province, it was our customary privilege to offer ashurer on the first day. According to tradition, Houssein was killed in the desert and died in thirst, crying out for water. Therefore good Moslems do not drink much water during this month, and only drink from clay pots. Some devout old women hardly drink at all.

Source: *When I Was a Boy in Turkey* by Ahmed Sabri Bey. Boston: Lothrop, Lee & Shepard Co., 1924, pp. 79-80.

West Africa

'Ashūrā

Ten Muharram, 'Ashūrā, in West Africa

The first event of the Islamic year is the 10th night of Muharram (the 'Ashūrā) to which African practices connected with the New Year have cohered, although, since it is continually moving round the year, it has been disconnected from the agriculatural season. The pious fast for from one to three days and most prepare for it by a short fast ablutions, and a purge to purify the body. Symbolic rites to ensure prosperity during the new year are universal. When the sun has set everyone eats all he possibly can and poor people are invited to participate, for no one must go empty that night so that a prosperous year may be ensured. Hausa have the custom (*jūva bai*) of providing every member of the household with a fowl or goat's head which each must eat with his back turned to the others. Peoples of Senegal, Guinée, and Sierra Leone cook and eat the dried head and feet of the ram slaughtered at the Tabaski feast (an animist survival—linking the new year to the old and drawing the blessing of the sacrifice into the new year?). Susu (and many others) make an offering (*la kayanye*) at the time of the last prayer of the year, and on New Year's Day young men and girls immerse themselves in a river seven times. Many believe that on this night God counts all earth-dwellers and designates those who are to die during the year. With the Islamic lustrations is associated a customary ceremony of purification by fire. Songhay, after ablutions, pass and repass over a small fire shouting, '*Yesi hirow*' ('The New Year has entered'). After the feast many

(Hausa, Nupe, Mandinka, Dyula) have torchlight processions and contests between age-groups.

When day comes special prayers are offered in all mosques.

Source: *Islam in West Africa* by J. Spencer Trimingham. Oxford: Clarendon Press, 1959, pp. 76-77.

For more on Muharram see: "The Tenth of Muharram" in *Muhammaden Festivals* by Jon Grunebaum. New York: Henry Scuman, 1951, pp. 85-94. (Drawn from late 19th-century sources.); *Persian Belief and Customs* by Henri Masse. New Haven: Human Relations Area Files, 1951. Translated from Croyances et coutumes Persanes suivies de contes et chansons populaire. 2 vols. Paris: Librarie Orientale et Americaine, 1938, pp. 109-128; "Shia Muslim Processional Performances" by Peter Chelkowski in *The Drama Review,* 29 (3) (Fall 1985), 18-30; TA'ZIYEH: *Ritual and Drama in Iran* by Peter Chelkowski. New York: New York Univ., 1979; *A Street in Marrakech, A Personal Encounter with the Lives of Moroccan Women* by Elizabeth Warnock Fernea. Garden City, N.Y.: Anchor/Doubleday, 1980, pp. 217-219.

July 14
Bastille Day

Celebrated in France and her territories, July 14 commemorates the day in 1789 when the Parisian populace overthrew Louis XVI, taking the Bastille by storm. The day is celebrated with parades, torchlight processions, fireworks, and the flying of flags.

France

Bastille Day in Paris c. 1929

July 14, anniversary of the capture of the Bastille (in 1789), is celebrated always to date. It is indeed supplemented—as are all true fêtes—by a preface and an epilogue. Actually, this fête lasts three nights and a day.

On the 13th, in the evening, but well before nightfall, orchestras, of various composition, according to the wealth of the district committee which has collected them, seize the cross-roads. Platforms have been erected, with coloured fairy-lamps, and draped with strips of red, white and blue. For three nights and most of one day a jazz band or a mixture of a cornet, trombone, clarinet, and a big drum unwearyingly pours forth a rather scanty repertoire—tangos, blues, fox-trots, one-steps, and javas. Let these bandsmen earn their money never so zealously and never so conscientiously, they will not succeed in tiring out their dancers. Let the street be cobbled, uneven, slippery, or dry, hemmed in by the encroachments of the neighbouring cafés which, this evening, shamelessly invade two-thirds of the road—there is always a crowd. At dawn, when the neighbours who either have not wished or have not been able to escape, try to go to sleep, there will always be some devotees to cry 'One more!—the last!' But the bandsmen know well that if they show the slightest weakness, it will be by no means 'the last'. Their collars soaked, their heads splitting, and feeling rather sick (for they have been refreshing themselves throughout the night on cheap wine, beer, and lemonade), both dance-band and dancers go off to sleep an hour or two, to be back on the spot in the early afternoon.

The parade

Since the War there has only been a simple military demonstration on the Place de l'Etoile, before the tomb of the Unknown Warrior. The President of the Republic, the Cabinet, the Presidents of the Chambers, stand with bowed heads at the sacred slab. Then a detachment of all arms marches past the Arc de Triomphe while military airmen do evolutions in the sky. The Champs Elysées, the Place de l'Etoile, are covered with a dense crowd. Windows and house-roofs are turned into grand-stands. Applause and acclamations pour in from afar on the troops. This lasts an hour, and then all is over.

The ball

In the evening, while the balls start again, and the illuminations of the buildings increase yet more the luminous halo which lights up the Paris sky, fireworks are let off, at one and the same moment, on the hill of Montmartre, at Buttes-Chaumont, on the Pont-Neuf, in the Parc Montsouris, at the angle of Ile St.-Louis, and on the Auteuil viaduct. They attract an enormous crowd, especially in the artisan quarters. When the last Roman candle and the last 'bouquet' have plunged into the void, the crowd goes back to dance and drink; no sleeping that night, nor the night after, so long as the orchestras keep going, as the dancers have a kick left in them, as the last cask or jar have so much as a drop left.

Source: *A Guide to French Fetes* by E.I. Robson. London: Methuen, 1930, pp. 41-42.

Bastille Day in Besançon, c. 1900

The street is already full of people, and the fresh air of dawn seems in effervescence. Big flags flip and flap at every window and balcony, even at the garrets; flags of red, white, and blue, the national colors, also of black, yellow, and red, the city colors, all mixed up. Fresh green garlands of oak-leaves, and of roses, balance in the air from house to house.

A carpet of flowers—marguerites, blue cornflowers and red poppies—hangs from our balcony; the whole family and the two servants worked at it feverishly the whole day before. Late in the night, Father himself fixed a city flag at all the other windows, and garlands were hung in between. I wished the flowers would never fade, and I so loved the flapping of the flags.

Bands of peasants, dressed up in their best, mounted on decorated farm-wagons, gay with flags and flowers, or on horses caparisoned from nose to tail, rush noisily, with laughter, songs, and cracking of whips, down the street. They come from far, and have been rolling the whole night to see the Grand Review of soldiers at Chamars, in the great park. One must be there, very early, in order to have even a standing-place, for the Review begins at seven o'clock.

Soon the soldiers of the citadel come down, too; their blaring trumpets and rolling drums shake the air, their steps, the soil.

The bayonets, the sabres, the buttons, the buckles, even the polish of the boots, flash rhythmically to the music. From our window it is a wonderful sight to behold.

Then comes the moving ceremony of the bestowing of decorations for those who have distinguished themselves for patriotic service, and the decoration of the flags of regiments which have achieved some signal distinction. This goes on until noon.

The heat beats down, but no one feels it. Boom! Boom! The cannon's roar closes the Review.

The scramble in the street is great. Everybody rushes home for a copious lunch, and joy sits around the table. We always had friends with us for that day, and invariably my Uncle Louis, General of the Algerian Spahis, one of the most famous cavalry corps of the French colonial army.

"Mother, shall we go and see the menagerie, the booths, and the side-shows at the Fair in the Park Micaud? And may we look at the obstacle races, the climbing of the greased pole, the crossing of the river on a rolling log, and all funny things?"

"Yes, with Adèle, Fanny, and Nounou. I'll stay home with your father; he needs a rest. You know he has to supervise the illuminations of this evening."

The illuminations were a great responsibility upon Father's head. All the public buildings, squares, parks, bridges, public fountains, and statues were in his charge, and, really, on that night, Besançon looked like a fairy place.

Boom! Boom! The sunset gun! The play of the lights begins. The town-hall, the prefecture, the Palace of Justice, are ablaze with millions of tiny gas-jets. The grass and the flower-beds in the parks are strewn with burning candles, each one a star in a colored glass. In the trees hang, high and low, garlands and garlands of Chinese lanterns. The fountains reflect light, and the statues seem alive. The river is rolling fire, and precious gems fall from the sparkling bridges. And, therewith, upon the multiple and joyous faces of the compact moving crowd, the glare of red and green Bengal Fires, the lightning of golden fireworks—it is bewildering! I walk as in a dream. And all that beauty was Father's work and idea! I was infinitely proud of it.

The joy of the festival increased from hour to hour, music, crackers, singing everywhere, and, after supper, dancing in the open air on every public place. Late, late in the night, the streets still resounded with the words of our National Hymn: "*Aux armes, Citoyens!*" "*Allons, enfants de la patrie!*" O Great Marseillaise, you sing in every heart in France, and you have gone all round the world!

Source: *When I Was a Girl in France* by Georgette Beuret. Boston: Lothrop, Lee & Shepard Co., 1916, pp. 136-141.

New Caledonia

Bastille Day in the Pacific

This greatest national holiday in France is also celebrated in Tahiti, New Hebrides, Wallis and Futuna, all French territories in the Pacific. . . .

In Noumea, capital city of New Caledonia, the celebration begins on the eve of Bastille Day with a torchlight parade around the city. Everyone takes part; military bands in dress uniform, men, women and children. The majority are French and Melanesian, but there are also groups from Polynesia, Vietnam, Indonesia, Martinique, New Zealand, Australia and Europe.

Native women wear missionary-style long-sleeved dresses with floral patterns, while men and children wear *pareos* ("skirts") of bright printed cotton. The fervor of the parade continues into the night with street dancing and partying.

Bastille Day is given over to food fairs, carnival amusements for the children, and sports events. Teams from other islands come to Noumea to compete in soccer, cricket, basketball, volleyball and water skiing.

Source: *Celebrations: Asia and the Pacific* by Gene Sawyer. Honolulu: Friends of the East-West Center, 1978, p. 55.

Tahiti

Tiurai (Bastille Day Fête)

Competition and merry-making

[T]he Tiurai has been held annually since 1881. Although its distant roots may be in Polynesian harvest festivals, its more recent predecessor was the birthday celebrations of the French Emperor Napoléon III on August 15, celebrated annually until 1870. Whereas in France the fête is celebrated primarily on July 14, in Tahiti and the rest of French Polynesia it is celebrated for much of the month of July.

Competition has become the key factor for the festival participants, while merry-making liberally laced with food and drink is most important for the general populace. Rather than the high-minded ideals of the South Pacific Festival, Tiurai is celebration *par excellence*. Beginning with the more European accoutrements, including a parade, visits to the Governor's residence, horse races, and a grand ball, the fête moves on to more Polynesian activities including outrigger canoe races and the reenactment of the enthronement of a Tahitian high chief in an outdoor temple complex. The days follow with competitions of javelin throwing, plaiting of mats, copra preparation, and races of fruit carriers, but the most important part of the Tiurai begins each evening at 9:00 P.M.—the *spectacle folklorique*. This competition of music and dance draws performing groups from throughout French Polynesia—Tahiti and other Society Islands, the Austral Islands, Marquesas Islands, Tuamotu Islands, and Mangareva—as well as from the Cook Islands and occasionally

Easter Island. As they are at the South Pacific Festival, the performances are in the local vernacular, but these languages (and cultures) are closely related and the intent of the performance is immediately understood. Indeed, widespread cultural borrowing of myths and legends as well as dance movements is a feature of this *spectacle folklorique*. And a spectacle it is.

Although the dance troupes may perform together throughout the year, they begin to put together their new repertoire for the Tiurai some months before July under the direction of a choreographer who may also be the group leader. The choreographer, working alone or with others of the troupe, often takes as a starting point a myth, legend, or historical event and forms his outline around it. The performances have a standardized form and include one or more of each major Tahitian dance genre—*'ōte'a, 'aparima, hivinau,* and *pā'ō'ā,* and, if there is an appropriate singing group associated with the dance troupe, *'utē* are included.

Source: ''Pacific Festivals and Ethnic Identity'' by Adrienne L. Kaeppler in *Time Out of Time: Essays on the Festival* by Alessandro Falassi. Albuquerque: Univ. of New Mexico, 1986, pp. 165-166.

July 15

St. Swithin's Day

A day to honor St. Swithin, who became bishop of Winchester in 852. He was made a chaplain to Egbert, king of the West Saxons and was tutor to the young prince Ethelwolf. Swithin was born in Wessex and spent his youth at Old Abbey in Winchester.

Great Britain

Weather forecasting

St. Swithin, bishop of Winchester, died in 862. He requested burial outside the church. When attempts were made to move his body inside the church after his canonization a torrential rain lasting 40 days occurred. His body was left where it was. His day is seen as a weather forecast day. If it rains on St. Swithin's Day, it will rain for 40 days. If not, it will be fair for 40 days.

St. Swithin's Day weather chants

St. Swithun's Day, if thou dost rain
For forty days it will remain
St. Swithun's Day, if thou be fair
For forty days 'twill rain nae mair.

If you live in apple-orchard country you must remember that—

"If it rain on St. Swithun's
The apples be christened."

After that the early ripening varieties may be picked.

Source: *Happy Holidays* by Eleanor Graham. New York: E.P. Dutton, 1933, p. 247.

July 15

Virgin of Carmen

Day of celebration for the Virgin of Carmen.

Mexico

A fiesta for the Virgin of Carmen in Santa Cruz Etla, c. 1945

"Oh, you must know the Virgin of Carmen, Doña Elena, *pues* she is the Virgin who lives at Carmen. We have a statue of her in the San Pablo church. Last year the mother of this family, Doña Socorro, my little godmother, was very sick. All of us prayed. Don Bernabé promised that he would give the *mayordomia* to the Virgin on her day, July 15, if Doña Socorro got better. Certainly she got better."

Hence, the unusually loud rockets were paid for by this family, as well as the mass itself and the decorations in the church. When we got inside, the church was lighted with many expensive candles and strung with pink and white crepe paper. There were flowers in all seven saints' niches, and many lilies in front of the blue and white Virgin. There are no seats or benches in the San Pablo church; everyone kneels on the tile floor. There were about sixty people kneeling there that day, including twenty-five from Santa Cruz. In front of the church, special holy musicians, a piper and a drummer, the most primitive, pre-conquest musicians I ever heard in the Etla region, were playing an endless, plaintive tune. Every five or ten minutes the "rocket-setter-offer" who was with them would put some black powder in a small clay dish, light it with a charcoal ember at the end of long wooden tongs, and turn to run quickly as it exploded.

When we came out of mass, we followed the "holy" musicians up the hill to the house of Don Bernabé. Here we found that Doña Sista, wife of the then president of the Santa Cruz municipality, and as such obligated to help in San Pablo, had already been there two days grinding chile into *mole* and making tortillas, while Don Bartolo, the Santa Cruz president, having contributed young goats, was helping in the butchering of a hog. Now at 6:00 A.M. they were both helping Don Bernabé serve chocolate out in the houseyard for all the visitors from the mass.

As a special guest of Santa Cruz Etla, I was ushered inside the one-room adobe house. Here two long tables from the San Pablo school had been set up and covered with embroidered altar cloths. Two tortillas apiece were given to each guest with the chocolate, which was served in *jicaras,* small painted gourds. No one washed out the gourds; they were just drained of chocolate and passed on to someone else. The chocolate was made with cocoa, crude brown sugar (*panela*), and wheat flour gruel (*atole*), all boiled up together. Really it didn't taste very good.

It was three o'clock when I went back with Esperanza, Joel, and Sofia. By the time we arrived, all the pork, *mole* sauce, and beans were gone, fed to the hundred or more people who had come from both towns. Now they were serving pulque, that sour beer made from the century plant. They had mixed it with the *panela*. Esperanza thought it was the finest *dulce,* or sweetmeat, she had ever tasted, so I was glad to give her my full *jicara.* I was more than contented with three bottles of the strawberry pop which had been the *gasto,* or contribution, of Don Martin's family. (The cultural missions list does not include "the use of strawberry pop" as an improvement for rural Mexico; but the quantities of it consumed are surely an indication of the modernization and prosperity of any community, although it was being edged out in popularity by Pepsi-Cola at Don Martin's store in 1954.)

The women were still working in the bamboo kitchen outside, washing up the ten-gallon water jars in which they had cooked the pork. The babies were parked in a corner, asleep on a *petate.* Esperanza sat with the young women outside in the houseyard on other *petates,* and I joined them, even though the only place left to sit was right under the noses of Don Bernabé's oxen, which had been yoked together and tethered close for the day in order to keep them quiet while the rockets went off. Inside the dark little house, among the pigs' feet, the San Pablo Etla band, two clarinets, a bass viol, and our Don Fausto at the guitar, kept playing all day, dance music mostly, while occasionally people danced between the *petates* spread outside. Up on the hill behind the house, from sunrise to sunset, the "holy" musicians continued also to play, the piper with his shrill little four-note pipe, such as one associates with Inca llama herders, and the drummer with two Indian-type skin drums, as well as the famous "rocket-setter-offer," all well paid by Don Bernabé to provide the music that the Virgin of Carmen particularly liked for the entire day. They took up their stand on the hillside trail and kept up their mournful little refrain hour after hour, eight notes up and down the pipe, then four hard beats on each drum. The rocket-setter-offer had to retire when he ran out of powder, but the piper and drummer never gave up.

The dance band inside the house, close to the pulque, stopped to rest and drink and chat quite often. Whenever the dance music stopped, the piper and the drummer would come down from the trail into the houseyard and play more and more loudly nearer and nearer the door of the hut. When the dancers would start again, the primitive piper would wrap himself in his *sarape* up to his eyes, and stalk off up the trail to take up a position behind the house until the dance band stopped to drink once more. I saw this happen, like a repeated movie, at least six times during the afternoon. When it became too dark for Don Fausto's friends to play inside the house, they moved outdoors onto the ground in the late afternoon light. Set face to face like this with "modern" music, the piper and the drummer gave up and went home.

Source: *Santa Cruz of the Etla Hills* by Helen Miller Bailey. Gainesville, Univ. of Florida Press, 1958, pp. 119-122.

Ninth of Av (July-August)

Tish-Ah Be-Av

The period from 17th Tammuz to Tish-Ah Be-Av is referred to as the Three Weeks. It is a period of mourning for the destruction of the first and second temples in Jerusalem. The First Temple was destroyed by the Babylonians in 587 B.C. The Second Temple was destroyed by the Romans in A.D. 70. Tish-Ah Be-Av, the final day of this mourning period, is a fast day. Because Tish-Ah Be-Av commemorates the exile of the Jewish people, some feel that since the founding of the Jewish State of Israel in 1948 this day should become a day of rejoicing rather than mourning. Others disagree.

For more on Tish-Ah Be-Av see: ''The Three Weeks'' in *The Jewish Holdays: A Guide and Commentary* by Michael Strassfeld. New York: Harper & Row, 1985, pp. 85-93.

Iran

Ninth of Ab in Iran

On the eve of the fast a special meal is made of rice, beans, and hard-boiled eggs dipped in ashes. A pinch of ashes is rubbed on the forehead at the close of the meal. The Book of Lamentations is read by candlelight, and at the close of the reading, the candles are put out. The head of the house gives family members a bit of money to put under their pillows that night. In the morning this will be given to the poor. The next day the Book of Job is read in Persian. At the time for the *minha,* everyone assembles in the synagogue courtyard for the ritual slaughter of a sheep. This sheep has been purchased with an ''Atonement Offering'' to which everyone has contributed. All the men of the synagogue put their hands on the sheep as the prayer is offered before the sacrifice.

Source: *One People: The Story of the Eastern Jews* by Devora and Menachem Hacoben. New York: Sabra, 1969, p. 34.

Morocco

Tish'a b'Av

Observance in Morocco

The days between the seventeenth of lammuz and the ninth of Ab were keenly felt in the *mellah*. Children began fasting at the age of nine. On *Tish'a b'Av* night the entire family slept on the bare floor. To the prescribed Lamentations there was added a passage commemorating the expulsion from Spain, many of the forebears of those reciting it had been among the exiles.

Tunisia

Ninth of Ab in Tunis

The ninth of Ab was the culmination of weeks of mourning, not only for Zion but for the Tunisian community in its days of trial. Lamentations commemorating these days were composed in the vernacular by the Tunisian Jews. In the morning of the fast day, the Torah Scroll was placed on a low, black-covered bench, rather than on the reading table. The men came to prayers with ashes on their foreheads, while the women went to the cemeteries to pray at the graves of the sages. Since tradition had it that the messiah was born on the day that the Temple fell, the women cleaned and whitewashed their homes, to express their belief in his coming.

Yemen

Ninth of Ab in Yemen

The ''three weeks'' between the seventeenth of Tammuz and the ninth of Ab were observed in mourning. No business ventures were initiated during this period, which was regarded as being persecution-prone. Meat was permissible until the last meal before the fast. Everyone fasted most punctilliously—the weak, the ill, the pregnant. The ninth of Ab fast gave full expression to the yearning of the Yemenite community for the return to its ancestral home, and it also voiced the pent-up pain of life in that diaspora. Lamentations was read in the dim light of small candles, and the wailing in the synagogue was like mourning for the dead. The Scrolls of the Torah were decked in black. As the fast drew to its close, all spirits were uplifted. The final parting words were: ''May the mourners for Zion be given splendor in the place of ashes'' and each worshipper went home with hope and faith in his heart.

Source: *One People: The Story of the Eastern Jews* by Devora and Menachem Hacohen. New York: Sabra, 1969, pp. 34, 67, 90, 148.

July 25

St. James's Day / Fiesta de Santiago

St. James is the patron saint of Spain (Santiago). After being beheaded in Palestine, his body was set adrift in a boat whence it was guided by angels to Compostela, Spain. Eight hundred years later a hermit discovered the grave of the saint surrounded by heavenly lights. The feast is a celebration of the anniversary of this event.

Great Britain

St. James's Day grottoes

In the poorer districts of London it was once a popular custom of children to construct small grottoes of oyster shells on St. James's Day. These were constructed at the edge of the sidewalk and people were asked for a donation with phrases such as, "Penny for the grotter," or "Please sir, remember the grotter." These children's grottoes were reported to be a nuisance by *The Times* in 1957. The grottoes are made of sand and earth and decorated with broken glass, stones, shells, flowers, and moss.

Source: *Lore and Language of Schoolchildren* by Peter and Iona Opie. Oxford: Oxford Univ. Press, 1959, pp. 266-267.

Puerto Rico

The Fiesta de Santiago in Loiz Aldea

On this festival day the villagers take on characters from the battle of St. James against the Moors. Some wear white face, dressed as Spanish Conquistadors; others impersonate the Moors, with grotesque carved, horned masks. Still others are clowns and "crazy women" (men dressed as women).

Castor Ayala, the mask maker

Castor Ayala of Medianias carves the unusual coconut husk masks worn at this festival. Though he is black, his artistry was inspired by the "spirit of the Indian." And he told this story: "One morning, about five o'clock, my neighbor saw an Indian standing at the gate, his hands across his chest. He was smoking a pipe and had great feathers in the back of his head and part of his head was shaved. She called her sister and she saw the same thing. They couldn't work that day, because they were shaking and had a fever. They told me and I joked, 'Ha, don't worry. That's my watchman, don't get afraid.' Then I went to Guayama, and the spiritualist there say she see the same thing. About five different [spiritualist] ladies in different parts of the island say the same.

"One of them told me, 'The Indian was your father in ancient times, and he is by your side always. Don't you feel him by your side when you are alone?"

" 'Yes,' I said. 'I don't see him, but I feel he is there.'

"She said, 'Everything you design is not from you. Your hand is directed by him.' "

Source: *The Island: The Worlds of Puerto Rico* by Stan Seiner. New York: Harper & Row, 1974, pp. 63-65.

For more information on St. James's Day see: "St. James's Day, July 25" in *Folklore of American Holidays* edited by Hennig Cohen and Tristram Potter Coffin. 2nd ed. Detroit: Gale Research, 1991.

July 26

St. Anne's Day

Canada

Honoring St. Anne, the mother of Mary

St. Anne, the mother of Mary, was a favorite saint in Brittany and England. A chapel built in 1658 at Beaupré on the St. Lawrence River near Quebec City is the goal of over 15,000 pilgrims on July 26. Candlelight processions and a blessing of the sick occur. At the same time gypsy families from all over Canada and the United States arrive to celebrate what they call Santana on the church grounds. Each camping family prepares a *slava* feast in honor of St. Anne and there is much visiting among families.

Source: *Let's Celebrate!* by Caroline Parry. Toronto: Kids Can Press, 1987, pp. 168-170.

For more on St. Anne's Day see: Angelo, My Love. RCA/ Columbia, 1983. Film. (Shows ethnographic scenes of gypsy participation in Santana at Beaupré.)

July 26

Pardon De Ste. Ann d'Auray

France

The pilgrimage to attend a "pardon" in Brittany

Of even greater interest is the fervor with which Bretons enter into their pilgrimages. Those among them who leave their familiar horizons do not hesitate to undertake long and expensive voyages to solicit a favor, accomplish a vow or just pay homage to some renowned sanctuary. Some "Pardons," such as the one held at Ste. Ann d'Auray on July 26, will draw over 20,000 people. They come on foot, in cavalcades of cars, busloads—all singing their favorite hymns. It is like this, too, for the Pardon of Ste. Anne-de-la-Palud on the last Sunday in August. Pilgrims can be found everywhere, and those who must sleep under the stars for lack of accommodations can be multiplied without end since most towns and cities can boast of at least one Pardon during the year.

All in all, the Pardon remains the feast par excellence. The solemn ceremonies of the morning and afternoon, the famous procession which displays the delegations of 20 or more parishes with their flamboyant banners, the fire set to the "bucher" (stump of tree) by the clergyman, the prayers to the saints and their relics, the visits to the cemeteries and the bone-chapels, the visit to the sacred fountain are all functions of a program which remains purely religious. And if, at times, there are scenes more spirited than spiritual, the real sense of pilgrimage, when people come to honor the patron saint of the locality, to ask for new favors or the continuation of the old, is never lost.

Source: *The Breton and His World: Requiem for a Culture.* Compiled and translated by Gabrielle L. Coffee. Mobile, Alabama: The Madaloni Press, 1985, pp. 53-54.

July 29
Ólavsoka

Olav of Norway, 995-1030, was a descendant of King Harold of Norway. After spending his youth in piracy, he was baptized in Rouen (1013) and helped Ethelred of England against the Danes. In 1016 he became king of Norway and brought missionaries to Christianize his country. Because his harsh measures were disliked, he was driven from the country and died in battle attempting to regain his throne. He is considered the champion of national independence in Norway.

Faroe Islands

Celebrating St. Olaf's Wake

In the Faroe Islands St. Olaf's Day is celebrated as Ólavsoka, St. Olaf's Wake. Parliament opens on this day amid pageantry. Celebrations take place on the eve of Ólavsoka, July 28, and throughout the day on July 29.

Ólavsoka in Tórshavn

On July 28 in Tórshavn, the capital of the Faroe Islands, the town remains brightly lit as the long evening fades. From down by the harbor, up past the little green in front of the parliament-house, and on up to the theater, the main street is festooned with flags and colored lights. The theater has been turned into a dance hall, where people will dance all night to the heroic ballads which have been remembered in the Faroes since medieval times; downtown, young people are at a rock concert; in between the two, a few amusement stands rather grandiosely called a ''Tivoli'' are doing a thriving business; and from one end of the street to the other people are wandering back and forth: young people are courting; older couples are strolling, sometimes with a child or two in tow, greeting friends and taking in the sights and dropping into acquaintances' homes for a chat; people of all sorts are pausing to hear streetcorner preachers exhort them to be saved; and men—alone or in twos and threes—are lurching back and forth, drunk and getting drunker, singing snatches of song and finally passing out. During the day you may have taken in an art exhibit in the new national gallery up on the edge of town, or joined the spectators at one of the many sporting events. Tomorrow there will be more sports—a rowing-race in the harbor, a soccer match on the field across the road from the art gallery, a pony-race on a stretch of dirt road outside town. . . . In the morning the teams assembled on the green by the parliament-house, heard speeches and paraded off.

The occasion for all this revelry is the opening session of the Faroese parliament or Logting. Tomorrow morning there will be another sort of procession—a parade of dignitaries. The head of the Faroese clergy, the members of the Logting, and the chief representatives of the Danish state will parade through lines of spectators from the parliament-house to the church. There they will hear a sermon before parading back again to open the parliamentary session. And then there will be more sports, more preaching, more strolling up and down, more dancing in the dance-hall, another rock concert, and more drinking—until morning. Then, groggy, people will begin boarding ferries for the trip back to their home villages.

It is Ólavsoka, St. Olaf's Wake, the 29th of July, the Faroese national holiday. What can we make of it?

Among its many striking contrasts, Ólavsoka obviously includes both old fashioned and modern activities. Indeed, in a sense the whole occasion is ancient, for the Logting is descended from an althing, or parliament and court attended by all free men, which probably began in about the year 900 to meet at midsummer in Tórshavn on a rocky spit called the Tinganes.

Source: ''Ólavsoka: The Faroese National Holiday'' by Jonathan Wylie in *Studies in Society and History,* 24 (3), 438.

Moon 7, Day 7 (July-August)

The Birthday of the Seven Old Maids

This is a day to honor the seven daughters of the god of the hearth, Tsao Shen. They are the protectors of children. The youngest is the Spinning Maid, whose feast falls on this night.

Taiwan

Seeking protection for children

The seven old maids, Chhit-niu-ma, are patrons of children from their birth until their sixteenth year. Their aid may be solicited to conceive a child or for the good health of one's children.

To invoke their aid one must make a vow to do charitable work, give an opera, or such. The banner of the Eight Immortals is hung over the door and a banquet is given for relatives and neighbors. Also a puppet show or opera is sponsored at the home or at a temple. The family must ''kill a pig and fell a goat'' and do a work of mercy. If a child protected by the seven sisters lives to be sixteen, then on the seventh day of the seventh month, the vow must be fulfilled by killing a pig.

Source: *Taiwan Feasts and Customs* by Michael R. Saso. Hsinchu, Taiwan: Chabanel Language Institute, pp. 61-62.

Moon 7, Day 7 (July-August)

Chhit Sek / Chilsuk / Double Seventh

An auspicious day, the seventh day of the seventh moon is a "double seventh." On this night the Heavenly Spinning Maid meets her lover, the Cowherd, according to legend.

Hong Kong

Trays for the Seven Sisters

On the evening of one such festival, the skies had cleared after a three-hour thunderstorm and, by nightfall, all the side-streets were thronged with sight-seers. The chief offering to the Seven Sisters was a circular tray whose centrepiece depicted the meeting of the Cowherd and the Weaving Lady, who stood on a bridge spanning a stream in which waded the Magic Buffalo led by the Cowherd. In the background were the six sisters. Round the tray were the ornaments and toilet requisites for all seven; a fan, mirror, powder puff, bracelets and cosmetics, sometimes a flute, and always paper flowers for the hair, and a comb for dressing it. The trays varied from the cheapest variety in paper, on which the emblems were printed in colour, to huge electrically illuminated discs, hung on shop frontages, with mechanical tableaux in the centre. Some were fifteen to twenty feet across. Hanging at the side were elaborately painted paper dresses of Ming period style for the sisters, and a black and gold costume for the Cowherd. The altar, set just outside, or immediately within the doorway, was furnished with the usual five vessels, and three thick sticks of incense smouldered in the burner. In front were piles of fruit and nuts. Oranges lent a bright spot of colour. Green melons, bananas, dragons' eyes, and carambolas, regardless of price, formed part of the offerings. On one altar a white porcelain bowl filled with pure water, on which floated two pummelo leaves, symbolised the ritual bath for the bride. That Chinese religious ideas move with the times is demonstrated by the fact that an aeroplane is occasionally provided to ensure the meeting of the Celestial Lovers in the case when the weather is cloudy, and the magpies cannot form the bridge. Similarly at funerals a cardboard motorcar has replaced the old Peking cart for those Chinese whose affluence enabled them to enjoy the comfort of a limousine during their lifetime.

Perhaps the prettiest display consisted of a huge illuminated tray hung above the altar which was set on a balcony in front of the ground entrance to a building. As there was no house opposite, the effect of the lighting was enhanced, and crowds of sight-seers stood below, or on the steep staircase. An enormous roast pig was the centrepiece of the table, which groaned with its load of fruit. Nothing for the comfort of the seven sisters had been omitted, for they were even provided with a cigarette and a lipstick apiece. The outlay for all this magnificence was considerable, and had been contributed by six girls, none of whom belonged to any guild. As a rule the maidens form clubs, according to their trade, and contribute a small monthly sum from their earnings. Should a girl marry after she has agreed to subscribe, she must continue her payments till the next festival, in which she takes part as an unmarried woman. Should a child be born during the period, a fine is levied, in eggs for a girl baby, with a chicken in addition for a boy.

Source: *Chinese Creeds and Customs* by V. R. Burkhardt. Hong Kong: South China Morning Post, 1982, pp. 41-42.

Korea

Gyunoo and Jingny O, Herdboy and Weaving Maid

Young girls and unmarried women bow to the two stars, Herdboy (Altair) and Weaver (Vega) on this night and pray for improvement in sewing. Scholars drink wine and write poems to the star lovers.

Only a few magpies are seen on this night as all have made the voyage to the Milky Way to form a bridge for the two lovers to cross. In the morning they are everywhere to be seen, baldheaded because the Herdboy and the Weaving maid walked on them the night before. Rain falling on this night represents tears of joy at their meeting and tears of grief at their farewell.

Source: *Folk Customs and Family Life* by Tae Hung Ha. Seoul, Korea: Yonsei, 1958, p. 890.

People's Republic of China

Cleaning on Double Seventh

In non-Buddhist families, general housecleaning is postponed until after the great summer rains. The festival of the "double seven" (seventh day of the seventh month) is the day when the good housewife cleans the house, airing all clothes and books in the courtyard. This is a day which is especially lucky for housewives, as it is the day when the fairies travel around. On this day there must be no sunshine to spoil the books and dresses.

When the cowherd and spinning maid visit, there is no sun

And as the two are bashful, there is always a thick cover of clouds to conceal their happy meeting from the eyes of mortals. A rain which might fall during the night is the tears of the separating couple. The next day, you will see again the two stars on either side of the Milky Way.

Source: *Chinese Festivals* by Wolfram Eberhard. New York: Henry Schuman, 1952, pp. 143-144.

The evening of a small girl in Wuch'ang, Hupeh Province, c. 1920

The evening of the seventh day of the seventh month is the Evening of the Small Girl, and on this evening Hsing and I had to make sacrifices to the goddess of Weaving and Handicrafts, the Heavenly Weaver, Ch'i Ch'iao. We had to ask to be made clever at handicrafts. Mother said that every girl should be able to weave and embroider.

This evening a sacrificial table was set up after dinner on the balcony. Mother put out various ladies' toilet articles such as a comb, a mirror, cosmetics, artificial flowers, and so on, so that the Heavenly Weaver could make herself pretty; and also scissors, a needle and thread—the tools of a clever needlewoman—and little cakes and fruits, and, of course, candles. I had to light the candles and bow before the Heavenly Weaver, and then try, by the light of the moon—or, if it was cloudy, by the gentle light of the candles—to thread the needle. Little girls in China, from princesses to shepherdesses, had done this from earliest times.

Mother told me that the Heavenly Weaver would cross the Heavenly River in the night to rejoin for a short time the Heavenly Cowherd. Then, many, many magpies would come and build a bridge across the Heavenly River. Mother pointed to the sky and showed me the Milky Way, which was the Heavenly River, and told me that the star to the east of it was the Heavenly Weaver, and the star to the west the Heavenly Cowherd. The Weaver and the Cowherd were in love, but it was granted to them to meet only once a year on the night of the seventh day of the seventh month. That was why it usually rained gently on this night, light, warm rain: the raindrops were the tears of the Heavenly Weaver.

Source: *The Lotus Pool* by Chow Chung-cheng. New York: Appleton-Century Crofts, 1961, p. 82.

Taiwan

Chhit Sek

Constellations

The second celebration of the day is the meeting of the spinning girl and the oxherd boy, who are represented by the constellations Lyra and Aquila, respectively. They are the patrons of courtship and faithfulness in marriage. The feast in their honor is called Chhit sek or "seventh evening."

Taiwanese versions of the spinning-girl legend

The original legend tells how the spinning girl was banished from heaven to earth for a period of three years, where she met the oxherd boy and married him. After the term of banishment was finished, she returned to heaven, but the love of the oxherd boy for her was so great that he tried to pursue her. He was stopped by the "great silver river of the sky," i.e., the milky way, and could not find her. Seeing the plight of the two lovers, the Jade Emperor allowed all the crows from earth to fly up and build a bridge across the milky way, so that they might meet once a year. The evening of the seventh day, seventh month, is the time for their annual meeting. But if it rains, the crows cannot fly up, and the meeting must be postponed another year.

Another version of the story says that the spinning maid came down to earth with her other six sisters, and were swimming in a stream when the oxherd boy saw them. Attracted by the spinning girl, the oxherd boy proposed to her, and she agreed to stay on earth with him. So they lived happily for three years, while the heavenly spinning was unattended. The Jade Emperor therefore decreed that the spinning girl must return to her work in heaven. When the oxherd boy tried to follow her, he was stopped by the heavenly river, and only allowed to cross it once a year, so as not to disturb the spinning girl from her weaving. Once a year, on this night, the crows and magpies all fly up to heaven and build a bridge for them across the milky way. Some say that a slight rain will keep the crows from flying, others hold that rain on the evening of the seventh means that the spinning girl is crying, because she must be separated from her lover for another year.

The Taiwanese, in much more humorous vein, tell the story in another fashion. The oxherd boy, they say, is very lazy. For a whole year he does not wash the dishes in the sink, leaving them for the spinning girl to wash when she comes on her annual visit. A rainfall on this night means that the spinning girl is crying at the sight of all the dishes, for she must spend the shole [whole] night cleaning them.

Celebrating Chhit sek

In order to celebrate the feast, the young ladies of the house are supposed to lay out a table of offerings under the moon. The table top includes incense, fresh flowers, fruit, face powder, and other cosmetics. After praying, the powder is thrown into the air, or onto the roof-top, as a kind of offering to the spinning girl. They [sic] young ladies of the family also try to thread a needle by the light of the moon, thus assuring their capabilities at embroidery and household management in the future.

Source: *Taiwan Feasts and Customs* by Michael R. Saso. Hsrinchu, Taiwan: Chabanel Language Institute, pp. 62-64.

Moon 7, Day 7 (July-August)

Tanabata

Tanabata, the Star Festival, falls on the seventh day of the seventh moon but is now celebrated on July 7. On this night the Weaving Girl and the Herd Boy, lovers separated eternally by the Milky Way, may cross the heavenly river and visit. A flock of magpies form a bridge for them. Poems are written in the honor of these lovers and hung decoratively on a bamboo set in the yard or home. Ceremonial foods may be laid out, and the evening may be a festive occasion.

Japan

The legend of the weaver maiden

The festival is based on a legend of which there exist several renderings in China and Korea, widely divergent as to details but all founded on the same principle. . . . the festival obtained a great hold over the entire population, and continues to be faithfully observed, at least in rural districts.

The daughter of the Celestial Emperor, Tentei, lived on the eastern embankment of the River of Heaven (the Milky Way), where she was dutifully engaged in weaving the cloth needed by the many gods in her father's mansion. Day and night she sat at her loom, rapidly shooting the shuttle and clapping the reed. So absorbed was she in her work that she was only known as Shokujo, the Weaving Girl.

When reaching maturity, her father chose a husband for her in the person of a herdsman, Kengyū, the "Ox-Puller," who ruled on the western side of the river where he pastured his only beast. The two young people fell deeply in love with each other, indeed, their honeymoon lasted so long that they neglected their duties altogether, the ox grew thin, and the gods began to grumble about thier lack of clothing. Tentei, in a fit of anger, as punishement condemned the couple to again live apart on the opposite embankments, permitting them to meet only once a year, on the 7th night of the 7th moon.

But the River of Heaven is broad and swift, and no bridge spans it. So when the night of meeting arrives, the compassionate magpies flock together and form a path with their extended wings over which the lady can walk, to meet her husband.

Celebrating Tanabata

Fourth among the five big festivals, the *gosekku* of Japan, comes *tanabata* on the 7th day of the 7th lunar month, which usually fell on a date in August, during the hottest weather. If you go into the country on that day, you may still find rows of freshly cut bamboo stuck into the ground in front of the houses, or affixed to doors and eaves. They will be adorned with numerous pieces of gaily coloured paper: neat strips which twirl on a thread, and which, closer inspection will show, are covered with inscriptions, poems in fact. They are all in praise of Tanabata, the Weaver Princess. On the eve of the festival the children sat around a table and with the help of their elders tried to compose them, as fine ones as possible; and where the poetical vein was insufficient they had recourse to well-known anthologies. Provided with India-ink and brush, they then laboriously traced the characters in their best hand on the *goshiki no kami,* the "papers of five colours"—green and yellow, red and white, and dark blue as a substitute for the primary black.

In the morning, very early, these flattering outpours are then attached to the bamboos, to add to the festive atmosphere of the day. It is but natural that people should eschew work and dress better than usual: yet there is no noticeable increase in communal activity.

It is in the evening, well after sun-down, that the festival truly begins. A low stand will be set out on mattings, in the open, flanked by similarly ornamented bamboo twigs, and loaded with *sake* and various auspicious foods for the deities, offered on the usual *sambō* (ceremonial tray), while a few festive lanterns will enliven the "altar." In the more cultured households, a *koto* (harp) and a flute may also be laid out, to suggest the "harmony" of music, the *koto* being the feminine and the flute the masculine instrument *par excellence,* and together forming a melodious duet. Similarly, husband and wife should live in harmony, the manly flute leading with the tune, the gentler *koto* accompanying and supporting it with multiple chords. Perhaps there will be "offerings" of a *kimono* spread over a lacquered rack, a spool of coloured thread, some imitation gold coins. It is even said that there used to be special *tanabata*-needles with five eyes, to be threaded with threads of five different colours—amuletic for proficiency in sewing. And there will be incense, simple flowers, and the leaves of the *kaji* mulberry. Nearby, on the well-known broad benches on which the Japanese squat to enjoy the summer breeze in front of their homes, the family will sit and fan themselves and enjoy a pleasant evening.

Source: *The Five Sacred Festivals of Ancient Japan: Their Symbolism & Historical Development* by V. A. Casal. Tokyo: Sophia University and Charles E. Tuttle Co., 1967. pp. 79-94.

(Casal discusses the history of this holiday and variants of the "Weaver Maiden" legend.)

Tanabata Matsuri, c. 1980

Tuesday was *Tanabata Matsuri* (65), and the hottest day so far this year. Although we prayed for a clear evening, we were disappointed. Hajime stayed up long past his bedtime hoping to see the stars in the Milky Way, but finally he could not keep his eyes open any longer. His calligraphy has improved tremendously (66), and I think he believes that the stars may have had something to do with that. I know I did, and I remember how kind and encouraging you were to me when I was that age. School will soon be over, and Hajime is looking forward to his vacation. We have found a resort on the Izu Peninsula near Shimoda and plan to drive down together with Toshiro-san in the Mazda for a few days. I think it will be educational for Hajime to visit Shimoda.

Until the Meiji period, *Tanabata Matsuri* was observed on the seventh night of the seventh month of the lunar calendar. It is now celebrated on July 7, according to the Gregorian calendar. Schoolchildren write on paper strips and offer examples of their calligraphy to the two stars, and bamboo branches hung with poems written on colored strips of paper (*tanzaku*) are placed in front of houses or garden gates. On July 8, children take their decorated bamboo branches to the nearest stream for the current to carry away.

Source: *Letters from Sachiko: A Japanese Woman's View of Life in the Land of the Economic Miracle* by James Trager. New York: Atheneum, 1982, pp. 111, 207. (From letters to his Japanese wife from her sister.)

Tanabata Sohmen

Sohmen are thin wheat flour noodles which are normally eaten cold during the summer months, a time when the appetite tends to suffer because of the heat. Eaten after dipping in soy based sauce, sohmen can serve as a refreshing summer snack.

Amanogawa (the Milky Way) is the name given to a sohmen dish that is specially made on the seventh of July each year when the Milky Way is most clearly visible in Japan. It is also on this day, called Tanabata, when the Japanese can 'wish on a star' to make their dreams come true.

Milky Way Sohmen

Ingredients (to serve 4)
3 bunches dried sohmen
6 tablespoons gelatin
2-3 spring onions
4 cups water
4 tablespoons soy sauce
3 tablespoons mirin
1 tablespoon concentrated Japanese soup stock (or aspic jelly)
Some cotton string or elastic bands

Directions
1. Boil the water and dissolve the gelatin. Add the mirin and soy sauce.
2. Tightly tie the ends of the sohmen with the string or elastic bands. Boil with plenty of water for a total of 2-3 minutes. Remove and wash well. Allow to drain.
3. Cut the string and arrange the sohmen neatly in the bottom of a tin dish. Pour over 2/3 of the gelatin mixture and allow to stand.
4. Wash and chop up the spring onions. Sprinkle over the gelatin soup in the tin. Pour on the rest of the mixture, allow to cool and chill in the refrigerator. Cut into 7cm x 4cm pieces to serve.

Source: *A Taste of Japan* edited by Itsuko Hamada. Japan Air Lines Co., Ltd., 1950, p. 83.

Moon 7, Days 13-15 (July-August)

Obon

Obon is held during July or August. Each temple sets the date for its bon-odori dance. Obon includes visits to family graves, the return of family members to their birthplace, special foods offered in honor of the ancestors, and a lantern hung outside to guide home the spirits of the dead. The festival is held in honor of the dead and prayers are offered for their repose. The bon-odori dances are festive occasions that may include the selling of snacks and knicknacks by vendors.

Japan

Bon Odori in Miyamoto-cho neighborhood, Tokyo, c. 1980

The midsummer Bon Odori, one of the few joint projects of Miyamoto-chō's chōkai and shōtenkai, provides another major recreational opportunity. This popular event, held for two nights each July on the playground of the elementary school, attracts about 300 children and adults each evening for several hours of folk-dancing to recorded music. Children seem to prefer the Western-style folk tunes they learn in school, but local dance troupes of middle-aged women perform more old-fashioned dances on a wooden stage, which men from the two associations erect in the center of the playground. The "sale" of plastic lanterns—about 150 of which are hung around the stage and in long strings from the stage to the outer edges of the playing field—pays for the Bon Odori and usually earns a small surplus for the chōkai and the shōtenkai. Local merchants buy one or more small lanterns with their shop names painted on them for a contribution of 1,000 yen per lantern; larger lanterns, bought primarily by local politicians and local bank branches, cost the donors 10,000 yen apiece. The plastic lanterns are reused (and resold) from year to year, so the Bon Odori's major expenses are the electricity for the lanterns and the public-address system, and the hundreds of ice cream bars chōkai leaders distribute to throngs of clamoring kids at the end of the evenings.

Source: *Neighborhood Tokyo* by Theodore C. Bestor. Stanford, Calif.: Stanford Univ. Press, 1989, p. 157.

Ura Bon in Nineteenth-century Nagaoka

Ura Bon—(A Welcome to Souls Returned)—was our festival to celebrate the annual visit of O Shorai Sama, a term used to represent the combined spirits of all our ancestors. It was the most dearly loved of our festivals, for we believed that our ancestors never lost their loving interest in us, and this yearly visit kept fresh in all our hearts a cheerful and affectionate nearness to the dear ones gone.

In preparing for the arrival of O Shorai Sama the only standards were cleanliness and simplicity; everything being done in an odd primitive fashion, not elaborated, even in the slightest degree, from Bon festivals of the most ancient time.

For several days everyone had been busy. Jiya and another man had trimmed the trees and hedges, had swept all the ground, even under the house, and had carefully washed off the stepping stones in the garden. The floor mats were taken out and whipped dustless with bamboo switches, Kin and Toshi, in the meantime, making the air resound with the "pata-pata-pata" of paper dusters against the *shoji,* and the long-drawn-out "see-wee-is-shi" of steaming hot padded cloths pushed up and down the polished porch floors. All the woodwork in the house—the broad ceiling boards, the hundreds of tiny white bars crossing the paper doors, the carved ventilators, and the mirror-like post and platform of the *tokonomas*—was wiped off with hot water; then every little broken place in the rice-paper *shoji* was mended, and finally the entire house, from thatch to the under-floor ice-box, was as fresh and clean as rain-water falling from the sky.

Mother brought from the godown a rare old *kakemono,* one of Father's treasures, and after it was hung Kin placed beneath it our handsomest bronze vase holding a big loose bunch of the seven grasses of autumn—althea, pampas, convolvulus, wild pink, and three kinds of asters, purple, yellow, and white. These are mostly flowers, but Japanese designate all plants that grow from the ground in slender, blade-like leaves, as grasses.

The shrine was, of course, the most important of all, as it was there the spirit guest lived during the days of the visit. Jiya had gone to the pond before dawn to get lotus blossoms, for it is only with the first rays of sunrise that the "puff" comes, which opens the pale green buds into snowy beauty. Before he returned, the shrine had been emptied and cleaned, and the bronze Buddha reverentially dusted and returned to his place on the gilded lotus. The tablet holding the ancestors' names, and Father's picture, which Mother always kept in the shrine, were wiped off carefully, the brass open-work "everlasting-light" lantern filled afresh with rape-seed oil, the incense burner, the candle stands, the sacred books, and our rosaries, all arranged in place, and the ugly fish-mouth wooden drum, which is typical of woman's submissive position, rubbed until the worn place on the red lacquer was a shiny brown. Then Jiya covered the floor before the shrine with a fresh, rudely woven mat of pampas grass and placed on either side a vase holding bunches of the seven grasses of autumn.

But the most interesting time of all came when Honourable Grandmother and I sat down before the shrine to prepare the decorations of welcome. I always loved to help her do this. Ishi and Toshi brought us some odd-shaped vegetables they had found in the garden, a handful of dried hemp stems from which the bark had been removed, and yards and yards of *somen*—a sort of soft, pliable macaroni. Honourable Grandmother took a crooked-necked cucumber, one end of which was shaped something like a lifted head, and made it into a horse, using corn silk for mane and tail and hemp stems for stiff little legs. Of a small, plump eggplant she made a water buffalo, with horns and legs of hemp stems, and twisting some half-dried *somen* into harness for both little animals, she placed them in the shrine. I made several horses and buffaloes too. While we were working, Jiya came in with some small lotus leaves, the edges of which were beginning to dry and turn up like little curved dishes, and a few very small yellow and red balls, a new kind of fruit, which I now know were tomatoes.

After Ishi had filled the lotus-leaf dishes with vegetables and every kind of fruit except the furry peach, Honourable Grandmother looped the *somen* across the top of the shrine in a series of graceful festoons, hanging on it at intervals small purple eggplants and the tiny yellow and red tomatoes.

Then Ishi brought the kitchen "row-of-steps," and climbing up, hung the white Bon lantern high above everything. It was only a white paper cube, twisted about with a braid of paper having loose ends; but when it was lighted the heat made it constantly whirl, and the many ends of paper rising, falling, and waving looked like a flock of tiny fluttering birds. It was very beautiful.

Just before sunset we were all ready, for twilight was the hour of welcome. O Shorai Sama was always spoken of as a vague, impersonal figure who came riding on a snow-white steed from "the land of darkness, the shores of the unknown, the place of the dead."

Like all children I had always looked forward with pleasure to the visit of the ancestors, but after Father's death, I felt a deep personal interest, and my heart was beating with excitement, as the family met at the shrine. Each one, even the servants, wore a new dress—simple and inexpensive, but new. As twilight deepened, the shrine lantern was lighted, the *shoji* pushed back, and the entrance doors opened; thus leaving a free path from the outside road all the way to the shrine.

Then we started, walking two by two through the open door, across the hall, down the step of the "shoe-off" place and along the stone walk to the big entrance gates, which were open wide. In the centre of the gateway Jiya had criss-crossed a little pile of hemp stems—just thirteen—around a tiny heap of fluffy dried grass. When we reached this we parted, Jiya and Yoshita going on one side of the path, and on the other, Honourable Grandmother, Mother, myself, and Ishi, Kin, and Toshi. Then, all respectfully stooping, we bowed our heads and waited. Brother was in Tokyo, so Honourable Grandmother, with Ishi's help, struck the fire of purity with flint and steel, and the dropping sparks lighted the hemp stems into a blaze of welcome.

All the town was silent and dusky except for hundreds of tiny fires, for one was blazing at every gateway. As I bowed, my longing heart seemed to pull my father to me. Through the distance I could hear the sound of soft, galloping feet, and I knew the snow-white steed was nearing. The moment's blaze of the hemp-stem fire was dying, a faint breath of warm August wind struck my cheek, and peace crept into my heart. Slowly we rose and with bowed heads walked back, on the outside edges of the path, two by two—but wide apart—leaving the sacred space of the walk between. When we reached the shrine Mother struck the gong and we all bowed with the dignified cheerfulness of our usual greeting to a welcome guest. We seemed so few since even the year before, and how cordially our hearts welcomed the presence which we knew would bring into our home cheerful companionship for the happy and helpful comfort for the sorrowful.

The next two days the town was full of lanterns. Everybody carried one, every house was decorated with them, every street was lined with them, and at night the cemeteries were filled with glow-worm lights; for every grave had above it a tiny white lantern swinging from an arch made from stems of pampas grass. It was a happy time for all Japan, and the one day in the year when no life was taken of fish, fowl, or even insect. The fishermen idly wandered about arrayed in holiday garments, the chickens cackled and crowed in their bamboo cages, and the little crickets, which children love to keep in tiny cages, sang their shrill song in the trees without the approach of a single sticky-topped pole. And charity extended loving arms to the farthest limit. No priest passed with an empty begging bowl; pampas-woven baskets of food were hidden beneath lotus leaves on the graves, waiting for the poor to carry away when the Bon lights had burned out; and even the sinners in hell, if their hearts longed for salvation, were given another chance during the merciful days of Bon.

Our home was filled with an atmosphere of pleasant thoughts, unselfish acts, and happy laughter; for we felt that our kind guests enjoyed our simple pleasures of new clothes, company courtesies, and our daily feasts with them of the shrine food consisting of fruits, vegetables, and rice dumplings. Honourable Grandmother's face grew more peaceful each hour, Mother's beamed with calm content, the servants were chattering and smiling all the time, and my heart was full of quiet joy.

In the shadows before sunrise of the fourth day, Jiya went for lotus blossoms, and Mother placed fresh food before the shrine. When the brightening air outside began to quarrel with the soft white lantern inside we gathered for the farewell.

The past days had been happy ones and I think we all felt sad when, after the last deep bows, Mother rose and lifted the pampas mat from before the shrine. She doubled and flattened it, then tied the ends with grass, thus forming a rude little canoe, and fixed a hemp-stem arch in the centre. The lotus-leaf dishes of food were placed within, and some balls of rice and uncooked dough added, as O Shorai Sama's gift to the birds. Then the little vegetable animals and all the decorations of the shrine were put in, the white fluttering lantern was swung from the arch, and, with Jiya carrying the little canoe, Mother and I, followed by Ishi and Toshi, went to the river.

Morning was just dawning, but the streets were full of people and the air crowded with circling birds who seemed to know that a treat was before them. When we reached the bank, all except Jiya took their places on the bridge and watched him make his way down the slippery steps cut in the bank, and join the throng below. Each person was holding a little canoe with its burden of food and tiny swinging lantern.

''Look,'' whispered Ishi, as Jiya lifted his hands to strike the flint and steel to light our little lantern, ''our honourable ancestors will embark on the first tide warmed by the sunrise.''

The silence was unbroken except for the loud cries of the birds, then a sudden ray of sunlight shot across a distant mountain and hundreds of figures stooped and launched the little canoes. All stood watching as they whirled and drifted along in the midst of the storm of darting birds screaming their thanks. One upset.

''My O Shorai Sama has stepped off and is now in the unknown land!'' said an old lady, and waiting no longer, she climbed the bank and contentedly made her way home.

As daylight brightened we could see the little boats far in the distance rising and falling, the tiny white lanterns swinging back and forth. We waited until the sun broke into brilliance; then, as the light came racing down the mountain-side, a soft, deep murmur rose from the bowing figures all along the shores.

''Farewell, O Shorai Sama,'' we all gently called. ''Come again next year. We will be waiting to welcome you!''

The crowd scattered, and with satisfied faces, made their way homeward.

Source: *The Daughter of the Samurai* by Etsu Inagaki Sugimoto. Rutland, Vt.: Charles E. Tuttle, 1926, c. 1966, pp. 73-81.

Bon dances for the tourists, Sado Island, c. 1970

After supper nearly everyone in the hotel changed into a kimono provided by the hotel as if all were in a kind of uniform for some special purpose. I felt sorry that I was the only one to be different, not that I did not care to change, but I had difficulty in walking with clogs. I was then invited to join the rest for a bus ride to a local theater where a series of typical local dances would be performed. The young man who could speak some English came to sit by me in the bus, explaining to me that this was the season for the Bon dance and Sado Islanders were particularly good at this dance. The theater was small and cozy. Many seats were already occupied but everyone from our bus, including myself, found a place also. The young man sat by my side and kept telling me to watch the graceful movement of the hands, arms, and legs of each dancer while he raised his own hands to give a demonstration. I appreciated his help and friendliness. He then told me that all the dancers on the stage were men, and that the song the musician sang was the famous Okesa ballad. After a pause a new dance and new song were presented. The difference between one dance and another as well as from one song to another must be very subtle, for I could not easily distinguish between them. On returning to the hotel, I found a squarish wooden structure in the center of the hotel grounds with many lanterns lit up all around. Many people were already dancing around the structure while music played through a loudspeaker. I was urged to join the dance but could not, so the young man went in himself. Though the Bon festival has its origin from Indian Buddhism, no one knows whether it came to China as a Buddhist All Souls'. It must then have been introduced to Japan from China via Korea. It has gradually become a merrymaking holiday for all Japanese.

Source: *The Silent Traveller in Japan* by Chiang Yee. New York: W. W. Norton, 1972, pp. 333-334. (Observations by a Chinese scholar, artist, and world traveler.)

O-Bon week, c. 1920

We had a good many calls during O Bon week—and of course many gifts, all simple and most of them full of associations of the time. It certainly was a gift-giving time—even the vendors who made their daily round along our road each brought some simple gift in memory of O Bon. The vegetable man left behind him a blue-and-white towel with an artistic design of a big turnip in the center, from which curved out graceful branches, twisting into the name of the business house. The fish man left two fans with pictures of blue splashing water and swimming fish. The gift of the meat man was a fan with a foreign scene partly cut through the paper, leaving only the bamboo ribs. It was a beautiful thing. The sake boy left a little rice-paper bag of sugar, handy for afternoon lemonades. Fans are so appropriate for these summer days, that a number of vendors sent fans, each business being represented in the decoration. The iceman's gift had a picture of icebergs and frosty hillsides. Our rice dealer sent one of a farmer in his raincoat and big hat. He was wading through a mountain stream on the edge of a forest with a view of rice fields beyond. It was a cool, inviting picture.

Mother remembered everybody, especially the small vendors who carry their shops about with them, and so our O Bon was a pleasant season of giving and receiving. There is something that touches the heart in all the pleasant greetings and exchange of simple little gifts. It's like a Christmas that has come in summer time.

Vegetable animals at O-Bon

Once when I was a very little girl and had gone on a visit to my grandmother, I was standing before her shrine looking at the odd little animals made of wee eggplants and crooked cucumbers, which are always used for shrine decoration at O Bon Festival time.

Source: *Chiyo's Return* by Chiyono Sugimoto Kiyooka. Garden City, N.Y.: Doubleday, Doran & Co., 1936, pp. 239-240.

Floating the okuri-dango

O-Bon was almost over. It had been a good time, a happy time of prayer and feasting and rejoicing. That night's Bon-odori, or Dance of Rejoicing—a merry, graceful folk dance filled with handclaps and posturings—brought yound and old to the playground by the waterfront, and its drumbeat and flute shrill could be heard all over town. At midnight, each family gathered the okuri-dango that had been offered at the altars and reverently carried them to the waterfront. There, each family had a miniature boat made of rice straw, two or three feet long, and equipped with a rice-straw sail. The rice balls were placed aboard these boats to sustain the spirits on their outward journey. A small paper lantern lighted the bow of each miniature boat, while joss sticks burned fragrantly at the stern. An offshore breeze wafted the sacred Lilliputian fleet into the darkness of Togura Bay and on to the mysterious world of Meido.

Source: *The Lovely World of Richi-San* by Allan R. Bosworth. New York: Harper & Row, 1958, p. 65.

For more on Obon see: ''Bon Matsuri or Festival of Lanterns,'' in *Japanese Festivals* by Helen Bauer and Sherwin Carlquest. Garden City, N.Y.: Doubleday, 1965, pp. 59-65.; *The Japanese Bon Dance in Hawaii* by Judy Van Zile. Hawaii: Press Pacifica, 1982; ''Obon, Festival of the Dead'' in *Folklore of American Holidays* edited by Hennig Cohen and Tristram Potter Coffin. 2nd ed. Detroit: Gale Research, 1991; *Village Japan* by Richard K. Beardsley, John W. Hall, and Robert E. Ward. Chicago: Univ. of Chicago Press, 1959, pp. 455-456.

Moon 7, Day 15 (July-August)

Chung Yüan / Yue Laan / The Hungry Ghost Festival

On this day souls from Buddhist and Taoist purgatory roam the earth. Food is laid out for the spirits, prayers are said, and lanterns are floated to guide them to a resting place.

People's Republic of China

Chieh Tsu (Receiving Ancestors Festival)

Kao Yao village, Yunnan Province, 1938

On the 13th, each family was busy acquiring food for the elaborate meals that were expected and also buying gold-silver paper money as well as green paper, and red, from which to cut symbolic clothing for the dead. These were of curious shape which can be shown by their outline. People furthermore made what looked like tiny lanterns from paper flowers but were actually representations of sedan chairs only a few inches tall. For the evening meals, the women (or occasionally the men) cooked pork and rice and placed it with pears, pomegranates, and wine on a tray which at sundown the head of the family carried out and put down on the street near the door. Then he burned incense and kowtowed three times, the other members of the family not participating. After that obeisance, he burned gold-silver paper money and prayed to his deceased ancestors, "Grandfathers and grandmothers, father and mother, please return home." Naturally the latter were not named in cases where they were still alive. Then the head of the family picked up the tray with the food and drink offerings and carried it into the house, putting it on a table against the wall on which the symbolic red and green paper clothing had been stuck with some paste made from wheat flour and water. The table had been decorated earlier with an incense holder and two red candles, while two or three chairs had been placed facing it. These were reserved for the ancestors and none of the surviving family sat on them. With the offerings deposited, the head of the family again kowtowed three times. Afterward the empty chairs were pushed up to the table, while all the members of the family feasted.

Before breakfast and dinner of the 14th and the 15th, usually a son in the family placed rice on the table under the paper clothing and kowtowed three times. This was never done after eating for such an inversion of the ceremonial order of procedure would show disrespect. During the three days of the Receiving Ancestors Feast, the men gathered in the teahouses and the women sewed. A few families visited the tombs, especially if they missed doing so at the Planting Trees Festival. The delayed rites would then be carried out, but such procrastination was rare. The period was a serious one and not given over to such pleasures as were enjoyed at New Year's.

Finally, after supper on the 15th, the head of the family put a great deal of gold-silver paper money in baskets, covering them with the symbolic red or green paper clothing pulled from the wall as well as the flower sedan chairs, and then carried the baskets into the street and put them down near the door. There he burned everything repeating, "Good-by, go quickly," to his ancestors, afterward kowtowing a final three times.

As an ultimate gesture to the deceased came the floating of burning lamps on the lake, but this finale to the festival had been banned by government authority as superstition and consequently had not been performed for many years. Pi, the schoolteacher, had never seen it. Perhaps because of the presence of "the foreigner," it was adjudged safe to perform the ceremony once more, which happy decision enabled us to include it in the empirical record of the Huo Pa Festival which follows.

Source: *Village Life in Old China: A Community Study of Kao Yao Yunnan* by Cornelius Osgood. New York: Ronald Press, 1963. (From 1938 field research by a Yale University anthropologist.)

Feast of the spirits in Wuch'ang, Hupeh Province, c. 1920

According to the old Chinese calendar, the fifteenth day of the seventh month is the Feast of the Spirits. Father allowed Buddhist monks and Taoist priests to come to our house on that evening to perform a ceremony at which little rolls, intended for the spirits, were tossed in the air by the monks and priests. They recited hymns and threw little rolls in the air until late into the night. The feast was not only for the spirits, but also for us children—I always wished I could catch the rolls when they fell.

Source: *The Lotus Pool* by Chow Chung-cheng. New York: Appleton-Century Crofts, 1961, p. 20.

Taiwan

Releasing the suffering souls

The Taiwanese call this day the "opening of the gates of Hell." It is the day on which the souls of those suffering in Buddhist or Taoist purgatory are allowed to roam freely about the earth. A banquet must be prepared for them, which serves to alleviate their sufferings and sometimes effect an early release from punishment. The giving of a banquet-sacrifice with prayers and incense is called "phó-tō", releasing the souls from suffering. The gates of Hell are supposed to remain open until the 30th of the seventh month, which is the birthday of Te-chông ông the Buddhist saint who presides over the infernal regions and tries to release suffering souls from their torments.

This is a busy day for the Ch'eng Huang and all of his official court, as well as the deities of other city temples. They are usually carried around the city in procession, to see that the hungry ghosts do not misbehave, or harm their mortal hosts. Figures of the two generals Fan and Hsieh, who were mentioned as guardians of the entrance to Hell, are left in various places around the city to watch over the spirits as a sort of ghostly policemen. A large dragon is sometimes carried around the streets. . . . The souls of those who die an unnatural death, such as by sudden accident or drowning, as well as those souls who have no family to offer the ancestor rites or who were not buried properly, are supposed to wander about the earth until properly conducted to the nether world or the Western heavens. This is the day for performing the rites for such ghosts without a family. Food is laid out before each house, incense and paper money burned, to satisfy their needs. Lanterns are floated on rivers, and processions with lanterns formed along river banks, to conduct the souls of those who have drowned to a final resting place.

Source: *Taiwan Feasts and Customs* by Michael R. Saso. Hsinchu, Taiwan: Chabanel Language Institute, pp. 65-66.

Vietnam

Trung Nguyen (Wandering Souls' Day)

Food and prayer

This is the second largest festival of the year, (Tet is first.) Though it falls on the 15th day of the seventh month, its celebration may be held at any convenient time during the latter half of the month. The festival is celebrated throughout the country, in Buddhist Pagodas, homes, businesses, factories, government offices, and Armed Forces units. It is not just a Buddhist holiday, but one celebrated by all Vietnamese who believe in the existence of God, good and evil.

They believe that sinful souls can be absolved of their punishment and delivered from hell through prayers said by the living on the first and 15 of every month. Wandering Souls' Day however, is believed to be the best time for priests and relatives to secure general amnesty for all the souls. On this day, the gates of hell are said to be opened at sunset and the souls there fly out, unclothed and hungry. Those who have relatives fly back to their homes and villages and find plenty of food on their family altars.

Those who have no relatives or have been forsaken by the living, are doomed to wander helplessly through the air on black clouds, over the rivers and from tree to tree. They are the sad "wandering souls" who are in need of food and prayer. This is why additional altars full of offerings are placed in pagodas and many public places.

During the ceremony, huge tables are covered with offerings which basically consist of three kinds of meat: boiled chicken, roast pork, and crabs; and five fruits. Other foods may be included such as sticky rice cakes, vermicelli soup, and meat rolls to satisfy the appetite of the wandering souls who are supposed to be hungry the year round.

Money and clothes made of votive papers are also burned at this time.

Source: *Customs and Culture of Vietnam* by Ann Caddell Crawford. Rutland, Vt.: Charles E. Tuttle, 1966, pp. 196-197.

For more information on The Hungry Ghosts Festival see: "The Festival of the Hungry Ghosts" in *Chinese Creeds and Customs* by V.R. Burkhardt. Hong Kong: South China Morning Post, 1982, pp. 42-57; "The Feast of Souls" in *Chinese Festivals* by Wolfram Eberhard. New York: Henry Schuman, 1952, pp. 129-133.

First Day of Shrawan, Darkening Fortnight (July-August)

Gai Jatra (The Procession of Sacred Cows)

Families suffering a death during the preceding year sponsor Gai Jatra, a cow procession. In some villages each family processes individually; in others all gather to process together. Later in the day a masquerading atmosphere enters and anyone who wants may parade in costume to clown and lampoon the social order.

Nepal

Gai Jatra in Tikanpor village, c. 1971

On Gai Jatra day the entire bereaved family and clan gathered in a small upstairs room around two young boys ornately costumed to represent cows. From vividly coloured woven cane caps two bamboo sticks protruded, topped with brilliant circular festoons signifying the horns, between which the white paper mask of a cow was fixed. Garlands of flowers and jewellery hung about the boy's necks. Draped around their waists over flowered sari skirts and trailing the floor were widths of white cloth representing tails. Their dark sombre eyes, ringed with lampblack, looked enormous above perspiration-streaked dabs of yellow on their cheeks.

In a haze of burning incense and smoking cotton wicks an old priest intoned a prayer from a frayed holy book while sprinkling the 'cows' with holy water, rice, red powder and flower petals. In the background the ageing mother sobbed hoarsely, while mourning women murmured prayers. Suddenly a drum sounded outside and the smoke-permeated crowd clomped down the ladder stairs in procession, out across the muddy courtyard, up slippery stepping stones and a narrow footpath leading through the village. Behind trooped the grieving relatives, neighbours and a band of musicians blowing horns, clashing cymbals and frantically beating drums. Bringing up the rear was a gaily costumed troupe of 'actors' to perform rice-planting pantomimes at each halt along the route.

At the temples of Narayan, Ganesh, and Natisuri (the goddess of music and dancing), and at countless homes the procession paused for an outdoor performance, receiving from each household scraps of food and some rice-beer. Needless to say, things became livelier as the morning progressed. . . .

Source: *The Festivals of Nepal* by Mary M. Anderson. London: Allen & Unwin, 1971, p. 101.

For more on Gai Jatra in Nepal see: "Gai Jatra: The Procession of Sacred Cows" in *The Festivals of Nepal* by Mary M. Anderson. London: Allen & Unwin, 1971, pp. 99-104; "Gaijatra: The Festival of Holy Cows," in *The Nepal Festivals, Part I* by Dhurba K. Deep. Bhotahity, Kathmandu: Ratna Pustak Bhandar, 1978, pp. 57-60.

Fourteenth Day of Dark Fortnight Shrawan (July-August)

Ghanta Karna

In Nepal this day is the celebration of the victory over Ghanta Karna, a dread demon named Bell Ears (Ghanta Karna) because he wore jingling bells in his ears to prevent the name of Lord Vishnu ever reaching his senses. He roamed the land wreaking havoc, until a god in the form of a frog tricked Ghanta Karna into leaping after him into a well. The people then clubbed him to death and dragged his corpse to the river for cremation. On this day the cremation of Ghanta Karna is reenacted. Because boys play a major role in the activities of the day, it is sometimes called "The Festival of Boys."

Nepal

The Ghantakarna effigy

On this day the effigy of the monster made of reeds at every crossing of the roads is set up. Every neighbourhood has thus one of these monster effigies and a big bunch of boys to look after that. Small boys are the most enthusiastic sponsors of this particular street show. From the very early morning on this day quite a number of kids are seen standing round the effigy in the street and collecting the Jagats (a kind of ceremonial toll) from the passersby. When they see a car coming or any other vehicles they all jump up with a big cry and block the road shouting at the tone of their voice, 'Jagat, Jagat.' They don't let the driver go until he pays the toll.

Kids are busy all day long collecting tolls, buying things necessary for the funeral of Ghantakarna and doing make-ups on the effigy. When the evening falls they tie up the effigy with a strong rope and kick it several times in disgust and then drag it away shouting wild slogans until they reach a river where they throw it away into the water. Quite a battalion of kids join this drag-away-parade holding straw lamps in their hands which looks quite colourful in the evening. Then the kids all the way home come singing a kind of victory song.

Effigy as observed in Kathmandu c. 1971

During the afternoon, effigies of Ghanta Karna are erected at cross-roads around the city, and outlying villages as well, made from leafy bamboo poles, bound near the top to form a tall tent-shaped structure. A vividly painted, glowering demon's face is affixed to the body, and a pumpkin marked with evil sexual organs is placed at its feet. People come to hang tiny cloth devil dolls on the effigy, and toss coins to it, hoping thereby to avoid the ravages of disease and the wrath of evil forces.

Iron to ward off evil

Some people drive the iron nails on the lintels of their door ways to check the devils from entering their houses. Iron nails are considered very good safeguards against evil spirits.

Another interesting aspect of this festival is the wearing of iron rings on this day. Many people wear the iron rings on this day to safeguard themselves from the attack of the evil spirits. This is a big day for the kids to make money, as well as merriment. They do a very good ring business on this day and fill out their pockets with candy. As the traditional belief would have it those who wear the iron ring on this day will not suffer from evil spirits for the whole year.

Hanging tiny effigy dolls on the Ghantakarna

Little girls hang up the dolls on the effigy of Ghantakarna to keep the monster away. Girls do this to make themselves feel safe and sound.

The Ghantakarna substitute in Kathmandu

The way Kathmanduites celebrate is quite fascinating. Kathmandu picks up a boy from the lowest class family who is strong and skilful enough to act as secondary scapegoat. He is kept almost naked and his face painted to make him look like a devil. Then he goes on his round to collect the tolls from door to door followed by a big bunch of the enthusiastic kids. When he approaches a door or a shop, holding out his hands he says, 'My grandfather is gone; help me with some money for his funeral." Everybody laughs at him when he says this. He is regarded as the closest relative of the Ghantakarna and so supposed to arrange everything required for the cremation of his dead grandfather. When it gets dark he undergoes the funeral rites. All the kids of the respective neighbourhood will be present there to see the scene. The first thing he will do is to go round the so called dead body of the Ghantakarna three times which is a big honour for the dead then he sets fire on the Ghantakarna amidst loud clappings and clamours of the people. After this he will be seated on the top of the effigy and the kids shouting all kinds of ugly words at him drag away the effigy down to the river and throw it away into the water. Thus the festival comes to the end.

Source: *Festivals of India* by Brijendra Nath Sharma. New Delhi: Abhinav, 1978, pp. 45-47, 93.

For more on Ghanta Karna see: ''Ghantakarna: The Festival of Boys'' in *The Nepal Festivals, Part 1* by Dhurba K. Deep. Bhotahity, Kathmandu: Ratna Pustak Bhandar, 1978, pp. 44-47. (Deep is a prominent Nepali poet and scholar.); ''Ghanta Karna: The Night of the Devil'' in *The Festivals of Nepal* by Mary M. Anderson. London: Allen & Unwin, 1971, pp. 72-76.

Full Moon, Shrawan (July-August)

Janai Purnima / Raksha Bandhan

This is the day on which Brahmans and Chetri men annually change the Janai, a sacred thread worn around the neck and underarm. Men, women, and children of all castes, Hindu and Buddhist alike, have the Raksha Bandham tied about their wrist on this day. It is worn for three months until Laxmi Puja.

The priest visits the home on Janai Purni to perform the ceremony of blessing the new thread and installing it on the body. When removed during Laxmi Puja, the thread is tied to the tail of a sacred cow. It is possible to get across the River Ghaitarna after death if a sacred cow will let you cling to her tail and pull you across.

India

Tying the *rakhi*

The Raksha Bandhan festival is celebrated specially in Northern India in the month of Shravana (July-August). The word *Raksha* signifies protection. The festival is also called Saluno, corrupted from the Persian word *Sal-i-nu,* which means the New Year.

Girls and married women tie a *rakhi,* made of a few twisted golden or simple yellow threads, on the wrist of the right hand of their brothers, for their welfare, and also for protection from any evil influence and in return receive cash and gifts. This is an age-old festival, which strengthens the bond of love between brothers and sisters.

On this day, members of a Hindu family bathe very early and go to the market to purchase beautiful *rakhis* from the colourful stalls, which spring up everywhere. The males clothed in their best and females in their bright costumes first offer prayers to their family deity. In some places, before tying the *rakhi,* barley saplings are put on the ears of the brothers. A man considers it a privilege to be chosen as brother by a girl, who ties a *rakhi* on his wrist. If the brother is not at hand, the *rakhi* is sent to him by post or through some person and in return, the sister receives various kinds of gifts and cash. Women tie *rakhis* to close friends and neighbours also.

Source: *Festivals of India* by Brijendra Nath Sharma. New Delhi: Abhinav, 1978, p. 93.

Bhrātridwitiya, the Brother's Festival

Born on the eve of the Bhrātridwitiya, the brother's festival, according to the Hindu calendar, I have felt more and more my indebtedness to my sisters. The passing of years, instead of defacing that sense, has intensified it to such a degree that I can realize the beauty and the utility of such a festival. On this occasion, it is said that Yama, the Lord of Death, takes a vacation that he may accept his sister Jamuna's invitation to a feast. So, following her example, every sister in our Hindu homes observes a beautiful practice. She puts with the tip of her finger a small piece of sandal-wood paste on her brother's forehead. Along with it she breathes a prayer: "As Yama, the Lord of Death, is deathless, so may my brother, also, be deathless!" She blows the conch shell, the herald of auspicious moments. In case the brother is absent in a different part of the country, she puts on the wall a mark, intended for the brother.

If the brother is younger than his sister, he makes his *pronām* (touching the feet with one hand and placing it on his head). If he is the elder, the sister, in the same way, salutes him. She makes gifts of food, spices, and clothing. This simple but impressive ceremony is performed year after year in the homes of India. Such a ceremony marks the intensity of relationship between brothers and sisters in Hindu homes.

Several centuries ago a Hindu princess (of Rajputāna in central India) sent a silken cord to the then Mohammedan emperor at Delhi, Sultān Bābar. She was in great danger, and in the absence of a brother needed a brother's help very badly. That *rākhi* (the silken cord), symbolic of respect and affection between brothers and sisters, was mightier than peace and good-will established between rival houses even by the sword and the loss of many lives. The Mohammedan prince, upon learning the meaning of the silken cord, responded immediately to the call for help from a Hindu sister—a sister by adoption. He did not shrink from helping her because of her difference in birth, language, and religion. Above all else was the appeal of brotherliness, of sisterliness.

Source: *When I Was a Boy in India* by Satyandanda Roy. Boston: Lothrop, Lee & Shepard Co., 1924, pp. 5-7.

Nepal

Janai and Rakshya Bandhan threads

This festival which is celebrated by the entire Nepalese people is popularly known by so many nick-names like Gunpunhi, Kwatipuni, Rishi-tarpani, etc. And this is one of the most widely celebrated common festivals of the Buddhists and the Hindus. On this day one can see several Hindus going to the Buddhist temples and the Buddhists to the Hindu temples.

One of the main features of this festival is the binding of Rakshya Bandhan (a sort of safety-band) round one's wrist and the changing of the Janai (sacred threads) which the Brahmins and the Chhetris wear round their neck. The Janai which is a three-stringed thread necklace, is said to symbolize the three basic qualities of Nature known as *rajasic, tamasic* and *sattwic*.

It is also said to represent the Hindu trinity of Brahma, Vishnu and Shiva. The wearing of the Janai by Brahmins is said to symbolically remind one of their thorough knowledge of the Vedas and their non-dualistic approach to the realisation of God.

Another aspect of this festival is the wearing of (the Rakshya Bandhan, golden coloured thread round one's wrist. This ritual band is believed to protect those who wear it from all kinds of ills and evils. One is supposed to wear it until the Luxmi puja which falls in Kartik (Oct.). It is always the Brahmins who tie up this holy protective band round one's wrist with the chantings of mantra.

Nine temples, nine dresses, nine dishes, nine instruments

Another interesting aspect of this festival is the exhibition of religious art treasures which one can go and see almost at every Buddhist monastery in the Kathmandu Valley. The life size statues of the Buddhas and Bodhisattwas and the traditional tankas and tapestries depicting the life history of Lord Buddha are the main attractions of the exhibition. If one is to follow the age old tradition still preserved in Nepal on this auspicious day one should go and visit nine different Buddhist monasteries changing nine different dresses on this particular day. He is also advised to have the nine different dishes on the same day to celebrate the occasion.

Another interesting feature of this festival is the musical performance of the Naubaja, meaning nine different kinds of the traditional Nepalese musical instruments, which takes place in the evening at the temple of Kumbheswara in Patan.

Source: *The Nepal Festivals, Part 1* by Ohurba K. Deep. Bhotahity, Kathmandu: Ratna Pustak Bhandar, 1978, pp. 61-64.

For more on Janai Purnima see: ''Janai Purni or Raksha Bandhan: The Sacred Thread Festival'' in *The Festivals of Nepal* by Mary M. Anderson. London: Allen & Unwin, 1971, pp. 93-99 (The author includes details of rites at Kumbeshwar Pond in Patan and at Gosainkund Lake.); ''Janai Purnima: The Sacred Thread Festival'' in *The Nepal Festivals, Part 1* by Dhurba K. Deep. Bhotahity, Kathmandu: Ratna Pustak Bhandar, 1978, pp. 52-56. (Deep is a prominent Nepali poet and scholar.)

Esala (July-August)

Kandy Esala Perahera

This Ceylonese festival originally honored the deities Natha, Vishnu, Kataragama, and Pattini. Since 1775 the festival has honored the Sacred Tooth of Lord Buddha as well. This tooth is housed in the Temple of the Tooth in Kandy. The tooth is carried in procession in a golden casket atop a magnificent elephant. The procession is held nightly, with a daytime procession on the tenth and last day of the festival.

Ceylon

The procession

This procession is about a mile long, consisting of thousands of participants, gaily dressed intermingling with groups of dancers, all gesticulating around nearly eighty elephants by the dim red light of a thousand torches. In every section of the Perahera the leadership is taken by a Kandyan Chieftain in his traditional regalia to the accompaniment of drummers and Kandyan dancers.

The five Perahera

The Perahera procession consists of five separate Peraheras,

(1) Dalada Maligawa Perahera
(2) The Natha Devala Perahera
(3) The Maha Vishnu Devale Perahera
(4) The Kataragama Devale Perahera
(5) The Pattini Devale Perahera

The Maligawa Perahera

The Maligawa Perahera is led by whip crackers cracking their whips. The whip crackers usually praticipate [sic] in the Perahera from the commencement of the Randoli Perahera.

(b) The flag bearers carrying the standards of the different Provinces and the Temples walk in single file on either side of the road following the whip crackers.

(c) On the back of the first elephant in the procession a man carries the Buddhist flag which signifies that this is a Buddhist pageant.

(d) Peramunarala comes next. He rides an elephant attired in kandyan costume with a creamy beared flowing in the breeze carrying a parcel wrapped up with a silk handkerchief.

(e) Next comes the 'Hewisi Band' (Hewisi tom-tom beaters) which is led by Malagammana.

(f) Gajanayake Nilame comes next. He, too, is dressed in typical kandyan attire with a long black beard and carrying a silver goad (henduwa). Gajanayake means—leader of the elephants.

(g) The Maligawa tusker 'Raja' carrying the golden casket containing the sacred relics is in the centre with two other tuskers on either side at the tail-end portion of the Dalada Perahera. A canopy is held above the golden casket with white cloth spread before its path as a mark of respect.

(h) The Maligawa tusker 'Raja' is followed by the Diyawadana Nilame (the lay custodian of the Sacred Tooth Relic) in a beautifully worked out kandyan costume worn by kandyan chieftans of yore; keeping strides to the rhythm of beating of drums and kandyan dancing.

Raja the tusker

The stately and magnificient walk of 'Raja' (Senior) every one admires and it looks as if he is keeping strides to the accompaniment and rhythm created by the beating of drums, horane (clarionet) and the jingling sound created by the kaadyan dancers who dance around him. At times it looks as if he is keeping strides with the Diyawadana Nilame who follows him, as at the nick of time when the dancers are about to commence dancing he halts almost every fifteen yards and keeps on gazing at the crowds lined along the streets in Kandy.

Elephant Stampede

When the 'elephant stampede' took place in the Esala Perahera of 1959, 'Raja' was almost opposite Queen's Hotel, and when instructions came from the Diyawadana Nilame the late C. B. Nugawela Dissawa to turn back the Perahera, 'Raja' turned back with the casket (Karanduwa) carrying the Sacred Relics and in a melancholy mood amongst the disorderly crowd went back to the Sri Dalada Maligawa premises and assisted the custodians of the Sacred Relics to deposit same.

After the Perahera

On the final day, the Perahera is held in the day-time with a ritual called the 'water-cutting' ceremony. Following the Day-perahera the 'Waliyak-mangalya' continues for seven nights in the Maha Vishnu Devale to safeguard the participants of the Esala Perahera (inclusive of elephants) against the 'Evil Eye and Evil Mouth' of the onlookers. During the seven nights of the 'Waliyak Mangalya' thousands of devotees throng the Maha Vishnu Devale to pay homage to Lord Vishnu and to make generous contributions to safeguard them against evil spirits throughout the coming year.

Source: *The Kandy Esala Perahera (Asia's Most Spectacular Pageant)* by M. B. Dassanayake. Kandy: Kandy Printers, 1970, pp. 6, 21-22, 32.

For more on The Kandy Esala Perahera see: *Kandy Esala Maha Perahera and Its Connected Ceremonies* by K. M. L. B. Senaratne. A Diviya Book, no date; "The Perahera Processions of Ceylon" by G. H. G. Burroughs in *National Geographic Magazine*, July 1932, 90-100.

Third Day of Shrawan, Dark Fortnight (July-August)

Marya

A procession wends from shrine to shrine through the city of Patan. Oil butter lamps to Lord Buddha are the dominant offering. The festival celebrates Lord Buddha's triumph over the tempting Maras. They finally came to worship him on this day.

Nepal

The shrine-walkers

The number of the shrine-walkers who colourfully form this impressive parade is around three to four thousands. Men and women both participate in this festival. They carry varieties of interesting gifts to make offerings to Lord Buddha. The offerings of rice grains, flowers, red powders, sweets, incense and *guru patra* (a gift cup for guru) are quite common tin [sic] the scene. However, the offering of oil or butter lamps to Lord Buddha on this auspicious day is a dominant feature.

The masked Maras

All those devil dancers and the apsara actors and several other funny mask-wearers who are the part and parcel of this festival parade are said to represent the Maras. This parade is always accompanied by several groups of musicians playing various kinds of traditional Nepalese musical instruments.

The most enjoyable part of this festival parade for the children is the devil dancers and funny mask-wearers. Quite a number of them are clad from head to foot all in worn-out sacks and rags. Whenever they come across the inquisitive kids they suddenly jumping [sic] in a dramatic way try to scare them away.

Source: *The Nepal Festivals, Part 1* by Ohurba K. Deep. Bhotahity, Kathmandu: Ratna Pustak Bhandar, 1978, pp. 61-64.

Fifth Day of Shrawan, Brightening Fortnight (July-August)

Naga Panchami

A day of respect for nagas. Snakes are believed to have their own underground kingdom. Nagas can give wealth and bring rains. Displeased nagas can cause famine or collapse of one's home.

India

Snake festival

The festival of Naga Panchami is celebrated throughout the country in the month of Shravana (July-August). It is the main festival observed in honour of snakes, whose worship as a folk cult has existed in India since very early times. Mathura in Uttar Pradesh and Rajgir in Bihar were great centres of Naga worship in ancient period. Several images of Nagas or cobras executed in stone have been unearthed from different places, which prove the popularity of their worship in that remote age.

On Naga Panchami, people observe fast and worship cobras. If cobras are not available, huge cloth effigies of mythical serpents are made and displayed publicly for worship. Besides these, cobra images of metal, stone and clay as well as those drawn or painted on cloth or paper are worshipped. The devotees offer milk and flowers to the cobras and coins to the snake-charmers, who specially visit the towns on this particular day.

People also visit the temples of Siva at Varanasi, Vaidyanatha, Ujjain and other places with various kinds of offerings. Since Siva wears snakes as his ornaments (*sarpabhushanam*), hence he is also to be worshipped on this day. In the temples of Siva, hundreds of newly captured cobras are brought by the trappers and released before the god. The worshippers then empty their pots of milk over the heads of the cobras. By doing so every year, it is believed that harm by serpents can be averted throughout life. At the end of the day after some show of serpent dances in an open field, they are released into freedom.

Source: *Festivals of India* by Brijendra Nath Sharma. New Delhi: Abhinav, 1978, p. 93.

Nepal

Naga Panchami in the Puranas

On this particular day the serpent worship begins with the posting of colourful portraits of nagas (serpents) on the walls above the main doorways. Sweets and cereals and cow's milk are offered to the nagas and prayed [to] for peace and prosperity.

The puranas have plenty of verses devoted to the nagas. The Garuda Purana says that the worshipping of the nagas on the Nagapanchami Day brings peace and prosperity to the worshippers. The Skanda Purana also speaks almost in the same tone. The Narad Purana says that if one offers the cow's milk to the snakes on this day he is sure to be safe from snakebites for the whole year. The Bhavishya Purana assuring the aspirants says that one who worships the nagas with single-minded devotion will always be able to keep the thunder away.

Source: *The Nepal Festivals, Part 1* by Ohurba K. Deep. Bhotahity, Kathmandu: Ratna Pustak Bhandar, 1978, pp. 61-64.

For more on Naga Panchami see: ''Naga Panchami: The Day of the Snake Gods'' in *The Festivals of Nepal* by Mary M. Anderson. London: Allen & Unwin, 1971, pp. 85-92; ''Nagapanchami: The Serpent's Day'' in *The Nepal Festivals, Part 1* by Dhurba K. Deep. Bhotahity, Kathmandu: Ratna Pustak Bhandar, 1978. (Deep is a prominent Nepali poet and scholar.)

Shravana or Bhadra (June-July or August-September)

Pola and Hadaga

Pola and Hadaga are agricultural festivals popular mainly in Maharashtra. The actual dates vary from region to region, taking place either in Shravana (June-July) or Bhadra (August-September).

India

Maharashtra agricultural festivals

The Pola and Hadaga festivals concerning the cultivation of land are mainly celebrated in Maharashtra. The former is observed by the agriculturists in the month of Shravana (July-August) to honour the bullocks, which are mainly helpful in the cultivation of fields. And the latter is observed in Asvina (September-October) by the girls, who celebrate it by singing, dancing and wishing a good crop and timely rain for cultivation.

In Satara District, the Pola festival is observed in the month of Asadha (June-July) and in Poona and Sholapur, it is celebrated in Bhadra (August-September). On the festival day, a farmer worships his bullocks. He gets up early in the morning, and after bath thoroughly washes his bullocks and decorates them with different colours. Oil is applied to their horns, to make them shine. Garlands of flowers and ringing bells are tied around their necks, while small bells are fastened to their legs. Their *aratis* (lighted camphor) are performed and they are nicely fed with sweetened pulse flour called *puram.* In the evening, the bullocks are taken out in a grand procession to the accompaniment of beating of drums and different kinds of music. Races of bullocks and bullock-carts are also specially arranged on this occasion. Small children worship clay figurines of the bullocks and carry them from door to door to earn something in cash.

The girls of a family, while celebrating the Hadaga festival, prepare pictures of elephants on the ground or on the wooden planks and decorate them with different types of coloured powder. They then jointly sing and dance around them at different times for about 16 days. Sweets are distributed and feasts are arranged, at which friends and relatives are invited.

Source: *Festivals of India* by Brijendra Nath Sharma. New Delhi: Abhinav, 1978, p. 93.

Third and Fourth Days of Shrawan (July-August)

Teej

This is a women's festival in honor of Parvati. It occurs at the beginning of the monsoon season and is called "Green Teej." Women visit their parents' home and are sent gifts by their parents.

India

Teej in Rajasthan

Teej is a day for women to worship Goddess Pārvati. On this day long ago she was reunited with her long separated husband, Lord Siva. According to mythology, she declared this day holy and proclaimed that whoever invokes her on this day will be blessed with whatever one desires. On these two days married women worship the Goddess for long and happy married lives, and the peace and prosperity of their children. Wearing green, red, or yellow dresses hands and feet painted in delicate designs of red *henna,* they worship Pārvati and sing songs in her praise. Afterwards they amuse themselves on swings. This celebration has special meaning for a newly married woman who does this worship very religiously. Devotion to the Goddess and self-decoration of women are the two dominant themes of the festival. On this occasion parents send gifts to their married daughters, which is called *sindhara.*

Literally *sindhara* is from the Sanskrit word *sringar* which means the decoration of women and their charming beauty. These gifts include sweets, *henna,* new bangles, and a new dress. The rich send expensive gifts. The unmarried girls also receive new clothes and articles of decoration. Special festival food is prepared for sisters and daughters of the family to enjoy together. According to tradition the married girls go to their parents' house on this occasion. Sometimes they cannot go due to certain reasons. The brothers put up swings for their sisters. Thus Teej reunites married women with their parents' families. Much merrymaking is done by the women folk during this festival, perhaps the reason for its great following.

Gaiety and merrymaking give this festival tremendous importance. It is a monsoon festival. In India, especially in the deserts of Rajasthan, a good monsoon means hundreds of auspicious things, a bumper harvest, and a good life ahead. Thus this day expresses the happiness and enjoyment of the people. All this is reflected in specially cooked food, new clothes, new decorations in the form of bangles of glass and lacquer with colorful designs, *henna* paint, putting on collyrium in the eyes and the *tikka* (red dot) on the forehead, wearing of the best pieces of jewelry, etc. These things symbolize a woman's happy married life. Therefore to wear them at the time of worshipping Devi Pārvati has great significance. It is a sort of wish to have these decorations always in the life of the worshiper. "As today is, so should all my life be" is one of the boons asked from the Goddess on this day. Pārvati is the patron Goddess of Hindu women. From the Vedic era to the modern age she has been very popular, in the urban as well as in the rural areas, as a protector of family health and happiness.

Putting *henna* on hands and feet is done to express the auspicious festive mood. It is supposed to bring good luck to the person and it also symbolizes happiness. The most popular designs made on this festival are those of *lehariya* (vertical lines of *henna* on palms), *ghevar* (the form of a round sweet dish specially made for this festival) and *chaupar* (design of a game of dice), besides other regular designs of flowers and leaves. It is a great art with its own symbols. The design of vertical lines is also found on the clothes typically worn in this season. It depicts the showers, the falling of rain. Besides its religious meaning, *henna* also has medicinal properties for cooling the skin of the body.

I have observed this festival since childhood. I have attended the morning *puja* as well as the evening procession. In our house we worship the Goddess Pārvati to be blessed with a happy married family life. (In Hindu belief conjugal bliss is not complete until the couple has children.) I have personally received special Teej *sindhara* for my first Teej after my engagement. Even today my parents and in-laws send me money to buy sweets and clothes for this auspicious occasion. Beside new bangles and clothes, one's best ornaments are worn to celebrate this day. The place of worship is cleaned, good festive food is cooked consisting of poori-puffed fried bread made from whole wheat flour, the best vegetables, sweets and curd *raita* with gram flour fried drippings or cucumber, onions, tomatoes, and so forth. A day earlier a woman washes her hair and oil is put in the hair, and *henna* is applied to hands and feet. All these are part of this celebration.

Teej swinging

Swinging on this occasion has special meaning. In folklore and mythology the swinging is done by gods and goddesses because they also have fun and frolic like human beings. Primarily this festival is for women and girls so only they do this swinging. But small boys also swing. Out of the whole year's hard life studded with personal sacrifice, Hinduism does provide for the women some particular occasions for enjoyment, entertainment, and carefree relaxed moments. According to folklore the gods and goddesses come to earth to swing during the Teej festival. One song says:

> On the branch of the magnolia tree I have put a swing,
> Its rope is of silk, I have put a swing,
>
> On the branch of the magnolia tree I have put a swing,
> Its plank is of sandal wood, I have put a swing,
>
> To swing on my swing, the Sun and Moon have come,
> They have brought their queens to swing on my swing,
>
> While swinging they stopped and said, we like red bangles.
> Their mothers will buy them red bangles, I have put a swing. . . .

Teej processions

On the third and fourth days of Shrawan, processions of Teej go their way with great pomp from the palaces of Jaipur and Bundi through the main bazaars of these two towns. Images of Pārvati made of solid gold and pure silver are taken out in silver palanquins. They are escorted by bedecked elephants, horses, bullocks, and camels. . . . To watch the procession is considered auspicious and lucky, hence thousands of people come to Jaipur and Bundi to watch it as a religious obligation. A folk song sung during this time illustrates this point, where a wife tells her husband that:

> O Bhanwar! the Teej of *sawan* has come, let me go to Jaipur.
> In Jaipur let me bathe in Galtaji, let me roam in Ramniwas garden.
> O fair woman! In Jaipur you will be pushed around in the crowd.
> Forget going to Jaipur.

If one observes this festival in the pink city of Jaipur, one will surely understand the mystery and popularity of Teej. Common folk are bewitched by the size of huge crowds which convene to watch the procession of the Goddess. They may wait for long hours to observe all of the ceremonial activities. The togetherness of a big crowd attracts others to come and watch this procession. The fervor of the crowd is to be seen to be believed.

To the villagers who come from a quiet area, the lighting, decorations, the novelties in the shops, the fashion, the city carts with sweet delicacies, all present a unique experience in itself. They make the visit to this festival an otherworldly event.

Source: "The Monsoon Festival Teej in Rajasthan" by Manju Bhatnagar in *Asian Folklore Studies* 47, 63-72. (Article by a Rajasthan woman.)

July/August

Imechi Festival

This festival is a time of household worship in Igbo homes. Fowls are sacrificed at the chi tree. Feasting and dancing follow.

Igbo (Nigeria)

Meals during the Imechi Festival

This major festival celebrated by every household—the husband and wife, their children and children's children normally takes places in the fifth month of the Igbo calendar. As it is celebrated usually during the period of scarcity the main meals at this time include breadfruit (ukwa), sliced cassava, cassava foufou and ighu sliced three-leafed yam). Fowls are sacrificed at the foot of the *chi* tree, in many areas, the *oha chi,* and a few others, the *ogbu chi*. When a daughter is married and is setting up her own chi, it is incumbent on her mother to go and inaugurate the chi and while going she will take plenty of food to be eaten by all the guests invited. On the other hand a daughter is expected every year to attend her parents' chi festival with a fowl and some yams. There are ritual observances feasting at the chi shrine during the festival. There is also chanting and dancing and general rejoicing.

Source: ''Standardizing Igbo Festivals'' by Nnabuenyi Ugonna in *Nigeria Magazine* 136 (1981), p. 26.

Full Moon in Summer

Tea Meetings

A fancy ''court'' is held for a ''King and Queen'' on a full moon night in summer in Nevis. Various audience members come costumed and prepared to perform for the royalty and their court.

Nevis

The Nevis Tea Meeting, c. 1965

The Nevis *Tea Meeting* is a remarkable combination of pageant, mock fertility ritual, variety show, and organized mayhem. The proceedings probably developed most immediately out of fund-raising church events introduced in the nineteenth century, and are still to be encountered on a number of other islands in the British West Indies, but in many different forms. . . . Until recently, Tea Meetings were held often on Nevis on summer evenings during the full of the moon. A hall is engaged and a King and Queen and their court are chosen. Costumes are carefully prepared for the royalty and for the other performers. The night of the performance, the King and Queen are called for by a fife and drum (Big Drum) band. They go to the place of meeting where the rest of the community has gathered. Then they sit on the stage while members of the audience come up and perform some prepared routine—a song, poem, dialogue, speech, or dance, done by one or two performers, or a team song and dance such as *Japanese Fan Drill* or *Baby Drill*. The participants wear costumes appropriate to whatever role they are playing. In the middle of the evening tea (cocoa, or some other hot drink) is served, and some ceremonial cakes, fruit hanging from a *harbor* (sic), and kisses from the King and Queen are ritualistically auctioned. Then the King, the Queen, and members of the court make elaborate and ironic speeches. This is followed by other acts from the audience, which continue until dawn if the meeting is a good one. In the back sit the scoffers who make loud and often obscene comments about the performers and their routines.

Source: ''Patterns of Performance in the British West Indies'' by Roger Abrahams in *Afro-American Anthropology: Contemporary Perspectives*. Edited by Norman E. Whitten, Jr. and John F. Szwed. New York: The Free Press, 1970, pp. 163-179.

Early August

Llama Ch'uyay

The Bolivian ritual Llama Ch'uyay is preferably performed on the eve of Agustu (August First). This is the day when the earth is at her liveliest and most sensitive.

Bolivia

Llama Ch'uyay in Sonqo, Bolivia c. 1975

During the *Llama Ch'uyay,* the llamas are force-fed their *hampi* (medicine) of *chicha, trago,* sugar, soup broth, barley mash, ground *canihua,* and special herbs (*t'urpay, lloque lloque, ch'iri ch'iri, molle, t'ullma, chankaka,* and *yawar chanka*). Families who own horses usually perform the same ritual for them on the feast of Santiago, 25 July.

In the early afternoon of 6 August 1975, Francisco Quispe and his son-in-law Apolinar prepared colored tassels called *t'ikas* (flowers) to decorate the animals. As the two men cut and tied the yarn, they sat in front of the woven sack and *unkhuña* (coca-carrying cloth) they had used while preparing a *despacho* the previous night. Their chewed coca wads went into the sack. Meanwhile Sista, Gavina, and Cipriana (Francisco's daughter and two daughters-in-law) prepared the llamas' *hampi* in a big pot.

Preparations completed, we adjourned to the corral with Francisco and his extended family: daughter Sista and Apolinar, stepsons Julian and Erasmo, and their wives Gavina and Cipriana. Francisco's wife Maria was housebound with her terminal illness. Julian Quintanilla, a friend of Apolinar's, joined us.

Although the day was miserably cold and drizzly, we had to keep the llamas company in the corral, where we sat stoically chewing coca from the ritual cloth, drinking *chicha* and *trago,* and smoking cigarettes. Someone should have been playing "Sargento," a traditional piece for flute and drum played during Carnival and animal *ch'uyays,* but the bad weather dampened our musical inspiration. Instead, they called for the tape recording I had made during the *Uwiha Ch'uyay* (Sheep Festival) the previous June and played it over and over again. The hours wore on and the batteries wore out, but "Sargento" wheezed on.

Shortly before sundown, Julian and Apolinar removed their sandals and began to debate which male animal was the *machu llama* (old llama), or stud. Francisco pointed out the largest male, but the younger men preferred a smaller and older one. Once the men had grabbed the unruly animal, they forced three bottles of "medicine" down its throat and decorated it with tassels. Then they went on to repeat the procedure for the herd of six adult llamas and one baby. They forced as much of the medicinal brew as possible down the llamas' throats; the biggest male consumed five and one-half bottles, the baby one-half. Although three or more bottles were desirable for force-feeding a llama, five bottles were usually considered unlucky, and the men went to a lot of trouble to get the large llama to drink the last half bottle.

While the men were force-feeding and decorating the llamas, they were themselves continuously fed *chicha* and *trago* by the women. By the time they had finished, men and llamas together were stumbling around tipsily.

The herd duly decorated and surfeited with "medicine," we turned to the most dramatic of Sonqo's libations, the *ch'uyay* proper, which entails throwing whole containers of *chicha* onto the herd in a grand sweeping motion. Francisco used traditional wooden goblets called *qeros* for his *Llama Ch'uyay,* whereas Luis used yellow plastic teacups—prized new purchases from Cuzco—for his *Uwiha Ch'uyay* in 1975, and in 1980 did his *Llama Ch'uyay* out of the same bottle he had just used to force-feed the llamas.

The *ch'uyay* completed, we plunged into *hallpachikuy* forced coca chewing), cramming one another's mouths with coca and eventually depositing the wads in the woven sack.

Source: *The Hold Life Has: Coca and Cultural Identity in an Andean Community* by Catherine J. Allen. Washington: Smithsonian Institute Press, 1988, pp. 166-167.

August 1

Feast of the Progress of the Precious and Vivifying Cross

This is a Greek religious festival.

Macedonia

Bonfire-jumping

August begins with the Feast of the Progress of the Precious and Vivifying Cross. Bonfires are the order of the evening. The boys jump over them shouting in vigorous, but sadly unenlightening terms: ''Dig up! bury!'' whom or what, they know not. This exclamation supplies the name by which the custom is known at Melenik. At Shatista, in Western Macedonia, the same fires are called bush-fires, and at Berat, in Albania, *Trikka*. The evening is a Meat-Feast, a preparation for, and a fortification against a fortnight's fast, which again in its turn is a prelude to the Feast of the Repose of the Virgin.

Source: *Macedonian Folklore* by G. F. Abbott. Cambridge: Cambridge Univ. Press, 1903, p. 61.

August 1

Honey Day

This is is the day for blessing honey and horses in prerevolutionary Russia.

Russia

The blessings at church and at the river

On all days dedicated to the Redeemer, things from the fields are brought to the church to be blessed; there is a procession on August 1st, and all horses are driven up to be sprinkled with holy water. Is there a river in the village, the priest blesses it and the horses are driven into it. Bee-keepers bring the first cells of honey to church to be blessed, and that is why August 1st is called "Honey Day."

Source: *Home Life in Russia* by A. S. Rappoport. New York: Macmillan, 1913, p. 51.

August 1

Lammas

Lammas is a pagan first-fruits rite converted to Christian usage. The mass loaf ''Hlaf-mass'' became ''Lammas.''

Great Britain

The "Gule of August" and a Lammas chant

There used to be four great festivals kept in Britain in pagan times. They were about November 1st, February 1st, May 1st and August 1st. The ''Gule [Festival] of August,'' the last one was called. It was a dedication of the first fruits of the earth. Christianity did not interrupt the keeping of this festival and only changed its ritual a little. The first fruits were still the important matter, though offering of them was now made to the church in the form of loaves baked from the first ripe ears of corn. The name then became Hlaf-mass (loaf-mass), and so down the centuries it has become Lammas; just as Llafdige, the kneader of the loaf, has become lady and Hlaford, guardian of the loaf, lord.

Now Lammas comes in
Our harvest begins.
We have now to endeavour to get the corn in.
We reap and we mow,
And stoutly we blow
And cut down the corn that sweetly did grow.

Source: *Happy Holidays* by Eleanor Graham. New York: E. P. Dutton, 1933, p. 174.

August 1
Lúghnasa

A pre-Christian festival, Lúghnasa rites were associated with hilltops and with water. As late as the nineteenth century over a hundred hilltop sites in Ireland were still visited on August 1 for berrying and picnicking or for pilgrimage.

Ireland

Lúghnasa Traditions

The mid-point of the summer half-year was celebrated in the festival of *Lúghnasa,* originally on August first. It was a half-way festival also in another sense, for while *Bealtaine* remained frankly pagan and *Samhna* was largely won over by the festival of All Saints, *Lúghnasa* was characterized by a mixture of pagan and Christian rites. This applied also to the corresponding mid-winter festival of St. Brigid, held on February first. *Lúghnasa* was also a time for fairs often known as Lammas or gooseberry fairs. It was formerly, perhaps, the time when visits were made by those left in charge of the winter homestead to the young folk tending the flocks and herds in the hills or by some lake in the bogs. *Lúghnasa* rites are especially associated with hill tops and with water, but while many places were visited merely for berry picking and picnicking, some of them had long been taken over by the Catholic Church and turned into pilgrimage sites. Thousands of pious pilgrims still make the arduous ascent of the Reek (Croagh Patrick in County Mayo) on the Sunday before the first day of August. It is Ireland's holiest mountain, and its pilgrimage is made on the most celebrated Sunday of the year. Many Patrician legends have gathered around it since the seventh century, but other traditions clearly have pagan associations. The fact that its popularity waned in the second half of the nineteenth century—before its artificial revival in the present century—suggests that the driving force in its secular popularity had been commemoration of a seasonal festival.

It was a first-fruits festival, marked by the gathering of bilberries and by many ritual performances which have been carefully collected and analyzed by Maire MacNeill, who counted over a hundred such hilltop assemblies in nineteenth-century Ireland, and listed nearly a hundred local names, in Irish and English, applied to the day of the festival, e.g., Harvest Sunday, Garland Sunday, Height Sunday, Bilberry Sunday. Its fame rested partly on the guarantee of plenty as fruits began to ripen and harvests turn to gold towards the end of "the hungry month," when the previous year's harvest had been exhausted. It could well be that other processional gatherings such as the notorious Orange Marches which, taking place in "the hungry months," had led to periodic outbursts of violence, have origins that are older that Orangeism. They, too, have their associated bonfires.

Source: *Views of the Irish Peasantry 1800-1916* edited by Daniel J. Casey and Robert E. Rhodes. Hamden, Conn.: Archon Books, 1977, pp. 52-53.

A nineteenth-century Lughnasa

As I remember it, I heard the old people say that it was on the first Sunday of the month of Lughnasa they used to have a great day on the tops of the hills about here looking for bilberries. This Sunday was set out specially for the young people to go off to the hills as soon as the mid-day meal was eaten and they would not return again until twilight had fallen.

When they returned with their gathering of bilberries they had a strange custom. They all sat down on the hill-top and the boys began to make bracelets of bilberries for the girls. They had brought short threads in their pockets for the purpose. They would pick hard stalks on their way to the hill and with these they would put thread through the bilberries. Each man would compete with another as to which would make the best and prettiest bracelet for his own girl.

When that was done, a man or maybe a girl would be named to sing a song. The melody would begin then and would go round from one to another, and anyone who had a note of music at all in his or her head would have to keep the fun going. They used to tell stories and plenty of verses as well. After the singing they would begin the dancing. According to the old talk, they had no instrument for music at all; they had to make do with lilting. In those days boys and girls were good at lilting and they would make enough music for those who were dancing.

Source: *The Festival of Lughnasa: A Study of the Survival of the Celtic Festival of the Beginning of Harvest* by Maire MacNeil. Oxford: Oxford Univ. Press, 1962, p. 141.

Lughnasa customs in early Ireland

On the last Sunday in July the ancient festival of Lughnasa was celebrated and this marked the start of the harvesting. On that Sunday people travelled to the top of hills and there they held various kinds of celebrations. Visits to holy wells were common on all festive days. Lughnasa has now been turned into a religious festival in some areas and so thousands climb Croagh

Patrick in Co. Mayo to pray on the spot where the national patron saint is reputed to have prayed.

Source: *Life & Tradition in Rural Ireland* by Timothy P. O'Neill. London: J. M. Dent & Sons Ltd., 1977, p. 64.

For more information on Lughnasa see: *The Festival of Lughnasa* by Maire MacNeil. Oxford Univ. Press, 1962.

August 6
Transfiguration of Christ

This is a celebration of the Transfiguration of Christ on Mount Tabor in the presence of SS. Peter, James, and John.

Armenia

Vartavar/Aylagerbootyoon

Vartavar, or Aylagerbootyoon celebrates the Transfiguration of Christ ninety-eight days after Easter, instead of on August 6

The Armenian celebration of the Transfiguration usually fell in July rather than August. In July, Armenians were often in high pastures with their flocks, and people would sprinkle each other with water and dunk each other in streams. For young people who met for the first time on this day, it was a lucky meeting.

Source: *Armenian Village Life Before 1914* by Susie Hoogasian Villa and Mary Kilbourne Matoosian. Detroit: Wayne State, 1982, pp. 141-142.

Day of the Transfiguration drenching in Armenia

On the Day of the Transfiguration of Christ our custom is to throw cold water on each other. We do this amid great laughter and joy. On this day people usually wear their old clothes. I have seen many forgetful persons (wearing new clothes) thoroughly drenched. It is a very amusing picture to see young men dashing pails of water upon each other. On this day, also, we build bonfires, and dance around them. Many young men consider it great fun and a clever thing to jump over the bonfire, but through such daring there have been those who have fallen into the fire and been badly burned.

Source: *When I Was a Boy in Armenia* by Manoog Der Alexanian. Boston: Lothrop, Lee & Shepard Co., 1926, pp. 120-121.

El Salvador

El Salvador del Mundo festival

A festival in honor of the transfiguration of Christ as he stood before the apostles Peter, James, and John on Mount Tabor. The capital, San Salvador, hosts parades, dances, and fairs. On August 5, climax of the festival, the statue of El Salvador del Mundo processes through the city.

August celebrations at the Transfiguratión del Señor

The *Fiestas Agostinas* (August feasts) are famous throughout Central America. Beginning in 1525, almost as soon as the city was established, a simple parade featuring the Royal Standard took place on August 6. However, the festivity developed rapidly during the eighteenth century, when the above-named Garcia, a member of the Third Order of Franciscans, a sculptor and a painter, carved this image to fulfil a vow. Beginning in 1777, this good man endeavored to celebrate the feast with pomp and ceremony, privately defraying most of the expenses until his death in 1805. After that date, the municipality assumed the task and appointed sixteen stewardesses to have charge of the decorations for a period of six years. During the first year (1808), the celebrations were the same as formerly, but the next year one of the stewardesses, Dominga Mayorga, organized a pageant (*entrada*) with a float covered with wild flowers on which the famous *Salvador del Mundo* was carried. Every year after that a different allegorical float was made. The next step was a litter of wood and tinsel, with sundry decorations, on which the sacred image was carried around the *Plaza de Armas;* on one side the figure was unveiled: *El Descubrimiento.* Every year something has been added to the procession. Now the sacred image is hidden in a much decorated shell (*granada*), which at the corner of the *Parque Dueñas* is opened for *El Descubrimiento.* It is a breathtaking sight to watch the multitude kneel at a given signal as the sacred figure is revealed, and the procession then continues on its way back toward the Cathedral.

The present-day float is enormous and so tall that electric wires must be cut to allow it to pass. Popular legend says that in the year that the figure by some mischance happens to fall, some catastrophe is in store for the country, specifically the president. The men who carry the float do it so as to fulfil a vow, and it is a penitence indeed on a hot day.

The colonial *entradas* are still celebrated by the *Capitana* or stewardess of each district of the city; according to her means she invites friends to participate, and to gather at her house to celebrate; the festive board groans under different kinds of sweetmeats, and everyone receives a present: little baskets of candies, artificial flowers, and the like, and then they go into the street to admire the decorated float that their district contributes toward the great procession.

Up and down the streets, Indians perform typical dances:

Historia, Los Moros, El Torito, and others to the tune of the Indian fife and drum. Society disports itself at the clubs with dances and festivities. Military parades, races, and fireworks contribute toward the noise at this time of year. Repeatedly the attempt has been made to transfer the celebrations to the dry season instead of the August rainy season, but the custom is so entrenched that the people refused to take part in any festivities that did not take place in August on the day of the *Transfiguración del Señor*.

Source: *Four Keys to El Salvador* by Lilly de Jongh Osborne. New York: Funk & Wagnalls, 1956, pp. 156-158.

Greece

Night-long vigil

Metamorphosis Too Soteros

In Greece, this celebration is observed in special church services. At the Chapel of the Transfiguration on Mount Athos a night-long vigil is kept.

Russia

Apple blessing in peasant Russia

On the feast of the Transfiguration, August 6th, apples are taken into the church to be blessed, and apples are tasted that day. It is held a sin to eat apples before August 6th.

Source: *Home Life in Russia* by A. S. Rappoport. New York: Macmillan, 1913, p. 51.

Syria

Id Al-Tajalli

Special commemoration

Special church services commemorate the transfiguration.

August 10

Día De San Lorenzo

This is a day in honor of St. Laurence of Rome. St. Laurence died in 258. He was one of the Deacons of Pope Sixtus II and was put to death by being roasted alive on a gridiron three days after the martyrdom of that Pope. St. Laurence was buried on the Via Tiburtina at the Campus Veranus, where his basilica now stands.

Mexico

Festival of San Lorenzo in Zinacantan

San Lorenzo's day is August 10, but this fiesta is for the patron saint of Zinacantan, and it lasts five days—from August 7, when the band arrives and vendors set up their stands in the market and the Mayordomos renew their house altar decorations, to August 11, when the saints that have been ''visiting'' from other villages return to their homes. While San Lorenzo is the patron saint, there is little distinctive ritual during this fiesta. . . The only distinctive additional performers are the *Capitanes* who are costumed in brown skull caps from which red feathers dangle, a rolled red turban tied around their heads, and a blue kerchief around their necks, plus an everyday shirt under an old, torn black suit jacket and blue or green breeches which meet the red stockings below the knees. They carry bright scarves in their right hands, and gold paint streaks their faces. They accompany the processions meeting the six saints which visit from other villages and perform their dance at ritual stops and later at visits to cargoholders' houses throughout the fiesta. The dance is done by the Capitanes facing each other, and making rhythmic hops on one foot while the other foot is extended in front off the ground. At intervals of a few minutes, the Capitanes throw their scarves over their shoulders with a shout and exchange places, now hopping on the foot that had been lifted, and extending the other foot.

Otherwise, the fiesta is noted for the largest number of Zinacantecos, as well as residents of other villages, many of whom accompany the visiting saints, that attend the fiesta. The fiesta comes at a period in the agricultural cycle when the heavy work of the second weeding in the cornfields has been finished and when both fresh corn and many fruits are available. I would estimate that more than 5000 people attend to watch the ceremonies especially the spectacular fireworks and to trade in the market where there is a brisk exchange of Highland and Lowland products.

Source: *The Zinacantecos of Mexico: A Modern Maya Way of Life* by Evan Z. Vogt. New York: Holt, Rinehart and Winston, 1970, p. 89.

August 10-12

Puck's Fair

This is a three-day event of great antiquity held in Killorglin in County Kerry. The days are Gathering Day, Puck's Fair Day, and Scattering Day.

Ireland

Puck's Fair, an Irish tradition

At Killorglin in County Kerry, Puck's Fair, a traditional gathering, survives to this day. The events take place on three days, Gathering Day, Puck's Fair Day, and Scattering Day. A large puck (male) goat is decorated with ribbons and paraded through the streets on the first day. He is enthroned on a three-story platform in the town square to preside over the fair (in a large enclosure). On the second day a livestock fair is held. On Scattering Day (Children's Day) King Puck is piped out of town.

Source: *International What's What When and Where* by Ardith Nehrt. Columbus, Ohio: Shawnee, 1065, p. 95.

Gypsies at Puck Fair

When I was nine years old we were travelling the Counties Kerry, Cork, Clare and Galway, meeting other Travellers on our travels at fairs, and especially at Ballinasloe Fair. Hundreds of Travellers come to that fair, selling horses, donkeys, wagons, carts, swapping and dealing, and telling fortunes, playing musical instruments. For a full week the fair would be on. Spangel Hill Fair in the County Clare is a very big fair, and then of course there is Puck Fair, County Kerry. In Puck Fair all the wagons are camped on the roadside. Hardly any of the Travellers go to bed during the fair. The Travellers have been attending these fairs for hundreds of years. And there are great legends about them:

> The hand that kills King Puck
> Will wither like the dew.
> The blade that cuts his whiskers
> Will pierce your heart too.
> The rope that hangs old Puck,
> Will execute its maker . . .

Old King Puck is a goat and he'd be crowned King Puck during the fair. It is also said that the single girl that goes to Puck Fair will leave it doubled.

In the night around the camp fires you would hear some of the best Irish traditional music that ever was played; reels, jigs, horn-pipes, airs, marches, and old Irish waltzes—'The Galway Snare', 'Father Murphy', 'Sullivan John', 'The Jolly Tinker', 'The Catcherman', 'Ellen Brown', 'Banclothy', 'The Maid in the Garret', 'Seven Drunken Nights', 'Heather Ale', 'Flower of Sweet Strabone', 'Lalley Mountain', 'The Beggar Man', 'John Mitchell', and many more different names of songs: 'The Maid of Mount Scisco', 'The Sligo Maid', 'The Maid behind the Bar', 'Rakish Paddy', 'Georgie Whites', 'The Washer Woman', 'Pigeon on the Gate', 'Down the Broom', 'Battering Ram', and 'Sally Gardens', 'Hornpipes', 'The Black Bird', 'The Cork Hornpipe', 'The Dawn of the Day', 'Wearing of the Green', 'Kelly from Killarney', and many more.

Source: *Gypsies* by Jeremy Sanford. London: Secker & Warburg, 1973, p. 125.

August 15

The Assumption of the Virgin

The Assumption of the Virgin has been celebrated by Roman Catholics since the fourth century. "Assumption" refers to the belief that the Body of Mary was united with her soul in heaven rather than disintegrating on earth.

Armenia

Verapoghoom (Assumption of the Virgin Mary)/ Haghoghy Ortnootyoon (Blessing of the Grapes)

Blessing of the first fruits

On the Sunday nearest to August 15 the harvest's first fruits were blessed in church.

Brazil

Nossa Senhora dos Navegantes

Nosa Senhora dos Navegantes in São Paulo, Brazil

In southern Brazil August 15 is known as the day of Our Lady of the Navigators. Water pageants are held, with canoes decorated with flowers and colored paper. Each holds a captain, a purser, three musicians, and two rowers. They travel to various villages and small settlements, entertaining and collecting contributions. They may be feasted and spend the night en route. In towns a church procession featuring musicians portraying the Three Wise Men may take place.

Source: *Fiesta Time in Latin America* by Jean Milne. Los Angeles: The Ward Ritchie Press, 1965, p. 132.

Canada

Tintamarre

The Acadians in the Maritimes celebrate their national holiday on August 15, feast day of their patron saint, Our Lady of Assumption. At exactly six p.m. on this date, *tintamarre* breaks out, a bedlam of pot and pan banging, drum beating, and whistle blowing. On the Sunday nearest August 15, church services are held and a blessing of the fleet occurs. Decorated boats sail past the dock and the officiating priest.

Source: *Let's Celebrate* by Caroline Parry. Toronto: Kids Can Press, 1987, pp. 186-187.

Ethiopia

Whipping contests and bonfires

In August, finally, the sixteen-day fast in honor of the Assumption of Mary is observed by everyone older than six or seven years.

On the thirteenth day of that fast occurs the strange holiday of Buhē. Before and during this day, which is marked by the baking of special *dābo* for the shepherds, the countryside crackles with the reports of shepherds' whips. In this season when the humid air lends an explosive sound, the shepherds crack their whips for fun; but older boys and men join in great whipping battles on Buhē, in which two teams lash each other until the members of one can stand it no more. On the evenings of Buhē, small bonfires are lit all over the countryside, and more *dābo* is eaten and whips cracked. A few days later the fast of the Assumption is over. Young and old look forward to the end of the rains and the festivities that commence with the new year.

Source: *Wax & Gold: Tradition and Innovation in Ethiopian Culture* by Donald N. Levine. Chicago: Univ. of Chicago Press, 1965, p. 64.

Sicily

The Assumption festa in Messina, Sicily

This festa lasts for two weeks and includes a fair, water sports, and folksong/dance programs. Homes, city, and harbor are illuminated. A fireworks show takes place on the night of the fifteenth. The main feature of the festival is a huge pyramidal float bearing angels, with Christ at the top, holding the Madonna's soul in his hand. At one time all of the heavenly beings were portrayed by humans. The girl playing the Madonna was allowed to pardon one condemned criminal each year. Giganti, huge papier-mâché figures with men inside tour the streets.

They were once said to symbolize the mythical founders of Messina, Zancleo and his queen.

Source: *Festivals and Folkways of Italy* by Frances Toor. New York: Crown, 1953, p. 78.

Spain

El Día de la Asunción

Good-luck charms

An image of the Virgin is erected in the church on this day and resides there until the octave a week later. Street processions may occur as well. In Puebla de Guzmán (Huelva) people nail a small olive branch and wheat heads to their wall on this day. If this is not done, the home will lack both peace and bread all year long.

Source: *Culture and Conquest* by George M. Foster. Chicago: Quadrangle Books, 1960, p. 199.

The Assumption Play of Elche

During the middle ages a chest washed up on the shore at Santa Pola containing an image of the Virgin and the text for a mystery play written in Valencian. The play is performed at the Assumption each year.

The assumption play at Elche, c. 1968

In the late afternoon of 14 August, the actors walked solemnly to the church behind the two little boys who represented the Virgin Mary and Mary Salome, accompanied by angels carrying cushions for them to kneel upon. The Virgin and her escort paused at the door, waiting for their cue. Then they advanced into and through the church.

On the stage before the altar the Virgin sang in front of 'Gethsemane', 'Calvary' and the 'Holy Sepulchre', declaring that she wished to die and join her son in heaven. At that moment 'heaven' opened and disclosed the angel-messenger in his pomegranate. He had come to tell her that her wish had been granted. The Virgin then asked for one more favor: could she see the Apostles once more before she died? The angel, after presenting her with a palm branch and granting her this wish too, slowly ascended to heaven.

On the second day, the Apostles, presided by St Peter, entered the church singing to surround the Virgin's death-bed in fulfilment of the angel's promise, and later to bury her. Then a noisy band of Jews marched in to take possession of the body. A mock but quite realistic battle broke out on the gangway, but in the end the Jews were overcome and converted whereupon they all proceeded amicably to bury the Virgin, singing psalms in her honour.

Then heaven opened again and four guitar-strumming angels, kneeling on a narrow two-tier platform were gradually lowered to the Virgin's tomb. After taking the image of the Virgin in their arms—it represented her soul—they slowly embarked on their heavenward journey.

Suddenly the church doors were thrown wide open and the angels paused in mid-air as St. Thomas made his dramatic late entry. (According to the apocryphal gospels from which the archaic text is taken, he was preaching in far-away India when he received his celestial summons.) He flung himself on his knees with outstretched arms and eyes raised and sung a moving apology to the Virgin for his involuntary delay. This is one of the most lovely arias of the Mystery. A thrill went through me and, I believe, the entire audience-congregation. St. Thomas was in excellent voice. And his emotion was so genuine that it communicated itself to us all. 'Gee!' exclaimed the American journalist beside me in the visitors' gallery, that guy's got a wonderful voice!' I nodded proudly.

When the aria was over the angels continued their interrupted ascent. Yet another vision emerged from the trapdoor: God and two flanking angels (representing the Trinity) come to receive and welcome the Virgin to heaven. God was represented by the parish priest . . . his job in Elche is no sinecure. He crowned the Virgin, the organ burst into an exultant apotheosis, bells rang, squibs were let off outside and the entire congregation rose to its feet clapping and shouting ecstatically: *Viva la Virgen!*

The angel-lowering device

The church was transformed into a theatre for the annual event: in front of the altar was a wooden platform, open in the centre for the gangway leading to the main door from where the actors would make their appearance. A blue canvas representing the sky was stretched across the dome, with a small sliding door for communication between heaven and earth.

I climbed up the tower stairs to the wide terrace which surrounds the church at the base of the dome, on the same level as the canvas sky, to watch the angel preparing for his sixty-yard descent through the trapdoor. Heaven, I found, was full of contraptions: above the blue canvas was a platform for the operators. Above it was a wheel connected to a pulley on the terrace outside. Round it, a thick rope was attached to a large model pomegranate divided into several panels. This rope, wrapped in red and white cotton bands to make it less slippery to handle, was being manipulated by six men with strong, muscular arms.

Before the angel arrived on the scene from his dressing-room on the terrace, I peeped through the trapdoor into the church; it made me feel giddy and I quickly drew back. The choirmaster walked up with the angel: a mischievous-looking boy disguised in a wig of golden ringlets, a long white tunic and large wings; he gave him his final instructions while the men placed an iron belt round the angel fastened by six metal strips to a tiny foothold inside the pomegranate. This fearsome object opens out a few seconds after it has been lowered through the trapdoor leaving the angel alone on his foothold in the forbidding void. 'Now,' said the choirmaster casually as the first chords burst from the organ in the church below, 'down you go. Look straight ahead of you. Never, never look down. Sing well.

Nobody is going to eat you.' The angel grinned. He looked quite unflappable.

The panels of the pomegranate close upon him. The trapdoor slid open and the six operators sprung into action. Two lay full length on the platform upon their stomachs, two towered above them and two stood by the wheel outside. Very slowly and carefully, with almost feminine delicacy, they lowered the rope inch by inch; it requires a tremendous effort to prevent it from twisting and the men sweated profusely. But all went well. The pomegranate opened slowly and smoothly, revealing its glittering silver interior to the crowds below, the angel glued his blue eyes straight ahead of him as he had been told, and began to intone his archaic little song: *a-aaa-aaa-aaa. . . .*

Source: ''The Assumption Play of Elche'' in *Spanish Fiestas* by Nina Epton. New York: A. S. Barnes, 1968, pp. 164-171.

For more information on Assumption see: ''Assumption Day, August 15'' in *Folklore of American Holidays* edited by Hennig Cohen and Tristram Potter Coffin. 2nd ed. Detroit: Gale Research, 1991.

August 20

Saint Stephen's Fete

The Magyar king Vaik, who came to the throne in 997, applied for the title of Apostolic King to Pope Sylvester II and was crowned in Budapest in 1000 under the Christian name of Stephen. He founded churches, schools, and convents throughout Hungary and left the country completely converted to Christianity by his death in 1036, having quelled an uprising of the "Old Magyar Religion." One of his hands was amputated and embalmed after death, and encased as a relic in the Royal Palace in Buda. On August 20 the relic was carried in procession to Matthias Church for services.

Hungary

Saint Stephen's Fete in Budapest, c. 1906

At seven promptly the procession emerged from the Palace gateway. It was headed by several hundred children, the girls dressed in white, chanting as they walked along, and carrying many banners on which religious subjects were portrayed. The banners were a feature of the entire procession, as there was a great number of them throughout the line, some very beautiful. Those carried by the children were small and plain, with a picture of a saint on a simple background of some colored material. Later they became more elaborate, and those carried immediately in front of the reliquary were of the most splendid colored brocaded silk, the pictures being magnificent examples of hand embroidery. Behind the children were many religious societies, of both men and women, some wearing special regalias. These also were chanting or repeating prayers in concert, generally led by a priest in full vestments. A battalion of infantry formed the guard of honor and was preceded by a full regimental band. They marched with slow, measured step, the music being of a solemn and churchly nature. Immediately following the military came the priests from the different churches of the two cities, attended by their assistants and acolytes, all in their highest robes and vestments.

The dropping on the knees of many of the spectators and the bowing of heads and crossing of themselves by others announced the approach of the reliquary. Preceded by magnificent banners and by the Archbishop of Budapest, it was borne high in air, so that all might see. It stood on a carved framework, which was elaborately covered with gilding and embroidery, and was carried on the shoulders of four richly robed priests. On each side walked two royal heralds who represented the King as special guardians of the relic. They were magnificent persons, in crimson velvet, bearing the royal arms of Hungary embroidered in gold on their chests and backs and carrying golden staffs of office richly ornamented. A special guard of honor marched in single file on the outer edge of the immediate escort of the reliquary. This was composed of a detachment of the celebrated Hungarian Palace Guard, the most theatrically dressed troops in all Europe. Their uniforms were a queer combination of past and present. A polished steel helmet of ancient pattern, crowned by a single eagle's feather, surmounted a most modern-cut scarlet uniform, richly braided with silver cord. Their boots were of brilliant yellow leather, and for arms they carried a modern saber, with the long polished steel halberds of centuries ago. The relic was carried past with many signs of reverence and veneration from the spectators and mid a silence that was broken only by the murmurs of lowly spoken prayers.

Immediately behind the reliquary came the nobles and gentlemen, whose costumes I have already endeavored to describe. Individually as they arrived they were unique and showy, but massed together they made a picture of novelty and color to which no camera could do justice. They were followed by many army officers in full uniform and by the already-described chasseurs, who massed together were but little less brilliant and interesting than the gorgeously arrayed group that had preceded them. Another detachment of infantry brought the splendid cortege to a close.

The procession wended its way through the crowded streets to Matthias Church, where but a small portion of the escort and only those of the highest rank were admitted, as the interior is not large. Around the church was an immense concourse of people, who joined in the service with responses and chanting, as it proceeded inside, priests being stationed at different points to lead them at the proper time. The service lasts some three hours. . . .

After the service had finished, the procession was again formed in the same order as before, and the reliquary escorted back to its resting place in the Royal Chapel, where it mains until the next 20th of August. The crowd in the streets had waited patiently for another glimpse of the sacred relic, and the same scenes of devotion and veneration were enacted on its return. The religious part of the day being over, the afternoon and evening were devoted to pleasure and merry-making. In the squares and streets near the palace and church, booths had been erected for the sale of merchandise, refreshments, and souvenirs. The latter were all of a religious nature—pictures of saints, sacred medals, shrines, etc., in which the effigy of Saint Stephen always held the place of honor. Later in the day there were music and dancing in different parts of the city, the principal point of gaity being the *Stadtwaldchen*, or public garden, where cafés, shows, and other forms of amusement kept the citizens and visitors entertained until a late hour.

Source: ''Saint Stephen's Fete in Budapest'' by De Witt Clinton Falls in *The National Geographic Magazine*. XVIII (8)(August 1907), 54.

Circa August 24

Waratambar

A Thanksgiving day in the Christian tradition is observed throughout New Guinea during August. The date varies in different provinces, falling on August 24 in New Ireland.

Papua New Guinea

Thanksgiving in New Ireland

In a population of some two million, about half of the people of Papua New Guinea are Christians.

Waratambar, or Thanksgiving Day, is observed on different dates in August in different provinces. In New Ireland, several hundred miles north of Port Moresby, the date is the twenty-fourth.

It is, literally, a day of thanksgiving to the Lord for what Christianity has done for peoples throughout the world; for having given them comfort in time of misfortune, faith in prayer, and the hope of salvation.

In the villages, farmers and their families leave their work in the fields, on coconut plantations and fishing grounds, and gather to take part in the singing and dancing.

Their songs are in appreciation of nature and express a closeness with all creatures of the land. Their dances dramatize historical accounts of tribal wars. Some dances have comic characters, others represent Good and Evil. Costumes are made by hand of ferns, moss, leaves, flowers.

It's a time to unite with families, and to strengthen bonds of love and friendship.

Source: *Celebrations: Asia and the Pacific* by Gene Sawyer. Honolulu: Friends of the East-West Center, 1978, p. 63.

End of August
Umhlanga

Umhlanga is a week-long coming-of-age ceremony for young girls. They come to the royal city of Lobamba from throughout Swaziland. There they spend several days gathering reeds along the riverbank. On the sixth day they bring the reeds to the Queen of Swaziland and perform a difficult dance for her, tossing the reeds high into the air. The next day the girls use reeds to rebuild the screens around the Queen's compound. On the final day the festival concludes with feasting and dancing.

Swaziland

The Reed Dance

This is not a sacred ceremony and takes place at the end of August. In this ceremony, the Swazi maidens show respect for the Queen Mother by bringing reeds from all over Swaziland for the building of the symbolic screens round the Queen Mother's kraal. This tends to be strictly a feminine occasion where the girls who have remained chaste, may demonstrate their nubility. The dance climaxes when the girls, dressed in beautiful anklets, bracelets, necklaces and bead skirts bring their reeds to the Queen's kraal and do a slow dance, in perfect time, past the entrance of the royal village at Lobamba, to the cattle kraal behind. On the final day, the girls dance for the Queen Mother and the festival ends with feasting and rejoicing. Visitors are welcome to the Umhlanga or Reed Dance.

Source: *Swaziland* by Dirk Schwager. Mbabane, Swaziland: MacMilla Boleswa, p. 96.

Photrobot, Twelfth Day Waning Moon (August-September)

Prachum Ben

The fifteen days from day 1 to 15 of the waning moon of Photrobot are reserved for rituals of the dead. The skies are overcast at this rainy season and during the increasingly dark shifts of this fifteen-day period Yama, God of the Underworld, releases the souls to visit among the living. If these visitors do not find proper offerings at the shrines they might cause ill to their families. This period is called Kan-Ben. *Ben* refers to the rice balls offered to the dead.

Cambodia

Ben offerings

These days *ben* are made of glutinous rice mixed with coconut milk and other ingredients, depending on local custom. They are arranged on a platter around a centerpiece, the *bay battor,* which is placed on a pedestal. The *bày bettbór* is of the same rice as the *ben* but is formed into a cone. Flags, flowers, and joss sticks decorate the top.

Source: "La Quinzaine des Morts" in *Cérémonies des Douze Mois.* Translated by editor. Commission Des Moeurs St Coutumbres Du Cambodge, no date, pp. 47-56.

Prachum Ben in Cambodia, c. 1960

See Mong was in a most genial mood, and clearly *Prachum Ben* was one of the happiest of Khmer festivals. The special *ben* cakes, wrapped in banana leaves, looked like big green sausages. See Mong put me in charge of the cakes, which mounted into a great heap at the end of his verandah. He was surrounded by hundreds of his former pupils and ex-monks who had come from all parts of Cambodia to greet him. Most of them brought presents of food, and soon See Mong was surrounded with thirty or more dinner pails each containing tier upon tier of the choicest Khmer dishes. After lunch we started the ceremony of *bangskol.* A small table was set in front of See Mong on which he placed the bones of people's ancestors. Then he went into a back room and emerged carrying two triangular containers. "This is my father and mother," he said, "and these are my grandparents." Although most of the ancestors were contained in oval china flasks, some had been mislaid. Where no relics were forthcoming, the people wrote the names on a piece of paper and asked See Mong to *bangskol* the names. The other monks sat in a double line next to See Mong, while an *achar* collected money. See Mong glanced down the list of people he had been asked to *bangskol* and then walked over to where one of the novices was sitting. "What about your grandparents?" asked See Mong with a twinkle in his eye. The novice said he had none. "But you must know their names," said See Mong. "I don't," said the novice, blushing. "Nobody ever told me."

See Mong turned round to address the people. I could not understand all that he said, but he spoke of the monastery and the work done by his father, who—he said—had been head monk before him. A moment earlier he had been joking about the novice's grandparents. Now he suddenly moved his audience with quiet pathos, so that we all listened in dead silence. The actual *bangskol* seemed to consist of a few prayers. Separate ceremonies had to be held at the various tombs which surrounded the *vihara.* But now the sun was very hot and the monks were reluctant to carry on. "Come on," said the *achar.* "There are lots more to do yet." At one tomb *bangskol* prayers had to be said four times, since the ashes of a different family were interred on each side. The north side of one tomb was shared by three families, and a separate *bangskol* had to be done for each one.

Source: *Mistapim in Cambodia* by Christopher Pim. London: Hodder & Stoughton, 1960, pp. 161-162. (For more on Prauchum Ben see pp. 159-167.

Ninth Month (August-September)

Ho Khao Padap Dinh (Feast of the Dead)

This is a day to commemorate the dead.

Laos

Ho Khao Padap Dinh, Feast of the Dead

Ho Khao Padap Dinh (Feast of the Dead) occurs in the ninth month (August and September). Its origin is Buddha's commandment to honor the dead with gifts, prayers, and thoughts. There are, as usual, gifts to the *sangha*.

Source: *Laos: A Country Study* by Donald P. Whitaker et al. Foreign Area Studies. Washington, D.C.: The American University, 1971, p. 122.

Moon 8, Day 15 (August-September)

Mid-Autumn Feast / Chung Ch'Iu / Chusok / Tiong-Chhiu Choeh / Trung Thu

On this day, Thai-im niu-niu, the Goddess of the Moon, is honored. Mooncakes are eaten and given to friends. The full moon is viewed in the evening.

China

A civil servant's daughter celebrates the Autumn moon in Wuch'ang

In the eighth month the heat was oppressive. Mother said that the heat of autumn was worse than the heat of summer: it was called the 'Autumn Tiger.' The cicadas came no more, but other similar insects came in their place and sang, not in chorus, but singly. These insects told us that autumn had come and that it would soon be growing cooler.

The feast of the middle of autumn fell on the fifteenth day of the eighth month. It was a moon feast, and a sacrifice was made to the moon in the evening. The first autumn moon is particularly round and white, and one had to gaze at it and admire it. Mooncakes, as round as the moon itself, were sold everywhere and exchanged as presents.

Our tutor had us write poems about the moon. The evening was fresh, and the whole family felt happy in the bright moonlight. The long days of summer were over and the autumn winds were beginning to blow. Now the crickets began to sing their quiet song, and we felt a gentle melancholy.

Source: *The Lotus Pool* by Chow Chung-cheng. New York: Appleton-Century-Crofts, 1961, pp. 82-83.

A visit from the Buddha

One evening the Buddha, accompanied by several of his disciples, came to the garden. They sat at his feet and listened to his recitation of the sutras. So passed a night and a day until the scorching sun stood in the sky and the cicadas shrilled. It was the time when every creature sought the shade and every traveller suffered from the heat.

Buddha assumed the form of a Brahman and called out sorrowfully: "I am alone, my friends have abandoned me and I am hungry and thirsty. Believers come and help me!" The small animals of the forest heard his call and one after another hastened to his side.

They begged him to stay and accept their hospitality. Each brought such food as it could. The otter brought seven fishes and said: "Take these and stay with us. The jackal brought part of his prey and asked Buddha to honor them with his presence and be their teacher. Then came the turn of the rabbit. He modestly stepped forward, his hands empty. "Master! I have grown up in the woods. Herbs and grasses are my food. I have nothing else to offer you but my body. Bless us and rest here, and let me feed you on my flesh, for there is nothing else I can give you." Just then the rabbit caught sight of some magic coal, coal that burns without smoke. Just as he was about to jump into the flames, he stopped suddenly and picked the tiny insects out of its fur, saying: "I may give my body to the saint, but I have no right to take your lives." Setting the insects carefully on the ground, the rabbit threw himself into the fire.

Buddha resumed his own form and praised the sacrifice: "He who forgets himself, the most modest of all earthly creatures, shall reach the Ocean of Eternal Peace! All men should learn from him and be as compassionate and helpful as he!" Buddha then gave instuctions that the likeness of the rabbit should adorn the moon and thus remain a shining example for all time. And thanks to their holy friend, all the animals in the forest were placed in the world of saints.

Daoism, the indigenous religion of China, adopted the rabbit in the moon along with many other concepts that originated in Buddhism. They called it the Jade Rabbit and pictured it with short front paws, very long back legs and a short tail. It is said to stand under a magical cassia tree on the moon making pills of immortality, also known as the jade elixir.

Keeping the Jade Rabbit company in the Moon Palace is an immortal by the name of Wu Gang. This unfortunate being had been exiled by the Jade Emperor (the supreme deity in the Daoist cosmology) with the stipulation that amnesty could be extended only when he had succeeded in felling the cassia tree. Yet each time Wu Gang struck with his ax, the tree healed the cut immediately, dooming him to eternal futility.

Among the Chinese people, perhaps the most popular of all the tales connected with Mid-Autumn Festival is that of Chang E, the Moon Lady, who turned into a three-legged toad when she ascended to the moon. Like the story of the rabbit, this one also originated in India. From the earliest times the various elements of this myth have been interwoven: the moon, the female essence (*yin*), water, and amphibians (the toad). This tale, then, is told and retold at Mid-Autumn Festival.

Legend of Chang E

Chang E and her husband Hou Yi, the miraculous archer, lived during the reign of the legendary Emperor Yao (about 2000 B.C.). Hou Yi was a most capable member of the Emperial Guard who wielded a magic bow and shot magic arrows. One day ten suns appeared in the sky. People on earth could not stand the heat and drought which continued for years on end. The emperor called Hou Yi before him and ordered him to shoot the extra suns out of the sky to succor the populace. Bringing all his skill to bear, Hou Yi knocked nine of them down leaving only the one.

After this Hou Yi's fame spread even to the Queen Mother of the West (Xi Wang Mu) in the far-off Kunlun Mountains. She summoned him to her fairy palace to reward him with the pill of immortality, first warning him: "You must not eat the pill immediately. First prepare yourself through praying and fasting for twelve months." Being a careful man, he took her advice to heart and set about his preparations, first hiding the pill in his house. Unfortunately, he was called away suddenly on an urgent mission. In his absence, his wife Chang E noticed a soft light and sweet odor emanating from a corner of the room. Taking the pill in her hand, she just could not refrain from taking a taste. The moment she swallowed it the law of gravity lost its power over her—she could fly! Not too long afterwards she heard her husband returning and flew in terror out the window. Bow and arrow in hand, Hou Yi pursued her across half the sky, but a strong wind drove him back. Chang E flew all the way to the moon, but when she arrived, she was panting so hard from her exertions that she spit out the pill casing, which turned instantly into a jade rabbit. She herself became a three-legged toad. Ever since she has lived on the moon and continued to ward off the magic arrows Hou Yi shoots after. Her husband built himself a palace on the sun and they see each other on the 15th of every month. Chang E and Hou Yi symbolizing respectively the sun and the moon, have come to be regarded as embodying *yin* and *yang,* the negative and positive, dark and light, feminine and masculine, duality which governs the universe.

Source: "The Moon Festival" in *Chinese Creeds and Customs* by V. R. Burkhardt. Hong Kong: South China Morning Post, 1982, pp. 62-67.

Festival of the Moon

In the eighth month comes the Festival of the Moon, answering to the Harvest Festival in Western countries. What are called "moon-cakes" are sold at this season. If the year has been productive there will be a great deal of rejoicing. Presents are interchanged at this time as also at other festival seasons. As the moon becomes gradually full there appears in it to the Chinese eye a man who is climbing a tree. The full moon is greeted with much ceremony, and the night on which the luminary appears its brightest is passed in feasting and rejoicing.

Source: *When I Was a Boy in China* by Yan Phou Lee. Boston: Lothrop, Lee & Shepard Co., 1887, p. 80.

Fantastic paper lanterns

Next, in order of time, comes the Feast of Lanterns. The main feature of this fête, as the name implies, is a procession with lanterns of all shapes and kinds. Soon after nightfall, men and boys get in line, each carrying upon a bamboo pole a great paper bird, or quadruped, or fish, inside of which candles are lit. Very fantastic shapes sometimes are seen, and mythological books are ransacked to procure strange creatures.

Imagine three or four hundred of these lanterns passing before you, all brilliant with rich colors. Sandal-wood is burnt in censers carried in small movable pavilions, while bands of music mingle their racket with the applause of the spectators and the jokes of the men in the procession.

Last of all an immense and terrible dragon about forty feet in length is borne along supported on bamboo poles by a dozen or twenty men.

There is another procession similar to this in the fourth month, only it takes place in the daytime instead of at night, and the large number and variety of lanterns are wanting.

Source: *When I Was a Boy in China* by Yan Phou Lee. Boston: Lothrop, Lee & Shepard Co., 1887, pp. 78-80.

Hong Kong

Chung Ch'iu

Festival food

In traditional China the Mid-Autumn festival was especially a woman's occasion, befitting the essentially female (*Yin*) Moon. In each family a special table was set up facing the moon out of doors with dishes of round fruit (round for the fullness of the moon) such as apples, oranges, peaches, or pomegranates (the last being particularly propitious since their many seeds symbolise many sons) and, of course, moon cakes. Rice, wine and tea would be offered too, together with several suits of paper clothing and many ingots of *spirit money* in gold and silver paper.

Today these rites are less commonly performed, but the evening is still marked by a family dinner at home. In recent years it has become the custom to take the young children to the nearest park after dinner and settle down with them on the ground to light small candles, nibble moon cakes, and enjoy the moon. Wealthier families often hold moon parties on this date.

From about 7:00 p.m. onwards Victoria Park, Causeway Bay, Stanley Beach, and many other open spaces present a charming scene of family parties picnicking quietly on the ground, surrounded by lighted candles and small lanterns. Religious papershops all over Hong Kong have paper lanterns for sale at this season. Moon cakes are available from bakeries, supermarkets, stores, and some restaurants from about the end of August.

Source: *Chinese Festivals in Hong Kong* by Joan Law and Barbara E. Ward. Hong Kong: A South China Morning Post Production, 1982, p. 68.

The moon festival in Hong Kong, c. 1982

The altar for the Moon Festival must be arranged by the younger female members of the family, under the supervision of the "Old Lady". It is set in the open air, and on it are placed five dishes of round fruits, such as apples, peaches, and pomegranates, whose seeds betoken many sons, grapes and small melons. The shape not only symbolises the moon, but betokens family unity. The moon cakes are an essential part of the feast. Baked of a greyish (moon-coloured) flour, they are piled thirteen in a pyramid, for in a full year there are thirteen lunar months. Odd numbers are always lucky, and they represent a complete circle of happiness.

One of the offerings at the festival in Hong Kong is a brown seed, called Ling Ke, or water calthrops, about two and a half inches across the tips of what resemble buffalo's horns. It is exactly like the conventionalised Chinese bat, a lucky emblem, which probably accounts for its presence. It is sometimes employed in art, carved in jade or modelled, as the knob on the top of a tea-pot lid, the sides being decorated with snails and water chestnuts. At this time of year it also forms a child's toy, pierced with a hole, and having a string run through to whirl it.

Three cups of tea form the liquid refreshment, and in the centre of the table which serves as altar is a sand-filled receptacle for candles and sticks of incense. The Moon's consort is honoured at the same time by the provision of a cardboard effigy combining the characters for sun and moon in complementary colours of red and green. Suits of paper clothes are offered to the divinity and her consort. These have a gilt and red crown, mounted on bamboo, a red apron with gold embroidery, and a sort of square-necked bodice. On the left breast is the Chinese character for the sun, and on the right that for the moon. Below are the representations of two attendant maidens, each holding a lotus. No particular reverence is shown to these offerings, and a certain amount of horse-play often takes place whilst the preparations are being made with one girl putting the crown on the head of another during the folding of the gold and silver paper to represent ingots of metal.

The actual ceremony is very short. The women go forward one after the other, and make their three bows, offering two lighted candles, whilst bundles of ignited incense sticks are planted in the family burner. The portrait of the Moon Rabbit is pasted on the wall, sitting under his cassia tree and compounding the elixir of life on the head of the famous toad. After he has received his salutations, he is taken down and burned, so that he may return to his usual habitation. Someone sets fire to a cardboard bowl containing the clothing and money sacrifices and, as the flames die down, bundles of crackers are thrown in the blaze, whose explosion scatters the ashes to the four winds of heaven. The remainder of the evening is spent in consuming the fruit and moon-cakes which are an essential part of the feast, as are poultry and roast pigs, and Chinese bacon, cured with sugar, and packed in long strips.

In wealthier houses moon-viewing parties are arranged with a banquet at midnight, when the planet is high in the sky, accompanied by blind musicians singing the famous poems of Li T'ai Po.

The Moon's birthday is an occasion to consult the future and, as she influences matrimonial prospects, young ladies are naturally curious about their fate. They slip away one by one and burn their sticks of incense, whispering their question. Hiding behind the gate they listen to the chance conversation of the passers-by, the answer, lucky or unlucky, being deduced from the first phrase they let fall. Most of the requests have some bearing on matrimonial prospects, and are addressed to the Yueh Lao-yeh, an old man in the Moon, who shares the tenancy with the Rabbit and Three-legged Toad. Chinese maidens burn their candles to the old matchmaker, hoping he will reveal the house to which the red chair will eventually carry them.

The blind musicians, whose presence adds greatly to the charm of any party on the night of the Moon Festival, number about a hundred, and have formed a sort of colony near West Point and Kennedy Town.

It is essentially an open air entertainment, with the verandah facing the moon, and the lawn glowing with the soft light of the decorative lanterns. Candles should be used for illumination, as some of the more elaborate lamps depend for the movement of their silhouettes on the draught created by the flame, and neons are harsh competitors with the September moonlight.

Source: *Chinese Creeds and Customs* by V. R. Burkhardt. Hong Kong: South China Morning Post, 1982, pp. 64-65.

Korea

Chusok (Hangawi)

Harvest festivities

The fifteenth of the Eighth Moon is Hangawi or Chusok (Autumn Night). This is the fairest of the twelve full moons, one of the three great days of the year. Families go to the hills for an outdoor day of sports. Farmers rest and enjoy the fruits of their harvests. Wine, cakes, and fresh fruits such as jujube berries, pears, persimmons, chestnuts, and pinenuts are enjoyed and are offered to family shrines. Graves are visited also on this day. In some places wrestling contests are popular, and in the evening hemp-spinning contests for the women may be held. If the grain is not ripe yet at this time, the festival may be postponed to the ninth day of the Ninth Moon.

Source: *Folk Customs and Family Life* by Tae Hung Ha. Seoul, Korea: Yonsei, 1958, pp. 44-45.

Chusok, c. 1952

It all started on the previous market day, when there was a bumper crowd and a booming trade. More cows, more apples, more seaweed, more fish, more quacks, more people. It was practically a festival in itself. It met a harassed young teacher, using a schoolboy as intermediary, trying to bargain for a chicken.

The village bank was crowded; you could scarcely get into the post office for the rush. The word *myongjol* (festival) was on everyone's lips.

Then came the preparations in the kitchen, especially of the little half-moon-shaped rice cakes, stuffed with beans and flavoured with pine needles, which are the appropriate thing for the time.

And there was travelling. Student sons and daughters came home; some families sent representatives away to visit "the big house" (the senior house of that branch of the family). One young man told me that really only the children can enjoy Chusok, but he had patently caught the excitement himself.

Meanwhile the moon, the cause of it all, was nearing her perfection. Michael and I went to the top of the old beacon hill to get the best view. As she rode clear in a flawless sky, dusting the undulating hills with platinum and reflected in the ruffled pool at our feet, it was easy to dream of Yao and Shun.

From every valley around, voices rose clear in the night air. One young man was singing his heart out in a sentimental Irish song. In another direction a group were crooning Korean songs. But from hamlet after hamlet came the insistent throbbing rhythm of the farmers' bands: gongs, pipes, and cymbals. Some children's voices were raised in a festival game. Politics and war seemed so unreal that even the winking lights of the distant aerodrome became just a part of the beauty of the scene.

Come the morning of the feast, the shops are all shut. It is one of those rare days when the village wears a Sunday-morning air. Everyone wears his best, whether it be a carefully ironed Korean coat or a dapper Western suit. Even the men who usually wear grubby Western trousers turn out in Korean clothes with gay ankle ribbons and waistcoats of flowered silk. The women wear their national dress almost without exception.

The day's first duty is to the dead. The burial places have all been cleared of the summer's growth of weeds, and non-Christians go to sacrifice at the newer graves.

Source: *Korean Works and Days: Notes from a Country Priest* by Richard Rutt. Rutland, Vt.: Charles E. Tuttle, 1952, pp. 124-125. (Missionary observations.)

Merry-go-round

It is also called Chu-sok, Ka-wit-nal or Han-ka-wi. "Sok" in the word "Chu-sok" means a moon-bright evening. Folk festivities on this day include "Kang-kang-soo-wol-lae." The merry-go-round under the full moon elevates the festive mood of the day. The origin of Chu-sok traces far back to the old days.

Source: *Customs and Manners in Korea* by Chun Shin-yong. Seoul, Korea: Si-sa-yong-o-sa, Inc., 1982, p. 36.

Taiwan

Tiong-Chhiu Choeh

The Moon Maid

The Moon Maid is honored by laying out a table with tea, fruit, mooncakes, and burning incense. Paper money is burned, and a vow made, efficacious for curing sickness and granting off-spring. The Moon Maid is supposed to have been the wife of the famous legendary archer, Ho I. Her husband was given a pill which would cause longevity when eaten. But the Moon Maid found the pill and ate it first, whereupon she floated up to the moon and is there still. Some say that she was turned into a toad for her wicked act of stealing from her husband.

This story of the Moon Maid seems to date from the Han Dynasty (206 B.C.–220 A.D.). Her name was either Ch'ang O or Heng O, and her husband the divine archer Hsi Ho was the driver of the sun chariot, while she was the custodian of the moon.

Moon cakes

Moon cakes or "mid-autumn cakes" are a mixture of fruit and other sweets wrapped up in a thin crust in the shape of a full moon, about two or three inches in diameter and a half-inch thick. According to a long established custom they must be exchanged with relatives and friends on the days preceding the Autumn festival. The T'u-ti Kung, god of the soil, one's own employer in the business world, and foreign friends are also presented with a box of moon cakes for the occasion. In the olden days when a confucian scholar was hired to teach in the family school, the teacher presented moon cakes to each of his students, and was given a "red envelope" with money in it as a return gift.

Lanterns

On the night of the 15th, each family lights the four lanterns, hanging two on either side of the "The kong" incense pot, in the main hall of the residence. Two of these large lanterns bear the family name usually with the inscription "may boys increase," while the other two lanterns are in commemoration of the marriage of the mother and father of the family. The banner of the eight immortals is hung over the main hall, and the whole family comes together for a banquet. To the Chinese the full moon signifies completeness, the entire family gathered together in happiness. Many Chinese poets have used this theme of full moon and family togetherness to great effect.

Riddle competitions and other amusements

Among other traditions connected with the mid-autumn moon festival are the composing of riddles and rhymes by the literati, the meaning of which must be guessed by the participants; the practice of staying up all night at games or gambling, since "the later one sleeps the greater one's fortune" on the night of the autumn moon; and finally the "listening to incense" as was done on the lantern festival can be performed on this night too, to discover if one's next child is to be a boy or a girl.

Source: *Taiwan Feasts and Customs* by Michael R. Saso. Hsinchu, Taiwan: Chabanel Language Institute, pp. 70-71.

Vietnam

Trung Thu

A festival for children

This is a delightful festival for children and most pleasant for the adults to watch. Many weeks before the festival, bakers are busy making hundreds of thousands of moon cakes of sticky rice and filled with all kinds of unusual fillings such as peanuts, sugar, lotus seed, duck-egg yolks, raisins, watermelon seed, etc. They are baked and sold in colorful boxes. Expensive ones in ornate boxes are presented as gifts.

Also made in advance are colorful lanterns made in the form of boats, dragons, hares, toads, lobsters, unicorns, carp, etc. These are sold for weeks on the streets of every village and city. The children begin playing with them long before the holiday. They light little candles and place them inside the lanterns made of cellophane paper and swing them around on sticks, all in the darkness of the evening. It is one of the most beautiful sights to see in Vietnam during the year.

On the night of the festival, children form a procession and go through the streets holding their lighted lanterns and performing the dances of the unicorn to the accompaniment of drums and cymbals.

There are many legendary origins of the festival, but the one most accepted in Vietnam is that it began during the reign of Emperor Minh-Hoang of the Duong-Dynasty. Legend says that he took his empress, Duong-Quy-Pho, to a lake called Thai Dick on the 15th day of the 8th lunar month where they admired the moon. When the moon was at its brightest, the emperor composed a poem and explained it to his wife. He loved to read the verses in the moonlight.

Source: *Customs and Culture of Vietnam* by Ann Caddell Crawford. Rutland, Vt.: Charles E. Tuttle, 1966, p. 200.

For more on the Mid-Autumn Festival see: "Games at the Mid-Autumn Festival in Kuangtun" by Chao Wei-Pang in *Folklore Studies,* Museum of Oriental Ethnology, III (1) (1944), 1-15 (this article describes divination games. One player becomes possessed of a spirit and answers questions about the future.); *Folklore of American Holidays* edited by Hennig Cohen and Tristram Potter Coffin. 2nd ed. Detroit: Gale Research, 1991; "The Midautumn Festival" in *Chinese Festivals* by Wolfram Eberhard. New York: Henry Schuman, 1952, pp. 97-112; "The Moon Festival" in *Chinese Creeds and Customs* by V. R. Burkhardt. Hong Kong: South China Morning Post, 1982.

Moon 8, Day 16 (August-September)

Birthday of Ts'oi: T'in Tai Seng Yeh

This day is a celebration of the Sun Wu-Kung, the Monkey God.

Singapore

Celebrating the birthday of the Monkey God

His excellency the Monkey God, (Ts'oi T'in Tai Seng Yeh), is prominent among Chinese temple deities in Singapore. There are always mediums attached to his shrines. Most of these places of worship are most unpretentious to look at and may be nothing more than dilapidated shophouses or attap huts, but they are centres of a cult which shews no sign of diminishing its hold over Chinese worshippers.

For those interested, the birthday of the Monkey God is celebrated annually in Singapore on the sixteenth day of the eighth moon. The celebrations generally last two days.

Source: *Chinese Temples in Singapore* by Leon Comber. Singapore: Eastern University Press, 1958, p. 35.

Bhadra (August-September)

Ganesh Chauthi

During the Tij fast, this is a day to honor the elephant-headed god Ganesh. It occurs on the fourth day of the bright lunar fortnight.

India

The elephant-headed god, Ganesh

According to some *Puranas,* Parvati, before taking her bath inside, put her son Ganesa as sentinel at the door to prevent the entry of anyone in the house. In the meantime, Siva reached there and wanted to enter the house, but Ganesa prevented him. Siva felt humiliated and in anger cut down the neck of Ganesa. When Parvati saw this, she wept bitterly and requested Siva to bring Ganesa back to life. Siva agreed to this and brought the head of an elephant and fixed it on Ganesa. Since then, he is worshipped as an elephant-headed god, by all Hindus.

Ganesa is not only the god of wisdom and success but also the remover of all the obstacles (*vighna*). Hence, he is also known as Vighnesa or Vighneswara. In most of the Hindu homes, an idol of Ganesa is installed over the main doorway, to ward off every evil. He is propitiated at the commencement of every important endeavour, be it construction work, marriage or the starting of a new account book. The people bow or pay their obeisance by uttering 'Shri Ganesayanamah' (i.e., I bow to Lord Ganesa).

Ganesh Chaturthi Day

On Ganesa Chaturthi day, people wake up early in the morning and after bath they collect various articles for the worship of Vinayaka. Then at mid-day, they worship the image of the god made with clay with various offerings including sweet-balls. Later the beautifully decorated images are taken out in processions to the accompaniment of religious songs and music. These images are worshipped regularly for several days for gaming the blessings of the god and later they are immersed in the sea or river. *Modokas* or sweet-balls are distributed as *prasada* to all the devotees and the members of the household.

In Maharashtra, the festival is celebrated with great pomp and show and icons of the god are separately worshipped in every home. In Konkan, people visit each other's house at the performance of *arati* and take out the images on heads in processions.

In the Manakul Vinayakar temple at Pondicherry, the temple fesival known as the annual Brahmotsava is regularly celebrated by thousands of devotees for ten days.

Source: *The Festivals of India* by Brijendra Nath Sharma. New Delhi: Abhinav, 1978, pp. 107-108.

Nepal

Staying indoors on Ganesh Chauthi night

After dark, everyone must stay inside on this evening. Catching sight of the ill-omened crescent moon would bring disaster. This is, however, an auspicious night for thieves.

Source: "Ganesh Chata: The Elephant God Curses the Moon" in *The Festivals of Nepal* by Mary M. Anderson. London: Allen & Unwin, 1971, pp. 121-126.

Installing Ganapati idols in Maharashtra

Much ahead of Ganesh Chaturthi, localities or groups of people start organising themselves with a view to putting up the Idol of Ganapati on their behalf. Artists with long history and reputation of making Hindu idols throng to Maharashtra on this occasion and set up temporary workshops to meet the ever-growing demand for Ganapati idols. Colourful and artistic idols created by the devotional fervour of the artists range from one foot to over thirty feet in height and from rupees two to rupees ten thousand [sic]. The idol installed . . . in Parel, Bombay is so huge that it is transported in parts and then assembled on the site. On Ganesh Chaturthi Day Mandals or groups of people bring the idols in a procession amidst loud singing of bhajans and drum beating to the place of installation, the idols are installed on highly decorated and lighted rostrums with religious ceremonies performed by pundits. From now onwards it is a feast of artistic, cultural and literary programmes arranged all over Maharashtra.

Each group vies with one another in making the celebration as grand as possible. The whole atmosphere is charged with great elation, enthusiasm and activity. The whole of Maharashtra is out on streets every evening to see the grandeur of Ganesha idols installed in its towns. With some eighty thousand idols installed publicly there are some three million idols installed privately in the homes of Maharashtra.

Immersion of the idol

The dampness of the rainy season is relieved by the ten day long worship of Lord Ganesha in the warmth and devotion of the devotees [*sic*]. The tenth day is marked by the immersion ceremony of the idol. In the evening all the idols are lined up to be carried in a procession through the city to the place of immersion. The idols are carried on rick-shaws, bullock carts, old convertible ford cars and trucks, the services of which are supplied free as a gesture of devetion [*sic*] to Lord Ganesha, attended with music and cries of "Ganpati Bappa Moriya: Pudhcha varshi Lavkar ya", invoking the blessings of Ganesha and wishing his return the next year soon. People sing and dance in religious frenzy sprinkling and applying Gulal on those around. The immersion is generally done on the banks of rivers, lakes or ponds. Wherever there are no rivers, lakes or ponds the immersion is also done in the wells. This ceremony is also performed with all the religious rites by a pundit chanting mantras. As the idols are immersed a serene quiet reigns over the region as if in a state of rejuvenating catharsis experiencing the sublime.

Source: "Ganeshotsava of Maharashtra" by Prof. O. P. Bhatnagar in *Popular Festivals of India,* edited by Sunil Kumar Nag. Calcutta, India: Golden Books of India, 1983, pp. 36-37.

A family Pūjā for Ganesh in Poona, c. 1954

On the morning of the fourth day of the "bright half" of Bhādrapada in the Hindu calendar, a statuette of Ganeśa, or Ganapati, is installed in most of the homes at Poona. (In some other parts of India a Ganeśa festival is celebrated in the month of Vaiśākha—April-May.) The statuettes, made of hand-painted pottery, are bought in the market and may cost from four annas (roughly five cents) to one rupee (about twenty cents). Some wealthy families spend as much as ten rupees for an elaborate statue of Ganapati, but this, of course, is not common.

If the family has a special shrine for its family deity, the statuette is placed there, and a *pūjā,* or religious worship, is offered to Ganeśa. If the head of the family is a Brahman and knows the Sanskrit prayers and hymns required by the occasion, he may perform the Ganeśa *pūjā* himself. But since this kind of learning is rare nowadays, the family is more apt to call upon the services of a *purohit,* or priest. The latter goes from family to family on this day, performing his part of the ceremony which consists in reciting Sanskrit prayers and hymns from the Vedas and giving instructions to the family representative (a male member of the family but not necessarily the family head), who bathes, "feeds," and clothes the Ganeśa statue. Many families cannot afford to pay a *purohit*. Their *pūjā* will consist of a prayer, an *āralī* or offering of lights, the giving of flowers, and the singing of a simple song to Ganeśa.

Source: "The Changing Character of a Hindu Festival" by Victor Barnouw in *American Anthropologist* 56 (1954), 75-76.

Bhadra (August-September)

Gokarna Aunsi

This is a day to honor fathers, both living and dead. All who can visit Gokarna, near Kathmandu, pay tribute to their dead fathers at the Shiva Lingam there. Those with living fathers visit their homes, bring sweets, and share a feast. This occurs on the last day of the dark fortnight.

Nepal

Offerings

Pilgrimage is made to Gokarneswar Mahadev to worship at the Shiva Lingam there if possible. Worshippers bathe in the shallow waters there and leave offerings. *Pindas,* small rice balls, are offered to the souls of the dead by immersing them in the river or by giving them to a sacred cow. Those unable to travel to Gokarna may bathe in nearer streams.

For more on Gokarna Aunsi see: ''Gokarna Aunsi: Nepalese Father's Day'' in *The Festivals of Nepal* by Mary M. Anderson. London: Allen & Unwin, 1971, pp. 112-115.; ''Gokarna Auncy: The ceremonial Father's Day'' in *The Nepal Fesivals, Part 1* by Dhurba K. Deep. Bhotahity, Kathmandu: Ratna Pustak Bhandar, 1978. (Deep is a prominent Nepali poet and scholar.)

Bhadon (August-September)

Halashasti

Halashasti is an agricultural festival honoring the *hala* (plough). Lord Shiva is asked to bless the agricultural life of the family.

India

A day of worship and fasting

The farmers and peasants of India annually celebrate the festival of Halashasti in the month of Bhadon (August-September).

The agriculturists worship the *hala* (plough), the main implement used by them for ploughing their fields and specially its iron blade by applying powdered rice and turmeric and decorating it with garland of flowers. They do not plough their lands on the day of the festival. They observe fast that day and terminate it in the evening after worshipping Lord Siva and gaining his blessings for the welfare of their families and for better crops in the coming year. A grand feast is enjoyed in the evening by one and all.

Source: *The Festivals of India* by Brijendra Nath Sharma. New Delhi: Abhinav, 1978, p. 106.

Bhadra-Asvina (September)

Indra Jatra

This is an eight-day celebration commemorating the visit of Lord Indra to the Kathmandu Valley. During this time, Kumari Jatra occurs, the festival of the child goddess possessed of Kumari. This occurs on the twelfth day of the waxing moon.

Nepal

Indra Jatra in Kathmandu

Indra Jatra begins with the raising of the banner of Indra at the old palace at Hanuman Dhoka. This signifies that Lord Indra has come to the valley. Families who have had a death within the year process through the streets on this night. All homes have been cleaned, decorated, and illuminated wich butter lamps. Those marching in memory of their deceased carry burning incense. They may offer lighted oil lamps to shrines as they pass. Hymns for the dead are chanted. The procession takes a winding route requiring about three hours to complete.

The nights of Indra Jatra

Each night during Indra Jatra, the shrines and palaces at Hanuman Dhoka square are lit with oil lamps. An enactment of the ten earthly incarnations of Lord Vishnu is performed in the square during these evenings, and folk dramas and dances are performed.

Kumari Jayanti

On the afternoon of the day before the full moon, the vestal virgin Kumari appears. A new Kumari is chosen every ten years and raised in confinement, as an incarnation of the goddess. The child goddess appears to the public at this festival.

Beer from the mouth of Bhairab

As the Kumari procession passes the blue statue of Akash Bhairab and the twelve-foot mask of White Bhairab at his temple, rice beer flows from the god's mouths. Those who catch a drop of this liquid are blessed. Most blessed of all are those who catch the tiny live fish that flow in the beer.

Source: *The Festivals of Nepal* by Mary M. Anderson. London: Allen & Unwin, 1971, pp. 127-133.

Bhadra (August-September)

Janmashtami

This is a day in honor of Lord Krishna's birthday. It occurs during the new moon sighting.

India

Janmashtami celebrations

The popular festival of Janmashtami is observed in the month of Bhadra (August-September), throughout India, at midnight, at the appearance of the moon. It is joyously celebrated in honour of Lord Krishna, the eighth incarnation of Vishnu, who was born on this day at Mathura in Uttar Pradesh.

On this festival day, all temples and Hindu homes are beautifully and tastefully decorated to welcome the birth of the divine child, Krishna. In many houses, *jhankis* are arranged, which show various important incidents from Krishna's life. His image is placed on a swing in a decorated *mandapa*. Every member of a family including children observe fast for the whole day and break it when the moon is visible at midnight. At that time, first the small image of crawling Krishna is bathed in the *charnamrita* (curd mixed with milk, dry fruits and leaves of *tulsi* plant) and then the *arati* is performed. The *prasada* is distributed to all present and thus the day-long fast is broken. Religious songs and hymns in praise of the god are sung and the *Bhagavata Purana* and the *Gita* are recited by one and all. Men, women and children visit temples for the sacred *darshana* of Krishna.

Source: *The Festivals of India* by Brijendra Nath Sharma. New Delhi, Abhinav, 1978, pp. 93-94.

Bhadra (August-September)

Krishna Jayanti (Lord Krishna's Birthday)

This is Krishna's Eighth, the day of his birth. Devotees visit his temples and his birth is celebrated widely. It occurs on the eighth day of the dark lunar fortnight.

Nepal

Celebrating Krishna's birth

During the seventh day of the dark lunar fortnight of Bhadra worshippers carry Krishna images through the streets. They are dressed ornately and hung with garlands. Musicians accompany the processions and banners are carried with the words ''Krishna is God!'' Colored pictures of Krishna's adventures are posted on walls and Krishna images are set in places of honor in alcoves covered with flowers and jewelry. Pundits on the streets and in temple grounds sit cross-legged on cloth-covered benches to read the story of Krishna to listeners. In the evening women converge on the temple of Krishna Mandir in Old Patan to keep vigil throughout the night of Krishna's birth.

Source: *The Festivals of Nepal* by Mary M. Anderson. London: Allen & Unwin, 1971, p. 107.

Devotees' Dance

Not surprising the scene of devotees dancing on the occasion of the birthday of Lord Krishna, is one of the most enjoyable highlights of the celebration. Krishnasastami falls on the 8th day of the dark fortnight of the month of Bhadra. Devotees of Krishna, particularly women, from the countryside on this day get up early in the morning and set out for their pilgrimage trip to the Krishna Temple situated at Durbar Square in Lalitpur. The central venue for all kinds of religious singing and dancing on this auspicious day is the surroundings of the same Krishna Temple known for the intricate art works on the stone.

One of the most colourful features of Krishna's birthday celebration is the country-women's enthusiastic participation in the traditional dance performances that take around the temple mentioned above. This street show begins from early in the morning and goes on till late at night. The women devotee's [sic] dancing on this day around the temple is usually accompanied by male *wadal* drummers from the countryside.

Source: *The Nepal Festivals, Part 1* by Dhurba K. Deep. Bhotahity, Kathmandu: Ratna Pustak Bhandar, 1978, p. 67.

For more information see: ''Krishna Jayanti: Lord Krishna is Born on Earth'' in *The Festivals of Nepal* by Mary M. Anderson. London: Allen & Unwin, 1971, pp. 105-111. (Anderson lived in Nepal for five years.); ''Krishnastami: Lord Krishna's Birthday'' in *The Nepal Festivals, Part 1* by Dhurba K. Deep. Bhotahity, Kathmandu: Ratna Pustak Bhandar, 1978, pp. 65-68. (Deep is a prominent Nepali poet and a scholar.)

Bhadra (August-September)

Khordad-Sal

The birth of the Prophet Spitaman Zarathustra.

Parsi

The Khordad-Sal festival

The Khordad-Sal festival is also one of the most important festivals of the Parsis. It is observed in the month of Bhadra (August-September), on the sixth day, *Khordad*.

The birth ceremony of the Prophet Spitaman Zarathustra also known as Zoroaster, who was born in the beginning of the first millennium B.C., is observed very devotionally on this day. A grand feast is celebrated on the sixth day of Parsi month, *Farvardin,* in every home. People dressed in their best dress visit the fire-temples for prayers and later greet each other at social gatherings.

Source: *The Festivals of India* by Brijendra Nath Sharma. New Delhi: Abhinan, 1978, p. 97.

Shrawan-Bhadra (August)

Panchadaan

Within Nepal, this festival occurs on the third day, dark fortnight of Bhadra in Kathmandu and Bhadgaon, and on the eighth day, bright fortnight of Shrawan in Patan and elsewhere in Nepal.

Nepal

Alms giving

One of the main features of this festival is the giving away of alms to the Buddhist beggars. As a very old custom would have it, on this particular day all the Buddhists, rich or poor, go door-to-door in a sizeable group to beg for alms. Such a group of Buddhist beggars is generally regarded as the mission of Lord Buddha himself and treated very well when they are received in the Nepalese homes for the alms-giving ceremony. Giving away of the alms to such Buddhists on this day seems to have been widely recognized by the Nepalese people. There are several Hindus who also give away some foodgrains in charity to the Buddhist beggars on this day. There are many religious trusts devoted to this giving-away ceremony. The Buddhist monasteries are the places where even the non-Buddhist people can be seen giving away the foodgrains to the Buddhist beggars. The Dangatha chapter of Kapidawdan, a very old Buddhist text says that those who give away food and clothes to the saints and sadhus on this day would be blessed with seven great gifts in return viz., health, happiness, longevity, wisdom, wealth, fame and children.

Source: *The Nepal Festivals, Part 1* by Dhurba K. Deep. Bhotahity, Kathmandu: Ratna Pustak Bhandar, 1978, p. 70.

Bhadon (August-September)

Paryushana

In this Jain festival, forgiveness is asked of others and virtues are practiced.

India (Jain)

The Paryushana Jaina

The Paryushana Jaina festival is celebrated all over India in the month of Bhadon (August-September) on different dates. It is an eight-day festival for the Svetambara Jainas and on its termination, the ten-day celebrations of the Digambara Jainas begin.

Like most of the other Jaina festivals, it is also celebrated by more intense practice of ten cardinal virtues viz. 1. Forgiveness, 2. Charity, 3. Simplicity, 4. Contentment, 5. Truthfulness, 6. Self-restraint, 7. Fasting, 8. Detachment, 9. Humility and 10. Continence.

During the festival, the offender asks for forgiveness from those whom he has ever offended on some occasion or the other. During this time, lost friendship is thus restored. Every one is expected to dress nicely and in clean clothes at the time of the festival.

Source: *The Festivals of India* by Brijendra Nath Sharma. New Delhi: Abhinav, 1978, pp. 103-104.

Various Dates

Harvest festivals

This section includes harvest festivals. While most occur during August through October, harvest festivals from throughout the calendar are included here. In particular, note the Yam festivals of African cultures, which occur sometime in late summer or early fall, depending on the crop condition and the propensities of the gods.

Angola

The Feast of Nganja

Every year when the harvest is ripe in Angola—that is, in the month of April—the children from about eight years to twelve invite each other saying, "On Monday (or another day) we will eat the feast of *Nganja.*"

On the day named, they all go out to their family fields, each to his own, to gather some fresh ripe corn. Later they meet in a beautiful part of the woods near a little stream. In small groups, they light fires and roast corn on the cob. While they are roasting the corn or starting to eat it they have to be always on the watch, because someone may suddenly come to rob them of the corn. For, in the twinkling of an eye, someone jumps up, leaves his fire and corn, and rushes to grab the corn of another group. That is where the fun of this feast lies, in the excitement of mutual robbing and plundering. The children run and shout and laugh, although some are sad because they lose their ears of roasted corn and gain none.

The feast of Okambondondo

This feast may be held several times in the year, usually during the months of February, March, and April, the harvest months in Angola. The children invite all of their own age or group saying, "On such and such a day we will have *Okambondondo.*" Often those from six years to ten hold their feast in one place, and those from eleven to fifteen in another. And often those from sixteen up have a feast of their own.

The feast lasts all night. The girls bring cornmeal and corn and beans, and the boys bring dried fish or meat. The children borrow the big pots from the owner of the kitchen where they plan to hold the feast. In the evening, they play games and tell folk stories. Then the boys go to sleep in their house, and the girls sleep in their kitchen. But about one or two o'clock in the morning, the girls get up and make the cornmeal mush, and prepare the cracked corn porridge, and the bean and meat relish. They run to waken the boys and call them to the feast in the kitchen. They all eat together and then go to the village common to play and sing. They sing a special song, "We have eaten our *Okambondondo* in the night." One group sings the first five words, and the others add "in the night." When the first streaks of dawn show they get together all the food they have left and carry it to their own homes for their parents to taste of the feast. Tired children? Of course! But they are allowed to sleep late the next day.

Source: *Children's Festivals from Many Lands* by Nina Millen. New York: Friendship Press, 1964, pp. 17-19.

Barbados

Crop Over

This was formerly a festival of slaves at the end of sugar-cane harvest. It was revived in 1973 as a civic festival. It takes place during the last three weeks of June through the first week of July.

Crop Over in the 1800s

The procession of carts bringing in the last load of canes signaled the beginning of the celebration. The first cart, led by a woman dressed in white, her head tied in a bandana with a flower tucked into its folds, swung into the mill yard, followed by all the carts and all the people involved in harvesting and transporting the sugar cane.

The animals and carts were decorated with a profusion of colorful blooms, and all the people wore flowers in their headdresses, even the men. Canes on some of the carts were tied with gaily colored bandanas that danced in the wind like flags. One cart carried an effigy of "Mr. Harding," who symbolized hard times and represented all cruel gangdrivers. He was made from sugar cane refuse and dressed in an old black coat, top hat, and mask.

The procession would wend its way around the mill yard two or three times, to the enthusiastic cheers of the laborers. The windmill, usually weatherbeaten yet stately and impressive, was also decorated for the occasion.

As the procession around the mill yard came to a halt, an old and respected laborer or a headman would make a speech of thanks to the plantation owner or manager, who would reply. Speeches over, the laborers helped themselves to the fare provided. There were big estate tubs filled with black strap or sweet liquor, rumbullion, or "kill-devil," as rum was called in those days, salted pork, bread, pone, and cassava cakes known as hats because of their shape; and salt fish cutters and, as years went by, ham cutters and "falernum."

There were games, contests, dancing, and singing—and an occasional fight provoked by that green-eyed monster, jealousy. There was a greased pole with money at the top for whoever reached it first, and a partially greased rope attached to the tail tree of the mill, with a reward at the top of the rope for the first person to climb it. Another amusing contest was the scramble for a young greased pig, which was awarded to its captor.

The "stick licking" bout was an exhibition in the art of self-defense somewhat like fencing. The sticks were usually a little longer than the average walking cane and made from the toughest wood available. A stick with good "licking" potential was known as an *ockyuh*.

The effigy of Mr. Harding was burned to the singing of the song "Hold Fast, Old Ned at the Door"; Ned was the personification of the lean and difficult times ahead for the laborers before the next crop season.

Crop Over today

Crop Over occurs on the completion of the cane harvesting season during the final three weeks of June and spills into the first weekend of July. The early portion of the festival is dominated by events in the rural areas: fairs, cane-cutting competitions, open-air concerts, "stick licking," native dancing, and handicraft and art displays.

On the first Saturday in July, Crop Over moves to the Bridgetown market. Barbados' capital is then transformed into a traffic-free bazaar, where thousands of strollers converge to purchase a vast range of items ordinarily sold only in markets and handicraft outlets and to listen to the bands. The market place is also the setting for such offbeat competitions as a coconut milk drinking contest.

Sunday is the Cohobblepot, a contest at the National Stadium to name the Crop Over Queen, accompanied by a great variety of cultural events.

The finale on Monday is a public holiday known as the Kadooment. It opens with the judging at the stadium of scores of costumed bands depicting various aspects of Bajan life. The imaginative, colorful bands may portray anything from Arawak Indians to a cricket game. And their numbers can range from one to one thousand.

After the judging Kadooment shifts to the streets. Accompanied by the contagious music of the steel pans, the bands and followers road march and dance the five-mile distance from the National Stadium to the Garrison Savannah. At the Savannah a huge effigy of Mr. Harding—coattails, top hat, and all—has been mounted. The effigy is set afire and pelted with stones until "hard times" are destroyed, and the curtain is rung down on Crop Over, twentieth century style.

Source: "Crop Over" by Flora Spencer. *Américas,* 32 (5) (May 1980), 51-56.

Cambodia

A Cambodian harvest feast, c. 1963

Bartoli's jeep jogged us through open forests and hilly fields of tall white-tufted elephant grass to nearby Phum Thuy. The village looked almost deserted, but strange gong music told us the town was celebrating. A private party?

"Certainly not," the headman, Knai Tnail, assured us. "We are only thanking the spirits of the harvest." Behind us, in the community storehouse, giant rattan bins overflowed with grain.

"It is the happiest time of the year," said Tnail. "The rice is in. The skies are clouding for the rains. There is plenty of pork to eat, and wine. Come join the feasting."

We followed our host. He had a high forehead, large eyes, delicate features, and skin the color of well-polished leather. Only a loincloth draped his spare frame. He smoked a bizarre pipe, a bamboo bowl wrapped with wire on a copper stem. Nearly 40 villagers were crowded into his small house, eating heaping plates of pork, bamboo sprouts, sweet manioc, melons, blood soup, and roast lizard. The men took turns sipping from long reeds poked into crocks of fermenting rice. I found the drink palatable and cold—but strong. A few relaxing sips calmed any fears I had about the food.

Just before sundown the gongs stopped. The village was quiet except for a squawking parrot, the click-clacking of wooden cowbells, and a distant elephant munching bamboo.

Source: "Cambodia, Indochina's 'Neutral' Corner" by Thomas J. Abercrombie in *National Geographic Magazine,* October, 1964, 126 (4), 543.

Cameroon

Evamelunga in Christian churches

The Christians in Cameroon celebrate their Thanksgiving Day, *Evamelunga,* on September 8. On that morning, the little chapels made of bark and the big thatched churches are decked with bright flowers and green palms. The call drum beats out the invitation to all to come to the meeting.

Children and parents put on their best beads and their gayest clothes and crowd into the churches, singing as they go. Choirs and school choruses fill the air with music. And why do they give thanks? Because over seventy-five years ago the first missionary came to their forests and told them the story of Jesus. It is the coming of the good news to their country that they celebrate.

They call the festival *Evamelunga*, "The Taking Away of the Burden of Sin." And so in their festival of rejoicing they tell one another why they are glad. A schoolboy is thankful that he has been taught to read God's Book. A mother is grateful because she is no longer afraid of witchcraft. And all give thanks to God that they have heard about Jesus.

When the meeting is over, there is feasting and singing and laughter far into the night—for the festival of Thanksgiving is a festival of joy.

Source: *Children's Festivals from Many Lands* by Nina Millen. New York: Friendship Press, 1964, p. 39.

Cameroon (Bamum)

Historical descriptions of the Nja festival of the Bamum

One of the most important annual festivals at the royal court was the festival of Nja, celebrated during the dry season in December or early January. According to the recent testimony in Bamum, it last occurred in the 1920s. Therefore, the information cited here stems from reconstruction, not from direct observation.

The Nja festival was a display of royal riches and a visual representation of the Bamum political and social structure. Groups of dancers and musicians representing particular segments in the Bamum hierarchy performed in elaborate masquerades that featured zoomorphic and anthropomorphic helmet masks and crests. Today, the festival is fondly remembered as the day of beauty and the highlight of the year. Compared with the enthusiastic oral testimony recently collected on Nja, the lack of references to the festival in German accounts from the years when it was still taking place is astonishing. Only Wuhramann mentions Nja in some detail.

On the day of the [Nja], the royal wives and all the seed of the royal house and the court guards adorn themselves and go dancing. Those children that are still very little and can be carried on the shoulders also dance along. The older royal children beat the drum; the royal wives and the free noblemen dance around the earth seat [the slightly raised area in front of the palace], the king dances, too, and thirty court guards are before him. People come and sound the trumpets and the king gives them gifts. When he wants to leave, he administers an oath to the free noblemen. Then the [Nja] is over.

The photographic record of Nja by several photographers is an excellent source of information on some of the visual aspects of the festival. When the festival began in the morning, people from all over Bamum country assembled in the dancing field. They were clad in their most beautiful finery and adorned with emblems of rank. The beaded thrones of the king and the queen mother were placed in front of the central entrance of the palace, and soon both of them emerged. The king was dressed in his Nja costume, a most luxurious and lavish ensemble of cloth, beaded jewelry, and prestige weapons. No verbal description matches the photographs of one such costume, which Ankermann photographed and described in the spring of 1908. In this instance, the combination of inventory-taking photography and a systematic verbal description according to the standards of contemporary German cultural anthropology created a document remarkable in its detail.

> Njoya himself possesses some curious dance jewelry, which essentially consists of the following pieces:
>
> 1. A crown, very big and so heavy that it has to be held by a man standing behind the dancer. It exhibits several rows of animals one on top of the other, according to Njoya [they are] flying foxes with long ears, above and below a thick horizontal ring. At the top it is closed off by a horizontal round disc, crowned by a large feather tuft. Everything is embroidered with beads.
> 2. The face is framed by a bead beard.
> 3. Around his neck he wears a large beaded piece with lion or leopard [teeth] on the outer border that hangs down over his belly.
> 4. A very thick bead ring, from which hung two long bead-edged pelt strips, encircled the hips. In addition there hung from this hip ring (a) the dance loincloth which almost touched the ground, similar to those of the dancers, and (b) two very long "wings" of black patterned cotton cloth on either side which have to be carried by many men during the dance.
> 5. Over the hip band lies a second, thinner bead belt terminating in two serpent heads.
> 6. He wears bead bands of various forms around the arms and ankles.
> 7. In his right hand he carries a sword with an openwork blade and a bead-covered handle terminating in an animal head. The scabbard is embroidered with beads in a spider motif with dangling bead strands.
> 8. In his left hand he holds a fly whisk whose handle terminates in an animal head and is covered with beads.

This stately outfit projected the splendor of kingship. The accumulation of the different materials in extravagant configurations enhanced the persona of the king, making him the ultimate symbol of Bamum success and superiority and transforming him into a work of art. Some parts of the elaborate costume have been preserved in the Bamum Palace Museum, including the sword and its beaded scabbard and the beaded belt with the huge cloth "wings".

The highlights of the festival were the masks passing in review and the dances of the king, the groups of palace retainers, the nobles known as the councilors of the land, and the princes descended from ancient kings. The palace retainers were the only masked participants. They wore helmet masks or crests on their heads, among them buffalo masks, bird crests, ram crests, elephant masks, a crocodile crest, and anthropomorphic helmet masks. . . . With the exception of the leading buffalo mask and the crocodile crest, most masks could be danced by any retainer. Bird masqueraders moved vigorously, so that the wings of the bird crest, which were only loosely tied to the crest's body, would flap up and down. The masqueraders filed by the king, the queen mother, and the crowd of spectators. The masks, numbering more than one hundred, followed a prescribed sequence, but nowadays there is little information about the choreography.

What was the significance of Nja in the Bamum annual ritual cycle? Tardits links Nja with the large harvest festivals in other states of the Grassfields, even though it took place in the middle of the dry season and seemed to have no direct association with agricultural activities. Such activities ceased with the harvest at the end of the rainy season in October and began again with planting when the new rains fell in April. Nja celebrated the abundance of food and material wealth, physical beauty, and individual achievement in the Bamum state. It also articulated Bamum political and social structure through the performances of specific groups of actors. The elite of the kingdom—the king, the queen mother, the princes and princesses, and the retainers—were represented in this dramatic presentation. The retainers, the pillars of royal power who supported the king against the claims of his brothers, were the only participants disguised with masks.

Source: *Images from Bamum: German Colonial Photography at the Court of King Njoya, Cameroon, West Africa, 1902-1915* by Christraud M. Geary. Washington D.C.: Published for the National Museum of African Art by the Smithsonian Institution Press, 1988, pp. 105-106. (See *Images from Bamum* for photographs of the festival.)

Czechoslovakia

Posviceni and Obzinky

There are two harvest celebrations in Czechoslovakia at Thanksgiving time. *Posviceni* is the church consecration of the harvest and *Obzinky* is the secular celebration.

Wreaths made of rye straw, field flowers, and ears of corn are placed on the heads of pretty girls. After the ceremony, these wreaths are not destroyed, but are saved until the next harvest.

A typical feast includes roast pig, roast goose, kolaches filled with prunes, sweet yellow cottage cheese, poppy seed filling, or apricot jam, beer (*pivo*) and a prune liquor, (*slivovice*).

Source: *Czechoslovak Culture* compiled by Pat Martin. Iowa City, Iowa: Penfield Press, 1989, p. 117.

Czechoslovakian harvest customs

In Czechoslovakia there are two harvest celebrations, one of which Posviceni, is the church consecration of the harvest. The other, Obzinky, is secular in nature. When the harvesting is over, the farm laborers make a wreath of ears of wheat, or rye and field flowers. It is usually placed on the head of the prettiest of the girls, who then with the other harvesters, accompanied by music and song, proceeds to the home of the land owner to whom the wreath is offered. It is held in high honor and usually kept until next harvest. After the ceremony there is dancing and feasting at the farmowner's expense. At this feast are usually served roast pig, roast goose and the famous Kolace, cakes square in shape and filled with plum jam or sweetened cheese, or poppy-seeds.

In some sections of Czechoslovakia, instead of a wreath, or in addition to a wreath, the last sheaf harvested is dressed as an old woman, the *Baba,* and borne in state to the home of the landlord where it occupies a place of honor till Christmas or, in some places, till the next harvest. In Moravia an old woman, or perhaps the woman who bound the last sheaf, is actually wrapped up in the sheaf—but she is not kept there till the next harvest.

Source: *Foreign Festival Customs* by Marian Schibsby & Hanny Cohrsen. New York: American Council for Nationalities Service, 1974, p. 48.

Denmark

Nineteenth-century harvest customs

Connected with the work in the field and the harvesting of the corn were several customs that revealed the peasants' interest in the crops. Some stalks were left standing in the field so that it should not be empty, the idea being that it should be filled with crops again in the year to come. The last sheaf in the field was made extra large and heavy, if necessary by binding a stone inside it, in the hope that the new crop would also be big and heavy. These performances may be regarded as magic rites. The reapers vied with one another not to be last finished, both among themselves and as regards the neighbours, and so there was no mistaking when the end was reached, for the last sheaf to be tied was decorated in various ways. It was nothing uncommon for it to be given human form, sometimes emphasized by garbing it in old clothes. It was then placed in a conspicuous position in the field and the reapers gave it a cheer to let the neighbours know that the crops were harvested. When later the corn was carted home, the last sheaf came on the last load, which would be decorated to celebrate the ending of the harvest.

The unfortunate farmer who had got behind in his harvesting ran the risk of getting a ''harvest helper'', a dressed-up doll with a jocular or mocking letter, put up in his field by his more lucky neighbours. The harvest season was brought to a close with a ''harvest home'' at the farm, to which all were invited, though it was not always held immediately. It might be left till later in the year when the big killings of fat pigs were ended and when supplies of fresh meat were more plentiful.

Source: *Danish Peasant Culture*. Copenhagen: Danish National Museum, 1955, p. 62.

Ghana (Abron)

Odiwera: the first-fruits festival

In addition to life-crises ceremonies, the Abron celebrate three major fixed religious events. These are the great yam festival (Odiwera), in October, the Adae or tribute to the ancestors, and the Fofyé, or tribute to local gods and the punungo of dead priests. The yam festival combines a first-fruit ritual, during which the taboo on eating yams is lifted, with ancestor worship, and is by far the most elaborate ceremony. It unfolds in various villages by turn, according to a fixed chronology. The festival begins where an ancient chief is said to have first tasted the yam, proving it was edible. According to legend, long ago a hunter walking through the bush found a yam. When he saw it, he took it home. After some days, he noticed an animal eating it. He went to the chief of Guendé and told him what he had seen. The chief of Guendé then took the yam and cooked it. The people waited forty days and nights, and when they saw that their chief did not die they knew that the yam was good to eat. And so the yam festival is held every year at Guendé, and it is the chief of Guendé who eats the yam before the King.

Another story says that after the chief ate the yam it was then given to the children of the village as a further test. After another week with no bad results, the yam was accepted as fit to eat by all. Today a children's yam festival may follow the one at Guendé, but it does not occur every year and is not an obligatory part of the festival.

Forty days after the Guendé fete, the new yams are taken to the temple of Tano, where they are offered, along with sheep and goats to that deity. A week later, yams are offered to the punungo bo bokogo of each household. These offerings take place in the context of local yam festivals, one of which is usually held in the village of the King. After the final yam festival, the tuber is declared ready for eating.

Source: *When the Spider Danced: Notes from an African Village* by Alexander Alland, Jr. Garden City, N.Y.: Anchor Press/Doubleday, 1975, p. 105.

Ghana (Aburi)

Yam Festival on ninth Awukudae

From the beginning of the eighth Awukudae (September-October), a ban is placed on introducing the new yam into town. The first harvested yams must be offered to God before being enjoyed by man. Merrymaking and elaborate funerals are forbidden during this period. In fact death during this period, from eighth to ninth Awukudae, is taboo.

Aburi yam festival at Akuapem

On the chosen day the priest, who has been in seclusion for forty days, dons white robes and carries the new yam through the streets. At given points he stops and slices three pieces from the yam. If they fall face up, with the skin down, good luck will follow. Should they fall face down, calamity is portended.

After the priest makes his rounds, the yam is ceremonially served to the gods at their grove. A sheep is sacrificed and prepared with the new yam. Singing and dancing in honor of the god Ntoa take place in the streets.

Source: *Festivals of Ghana* by A. A. Opoku. Accra: Ghana Publishing Corporation, 1970, pp. 28-32.

Ghana (Akan)

Odwira on ninth Adae

Odwira is celebrated at the time of the ninth Adae (the Adae being a religious ceremonial event held every forty days during the year). The period from the eighth Adae to the ninth Adae (between August and October) is known as Adarbutuw. Singing, dancing, noisemaking, and noisy funerals or processions are forbidden, nor may anyone enter the stool-house (ritual center) during this period. Lesser chiefs are expected to attend the Odwira at Akropong, the capital, but will have their own local Odwira as well, perhaps at a different time.

Odwira in Akuapem, c. 1970

Odwira is a week-long festival. On Monday the path to the royal mausoleum at Amamprobi is cleared. On Tuesday the new yam is eaten for the first time. The priests carry the new yam through the streets and offer it to the gods, while the chief sexton (Adumhene) invokes Odwira at the royal mausoleum. Wednesday is a day of fasting for the dead. Drinking and drumming take place on this day. Thursday is the feast day. The spirits are feasted first with saltless mashed yam, boiled eggs, and drinking water. On the evening of this day a sacred procession to ceremonially cleanse the sacred stools takes place. All must stay indoors while this procession goes to the stream, conducts its ablutions, and returns. On Friday, the high chief holds court and is visited by subchiefs and their retinue. The chiefs then parade the streets in their finery, processing to the town square, where a court is set up and singing and dancing occur.

Source: *Festivals of Ghana* by A. A. Opoku. Accra: Ghana Publishing Corporation, 1970, pp. 12-13. (See also "Adae" and "Odwira in Akwamu" in this source.)

The Akan calendar

As harvest celebrations, the Odwira or Yam festivals are traditionally observed between August and October to mark the conclusion of the harvest season . . . because the dates for the festivals are determined according to the nine monthly cycles of 40 days each, their timing could fall anywhere between a period of several months.

All Akan groups observe an annual calendar that is composed of multiples of 40-day cycles known as *adaduanan* (literally 40 days). The beginning point of the annual cycle is a major festival such as the Odwira, yam or other harvest festivals celebrated by most Akan groups.

Following the focal point festival, the year is composed of nine "monthly" cycles of forty days each, and on the ninth the year has turned full cycle. Thus, the succeeding harvest celebration constitutes the anniversary (afenhyia) of that event.

The Asante Yam festival has been combined with the annual Odwira, while among many coastal Akan groups whose staple food is not yam, parallel harvest-like celebrations can be found such as the Bakatue of Elmina, the Afahye of Cape Coast and the *Aboakyer* of the Efutu of Winneba. All these celebrations share identical characteristics and significance: they are times of general festivities; they are connected with first fruits (Fante *afahye* is derived from *afa,* festival and *hye,* to fix or appoint a day); they are synonymous with the beginning of the new year; and they are occasions for the propriation of the ancestors. Because of space limitations more detailed attention here will be given only to the Asante Odwira and its place in the ritual *adaduanan* calendrical system as a model for other identical Akan structures.

Source: "Time, the Calendar, and History Among the Akan of Ghana" by Joseph K. Adjaye in *International Migration Review* xxi (2) (Summer, 1987), 79-81.

Ghanian harvest dishes

The calendars of Ghana and Nigeria are crowded with festivals to celebrate important happenings, and these include harvests of yams or rice. Usually such festivals in a village will include libations poured to the dead, feasting, dancing, drumming and a formal reception by the chief.

At a Yoruba yam harvest festival, a fine piece of yam is offered to the ancestors along with salt, palm oil, a goat or a chicken.

The Hausa New Year's is "the feast of the full stomach" at which revelers eat all the chicken or meat they can hold.

A special corn harvest festival dish in Ghana would be Kpokpoi. Soured corn dough, prepared as for Kenkey, is steamed to a jelly-like state. This is achieved by setting the steamer over boiling water, sprinkling in a layer of the corn mixture, letting it cook, then adding another layer, and when that is cooked, adding a third, and so on. When the whole is finished, it is turned into a bowl and stirred to eradicate lumps. Then okra, which has been sliced, cooked and mashed, is mixed into the corn and palm oil is stirred in. This is usually eaten as a side dish with a soup or stew made of palm butter.

An easier Ghanaian harvest festival dish is:

Oto

1 pound yam per person (African size helping)
salt to taste
3 tablespoons palm oil per person
1 hard-boiled egg per person

Peel and cut up yam in small pieces. Boil in salted water until tender. Drain and mash smooth. Add salt and oil and mix thoroughly. Spoon out individual portions and set a peeled hard-boiled egg on top of each helping.

Source: *A West African Cook Book* by Ellen Gibson Wilson. New York: M. Evans, 1971, p. 247.

Ghana (Asante)

Historical background of the Odwira

The Asante Odwira appears more structured and institutionalized than those of other Akan groups, and right from the beginning it and related calendrical matters were a subject to which the Asante Kings gave a great deal of attention. The Odwira seems to have been instituted by the Asante King Osei Tutu during the early years of the kingdom in the late seventeenth century as a yearly meeting to reinforce the subordination of the chiefs of the newly subjugated provinces to the king's authority. It also provided an occasion for sanctifying the spirits of past kings and for offering thanksgiving to the ancestors in appreciation of bountiful harvests. Towards the end of the usually long period of celebrations, the annual meeting of the Asantemanhyiamu (Council of State) was convened to deal with all major judicial and legislative matters of state.

Odwira moved to November-January

The Odwira was held apparently between August and October until Asantehene Kofi Kakari (1867-1874) moved it from this wet period to the drier period from November to January when travelling is much easier.

The Odwira celebration was suspended in 1896 when the British, in a move to colonize Asante, exiled the Asantehene, Agyeman Prempeh I.

The Odwira itself is not a single event as such, but a sequence of events and celebrations that span an entire *adaduanan* period and climaxes in the final week. Within this 40-day period specific days are set aside for various activities, functions and observances including libations on and offerings of ritual food to blackened stools, invocations of spirits and consecrations of ceremonial swords.

Source: "Time, the Calendar, and History Among the Akan of Ghana" by Joseph K. Adjaye in *International Migration Review* xxi (2) (Summer, 1987), 71-100, 82.

Ghana (Ewe)

Yam Festival

Only those Ewe who live in the hinterlands continue to celebrate the Yam Festival. This is a harvest festival, an offering of first fruits to the gods.

Yam festival at Peki in the Volta Region

The Tuesday before the Friday of the Yam Festival is a day of purification for the community. Towns are swept and weeded; houses are cleaned. After sunset, every fireplace is put out and the fireplace cleaned of ashes, which are deposited by the women in a huge communal pile in the village road. The men, meantime, are meeting with the priest, who ritually ties a chicken and a frog to blades of an oil palm shoot. The group processes through town with this *atidzie* bundle, chanting. The priest dips a ritual spray into a calabash of water and afia leaves, and sprinkles in all directions as they process. All lights along the way must be put out as the procession passes. The *atidzie* bundle is ritually laid on the ash heap in the main road, and prayers are offered that no evil shall pass over this *atidzie* bundle and enter the town.

On Thursday yams are dug for the first time from the fields. But these are hidden in the bushes, since they cannot be brought into town until Friday. From dusk to 8 p.m. on Thursday and from dawn to 8 a.m. on Friday the yams are carried into town. Singing songs of the new yam harvest, onlookers run after the farmers and pound the yams they like, gently with their fists.

On Friday morning, the chief of each Peki town sends to the chief priest a chicken and two yams. The priest prepares these as a yam *fufu* meal for all to partake. Plain and red (mixed with palm oil) mashed yams have been sprinkled over the shrine for the ancestral spirits. No one must eat of this ritual food. Anyone doing so would die, should he ever eat a garden-egg again. On this festive day, the chief priest cuts the head from a yam and plants it in a mound in a corner of the shrine. This, when sprouted, will be the first yam of the next season. As soon as it grows, the priest splits it and presents it to the shrine spirits as the "first fruit" of the season. Thus the spirits can be first to taste the yam of the new year.

People visit friends on this day to wish a good new year. Prize yams are displayed at each house. The main feast of the day is yam *fufu,* served with a soup prepared with smoked river fish, chicken, or goat. Drumming, dancing, and games fill the afternoon. Top spinning, palm leaf bundle throwing, and somersaulting are popular.

The festivities continue for a week. The following Thursday just after dusk, a male of the household takes a brand from the fireplace and waves it about every corner of the house to drive out evil spirits. The brand is then raced out of town with a shout and tossed into the branches of the tallest tree he can find. This ends the festival.

Source: *Festivals of Ghana* by A. A. Opoku. Accra: Ghana Publishing Corp., 1970, pp. 63-69.

Ghana (Ga)

Homowo/Hunger Hooting Festival

Between August and September this festival commemorates a fine harvest that blessed the Ga in ancient times following their long and harrowing travels in famine to their present home in Ghana.

Ga Homowo celebrations

As in days of old, people living in neighboring villages such as Abokobi, Dodowa, Boi, etc., travel to the city for the festival. As though by mutual decision, the villagers dress alike. They no longer travel on foot but in lorries or Mammy trucks that were decorated with flags and strips of the cloth the villagers wear. The drivers honk their horns intermittently while "*Kpa*" (a deity of the people of Labadi) songs on current events are sung. They get off the lorries on the outskirts of the city. Accra, carrying on their heads their harvest of foodstuffs like okra, corn, pepper, tomatoes and onions in baskets or bowls that are decorated with either strung pepper, tigernuts or garden eggs. People gather by the sides of the road, shouting, "*Soobii, Soobii*" "Thursday people," since the first travelers arrived in the city on a Thursday). The new arrivals join the villagers in a procession and dance to songs that explain "*Nmaayi eye*" "*Nmaa eswere*" and "*Nmaayi eye*" (the harvest is white, the harvest is plentiful, the harvest is white).

The town gradually works itself up for the great day. For the Hunger-Hooting Festival, the Ga have open house. People are free to walk into a house and be sure of a meal of *Kpokpei,* the festal food. The preparation of the food starts the night before. Fish, already smoked, is cleaned: different species of fish—brim, herring, *tsile*—are used. It is a time when fish is in abundance. The corn soaks for three days before it is milled and made into dough. The palm nuts for the soup are cooked and pounded. Every household is up quite early in the morning to be sure that the meal is ready before mid-day. People squat around bowls of *kpokpei* and palm-nut soup and eat the festal food together.

The chiefs and elders go around the town and to places like cemeteries, the royal mausoleum, and houses where distinguished people have been buried—e.g., the Christiangborg Castle, where the Labadi (a Ga town) leader Akodzeram was buried, and the Ussher Fort Prisons in Accra, which is an old cemetary. They sprinkled white and red *kpokpei* around for the souls of the departed ancestors and for the deities. An attendant holds a bowl of festal food while the chief or elder does the sprinkling. Around his waist, the chief has a rustic brown cloth tied with a strip of another cloth to keep it in place; he has a matching cloth tied around his head. At Ussher Fort Prisons, the warders are treated to a meal. The chief literally puts the food into their mouths.

People continue in the festive mood well into the night. Food is plentiful—enough to last for almost a week in a number of homes. Hunger is indeed hooted at, and the new year is ushered in.

The next day after the feasting people dress in their best clothes and go to the houses of relatives and friends to exchange New Year Greetings, accompanied by words of wisdom, drinking, reconciliations and merrymaking. Greetings go with handshaking:

	Response
Noowala Noowala	Yao
Long life long life	*Amen*
Afi naa akpe wo	Yao
May the new year bring us together	*Amen*
Gbii kpaanyo anina wo	Yao
May we live to see the eighth day	*Amen*
Woye Gbo ni woye Gboenaa	Yao
May we eat the fruits of Gbo and that of Gboenaa (seasons)	*Amen*
Wofee moomo	Yao
May we live long (be grey, old)	*Amen*
Alonte din ko aka-fo woten	Yao
May no black cat (ill omen) come between us	*Amen*
Wosee afi bene wotrashi neke nonu noon	Yao
May sit like this the next year (celebration, anniversary)	*Amen*
Tswa Tswa tswa Omanye aba	Yao
Hail; Hail! Hail! let there be blessing (peace)	*Amen*

Some people mourn departed friends and relatives—weeping one minute and in jubilation the next—in recognition of all that has gone by, hopeful of a better year.

Source: ''Hunger-Hooting Festival in Ghana'' by Sophia D. Lokko in *The Drama Review* 25 (4) (T92) (Winter), 1981, 49-50. (Author teaches at the University of Ghana. See the above for discussion of other rites in the harvest cycle as well.)

The homowo season

The homowo cycle begins in early May with the rains when the priests ritually sow corn and end in late September with the harvest. The Koyeligbi, Day of Feasting, of Homowo, however, falls in August. In Ga Masi or Accra it is celebrated on a Saturday, but in Osu, Labadi, Teshie, Nungua, Kpone, Prampram, and Ningo it falls on a Tuesday ten days later. In Tema it is celebrated on Friday.

Ga Masi Homowo Day, c. 1970

Ga who have moved away return to their hometown for this festival. They are called Soobii, Thursday people, because they arrive home on Thursday. They assemble outside of town and march into town in groups, singing and carrying loads decorated with produce. Each of the seven quarters of Ga Masi has a group; all march together to a central point and then divide and go to their respective areas.

Returning by truck

In other towns, where Homowo Day is on a Tuesday, villagers return home on Monday by truck. The trucks are decorated and the groups enter in fancy clothing, singing Kpa songs.

The yam festival

The day after the Soobii arrive is the yam festival and also the day of twins. Twins are dressed in white and feted on this day. They ceremoniously carry the feast's leftovers to the seashore at sunset.

Homowo preparations

Milled corn, palm oil, and fish are prepared for the feast. Hearths and lintels are cleaned and painted with red clay. A palm soup and *kpokpoi* or *ko,* are prepared. The latter is made from steamed, unleavened corn dough mashed and mixed with palm oil. It is eaten with palm soup, served in clay bowls. The *kpokpoi* is sprinkled at the doorsteps before eating as an offering for the departed spirits of the household. The chiefs or Mantsemei go from house to house sprinkling *kpokpoi*. The menfolk vie for the food of the feast, which is served in a communal bowl. A fun scramble for the best bits takes place, with children snatching food out from under their father's noses, while the women laugh and cheer the children on.

Visiting

The day following Homowo Day is a time for visiting relatives and friends to exchange Noowala greetings. It is the time to settle misunderstandings in the community.

Kpa Day

Kpa Day is celebrated on Noowala Day at Labadi and on the Sunday after Noowala at Teshie. On Kpa Day people in uniform sing and dance through the town. The young sing of fantastic deeds and sometimes of not-so-fantastic deeds, just to poke fun.

Source: *Festivals of Ghana* by A. A. Opoku. Accra: Ghana Publishing Corp., 1970, pp. 51-56.

Hungary

Szuret (Grape Harvest)

The gathering of the grapes—the szuret, it is called—the last of the great outdoor tasks in Hungary, is the occasion for special gaiety. It is looked forward to eagerly by the young people; most of the peasant marriages take place after this festival. According to ancient custom the gatherers of the grapes fashion an enormous ''bouquet'' out of grapes. This is carried in procession on a pole by two men. Gypsies go in front playing gay dance tunes and next follow usually clowns or actors who perform comic stunts. Then come the gatherers of the grapes and finally, surrounding the grape bouquet, a bevy of girls dressed in white and with flower wreaths on their heads. In festive procession they pass through the village, dancing, singing and drinking the health of every person they meet. When they reach the home of the owner of the vineyard, they hang the big cluster of grapes from the ceiling and then follow feasting and more dancing.

While the grapes are being gathered, or later, during the dancing, a traditional game of ''robber'' takes place. Several men are appointed to guard the grapes; the others then endeavor to steal the fruit from the vines or from the ''bouquet'' without being caught. If caught, the thief is dragged before a ''judge'' and made to pay some forfeit, usually to dance a solo dance amid the jeers of his companions, to sing a song, or to perform a ridiculous pantomime.

Source: *Foreign Festival Customs* by Marian Schibsby & Hanny Cohrsen. New York: American Council for Nationalities Service, 1974, pp. 51-52.

Wheat harvest

Later in the summer when the wheat is harvested, the second festival occurs. Modern agricultural methods have done away with the old harvest-home customs in most sections of the country, but they still linger in the remoter districts. In Transylvania, where the owner of a farm still relies chiefly upon the labor of friends and neighbors for the gathering of his crops, the harvest is an occasion for mirth and feasting as well as work. When the last sheaf is harvested, a wreath of wheat and wild flowers is carried to the farmer's house by girls dressed in their most colorful costumes. It is still customary to lie in ambush for this procession and to drench them and the harvest wreath thoroughly with water, to ensure a rich harvest for the coming year. Another custom that still survives is this: on the landowner's first appearance in the harvest field, the harvesters seize him and tie him securely with a straw rope. He has to pay ransom for his release.

When the procession arrives at the farm house, poems are recited in honor of the farmer. Then the wreath is hung in a place of honor where it remains until next harvest. After that follow a bountiful feast and dancing usually to the music of a gypsy band. Gingerbread cookies made especially for this festival are lavishly distributed among the guests. They are usually highly ornamented and moulded into the shape of animals, human beings, hearts, etc. The gingerbread cookies of Hungary are considered an interesting manifestation of the folk art of that country.

Source: *Foreign Festival Customs* by Marian Schibsby & Hanny Cohrsen. New York: American Council for Nationalities Service, 1974, p. 51.

Ireland

Harvest knots in early Irish tradition

The end of the harvest was also celebrated in various ways, and the cutting of the last sheaf was a complex folk festival of great antiquity in northern areas. In Co. Offaly beautiful harvest knots were woven from straw and worn by both men and women.

Source: *Life & Tradition in Rural Ireland* by Timothy P. O'Neill. London: J. M. Dent & Sons, Ltd., 1977, p. 101.

A dish to celebrate the first potatoes of the year

The first meal from the crop of early potatoes was an occasion of great excitement and a special meal was prepared. A basket of potatoes was dug and with the tender skins peeled or rubbed off they were placed in a three-legged pot and boiled over the open fire. The water was then drained off and the potatoes were mashed using a pounder or beetle. Milk, salt, onions and in some places vegetables or spices were added, and a large hole was made in the middle and filled with butter which melted quickly. The food was then ready for eating. This dish in different varieties was known all over Ireland—in the midlands it was known as *calcannon,* while in Donegal it was *bruitin*. The pecking hens, who were usually given what was left in the pot after meal times, quite often had lean times on days when this dish was served.

Source: *Life & Tradition in Rural Ireland* by Timothy P. O'Neill. London: J. M. Dent & Sons, Ltd., 1977, p. 65.

Ivory Coast

Yam Festival

Throughout the Ivory Coast, Dan, Wobe, Senoufo, Baoule, Bete, and Lobi celebrate the harvest. Religious ceremonies are accompanied by masked dancers in raffia and bright cloth who represent gods and ancestors.

Source: *Hi Neighbor. Book 6*. New York: U.S. Committee for UNICEF/Hasting House, 1962, p. 15.

Ivory Coast (Abron)

Odiwera legends

In addition to life-crises ceremonies, the Abron celebrate three major fixed religious events. These are the great yam festival (Odiwera), in October, the Adae, or tribute to the ancestors, and the Fofyé, or tribute to local gods and the punungo of dead priests. The yam festival combines a first-fruit ritual, during which the taboo on eating yams is lifted, with ancestor worship, and is by far the most elaborate ceremony. It unfolds in various villages by turn, according to a fixed chronology. The festival begins where an ancient chief is said to have first tasted the yam, proving it was edible. According to legend, long ago a hunter walking through the bush found a yam. When he saw it, he took it home. After some days, he noticed an animal eating it. He went to the chief of Guendé and told him what he had seen. The chief of Guendé then took the yam and cooked it. The people waited forty days and nights, and when they saw that their chief did not die they knew that the yam was good to eat. And so the yam festival is held every year at Guendé, and it is the chief of Guendé who eats the yam before the King.

Another story says that after the chief ate the yam it was then given to the children of the village as a further test. After another week with no bad results, the yam was accepted as fit to eat by all. Today a children's yam festival may follow the one at Guendé, but it does not occur every year and is not an obligatory part of the festival.

Forty days after the Guendé fete, the new yams are taken to the temple of Tano, where they are offered, along with sheep and goats, to that deity. A week later, yams are offered to the punungo bo bokogo of each household. These offerings take place in the context of local yam festivals, one of which is usually held in the village of the King. After the final yam festival, the tuber is declared ready for eating.

Source: *When the Spider Danced: Notes from an African Village* by Alexander Alland, Jr. Garden City, N.Y.: Anchor Press/Doubleday, 1975, pp. 105-106.

Ivory Coast (Baoulé)

The klo dance

A Baoulé dance called the *klo* takes place in the harvest season in the fall, and seems much like our Halloween. Groups of boys from about five to eleven years old gather together, dressed in strips of palm leaves that cover their faces and bodies to the ground. They move from house to house in a sort of dance accompanied by the sound of sticks beaten together, and ask the housewives for treats of yams, manioc, or peanuts. If they are given something, they sing songs of thanks. If they receive nothing, they sing teasing songs and scold the woman and her house. Afterward all the boys go into the bush to eat what they have been given.

Source: *Hi Neighbor, Book 6*. New York: Hastings House/ U.S. Committee for UNICEF, 1963, p. 16.

Ladakh

A harvest mandala

In the main shrine-room of the monastery, in the corner, around a large white marble circle that had been raised slightly on a platform, seven monks were sitting. They were holding silver instruments in their hands, silver funnels that tapered to a point, and by their sides were heaps of what looked at first like glass beads, green, yellow, blue heaps, small iridescent mountain that shone in the candlelight.

'What are they doing?'

'They are making a mandala. The white marble circle is the Emptiness, Sunyata, from which all form comes, and in which all form is inherent. Through the small silver funnels the monks will place, in an ancient pattern, the stone colours heaped by their sides. When the mandala is ready it will be blessed by the Rinpoche of Spituk, the Bakula Rinpoche, and then all the colour will be scraped from it again, and only the white marble circle remain.'

'And this happens every year?'

'Every year. It is one of the most sacred rituals of the year. It falls always near harvest. As the fields ripen, the mandala is prepared. Ladakh turns gold in the sun, and the mandala, the sacred diagram of Reality, is revealed. Through the making of the mandala, the whole of Ladakh is charged with a sacred power. The mandala is always present; Reality is a mandala, of which each of us is the centre. So when the Rinpoche blesses this mandala, he is blessing the whole of this world through it.'

The monks had seen us, and were waving to us to come closer, to come and sit by them. Two chipped white cups were filled with Tibetan tea for us; and two lumps of tsampa placed by each cup. When we sat down, the youngest monk, who was sitting next to Helena, took her lump of tsampa, and made a small Buddha in meditation out of it, with long arms and a pot belly. He lifted it solemnly into the air. Everyone laughed. 'Eat it!' he said. 'Be happy.'

The monks worked in bursts, each in his own rhythm. They talked or chanted as they worked. Sometimes one of them would yawn and leave the circle to lie down for a quarter of an hour on one of the benches.

Source: *A Journey in Ladakh* by Andrew Harvey. Boston: Houghton Mifflin, 1983, p. 11.

Lithuania

Nubaigai (Grain Harvest)

The end of the harvest brings to Lithuania one of its most joyous festivals, the ''nubaigai''. At that time landowners keep open house for all who have helped in the harvesting and for their families. An abundant feast is prepared, and dancing, games and merrymaking last till late at night. At the harvest season the Lithuanian farmers formerly killed a cock and a hen, without bloodshed, the survival of a harvest sacrifice. The fowl were then eaten by the family; no servants were allowed to be present on this occasion.

A number of quaint harvest customs have survived. In Lithuania also the last sheaf dressed as an old woman, the Boba, is borne in triumphal procession to the farm; sometimes the person who bound the last sheaf is wrapped up in it. Here also every effort is made by the farmer and his family to drench the Boba with water so as to ensure plenty of rain for next year's crop. The harvest wreath also as a rule features in the Lithuanian celebration but the mode of presenting it is somewhat unusual. The prettiest of the girls walks at the head of the procession, carrying the wreath on a plate covered with a white linen cloth. As the reapers advance they sing an old song, telling how they rescued the master's crop from a huge bison—probably a symbol of winter—that would have devoured it and how they have brought the rye safely to his barn. On entering the farmyard, they change to songs in honor of the master and his family. Then the wreath is presented and the master thanks everybody and gives a gift to every girl in the procession. One of the harvesters usually delivers a speech; according to tradition the speech must end with a meaningless jumble of Latin and French or Polish words, though to be a satire on the use of foreign languages by the great landed proprietors in Lithuania. The following translation of an ancient Lithuanian harvest speech or poem will be of interest:

> "From deep forests, from trackless swamps, pursued by famine, we wandered about in search of a valley, strewn with flowers, silvered by rye, gilded by wheat. We wandered through dark woods and birch groves, over treacherous bogs, over inumerable bees' nests and over the lairs of bears. We suffered from cold and rain and no one showed us pity. At last an old bear had the kindness to tell us: 'Keep on going. Go where your feet carry you. Go where the finches fly and you will come to (here the name of the master is inserted) who lives on a farm surrounded by tall maples and who has immense acres sown with corn and only a few laborers in the house. Go to him, help him to harvest his corn, and he will give you enough to eat and drink.' We came to thee, gracious master. We have harvested thy corn and now we bring thee a wreath, not of gold or silver, but of rye like diamonds, of wheat like amber. Clarissime, eminentissime, Vestra dominatis, oratis, vocatis—."

Source: *Foreign Festival Customs* by Marian Schibsby & Hanny Cohrsen. New York: American Council for Nationalities Service, 1974, pp. 54-55.

Mexico (Maya)

The Dinner-of-the-Milpa in Chan Kom, Yucatan

The ceremony of this name (u hanli col) is the most important of all agricultural rituals performed by and for the individual agriculturalist. It requires the services of the h-men; it demands the aid of a group of male friends; and it consumes several hours of time and a considerable quantity of food and drink. By performing it the agriculturalist establishes satisfactory relations with the chaacs, balams and kuilob kaaxob. The ceremony secures him wealth and health: the beneficence of the yuntzilob assures him a good harvest; and if it be omitted, they will bring sickness upon him. It is recognized that one should perform the ceremony every four years, at a time when the maize is just ripening. . . . the h-men begins by clearing a piece of land 15 or 20 meters square. As this ceremony is performed at the initiative of some one man, the clearing is made in the yard of his house. The usual altar is erected, covered with habin leaves and provided with a small wooden cross. The h-men begins by offering zaca to the gods, asperging the altar with it using a leaf of habin, and reciting a prayer which invites the yuntzilob to the feast that they are about to prepare.

The owner of the house has asked some of his friends to help him. The h-men now directs these men to prepare the earth-oven and he supervises the preparation of the sacred breadstuffs. In this work the laymen are engaged for an hour or more, mixing the meal with water, patting out the cakes, inserting the squash seed and other special ingredients and grouping them into the specified piles. This is play, not work nor prayer.

While the sacred breads are baking, the h-men offers balche to the gods. This has been prepared three days in advance of the ceremony, so that it may have reached the desired degree of fermentation. As is almost invariably the case in offering balche, the liquor is placed in thirteen of those vessels known as homa and these are placed on the altar. When this is done (and again from time to time during the rest of the ceremony) balche is sprinkled on the cross and on the altar itself with a half-folded leaf of habin employed as a scoop. This is done because balche has the quality of sanctifying and cleansing from impurity and evil anything with which it comes in contact.

The h-men recites a prayer inviting the gods to come and partake of the liquor. After a pause to allow the deities to do this, the balche is distributed among those present. No one may refuse to drink at least a little. Each recipient returns thanks in the phrase always employed in the distribution of sacred food and drink: ox tezcuntabac tech, tat ("Thrice be saluted, sir").

The second dedicatory act is the consecration and offering of fowl. . . . In some cases the h-men directs the giver of the ceremony to hold the fowl while he consecrates them. One h-men appoints four persons, whom he calls Chaacs, each one of whom holds a leg or a wing of the fowl while it is ritually killed. The consecration is accomplished by the recitation of a short prayer by the h-men while he puts balche down the victim's beak with a scoop of habin. As the prayer concludes, the assistant (or the four Chaacs) kills the fowl, the hens by wringing their necks, and the turkeys by cutting tongue or throat and allowing them to bleed to death.

At this point in the ceremonies another interval occurs, during which the laymen gather in a group to pluck and cut up the fowl. When this has been done, they carry the dismembered birds into the house, where the women (led usually by the wife of the man who is giving the ceremony) have gathered to prepare the broth (kol) which forms an essential part of all the food offerings to the gods. During the ceremonies the women must not approach the place where the h-men's activities center, but inside the house they are enjoying the social pleasures incidental to the cooperative preparation of festal foods.

The ritual continues with offering of the ritual foods to the spirits of the four corners of the sky.

Source: *Chan Kom: A Mayan Village* by Robert Redfield and Alfonso Villa Rojas. Chicago: The Univ. of Chicago Press, 1939, pp. 135-136.

Niger (Songhay)

The "eating the new millet" ceremony of the Songhay

Zimas organise a third farming ceremony after the harvest, called "eating the new millet." At this—a celebration of thanksgiving held by the possession troupe—the spirits are invited to sample the new millet.

Source: *Fusion of the Worlds: An Ethnography of Possession Among the Songhay of Niger* by Paul Stoller. Chicago: University of Chicago, 1989, p. 131. (For more information on

Songhay spirits and possession troupes see *Fusion of the Worlds.*)

Nigeria

New Yam festival customs

New Yam festival is celebrated in almost all the ethnic groups of Nigeria. It takes place usually, about the end of June, and it is celebrated annually. In most areas, to eat new yam before this festival is taboo. A day is usually set aside for this festival by the chief priest of the god of harvest. The day is designated a public holiday by the community. Very early on this day, the high priest kills a goat in the fetish place and pours the blood on the symbol that represents the god of harvest. After this the carcass is cooked and vegetable soup is made of it. Yam is boiled and pounded to make foofoo. Everybody gathers around the market place and the chief priest after incantations and prayers about the past season, prays for a better harvest in the coming season. After this the high priest declares the feast open by eating the pounded yam and the soup first before any other person. After this there is a lot of dancing, drinking and merry-making as the new yam is being eaten. After this festival, the new yam can then be eaten by any member of the community.

Source: ''Festivals in Nigeria: A Bibliography'' by G. D. Ekpenyong (MRS) in *Nigeria Magazine* (136) (1981), 33.

Nigeria (Dakkarkari)

The Uhola Festival

Two months after the *Dbitti* ceremony (mid-October), the chief and his council of elders call a meeting to decide on a date for 'house cleaning' in the preparation for the 'big' festival. People from the farmlands are expected to come home for the purpose of keeping [the] environment clean. Members of the *Golmo* institution help clean the community—the hills are cleared and burnt, the shrines are kept in order, the chiefs' compounds and the surroundings [sic] are neatly kept. Drinking of local beer (M'kya) dominates these days of environmental sanitation. When the 'cleaning' exercise is over, the chief invites all the elders to decide on a convenient date for the *Uhola* celebration. The date fixed does not normally exceed 30 days after the 'cleaning' period. Like the Sallah festival, the chosen date should coincide with the new moon. About four weeks to the celebration, the *Yadato*—boys from rich families—go through the process of fattening. They are kept in seclusion for four weeks. They are properly fed and encouraged to take full rest.

First Day of Festival

On the first day of the festival, all the Dakkarkaris living in neighbouring towns and in the farmlands begin to troop into the old town of Dabai amidst music, dancing and merrymaking. Some participants appear in comic attires to amuse the spectators. The *Yadato* is expected on this day to dance in front of the chiefs' palace, and in front of recognised elders' homes, presenting them (chiefs) with *Uhola* gifts. They then move on to the village square to dance and sing satirical songs. The songs shower well-aimed barbs at their mates who have not lived up to the expectations in the community—heady women, pregnant girls who have no husbands, prostitutes, lazy and irresponsible men are all singled out for satirical attacks. Socio-political issues are not left out either. In a particular festival I watched on the 11th December, 1984, Buharis' government was seriously ridiculed. Wherever a *Yadato* is found, a pageant of followers and musicians is found too. One of the followers carries a long, straight and very smooth ludian Bamboo.

Costumes

The male *Yadato* wears a traditional costume called *Doro* and *Ubada* (short skirt) made of animal skin. The costume comprises a long and loose multi-coloured skirt cut into stripes. The *Yadato* also wears a coloured straw hat decorated with numerous small mirrors: neckscarf, and carries a hand fan.

The female *Yadato* wears a costume known as *O'getti, Zgida and Ubada.* Most of the girls wear decorated head-pieces, decorated straw hat, necklace and neck scarf. Both hands and waist are decorated with several beads. She wears a white metal anklet and white fur on the left leg. Several mirrors are seen round the body, and umbrella in hand. The female *Yadato* appears in the arena bare-body except for the brassiere which covers the bossom [sic] Some of them wear shoes with fanciful socks. Their dance steps are slow but graceful.

The second day is devoted to dance, merrymaking, exchange of gifts and wrestling. The wrestling contest is done in the village square. The wrestlers wear black animal hides over short trousers with cowrie shells around their waist. The black hide is further covered with red-stripped animal skin. The elders serve as organisers and referees in the match. Girls hold up several handkerchiefs to cheer their admirers. They clean off sweat with towels and dust their (wrestlers) faces with talcum powder. When a wrestler throws an opponent in the match, his supporters carry him shoulder high, and the victor receives an instant prize from the chief. The match is often arranged in such a manner that one Dakkarkari community wrestles against the other. This is where the real festival ends. But elderly people do normally continue in the wrestling; people may present speeches, prizes and awards are given to those who deserve them. This goes on for about four more days until the magiro priest declares the festival closed.

After the festival, the girls move into their respective husbands' homes, while the boys go into *golmo.* No girl participates in the *Uhola* without a prospective husband who must have completed his *golmo,* a form of farm labour in lieu of bride-price as hinted before. *Golmo* is a way of life in Dakkarkiri culture.

Source: ''The Uhola Festival in Sokoto State'' by P. J. Ebewo in *Nigeria Magazine* 55 (1) (January-March 1987), 16-18.

Nigeria (Ibo)

Onwasato Festival

The Onwasato festival still takes place about the month of August and formally marks the beginning of the harvesting period. It is celebrated with great feasting, when new crops, particularly of yam, are eaten. The highlight of the ceremony is the thanksgiving ritual procedure. Every family is expected to kill at least a fowl. The senior member of the family kills the fowl in his Obu (the father's sitting-house), sprinkles its blood on the Okpensi (the symbol of the family), and lifts his voice in thanksgiving to the ancestors of the family. He prays that they should continue to protect the family and give them the ability to live, to accumulate more wealth, and to build a greater community. Next, the feathers of the fowl are removed, not inside but outside the compound, and sprinkled on the threshold. This is done to demonstrate the determination of the people to forsake all evil in the coming season. Of the fowls killed for the occasion, at least one is roasted and reserved, while others are consumed at the day's feasting. The second day, the roasted fowls are produced by every family, and all the members of the extended family meet in the Obu of the senior elder to share them. As custom provides, particular parts of the fowl go to elders and women. This procedure is called Inya Okuku (handing round of fowl).

Source: *A Nigerian Villager in Two Worlds* by Dilim Okafor-Omali. London: Faber & Faber, 1936, p. 57.

Mgbu Mgbu Uzo, c. 1939

The account had been as follows: 'The ceremony of *Mgbu Mgbu Uzo* is the women's festival [before the eating of the new yams] as *Oru Owerri* is that of the men, and takes place after the latter. By this time [i.e. end of July] the corn the people will have been eating has become a little hard and over-ripe. On a certain day, the women, helped by their children, gather a quantity of corn cobs, strip them and boil the corn that same evening, in large cooking-pots. Only married women [that is to say, non-Owerrians, Owerri being exogamous] are allowed to cook the corn. When the cooking is nearly finished, unmarried girls and married Owerri women who have come on a visit [that is to say all 'daughters' of Owerri] stand by the kitchen door and beg for some of the corn. They are given small portions and the ones who get it first and find it well cooked run out into the yards, their spoons in their hands, calling: "Mine is done! Mine is good!" Although it often happens that it rains on that evening [July is well in the middle of the rains] they run round all the same. Next morning the married women mix the corn with oil, etc., and the day is spent feasting on this corn, men and women together, but the men will have been invited by the women, in the same way that on *Oru Owerri* the women were invited by the men. A special dish of corn will be passed round among the Christians as they will not want to give a portion of it as a sacrifice [I think, to the ancestors], as the others do. On the next morning, the married women take a little of this same cooked corn in small earthen pots, and go out to their farms where they throw small portions of it over their yam crops, saying to the yams: "We have been eating corn all this time and it has done us no harm. Now we come to present you with some of it and may you not hurt us when we eat you any more than the corn has done." They then dig up three or four yams and carry them home. They could eat them at once but it is preferable to wait a month or so as they are rather moist and nasty when first dug up. On the day the corn is being mixed and eaten, no one must draw water from, nor go near, the stream sacred to the female spirit Nworie, as she would not like it, and also all the snakes that live in or near the stream are out having a holiday.

Source: *African Women: A Study of the Ibo of Nigeria* by Sylvia Leith-Ross. London: Faber & Faber, 1939, pp. 216-217.

Nigeria (Igbo)

New Yam Festival (Iri ji Ohuru)

This is the festival commemorating the apotheosis of Ahiajoku, the god of yam. The significance of the yam crop to the Igbo is demonstrated by the fact that the traditional Igbo man's next request after asking God for abundance of children is the possession of yams. Many taboos surround the yam, a crop that is indeed sacred to the Igbo. In the past anybody who stole yam was put to death because he had desecrated the land. With the passage of time the Igbo no longer put to death yam stealers but banish them from the land.

The question had been asked why the yam is revered in Igbo culture. There is a myth that at first *Ahiajoku* was the son of eponymous Igbo. And once upon a time there was famine in Igbo land and the children of Igbo were dying out. Chukwu asked Igbo to sacrifice his son Ahiajoku and Ada, his daughter, in order to save his other children. Ahiajoku and Ada were killed and God directed that their flesh should be cut into pieces and buried in several mounds and this was done. In a few days yams germinated from the flesh of Ahiajoku and cocoyams from the flesh of Ada and God asked Igbo and his remaining sons to farm the two crops. Eventually Igbo and his children survived by eating these.

The Igbo therefore regard the yam as a human being sacrificed so that other human beings may survive. Ahiajoku is thus seen as a redeemer and his festival is celebrated with pomp and pageantry

The significance of the Ahiajoku myth in Igbo philosophy of life can hardly be over-emphasised. There is in this myth the only instance in Igbo belief of deification of a human hero. After the immolation of Ahiajoku, his spirit becomes the God of yam. Also, the myth symbolises the Igbo belief that they are the children of God because God communicated with their eponymous ancestor. Besides, it demonstrates the significance of sacrifice in Igbo religion and that the more precious the sacrificial victim the more abundant the reward obtainable from God.

In the New Yam Festival the myth of the immolation of Ahiajoku is re-enacted. The individual householder is his own priest. He places four or eight new yams on the ground near an *ogirisi* shrine and after some incantatory prayer cuts little portions off the head and tail of the yams thus re-enacting the killing of Ahiajoku. The yams are then cooked with palm oil, water and chicken, the meal representing the body and blood of Ahiajoku. During the sacrificial meal (oriri) the participants eat, as it were, the flesh and drink the blood of Ahiajoku.

Another significance of the New Yam Festival is that it marks the transition from the period of scarcity to the period of plenty. The period of scarcity, in religious terms, could be looked upon as the period of fasting, prayer, penance and mourning and the festival marks the period of resuscitation, of hope and plenty, a period of rejoicing.

Source: ''Standardizing Igbo Festivals'' by Nnabuenyi Ugonna in *Nigeria Magazine* 136 (1981), 28.

Ogwugwu Festival

Between the first and third months of the Igbo calendar year many important festivals are celebrated and although the planting season has begun there is still plenty of food. By the fourth month however not only are all the yams planted but those reserved are consumed and the period of scarcity sets in. In fact the fourth month has given a name to this period of scarcity which lasts until after the new yam festival in August/September. It is called Onwaino or Ugali.

Beginning from the end of the fifth month a series of festivals culminating in the new yam festival will be celebrated. These include *ime Ogwugwu* (Ogwugwu Festival). *Ogwugwu* is the madona of Igbo religion and the symbol of the Great Mother. She inspires both love and fear. She protects her children at all costs but can be ruthless in her anger. Ogwugwu Ukpo and Ogwugwu Okija, for instance, can destroy utterly anybody that swears falsely by them. On the other hand, it is believed that the goddess, Ogwugwu, can intercede most successfully for her wards before the council of spirits that is bent on doing harm to the wards. Ogwugwu goddess should not be confused with Nne Ala (Earth goddess). The Ogwugwu Festival is predictably a period of great celebration.

Source: ''Standardizing Igbo Festivals'' by Nnabuenyi Ugonna in *Nigeria Magazine* 136 (1981), 26.

Nigeria (Yoruba)

New Yam Festival

One of the most important crops of the Yoruba is yams. They are a staple in the Yoruba diet, and much depends upon their bounty. Because orisa, ancestors, and humans are mutually interrelated, all are involved in the success or failure of the crops. The harvest festival provides a context for the establishment and maintenance of these relationships; the roles of the people and the sacred powers are particularly important for the destiny of the crops.

One such festival is the New Yam festival, known in some parts of Yorubaland as Eje. In this annual festival the god of the sea, Malokun, plays an important role, but many other types and levels of religious power play a part as well. In fact, the entire range of religious power from the ancestors to the gods becomes involved in this celebration.

The festival lasts for two days and consists of a number of activities: purification rites, presentation rites, divining rites, and thanksgiving rites. On the first day it is important to ritually purify the areas in which the rites will take place. Two such places are the sacred grove and the sacred shrine. After these areas have been purified, the rest of the festival may proceed. The yams have already been taken to the oba's farm, where they have been placed in heaps. These yams must be presented in a ritual manner to the appropriate religious powers. Some of them are placed at the shrine of the orisa Malokun. Upon their arrival, which is announced in a loud voice, the people congregate together to joyously welcome the new harvest. A new year is about to be born, and the priest of the shrine prays it will be a good and successful one.

On the night of the first day of Eje, after the yams have been installed in the shrine, the people remain outside, where they give continual thanks to the religious powers generally and address the ancestors specifically, making offerings of palm wine and kola nuts to them.

But although the yams are already in the shrine, they have not yet been formally offered in sacrifice and have not played a role in divination. The ritual of presentation to the orisa involves a number of elements. First is the requirement that both oba and priests purify themselves by fasting throughout the day. On the morning of the second day the oba, dressed in a white garment, makes an offering of a white kola nut and a white pigeon and prays with the priests to Malokun. This is followed by a procession to the shrine, where the yams are now presented to the religious powers, namely, Malokun and the ancestors.

One of the high points of the festival is the divination rite that will determine the destiny of the life of the community, especially the success or failure of the crops in the following year. In this rite one of the recently harvested yams is taken and divided into two parts. They are cast, and if one falls face up and the other face down everybody is pleased, for this is a positive sign. If both fall either face downward or face upward there is concern, for it indicates problems ahead.

Another ceremony, also involving divination, then takes place in the other sacred area, the grove. The people all move in a procession to the grove, where, once again, a yam is divided and its two parts cast in an act of divination. And once again there is rejoicing if the signs are positive and concern if they are negative. The people and the priests then proceed to the palace, where they are met by the oba, who then joins the procession and leads them in a dance through the town. An important part of this dancing procession is the stops it makes at each of the shrines of the many divinities worshipped in the town. Sacrifices are made to the orisa venerated at each shrine. The fast of oba and priests is then broken, and a general celebration begins. The town has been purified, the yams have been presented; the future has been divined; the orisa and the ancestors have been served; and the new year has begun when new crops can be planted with confidence that the act of divination has ensured their destiny.

Source: *Religions of Africa: Traditions in Transformation* by E. Thomas Lawson. San Francisco: Harper & Row, 1984, pp. 70-71.

For more on the Yam Festival see: *Arrow of God* by Chinua Achebe. New York: John Day, 1967. (Account of the disasters that befall the chief priest of an Eastern Nigerian Ibo village, and the dilemma he faces when unable to announce the New Yam festival at the necessary time.)

Nigeria, Benin (Yoruba)

New Yam Festival at Ondo's shrine in Pobe

Movement 1: *The Placing of raw new yam at Ondo's shrine*

The new yam festival is an important festival in Pobe and every inhabitant is deeply involved in it. The festival begins at 8:00–9:00 p.m. the day before the ceremonies proper, and it usually falls in the month of August whenever the new yam appears. On the eve of the festival, a small yam tuber is provided. This yam must be removed from the ridge with hands, a knife or cutlass must not be used. It is then covered from the public eye and given to *Atele,* the officiating priest. *Atele* at night, without light, goes to place the yam tuber at Ondo's shrine paying homage to the deity saying that the placing of this new yam signals the beginning of a new year. He then asks *Ondo* to give protection, prosterity, happiness, wealth and health to the community, its *Oba* and chiefs.

Movement II *The placing of the boiled new yam at Ondo's shrine*

The sacrifice of the raw yam tuber always falls on the eve of the grand worship. Thus, the following day, when the worship might have been over, the head of *Elegbe ila* announces that the festival or sacrifice of the boiled yam to *Ondo* would take place in eight days time. Thus the festival coincides with the grand worship.

But late in the night two days after the placing of the raw yam, priests, Chiefs, and notables make for the shrine with large calabashes of yam, covering themselves up talking to nobody and carrying no light except swords. No gongs were sounded. On arrival at the shrine, the priest placing the boiled yam at *Ondo's* shrine says: *Tutu ni n'ejo sise ki n'ejo*—You alone eat the raw yam but the boiled one we can eat with you without fear.'' It is only then that they could begin to eat. It is taboo to eat yam before offering it to Ondo, the aftermath is death.

Movement III (*Eight days after*)

In the morning before the *Eegu* shrine, *bata igba* is beaten and gongs are sounded with frenzy calling the old men and women, chiefs, *elegbe ila* etc. to come. One by one they arrive, some carrying hoes; others their cutlasses and all begin to clear the path leading to the sluggish *Iseko* stream. As people are busy clearing the path, *Aro* appears, he is usually the last man to show up. He goes to the palace and out of the many yam tubers in the palace he takes three which he displays for everybody to see. On arrival at the *Iseko* stream, chiefs carrying their wands of office immerse them in the streams to cleanse them, those who have just used their hoes and cutlasses to clear the path to the stream also wash these implements. It is a symbolic gesture of washing away the yesteryear and of embracing the maiden year with all its blessings and joys. They then proceed to the other extreme of the *Ondo* grove running alongside the Islamic school. Although there are no weeds there, participants must pretend that they are really clearing the ground with their hoes. They also rake the air with their sticks. All this they do from *aitan ola* (the sacred refuse) via *Ita Pobe* (the market square) to the palace just right in front. They then clap their hands to tell the oba of their arrival and to greet him. The oba, comes out to wish his people a good festival and many more in the future. Then the people disperse home.

Movement IV: *Yam tubers as presents*

Each family depending on how many yam tubers they have reaped begin to give them out as presents. They send some to the *Oba,* to his chiefs, to priests and priestesses. Yams are also sent to parents, relatives friends, inlaws etc. On this occasion, the divisive issues of religious and political credo do not come in. Everybody sends out yams and receives sometimes even more than he gives out. It is the townspeople's version of the European custom of distributing cards during the Christmas and New Year periods.

Movement V: *Distribution of Yams*

In the evening of the distribution of yams, around 7 p.m. big yam pots are placed on the heath at the oba's palace, at the priests' and chiefs' houses. Children are then engaged to poke the fire till dawn. they are given very tiny yams to roast and eat when they are about their nocturnal duties.

The second day of the festival

In the morning chiefs, priests and priestesses go to the palace to cut the boiled yams into slices, put them in calabashes, pour palm oil on them and cover up the calabashes with their appropriate lids. Meanwhile the sweeping ritual is going on at the palace, the market square and the grove. The priestesses who are to fetch water must have been on their way carrying small pots or guards on their heads. They go to the same *Iseko* stream talking to nobody and meeting nobody on the way. They should be the first group to arrive at the stream to fetch the 'new' water, and nobody should help them lift their pots onto their heads. Having finished preparing the calabashes (*igba i Ketu*) at the palace, princes, priests, chiefs etc head for the grove and lay out these calabashes in front of the shrines, *Elegbaa* is the first to be given his own share by the chief priest, then it is *Okere's* turn. The chief priest, accompanied by a notable who will help him take one of the covered calabashes in and out of the shrine, goes in to pay homage and pour libation on the ground and sacrifice some yam, sucks palm-oil from his fingers and finally goes out. As usual, the *Okere* priest remains at a short distance from his female deity, he watches the rites going on. The chief priest, in the same way, offers morsels of yams to *Ondo* appealing to him to listen to the supplications of his people.

Okere's nominal role is again stressed at this point. He cannot at the grove worship his god but he can worship any other god(s) in his house. His title and the presence of his *orisa* at the grove are somewhat formalistic in an essentially patriarchal society. Nowadays, things are already losing their sacredness, worshippers are becoming too lazy to accept the demands of elaborateness in rituals. In actual fact, *Okere* has no business at the grove, he normally has no duty to perform there; even he should not be there at all. She is a farmstead goddess. Only when possessed does her priest come to the town screaming like the Greek Cassandra telling the townspeople his visions, and only when he goes back to the countryside or farmstead does his spiritual possession leave him.

On the festival day there are usually as many garnished calabashes as there are family lineages and rich influential people. The day is always a day of 'superfluity', of waste, of hillocks of yams with which eagles in the olden days used to regale themselves. And all the *Orisa* in the town are worshipped and given their share of yam suffused with palm oil.

The worshipping community now retire to the grove. At the grove are tortuous paths leading to the innermost clearings. In each of them must have been placed, calabashes of yams. *Elegbe ila,* the notables, priests and priestesses withdraw into their respective clearings to eat. Everybody eats to his full. Then the people begin to throw morsels of yams at one another. This is not fight or violence, it is a gesture of joy in the middle of abundance. Old men and women are all involved in the throwing ritual. But nowadays the custom of throwing yam morsels has been vitiated by a certain person called Bangudu. Instead of throwing yam morsels, as a ritual reciprocal gesture, at a fellow worshipper he would throw angular stones. In his iconoclastic impulses he has been followed by some rascally young ones. The erstwhile traditional ritual gesture of nature's abundance and exuberance has been turned into a bilious pitched battle which outlasts the festivals. Old people have reacted against this profanation; the malpractice has been somewhat abandoned. When a hot morsel hits you hard on the back, you now reciprocate with volleys of slaps or blows. This seemingly hostile gesture is accepted by *Ondo.* Bacchanalian exuberance and intoxication is a sign of well-being, *'Kayo Kanya'*—regale oneself to intoxication—as a popular expression goes.

The rounds of the *aposi* are now counted; the yam festival now follows the regular grand worship. Sacrifices of yam are offered in turns to the gods.

In the evening, people dance *Efe*(') till dawn. At 6.00 a.m. or so, women are sent away from the arena, *Gelede* drums are taken in and the smallish drums called *Asiele* is beaten. Women can dance to this drum but it is essentially meant for men. In turns men come out and dance alone for some time amidst cheers from the participants. Priests and priestesses also present here, dance a little. The chief priest alone sings and they all withdraw but the gathering continues dancing until they are tired.

The following *Obada* market (the royal market) which the people anxiously wait for is meant to serve as a relaxation. The market is held but at about 2.00 p.m., *aje* drums call them back to the dancing arena. It is a dance meant only for priests and priestesses and their novices. After their departure, the *'Omo Ode'*—those who have no real chieftancy titles but who are nonetheless important in the spiritual live-wire of the community come out to dance *'Awo'*.

Eight days after, boiled yams are prepared and taken to the grove. The arena is swept as usual. In a circular form of about four metres radius, priests and priestesses litter thick layers of yam morsels. *Ondo* is then called upon to protect them and hear their prayers. As usual, *aposi* is beaten; participants begin to dance round the yam littered circle. Between the 9th and 13th rounds of *Aposi,* any of the three priestly gods is possessed, or even all of them are possessed. They divulge their visions and that would be the end of the worship.

This particular ritual is repeated, the third time eight days after. On the second day of the last ritual comes the *'Kari igba Ko'*—the end of the calabashes festival. *Babalawos* are called in to the place to probe into the future by consulting *Orunmila* and tell the community what the new year has in stock. The role of the *Babalawos* brings in the grand finale of the festival. It is they who see into the future and say what sacrifices to perform to ward off all evils.

The grand worship and the low worship, as usual, alternate with each other till the advent of the dry yam festival which usually falls five months after the new yam festival. In the case of the dry yam festival, *Gelede* is performed at three intervals. There are no *Asiele, Aje Awo* but all the other ritual details are present. And in all these worships, Ondo's relevance to the spiritual cohesion, socio-cultural integrity of the community is always emphasised.

Source: ''Ritual Drama and Yam Festival in Western Nigeria: The Case of Ondo in Pobe'' by B. M. Ibi Tokun in *Nigeria Magazine* 145 (1983), 3-9.

Nigeria, Oyo State (Yoruba)

Egbodo Oba Ooni

24 days after the ''Oro Ayigun'' festival comes this festival. This festival is very significant and impressive. It comes up late in June every year. It is a festival of Ifa oracle. It is the Yoruba oracle of divination and of herbal medicine. Ifa priests are the interpreters of ''Orunmila''. The festival involves the great mystery of Ifa at the sacred grove of ''Igbo Ijawe Ifa'' situated at ''Osara shrine''. This festival of the New Yam marks the beginning of the Yoruba calendar year. The colourful robes of the priests ''*Awos*'' include rich hand woven clothes. They also wear a kind of sacred chain of office with triangular beaded pendant hanging from neck on beaded cord, showing the rank of the priests' offices. They also carry horse tails ''*Irukere Akun*'' the leader of the ''*Awos*'', the priests is the Araba of Ifa, who leads all ritual processions and sacrifices in the shrine at ''Oke

tase.'' A total of eleven ''*Awos*'' (priests) take significant positions during this festival, they include the following in order of their seniority:—The Araba, the Agbongbon; the Akode; the Aseda; the Megbon; the Agasinyowa; the Afedigba; the Tedimola; the Adifalu; the Oluwo Gidi—Ogbo and the Olore Iharefa.

''Ilaja Isu Titun''

This festival takes place annually on the same day with the Oke Agbonniregun festival at Ijio. The chief priest of this festival is Chief Obajio. It is in commemoration of the date on which the new yams are officially approved for introduction to the city of Ile-Ife by Oranfe.

Igun Efon Festival

Obalufon was the son of Olofin Osangangan Obamakin. He was popularly known as ''Obalufon Ogbo-gbo-dirin''. He grew to a very old age, and was one of the reigning Oba Ooni of Ile-Ife. He was deified after his death and has since then been worshipped as one of the deities of Ile-Ife. He was the first Oba Ooni to wear beaded crown. The festival of ''IGUN EFON'' has since been earmarked in commemoration of the time he ''Obalufon'' ate new yam. During this festival, the Oba Ooni will send to Chief Obalara (Obalufon's descendant) one cock, two dried fishes, rats and four ''abata'' kolanuts for ritual ceremony to Obalufon.

Ogijan Festival

This festival is to commemorate the period the powerful Prince ''Ogijan'' used to eat new yams. In recognition of the powerful position held by that great prince, all the Dukes and Duchesses known as ''*soko* and *Wagbodu*'' virtually observe the festival annually.

Igun ''Ekun'' ''Ajinida'' Festival

This festival is observed annually by the reigning Oba Ooni in commemoration of the past Oba Oonis. During this festival, all the princes and princesses are feasted.

Igun Luwo Festival

It is a festival set aside to commemorate the time of eating new yam by the powerful Queen who first tarred the Oduduwa Empire with potshiels. She was very wealthy. In remembrance of her deed, the women in the ''Owodo'' Compound in Okerewe slaughter rams in the shrine of the great Queen. All the men of the quarters also have the day as a special day for jubilation. On the day of the festival, the Oba Ooni will send one ram through Chief Eredumi to the ''Igbo-Odi'' to be sacrificed to all the past Oonis. Following this festival is the Olojo festival.

Source: ''Ife Traditional Festivals: A Dialectical Hermenuetics'' in *Nigeria Magazine* 55 (3) (July-September 1987), 43-44.

Egungun Festival in Oyo State

Most Yoruba celebrate their yearly Egungun festival during the short dry season between rains. . . . In Oyo state, when the masks come out, it has already been raining for three months and the harvesting of first crops is not far distant. . . . Suddenly the clamor of Bata drums announces the visit of a great Agba masquerade to the owner of the house, who will receive the impressive guest in a private shrine room on the first floor. You jump up and peer over the stairwell. Maybe you catch a glimpse of its bulk or hear its thick, gravelly voice bestowing blessings, but chances are all you'll see are its numerous retainers. Evenings, along the street will come acrobats and satirists of the cult. They perform—turn themselves inside out, dragging their strange sackcloth in the dust. Some dart erratically after pretended miscreants. They are accompanied by young men wielding branched sticks flexible as willow wands. They are like trick-or-treat pranksters. You dash them small amounts of money, and they dance off to the adjoining compound. Then the day comes when the great old ones all convene to greet the traditional ruler, the Oba. Several Bata drum threesomes are playing at once. The yard is so tightly packed with celebrants that it is difficult to see what's going on. From the crotch of a nearby tree looking down: their huge cowrie-studded heads rise like snowy hillocks above the colorfully coiffed crowds.

It is these great old ones, the Agba Egungun, those who carry heavy ''loads'' on their heads, who are of primary metaphysical importance in the cult. . . . These living ghosts of lineage founders,. . .have names, which permit a distinguishable ''character'' to be acted out by the hidden impersonator. Even propped on poles in a hidden shrine room awaiting the next outing, these Agba costumes get to seem like weird great-uncles, to be recognized and greeted with respectful affection. The Agba I know in this way are Jenju (A-restless-person-who-devours-in-the-bush), Ologbojo (The-bard-who-controls-rain), and grandmother L'Aiye Wu, Egungun Ode, Orisha Oya (Witches-please-me, Egungun-of-the-bush, Orisha-Oya).

They come on like beggars in a grand comic opera: top to bottom accomodated in a cumbrous multilayered garment made up of panels of bright cloth, some of it patchworked, edged with red rick-rack borders that express both lightning energy and the dynamism of surface boundaries. Some of the strips are pure ''Grant-I-may-live-long'' crimson. This red is apotropaic against death, empowering their defiant return to this world. Some of the strips are snakeskins and pelts of powerful animals like the leopard. Still others—the blue brocades, the purple velvets, the gold satins—signal lineage wealth. Although the lappeted construction of this spirit tent in motion is thought by some connoisseurs of Egungun to derive from the palanquins in which Bariba kings used to make concealed public appearances, although the stunning appliquéd segments and the borders are tributes to the sartorial imaginations of Hausa tailors hired to make them, whatever the artistic models—all are at the service of the spiritual conception to be realized. When the attendants clear space for these costumes to dance in the open, strips of the very fabric of existence fly out whirligig-fashion in praise of Oya. What seemed strata of something oppressively solid are revealed to be naught but an explosion of boundaries.

The faceless face of these senior Egungun is a rectangular

window covered with woven mesh, often black-and-white striped, occasionally beaded. Atop the head a mask or masks of clay or wood may be set among spiky animal horns. Alternatively, animal skulls thickly encrusted with dried pond mud, blood, indigo, and herbal medicines may be displayed together with horns and clusters of small sticks (like Roman fasces) on a sort of mortarboard tray—as if these masquerades were carrying summations of sacrificial offerings. (The animal skulls are most often of the monkey sacred to the cult.) Here and there brilliant white cowrie shells decorate the "offerings." There is an alternate domed head construction: a mound of resinous medicine so thickly paved with cowries that the beholder imagines cells of a giant brain beneath it.

Attendants of the masquerades keep back the crowd with switches known as *isan,* made from the flexible stems of the *atori* bush, which are of more importance than at first appears. Unlike the switches that African elders routinely pick up to discipline unruly boys, the *isan* are ritually incised. They dramatize the existence of a repellent magnetic field already created by the apotropaic cloth (which in the old days it was death to touch) and intensified by chants activating medicinal preparations applied to the carrier during his costuming.

Source: *Oya; In Praise of the Goddess* by Judith Gleason. Boston & London: Shambhala, 1987, pp. 77-79.

Norway

Tying a harvest cross

It was sometime during the eighteenth century. One autumn Old Tore and Marte, who lived on Austaana in Kvitseid, had much trouble getting help to bring in the harvest. Their big, beautiful field was so ripe that the grain was dropping to the ground, and there was not a single person they could hire to do the mowing. They thought they might have to ask their neighbors for help, as they often did in those days whenever they were in a hurry with a job.

So Tore and Marte brewed and baked, as if they were preparing for a great feast. They brewed in the workhouse, and the evening before the neighbors were expected to come and help, the beer stood ready in a vat. But during the night, they heard the sound of cutting and tying in the field, and the sound of many feet shuffling and walking in the workhouse. And they heard voices mumbling and talking:

> Everybody can mow,
> but nobody can tie the cross.
> We tie it straight,
> and soon we can quit.

The next morning the folk on Austaana got a big surprise—the whole big field had been cut. But the sheaves had been tied in a way that no one in the village had seen before. Ever since that time, it has been called a "straight tie." The usual tie was in the shape of a cross, but the *tusse* could not tie that way.

When Tore and Marte went into the workhouse to fetch the beer, they found it was all gone except for a little bit of the dregs. The *tusse* had drunk the beer in payment for their labor. But when Marte flushed the dregs from the vat, she found three or four silver spoons on the bottom, which the *tusse* had left there. The spoons have been passed down on the farm from generation to generation, and they are engraved with Tore's name.

One of the few fixed epic patterns in legends about the invisible aiding humans concerns the harvesting of the grain. The invisible cut the grain, but they cannot tie the sheaves in the shape of the cross because of the religious power associated with that shape. Traditionally sheaves were tied crosswise until the more efficient straight tie was introduced from Jutland, Denmark. In legendary tradition, this innovation is attributed to the *tusse*.

(Collected by Kjetil A. Flatin in Seljord, Telemark (Norway). Printed in Flatin, *Tussar og trolldom* (1930), 41-42.)

Source: *Scandinavian Folk Belief and Legend* edited by Reimund Kuideland and Henning K. Sehmsdorf. Minneapolis: Univ. of Minnesota Press, 1988, pp. 223-224.

Potato Digging Vacation

Each fall a vacation period was held in Norway for all school children to turn out and help get in the potato crop. This was called "Potato-Digging Vacation" and was looked forward to by the children as their last holiday before Christmas. To town children, of course, it actually was a vacation. For farm children it meant hard work.

Boredom during potato-digging vacation, c. 1920

"Potato-Digging Vacation" began with rain and ended with rain, and the boys were bored and cross. They could not find anything to do themselves, and nothing that Mother and Thea suggested was any fun.

"You ought to be ashamed of yourselves." Thea said. "In the country the children have to go out and dig potatoes rain or shine. You don't even do so much as help straighten up the garden for your mother."

What she said was so true. At all the farms around the little town, grownups and children alike were out in the muddy potato fields, bent over the long rows of potato vines, with gunny sacks over their heads to ward off the pouring rain.

Source: *Happy Times in Norway* by Sigrid Undset. New York: Alfred A. Knopf, 1942, p. 3.

Papua New Guinea (Bundi)

Pig Festival

One of the largest and most complex events in the Bundi area is the pig festival. It would be futile to list all the events that take place during a pig festival in an attempt to illustrate the magnitude of such an occasion. It is true, however, that marriage ceremonies, initiation ceremonies, bride-price payments, *tu poi* payments, *kuieiagi* payments, trade and exchange, courtship, menstruation ceremonies, sing sings and presentations may all occur during the festive period. Behind the scenes there are myriad discussions and debates and complex networks in which fortunes are amassed, redistributed and amassed again. Each man in a tribe has a number of trading partners to whom he is in debt or credit. The pig festival, therefore, is also a time when every man in the tribe must endeavour to settle his outstanding debts.

One of four Bundi sing sing types: *Sing sing kanam*

The *kanam* is one of the most strenuous of all the *sing sings* and is very pleasing for the spectators. Originating in the Madang area, the *kanam* was traded up through the Ramu to the Bundi people. The word *kanam* means 'acting' and it depicts the life of the animals and birds that live in the dense forest. Through the *kanam* the dancers show how animals live and move, and how the sun, moon and water affect their behaviour. The *kanam* begins at night, and the performance corresponds to the habits of certain animals at that particular time of day or night. So the dance changes continually as the night passes and breaks into day.

The dancers usually dress with many leaves and few feathers, as the violent activity of the *kanam* rapidly destroys the plumes. A solid beat from the *kundu* drums accompanies the actions of the dancers. Females also perform in the *sing sings,* but the male dancers play the major roles. According to the Ramu people, the *kanam* may be performed at any time, but in the Bundi society *kanam* is usually performed at large parties, at weddings and at pig festivals.

Source: *Bundi: The Culture of a Papau New Guinean People* by David G. Fitz-Patrick and John Kimbuna. New York: Ryebuck Publishing, 1983, pp. 106, 129, 126. (See chapter 6, "Sing Sing," pp. 125-129.)

Papua New Guinea (Kapauku Papuan)

Juwo/Pig Feast

The Juwo, pig feast, c. 1962

By far the most spectacular and elaborate Kapauku ceremony is *juwo,* "the pig feast." This is a rather protracted affair comprising several major events and innumerable night dancing parties. The whole cycle of a pig feast usually lasts several months. It starts with the decision of a rich man, preferably a headman, to sponsor a feast.

As the day of the main and final feast draws close, the dances in the *ema* become more and more frequent. Some nights are reserved for the women, when they dance and sing the *ugaa* songs, and the men provide light with the torches. The dancing intensity culminates during the night preceding *juwo degii naago* "the main feast." During the first half of the night the men dance and sing, and the women provide the torchlight; in the second half of the night the roles are reversed. After sunrise, as soon as the heavy dew on the grass and foliage dries out, the sponsors of the feast appear with their pigs. The animals are slaughtered with bows and arrows, or are sometimes clubbed to death, and the butchering begins. The cut pieces of meat and entrails are stored in small partitions in the back of the *juwo owa,* "the feast house," where the people usually go in order to buy it from the pig owners.

A Kapauku pig feast is an impressive affair. On such an occasion there may be as many as 2,000 visitors, and the slaughtered pigs may be counted in the hundreds. The trade turnover, in terms of shell money, may be quite considerable. Generally it can be said that the greater the number of visitors and slaughtered pigs, the greater the prestige the sponsors of the feast will acquire. Successful feasts are talked over and remembered by the people for years. Because of its social and political consequences a Kapauku pig feast, although a trading ceremony in nature, surpasses in its significance the scope of economy and becomes one of the central events around which Kapauku public affairs are patterned.

Source: *The Kapauku Paplans of West New Guinea* by Leopold Pospisil. New York: Holt, Rinehart and Winston, 1963, pp. 71-73, 76-77.

Poland

Dozynki (Okrezne)

There is also in Poland a secular harvest festival called "Dozynki", or, more rarely, "Okrezne". When the harvesting is over, the farmworkers gather around a small stack of grain which has been left standing in the field and celebrate an ancient rite known as "the decoration of the quail" or "the decoration of the goat". The grain is divided into three parts, each part is plaited like a braid and the three braids tied together to form a tripod. The ground under the tripod is covered with a cloth of pure flax linen and on this cloth are placed a loaf of bread, some salt and several copper coins, from immemorial times the symbols of affluence and a plentiful harvest. Thereupon the harvesters proceed to plough the ground around the tripod. The ploughing may be literal or symbolic. If the latter, a young girl who has worked in the fields for the first time this harvest is swung by hands and feet above and around the stack of grain, "ploughing" it, and being initiated at the same time.

After the "decoration of the quail", the harvesters march under song and music to the home of the landowner. They bear with them large wreaths fashioned of grain and wild flowers; sometimes branches of hazelnut are also woven into the wreaths. At the house the master and mistress with their children and guest await the procession. The wreaths are presented and then hung in the hall of the manor where they remain until the following harvest. Then the master, or his eldest son, dances with the girl who has most distinguished herself during the harvest; and the mistress dances with the most industrious of the men reapers.

After that, all are invited to a supper consisting usually of meat, bread, cakes, apples, brandy and the traditional Polish honey-wine.

In the district of Cracow the woman who binds the last sheaf is known as the Baba, or old woman. She is wrapped up in the sheaf so that only her head projects, and then taken in a harvest wagon to the farm house where she is drenched with water by the whole family. She remains in the sheaf till the harvest dance is over and all through the year she is called Baba.

In Poland, as in most other countries, farm machinery has largely replaced manual labor and incidentally has to a considerable extent done away with the old colorful customs. In an effort to preserve them and to renew their importance, President Moscicki for some years celebrated "Dozynki" at his country estate at Spala. On these occasions persons from all sections of Poland gathered in the spacious grounds at Spala to pay homage to the nation's foremost farmer and President. The magazine "Poland" in the issue for October 1930 thus described the Dozynki procession of that year:

> "At one o'clock on Sunday the President went out on the balcony of the palace to receive the representatives of the various peasant groups. In spite of a steady downpour of rain this file of determined folk passed before their Chief Harvester for more than an hour. During the first half hour, delegations from all over Poland filed passed, dressed in their distinctive and colorful costumes. The larger groups were preceded by orchestras which have played those stirring melodies which have come down to them from generation to generation. Then came peasants from different sections of Poland bearing wreaths, and following these a group of harvesters representing Poland as a whole. This last delegation was led by a woman who wore a wreath on her head and carried in her hands a live cock, an old Slavonic symbol of good will. Threshers added to the rural effect, and a peasant orchestra played a rhythmic accompaniment for the procession. Next passed a wagon driven by a farmer from Spala itself and bearing three bags of flour and a kneading trough. An old woman proudly carried on a wooden tray her own manufacture, a loaf of bread covered with a linen cloth. Then came a Wolyniak with a comb of honey on the same kind of tray. Next were groups from Spala and from Cracow and the Tatra district, the latter wearing the brightly embroidered woolen costume of the Goral. All through the entire procession the President stood there in the pouring rain. He conversed briefly with the leader of each delegation, and received graciously from each an offering of wreaths and bread, visible tokens of Nature's bounty.
>
> "Next the band struck up martial music and groups filed past symbolizing various phases of agriculture. Farmer Polescuk, clad in rough linen, led, driving his two horses hitched to a plow that was held by a robust peasant. An elderly woman in Kurpian dress, adorned with amber beads of her own manufacture followed, carrying a consecrated candle. Three sowers, a Wolyniak, a Lubliniak, and a Kujawiak, were next in order. Four young boys dressed to represent the four most characteristic districts of Poland came next. Wearing the colors of the Cracow district, a man drove past with a harrow. Reapers and binders from different sections displayed their costumes. Three peasant woman, a Wolynianka, a Lowiczanka, and a Goralka, followed with their rakes. To give a more modern touch, a mechanical binder was drawn past by two horses. A horse rake, still quite a novelty in Poland, and driven by a brilliantly attired peasant, continued the procession. A ladder wagon filled with hay brought this part of the program to a close. The girls rode on the hay and a group of Mazovian peasants surrounded the wagon.
>
> "At three-thirty in the great hall near the stadium the ceremony of delivery of ornate wreaths by the delegates of the districts took place. Among the scores presented were some of real artistic merit. The Wielkopolski wreath was adorned with an eagle artistically made of heads of grain. Ancient village songs were sung as an accompaniment to the ceremony of presentation. Especially stirring was the song of the full-voiced Wolynians, whose magnificent rendition was worthy of a trained choir."

Source: *Foreign Festival Customs* by Marian Schibsby & Hanny Cohrsen. New York: American Council for Nationalities Service, 1974, pp. 55-56.

Ponape

The Ponape feast as a means of acquiring title

The polity of Ponape, a high island in the Eastern Caroline Islands, was organised into five states before colonial contact. Each state, called *wehi,* was (and remains) a territorial entity organised politically in two ranked lines of chiefs. The highest ranking chief, the ritual chief, is the Nahnmwarki, head of one line. The other line is headed by the Nahnken, who is more of an implementer of chiefly policy, and who can intercede with the Nahnmwarki on behalf of people of lower rank. Each status in each of these two lines is labelled, i.e., is a title. The Nahnmwarki controls the allocation of state titles, and he can award and remove almost any title at his discretion.

Every title is gotten and maintained through personal effort. Men aspiring to higher titles get them through competition with other aspirants, titles being awarded by section and state chiefs in recognition of extraordinary service and achievement. Typically, competition is channelled through feasts, either section or state feasts. Although feasts are not the only avenue of competition in rendering service, they are certainly the best-documented ones. Men compete in providing kava root, pigs, yams, pit breadfruit, and other agricultural products for the chiefs of these feasts. The chiefs will, in turn, redistribute most (but not all) of the produce in the form of food and drink during the feast, the size of an individual's portion being proportional to his rank. The spectacular size of one's yam or a new variety of yam presented to the chief may so distinguish one's effort that the chief rewards that effort with a higher title. The higher one's title, the more deference one gets from an increasing number of lower-ranked people.

The winter months of each year are a time of intensive feasting on Ponape. Carefully cultivated yams, taro, and tapioca are harvested. Pigs, dogs, and chickens are bought, exchanged, and slaughtered. Debts are incurred and debts paid as people gather the items of food that will, with good fortune and good timing, bring ritual titles to some and validate titles for others. Some of the feasts are statewide, and one can hear the exuberant cries of men and women as they stand amid a pile of food on the back of a pick-up truck on the way to the feasting site. Other feasts are more local, quieter affairs involving section (but still prestigious) titles. While the mood is always festive, vibrant, and playful, underlying the celebrations for many people is an intensity that is deadly serious—their positions in an ancient social order is at stake.

During a feast in Kiti in 1977, the Nahnmwarki received a pig weighing 375 pounds. Its market value at the time was $1.10 per pound. The Nahnmwarki held the pig back from slaughter, as is his right. One man asked the Nahnmwarki for the pig, giving him $50. The Nahnmwarki assented, and the man took the pig. I commented to the informants (five of them) that it was a strange sort of sale that lost the Nahnmwarki over $350. The informants denied that it was a sale, explaining that the money was a token of the man's intention to give a feast for the Nahnmwarki within the next two years.

It was not a market exchange, in other words. The money was not being used as a general purpose measure of value as is typical of market exchange. The dollars had become, in this context, "special purpose money".

Source: "Strange Feast: Negotiating Identities on Ponape" by Michael D. Lieber in *The Journal of the Polynesian Society,* 93 (2) (June 1984), 141-173.

Roumania

Corn Husking

Curătat (corn husking), c. 1930

"The husking of the corn. To-morrow night, or perhaps the night after, Gheorghe Tamas will have gathered all his corn. All the village will go to help him clean it. Soon all the corn will be in, then every night there will be a *curatat.* You will see."

At the entrance to Gheorghe's yard I paused a moment in the shadows. Along one side of it stood his house, and across the moonlit yard facing the roadway was a barn open on one side. On its wall was a lamp throwing into grotesque relief the men and women crowded on a vast heap of corncobs. In a corner two *tigani* made music, one, with a fiddle, was standing singing and swaying, the other, half-hidden, plucked at a lute. The movements of the huskers as they tore the cobs free from the sheaths and threw then out on the growing pile in the yard made a symphony of dark, dancing shadows.

But never for a moment did the work flag. Sometimes when the *tigani* played a favourite song, we beat time with the corn cobs. The chatter and the singing went on while the heap on which we sat sank lower and lower as the pile of naked cobs mounted in the yard. Round and round went the *tuica,* merrier and merrier were the workers.

> Then comes autumn, rich with vintage,
> Happily the world rejoices,
> He who works will want for nothing
> When the heavy winter falls.

sang the *tigan.* Then lest anyone should think he was becoming serious, he roared with laughter and, throwing down his fiddle, began to act a two part comedy, changing his voice back and forth from a deep bass to a thin falsetto while his companion strummed an accompaniment.

Ten, eleven, twelve o'clock, the hours slipped by. Many of the people had been at the husking for two hours before I had come. Surely Gheorghe Tamas would have enough and to spare for his mamaliga and his bread. But the fun and good humour never abated. What they were doing for Gheorghe Tamas to-night he and others would be doing for them for many nights to come. No money passes for the labour but to the *tigani.* Gheorghe was paying for them; and we were there to help him, hired for the songs, for the pleasure of gathering together in good company and for the dancing presently. To-morrow night one of us will be paying the *tigani,* while Gheorghe comes with his family to help another's husking. So it will go on all round the village till every one's corn is safely unsheathed and stored.

Source: *Romanian Furrow* by D. J. Hall. London: George G. Harrap, 1933, pp. 51-53.

Sarawak (Berawan)

Decline of the Bungan harvest festival

[In February 1973,] the days prior to the festival were busy with preparations, principally to ensure that there would be enough food and rice wine. Early on the appointed day, women were busy setting up tables at two places on the longhouse veranda, both decorated with cloths, artificial flowers, and valuable brassware. The resemblance to an altar was obvious. On the tables were those offerings that Sadi Pejong enumerates at the beginning of his prayer—special delicacies, rice wine, tobacco. By nine o'clock about fifty people were seated around the table outside Sadi Pejong's room, much less than the total Bungan congregation but including the heads of most households. Other adherents joined in later in the day. The proceedings began with a prayer by Sadi Pejong, the prayer that is recorded in this chapter. It was the longest that I ever heard, and dealt exhaustively with all aspects of longhouse welfare. It was received attentively, in contrast to the irreverent chatter that often accompanies prayers at Long Teru. The atmosphere was indeed similar to a prayer meeting of the Christians, but that was to change as the day wore on.

One distinctly non-Christian element was the sacrificial chicken, which Sadi Pejong waved about by its feet during his prayer, charging it with messages for both the Creator Spirit and Bungan together. This combination distinguishes Sadi Pejong's version of Bungan from that of neighboring Kayan and Kenyah adherents. The latter have retired their male supreme deities, who are regarded as having little interest in the affairs of men anymore, and address their prayers instead to the friendly figure of "grandmother Bungan." If Sadi Pejong had done the same, he would have been left with a goddess lacking a counterpart in

Berawan cosmology. His compromise was to retain the properly Berawan Creator Spirit in addition to Bungan, and indeed to give him priority over her. Lesser spirit agencies, usually talked about in terms of the harm that they might do, were not addressed directly. Instead, the Creator and Bungan were asked to intervene to control them. The ancestral spirits, so prominent in the prayers of papi' lamèng at Long Teru, were inconspicuous in Sadi Pejong's prayer.

Once he had completed the prayer and sacrificed the chicken, Sadi Pejong beckoned other leading men in the community to join him. This they did with gusto, raising their voices to a crescendo of prayer, and finally merging them in a loud humming noise. This is the sound that the crowd at a party makes to encourage some individual who is currently the center of attention to down his glass of rice wine in one go. The procedure was repeated five times, causing everyone to become more animated. Bottles of rice wine circulated freely among the crowds until it was time to move over to the other table of offerings. This table was set up outside the room of Sadi Pejong's most important backer, Sadi Ulau, a man of impeccable pedigree who nevertheless preferred to let others take the lead in day-to-day affairs. There the prayers were repeated, first by Sadi Pejong alone (but briefly this time), and then by the senior men together, who were joined by a couple of latecomers. Everyone drank more rice wine before the party moved off to a third location, inside the apartment of a staunchly Bungan family. The party traveled from there to a fourth location, and then to a fifth, always saying prayers—though successively less formal at each stop—and always drinking plenty of rice wine.

By early afternoon an easy sociality was well established, with knots of people wandering from room to room to sample the food prepared for the occasion, to drink, and to chat. The early starters, Sadi Pejong included, retired to take a nap before the evening's events, but not before a pig had been sacrificed with due ceremony before the *kaju uran* (*kaju* means "wood," *uran* is untranslatable). This mysterious structure, mentioned several times by Sadi Pejong in his prayer, consisted of a carved post set up outside the longhouse in front of the apartment of Sadi Ulau. The original *kaju uran* was built by a prestigious ancestor of Sadi Ulau, who had received the inspiration for it in a dream. The structure has been renewed every decade or so, in effect proclaiming the superior social status of its owners.

That evening, and far into the night, kerosene lanterns burned brightly along the veranda. An elaborate party had been organized with all manner of games to amuse young and old. Despite the disapproving presence of a Christian missionary, almost everyone was successfully drawn into the festivities. Over a filled glass, convert and conservative alike agreed that the only important value was neighborliness. The festivities continued the next day. Though the festival of Bungan was completed, it was followed by a wedding, and then a *kumaan selamat*, initiating an informal ritual season.

Source: *Where Are You Spirits* by Peter Metcalf. Washington and London: Smithsonian, 1989, pp. 217-219.

Papi' lamèng food sharing

In 1972, the people of Long Teru decided to coordinate papi lamèng with a state-wide public holiday called Gawai Dayak, which is intended to honor interior folk. There is, of course, no reason why upriver farmers should concern themselves with a bank holiday, but there was a desire to participate, however indirectly, in a national event. In subsequent years, the coordination has not been repeated, indicating a progressive disenchantment with state politics.

The prayers in this chapter were made on the previous day, near the mouth of the Bunok stream. After some confusion, with people changing their minds about whether to come or not, a canoe set out with a dozen passengers, including Tama Jok and Tama Aweng, our prayer makers, and Gumbang Lawai, who is the son-in-law of the last major leader of the Long Teru community, Oyang Ajang, and the son of the leader before him, Penghulu Lawai. Gumbang Lawai is the obvious person to emerge as the next major leader of Long Teru, but he spends much of his time away earning money in the lumber camps. Nevertheless, he is the man entrusted with supervising the fishing operations in Bunok. The canoe also contained provisions for the event.

When we arrived at the chosen spot at about noon, a prayer station was rapidly constructed. Tama Aweng was the first to make piat, but his prayer was split into two parts. First he prayed, waving a chicken around. Then Tama Jok spoke, using the same chicken. When Tama Aweng finally immolated the bird, he began his prayer anew over a pig that lay trussed at his feet. . . . almost everybody present joins in, producing a veritable crescendo of píat in the moments before the pig was decapitated. Its blood was splashed on the sticks of the prayer station, augmented with that of a couple more chickens, and dabbed onto the participants.

After this climax, the tensions evaporated. A fire was lit so the pig could be roasted on the spot. Unfortunately, it began to rain while the cooking was in progress, and we made a rather miserable picnic of half-cooked pork and pungent rice wine. On the way back, Gumbang stopped at several fishing sites along the Bunok to see if all was well. One or two showed evidence of illegal manipulation of the river bed to increase catches at other people's expense. Gumbang waded around in the river, pulling out driftwood that may or may not have been stuck into the riverbed on purpose. There was a lot of joking directed at those suspected of cheating, but I was warned not to say anything about this back at the longhouse. An unsupported charge would cause much bad feeling. We arrived back at the longhouse after sundown to find festivities in full swing.

On the next day, perhaps a dozen men made prayers in front of different tapo'. The contents of their prayers were entirely similar to those offered at Long Bunok, and all displayed skill at píat. The recordings are hard to make out, however, because of the noisy, excited crowds that surrounded every speaker. At some stations, old swords and shields and other military equipment were stacked and sprinkled with blood, so as to gain further strength from the spirits. At climactic moments, women brought water to splash on the crowd. . . .

While all this was in progress outside, a crowd inside, mostly women, took this auspicious opportunity to chase malign influences from the longhouse. They began at the downriver end of the house, standing shoulder to shoulder in a line, each person armed with a canoe paddle or a rice pounder. At a signal, they advanced in a phalanx, pounding furiously on the raised wooden floor of the house. As they passed by each room, a contingent would fall out to sweep through it too, and then rejoin the main body. This numbing din is intended to scare away all evil spirits. Three times they swept up and down the veranda.

The last sacrifice occurred outside the room of Gumbang Lawai at about noon. The victim was of the most valuable kind, a large black pig. Several voices were raised in píat, and a general splashing of water followed. When the final climax was over, people drifted away to resume drinking in one or another room of the longhouse.

Source: *Where Are You/Spirits* by Peter Metcalf. Washington and London, Smithsonian Institution Press, 1989, pp. 99-102.

Sierra Leone

Awoojoh

Thanksgiving in Sierra Leone may come at any time of the year. The Awoojoh is a feast denoting gratitude for some good fortune. The thanks are directed to the spirits of the ancestors, whom both Christians and other religionists regard as having a special interest in them and a usually benevolent effect upon their luck.

The practice of holding a thanksgiving feast originated with the Yoruba, who came to Sierra Leone from Nigeria. But Christian Creoles and Muslim Akus also give them. Because these are very elaborate occasions, it requires a person of some substance to put one on. One of our Creole friends gave a memorable Awoojoh after two notable events in his life: First, he had just got a very good job and second, he had been thrown from a motorcycle without being killed.

The guests include all of one's friends and relatives and, in a small community, almost the whole village as well. The day begins with a family visit to the relatives' graves, where a libation—fresh water or liquor—is poured and the dead are invited to the gathering. Two kola nuts, one red and one white, are split and the four pieces cast upon the grave. The way they fall can be read as a message from the ancestors. For example, a friendly ancestral nod may be indicated if two pieces of kola nut fall with the hollow sides up and two with the hollow sides down. Then everyone will clap hands and cry, "Thank God!"

Similar rites at the graveside may be performed at other times, such as on Good Friday, Easter, Christmas and New Year's Day. The graves are first decorated and tended. Then follow the libation, prayers, and speeches addressed to the dead.

At an Awoojoh, the family returns to the house from the cemetary and in the course of the ensuing conversation, any family quarrels will be settled. This is an essential preliminary to the feast.

Meanwhile, of course, the cooking has been underway for hours, if not days. A sheep and some chickens will have been slaughtered and mountains of rice, beans, plantains, onions, peppers, tomatoes, sweet potatoes and other vegetables will have been laid in. Supplies of palm oil, palm wine, sweet wine, beer and, perhaps, rum are on hand. The centerpiece of the great meal is a particularly elaborate stew, "cooked for the dead."

When all the food is ready, a portion of this main dish is set out for the ancestors. The eldest member of the family and the person who is giving the feast address the hovering spirits. A part of the ancestral serving may be thrown out for the vultures, who are an embodiment of departed souls. Then the general eating and drinking commence.

In addition to this stew, an Awoojah will undoubtedly feature such popular African dishes as fried bean cakes, fried plantains and rice bread. From Mrs. Muriel Davies of Sierra Leone, we have this recipe for Awoojoh Beans:

AWOOJOH BEANS

2 cups cooked beans
2 onions
1 cup red palm oil
2 teaspoons ground red pepper
salt to taste
2 ripe plantains
4 sweet potatoes

Drain the beans of the water in which they have boiled. Fry the onion, chopped finely, in half of the hot palm oil. Season with pepper and salt. Add the beans and simmer 30 minutes, stirring occasionally. Peel the plantains and sweet potatoes and slice both. Fry them in the rest of the palm oil and serve with the beans.

Source: *A West African Cook Book* by Ellen Gibson Wilson. New York: M. Evans, 1971, pp. 238-240.

South Africa (Zulu)

The ritual eating of first fruits

Although now obsolete as a national event, the festival of the first fruits must, in the past, have played a significant role in Zulu society . . . people underline that food from the fields was (and still today among Swazi is) not to be eaten until the rituals of the festival have been completed, including the speaking out in the hatred songs. An informant from Swaziland said in January 1969: "Those words of hatred are spoken before there is eating. If a person eats before everything is done (i.e. the rituals), he is behaving very badly. He is called *umisakatsi* (equivalent to Zulu *umthakathi*) because he behaves in a very bad way. The eating of the food is the last thing done."

Source: "The First Fruits Festival" in *Zulu Thought-Patterns* *and Symbolism* by Axel-Ivar Berglund. Uppsala, Sweden: Swedish Institute of Missionary Research, 1976, pp. 325-327.

Swaziland

The Nowala ceremonies

The King of Swaziland, the *Ngwenyama* (''Lion''), has a status far greater than that of most contemporary monarchs, since tradition endows him with mystical characteristics. He is the embodiment of the nation, his health is the nation's prosperity, his fertility is that of the nation's soil. He is therefore expected to have a large number of wives and to beget many children.

The most important and sacred of the Swazi ceremonies is the Newala, which takes place in December and January each year. Spread over a period lasting almost a month, the Newala is the ''first fruits'' ceremony, before which everybody is forbidden to eat certain new crops. It is also a mystical ceremony of kingship which binds the nation together and renews its strength for the coming year.

At the new moon of the month before the Newala a party of Swazi water officials (*bemanti*) set off for the seashore where they gather foam from the wavetops. They also collect water from the major rivers and certain plants from the Lubombo Mountains. The day before the bemanti set off, the King goes into seclusion.

The main Newala ceremony is preceded by the gathering of the sacred lusekwane shrub (a species of acacia) at Gunundvwini, on the night of the full moon. Youths from all over Swaziland meet at Lozithehlezi and, escorted by older men from the regiments, make the 25-mile march to Gunundvwini in the afternoon, arriving before sunset. When the full moon appears on the eastern horizon the order is given to the boys each to cut the largest lusekwane branch he can carry. Before dawn, the party reaches Lobamba and after sunrise the lusekwane is delivered in the cattle byre [pen].

The youths who fetch the lusekwane must have reached puberty and are expected to be pure: it is said that the leaves will wither in the hands of any who has intrigued with a married woman or made a girl pregnant. Boys who are too young to fetch the lusekwane collect pieces of the mbonvo shrub which grows . . . in the vicinity of Lobamba.

The following day, the Newala continues. A black ox is driven out of the sacred enclosure (*nhlambelo*). The young men catch it and carry it back into the nhlambelo where it is slaughtered.

In the afternoon of the next day official guests are present. The King meets the guests of honor and then takes his place in the center of the dancing warriors. The Queen Mother appears, accompanied by the senior women of her household, and joins in the proceedings. A drink of traditional beer is handed to the guests.

The climax of the Newala approaches. The warriors, chanting sacred songs, dance round the nhlambelo, surging backwards and forwards in attempts to persuade the King to return to his people. After pretending reluctance, the King emerges from the nhlambelo, his face smeared with black medicines, his body covered in bright green grass, his head dressed with large black plumes and a belt of silver monkey skin around his waist.

The King then dances before his regiment and his people. The dance, it is said, is one that only a king can improvise. At one stage the King eats a part of a special pumpkin, the *luselwa*, and tosses the remains to one of his warriors. This is a sign that the new crops may be eaten by everyone.

The great day is over but the Newala is not quite finished. The next day is a day of taboos (*sitila*) for everybody. No work must be done. Everyone must rise early. On the sixth and last day, the warriors march up the hills behind Lobamba and collect materials for a large fire in the cattle byre. The fire represents the burning of the past year. Rain is expected to fall to quench the flames—it often does! The last day of the Newala ends with feasting and dancing. The new year of the nation has begun.

Source: *Africa: South of the Sahara* by James I. Clark. Evanston, Illinois: McDougal, Little, & Co., 1982, pp. 87-88. (Citing ''A Swaziland Source.'')

The Incwala ceremonies

The *Incwala* is a sacred period set apart from the profane and mundane routine of normal life. It extends for roughly three weeks of each year, and is divided into the Little *Incwala*, which lasts two days, beginning when the sun reaches its southern summer solstice and the moon is dark, and the Big *Incwala*, which lasts six days from the night of the full moon. In the interim period, sacred songs and dances of the Little *Incwala* are performed in key villages throughout the territory. It is believed that wrong timing will bring national disaster that can only be circumvented by elaborate counter-ritual, a common cultural device to make people abide by tradition, yet not automatically accept calamity.

The honor of opening the *Incwala* is bestowed on the oldest regiment. Thereafter, other participants join in, taking their places according to rank and sex. The stage is the open cattle pen of the capital, but the main rites are enacted in secret in the king's sanctuary. The public contributes by performing sacred songs and dances. As the sun sets in a moonless night, the formation of the dances changes from the crescent of a new moon to the circle of the full moon. Princes and foreigners are dismissed as the warriors chant a new song that is associated with other important events of kingship—a king's marriage to his main ritual wife, the return of ancestral cattle from the royal grave, the burial of kings. It is a key song of the *Incwala*.

Jjiya oh o o King, alas for your fate
Jjiya oh o o King, they reject thee
Jjiya oh o o King, they hate thee.

Suddenly the chief councilor commands "Silence," and the singing ceases while the king spits powerful medicine, first to the east, then to the west, and the crowd is given the signal to shout, "He stabs it!" Informants explained that "Our Bull (Our King) had produced the desired effect: he had triumphed and was strengthening the earth." He has broken off the old year and is preparing for the new." This climaxes the opening of the ceremony. The people then sing a final song comparable to a national anthem, praising the king as "the Bull, the Lion, the Inexplicable, the Great Mountain." At dawn of the following day, the ceremony is repeated. Afterwards, warriors go to weed the queen mother's garden, for which service they are rewarded with a feast of meat. The Little *Incwala* is over, and the men may return to their homes until the moon is "ripe."

On the first day of the Big *Incwala*, the regiment of pure unmarried youths is sent to cut branches of a magic tree with which to enclose the king's sanctuary. Swazi believe that if the branches are cut by anyone who has violated the moral code of his age group, the leaves will wither. Such branches must be cast out and the culprit ostracized and even attacked, not so much for his sexual violations as for his willingness to endanger the well-being of the state. The tree is quick-growing, with leaves that remain green for many weeks, when cut by the virtuous. The cutting must begin as the full moon rises, to the rhythm of a new sacred song—a sacred lullaby—the theme song of the second stage of the drama. The qualities of quick growth, greenness, toughness, and fertility characterize most elements of the *Incwala* ritual.

On the morning of the second day, the youths return, bearing their wands proudly aloft and chanting the lullaby. The councilors surround the sanctuary with the mystic greenery, behind which the powers of the king will be symbolically reborn.

The main event of the third day is the "killing of the bull," the symbol of potency. The king strikes a specially selected black bull with a rod doctored for fertility and "awakening," and the pure youths must catch the animal, throw it to the ground, pummel it with their bare hands, and drag it into the sanctuary where it is sacrificed. Parts of the carcass are used for royal medicine the remainder is an offering to the ancestors.

The "Day of the Bull" fortifies the king for the "Great Day" when he appears in his most terrifying image and symbolically overcomes the hostility of princely rivals. In the morning he bites "doctored" green foods of the new year; his mother and others follow suit, their medicines graded by status. Later in the day, under the blazing sun, all the people, in full *Incwala* dress, and with the king in their midst, dance and sing the *Incwala*. Towards sunset the king leaves them; when he re-emerges he is unrecognizable—a mythical creature—clothed in a fantastic costume of sharp-edged green grass and skins of powerful wild animals, his body gleaming with black unguents. The princes approach and alternately drive him from them into the sanctuary and beseech him to return. Behind them the people sing and dance. All members of the royal Dlamini clan and all "foreigners" (seen as potential enemies) are ordered from the cattle byre; the king remains and dances with his loyal supporters and common subjects. Tension mounts as he sways backwards and forwards. At the climax he appears holding in his hand a vivid-green gourd, known as the "Gourd of Embo" (the north), the place of Dlamini origin. Although picked the previous year, the gourd is still green. The king throws it lightly on the horizontally placed shield of a selected agemate, who must not let the fruit, sacred vessel of the past of continuity, touch the ground. The old year has been discarded; the king has proved his strength, and the people are prepared for the future.

Source: *The Swazi: A South African Kingdom* by Hilda Kuper. New York: Holt, Rinehart and Winston, 1963, pp. 69-70.

Syria

Harvesting customs

In Syria after the wheat is harvested, a part of it is boiled before being stored. In some villages a huge brass cauldron is placed in the public square for the use of all the people and fire is kept burning under it day and night during the harvest season. On others, the boiling of the wheat takes place within the home, but even here it is largely a community affair.

The young girls of the neighborhood are invited to help on the day a family boils its wheat for store. They are divided into two groups; one group brings the wheat from the huge pile—sometimes it contains 20 to 30 bushels—to the big cauldron; they carry it in small brass vessels balanced on their heads. The other group goes to the spring to fetch water in which to boil the wheat; the water jars are likewise carried on the heads of the girls. Both processions are attended by a man carrying a lighted lantern.

After grain and water are mixed in the big cauldron, a fire is started underneath it. Then in the firelight the helpers dance and sing and play games until the wheat is cooked. A bowl of the cooked wheat into which nuts and sweets have been stirred, serves as refreshments.

Source: *Foreign Festival Customs* by Marian Schibsby & Hanny Cohrsen. New York: American Council for Nationalities Service, 1974, p. 54.

Tanzania, Mozambique, Malawi, Zambia, Zimbabwe (Makonde)

Midimu Ceremony

The Makonde people live in Tanzania in the regions of Newala, Mtwara and some areas of Lindi, as well as in the Tunduru region of Mozambique. Originally they lived in several regions of Malawi, Zambia and Zimbabwe. The migration of this large population into the areas where they live now has been taking place in successive waves over the past three hundred years.

Between June and October, during the dry season, some of the men who live in the Makonde villages tell their families that they have to go away, that they have been "called" to make a long journey. A farewell ceremony is held in public, and then, for ten to fifteen days, the men disappear. While they are away, various danced and masked ceremonies take place, including those known as the "Midimu."

The Midimu ceremony begins at night during the period when the moon moves from the quarter to its half phase. It usually follows some felicitous event such as a bountiful harvest, a large haul of fish, a good hunt, or the preparation of new farmlands, but principally, the Midimu celebrates the termination of the initiation period of both the boys and the girls. (In the Makonde villages the initiation period lasts for three years.) Torches burn; drums resound. All the villagers come outside to join in the festivities. In general, the feast continues without stopping for three days and three nights. At the end of the third night, the masks visit the house of each new initiate and, after having performed various danced myths on the threshold, are given honey, meat, jewelry and sometimes money. The feast is over. The Midimu spirit leaves the village; the masks return to the forest.

Professional dancers and musicians participate in the masked dances of the Midimu that, over a very short period of time, are given consecutively in six or seven villages. At the end of their tour" the dancer, who must never be recognized, "return" home. In their villages everyone knows why they have been away, but nobody ever brings up the question.

Source: "Masked Dances and Ritual in Tanzania, Mozambique and Zambia" by Francoise Grund-Khaznader in *The Drama Review* 25 (4) (T92) (Winter 1981), 25-27.

Tanzania (Zinza)

First-Fruits Ceremony

At the beginning of the long rains in March, a tiny plot of land is selected and dedicated to Kihazi. The female medium of the family, (Kihazi and Nyabayombe traditionally possess women only) as well as the family and kinsmen and neighbours, gather together at this plot. Here the family head (or the wife of a neighbour), invokes Kihazi who then possesses her medium, presents herself and says that she wants her hoe as she is about to cultivate her plot. The family head hands 'the hoe of Kihazi' to the medium, informs Kihazi of the act, and urges her to cultivate and let them receive an abundant harvest. After Kihazi-in-medium has finished hoeing the plot, she sows in it various kinds of seeds, such as millet, maize and beans.

When the crops on this plot, like the crops in general, have ripened by the beginning of July, a meal of food and beer is prepared, made from the crops of Kihazi and mixed with some of the crops from the food gardens of the family. When this meal is ready, the food and beer are placed in front of the medium who is then possessed by the most important *mbandwa* in the following of Ryangombe. Nyabayombe-in-medium then gives food and drink to the cult group. After they have tasted the food and beer, this group expresses their gratitude, they thank her for having given them food. The response of the spirits-in-medium to the expression of gratitude is the spraying out of beer on the members of the cult group, that is, an act of blessing complemented by verbal well-wishing to the effect that the group will continue to live in 'peace'.

It should be added that the offering of the new crops is not a first-fruit offering in the sense that a part, however small, of the harvest has to be offered to the *mbandwa* spirits before people may prepare from it food for themselves. As we have seen, the real first-fruit offering of the Zinza is the libation to the ancestors of the first beer made from the new millet. This ritual expresses to the *mbandwa,* and particularly Kihazi and Nyabayombe, the gratitude for the food which they have given to people.

Source: *Religion and Misfortune* by Svein Bjerke. Oslo: Universitetsforlaget, 1981, pp. 240-241.

Uganda (Dodoth)

Lara, a season of harvest and parties

Being the time of plenty, Lara is the season of parties, celebrations, and feasts. Women brew grain into delicious sour beer, thick as cereal, served hot enough to steam. A man may ask his friends to help him with some heavy work—moving a roof, for instance—and then repay his friends in beer, so Lara is the season for accomplishing things. But a man may serve drinks to visitors just for pleasure. Sometimes twenty or thirty men may meet under an etem tree to hear their host's opinions while trying his beer. Or a man might give a small party for a few close friends in the court of one of his wives, where privacy assures that passersby will not join the group to drink up everything, where men and women can sit together informally, passing a warm calabash among them, spending the afternoon. There is an air of relaxation toward the end of harvest. The grain is in the granaries, and the dry, headless stalks rustle in the fields. At this season, for once in all the year, the thornbush fences that surround the fields are opened and the livestock is let into the canes. Thus the fields are cleared for next spring's planting, and the cattle have their harvest festival too.

Threshing bees

Threshing can go on until evening, when, from the top of a hill, one can see all of the threshing floors of a neighborhood surrounded by smoldering, glowing rings as the people set the chaff on fire. Even after dark, you can hear the rhythmic thumping of the flails and now and then you can hear laughter and singing too. Sometimes, to speed the work, the men flail also, and sometimes many people thresh together, as the families in a neighborhood take turns helping each other, doing one harvest at a time. These threshing bees are gay occasions: it is cooler at night, and more pleasant because the men are there.

Source: *Warrior Herdsmen* by Elizabeth Marshall Thomas. New York: Alfred A. Knopf, 1965, pp. 184-185. (Anthropological writer.)

Uganda (Sebei)

Misisi

A ritual feast, the misisi is held by the Sebei after the millet harvest each year. An adaptation of the feast, called "mukutanik," takes place now at Christmas.

The misisi beer feast

A ritual called *misisi* takes place annually after millet has been harvested. On the escarpment, the ceremony occurs in the month called Twamo (about October) but it is earlier on the plains, where millet ripens sooner. Millet is spread on the ground to dry, and the stalks are later picked up and placed in granaries. The word *misisi* refers to the grain that falls off the ears and remains on the ground because it is too small to be gathered and stored. By extension, it refers also to the cobs of maize that are too small to be worth storing. The *misisi* beer was made of this grain, though, if insufficient, it could be supplemented from the granary.

The essence of the *misisi* ritual is a small feast to which specific close relatives are invited, its purpose being, according to one informant, to strengthen the friendship among those who share the feast. This purpose takes on special meaning when we examine the guest list proper to *misisi*: an age-set mate, a *tilyet,* sister's daughter's husband and his brothers, and, for each wife, her father, brothers, mother's brother, and their wives, and her daughter's husband. These kin may all be characterized as persons with whom there is a sense of mutual obligation and respect, but also a certain degree of tension. Thus, both the uncle to whom the man has given the *kamama* payment in brideprice and the nephew from whom he receives such payment are included, as well as the son-in-law and father-in-law from or to whom the basic brideprice payments are made. From the woman's standpoint, the son-in-law is a relationship of deep respect. Little wonder then that the songs they sing around the beer pot are all circumspect, not those sung during initiations.

The *misisi* feast includes, in addition to beer, maize meal steamed plantains (*matoke*) and some meat, a bullock, if the host is rich, or a ram or chickens. There is no anointing with chyme. The ritual aspects are limited to libations of beer for the good and bad spirits; the libation should be poured by the host's father but may be poured by any elder who, after offering it to the *oyik,* drinks from the libation gourd (*mwendet*) and hands it to a friend, who then becomes the other man's guest. "By brewing this beer, we say that there has been darkness and now light is coming with the new crops." The libation is accompanied by such words as, "Please accept this beer; I am still alive and let us enjoy it together." The good spirits are offered beer inside the house or kraal and are mentioned by name; they include the host's fathers, brothers, mothers, mothers' brothers, grandparents, fathers-in-law, brothers-in-law, and all the deceased members of the host's clan whose names are known and who have living descendants. A failure to mention an ancestor might annoy the spirit. Libations are poured for the evil spirits away from the house or kraal, using the left instead of the right hand. Evil spirits may also be mentioned by name and will include those relatives who have died without progeny and are therefore jealous, or those who cursed a kinsman when he was alive. They are thus placated but kept at a distance.

Source: *Culture and Behavior of the Sebei: A Study in Continuity and Adaptation* by Walter Goldschmidt. Berkeley: Univ. of California, 1976, pp. 161-162.

U.S.S.R. (Chukchi)

Reindeer Slaughtering

The first and second autumn slaughterings of reindeer were the reindeer-breeders' chief festivals. On these days the herdsmen drove the herd to the summer camp and the women made a fire. The herd was met with loud shouts and shots, which were to frighten off the evil spirits. This was followed by a sacrificial ceremony, in which bits of food were scattered. The men separated reindeer from the herd and killed them, selecting mainly young calves. After that came the ritual of anointment of people and sleds with blood. The meat was brought into the cold part of the yaranga and cooked. After eating, all members of the family took turns for the rest of the day in striking the tambourine. Such holidays were often attended by coastal Chukchi and Eskimos, who brought the reindeer-breeders products of sea hunting in exchange for reindeer skins and meat. The number of reindeer killed and bartered and the number of guests from the coast depended entirely on the degree of the reindeer-breeder's wealth. Races were usually held during such festivals.

Source: *The Peoples of Siberia* edited by M. G. Levine and L. P. Potapov. Chicago: Univ. of Chicago Press, 1964, p. 823.

August-September

Agwunsi Festival

This is a ritual of Agwunsi, god of Healing and Divination. Dibia who have healed patients are sent animals on this day.

Nigeria (Igbo)

Honoring the patron of doctors

Another important festival at this time is the Agwunsi Ritual. The god of Healing and Divination, Agwunsi, controls the human psyche. If a person behaves abnormally the Igbo will ask if he is being disturbed by Agwunsi. This deity is the patron of all doctors for he gives potency to herbs and all medical formulae, etc.

On the Agwunsi feast day, healed patients send animals to the dibia that gave them medicine. The festival is not as important as the Ogwugwu celebration and this is why the Igbo say ''Agaghi m ahapu ebe a na-eme Ogwugwu, jewe ebe a na-eme Agwunsi''—I will not decline the invitation to an Ogwugwu festival in preference to an Agwunsi one.

Source: ''Standardizing Igbo Festivals'' by Nnabuenyi Ugonna in *Nigeria Magazine* 136 (1981) 26.

August-September

Insect-Hearing Festival

Pet crickets and other insects are released from their cages on a day in late August or early September.

Japan

Ceremony of "freeing the insects," c. 1965

A picturesque rite that has come down from feudal days. This is a pastime held in temple and shrine precincts, public parks, and many gardens at the time when the "seven grasses of summer" are in full bloom. People gather in chosen spots where they take insects in tiny bamboo cages, some of which are purchased from insect vendors for the ceremony of "freeing the insects." As the insects are set free, the liberator waits for them to get their bearings, realize their freedom, and then listen to them as they burst forth with their chirpings. There is a festival on May 28 at which time the insect vendor sells his wares. People seem to enjoy keeping the insects close at hand during the summer months in order to enjoy their sounds during the evenings. This custom is probably much more prevalent in rural areas.

Source: *Japanese Festivals* by Helen Bauer and Sherwin Carlquist. Garden City, New York: Doubleday, 1965, p. 185.

Circa September

Okpesi Festival

The Okpesi ceremony, also called Itensi, must be performed by every male Igbo child whose father has already joined the ancestors. This ceremony to honor the ancestors is held annually.

Nigeria (Igbo)

The Okpesi Festival honors ancestors

Now follow the ceremonies in honour of the ancestors. In many areas every child whose father has joined the ancestors has to perform the okpesi ceremony also called Itensi. This festival has been a source of major conflicts between Christians and traditional believers. The Okpesi Festival is symbolic of the communion between us and our ancestors, ndioki, and it is strongly believed by Igbo traditionalists that failure to perform this annual rite will spell disaster not only to the erring individual but to the whole community.

The Okpesi Festival, like any typical Igbo festival has a ritual, sacrificial phase during which cocks are sacrificed to the ancestors, the blood of the victims being spread on wooden altars erected for the purpose, and a feasting phase in which festal communion is achieved among the living (hosts and guests) on the one hand and between the living and the dead on the other.

Source: ''Standardizing Igbo Festivals'' by Nnabuenyi Ugonna in *Nigeria Magazine* 136 (1981) 26-28.

September 8

National Festival

Andorra

Honoring patron saint of Andorra

A celebration in honor of the treaty of 1278, giving Andorra independence from Spanish and French overlords. Jungfrau von Meritxell, patron saint of Andorra, is honored on this day. Pilgrims arrive early, climbing the hill to her sanctuary near Encamp and Canillo villages. Her wooden statue was found on this spot by a shepherd, beside a rose bush blooming in the snow. Bars are set up at the many hillside springs. There drinks are cooled, and after the sermon, lamb grilled on slabs of slate is served. Dancing follows.

September 8

Nativity of the Virgin

This is a feast day in honor of the Nativity of the Virgin Mary.

Italy

A celebration in Florence

On the eve of The Nativity of the Virgin children in Florence carry paper lanterns that they have made. They are constructed of paper and painted, and each holds a candle. The boating clubs have adopted this festival by adorning their boats with lanterns, and a pageant takes place with prizes for the most attractively decorated boat.

Source: *Festivals and Folkways of Italy* by Frances Toor. New York: Crown, 1958, p. 244.

Malta

The Vittoria

A commemoration of the defeat of the Turks

This day, dedicated to the nativity of the Virgin Mary, is also a commemoration of the defeat of the Turks under Suleiman the Magnificent by the Knights of St. John of Jerusalem at Malta in 1565, and the lifting of the siege against the Axis powers in 1943. A regatta is held at the capital, Yalletta, and children compete in climbing the greased pole of a barge in the Grand Harbour to reach the knight's red and white cross banner.

Source: ''Malta & Gozo: Events Calendar '90'' National Tourism Organization, 1990.

First and Second Days of Tishri (September-October)

Rosh Hashana

On this first day of the New Year, God sits in judgment over all men. The shofar, made of a ram's horn, is blown in the synagogue to signal God's sovereignty. A family meal on the first night of Rosh Hashana features apples dipped in honey eaten with the blessing, ''A good and sweet year.'' On the second night a new fruit not yet eaten this season should be eaten. After the afternoon meal on the first day, the community may congregate by a river to symbolically toss its sins into the water. Dates of this celebration: September 9, 1991; September 28, 1992; September 16, 1993; September 6, 1994; September 25, 1995.

Iran

Rosh Hashanah in Persia

The two days of Rosh Hashanah were semifast days, no food or drink being taken until after prayers. In the synagogue the cantor recited prayers both in Hebrew and in Persian. A clear flowing tone from the shofar promised a good year, a quavering tone bode ill. The Psalms were recited in the afternoon. On Rosh Hashanah eve one was released from vows made unreasonably and charities were distributed. The meal on that night included fruits and vegetables whose name, shape, or taste symbolized a good year: beets, ''so that our enemies may be beaten'' (*selek* and *salek* in Hebrew); apples in sugar for ''a sweet year''; a pomegranate to signify a multiplicity of rights; fish for fertility; and a lamb's head ''so that we be the head and not the tail.''

Source: *One People: The Story of the Eastern Jews* by Devorah and Menachem Hacohen. New York: Sabra, 1969, p. 71.

Libya

Rosh Hashanna in Libya

On Hoshanna Rabba eve everyone ate broiled lamb lung and liver. In the synagogue the next morning, men tapped each other with willow twigs.

Source: *One People: The Story of the Eastern Jews* by Devorah and Menachem Hacohen. New York: Sabra, 1969, pp. 34-35, 102.

For more on Rosh Hashana see: ''Rosh Ha-shanah'' in *Burning Candles* by Bella Chagall. New York: Shocken, 1946, pp. 73-81; ''Rosh Hashanah'' in *Folklore of American Holidays* edited by Hennig Cohen and Tristram Potter Coffin. 2nd ed. Detroit: Gale Research, 1991, pp. 350-351.

September 11

Coptic New Year

This is a celebration of the new year in the Coptic Orthodox Church.

Canada

Egyptian-Canadian celebrations

Egyptian-Canadians celebrate the New Year on this date when the Dog Star, Sirius (Sothis to Egyptians), reappears in the sky of Egypt. This was a signal that the Nile flooding was approaching and a new planting year would commence.

The martyrs of the Coptic Orthodox church are remembered on this day. Vestments and altar clothes are red, to recall the blood the martyrs spilled. Red dates are eaten to signify thier red blood, the white meat of the date is symbolic of the purity of the martyrs' hearts, the hard pit represents their faith.

Source: *Let's Celebrate* by Caroline Parry. Toronto: Kids Can Press, 1987, pp. 206-207.

September 11

Enkutatash (New Year)

This is The Ethiopian New Year, which coincides with the feast of St. John the Baptist. This is the first day of the Ethiopian month Maskarem.

Ethiopia (Amhara)

Children's singing troupes and feasting

The new year falls on St. John's Day in September. For this occasion the floor of the peasant's home is strewn with freshly cut grass, tall and green after the long rains. Children go singing from house to house in small bands, or take bunches of wild flowers to relatives, in hopes of getting a bit of *dābo* [roasted grain]. In most homes an animal is slaughtered—in some areas superstition decrees that it be a white-headed lamb or a red chicken—and there is much eating and drinking, the basic activity of every holiday.

Source: *Wax & Gold: Tradition and Innovation in Ethiopian Culture* by Donald N. Levina. Chicago: Univ. of Chicago Press, 1965, pp. 61-62.

Prayers, wildflowers, and dabo at Enkutatash

The first day of Maskarem, September 11 on the Gregorian calendar (September 12 in leap year), is Enkutatash, or New Year's Day. It coincides with the end of the ''big rains'' and the greening of the countryside. It is also the feast of Saint John the Baptist. At the churches there are prayers, songs, and processions. In the villages, the children visit their neighbors and relatives with bunches of wildflowers and are given a handful of *dabo* as a treat.

Source: *Ethiopia: Land of the Lion* by Lila Perl. New York: William Morrow, 1972, p. 72.

New Year in Ethiopia

On September 10th, the day before the New Year, Almaze and the other girls of her village go to the fields to gather flowers. They make these into many tiny bouquets to be ready for the next day. Filled with excitement, the girls awaken early on New Year's Day and dress in the costume of their country. Carrying their tiny bouquets, they gather in front of their houses. Together they go from house to house singing and bringing good wishes for the New Year. At each house they are invited in, receiving presents in return for their good wishes. To say ''thank you,'' each girl leaves a bouquet.

The boys too have their way of celebrating the New Year. Before sunset on New Year's Eve, Almaze's brother Kebede and his friends make bundles of branches. Grown-ups soon join them. As the sun goes down they set fire to the branches to light their way. Off they go to pay calls at every house in the village. As they walk they sing a happy New Year song. At each house people come out and join in the singing. The singers receive presents, usually coins, to help start the New Year off in a happy way.

Source: *UNICEF'S Festival Book* by Judith Spiegelman. New York: United States Committee for UNICEF, 1966.

September 14
Holy Cross Day

This is a commemoration of the discovery of the cross on which Jesus died. St. Helena, Mother of Constantine the Great, discovered the holy cross. May 3 and September 27 are celebrated as Holy Cross days in other branches of the church.

Syria

Visiting the vineyards

On Holy Cross Day, September 14th, when the grapes are ripe, the ''Feast of the Crucifix'' is celebrated in Syria. On that day the villagers go into their vineyards prepared for a day's outing. Each family divides into two groups; one, consisting chiefly of the younger memebers, cuts the grapes and loads them into boxes; these are then taken to a big plot of ground where every family has been assigned definite space and where other members of the family await their coming. They dip the grapes into a mixture of alkali and olive oil and then spread them out to dry. During the gathering of the grapes, the poor of the neighborhood and the Bedouins come with bags begging a share of the grapes and gleaning those left unpicked on the vines. At the end of the day the families assemble in the vineyards for dancing and feasting.

Source: *Foreign Festival Customs* by Marian Schibsby & Hanny Cohrsen. New York: American Council for Nationalities Service, 1974, p. 58.

For more information see: ''Recovery of the Cross, September 14'' in *Folklore of American Holidays* edited by Hennig Cohen and Tristram Potter Coffin. 2nd ed. Detroit: Gale Research, 1991, pp. 337-338.

September 15

Keirō no Hi (Respect for the Elderly Day)

This national holiday honors the elderly.

Japan

Gifts for the elderly

In the past the chōkai and its women's group also sponsored parties for elderly residents on the national holiday, Keirō no Hi (Respect for the Elderly Day, September 15), but in recent years they have stopped holding the parties because poor health prevents so many of the old people from attending. Instead, to try to benefit all the elderly, the chōkai and the fujinbu now present a gift to every resident over the age of seventy; one year they gave sets of underclothing sewn by the fujinbu women, along with amulets from the local Buddhist temple to protect against incontinence.

Source: *Neighborhood Tokyo* by Theodore C. Bestor. Stanford, Calif.: Stanford Univ. Press, 1989, p. 158.

Tenth Day of Tishri

Yom Kippur

This Day of Atonement is marked by a twenty-four-hour fast and prayers for forgiveness. Bathing and wearing leather shoes are also prohibited. On the eve of Yom Kippur the entire community congregates in the synagogue. The men wear prayer shawls and kittles, snow white robes reflecting the purity of the day. As night falls the cantor begins the Kol Nidre, signifying the absolution for unkept vows. Yom Kippur dates are September 18, 1991; October 7, 1992; September 25, 1993; September 15, 1994; October 4, 1995.

Iran

Yom Kippur in Persia

The *kapara,* atonement offering, on Yom Kippur was important. Males offered a rooster, females a hen. A pregnant woman would offer a hen for herself and a rooster or hen for her unborn. After the *kaparot* prayer, the chicken was given to the *shochet* to be killed. The women plucked the feathers for bedding. Some of the meat was given to the poor, the rest consumed prior to the fast.

The men took seven ritual dips at the bathhouse and then went to the synagogue for the Penitential flagelations. The Mula passed a thong over their bare backs while reciting prayers. The men remained in the synagogue all night after the Kol Nidre, reciting Psalms and the "Crown of Sovereignty" of Ibn-Gabirol in Persian. On Yom Kippur day the entire families attended the synagogue. At nightfall the congregation held *kiddush levana,* blessing of the moon, outside in the yard, and new year good wishes were given.

Israel

Yom Kippur in Jerusalem

Today, in Jerusalem, a soft siren is sounded in the evening. It signals the start of Yom Kippur. Within seconds, the streets fill with people dressed in white, holding prayer books. They are headed for the synagogue. They pause to embrace friends and neighbors and say *Hatimah Tovah!*—"may you be well-inscribed"—and continue on their way. In Jewish communities all around the world people joyfully celebrate their cherished holidays, remembering their past, and praying for a future of peace.

Source: *Sound the Shofar* by Miriam Chaikin. New York: Clarion Books, 1986, p. 84.

Tunisia

Yom Kippur in Tunis

At Kol Nidre the synagogue was illuminated with hundreds of candles. To intensify their atonement many would stand on hard chickpeas during the prayers. At the end of the fast *bulu* was eaten, a pastry of flour, eggs, and raisins. Friends were visited for *jufra,* forgiveness, and family elders were visited for their blessing.

Source: *One People: The Story of the Eastern Jews* by Devora and Menchem Hacohen. New York: Sabra, 1969, pp. 33, 88.

Yemen

Yom Kippur in Yemen

Preparations for the Yom Kippur fast were a serious matter. A large meal was eaten at forenoon, followed by the pre-fast meal after the afternoon prayers; this meal usually consisted of buttered bread, honey and much fruit, particularly grapes and pomegranates.

The Yom Kippur vestments were predominantly of white silk; on their feet, the Yemenites wore rope sandals or else they went barefoot. Many spent the entire night in the synagogue. At *minha* time everyone went home to exchange the white silk vestment for the regular Sabbath attire, along with a quince with which to break the fast after the *shofar* blast had announced the end of the Day of Atonement.

Source: *One People: The Story of the Eastern Jews* by Devora and Menachem Hacohen. New York: Sabra, 1969, p. 143.

For more on Yom Kippur see: "Day of Atonement" in *Burning Candles* by Bella Chagall. New York: Shocken, 1946, pp. 82-88; "Days of Awe" in *A Walker in Jerusalem* by Samuel Heilman. New York: Summit, 1980; *My Life* by Marc Chagall. New York: Orien Press, 1960, p. 37.

12 Rabi-ul Awal (August-October)

Ma-ulid

Ma-ulid, on the twelfth day of Rabi ul-Awal, is a celebration of the birth of Mohammed. Conservative Muslim groups such as the Wahhabis disapprove of the celebration of any human being, even Mohammed. This is considered a wavering from the single-minded worship of God. Other sects, however, make a great holiday of this. Shiites celebrate other birthdays as well throughout the year, for example, the birthdays of Ali, Fatima, and Hasan and Husain. Ma-ulid dates: September 21, 1991; September 10, 1992; August 30, 1993; August 19, 1994; August 9, 1995.

Egypt

Maulid

Sufi prevalence in Egypt, maulid in Cairo

Egypt has long been the home of many Sufi orders (singular, *tariqa,* plural, *turuq*), some of which were established as early as the thirteenth century. Until recent years, the majority of Egyptian males belonged to one or more of these orders, and 60 such orders still survive.

While the Sufi orders are a part of the orthodox life of Moslems, the worship of saints, prevalent throughout the Islamic world, has no such sanction. Nevertheless, the Egyptians have hundreds of saints, and Muhammad has become the first of them. His *maulid,* or birthday, is gaily celebrated by the illumination of Cairo and by ceremonies and performances, including a dhikr.

Source: *United Arab Republic: Egypt* by Donald N. Wilber. New Haven: HRAF Press, 1969, pp. 71-72.

Mawlid an-Nabawi in Kafr el-Elow village, c. 1970

The villagers of Kafr el-Elow begin celebrations four days before the twelfth of Rabi al-Awal. Homes are decorated and the wealthy build big tents near their homes where male guests eat the holiday meals and carry out the rituals of the holiday. Recitations from the Koran dealing with the life of Mohammad are broadcast over microphones throughout the village. Various brotherhoods also sponsor festivities on this occasion. In addition to reciting from the Koran, the members march back and forth in two parallel lines chanting, "Zikr Allah, al hayy al gayyum, al tawheed lil-lah," "The name of God, the compassionate and merciful, who is living and present everywhere, God, he is the one." On the second evening of the celebration, the day preceding Mohammad's birthday, the religious brotherhoods process with flagbearers and a band, chanting praises to Mohammad.

Families hold a feast on the prophet's birthday itself. Cotton candy and *arusa,* a brightly colored candy doll, are sold at this time. A few individuals go to Cairo's Essit Zainab Mosque for this celebration and rent a spot in one of the big tents erected there for this holiday.

Source: *Kafr El-Elow: An Egyptian Village in Transition* by Hani Fakhouri. Prospect Heights, Ill.: Waveland Press, 1972, pp. 85-86.

Indonesia

Sekartan

Mohammed's birthday in Jogjakarta, c. 1960

When they had finished I went with some of them through the palace grounds to a forecourt bounded by high walls, where the sultan's gamelans were being played to celebrate the festival of Sekartan, Mohammed's birthday. The great space was crowded like a marketplace with thousands of people gathered round a brightly lit pavilion ablaze with hanging oil lamps and candelabra holding flares and torches and the lights from scores of food stalls.

The two royal gamelans, one on either side of the pavilion, played alternately, each group of players dressed in the sultan's uniform, tight turban, jacket, and patterned sarong. They had started at sundown and would play until close to midnight without interruption, watched by thousands of townspeople sitting on the ground, while others walked about the forecourt among the food sellers or gathered in groups by the high walls, talking. . . .

A little before midnight, a hundred young men wearing pantaloons, maroon tunics, and red tabooshes, came with litters and long poles to carry the gamelans to the mosque, where for a week they would play all night in honor of the prophet. More men came with flaming torches and others with spears, all dressed in the sultan's uniform, and for a while there was the confusion of forming all into a procession, which eventually set off along a winding lane made by the people and led along the edge of the palace wall, past an open bazaar, to an old and honored mosque.

Strangely, at the head of this cavalcade of holy instruments went a quartet of fifes and drums, playing a merry jig that surely must have first been heard in Raffles' time. . . .

After the fife band, stepping lively, came spearmen and torch-bearers, then twelve men with baskets of food, then one of the sultan's brothers dressed richly (deputizing for His Highness, who had been called to Jakarta by the President), and the chief Iman of the mosque, wearing white and with a heavy gold chain hung about him, then other dignitaries, followed by the holy gongs, under umbrellas and the other instruments of the gamelan carried upon the shoulders of the young men in their maroon tunics. When the procession had passed the people followed after it, but being tired I went to the hotel.

Source: *Five Journeys from Jakarta: Inside Sukarno's Indonesia* by Maslyn Williams. New York: William Morrow, 1965, pp. 288-289.

Indonesia (Sumatra)

Maulud Nabi

A dish for Maulud Nabi: Lemang, glutinous rice cooked in bamboo

This is a Sumatran equivalent of Lontong or Ketupat, and like them it is associated with a major feast of the Islamic year—in this case, *Maulud Nabi* or the Prophet's birthday. We eat it then with Rendang, and neighbours send little packets of Lemang to each other rather as, elsewhere, they might exchange Christmas cards. The Javanese do the same with Ketupat at Lebaran. Throughout the rest of the year, however, Lemang is regarded as a sweet dish and is eaten with kolak, bananas, or durian in season.

It is made from glutinous rice, cooked with thick santen (coconut milk) in segments of bamboo: not just any bamboo, but specifically *Schizostacayum zollengeri,* which we call *telang.* This variety has very thin walls, which let the heat penetrate, and unusually long internodes. The cook may prepare 15 or 20 or more of these bamboo cylinders, 50 cm long and 5 cm across, open at the top and lined with banana leaf. The rice is usually white, but red and black glutinous rice are also used. It is first soaked for several hours, then dried. Each length of bamboo is filled about one-third full of rice, and is topped up with thick, slightly-salted santen. A banana-leaf lid is tied down firmly over the mouth of the tube. A wooden crossbar is rigged over a low fire and the bamboos are placed so that they lean against it, even numbers on one side and odd numbers on the other, like the rafters of a little house. Cooking takes up to 2 hours, with the rice swelling as it absorbs the santen to make a soft, firm mass. When it is cooked, the Lemang is shaken and slid from the tubes, unwrapped from its banana-leaf coverings and sliced into good chunky rounds.

Source: *Indonesian Food and Cookery* by Sri Owen. London: Prospect Books, 1980, p. 105.

Iran

Mohammed's birthday in Teheran, c. 1945

It was the eve of Mohammad's birthday, the seventeenth of the month of Rabi'ul Awwal of the Hegira Lunar Calendar. Mohammad's birthday is to Moslems something like Thanksgiving is to Americans. "The earth is the Lord's, and the fulness thereof." Everything which man has, has been given him by God. It is the custom in my country to take meat to the poor people on this special day so that all may share in gratitude to God.

Early Zahra spoke of taking a barbecued lamb to the people in a near-by village. . . . The whole lamb is purchased dressed and ready for cooking. It is placed in a great earthenware vessel over a charcoal fire. With it are water, tomato, onion, herbs. All day long it cooks, sending out delicious fragrance.

Late afternoon we went in the family car to this village, maybe ten, maybe twelve miles from Teheran.

Source: *Reveille for a Persian Village* by Najmeh Najafi and Helen Hinckley. New York: Harper, 1958, pp. 2-3.

Kenya

Maulidi

Traditional Maulidi music in Lamu

Maulidi, the celebration of the birth of the prophet, is particularly magnificent on the small island of Lamu. Music for festivals and celebrations is often provided by a tarabu, a small group of musicians playing haunting music as a backdrop to epic songs or poetry.

Source: *Fielding's Africa South of the Sahara* by Sheery A. Suttles and Billy Suttles-Graham. New York: Fielding Travel Books/William Morrow, 1986, p. 197.

Recitation of the Maulidi

One of the most important rituals in Lamu, and indeed in all of East Africa, was the recitation of the *Maulidi,* the celebration of the Prophet's birth. We do not know for sure how or when that celebration was first introduced to Lamu. We do know that there were two ways of reciting the Maulidi: one type of Maulidi was recited by the more advantaged wangwana, i.e., the Wa Yumbili Pembe, the Wa Yumbili Ngombe, and the newcomers; the other

Maulidi was recited by the lesser wangwana, the Wa Yumbili Ponde.

In the month of *Rabi' al Awwal,* the month in which the Prophet was born, the ruler of Lamu summoned the preachers to come to the Maskiti Pwani to read the Maulidi. The mosque was decorated and painted especially for that occasion, and only the higher groups of wangwana were allowed to attend. This was the beginning of a series of Maulidi celebrations.

The Maulidi Barzanji was a ''private'' ritual. The only people who were able to read it were either the 'ulama, the mwenye chouni, or the khatibs.

The recitation of this Maulidi was a solemn affair; it was read in a low voice with everyone sitting quietly in a place corresponding to his social position. If the ruler were present, he sat at the reciter's right hand, with the minister at his left. Next came the old people from each social group, who sat accordingly. Thus this Maulidi was simple and well-organized, and the behavior of the participants highly controlled.

The other Maulidi celebrations however, were quite different. On the mainland the slaves created their own Maulidi. . . . The two groups living in Lamu who were not able to use the Maulidi Barzanji were the Wa Yumbili Ponde and the Comoro Island people, and so these two groups celebrated their own Maulidi. Instead of having a private Maulidi, they used to read theirs out in the streets inside their mtaa, with all of the people of the mtaa contributing their efforts. The main street was cleaned and decorated for the occasion. After the last prayer at night, they gathered in their mtaa, sitting on mats spread on the ground, and the oldest person from that mtaa would read the Fatiha, burn incense, and bless the Prophet. After finishing, someone might stand and praise the Prophet in Swahili verse which he had prepared especially for the occasion. Another might continue with another verse, also praising the Prophet. This ritual would last for two or three hours. Then, the best poet of the group would stand and describe the world before the Prophet; when he reached the point of the Prophet's birth, all the people would stand up and sing together a Swahili poem welcoming the Prophet's birth. After that, they would sit down again, and the old man who opened the ceremony would read the Fatiha and make invocations in Swahili, ending the ritual. This Maulidi was called *Maulidi ya Rama*—the shaking Maulidi.

The Comoro Island people performed this Maulidi, and they invited the Wa Yumbili Ponde to attend, and the Wa Yumbili Ponde reciprocated.

Source: *The Sacred Meadows: A Structural Analysis of Religious Symbolism in an East African Town* by Abdul Hamid M. el Zein. Chicago: Northwestern Univ., 1974, pp. 40-41. (See this source for detailed description of the Maulidi readings.)

Libya

Ma'ulid Annabi

School holiday

The birthday of the Prophet Mohammed is an official holiday, with schools and offices closed. School children celebrate with athletic contests and parties. There are fireworks in the evening.

Making a Khumaisa for Ma'ulid Annabi

A *khumaisa* (koo-my-SAH) is a hand-like symbol seen everywhere on the occasion of the Prophet's birthday. Libyan school children work on these much the way American boys and girls make *crèches* and decorate Christmas trees. In fact many of the decorations—glass balls and bells, gilded pine cones, silver paper cutouts and tinsel—are the same. The *khumaisa,* like the star on a Christmas tree, may be small or large.

A small one can be made using a round paper ice-cream carton as a foundation. This should be covered with bright-colored tissue paper or crepe paper, bound with gold or silver ribbon at the base. This foundation is covered entirely with tissue-paper (or crepe-paper) rosettes which can either be glued on or sewn on a string and wrapped around the carton. The rosettes may be all one color or in rows of alternating colors. The whole thing is hung with tinsel and other Christmas-tree decorations. On top is placed the *khumaisa* itself. This can be cut out of wood or cardboard or made from a Tinkertoy spool and five sticks, each covered with a cylinder of colored paper.

Source: *Hi Neighbor. Book 8.* New York: Hastings House/ U.S. Committee for UNICEF, 1965, pp. 27, 31-32.

South Africa (Cape Malay)

Moulidi-n-nabi

The men prepare buriyani for Moulidu-n-nabi

The special dish *buriyani* is prepared by the Malay men, not the women, on this occasion. The dish consists of rice and a mixture of diced mutton with onions, tomatoes, and spices, as well as hard-boiled eggs, layered in a pot. The pot is sealed and cooked over a slow charcoal fire for hours. The women, meanwhile, gather at each other's homes to have tea and sweets.

Source: *African Cooking* by Laurens Van Der Post and the Editors of Time-Life Books. New York: Time-Life Books, 1970, pp. 133-134.

Turkey

Birthday of Mohammed

On the twelfth day of Rabi-ul-Avel, the third month, is the

birthday of Mohammed. The town-crier goes about informing the inhabitants that at two hours after midday prayers a rich citizen invites them all to the mosque. When everybody is assembled in the mosque, songs celebrating the birth of Mohammed are sung. These songs are over four hundred years old and were written by the famous Turkish poet Souleiman Cheliby. After some singing, the hodja dressed in white brings forth on a small table a package of silk handkerchiefs. There are forty in all, and in the very center is a small glass vial supposedly containing a hair from Mohammed's beard. As the hodja removes the handkerchiefs, the people sing. When the handkerchiefs are all removed and the vial finally exposed, each one comes forward, kisses the vial and touches his forehead with it. After this ceremony is completed, sweet sirups are offered to all at the expense of the wealthy man who is host for the day. The reason sirups are drunk is because, according to a tradition, Emina, the mother of Mohammed, was given sirups by an angel and immediately after she drank them Mohammed was born. At night the minarets of all the mosques are illuminated with many lamps. During the remainder of this month and the whole of the next the songs in the mosque are repeated daily and a different citizen acts as host every day, providing the necessary sweet sirups. Thus the people are entertained.

Source: *When I Was a Boy in Turkey* by Ahmed Sabri Bey. Boston: Lothrop, Lee & Shepard Co., 1924, pp. 81-82.

Upper Volta, Dagomba (Mande-Dyula)

Damba

Tribal influence on Islamic traditions

Further, some features of Islam in Dagomba suggest a Mande-Dyula rather than a Hausa influence. Take, for example, the most important national festival of Islamic origin, the *Damba* festival commemorating the Prophet's birthday. The name *Damba,* as in Gonja, is of Mande-Dyula origin. Names of other festivals have been translated into Dagbane, but they provide clear parallels to festivals in Gonja. In general, one may suggest that Islamic elements have been incorporated into the Dagomba culture in much the same way as in Gonja. In Hausaland, in Nupe, and in Borgu this festival is known as Gane.

Source: *Muslims and Chiefs in West Africa* by Nehemia Levtzion. Oxford: Clarendon, 1968, pp. 89-98.

West Africa

Birthday of Mohammed

The next festival is the Prophet's birthday on 12th Rabi'al-Awwal (19th in Hausaland). This is little celebrated by the people except in Bornu, but clergy gather in the mosques and hold recitals of the *Ishi rīniyyāt* of al-Fazāzī, the *Takhmīs* of the same poem by Abū Baki; Muhammad Ibn Muhīb, and the *Dalā' il al-Kharāt.* In Futa Jalon the *karamokos* keep it as a day of fast and prayer and recite poems in Fulfulde in honour of the Prophet. Dyula keep it as a festival day when young men parade with arms and war equipment 'to guard the Prophet from his enemies'. The 26th Rajab, 'when the Prophet accompanied by an angel-guide visited the seven heavens and seven hells' is observed by some clerics and is a recognized school holiday. On the 14th Sha'bān prayers are recited for deceased kinsfolk but graves are not visited.

(Mandinka and Dyula *dō-mba ma,* 'day of the great dance', *anabi dō,* 'the Prophet's day', Moorish Arabic *mūlūd;* Masina region *mūlūd dō-mba;* Soninke *modinu n'tiale;* Tuareg *gāns;* Kanuri-Teda *gāni* and *lebi lowel;* Hausa *sallar gānē* or *sallar tākūtaha;* Wolof *gāmu;* Songhay *almudu dyinger, hay dyinger* [birth festival] or *hay tyidyi* [birth night].)

Source: *Islam in West Africa* by J. Spencer Trimingham. Oxford: Clarendon Press, 1959, p. 78.

Circa September 21-22

Autumnal Equinox

In the Northern Hemisphere the Autumnal Equinox occurs about September 22. After this date the nights are longer than the days. In the Southern Hemisphere the reverse is true and spring commences. The day is celebrated in many cultures with special rituals or festivities.

Assam

Kati Bihu

Kati Bihu rituals and lamps

Kati Bihu . . . is the poor Bihu, as there is no feasting in it. It is a one-day affair associated with the worship of the tulasi plant, supposed to be Vishnu's wife, and certain rituals performed for the well-being of paddy fields. On this day a small banana tree is planted beside the sacred tulasi in the yard and in the evening earthen lamps (*chaki*) are put at the foot of the tulasi and on the body of the banana on shelves made of bamboo sticks. Lamps are also put at the granary, in the garden and in the fields.

Offering of *naibedya,* consisting of gram, pulse, uncooked rice, banana, etc., at the foot of the tulasi and holding of *nam-prasanga* (*kirtana*) prayer are other features of the evening. This prayer, rather singing of hymns is more often done by women and children. They sing:

> Tulasi, O Mother Tulasi,
> you are Govinda's favourite,
> which way has Krishna gone do tell us,
> Mother, tell us quickly.

A feature of Kati Bihu . . . is the lighting of the sky-lamp as in other parts of India, though the custom is not widespread in Assam. This lamp hanging from the tip of a tall bamboo is supposed to show the souls of dead persons the way to heaven or to enable one to attain the abode of Vishnu.

Source: *The Springtime Bihu of Assam* by Praphulladatta Goswami. Gauhati, Assam: Lawyer's Bookstall, 1966, pp. 1-23. (Goswami discusses various Bihu customs and dwells particularly on Bihu dance and song. Some historical information on Bihu is included.)

Japan

Higan

Visiting grave sites

Higan are celebrated at both the Autumn and Vernal equinoxes. The official holiday, Subun No Hi, dates from 1946. This replaces the Imperial Ancestor Worship known as Suki Korei Sai. On the higan graves are visited and ancestors honored.

Higan, c. 1965

At this time Buddhist temples hold services in honor of the dead. Cemeteries are visited for a biannual grave cleaning and to pay respects to the departed.

Source: *Japanese Festivals* by Helen Bauer and Sherwin Carlquist. Garden City, N.Y.: Doubleday, 1965, p. 190.

Higan in Niike village, c. 1958

Memorial tablets of the household ancestors are taken out from the [storehouse] to be honored in the [household] *tokonoma* four times each year, at the two higan of the equinox, at New Year, and at Obon. Each household performs these special rituals at this time.

Source: *Village Japan* by Richard K. Beardsley, John W. Hall, and Robert E. Ward. Chicago: Univ. of Chicago Press, 1958, p. 455.

Circa September 21-22

Jūgowa (Autumnal Equinox)

A thanksgiving offering at the equinox. According to anthropologist Clarence Glacken the actual date of the celebration varies, being set by each village, but occurs at the time of the full moon (eighth month, fifteenth day).

Okinawa

Making paper money for the dead by using coin impressions

In one private observance, an old woman placed two bowls of rice, dyed pink (*someiko*) on the alcove of the first room. After placing the rice on the alcove, she went to the Buddhist god shelf in the second room where she lit charcoal sticks. Then, sitting before the god shelf, she ignited three strips of paper with a charcoal stick. These provide pocket money for the dead. The paper had previously been prepared by placing an aluminum Japanese 10 *sen* coin (minted before the war) on the paper and tapping the coin sharply with a hammer to make the impression on the paper. The embers were quenched with a little *sake*. A wash basin with two strips of wood laid diagonally across its top was used for the burning to eliminate the danger of fire. The old lady's granddaughter held the paper on the wood strips with a pair of chopsticks. The old lady then offered three prayers in a scarcely audible voice, the first two with bowed head, the last with her face to the god shelf. Then she served a meal of rice, dyed pink, fish fritters, and *sake,* though she did not partake of the drink.

Providing pocket money for the dead by tapping an impression of a coin on a strip of paper is now practiced only by the very old. In Hanashiro and Hatsuda, this custom is rarely observed. Formerly, in Hanashiro, everyone offered pocket money on New Year, *O-Bon,* and the equinoctial festivals.

Source: *Studies of Okinawan Village Life* by Clarence J. Clacken. Scientific Investigations in the Ryukyu Islands (SIRI) Report no. 4. Washington D.C.: Pacific Science Board Council, 1953, pp. 324-325. (Source details a parade held in 1951 and a full moon evening celebration in Minatogawa held at Jugowa.)

Seven Days, Beginning Fifteenth of Tishri (October-November)

Sukkot

This seven-day harvest festival begins on the full moon of Tishri. Originally called the Feast of the Ingathering, the festival is now known as Sukkot. The temporary trellis-roofed hut in which the holiday is celebrated is called a *sukkot*. Levitious 23:40 says, "on the first day you shall take the fruit of goodly trees (citron-ethrog), branches of palm (lulau), boughs of leafy trees (myrtle), and willows of the brook, and you shall rejoice before the Lord your God seven days." These *lulavim* and *ethrogim* are blessed in the synagogue and in the home Sukkot ceremony. Dates for Sukkot are September 23, 1991; October 12, 1992; September 30, 1993; September 20, 1994; and October 9, 1995.

Bukhara

Succot in Bukhara

Bucharan Jews decorated their booths with paper garlands and hung the walls with tapestries. The ground was covered with thick carpets. "Elijah's Chair" was set out to welcome the Patriarchs, who visit the booth in spirit. The chair was decorated with silks and held sacred books.

Source: *One People: The Story of the Eastern Jews* by Devora and Menachem Hacohen. New York: Sabra, 1969, p. 144.

Ethiopia

Feast of Tabernacles

Falasha spread floors with palms and willows

The Feast of Tabernacles (in Ethiopic *bä alä mäsällät*) is celebrated from the fifteenth to the twenty-second of the seventh moon in commemoration of the exodus of the Jews from Egypt and corresponds to the Jewish Feast of Tabernacles. There are special prayers, but the Falashas do not make the booths required by Scripture. The reason given for the disregard of the ordinance is that the huts in which they live may be regarded as booths symbolical of Israel's sojourn in the wilderness. They spread leaves of various trees, such as the palm or a variety of weeping willow, over the floors of their houses and the synagogue.

Source: *Falasha Anthology: The Black Jews of Ethiopia* by Wolf Leslau. New York: Schocken, 1951, p. xxxii.

Iran

Succot in Persia

Each compound built a communal succa. Construction began after the post-Yom Kippur meal. Materials for the *succa* were stored away from year to year. Each person removed shoes before entering the *succa*. Nothing was eaten outside the *succa* during the festival. *Etrog* and *lulav* were also shared among families, as they were too expensive for individual families to purchase. Dancing with the Torah in procession occurred every evening, so Simchat Torah actually commenced with Succot itself. Nuts and candies were tossed at the "Torah Bridegroom" and "Genesis Bridegroom" as they recited their portions from the Bible.

Source: *One People: The Story of the Eastern Jews* by Devora and Menachem Hacohen. New York: Sabra, 1969, p. 144.

Israel

Sukkot in Jerusalem

The days between Yom Kippur and Sukkot are festive in Israel. Everyone is busy buying the arba'ah minim and building sukkot. Jerusalem's main market looks like a carnival, with many people carefully selecting the most stately lulav and the lumpiest lemon-shaped etrog they can afford. In addition to the many lulav and etrog stands, there are also portable sukkot for sale, branches for the sekhakh, and special pictures to decorate the sukkah.

The Israeli sekhakh is usually made of carob tree branches and oleander entwined with palm branches—the same sekhakh that was used in Israel two thousand years ago. The tasty carob fruit hangs between the colorful oleander flowers. The walls of many sukkot are decorated with fine rugs and special paintings that are meant only for this holiday.

In Jerusalem, a prize is awarded for the most beautiful sukkah in the city. Because there are Jews in Jerusalem who come from all over the world, there is a variety of different sukkot and customs. *Kurdish* Jews sit on pillows around a low table in the sukkah, while *Sephardic* Jews prepare a fancy chair for the Ushpizin. They cover it with fine cloth and place sacred books on it. All these customs reflect the wish to fulfill the mitzvah of making the frail sukkah beautiful.

Most people in Jerusalem live in apartments, so many of them build their sukkot on balconies. Others build them in small yards, on roofs, or on sidewalks. The sekkakh must not have anything over it, not even a tree, so apartment buildings in Israel have balconies without overhangs. Each balcony is open to the sky.

Source: *Sukkot: A Time to Rejoice* by Malka Drucker. New York: Holiday House, 1982, p. 51.

Yemen

Succot in Yemen

Many houses were built with one room without a ceiling to serve as the *succa*. The room was covered with mats during the rest of the year. Durra, corn stalks, or green cacti leaves formed the *succot*. The floor was covered with mats and carpets. Bowls of myrtle leaves were hung in the corners.

Two kinds of *etrogin* grow in Yemen. An edible etrogin which can weigh as much as fifteen pounds is found there. But a smaller, inedible etrogin is used for Succot. Some fathers would provide lulav and etrog for each son who could hold them.

Several families might buy an ox or sheep communally for the feast. Everyone slept in the succa during the festival nights.

Source: *One People: The Story of the Eastern Jews* by Devora and Menachem Hacohen. New York: Sabra, 1969, p. 144.

For more on Sukkot see: ''Sukkot: Creating Shelter'' in *The Jewish Holidays: A Guide and Commentary* by Michael Strassfeld. New York: Harper & Row, 1985, pp. 125-148. (Contains plans for building a sukkot.); ''Sukkot'' in *Burning Lights* by Bella Chagall. New York: Shocken, 1946, pp. 95-114.

September 27

Maskal (Meskel, Masqal)

''The Feast of Finding the True Cross'' is a day to commemorate the finding of Jesus' cross by Saint Helena, mother of the Roman Emperor Constantine, in the fourth century. *Maskal* means ''cross.'' Holy Cross Day is also celebrated on May 3 and September 14 in other branches of the church.

Ethiopia

Building the demera

[The] Festival of Masqual . . . celebrat[es] the discovery of the true Cross by Empress Helena. By this time the heavy rains have subsided, and the air is filled with something of the spirit of spring. (Although Ethiopia lies north of the equator the summer rainy season is known as ''winter'' because of its coldness.) The landscape is colored by acres of yellow wildflowers, which are cut and fastened to the poles each family brings to a central clearing where a huge bonfire is built. In late afternoon, after the tepee of poles has been constructed, the priests begin the ceremony by intoning appropriate chants. Then each status group circles the poles three times, in honor of the Trinity—first the local lord, then the clergy, the lesser nobility, the peasant men, women, and finally the children. In the evening the festival takes a more secular turn. The bonfire is lit, and the young [men] dance around it shouting their war chants. As the fire blazes on, these fellows seize burning brands and playfully hurl them at one another.

Source: *Wax & Gold: Tradition and Innovation in Ethiopian Culture* by Donald N. Levine. Chicago: Univ. of Chicago Press, 1965, p. 62.

Maskal celebrations

By this time of year the golden Maskal daisies cover the slopes and meadows of the Ethiopian countryside. On the eve of Maskal, in every town and village, a *demera* is built, a tall conical arrangement of wooden poles decorated with golden daisies. The completed *demera* is blessed with incense and a procession of villagers or townspeople, led by the priests and other clergy, circles the *demera* three times. Then, as dusk falls, the *demera* is set aflame to symbolize the flame of burning incense that guided Saint Helena to the exact location of the true cross in Jerusalem.

Many lambs and chickens are slaughtered for the feast, and singing and dancing continue far into the night. On the following day, Maskal, people draw a cross on their foreheads with the charcoal from the dead fires of the previous night, feasting resumes, and the day is spent in visiting and merry-making.

Source: *Ethiopia: Land of the Lion* by Lila Perl. New York: William Morrow, 1972, pp. 72-73.

A Meskel visit

On the third day of Meskel, the day called *nik-bar,* Zemwet came to visit Kerwagé . . . to give her the customary holiday greetings. . . . It was the end of the rainy season and the sky seemed to shimmer; there was not one speck of cloud. The wild flowers blossoming in clusters beside the path looked as though they were showing their teeth in laughter. The grassless yard in front of Bala's house had been scraped and made neat for Meskel, and the flat gray stepping stones had been scrubbed. . . . The doormat was new and had been bought especially for the holidays. The Meskel meat could be seen through the partition and the loft was piled high with damp white firewood. The walls had been freshly whitewashed, and the black jugs and bowls and platters hanging in a row on the wall were shiny, some of them new and others newly polished.

''I am happy that you are in good health to see this Meskel,'' said Zemwet, the customary holidays greeting. She kissed Bala on both shoulders and the forehead and kissed Kerwagé on both shoulders. Kerwagé rose and responded:

''May we again have a good year!'' She kissed Zemwet's shoulders. Then Theresa took the little bowl of butter Zemwet had brought as a Meskel gift, and put it behind the partition on the floor beneath the hanging meat. She returned and kissed Zemwet's cheeks, and Shinega got up and kissed her cheeks, too. Theresa poured beer into a clay glass and presented it to the guest. Zemwet took two swallows and pronounced judiciously: ''Even if it weren't Meskel, I would have come only for this beer!''

Source: *Shinega's Village: Scenes of Ethiopian Life* by Sahle Sellassie. Translated from the Chaha by Wolf Leslau. Berkeley: Univ. of California, 1964, pp. 60-61.

September 29
St. Michael's Day

This day is the Feast of St. Michael the Archangel, patron saint of soldiers, Normans, horses, and high places. Goose is the favored dish at this time in Northern Europe. St. Michael's Day is also celebrated elsewhere on the first Sunday of October and on November 8.

Bolivia
Fiesta De San Miguel

Fiesta de San Miguel in Taypi, in 1982

After Mass and a brief, somewhat disorganized procession around the church to bless its four sides, the priest went back to La Paz and the secular part of the fiesta began.

Two dance groups participated: one from Taypi called Potolos, the other called Kullawas from a neighboring community, Ranikera, situated at about three hours walking distance. It was said that in earlier years there had been four to six dance groups, but with rising costs it had become too expensive.

The members of the two groups wore special, colorful, rented costumes, different from those of the other group, so that they could easily be distinguished from one another. For the Taypi group the men's costume consisted of black and white striped trousers with wide embroidered trimmings at the bottom, a white richly embroidered shirt and a yellow jacket with a black ornamented ribbon at the front and around the sleeves. Around their neck the men wore a red, white and black striped scarf and on top a white hat with multi-colored feathers and yarn tassels.

The women dancers wore blue or purple dresses of heavy, woolen fabric with long sleeves, all richly decorated. Over their shoulders they wore a white *manta,* with multicolored adornments and the daily carrying cloth, *awayo,* this day holding only a symbolic burden. They wore hats similar to those of the men and in their hands a *tari*. Little items needed for the day can be carried in this small piece of cloth, patterned and woven like an *awayo*. These small bundles were also used as ornamental devices in some of the dances.

At the onset of the fiesta there was a certain degree of interaction between the members of the two communities. Participants from Ranikera joined the Taypis for the religious ceremonies and the two dance groups performed at the same time, though not literally together, at the very opening part of the dancing. From then on, the two groups socialized, rested and ate separately at all times. Each group withdrew to opposite corners of the huge square—seemingly as far away from each other as possible.

Thus, the fiesta rituals can be said to emphasize the existence of distinct boundaries around separate groups, and at the same time, symbolically remove or allow the crossing of those boundaries. It follows then that the fiesta demonstrates two mutually opposed principles: boundary maintenance and boundary crossing.

Fiesta meals of the Taypi group

On the main day of the fiesta five meals were served before 3 P.M. Fiesta meals are prepared with more costly ingredients than regular meals. Some of these ingredients have been saved for the special occasion. Meat, rare on the daily menu, and plenty of the most appreciated potatoes, *ch'uñu* and *tunta,* are included in many of the dishes. No effort is spared to make the meals memorable.

The 12 o'clock lunch, *Papas a la huancayna,* was the first community meal to be served to the Taypis in the square that day. It was sponsored by the *padrinos* of the day. The dish is time-consuming to make and contains such uncommon ingredients as ground peanuts and milk, simmered into a sauce, which is poured over pre-boiled potatoes and lettuce.

After about an hour of dancing following the first community meal the next one, a dish named *Fricasé,* was served. The new *preste,* Sergio, and his wife, Antonia, were the hosts of this third meal of the day. *Fricasé* is a heavy soup reminiscent of a stew, and the main ingredients, potatoes, *ch'uñu, tunta* and pork (spiced with hot pepper, garlic, oregano, cumin, pepper and salt) are added in chunks and not cut up, minced nor mashed.

The second and third meals, which had been prepared for days in advance at the hosting homes, were carried to the square while still hot. A group of women helped to place portions of food on individual plates, which were quickly passed around by running *sirwisuyos,* male "waiters". These men brought the empty plates back, and when refilled passed them around to new eaters, although strictly to persons affiliated with Taypi. The people from neighboring communities, who were watching from outside the abode wall, were never asked to share in the dancing nor in the eating.

The communal eating continued after another hour of dancing in the blazing sunshine, when the entire group of Taypi dancers and their supporters were invited to the homestead of Severo's parents at 20 minutes walking distance. In a meadow adjacent to the buildings the meal was served in the same manner as before. The hearty dish, *Guiso de cordero,* contained lamb, potatoes, *ch'uñu,* onion, carrots and spices such as bay leaves and hot pepper.

A new type of communal eating commenced shortly thereafter: several women from different Taypi farmsteads, who had relatives among the dancers, arrived with their *awayos* filled with food. The cloths were spread on the ground, and a number of heaps of various kinds of boiled, cold potatoes were piled on each one, with small bowls of hot, spicy *llajua*-sauce for dipping the potatoes placed in the center. Desired guests were invited with gestures and verbal calls. The entire meadow was eventually filled with dozens of dispersed groups sitting or lying around. After a short rest the party marched back to the square, where the dancing and drinking continued throughout the rest of the day. No more collective meals were served that day.

Source: *Food and Culture among Bolivian Aymara: Symbolic Expressions of Social Relations* by Mick Johnson. Uppsala, Sweden: Univ. of Uppsala, 1986, pp. 146-151. (For more information see "The Fiesta de San Miguel in Taypi" in this source, pp. 144-156.)

Estonia

Mihkli Paev

Summer work ended, laborers returned to their homes, and school started.

Great Britain

Michaelmas

A day to settle debts

Michaelmas is one of the "quarter days" in the south of England, a time to settle rents and bills and fire or hire farm hands in the past. The Michaelmas goose, at its fattest this time of year, is enjoyed.

Blackberries unlucky after Michaelmas

It is very unlucky . . . to eat blackberries at or after Michaelmas (or, some say, after Old Michaelmas, 10 October) because the Devil then spits—or worse—on them, presumably to spite his rival.

Source: *The Customs and Ceremonies of Britain* by Charles Kightly. London: Thames and Hudson, 1986, p. 163.

Hungary

Szent Mihaly Napja

On this day servants received pay and winter clothes.

Ireland

A Michaelmas goose

If you eat goose on Michaelmas Day you will never want for money during the coming year. Geese are just ready for eating at this time of year, being fattened and tender. Irish traditionally stuff the goose with potato to cut the grease and absorb the rich flavor. In the eighteenth and nineteenth centuries onion sauce was served with the goose. Onions were cooked in a mixture of half milk and half water with a slice of turnip. These were then mashed, mixed with butter, nutmeg, salt, and pepper and a little cream, and mashed again. Today apple sauce is the more traditional goose topping.

Source: *A Taste of Ireland: Irish Traditional Foods* by Theodora Fitzgibbon. New York: Avenel Books, 1978, p. 105.

Moon 9, Day 9 (September-October)

Double Ninth

This is a day for climbing hills to picnic. Kite flying takes place in some areas. In parts of Southern China this is also the autumn day for grave visiting.

Hong Kong

Burning of the clothes in Hong Kong

Apart from the actual visit to the cemetery, All Souls Day is observed in the home by the ceremony of the "Burning of the Clothes". Winter has now set in, and the dead are in need of warmer garments and other household necessaries. Imitations of wadded garments, and notes on the Bank of Hell for current expenses, are addressed to the spirits for whom they are intended. A sort of Bill of Lading is drawn up and signed in the presence of witnesses, stipulating that on its arrival in Hades, it shall be handed over to the addressee. The Deed contains a list of everything included, money, clothing, paper servants, etc., and it is burned along with them, so that the contributors have every confidence that their gifts will reach the proper destination. An extra parcel is often made up to propitiate any hungry spirits who may be infesting the route like footpads, partly from a sense of charity towards these neglected souls, and partly as an insurance against pilferage on the journey.

Source: *Chinese Creeds and Customs* by V.R. Burkhardt. Hong Kong: South China Morning Post, 1982, p. 72.

People's Republic of China

Ch'ung Yang

Celebrating in Peking, c. 1930

On the ninth day of the ninth moon, Ch'ung Yang, one was supposed to climb mountains, have picnics, fly kites, eat crab and drink some warm wine, which presented certain difficulties for northern city dwellers, as there were no mountains for miles around, and as yet very little wind for flying kites. One was not allowed to picnic on Coal Hill, the nearest approach to a high place available, nor to fly kites from it, but at least we could go to the highest place in the garden, the "man-made hill," and enjoy some warm wine impregnated with chrysanthemum petals. . . .

We ate special *teng-kao* cakes at this time, a kind of pastry made of glutinous rice, filled with meat and flat in shape, which was made in a mold and then steamed. In the old days these customs had a particular significance for the official classes, as the chrysanthemum symbolized endurance and the word cake, by punning association, could also mean "promotion." Chrysanthemum-viewing parties were held by the Imperial Court in the grounds of the Forbidden City, and literati vied with one another in composing poems while sipping the life-lengthening wine.

My parents usually gave a family dinner party on the day of the Double Ninth, which took advantage of whatever fruits were in season and had no embargoes imposed by religion on meat or fish.

Source: *The Mandarin Way* by Cecilia Sun Yun Ching. Boston: Little, Brown, and Co., 1974, p. 187.

Kite flying on the Double Ninth in Fukien

In the North the month for flying kites is March, but in Fukien the Double Ninth is consecrated to this diversion. Given fine weather, huge crowds congregate on the hill-tops round Foochow to witness the contests, and special police are mobilised to prevent clan fights, which are liable to result from disputes among the competitors. The Festival kites are enormous, needing several hands to manipulate, and are the property of guilds, and private clubs formed by the gentry. It is part of the game to bring down a rival kite, and knives are sometimes attached to sever the strings. On a favourable day the sky is full of butterflies, dragons, frogs and centipedes, fluttering and wriggling as they dip and mount in the breeze. As the Chinese like noise, a musical accompaniment is provided by the attachment of Aeolian harps, called Yao ch'in, gourd-shaped frames of bamboo, with slivers of the same plant stretched across to form the strings. The Chinese are loath to admit that the musical accompaniment is merely a refinement which adds to the pleasure of the sport, so they have been obliged to invent a legend to account for its origin. During the reign of the first Han Emperor, a general on the losing side found himself surrounded, and threatened with annihilation. Like Gideon with the pots and candles, he devised a ruse to scare his enemies, and broke his way through by attaching Aeolian harps to kites, whose eerie whistlings from the skies deluded the host of Han into the belief that they were being attacked by supernatural powers.

Source: *Chinese Creeds and Customs* by V.R. Burkhardt. Hong Kong: South China Morning Post, 1982, p. 70.

Taiwan

Double-yang (Tiong-iong Choeh)

The day is called "Double-yang" because the number "9" is a special number dedicated to the "yang" principle of the sun. So also the day is called the "double ninth". . . . It is connected with a story from the later Han Dynasty about a famous magician and hero-doctor named Fei Ch'ang-fang (A.D. 25-220) and his friend Huan Ch'ing. The Taiwanese version of the story says that Huan Ch'ing was Fei's disciple, and one day was told by his master that on the ninth day of the ninth month he and all his family would be destroyed unless they went up to a high mountain, and brought with them the berries from the pepper-acacia tree. Huan obeyed, and when he returned to his house in the evening, he found that everything that had remained in the house was slain, including the pigs, cattle, and chickens.

The common man gives a banquet on this day, and many go into the hills for a walk or a picnic. The Taowanese say that the main purpose of the day is to "drink wine and enjoy from a mountain top." The day is also called the "Climbing up on high" festival, "Teng-ko Choeh."

Source: *Taiwan Feasts and Customs* by Michael R. Saso. Hsincu, Taiwan: Chabanel Language Institute, pp. 72-73.

Moon 9, Day 9 (September-October)

Chrysanthemum Day

This is one of the five sacred festivals of Ancient Japan. A wondrous display of chyrsanthemum varieties was held on this day. Figures constructed of trained chrysanthemums were displayed. Chrysanthemum wine was drunk, and in Korea, chrysanthemum cakes were eaten.

Japan

Foodstuff

Choyo, Chrysanthemum Festival, is the last of the five festivals of the ''*gosekku*''. . . . Rice boiled with chestnuts is eaten and *kiku-sake,* a wine sweetened and flavored with chrysanthemums, is drunk to celebrate the occasion in many families.

Cotton nursing of the chrysanthemum

A very interesting custom growing up with this festival is that of putting cotton wool on the chrysanthemum flowers on the eve of the festival day. The next morning the cotton, now wet with either dew or frost, is removed and the body wiped with it. This is knows as ''cotton nursing of the chrysanthemum'' and shows a desire both to protect the flowers and to use the dew of the early frosts to cure the ailments of mankind.

Source: *Japanese Festival and Calendar Lore* by William Hugh Erskine. Tokyo: Kyo Bun Kwan, 1933, pp. 109-110.

Jugoya, chrysanthemum displays in Ancient Japan

The figures, over man-size, had very lifelike heads, hands and feet, made of wax or paste; but their costumes, apart from the smallest trimmings, were completely and most cunningly composed of tiny chrysanthemums, varying in size and colour according to the realistic demands. The figure's body consists of a fragile network woven of bamboo or wire, sustained in the desired pose. The plants are grown within this frame, and the boughs trained in such a way that the blossoms will form just on its surface, covering the structure completely with a smooth, velvety coat. If the effect looks somewhat incongruous to a real flower lover, full credit must nevertheless be given to the skill with which living plants are utilized for these *tableaux*. Part of the ''stage background'' may be equally composed of floral objects, such as boats, bridges and so forth, while huts and temples, castles and hills will be of wood or painted on a backdrop.

The cost of producing such puppets and scenes was so high that a considerable entrance-fee had to be exacted; nevertheless the lengthy meandering paths through the grounds were thronged for weeks, and at one time Edo had more than fifty places where these flower-displays were held. *Kiku ningyō* exhibitions were still frequent in the parks of big cities some years ago, although rapidly decreasing because of the growing cost on the one hand, and a lesser interest in ''old-fashioned amusements'' on the other.

Ninth day of the ninth month, c. 1967

For ages past, the 9th day of the 9th month has now been principally a day of congratulatory visits to one's superiors, and in no way comparable to any of the other festivals. It had little to do with family, except perhaps in the remoter regions. The actual chrysanthemum festival extends over practically the whole month or far into the tenth month, depending on the climate, and had to do with the viewing and enjoying of the wonderful floral displays. Yet even these viewings were far more sedate, more formal, than the viewings of the cherry-blossoms in spring or of the maple-leaves when they began to turn red after the first frosts. On both these occasions the populace made merry with picnics, *sake*-drinking, dancing and songs, sitting under the colourful trees. The chrysanthemum festival was a quiet promenade from booth to booth, standing in admiration before each plant. There was no exuberance.

Source: *The Five Sacred Festivals of Ancient Japan: Their Symbolism & Historical Development* by U.A. Casal. Tokyo: Sophia University and Charles E. Tuttle Co., 1967, pp. 95-105. (Casal was a Swiss businessman who lived for 50 years in Kobe.)

A visit to a turn-of-the-century Chrysanthemum Show

Yoshi-san and his Grandmother go to visit the great temple at Shiba. They walk up its steep stairs, and arrive at the lacquered threshold. Here they place aside their wooden clogs, throw a few coins into a huge box standing on the floor. It is covered with a wooden grating so constructed as to prevent pilfering hands afterward removing the coin. Then they pull a thick rope attached to a big brass bell like an exaggerated sheep-bell, hanging from the ceiling, but which gives forth but a feeble, tinkling sound. To insure the god's attention, this is supplemented with three distinct claps of the hands, which are afterward clasped in prayer for a short interval; two more claps mark the conclusion. Then, resuming their clogs, they clatter down the steep, copper-bound temple steps into the grounds. Here are stalls innumerable of toys, fruit, fish-cakes, birds, tobacco-pipes, ironmongery, and rice, and scattered amidst the stalls are tea-houses, peep-shows, and other places of amusement. Of these the great attraction is a newly-opened chrysanthemum show.

The chrysanthemums are trained to represent figures. Here is a celebrated warrior, Kato Kiyomasa by name, who lived about the year 1600, when the eminent Hashiba (Hidéyoshi) ruled Japan. Near the end of his reign Hashiba, wishing to invade China, but being himself unable to command the expedition, intrusted the leadership of the fleet and army to Kiyomasa. They embarked, reached Korea, where a fierce battle was fought and victory gained by Kiyomasa. When, however, he returned to Japan, he found Hidéyoshi had died, and the expedition was therefore recalled. Tales of the liberality and generosity of the Chief, and how he, single-handed, had slain a large and wild tiger with the spear that he is represented as holding, led to his being at length addressed as a god. His face is modelled in plaster and painted, and the yellow chrysanthemum blossoms may be supposed to be gold bosses on the verdant armor.

Next they looked at eccentric varieties of this autumn flower, such as those having the petals longer and more curly than usual. To show off the flowers every branch was tied to a stick, which caused Yoshi-san to think the bushes looked a little stiff and ugly. Near the warrior was a chrysanthemum-robed lady, Benten, standing in a flowery sailing-boat that is supposed to contain a cargo of jewels. Three rabbits farther on appeared to be chatting together. Perhaps the best group of all was old Fukurokujin, with white beard and bald head. He was conversing with two of the graceful waterfowl so constantly seen in Japanese decorations. He is the god of luck, and has a reputation for liking good cheer. This is suggested by a gourd, a usual form of wine-bottle, that is suspended to his cane, whilst another gourd contains homilies. He was said to be so tender-hearted that even timid wild fowl were not afraid of him.

Source: *Child-Life in Japan and Japanese Child Stories* by Mrs. M. Chaplin Ayrton. Boston: D.C. Heath, 1901, pp. 30-31.

For further study see: *The Five Sacred Festivals of Ancient Japan: Their Symbolism & Historical Development* by U. A. Casal. Tokyo: Sophia University and Charles E. Tuttle Co., 1967. (Entire chapter on topic, pp. 95-105.); *Japanese Festival and Calendar Lore* by William Hugh Erskine. Tokyo: Kyo Bun Kwan, 1933, pp. 124-131. (Detailed description of the figures in the Hirakata Chrysanthemum Doll Show. Pages 109-111 discuss the Choyo Chrysanthemum Festival on September 9.)

Korea

Chrysanthemum Cakes

On the ninth day of the Ninth Moon people in every house eat chrysanthemum cakes as they eat azalea cakes on the third day of the Third Moon. Chrysanthemum cake is a kind of dumpling made from mixing yellow chrysanthemum petals with rice flour. Honey water, with mandarin oranges, pears, pomogranates and pinenuts floating in it, is drunk. Numbers go to view the crimson maple leaves, and men of letters and painters visit places noted for autumn foliage where, with sweet smelling chrysanthemum petals in their wine cups, they write and read poems and paint pictures.

Source: *Folk Customs and Family Life* by Tae Hung Ha. Seoul, Korea: Yonsei, 1958, p. 37.

Okinawa

Chrysanthemum day in Okinawa

Chrysanthemum day, the ninth day of the ninth month (October 9, 1951), is a very minor holiday. A chrysanthemum is put in *sake,* and the flask is placed on the god shelf. A leaf of the plant is put in the *sake* when it is drunk. People at this time wish one another good health. The festival is only spottily observed.

Source: *Studies of Okinawan Village Life* by Clarence J. Clacken. Scientific Investigations in the Ryuky Islands (SIRI) Report no. 4. Washington, D.C.: Pacific Science Board Council, 1953, p. 326.

Moon 9, Day 9

Festival of the Nine Imperial Gods

Singapore

Festival of the Nine Imperial Gods in Singapore

In the China of the past, on the ninth day of the ninth month people would fast and climb the mountains to cleanse themselves from whatever evil had gotten attached to them during the preceding year. In the Singapore of today, people of Chinese descent celebrate the Festival of the Nine Imperial Gods during the first nine days of the ninth month.

For centuries, Chinese have upheld the belief that the Nine Imperial Gods—*T'ien ying, T'ien jen, T'ien chu, T'ien hsin, T'ien ch'in, T'ien fu, T'ien ch'ung, T'ien jui*, and *T'ien p'eng*—reside in the northern heavens, each on one of the seven stars of the Big Dipper (*Ursa Major*) and the remaining two gods on two stars nearby. These two stars are invisible. They are stars of transformation which are visible only to the eyes of immortals.

The main focus of activities around the Nine Imperial Gods is the festival during the first nine days of the ninth lunar month. Devotees will keep a vegetarian diet for one up to twelve days depending on the depth of their involvement and the degree of their piety.

The first day of the festival is marked by a procession to a river or the sea, whatever is closest to the temple, in order to "fetch the Nine Imperial Gods." (It should be remembered that the mother of these gods was originally a water spirit). When asked why the gods have to be fetched from a river, devotees may tell the following story:

During the Ch'ing Dynasty (1644-1912 A.D.), a rich man, head of a gentry family, invited many noblemen and wealthy people for dinner to celebrate his birthday. When a leprous beggar appeared, the guests showed their disgust and wanted to leave. The beggar advised to let the guests go, he would stay with the host overnight. The next morning it was discovered that the dikes had burst and that all those who had left during the night, had drowned in the ensuing flood. The host family and his property, however, remained untouched by the raging waters. The beggar then revealed that he was one of the Nine Imperial Gods who have power over rivers and seas and who control life and death.

When the procession has reached the sea or a river, a Taoist priest invokes the spirits of the Nine Imperial Gods and invites them to descend into an urn with burning benzoin. It is believed that when the sacred ashes start to burn vigorously, the spirits have entered the flames. The urn is then put on a sedan chair and ceremoniously carried to the temple where it is kept at a secret place away from public view. The temple committee of the Tou Mu Kong Temple, Upper Serangoon Road, though, has decided to place the urn at the entrance of the central hall, so that all worshippers can pay homage to the deities when entering the sacred enclosure. In this case, secrecy is retained by permanently keeping another urn with ashes in a small pagoda behind the temple where only Taoist priests and Buddhist monks are permitted to enter.

After the ritual fetching the gods from the river, devotees start to crowd through the temple doors which have already been opened at dawn. A bamboo pole with a yellow flag on top has been erected in front of the temple. Nine oil lamps, each representing one of the Nine Imperial Gods, are hung from another bamboo pole which is tied crosswise to the first pole just below the yellow flag. Every morning and every afternoon at 5 o'clock, blessed water is sprinkled on the ground directly below these lamps to purify the site. Gongs are sounded to summon the gods and a temple committee member lowers the lamps, then hoists them again when the gods are supposed to have arrived. Mr. Sou Huat San, in his end twenties, who serves the Hong San Temple, told me that if one of the lights should suddenly flare up or explode, this indicates an impending disaster. He was quickly interrupted by other members who, in Hokkien and Teochew, told him to keep quiet and explained that such things rarely occur.

A bridge is put up on the temple grounds for the festival. Devotees cross this bridge before they enter the temple. This "rite of passage" symbolizes the belief that the evils of the past year are left behind and that the worshippers enter a better future. Midway on the bridge, a temple committee member stamps the devotees' blouses or shirts just below the neck with a crimson stamp bearing the insignia of the deities. The red stamp seals the promise of the deities and is thought to ward off evil. At the end of the bridge crossing, the devotees receive yellow charm papers for more protection. These papers, on which the medium of the temple has painted divinely inspired characters, may be burnt. Their ashes, will then be mixed with water, and drunk to internalize the blessings. Or the charm papers may be folded up and worn as amulets or they may be affixed to the walls of the devotees' houses. In addition, yellow threads may be tied to the wrists of devotees, another precaution to avert evil. That means, the *ch'i* ("life force") of the devotees is prevented from escaping, evil influences are kept out and the threads, like the red stamp, also seal the promises of the deities. In return for the blessings, the devotees make donations in red envelopes (*ang pows*) and bring wax candles—some of these candles are up to nine feet tall—and thick incense sticks made out of sandalwood dust. Candles and incense sticks are frequently decorated with dragons and phoenixes. Fruit, rice and other food offerings are placed on the altar. These food offerings will be distributed among the devotees after the ceremonies and taken home for consumption. Some of the blessed rice will be added to the devotees' daily meals during the year.

Temples may put on *wayang* shows during the nine days of the Festival of the Nine Imperial Gods in Singapore. That means, Chinese operas are performed. The plot of such operas may unfold for two up to nine nights. Lion dancers and athletes may be asked to make an appearance. These shows are meant to entertain the deities while they are present in the temple. The worshippers keep coming and going, most of them using the opportunity to chat with other devotees they have not seen for a long time. Only a few settle down to enjoy the *wayang* for any appreciable period of time.

On the sixth day, temple compounds or the space where the festival is being celebrated are once again ritually purified with blessed water. For the Tou Mu Kong Temple, this water is drawn from the Kangkar River at the end of Upper Serangoon Road. At the Leong Nan Buddhist Temple this ritual is omitted and the festival is celebrated comtinuously for the whole nine days. The committee of this temple invites at least forty monks to conduct the ceremonial chanting. When the monks take a rest, the gap is filled with taperecorded chanting.

With more lion dancers, stilt walkers and musicians playing drums, cymbals, and gongs, the festival builds up to a climax on the ninth day. At the Tou Mu Kong Temple, a procession starts from the Upper Serangoon-Yio Chu Kang Junction to Kangkar at night. The procession is preceded by forty boys, each holding a colorful banner. The devotees carry joss sticks. They board trucks, buses, cars, and taxis to follow the gods. The sacred urn with the burning ashes, in which the Nine Imperial Gods are supposed to reside, is brought out of the temple and put on one of the sedan chairs. Other chairs may carry statues of the deities.

As soon as the chairs leave the temple, they begin to sway and to rock. Their bearers charge with the chairs into the crowd, running back and forth. Devotees bathe themselves in the thick smoke coming from the hundreds of joss sticks. Women may wave the smoke into their handbags. Then the chairs are put on trucks and everybody moves to a vacant lot at Kangkar where an altar has been erected and a Taoist priest is waiting.

A *chai koo* (''vegetarian nun'') steps in front of the priest and performs a slow ritual dance, bending back, upright and sideways, rolling her hands ever so slowly above each other. The movements remind of *Tai chi Chuan*. Thus the nun is bidding the Nine Imperial Gods farewell, sending them off and wishing them a pleasant journey back to their stellar thrones.

The ritual lasts about one hour. During this time the assembly remains kneeling. Then the urn is carried to the Serangoon River. The Taoist priest, holding a yellow tablet, leads the way. When the procession reaches the fishing village at Kangkar, the people living there are already asleep because they have to get up at 3 a.m. to prepare the fish they caught for the daily auction. Their boats line the bank two or three deep. The jetty is decorated with burning candles right to the water and the Taoist priest launches the small boat on which the gods will sail home. The flaming urn is now put into the boat. The crowd remains silent, waiting for the boat to move which will indicate the gods' departure. When, after some time, the boat still has not moved and the priest as well as the boys with their banners have left, some of the fishermen may leap into their boats and turn on their engines. Then the water begins to churn and the gods are on their way.

The Nine Imperial Gods in Gelang Serai

The community of Gelang Serai, sponsoring the Leong Nan Temple, celebrated the Festival of the Nine Imperial Gods from the first to the tenth of October, 1978, at Katong, Mountbatten Road. Permission to use this parksite had been granted by the Singapore Bus Administration and the Physical Education Office of the Republic of Singapore.

On one side of the huge area, a temple tent had been put up. Large crowds came daily to pay respect to the statues of Amitābha Buddha, Kuan Yin, Kuan Kong, three of the Nine Imperial Gods (the second being the most important for this community), and the nine sedan chairs for the deities. Devotees kept coming to the temple tent. They placed their joss sticks, candles, and fruit on the different altars. Mediums were also available for consultation.

On the eighth day, the temple committee served a ceremonial dinner for ten thousand of their community members. Ten huge tents had been put up, each containing ten rows of ten tables which each seated ten guests. While everybody was waiting for the tasty vegetarian meal of many courses which had been prepared by fifteen caterers, the ceremony started with the chanted blessings of *Theravāda* monks who had been recruited from local Ceylonese and Thai temples. After thirty minutes of chanted blessings from the Pāli Canon, the interest of the crowd diminished and dragons, held up by fifteen or more men, began to dance in the aisles, breathing fire when the dragon ''tamer'' threw a chemical substance on the fire ball he carried on a stick which he also used to lead the way for the dragon. Athletes began to somersault and lions danced on the stage on the opposite side of the huge site. A Chinese opera was performed on the stage on the right end of the area, while the temple tent stood on the left end.

The Theravāda monks left their platform in a hurry, when the main medium, an elderly, stately woman clad as Kuan Yin, emerged from the temple tent. Waving swords and banners, the medium began to consecrate the site. Considering the size of the huge area, it was an admirable task which took almost one hour. She symbolically fought with the lion, subduing the animal, and she exorcised the entire space whirling a large pole which had two fire balls attached to each end.

During the dinner, representatives of the city, members of other communities, and guests of honor delivered seemingly endless speeches. The nine sedan chairs danced through the aisles. With these illuminated chairs, the gods, though invisible, made their presence felt. At the end of the long program, the medium signed a paper scroll with one hundred and eight panels. While members of the community sang Buddhist chants, she painted the characters with a brush in red. Her writing was supposed to be divinely inspired and did not necessarily resemble any known Chinese characters. The scroll with the one hundred and eight panels was then placed in the Leong Nan Temple to protect the community during the coming year.

Source: ''The Nine Imperial Gods in Singapore'' by Ruth-Inge Heinze in *Asian Folklore Studies,* XL (1) (1981), 151-165.

Bright Fortnight, Asvina (September-October)

Durga Puja / Dasain / Dussehra / Durgotsava

This is a ten-day festival. The first nine nights are called Navaranti and are dedicated each to a different aspect of the Goddess Durga. The Ramayana is read or performed. The festival culminates on the tenth day with processions and ritual.

India

Navaratri worship of Durga

The festival besides other minor functions comprises the worship of goddess Durga during *Navaratri*, the *Rama-lila*, *Vijayadasami* and *Maha-Ashtami*. It commemorates the victory of Durga Mahishasuramardini over the buffalo-demon Mahishasura and also the victory of Lord Rama over Ravana, the ten-headed king of Lanka. Thus, the various celebrations of the festival show the victory of virtue over evil.

Among the Hindu festivals, Durga *puja* is unique. During *Navaratri* (nine-day worship) *Durga Saptasati* is recited by the devout people. During the festival days the people visit different temples to hear the recitation of the *Durga Saptasati* and also to have *darshana* of the goddess. *Aratis*, the rising crescendo of the drums, cymbals and bells and also the performance of dances before the image of Mahishasuramardini are some of the highlights of the worship.

During *Navaratri* she is adorned under different nine names viz. 1. Shailaputri, 2. Brahmacharini, 3. Chandraghanta, 4. Kushmanda, 5. Skandamata, 6. Katyani, 7. Kalaratri, 8. Mahagauri and 9. Siddhatri.

Durga's worship in various forms throughout India

The worship of Durga is widespread. In Punjab, Navaratri is considered a period of fast. In Gujarat every evening during the nine nights women perform the *Garba* dance. They joyfully dance around an earthen lamp, placed on a stand, singing and clapping hands in rhythmic movements.

In Tamil Nadu, the first three days of this festival are dedicated to goddess Lakshmi, the next three days to Sakti (Durga) and the last three days to goddess Saraswati. Every home has a display of *Kolu*. A decorated platform is prepared and covered with dolls and clay figurines, representing gods and goddesses. In the main room a *kalasa* or a pitcher made of silver, copper or clay with a coconut on it, symbolising goddess Durga is placed and girls sing and dance before it. Gifts are exchanged on this occasion.

In Uttar Pradesh, people wearing colourful clothes celebrate this festival with great joy.

Durga worship is specially popular in Bengal. Both Hindus and non-Hindus worship her in the form of Kali. In pre-independence days, even the people of the European community in Calcutta used to offer obeisance to goddess Kali. After nine nights (*Navaratri*) of fast and worship, the images of Durga are taken out in procession and immersed in some tank, river or sea.

Vijayadasmi, last day of Dussehra

On Vijayadasmi day, which is the last day of the Dussehra festival, the worship of gods, specially Lord Rama, is done with fervour and prayers and oblations are offered in every Hindu home. Important articles of the household are placed at the place of worship. The *noratras* (small fresh offshoots of barley plants, which are sowed in every house on the first day of the festival) are put on them as an auspicious act. The men and specially children put them after worship in their caps, on ears and in the books, etc. Poor persons and the middle-class Brahmanas carrying *noratras* go to wealthy people to offer them the stalks of *noratras* and get alms in return.

Dussehra as a royal festival

Though the Dussehra festival is tastefully celebrated by the people of all the classes, it is chiefly a royal festival. Durga being the presiding genius of all militant activities, she was assiduously courted by the Kshatriya kings desiring success in arms. The kings planned their military operations generally on the tenth day of Dussehra—the day when Rama secured his victory over his formidable foe Ravana.

Source: *Festivals of India* by Brijendra Nath Sharma. New Delhi: Abhinav Publishing, 1978, pp. 109-111.

The Ramayana during Navarati

In the South it is customary to recite the full text of the *Valmiki Ramayana* or the *Devimahatmya Purana* during the Navaratri days. In Maharashtra, to cross the village boundaries, known as *Shilanghan*, obviously the same as *Simollanghana*, is a common practice. Some people commemorate the heroism of Shivaji when they parade the roads crying 'Shivaji Ki Jai'.

In other parts of India, Ramalila which dramatizes the epic of Rama is the main item of public celebration. On the tenth day large colourful effigies of Rama's principal enemy, the ten-headed demon Ravana, his son Meghnada and brother Kumbhakarna are burnt in the night. In Varanasi the *Ramalila* is staged for one full month. The festival ends with the enactment of Bharatamilapa i.e. Rama's return to Ayodhya along with his wife Sita and brother Lakshmana and his meeting with Bharat the brother in waiting. This happy event is soleminized with the display of fireworks, etc. In Delhi a long and colourful *Ramalila* precession is a great attraction and the ground where the procession terminates and the *lila* is staged is called '*Ramlila Maidan*'. Allegorically the *Ramalila* is eulogized as the victory of good over evil.

Source: *Our Cultural Fabric: Festivals of India.* Ministry of Education and Social Welfare, Government of India, 1977, p. 27.

Dussehra in North India, Kulu Valley, and Mysore

In North India, vivid portrayals of the battle between Rama and Ravana are given by masked dancers who go on elaborate floats in a procession through the cities.

The tenth day is the culminating point of the festival. Colossal paste-board effigies of the three principal demons of the *Ramayana*—the ten-headed Ravana, Meghnada and Kumbhakarna—are erected. These are packed with crackers and explosives. The festivities conclude with Rama shooting fiery arrows into the effigies, which explode the crackers inside them.

In Bengal, beautiful idols of Durga are worshipped for nine days and on the ninth day taken out in a procession for immersion in a river or a pond. In the Kulu valley in the Himalayas, the hill people celebrate Dussehra with a colourful mass ceremony in which village-gods are taken out in processions and an animal is offered in ritual sacrifice to the gods.

Also famous is the Dussehra of Mysore, where caparisoned elephants lead a colourful procession through the gaily decorated streets of Mysore city.

Source: *Festivals of India.* Publications Division, Ministry of Information and Broadcasting, Government of India, 1956, pp. 15-16.

The mass contact element of Durga Puja

Durga Puja in Bengal during the last thirty or forty years has assumed the character of more or less community affair rather than an individualised or a private one. Formerly Durga Puja used to be held in the courtyard of a country gentleman or a rich townsman more or less as a private religious ceremony and only the very kith and kin and near-neighbours of the organiser concerned used to share in its joys and merry-makings. It was strictly a matter of individualised concern then without the involvement of the communtiy in its activities.

But not so now. In this part of the country, particularly in the cities, notably Calcutta, Durga Puja is increasingly putting on the garb of a community festival with mass contact forming one of its most essential features or components.

Durga Puja as a source of livelihood

A Sarbajaneen Puja has so many paraphernalia attached to its mirthful pageantry that it has now turned out to be the source of livelihood, at least temporarily, of so many men engaged in different professions. Right from the image-makers and the clay-modellers down to the decorators, hawkers, vendors, stall-holders, cloth-dealers tailors, musical bands, suppliers of umpteen number of small items of articles required in a puja, florists, confectioners, grocers, purohits, volunteers, etc., etc., what a vast amount of man power of diverse variation is needed to see through the performance of a Sarbajaneen Puja to its successful conclusion. As a matter of fact, Sarbajaneen Puja has nowadays become a mini-industry by its own right opening out so many ways of deriving pecuniary gain from its multi-pronged source of income.

Source: ''Festivals and Mass Contacts'' by Narayan Chaudhuri in *Popular Festivals of India* edited by Sunil Kumar Nag. Calcutta: Golden Books of India, 1983, p. 18.

India (Bengal)

Durga Puja in a Bengali home, c. 1910

The chief Hindu festival of the year (in Bengal) is known as the Durgā Pujā or Durgotsav. The great goddess Durgā, with her arms extended riding on a lion, killing an Asura (demon) with a spear, and surrounded by her whole family, visits the Hindu home every October in order to receive the worship of her devotees. The festival is known by different names in other parts of India, but the worship is conducted with more pomp and solemnity in Bengal than in any other part of India. The Pujā season is marked by great rejoicing. The Hindus refer to the occasion as the coming of the mother. Two weeks before the festival, beggars and singers go around chanting the Agamani (or coming in advance) hymns. These hymns are all marked by a human touch which appeals immediately to the listeners. It is hard for anybody born and brought up in Bengal to resist their appeal.

People dress in their best clothing and meet their friends with the utmost cordiality. Members of the same family living in different parts of the country come together under the old family roof and hold their annual reunions. The goddess Durgā is said to have been worshipped by the epic-hero Sri Rāmachandra before and after his successful expedition against Rāvana—the ten-headed demon king of Lankā (Ceylon).

The worship of Durgā is continued for four days at the end of which the image is thrown into the river or the village tank. In some homes the building of the image begins at least a month before the date specified in the almanac, if not earlier. The image is made out of clay and different kinds of paints, and numerous tinsels made of zinc, lead, or tin.

Children enjoy the festival most, not only because they have, on that occasion, new clothes to wear and good food to eat, but because they can buy toys and receive presents from others, too. Theatres, concerts, professional dancing and singing form parts of the program. The Durgā Pujā, like the Christmas season of the West, is the festival for rich and poor, high and low, learned and illiterate.

The last day when the image is thrown into the river Ganges (or into some tank, if the Ganges is not near) is the day of universal rejoicing and reunion. People greet each other; embrace each other. The younger ones "take the dust" of the elders' feet as a mark of respect for age and relationship. Everybody is supposed to eat something sweet ("sweetening his mouth," as it is called) and to drink a small glassful of *siddhi* or *bhāng* (a kind of narcotic called Indian hemp). Many past enmities are forgiven and forgotten on this occasion. Like the Christmas season, peace and good-will reign.

Animals (goats and a few buffaloes) are sacrificed before the image of the goddess in some houses. But there are homes where vegetables and fruits have been substituted for the animal sacrifices.

Source: *When I Was a Boy in India* by Satyananda Roy. Boston: Lothrop, Lee & Shepard Co., 1924, pp. 183-185.

For more on Durga Puja see: *The City of Joy* by Dominique LaPierre. Translated by Kathryn Spink. Garden City, N.Y.: Doubleday, 1985, pp. 197-200; *The Play of the Gods: Locality, Ideology, Structure, and Time in the Festivals of a Bengali Town* by Ákos Östör. Chicago: Univ. of Chicago Press, 1980.

Nepal

Dasain

The first of Dasain

On this day, called Ghatasthapana, the holy water vessel representing the Goddess Durga is placed in the prayer room. It is filled with holy water and is covered on the outside with cowdung designs. Grains are sown in the dung and piles of sand surrounding the holy jug are also sown. A puja is performed before the holy jug and each day Durga is worshipped here. The . . . sand [is] dampened with holy water each day and kept from the light. By the tenth of Dasain the seeds have sprouted. These pale yellow *jamara* are picked in small bunches and placed on the heads of children by parents as a token of Durga's blessing. Jamara sprouts are worn in the hair or behind the ears as a Dasain symbol toward the end of Dasain.

The eighth, a black night

On Kalratri, the Black Night, hundreds of animals are sacrificed at Durga's temples. On the ninth night, Maha Nawami sacrifices are made in particular for vehicles and carpenters. Blood from the sacrifices is applied to the wheels of cars along with red powder and flowers. A goat is sacrificed for each airplane of The Royal Nepal Airlines each year. Vishwa Karma, The Great Carpenter, is applied to also on this day and all tools must have a day of rest.

The Tenth, Vijaya Dasami

On the Great Tenth Day of Victory, Vijaya Dasami, Lord Rama killed the demon Ravana and Durga appeared riding a lion to vanquish Mahisaura. Hindus visit their elders on this day to receive a Tika blessing (dot of red paste placed on the forehead).

Source: *The Festivals of Nepal*, by Mary M. Anderson. London: Allen & Unwin, 1971, pp. 143, 145, 147. (For more on Dasain in Nepal see: "Dasain or Durga Puja: The Universal Mother-Goddess Triumphs Over Evil" in *The Festivals of Nepal*, pp. 143-154.)

Asvina (September-October)

Pitra Visarjana Amavasya

This is a day of remembring ancestors.

India

A remembrance of ancestors

The eldest son or some other elder member of the family performs certain religious ceremonies and offers oblations for the departed members of the family. On each day of the fortnight of *Pitra Paksha,* water is offered in honour of the departed ancestors and also in honour of the one who had died during the preceding year, as by doing so the new soul may join the already departed souls. Brahmanas and their wives are invited and food, specially *khir* (rice boiled in milk) is offered to them, with the belief that whatever is offered to them would reach the souls of the departed family members and they would feel satisfied and rest peacefully in the heaven.

During this period of about two weeks, no male member of the family shaves. Besides this, the wearing of new clothes, the cutting of hair and the paring of the nails are also not allowed.

Source: *Festivals of India* by Brijendra Nath Sharma. New Delhi: Abhinav Publishing, 1978, p. 37.

First Sunday in October
Mikkelin Paiva (St. Michael's Day)

This harvest festival is held on the first Sunday in October, but celebrates St. Michael's Day, which is held on September 29 in other countries.

Finland

Mikkelin Paiva

The first Sunday in October the churches in Finland offer prayers for the safe gathering of the harvest. It is known as ''Mikkelin paiva'' (St. Michael's Day), and in the country districts it is a day of much importance. On this day servants are hired and labor contracts concluded for the following year. A day or so before Sunday, candle-light dances are held at which the harvesters celebrate the end of their arduous labors.

Before the custom of giving thanks for the harvest on ''Mikkelin paiva'' came into existence, there was throughout Finland a celebration known as ''Kekri''. Like so many harvest festivals, it had no fixed date but was celebrated by each landowner as soon as his crops were safely in the barns. The festival was probably originally some form of pagan ancestor worship. The ''Kekri'' were the spirits of the dead who were believed to be interested in the farm work and to help with it. When the harvest was over, in gratitude for their services during the year and to preserve their good will, a feast was prepared for them, usually in the stables, as the ''Kekri'' were supposed to be especially helpful with the horses and cattle. With the coming of Christianity the ''Kekri'' festival became a part of ''Mikkelin paiva.''

Source: *Foreign Festival Customs* by Marian Schibsby & Hanny Cohrsen. New York: American Council for Nationalities Service, 1974, pp. 57-58.

First Sunday in October

La Fiesta de Agua

This is a ritual cleansing festival held at San Pedro de Casta, Peru.

Peru

La Fiesta de Aqua

This is the day on which the water is let loose, the gates of the river Carhuayumac are opened, to let the water course freshly through the irrigation ditches which have been cleaned and restored in the preceeding weeks. It is also the day of the impressive parade of horsemen which symbolizes the rapid arrival of the water to the town.

Near La Toma, the river gate, is a cave where Pariapunko resides, the God of the Water. The Mayor of the festival enters this cave and fervently suplicates Pariapunko to flood much water onto the Community. Pariapunko is offered coca, cigarettes, and chica.

After this all gather at a cross, made of branches. A second cross, made of wood, fastened into a stone pedestal, is considered the Cross of La Toma.

At this point La Toma is opened and a sky rocket is let off to signal that the new water has been released. The procession then begins before the new water. The Michiko of the Carhuayumac stops to receive the purified liquid and carries the water quickly to the fountain of Huanaquirma. Calling continually:

> ''Ay agüita de mi vida,
> qué te pasa?
> Por qué te vas bajando día a día?
> Linda Cunyac, nos das la vida a nosotros.''

At the same time the Functionaries ride parallel to the water ''lifting it up'' and singing walinas.

In this way the water is accompanied down its course, reaching the gorge of Carhuayumac on Wednesday.

Source: ''Ritual de la Fiesta del Agua en San Pedro de Casta Peru'' by Oliverio Llanos and George P. Osterling in *Journal of Latin American Lore* 8 (1) (1982), 115-150, 133, 136-137.

Second Sunday of October

Lotu-A-Tamaiti

White Sunday is a special Samoan day to honor children. They all arrive at church bedecked in pristine white, and the children provide the service on this Sunday.

Samoa

White Sunday honors children

All Christian churches in Samoa celebrate this day (''White Sunday'') in honor of children.

Church bells call over quiet towns and villages at eight o'clock in the morning for the first service. Along roads and pathways, children line up and begin to walk toward the church. Parents already fill the seats inside the church and are waiting.

The children are a vision of white. Every child is dressed in white and there's a ring of white frangipani blossoms on each dark head, like a halo. As they walk they carry banners and sing hymns.

There is no sermon by a minister at this service. Instead, the children take the stage. For weeks they have been rehearsing parts in Biblical plays at school and at home. Now they present, in turn, short dramatizations of such parables as those of the good samaritan, Noah's ark, and the prodigal son. These playlets go on throughout the morning.

After the service the children are rewarded. At home, every family has prepared a feast, having collected firewood and obtained a pig, bananas and taro, coconuts from nearby plantations, and cakes from the village store. The children are served by their parents, a once-a-year happening because on all other days the adults eat first. The children are allowed to eat all they want, and, in retrospect, they consider it the happiest day of their lives.

Source: *Celebrations: Asia and the Pacific* by Gene Sawyer. Honolulu: Friends of the East-West Center, 1978, p. 78.

Moveable: October or Later (after Rainy Season)

Antrosht (Mother's Day)

Antrosht is a day for children to visit their family homes. Special foods are prepared and songs celebrating the family heritage are sung. The celebration lasts two or three days.

Ethiopia

Antrosht in Gurage province, c. 1946

The Mother's Day is called Antrosht. It is celebrated once a year, some time after the rainy season. On that day boys and girls come from all over the places to pay visit to their parents. When the girls come, they bring butter, cheese, vegetables, various spices and everything that is necessary for the preparation of the vegetable hash. The day they arrive they make the hash in their parents' house and eat it for their evening meal. It is the mother who distributes the hash to the family. If, for some reason, the mother is absent the eldest sister distributes it.

The boys, when they come, bring with them a bull or a lamb. They slaughter it the next day and the mother provides butter and all the things which are necessary for the meat hash. Particular dishes are prepared and eaten on that day, such as a dish called *ze mamoq̌at,* all kinds of hash, and various kinds of bread, such as millet-bread, the bread made of the flour of the *äsät*-plant. . . .

The mother and the girls anoint their heads and their breasts with butter. The boys and girls sing songs celebrating the heroes of their family and of their tribe.

The festival of Antrosht lasts two or three days. When they go and come, the children kiss their parents and receive their blessings.

Source: ''Mother's Day in Ethiopia'' by Wolf Leslau in *Journal of the American Folklore Society* 61 (242) (October-December 1948), 394-395. (From a Chaha-speaking informant.)

Twenty-fourth and Twenty-fifth Days of Tishri (September-October)

Simhat Torah and Is'ru Chag

Simhat Torah marks the completion of the reading of the Torah and the beginning of the next annual cycle of reading. The scrolls of the Torah are removed from the Ark and carried aloft through seven joyous circuits of the synagogue, accompanied by singing and dancing.

Is'ru Chag, the day following Simhat Torah, begins the new reading of the Torah with celebration. Musical instruments, forbidden on Simhat Torah, are now employed. Dates for Simhat Torah are October 1, 1991; October 20, 1992; October 8, 1993; September 28, 1994; and October 17, 1995.

Israel

Simhat Torah in Israel

Because Israeli schools are closed during Sukkot, many families go on camping trips, but they return in time for Simhat Torah. . . . Shemini Atzeret and Simhat Torah are observed on the same day by Israelis. Simhat Torah is celebrated in much the same way as in America, but the flag and apple have a special meaning: The apple is the fruit of Israel's harvest, and the flag is the flag of Israeli independence.

Source: *Sukkot: A Time to Rejoice* by Malka Drucker. New York: Holiday House, 1982, p. 52.

Kurdistan

Simchat-Torah in Kurdistan

Simchat-Torah brought to all the Jews their highest moments of ecstasy. As the men went around and around in the *hakafot,* the women sprayed them with fragrant water. The small children, prayer books in hand, were carried aloft on their fathers' shoulders.

Source: *One People: The Story of the Eastern Jews* by Devora and Menachem Hacohen. New York: Sabra Books/Funk and Wagnalls, 1969, p. 20.

U.S.S.R.

Simhat Torah in the U.S.S.R.

Soviet Jews are a miracle in modern Jewish history. They are the relatives of the Eastern European Jews who became the majority of the American Jewish community. American Jews have enjoyed religious freedom but the Jews who have remained in Russia have suffered. For generations they have not been allowed to study Torah or pray together. Because of being Jewish, they have been kept from going to college, worshipping freely, and leaving Russia. It is therefore a miracle that Simhat Torah has become the one brave public expression of their Jewishness. Once a year, Soviet Jews affirm their connection to one another, to their history, and to Jews all over the world. Since they cannot escape their Jewishness in Russia, they have made it their strength. Tens of thousands of Jews stand in Red Square in Moscow and sing the Israeli national anthem, "*ha-Tikvah,*" which means "The Hope."

Source: *Sukkot: A Time to Rejoice* by Malka Drucker. New York: Holiday House, 1982, p. 52.

For more on Simchat Torah and Isru Ch'ag see: "Echoes of Celebration" in *A Walker in Jerusalem* by Samuel Heilma. New York: Summit, 1980; "Simchat Torah" in *Burning Candles* by Bella Chagall. New York: Shocken, 1946, pp. 106-113.

October 5

Han'gul Day

This day commemorates the invention of the Korean alphabet by King Sejong in 1446. Han'gul is a 28-letter phonetic alphabet.

Korea

Han'gul observances

Han'gul Day is observed throughout Korea. In schools, the children compete for prizes in calligraphic contests.

The annual Grand Cultural Festival is held for three days in Yoju, Kyonggi, to celebrate the proclamation of *Han'gul*.

Ceremonies are also held at King Sejong Memorial Center near Seoul. The Center was completed in 1973—a handsome structure with display rooms, an auditorium, conference halls and a library. On permanent view are over six hundred reference items on *Han'gul,* Korean court music, scientific equipment invented during the reign of King Sejong, and paintings that illustrate his life and achievements.

Source: *Celebrations: Asia and the Pacific* by Gene Sawyer. Honolulu: Friends of the East-West Center, 1978, p. 75.

October 7

Virgen del Rosario

This is a day of honor for the Virgen of Rosario.

Mexico

Fiesta for the Virgen del Rosario in Zinacantan

The last fiesta of the year of special character and significance is the ceremony for the Virgen del Rosario whose image is kept in the chapel in the hamlet of Salinas, or *Ats'am* (''Salt''), where the sacred salt well is located. On the Sunday before October 7 (the actual day of this saint in the Catholic calendar), the image is brought from Salinas to Zinacantan Center, and a three-day major ceremony . . . takes place. Then the Mayordomos Reyes from Zinacantan Center together with their families and assistants accompany the image back to Salinas and perform a five-day ceremony there. The climax of the ceremony is a special offering to the sacred salt well. Each Mayordomo Rey prepares a special censor (that has been especially made for this ceremony) with copal incense; the two burning censers are then lowered into the salt well and the top is covered over and wrapped up with reed mats. Then the Mayordomos Reyes and their wives dance (supposedly without stopping except to eat and drink rum) for three days and nights to pay homage to the Virgen del Rosario and her sacred salt well. During the ceremony other members of the hierarchy, including the Alcaldes, Regidores, and Mayordomos, also make a pilgrimage to Salinas to offer candles and pray. At the end, the exhausted Mayordomos Reyes and their wives and assistants return to Zinacantan, with the assurance that the Virgen has been well entertained and will permit her salt to be brought to the Hermitage of Esquipulas and distributed to the cargoholders during the course of the coming year.

Source: *The Zinacantecos of Mexico: A Modern Maya Way of Life* by Evan Z. Vogt. New York: Holt, Rinehart and Winston, 1970, p. 90.

October 17

Romería of Our Lady of Valme

The romería involves a picnicking, camping, cross-country pilgrimage. Romerías take place in many Spanish communities. The Romería of Our Lady of Valme gives the flavor of the event. Some romerías are overnight events. The Romería del Rocio of Huelva, for example, begins on the Thursday before Whitsunday and ends on Whitmonday.

Other romerías include: The Virgen de la Cabeza, at the end of April in Andalucía; The Virgen de la Pena, on the last Sunday in April at Puebla de Guzman, Huelva; Vjve, April 30 in Navarra (a twelve-mile silent romería commencing at midnight, executed by twelve members of the Brotherhood of the Holy Apostles of La Falla); the Romería del Rocio, Whitsunday at Huelva; the Romería of Pedro Bernardo, September 5 to 17 in Ávila; La Dandelada, the second Sunday in September in Ávila.

Spain

The Romería of Our Lady of Valme in Dos Hermanas near Sevilla, c. 1966

The image of Our Lady of Valme is kept in the parish church of Dos Hermanas, near Sevilla, except for her one-day visit to the shrine of Valme, on a hillock overlooking Sevilla. It was on this spot that King Ferdinand III is said to have halted before marching on to regain Sevilla from the Moors, and where he invoked the assistance of the Queen of Heaven, exclaiming: *Valme, Señora, Valme!* He promised that if she did help him in his venture he would build her a sanctuary in memory of the event.

Dos Hermanas is one of several carefully whitewashed villages that surround Sevilla like poor but respectable relations. It exports olives and has no art treasures to display but it is determined to at least present a well-scrubbed face to the occasional traveller who passes through it on his way to the capital of the province.

Outside the parish church the crowds wait expectantly for the *salida,* the ceremonial departure of Our Lady of Valme, accompanied by decorated floats and Andalusian *grupas,* superb in their flamboyant regional costume.

The members of a local Brotherhood, also on horseback, each carrying a silver mace, precede the canopied ox-cart which bears the smiling image of Our Lady, elegantly attired in a blue velvet cloak. She is surrounded by vases of Madonna lilies and the cartwheels are so heavily stuffed with flowers and foliage that they can hardly turn.

An attempt is made to transform the clumsy, fawn-coloured oxen into creatures less obviously workaday and rustic; their horns are painted and gilded, their yoke adorned and floral garlands hung round their massive necks. The effect, from a distance, is one of Minoan splendour.

The pilgrims follow the image-bearing cart on foot over dusty tracks between fields; behind them come the gay carriages full of girls and boys, singing to the accompaniment of tambourines and hand-clapping, and the cavaliers with their full-skirted ladies behind them; two small boys on a pony drew good-natured laughter: 'Are you afraid of riding a horse?' shouted a man in the crowd.

A priest passed by on horseback, and a hatless girl in jodhpurs.

One cart, full of noisy youths, was labelled 'The Vegetarians' and adorned with vegetables; another all-male-filled cart, drawn by a donkey, carried a notice: 'Don't make too much noise—our little donkey has a sore head.'

Flowers, carrots, songs, tambourines—all seemed to be equally acceptable to Our Lady of Valme, who continued to smile delightedly at the motley scene arranged in her honour. From time to time fireworks were let off so that the motorist pilgrims waiting at Valme could gauge the progress of the procession, which took three hours to reach the sanctuary.

The last few yards were the most exciting. The crowds almost stopped the procession, the cavaliers advanced to form a semi-circle at the gates of the sanctuary, the door was flung open and people surged inside in a wave of enthusiasm. . . . A pair of strong arms grasped the image of Our Lady firmly by the shoulders and turned her round for all to see. She sparkled happily in the sunshine as the crowds surged round her. *Viva, viva Nuestra Señora de Valme!* they cried again.

Then she was borne inside the church, shoulder high. The priest began to intone Mass. Outside, groups of girls and boys twirled in a spontaneous *sevillana;* castanets clicked, guitars twanged. There would be dancing and singing, praying and drinking, until sunset, when Our Lady of Valme would be escorted back to her home at Dos Hermanas.

Source: *Spanish Fiestas* by Nina Epton. New York: A.S. Barnes, 1968, pp. 201-202.

On the appeal of romerías

The processional pilgrimage of the *romería,* for example, bases its emotive appeal on the natural beauties of the countryside surrounding the sanctuary. In the *Romería de la Pastora* of Cantillana (Sevilla), the people returning from the sanctuary with their Virgin deliberately slow down the procession in order to cross the river at nightfall, at the right moment, those on horseback ignite flares that illuminate the silver accouterments of the ''sinless one'' while the shimmering waters mirror the whole *tableau vivant*—''the effect is overwhelmingly beautiful.''

Source: *Violence and Piety in Spanish Folklore* by Timothy Mitchell. Philadelphia: Univ. of Pennsylvania Press, 1988, p. 115.

For more information on romerías see: ''Spring Romerías,'' pp. 53-61, ''Autumn Romerías,'' pp. 200-203, and ''Romería del Rocio,'' pp. 85-88 in *Spanish Festivals* by Nina Epton. New York: A.S. Barnes, 1968.

October 18

St. Luke's Day

This day honors St. Luke, who wrote one of the Four Gospels. Luke also wrote the Acts of the Apostles. He was one of the few non-Jews close to Jesus. Tradition says that he was an artist, thus he is the patron saint of artists. He is also patron saint of doctors and surgeons.

Great Britain

The Charlton Fair on St. Luke's Day

St. Luke's special flower is the Marygold,
His symbol is a horned ox.

ST. LUKE is apt to be forgotten unless he reminds us by bringing some golden days out of his horn for us and, amid the chilly on-coming of winter, makes us a present of what we like to call "St. Luke's Summer."

It is for him, however, that the Great Charlton Fair is called "Horn Fair." It is held on October 18th, and every booth has a pair of horns stuck up in front. Rams' horns are for sale there and even the gingerbread is adorned with gilt horns. In those parts there is a common saying that—

"All is fair
At Horn Fair."

St. Luke's charms

He has two charms for those who would use them. The first is intricate. It requires that you shall take some marjoram and thyme and a little wormwood. Dry these before the fire and rub them to a powder, which must be sifted through fine linen. Simmer the sifted powder over a slow fire with virgin honey, white wine vinegar. Let it cool and then anoint the hands, lips and chest while lying down, ready for the night. Repeat thrice:

"St. Luke, St. Luke, be kind to me
In dreams let me my true love see."

The second of St. Luke's charms is this. You must find a peascod with nine full peas on it. Take out the peas and put in a thin slip of paper, on which you have written small,

"Come, my dear,
And do not fear."

Close the peascod and lay it under the door. The Christian name of the next person to pass through the door will be the name of the man you will marry.

Source: *Happy Holidays* by Eleanor Graham. New York: E.P. Dutton, 1933, pp. 208-209.

October 25

St. Crispin and St. Crispinian's Day

These two brother shoemakers were beheaded at Soissons in France under Diocletian. They were popular during the Middle Ages and are the patron saints of shoemakers.

Great Britain

A shoemaker's festival

Until the late nineteenth century traces of the shoemaker's craft's festival on October 25 remained. In Cross Keys in Shropshire and at Ross cobblers still took the day off then, and boys sang:

> The twenty-fifth of October
> Cursed be the cobbler
> Who goes to bed sober.

Source: *The Folklore of the Welsh Border* by Jacqueline Simpson. Totoway, New Jersey: Rowman and Littlefield, 1976, p. 165.

October 26

St. Demetrius' Day

St. Demetrius is the patron saint of Salonika. He was martyred there in A.D. 306. This day marks the beginning of the winter season for farmers. Winter contracts are signed on this day. The usual spell of good weather after this date is called "the little summer" or "the summer of St. Demetrius."

Greece

St. Demetrius' day in Greece, c. 1960

This is an occasion for opening and tasting the season's new wines. Since Demetrius is a popular Greek name, many name day celebrations are held on this day as well. This is now also the celebration of the liberation of Salonika from the Turks in 1912, so the day is a political triumph in Salonika.

An early St. Demetrius custom in Thrace

In Tzando, Thrace on the eve of Saint Demetrius' Day, a camel constructed of boards, cloths, and sheepskins made the rounds of the village at sunset. Two men inside operated the camel, and other costumed friends accompanied them. They wished each houswife a prosperous year and were given small gifts of wheat or wine in return.

Source: *Greek Calendar Customs* by George A. Megas. Athens: B. & M. Rhodis, 1963, pp. 19-20.

October 28

Thanksgiving

This is a day of Thanksgiving in Czechoslovakia. The holiday consists of church services on the first day followed by dancing and feasting that continues into the second day.

Czechoslovakia

Thanksgiving foods

"On our Thanksgiving, which is earlier than here, October 28, Czechs have roast goose, liver dumpling soup, sauerkraut, dumplings, and apple strudel. Lots of people eat raw sauerkraut; it is so delicious. You've got to know how to prepare it. We put in onion, cut very fine, and a tiny bit of olive oil, lemon juice, pepper, and sugar and salt. And you never rinse it, ever! It's a big mistake to rinse it; you rinse the good out of it. And this makes it sweet and sour.

"Thanksgiving is two days," Barbara continues. "The first day you go to church, and the second day you dance, and maybe another day after that. And people won't think they are having Thanksgiving without *klobásy,* sausages. To make them you take lean veal and lean pork, half and half, and grate in finely cut onions, garlic, and pepper that is pounded, not ground. You mix this with dry white wine, and a very few bread crumbs to hold it together. People were so particular that they baked bread especially for these bread crumbs. Then with a machine you put it in the casings, half a yard long, and tie the casings in spirals. You put a little piece of special sharp wood, a skewer, in the sausage to hold it together, and then they are fried in wine. This is the best thing out of the whole world! And that rye bread they bake is round and flat, baked very slowly, and thick and crisp. It is most important for it to be crisp. They don't make fancy sweet bread; bread should be bread!"

Source: *The International Grandmother's Cookbook* by Eileen Weppner. Boulder, Colorado: Blue Mountain Arts, 1974, p. 57. (Barbara Trousil, who, coming from near Prague, settled in Chicago in 1946).

October 28

Punkie Night

A custom of some antiquity, which remains popular in some areas of Great Britain. Children carve lanterns from mangolds (beets) or other vegetable roots and go from house to house begging pennies. This occurs on October 28 or 29, or on the fourth Thursday of October.

Great Britain

"Punkie night" at Lopen and Hinton St. George, c. 1972

This event takes place on October 28th. The children go into the fields and get mangolds, on which they carve pretty scenes, a mask, a design or something. They hollow them out and put a candle inside, and go round the village for pennies. They sing, or rather chant;

> 'It's punkie night tonight
> It's punkie night tonight.'

Although this festival is observed in other places in England, it is only at Hinton that it is on October 28th, because in the olden days this was the date of the fair down at Lopen and Chinnock. Once the men of the village went down there, and got rather tight, and lost their way in the fields. They carved themselves lanterns to see the way home. Meanwhile the women of the village were hunting for them with scarlet cloaks, and trying to fetch them home. . . .

The men went to the fair at Chiselborough, and because they were so long coming back, their womenfolk and children went out and made lanterns from mangolds to search for the men. . . .

This had been the custom ever since the informant could remember. The children would go round singing the song, 'It's punkie night tonight', and collect money that they would share out to buy fireworks. The story of how it originated was that one night a gang of men went over to Chiselborough Fair, and it was so dark that they could not see their way home. They scooped out mangolds, and put candles in them, and that is how they reckon the custom originated. Variations to mangolds are vegetable marrows. In Hinton they now give prizes for the best punkie. The informant knew of no other village that did this.

The information collected and printed above shows the usual local variations in details. The custom has previously been recorded as taking place at Hinton St. George and Long Sutton, but not at Lopen. The punkie is distinguished by the ingenuity and complexity of design being greater than is exhibited in the usual mangelwurzel lanterns found elsewhere.

The date and the nature of the custom are made plain by the above accounts. While the 28th or 29th October is claimed as the authentic Punkie Night, the fourth Thursday in October is now chosen at Hinton. Such standardization is obviously more convenient. However at Lopen the custom seems to be less strictly adhered to, and the date varies, becoming confused with Hallowe'en and November 5th. One informant at Lopen told me that the children used Punkie Night to go round and collect money for fire works.

At Hinton St. George the custom is now an event of local importance. A procession carrying punkies, chanting the song goes through the streets, and a local person is asked to judge the punkies, a prize being given for the best.

Source: "Punkies" by K. Palmer in *Folklore* 83 (Autumn 1972), 240-244.

October 31

All Hallow's Eve / All Saints' Eve

Rites for honoring the dead on All Saints' Day and All Souls' Day begin on the Eve of November 1 in many places. In a few cultures All Hallow's Eve is a time for pranking. All Saints' Day was originally a pagan festival of the dead that began at sundown.

Great Britain

Guy Fawkes and Halloween mix in Sheffield in 1973

An observer of the autumn scene on the streets of Sheffield in 1973 reported:

> I was walking home from work about 5.30. Outside the shops opposite the Drama Studio in Glossop Road a boy was sitting with a guy. A girl was running round with a turnip lantern saying, 'Spare a penny for the Guy, mister?' Is Hallowe'en now merging with Bonfire Night?

The answer to that question apparently is yes, although whether this is a new development and whether children would agree that two really different things are 'merging' are additional questions that should be asked. Perhaps Hallowe'en and Guy Fawkes activities have always been connected, in the eyes of the children, and the assigning of definite dates to one or the other kind of activities has resulted more from adults' rage for order than from the thoughts and practices of children. Indeed, some evidence already discussed elsewhere, and much more to follow this essay, suggests that children perceive a single, more or less coherent season of events, rather than separate days of Hallowe'en (October 31) and Bonfire Night (November 5). This may be the most important insight resulting from the questionnaire on autumn traditions administered to 649 Sheffield schoolchildren in the autumn of 1981. If it is true, it forces a reconsideration of the nature and function of two of the most universally observed events in the English folk calendar.

My earlier essays have offered abundant additional evidence that the Hallowe'en and Guy Fawkes traditions are indeed linked in the experience of those who participate in them. Some children indulge in mischief from Hallowe'en to November 4. Others report singing Hallowe'en songs, especially 'Witches of Hallowe'en,' on Bonfire Night and bonfire songs, especially 'Build a Bonfire,' while caking or trick-or-treating at Hallowe'en. Rachel, 11, represents this merged use of song best, since she also refers to the 'mischiefing' or trick-or-treating that she did on October 30 and 31 as 'bonfire singing.' Many people eat the same traditional foods throughout the wek that encompasses these days. Turnips, or even pumpkin pie, may alter the menu on October 31, and roast chestnuts on November 5, but people quite consistently report eating parkin, flapjack, toffee apples, baked potatoes, and hot dogs as 'special' foods during those days. Similarly the setting off of fireworks punctuates the evenings of this week, although, of course, the grand climax of explosive energy occurs on November 5.

In addition to these explicit connections between the two days, one can also perceive in the inherent nature of activities associated with Hallowe'en and Guy Fawkes certain repeated kinds of practices that give a consistent, unifying rhythm to the season. Except for guying, which can be done during the day, most of the crucial activities—scaring, trickery, caking, bonfire, fireworks—occur after sundown. It is a night-time festival. And the nights are punctuated by fires—from the candles in the turnip lanterns, the fireworks in the sky, and the bonfire on the field. Children also fashion disguises throughout the week, first in the turnip lantern, then in their own disguise for caking or trick-or-treat, and finally in the elaborate Guy Fawkes figure. The typical pattern of movement for the week is the procession from house to house. It begins with caking or trick-or-treat, includes guying from house house to house or pub to pub, and frequently also includes house-visitation for wood to burn on the fire, or, frequently by the grown-ups, for money for fireworks or food for the buffet. Even most mischief is part of house-visitation. In particular, hedge-hopping and cat-walking (i.e. sneaking across walls or hedges into people's gardens, sometimes moving on hands and knees) represent visitations that are unwelcomed and unannounced, sometimes even unperceived. Most of the tricks could at this season . . . be called 'threshold' tricks, since they are located on the porches, or at the doorways, windows, letter boxes or knockers of houses involved in a kind of aborted visitation. These tricks parody the goodwill visitations made by the singers, cakers, and trick-or-treaters. The visiting of rival bonfires, with the intention of nicking wood, is even a kind of house-visitation, this time the children to their peers rather than to adults. All of these related activities function as subtle, unperceived, reinforcements of the sense of unity that some children apparently respond to in late October and early November.

Source: "Trickster on the Threshold: An Interpretation of Children's Autumn Traditions" by Ervin Beck in *Folklore* 96 (i) (1985), 24-25.

A Halloween "caking" song

The most traditional song used in Halloweening is the "caking" song—usually pronounced "cakin" and often spelled "kaking." This is found especially among children in the villages served by the Bolsterstone and Bradfield schools, where house-to-house visitation accompanied by singing by the child visitors and by gift-giving by the adult householders is a longstanding tradition, usually thought to be associated with November 1st, the eve of All Souls' Day. As I have discussed elsewhere, however, the gradually increasing importance of October 31st, or Halloween, as a time for children's nocturnal activity—whether mischief—or solicitation of gifts—has tended to move the caking convention away from November 1st and toward October 31st. Consequently, the caking song is being regarded as a Halloween song much more than it used to be.

The typical version from the village of Stannington resembles the caking song that the Opies recorded for nearby Stocksbridge and the Christmas song that they recorded for other parts of England:

> Cake, cake, copper, copper.
> Cake, cake, copper, copper.
> Have you got a penny
> For the old man's hat?
> If you haven't got a penny
> A hapenny will do.
> If you haven't got a hapenny.
> God bless you.
>
> Nicola Ball, eleven, Bradfield Comprehensive School.

A student from Worrall knows a variant line that adapts the traditional rhyme to the more threatening convention of trick-or-treat (discussed below):

> If you haven't got a hapenny,
> A window'll go through.
>
> Hellen Bullivant, sixteen, Bradfield Comprehensive School.

The children in the survey who use this rhyme do not sing it to a tune. Rather, they tend to chant the first few lines in a sing-song fashion and then recite the rest, as Nicola did. She delivered her rhyme with a crisp, strictly observed rhythm. Although she began her recitation with a kind of tune, it eventually levelled off to normal speech patterns.

A TV tune adapted as folk rhyme by children

The most popular rhyme for Halloweening seems to be the song, "Witches of Halloween", which has been popularised through its use on the BBC TV programme, "Words and Pictures". Children report having learned the song from the televised broadcast, from its videotaped reshowing in schoolrooms, or directly from school teachers or friends. The original version of the song, as composed by Cynthia Raza, is as follows:

> We're witches of Halloween—Woo-oo,
> The ugliest you've ever seen—Woo-oo,
> We fly around at night
> And give you such a fright,
> We're witches of Halloween—Woo-oo.
>
> We're witches of Halloween—Woo-oo,
> Our faces are crooked and green—Woo-oo,
> We have black pointed hats
> And wicked witches' cats,
> We're witches of Halloween—Woo-oo.

Of course, few schoolchildren reproduce this text and tune perfectly in their informal use of it during Halloween activities. Variants abound. For instance, other forms of line two include, "They are all dirty and green" and "And we're known to be very dim". Other versions of lines three and four are, "We'll scare you in the night / And give you such a fright" and "We'll hide on the stair / And chase you everywhere".

In addition to the complex rhythmic and musical features to be commented on later, the facts of the song's composition and transmission by television obviously place it within academic or popular, rather than folk, culture. Even so, in content and imagery it is not far removed from a traditional Halloween verse recorded in Scotland by the Opies:

> This is the nicht o' Halloween
> When the witches can be seen,
> Some are black and some are green,
> And some the colour o' a turkey bean.

Children, of course, are undisturbed—perhaps even pleased—by the song's origin in mass media. Attracted by its catchy tune and its concern for witches, which so fascinates them about Halloween, children are in the process of adopting it and transforming it into something of their own creation. Although they know other similar Halloween songs from classroom or television, this is the only one to be both widely reported and to have developed a significant number of variants.

Many children sing this song before people open the door on Halloween night. "Because people like to hear it", Deborah says. "Because I am quite shy of singing to somebody's face", says Vanessa, eleven. "To attract attention", says Sharon, fourteen. Deborah learned this song six years ago while trick-or-treating with her family. She says, "When we went trick-a-treating some boys were singing a different one and when they heard it (her song) they began to sing it". Lisa, twelve, has known the song for seven years and "taught this rhyme to my friends by writing it down and then I asked them to sing it to me and I sing it to them afterwards".

Mark, seven, sings the song while he walks around scaring people at their windows. Lisa also sings the song "just before we light the bonfire" on Bonfire Night. Natalie, nine, uses the song "when I go Halloween singing, and sometimes I sing it at bonfire night when we stand around the bonfire".

From soul-cakes to "kaying"

In the village of Bolsterstone, the Loxley variant is sometimes used with the lines, "All in my stocking / All in my shoe", which is the wording recorded by A Wortley in Sheffield around 1900. The Bolsterstone variant, which is shorter and less witty than the Loxley song, normally begins with, "Kay Kay Kay. Kay Kay Kay." These words represent, of course, a reinterpretation of the traditional "Cake, cake, cake", as a result of the now lost association between what children do and the "soul cakes'' earlier given house-visitors in exchange for their promise to say prayers for the dead on November 2nd, All Souls Day. Most children today who say ''Kay kay kay'' are unaware of the connection between their nonsense word and its standard English origin. When asked whether she goes ''caking'', one eleven-year-old girls said that she did not, but then soon added that she does go ''kay-kaying''. The only Bolsterstone child who ventured to explain what ''Kay kay kay'' means said that it meant, ''Oh! Oh! Oh!'', which transforms the opening exclamation into a woeful preface to the complaint, ''Hole in my stocking, hole in my shoe.''

Source: ''Rhymes and Songs for Halloween and Bonfire Night'' by Ervin Beck in *Lore and Language* 4 (2) (July 1985), 1-2.

Halloween charms

1. Go up to your bedroom secretly and take off your shoes. Place them at right angles to one another and repeat these words:

> ''I cross my shoes in the shape of a T.
> Hoping this night my true love to see.
> Not in his best or worst array
> But in the clothes of everyday.''

Look over your right shoulder and you may, indeed, see him.

2. Go alone into a dark room where there is a looking glass. Eat an apple before it and at the last mouthful the face of your future husband will be seen peeping over your shoulder.

3. Roast nuts in the fire, naming them for each person present. The future is shown by the behaviour of the nuts. If the nut burns quietly life will be even and uneventful. If they pop right out of the grate, it may mean that the person will travel. If they stay in the grate but pop and explode[,] the owner of the nut will have an exciting time in her own country. If the nuts burn right up, the owner will not get her wish.

4. If a girl should want to know how to decide between two suitors she must get an apple and eat it, but from the core she must take out two pips. Naming them after the two men she must stick them one on either cheek and wait to see which falls off first. The one that remains on her cheek is the best choice, as he will remain faithful.

5. Pare an apple and throw the parings over the left shoulder. Turn round and see what form the peel has taken. It may be the initial name of the man you are to marry.

6. Place three saucers on a table. In one put clean water, in the second dirty water, and the third leave empty. Each member of the party is blindfolded and sent to make her or his own way to the table and see which saucer she or he finds. Their fate is told by their chance selection of a saucer.

Red to protect at Halloween

> ''Rowan tree and red thread
> Gar the witches dance their dead.''
> (I.e., till they are dead.)

If you are nervous of being bewitched or ill-wished or snatched away then wear something red or better still a branch of the rowan tree with its red berries on. Red is a dangerous colour for these supernatural beings, and they fight shy of it and shun those who wear it.

The devil in church on Halloween

It used to be thought that if you were brave enough to go and look through the windows of a church at midnight on Hallowe'en you would see an unearthly light there and the devil, himself, in the pulpit reading out the names of those who would be his before the next Hallowe'en!

Games for Halloween

1. Apples are suspended from a beam by strings. Each person has to try to catch one, using the mouth only. The hands should, really, be tied behind securely.

2. *Bob Apple.*—A number of apples are floated in a tub and the assembled company must extract as many as they can, again with the mouth only. Of course, the apples with stalks are managed fairly easily and are picked up first. The real scramble begins when the last few stalkless ones are all that are left and the competitors must either be prepared to get very wet going after their prey or be very clever in sucking up the apples and so catching them.

3. *Snap-dragon.*—This is one of the jolliest things to do. A broad shallow basin is needed and in that are put some raisins. Brandy is poured over and lit. The lights in the room should be out so that there is only the firelight and the strange flickering flame of the burning spirit. The company must snatch ''a brand from the burning,'' a raisin that is, and how they do it and what is their reward give fair means for character judging and forecasting. A timid person may refuse to try at all; one who is timid but persevering may try and fail. The rash fly right in and pull out their plums regardless of the flames. The cautious may get their prize but are likely to get burned in the effort.

Source: *Happy Holidays* by Eleanor Graham. New York: E.P. Dutton, 1933, pp. 214-217.

Ireland

All Hallow's Eve

Strawboys on Hallow Eve in Ireland

On Hallow Eve Night the spirits of the dead rise and go on the earth, girls at the hearth play at divining the identities of future mates, and in the past boys dressed in suits of white straw and caroused over the hills in the company of the dead, attacking the homes of men who kept their daughters from the cohort of bachelors. Into the girls' kitchens the ''strawboys'' broke, demanding a dance, a pantomime of procreation, and stealing food, life's resource, from the home.

Boys dressed in straw processed in some localities at Saint Brigid's and May Day. In our District they came on another of the Quarter Days, Hallow Eve, and they came violently. At a wedding the strawboys' captain demanded a last dance for the bachelors from the new bride. On Hallow Eve bachelors in straw dresses disrupted the home, unhinging the gates, dismantling the cart, and stuffing up the chimneys of the man whose eligible daughters had not been released to courtship or the man against whom the strawboys' leader held personal spite.

Source: *Passing the Time in Ballymenone* by Henry Glassie. Philadelphia: Univ. of Pennsylvania, 1982, pp. 492, 778.

Boxty, a traditional dish for All Hallow's Eve

In the northern counties such as Cavan and Donegal, the chant runs, "Boxty on the griddle, Boxty in the pan, If you don't eat Boxty, you'll never get a man." Boxty is served traditionally on the eve of All Saints' Day. To make boxty in the pan use equal amounts of raw potatoes, cooked mashed potatoes, and flour. Grate the raw potatoes and wring out the liquid, strain off the water leaving only the starch. Mix this with the grated and cooked potatoes and the flour; add salt and pepper and melted butter or fat. Knead, make into round flat cakes, cross each, and bake. They are served, split open, with butter. By adding baking soda and enough milk to make into a batter, the mixture can be dropped onto a griddle and fried as boxty pancakes. Sugar may be sprinkled on these pancakes, served with butter.

Source: *A Taste of Ireland: Irish Traditional Foods* by Theodora Fitzgibbon. New York: Avenel Books, 1978, p. 12.

Halloween customs in early Ireland

The other holiday on which food played an important role was Halloween, or the day before the first day of winter. The usual festive foods were eaten and various games associated with apples, nuts and seasonal foods were played. Barmbrack was eaten and many of the games involved fortune telling by chance; the person who happened to get the ring in the barmbrack would be the first to marry. Nuts were placed by different members of the family on the hearth and those placing them agreed that whichever nut jumped first would indicate the first person to leave home; other divination games were also played. Halloween was a holiday which, though joyful, was tinged with foreboding. It was a time to remember dead relatives and friends, and it was believed to be a time when spirits good and bad were abroad. The long, dark winter was approaching and it was a time when people prepared for the hardship of the winter months.

Source: *Life & Tradition in Rural Ireland* by Timothy P. O'Neill. London: J.M. Dent & Sons, Ltd., 1977, p. 64.

Snap Apple Night

As summer turned to autumn we stored the best apples for Hallowe'en, or Snap Apple Night as we called it. We diligently watched the nut trees, hoping that they would be ripe in time, but ripe or not we always picked them. These trees were tall with high, arching branches far from the ground, so it took all our climbing skills to conquer them. We climbed to the top and then as far out along the swaying branches as we dared, while we swung up and down at precarious angles, grasping bunches of nuts and throwing them down to the collector on the ground. Finally, gallons full, we slithered to the ground and danced home through the gathering dusk, scratched but triumphant. That night we cracked our nuts with a stone on the flagstone before the fire while apples swung from cords tied to the meat hooks on the rafters of the kitchen or floated in the timber tub of water in the middle of the floor.

Source: *To School Through the Fields: An Irish Country Childhood* by Alice Taylor. New York: St. Martin's Press, 1988, p. 48.

Philippines

Observations in the barrio by a Manila dentist

I HAVE DISCOVERED that the eve of All Saints Day is a time for fun in the barrio, so I asked Poldo more about what young people do during *Undas*.

Poldo said, "It may include telling stories, portraying apparitions, the smell of cypress or candle, footsteps in the night, *tikbalang* (a combination of horse and human forms), *tiyanak* (restless soul of a child that died unbaptized). Stories about persons who died and came back to tell the tale."

There was the story of a man who died and who had expressed the wish that he should not be placed in a niche. The family insisted on placing him in one but a month later the niche cracked. Children crowded together to listen and huddled under blankets.

Youngsters may organize themselves into singing groups to collect funds or raise money. *Nangangaluluwa,* the root word of which literally means soul. The singers are supposed to represent the souls of the dead, singing the songs of the dead souls.

As the popular hallowe'en song goes:

> *Kaluluwa ka ming tambing, Sa purgatoryo ka mi galing,*
> *Doon po ang gawa na min, Araw gabi manalangin.*
> *Kung ka mi po ay lili musan, Dali-daliin po la mang,*
> *Baka ka mi mapagsarhan, Ng pinto ng kalangitan.*
> (Ordinary souls we are, from Purgatory we have come
> And there we are duty-bound to pray by night and day.
> If alms you are to give, be in a hurry please
> For the door of heaven may close on us forever.)

Hallowe'en is also a time for stealing eggs, chickens, and other small farm animals and fruits. Sometimes whole bamboo stairs and other movable household items are carried away and the spirits of the dead are blamed for the theft.

Some homes do not open up to give "alms" after the singing of these songs. Sometimes they don't want to give, so they feign sleep. Generally, the "soul of the dead" then settles for alms in kind and they help themselves to the chickens, eggs, etc. Thus the petty stealing is justified.

Source: *My Friends in the Barrio* by Dr. Juan M. Flavier. Quezon City: New Day, 1974, p. 18.

Scotland

All Hallow's Eve in Scotland

By the age of nine I could knock out a fair tune on my 48 bass accordian. That year I was allowed to go guising with the shiny crimson and chromium-plated instrument. ''Don't fall on the stairs and drop your accordion''. I can still hear the words of warning ringing in my ears.

It's great fun dressing up or disguising on Hallowe'en night. Pirates, clowns, witches and a host of others come to life on the eve of All Hallows, or All Saints' day, the last day of October. It's even more fun doing your party piece and getting a small reward.

Our group went into tenement buildings. A sharp knock on the door and we chanted ''Would you like any guisers?'' I decided a more theatrical approach was needed. As the doors opened, I let go a loud chord from my squeezebox. It reverberated against the walls, which were often tiled shoulder-high.

But nights of saying the same silly jokes (clean ones, of course) or singing the same little song would end with our safe return to count the spoils. ''Be in by eight o'clock. You have school tomorrow''.

Two shiny apples, a handful of nuts and maybe three shillings in brown coins, with the odd silver sixpence among the loose change, and our pocket money had multiplied fourfold in one night. Oh to have Hallowe'en more often!

Hallowe'en is a time of parties for young and old alike. Bobbing for apples floating in a tub or pail involves trying to spear the fruit with a fork dropped from clenched teeth as the punter leans over the back of a chair ready to pick up the spoils.

Fortune-telling and ghost stories go hand in hand with pots of creamed potatoes containing silver trinkets or small coins. Find the treasure as you wade your way through the fluffy mash served on a cardboard plate.

Source: ''Hobgoblin nor Foul Fiend'' by Douglas M. Scott in *Scottish World* (October, 1989), 42.

Halloween pranking

A favourite ploy is to go bundering at the doors and puff smoke into the dwelling-houses. In Moray this ceremony is known as ''burning the reekie mehr''.

Burning the Reekie Mehr.—Take a cabbage or kail stock, scoop out the centre, and fill the hollow with tow. (This is the ''mehr''. ''Reekie'', of course, means smokie.) Choose your scene of action; then set fire to one end of the mehr, apply the lighted end to the key-hole of a door, blow lustily at the other end, and you will send a column of smoke into the house.

When you tire of this, climb up to the roof and stop the chimney with turf, thus turning back the smoke. It is advisable to have a rope handy for a speedy descent.

Window-tapping.—Take two pieces of string, one long, one short. Tie an end of the long one to a pin, and about an inch from the pin tie the short string to the long one, then fix a small stone or a button to the other end of the short string. Fix the pin in the wood on the outside of the window, and, holding the free end of the long string in your hand, take up a position some distance from the window. Pull the string gently towards you and immediately slacken it. Every time this is done, the stone or button strikes the window. Should the occupants come out to investigate, pull the string hard, and the pin will come away. Repeat the performance as soon as they go in, and thus keep on annoying them.

Sham Window-Smashing.—Two lads stealthily approach a window, one of them carrying a bottle. One of them strikes the window with his hand, and the second instantly smashes the bottle against the wall of the house. Those inside rush to the window, convinced that it has been smashed.

Halloween bonfire

In Aberdeenshire, up to our own time, the fomula used by the lads who went about collecting fuel for their Hallowe'en bonfire was, ''Gie's a peat to burn the witches!'' (The needfire, which was created by the violent friction of two pieces of wood, was regarded as a sovereign remedy for witchcraft, for it was believed that the witches hovering unseen in the air were consumed by the purifying flame.) Once the fire got going, the lads kept tossing the burning mass while the younger ones danced round the fire or ran through the smoke shouting, ''Fire! Fire! Burn the witches!'' The ashes were scattered far and wide, scaring away all evil powers and fertilising the fields; and hardly had the last spark died when the cry was raised, ''The de'il tak' the hindmost!'' and they would run for their lives.

Directions for making a turnip lantern

To make a lantern, choose a large round turnip. From the top, cut off a thick slice—about a quarter of the whole—and scoop out the inside, preferably with a spoon, taking care not to break the skin.

The ''shell'' should be as thin as possible, but a stump must be left at the bottom and hollowed out to serve as a socket. Now take a sharp pen-knife and carve on the turnip a man-in-the-moon face, a skull and cross-bones, or other device. Then get a candle, plain or coloured as desired, and set it firmly in the socket. Make two holes near the top, one at each side of the handle. It should be long enough to prevent any risk of burning one's hand. Alternatively, the lantern may be suspended from a forked stick.

When the lantern is lit, there is a soft, luminous glow, and the device you have carved stands out clearly. There is room here for considerable artistry.

To make a kail-runt torch, strip a colewort stem of its leaves, hollow it out and insert a candle.

Source: *Hallowe'en: Its Origin, Rites, and Ceremonies in the Scottish Tradition* by F. Marian McNeill. Edinburgh: The Albyn Press, 1970, pp. 24-25, 34-35.

Halloween in Scotland, c. 1920

"Halloween," as we called it in Scotland, was a hilarious time. The "Gallotians," a sort of masqueraders, in old costumes and blackened faces, went around the homes. They had wooden swords, old pots for helmets, and a crude play with mimic sword-fighting, ending in a mock death.

Then an old, patchwork-clad man with a mask, said:

> "Here comes I, old Keek-um-funny,
> I'm the man that lifts the money."

Then passed his hat round for coppers.

At Halloween parties apples were put in a tub of water and whirled round quickly. We stood on a chair, with a fork between our teeth, dropped it into the whirling apple circle. If lucky, we got an apple.

Scones smeared with molasses on one side would be suspended by a string from the roof. With hands behind our backs we tried to snatch bites out of the swinging scones. After several trials our faces were sweet but unkissable.

Halloween parties ended around a big pot of "champit taties," mashed potatoes. Beaten into them were a button, a ring, and a thimble. Lights were put out, we ate in the dark. If a boy got the button, he would be a bachelor, a girl the thimble, she would sew all her life and never get married. The ring meant marriage and happiness some future day.

There were some rhymes about Halloween which were recited as we swung our turnip lanterns. Big Swedish turnips hollowed out and a candle lit in the inside. One of them ran:

> "Halloween a nicht—a teen
> A can'al an' a custok."

Out in the country and especially among the Celtic Highlanders they have many customs we heard about. Witches, fairies, elves and other eerie folk had grand reviews on Halloween, they believed. And the pulling of stock or plant of kail, crossing the graveyard at midnight, sowing hemp, all have something to do with them. We never practised any of these customs except burning nuts, and the three dishes.

Three dishes with dirty water in one, clean in another, the third empty, were set out. A girl, blindfolded, was led in front. If by chance she put her hand in the clean water, she would be married, if in foul water, widowhood lay ahead, and if the empty dish, she would never be married.

Before going home from a Halloween party we stood in a ring, joined hands and sang "Auld Lang Syne."

> "Should auld acquaintance be forgot
> An' never brought tae mind."

Indeed all our parties ended with that song.

Source: *When I Was a Boy in Scotland* by George McPherson Hunter. Boston: Lothrop, Lee & Shepard Co., 1920, pp. 62-65.

For more information see: *Hallowe'en: Its Origin, Rites and Ceremonies in the Scottish Tradition* by F. Marian McNeill. Edinburgh: The Albyn Press, 1970.

Wales

A Halloween omen in North Wales

In North Wales families used to combine to make a bonfire between them in some conspicuous place near the house. Everyone of the families threw into the ashes a white stone marked in some distinguishing way. Next morning these stones were searched for anxiously, for if any were missing the owners would die in the coming year, it was believed.

Source: *Happy Holidays* by Eleanor Graham. New York: E.P. Dutton, 1933, p. 215.

For more information on Halloween, All Saints', and All Souls' Day in the United States see: *Folklore of American Holidays* edited by Hennig Cohen and Tristram Potter Coffin. 2nd ed. Detroit: Gale Research, 1991.

October 31

November Eve

Ireland

November Eve, a holiday for the daoine sidhe (fairies)

The *daoine sidhe* celebrate three festivals during the year. As we have our Christmas, New Year and Easter, they have their November Eve, May Eve and Midsummer Eve.

I learned something of these festivals one Halloween night sitting around a log fire with a group of schoolchums, listening to the stories that fell from the lips of Mr. Griffith, our history teacher at Mount Saint Benedict.

On November Eve, he would have it, the *daoine sidhe* are particularly sad for on that night they open the graves of the dead and dance with ghosts on graveyard tombstones. They endeavor on this night, above all other nights, to capture a mortal musician and have him play for them.

It is on November Eve, also, the Puca, a very famous fairy, comes down from the mountains, putting his curse on the blackberries, rendering them unfit to eat after that date.

The Puca comes in various forms; sometimes as a donkey, sometimes a horse, sometimes an eagle, but whatever his shape or form, if kindly spoken to, the Puca will answer all manner of important questions concerning happenings of the coming year.

Source: *When I Was a Boy in Ireland* by Alan M. Buck. New York: Lothrop, Lee & Shepard Co., 1936, p. 92.

Month 10 (September-October)

Ho Khao Slak

This is a time for bringing offerings to monks during their Lenten retreat. Individuals may draw the name of a specific monk to whom they bring a present. Food, flowers, and some of the eight articles which monks are allowed to own may be given. A robe, for example, may be folded intricately and adorned as a gift.

Laos

Related to the Ho Khao Padap Dinh is the festival of Ho Khao Slak, in the tenth month (September and October). It also involves offerings to the *sangha*. The sources of the offerings are decided by lot. This has also been a traditional time for giving children gifts of toys, sweets, and other good things to eat.

Source: *Laos: A Country Study* by Donald P. Whitaker et al. Foreign Area Studies. Washington, D.C.: The American University, 1971, p. 122.

Wagyut Moon, Day 15 (Circa October)

Ok Pansa / Ok Vatsa / Thadingyut

This is the end of the Buddhist fasting and retreat period (lent) and the beginning of the Kathin season. Kathins are pilgrimages to various temples to feed the monks and offer them gifts. Robes and other necessities are given to the priests. They are folded and arranged in a beautiful fashion. This period of Kathins continues until the full moon of the twelfth month.

Burma / Myanmar

Thadingyut

Festival of lights

At end of Lent, this is a festival of lights marking the month in which Buddha descended to earth along a path illuminated by many lights. This comes at the end of the rainy season and is a time of delight. Homes and shops are illuminated. Tiny lighted rafts are set adrift on waters, and fireworks and fire balloons may be set off.

Temple visits

. . .And without fail they go to the pagoda.

They go as a family, taking food to priests and paying homage. Men buy a packet of gold leaf at the entrance and offer it by rubbing it on an image. Women, however, are not allowed such close contact, so each woman goes to her own special corner on the pagoda platform. There are seven corners, each named for a day of the week, and each woman chooses her corner by the day on which she was born. Here she offers fresh flowers, usually lotus, and lights candles.

Source: *Celebrations: Asia and the Pacific* by Gene Sawyer. Honolulu: Friends of the East-West Center, 1978, p. 73.

Thadingyut in Mandalay, c. 1909

. . . the illumination, called taungpyi pwè, of the pagodas and the town. In Rangoon a very fine effect is produced by hanging the Sule Pagoda, in Fytche Square, all round with Chinese lanterns, from the base up to the top of the thabeit-hmauk, where the body of the shrine begins to narrow into the spire. The rings of coloured light narrowing upwards in a veritable pyramid of fire, produce one of the finest sights of the kind to be seen in the country. The street lamps, however, somewhat handicap the simple means of illumination open to the inhabitants, and to see the illumination of a town at its best one must go to a place where there are no street lamps. There all the pagodas and many of the private houses are lighted up, and the contrast to the ordinary gloom is startling. Candles are placed on posts at intervals of ten paces in every street, and the sè-eing gaungs have very plain-worded instructions as to what will happen to them if any of the lights in front of the ten houses of which they have charge go out. Mandalay Hill at such a time was a fine sight and still is, though it is no more a royal town. The two covered ways which lead up the steep uneven sides to the pagoda and the richly gilt Gautama on the top, look like streams of flame, or fiery serpents from the haunted nat-taung, under the shade of the Shan hills.

Legend of the fire rafts

At the same season there is an illumination on the river. As soon as it is dark the villagers row out into the middle of the stream and set adrift a multitude of little oil-lamps, each fastened to a little float of bamboo or plantain stems. The lamps are simply little earthenware cups filled with oil, and each supplied with a small piece of cotton for a wick. Thousands of them are sent out by a single village, and the sight from a steamer suddenly rounding a bend and coming upon a bank of these little stars of light afloat on the river is very singular. In the distance it looks like a regular sea of flame, and as there is plenty of oil, on the night of the full moon there is a constant succession of these shoals of twinkling lights floating down the whole length of the Irrawaddy from above Bhamaw to China Buckeer, every village sending its contingent.

This ceremony, called ye-hpaung hmyaw thi, or mi-hpaung hmyaw thi, launching water or fire rafts, is in remembrance of a universally honoured payā-ngè, a lesser divinity called Shin Upago, who lives down at the bottom of the river in a kyi-pyathat, a brazen spire, where he zealously keeps the sacred days. In a former existence he carried off the clothes of a bather, and for this mischievous pleasantry is condemned to remain in his present quarters till Arimadeya, the next Buddha, shall come. Then he will be set free.

Source: "The End of Lent" in *The Burman: His Life and Nations*. London: MacMillan, 1910, pp. 223-230.

Thadingyut history

Thadingyut Fullmoon Day is the day on which Buddha completed the preaching of the Abhidhamma and is also known as Abhidhamma Day.

In the year 109 Buddha spent his seventh lent period in Tavatimsa preaching the Abhidhamma to Santussita nat who was once his mother and the nat and brahma of the universe who had come to pay respect. He began on Wazo Fullmoon Day, preaching a day and night throughout the lent period of three months and finished it on Thadingyut Fullmoon Day. In the early part of Thadingyut fullmoon night, Buddha stepped down from the summit of Mt. Meru. where Tavatimsa is, using the ruby stairways out of the three, gold, ruby and silver, created in respect by the king of the gods.

At Sankassanagara, a crowd which filled a space of 36 yuzana, greeted the Buddha with lighted oil lamps and fragrant flowers.

In commemoration of the welcoming of Buddha on Thadingyut fullmoon night the festival of lights is celebrated with illuminations.

On this day, Buddhists go to the monasteries and pagodas where they observe the precepts, give in charity, meditate and perform other acts of merit.

Source: Embassy of the Union of Myanmar.

Laos

Boun Ok Vatsa

The Festival of the Waters

Boun Ok Vatsa, at the end of the period of retreat in the eleventh month (October), is an occasion of general rejoicing. The bonzes recite the *patimokkha,* confess their evil and careless thoughts, and leave the *wat* for pilgrimages. They are given new mats, robes, begging bowls, and serving sets for betel.

Also known as the Festival of the Waters, the Boun Ok Vatsa is a time for decorating homes and the *wat,* for processions, and for pirogue races on the rivers. Nominally, all is organized for the *naga* and tutelary spirits, and there are ceremonies for the ousting of the evil *phi,* who have been lurking in the houses during the rainy season.

Source: *Laos: A Country Study* by Donald P. Whitaker et al. Foreign Area Studies. Washington, D.C.: The American University, 1971, p. 123.

Thailand

An American visitor attends a Katin near Bangkok, c. 1960

We climbed the steps into the temple and found an impressive array of twenty saffron-robed priests awaiting their gifts and food. The glow of their saffron against the soaring, fluted temple doors caused me to catch my breath in awe.

The Thai settled into excited huddles of conversation on the floor of the temple. Our hostess bustled and supervised. . . . Food was ladled out of pots and kettles. No attempt was made to reheat it; Thai food is as hot as Hades in spices but never in temperature.

The priests stopped eating at eleven and we watched as the food remaining on their plates was scooped back into community kettles and redistributed to the crowd.

Following the meal the presents were given to the priests and many photographs were taken. The main presents at a katin . . . had mammoth, wedding cake-like exteriors, bathed in gilt and hung with things that tinkled and streamers that streamed.

Boat races

People were beginning to leave the temple and I thought this meant return, but it meant that the boat races were about to begin. These were so exciting that I began to realize with the Thai that good time is long. Wild, Dayak-like people appeared in front of the wat in long, hand-carved racing canoes. They were dressed in vivid pakimas with colored bands around their heads and except for the bizarre environment and dress I was struck by the resemblance to a university crew race. The races lasted for hours.

Source: *Mai Pen Rai Mean Never Mind* by Carol Hollinger. Boston: Houghton Mifflin, 1965, pp. 173-176.

For more on end of Lent see: ''The End of Buddhist Lent'' by Phya Anuman Rajadhon in *The Journal of Siam Society,* XLII (2) (January 1955).

Moon 10, Day 1 (October-November)

Sending the Winter Dress

This is the third time during the year at which visits are made to ancestral tombs. The dead are presented with winter garments at this time. Visits to graves are also made at Chung Yuan (Moon 7, Day 15) and Ch'ing Ming (April 5 or 6).

China

Winter clothing for the dead

The garments are imitations, made of paper and well packed into parcels bearing the names of the recipients. Some paper money is usually added to the package. Careful descendants even draw up a deed in which every piece of dress and each gift if mentioned, the whole document being signed and counter-signed by witnesses; thus there can be no misunderstanding between the living and the dead.

The gifts are exhibited in the home and the ancestors are invited to take them spiritually. The actual ''sending'' of the gifts takes place in an open place in the courtyard or near the tombs, when they are burned.

Source: *Chinese Festivals* by Wolfram Eberhard. New York: Henry Schuman, 1952, pp. 135-136.

Tibetan Moon 10, Day 25 (October-November)

Sang-joe

Sang-joe is the anniversary of the death of Je-Tsong-Kha-Pa, the Lamaist reformer. The festival lasts two weeks and includes dancing, feasting, and the collection of alms by monks. Holy texts were read in the monastery every night from midnight to dawn.

Tibet

Sang-joe in Lhasa 1902

This may be called the "Festival of Lights," every roof in Lhasa and in all the adjoining villages blazing with lights set burning in honor of the occasion. Hundreds, even thousands of such butter-fed lights were burning on the roofs of monasteries, and presented a unique sight, such as is rarely-seen in other parts of the world.

The Sang-joe is one of the most popular festivals, and lasts for two weeks. It is the season when the Tibetans, priests and laymen, give themselves up to great rejoicing, when dancing, singing and feasting are the order of the day, and when people put on their gala dresses.

Source: *Three Years in Tibet* by Ekai Kawaguchi. Adyar, Madras: The Theosophist Office, 1909, pp. 467-468.

Kartiki (October-November)

Diwali / Deepavali / Tihar

Diwali takes place at the dark of the moon, usually eighteen days after Dasera. Diwali has different connotations in the various regions of India. In some areas Diwali is a renewal of life. Old lamps are thrown out and a newly made pottery lamp is put on the manure pile. These lamps signal renewal and also guide the souls of the dead to heaven. In West Bengal, Diwali is a Kali festival. In Maharashtra, Diwali is a festival to ward off King Bali, ruler of the underworld. In the Punjab, Diwali celebrates the coronation of Prince Rama. Lamps are lit to guide ancestors on their visits to the homes at this time, as well. In Gujerat, Diwali is associated with Lakshmi, goddess of wealth. Shopkeepers close their accounts at this time.

India

Diwali

A festival of lights in honor of the goddess Lakshmi

Every Hindu home is white-washed and properly cleaned a few days before Diwali. On the evening of the Diwali day, Lakshmi, the goddess of wealth, is worshipped along with Ganesa. Then people illuminate their houses, courtyards, outer walls, roofs, gates and gardens, etc., with oil-filled little earthen lamps, candles or electric bulbs. Some buildings blaze with neon lights. It is also customary to leave an open lamp of burnt clay filled with *ghee* or clarified butter throughout the night at the place of worship for the welcome of goddess Lakshmi. Fireworks are also displayed in front of almost every house to ward off evil spirits from that area.

The markets, streets and all the public places are decked with small glittering lamps. Diwali heralds the approach of winter and winter crops are sown.

On this night, when the people of [the] rest of India worship Lakshmi, the Bengali worship Kali. Spectacular images of Kali are installed, adorned and worshipped before immersion in a tank, river or sea.

Source: *Festivals of India* by Brijendra Nath Sharma. New Delhi: Abhinav Publishing, 1978, p. 118.

Deepavali fireworks

DEEPAVALI, the Festival of Lights approached. It is a festival mainly for the children, but of course everyone who can takes part. I twisted cotton wicks, soaked them in oil and placed them in mud saucers ready to be lit at night. To the children I handed out two annas apiece, to be spent on fireworks. I had never been able to do so before—in previous years we had contented ourselves with watching other people's fireworks or with going down to the bonfire in the village, and even now I felt qualms about wasting money on such quickly spent pleasures; but their rapturous faces overcame my misgivings. It is only once, I thought, a memory.

As it grew dark we lit the tapers and wicks and encircled our dwelling with light. A feathery breeze was stirring, setting the flames leaping and dancing, their reflections in the black glistening oil cavorting too. In the town and in the houses nearby, hundreds of small beacons were beginning to flash; now and then a rocket would tear into the sky, break and pour out its riches like precious jewels into the darkness. As the night went on, the crackle and spit of exploding fireworks increased. The children had bought boxes of coloured matches and strings of patt-has and a few pice worth of crackers, like small nuts, which split in two with a loud bang amid a shower of sparks when lit.

A Deepavali bonfire

There was a great noise everywhere. Men, women and children from the tannery and the fields had come out, many of them in new clothes such as we too had donned, the girls and women with flowers in their hair and glass bangles at their wrists and silver rings on their toes; and those who could afford it wore silver golsu clasped round their ankles and studded belts around their waists.

In the centre of the town the bonfire was beginning to smoulder. For many weeks the children had been collecting firewood, rags, leaves and brushwood, and the result was a huge pile like an enormous ant hill, into which the flames ate fiercely, hissing and crackling and rearing up as they fed on the bits of camphor and oil-soaked rags that people threw in.

Drums had begun to beat, the fire was blazing fiercely, great long orange tongues consuming the fuel and thrusting upwards and sometimes outwards as if to engulf the watchers. As each searching flame licked round, the crowd leaned away from its grasp, straightening as the wind and the flames changed direction; so that there was a constant swaying movement like the waving of river grasses. The heat was intense—faces gleamed ruddy in the firelight, one or two women had drawn their saris across their eyes.

Leaping, roaring to climax, then the strength taken from fury, a quietening. Slowly, one by one, the flames gave up their colour and dropped, until at last there were none left—only a glowing heap, ashen-edged. The drum beats died to a murmur. The scent of jasmine flowers mingled with the fumes of camphor and oil, and a new smell, that of toddy, which several of the men had been drinking—many to excess, for they were lurching about loud-mouthed and more than ordinarily merry. I looked about for my family and at last saw my husband. He seemed to have gone mad. He had one son seated on his shoulders and one son at each hip, and was bounding about on the fringes of the crowd to the peril of my children and the amusement of the people. I fought my way to him. "Have you taken leave of your senses" I cried out above the din.

"No; only of my cares," he shouted gaily, capering about with the children clinging delightedly to him. "Do you not feel joy in the air?"

Source: *Nectar in a Sieve* by Karmala Markandaya. New York: John Day, 1954, pp. 58-59.

Tika Festival

The Tika festival is colourfully observed in Punjab and Haryana in the month of Kartika (October-November).

On the day following Diwali, women, dressed nicely, prepare a paste of saffron and rice and apply it on the forehead of their brothers as a mark for protection.

Source: *Festivals of India* by Brijendra Nath Sharma. New Delhi: Abhinav Publishing, 1978, p. 119.

India (Jain)

Deva Diwali

The Jains honor their founder, Mahavira

The Jaina festival of Deva Diwali is observed in honour of Jaina deities and the final liberation or emancipation of Lord Mahavira, the 24th Tirthankara, who died on this day at the age of 72 at Pavapuri in Bihar. He is worshipped by all the Jainas at midnight and early next morning. Sacred scriptures are recited and the houses are beautifully illuminated. The festival is specially celebrated at Mount Girnar, near Junagadh in Gujarat, where thousands of pilgrims from different places come on this day to the foot of the sacred hill for circumambulation. Some Jainas also observe a full-day fast and visit the shrines of the deity situated in their towns.

Both Digambaras and Svetambaras reach there in the later half of the night carrying bowls of *laddus* and stay there till the early dawn of the next day. Several maunds of sweets are thus offered to the foot-prints of Mahavira, which are later on distributed as *prasada* to all the devotees assembled there.

Source: *Festivals of India* by Brijendra Nath Sharma. New Delhi: Abhinav Publishing, 1978, p. 119.

The passing of Mahavira

We have seen that Mahavira passed into the state of beatitude in the city of Pava while he was staying as the guest of the king. Jain legends, especially those of the Swetambaras, vividly describe his last days. All the kings of the world, we are told, came to Pava to witness the passing away of the Tirthankara. The dying saint continuously preached to the kings as well as to his disciples for six days on the Jain way of life and righteous living. In the meantime, the kings and the people were constructing a magnificent hall and a lion-throne of diamonds. On the seventh evening he mounted the throne, when the throne and the hall became suddenly illuminated by a supernatural light. Throughout the night the Tirthankara preached and when the last of the enraptured audience fell asleep, Mahavira passed into the supreme state, in the presence of thousands of people but unseen by any one. When the people woke up, they saw the mortal remains of the Tirthankara. 'Since the light of the world has gone out,' said the leaders of the congregation, 'let us light the city and the palace.' So during that day and the night, the people of Pava illuminated every building and street with wick and torch lights.

Source: *Festivals and Holidays of India* by Paul Thomas. Bombay: D.B. Taraporevaia & Co., 1971, p. 76.

Malaya

Deepavali

Deepavali in the home

The festivities for *Deepavali* are mainly domestic in character. On the auspicious fourteenth day, the people get up at 4 o'clock in the morning and take a ritual bath at the hour of sunrise. At the same time they light a lamp and worship Lakshmi the Goddess of wealth. Then offerings consisting of oil, fruits, betel and arecanut, and sweet-meats are presented to Vishnu and Lakshmi. The lady of the house anoints her husband's head with the sacred oil. This oil is held to have Lakshmi in it, as in the water which is used for that day's bath there is the goddess *Ganga*. The bath taken on that day would be equivalent in merit to a bath in the sacred river Ganges. After daybreak the other festivities begin. New clothes are worn and visits exchanged with friends and neighbors. Gifts and fruits and betel are exchanged. Varieties of food are cooked and eaten. On this day there are no taboos against meat-eating, as there are on many other Hindu holidays. Generally feasts are prepared with different kinds of meat. In the night houses are lit up with rows of tiny oil lamps.

Deepavali as the New Year

For the northern Indians, *Deepavali* marks the beginning of a

New Year reckoned according to the *Vickrama* Era. This is one of many Hindu systems of dating and was begun by a legendary King Vickramaditya of Ujjain. Here the year begins with the first day of the month *Kartik* (October-November), the date when this King is said to have been crowned. This is why for north Indians, the day of the new moon and the day following are the important days for celebrating *Deepavali*.

Sikhs join in celebrations

Because it is a national Indian festival, the Sikhs too join in the celebrations. For them, the festival is divested of all religious significance and they celebrate it on its purely secular side. New clothes, delicious food and visiting friends are the main aspects of their celebrations.

Deepavali in cosmopolitan Malaya

In cosmopolitan Malaya, much of the religious significance of *Deepavali* has been lost even on the Hindus, though it is celebrated as an important festival. It is one of the few Indian festivals for which a public holiday is declared, thus enabling Indians and their friends to enjoy themselves. Hindus invite friends of other communities and feast them on this occasion. Much food and wine are consumed. In the estates, the Indian labourers celebrate *Deepavali* with gaity. Goats are slaughtered and the meat is distributed among participating families. In the evenings the entire population moves to the nearest town, generally to the Tamil cinema. Cinemas put up special Deepavali shows of Tamil pictures.

Ceremony of the account ledgers

North Indian merchants generally close accounts on this day and ceremonially open new account books for the next year. Account books are subject to a special *pooja*. The holy letter *Sri* is written in triangular pattern on the books and these are placed before a picture of the Goddess Lakshmi and *pooja* offered so that the Goddess of wealth will multiply the profits for the following year. There is a belief that this is a lucky day for gambling and this is indulged in by some.

Source: *Indian Festivals in Malaya* by S. Arasaratnam. Kuala Lumpur: Dept. of Indian Studies, University of Malaya, 1966, pp. 39-40.

Mauritius

Divali

Divali is the gayest of all Hindu festivals. Celebrated in October it marks the victory of Rama over Ravana and also commemorates Krishna's destruction of the demon Narakasuran. Clay oil lamps are placed in front of every home turning the island into a fairlyland of flickering lights.

Source: Embassy of Mauritius.

Nepal

Tihar (Diwali)

Festival of honoring

This is a multifaceted New Year festival of lights. On day 3 Laxmi, goddess of wealth, visits homes where lights burn to welcome her. On day 5 sisters honor their brothers. Day 1 honors the crow, day 2 the dog, day 3 the sacred cow, and day 4 the bullock. On day 4 mandalas are prepared to honor each family member and the God of Death.

For more information on Diwali see: "Diwali" in *Joy Through the World*. An Allen D. Bragdon Book. New York: U.S. Committee for UNICEF/Dodd, Mead, & Company, 1985, pp. 8-17; "Diwali" in *Hindu Festivals* by Swasti Mitter. Vero Beach, Florida: Rourke, 1989, pp. 22-27; "Tihar or Diwali: Goddess Laxmi's Festival of Lights" in *Festivals of Nepal* by Mary K. Anderson. London: Allen & Unwin, 1972, pp. 164-174.

Kartika (October-November)

Karwachoth

This is a festival of married women observed in Hindu families during the month of Kartika. Karwachoth day is a fasting day for married women.

India

Married women worship Siva and Parvati

The Karwachoth festival is observed in all Hindu families exclusively by married women in the month of Kartika (October-November). Virgins and widows are not permitted to celebrate it. On this day, married women observe a full-day fast. At dawn they take bath and wear new clothes and thereafter collect various articles including Karwa (an earthen pot with a spout) decorated with coloured rice paste and offer worship to god Siva and goddess Parvati for the welfare, prosperity and longevity of their husbands. During day-time, the women draw sketches on the floor of the courtyard depicting the emblems of sun, moon and *karwa*. At night when the moon becomes visible, water along with flowers is offered and the fast is broken. On this festive occasion, the mother blesses her married daughter and presents her ornaments, garments and sweetmeats. An elderly woman of the house tells the story of Karwachoth before the fast is terminated.

Source: *Festivals of India* by Brijendra Nath Sharma. New Delhi: Abhinav Publishing, 1978, p. 27.

Circa Early November (Near End of Rainy Season)

Sango Festival

A seven-day festival of the Sango cult of Oyo. Sango, the third Alafin of Oyo, moved the capital of Nigeria from Oko to Oyo, established supremacy through warfare over other peoples, and then pledged himself to peace. Sango hanged himself under tragic circumstances and was immediately deified. He is identified with thunder and lightning.

Nigeria (Yoruba)

Sango as celebrated in Ede, Nigeria, c. 1955

Sango is one of the most popular and powerful cults among the Oyo. He is still associated with thunder and therefore with rain magic. Like all orisa he brings fertility to women. One of his special functions is to kill liars and thieves.

The cult has penetrated all parts of Yoruba country, and recently (within the last ten years or so) it has even gained a footing in Benin. There is much solidarity among the worshippers and members often travel for miles to attend each other's festivals. That of Ede, for example, is attended by worshippers from about a dozen surrounding towns and villages.

Normally, every fourth day is set aside for his worship. Every worshipper has his own little shrine in his house and he begins the day with divination with the bitter kola nut. The nut is split in the middle and then thrown to the ground. If one half faces upwards and the other downwards then Sango's answer is positive and there will be rejoicing. If on the other hand, both faces turn downwards or both upwards, the answer is not quite satisfactory and further questioning will follow 'Are you angry?' 'Have I forgotten such and such a sacrifice?' 'Is it because I quarrelled with such and such a person?' And so on until a positive answer is obtained.

Having performed his private ceremony at home the worshipper then proceeds to a larger shrine belonging to an important priest in the town where he will meet many other worshippers. After a further divination the old women among them will sing the praise names of the god.

These Oriki go into many hundreds and they vary slightly from town to town.

The annual festival of Sango takes place towards the end of the rainy season round about the beginning of November. The precise date is always announced twenty-eight days in advance, and this announcement is in itself a minor festival. The Timi sits in state in his palace and the Sango worshippers dance the famous Lanku dance. Lanku is a vigorous dance which is always played by the bata drums which are sacred to Sango.

The principal festival lasts for seven days and it starts in the morning with various ceremonies connected with rain magic. It is absolutely essential that no rain should fall during these seven days. What this means can only be realised if it is remembered that the ceremonies take place towards the end of the rainy season, when thunderstorms are the rule during the afternoons. Whatever the reason it must be stated that in four successive years rain has never interfered with the ceremonies.

The women go in procession to the river and at a special place a calabash containing special medicines is sunk into the depths. From that day onwards the level of the river is supposed to go down and the dry season to begin. In four successive years the dry season has, in fact, commenced with the sinking of the calabash.

While this ceremony takes place the Timi proceeds in great pomp to a place near the river to meet the worshippers. He rides under the state umbrella and is accompanied by a huge crowd as well as by a large orchestra of drummers and the royal trumpeters.

In the afternoon of that day the women of the palace gather together to perform a strange music which is played only once a year. They start with the praise names of Sango then go to the first Timi, the founder of the town and continue through the list of twenty-two rulers until they come to the present king.

During the rest of the week the Sango worshippers give performances of dances and tricks before the Timi. A huge crowd gathers in the market place but the performances are really meant for the god himself rather than for the human audience. The Sango worshippers are extremely conscious of the god's tragic nature and they desire on this occasion to entertain him and make him happy.

The principal performer each day must 'carry' the god. That is to say he must fall into a self-induced state of possession, during which he will speak with the voice of Sango. He dances with incredible energy whilst in this state and he appears to be insensitive to pain.

A Sango festival is concluded on the seventh day with a procession of fire. One of the worshippers carries a large pot on his head in which is burning a sacred flame. This flame must be carried so that the blessing of Sango can be brought to all parts of the town.

Source: *A Year of Sacred Festivals in One Yoruba Town* by Ulli Beier. Lagos, Nigeria: Nigeria Magazine, 1959, pp. 71-72.

Circa November

The Seal Festival

A festival at the close of the seal-hunting season, to implore the animals that were killed to return to the sea and to return next year and bring their relatives with them.

U.S.S.R. (Koryak)

An autumn festival for sea animals

After the closing of the autumn sea hunting season (in November) the coastal Koryaks held the ''seal festival'' (in olden times it was the ''whale festival''). The participants in the celebration pleaded with the animals killed during the hunt to return to the sea and let themselves be caught again next year, and also to bring along their relatives with them. The dead animals were replaced by zoomorphic representations made of seaweed.

Source: *The Peoples of Siberia* edited by M.G. Levin and L.P. Potapov. Chicago: Univ. of Chicago Press, 1964, p. 868.

Moon 8, Day 29 (November)

Seged

This is a religious festival of unclear origin celebrated only by Falasha (Ethiopian Jews). Six thousand people were reported to attend the Seged ceremonies in Ambover in 1971.

Ethiopia (Falasha)

Seged, c. 1982

People arrive from the surrounding villages and the participants assemble outside the prayerhouse. The priests come out with the *Orit* (the Bible in Geez, written on parchment), the most holy book of the Falashas, wrapped in colourful cloth. Several books are carried along. When all the pilgrims from the other villages have arrived, preparations are made to ascend the nearby hill, where the ritual is to be held. A trumpet or metal horn is sounded after which the procession, headed by the priests, moves toward the top of the hill. This hill is a ''clean place,'' where non-Falashas may not tread. On their way up, the priests are followed by the *debteras* and *diyaqons;* after them come the elders and finally the rest of the people. Everyone is wearing clean, preferably white clothes with coloured fringes (e.g., the *gäbis* or *qamis*) and everyone has kept him/herself in a state of purity (i.e., no sexual intercourse during seven days before the celebration, no bodily contact with non-Falashas). The priests wear, in addition to their white clothes, a dark velvet cloak (the *kabba*), their priestly headcover (*shash*). *Debteras* and *diyaqons* hold coloured umbrellas (*jantela*) and cymbals (*tsenaka*).

During the ascension of the hill, the priests sing prayers, beginning with the ''*Berhan säräqä läsadqane*'' prayer, often said at the beginning of a service. Now and then they are accompanied by the cymbals and by the typical ululating sounds (cries of joy on ceremonial occasions) by the women. The people, while ascending the hill, also take a stone with them, which they carry on their head or shoulder. When they have arrived on the top of the hill, they place the stone on an already existing circular wall of stones which marks the ''holy area'' where the *Orit* will be placed. When the whole party has arrived at the top, it divides into three groups: priests move in the circle, men place themselves at their right, women and smaller children at the left. The priests then place the holy books they have brought in the middle of the circle, where a bunch of fresh leaves, from bushes growing on the hill, or pieces of coloured cloth, are spread out. After this, the people place their stones on the wall and then the actual service starts.

At a certain point in the service, the so-called *ëmen* or *ammeyan* ceremony is held, a commemoration of the dead. People who wish to honor their dead relatives take a haulm of *t'eff* or *mushela* (two staple grains used by the Falashas) to the priests, who say a benediction over it. One then takes a grain for every relative one wishes to commemorate, evoking the name of the deceased and saying a few words in remembrance. The grain is then put on the stone wall with the wish that God may take care of the dead, will allow them a good life in Heaven, and that the living may inherit their strength. These are personally worded appeals, without circumscribed formulas. Often therefore, a personal vow is said with it. The seeds are then thrown into the ''holy circle'' and the remaining haulms are put on top of the stone wall, preferably on the stone which has been carried that day. Birds that will arrive later on to eat or take away the grains are considered to be sent by God to take the offering. Prayers conclude this ceremony.

The next part of the service starts with the reading of texts from the *Orit* in Geez. After the reading they are translated into Amharic. Parts which are read are from the books of Exodus, Leviticus, and Deuteronomy, as well as from Nehemiah and Ezra.

When the final prayers are said, the faithful give some money. This is put on stones within the holy circle. It is given ''for God and for the *Orit*'' and it will be used by the priests for themselves and for the prayerhouse. Everyone is supposed to give according to his/her ability.

The priests and their assistants then wrap the holy books in their cloth, take them up and start the procession down the hill towards the prayerhouse. The priests enter the prayerhouse, the rest of the people assemble near special huts made of leaves and branches (the *das*), built for the occasion. From here the food for the communal meal will be distributed. The priests come out of the prayerhouse, say benedictions over the food and beer and break the fast. This is in the afternoon. The women distribute the *indjära* (bread), the *kay wot* (meatstew), and the *t'alla* (beer). The meal is the start of a more joyous celebration with songs, dance, and music, played by non-Falasha musicians playing *masänqos* (one-stringed bowed lutes). These non-religious festivities continue throughout the night, in private homes. During the meal and the ensuing conversations the elders of the various Falasha villages deliberate about common affairs and problems of their communities, in which priests also participate. Some people already return home that evening, others depart the following day.

Source: ''Seged Celebration in Ethiopia and Israel: Continuity and Change of a Falasha Religious Holiday'' by J. Abbink in *Anthropos* 78 (1983), 793-795.

November

Tori-no-ichi

This is a Shinto celebration held at shrines dedicated to "The Great Bird," the sacred crow that perched on the long-bow of the first Mikado and guided him out of the wilderness by the light from its shining wings.

Japan

A crowded street during Tori-no-ichi

"Why is it called 'Eagle Market'?" I asked, as our taxi slowly made its way along the crowded street. "And why do they have rakes as souvenirs?"

"Bird Fair is just as good a name," replied Takezo San, "but the men who favor Bird Shrines are always watching out for riches, and so they take the eagle as a good-luck symbol, because it is the strongest and flies the highest of all birds. Now everybody calls a Bird Shrine fair an 'Eagle Market'."

Takezo San didn't say anything about the rakes, but the crowd was so big and noisy that I didn't ask any more questions. I just looked.

Perhaps it is as well for me to say right here that Mother told me after I got home that the real name of the festival is "*Tori-no-ichi*—Bird Fair—" which on account of a curious play on words, so common in the Japanese language, signifies *gain;* and as most of the influential members of this sect are speculators and wealthy merchants, they accept as the mascot of the market a "*kumade*"—bear hand—which is an ordinary bamboo rake, so called because its widespread prongs resemble the outreaching clutching claws of a bear's hand. It is supposed, in the lore of the market, that to own one will give its possessor the magic power to pull to him any treasure he may desire; thus few people leave the fair without carrying at least one rake home with them.

This explains why so many people on the streets were carrying bamboo rakes, and why the one thing always seen in an Eagle Market, first and last and everywhere, is bamboo rakes—just the kind used in everyone's garden, only these are prettier and finer made. Each rake had fastened on it somewhere, or dangling from its sides, many good-luck emblems, and in the very center of each is always the smiling mask of Okame, the Goddess of good nature, or as she is frequently called, the "Laughing Goddess."

He pointed up to a huge gayly ornamented rake towering almost directly over us. It was swinging around in a most top-heavy manner from the midst of a party of men and girls clustered about those who were carrying it.

"It advertises a famous tea house," Takezo San said. "They've had it made on purpose for the Eagle Market, and now they're carrying it so that everybody can see. They'll use it as an advertisement for a year to come."

The rake was so large and heavy that it took three sturdy men to carry it, and they changed shoulders every five minutes or so. Whenever they stopped, everybody near them stopped, too, to watch the jolly party. The carriers were large men in blue coolie coats having the name of a well-known tea house in big white characters on the back and neck bands. In the group were a number of beautifully dressed laughing girls in gay colors and elaborately dressed hair with flower hairpins. They had tiny rakes stuck in their hair, in the tops of their sashes, and in the neck folds of their dresses; and each one carried several in her hands. Afterward I was told that they were geisha girls.

This big, overloaded rake on top of the tall bamboo pole was the most elaborately ornamented of any that we saw all afternoon, and the emblems of good luck were all rich and beautiful. There was a plump income book—exactly the kind one sees hanging from the corner of the desk in every shop, only this was huge in size and made of brocade with silver mountings. Swinging beside it were a lot of coral branches on a bunch of gold and silver coins, an immense gilded key, supposed to be the magic key that unlocks the door of fate, the "invisible coat" that hides the wearer from the evil of sickness, and the wonderful hammer that has power to pound out your heart's wish from the fortune bag of the god of wealth. All these things I recognized from the fairy tales, but there were a lot of other emblems that I didn't understand, and there was no time to ask Takezo San. But the most prominent thing of all, right in the center of the jingling, teetering rake, was the merry, roguish face of Okame, the Goddess of Laughter.

"That rake is probably the costliest thing in the fair," said Takezo San. "It was made by the finest paper-paste worker in Tokyo. There's his name on it."

"I want a good-luck rake!" I cried. "A little one. I want to buy it myself!"

Source: *Chiyo's Return* by Chiyono Sugimoto Kiyooka. Garden City, N.Y.: Doubleday, Doran & Company, 1936, pp. 327-328.

Late Autumn

Keretkun Festival

The people of the Soviet Union celebrate a two-to three-day festival held in late autumn for the "owner" of all sea animals.

U.S.S.R. (Chukchi)

Family rituals

The Keretkun festival was held in honor of the "owner" of all the sea animals. It took place in late autumn and lasted 2-3 days and nights, depending on the wealth of the given family. It was celebrated inside the yaranga. The objects used in the celebration included a special net of reindeer tendons ("Keretkun's net"), painted oars, statuettes of birds, and an image of Keretkun in the form of a small manlike figure made of wood. The family celebrating the festival dressed in clothing of walrus intestines and special headdresses. Among other holiday dishes, there was always a gruel of ground roots with seal fat and deer meat. At the end of the festival the image of Keretkun was burned in the oil lamp, the floor was swept, the refuse and remains of the sacrifices were gathered and thrown into the sea, thereby—it was believed—returning all the killed animals to the sea.

During rituals, the Chukchi customarily used the tambourine which every family owned. The Chukchi tambourine was narrow-rimmed, round, 40-50 centimeters in diameter, with a handle attached. The stick was made of whale-barb or wood.

The shamans did not have special costumes, but could be distinguished only by the large number of amulets and tassels sewn to their clothing. A distinguishing feature of shamanistic performance among the Chukchi was ventriloquism; the shaman also performed various tricks (such as piercing himself with a knife, etc.).

Source: *The Peoples of Siberia* edited by M.G. Levine and L.P. Potapov. Chicago: Univ. of Chicago Press, 1964, p. 823.

November 1

All Saints' Day

This is a day to honor all saints. The day was proclaimed in the seventh century by Pope Boniface IV to supersede a pagan festival of the dead on this day. The Gaelic Samhain, summer-end festival also came at this time. In practice, All Saints' Day and the succeeding day, All Souls' Day, usually meld into a two- or three-day festival honoring the dead.

Belgium

Aller Heiligen Dag

Aller Heiligen Dag in Belgium

The feast of All Saints is of great importance all over Belgium, both in Flanders and Wallonia. No one who even pretends to be any kind of a Christian is absent from Mass on that day, for this is the triumphal feast of the dead, and the strong familial cast to all Belgian society impels everyone with any regard at all for his parents and kin to be present on that day to pray for the repose of their souls. On this day, too, all towns and villages are depopulated, as everyone goes to refurbish and repair the family tombs and to decorate them with flowers.

Source: *Chateau-Gerard: The Life and Times of a Walloon Village* by Harry Holbert Turney-High. Columbia: Univ. of South Carolina Press, 1953, p. 256.

Bolivia

Kawsasqanchis (Our Living with the Dead)

Kawsasqanchis in Sonqo, Bolivia, c. 1980

November First, the day souls of dead *Runakuna* return to visit their relatives, is called *Kawsasqanchis* (Our Living; the word groups the dead with the living through the inclusive suffix *-nchis*). On the following day, *Kachaypari* (Send Off), the souls are sent on their way by the pounding feet of many dancers, as *Runakuna* dance intermittently in and around their houses. All the dead come—the good souls from *Tay-tanchis Laru* (Our Father's Side) and the *kukuchis* from the Snowy Mountains. Rufina described to Felicha how "pretty and green" the souls were as they hovered around the rafters. Later she was to tell me that her fatal illness began on All Souls' Day.

Kawsasqanchis is spent preparing and consuming holiday food in a cheerful mood resembling our Thanksgiving. Each family stays home to cook and eat in its own house, for if a soul were to find its relatives not at home it would go off "*renegaspa*" ("complaining") to another house. A special table (or a corner of the bed if a table is lacking) is set up for the souls' meal, and large portions of food are placed there before the family helps themselves to any. The same table is set up during the funeral wake held eight days after a death. The deceased one partakes of the special food and goes on its way.

Certain foods are prescribed for the souls' table, including boiled beans, patties made from ground *qhaya* (dehydrated *oca*) and water, a bowl of *quinoa* (a high-altitude grain) containing a hardboiled egg, and very large potatoes baked in the ground (*papa watia*). On the assumption that the dead share the tastes of the living, the souls also receive a fancy dinner plate of pancakes, noodles, two kinds of meat (usually lamb and pork), and coffee or hot chocolate with a piece of bread. A candle and a bottle of *trago* also go on the table, and families with access to *qantu* bushes drape the table with garlands of *qantus*, the flower of the dead, and sprinkle the bell-shaped blossoms over the meal.

Food preparations are completed by late afternoon. For the rest of the day and the evening, *Runakuna* sit next to the table, alternately eating and chewing coca. Their *k'intus* are blown to "*Almakuna, Machula Aulanchis,*" whose day it is.

But what of the real food sitting on the table? I thought that it might be burned, recalling that the *despacho* feeds the *Tirakuna* through burning, but Luis explained that the food passes to the souls differently: he needed a *mihuq* (eater), who would consume the food while saying prayers for the dead.

Those who have eaten a share [of the funeral feast] believe that they are eating on behalf of the stomach of the dead man and they will say, "I don't feel satisfied these days. It's said we are eating on behalf of the dead man's stomach."

Source: *The Hold Life Has: Coca and Cultural Identity in an Andean Community*. Washington and London: Smithsonian Institution Press, 1988, pp. 164-165.

Germany

Allerheiligen

Allerheiligen remembers all the saints who are not honored with a day of their own. In Marchfeld, in Austria, a woven straw decoration (Heiligenstritzel) is put outside the door to show that the harvest is in safely.

Source: *German Festivals and Customs* by Jennifer M. Russ. London: Oswald Wolff, 1952, p. 78.

Mexico

El Diá de los Santos

Remembrances in Santa Cruz, Mexico, c. 1945

The first two days of November, the feast of *Todos los Santos,* or All Saints, is a very important time in Mexico. In the two weeks before November first, when the harvest is in, all the able-bodied young men go to the sierra to cut a great deal of wood and make cash money. This money is all spent in the market on Saturday before Halloween, spent on fruit and hard candies, sugar and chocolate, and special frosted cookies with skulls on them. Each family fills at least two burro panniers with these riches, depending on how many dead people they have in their families. I use that expression "have" on purpose, because the dead children are always counted among the living children when families are listed. "I have twelve children" may mean five living and seven dead.

On the night of October 31, all the families kill chickens, turkeys, or hogs, and the women work hard grinding chiles for *mole*. That night they set up tables, or *petates* if they have no tables, on the floor below the family altars. A place is set on the table or *petate* with a dish of food, a lighted candle, and a bouquet of flowers for each person who has died out of that household. In Doña Patrocina's house they had to do this for her husband, his parents, her own dead children, and all the relatives and lost children of La Abuelita (and now, of course, for La Abuelita herself and for Esperanza's dead children). The little dead children will come and eat in the night, and the grown-up dead the next day. Throughout the first day of November families visit each other to see the familiar dead friends and to pay their respect, though food and refreshments are served for the dead only. I have never been in Santa Cruz at any such festival; and I have only the vivid description of my friend, the first teacher in Santa Cruz, to go by. Twice during the six years she taught there, she saw the people of Santa Cruz dress up a bride and a groom, a father and a mother, a boy child and a girl child, and have them visit in a group at each household to represent all the dead people of all ages.

Supposedly the food is eaten, or at least the essence of it is consumed, by the spirits before dark on November first. then all the ghosts go back to the burial grounds, and the living members of the family eat the delicacies. On the morning of November 2, more *mole* is made and a tortilla full of chicken *mole* is taken to each grave of a person dead in the last year or so. Flowers and hard candy and the special frosted cookies are left on every grave connected with the family. This is the day when La Abuelita went to visit her beloved dead. Weeds are pulled, the graves cleared of the faded paper flowers from the year before, and shrubs and flower cuttings planted.

Source: *Santa Cruz of the Etla Hills* by Helen Miller Bailey. Gainesville: Univ. of Florida Press, 1958, pp. 122-123.

Remembering the children

In the homes, the children are remembered by preparing an altar decorated with flowers. The families that have lost a child are visited by relatives and friends who participate in the ceremony which consists of a meal and perhaps some prayers. The meal includes a *tamal* seasoned with seeds which symbolized happiness. The parents of the dead child place toys and foods that children like on the altar.

Source: "Day of the Dead" by Luis Leal in *Día de los Muertos: An Illustrated Essay and Bibliography*. Univ. of California, Santa Barbara: Center for Chicano Studies and Colección Tloque Nahuaque, University Library, 1983, pp. 1-2.

Philippines

Cemetery visits

By definition All Saints Day is a feast observed in honor of the dead. The common term is *Undas*. And the closest origin I have heard is the Spanish phrase "Honras de funebre"—literally, to honor the funeral. Actually it is more a feast for the living.

The arch at an entrance to a cemetery in the barrio boldly states: "To honor the dead is to serve the living."

On All Saints Day, Poldo's extended family holds a family reunion. The tomb of the dead is whitewashed, the weeds are uprooted, plastic flowers are displayed, and candles are lighted. But the highlights of activities are the meeting of relatives and friends from out of town, the eating of sweets and other delicacies piled on the table.

"Do you clean up at the cemetery?" I asked Poldo.

"*Pag hindi mo nilinis ang pantyon dadalawin ka ng patay* (If you do not clean the tomb, you will be visited by the dead)!"

One of the most common reasons for unexplained illness in the barrio is attributed by the *aibuiaryo* (herb doctor) to the failure to remember a relative's tomb.

Source: *My Friends in the Barrios* by Dr. Juan M. Flavier. Quezon City: New Day, 1974, p. 19.

Trinidad

Feeding the dead in Trinidad, c. 1946

All Saints' Day, though formally more important to Catholics and Anglicans than to members of other sects, is an occasion when the dead are widely feted. Their graves are weeded, and covered with flowers, "nice, nice," and candles are placed about them. At home, during the afternoon, a table is festively set with dishes, glasses, knives, forks, and spoons, and decorated at the outer edges with strands of "cotton" from the silk-cotton tree, "pulled out nice, so you can see through it when it's held up, so they can get themselves a kerchief if they wants to wipe their faces."

At about sundown, the family go to the graveyard, leaving the house unlocked. "Nobody goin' into your house that night!" The candles on the graves are lighted, and the dead are addressed. "Ask them for anything." On returning to the house, a lighted candle is placed before the door, and a bouquet of flowers. "Rap on the door three times," and as the first one enters, he says, "Good night, good night. Who is here? I come, I come." Then the family seat themselves about the table, and say; "We, weself go now drink a little rum in the bottle on the table," and say again, "This dinner is for you, so we sit to help you enjoy it."

As the family sit chatting, they become drowsy and, as in a dream, hear voices say, "We come. We eat. We drink. We thank you all. We merry. We glad. You hear de stick break, that we"—that is, in passing a bush on the way from a grave, when a twig breaks, a person turns and hears a laugh, and he knows, "that my dead telling they friends, 'That my family.' "

When those about the table awake, they take a little rum, pour it on their hands, wet their faces with it, and eat the food before them, even though, since it was prepared for the dead, it is unsalted. As they eat, they say "Aunt—or uncle, or grandfather, or mother or father—we eating this food. We hope you always here to prevent us from harm." Then the family hear a "growl." "They glad." When the candles are burned out, the family go to bed, but in the morning the wax is put in a small box and saved as a remedy to cure a cold, or a rheumatic hand or foot, or other ailment.

Source: *Trinidad Village* by Melvill J. Herskovits and Frances S. Herskovits. New York: Alfred A. Knopf, 1947, pp. 156-157.

For more on All Saints' Day see: "Halloween, All Saints', and All Souls' Days" in *Folklore of American Holidays* edited by Hennig Cohen and Tristram Potter Coffin. 2nd ed. Detroit: Gale Research, 1991; *The Masked Media: Aymara Fiestas and Social Interaction in the Bolivian Highlands* by Hans C. Buechler. The Hague: Mouton, 1980, pp. 79-90.

November 2

All Souls' Day

This is a day to honor the dead. Graves are visited and cleaned. Food is generally offered to the dead souls, who return on this day to visit the living.

Colombia

Día de los Angelitos (Day of the Little Angels) in Aritama, Colombia, a mestizo community, c. 1960

After noon on November 2 one of the members of the dance groups goes from house to house carrying a wooden cross about forty centimeters high and covered with flowers. A boy runs behind him ringing a bell. Children join the group and troup from door to door calling, "Casa de teja (house of the tile roof) / Donde vive una vieja (Where lives an old woman) / Casa de rosa (house of roses) / Donde vive la hermosa (Where lives the beautiful) / Casa de pino (house of pine) / Donde vive un mezquino (where lives the stingy)." At each house they sing, "Angelitos somos, Del cielo venimos, Pidiendo limosnas, Para nosotros mismos" ("Angels are we, from heaven we come, asking alms, for ourselves.") From the houses people throw fruit for the children. In past times the children took this food to the church and cooked it, spending the night cooking and eating, and tolling the church bell, as the feast was thought to be shared by the souls of Purgatory. Nowadays the children take the food home and share it with their families.

Source: *The People of Aritama: The Cultural Personality of a Colombian Mestizo Village* by Gerardo and Alicia Reichel-Dolmatoff. Chicago: Univ. of Chicago Press, 1961, pp. 374-375.

Germany

Allerseelen

Tending the graves and the caretaking of souls on Allerseelen

This is a day to decorate graves and light candles for the souls of departed relatives. At noon, church bells may ring for an hour, freeing the souls until the noon bell rings the next day. No knife should be left with blade upturned, lest the souls hurt themselves. Nor should a pan stand empty over heat. The stove must be kept lit, however, to warm them. Bowls of butter and fat may be left to soothe the dead's wounds, and cold milk is laid out to cool their souls. At one time children, servants, and the poor were given bread on All Souls' Day. Godparents gave their godchildren specially shaped pastries, *Seelenwecken,* on this day, and children once went from house to house chanting All Souls' Day rhymes and receiving special breads.

Source: *German Festivals and Customs* by Jennifer M. Russ. London: Oswald Wolff, 1982, p. 78.

Italy

Giorno dei Morti

A visit to the cemetery in Brescia, Italy, c. 1900

The grand day . . . is the second of November, *Giorno dei morti,* Dead Day.

That day is celebrated as a regular fair day; all the bakers and *pasticcieri* make a bread that is called *pane dei morti,* dead bread.

The bakers' bread is made of Indian meal and *milio,* bird seed. The *pasticcieri* bread tastes like American pound cake. The bakers send their bread to all their customers.

Early that November morning all the people are out, going toward the cemetery; rich and poor, young and old, all carry some flower-token to their departed friends.

As the cypresses are placed about twelve feet apart on the avenue, between each two cypresses (that day) you find a stand of some kind. There you can buy everything you desire, to use or to wear.

The chestnut man, woman, and boy are there; so is the man with his toys, the florist with his flower designs, the man that will make you up tresses to put in your locket and ring, or make you a picture with the hair of your father, mother or friend, to hang up in front of their tombs. There too is the candle-man who will sell a quarter-of-an-inch candle to a ten-inch candle, all decorated with gold, and white, red and green. Then there is the plaster-figure man; he has all sorts of things—large and small figures, small lambs, cows, horses, and small monuments; so if you are too poor to have a marble monument for your dead you can buy one of his, that will last at least until the next *Giorno dei morti.*

The inside of our cemetery is like a beautiful garden. That day the rich monuments are covered with expensive flowers, made up in all kind of designs; and when night comes you would think yourself in a fairy land, as under the gallery burn the five-foot torches; and as each monument has about half a dozen of them burning brightly you can read the inscriptions on them very easily. Then there are the other large monuments all over the grounds and the church; they are illuminated all around. And as the poor people have only a stone slab in the grounds they place thereon flower-pots in bloom, and in front or at the back they put a candle; but more often they hang an oil lantern.

On this day and night all we children attended the show. We provided ourselves with twine, matches and scissors, and walked all over the ground, looking to our right and left; if we saw any of the lanterns crooked we would go and straighten them and fasten them with our twine, and we would tie up all the garlands that got loose; we snuffed the candles, and guided strangers to certain graves, that in the midst of such a crowd they lost sight of.

At the end of that day we went home tired and greased, but we enjoyed it very much.

Source: *When I Was a Girl in Italy* by Marietta Ambrosi. Boston: Lothrop, Lee & Shepard Co., 1906, p. 116-118.

Giorno Dei Morti, a time of gift-giving in Sicily

On the morning of il Giorno dei Morti children wake to find presents that are believed to be left by their dead relatives. In Agrigento children may leave a tray on the dining room table with their names and the lists of presents they want. If they have been good they may receive those gifts.

In Palermo candy dolls, *pupi de cera,* are given as presents at this time. They are decorated with gold and silver tinsel and are sold only from early September until November 2. They range from two to ten inches tall and are made as knights, dancing ladies, Garibaldi on horseback, brides and grooms, or other characters.

Source: *Festivals and Folkways of Italy* by Frances Toor. New York: Crown, 1953, pp. 15-16.

Mexico

El Dia de los Muertos

November 1 is El Día de los Santos, All Saints' Day, and is dedicated to the children who have died. November 2, El Día de los Difuntos or El Día de los Muertos (Day of the Dead), is for mourning adults who have died.

Remembering the dead

On the 2nd of November, the ceremony for the adults who have died is the same [as November 1], except that the offerings include a special kind of bread for the dead called *pan de muerto,* a sweet bread decorated with skulls and crosses.

Since this is a celebration of the people, the presence of death is manifested in the form of folkloric objects. In 1898 the anthropologist, Franz Boas, published a list of more than 100 objects representative of the dead, among them candies made of white sugar in the form of skulls, crosses, coffins, tombs, spirits, animals, fruits, and birds; wooden or clay toys in the form of coffins lined in black; wire skeletons painted white in the form of devils, dancers, musicians, bullfighters, drunkards, salesmen, *charros* or Mexican horsemen, and other popular types; funeral processions accompanied by priests and altar boys; as well as tables set with skulls, candles, food, and drink.

On the 2nd of November in the bakery shops one can buy *pan de muerto* in various forms, such as human beings and animals; in the candy shops they sell candy in the same forms, decorated with skulls. For the children there are white masks, skeletons, or toys in the form of a coffin from which a skeleton jumps out when a string is pulled, and skeletons that dance when the little boards from which they hang are pressed.

The main activity on the 2nd of November is, of course, the visit to the cemetery to bring offerings to the dead. This custom is becoming out-dated in the cities but is kept alive in the provinces and the countryside.

Calaveras, satiric newspapers

Another important activity that occurs only on the *Dia de los muertos* is the publication of the so-called *calaveras* on sheets of paper or in newspapers and magazines. The word *calavera,* besides meaning "skull" and "corpse," also carries another special meaning, that of the satiric poetry which is published on this particular day. Writers take advantage of this time to joke about their superiors whether they be government officials, businessmen, or employees like the police. No one escapes this yearly criticism, not even the priests.

Source: "Day of the Dead" by Luis Leal in *Día de los Muertos: An Illustrated Essay and Bibliography*. Univ. of California, Santa Barbara: Center for Chicano Studies and Colección Tloque Nahuaque, University Library, 1983, pp. 2, 5.

Día de Los Muertos in a Zapotecan family of Xochimilco barrio in Oaxaca

On October 31, most of the people stay up all night. They prepare tamales for the next days; and it is a long complicated and delicate process. The *masa* (corn dough) must be very, very light so that a bit of it will float in a cup of water instead of sinking to the bottom. Without the convenience of electric mixers this means long and hard hand beating, and many tamales must be made for all the guests, living and dead, who will come. The feather-light corn dough is wrapped in individual packages made of corn husks and tied at the ends with a small strip of the husk. Then, at the moment the tamales are thrown into the clay pot to steam, the boys and men outside set off firecrackers to celebrate the event. Other foods are cooked on that night too, such as the rich, near-black Oaxacan *mole,* red *moles,* and chiles.

The altar must be prepared on this night as well. All the relatives in the household help to set up the display to honor the beloved spirits.

It is worthwhile to digress a moment to describe the appearance of the altar itself in this household. A large wooden table has been placed at one end of the room. (However, at Xoxo and Santiago Ixtaltepec and other nearby villages we noticed that some individuals had heavy adobe or cement altars built into their homes.) On the clean white wall behind the table, someone had arched two long canes to form an arc framing the many holy pictures hanging there. Cherished prints of the Sacred Heart, the Virgin of Guadalupe (Mexico's patroness), Our Lady and the Child Jesus and other indistinguishable pictures were enshrined. Some had small bunches of yellow *semposuchils* attached to the frames. Sprays of cultivated *semposuchil* and coxcomb festooned the table, and a huge bouquet of wild marigolds stood in front of it on the floor. As well as flowers, large white tapers, small, fat vigil candles, incense, and a large cardboard *calavera,* or skull, sat on the altar. Fragrant fruits such as limes, oranges and bananas were piled here and there; and loaves of bread of the dead and tablets of chocolate gave evidence of the work of the evening.

All the tasks had to be done through the night, said our Zapotec informant, for at about 4:00 A.M. the spirits of the children would arrive. At the present time they put the children's miniature things on the same altar that would be used to honor adults, but formerly, in a larger house, they had a separate altar in the corner for the children. Each expected child spirit has its own tiny candle in a miniature clay candle holder. At Santa Lucia, Oaxaca, we saw a children's altar which was also considered the altar belonging to the living child of the family. It featured an array of tiny toys and paper goods, little apples, flowers and miniature loaves as well as candles.

When the little spirits arrive the only evidence may be a fluttering of their candle flames or a bit of fruit dropping from the pile, our informant confided. After they leave at 8:00 A.M., the morning of November 1 (the same morning they arrived), the family snuffs out the tiny candles and takes them off the altar.

The adult spirits then arrive at 3:00 P.M. The family has carefully placed large candles in normally-sized holders for them. Everyone hopes that they will be pleased with the gifts of food and drink set out before them. They may go away weeping if nothing is offered. Our Zapotec friend tells the story of a thoughtless woman who left her father-in-law only an old olla of dry corn. His son, arriving home from a long journey, found his father's spirit leaving the house in disgust with marks of blows from the corn cobs on his arms.

Evil fortune falls on humans who dare to eat the food on the altar before the spirits come to take its essence, for they feel that the angry adult spirits may come and tie their feet up before they wake.

In the evening, about 8:00 P.M., the family prays the rosary in front of the altar in honor of the deceased ones. On this night visitors and relatives come by to pray, talk, and offer a gift to the "souls". Many years ago, said the old mother from Xochimilco *barrio,* the visitors sometimes came in costumes, but this is no longer true. Guests and relatives come by with gifts called "Muertos" (dead ones). If the visitors include a *compadre* or *comadre* (godfather or godmother) to someone in the family they usually bring tortillas, an earthenware jar of black *mole,* fruits, nuts, flowers, and a candle, all wrapped in individual spotless napkins and carried in a basket.

As people come by to visit and offer *muertos,* the talk often turns to the dead ones being honored that evening. By the flickering lights of the altar in an otherwise dark house, the perfect setting is created for ghostly stories. Children gather around, shivering with fear and delight to hear their elders tell them.

On the morning of the second of November, All Souls' Day in the Catholic calendar, there are three masses for those in Xochimilco barrio—one at 6:30 A.M., one at 7:00 A.M., and one at 8:00 A.M. Promptly at 8:00 A.M. the adult spirts leave for their own world, and the family again snuffs out the candles. Prayers for the dead may go on all day, however.

Since the dead are officially gone, people may remove food from the altar and take it around to friends. Before this no one dares take the food that belongs to the spirits.

In the evening some cemeteries slowly fill with people. They carry flowers and candles to decorate the graves of the dead. At the little cemetery of San Felipe del Agua near Oaxaca City, there is a painted wooden altar in the center of the graveyard. It is filled with flowers and candles, offered by the faithful on the night of All Souls'. A tiny old Zapotec woman lights copal incense in a three-legged clay burner in front of one flower-decked grave. The most ornamented graves are those of little children. Everything there is in miniature. Among the flowers are tiny ollas, toys, minuscule candles in little holders, and cardboard tombs (*tumbitas*).

At the few unattended gravestones small children play the traditional board games—El Ancla and La Oca, by the waning light of a single vigil candle.

The older people complain that things are changing, that many young people today make fun of the customs, and get drunk at the cemetery. As we went on to Santiago Ixtaltepec on the night of November 2, we found all behavior most solemn and decorous. While clusters of people spoke in quiet tones, and children played El Ancla on the empty stones, others waited patiently near the tomb of a "soul". The responses, or prayers for the dead, were being chanted at this cemetery over each grave. A lay prayer leader intoned the responses and sprinkled holy water over each grave. He was accompanied by a whole band, consisting of trombone, bass fiddle, trumpet, clarinet, drum, cymbals and other instruments. Each family gave the singer and musicians a gift of food when they finished. The gifts would be divided among all equally after they finished the prayers at about midnight.

Close to midnight the musicians gathered in the middle of the *panteon* to play "Las Golondrinas" (The Swallows) and "Dios Nunca Muere" (God Never Dies). Then slowly the families collected their baskets and candles and left the little cemetery.

By the next day, November 3, the Days of the Dead and All Saints' is officially over. At Xochimilco barrio, the altar is not dismantled until the fourth, however. Fruits and candies can be enjoyed by everyone since the spirits have left the earthly part they can no longer enjoy. The cardboard games, coffin bearers, and calaveras of paper are stored away for the next year. The grave decorations at Xochimilco cemetery remain until the thirtieth of November.

Source: *Laughing Souls: The Day of the Dead in Oaxaca, Mexico* by Judith Strupp Green. San Diego Museum of Man, Balboa Park. Popular Series no. 1, May, 1969.

Día de los Muertos in Juárez, Mexico

Most colorful of the elements associated with Dia de los Muertos is the custom of tending to the graves of loved ones. As noted above, there has been a blending of the two days, but one distinction lives on. All Saints' Day is also called *Día de los Angelitos* (Day of the Little Angels), and on that day the graves of children get special attention. In 1980, when November 1 fell on a Saturday, I was surprised on visiting a Juárez cemetery to note that there was little activity, and that generally only children's graves were being decorated. Everyone I asked told me that this was the children's day; All Souls' Day was for the rest of the people, and that the following day would see the graveyard crowded—and it was so.

After breakfast on the chosen day, and perhaps after a visit to the neighborhood church where a candle is lighted in memory of departed family members, people descend on the graveyards carrying flowers and hoes, rakes, and other tools for the cleaning up of the grave sites. Many graveyards where Mexican-Americans are buried do not have the luxury of perpetual care; similarly, many small town and rural Anglo cemeteries do not, and have regularly scheduled dates, usually Saturdays, when the people turn out to cut weeds, mow the grass, etc. But the special days for Mexican-Americans are far more than just grave-cleaning. In Juárez, where our family goes each year to fulfill our duties to the dead, the custom is seen in a fuller state. It is truly a holiday time: people bring lunches, paint to decorate crosses and headstones, and new plastic or metal crosses or *coronas* (wreaths), and urchins scurry about carrying plastic jugs of water for the families to sprinkle the graves and water the flowers they have brought, often from their own yards, although flower-sellers do a big business too. Outside the gates of the *camposanto* (holy ground, cemetery), taco vendors and sellers of sugar cane and soft drinks are also present. Inside, after the graves are scraped and re-mounded, weeds pulled and flowers arranged—often in patterns that are quite artistic—the families settle down for a picnic at the family grave site, with no sense of impropriety, even sitting on grave slabs—while at an adjoining grave, the family may be kneeling in prayer.

Source: *Mexican-American Folklore* by John O. West. Little Rock: August House, 1988, p. 158.

Día de Muertos in Mexico City, c. 1910

"Dia de Muertos" (All Souls' Day) is greatly observed in Mexico City by persons visiting the cemeteries and decorating the graves of departed relatives or friends with beautiful wreaths and flowers. The resting-places of the dead are crowded, all the tramways that lead to the different cemeteries are full of passengers all day long, coming and going. During the day preceding and the day after, as well as "Dia de Muertos," booths are erected, sometimes near the Zocalo or Alameda, where peculiar toys and sweet-meats are sold in shapes of skulls, tombs, etc., all of funereal aspect, but which strange to say do not frighten the children, who buy these queer toys and take home to play with them. A bread is also sold called "pan de muerto" (dead man's bread), made into these weird shapes.

At every theatre the drama, "Don Juan Tenorio," is given for a few days around All Souls' Day and also on that particular day. The play is in verse and written by Zorrilla, a well-known Spanish author. It is a weird and allegorical play, describing a young man whose great reputation for his numerous successful love affairs and duels was known everywhere. Suddenly he falls really in love with Doña Ines. This girl is sent to a convent, to become a nun, by her father, so that Don Juan cannot pursue her, but the insistent lover manages to send her letters full of his great devotion and finally carries her off, even though a nun, to a castle by the sea. He has duels with her father, brother, and others, killing them all, and from grief Doña Ines dies. He visits her tomb, and there while praying for her and God's forgiveness, the ghosts of all those he killed appear and demand his condemnation. The spirit of Doña Ines prays for his pardon and they are reunited finally in heaven and Paradise. The verses are beautiful in sweetness and originality. This play is given every year in nearly every Latin-American country and Spain during "Dia de Muertos," so that it is considered one of the most popular and well-known plays in Spanish-speaking cities. Perhaps "Don Juan Tenorio" has been given more than any other play in the world. In these countries the name "Tenorio" is greatly used, being often applied to the men who have many love affairs.

Source: *When I Was a Girl in Mexico* by Mercedes Godoy. Boston: Lothrop, Lee & Shepard Co., 1919, pp. 51-53.

For more information on El Día de los Muertos see: *Día de Los Muertos: An Illustrated Essay and Bibliography*. University of California, Santa Barbara: Center for Chicano Studies and Colección Tloque Nahuaqua, University Library, 1983; *Laughing Souls: The Days of the Dead in Oaxaca, Mexico* by Judith Strupp Green. San Diego Museum of Man, Balboa Park. Popular Series no. 1, May, 1969; *Mexican American Folklore* by John O. West. Little Rock: August House, 1988, pp. 150-160; *A Treasury of Mexican Folkways* by Frances Toor. New York: Crown, 1947; *Vive Tu Recuerdo: Living Traditions in the Mexican Days of the Dead* by Robert V. Childs and Patricia B. Altman. Museum of Cultural History, Univ. of California, Los Angeles. Monograph Series no. 17, 1982.

Northern Marianas (Chamorros)

Grave-tending in the Northern Marianas, Chamorros communities

On All Souls' Day (2 Nov.), cemeteries are visited, and the graves cleaned and adorned with candles and flowers.

Source: *Micronesia Handbook: Guide to an American Lake* by David Stanley. Chico, Calif.: Moon, 1985, p. 167.

November 3

St. Hubert's Day

This day is named after St. Hubertus Van Luik or St. Hubert of Liége. After the murder of St. Lambert at Liége in 705, St. Hubert had St. Lambert's bones transferred to Liége and made Liége the center of his diocese. St. Hubert is regarded as patron and founder of Liége.

Belgium (Wallonia)

A cure for rabies

. . . bread [is] blessed at St. Croix Church in Liege on St. Hubert's day and fed to the dogs to protect them from hydrophobia.

Source: *Chateau-Gerard: The Life and Times of a Walloon Village* by Harry Holbert Turney-High. Columbia: Univ. of South Carolina Press, 1953, p. 259.

November 5
Bonfire Night

Canada (Newfoundland)

Village-dwellers on the coast of Newfoundland light bonfires on this night. Young people compete in building the biggest fire. Though the fires are a descendant of Guy Fawkes Day bonfires, ''Guys'' (effigies) are seldom a part of these big bonfire nights in Newfoundland.

Source: *Let's Celebrate!* by Caroline Parry. Toronto: Kids Can Press, 1987, pp. 236-237.

November 5

Guy Fawkes Night

On November 5, 1605, Guy Fawkes was discovered in the cellar of parliament with thirty-six barrels of gunpowder. He planned to blow up parliament the next day during its opening. The breaking of this "gunpowder plot" was celebrated with Thanksgiving church services every November 5 until 1859. Since that time, the burning of an effigy of Guy Fawkes has become the main attraction of this holiday.

Great Britain

Begging with the "Guy" in England

The "Guy" may be an elaborate effigy clothed in the period of Guy Fawkes or simply a bundle of rags. It is trotted around the streets by bands of children who chant and collect money. They may chant verses like "Please to remember the fifth of November, / Gunpowder treason and plot, / I see no reason why gunpowder treason, / Should ever be forgot" or "Guy, guy, guy, / Poke him in the eye, / Put him on the bonfire, / And there let him die." Bonfires are built that night and the "Guys" are burnt amid celebration. Sausages may be toasted on the bonfire and potatoes roasted in the embers. Special foods such as Bonfire Parkin (a heavy cake made of oatmeal, molasses, and ginger) and Plot Toffee are popular in Yorkshire.

Source: *The Customs and Ceremonies of Britain* by Charles Kightly. London: Thames and Hudson, 1986, pp. 130-131.

New Zealand

Guy Fawkes Day in Christchurch

The longest example of a Guy Fawkes rhyme comes from Christchurch of 1920:

> Please to remember the fifth of November,
> The gunpowder treason and plot.
> I see no reason why the gunpowder treason
> Should ever be forgot.
> Four and twenty barrels lain down below,
> Blow old England overflow.
> Happy was the night, happy was the day,
> See old Guy Fawkes going to his den
> With a dark lantern and a candle in his hand.
> Get out! Get out! you dirty ole man!
> Holla, Holla, boys, make the bells ring.
> Holla, Holla, boys, God Save the King.
> A pound of cheese to choke him,
> A bottle of beer to wash it down,
> A jolly good fire to roast him.
> Christmas is coming, the pigs are getting fat,
> Please put a penny in the old man's hat.
> If you haven't got a penny, a hapenny will do
> If you haven't got a hapenny, God Bless You.

The informant claims that as children they would never get their money unless they were able to chant masterfully this particular rhyme from beginning to end. Often they would be lined up beside their "Guys" and the money was given to the child able to say his rhyme the best—and that generally meant the loudest. He remembers also the pennies that were thrown down to the crowd of children from the Express Building in Christchurch. This practice, and the following one, is reported also from other centers. Certain adults delighted in heating the pennies on a shovel held over the fire. These were thrown out with the other pennies, much to the consternation of the children who were striving to catch them or pick them up. Generally the children would pick them up irrespective of the burn, or kick them into the gutter to cool in the water. Many carried the scars—burns—of Guy Fawkes for many weeks after. Another trick was to wrap a penny in silver paper so that it would look like a half-crown flying down. And pennies were occasionally dipped in hot lead with similar intent. One Christchurch informant had a trick by which he was always successful in getting many of the pennies thrown down. As the pennies fell he would run forward, jabbing at the bending children with an open safety pin. As they recoiled he would seize the coins.

Guy Fawkes Day in Wellington in 1949

The following comment in the *Evening Post,* Wellington, May, 11, 1949, is a fairly accurate description of what had happened:

Guy Fawkes Day seems to be another honourable institution that is now on the decline. It seemed so this morning when a few desultory small boys roamed the streets seeking a few pennies to buy the traditional fireworks. "A penny for the guy, Mister?" was about the best that could be heard from most collectors. Gone are the good old songs and chants. . . . Bands of juvenile pirates complete with hideous masks swarmed about the trams at Courtenay Place for a while this morning like beggars in an Eastern Market. They did some brisk business too. A few scooters, carts, and prams were decorated with the conventional stuffed sugar bags and old hats and coats, and these made some attempt at the time-honoured parading that precedes the real Guy Fawkes Festival.

Source: *The Games of New Zealand Children* by Brian Sutton-Smith. Berkeley: Univ. of California, 1959, pp. 206-207.

Circa November 6-8

Water Festival

Cambodia/Kampuchea/Khmer Republic

This festival formerly celebrated the king's birthday. It now commemorates the reversal of current in the Tonle Sap, a large lake area that feeds the Mekong.

November 7

Anniversary of the Great October Socialist Revolution

U.S.S.R.

A commemoration of the popular uprising in Russia in 1917 and the coming to power of the Communist Party. The revolution took place on October 25 (Julian calendar). November 7 is the Gregorian calendar date.

November 8

St. Michael's Day

Michael is known as a prince, greatest of all angels in Hebraic tradition. His day is celebrated on November 8 in Greek Orthodox religion and on September 29 in the Western Church.

Ethiopia (Amhara)

Rituals for the day of St. Michael (Mikā'ēl)

In November the monthly St. Michael's Day is honored with special celebrations. The peasants travel distances to attend the ceremonies at any church consecrated to "Mikā'ēl." Holy water and hot springs sanctified by Mikā'ēl's name are drunk and bathed in by those with many kinds of disease. The rituals involve carrying the Mikā'ēl *tābot* ("holy ark") out of the church and elaborate chanting and dancing by the clergy. After the *tābot* has been returned, in a procession in which the laymen follow shouldering their rifles (undoubtedly spears in older times), folk dancing and singing go on until late afternoon. This provides an occasion for the more enterprising adolescent male to spot a potential bride, about whom he may diffidently ask his father to make inquiries.

Source: *Wax & Gold: Tradition and Innovation in Ethiopian Culture* by Donald N. Levine. Chicago: Univ. of Chicago Press, 1965, p. 62.

November 11

St. Martin's Day

Martin of Tours, a Hungarian army officer, cut his cloak in half to share with a seminaked beggar. This took place at Amiens, France, in the year 337. Martin later became Bishop of Tours. In some areas, protestants associate the day with Martin Luther, who was born on November 10.

Denmark

Mortensaftenn

This is a thanksgiving day in honor of St. Martin of Tours, patron of the harvest. It is a time of family reunions.

Germany

Martinstag

This day is known in Germany as Martinstag. It is celebrated by Catholics for Bishop Martin of Tours. Protestants celebrate the day in honor of Martin Luther.

The *Martinsgans* (Martin Goose)

Martinsgans appears on restaurant menus in late autumn and is a specialty of St. Martin's Day. St. Martin is said to have tried to hide in a flock of geese, because he felt unworthy to be made Bishop of Tours. The geese cackled and gave him away.

Martinmas fires

Martinmas fires on the eve of St. Martin's Day were once popular. They still are found in areas along the Rhine and the Moselle. One can rid oneself of personal blemishes or mistakes by dancing round the fire on this night.

Lantern parades and *Martinsmännchen*

Children used to go through the streets carrying lanterns and singing *Martinslieder* or reciting rhymes. They were given special breads shaped like men (*Martinsmännchen*) holding a clay pipe. Children still form lantern parades, but these are no longer associated specifically with St. Martin's Day.

Source: *German Festivals and Customs* by Jennifer M. Russ. London: Oswald Wolff, 1982, pp. 75-76.

St. Martin's Day remnant in lantern parades

Today, the parades are held at various dates in the fall, but originally they were all held on the 11th of November, "Martinstag" (St. Martin's Day). Bishop Martin of Tours, who died around 400 A.D. is the Catholic saint of November 11th. It is not clear why lantern marches—even fires in earlier times—were held on this day. It may be that the "trick-or-treating" excursions which were customary on that day simply needed artificial light because of the early dark. Instead of today's paper lanterns, hollowed out pumpkins or turnips with bizarre carved faces—very much like American Halloween pumpkins—were used in Germany in earlier times, too. There were also parades with ghastly made-up figures on this day. Already at a relatively early date the pupils had to sing in the city parades. In former centuries, these parades were popular primarily in north-western Germany and the Rhineland.

Although St. Martin is a Catholic saint, Protestants did not have to forego celebrating this day. Martin Luther was born on the 10th of November, 1483, and was baptized on St. Martin's Day (that is where he got his first name). After the Reformation, Martin's Day customs were simply antedated to the 10th of November, Luther's birthday, particularly in the central regions of Germany.

The old custom vanished at first in the big cities, but it was also in the big cities, viz. in the city kindergartens, that the new custom of the lantern parades originated. For the kindergartens, lantern parades are interesting for various reasons: when children make their own lanterns, they can pracitice their creativity, they become acquainted with paper and scissors, and they learn to be proud of their creation. And if the children parade with their lanterns during the early darkness of fall, the whole kindergarten shows itself to the parents and to the community. The children enjoy the performance, and the younger ones are given an opportunity to integrate with the group.

Throughout the fall, however, you can also see individual mothers with their children carrying paper lanterns in the streets. This is partly a relic of the old custom, partly a consequence of the new custom of the lantern marches.

Source: *German Holidays and Folk Customs* by Dieter Kramer. Hamburg: Atlantik-Brucke, 1972, pp. 40-41.

Great Britain

Martinmas

Known in England as Martinmas, this is the Feast of St. Martin of Tours. Martinmas was once a "quarter day" (in the North of England) when feudal dues were collected and hiring fairs were held. More recently the day is associated with the armistice of World War I, which occurred at 11 A.M. on November 11, 1918. Services are held to commemorate the war dead on the Sunday following November 11, Remembrance Sunday.

Source: *Customs and Ceremonies of Britain* by Charles Kightly. London: Thames and Hudson, 1987.

A St. Martin's legend

It happened that he was once obliged to go to Rome and set off thither on foot. On the way he met the Devil, who taunted him with his lowly state and jeered at him for trudging along thus instead of driving in a carriage suitable to his rank as a bishop. St. Martin, with great presence of mind, changed the Devil into a mule and leapt on his back and rode off on his way. Whenever the steed attempted to slacken speed, St. Martin goaded it on by making the sign of the cross. At last, thoroughly beaten, the Devil cried out:

> "Signa te signa; temere me tangis et angis:
> Roma tibi subito motibus ibit amor."

These lines are curious because each reads the same whether you start from the left and read to right or from right to left. That is what is called a pallindrome.

(The English is roughly, "Cross, cross thyself. Thou plaguest and vexest me without necessity for owing to my exertions thou wilt soon reach Rome, thy desired goal.")

A Martinmas saying

> "If you raise your glass
> At Martinmas.
> Wine will be yours
> Throughout the year."

Source: *Happy Holidays* by Eleanor Graham. New York: E.P. Dutton, 1933, p. 241.

Ireland

Early Irish St. Martin's Eve customs

In some areas, notably Galway, on St. Martin's Eve (10th November) cocks were killed and blood sprinkled on the doors of houses. This was probably a survival from a period when animals were killed before the winter when fodder was difficult to obtain. It is yet another interesting example of the way in which religion and agriculture were mixed in Irish folk festivals.

Source: *Life & Tradition in Rural Ireland* by Timothy P. O'Neill. London: J.M. Dent & Sons Ltd., 1977, p. 64.

The Netherlands

St. Martin's Day in Holland, c. 1910

St. Martin was celebrated on November eleventh, but only in such villages and towns as had preserved ancient customs. On the evening of the eleventh, soon after we had come out of school and it was dark, we gathered a lot of dry twigs and shavings, and if possible, we procured a tarred barrel. We toted these things to a meadow right back of the village. There we built a fire and we danced and shouted around it as if we had been wild Indians. Father used to tell us of a boy who ran right through the flames of a St. Martin's fire, scorching his hair and clothes. I deplored the degenerate days I had been born in, for there was not a single boy among us children who had the courage to follow this hero's example.

When the fire was out, we walked two or three abreast, holding Chinese lanterns or a candle stuck in a turnip with a paper bag around it, somewhat resembling your pumpkins on Hallowe'en. Some of the boys had firecrackers. We sang many school songs and also a ditty about St. Martin being very cold and needing fire-wood, while we were serenading some of the village people and the nearest farmers, who rewarded us with a few cents. Later we went to the baker and bought cookies and sweets for the money and divided this amongst ourselves. Thus the fun ended.

Source: *When I Was a Girl in Holland* by Cornelia de Groot. Boston: Lothrop, Lee & Shepard Co., 1917, pp. 78-79.

Portugal

Feast of Sao Martinho

St. Martin's Day is celebrated with roasted chestnuts, red wine, and a freshly butchered pig.

Source: *A Portuguese Rural Society* by José Cutileiro. Oxford: Clarendon, 1971, p. 257.

Sweden

Marten Gas (Martin Goose) in Sweden

This festival, originally in memory of Saint Martin of Tours, has come to be associated also with Martin Luther, whose day is celebrated the day before. The day marked the end of autumn work and the beginning of winter activities. Goose banquets are served in homes and restaurants. They begin with *swartsoppa* (blacksoup), a bisque of goose-blood and spices. St. Martin's

Day traditions are especially stong in Skane, the southernmost province of Sweden.

Martin's Goose Day, c. 1910

One rather interesting feast-day came on November tenth and was known as Martin's Goose Day, celebrated in honor of Martin Luther. A goose was killed in each household which could afford to have a feast and entertain guests. In a manner, this feast-day corresponded to the American Thanksgiving Day, for the thoughtful farmer no doubt felt grateful to God for the harvest, and celebrated by eating the apple-and-prune-stuffed roasted goose and other good things served on this day.

This time of the year the Swedish peasants usually devoted their evenings to ''brushing up'' their Catechism and Bible History knowledge. For soon the *Kyrkoherde,* or parish priest, would appear in each village and conduct quizzes regarding the religious knowledge of his flock. A strict record of each parishioner was kept. Those who fell below a certain standard would not be permitted to partake of the Lord's Supper during the following year, and such a person was regarded as an outcast until his lack of religious knowledge had been remedied.

In later years, this quizzing system was abandoned, although it was an excellent practice which helped the priest to keep in closer touch with his people. Then there were the social elements also: rich and poor alike looked forward to these household examinations, because it was usually the most prominent farmer in each village who opened his house for the occasion. And, after the ordeal was over, all who attended were treated to a sumptuous feast, with the *Kyrkoherde* leading the way.

Before everybody sat down to do full justice to the meal itself, the *smörgas-bord* greeted the eyes of the hungry ones. This institution is a kind of unwieldy, multiple *hors-d'oeuvre,* or appetizer. The *smörgas-bord* always precedes any formal meal. The men and women helped themselves to the various spiced and thinly sliced smoked home-made sausages, cold tongue, pickled herring, jellied eel, smoked salmon and anchovy, tiny, delicious meat balls, rich cheese, breads of many kinds, butter and preserves, etc. A well-planned and prettily arranged *smörgas-bord* resembles a colorful exhibition of delicatessen stuff at a food show.

Source: *When I Was a Girl in Sweden* by Anna-Mia Hertzman. Boston: Lothrop, Lee & Shepard Co., 1926, pp. 121-122.

November 11

St. Mennas' Day

A day to honor St. Mennas. Mennas was born in Egypt and may have been a camel driver before enlisting in the Roman army. When his legion reached Phrygia the persecution of Christians under Diocletian began. Mennas, who was a Christian, deserted and hid in a mountain cave. During the annual games in the arena at Cotyaeum in Phrygia, Mennas entered the arena and announced that he was a Christian. He was tortured but would not recant, so was beheaded. He died in A.D. 295.

A second St. Mennas also shares this day. This saint was a Greek from Asia Minor who became a hermit in the Abruzzi, probably at Santomena (Sanctus Menna) in the diocese of Conza. St. Gregory the Great described the miracles and virtues of this St. Mennas, who died in the sixth century.

Greece

St. Mennas aids shepherds

St. Mennas has the special power to reveal where lost or stolen objects lie. Shepherds invoke his power to find lost sheep and to protect against wolves. A shepherd's wife does not use scissors on this day but winds a thread around the scissors' mouth. This symbolizes keeping the mouth of the wolf closed. It is also believed to keep shut the mouth of the village gossip.

A St. Mennas' Day proverb

"I (winter) send word of my coming on St. Mennas' Day, and I arrive on St. Philip's Day." This is the onset of the winter season.

Source: *Greek Calendar Customs* by George A. Megas. Athens: B. & M. Rhodis, 1963, p. 21.

November 15

Shichi-go-san (Seven-Five-Three)

Three-year-old children, five-year-old sons, and seven-year-old daughters may be taken to a local shrine for blessing.

Japan

Thousand-year candy

Japanese children who are seven, five and three years old dress in their best clothes and and are taken to a shrine by their parents to be blessed. The children are all given long sacks full of pink candy, called ''thousand-year candy.'' It is supposed to bring them good luck and a long life.

Source: *Visit with Us in Japan* by Joan Pross Larson. Englewood Cliffs, N.J.: Prentice-Hall, 1964, p. 65.

Shichi-go-san in Miyamoto-cho, Tokyo, c. 1980

The shrine comes briefly alive in November for Shichigosan, when children aged three, five, and seven, dressed in their finest clothing, are presented to the deity. Accompanied by mothers and grandmothers dressed in their best kimono[s], and by proud fathers carrying cameras or video recorders, the children receive blessings from the priest and a bag of candy from the ujiko sōdai who collects the parents' donations.

Source: *Neighborhood Tokyo* by Theodore C. Bestor. Stanford, Calif.: Stanford Univ. Press, 1989, p. 157.

Shichi-go-san, c. 1933

At this time all children of three years of age, boys of five and girls of seven, go to the shrine for a blessing, seeking health, wealth and long life from the guardian gods of the family. The change of the hair dressing, the putting on of the skirtlike trousers by the boys, in the ''*Hakamagi,*'' trousers-wearing ceremony, and the putting on of the sash like mother or big sister wears, in the ceremony called ''*obi-toki,*'' wearing of *obi* or sash makes it a great day in the child's life.

Source: *Japanese Festival and Calendar Lore* by William Hugh Erskine. Tokyo: Kyo Bun Kwan, 1933, p. 27.

Shichi-go-san, c. 1920

Of course New Year's Day brings a new birthday to everybody, old and young, but the November fifteenth celebration is for children only; and not all children, either—though everyone has his chance in time. It is exclusively for little girls of seven and three years old, and little boys of five.

On this day every Shinto shrine in Japan is prepared and waiting for its many little guests. The streets are full of children, all dressed in their best, each child being taken by mother or servant to the special shrine where it was registered at birth.

Shortly after I had begun to think about the lucky numbers it was time for the November fifteenth day and Mother and I walked through the crowded street toward a small shrine not far from our home. Most people were walking, but there were a number of autos filled with children. They looked like bouquets of lovely flowers, mostly scarlet—as that is the color for little girls—but mingled in was a generous sprinkling of little boys in their gray skirts and coats of ceremonious black. Here and there was a jinrikisha pulled by a smiling runner in a new coat. One had three children merrily huddled in together, with a smart-looking servant walking beside it. Every child on the street was carrying, or having carried for it by someone else, one or more black-and-white, big-eyed, scarlet-collared toy dogs—the good-luck guardian for little children.

It was a gay scene, for everybody was smiling and hurrying. We smiled, too, but we did not hurry. We walked slowly, watching the passing crowd. One mother had a gaily dressed little tot of three, toddling along beside her, with a tiny dog held upside down. Another, with two little girls of seven and three, was followed by a servant carrying an armful of toy dogs of every size, everyone with a scarlet collar having a pleated ruffle around it.

Then came along a lucky mother who had children of all three ages; the son of five years striding along proudly, as should the young master of the home, in his silk pleated skirt and loose-sleeved crest coat. Beside him walked his seven-year-old sister, wearing her first ''grown-up dress'' of orange crêpe with a pattern of chrysanthemums and a sash of red-and-gold brocade. In her black hair was a gorgeous tinsel hairpin and as she passed I heard the ''tinkle-tinkle'' of tiny bells hidden in the hollow of her red-lacquer shoes, and saw, hanging from her left side, close to the big stiff bow of her sash, a plump little bag of gold brocade. It held a bit of priestly writing which had been given her on her first visit to the shrine at eight days old and was considered a protection from evil.

Following close behind the mother and children was a maid

carrying on her back the little sister of three years, in a bright, big-flowered kimono and her first stiff sash. She, also, had a guardian bag, a bright bit of color swinging at her side. Brother's was hidden by his loose crest coat.

Each child held, clasped tight in its arms, a large toy dog with a capelike collar of scarlet crêpe, but the little sister's was of smaller size and it had no collar; only a red band on which hung a tiny bell. A man followed, tall and erect—probably their neighborhood carpenter who offered to be a retainer on this important day, to carry the many faithful dumb attendants, the gifts of relations and friends. Toy dogs were all over him—tied on his shoulders, his belt, his arms, his neck—all black and white, all with staring eyes and scarlet collars. And they were of every size from one dangling from his finger to a great, square, big-eyed creature at least eighteen inches high.

Finally we reached the shrine and found just within the entrance a number of busy gentlemen, some of whom were acquaintances of ours. They were prominent members of the shrine who had offered their services today, and with astonishing system and dispatch were getting the many names registered, all in groups of ten. When the children were all seated on the matted floor, with the older people in the rear, it was a pretty sight—a mass of gay colors and big-eyed toy dogs, of black heads and flower hairpins, of proud little boy faces and sweet little girl faces all upturned to the altar toward a small eight-sided mirror and some sacred *sakaki* branches. That was all, but they proclaimed that the place was holy.

The priest, stately in a stiff robe and over-garments of rainbow-colored gauze, with a lacquer belt and high lacquer crown, appeared before the altar and, lifting a sakaki branch high in both hands, he waved it in slow, swinging circles as he recited the "*notto*"—the old mythical Shinto ritual. It was broken at intervals by the dull beat of a wooden drum and the shrill, mournful music of the *sho*—a flute similar to the pipes of the god Pan. The ceremony was beautiful and impressive, but very short. At its close priest attendants entered carrying white boxlike trays holding pyramids of small white paper packages—two for each child. One contained little cakes in the form of the Shinto emblems—the mirror, the sword, and the jewel; and the other a small quantity of raw rice—sacred because it had been before the altar. This was for the mothers to take home to mix with the rice for the evening meal, where each of the family, before lifting the chopsticks to eat, would bow a pleasant "Congratulations!" to each lucky little brother or sister of the ages of seven, five, or three.

That evening Mother explained to me the origin of this universal respect for these special numbers.

The story goes to the olden, olden, olden time when the Sun goddess, indignant at her brother's disrespectful conduct, hid herself in a cave. This left the world in darkness. The troubled gods gathered in front of the closed rock, and the goddess of good nature merrily danced on the hollow, echoing trunk of a fallen tree, which caused such shouts of laughter from the gods that the Sun goddess peeped out to see what it was all about. When the first ray of her brilliant presence lighted the world again, a quick-thinking god hastily twisted a rope of rice straw and, slipping unseen behind her, he stretched the rope across the front of the cave so that she could not retreat. Thus was the blessing of sunlight saved to the world.

Source: *Chiyo's Return* by Chiyono Sugimoto Kiyooka. Garden City, N.Y.: Doubleday, Doran & Co., 1936, pp. 305-307.

Circa November 15

Haile Selassie's Coronation Day

A feast of the occasion of Haile Selassie's (Ras Tafari) coronation, this day is celebrated as a major holiday by Jamaican Ras Tafarians.

Jamaica (Ras Tafarian)

Haile Selassie's coronation celebration in 1953

Ras Tafarians do not celebrate Christmas because they believe that Christ was born on April 1st. The latter date is regarded by them as the beginning of the year, and ceremonies are held during the day and in the evening. Emancipation Day, a Jamaican holiday, is not observed by Ras Tafarians because they hold that black men have not yet been emancipated. The anniversary of Haile Selassie's Coronation Day provides the occasion for the most important special celebration during the year. In 1953, this ceremony occurred on November 15. The evening programme began with the singing of "When I Go to Zion I'll Never Leave Again."

When I go to Zion I'll never leave again.
When I go to Zion I'll never leave again.
I am going to the mansion
King Rasta come and prepare.
When I go to Zion I'll never leave again.

A special orchestra, which included the following instruments—two rhumba boxes, hree guitars, two saxophones, one violin, one banjo, tambourines, and rattles—accompanied the singing. Special recitations, and songs by individuals and a quartette were presented. Ten babies were dedicated to Ras Tafari, and a godfather and godmother were appointed for each baby. During this part of the ceremony, each mother handed her child to a male assistant of the Leader. This official took the baby in his arms, gently raised and lowered it several times, smiled and said: "The King (Ras Tafari) bless thee, keep thee, and make his face to shine upon thee, and give thee peace and life everlasting." Two collections were taken for the babies and the money was divided equally among the mothers. On this occasion ten speeches were delivered throughout the programme. We shall cite only one speech "Mr. S. is a brave man to come here, but remember that Satan is a brave man too. The Anglo-Saxons teach us ignorancy. Black man, be reasonable. Can you have a Queen without a King? I know that the Queen who is coming here doesn't care for me, so why should I adore her? The only future destination is with Ras Tafari. Where was God when the white man was raping India, Egypt and other countries? Haile Selassie is Jesus Christ reincarnated. He has a legion of angels [presumably his officials] around him. We are celebrating the coronation of Jesus Christ tonight, and for that we make no apology and no compromise. Mau Mau is a war between black men and white men. The white men throw bombs on the Mau Mau, but they can't hurt them because Haile Selassie controls the bomb. Mau Mau don't have guns; they use bows and arrows. The white man tells us to wait until Jesus comes, but we're not going to wait. The Minister of Education is going to prison. Our only hope is to go back to Africa. In the near future we are going back to our Homeland." The speech was followed by a brief song:

I shall not die but I shall live
Forever with the Lord.
In these days I heard
These prophets saying
I shall live forever with the Lord.

At the end of several hours of celebration, which included the serving of cakes and aerated water, an important business meeting was held.

Source: *Religious Cults of the Caribbean: Trinidad, Jamaica, and Haiti* by George Eaton Simpson. Rio Piedras, Puerto Rico: Institute of Caribbean Studies, 1970, pp. 217-218.

November 18

Feast of St. Plato the Martyr

This day honors the popular Greek saint, known as St. Plane-tree.

Macedonia

St. Plane-tree Day as a weather omen

On the 18th is held the Feast of St. Plato the Martyr, whose name ingenious ignorance has transformed into St. Plane-tree. This is a very important date in the weather-lore of the coast especially. It is said that this holy day witnesses all known kinds of meteorological vicissitude. But the weather which finally prevails at sundown is the one which will last through the Advent or 'the Forty Days.' So deeply-rooted is this belief that a learned farmer tried very earnestly to persuade me that the failure of Napoleon's Moscow campaign was due to the omens taken by the Russian Emperor and his counsellors from a careful observation of the weather on St. Plane-tree's Day. "The Tsar on hearing of Napoleon's approach called together his Council of State.

'What are we to do, gentlement?' asked His Majesty.

'Wait for St. Plane-tree most serene master,' answered the President of the Council.

The Tsar followed this sensible advice, and saved his empire." Not a bad paraphrase of Nicholas the First's dictum: "Generals January and February will fight for us," and a good example of the mythopoeic faculty of the people.

Source: *Macedonian Folklore* by G.F. Abbott. Cambridge: Cambridge: Univ. Press, 1903, p. 67.

November 21

Presentation of the Virgin Mary in the Temple

In ancient Greece, seeds were offered to Demeter at this time of year. Customs connected with the sowing of winter seeds now occur on this day.

Greece

The halfway point in winter sowing

By this date, farmers should have sown half their land. The feast is known as Our Lady Mesosporitissa (half). It is also called Our Lady Polysporitissa (varied), because a dish made of several varieties of corn is served on this day. Plates of the dish are sent to friends with well wishes for the crop. On this day, handfuls of grain are thrown into fountains or wells as the throwers say, "As the water flows, so may riches flow."

Weather lore

In Anatolia it is said that if on this day the Pleiades are seen to set below the horizon, the weather will remain unchanged for forty days. In Macedonia it is believed that seed sown before November 21 will sprout after a day or two. Seed sown after this date will not sprout for forty days.

Source: *Greek Calendar Customs* by George A. Megas. Athens: B. & M. Rhodis, 1963, p. 22.

November 25

St. Catherine's Day / Santa Catarina

Catherine, a wealthy Christian girl, was carried off from Alexandria by the Emperor Maxentius in the year 305. She refused pagan conversion and instead converted to Christianity the fifty pagan philosophers brought to persuade her against her faith. The Emperor had the fifty put to death. His own wife, Faustina, was also converted to Christianity while visiting Catherine in prison, as was Porphyrius, a guard, who himself converted two hundred other guards. Maxentius had them all killed and set Catherine on a wheel covered with razors. The wheel broke, however, and injured the onlookers. Catherine was later beheaded.

Canada

St. Catherine's Day/La Tire Sainte-Catherine

Toffee-pulling

To French Canadians November 25 is the day for *La Tire Sainte-Catherine*. A seventeenth-century teacher, Marguerite Bourgeoys, let her students pull (*tire*) toffee in honor of St. Catherine and the custom stuck.

Source: *Let's Celebrate!* by Caroline Parry. Toronto: Kids Can Press, 1987, p. 243. (Contains a Sainte-Catherine's Day toffee recipe.)

El Salvador

Santa Catarina

St. Catherine's Day in Apopa

A *velaciones* is held on the twenty-second of the month at one of the larger homes to honor the saint and collect money for the fiesta. An altar for the saint is prepared with greenery, flowers, lanterns, and paper flags. Garlands and paper chains decorate the room. After a brief religious cermony at the altar, refreshments are served and dancing begins.

Source: *Fiesta Time in Latin America* by Jean Milne. Los Angeles: The Ward Ritchie Press, 1965, p. 170.

France

Patron of unmarried women

Unmarried girls of twenty-five wore white paper caps in honor of St. Catherine, patron of unmarried women. ''Coiffer Sainte-Catherine'' is an expression suggesting that a girl who wears St. Catherine's cap will remain an old maid. Parisian midinettes, sewing girls, held a procession on this day. Today the day is recalled in Parisian fashion houses and dressmaking firms.

Source: *A Guide to Frence Fêtes* by E. I. Robson. London: Methuen, 1930, p. 69.

November 30

St. Andrew's Day

Andrew the Apostle was the first disciple called by Christ. He was crucified on an X-shaped cross in A.D. 60. Andrew and his brother Simon Peter were fishermen.

Austria

St. Andrew's branches

In Austrian Silesia, the peasant women to this day sally forth at twelve o'clock at night on St. Andrew's Day to pluck a branch of the apricot-tree, which is put in water so that it may flower at Christmas-time. With this flowering branch they go to the Christmas Mass and it gives them the faculty of discerning all the witches whilst the clergyman is saying the blessing; each witch is seen carrying a wooden pail on her head. In some parts of Austria, every member of the family cuts a branch of cherry, apricot, or pear-tree on the day of St. Barbara. Poor people offer them for sale under the name of ''Barbara branches''. In order that each may recognise their own branch, they are all marked, and then put into a dish with water, and placed on the stove. The water is renewed every second day. About Christmas-time, white blossoms burst forth, and the one whose branch blooms first or best may expect some good luck in the following year. In the Tyrol they even try to force a cherry-tree into blossom in the open air.

Source: ''German Christmas and the Christmas-Tree'' by Alexander Tille in *Folklore* III (December, 1892), 72.

Peru

Día de San Andrés

San Andrés in Pacariqtambo, c. 1985

The planting season ends officially with the celebration of the day of San Andrés, on November 30; except for two nonindigenous cash crops, wheat and barley (which are planted in early December), most crops are, in fact, planted by the time of San Andrés. On the occasion of this festival, the eight community crosses, each of which belongs to one of the first four ayllus of the two moieties, are taken from the church in Pacariqtambo and erected on mountaintops overlooking the newly planted fields. The crosses, which are considered to guard the crops from hail, remain on the mountaintops until Cruz Velakuy (May 3), just before the harvest begins. The San Andrés festival is the responsibility of the *moieties,* not of any single ayllu. The actual celebration, in terms of the preparation of corn beer, hiring musicians, and so on, alternates between the moieties from one year to the next; one year it is sponsored by Hanansayaq, the next year by Hurinsayaq.

Source: ''Calendrical Cycles and Their Projections'' by Gary Upton in *Journal of Latin American Lore* 12:1 (1986), 54.

Sami

St. Andrew's Day is the Laplanders' principal feast and this is the occasion generally chosen for weddings which take place in happy and colorful surroundings and the participation of the entire populace of the district. New acquaintances and friendships are made and the young people have a wonderful opportunity of searching among the crowd for the face of the ideal companion. . . .

Source: *Lapponia* by Dino Sassi. Oslo: Mittet, 1982, p. 72.

Scotland

St. Andrew's Day in Scotland, c. 1986

St. Andrew is the patron saint of Scotland. This was once an important patriotic festival for Scotland. It is now overshadowed by Burns's Night. The day is marked with ceilidhs, piping, and the bringing in of the haggis.

Source: *The Customs and Ceremonies of Britain* by Charles Kightly. London: Thames and Hudson, 1986, p. 201.

For more information on St. Andrew's Day see: *Folklore of American Holidays* edited by Hennig Cohen and Tristram Potter Coffin. 2nd ed. Detroit: Gale Research, 1991, p. 395.

Month 12 (November)

Boun Phan Vet

This festival honors Prince Vessantara, an incarnation of the Lord Buddha. The holiday is celebrated at different times in different localities. In Vientiane the holiday takes on the status of a national rite and is held in the twelfth month to honor a repository of the Buddha's relics at That Luang temple.

Laos

National rites

Boun Phan Vet, in the twelfth month (November), also has its origin in the sacred texts. At this time certain national rites are held in That Luang, the temple located nearly two miles from Vientiane that is the traditional repository of relics of the Buddha. These rites commemorate Lao origins and historical events, but they are not always celebrated outside the capital. Outside Vientiane, the Boun Phan Vet is celebrated at different times in different communities, as a feast in honor of Prince Vessantara, an earlier incarnation of the Buddha. The prince, who exemplified perfect charity and detachment, is honored by the ordination of village males into the *sangha*. Also during his festival dramas and lovesong contests are held in the *wat* courtyard. There are also village cockfights and banquets and various social gatherings involving hospitality by villagers to friends and kinsmen from villages that are not celebrating the festival on that date. Such hospitality is often reciprocated.

Source: *Laos: A Country Study* by Donald P. Whitaker et al. Foreign Area Studies, Washington, D.C.: The American University, 1971, p. 123.

Balloon lanterns, c. 1900

In northern Laos, balloons are constructed out of paper which is either made locally or imported from China. They are cylindro-spherical in shape and a little gondola of rattan cane is suspended from them by a cotton thread. In the gondola there is an oil cup filled with lard and provided with two or three cotton wicks, and these are lit in order to keep the air in the balloons hot for a given length of time.

Since they are generally launched in the evening at the time of the great holiday of the twelfth month (October-November), the absence of wind makes it possible to follow their aerial course as long as the cotton wicks continue to give off light.

Source: *Le Laos* by Lucien Reimach. Human Relations Area Files translated. Paris: A. Charles, Librarie-Editeur, 1901, p. 149.

Circa November

Loi Krathong

This is a thanksgiving for the gift of waters to Me Khongkha, Mother of the Waters. *Loi* means "to float." *Krathong* means "leaf cup" or "bowl." Paper or leaf bowls, shaped like the lotus, are floated on the waters this night. Each contains a candle, four joss sticks, and flowers. They are set on the water and float slowly away. Nang Nophames, wife of King Ramakhamhaeng of Sukhotai, is said to have originated this custom about eight hundred years ago.

Thailand

Loi Krathong, c. 1950

Originally it was a Brahman ceremony; today, some Thai contend that it is performed to atone for the sin of boating over the footprints or images of Buddha which may be imbedded in the sands of the waterways; others that it is a ritual to appease the river spirits. It is no longer celebrated widely in the Bangkok region but is still a major festival in the north. In 1948, the royal government sought to revive the festival in regions where it had become moribund by sponsoring contests in the provincial capitals and awarding prizes for the most original and beautiful boats.

All villages where the festival is held decorate houses and the *wat* with colored streamers and lights. Villages that are not on rivers or canals stress this part of the festival and make elaborate lamps shaped like animals, birds, dragons, airplanes, and so forth; these villages also float illuminated boats on irrigation ditches, and young people often trek to the nearest large waterway to float their boats. Villages on waterways are also gaily decorated, but they give particular attention to their boats, making them in the shape of battleships, gondolas, rafts, airplanes, dragons, or whatever image happens to catch the maker's fancy.

On each of the three days of *Loi Katong* the monks (who are forbidden to take part in the floating of the boats—though this rule in villages on waterways is honored more in the breach than in the observance) conduct morning, afternoon, and evening services in the *wat*. The village elders, the women and girls attend all of these services, but men and boys usually attend only the evening service, at which time the *wat* takes on a festive air. Drums and gongs are beaten before and after the service; firecrackers are exploded in the *wat,* and the faithful gossip, flirt, and court, and drift in and out of the temple, where the monks chant until midnight. Festivities go on until dawn.

Source: *Village Life in Modern Thailand* by John E. deYoung. Berkeley: Univ. of California, 1955, pp. 139-140.

Loi Krathong in Bangkhuad village

Lojkrathong (Floating Leafcup): This festival is for the entire community and employs the clergy only briefly. The *krathong* is held at the end of the rainy season on the 15th day of the waxing moon in the 12th lunar month (November).

According to the Bangkhuad farmer, the purpose of the *krathong* is two-fold: it is a tribute paid to the *thewada* of the river called *Phramaskhongkha,* and also a tribute to the snake, *Phrajanag,* who resides at the bottom of the canal. The legend states that *Phrajanag* literally followed in the Buddha's footsteps and succeeded in reaching Nirvana.

In the morning, all the households are busily preparing their *krathongs*. The trunk of the banana tree is cut, transversely, into one inch slices. These serve as the hulls or bases of the *krathong*. The banana leaf is cut into strips, folded in various ways, and attached to the sides of the base in such a way as to resemble birds, boats, or lotus plants. Inside the *krathong* are placed flowers, joss sticks, candles, popcorn, and money—one *satang* for each year of age of the maker. Some farmers also place a small mud snake inside.

The festival starts in the early evening. Since it is a holy day, many of the elders have already gathered at the *wihan*. The other members of the village gather there at 6:00, each with at least one *krathong* and many with two or more. Five monks perform a special chant called *Mahachad,* which depicts the story of the king who gave on holy days during the Lenten period. The candle remains in the *bod* at all times.

Source: *Bangkhuad: A Community Study in Thailand* by Howard Keva Kaufman. Locust Valley, N.Y.: J.J. Augustin, 1960, pp. 195-196.

Loi Krathong markets

If you go into a market just a few days before the full moon of October and November, you will see in some stalls or shops, displayed apart from other things, a number of krathong or leaf cups specially made for sale in this season. . . . Generally, some of them are in the shape of a bird or a boat. They are more of a toy than a krathong, and have only made their appearance in recent years. These are confined mainly to the town people. The country-folk usually have their own home-made krathong for the occasion, and perhaps there may be one or two progressive folk who make them in the shape of a bird or boat for the merriment of their children. Usually in a krathong, apart from a candle and one or more incense sticks, a small coin, say a one or five stang piece, is also put in, and sometimes a mouthful of betal nut and betal leaf for chewing purposes is added. . . .

In the evening when the full moon begins to rise on October and November, the people, mostly old women and matrons with their children, carry one or two krathongs to the edge of brimful running water. After the candle and incense sticks in the krathong are lighted, they let it go gently on the surface of the placid waters. A few folk will sometimes raise their hands in worship to the floating krathong. They watch the krathong as they float sluggishly along the water for sometime until they float far away or out of sight. The children to while away the time play with water fire-works. The fireworks, apart from amusement, are a part of any celebration secularly and religiously. We light fireworks sometimes in the same spirit as we light candles as an act of worship.

The floating krathong usually has a short life. As it floats far away from its starting place, the children further down stream will, in most cases, swim out to snatch the krathong. If it is a beautiful one there may be a scramble for it. They will perhaps ignore the common ones, but will not forget to snatch up the small coin, if any, in the krathong. It is an aesthetic pleasure to see many krathongs with their flickering candle lights bobbing gently up and down, borne along the silent and placid flooded waters under the light of a full moon. Of course, I speak of this in the days there were no motor boats and outboards to disturb the peaceful waters with their waves and unpleasant sounds.

As can be gathered from the above description, there is nothing in the nature of a ritual and ceremonial act attached to the Loi Krathong. You simply light the candle and incense sticks and let loose all in the water. That is all you have to do. But the small coin that is put in, and the lighting of the candle and incense sticks betray that there must be a cult of some kind.

If you ask the people for an explanation, the elder ones will tell you that the Loi Krathong is an act of remission to the Goddess Me Khongkha, the Mother of Water. Khongkha is the same word as the Indian "Ganga" or "Ganges", but in Siamese, it means water in general. They will further explain that in spite of the Mother's bountiful gift of water to man, he sometimes has polluted her water in various ways, therefore it is only proper to ask her pardon. It is an explanation which, if not plausible, is one which the simple believing folk can explain. But why do it in two consecutive months? Another explanation is that the Lord Buddha printed his foot on the sand shore of the Nammada River or the Nerbudda River of India in the Deccan by request of the King of Naga, who wanted to worship the Lord Buddha's foot-print when the Lord had gone. The Loi Krathong is therefore an act of worship of His foot-print which is a far cry from here to India. This is a religious but apocryphal explanation as to the origin of Loi Krathong which is not to be found in the Buddhist scriptures. It is in one way useful to preserve any tradition if a touch of religious explanation be given to it. There is another explanation in the nature of a folktale of the Buddhist Jataka kind, which long story I need not go into for it will interest folklorists only. The Chiangmai folk of Northern Thailand have a different explanation for the origin of Loi Krathong which is, I think, identical with the Burmese.

H.M. King Chulalongkorn says in his book that the Loi Krathong has nothing to do with any recognized ceremony or rite. It is merely a matter or rejoicing in which all the people take part and is not only for royalty; moreover it is concerned with neither Buddhist nor Brahmin ceremony. His Majesty thought that the Loi Krathong had some connection with the floating lanterns as observed by Siamese kings in the north when Sukhothai was the capital some six or seven hundred years ago. It was described ornately in a book written by Nang Nophamat, a beautiful and learned lady of the court of King Phra Ruang of Sukhothai's capital. The lady was the daughter of a Brahmin family priest attached to the Court. She said that in the twelfth month (she said nothing of the eleventh month) i.e. in November, the country was flooded. The king and his court went for a picnic on the river to witness the people enjoying themselves during the water festival at night. Nothing is said of the Loi Krathong of the people, but it can be taken as a fact that it took place. The krathong was most probably in the same shape as that which we see at the present day, for Lady Nophamat told in her book that she had introduced a new kind of krathong in a shape of a big lotus flower and many other styles for the king to float in the running stream, no doubt for his enjoyment. She further initiated certain recitations and songs to be sung for the king on the occasion.

Source: *Essays on Thai Folklore* by Phya Anuman Rajadhon. Bangkok: Thai Inter-Religious Commission for Development & Sathirakoses Nagapradipa Foundation, 1988, pp. 54-56.

For more on Loi Krathong see: "Thailand" in *Joy Through the World.* U.S. Committee for UNICEF. New York: Dodd, Mead, & Co., 1985. (Contains directions for folding a Krathong.); "Loy Krathong" by Napa Bhongbhibhat in *More Festivals in Asia* by Asian Cultural Centre for UNESCO. Tokyo: Kodansha, 1975, pp. 55-60. (Children's story.)

Tasaungmon Full Moon

Tawadeintha / Tazaungdaing

This is a commemoration of the return of Gautama Buddha from his visit to heavenly Tawadeintha to visit his mother's reincarnated spirit. He journeyed to her realm to share the wisdom he had attained through enlightenment. The holy men of that realm held tapers to light his way back to earth, lining his path on either side. As at Thadingyut, homes and shops are again illuminated.

Burma / Myanmar

Tazaungdine festival

The Tazaungdine festival is held on Tazaungmon Fullmoon Day. Lights are offered through the sending up of fire balloons and the lighting of multi-coloured illuminations. The Samannaphala Sutta is usually recited. Monk's robes are woven overnight, kathina robes are offered, charitable and other meritorious acts are performed.

Fire balloons are sent up and illuminations are lighted in dedication to the Sulamani Pagoda in Tavatimsa, a pagoda which is much revered by Buddhists.

On fullmoon night, the Buddha preached the discourse on the advantages of the life of a monk to King Ajatasattu. In celebration of this, the Sutta is recited on Tazaungmon fullmoon night.

While Buddha was residing at Nigrodha monastery in Kappilavastu, His Stepmother Mahapazapati Gautami offered him a robe woven by herself. On that occasion Buddha said that offering robes to the Sagha was offering robes to the Buddha. In celebration of the offering of that robe there rose the tradition of weaving robes overnight and offering them.

While Buddha was staying at the Zetawunna monastery in Savatthi, the thirty Buddhavati brother monks left Saketa at the end of the Retreat and made their way to Buddha. On their journey they were caught in heavy rain and spattered with mud but they had no robes to change. Beginning with this occasion, Buddha permitted the offering of kathina robes during the period from the first waning of Thadingyut to the first waning of Tazaungmon. Ceremonies to offer kathina robes were initiated at that time.

Source: Embassy of the Union of Myanmar.

A weaving contest and the offering of Kathin robes

Similar to the Thadingyut Festival, the Tazaungdaing Festival features colorful illuminations throughout the cities, but does not have the religious significance of Thadingyut. The celebration of the full-moon night of Tazaungdaing, the Burmese eighth moon, is known to have been held in the country even before the spread of Buddhism. It is regarded as an occasion to honor the God of Lights (the moon is believed to be its brightest at this time), and is the night when Vishnu, one of the great Hindu gods, awakens from his long sleep. Vishnu is honored on the full-moon night with offerings of incense, sweet meats, and lights in a pre-Buddhist custom.

Although Tazaungdaing celebrations are non-Buddhist in origin, Burmese Buddhists give the occasion religious meaning. According to legend, on the evening before Prince Siddhartha gained enlightenment, his mother sensed that he was about to discard the royal robes of birth and put on the monk's garments. His mother, Maidawmi Nat, wanted to provide the yellow robes of the monkhood for her son, but had only one night in which to prepare them. She spent the entire night weaving the vestments, and by dawn of the next day they were ready. She delivered the robes by heavenly messenger as an offering to her son.

To commemorate Maidawmi Nat's speedy, sacred achievement, Rangoon's great Shwe Dagon Pagoda hosts an annual *Matho Thingan* (*matho* means "not stale, fresh") weaving contest.

Another activity of the festival is the offering of *Kathin* robes to the monks. *Kathin* robes are specially named because they replace the soiled robes used during the rainy season. This offering ceremony begins on the first waning day of Thadingyut and continues until the full-moon night of Tazaungmon. Since the Tazaungdaing Festival occurs during the end of this period, the offering of *Kathin* robes is most intense during this festival.

Source: *Southeast Asia: A Cultural Study Through Celebration* by Phil Scanion, Jr., De Kalb, Ill.: Northern Illinois Univ., 1985, pp. 126-177.

Legend of the fire-balloons

Of a similar character to this illuminating of the pagodas, the town, and the river, is the letting loose of fire-balloons, from the end of Lent to the Tawadeintha festival in Tasaungmôn. The balloons are sometimes very big, but they are simple enough structures. A bamboo framework is covered over with the thick, coarse, home-made paper manufactured from the bark of the mahlaingbin (*Brousso-netia papyrifera*), which also supplies the material for the black parabaik note-books. At the bottom, across the open mouth of the balloon, is a little platform, on which pitch is heaped, and with torches attached to it. The balloon is then tethered to the ground. The torches and resinous matter are lighted, and when the strain on the stays is considered sufficient, they are cut, and the balloon goes off. They are dangerous in large towns, and are forbidden there, but the Burman considers that the law applies only to the ground round the town, and dozens are let off every year from spots only a hundred yards or so outside of municipal limits. Not unseldom dôn, rockets, and other kinds of fireworks are attached to them, not by any means tending to make them safer for the houses below. This mi-eing byan, as it is called, is in honour of the Sula-mani paya, a pagoda erected in Tawadeintha, over Mount Myinmo, by the Thagya, king of the Nat-déwas. When Prince Theidat left his palace, his wife, and forsook all to become a Buddha, he rode as far as the river Anawma and leaped over it on his famous steed Kantika. Then he drew his sword, cut off his long hair and threw it into the air, where it remained suspended, till the Tha-gya-min carried it off in a basket and had his Sula-mani shrine built over it. Hence the offering of fire-balloons.

Source: "The End of Lent" in *The Burman: His Life and Times*. London: Macmillan, 1910, pp. 223-230.

Sunday before Advent (Early December)

Stir-Up Sunday

The Sunday before Advent was traditionally known as the day to "stir up" the Christmas pudding in England.

Great Britain

A day for stirring up the Christmas pudding

The collect of the Church of England for this Sunday begins, "Stir up, we beseech thee, O Lord, the wills of thy faithful people, that they plenteously bring forth the fruit of good works. . . ." This prayer was parodied by the choirboys: "Stir up, we beseech thee, the pudding in the pot. And when we do get home tonight, we'll eat it up all hot."

The Christmas pudding is traditionally "stirred up" on this day. All family members must take a hand in the stirring, and a special wooden spoon (in honor of Christ's crib) is used. The stirring must be in a clockwise direction, with eyes shut, while making a secret wish.

Source: *The Customs and Ceremonies of Britain* by Charles Kightly. London: Thames and Hudson, 1986, p. 211.

The Four Weeks before Christmas, Beginning on a Sunday

Advent Season

Austria

Lighting the Advent candle

In the afternoon of the first Sunday of Advent, around vesper time, the whole family—and this always means ''family'' in the larger sense of the word, including all the members of the household—meets in the living room. The Advent wreath hangs suspended from the ceiling on four red ribbons; the Advent candle stands in the middle of the table or on a little stand on the side. Solemnly the father lights one candle on the Advent wreath, and, for the first time, the big Advent candle. Then he reads the Gospel of the first Sunday of Advent. After this the special song of Advent is intoned for the first time, the ancient ''Ye heavens, dew drop from above, and rain ye clouds the Just One. . . .''

Source: *Around the Year with the Trapp Family* by Marie Augusta Trapp. New York: Pantheon, 1955, p. 19. (See pp. 15-17 for directions on making an Advent wreath.)

Germany

The Advent wreath in Berlin, c. 1936

The Advent wreath is hung before the first Sunday in Advent. One more of its four candles is lit each Sunday during Advent. The wreath is preferably made of balsam and can be hung in a doorway. The wreath is suspended on four sides and hangs flat, parallel to the floor, the candles standing up from it.

Source: Winifred Jaegger, Kirkland, Washington.

Sweden

Advent candles in Sweden

On the first Sunday in Advent, all Swedish families take out a special candlestick. Traditionally, it is an oblong brass container with holders for four candles in a row. The candles are always white and often hand-dipped. Bedded down around their base are moss and lichen from the forest.

One candle is lit on Advent Sunday and allowed to burn down a little way. On the Second Sunday, both the first candle and the next are lit for a while; and so on until, on the Fourth Sunday, the candles look like a small row of organ pipes. Their four-fold light means that Christmas is almost here.

Source: *Round the Swedish Year* by Lorna Downman, Paul Britten Austin, and Anthony Barid. Stockholm: The Swedish Institute/Bokförlaget, 1967, p. 69.

Early December (Variable)

Bear Festival

A young bear, two or three years old, is baited and ceremoniously killed. Dancing and feasting accompany his send-off to the spirit world.

Japan (Ainu)

An invitation is issued in 1888

"I, So-and-So, am about to send away the dear little divine one whose home is among the mountains. My friends and masters, come ye to the feast and we will unite in the great joy of sending him off. Come!"

A ceremony takes place for the bear

As for the men, they do worship and perform dancing before the divine one, while the women and children clap their hands, sing songs, and take part in the dancing.

The bear is killed ceremoniously and arranged for his feast

"Then," my friend added, "when the old men have placed their crowns on their heads, they dance, and, the head of the divine cub having been nicely arranged and many fetishes presented to him, he is given some of his own cooked meat and broth to eat. And a little of his own blood is also set before him. After waiting a short time, when all are quite silent, the headman worships, saying, 'O divine One, we present Thee with these fetishes, cakes and dried fish. Take them to thy parents and say, "I have been brought up by an Ainu father and mother, and have been kept free from harm and trouble. I am now grown big and am come back to you. I have also brought cakes, dried fish, and fetishes with me. Let us rejoice." If you say this to them they will be glad.'"

So we find the idea of a death is emphatically denied. The animal is not killed, but his living spirit is sent away to its heaven in the mountains. There he once more enjoys the society of his parents and friends. After a time there he is supposed to be reincarnated and to return to this earth as another cub.

Source: *Ainu Life and Lore: Echoes of a Departing Race* by John Batchelor. Tokyo: Kyobunkwan, 1927, pp. 205-206, 209-211.

December to August, Biannually

Odo

This festival marks the return of the dead to their own realm after their biannual visit to the living.

Nigeria (Igbo)

The Odo festival, a farewell party for the dead

Odo is the name of the traditional festival that marks the mass return of the dead in the Northern Igbo villages, particularly the Enugu and Nsukka districts. Odo is also a general name for the dead returnees. It is generally the dead males who return, but occasionally female characters are found. Men, however, act both male and female roles.

Celebration of the Odo festival is a happy but expensive affair for the living. The festival, which lasts in some places from December to August, can be divided into three phases: the return of the odo, their stay with the living, and their departure. The first phase, characterized by ritual celebrations and festivity, welcomes the odo into the community. Between the arrival and departure of the odo is a long time span—six months or more—during which the returnee-spirits stay and interact with the living through visits to personal and ancestral homes. These visits are marked by lavish entertainment. Finally, when the odo are due to depart from the living, they give their last-minute blessings to those they are leaving behind and receive requests for favors: the living relatives offer more entertainment and gifts. This departure is a very emotional, sad affair, comparable to taking leave of one's family before a sojourn to another country. It will be another two years before the odo visit again.

The Odo festival is a communal affair. Although it is the men who initiate and regulate its activities, the women are very much involved in its successful celebration. Women cook the food and provide other edibles during the festival; during the dramatic performances, they function as chorus performers and sometimes as spectators. During an Odo year, those citizens residing away from the village come home to renew their solidarity and to make contact with their roots. Performances take place at the return and staying stages of the odo journey. (They are called *Igo-Odo* [Homage to Odo] in places where the performance coincides with the return, and *Izu Ahia Odo* [Market Outing of Odo] in villages where the performance occurs some weeks after the return.) They are times for public holidays and merriment. Guests and other visitors go to the village sponsoring the performance to enjoy the splendor and drama of the Odo festival theatre.

The Odo performer

Odo characters reflect the social hierachy within the community. They range from highly respected, titled elderly men to young adults and children. The world of the dead is structured socially like that of the living. There are six categories: elderly, titled odo, youthful, masculine odo, female odo (young and old types), child infant odo, spirit odo and animal odo. Character types are easily identified by their costumes and their manner of interaction with the spectators.

Eworo Odicha, from Ukehe, is one such elderly odo character. His importance is symbolized by his elaborate costume and the large following he commands. He carries an elaborately carved wooden headpiece backed with leopard skin, and body masks of the finest plant fiber. Okikpe, another elderly odo from Aku (called Okwu-ikpe in parts of Udi area) is about eleven feet tall. He is not one of the recent dead but an ancestor whose role as protector and impartial judge of the living has been sanctioned by the people for generations.

The entrance of these ancestor odo into the performance arena is greeted with cheers, jubilation, ululation, and a volley of gunshots. Okikpe is received by the Umada (daughters of the land, in this case especially the very aged ones) with chants of praise and heroic rhetorical invocations. As Okikpe walks majestically through the jubilant crowds of spectators and performers, titled men invoke his ancestral deeds with their elephant-tusk horns. His language is not intelligible to the ordinary person; he communicates through the medium of a diviner, the link between human beings and spirits.

Odo costumes are made largely from plant fiber, leaves, beads and feathers. In the opening phase, these costumes generally look fresh and elegant. However, weeks after the return, the costumes begin to fade and dry. The people describe this as the ageing of the odo. As a result, some odo return, perform for a few days and are never seen again. Cloth costumes are, however, becoming increasingly common in contemporary Odo plays to offset problems created by rapid ageing. Age and function determine the type of costume worn by each odo. The elderly odo are usually elaborately costumed in long gowns of multicolored striped silken cloth, while the young ones dress smartly in short skirts to facilitate agile movement. The elderly carry staffs and fans, while the youth carry long whips and swords for communal protection.

Odo music

Odo music includes drumming, songs, and dance. Drumming in this festival theatre is highly esoteric. The odo play their own xylophones, drums, and rattles. Odo music is called *obilenu* music, literally "that which lives above." Metaphorically, the music issues from the spheres. Thus the obilenu house has two floors—the upper floor or music chamber, where the odo themselves play, and the lower floor, a storeroom for Odo cult instruments and paraphernalia. The soft music seems to come from another world.

During the communal open performance, the human participants sing heroic songs in praise of their ancestors and the arriving odo. Sometimes the odo sing, and the human performers answer in a chorus. There are songs of praise, didactic songs and expository or satiric songs.

Source: "Odo: The Mass Return of the Masked Dead Among the Nsukka-Igbo" by J.N. Ndukaku Amankulor in *The Drama Review,* 26 (4) (Winter 1982), 46-58.

Eight Days Beginning on 25 Kislev (Usually in December)

Hanukkah

This holiday commemorates the victory of Judah Maccabee over the Syrians. When his people repossessed their temple they found only a small amount of oil for the temple lamp. This oil miraculously burned for eight days. Hanukkah dates are December 2, 1991; December 25, 1992; December 9, 1993; November 28, 1994; and December 18, 1995.

Israel

Hanukkah in Israel

Hanukkah is a national holiday in Israel, jsut as the Fourth of July is a national holiday in the United States. It is a great public festival, and the spirit of the Maccabees is everywhere. Before Hanukkah, students have parties, present plays, and sing Hanukkah songs. During Hanukkah, schools close, menorahs are lit on top of tall buildings, and parties go on everywhere. Dreidel, called *sevivon* in Hebrew, is played as it is here, but with one exception. The letters are *nun, gimmel, he,* and *pe,* to stand for *Nes gadol hayah po*—"A great miracle happened here."

The highlight of the national celebration is a relay race from Modin. Burning torches are carried to Jerusalem's Western Wall, which is all that is left of the Temple. One runner begins in Modin, passes the torch to another along the way, until finally a torchbearer reaches the wall. He gives the torch to the chief rabbi, who uses it to light the first light of the giant hanukkiyyah.

Source: *Hanukkah: Eight Nights, Eight Lights* by Malka Drucker. New York: Holiday House, 1980, p. 76.

Iran

Chanukah in Persia

Children of the poor went from door to door for gifts, in exchange, they burned a wisp of grass to discourage the evil eye from each house. On the last of the eight nights, the father brought in a large tray full of nuts and roasted seeds. The children grabbed handfuls to eat in cheder the next day.

Source: *One People: The Story of the Eastern Jews* by Devora and Menachem Hacohen. New York: Sabra Books/Funk and Wagnalls, 1969, p. 35.

Tunisia

Preparation of the menorah

The menorah was prepared by the mother or grandmother of the house and hung on the doorpost opposite the mezuza. It remained there until Purim. On Rosh Hodesh Tevet, during Chanukah, the girls received gifts from their parents, and brides, from their bridegrooms. This was called the "New Moon of the Daughters."

Source: *One People: The Story of the Eastern Jews* by Devora and Menachem Hacohen. New York: Sabra Books/Funk and Wagnalls, 1969, pp. 35, 89.

For more on Hanukkah see: "Hanukkah" in *Folklore of American Holidays* edited by Hening Cohen and Tristram Potter Coffin. 2nd ed. Detroit: Gale Research, 1991; "Hanukkah" in *The Jewish Party Book: A Contemporary Guide to Customs, Crafts, and Foods* by Mae Shafter Rockland. New York: Schocken, 1978, pp. 127-151.

December 4

St. Barbara's Day

This is the day to honor St. Barbara. St. Barbara was the daughter of Dioscorus, who lived at Heliopolis in Syria. He locked Barbara in a high tower to prevent her from continuing in her Christian faith. When she persisted, he turned her over to the pagan authorities. She was tortured but refused to recant. Dioscorus himself was ordered to slay his daughter. He took her up into a mountain and killed her with a sword. On his way back down the mountain Dioscorus was struck by lightning and killed. St. Barbara is a protector from lightning and from sudden death.

Germany

The miner's saint

An older-established group of workers, the mining community, cultivated and brought about the rapid spread of another custom. The 4th of December was and still is a special day for miners as has already been mentioned, this is St. Barbara's Day. She became the patron saint of miners in commemoration of her painful martyrdom. Legend reports that her father, a heathen, did not want her to become a Christian. When he discovered that she had nevertheless gone ahead and acted against his will, he dragged her before the Roman tribunal which condemned Barbara to death. No-one was ready though to execute this delicate girl. Her enraged father then cut off Barbara's head himself. No sooner had he done this terrible deed than there was a mighty clap of thunder, and a flash of lightning out of a clear sky struck down this man who had murdered his own child. For that reason Barbara became patron saint of all vocations concerned with fire and explosions—the fire brigade, the artillery, and miners.

On the 4th of December, miners honour Barbara by putting freshly cut cherry, elder, or peat branches into a jug filled with water and keep this in a warm place. The branches must have vigorous buds so that they will blossom and turn green on Christmas Eve to the day. People say that when these branches do blossom for Christmas, misfortune will stay away from the house in the coming year.

Source: *Christmas in Germany* by Josef Ruland. Translated by Timothy Neville. Bonn: Hohwacht, 1978, p. 56.

Syria

St. Barbara's Day in Syria

The holiday season in Syria differs considerably from that in most other countries. It begins on Saint Barbara's Day, December 4, and continues until Epiphany, January 6. Saint Barbara was outstanding in goodness, so that her faith and love made her an example to the children. On this eve, sacred to her memory, a table of sweetmeats is arranged, prepared from nuts, sugar, honey, and wheat, the latter in memory of the dead and signifying the resurrection of the soul. Little children are taught lessons of unselfishness and thoughtfulness for the less fortunate. A prosperous family will help several others into which sorrow and poverty have come. To homes in which loved ones have passed away, sweetmeats are sent, and to the houses of the poor the children bring their cakes with the greeting: "May God bless you and bring you happiness every year. Father and Mother beg you to accept these gifts from us." At a social hour of dancing, singing, and games, wheat is cooked and flavored with sugar, rose water, and candy. The girls at the party, as a sign that they have learned the lesson of the good Saint Barbara, come one by one to an elderly woman who anoints their eyes with a salve. The above will be clearer if we quote completely the story of Saint Barbara as it has been translated:

> Barbara, the saint, was elected of God.
> She gave her bread to the poor.
> Her miserly father rebuked her
> And threatened her with his sword.
> When he caught her with the bread in her lap
> She cried unto God in her fear.
> God turned the sword in her father's hand
> Into a crochet needle.
> When her father demanded to see
> What she concealed in her lap,
> She cried unto God for help
> And the bread in her lap turned to roses.

Source: *Christmas Customs around the World* by Herbert H. Wernecke. Philadelphia: The Westminster Press, 1959, p. 120.

December 6

St. Nicholas' Day

St. Nicholas was bishop of Myra in southwest Asia Minor in the fourth century. He persuaded the governor to refrain from killing three innocent men, and forced him to confess his sin in taking a bribe to kill these men. Nicholas probably was imprisoned during the persecutions of Emperor Diocletian.

The Emperor Justinian built a church in St. Nicholas' honor in sixth-century Constantinople. His shrine at Myra was a center of pilgrimages until 1087, when Italian sailors stole his remains and brought them to Bari. St. Nicholas is patron saint of Greece and Russia. He rescued sailors in his lifetime and is also patron of seafarers. His feast on December 6 was occasion for election of a Boy Bishop in the Middle Ages. This child Bishop would reign until the Feast of the Holy Innocents on December 28. St. Nicholas remains the patron of children and sailors.

Austria

An Austrian family welcomes St. Nicholas

While in some places the children only put their shoes on the window sill on the eve of St. Nicholas' Day and find them filled with candies, cookies, oranges, and dried fruit the next morning (but only the good ones; the bad ones find a switch), in other parts St. Nicholas comes in person. He always did in our house. On the eve of December 5th the whole family would gather in the living room with great expectancy. By the time the much-expected knock at the door could be heard, one could almost hear the anxious heartbeat of the little ones. The holy bishop, in his pontifical vestments, accompanied by Krampus, would enter the room while everybody stood up reverently. St. Nicholas always carried a thick book in which the Guardian Angels make their entries throughout the year. That's why the saint has such an an astonishing knowledge about everybody. He calls each member of the household forward, rewarding the good and admonishing the less good. The good children will get a package of sweets, whereas Krampus aims at the legs of the children who did not deserve one. After everyone has received his due, the holy bishop addresses a few words of general admonition to the whole family, acting as a precursor to the One Who is to come, drawing their thoughts toward Christmas, asking them to prepare their hearts for the coming of the Holy Child. After giving his blessing, he takes his leave, accompanied reverently by the mother, who opens the door for him. Soon afterwards the father, who, oddly enough, usually misses this august visit, will come home, and he has to hear everything about it from the youngest in the house.

In the old home this beloved bishop's attire was stored away in the attic to be used every year on the evening before his feast.

Speculatius

"St. Nicholas smells of Christmas, don't you think, Mother?" one of my little girls said once, meaning that on December 5th the whole house was filled with the same good smell as it would be in the days just before Christmas. For this day there is a special kind of cookie called *Speculatius.* The dough is rolled very thin and then cut in the shape of St. Nicholas, and these little figures are then decorated with icing in different colors and candied fruit. And just as we are sharing with the reader our ancient songs and customs, I believe we should also share those ancient recipes that have come down to us through the centuries. So here is the recipe for *Speculatius* (St. Nicholas). It comes from Holland.

Speculatius

1 cup butter
1 cup lard
2 cups brown sugar
1/2 cup sour cream
1/2 tsp. soda
4 tsp. cinnamon
1/2 tsp. nutmeg
1/2 tsp cloves
4 1/2 cups sifted flour
1/2 cup chopped nuts

Cream the butter, lard, and sugar. Add sour cream alternately with sifted dry ingredients. Stir in nuts. Knead the dough into rolls. Wrap the rolls in waxed paper and chill in the refrigerator overnight. Roll the dough very thin and cut it into shapes. Bake in moderate oven 10 to 15 minutes.

Source: *Around the Year with the Trapp Family* by Maria Augusta Trapp. New York: Pantheon, 1955, pp. 31-32.

Belgium

Sint Nikolaas Vooravon (St. Nicholas Eve)

A commercialized St. Nicholas

The next festival which sets all children in almost unendurable excitement has diffused into Wallonia from Flanders long ago. This is the feast of St. Nicholas. Gifts are not given them on Christmas, this day being strictly a religious feast, as in other French-speaking countries. But if some traditionalist is outdone with the commercializing of Christmas in modern America, he had better stay away from Belgium anytime before or during December 6, the festival of Nicholas, Bishop of Myra. Belgium is a nation of keen businessmen, and the merchants capitalize on St. Nicholas in ways which might even shame a Chicago or New York department store. One such establishment in Brussels completely snarled traffic by announcing that St. Nicholas would arrive that year by helicopter. He was to alight in the park of the Botanical Gardens and from there proceed in solemn procession to the store's toy department for enthronement and personal greeting of all ''good'' little boys and girls.

In Chateau-Gerard village, disparaging remarks for American Santa in Wallonia

Then the Saint visited the schools, clad in the garments of a modern Catholic bishop but with the vast Santa Claus cotton beard, and asked all the children if they had been *sage* during the year, and, upon receiving the universal affirmative reply, distributed gifts which the parents had provided. Even the younger children thought that their St. Nicholas appeared rather tawdry, while the older ones recognized the voice behind the beard as that of the janitor who had reprimanded them and thumped them many times during the year. Belgians think poorly of the American Santa Claus, saying that this alleged saint with the red, furred suit, is a German who deserted a large family of children to become a mountain hermit, and therefore deserves little devotion from children. Nicholas of Myra was quite another character, of course.

Source: *Chateau-Gerard: The Life and Times of a Walloon Village* by Harry Holbert Turney-High. Columbia: Univ. of South Carolina Press, 1953, pp. 236-237.

St. Nicholas' Day in Belgium, c. 1910

St. Nicholas day, however, which falls on the sixth of December, was always a great event. Then we had our basket put under the chimney, and in the morning it was filled with all kinds of candy and playthings. At school, too, we would find that the schoolmaster had put some candy and either a new pencil or penholder in our desks.

Source: *When I Was a Boy in Belgium* by Robert Jonckheere. Boston: Lothrop, Lee & Shepard Co., 1915, p. 39.

Czechoslovakia (Bohemia)

St. Nicholas' Eve

In Bohemia it appears that the present-giving occasion originally occurred much earlier in the month, on the eve of St. Nicholas' Day, December the 5th. Though it is not a public holiday, customs connected with this day are still widely observed, especially in families with smaller children. Towards the evening a group of three or more grownups or youngsters representing a devil (čert), an angel (anděl) and St. Nicholas (Mikuláš)—his attire strongly resembling that of Santa Claus—visit homes in the neighbourhood. The devil, rattling chains, gives the naughtiest of the children a lash, which can be either playful or serious, with a bundle of gilt branches—or more recently sometimes gilt misletoe—while the angel and St. Nicholas praise the good children. Often the parents arrange for St. Nicholas to share out presents of sweets and fruit, but the custom is frequently kept that the children hang a stocking outside the window to find it on the following morning filled with chocolates and little presents—possibly a few pieces of coal and carrots for the naughty ones—decorated with a few gilt twigs.

Source: ''Christmas in Bohemia—Traditional and Present Day'' by Miriam Jelinkova in *Lore and Language* 2 (January 1970), pp. 9-10.

Germany

Nikolaustag, St. Nicholas' Day

Filling the shoe

A shoe is put outside the bedroom door or window or by the fireplace on the evening of December 5. It is found filled with candies, nuts, and fruits in the morning. St. Nicholas brings these presents. He comes clothed in a red gown, with white beard, boots, and sack. He carries a staff and a book of sins, in which the children's misdeeds are written. He is sometimes accompanied by Knecht Ruprecht (Krampus, Pelzmarte, Klaubauf, Hans Muff, Butz, Buller, or Pulterklas) who has the task of punishing the wicked children. A switch is found in the shoe of those who have been bad, though nowadays, the children are more apt to find a *Wundererrute* (miracle stick) covered with dangling candies. In southern Germany, St. Nicholas may be accompanied by a female companion who metes out the punishments.

Source: *German Festivals and Customs* by Jennifer M. Russ. London: Oswald Wolff, 1982, pp. 8-9.

Knecht Ruprecht in the Frankfurt area, c. 1940

Knecht Ruprecht used to arrive at the home on St. Nicholas Eve carrying toys and a bunch of switches. He would threaten bad children with switching and present those who had been good with toys. Children tried very hard to be good for a month or so before this night. Rosemarie Peterson recalls being quite frightened of Knecht Ruprecht's visits. Strangely, a certain uncle always just happened to be out of the room at the moment Knetch Ruprecht arrived. Only when she was older did Rosemarie connect that uncle with the costumed visitor who knocked on their door.

Source: Rosemarie Peterson, Kirkland, Washington.

The Netherlands

St. Nicholas

Saint Nicholas was a dearly loved bishop, whose generosity with children was well-known, and word of this spread to many countries. His pockets were always full of sweetmeats. On his feast day he visits children and brings presents. In return children write poems for him and leave them in their empty clogs by the sitting-room fireplace. The Saint is accompanied by Spanish blackamoor servants in medieval costumes. They are called 'Black Peters' and carry bundles of switches to beat naughty children. Saint Nicholas is pictured as a whitebearded old gentleman, in bishop's red robes and gold mitre. He carries a shepherd's staff.

St. Nicholas' parade in Amsterdam

In Amsterdam St Nicholas Church is not only named after the traditional protector of children but because Nicholas is also the patron saint of sailors. Each December a parade, led by a 'Saint Nicholas', with his entourage of 'Black Peters', marches to the Royal Palace. There is then a discussion with the Mayor about children's behaviour during the preceding year.

St. Nicholas arrives at Enschede town

The parade, led by the old Saint in his long red robes while his blackamoors threw sweets to the children as they passed. The mayor received the Saint and told him how good the Enschede children had been for the last 12 months. Whereupon the Saint turned to the people and made a speech. He congratulated the children on their excellent behaviour and said he would visit them at their individual homes later that night and deliver presents. On the night of 5 December a sack of gifts is put through the front door and the hallway is showered with sweets. After the parcels are opened the family sit down to a table covered with Christmas fare; chocolate and pastry letters filled with almond paste, cakes and various kinds of sweetmeats.

Source: *Holland* by Nina Nelson. New York: Hastings House, 1970, pp. 22-24.

Sinterklaas-Avond (St. Nicholas Eve)

Three weeks before his day, St. Nicholas arrives in Amsterdam by ship. He rides a huge white horse and descends to be greeted by the Lord Mayor, and then leads a parade to the city's main square where the Royal Family receives him. Zwarte Piet, Black Peter, accompanies him. Peter wears an embroidered tunic, puffed trousers, and a plumed cap. He carries a big red book, wherein are written the behavior reports on all children. He also brings a handful of birch rods to punish bad children, and a sack of treats for those who have been good. An especially naughty child might be stuffed into Zwarte Piet's bag and carried back to Spain with him for punishment. For several days the children put out their shoes at night with straw and carrots for St. Nicholas' horse, in hopes that Zwarte Piet will discover this and refill the shoes with presents from Sinterklaas.

On Sinterklaas Avond itself (St. Nicholas' Eve) a festive dinner is held. Sinterklaas and Zwarte Piet may drop by in person to give mock lectures to everyone present on their behavior during the past year, or they may simply knock, open the door, and toss candies inside. After dinner, gifts are opened. The value of the gift is less important than the clever poem that accompanies it or the way in which it is camouflaged or hidden. Clues may lead children to presents hidden around the house, or a present may be wrapped in many layers or in boxes of misleading size. Each giver takes pains over the humorous verse enclosed. These verses are read aloud and represent much of the evening's fun.

Source: *Joy through the World.* United States Committee for UNICEF, New York: Dodd, Mead & Co., 1985.

St. Nicholas' Day in Holland, c. 1910

The day of days to us, was the sixth of December, St. Nicholas Day. St. Nicholas was once a bishop in Spain and beloved by all for his good deeds. That was many hundreds of years ago, but since then he is supposed to come from Spain with his black servant each December.

He is said to ride on a white horse through the air, and on the eve of the sixth, his feast day, to jump from roof to roof, where he descends through the chimney into the house. There he finds, standing in a row, the children's baskets with a tuft of hay for his horse in each of them, and he fills them with sweets and toys if the little ones have been good, with a turf and salt if they have been bad or are becoming too big to be thus remembered by him. Then he hides the baskets somewhere in the room. Noiselessly, he now climbs up through the chimney, mounts his waiting charger and visits another house.

Several mornings before the great event we would find a sort of giner-cake called "taai-taai," in the form of a woman at the churn, Adam and Eve under the apple-tree, of a boy or a girl, or some animal, in our stockings as we awoke. In the evening, especially on the eve of the sixth, St. Nicholas himself, dressed in a long tabard with mitre on his head, followed by his black servant who carried a bag, would enter the living-room. Sometimes the good saint was dressed up so unsaintlike, resembling more a tramp-burglar than a bishop, that we little ones were frightened and hid behind mother's chair, although we quite well knew there was no such thing as a "Sinterklaas," as we called him in Frisian. He would ask whether we had been good or bad; if bad, his servant would take us along in the bag and carry us to the attic where he was supposed to keep a mill; and in this mill he would grind us to pepernoten or peppernuts, the tiny gingerbread cookies. Of course, mother always said we had been good children, and then he would open the bag and throw handfuls of pepernoten on the floor. We forgot our fear, and coming out of our hiding-places, we picked up the cookies, finding them in every corner of the room.

Early in the morning of the sixth we awoke, and in our nightclothes and on bare feet we would run into the very cold front-room and hunt for the baskets. They were hidden in some corner, behind a piece of furniture or in a closet. As soon as we had found them we carried them into the warm living-room and there we examined the contents, consisting of one toy or a book for each of us, and several figures, some large, others small, of taai-taai, the brown, flat, tough cake, of which we were so fond, and which was made by the bakers all through the country on this feast of St. Nicholas only. There was always a girl a couple of feet tall, for a boy, and a boy for a girl, and these we hung against the wall and kept for weeks sometimes. The others lasted only a few days.

Then there were figures and letters made of a sweeter kind of cake, more pepernoten, cookies, letters of sweet chocolate, and hearts of a very sweet pink or white candy, and the initial of our given name made of a deliciously light pastry, the filling of which was made of almonds and other ingredients. We called it "marsepyn." It was very rich and by every one considered a great delicacy. We also received a flat cake, resembling a pancake; it was sweet and decorated with gold tinsels.

We went to school early that morning to tell other children of the treasures we had received and to make comparisons. Now, for years we had known the truth about St. Nicholas; I had discovered it at the age of six, but the little comedy was kept up each year, just as a child may talk to a doll while knowing very well that it is not alive and cannot hear. And our fear of St. Nicholas when he was dressed so disreputably and growled so fiercely, was genuine, although we did not believe in him.

In school, the younger children sang a song in his honor and the teacher also gave them each a figure of taai-taai.

On the eve of St. Nicholas, many grown-ups and also some of the older children went to the baker to listen to the results of the raffle which he had been conducting. Our family usually won at least one prize, and sometimes two. These were several letters of marsepyn, taai-taai, big cakes, gigantic loaves of bread with currants, or other sweets. Small shopkeepers held raffles of toys, dry-goods and other things.

The baker that evening also conducted a sort of gambling hall in his bakery. Young and old were throwing dice to win more taai-taai and more sweets. These people never even played cards, yet at such a time some of them would not stop until all their available cash was gone and they had nothing to show for their folly but heaps of cakes and tarts and other sweet stuff. It was a very good day for the bakers. A few years ago, a law was passed, prohibiting this raffling and dice-throwing.

We children did some impersonating St. Nicholas on our own account, too. A couple of evenings before St. Nicholas Eve we dressed up in old clothes that belonged to our mothers and older sisters, and tied before our faces masks of paper which we had cut out and colored ourselves. We put on long gloves, and, supplied with a big bag of pepernoten, went to a few of the poorest homes where there were several little tots, and, opening the front door carefully, threw handfuls of the confectionery on the floor. We must have been a queer lot of Sinterklaases, and I am sure that the fun it gave us must have far exceeded in magnitude the good and pleasure the poor children derived from the few pepernoten.

Source: *When I Was a Girl in Holland* by Cornelia de Groot. Boston: Lothrop, Lee & Shepard Co., 1917, pp. 80-85.

Spain (Basque)

The Boy Bishop makes his rounds

In Oyarzun he was forbidden in 1688 on account of the arms his retinue saw fit to carry, nevertheless he still goes out on December 6th singing—

'Samikolas tikiya
gure ganbaran aziya,'

which when well regarded resolves into nothing more than—

Little St. Nicholas
Growing up in our loft. . . .

At Mondragon he runs singing all night; at Segura he wears mitre and gloves, and is given a seat in the sanctuary during Mass. Afterwards he sits on a mule with a man to hold him on, so little a St. Nicholas is he, and off they go collecting, attendant boys shouting—

'Bota, bota, Jaingoiko duta. . . .'
Throw, throw, God will recompense you.

In Alava the same company announces itself with a line borrowed from Santander wassailers, dropping with a bump from celestial heights to the larder,

'Angels are we, from Heaven we come,
Rashers and bacon we ask;
And if you won't give your hens shall pay.'

Whereupon, if gifts are not forthcoming, they help themselves from the henhouse.

Source: *Pyrenean Festivals* by Violet Afford. London: Chatto and Windus, 1937, p. 198.

Syria

St. Nicholas Thaumaturgus

A special Mass for St. Nicholas Thaumaturgus

On December 6, a special mass is said in the churches for Saint Nicholas Thaumaturgus, the Wonder-Worker. The stories that have gathered around him relate him to our modern Santa Claus.

Source: *Christmas Customs around the World* by Herbert H. Wernecke. Philadelphia: The Westminster Press, 1959, p. 120.

December 7

La Quema del Diablo

''Burning the Devil'' takes place from the start of Advent until December 7 in Guatemala. Men costumed as devils terrorize the highland towns. The season culminates with the burning of trash in the streets on December 7.

Guatemala

Burning the Devil in Guatemala

From Advent until December 7, men dressed as devils chase children through the streets of highland towns. The custom is celebrated with particular zest in San Cristóbal Totonicapán. The Burning of the Devil (La Quema del Diablo), December 7, is celebrated with the burning of trash in the streets of Guatemala City and highland towns. Christmas is preceded by nine days of posadas, house visits which re-enact the search of Joseph and Mary for shelter.

Source: *Guatemala Guide* by Paul Glassman. Champlain, N.Y.: Passport Press, 1988, p. 359.

Circa December 7-8

Itul

A prestigious Kuba dance festival held only with authorization from the King. The festival is held infrequently and its date varies.

Congo (Kuba)

The Itul, a rare festival of the Kuba, held in Mushenge

The most highly esteemed ritual is the *itul,* which only the king can authorize to be organized. As a rule, permission to sponsor this prestigious dance festival is granted only to the children of a king. The *itul* occurs only rarely because it is extremely costly.

The *itul* may occur in two different settings: when it is performed for the king, it takes place in the dance area of the palace called *bweng,* and when it is open to the entire population, it takes place in front of the palace in the plaza called *ibaantshi.* The ceremony at the palace is more refined because the wives of the king are professional dancers and singers.

Preparations for the ceremony are long and detailed, lasting in some cases for several months and involving many people. Durint this entire time, the participants are on the payroll of the sponsor of the dance. Once the important choice of the enemy-animal has been made, the plot for the dancers must be adapted, not only to the animal but also to incorporate a certain number of episodes, many of which are prescribed by tradition. The dancers last two days, with the evening of the first day devoted to lamentations over the destruction caused by the animal, and the afternoon of the second day dealing with its capture and killing. Each part lasts one or two hours.

On the first day, a dance is executed in the evening by women wearing wraparound skirts of red, the color of mourning among the Kuba. A chorus of women kneels at the center, performing the songs and supplying the rhythmical accompaniment, the latter partly achieved by beating calabashes on the sandy ground. Although drums rather than calabashes could be used, only the sons or grandsons of kings are authorized to touch them, and they must keep their eyes constantly on the ground or risk severe punishment. Accompanying the chorus and directing the dances is the lead singer, or *shwoong*. The dancers move counterclockwise around the chorus. To one side of their circle is a shelter where the king watches the spectacle and, to a certain extent, participates in it. To another side is the *ibul,* the den of the attacking animal. The audience, including the other wives of the king, their infant children, and a few high dignitaries and privileged guests, surrounds the dancers at a distance.

One of the important differences between the second day's ceremonies and those of the previous day is the color of the dancers' skirts, Instead of the furled and tightly hemmed skirts of red, the color of mourning, the dancers wear splendid and festive ones made of natural-colored raffia embroidered in black. On a background of geometrically arranged lines are certain embroidered motifs, simple in shape and randomly distributed over the cloth.

A gun salute starts the second ceremony. The circular dance resumes with the same melodies as the day before, but it is animated by livelier episodes. The furious animal shakes its den violently, with a friction drum sometimes used to represent its voice. This drum always evokes terror among the assembled people. It is a mysterious object, always unseen, and it is usually used to represent the voice of awe-inspiring spirits. Then, a group of women dances toward the *ibul* containing the restive animal to warn, ''Get ready, we are going to kill you!'' On their return, they are praised and embraced.

The most exciting moments are when the animal emerges from the *ibul,* which occurs fairly frequently. On its first appearance, the enemy, more splendidly attired than on the day before, salutes the king and takes a turn around the ring. At other times, defying weapons, it tries to attack a dancer, misses, and retreats to the *ibul.* In the last dramatic foray, the animal, which is in front of the king, grabs a woman. There is much disorder—a flurry of shrieks and gunshots. The animal is symbolically killed, presented to the king, and laid out rather roughly on a stretcher, which is hoisted on robust shoulders amid great tumult. This is the climax of the play and also its abrupt ending. The king immediately returns to the palace and the crowd disperses.

At the time of the 1974 ceremony, one dignitary said that if the Kuba residing in Kinshasa learned that an *itul* ceremony was taking place at Mushenge, they would all run to attend it. His statement indicates the importance of the event to the Kuba people. King Kwete Mbokashaang was trying to restore the traditional power threatened by modern secular life, and he could not have achieved greater success than by reviving the *itul* ceremony.

Source: ''The Itul Celebration of the Kuba'' by Joseph Cornet in *African Arts* XIII (3) (May 1980), 29-32.

December 8

La Inmaculada Concepción (The Immaculate Conception)

A festival day to celebrate the immaculate conception of the Virgin Mary.

Argentina

Argentinian fiestas of La Inmaculada Concepción

Several Argentine towns have fiestas on this day. The most popular is that of the Virgen del Valle, in Catamarca. This image was found by the Spaniards in 1620 in a cave near Catamarca. The face is dark and broad, with narrowed eyes, clearly Indian features. Each village in the provinces of Catamarca, Salta, Jujuy, Tucuman, and Santiago del Estero has a replica of this virgin. These are taken to Catamarca in procession for the December 8 festival. Some pilgrims travel on foot, quite a distance for those from provinces far removed. Many arrive in costume, playing native instruments, such as the *quena* and *charango,* and singing. Singing, dancing, and games take place during the festival. A procession is held on the eighth when the original image passes through town. Thousands of white handkerchiefs are tossed in the air as the statue passes.

Source: *Fiesta Time in Latin America* by Jean Milne. Los Angeles: The Ward Ritchie Press, 1965, pp. 177-178.

Bolivia

The fiesta of Concepción in the Sopocachi Alto barrio of La Paz

Two social classes, la Choolada (the higher class) and la Indiada (the lower class) take part in this fiesta. The Prestes (leaders) and their groups decorate two statues of the Virgin in the chapel in Sopocachi Alto on the afternoon before the fiesta. After this is finished, the group relaxes and the men drink *chicha* while the women chew coca until Mass at 7:00 P.M. After Mass, brass bands perform in the streets. The next day the festivities continue with brass band playing, dancing in the streets, and treats. The plaza fills with decorated vehicles, vendors, dancers, and festival goers. One writer mentions a vehicle covered with handwoven cloths, to which had been sewn silver spoons, dinner plates, stuffed armadillos, dolls, and a stuffed vicuna. After Mass the Virgin is carried from the church in procession. Women throw confetti at the Virgin. The decorated cars and dance groups form a procession. Later the groups gather at their preste's home for more partying.

Source: *The Masked Media: Aymara Fiestas and Social Interaction in the Bolivian Highlands* by Hans C. Buechler. The Hague: Mouton, 1980, pp. 182-183.

Honduras

La Inmaculada Concepción in Honduras

At Juticalpa in Honduras, this is a major festival, beginning several days before the eighth. Fireworks take place each night. One of the city's guilds sponsors each day's events. Prizes are given for competitions such as "Triangle," a balancing contest on ropes strung in the shape of a triangle. Greased pole climbing, greased pig chasing, sack races, and such as well as horse races, bicycle races, and bullfights may be held. Parades and masked costumed individuals are also part of the festival. On the seventh a horse parade is held, and the climax is, of course, the eighth, when the image herself is carried through the streets in religious processional.

Source: *Fiesta Time in Latin America* by Jean Milne. Los Angeles: Ward Ritchie Press, 1965, p. 176.

December 8

Needle Day

This is the final day to finish needlework for the year.

Japan

Needle Day in Tokyo, c. 1920

Inside the house, Aunt Sui and the girls, as well as the two maids, had scarcely had an hour's leisure since "Needle Day"—December 8th—when all the unfinished sewing of the year had to be hurried through. Since then every article in every room had been freshened into shiny newness, yet there were some little duties still left undone and everybody, even Mother and I, was put to work.

Source: *Chiyo's Return* by Chiyono Sugimoto Kiyooka. Garden City, N.Y.: Doubleday, Doran & Company, 1936, p. 239.

Second Sunday before Christmas

Materice (Mother's Day)

This is a day to honor mothers.

Yugoslavia

The mother hides small gifts under the mattress. Her children creep to her bed early in the morning, tie her legs with string, and demand presents as a ransom.

Source: *A Serbian Village* by Joel Martin Halpern. New York: Columbia, 1958, p. 243.

December 12
Our Lady of Guadalupe

El Salvador
Día del Indio

A "Day of the Indian" in honor of the Virgin of Guadalupe, patroness of the Indian. Families trim a cross with paper decorations and fruits and install it in their gardens.

Source: *Four Keys to El Salvador* by Lilly de Jongh Osborne. New York: Funk & Wagnalls, 1956, p. 158.

Mexico

"The Dark Madonna of the Hill of Tepeyac" appeared to woodcutter Juan Diego on December 9, 1531. She told him to fill his cloak with roses that miraculously appeared. When he presented them to the bishop the image of the Virgin was seen on the cloth. Thousands make pilgrimage to her shrine on her feast day. Singers serenade her at dawn, and gambling is popular on the hill behind her basilica. People with the name Guadalupe celebrate with name-day parties.

Source: *Fiesta Time in Latin America* by Jean Milne. Los Angeles: The Ward Ritchie Press, 1965, p. 179.

December 13

St. Lucy's Day

St. Lucy was thrown into a brothel by the pagan governor of Syracuse when a suitor, displeased at her decision to live a chaste, single life, reported her as a Christian. She preserved her honor even in the brothel, and when sent to be burned alive, the flames failed to harm her. She was killed by a sword thrust through the throat. According to some accounts, she tore out her own eyes in order to become ugly, but they were miraculously restored. She is known for healing eye diseases.

Finland

St. Lucia's Day

It begins at the crack of dawn when a young girl of the family acts as Lucia, the bringer of light. She rises before the rest of the house, dresses in a white robe, and crowns herself with a wreath of lighted candles. Then she wakens the others by serving them Saint Lucia buns and coffee in bed. She herself is feted at the hearty breakfast that follows.

Source: *Of Finnish Ways* by Aini Rajanen. Minneapolis: Dillon, 1981, p. 67.

Hungary

Planting the Christmas wheat

It is an ancient Hungarian custom to offer to the Infant in the manger the green sprouts of wheat.

Agriculture is the mainstay of the Hungarian nation and wheat is the symbol of sustenance and prosperity for this nation. It is therefore the most suitable gift for the newborn Saviour.

But it also has a meaning for everyone. The ''new wheat'' symobolizes the ''new bread'' in the natural order and also the ''New Bread of Life'' in the supernatural order; for it is from wheat that the altar bread is made which becomes the Holy Eucharist, the bread of our souls.

The wheat seeds are planted on the day of St. Lucy, the virgin martyr, December 13th. Kept in a moderately warm room and watered daily, the plant reaches its full growth by Christmas. The little daily care given to it is flavored with the joy of expectation for the approaching Christmas and spreads the spirit of cheerfulness as the tender plant reminds us of our spiritual rebirth through the mysteries of Christmas.

To plant the seeds, take a flower pot four or five inches in height and fill it with plain garden sod. Spread the seeds on the top and press gently, so that the seeds are covered with sod. Do not push them too deep.

Watered daily at the manger and paying its simple homage to the newborn Saviour, the plant will last until about January 6th.

''O all ye things that spring up in the earth, bless the Lord.'' (*Canticle of the Three Children*)

Source: *Around the Year with the Trapp Family* by Maria Augusta Trapp. New York: Pantheon, 1955, p. 34. (Reprinted by Maria Trapp from a Christmas card of the Hungarian order ''Sisters of Social Service.'')

Italy

Santa Lucia Day

Santa Lucia, born in Syracuse, Sicily in the third century was blinded and martyred by the Romans in A.D. 304. She is patroness of the blind. Her silver image is processed through the streets of Syracuse on her feast day. Boiled wheat is traditionally served.

Source: *A Calendar of Saints* by James Bentley. London: MacDonald & Evans, 1986, p. 239.

St. Lucia

The Caribbean island of St. Lucia celebrates the feast of her patron saint on this day.

Sweden

St. Lucia's Day

Morning rituals

Of the many Lucias who brighten December 13th, the little daughter at home is undoubtedly the most memorable. But on this darkest of mornings, each member of the family has his or her appointed role to play. Father's is to stay in bed, pretending to be fast asleep. Neither the titterings in the kitchen where Mother is busily dressing the family in long white robes—then a crown of candles for Lucia, coronets of silver tinsel for her sisters and tall white conical hats for the boys—nor the cheerful clink of coffee cups and saucers does he hear. Even the suspicious shuffling outside the bedroom door and the clearing of throats as the small procession tries to find the right note to start up the traditional Lucia song do not awaken him. Just to make sure, the youngest ''star boy'' pokes his tall hat round the door and as he does so, long shadows cast by the burning candles dance up the walls. But it's all right. Father is really and truly asleep!

He wakes up in heaven. Or so it seems. For his once dark bedroom is now filled with candlelight. White-robed figures stand beside his bed. One of them seems to be an angel with a halo of flames round her head and shining golden hair.

Then, as the last verse is sung, Lucia hands her father a cup of coffee. Father sits up, blinking, and the solemnity is over. Lucia's candles are blown out for, even with a wet handkerchief protecting her hair, there's always some danger. The toddler is relieved of his wobbly candle and the family seats itself on the bed. The special *lusse* buns are passed round. These are decorative flat saffron rolls with a currant at each of the four rounded corners. Ginger-bread hearts and stars follow.

Source: *Round the Swedish Year* by Lorna Downman, Paul Britten Austin, Anthony Baird. Stockholm: The Swedish Institute/Bokförlaget, 1967, pp. 77-78.

Ancient origins of St. Lucia's

December 13 was considered the longest night of the year under the old calendar. Creatures from the underworld were abroad on that night and early Norsemen feasted and drank to call back the sun god. They masked themselves in frightening costumes to scare away the underworld's creatures and took to the roads, making house calls. At homes they were given *branvin* (brandy) as ''lussesup'' (drink of light). Later this ''lussesup'' came to be served to the butcher who came to stick the Christmas pig on December 13.

Source: *Notes from a Scandinavian Parlor* by Florence Ekstrand. Seattle: Welcome Press, 1984, p. 86.

December 14

St. Spiridion Day

St. Spiridon was a shepherd who became Bishop of Tremithus in Cyprus. Diocletian had one of his eyes put out, and he was forced to labour in the mines. He survived and was one of the "Confessors of the Faith" at the council of Nicea.

Greece (Corfu)

St. Spiridon is venerated in Corfu

"It is Saint Spiridion, *kyria,*" she explained. "Today we may enter the church and kiss his feet."

Saint Spiridion was the patron saint of the island. His mummified body was enshrined in a silver coffin in the church, and once a year he was carried in procession round the town. He was very powerful, and could grant requests, cure illness, and do a number of other wonderful things for you if he happened to be in the right mood when asked. The islanders worshipped him, and every second male on the island was called Spiro in his honour. Today was a special day; apparently they would open the coffin and allow the faithful to kiss the slippered feet of the mummy, and make any request they cared to.

Inside, it was dark as a well, lit only by a bed of candles that bloomed like yellow crocuses along one wall. A bearded, tall-hatted priest clad in black robes flapped like a crow in the gloom, making the crowd form into a single line that filed down the church, past the great silver coffin and out through another door into the street. The coffin was standing upright, looking like a silver chrysalis, and at its lower end a portion had been removed so that the saint's feet, clad in the richly-embroidered slippers, peeped out. As each person reached the coffin he bent, kissed the feet, and murmured a prayer, while at the top of the sarcophagus the saint's black and withered face peered out of a glass panel with an expression of acute distaste.

Source: *My Family and Other Animals* by Gerald Durrell. New York: Viking, 1956, pp. 86-87.

December 16

Braaiveleis

This is a midwinter campout popular with Afrikaans farmers in earlier days. The custom survives as a simpler outdoor barbecue today.

South Africa (Afrikaans)

Braaiveleis was a midwinter campout. Farmers in earlier days would load family, food, and bedding on a wagon and trek off into the veld to rendezvous with other families for a camping party. December 16, anniversary of the defeat of the Zulu king Dingaan in 1838, was a popular day for this. These camp-outs included prayer meetings and political speeches. Today the *braaiveleis* is a much smaller outdoor adventure, such as a backyard barbecue, and occurs at any time during the year.

Source: *African Cooking* by Laurens Van der Post and The Editors of Time-Life Books. New York: Time-Life Books, 1970, pp. 190-191.

December 16-25

Cock Crow Mass

This begins the pre-Christmas season of daily morning masses.

Philippines

Cock Crow mass

The season starts with a Cock Crow Mass, followed by daily masses every morning until December 25.

Before the first mass, houses are decorated with star lanterns, called *parols*. They are made of translucent colored paper with bamboo frames and are lighted with candles or small electric bulbs. Streamers hanging from them represent star rays. The lanterns are put in windows and doorways to symbolize the star of Bethlehem.

An hour or so before dawn, a band marches through the streets to wake up the townspeople. Because it is still dark when they leave their homes, they light the way with their star lanterns.

Inside the church there is candlelight, and a very large star gleams at the entrance. The church choir sings Christmas music accompanied by castanets, tambourines and triangles. Priests preside over the mass and the congregation joins in carol singing.

After the service, everyone gathers in the plaza for breakfast or snacks. Vendors are waiting with their little carts to sell freshly baked cakes made of rice, coconut or corn.

Source: *Celebrations: Asia and the Pacific* by Gene Sawyer. Honolulu: Friends of the East-West Center, 1978, p. 94.

Sunday before Christmas

Očevi (Father's Day)

This is a day to honor fathers.

Yugoslavia

Children tease their fathers by tying them up in bed and demanding treats or coins. This resembles the Yugoslavian "Mother's Day," Materice, held on the second Sunday before Christmas.

Source: *A Serbian Village* by Joel Martin Halpern. New York: Columbia, 1958, p. 248.

December 18

St. Modesto's Day

This is a day to honor St. Modesto, patron of farmers.

Greece

The cattle's holiday

December 18 is called ''the oxen's feast.'' Farmers join to pay for a Mass and *kollyva* for the cattle. In Lemnos, the kollyva and holy water are given to the cattle mixed with their fodder. In Drymos, Macedonia the farmers give sanctified bread to their cattle after the mass and wish them ''Chronia polla,'' ''Happy returns of the day.'' At Telonia in Lesbos, the holy water is sprinkled on the fields to drive away locusts and disease. On this day all horses and oxen are given a day of rest.

Source: *Greek Calendar Customs* by George A. Megas. Athens: B. & M. Thodis, 1963, p. 27.

Circa December 21

Ysyakh

This is the celebration of the midnight sun. It is an official national holiday.

U.S.S.R. (Yakutsk Autonomous Soviet Socialist Republic)

Feasting and dancing in the arctic night

There is plenty of good boiled beef. Each diner spears big chunks of the beef on long wooden skewers and chews off mouthfuls of the meat. He washes it down with fermented mare's milk—a sort of sour buttermilk—called *kumiss,* which he drinks from a big carved wooden mug. Bottles of other things to drink appear on the long tables, but kumiss is the true drink of the Yakut people.

When everyone has had enough to eat and drink, the fun begins. Men and boys run foot races, and everyone joins in the dancing. For one dance, called the Hitching Post, a horse is tethered to a post in the middle of an open space. The dancers, young men and women, form a circle around the horse. As they move about the circle in dancing steps, they sing. Often they make up their own words to tell of their joy at having good health, good friends—at just being alive!

''What does the horse tethered out in the center have to do with the dance?'' a visitor asks.

Some of the men rub their chins and frown thoughtfully, but no one can give a real answer. The custom is so old that its meaning has been lost in the mists of tribal traditions.

There is no hurry about finishing up the dancing. At midnight the sky is still pale and glowing. It is then that the men line up on their mounts for the horse races. In winter they race dog and reindeer sledges, but they like horses too. So the crowd has a fine time racing and betting on the races, eating, drinking, and dancing, far into the arctic night.

Source: *A Parade of Soviet Holidays* by Jane Werner Watson. Champaign, Ill.: Garrard, 1974, pp. 64-65.

December 21

St. Thomas' Day

This is the day honoring St. Thomas the Apostle. He is best known for his doubt of Christ's godliness until after the resurrection. According to some accounts he preached the gospel in India and was martyred there.

Austria

Christmas baking begins

Finally, St. Thomas' Day, December 21st, arrives. Throughout the Austrian Alps this is the day when the *Kletzenbrot* has to be baked. *Kletzen* is the Tyrolean word for dried pears, but this bread contains a mixture of dried fruit. There will be one large loaf made for the family breakfast on Christmas morning, and an individual small loaf for every member of the household. This *Kletzenbrot* keeps forever, and it is as wholesome as it is delicious. Try it!

Kletzenbrot

2 cups whole wheat flour
1 cup white flour
2/3 cup brown sugar
3 tsp. baking powder
2 tsp. baking soda
1/4 tsp. salt
2 cups buttermilk
1 cup chopped nuts
1 cup chopped prunes
1 cup chopped figs
1 cup chopped dates
1/2 cup raisins
1/2 cup currants

Mix sifted dry ingredients in a bowl. Add buttermilk slowly and stir to a smooth dough. Mix in the nuts, raisins, and the rest. Bake in a hot oven for about an hour.

But not only *Kletzenbrot* is being baked—on St. Thomas' Day Christmas baking begins, and from now on the house will be filled with a cloud of delicious smells. Some of this Christmas baking—the choicest delicacies in the realm of cookies and candies—will be hung on the Christmas tree, which is altogether different from an American one. Of the many varieties we always preferred the cookies known as *Lebkuchen* (or *Lebzelten*). They got better with age, and they are responsible for the unique scent known in our family as "Christmas smell."

Source: *Around the Year with the Trapp Family* by Maria Augusta Trapp. New York: Pantheon, 1955, p. 31.

Belgium

Tricks played on teachers

On this day children may play tricks on their teachers. In the Ardennes school boys used to set fire to little paper roosters on this day, and at an even earlier date teachers gave students a live rooster to behead on this day.

Source: *Château-Gérard: The Life and Times of a Walloon Village* by Harry Holbert Turney-High. Columbia: University of South Carolina Press, 1953, p. 255.

Germany

Thomas donkeys, *Thomasplätzchen,* and *Hutzelbrot*

In Sauerland, the last person to wake on this day is a "Thomas Donkey" (*Thomasesel*). Cardboard donkey ears are worn, and this person is the butt of jokes all day. In the evening, round, iced currant buns, marked with a cross (*Thomasplätzchen*), are eaten. In Luneburg Heath, St. Thomas, rather than St. Nicholas, brings treats to the children. In earlier times, employers gave presents of food and money on this day. *Hutzelbrot* (*Klotzen, Kletzen, Schnitzbrot, Fruchtebrot*), made of pears and flour is baked on this day. The patron saint of shoemakers, the *Hutzelmann,* is believed to have invented *Hutzelbrot.*

Source: *German Festivals and Customs* by Jennifer M. Russ. London: Oswald Wolff, 1982, pp. 22-23.

Norway

St. Thomas takes away the ax

All Christmas preparations must be finished before St. Thomas' Day, December 21st. By that time sufficient wood had to be cut to last over the two weeks' celebration. If this were neglected, St. Thomas would come and take away the ax. Likewise, must all baking, brewing, and butchering be ready by that day, otherwise they will have some mishap with everything. A cake was put on a shelf for St. Thomas before five o'clock Christmas Eve.

Source: *When I Was a Boy in Norway* by Dr. J.O. Hall. Boston: Lothrop, Lee & Shepard Co., 1921, p. 155.

Circa December 22

The Winter Solstice

In the Northern Hemisphere the winter solstice is the shortest day of the year. After this date the days begin to lengthen and the light and warmth of the sun slowly return. The day is important in the religious cycles of many cultures. In the Southern Hemisphere this is the date of the summer solstice, the longest day of the year.

Hong Kong

Rites of the Emperor and home observances

Under the monarchy in China, it was the day on which the Emperor led the annual sacrifices at the Temple of Heaven in Peking. No foreigners were ever permitted to see this greatest of all Imperial ceremonies, and very few Chinese. Indeed, the ordinary people of the capital were obliged to stay at home and curtains were hung so that the Emperor's procession could pass along the main thoroughfares without danger of his being seen.

After the fall of the monarchy in 1912, the Imperial rites were abandoned, but in Hong Kong the people still treat the Winter Solstice as a day for staying home, making offerings to the *ancestors,* and enjoying a family dinner.

In many New Territories villages there are ceremonial offerings in the temples or *ancestral halls,* followed by a distribution of pork. The small shrines to T'o Tei Kung are not forgotten, and people also use this day for making offerings to spiritually powerful trees and rocks.

Source: *Chinese Festivals in Hong Kong* by Joan Law and Barbara E. Ward. Hong Kong: A South China Morning Post Production, 1982, p. 83.

India (Assam)

Magh Bihu

Magh Bihu celebrations

Magh Bihu, the harvest festival, has many parallels among agricultural people. In Assam its core is a fire ceremony observed on the Bihu or Samkranti day, not on the full moon of Phagun as in other arts of India but the Bihu eve or *Uruka* has its particular importance. On this day womenfolk get ready for the next day with *chira, pitha* and *laru, gur* and curd, the usual eatables taken at noon at Magh Bihu. Malefolk go to the lakes and rivers and catch fish and prepare for the communal feasts in the evening. On the Uruka day it is customary to take fish or meat at both meals. Then, cowherds and other young lads collect in a nearby field stubble, dried banana leaves and green bamboos and raise high temple-like structures known as *bhelaghar*. They construct a makeshift cottage close by and pass the night there. They collect Bihu cakes and rice, fish and other things, steal fuel and vegetables, and have their feast there. In urban areas fuel and sometimes furniture and gates are stolen to burn in bonfires. The number of bhelaghars depends on the size of the village and the number of its *khels*. Further, there are small family bhelaghars made by children.

On the first day of Magh, at crack of dawn, someone in the family ties bands of bamboo laths, jute or thatch around fruit-bearing trees, calls out to dogs and offers them rice, while womenfolk clean the house and cooking pans, throwing away the earthen ones. Then all take a purifying bath and put on washed clothes. The malefolk and children then move on to the communal bhelaghars, though first the family bhelaghars are burnt. Naibedya or offerings of chira, pitha, etc. are made to God near the bhelaghars, then to cries of God's name fire is set to the temple-like structures. Red flames warm up the people so long shivering in cold and the bamboo tubes burst like gun-fire. Brahmans or elderly persons give blessings and put marks of ash on the forehead. The half-burnt sticks and bamboos are scattered in the fields, sometimes a few pieces may be brought home to be thrown near fruit-bearing trees. The belief is that the ashes and half-burnt bamboos increase fertility of fields and gardens. Europeans who lighted Lenten and Midsummer fires also had this belief in the efficacy of ashes and embers as a means of fertility. Some of them also had the custom of tying bands of straw round tree-trunks to render them fruitful.

After the bhelaghars are burnt and the cottages are destoyed or burnt, people sit and to the accompaniment of *nagara* kettle-drums and *bhortals* or large cymbals hold a nam-prasanga. In fact, holding of nam-prasanga or singing of hymns begins from the evening of Uruka. Throughout this month, taken to be suitable for religious activities, it is usual to hold such nam-prasangas. In this aspect of the festival the influence of Vaishnavism is clear.

The noon is spent in eating food kept prepared earlier. This may be followed by accepting invitations. Another aspect of the festival is the holding of sport like wrestling, racing, jumping, egg-fighting, buffalo fighting, etc.

Source: *The Springtime Bihu of Assam* by Praphulladatta Goswami. Gauhati, Assam: Lawyer's Bookstall, 1966, pp. 1-23. (Goswami discusses various Bihu customs and dwells particularly on Bihu dance and song. Some historical information on Bihu is included.)

Japan

Toji

This period is observed in many shrines throughout Japan. Toji marks the time when the days begin to grow longer, the nights shorter. . . . The day brings particular joy to the farmers because the sun grows warmer and makes plants grow; so Toji is celebrated as a joyous day. There are traditional customs observed in some rural areas such as: taking citrus baths, eating pumpkins for good luck, taking a respite from work, making offerings to ancestors, and giving servants and workers a holiday. Shrines have great bonfires to encourage the early coming of the spring season (especially at Yoshida slope, Mount Fuji, or Togakushi, Nagano Prefecture).

Source: *Japanese Festivals* by Helen Bauer and Sherwin Carlquist. Garden City, N.Y.: Doubleday, 1965, p. 209.

Okinawa

Toji

The festival of the winter solstice, the longest night of the year (*toji*) is known, but Minatogawa was the only place in which its observance was noted. It is a home festival with prayers and the familiar offering of assorted foods to the ancestors.

Source: *Studies of Okinawan Village Life* by Clarence J. Glacken. Scientific Investigations in the Ryukyu Islands (SIRI). Report no. 4. Washington, D.C.: Pacific Science Board, National Research Council, 1953, p. 326.

Taiwan

Tang choeh î

At the winter solstice a feast is prepared for the door, well, and ancestor spirits. Thanks are given for past benefits and protection ensured for the future.

Tang choeh î (winter solstice balls)

Besides offering the "three meats" or "five meats", the burning of paper money and incense, the Taiwanese also prepare a special dish called "Tang choeh î" or "Winter solstice balls." These winter solstice balls are made of rice-dough rolled into the size of a small marshmallow, and boiled in sugar syrup. Half of them are dyed red, and when served up in steaming bowls, resemble large red and white cherries. 12 of the balls are rolled much larger than the others, and these are set aside to offer to the spirits and to the ancestors. They are called "Îbu" or "mother balls", the progenitors as it were, of their smaller and less honored counterparts.

When the feast has been prepared, 3 bowls of the sweetened solstice balls are placed before the ancestor shrine, and a section of the banquet table is moved directly in front of the family altar, so that the place reserved for the guest of honor is given to the ancestors. Then the various dishes are placed on the table, including the three or five kinds of meat; namely, pork, chicken, duck, goat, and some other kind, but usually not beef. Then incense is lighted, and paper money burned, while the "bai-bai" or prayers offering thanks and asking the gods protection are recited. Fire crackers can also be exploded. Thereupon the winter solstice balls are pasted on the lintels and doorposts, on the courtyard well, and on all the animal pens, to thank the gods and beg for further protection. The roundness and brightness of the ball suggests the fact that the sun is soon to come back for from this day on the days grow longer, and so an increasing prosperity is insured for the household members.

As with other rites and ceremonies, the past few years have seen a great simplification on Taiwan. In the more modern city family, the balls are no longer pasted about the house, nor on the door posts. One becomes a year older at Chinese New Year, and not on the winter solstice. The younger members of the family are more likely to consider the day as a feast in honor of the ancestors only, or simply a day for a banquet.

Winter solstice is a propitious day for making contracts and for renting arable land. Property can be safely mortgaged, possessions pawned, and the time limit for a contract decided. After the 16th of the last lunar month, such transactions are no longer permitted.

Source: *Taiwan Feasts and Customs* by Michael R. Saso. Hsinchu, Taiwan: Chabanel Language Institute, pp. 1-3.

December 23

St. Thorlak's Day

This is a day to honor St. Thorlak. Thorlak Thorhalli was born in Iceland in 1133. He became a deacon at the age of fifteen and a priest before the age of eighteen. He studied in Paris and Lincoln and returned to Iceland to become Bishop of Skalholt in 1177. He stamped out simony and incontinency and was canonized by the Althing in 1198. He died in 1193.

Iceland

Christmas preparations

On St. Thorlak's Day the preparations for the Christmas festivities reached a climax. In many places, for instance, the *hangiket* (smoked mutton) for Christmas was cooked this day. Also, clothes were washed and the house cleaned either on this date or just prior to it. In that connection the phrase *dry spell for the poor* was coined—which simply meant that poor people often did not have the change of bedsheets or even of underwear, so God in His grace gave them good drying weather (on St. Thorlak's Day or the days before) the few times they were washed.

In some places at least, there was a tradition of special food on St. Thorlak's Day. In particular, mention should be made of the skate, or rather skate hash, which was an almost unalterable dish on this day in the Western Fjords; in fact, it still is among many migrants from the region, as well as the remaining inhabitants. They consider the smell of the skate hash (similar to ammonia) to have been the first tangible proof that Christmas was coming at last.

Source: *Icelandic Feasts and Holidays: Celebrations, Past and Present* by Arni Bjornsson. Reykjavik: Iceland Review History Series, 1980, p. 76.

December 25
Christmas

This day commemorates the birth of the Christian Messiah, Jesus of Nazareth. Because of calendar changes, Eastern Orthodox countries still remember Christmas as occurring on January 6. That date is termed ''Old Christmas'' in some areas. Christmas celebrations range from a quiet religious observance to the rowdy carnivalesque masquerading of several Caribbean islands. The addition of a gift-bearing Santa Claus to the day originally set to celebrate the Christ Child's birth seems mainly connected with American and British traditions. Elsewhere, children receive their gifts on December 6 or January 6, though the influence of the Santa Claus tradition is felt in many places today.

Albania

Christmas in pre-Communist Albania

In the olden days in Albania, at the Christmas season, the table was set with a cloth, under which straw was laid, in memory of the humble birth of the Christ Child in a manger. The table was decorated with as many lighted candles as there were guests around it. It was loaded with good things to eat and the chief delicacy was a large cake, in which were many raisins and nuts and also a gold piece. It was believed that whoever found the gold piece would have good luck for the coming year.

Source: *Children's Festivals from Many Lands* by Nina Miller. New York: Friendship Press, 1964, p. 101.

Argentina

Los Tres Reyes

The Three Kings arrive on the eve of January 6, bringing gifts for the children. During the Christmas holidays they sit in state in a special toyland for children on the top floor of the Harrods department store in Buenos Aires. There children queue up to talk to Los Tres Reyes. Harrods, a British department store, has adapted the ''visit to Santa Claus'' to fit the Argentine gift-givers.

Source: Margaret MacDonald, observation in 1974.

Armenia

Christmas morning.

On Christmas morning all the Armenians go to church, and after dinner begin the customary visits and greetings of the season. Usually two of the members of the family stay at home to receive the visitors while the others make the calls; then they change their turn so that, during the three days of greeting, all neighbors are able to visit each other. The visitor enters the house saying, ''Greetings! Christ is born!'' The host replies, ''Greetings to the whole world!'' Upon this, the visitor is received with respect, and entertained with refreshments.

We have no Christmas tree and do not exchange presents on Christmas day. Our Santa Claus comes on New Year's Eve instead of Christmas Eve, for Christmas is a sacred day and is passed with greetings and festivals of joy.

Source: *When I Was a Boy in Armenia* by Manoog Der Alexanian. Boston: Lothrop, Lee & Shepard Co., 1926, pp. 118-119.

An Armenian Christmas dish

Christmas among Armenians is chiefly a religious feast; Gaghant Bab, the Armenian version of Santa Claus, does not make his appearance till New Year's, the season of mirth and feasting and exchange of gifts. Though Christmas Eve and Christmas Day are largely dedicated to religious worship, time is found nevertheless for the preparation and enjoyment of an elaborate meal at which the orthodox Armenian makes up for the week of fasting which has preceded Christmas Day. ''Anoush Abour'' (sweet soup) for which the recipe is given below is a traditional Christmas dish. . . .

Anoush Abour

2 lbs wheat grains
1 lb sugar
1 lb nut meats (walnuts, almonds)
1 tsp cinnamon
1 lb small raisins (seedless, light and dark)
2 tbs cornstarch
2 qts water

Wash wheat grains, cover with 2 qts of water and cook well until grains are split. Remove from fire and let stand for an hour. Add sugar, raisins, nut meats and cinnamon. Soften and dissolve cornstarch in a little lukewarm water and stir into grain mixture. Add more water as needed and cook for about five minutes. Pour into individual dishes. Serve cold.

Source: *Foreign Festival Customs* by Marian Schibsby & Hanny Cohrsen. New York: American Council for Nationalities Service, 1974, p. 59.

Australia

Christmas in Australia, c. 1958

Gifts are exchanged at the breakfast table in some families. Christmas services at the church follow. The Christmas dinner may be roast beef or a fowl. The Christmas Bush is popular for decorating homes; it is a bush with tiny flowers that grow in soft clusters. The Christmas Bell, a bell-shaped flower fringed in yellow, is also popular.

Carols by Candlelight

A Melbourne radio announcer, Norman Banks, started the tradition of Carols by Candlelight in 1937. According to the story, he passed an open window and saw an old woman sitting alone by the radio, holding a lighted candle and softly singing along with the Christmas carols. He started the community caroling tradition the next year, and it has become a national favorite event.

Source: *Christmas Customs around the World* by Herbert H. Wernecke. Philadelphia: The Westminster Press, 1959, p. 134; *Joy through the World.* The United States Committee for UNICEF. New York: Dodd, Mead, 1985.

An Australian ranch hand remembers Christmas, c. 1920

You might cut the pudding up for eating and find you have something there. We all got something when we had Christmas dinner. That was how we used to spend Christmas Day. It made a lot of fun. These days they do not bother much with Christmas on the stations. Some of them buy a lot of things and bring them in tins of cakes and puddings and all that. But in the early days they were mates out on the stations and the food was better than the kind you buy now. You had a big Christmas dinner in those days, and sports to follow till sundown.

There were foot races and a high jump. Everybody were invited in from Rosewood and Lissadell. Big boys and girls ran races over the yard. An obstacle race they called one, over the house and down, and there was a big prize for it. You won a good blooming white moleskin and white shirt, good sort of leggings and a good hat, a pound of tobacco, a couple of pounds of lollies, and a handkerchief and pocket knife. Anything you wanted was all laid out on the verandah and the winner came and picked them, and the second would come past. Ther were big prizes at those races.

Source: *Banggaiyerri: The Story of Jack Sullivan as Told by Bruce Shaw.* Canberra: Australian Institute of Aboriginal Studies, 1983, p. 78.

Australia / (Aborigines)

An Aborigines Christmas

Then came Christmas Eve, which was also the pay-day for our weekly work, and over the town the shop windows were decked out with green bushes and bits of coloured paper. Paper lanterns swayed from shop beams amidst a clutter of pack-saddles, horse-bells, and shining billy-cans, all of which added gaiety to the scene.

As I wandered through the bush, a night owl called from the trees and was answered by another nearby. Christmas Eve! And tomorrow was the day of all days! I never bathed the kiddies that night because they were too tired. Sleepy-eyed, they watched me hang out little calico bags for Santa to put their presents into, then they went to bed and were soon fast asleep.

Present after present came out of the sacks—dresses and rompers, hats and shoes, all of different colours. How Beattie's eyes stared when I told the old, old story of Santa coming down the chimney in the traditional manner! I had to change the mode of entry of the gift spirit to the doorway when she pointed out that our chimney was not open at the top, but covered with sheets of galvanised iron.

As we were having our breakfast, Drummer arrived breathless at the door, holding in his hands a box of fishing lines that he had found beside his camp fire. As the gift had been placed there as a result of a secret pact between Windanger and myself, I explained that on Christmas Eve 'somebody comes up to give children things'.

'For nothing,' said the incredulous Drummer. 'That not right!'

'Not for nothing,' Beattie chided him. 'Santa bring it on cart with different-kind bullock . . . they travel in sky and give present to boy and girl who are not cheeky to people.'

'But he leave no track,' sceptically replied Drummer, who believed in practical things. 'S'pose he come, must be he leave track.'

'Santa different,' Beattie remarked emphatically, and I noticed that Billy nodded his head in agreement with her.

Source: *Grief, Gaiety, and Aborigines* by W.E. (Bill) Harney. London: Robert Hale Limited, 1961, pp. 151-153.

Belize

John Canoe

Both Garifuna and non-Carib Blacks of Belize and neighboring parts of Guatamala enjoy the John Canoe masquerade. The John Canoe masqueraders dance from house to house on Christmas Day and Boxing Day. They wear cloth headwraps and wire-screen masks, which are painted white or pink and given staring eyes, red lips, black eyebrows, and, for males, a thin mustache. These whiteface masks were produced commercially during the nineteenth and early twentieth centuries but are now made by the performers. The John Canoe are accompanied by two drums and a female chorus.

Pia Manadi

Pia Manadi is a mime and dance drama that is performed during the Christmas-New Year season. Fife and drum as well as bass and snare accompany the drama. The pantomime somewhat resembles Caribbean versions of the English Doctor plays.

Source: "Jonkonnu and Other Christmas Masquerades" by Judith Bettelheim in *Caribbean Festival Arts* by John Nunley and Judith Bettelheim. Seattle: Univ. of Washington, 1988, pp. 68-69.

Belgium

Crèches of butter, bacon, hardware, and more

As Advent season draws to a close and Christmas approaches, the merchants all over the principality erect the crèche, or the birth scene of Christ in the stable in their windows. Of course a certain amount of advertising value is inherent in such decoration, but for the most part the great expenditure of time and money involved is without hope of return. The figures of the Holy Family and worshiping animals are not unusual. Some are fine; some are ordinary. The extraordinary feature of the window decorations is that each merchant builds the stable out of the thing he sells. In a land famous for pastries and candies, one might imagine the magnificent results, but when hardware sellers build the crèche of their goods, or haberdashers erect impressive stables out of cravats and neckties, the results are sometimes astounding. Those of the great Liege dressmakers, of the most sumptuous silks and laces, and those of the jewelers, are expectably splendid. But to find great stables of pure butter or cheese in the dairy windows is something else! It is hardly to be credited that one of the finest and most artistic stables in Liege was in a butcher's shop, woven out of strips of bacon and decorated with rings of Ardennes sausage, but that was the general opinion of the crowds. Naturally, an humble village like Château-Gérard could hardly be expected to reach Liege levels, but the merchants try their best, and that of the local baker whose holy house was of specially baked bread was particularly ingenious.

Living crèches, or full-sized stables with real animals and with the more personable parishioners acting as Joseph, Mary, and others, have long been a Liege custom. This spectacle is held at night and is a very popular sight with the strolling Liègeois.

Source: *Château-Gérard: The Life and Times of a Walloon Village* by Harry Holbert Turney-High. Columbia: Univ. of South Carolina Press, 1953, p. 257.

Brazil

Making Pesebres

Manger scenes are often made of bright-colored sawdust. Each day from Christmas until Epiphany (January 6), the figures are moved a step nearer to the Christ Child. Epiphany itself is celebrated with firecrackers and is the end of the Christmas season.

Source: *Christmas the World Over* by Daniel J. Foley. Philadelphia: Chilton, 1963, p. 100.

Bulgaria

Feasting, the yule-log, and carding

The winter festive cycle essentially includes rites which are meant to predict and evoke fertility, the development and multiplication of the farm animals and hence personal happiness and family prosperity.

Christmas is the greatest feast of this cycle. Its rites and customs can be classified in three groups: the dinner table, the fireplace and the carol singing.

Traditionally, the Christmas dinner table must be over-abundant so that the coming year may also be rich. The housewife kneads and bakes a ritual loaf of bread. The oldest man of the house burns incense over the table using the ploughshare and not forgetting to burn incense over the farm animals, as well. Then he breaks the loaf and hands a piece to each member of the family, putting aside a piece for the animals. After dinner there comes the fortune-telling: the main subjects are love, marriage, the weather and the harvest.

The Christmas fire is of special significance. A yule-log is put in it to burn there all night. If the fire dies out this is tantamount to bad luck for the family. From the unburnt wood they make wedges for the plough. The more sparks from the yule-log, the more lambs will be born in the following year.

Carol singing is the third important aspect of the feast. The participants are boys and occasionally men. In the daytime the children carry carol rods, pat adults on the back and say: "Christmas, Granny Christmas." The men give them walnuts, bacon and ring-shaped buns specially baked for the feast. The adult carol singers walk in groups and each group has a leader.

They wear their Sunday best and visit all houses chanting blessings.

Source: "Bulgarian Folk Feasts and Rites" by Sofia Press Agency in *Journal of Popular Culture* 19:1 (Summer 1985), 155-156.

Canada (Newfoundland)

The Twelve Days of Christmas and Mumming

The twelve days of Christmas in the parish are celebrated by freedom from work, and by a high degree of social interaction in the form of house-parties and visiting. A month or so before the Christmas season large brews of beer are made and set aside in kegs to age. The women make many fruit-cakes and large batches of cookies, and open jars of preserved moose, chicken, jams, and vegetables. A cow or a pig is usually slaughtered so that all visitors can be given a meal or a 'lunch'—a late evening meal—of the highest quality. Hospitality and generosity are strikingly displayed.

Starting with the end of fasting at Midnight Mass on December 25, the holidays begin. On returning from Mass, food and drink are consumed in full quantity, as presents from one member of the family to another are opened. Adults go to bed quite late, and children wake in the morning to find more gifts, these left by Santa Claus. From Christmas Day through the rest of the days of Christmas, visiting continues. Whole families go together to other houses, beginning usually with their immediate relatives and moving next to the neighbours living in the same village. These visits begin somewhat formally, but frequently wind up in partial or complete drunkenness among the men. . . . Mummers have always been known to go about at Christmas time in the parish, although no one has every heard of the mummers' play.

Mummers dress in household odds and ends: table cloths, burlap bags, hip boots, torn dresses, battered hats, woollen underwear, long coats, and gloves. Men usually dress as "generalized" women and women as "generalized" men. Shapes become blurred as the pile of coats, sweaters, table cloths, and padding reduce individual differences. Veils of various materials completely surround the head and are held in place by battered men's and women's hats. For mummers, a covered face is a necessity.

Mummers move from house to house in small groups of two to six, always after dark. Uninvited, they enter houses noisily without knocking, stamping their feet heavily as they approach the door and as they pass into the kitchen. Once inside, they begin a jogging, half-dance, half-shake that is the 'mummer's walk.' They often move about the room freely, and will sometimes even go into other parts of the house; they are aggressive and may nudge or jostle members of the household, or begin dancing with them or other mummers. They may make jokes about the family. Frequently, the mummers bring musical instruments and may play guitars or violins, or beat on breadpans. One or two mummers might step-dance if asked to do so.

As mummers reverse their sexual roles in their dress, so they reverse their speech. On deep gulps of breath, words are swallowed in a rapid monotone of short phrases.

When identification is positively made, mummers are expected to 'strip'—to remove their masks. Not to do so is considered an affront to the hosts, and even fellow mummers may try to force a reticent masker to reveal himself. If a host fails completely to identify a mummer, he may try to remove his mask forcibly, often leading to a scuffle that may become quite rough. A host may offer a drink to the mummer he fails to recognize; but it is generally felt that an unidentified person should pass on to another house without accepting food and drink.

But once a mummer has been identified he ceases his aggressive behaviour and takes a seat along the wall, returning to the usual demeanour of normal social encounters.

Source: "The Mask of Friendship: Mumming as a Ritual of Social Relations" by John Szwed in *Christmas Mumming in Newfoundland* by Herbert Halpert and G.M. Storey. Toronto: Univ. of Toronto Press for Memorial Univ. of Newfoundland, 1969, pp. 109-111.

Canada (Northwest Territories—Baffin Island)

The school Christmas party in Apex village on Baffin Island

The festive Christmas season begins with the Nanook School Christmas concert and feast, held on the last Friday evening before the holidays. Every household receives a hand-delivered invitation and every resident capable of locomotion attends. The gymnasium is transformed into a banquet hall for the occasion. Students painstakingly cover every available inch of the gym with decorations they have made—paper chains and tin foil stars hang from the rafters, and the walls are dressed with colourful paper bells, each with hand-lettered messages in Inuktitut and English.

After the recitals and singing comes the eating. People crowd around the tables to see what food is available and what neighbours have brought. Traditional food is a favourite. The raw, frozen char disappears as fast as it hits the serving tables, and those slow off the mark miss the caribou and seal.

But some southern traditions also hold sway, and Neil struggles valiantly in the school kitchen trying to keep pace with the demand for turkey. He will carve his way through a flock of birds before the evening is out. It is clear that every oven in Apex has been busy.

There is special pleasure this evening as community folk mix with friends and relatives just arrived from the out-post camps. Several families have travelled many hours by snowmobile along the sea ice to join in the Christmas celebrations. While most of the Inuit of the eastern Arctic have moved to permanent communities in the last 30 years, some remain in, or have returned to, outpost camps. These families come to town occasionally for supplies or to attend community events.

The excitement mounts as Santa arrives with a sackful of presents and the children's names are called one by one. Their mothers have been busy conspiring with our two teachers, buying and wrapping gifts appropriate for each child. Everyone is remembered. There are presents for the "big kids" who now attend classes in Iqaluit, and extra gifts for the unexpected arrivals and pre-schoolers.

The Sunday-before-Christmas church service in Apex village

On Sunday the tree in the church is trimmed with iced gingerbread and ribbon bows. The children somehow resist the temptation to take a bite from the cookie decorations, even during parts of the service when heads are bowed.

The regular service at St. Simon's is always in Inuktitut. Once a southerner has lived with the Inuit language for a while it becomes possible to follow the prayer book and hymnal, both written in the syllabic alphabet. As we near Christmas it becomes easier to follow the Inuktitut Bible readings. The story being told is an old one, familiar from many repetitions, the tale of a baby born in the simplest of circumstances and the community that gathered to celebrate his birth. Heard again in a new language and a fresh context, its universality is brought home.

Church in Apex is not distinct from the rest of community life. Children are allowed to play during the service. Some sit quietly and listen, others wander forward to sit on the lap of a relative in the choir. Babies peak from the hoods of their mother's *amautiq*, cry and gurgle, are nursed and changed as worship continues.

After the service, everyone shakes hands with our minister and the parishioners who assisted him. Handshaking here is different from the powerful grips customary in southern Canada. A light grip and a single up-down shake is the Inuit way. When the greetings are over, the congregation heads for tea and bread at the home of this week's volunteer. We usually get variations on bannock, cakes and yeasted bread, but when there has been good hunting there may be caribou stew, char, or even a whole seal.

Canada (Nova Scotia)

Belsnicking in the La Have Islands

The belsnickles began their visiting rounds shortly after dark on Christmas Eve. "The very minute the sun went down, we'd go in a barn or someplace and start to rig up." Once dressed, the belsnickles began their rounds, ringing their bells, blowing their horns, singing, occasionally shooting off firecrackers, and generally making their presence known.

When they reached a house, the belsnickles' chief method for requesting admission was to knock on the door, or more often a window, and call out "belsnickles allowed in?" Most people, apparently "was glad to have 'em come" and "let 'em right in," putting aside the nets they were knitting for the fifteen or twenty minutes that the belsnickles would stay. Very few families refused the mummers admittance—perhaps two or three at most—although every house in the community was visited. Those who refused were either very old people, finicky housekeepers who did not want their floors dirtied by the belsnickles' muddy boots, or families whose small children were so frightened by the belsnickles that their parents feared they "would get the fits."

Once inside the house, and with the encouragement of their hosts, the belsnickles launched into their special performance behavior, characteristically indecorous and licentious. This behavior was summed up by my informants with such phrases as, "you'd put on a little act," "just act the jackass," "carry on a little bit," or "act the fool." The performances usually involved grotesque singing and almost always clumsy, exaggerated step dancing, and were requested by the householders if not soon forthcoming. The dancing was done to the accompaniment of a mouth organ and occasionally a drum, with one member of the group stretching back the mouth of his mask to play while the others danced around the room: "they'd dance or make believe they was dancin'—jump around a little bit." Informants emphasized that it was not only the good dancers who danced, but everyone. One said, "they would just go through the performance—why they couldn't step dance." Another made the revealing comment that "any of us fellers that didn't dance, well, we danced just the same. We wouldn't dance at all if we wasn't dressed."

Besides the singing and dancing, the belsnickles engaged in other "foolish" antics. Some might pretend to be drunk and stagger around the room, while others simply jumped around wildly. Those dressed as women engaged in an exaggerated caricature of feminine behavior—"they was waltzin' around just like women."

A degree of sexual license also characterized the behavior of some of the bolder belsnickles, who would do such otherwise forbidden and daring things as sitting on a woman's knee and hugging her, "just to torment her," or making "as if they was going to kiss the girls."

The children's fears of the belsnickles were not assuaged by their parents, but reinforced still further by the use of the belsnickles as bogeymen during the rest of the year. Many of my informants recalled the threat, "the belsnickles will get you" to curtail their misbehavior as children. Two men in the community are remembered for teasing children by dressing up in long black oilskin coats and belsnickle masks when they saw them coming and scaring the wits out of them. The belsnickles themselves played upon the fears of the children as well as the anticipations of the adults by blowing their horns for several nights before Christmas Eve, "to show the belsnickles was around" and frighten the children. It required special boldness for a child to venture out of the house after dark around Christmas. Almost all my informants were teenagers themselves before they found out that the belsnickles were local people dressed up in costumes.

The net effect of all this was that when the belsnickles entered the house on Christmas Eve, the children were petrified. They took refuge under a table or in a cupboard, or hung onto their parents so "you couldn't tear 'em away." This, then, is the frame of mind in which they faced the belsnickles in their role as inquisitors.

Any of the belsnickles could act as inquisitors, and all those who were willing to use their voices did so in one or another of the houses they visited. The inquisitors would call the children of the house forward and ask if they had been good during the past year. Naturally, the children always replied in the affirmative—"we're good, we're good"—whereupon the inquisitors made them promise that they would be good during the coming year as well, and rewarded them with candy which was carried on their belsnicking rounds for this purpose.

Source: "Belsnicking in a Nova Scotia Community" by Richard Bauman in *Western Folklore* XXXI (4) (October 1972), 234-236.

Chile

Pesebres

The *pesebres* (crèches) of Chile take a variety of forms, created by folk artists of several villages. Some are carved of wood; others, of clay. Entire villages may be assembled, with mirrors for lakes and sawdust-mound hills. The more elaborate of these may be displayed in homes whose owners leave their doors open so that passersby can enter and enjoy worship briefly at the Niño Lindo. Those who stop may be treated with refreshments.

Source: *Folklore Chileno* by Oreste Plath. Santiago: Nascimento, 1969, pp. 351-352.

Czechoslovakia

The Christmas season

The merriment of Christmas begins December 6 in Czechoslovak communities, when Sv. Milulaš, also known as St. Nicholas or Santa Claus, arrives at the appointed place, accompanied by the angel and devil, both in costume.

One by one, the children are asked if they have said their prayers and if they have been good or bad children. The angel busily makes notes; the devil might rattle his chain. The child may be rewarded with candy or cookies from the angel. For everyone, it is a time of celebration and joy, a happy get-together.

The ensuing days are busy times of housecleaning and the baking of Christmas cookies and goodies. The Christmas tree is cut and decorated with sufficient secrecy that small children will find it a Christmas Eve surprise.

The Christmas Eve meal may begin with a prayer of thanks and a sharing of honey and *oplatky*, a thin wafer eaten as a symbol of family love and forgiveness for past quarrels or differences. Soup may be lentil, dumpling or fish. The dinner may include breaded fish, either mashed potatoes or potato salad, peas or variations, followed by fruit, Christmas cookies, kolaches or apple strudel.

Afterward, the gaily lighted and decorated Christmas tree, with the star or dove on top and presents and a creche beneath, is unveiled, a carol may be sung, and presents are unwrapped. The family may attend midnight Mass or Christmas morning services.

The traditional Christmas dinner features roast goose, dumplings, and sauerkraut. It is a time for visiting friends and exchanging Christmas greetings.

Source: *Czechoslovak Culture* compiled by Pat Martin. Iowa City, Iowa: Penfield Press, 1989, p. 117.

Czech Christmas meals

In Czechoslovakia the housewife begins her preparations for the Christmas meals fully one week beforehand. Everywhere there is bustle and joyful activity; the village is fragrant with the odor of delicious cooking. In most households the Christmas Eve meal is a meatless one and the day one of fasting. Even the children are urged to abstain from food and promised that, if they do, they will see the golden pigs at supper. It is hoped that their enjoyment of the supper outweighs their disappointment when the golden pigs turn out to be merely the flickerings of the lighted candles on walls and ceilings. Carp is the traditional Christmas Eve dish. It must be bought alive and kept alive until the moment when it is to be cleaned and cooked. Typical Christmas Eve and Christmas Day menus in Czechoslovakia are as follows:

Christmas Eve Supper

Fish Chowder
Fried Fish (hot)
Carp in black sauce (cold)
Pear barley gruel with mushrooms
Vdolky (see recipe)
Coffee, nuts, apples
Decorated ginger bread cookies

Christmas Dinner

Giblet soup with noodles
Roast goose with dumplings and sauerkraut, or
Roast suckling pig
Vanocka (braided coffee cake)
Kolacky
Coffee, nuts, apples
Decorated ginger bread cookies

Vdolky

Butter, size of an egg
2 cups milk
2 eggs
flour
1 cake yeast

pinch of salt
pinch of mace

Melt the butter in warm milk. Add the eggs (beaten), the salt, the mace and yeast and enough white flour to make a soft dough. Stir the mixture until very smooth; let it rise. Then put it on a floured board, roll it out and shape into good sized biscuits; let them rise. Then bake on both sides. Spread with prune marmelade and cottage cheese or thick sweet cream. Instead of baking the Vdolky, they may be fried in deep fat.

To make the prune marmalade, wash and boil one pound of prunes; then stone the prunes and press through a sieve. Boil the pulp awhile with a small piece of butter, grated lemon peel, cinnamon and one cup of sugar. If too thick, add a little prune juice or water. Let cool before rising.

Source: *Foreign Festival Customs* by Marian Schibsby & Hanny Cohrsen. New York: American Council for Nationalities Service, 1974, pp. 60-61.

Czechoslovakia (Bohemia)

"Generous Day" (Christmas Eve)

On the "Generous Day" itself the family usually spends the day packing presents, decorating the tree, always a real fir tree, with glass and tin-foil decorations, sweets, gilt chains, candles, and recently imitation snow. The children are encouraged to fast during the day by the promise of seeing the evening a "golden piglet" (zlaté prasátko)—a beautiful creature which is supposed to be seen only by children who have fully observed the fast—while the housewife prepares the main courses of the evening meal: fish soup, carp in sweet sauce with steamed dumplings, pork cutlets with potato salad. By dusk most families begin the meal around a table decorated with greenery, candles, ornamental chains and the like and at an opportune moment the sound of a bell announces that "Little Jesus" (Ježišek) has made his brief visit to the house. The family then assembles at the brightly lit tree, and under it are the wrapped presents and often a Nativity scene carved in wood or made of hardboard. Many of these, especially in country districts, have very beautiful traditional designs and may be very old. Some of the oldest of these are owned by provincial communities, and are displayed in the local church. Before unwrapping the gifts "brought by Little Jesus" many families will spend a short time lighting "sparklers" (priskavky) which are already hanging on the tree. They also sing carols and admire the tree. The evening ends late after continued feasting and rejoicing over presents.

Attending Midnight Mass is a living tradition even among non-believers; churches are filled to capacity, especially where there is a good organ and celebrated singers taking part in the mass, and every year the main radio station broadcasts a mass by the 18th century Czech composer Jan Ryba, based on folk carols.

Source: "Christmas in Bohemia—Traditional and Present Day" by Miriam Jelinkova in *Lore and Language* 2 (January 1970), 9-10. (See this article for Christmas superstitions also.)

Denmark

The Jule-nissen, in Ribe, c. 1880

I do not know how the forty years I have been away have dealt with "Jule-nissen," the Christmas elf of my childhood. He was pretty old then, gray and bent, and there were signs that his time was nearly over. So it may be that they have laid him away. I shall find out when I go over there next time. When I was a boy we never sat down to our Christmas Eve dinner until a bowl of rice and milk had been taken up to the attic, where he lived with the marten and its young, and kept an eye upon the house—saw that everything ran smoothly. I never met him myself, but I know the house-cat must have done so. No doubt they were well acquainted; for when in the morning I went in for the bowl, there it was, quite dry and licked clean, and the cat purring in the corner. So, being there all night, he must have seen and likely talked with him.

The Nisse was of the family, as you see, very much of it, and certainly not to be classed with the cattle. Yet they were his special concern; he kept them quiet, and saw to it, when the stable-man forgot, that they were properly bedded and cleaned and fed. He was very well known to the hands about the farm, and they said that he looked just like a little old man, all in gray and with a pointed red nightcap and long gray beard. He was always civilly treated, as he surely deserved to be, but Christmas was his great holiday, when he became part of it, indeed, and was made much of.

The sparrows' sheaf

The very sparrows that burrowed in the straw thatch, and did it no good, were not forgotten. A sheaf of rye was set out in the snow for them, so that on that night at least they should have shelter and warmth unchallenged, and plenty to eat. At all other times we were permitted to raid their nests and help ourselves to a sparrow roast, which was by long odds the greatest treat we had.

The stable animals kneel

All the animals knew perfectly well that the holiday had come, and kept it in their way. The watch-dog was unchained. In the midnight hour on the Holy Eve the cattle stood up in their stalls and bowed out of respect and reverence for Him who was laid in a manger when there was no room in the inn, and in that hour speech was given them, and they talked together. Claus, our neighbor's man, had seen and heard it, and every Christmas Eve I meant fully to go and be there when it happened; but always long before that I had been led away to bed, a very sleepy boy.

A fortnight of celebration

A whole fortnight we kept it. Real Christmas was from Little Christmas Eve, which was the night before the Holy Eve proper, till New Year. Then there was a week of supplementary festivities before things slipped back into their wonted groove. That was the time of parties and balls. The great ball of the year was on the day after Christmas. Second Christmas Day we called it, when all the quality attended at the club-house, where the Amtmand and the Burgomaster, the Bishop and the Rector of the Latin School, did the honors and received the people. That was the grandest of the town functions.

When we were not dancing or playing games, we literally ate our way through the two holiday weeks. Pastry by the mile did we eat, and general indigestion brooded over the town when it emerged into the white light of the new year. At any rate it ought to have done so. It is a prime article of faith with the Danes to this day that for any one to go out of a friend's house, or of anybody's house, in the Christmas season without partaking of its cheer, is to ''bear away their Yule,'' which no one must do on any account.

Christmas Eve, c. 1880

When it had had time to settle and all the kitchen work was done, Father took his seat at the end of the long table, with all the household gathered about, the servants included and the baby without fail, and read the story of The Child: ''And it came to pass in those days,'' while Mother hushed the baby. Then we sang together ''A Child is Born in Bethlehem,'' which was the simplest of our hymns, and also the one we children loved best, for it told of how in heaven we were to walk to church

> On sky-blue carpets, star-bedeckt,

We had no piano,—that was a luxury in those days,—and Father was not a singer, but he led on bravely with his tremulous bass and we all joined in, Ane the cook and Maria the housemaid furtively wiping their eyes with their aprons, for they were good and pious folk and this was their Christmas service. So we sang the ten verses to end, with their refrain ''Hallelujah! hallelujah,'' that always seemed to me to open the very gates of Yule.

And it did, literally; for when the last hallelujah died away the door of the spare room was flung wide and there stood the Christmas tree, all shining lights, and the baby was borne in, wide-eyed, to be the first, as was proper; for was not this The Child's holiday? Unconsciously we all gave way to those who were nearest Him, who had most recently come from His presence and were therefore in closest touch with the spirit of the holiday. So, when we joined hands and danced around the tree, Father held the baby, and we laughed and were happy as the little one crowed his joy and stretched the tiny arms toward the light.

The Wandering Jew passes at Christmas

Light and shadow, joy and sorrow, go hand in hand in the world. While we danced and made merry, there was one near for whom Christmas was but grief and loss. Out in the white fields he went from farm to farm, a solitary wanderer, the folklore had it, looking for plough or harrow on which to rest his weary limbs. It was the Wandering Jew, to whom this hope was given, that, if on that night of all in the year he could find some tool used in honest toil over which the sign of the cross had not been made, his wanderings would be at an end and the curse depart from him, to cleave thenceforward to the luckless farmer. He never found what he sought in my time. The thrifty husbandman had been over his field on the eve of the holiday with a watchful eye to his coming. When the bell in the distant church tower struck the midnight hour, belated travellers heard his sorrowful wail as he fled over the heath and vanished.

Source: *The Old Town* by Jacob A. Riis. New York: MacMillan, 1909, pp. 79-83, 92-96.

A feast for the invisible ones

Good fare had also to be provided for the invisible beings present especially on Christmas Night; so at many places it was the custom to leave the Christmas table as it was overnight, or perhaps for several days, to enable the invisible ones to help themselves. For the familiar spirit of the farm, the goblin, they made special provision, putting out a dish of porridge with a lump of butter in the middle. The goblin was the sponsor of the luck of the farm and in earlier times had nothing to do with the Christmas presents. The modern conception of the Christmas troll who comes with presents for the children is a later development from books, under the influence of foreign conceptions of Santa Claus, pere Noël, etc.

Source: *Danish Peasant Culture*. Copenhagen: Danish National Museum, 1955, p. 64.

Christmas, c. 1910

Now Christmas in Denmark is something widely different from what we know in America, the chief celebration centering around the night of the twenty-fourth of December, called Juleaften. On that night all stores will close at four or five o'clock and the family will gather around the huge table where the roasted goose stuffed with apples and prunes, is served. When the meal was finished, we would occupy ourselves with nuts and almonds, while Father and Mother retired to the drawing-room, where the huge Christmas-tree was being arranged, illuminated by numerous candles. Of course we would try to spy upon the preparations by peeping through the keyhole, which mostly proved ineffective, since Father had locked the door and put a cloth over the keyhole.

After what to us seemed an interminable waiting, our parents opened the door widely and ushered us in to the magnificently adorned tree. It teemed with lighted candles, angels' hair, cotton-snow, and flags, and from every bough were dangling gilded walnuts and pine-cones, small baskets filled with chocolate-drops and almonds, and the extremely toothsome marcipan.

Next the gifts were distributed. They lay under the tree, each present wrapped in paper or a box upon which was written the name of the receiver. When we had inspected our presents and played a while with them, we began to dance around the Juleträ. The dance consisted in forming a ring by seizing each other's hands and walking slowly around the tree, singing the old Christmas hymn: ''A child was born in Bethlehem,'' or ''Glade Jul,'' which latter one is sung to the old German tune ''Silent Night.''

When we had danced around the tree for about ten minutes we

began to plunder it, for, as it is told in the old song of Christmas, "First we must see it; afterwards we must eat it." But the tree was duly restored with all its fillings the ensuing day and remained thus till Christmas was considered a past thing for this time, which usually was on or about the sixth of January. In the country, however, they used to celebrate Jul till well into the middle of January. It being now close to midnight, we took a light supper, sitting up for some time afterwards. Christmas morning, we went to church early. No business was transacted during the two Christmas days, though all the theatres generally would open at four o'clock P.M. on the twenty-sixth offering a gala performance.

Let me not forget to tell that children celebrate the day before Christmas (December 23), which is called Lille Juleaften (Little Christmas Eve). On that day most baking is done, and in the country they begin the celebrations then.

Source: *When I Was a Boy in Denmark* by H. Trolle-Steenstrup. Boston: Lothrop, Lee & Shepard Co., 1923, pp. 202-205.

Estonia

Estonian Christmas Kringle

Kringle - Coffee Cake

2	yeast cakes
1 1/2	cup sifted flour
3/4	cup scalded milk lukewarm
	Grated rind of 1 lemon
2	tsp. vanilla
2	eggs separated
3/4	cup sugar
1	tsp. salt
3/4	cup soft butter
1/4	cup sugar
3 1/2	cup sifted flour
2	cups white raisins
1/2	cup thin sliced blanched almonds
	Confectioner's sugar

Put yeast cake and 1/4 cup sugar into a bowl and stir until mixture becomes liquid and smooth. Stir in alternately small amounts 1 1/2 cups flour and cooled milk. Beat until smooth. Sprinkle lightly with flour and set in warm place until bubbles form. Add lemon rind and vanilla. Put egg yolks into a bowl add sugar gradually and beat until light and foamy, stir in salt and butter. Add to first mixture. Stir in 1 cup of flour, beat until smooth. Beat egg whites until stiff but moist, fold into dough. Add remaining flour a little at a time. Beat until smooth and elastic. Press down in bowl. Sprinkle lightly with flour and set in warm place to rise. When double in bulk, add raisins and mix in thoroughly. Turn onto a floured board, form into a long strip. Place on greased cookie sheet. With hands continue to shape and stretch dough. When ends extend 6 or 7 inches beyond pan twist them together. Then attach ends to middle of the strip of dough. This gives two circles joined in the center. Brush with cream or milk. Sprinkle generously with sliced almonds. Set in warm place and let rise for 30 or 40 minutes. Bake in 325 degree oven for 40-45 minutes. Sprinkle with confectioner's sugar. Cool on cake rack. Let stand one day before cutting.

Source: *Foreign Festival Customs* by Marian Schibsby & Hanny Cohrsen. New York: American Council for Nationalities Service, 1974, p. 69.

Finland

The Christmas Goat, Joulupukki

Along comes Christmas Eve, and here the fun begins. Traditional activities are carried out in the home. There's the dinner, a special one that includes lipeä kala. This is horrible-smelling codfish, but if you can get close enough to eat it, you become addicted. There is also a Christmas ham and a special rice pudding in which, somewhere, there is *one* almond. The person who gets it is lucky in more ways than one. Not only does [he] or she get a special treat, but the year ahead will be filled with good fortune. (At one time it meant that if the recipient was a young girl, she would be married within the year, but this may not be considered all that lucky anymore.)

Christmas Eve is the time when the gifts are given out—and who does that? The Christmas goat, that's who. Yes, the Christmas goat. He is the descendant of an ancient pagan symbol, who somehow got promoted from the personification of the Devil's emissary to a jovial, boisterous figure in a shaggy fur coat who makes his appearance on a bicycle. His name is Joulupukki (Joulu is the word for Christmas, pronounced "Yule-oo"). Sometimes he appears as the familiar, white-bearded Santa Claus, who may arrive in a sled drawn by real, rather than airborne, reindeer. In either case, he goes through the rigamarole of asking if the children have been good and hands out the presents their parents have thoughtfully provided in secret.

Source: *Of Finnish Ways* by Ainu Rajanen. Minneapolis: Dillon, 1981, pp. 167-168.

"Little Christmases," dried cod, and "professional Santas"

But before that, 'Little Christmases' have begun. Every office, every club, society or group of any kind has its party, and some people find themselves obliged to attend about ten of these 'Little Christmases' in the space of two or three weeks. Once the real Christmas arrives, they are so sated with celebration that they accept without demur the austerity of some of their Christmas fare. For now they deliberately maintain the traditions which belong to the days when all were equal in poverty. Thus the Christmas food which was festive a century or more ago seems almost penal today. But still the Finns insist on eating on Christmas Eve a variety of dried cod whose chief characteristic is an all-pervading and particularly revolting smell, boiled rice, once a rare imported delicacy, and small prune pasties. The meal is fortunately redeemed by the excellent pork, interpolated between cod and rice, from the pig traditionally killed at Christmas. The less traditional side of the festival is represented by the professional Father Christmases, who advertise themselves in the newspapers as 'good' and 'reliable', and able to visit any number of homes on Christmas Eve. The less reliable among them have a tendency to drink deep on all their calls, with the result that by midnight the police stations in the larger towns are said to be full of merry gentlemen, all with long white beards, and all clad in scarlet robes.

Source: *The Finns and Their Country* by Wendy Hall. New York: Paul S. Eriksson, 1967, p. 59.

France

La Veillée du Petit Jésus (the Watch Night for the Baby Jesus) in Besançon, c. 1900

In France, the gift-day is on New Year's Day, Christmas being toy-day.

With us, the little Infant Jesus comes down the chimney in every home on that cold and starry night, and fills with bonbons, oranges, and toys, the little shoes—and sometimes big ones, too—which have been put in the fireplace the night before.

That night before—*la veillée du Petit Jésus,* the Watch Night—is perhaps sweeter in my memory than Christmas Day itself. After supper, all the family gathered in the drawing-room, in front of the chimney, blazing with a jolly wood fire and alone lighting the whole room.

The smell of a fresh green fir-tree floated in the air. The tree was there, behind a screen in the corner, but we were not permitted to look at it before morning. We were allowed, though, to sit on the carpet, oh, joy! while the grown-ups were on chairs. My dear old Aunt Fanny came from Montbeliard, my Uncle Louis—the old General—from Algiers, my eldest sister and her captain husband from Belfort, and my tall cousin Eugene, a young architect from Paris. All brought news and sweetmeats from those far-away places.

"And the Blessed Virgin went back to the altar, taking back her halo and her crown of Flowering Thorns."

"Oh, Nou-nou, it's a sweet story!" I exclaimed. "Give us just another one before going to bed, please!"

But what a noise!

Piff! Puff! Jim! Boom! Crack-crack!—the whole fireplace seemed to burst gaily!

"*La buche! La tronche de Nöel* (The Yule Log)," Goby and I screamed together.

And everybody, even Mother, knelt on the floor, picking up chocolates, bonbons, sweets, thrown out by the Yule Log—a big hollow branch of oak filled up with sweets and so arranged that the heat releases a spring and explodes a little powder. This had been placed on the fire by Cousin Eugene, unnoticed, during the telling of the stories. One may keep what one picks up, so everybody hurries, scrambles, and laughs.

Midnight! The bells toll madly, and the Watch is over, with its wonderful tales.

My family goes to the service of the Protestant Church, Nou-nou to the Cathedral, and we little ones, we go to bed, we are so tired and it is terribly cold outside.

Christmas morning in Besançon, c. 1900

The next morning, Christmas Morning, what a rush to the chimney.

"Ohé! A jumping-jack, Goby; a jumping-jack!"

"And I a Punchinello!"

"And a shepherd for me!"

"And I've got the shepherdess!"

"We'll make them play the comedy!" This we said together.

"And, look! A little earthen pot to play cooking with!"

"And I—I have the little stove!"

Nou-nou was there, looking and laughing with us.

Mother came in.

"Now, turn around and look!" she said, as the screen was put aside.

"*Oh, qu'il est beau, qu'il est beau!*"

That was the Christmas Tree which our eldest sisters had arranged for us, with silver and gold paper garlands, bright stars, globes, icicles, trinkets of all kinds, apples, pears, oranges, nuts, crackers, all hung from its bountiful branches. Hundreds of tiny candles were on it, ready to light it up in the evening. Our eyes were fascinated.

La Crèche Bisontine, a folk puppet play of Besançon

The Christmas joys were not over with Christmas Day. Far from it! The festival lasted until New Year's Day.

A quite special treat was and is still reserved for the little folks of Besançon—and the grown-ups, too: "La Crèche Bisontine," an incomparable puppet-show, a popular drama in the Besançon dialect, all about the birth of the little Infant Jesus. It is played every year, and has been so ever since the Middle Ages. The fancy of the popular tradition places the birth of the Divine Child as it were in Besançon itself, in a stable upon the hills.

Still, I see the tiny theatre, packed with people of all kinds: children poor and rich, soldiers, wealthy burghers, chimney-sweeps, bakers, even priests and nuns, all chatting, laughing, full of expectancy. Three traditional knocks on the floor of the stage, and the curtain rises.

A formidable "Ha!" resounds from the audience.

My two eyes and two ears are not enough to enable me to see and hear all that is going on.

There is the Star of Besançon, above the well-known mountains, the city asleep at their feet, the house of Barbisier—a legendary citizen, and, in the rocks of the citadel, the cell of Brother Blaise, a legendary hermit. Now come the angels of Besançon, calling the shepherds of the country, showing them the Star, and telling them the glorious news. Barbisier appears, waked by the singing, and wakes up his wife Naitouère. Both call to their neighbor, Verly. They all decide to go to the hermit and ask him about that wonderful Star. On the way, they meet Brother Danapoio, another monk, full of wisdom and mischief. Brother Blaise, looking through a telescope, tells them of the coming of the Three Kings, led by the Star. Then soon appear all the good people of Besançon: Sister Angèlique, Lawyer Bartolo, a coughing woman (*la tousseuse*), a potter, a doctor, a mischievous chimney-sweep, a milkman, a coquettish woman, and some soldiers. All that colorful and noisy crowd goes to pay its adoration to the Divine Babe in the stable up on the hill.

In the second act, a dreadful thing happens. The vain woman—who disturbs everybody and seeks only to be admired—is taken away by the Devil, who appears suddenly in a huge flame. The audience shrieks in horror at the top of its voice, I, more than any one else. Then arrive the Three Kings, with their gifts of gold, perfume, and fruits. One cannot imagine the funny meeting and dialogue between those Oriental Kings and the good people of Besançon; even with the ox and the ass. Nothing can translate it. The whole theatre is shaken with laughter. The children stamp with wild joy.

Then follows, in the third act, a beautiful sermon in the Church of La Madeleine, with the whole population listening to it, and, finally, a gorgeous procession across the bridge.

Oh, those puppets, so exquisitely and humanly grotesque! They really were alive for me, and when, later on, I heard that they had been replaced by real persons as actors, though all from Besançon, I felt a deep mourning in my heart.

Source: *When I Was a Girl in France* by Georgette Beuret. Boston: Lothrop, Lee & Shepard Co., 1916, pp. 155-156, 158-160.

Gambia and Senegal

The Lantern Festival

In contemporary urban Senegal and Gambia (Senegambia), Lanterns, also known as the Lantern festival or Fanal is held varyingly on Christmas Eve, during the Christmas-New Year holiday, or Ramadan. Lanterns is a secular festival that takes place in these different holy days because of historical circumstances, government regulations, and competitive activities. For example, during slavery Christmas was the time when slaves were permitted the leisure to entertain themselves and their masters. After Emancipation in Senegal and Gambia, there was no impetus to change the holiday, and a general festive spirit prevailed during the season. While Lanterns takes place during Christmas or Ramadan, it is not essentially religious.

Lanterns is characterized by the building of lanterns, which are most often constructed on a wooden frame and covered with elaborately patterned cut paper resembling fine filigree. They are traditionally illuminated by candles placed inside them. Lanterns can range in length from thirty centimeters to six meters. Sailing ships have been a traditional shape, although model houses, and more recently airplanes, cars, mosques, and other edifices from contemporary urban environments, have appeared. Although the earliest record of the style of the lanterns describes a boat, Hassan Nije indicates that the original form was a house, built in imitation of colonial houses. Other reports suggest that no one form is more important or traditional then others.

The lanterns are paraded in the streets and ultimately offered to important local residents for a monetary reward. Work associations formed for this purpose compete with one another to produce the most beautiful structure. These parades have now developed into formalized competitions, with monetary and achievement awards presented by government agencies.

Gamble claims that today the work associations that build lanterns are often largely Wolof and other reports from Senegal also associate the Wolof with the festival.

Over the past century the structure of the festival has changed only slightly. Today, moneyed individuals, political parties, local industries, and even tourists have replaced the colonial patrons. There are usually two types of lanterns. In one, individual lanterns are made in a variety of forms and are paraded by their owners, who hold then in the hand. The second type is the monumental lantern built by an organization of young people, which is either carried about by about eight men or placed on a wheeled platform that is pulled along the ground. It requires considerable planning and preparation. Work on it usually begins a month before Christmas Eve. Although most lanterns appear during the Christmas-New Year season, a major political rally or important national holiday may prompt the building and parading of a new one.

Source: ''The Lantern Festival in Senegambia'' by Judith Bettelheim in *African Arts* XVIII (2) (February 1985), 50-53.

Germany

Christmas markets

Christmas markets are a special feature of the Advent season. They sell presents, decorations, and Christmas foods. Some have developed into a fair with music, puppet shows, plays, and foodstalls selling such treats as mulled wine, sausages, roast chestnuts, pancakes, toffee apples, and balloons. St. Nicholas may grace the fair as well.

Knocking nights (Klöpfelnächte) in Bavaria

During the three Thursday evenings before Christmas, children may knock on doors for treats. They come masked, cracking whips, ringing cowbells, and throwing pebbles or beans at the windows to make a racket. Their chant begins "Klopfan . . . Klopfan . . ." "Knock . . . Knock . . ." In the Bavarian Forest the singers hold an upturned pitchfork in the doorway, on which the householder should impale some treat.

Rauschgoldengel

The gold foil angel that originated in Nuremberg is a popular Christmas symbol throughout Germany. Dollmaker Melchior Hauser is supposed to have originated the doll during the Thirty Years' War at the instructions of his deliriously ill daughter. Some say he made it after her death to comfort his bereaved wife. The doll has a pleated gold foil skirt, gold wings, and long golden hair.

Der Heilige Abend (Christmas Eve)

The Christmas tree is decorated behind closed doors, then a bell is rung to admit the children. The tree may be trimmed with candies, *Lebkuchen* (cookies cut into shapes of cars, men, trees, and so on). A variety of Christmas decorations are hung. Woven straw ornaments, painted wooden figures, glass baubles, toy birds, pinecones, and candles. Presents may be under the tree or on a special present table (*der Gabentisch*). Each person has a special decorated cardboard plate (*der bunte Teller*) holding candies and cookies just for that individual. The Christmas Story may be read before the tree and carols sung before the gifts are opened.

Juleklapp

Formerly the Christmas gift opening would begin with *Juleklapp*. A window or door would be opened and a present thrown into the room with the loud shout, "KLAPP!" The present was wrapped in many layers, each labeled for a certain member of the family. The person owning the inner layer would get the gift.

Source: *German Festivals and Customs* by Jennifer M. Russ. London: Oswald Wolff, 1982, pp. 16, 18, 24. (See this source for much more on German Christmas customs.)

Dresdner Christstollen (Dresden Christmas Stollen)

> 500 gr. raisins, 125 gr. currants, 100 gr. candied lemon peel, 100 gr. candied orange peel, 250 gr. almonds, 2 liqueur glasses of rum, 1 kg. flour, 120 gr. yeast, 350 gr. sugar, 1/4 l. milk, 375 gr. butter, 125 gr. butter for brushing on afterwards, 100 gr. icing sugar.

Pour the rum over the raisins, currants, finely chopped candied peel, and the peeled and chopped almonds. Stand overnight—covered. Crumble the yeast, and mix with the luke-warm milk. Add to the flour together with the soft butter and sugar, and knead into a smooth dough. Cover and leave to rise in a warm place for 20 minutes. Add the fruit that has been steeped in the rum. Knead thoroughly once again, and let the dough (covered) rise for another 30 minutes. Knead once more. Roll out on a surface covered with a little flour to make an oval slab about 3 cm. thick. Make a groove with a large rolling pin along the length of the centre of the dough, and then fold one half over the other. Let the Stollen rise for another 15 minutes on a greased baking tray. Bake for 20 minutes in an oven pre-heated to 200 degrees—and then for 70 Minutes at 175 degrees. If the Stollen gets too brown, cover with some greaseproof paper. Immediately after baking, brush the Stollen with melted butter and sprinkle thickly with icing sugar.

Source: *Christmas in Germany* by Josef Ruland. Translated by Timothy Neville. Bonn: Hohwacht, 1978.

Possible origins of the Christmas tree

The most popular idea nowadays is, that the custom is a remnant of the old tree-worship. Others believe it to be of Christian origin. The 24th of December is the day of Adam and Eve. From there to the tree bearing the fruit of knowledge it is not far. In the New Testament, Jesus is often called a branch of the root of David. These pictures were familiar to all classes in the Middle Ages. Some sought for the origin in the seven-branched candlestick of the Jewish temple, but not one of these assumptions is well founded. In legend we also find many tales relating to it. . . . Wherever you trace the origin of the Christmas-tree outside Germany, you will find that it has been introduced from the Fatherland. Up to the year 1840 Great Britain did not know it. It was the Prince Consort Albert of Sachsen-Coburg who brought it to the Court of St. James. From there it slowly found its way through the aristocracy and the wealthier merchant classes to the whole of the city of London. Nowadays the custom of having a Christmas-tree is very common all over England.

Christmas tree legends

One Christmas Eve, Luther, so the story goes, was wandering across country. Clear and pure the night sky arched overhead, bright with thousands of stars. The picture impressed itself stongly on his mind, and when he came home, he immediately went out and cut a fir-tree in a neighbouring wood, and covering it with small candles, placed it in the room, in order to give his little ones an idea of the nocturnal heavens, with their countless lights, from whence Jesus descended to the earth. But this legend is not yet a century old. It probably took its source from a picture by Schwerdtgeburth—"Luther taking Leave of his Family." Here the artist shows Luther's family around the Christmas-tree, but he has as little historical foundation for this as Scheffel has when he introduces a Christmas-tree into his *Ekkehard* in the tenth century.

In Lindenau, a suburb of Leipsic, a legend is told that the Christmas-tree was introduced there during the Thirty Years' War from Sweden. In the autumn of 1632, the battle of Lutzen had been fought, in which Gustavus Adolphus, King of Sweden, had been killed. For many months, wounded soldiers of the victorious Swedish army were quartered in the neighbourhood. In Lindenau there was a Swedish officer who had been shot through the hand, and who was nursed with great kindness by the people in the Protestant village. His wound healed quickly, and at Christmas-time he was well enough to leave; but, before going back to his own country, he wanted to thank the people in some tangible way, and so he asked the clergyman to allow him to arrange a Christmas-festival as he used to know it in his own northern home. He got the permission, and there, for the first time, a fir-tree covered with lights was seen in the old church. This story, like many others, seems to have no historical foundation. It is simply a charming little legend.

The Christmas tree in 1604

The oldest record we have of a Christmas-tree dates from 1604, in Strasburg, in Alsace. It is a description, by a citizen of that town, of all the peculiar customs prevalent there at that time, to which he gave the title of *Memorabilia quaedam Argentorati observata.* After describing how the church-service is conducted, he gives an account of a children's festival: "At Christmas-time each child is taught a hymn or a verse from the Bible, which the boys have to say on Christmas Day, and the girls on New Year's Day, after saying which each child receives one, two, three, or four farthings, and sometimes a small book. As a contrast to this, the writer later on describes the Christmas in the house of the citizen:

"At Christmas, a fir-tree is put into the room, on which are hung roses made of coloured paper, apples, wafers, tinsel, sweetmeats, etc. Usually a square frame is made around it." It is impossible to decipher the writing after this, as the paper is quite torn.

So in 1604 the Christmas-tree (but without candles) was already quite common in Strasburg. The next mention we find of the subject comes from the same place. In the years 1642-1646, Professor Dannhauer, D.D., in Strasburg, wrote a very learned book, entitled *Catechismusmilch* (The Milk of the Catechism). The professor was an orthodox Protestant; the Church was to him everything, secular life nothing. He was indignant that the people of Strasburg celebrated Christmas in their home, instead of devoting all their time to religious rites, and so he says: "Among other trifles with which they commemorate Christmas-time often more than with the word of God, is the Christmas, or fir-tree, which is erected at home. It is hung with dolls and sweetmeats, and afterwards shaken and plundered. Whence this custom came I do not know; it is child's-play. It would be much better to direct the children towards the spiritual tree of Jesus Christ."

In Iceland there goes the tale that once upon a time at Mödhrufell, in the Eyjafiord, a mountain-ash stood, which had sprung from the blood of two innocent persons who had been executed there. Every Christmas-night this tree was found covered with lights, which even the strongest gale could not extinguish. These lights were its wonderful blossoms.

In German folk-lore we find the legend about the blossoming-trees of Christmas amongst the peasantry as far back as the fifteenth century up to the present day. The oldest mention of it dates back to the year 1426. It is a letter of the Bishop of Bamberg, which is at present in the Court Library of Vienna. About 1430, a chronicle-writer of Nüremberg tells us the story with all its particulars: "Not far from Nüremberg there stood a wonderful tree. Every year in the coldest season, in the night of Christ's birth, this tree put forth blossoms and apples, as thick as a man's thumb. At this time our native land is usually covered with deep snow for two months before and after, and cold winds sweep across it. Therefore it caused great wonderment that at this holy time the apples came forth; so that several reliable people come from Nüremberg and the neighbourhood, and watch throughout the night to see if it is true." A similar tree is found in a place near Bamberg. During the sixteenth, seventeenth, and eighteenth centuries we have many similar records in Germany.

Source: "German Christmas and the Christmas Tree" by Alexander Tille in *Folklore* III (December 1892), 165-171.

Ghana (Abron)

A Protestant service at Gumeré in 1961

I had two invitations for Christmas Eve 1961: one from the Protestant missionaries to see their play in the early evening, and the other from the few Catholic Abron in Diassenpa to Midnight Mass in the new church at Lomo, Oppong's home town.

The Sparks had borrowed the use of a small building on the main street of Gumeré and had spread a few sheets on a wire running around the small, mud-walled porch. Costumes were fashioned from other scrap material and scenery from assorted tables and chairs. The scene was appropriately tropical and there was no difficulty collecting palm fronds and banana leaves to finish the décor. The play was lit by flashlights held by a few members of the audience. Actors were recruited from among converts' children, and although it was their debut, they had memorized their lines well and performed eagerly. The curtain parted to reveal the biblical characters, all black and half adult size or less. Mary and Joseph, dressed in white (the Abron color for priests), came before the door of the inn and were refused shelter by the owner. They were soon led to the stable by a "kindly servant," obviously aware of his coming place in history. The Holy Child was born between the acts and when the curtains opened again, the Three Kings, their heads turbaned in missionary family towels, presented their gifts to the Child. The play, translated into Kolongo by the pastor, came off without a hitch and was enjoyed by the rather large crowd of curious spectators. Although unfamiliar with the Bible, most of the audience were regular patrons of the local movie theater set up in the back yard of Alhaje Baba, the rich Moslem chief of Gumeré. The gentle story of Christ's birth was an undoubted change from the blood-and-thunder Indian potboilers. The sincere acting of the children was better than the pompous mannerisms of the professionals, to which they were accustomed. After the brief play, Pastor Sparks delivered a brief Christmas sermon stressing that Christ was neither black nor white, but, like "Syrian traders, a man of mixed parentage." By the time the service had ended, it was dark. I groped around the village looking for my friends and finally found them in the house of the local carpenter, a Ghana

Brong with whom I had drunk palm wine and who had made shelves for me. This man had the habit of calling me master,'' a term the British in West Africa had taught Africans to use in addressing white men. I had often explained the meaning of the term and tried to get him to use my first name. One day, I broke his habit. After he had addressed me as master, I began to punch him on his arms. ''Do not beat me, master,'' he said, partially in jest but surprised that I would hit him. ''If I am your master,'' I replied, ''then you are my slave and I may beat you.'' He and his friends roared with laughter, and after that we were better friends and used first names with each other.

A Catholic Mass in Lomo in 1961

I managed to get everyone into the car and we set off down the road to Lomo. The Mass was to be celebrated in a bower erected outside the partially completed church. Behind the bower, a large bonfire burned in a pit. The villagers, mostly Catholic, had gathered to warm themselves. It was the coldest night I could remember and, dressed in a light shirt and shorts, I was grateful for a chance to warm myself. When midnight came, the group assembled in the temporary chapel. The priest, a stooped old man with a white beard and white robes, stepped forward and began the Mass, assisted by village boys and the local church choir. Part of the Mass was in Latin, the rest in Kolongo. A good part of the congregation joined in a high whine characteristic of Kolongo and Abron singing. Sitting in the crowd was an effort for me, as I grew colder and colder, but the strange sound of this transplanted Roman ceremony was fascinating. Not only was the language African, but the whole tone, even the Latin, had been unconsciously translated by the singers into the local idiom. Yet the Mass was alien. The total effect must have been startling even to the non-believers present, for it was a performance set apart from the world known to any of us.

The Mass ended at two o'clock in the morning. The crowd broke up and reassembled around the still smoldering fire.

A Christmas Day masquerade in Tabgne in 1961

I arrived at Tabgne, near Diassenpa, at four o'clock to find a carnival in full progress. It was Christmas Day, and a time of celebration. The cooler winds of evening brought the people out into the market place and some drummers were performing. Men dressed in rags were dancing for the growing crowd. They were moving rapidly, jerking their bodies back and forth in a grotesque manner that looked like a cross between sexual intercourse and epilepsy. Occasionally, one of the dancers shouted an obscenity at the crowd. This was greeted with much laughter. As the drumming grew more intense, one of the dancers jumped on the back of another and forced him into a crouching position. They then began to gyrate together, with the first man pressing his midsection against the buttocks of the other. Then a third dancer jumped on the first and soon there was a line of men front to back, all pulsating one against the other. This time there was no ambiguity in their movement. The audience went wild, screaming approval and encouragement. The dance had become one big sexual joke, enjoyed by the participants and the onlookers together. Then, from another part of the village, two dancers appeared on enormous stilts. They wore cloth masks covered with red beads. Each step they took on their ten-foot-high stilts covered a couple of yards. As soon as they got within range of the drums, their steps fell in with the rhythm. The crowd, which had been watching the other dancers, gathered around. The stilt dancers came forward, moved toward each other, and with a halting grace performed a circle dance on the inside of the crowd. Their steps became more daring and their bodies moved so fluidly that I was sure that one would topple over, but they had complete control over their movements. Finally, one and then the other did a complete backbend without losing his balance. Their bodies tipped backward until their heads touched the tops of the stilts behind them, and then, with a rapid jerk of their bodies, both men righted themselves. The other dancers joined the circle, and the men on stilts, who strode in and out among them like cranes dancing with a group of sparrows, continued their acrobatic display.

These men were Fon, from Dahomey. Most of the time, they ply less spectacular professions. Many of them were itinerant masons and housebuilders who traveled throughout the ex-French territories in search of work. On holidays, they became entertainers and were known far and wide. They performed in public hoping for gifts of money from the audience, but also out of the enjoyment that came with an unmatched skill. Fon dancers start their training when they are children. Beginning with short stilts, they graduate slowly upward until the master stilt dancers can top fifteen feet. They then exaggerate their own prowess and boast of experts who can top twenty-five feet and step over the roofs of houses. They also believe that they are protected from falling by a special magic. Their Christmas celebration was the finale of two days in which the influence of Western culture mingled with the mosaic of local custom.

Source: *When the Spider Danced: Notes from an African Village* by Alexander Alland, Jr. Garden City, N.Y.: Anchor Press/Doubleday, 1975, pp. 135-136.

Great Britain

The Christmas dinner

Turkey is now the Christmas favorite, though goose, chicken, and roast beef were recently popular. The Christmas pudding, made on Stir-Up Sunday, is eaten on this day. Within it lucky coins may be hidden. Mince pies are also a Christmas treat and are exchanged between households and sent to friends. The party is made festive by the pulling of Christmas crackers.

Source: *The Customs and Ceremonies of Britain* by Charles Kightly. London: Thames and Hudson, 1986, p. 74.

Greece

Christmas kalendas in Greece

Early on the morning of Christmas Eve, children go from house to house singing *kalendas,* or carols. Boys sing, accompanied by small triangles and clay drums. The children are given buns or nuts in reward.

The Christmas bread

Christopsomo, Christ-bread, is baked on Christmas Eve. The large, sweet loaves are ornamented with an emblem of the family's life or profession. Special buns are baked for the livestock. Those baked for the cattle are crumbed, salted, and fed the animals to protect against illness.

The Christmas feast

The table is set with the *Christopsomo* and a pot of honey. Nuts and dried fruits are scattered around these. The husband makes the sign of the cross over the loaf with the knife, wishes everyone "Chronia polla" and cuts the loaf. The family begins the meal with the honey, then lifts the table three times. White beans and *kollya* broth are traditional at Christmas. Each person should take three spoonfuls of each. In Thrace, nine different dishes must be served.

The Kallikantzaroi

The Kallikantzaroi emerge from the bowels of the earth for twelve days each year, from Christmas to Epiphany. During the rest of the year they chop away at the tree that supports the earth. When they are nearly done, the Christ is born and the tree regrows. The spirits come to the earth's surface in a fury. A child born at Christmas is in danger of turning into a Kallikantzaroi. It must be bound in garlic and its toenails can be singed, since it cannot become a Kallikantzaroi without toenails.

To protect against Kallikantzaroi, the lower jaw of a pig can be hung behind the door, a handful of salt or an old shoe can be thrown into the fireplace, or a tuft of tangled flax can be hung over the door. The Kallikantzaroi will stop to disentangle the flax and count the threads and be caught by sunrise. The hearth is kept burning day and night during this period to keep the Kallikantzaroi away. A huge Twelve-Day-Log is brought in on Christmas Eve and sprinkled with dried fruit. Wild asparagus, pine, thistle, and other plants that burst or make thick smoke when thrown on the fire are effective in driving away the demons. At the blessing of the waters on Epiphany the Kallikantzaroi scurry away, not to return until the following Christmas.

Source: *Greek Calendar Customs* by Geroge A. Megas. Athens: B. & M. Rhodis, 1963, pp. 27-32.

Hungary

Christmas Eve dinner

On Christmas Eve, as soon as the first star gleams in the sky, the Hungarian family sits down to an abundant, though meatless meal. Cabbage soup, fish, noodles, cakes shaped like horseshoes and filled with poppy seed or walnuts, twisted Christmas bread, "bobajka" or dumplings sprinkled with poppy seed and sugar, strudel and nuts are traditional dishes for this occasion. The gaiety and feasting continue till near midnight, when people flock to church to attend the Christmas mass.

"Mezes-Makos Metelt"

1 lb flour
6 large potatoes
1/2 tsp salt
1/4 lb butter
4 oz poppy seed
1/4 lb sugar
2 tbs honey

Boil the potatoes, then peel. Place them on a board and mash well with a fork. Add salt and flour, taking care the mixture does not become too stiff. Knead mixture carefully, then roll out thin. Cut into strips 2 x 1/2 inches in size. Place in a deep pan of boiling water. When strips float to the top, remove them with strainer. Place them in cold water for about one minute. Melt butter in a pan and when hot lay strips in butter. Place in hot oven for five minutes. Mix the poppy seed with sugar and honey and pour mixture over noodles just before serving. Serve hot.

Source: *Foreign Festival Customs* by Marian Schibsby & Hanny Cohrsen. New York: American Council for Nationalities Service, 1974, pp. 62-63.

Iceland

Yuletide Lads

The recent custom by children to put their shoe in the window shortly before Christmas in the hope that it will be filled with sweets. As far as can be determined, this custom reached Iceland in the 1920s, probably from Germany. It was first mentioned in print in a children's Christmas poem written about 1940, and during the last few decades it has become widespread.

It seems most commonly to begin on the day when the Icelandic "Santas," the so-called Yuletide Lads, start coming down from the mountains, either thirteen or nine days before Christmas.

The Icelandic Santas, or, as they are more properly called, Yuletide Lads, are of an origin totally different from that of St. Nicholas. They are first mentioned in the 17th-century "Ballad of Gryla" by the Rev. Stefan Olafsson of Vallanes (in the East), one of the best poets of his time. Gryla was an ogre supposed to feed on unruly children and was much used to scare them with. In the poem, the Yuletide Lads are said to be the offspring of Gryla and her husband, Leppaludi, and are presented as extremely inimical to children, just like their parents:

They begat the Yuletide Lads;
as giants they are tall,
an evil stock and threatening

to children, one and all.

Ideas about the appearance of the Yuletide Lads changed as well. At first, they were considered ogres, but later affected human shape, though still big, ugly, and clumsy-looking. After the turn of the century, however, they began more and more to assume the appearance of the international Santa, both in terms of stature, clothing, and disposition. They became friends of children, brought them gifts, sang to them, and told them stories. Directly and indirectly, the mercantile class probably aided and abetted the development by using them in their Christmas advertisements. This evolution began in the towns and reached the countryside much later.

The Yuletide Lads were considered to be either nine, which is the number used in an old nursery rhyme, or 13, an idea that first appeared in print in Jon Arnason's *Folk and Fairy Tales* in 1864. In either case, one of them is supposed to come down from the mountains each day and the last one on Christmas Eve. They return to the mountains in the same way, the first leaving on Christmas Day. For that pattern, the number 13 fits better, since the last one must then leave on Twelfth Night, the last day of Christmas.

Those of their names that first saw print in the *Folk and Fairy Tales* naturally won the most permanent acceptance. There, they are known as Sheep-Cot Clod, Gully Gawk, Shorty, Spoon Licker, Pot Scraper, Bowl Licker, Hem Blower, Skyr Gobbler (*skyr* is an Icelandic dairy product similar to yogurt), Sausage Swiper, Window Peeper, Door Sniffer, Meat Hook, and Candle Beggar.

There are dozens of other names or variations of names of the Yuletide Lads, and some may still await collection. Indubitably, children's poems about them, written by various hands during the past half a century or so, as well as the Christmas "Children's Hour" of the State Broadcasting Service, may be credited with the fact that the Icelandic Yuletide Lads have retained both their number and names and have not been entirely replaced by St. Nicholas.

Source: *Icelandic Feasts and Holidays: Celebrations, Past and Present* by Arni Bjornsson. Translated by May and Hallberg Hallmundson. Reykjavik: Iceland Review History Series, 1980, pp. 73-74.

Christmas in Iceland, c. 1910

Christmas was a landmark of time; a great many things were connected with it. This and that should be done before Christmas, clothes had to be made, stockings, shoes, and mittens. The week before was a busy one. The baking of bread, cakes, and pastry was a very important task and I was glad when I could be used as a hand for that, either for helping mother, or the cook. But sometimes it happened that the hands were too numerous, as there were more than I who liked to be that. If the wheat flour was scarce, grain had to be ground for adding to it. . . .

Tallow candles were always made before Christmas. Mother had to provide the church with candles, and those which were placed on the altar had to have a special shape. They were called "*kóngakerti*" (king's-candles), and were three at the top, but leaning together in one stem at the bottom. I think they were the symbol of the three holy kings who saw the Star of Bethlehem. The candles were molded in a very primitive way, when I first remember, but later on mother got a real mold. . . .

Meat and sausages were cooked and roasted, cakes and pastry had been baked and bread of several kinds. Every room on the farm had been cleaned thoroughly. A big washing had been done. "*Fátkrapurkurinn*" (dry weather for the poor) had not failed to come this year, to dry the washing also for those who could not change their clothes unless they could wash them and get them dry the very last day before Christmas. At last Christmas had arrived, as we children called it. Christmas Eve was the most holy night in the year. After six o'clock nothing unnecessary had to be worked. Everybody got at least one new garment, for none wanted to *klōa köttinn* (clothe the cat) as we said they did who had nothing new on that evening. If some piece or other of work had not been finished, for instance if you had knitted only the half of a stocking, you were teased by the saying that you had that about your neck (*aō hafa um hálsinn.* I presume the beginning of that was that the bosses used, formerly, to threaten their lazy workers with hanging their half-finished work about their necks to make them ashamed.

I had put on my new dress, new stockings, and new slippers, and so had Tóta and the other children. We were so happy, and every one seemed to be happy. Even the cat and the dogs looked to be more gentle than usual, though they got none of the new things.

We were all assembled for the domestic service. Father took the books from the book-case. The whole atmosphere was filled with sacred peace and joy. A Christmas hymn was sung, the Christmas gospel was read, and a sermon; prayers were said, another hymn was sung, followed by silent prayer. Father broke the silence by saying, "God give you all a good time and happy Christmas." The others repeated that, rising and shaking hands with each other. We children kissed father and mother.

Father went into the guest-room for a bundle of candles. Every one got one of them for his own use. The Christmas candle was no surprise to us, but all the same, every year it played a big part in the enjoyment of that evening. Every nook and corner had to be lighted that evening. The table was laid and dinner eaten. Later on coffee was served, with chocolate for us children and those who wanted it. Cakes and pastry were in abundance.

The remainder of the evening was devoted to Bible study. Each one took his own Bible and read for himself. The children, who were unable to read, went to mother, and she told them about the Holy Child and what they had to do in order to imitate Him, and that they had to thank Him for the Christmas.

We went early to bed Christmas Eve with the intention to get up early next morning. When we awoke Christmas day, Oläf had prepared the coffee and brought it into the baostofa together with sugar, cream, and cakes and pastry. We got our coffee in bed, and no doubt we were not cheated of the due share of cakes.

The grown people went to church, if the weather was fine. At eleven years of age I was allowed to go with the others. What impressed my mind most was to look at the lights in the three big chandeliers of the church. . . .

Young and old people from the neighborhood were frequent guests at Yule-tide on Kálfsstadir. The older played cards, the younger played a game called *Jólaleikur*. Girls and boys were separated. The girls sat down in the guest-room, the boys went into the hall, and the door was shut. Then one girl "gave" to each a boy of those who were in the hall. The door was opened and in came the oldest boy. He looked at the girls for a while, and they tried to bewilder him and tease him. He bowed in front of one of them. If he happened to be the right one "given" to that girl, she bowed again, but if not, she clapped her hands, and all the rest with her, and the boy was turned out of the room. The next boy came in, and this was repeated till they all had entered the room and tried their luck. They who bowed to the girls they had been "given" to did not go again and had to keep silent to the other boys about who their matches had been. Some of them failed several times and had always to wait till their turn came again, and were never allowed to bow to more than one each turn. The least successful was put up at auction, which was the greatest fun of all.

Next it was the girls turn to stand in the hall, and the boys sat in the room. The game was repeated several times. Dancing was one of the favorite amusements, the music being that of the harmonica. Singing was also frequently practised and there were a number of musical plays. There is much folk-lore connected with Christmas. The fairies and giants and giantesses in the vicinity of the farmers often paid them visits at this special time, always for doing some harm.

It was the custom in olden days for both young and old to go to church on Christmas Eve, except one, who generally was a young woman. When the others returned, which was not till the next morning, this woman had either disappeared altogether, died, or became mad or insane. It was difficult to get any to stay at home where this had often håppened.

From a farm, where this had been the case, all went to church one Christmas Eve, except a young maiden, who recently had become a servant there, and probably knew nothing about what had happened the preceding years. When the people had started, she put a light here and there in the farmhouse. Then she sat down on her bed in the baostofa and commenced reading the Bible. Having done so for a while, she saw a crowd of people enter the baostofa. They were men, women and children. They bagan to dance. They spoke to the maiden and asked her repeatedly to join in the dancing, but she did not answer. They offered her beautiful presents, but she did not even look at them, and continued reading. Just before daybreak they left the farmhouse. When the people came home that morning, they were exceedingly glad to find the maiden all right. She told them her adventure, and they praised her for her steadfastness. After that she always stayed at home Christmas Eve, as long as she lived at that farm, and always did the same people visit her, and they never did any harm.

Source: *When I Was a Girl in Iceland* by Holmfridur Arnadottir. Boston: Lothrop, Lee & Shepard Co., 1919.

Iran (Persia)

Christmas in Azerbaijan, c. 1910

The Christians observe a Christmas fast by refraining from eating meat for twenty-five days. Easter is observed in the same way with the exception of a longer period of fasting, similar to the observance of Lent.

Christmas in the Province of Azerbajin falls in a cold and snowy season. Therefore it is celebrated on the housetops. On such occasions the boys of our village gathered in bunches to play marbles and Christmas eggs. One egg was hit on the end by another just as the boys pick eggs at Easter in this country. The one that broke had to be given to the boy that had the hardest egg. Once we discovered an egg that no one could break. This we found to be a china egg. Some smart boy who had made a trip to the city was the owner of the envied property. The presence of such an egg in our little village created a panic among the boys. We could never discover who had it because, when the owner had won about a hundred eggs he sold it to some one else with the idea, of course, of not giving himself away. Personally, I never was so fortunate as to possess it.

To guard against the china one we tested each other's eggs by tapping them against our teeth. By this method we sometimes discovered a china egg and also came to some conclusion as to which egg would break first.

There is no Santa Claus in Persia, and I do not believe the devout people would allow any one to introduce this good fairy into their Christmas festivities.

Source: *When I Was a Boy in Persia* by Yovel B. Mirza. Boston: Lothrop, Lee & Shepard Co., 1920, pp. 105-106.

Iraq

A Coptic Christmas in Iraq

On Christmas Eve Coptic families gather in the courtyard, holding lighted candles, while one of the children reads the story of the Nativity in Arabic. A bonfire of thorns is then lit. If the thorns all turn to ashes, good fortune will be in store for the family. Each person jumps over the ashes three times, making a wish.

On Christmas Day, a thorn fire is lit at the church. A procession of the Baby Jesus carried on a scarlet cushion follows. Last of all the Bishop touches a congregation member with "The Touch of Peace." This person passes it to the next, and so on throughout the congregation.

Source: *Christmas Customs around the World* by Herbert H. Wernecke. Philadelphia: The Westminster Press, 1959, pp. 120-121.

Ireland

Christmas Stampy

"They used to make a kind of bread with potatoes called 'Stampy'. They would grate the potatoes on a tin grater, and then squeeze them into a tub of water. From the water they would get the starch for the clothes. There was no such thing as a bastable in those days. The 'Stampy' was made on a breadtree, which was a kind of sloping board put before the fire to hold the bread, as you would make toast nowadays. 'Stampy' was usually only made for Christmas or November Night, unless you had a good supply of potatoes, when you might make it once a week.

Source: *The Tailor and Ansty* by Eric Cross. Dublin and Corck: Mercier Press, 1964, p. 33.

Christmas foods

Christmas in the popular mind is now the holiday most closely associated with feasting, and the turkey, which came to Europe at the same time as the potato, is now the most important item in the Christmas dinner. Though turkeys were known in Ireland since the seventeenth century they only became associated with the Christmas dinner in the present century, and this development was probably caused by the writing of English Victorian novelists. The traditional Christmas dish before the turkey was beef, either roasted or boiled, and spiced beef is still popular in some areas at Christmas. For the affluent, fowl were always popular and a goose or a chicken was regarded as a suitable Christmas delicacy. Puddings of various kinds have always been popular at Christmas and continue to be so. The nature of the Christmas food depended on the prosperity or otherwise of the family and on the customary dishes in the region; rye bread was always a traditional Christmas treat in Connemara. Christmas Day was the main day of celebration in the year but not by any means the only one.

Source: *Life & Tradition in Rural Ireland* by Timothy P. O'Neill. London: J.M. Dent & Sons, Ltd., 1977, p. 64.

Gathering holly for Christmas

For Christmas too the land provided what was needed, and the Sunday before we made our annual pilgrimmage to the wood for the red-berried holly. It was there in abundance as was the ivy and moss, together with strange, interesting pieces of dried-out timber. We gathered them all and tied them up in bundles with hay twine and we brought them home on our backs, holding firmly to the twine across our shoulders. They would all be used to make different decorations for Christmas. There was no money for shop decorations but we did not need them as all around us the countryside fulfilled our needs.

Source: *To School Through the Fields; An Irish Country Childhood* by Alice Taylor. New York: St. Martin's Press, 1988, p. 48.

Italy

The *Ceppo*

In Italian homes a *ceppo* is erected. This is a pyramid of shelves on which Christmas symbols may be displayed. It may be lit with candles and hold stars, angels, fruits, candies, or small gifts. On the lowest shelf is the presepio (crèche).

Source: *Joy through the World.* United States Committee for UNICEF; New York: Dodd, Mead & Co., 1985, p. 90.

A family Christmas in Brescia, Italy, c. 1900

The old folks prepare all the good things we are going to eat on the Christmas night after we have heard the mass, of which the first begins at midnight. The victuals are all cooked without fat, our fish being always cooked in olive oil.

We children, that night, try hard to keep our eyes open so as to go with the old people. Of course we fall asleep many times, although on that evening we always make up big parties and pass most of the evening sitting together under the chimney.

Our fireplaces are very large and high, with a very high step at each side of the chimney; and there are stone seats for the children and dogs.

Then they put, for Christmas night only, large branches of *ginepro* (juniper) on the fire; it smells very good, and it crackles beautifully.

To keep us children awake, they let us put big chestnuts (whole) in the hot cinders, and when they are roasted we all know it because they make a little explosion. The cinders get into our mouths and eyes; that is part of the fun. The old folks put large terra cotta bowls full of wine to get warm on the stone steps, and they soak in it baked pears and apples.

At half-past eleven we all start for the Vuomo, where the mass is going to be said. Our churches, as you know, are of stone and marble, but although they are never warmed you soon feel comfortable in them. They only keep a *braciere* (brasier) in the sacristy, to warm the hands of the priests.

On Christmas night the crowd is immense; we children get the worst of it, as most of the time we have to content ourselves with being buried between overcoats and petticoats; once in a while our folks will raise us up to get a peep, and then down we go again in the dark. We dare not keep our eyes always raised, because our folks all take snuff, and as they are very careless, they always let some of it drop; if you catch it once you remember it for a long while. Finally mass is finished and we run home to our chimney corner, preparing ourselves to eat the grand dinner. But alas! half an hour is all we can stand; the trial of the mass, the heat of the fire from our place is too much for us—one by one we droop as you might see plants do in a hot summer day in the fields.

Next day finds up very stupid, but by and by, at about two or three o'clock in the afternoon, we are up, preparing the stocking for the Magi. We hang our stocking at the side of the chimney, and go to sleep very early. The morning following finds us very bright and happy.

Well, winter goes by about the same; the only difference is we go to bed at eight and burn plain wood made up in *fascine* (fagots).

Source: *When I Was a Girl in Italy* by Marietta Ambrosi. Boston: Lothrop, Lee & Shepard Co., 1906, pp. 25-27.

American Santa and tree, Gesù Bambino, and the *presepio* (crèche)

Italian youngsters who nowadays anticipate gifts on Christmas as well as on Epiphany are taught that the Christmas donor is Gesù Bambino (Baby Jesus). The Vatican, through one of its publications, has expressed disapproval of Christmas trees and Santa Claus (known in Italian as Babbo Natale, or "Father Christmas"). The Sunday newspaper, *L'Osservatore della Domenica* (The Sunday Observer), in an editorial signed by an Italian priest, The Rev. Pirro Scavizzi, considered Santa Claus (described as an insidious form of "de-Christianization") worse than Christmas trees because the latter at least recall the spirit of the winter night when Jesus was born. The Befana was evaluated as not much better than Santa—"a monstrous figure." Children are "terrorized and nauseated" by warnings that they will receive no gifts from the witch or Santa if they are naughty. In the United States children are confused by seeing many Santas who "cannot and must not be accepted or tolerated by Christians." The Vatican publication denounced the effort to "inject into the fantasy of children the clumsy figure of a good (or bad) old man, substituting it for the sacred and gentle figure of the Christ child."

Unlike Santa's reindeer sleigh and the Befana's broomstick, the Baby Jesus makes his rounds on a donkey, distributing toys to sleeping children. (One Italian father told me that his children now believe in a more modernized and realistic way of Jesus' traveling. "They believe he drives a jeep, and that's why, instead of providing a handful of hay under the chimney for the donkey as do other children, mine provide a bottle of gasoline; this year my oldest boy suggested leaving some coupons which can be traded for gasoline.")

Italian youngsters write letters addressed to Gesù Bambino, Paradiso (Baby Jesus, Heaven) listing their wishes. Many children send or bring letters to Rome's Santa Maria in Aracoeli (St. Mary in the Altar of Heaven) Church where a famous, two-foot tall wooden Christ doll is kept. From time to time at any season the figure is rushed to the hospital bedside of an ill child because it is supposed to possess healing powers. Legend has it that the figure of the infant was carved by angels from the wood of an olive tree in the Garden of Gethsemane. Every afternoon from Christmas day to Epiphany, parents bring their offsprings to the church where one by one the youngsters recite a poem or sing a song, memorized for the occasion, to the Bambino in his Christmas manger. The figure is bedecked with jewels donated by persons who have asked or received favors and the idol's niche in a small chapel is lined with letters from devout children from all over the world.

Living *presepios* are enacted in schools and in some villages. The custom of the *presepio* was begun by St. Francis of Assisi, renowned for his gentle rapport with animals and birds, in the year 1223 at the town of Greccio in the Umbria Region of Italy.

Christmas foods

Since it is a Roman Catholic fast day, Christmas Eve fare consists of fish, and the traditional fish is eel. A Roman Christmas custom opens the wholesale food market for the sale of fish on the night of December 23, the only time of the year when the general public (rather than only merchants) is admitted. The most desirable eel is called *capitone,* a slithering three or four feet long, bred in lagoons near the mouth of the Po River.

Panettone, a towering loaf of cake with raisins and citron, is traditionally eaten on Christmas, and two Italian companies, Motta and Alemagna (the originator), have grown rich on this custom. The cakes are packed in attractive boxes with string handles and are given as gifts.

Zampognari and the Novena di Natale

Other Christmas season customs include: the arrival in Rome and other cities from Abruzzi Region hill towns of the *zampognari,* bagpipe players clad in rustic sheepskin jackets and thong-laced shoes, reminiscent of Bethlehem's shepherds, to play old tunes for gratuities, and the Novena di Natale, nine days of Christmas church services, which are major social events in small towns.

Source: *Main Street, Italy* by Irving R. Levine. Garden City, N.Y.: Doubleday, 1963, pp. 489-91.

Jamaica

Jonkonnu, traditionally performed at Christmas and New Year, is also featured now at political rallies and Independence Day celebrations.

"Root Jonkonnu" and "fancy dress" masquerade

In Jamaica today, there are two different kinds of Jonkonnu troupes, which I shall designate "root Jonkonnu" and "fancy dress," or Masquerade. I use *root* in keeping with the insistence of the local Jamaican vernacular, in which it connotes "peasant" to some people and "lower class" to others, but always emphasizes a strong Black presence; for example, reggae music and Rastafari religion are both considered to be root Jamaican. The performances of both types of Jonkonnu troupes are structurally the same—they use the same steps and follow the same performance pattern of a procession followed by a break out—but the quality of motion and the identity of the characters and the costumes are different.

In a fancy dress performance, Courtiers perform steps in a contained fashion, emphasizing movements that are straight up and down and to the side, and hip swings that cause their short "skirts" to flare out. The Amerindians in a root Jonkonnu performance do the very same steps, but with a different rhythm, and perhaps with a more pulsating movement of the hips and hands and more syncopation with the feet and knees. A typical procession of a fancy dress troupe begins with Courtiers followed by a King and Queen, perhaps preceded by a Flower Girl. Sailor Boy runs around the outside of the line, wielding a whip to keep the audience in line, and Babu, the East Indian cowherd with his long cattle prod, may accompany him. Pitchy Patchy also runs around the outside of the procession—like Sailor Boy and Babu, he is more exuberant than the courtly entourage.

In root Jonkonnu, the Courtiers are replaced by Amerindians and Warriors, the Amerindians distinguished by being more expressive than the Warriors, who are forceful but dignified. Flower Girl is replaced by Whore Girl, who raises her skirts to titillate the audience, or by Belly Woman, who shakes her belly to the rhythm of the music. Cowhead confronts the crowd, charging them and butting to keep people back. The inclusion of Cowhead and other animal characters is one of the most important differences between root Jonkonnu and fancy dress. They introduce a strong, rural or ''uncultured'' flavor into the performance. Fancy dress, on the other hand, seems more closely affiliated with a British plantation model.

Root Jonkonnu is associated with villages that are removed from major coastal towns.

Source: ''The Jonkonnu Festival in Jamaica'' by Judith Bettelheim in *The Journal of Ethnic Studies* 13:3, (1985) 85-99.

For more information see: ''Jonkonnu and Other Christmas Masquerades'' by Judith Bettelheim in *Caribbean Festival Arts* by John W. Nunley and Judith Bettelheim. Seattle: Univ. of Washington Press, 1988, pp. 39-83.

Japan

Postoccupation Christmas influence

Today Christmas is celebrated throughout the Japanese islands. In some urban shopping centers the decorations are up by mid-November; and news commentators quip about ''instant Christians'' who flock to the Ginza bars on Christmas Eve. In the rural areas as well there are youth-group parties and household gift-exchanges. A survey I conducted in central Nagano prefecture in 1960 found that (1) approximately half of the households in the sample, rural as well as urban, have a home Christmas celebration, and that (2) Christmas is the only holiday in a list of more than two dozen that has gained a significant number of adherents since the war.

The Christmas cake

Family Christmas foregatherings do not center around dinner, as in the American ideal, but rather upon mutual partaking of a Christmas cake. Many Anchiku housewives do indeed prepare ''something different'' (*kawatta mono*) for the Christmas meal, but this is just as likely to be raw fish or a rice curry as it is to be a Western dish. A few white-collar wives bake a chicken, but turkey is not available in Anchiku.

The Christmas cake also is called a ''decoration cake'' (*dekorēshon kēki,* a loan word), emphasizing its ridges and waves of thick frosting. The cake almost always is purchased, and in the cities some bakeries prepare a supply of cakes early in December and quick-freeze them until the sales demand mounts. In the Anchiku village where I lived, a local confectioner—who prepared only Japanese-style sweets—served as agent for an urban baker, and distributed mimeographed order blanks early in December. Decorated cake is not an item in the usual American popular Christmas, although we do have our fruitcakes and cookies of various derivations. So perhaps the precedent here is European, although none of the European forms I know of seems to correspond exactly with the Japanese form.

Stockings hung by the bathtub

Parents, peers, teachers, and the mass media collaborate to inform the young about Santa Claus and his visit. The stockings can not be hung by a fireplace in the typical Japanese house, so most parents place the presents by the children's pillows during the night. Some of the more literal-minded transfer Clement Moore's chimney motif to its closest Japanese counterpart, the pipe for the bathtub stove. And the stockings are hung by the bathtub with care. (The Japanese word *entotsu* is a generic for many forms of waste-gas conveying tube that are distinguished in English as chimney, smokestack, stovepipe, and so on.)

Santa Kurōsu no ojiisan

The Japanese call him ''Grandfather Santa Claus'' (*Santa Kurōsu no ojiisan*)—

Cards, trees, and parties

Christmas cards are used, but only sparingly, by American standards. School children often exchange them. They are of course appropriate to send to one's Western friends and acquaintances, but they are felt to be rather frivolous for ordinary adult intercourse; they cannot, for example, take the place of the New Year postcards. The latter are exchanged much the same as Christmas cards are exchanged in the U.S., and most families devote a good deal of time, money, and thought to them.

The Christmas tree also has a New Year's competitor. This is the ''gate-pine'' (*kadomatsu*) seen before nearly every Anchiku house from late December until mid-January. Gate-pine decor varies over a wide range: some families put up elaborate clusters of 10-foot firs and 25-foot bamboos, others merely paste on the doorpost a sheet of paper with a pine tree printed upon it. By contrast, Christmas trees usually are set up inside, and are sparsely decorated. The tree has fared somewhat better in competition than the card, and many families set up pine decor both for Christmas and separately for New Year's (a doubly unproductive use of precious timber which becomes a handy target for the complaints of literal-minded conservationists).

Christmas parties are held both by instrumental and by expressive social groups. These parties are a syncretism with "closing-the-year parties" (*bōnenkai*) long customary in December. But a *bōnenkai* tends to be a man's affair, with *sake*, group singing, and displays of masculine affection. Only professional women are allowed in the room: waitresses, geisha, entertainers. The Christmas party, on the other hand, provides a role for "proper" women. There is social dancing in place of the music of samisens, and often port wine is served rather than *sake*. Understandably enough, the Christmas party tends to be more favored than the *bōnenkai* in heterosexual groups such as office staffs, or the employees of a department store, or village youth clubs. This is one reason why some Japanese see Christmas as democratic.

Source: "The Japanese Popular Christmas: Coping With Modernity" by David W. Plath in *Journal of American Folklore*, 71 (302), (October-December 1963) 308-317.

Lappland

Seventeenth-century Lapp offerings to the Yule-tide people

At Christmastime the *joulo-herrar* were once thought to fly about the earth. As Christmas Eve was a fast, the food that would usually have been eaten on this night was set out for the Yule-Tide People. On Christmas Day a bit of each food that would be eaten in the feast that day was put into a little birch basket-boat. Warm fat was poured over it and it was hung in a tree at a short distance from the home. This resembles the Swedish habit of putting a bowl of rice pudding outside on Christmas Eve for Father Christmas.

Another Lapp custom of those days was the erection of a tree with only its central branches remaining. On this the heart, lungs, tongue and lips of a reindeer were hung, and the tree was smeared with the animal's blood.

Source: *Swedish Christmas*. Gottenburg: Tre Tryckare, 1955, pp. 155-156.

Lithuania

A Lithuanian Christmas feast

Among Lithuanians also the pig furnishes a considerable portion of the Christmas fare. A typical Christmas dinner menu is as follows: soup—clear beet boullion or mushroom soup; roast suckling pig with sauerkraut, pan-roast potatoes and baked apples; a spring salad consisting of lettuce, sliced radishes, scallions, cucumbers, and sour cream; and apple cake.

Roast Stuffed Suckling Pig:

1 suckling pig (8-10 lbs)
5 apples
2 onions (large)
1 quart bread crumbs
4 tbs melted butter
4 tbs chopped parsley
salt and pepper
sifted sage or ginger

Wash the pig inside and out with a weak solution of baking soda, paying special attention to head openings and mouth. Pour water off and lay pig in cold water for about 15 minutes. Dry thoroughly. Rub inside well with salt. If desired, pepper and sifted sage or ginger may also be rubbed on inside of pig. Mix bread crumbs with peeled and finely chopped apples, onions, chopped parsley and melted butter. Add salt and pepper to taste and enough milk to moisten mixture. Stuff the pig with this mixture. Sew openings of pig together. Cover the legs and ears with oiled paper and tie the legs back. Put corn cob in mouth to keep the jaws open. Place pig in roasting pan in a very hot oven until brown; then reduce heat to moderate until done. Baste frequently with plenty of fat. Do not allow any water or steam to form as it is likely to burst the skin and spoil the meat. Put the peeled potatoes in the roasting pan around the pig about 3/4 of an hour before the pig is done. Time required for cooking pig is about 10 to 12 minutes per pound. When done, insert a red apple in the mouth of the pig and place on a large platter on a bed of sauerkraut. Surround the pig with browned potatoes and baked apples.

Lithuanian Apple Cake

Grate or crumb a loaf of pumpernickel bread. Place a layer of the crumbs in a cake mould (preferably a mould with a center, such as an angel-cake mould). Sprinkle crumbs with sugar and pour over them enough melted butter to moisten them. Then add layer of sliced apple; if apples are tart, sprinkle sugar on them. Repeat process until cake mould is filled with alternating bread crumb and apple layers. Bake in oven until apple slices are tender. Turn apple cake out from mould onto a cake dish or platter. Serve hot or cold as preferred. Fill the center and surround the cake with whipped cream.

Source: *Foreign Festival Customs* by Marian Schibsby & Hanny Cohrsen. New York: American Council for Nationalities Service, 1974, p. 65.

Malaysia (Sarawak)

Christmas afloat in Sarawak

On Christmas Eve, in Sarawak, a service is held in the church, which stands on stilts at the edge of the water. At its close the young people, dressed in white and carrying lighted candles, climb down the notched pole that leads to the wharf below. They clamber into boats and paddle up and down the river, which serves as the village street. At the wharf of each member of the congregation, they stop and sing carols, ending with the greeting, "*Selamat hari Kristmas,*" "Merry Christmas." The householders are waiting for them and they set off firecrackers of every shape and size as their part of the ceremony. The singing goes on until midnight and then the young people return home for family celebrations.

Source: *Children's Festivals from Many Lands* by Nina Millen. New York: Friendship Press, 1964, p. 84-85.

Malta

Christmas Day (Public Holiday)

Yuletide in Malta is primarily the season for family parties. The highlight of the festivities is the midnight mass, when a child narrates the story of the nativity.

The statue of Baby Jesus, the Crib and the "Pasturi", as well as the more recently introduced Christmas Tree, still form part of the special Christmas decorations in Maltese homes. Streets and shop windows are not left wanting—they too receive the Christmas touch. During the Festive Season, celebrations take the most varied of forms.

Source: "Malta & Gozo: Events Calendar '90" National Tourism Organization, 1990.

Marshall Islands

Another festival involving singing and dancing locally is during Christmas. The singing and dancing groups are called "Jebta" a loan from the English word "chapter." It involves singing groups called "Jebta" trying to outdo the other with their songs and performances. The end result is everybody having fun and enjoyment.

Source: Alfred Capelle, Alele Museum, Republic of the Marshall Islands.

Mexico

Las Posadas

Each night for eight nights before Christmas the neighbors process to a different house. The children carry a small litter with figurines: Mary riding the burro, accompanied by Joseph and the Angel. Everyone carries lighted candles and sings as they walk through the streets. At a prearranged house they stop and sing, asking for lodging for the night. The owner of the house sings back, telling them to go away as everyone is asleep. He threatens to beat them, but at last opens the doors to let them in. Inside the house, all kneel at the manger to pray and sing. Afterwards the children ask in humorous verse for treats. Then comes food, dancing, and breaking of the piñata.

Source: *A Treasury of Mexican Folkways* by Frances Toor. New York: Crown, 1947, pp. 247-249.

The two Christ children in Zinacantan belief

At midnight on Christmas Eve, the birth of the Christ children (there are two in Zinacantan belief: one older brother and one younger brother) is reenacted in the church of San Sebastián. The two children are carried by their godparents—the Alcaldes, the Regidores, and the top civil officials from the Cabildo—to the church of San Lorenzo where they are placed in the creche and all come forward to venerate them to the resonant sound of turtle shell drums.

Source: *The Zinacantecos of Mexico: A Modern Maya Way of Life* by Evan Z. Vogt. New York: Holt, Rinehart and Winston, 1970, p. 86.

Christmas in Mexico City, 1910

The Christmas tree, the children's delight in the United States, is sometimes used in Mexico, but the "nacimiento," or birth of Christ, is the typical Christmas amusement for the Mexican children.

The figures of the child Jesus, the three Kings, St. Joseph, the Virgin, shepherds, and animals are made by the Indians in clay or wax, painted in brilliant colors. These are placed on a table or platform where a representation of the stable at Bethlehem is arranged, with moss and green to simulate hills, trees, and roads, while by using mirrors, lakes or ponds are shown. Scattered here and there are tiny houses, huts, and the shepherds and animals, the whole being illuminated with candles or electric lights. Some of these "nacimientos" are very artistic and elaborate, and are really worth seeing.

The "posadas" are evening parties given for a period of nine days at different friends' houses, the last being on Christmas day. When the invited guests meet at the house where the "posada" is held, they go in a procession accompanied with music, singing and carrying the child Jesus, as if they were asking for *posada* or lodging for it. Another group is stationed at one of the parlors and behind closed doors. They also sing some hymns and after a time the door is opened, and those seeking the posada are admitted. After this there is dancing and supper is served. A tray is also passed around with pretty souvenirs filled with candies for each guest, this being a feature of the "posada." Sometimes a "piñata" is broken. This is an earthen jar decorated with tissue-paper in all colors and shapes and filled with candies, nuts, and all kinds of sweetmeats. Each person or child in turn is blindfolded and with a stick tries to break this "piñata," but many times they miss it, or lose their way and go in another direction, so the rest have to run and get out of their way, or surely they would get a good hit on their head or body. When finally some one breaks the piñata, all rush and shout and try to get most of the candies and other things, these being quickly picked up from the floor by all participants. This amusement is nearly always used in all children's parties and I remember that I enjoyed it very much for its good fun.

Perhaps it is unnecessary for me to say that on Christmas eve the churches are crowded with people who go to the midnight mass, as is the case among the Catholics in the United States. In some instances there is a family gathering at the homes of those who have been present at the midnight mass, but of course while a child I had to forego this on account of the lateness of the hour when it was given. Furthermore these reunions are usually only for older persons.

Source: *When I Was a Girl in Mexico* by Mercedes Godoy. Boston: Lothrop, Lee & Shepard Co., 1919, pp. 56-59.

The Netherlands

Christmas in Holland, c. 1910

Our Christmas vacation lasted about ten days. Christmas was celebrated very quietly and for two days. The first day we went to church with our parents. I sat deep down in a big pew with my mother, and she gave me her cushion to sit on.

Under her feet mother had one of the ''stoven'' or foot-warmers.

At noon, on Christmas, we ate for dessert a lot of bread-pudding, and in the evening, also with our tea and coffee, big, long loaves of sweet bread so full of currants that you could not see anything but currants.

If the ice was strong, everybody went skating except those who were very pious; they considered it sinful to enjoy themselves on Christmas.

Source: *When I Was a Girl in Holland* by Cornelia de Groot. Boston: Lothrop, Lee & Shepard Co., 1917, pp. 73-75.

Nigeria

Christmas in Calabar

In Calabar, there are no great traditional festivals, so it is the Christian holy days—Christmas and Easter—which have become the popular festivals. New Year's Eve has also developed into a time for the manifestation of popular beliefs and practices.

Christmas is an important time for family reunions - relatives return from abroad or other parts of Nigeria. The dry season has just begun and favours outdoor festivities and celebrations. It is not only a time for church-going but also for traditional plays and masquerades; the various troupes move around the streets of Calabar with their colourful and dramatic costumes. The children join in the merriment by donning their own masks and performing for passers-by and friends in the hope of financial reward.

The Christmas period is also a busy time for a variety of religious gatherings such as conventions, crusades and retreats. While the majority of these evangelistic gatherings are staged by specific religious organizations, they may be considered as a forum for popular religion since they are organized in such a way (open air, ''neutral'' territory, over several days) as to allow non-members to participate. For some, these occasions represent a form of supplementary devotionalism, for others they may be a potential channel of conversion. In addition, there is the attraction of free food and accommodation, entertainment and social interaction with like-minded people.

Source: *Religion in Calabar: The Religious Life and History of a Nigerian Town* by Rosalind I. J. Hackett. Berlin/New York: Mouton de Gruyter, 1989, p. 271.

Norway

An immigrant's daughter describes Christmas customs in the old country

The farmers usually slaughtered a pig and a calf for the Christmas Season. Pressed meats and sausages were made and wives were known to spend days baking *flatbrod* (hardtack) and *lefse* (a thin potato roll). The house was scoured and polished and fresh curtains hung. The Christmas Eve table was set with the best cloth, dishes, and silver. The tree was brought in a day before and might be pine, fir, or, as in southern Norway, a holly.

Julaften (Christmas Eve)

Dinner was served around seven p.m. after chores were done. It would feature *Lutefisk,* a stockfish processed in lye and dried. It is rehydrated, and water must be changed several times for two or three days. Finally it is simmered for three minutes in boiling water. This must be handled carefully. It is drained and served with melted butter by Norwegians, cream sauce by Swedes. It looks like a plateful of Knox gelatin when served. Other dishes were: *potetes,* boiled; lefse, made with flour and potatoes, rolled thin and baked and served with butter or spread with cinnamon and sugar at the dessert table; flatbrod (flatbread, thin variety); melke suppe (milk soup), a little rice cooled in milk, thickened and seasoned with cinnamon; and homemade beer.

After dinner the family joined hands and walked round and round the Christmas tree singing carols. Gifts were then exchanged and around ten p.m. the coffee table was presented, loaded with all kinds of cookies, Goro, Fattigman (Poorman, a put-on as they are exceedingly rich), Berliner Kranser, and such.

Another traditional Christmas Eve meal could be: *Ribbesteak,* spareribs served with lingonberry sauce, potatoes, and cabbage. And for dessert *Risengrensgraut,* rice porridge served with sugar, cinnamon, and butter, and taken with a glass of cold milk. Or for dessert *Rommegraut* may be served, cream pudding made by boiling down cream until it is thick and served in its own fat.

Christmas morning breakfast is lefse; flatbrod; *julekage* (sweet bread with raison and citron, flavored with cardamom); *rulle-pulse,* a lamb and veal roll, spiced and pickled in brine; *sylte* (head cheese); and coffee.

A week before Christmas the farmers put a sheaf of oats on a pole, "Julenek," a symbolic sharing of their bounty with the birds.

Source: Emely Sather, Seattle, Washington.

Christmas Eve dinner

Christmas Eve dinner is at six o'clock and it is always rice porridge, boiled codfish, and red wine. At heart, the boys are not terrifically fond of either the rice porridge or that sour red wine. But that was what *they* had for Christmas Eve dinner in their home, because Mother's father had always had porridge and boiled codfish in *his* home. In many places in Norway people have clung to the customs of Catholic times and fasted thus on Christmas Eve, even though it was four hundred years since the country became Protestant. But Christmas Eve is always festive, for everyone dresses for dinner or comes to the table dressed in his very best, and the electric lights are turned off everywhere in the house, for this night there must be only the living light of candles, and there must be a candle in every nook and cranny.

The table was decorated with flowers and candles stood in the old English-plate candlesticks, and on the table around these Thea had laid a garland of spruce fir sprigs and heads of grain. And with a lot of sugar and cinnamon on it, and a lump of butter in the middle, the rice porridge did not taste so bad after all. Besides, there was always one almond in it, and the one who found the almond in his porridge would have luck all year.

Source: *Happy Times in Norway* by Sigrid Undset. New York: Alfred A. Knopf, 1942, p. 27.

The pagan yule

The celebration of Yule was practised in the northern countries long before they accepted the Christian religion.

This heathen celebration was a feast in honor of the sun, when, in January, it seemed to renew its strength and overcome the power of darkness (by rising high enough on the firmament to spread its golden rays over the country).

During the two weeks of this festival only the most necessary work was to be done. Implements with wheels, as wagons and the spinning-wheels, must rest. To let a wheel move was a sacrilege against the holy sun, as it might indicate that they wanted the sun-wheel to move faster.

At the end of the twelve holy days came the climax of the great festival. The days were getting longer and a huge wheel would be rolled from farm to farm.

When the Christian religion was introduced, Christmas was celebrated a couple of weeks earlier than Yule, and thenceforth heathen and Christian customs were mixed.

Peace for the animals

Fish, bird, and beast must have perfect peace during the two-weeks' celebration of Yule. Therefore, every trap and snare must be taken away, and even the fish-nets must be removed from the ocean and rivers.

The great Christmas peace,—resting over the whole creation—must be observed, or woe be unto the transgressor. Selma Lagerlöf tells a beautiful story about a bear that was kind enough to give Christmas lodging in its winter den to a farmer, who was lost in the storm.

But when the farmer returned the next day with his gun in order to kill the bear, the bear killed the man, and even his wife thought this was a righteous punishment, because her husband had attempted to kill the bear before the Christmas festival was over.

Christmas dinner, the lucky almond, and food for the dead

Christmas Eve dinner which usually consisted of short ribs, different kinds of bread and cake, and rice pudding. Into the rice pudding had been put *one* almond. The one who found this almond on his plate would be the first one to get married. Every one had to leave some pudding on his plate for the dead, who were certain to call during the night and get their share of the Christmas food. This was left on the table in great quantity and variety; but the dead do not eat like us mortals. They only want "the spirit of the food," hence when morning came everything looked as though it were untouched. It was, however, not only the good spirits that would visit the house Christmas night. The ghostly pranks of the evil spirits consisted in going from farm to farm and taking revenge on their enemies. This wild host brought fear and trembling wherever they went, for the transgressor was put through the most cruel punishment.

The Christmas goat

Even the Christmas ram or goats must be fed. In some places they would put some barley in a shoe and place it under the bed. Most of the time they could see that he had been eating a little during the night. But if the ram did not touch it, he was offended at something and would bring bad luck during the year. At a certain farm a cow died during the spring and the lady of the house was positive that it was her husband's fault because he had neglected to feed the Christmas ram.

In the parish, Elverum, they knew just where the Christmas ram lived. He moved from place to place during the winter until Christmas Eve, when he finally managed to get under the dining-room table. The last thing before they went to bed they would sweep very carefully under the table, and the first thing in the morning on Christmas day, they would see if the ram had left any grain there. If they found some it would be a good year, providing the grain was good. If this was poor, it would be a poor crop that year; but if they did not find any, it would be crop failure.

Feeding the animals on Christmas eve

But it is not only the supernatural beings that must be provided with extra food at Christmas. In some places they would give the domestic animals an extra meal about five o'clock Christmas

Eve. In feeding them they would say, ''Eat well, keep well; this is Christmas Eve.''

Then they would feed the cattle salt out of a cow-bell. This would help them next summer to come home from the pasture in the evening of their own accord.

Sheaves for the birds

. . . Sheaves of grain [were] put upon poles out in the yard, or on top of the barn. Then I knew that Norwegians were living there.

These sheaves are the largest and best that could be selected at threshing time. They should be put up on a spruce pole on which a large tuft of branches must be left at the top. This makes a nice place where the birds can rest after their meals. The snow should also be removed from a large circle on the lawn, and on this bare spot the birds will dance between meals, and thus get up their appetites for the next repast.

When everything was finished Christmas Eve, the dishes washed and the house set in order for Christmas day, and all the old brooms had been carefully hidden in order to prevent the witches from riding them Christmas night; when for a similar purpose the fire-shovel and tongs had been put away; then the head of the household would go out to see if there were many sparrows in the Christmas sheaf. If there were many, it would be a good corn year; but if a sparrow sat down in the sheaf before all the work connected with putting it up had been finished, it was an omen that some one in the family would soon die.

Shooting in Christmas

On Christmas Eve, when darkness had conquered the light, then the fear of evil beings crept upon one. In order to drive away the witches and other uncanny beings, they went out in the yard and fired a shot. This has been transformed into ''shooting in Christmas,'' or a Christmas salute. The young men go from farm to farm and sneak up close to the window while shooting, in order to make the people quake.

But they could not be offended, as such a visit was considered an honor, and the husbandman would go and invite them in for refreshments.

The Yule Log and other protective devices

As it was commonly believed that the witches would be riding around in the air on their brooms that evening, the people were afraid that they might come down the chimney. In order to prevent this they would burn dry spruce, which would send out so many sparks, that it would keep away the uninvited guests, or if one put salt in the fire it would serve the same purpose.

It was not considered safe to go to bed that evening without leaving a light burning, because all evil beings were usually active on this holy night. Sometimes they made an extra large candle that would last all night, and this they left burning on the hearth with a circle of salt around it. Both the candle and the salt were consecrated.

But in most places they would burn the ''Yule Log,'' as all evil shuns the bright light. This custom of burning the ''Yule Log'' was in olden times transferred from Norway into England.

Many other safety devices were resorted to on Christmas Eve. Steel had to be put over the stable and barn doors; and with a brush dipped in tar, the sign of the cross was made over the different doors.

These customs, mostly used in the rural districts, are now passing away; but of those that are still in use one might be mentioned.

They leave a light burning in the window all Christmas night as a sign that any traveler is welcome for food and shelter.

The table is set all the time during the two weeks of Christmas festivities, and visitors as well as members of the family can help themselves at any time to food and drinks.

Source: *When I Was a Boy in Norway* by Dr. J.O. Hall. Boston: Lothrop, Lee & Shepard Co., 1921, pp. 154-163.

Nyasaland (Malawi)

Christmas in a Nyasaland village, c. 1945

I was used only to the simple and modest manner in which we celebrated it in my own village. No exciting preparations. Too far away for Santa Claus. No Christmas trees, no cards either. But early on Christmas morning little children ran about in the village shouting, ''Christmas Box.'' Then families had their morning meals and cleaned themselves up. The believers, and nonbelievers if they wished, gathered together in a Church or a field. The pastor or maybe a local school teacher read the Testament, and then they gave thanks to their Maker for sacrificing His own Son to save them. The school children sang one or two carols, more often than not, ''Silent Night.'' A dance or a football game or some other game followed and usually lasted the rest of the day.

Source: *I Will Try* by Legson Kayira. New York: Doubleday, 1965, p. 215.

Peru

Christmas in the Andean community of Muquiyauyo, c. 1949

The Christmas fiesta lasted from December 28, with dancing in the plaza taking place every day. Christmas Eve the Misa de Gallo is held at midnight, and dawn Mass, the Misa de Aruora, is held on Christmas morning. From four hundred to six hundred people attend each of these, thronging the plaza outside the church after the church itself is filled. After the dawn Mass concludes, the plaza begins to fill with dance groups. Each group, with its band, takes up a place in the plaza and dances for a while, moves off to visit a member's home for a while, then returns for more dancing. Each group has two distinct dances, a mobile dance, which they use while moving through the streets, and a stationary dance, performed in one spot. Many groups share the plaza, with several bands playing at once. As many as six hundred dancers and spectators may crowd into the plaza at one time. A variety of foodstalls sell pastries, fruit, gelatin drinks, ice cream, *chicha* and *aguardiente* (alcoholic drinks), beer, and coca.

Source: *A Community in the Andes: Problems and Progress in Muquiyayo* by Richard N. Adams. Seattle: Univ. of Washington, 1959, pp. 190-191.

Philippines

Simbang-gabi, the nine *misas de gallo*

Starting on the dawn of the sixteenth of December, and on to the 24th, Filipinos celebrate nine days of early morning masses called "misas de gallo", or in Tagalog, "simbang-gabi".

At 4:00 in the morning, the crisp December air is rent by the ringing of the church bells. In the provinces, they still fire bamboo cannons to awaken the faithful and call them to mass.

In the early days, the Spanish missionaries had to resort to all forms of showmanship to attract the newly-baptized natives to church. These nine days of early morning masses may have been among these advertising gimmicks the missionaries used, to impress upon the new converts the significance of the Nativity. In rural communities, this gave an opportunity for the farmers to benefit from mass before going to their fields.

Now, the Filipinos in towns big and small rouse themselves at the first chiming of the bells, or the first whir of the alarm clock. They put on snuggies for which they may have shopped assiduously only the previous afternoon. Now to the Filipino, the dawn mass does not have the spiritual appeal it may have had for the early Filipino Christians. Now, the early morning mass is occasion for lovers' trysts, or parading around in winter costume, for snuggling close together by the fire of the *bibingkahan,* or holding hands under the table for the traditional after-mass snack of *salabat* and *puto bum-bong.*

During this period, young people keep their parties going on to the dawn hour, so they can hurry from their frugging (the girls bring out a veil from their jewelled evening bags, or, in the absence of one, a kleenex sheet will do), to the mass. The nightclubs extend their closing hours from three to four, so the hostesses can let their patrons bring them to church.

Source: *The Galleon Guide to Philippine Festivals* by Alfonso J. Aluit. Manila: Galleon, 1969, pp. 152-153.

Poland

The Wiglia on Christmas Eve

At the sighting of the first evening star, the Wiglia begins. A candle at the window lights the way for the Christ Child, and a place is set at the table for Him. Straw is laid under the tablecloth on this night to call to mind the manger. Salt and bread are placed on a plate, and money is placed under this, symbolizing the staffs of life and a hope for a prosperous future. Sheaves of grain are stood in the corners of the room as signs of a bounteous harvest to come. A large, unleaved wafer, the *Oplatek,* is broken among family members and shared with loving greetings and embraces. The wafer is stamped with nativity scenes and has been blessed by the priest. Family members who cannot return home for the feast may be sent a piece of the wafer in the mail as a token of family ties. Twelve dishes are served, in commemoration of the Twelve Apostles. All are without meat, as this is a fast day. They may include a clear beet soup with mushrooms, carp, *pierozhki,* and a grain pudding called *kutya.* Popyseed cakes and a twelve-fruit compote conclude the dinner.

Source: *Joy through the World.* United States Committee for UNICEF. New York: Dodd, Mead & Co., 1985, p. 72.

The King Herod play in Polish villages

The King Herod Play is a Christmas folk play that exists in a variety of versions and has been passed down for centuries from generation to generation by word of mouth. Its starting point is the biblical account of the wicked King Herod, who ordered the murder of all male infants in Bethlehem when threatened by the birth of Jesus. This episode provides a framework into which characters and events from Polish history are woven organically, including a Turkish soldier, a village Jew, a Polish cavalryman, a Field Marshal, the Devil, Death, and, in some versions, an angel, two gravediggers, the cavalryman's horse, and Rachel, the Jew's wife.

The King Herod Play has a tradition in several European countries, including East Germany, Czechoslovakia, and Rumania, and is part of a cycle of several Christmas folk plays. Numerous analogies between episodes of this play and medieval European drama have led scholars of folklore to postulate that it descended from a fragment of a Christmas mystery play. One source on the history of this tradition in Poland traces its origins to the crèche or *yaselko,* which was brought to Poland in the 13th century by Franciscan monks and displayed in the church at Christmas. The wax, clay, and wooden nativity scene figurines were eventually transformed into puppets. These puppets performed Christmas mystery plays, and the puppets as well as their performances came to be called *szopka.* When the monks themselves took the roles of the various personages, they created "living *szopka,*" which is a name still used in Poland to describe live performances of Christmas plays. . . . The players themselves and the tradition of performing this play came to be called *Herody,* which means simply "Herods." On Christmas Eve children are reminded that "the Herods are coming tonight."

In Poland, the King Herod Play survives most strongly today in villages near Cracow and Katowice. It survives in a variety of versions even within a single village and varies considerably from performance to performance. . . .

On Christmas Eve in Bojków every village cottage becomes a potential place of performance. After sharing the traditional Christmas Eve meal, families linger at the dinner table—grandparents, uncles, aunts, and cousins, as well as parents and children. Straw has been loosely scattered under the table in remembrance of the manger bed. Off to one side of the table stands the Christmas tree.

Suddenly, the caroling of a group of approaching "Herods" is heard amid the jangling of bells and the clanking of the Devil's chains. Conversation ceases. The children shriek in excitement and hide under their chairs. As the head of the household opens the door, the cavalryman steps forward and asks, "Will you accept King Herod into your house?" The host nods and welcomes them in. The Herods resume their caroling as they enter and group themselves into a chorus at the entrance to the dining room.

King Herod wears a silver-colored shirt loaned to him by a local police officer and gold and silver robes borrowed from the village priest. Around his neck hangs a large metal plaque with an embossed wingspread eagle—the national emblem of Poland. Black crayon marks above his lips form a mustache, and strands of black yarn glued to his chin create a beard. On his head sits a crown cut out of heavy scrap metal and loosely draped with strands of orange, white, and blue beads, and gold and silver sequins. The crown has been in the player's family since before World War II, surviving even their uprooting and resettlement after the war.

The Polish Cavalryman is dressed in his great uncle's army uniform, with white fringed epaulettes and medals and ribbons decorating his chest. A silver tinfoil stripe stretches down each side of his pants. The long metal sword that he carries at his side was used by one of his ancestors in the 1830 uprising against the Czar. On his head, he wears a tall, cylindrical cardboard hat. The Field Marshal and the Turk also wear military clothing. The Field Marshal wears a fireman's hat, while the Turk distinguishes himself by an elaborate headdress of gold-colored glass balls.

The Jew-Rabbi's costume consists of an over-sized suitcoat fastened at the waist by a towel, and a sheepskin mask to which a wispy silver-gray beard is attached. A pillow has been stuffed in his back to create a hunchback effect, and a battered black felt hat has been shoved on his head so low that it almost reaches his glasses. In his left hand, he carries a large "bible" as a symbol of his learnedness.

The Devil wears a black sheepskin coat turned inside out and a sheepskin mask covering his entire head. A red felt tongue protrudes at the mouth and ram's horns stick out from his head. The Devil carries a bell-tipped pitchfork and long chains which he rattles with every step.

Death is dressed in a white sheet and a skull-shaped mask, and carries a white wooden scythe.

As the chorus of players stands singing at the entrance to the room, the family members turn their chairs to face them. The play flows organically out of the caroling by opening with a carol prolog. The carol depicts the scene of Jesus' birth in Bethlehem—the catalyst for the play's action. After singing the carol, the players remain standing at the entrance to the room until each of their roles is called for.

First the Cavalryman steps forward and announces:

> King Herod rules in this house
> As he always has and always will.

King Herod orders the Cavalryman to:

> Go to the town of Bethlehem
> and cut off every little head—
> beginning with my own son.

A humorous interlude follows in which the Jew, acting the part of a clown, sings, dances, and cavorts among the spectators.

One of his songs goes as follows:

> My wife was Jewish
> and refused to eat pork,
> so she died of hunger,
> and I must hop for her soul's sake.

At this point a woman in the audience calls out, "Hop, Jew, hop," to which he replies, "Just a minute, Ma'am," and then hops about the room, shifting from one foot to the other, while the accordion urges him on and the spectators clap their hands. Sometimes the Jew continues to sing for as long as twenty minutes, depending on his mood and the response of the audience. Finally, the King orders him to leave. He does not leave the room but scampers about among the spectators. He grabs and kisses the girls, soiling their dresses with his coal-dust-covered hands, and "steals" vodka and cakes from the holiday table. Throughout the rest of the performance he remains among the spectators and continues to play pranks.

Next the Turk challenges the Cavalryman and mortally wounds him. The Devil and Death are called.

Death touches her wooden scythe to the King's neck. The King leans over and kneels on one knee, indicating that he has died. The Devil jumps about gleefully and offers to take his body, while Death agrees to take his soul. Together they take King Herod by his hands and lead him away. The story has ended.

The players reassemble to sing carol greetings of thanks to the host family wishing them "health and happiness, on earth as in heaven." The spectators do not clap, but instead treat the players as guests in their homes. As Mieczyslaw Koszka, the man who played King Herod for eight years in Bojków, explained: "The people who accept us into their homes on Christmas Eve do so warmly and sincerely. Afterwards, they share food and drink with us, wish us well, and invite us back the next year. Thus, our reward does not come from dry applause but from the good times we share together.''

(''Those good times are sometimes so merry that we do not make it beyond four or five houses,'' added the Devil—after asking me to turn off my tape recorder.)

As the Herods leave to go on to the next cottage, some of the children in the family follow them out the door and remain with them the entire evening. It is usually from among these early enthusiasts that a new group of Herods is formed, carrying on the tradition after the older Herods leave for army duty.

Source: ''Performance in Polish Villages'' by Marjorie Young in *The Drama Review* 18 (4) (T-64) (December 74), 6-9.

Portugal

Christmas in Vila Velha

Men and women from Vila Velha and the two nearby villages regularly attend Christmas Eve mass but nowadays hardly anyone comes from the more distant villages, although I was told that this was not so in the past. During the mass, women sit in the centre nave of the church, while some of the more respected men (the local doctor, one or two proprietários, the Junta clerk) sit in the front pews with their families. Other men stand at the back or take seats in the right nave of the church and go in and out during the mass. Since it is usually very cold at Christmas time, they stamp their feet on the stone floor, some talk in loud voices, some smoke, some are clearly intoxicated. When the mass is over, the priest holds up the image of the infant Jesus for the congregation to kiss. Women and children move forward first and form an orderly queue but when the men's turn comes, they rush up noisily to plant a perfunctory kiss on the foot of the image. After mass, everyone goes home to the traditional Christmas-eve supper.

Mass and supper mark the two moments of the Christmas celebration. The supper is strictly a family reunion and even families who do not attend the mass respect this traditional Christmas custom.

Source: *A Portuguese Rural Society* by Jose Cutileiro. Oxford: Clarendon, 1971, p. 252.

Puerto Rico

San José de la Navidad on Hispaniola

On the small island of Hispaniola, off Puerto Rico, the Church of San José presents an animated *nacimiento*. This mechanized toy village features tiny trains and various inhabitants going about their jobs. Children travel to this church at Christmas each year to see the wondrous miniature *nacimiento*.

Source: *Christmas the World Over* by Daniel J. Foley. Philadelphia: Chilton, 1963, p. 114.

Roumania

Making *turte* and threatening the fruit trees

The Christmas festivities begin on the twenty-fourth of December, the last of Advent, which is also a holiday. On that day *turte* are eaten in every household. This is a special kind of cake and is made of many layers of thin dough with melted sugar or honey and pounded walnut. Sometimes bruised hemp-seed is used instead of sugar. The *turte* are prepared on the previous day. In the midst of her kneading the dough, the housewife walks into the yard followed by her husband who holds an ax. They approach a tree and he threatens to cut it down. ''It seems to me this tree is useless; it bears no fruit,'' he says. The wife speaks up to save the tree. ''Oh, no,'' she says, ''I am sure it will be as full of fruit next summer as my fingers are full of dough.'' They pass on to the next tree where the dialogue is repeated, and so on until many trees are visited. The man threatens, the woman saves each tree that they want to coax into fruit-bearing.

While this is clearly a pagan ceremonial, the remnant of some old custom, the *turte* into which the dough is made is supposed to represent the swaddling clothes of the infant Christ. Thus are paganism and Christianity brought together.

Colinde singers, c. 1900

Boys are busy announcing Christmas from house to house with the greeting:

> Good-morning to Uncle *Ajun!*

We dress heavily, because the winters are usually severe, and begin our rounds before dawn. We carry long bags into which we pack the gifts that are offered us as we pass from house to house and repeat the old familiar greetings. Sometimes we add verses of our own and songs. We expect and usually receive some fruit or *colac* or a small gift of money. If we strike a house where the people are slow in coming forward with a gift we repeat the song again and again:

> Wake up, wake up, Great Lords,
> For we bring you great news, etc.

But if we are kept waiting too long, we are likely to break out with the chorus:

> Good-morning to Uncle Ajun:
> Do you give us, or do you not?

repeated several times.

If our patience was tried too long we knew and could use some humorous verses about stingy people. But sometimes all our strategy failed and we had to give up all hope and pass on to the next house to begin all over.

These greetings are called *colinde*. We began singing *colinde* on the evening of the twenty-fourth and kept them up regularly till midnight. On the thirty-first of December we changed our songs into verses appropriate for greeting the new year.

We banded ourselves into a group and learned to recite these verses, legends, and fanciful stories, under the leadership of an older boy with experience. The *colindae* are supposed to come from the Latin *calendae, festum calendarium*. Some of the verses are adaptations to Christian subjects. Other verses are quite foreign in spirit to the Christian religion. Most of them have been carried down orally from remote ages.

We chanted the verses together, according to tradition, always beginning each stanza with the same lines, over and over:

Asta sare-i sare mare,	This evening is a great evening,
Florile dalbe;	White flowers;
Sarea mare-a lui Craciun	It is the great Christmas Eve,
Florile dalbe!	White flowers!

and always ending each stanza with the same refrain:

Casa-i legea din batrani,	For such is the law (custom) of old,
Florile dalbe;	White flowers;
Din batrani din oameni buni,	From the old, the good men,
Florile dalbe!	White flowers!

. . . We knew a collection of many stories, making several hundred verses in all.

We were supposed to be messengers and to have come from distant lands. In these chants we related our experiences: whom met, what gifts we received and other fabulous happenings.

Every little while the boys broke out with the shout: *La ani si la multi ani! To the new year and to many years to come!* This gave us a chance to break our subject. Many of our *colinde* narrated fanciful stories about the moon, the sun, the stars. Even the Lord sometimes figured in our recitals. Whenever we could we brought into action the householder before whose window we were singing our carols. Usually we gave him the rôle of the hero of our tale.

The Star singers

The *colinde* we sang at night. But we were also busy during the daytime carrying from house to house *Steaua*, the Star. This is a plain, six-cornered star, made of wood which we carried around on a high wooden pole. We covered it with colored and gilt papers and frills to make it look pretty. We kept a small candle burning in the middle of our star and the light shining through the colored paper gave it a weird appearance. We also put many little bells all around the star and the pole and their merry jingle heralded our approach.

We carried the star from about the twenty-fourth of December till the end of the month. The custom is said to be a remnant of an old Roman festival, the *Atelanae* or *Satirae*.

The songs we recited while carrying the star had come down through tradition from past ages:

Who will receive
The beautiful star
With many corners
And tiny ones . . . etc.

and the melody was also traditional. . . .

Source: *When I Was a Boy in Roumania* by Dr. J.S. Van Teslaar. Boston: Lothrop, Lee & Shepard Co., 1917, p. 80.

St. Kitts and Nevis

Christmas masquerading on St. Kitts and Nevis

Masquerade troups consist of eight to twelve performers and three musicians who play bass drum, kettle drum, and fife. They are in colorful shirts, short aprons, and capes decorated with mirrors, beads, and ribbons. Small bells may be attached and circular headdresses of peacock feathers complete the costume. The Captain directs the troup with a crack from his whip as they perform a routine of dances. In 1986 they were seen to perform the Quadrille, the Fine, the Wild Mas, the Jig, the Waltz, and the Boillola.

This masquerade is performed almost identically in The Dominican Republic, where it arrived with immigrants from St. Kitts and Nevis.

Source: "Jonkonnu and Other Christmas Masquerades" by Judith Bettelheim in *Caribbean Festival Arts* by John W. Nunley and Judith Bettelheim. Seattle: Univ. of Washington, 1988, p. 81.

Sierra Leone

Boys' Alikali Devils in Bo, Sierra Leone

On the major Muslim and Christian holidays, groups of schoolboys parade in formation down the public streets of town with their *devils*, stopping to perform before any adults who might appreciate their efforts sufficiently to offer a dash (a gift, usually monetary). When a likely group of spectators is spotted, the boys form a semicircle facing the audience with the musicians behind the masker. A performance, lasting six to fifteen minutes, includes two or three dances by the *devil*, accompanied by a group of child musicians playing a variety of handcrafted instruments and a chorus singing songs drawn from the masking group's repertoire. During any one festival day, such a routine may be repeated twenty or thirty times, and a group can collect a considerable amount of money (the equivalent of an unskilled worker's wage for two or three days) and numerous followers.

These performances are sponsored by urban associations that are multi-ethnic, residentially based, and segregated by sex but not by religion or social status. Each group, composed of seven or eight boys aged seven to twelve, maintains order, both political and performative, through a nonhierarchical structure made up of seven officers. The "owner" of the *devil,* who keeps the costume in his home and is responsible for its maintenance, is the founder of the group. Internal harmony is the responsibility of the "headman," who also acts as spokesman in inter-group disputes. Often selecting both the festival route through town and the songs and dances for performance, he also collects the dashes. These he turns over to the "cashier," who safeguards membership fees and admirers' contributions and keeps a mental record of the accounts. The "controller" stations himself near the masker in readiness to re-arrange the costume should it become disturbed during dancing. If the group sports an aggressive *devil,* he also restrains the dancer, keeping him from going berserk. Although the possibility always exists in theory that maskers may run amok, usually the controller only has to manage smaller spectators who tend to close in on the *devil* in their eagerness to see the dance. This boy is also in charge of co-ordinating various elements in the performance, and if a group builds an enclosure in which to dress the masker, he selects the work detail for its construction. All members audition for the three performing positions, and by a process of elimination the group as a whole selects the head musician, who leads the dance music, the head singer, who supervises the chorus, and the dancer, who follows the musicians' lead and performs the Alikali dances particular to each of the four *devil* types.

The most common *devil* is the Jolly, whose *dressing,* or costume, consists of three basic parts: the body of the dancer is covered by a long-sleeved, loosely fitting shirt and a pair of full-length trousers; the head is hidden by a cloth hood with a circular inset of mesh or net over the face, through which the dancer can easily breathe and see; the hands and feet are covered by pairs of socks, or sometimes by gloves, matching if possible. The Jolly wears no headdress, and there are no other prescribed accessories to his costume, which is usually made from solid-color cotton cloth, although the face covering, most often of white gauze, is separately inset. Heavily gathered ruffles, often in a contrasting color, outline this inset and the legs or arms of the costume; the use of unusual color combinations, the addition of decorative fringe, belts, lace, and imitation fur contribute to the individual appearance of different Jolly *devils.*

The Jolly *devil* is said to be a jumper who turns about; his dance consists of a series of acrobatic stunts such as handstands, headstands, and somersaults. Most also run rapidly in circles with the body bent forward and inclined toward the earth. Individual variations that I witnessed included a "woman" dance, which involved the shaking of non-existent breasts and much *tumba* ("bottom") wiggling, and dances apparently influenced by the very popular kung fu movies shown in Bo, for they were punctuated with the sharp jabs and kicks typical of this form of self-defense.

Source: "Alikali Devils of Sierra Leone" by Jeanne Cannizzo in *African Arts* XII (4) (August 1979), 66-70.

South Africa

Christmas customs of South Africans of European ancestry

Christmas trees, mistletoe, and presents from Santa continue the European tradition in South Africa. Dinner, however, may be an outdoor lunch. Featured dishes might include turkey, roast beef, mince pies, suckling pig, tumeric rice with raisins, and plum pudding. Crackers and paper hats add to the festivities. In the afternoons there are games or other outdoor activities.

Source: *Christmas Customs around the World* by Herbert H. Wernecke. Philadelphia: The Westminster Press, 1959, p. 109.

Christmas in South Africa

Christmas in South Africa is celebrated on December 25, in much the same manner as the rest of the Christian world.

Christmas falls shortly after the winter solstice, when, in the Northern Hemisphere, the night is longest. The birth of Christ thus symbolizes the passing of the world's long night of preparation and the coming of a new day.

Midnight Mass on Christmas Eve, and church services on Christmas Day are well attended.

The pine trees (not available everywhere), with their evergreen needles and distinctive aroma, are a symbol of the never-changing loveliness of the Child of Bethlehem. They are festively decorated and placed in churches and public areas such as shopping malls, civic centres and urban recreational parks, and especially at home. Father Christmas (Santa Claus) is a popular figure.

The festive board also contributes to the sociable character of an essentially family festival, relating back to the Holy Family of Bethlehem.

Source: Embassy of South Africa, Washington, D.C.

Spain

Villancios, Spanish carols

Spanish carols talk of the Holy Family as if they were next door neighbors. Two examples:

> The Virgin is washing diapers
> She hangs them to dry on the rosemary bush.
> The little birds sing
> And the water rushes off laughing.
>
> St. Joseph kissed the Child Jesus on the cheek.
> The Infant Jesus said to him,
> "You are tickling me with your bristles."

The carols are accompanied by the *zambomba.* This is made of an earthen pot, with a piece of skin stretched over the open end.

A reed is inserted into the middle. The reed is rubbed up and down with a wet finger, producing a *rom, rom, rom* sound.

Source: *Spanish Fiestas* by Nina Epton. New York: A.S. Barnes, 1968, pp. 210-211.

Beating the Yule log for sweets in an Aran Basque community

The Yule log is brought in covered with a cloth. The father prays with the children; then all beat the log with sticks three times. The cloth is removed and the candles and cake it has brought the children are revealed. The log is called *Naddau Tidun.* This custom is popular in Catalonia and as far north as Poitou [France].

Source: *Pyrenean Festivals* by Violet Alford. London: Chatto and Windus, 1927, p. 97.

Surinam

A two-day holiday in Surinam

CHRISTMAS—Although the celebration of this festivity does not differ at all from other countries, we recognize *two* Christmas days, the 25th and the 26th of December. The first Christmasday is reserved for the family with the traditional Christmasdinner, a visit to Church, and exchanging of Christmas gifts, while the second day most families usually extend invitations to their friends for a Christmas party with dancing and eating and presents are being exchanged under [sic] the dearest friends.

Source: Embassy of the Republic of Surinam.

Sweden

The straw goat

Straw decorations are popular Christmas ornaments in Sweden. Angels, flowers, stars, and other symbols are woven of straw. A braided straw goat, the Christmas Goat, stands under the tree. At one time these straw goats were sent from farm to farm as Christmas greetings. They are thought to have descended from the billy goat of the God Thor, which was associated with midwinter festivals in pre-Christian times.

Source: *Round the Swedish Year* by Lorna Downman, Paul Britten Austin, and Anthony Baird. Stockholm: Swedish Institute/Bokförlaget, 1967, p. 82.

Christmas Eve in Sweden

Only when the tree has been fixed upright in its metal foot, and decorated, can the working part of Christmas Eve be regarded as over—or almost—and the merry-making and eating begin.

Decorating a Swedish tree never takes long. Most people prefer their tree to be its own ornamentation, with a few white candles here and there and perhaps a white or silver ornament hung to catch the light.

Now, surely, it's time to pitch into all that delicious food? Not quite. First the manger must be taken out of its box and set up on a suitable table. The odd, but beloved, assortment of animals is placed about on a paradoxical scene of cotton wool representing snow, and a blotting-paper carpet of delicate green grass (sown by a thoughtful mother in good time) not so much to represent the luscious vegetation of the sub-tropics, as a reminder of the glory of the Swedish spring.

Other symbols of hope, of looking forward to a new spring and another summer can be read in the potted bulbs taken out now and placed around the house. Set weeks ago and carefully tended for this moment, these pots of blue or pink hyacinths and dainty lilies-of-the-valley belong to Christmas and are cherished for their loveliness in the midst of darkness and cold. The red tulip has also become a part of Christmas and is by far the most common flower on sale at this time. Cratefuls are flown in yearly from Holland. And a miniature variety in its small pot or fragile birch-bark container is a welcome gift.

But—now we're ready! With a joining of hands and thumping of feet, the family sets off on a ring dance. Round the table—how festive it looks!—down the corridor, through each room, up the stairs and down again. In and out the line coils, to the somewhat breathless accompaniment of old Swedish carols.

And so, back to the kitchen where the Christmas meal awaits them. Someone switches on the large Star of Bethlehem in the window. Someone else lights the candles, not forgetting the tall candle in the centrepiece. A third turns off the electric light. There! For a minute, a hush descends as the special atmosphere that is Christmas fills the room. Flickering light on the red of the tablecloth, a faint suggestion of hyacinths and candlewax mixed with the sharper and spicier smell of the food on the table. Then, the spell is broken and the eating begins.

Plate in hand, each member of the family helps himself to the vast *smörgasbord* spread out before him. Beginning with one of the pickled herring dishes or some other fish savoury, the family works its way slowly and appreciatively for the next hour or two through the savouries and pastes and Swedish salads. Finally it's time for the *lutfisk* and boiled potatoes and, last of all, the rice dessert.

All hands help to stack the dishes and stuff what's left of the food back into the larder. Mother makes coffee and heaps a plate with Christmas cookies.

Urged on by the children's excitement, the grown-ups take their plates round a table. Even they find it hard to take their eyes from the large wickerwork basket overflowing with gifts. What are they waiting for?

Why, Father Christmas, of course!

There's a knock on the front door. A gasp of anticipation from the children. And then he comes in, a little bowed from the sackful of presents on his back. "Are there any good children in this house?'' he asks. Of course, there are! At least on Christmas Eve. With some attempt at disguising his voice father, uncle, or elder brother hands out a few presents to the younger children before he leaves ''to go on to the next house.''

Strictly speaking, the Swedish Father Christmas, or *jultomte,* is not at all our jolly, round-cheeked man but a skinny little person closely resembling the leprachauns of Ireland with whom he has much in common. Or even Puck. For the Swedish *tomte,* or Little Man, has existed since time immemorial. Useful around the farm if well treated, he easily became mischievous and a cause of adversity [if] crossed or neglected. And because midwinter was traditionally a dangerous season, full of evil influences, it was particularly necessary to treat this *tomte* well at that season by putting out food and drink for him. This idea continued on into Christian times. However, during the last few generations, the *jultomte* has become a gentler and more kindly person who distributes gifts rather than receives them. His physical appearance, however, is little changed. And even if he now appears dressed in red with a white beard, he is fairly skinny. Besides, it is still possible to buy small Father Christmases dressed in the age-old grey. Little wire figures, with or without beards; but not particularly jolly.

And now, on a busy Christmas Eve, this very nation has spent *hours* composing verses, rhymed and scanned, for their presents. Foibles and desires—both secret and otherwise—happenings during the year, all are brought out. And, of course, each present has to be read out loud before being handed over to the recipient.

Source: *Round the Swedish Year.* by Lorna Downman, Paul Britten Austin, and Anthony Baird. Stockholm: Swedish Institute/Bokförlaget, 1967, pp. 96-97.

A Swedish Christmas dance

One of the most melodious round dances nowadays mostly connected with Christmas is the old central-Swedish 'Judge-dance'. The circle goes round anti-clockwise whilst one member goes round clockwise inside, holding a lighted candle up to those who are dancing by. At the last line ''Har du drömt om din käraste i natt, skall du mot ljuset le'' he or she stops before one of them and if the latter cannot help smiling then he or she has to take a turn with the light.

> NU VILJA VI BEGYNNA EN DOMAREDANS
>
> We fain would like to start up a judge's dance now, but he's not at home for the present. All-those who in a judge's dance would step, must with hearts aflame be trip-ping All the dan-cers say: ''O! O! O!''
> All the dancers say: ''Well! Well! Well!'' If you dreamt of your dearest one last night. You'll smile upon the light.

Source: *Swedish Christmas.* Gothenburg: Tre Tayckare, p. 258.

Christmas in Sweden, c. 1910

Before the great feast, every Swedish home is scrubbed from attic to cellar. Not a speck of dirt or dust is left when the twilight of December twenty-third falls. *Jul-afton*—the day before Christmas—is also a great day. To us children it meant more than Christmas Day itself.

Early in the morning on December twenty-fourth, we were served coffee and *doppa* while we were still in bed, *doppa* literally meaning to dip in the coffee anything served with it, such as sweet rolls, rusks, or little dry cakes. This, our first breakfast, tasted delicious, for the night had been ''nippy,'' the porcelain stove may have cooled off, and our maid had no time to make a fresh fire. That morning after our coffee and *doppa,* we were allowed to enter the chamber in which our parents slept. We came in to wish them ''*Good Jul,*'' and then were usually invited to creep under the coverlets and cuddle up close to Mother while waiting for our room to get warm so we could dress.

As soon as we had dressed and said our morning prayers, we were set to work unwrapping the decorations for the Christmas tree. Of course, we had no glittering, multi-colored ornaments such as American boys and girls hang on their trees. We had a few meager treasures of tinted and blown glass, gold and silver stars, angels of wax and paper with gauzy wings and shimmering robes; but we used home-made ornaments, such as tiny baskets for nuts and bonbons woven of bright paper strips. Then, too, we had gilded pine and spruce cones, also silver and gold-painted walnuts; and what with the red apples and gingerbread figures and the candles, our Christmas tree looked lovely.

If the weather was nice, my sister Constance and I were allowed to come with Father to the spruce forest and help him select the prettiest tree.

He always made a pretty little ceremony out of this tree-cutting. After a perfect one had been found, he would walk up to the nearest and largest tree, doff his cap, bow low before it, and say in a deep solemn voice: ''Dear Father Spruce, I salute you. May we bring your pretty child to our house to help us celebrate Christmas?''

Soon it lay on the sled, and we would return to the city. Most people bought their trees in town, but Father always preferred to cut ours himself. Next thing, the fragrant dark-green pyramid was set up in its green-painted wooden base and we began decorating it.

Soon the most tantalizing odors penetrated from the kitchen, and we suddenly discovered that, we were so hungry, our mouths actually watered. In a short while Lotta, our maid, invited us to the kitchen to *doppa i grytan,* dip in the kettle.

On the stove stood a huge, burnished, copper kettle. In it had been boiling ever since early morning the entire head of a great pig, several sets of pigs' feet, beef tongues, various meat sausages, a whole ham, some salted beef, and pork. All these viands had been removed to several platters and stood steaming on the kitchen table ready to be carried into the dining-room where the Christmas table was spread and would remain so until after December twenty-sixth.

On the white, scrubbed kitchen table stood serving plates,

knives and forks, and some sliced *limpa*. Each participant in the *doppa* ceremony stuck his fork firmly into a slice of the *limpa,* then immersed it in the rich broth of the kettle until it was well soaked. It was then deftly flicked on the serving plate. Then one went into the dining-room where Father was busy slicing meat, ham, or tongue, distributing pigs' feet, or anything else desired from the Christmas kettle. There was also the huge, plump cheese to be cut and sampled; it was Father's task to cut into it and to eat the first slice, pronouncing it good.

Usually some friends came in for this meal to try the *Jul-ale,* wish the family "*Good Jul,*" and make plans for some sleighing party or other entertainment in which we could all take part.

All food had to be prepared on December twenty-fourth; for on the great day itself nobody was supposed to cook anything, except making the inevitable coffee.

After we had literally stuffed ourselves with the many good things on the table, we returned to our various tasks. How we enjoyed sealing up the gifts! Even after thirty years of absence from Sweden, the odor of sealing-wax brings back the most vivid memories of the Christmas joys of my childhood. Of course we had no gay tinselled cords or holly ribbons or pretty embossed Christmas seals in those days; we used red twine, red sealing-wax, and white paper for our packages.

But no package—no matter how humble—was complete unless it had a jolly jingle written on it. These little verses were supposed to be read aloud by the *Jul-gubbe* when the gifts were distributed, a person with a gift for rhyming being thereby given opportunity to express himself. . . .

The dinner on Christmas Eve is a stately meal. . . . After the fish course the main dish, *Jul-gröt,* is served. This dish is a rich, boiled rice-pudding, flavored with stick cinnamon and decorated with ground cinnamon and powdered sugar. In the center is a little lake of melted butter, and around the edge a deep ditch filled with honey. In the *Jul-gröt,* which is served with milk, a *lucky almond* is always buried.

But it is an immemorial custom that each person who is to partake of this special food must first *Rimma för Gröten,* that is, he must make up a nonsense rhyme—usually something complimentary to the hostess or the cook, or one's table neighbor.

Our own dinner is finished with "torta," nuts and fruit. Before the *Jul-gröt* is removed from the table, a generous portion is put into a dish with an extra lump of butter in the center. This is for the "Tomte-gubbe," or the "Good Luck Brownie," who is said to live in the attic of every well-ordered house in Sweden. The delicacy is placed in the attic stairway, and at midnight the "Tomte-gubbe" comes to have his feast. On Christmas morning, Lotta always showed me the empty dish. But the "lucky almond" in the *Jul-gröt!* Oh, with what eagerness we all looked for it in our individual dishes! The one who found it would be especially fortunate during the coming year.

After the dinner, we all joined hands and marched about the Christmas tree singing old folk-songs and ballads. Usually Father excused himself, saying that he had some important business to attend to. As we were romping and singing, there came a fearful pull on our door-bell. We all stood still, waiting.

Mother bravely went to the door. When she opened it and looked outside, there stood the *Jul-gubbe* as real as real could be. He entered the vestibule and stamped into the living-room. He slapped his arms; he puffed and he panted as if he had been running. He wore a mask showing only a pair of keen grey-blue eyes through holes cut for the purpose of seeing. But it was a pleasant ruddy mask, with long, curly whiskers of grey.

We children stood at a little distance, hardly daring to breathe, for usually the "Jul-gubbe" carried a great sack when he came to our house. In fear we wondered what had happened. Still, Mother did not seem upset about this unusual occurrence. Instead, she offered him a glass of the *Jul-ale* which he sipped slowly; and then, very deliberately, wiped his beard with the back of his gloved hand. He rose as if to go, for he bowed to Mother and was already at the door, when sister Margareta set up a lusty howl: "Mother, don't let him go! He always brought us presents other years."

Upon hearing this distressful plea, the *Jul-gubbe* gave a happy chuckle, and went out to the vestibule, where, to be sure, we all saw the huge sack filled to the bursting point with packages.

All of us remained quietly at home on Christmas Day. We children played with our new toys and read to each other out of our new story-books.

Next day the Christmas festivities began. In my country, there was senseless over-eating of rich food during this season, and among the men, much drinking. So, when finally the holidays were over—well past the middle of January—the people were half-sick and sluggish from the after-effects of too much food and drink.

Then there was the *Jul-brasa* or fire, to be kept lighted until the end of Saint Stephen's Day. This symbolized the return of the sun.

We also had a very pretty legend, possibly of Christian origin—that on Christmas night, the animals were given the power of speech for one hour. When Aunt Inga told me this, I immediately wanted to hear the animals talk, and so to give this fable credence, my aunt adroitly related a story of a servant girl who had also wanted to make sure that this really took place on Holy Night. So she hid herself in the cow-stable on Christmas Eve to witness the miracle, but alas, the next morning she discovered that she had lost her power of speech. It may be, said Aunt Inga, this had happened so that she could not tell human beings what the animals had been talking about.

Source: *When I Was a Girl in Sweden* by Anna-Mia Hertzman. Boston: Lothrop, Lee & Shepard Co., 1926, pp. 56-66.

Syria

Christmas in the Syrian Christian Church

A bonfire of vine stems is made in the middle of the church on Christmas Eve in honor of the Magi, who were cold from their long journey. The family attends Mass on Christmas Eve, and when they return home the father tells the story of the Christ Child, and all sing Christmas carols. Those who can do so make the pilgrimage to Bethlehem on this night.

Source: *Christmas Customs around the World* by Herbert H. Wernecke. Philadelphia: The Westminster Press, 1959, pp. 130-132.

Uganda (Sebei)

An October harvest ritual, *Misisi,* has been adapted as a Christmas ritual called *Mukutanik.* (A detailed description of *Misisi* is found in the autumn harvest section.)

Mukutanik feasting and beer drinking

This ritual somewhat changed in character, is now called *mukutanik* and takes place at Christmas. The change from *misisi* to *mukutanik* reflects a deemphasis upon the harvest, as such, and upon millet as a crop. The word *mukutanik* is built on the root word for a share or portion (*mukut*). A group of families establishes a pattern, and, on successive Christmases, each in turn serves as host, making the beer and providing the food. Each participant provides his share of grain for beer and food and may furnish shares for other guests. The hosts may invite two guests as compensation for their labor in making the beer. There is a lessened sense of obligation to particular kindred in this system, though many of those collaborating are related, just as was the case in the older *misisi,* and libations for the ancestors are not omitted. *Mukutanik* brings together neighbors rather than kindred.

The group of people around a *mukutanik* beer pot behaves differently from the participants around other beer pots, in that they tend to be quiet and subdued, singing songs in small groups but without the quarreling and boisterousness of a work party or other ceremonial pot. Christmas, incidentally, is a time when wives expect new clothes, and children, too, are given clothing. There is no other regular ceremonial associated with Christmas. The result is that adults have a quiet good time, but the children stand along the road, and at such other places where they congregate, with nothing to do.

Source: *Culture and Behavior of the Sebei: A Study in Continuity and Adaptation* by Walter Goldschmidt. Berkeley: Univ. of California Press, 1976, p. 162.

Upper Volta

Street nativities in Ouagadougou, Upper Volta

December in Upper Volta is the crystal clear, dry season of sunny, cool days. Because the millet and cotton harvests are in, money and good feeling abound. The season of celebrations has arrived, and each social group prepares its own events. Some two weeks before Christmas, Christian boys between the ages of five and fifteen are very busy around the entrance gates to their family compounds, building plinths of mud bricks. The nativities they construct atop them are to be ready on Christmas morning, when friends and neighbors will come out to admire them and express their pleasure by leaving a few francs in the bowl provided. These creations appear to be the manifestation of the newly developing children's culture, indicating the importance of a schooled generation and the impact of changing values upon it.

The nativities are fairly recent and localized. Upper Volta is made up overwhelmingly of Moslems and traditional believers, with Christians constituting only about ten percent of the population. Because most civil servants are Christian, the nativities are found in Ouagadougou, the government center. The idea seems to have been introduced sometime in the 1950s by the sisters in Catholic mission schools, who urged the children to make their own little crèches out of paper. Around 1955 small nativities made of six bricks set against houses or courtyard walls began to appear. Around 1960 children started placing these crèches out in the streets, near the entrance gates. This idea then spread rapidly all over the city. One boy's father explained, "When Christmas came to Ouagadougou in 1960, there were crèches (in the streets). Before that the only public celebrations we had were Id and Tabasci (Moslem holidays)."

What some designate as the original version of the street nativity can still be seen in all the *quartiers* of the city. It is a kind of economy model, made of mud bricks and with a peaked roof, set up against a wall on a platform that has little steps to the street level. It is painted white, and a Christmas greeting is written somewhere on it. This form stands up particularly well to the weather, and some are around after years. Others, particularly the free-standing models, tend to erode quickly, or, in some cases, the family recycles the material for another project. It seems that nativities are an ephemeral art. What remains by June the rains take away. The small figures inside tend to be very simple sculpted forms of earth or clay—always the Virgin and Child, usually some angels, frequently animals, and sometimes shepherds or kings. A few are painted. This general theme can be seen in all parts of Ouagadougou, but it is the embellishments on the theme that are so arresting.

In 1981, the most popular design in my own *quartier* of Zogona was the traditional round house with straw roof of the Mossi people, who are the predominant ethnic group in the Ouagadougou area and also constitute about fifty percent of the Voltaic population. The house portion is usually between thirty and sixty centimeters high and is set on a plinth that may be only several centimeters or a meter or so in height, most often rectangular but occasionally round or star-shaped. A masonry dome may be substituted for the thatch, providing another surface to decorate. If the boy has money to buy cement, he trowels on a layer over the mud brick, a local house-building technique called *crépissage*. These round houses are built about a meter in front of the compound wall, although a painted white panel on the wall behind it visually links it to the family property. This also provides another surface for brightly colored messages and pictures of Mary and Joseph, angels, birds, bells, stars, flowers, Voltaic flags, crosses, and hearts and arrows. Written statements include *Joyeux Noël, Bonne Fête, Soyez le Bienvenu, le Divin est né,* and on a few the English greeting "Merry Christmas."

Boys say they get their ideas from looking at pictures of European churches in books and magazines in their schools. Some crèches are little copies of village churches in Europe, but others are imaginative expressions that have little in common with a static photograph. All kinds of found materials enrich the construction. Bits of shiny metal outline doorways. Pieces of plastic packing material are strung like popcorn from tower to tower. Small bars of metal imitate the louvered windows so common in Upper Volta. Tinsel and plastic are much valued. Flashlight bulbs under colored glass provide nightime illumination, and it is becoming the fashion to plant millet around the base, creating a bright green grassy plot, a thing rarely seen in this arid country. Some of the artists have a gift for masonry, and being able to build a nativity several stories high is considered a fine accomplishment. Children greatly admire the more gaudy and individual expressions. There is also room for humor, as in the case of one *église*-crèche that had several small angels running up and down exterior stairways.

Source: "Street Nativities in Ouagadougou" by Priscilla Hinckly in *African Arts* XVI (3) (May 1983), 47-49.

Uruguay

Burning Judas at Christmastime, c. 1955

For several days before their bonfire, the children collect materials to make a "Judas" effigy. This effigy may be larger than the children themselves and may require two children to carry it or be trundled around on a cart. The "Judas" is taken around the neighborhood on begging trips as the children collect wood and coins for the bonfire party. On Christmas Eve or New Year's Eve, the effigy is burnt on a huge bonfire. Since this occurs on one of the hottest nights of the summer, the bonfire itself does not draw the participants especially close. Judas effigies may be burnt, as well, on the Eves of St. John and St. Peter. Since this falls in June, at the coldest time of the year, the bonfires are welcome.

Source: "*Un Vinten P'al Judas*" by Emilio Ramon Paradela. Montevideo: Bilbioteca de Anthropologia y Folklore, 1955.

U.S.S.R./Russia

Christmas gifts in Russia

In Russia Christmas gift exchanges were not a tradition. Godchildren sang carols to their godparents, the girls on Christmas Eve and the boys on early Christmas morning. A traditional dish of rice and wheat with nuts and a jug of home-brewed mead were presented to priests and godparents. This is the end of a forty-day fast for the pious Orthodox, during which fat, meat, and eggs are forbidden.

Source: *Life in Russia* by Michael Binyon. New York: Random House, 1983, p. 230.

Venezuela

Christmas Eve skating in Caracas

After midnight on Christmas Eve, the Avenida de los Caiboas fills with hundreds of teenaged rollerskaters. They skate for an hour or more, until a special early morning Mass. Folk music greets them at the church door. After Mass, they skate home and consume a hearty Christmas breakfast, featuring *hallacas*. This is a spiced meat pastry with cornmeal crust, wrapped in banana leaves and boiled.

Source: *Christmas the World Over* by Daniel J. Foley. Philadelphia: Chilton, 1963, p. 115.

Wales

Y Mari Lwyd visits

In West Glargan and Carmarthenshire (Dyfed), the Mari Lwyd still makes her rounds at Christmastime. This is a hobbyhorse figure with wooden stick body and a real horse's skull painted black, with snapping jaws and bottle-glass eyes. A man in a white sheet operates the horse. She is accompanied by mimers such as a Mare-Leader, a Sargeant, a fiddle-playing Merryman, or black-faced Punch and Judy characters. They carry on a Welsh verbal duel in verse at each house. If he householder wins the verbal duel by providing the most witty verse insults, the Mari must go elsewhere. If the Mari party win, the horse may enter and her party receives treats.

Source: *The Customs and Ceremonies of Britain* by Charles Kightly. London: Thames and Hudson, 1986, p. 157.

An ancient Welsh recipe for the Wassail bowl

FEW PEOPLE have the time nowadays to concoct a Wassail bowl, but for those with hardy stomachs and time on their hands, here is the recipe:

> Simmer a small quantity of the following spices in a teacup of water, viz:—Cardamums, cloves, nutmeg, mace, ginger, cin-

namon, and coriander. When done, put the spice to two, four, or six bottles of port, sherry, or madeira, with one pound and a half of fine loaf sugar pounded to four bottles, and set all on the fire in a clean bright saucepan; meanwhile, have yolks of twelve and whites of six eggs well whisked up in it. When the spiced and sugared wine is a little warm, take out one teacup; and so on for three or four cups; after which, when it boils, add the whole of the remainder, pouring it in gradually, and stirring it briskly all the time so as to froth it. The moment a fine froth is obtained, toss in twelve fine, soft, roasted apples (or crabs) and serve it hot. The spices for each bottle of wine: 10 grains of mace, 28 grains of cinnamon, 46 grains of cloves, 37 grains of cardamums, 12 grains of nutmeg, 48 grains of ginger, 49 grains of coriander seeds.

Source: *Holidays in Wales* by William H. Crawford, Jr. New York: Oxford, 1950, p. 27.

Zaire

Christmas in Zaire, c. 1964

The singing of carols and the dramatization of the Christmas story mark the festive season amont the Christians in Zaire's villages. A palm branch shelter is made for the Holy Family and decorated with flowers. When it is time for the play to begin, the drum beats out the call "Come, see, come, see." Visitors are greeted with a cheery "*Yo, yo! Yo, yo!*"

The whole village may take part in the drama, men and women lining up before the "tax collectors" at the start. Joseph and Mary appear and are told there is no room in any house for them. They go to the palm branch shelter. A cradle is there with a real baby in it. Soon shepherds appear with some live goats and they make their bows to the little family. Then come the Wise Men, wearing costumes of artistically twisted scarfs of bright colors and carrying black native pots and gourds.

Source: *Children's Festivals from Many Lands* by Nina Millen. New York: Friendship Press, 1964, p. 27.

Zimbabwe

Kisimusi in Rhodesia, c. 1964

In the Christian village home, the parents do their best to prepare as large a feast as possible, give gifts of clothing to their children, and candy to friends' children. Christmas Day begins with attendance at the early morning church service. The children usually participate in a song which they have practiced especially for this day.

Sometimes a feast is held for all the people of the church. The mothers then take turns preparing the church feast, so that others can attend the service. Everyone, old and young, streams from the church toward the home where the feast is being prepared, and those who are not helping sit down under a shady tree and wait to be served. There will be fresh roast ox or goat, if the village is prosperous, cornmeal porridge (very stiff), bread, jam, tea, and sugar. The men and boys are served first, then the women and girls. The church does not invite outsiders, but no one who passes by is turned away.

Source: *Children's Festivals from Many Lands* by Nina Millen. New York: Friendship Press, 1964, pp. 37-38.

Zululand

Christmas Celebrations

It is possible that the increasingly important role played by the party in connection with the Christian festival of Christmas in Zulu society may have roots in the obsolete festival of the first fruits. The party, if nothing more, is found everywhere, including among pagans. Parallels between the Christmas celebration, ritual celebrations and the annual feast of the first fruits of old are not lacking.

Much importance is attached to the fact that people get together at Christmas, particularly relatives and kinsmen. The annual holiday granted people who work in urban areas, industry and mines makes it possible for them to assemble. The presence of the men is a significant part of the Christmas party. "That is why Christmas is a great occasion. It is because of the getting together of all the people of the family.". . . Much attention is given to the preparation of a meal to which many assemble. Everywhere possible either a goat or some other animal is slaughtered. In Christian homes where importance is no longer attached to the choice of animal, a sheep may be slaughtered and, occasionally, even a pig.

The speaking out ritual which occurs at most Christmas parties has already been described. Along with the meat eaten at the festival, vegetables are served. It may be a coincidence that greens are obtainable at this time of the year, but I could not but make a note of a hostess once stressing very emphatically that the maize cobs which were placed before us on the table "are the first of the fields". I also made a note of the fact that the cobs were already fairly well ripened, many people eating fresh maize at a far earlier stage.

Zulu do not attend to graves as do many whites. Besides Easter, it appears that Christmas is one of the few occasions when flowers are placed on the graves.

Source: *Zulu Thought-Patterns and Symbolism* by Axel-Ivar Berglund. Uppsala, Sweden: Swedish Institute of Missionary Research, 1976, pp. 323-328.

For more on Christmas see: "The Afro-Jamaican Jonkonnu Festival: Playing the Forces and Operating the Cloth" by Judith Bettelheim. 2 vols. Dissertation. Yale University, 1979. (Much of this is restated in *Caribbean Festival Arts* by Judith Bettelheim and John Nunley. Seattle: University of Washington, 1988); *All Silver and No Brass: An Irish Christmas Mumming* by Henry Glassie. Bloomington: Indiana University Press, 1975; *The Australian Christmas* by Frank Cusack. Melbourne:

Heineman, 1966; "Celebrating Las Posadas in Los Angeles" in *Western Folklore,* 39 (1980), 71-105; "Christmas" in *Folklore of American Holidays* edited by Hennig Cohen and Tristram Potter Coffin. 2nd ed. Detroit: Gale Research, 1991; *Christmas: An Annotated Bibliography* by Sue Samuelson. New York: Garland, 1982; *Christmas Customs around the World* by Herbert H. Wernecke. Philadelphia: The Westminster Press, 1959; *Christmas: Its Origins and Associations.* London: Elliott Stock, 1902. Gale Reprint, 1968; *Christmas Mumming in Newfoundland.* Toronto: Univ. of Toronto Press, 1969; *Christmas the World Over* by Daniel J. Foley. Philadelphia: Chilton, 1963; *The Christmas Tree Book: History of the Christmas Tree and Antique Christmas Tree Ornaments* by P.V. Snyder. New York: Viking, 1977; *Christmastide: Its History, Festivals and Carols* by William Sandys. London: John Russell Smith, 1860; "German Christmas and the Christmas Tree" by Alexander Tille in *Folk-Lore,* 3 (1892), 166-182; *German Festivals and Customs* by Jennifer M. Russ. London: Oswald Wolff, 1982; *Joy Through the World.* United States Committee for UNICEF. New York: Dodd, Mead, 1985; *La Navidad en Bolivia* by Julia Elena Fortun de Ponce. La Paz: Collección Ethnografia y Folklore, Ministerio de Educación, 1957; *Les Noëls de France.* by Maurice Vioberg. Grenoble: B. Arthaud, 1934; *Once Upon a Christmas Time* by Thyra Ferre Bjorn. New York: Holt, Rinehart and Winston, 1964; *Swedish Christmas.* Gothenburg: Tre Tryckare, 1955.

December 26

Boxing Day

The day after Christmas is known as "Boxing Day" throughout the British Empire and is still an official holiday in many countries. Nowadays it is thought of as a day to throw out the Christmas boxes, but the original meaning comes from the small box passed for donations on this day. Tradesmen such as postmen and dustmen once received small boxes of holiday cash on the day after Christmas.

The Bahamas

Boxing Day Junkanoo in Nassau, c. 1986

An elaborate Junkanoo parade takes place in Nassau on Boxing Day. Special Junkanoo groups have worked for days preparing elaborate costumes made of crepe paper and gessoed cardboard. The parade of 1986 included giant sea creatures, giant Christmas effigies, and mythic figures. One group, the Saxon Superstars, featured a contemporary theme, "SOS—Save Our Species," with maché costumes of endangered Caribbean species such as iguana, parrots, wild boar, and giant frogs. Bands provide music for each group. By 10:00 A.M. the parade is completed and the costumes lie abandoned.

Source: "Jonkannu and Other Christmas Masquerades" by Judith Bettelheim in *Caribbean Festival Arts* by John W. Nunley and Judith Bettelheim. Seattle: Univ. of Washington, 1988, pp. 77-79.

Ireland

A Boxty recipe from Ballymenone

. . . boxty is delicious. "They're alot of work," Mrs. Cutler said, "They are too much work. But, the Lord, they were lovely." Boxty is so tasty that it became a special, ceremonial food, eaten on Hallow Eve and on Boxing Day. From that happy high point in the Christmas season, Mr. Flanagan feels the food took its name.

Every woman has a slightly different recipe for "boxty bread." The culture's homogeneity leaves room for personal diversity. But Ellen Cutler's is representative. First, peel thinly half a dozen of the biggest potatoes you have. Grate them, not your knuckles, on a can lid in which holes have been punched with a nail. Wring the gratings "oh, so tight until not one taste of water is left" in a strong cloth and mix them with salt and boiled mashed potatoes. Mary McBrien said to add the marzipanlike substance skimmed off the water, and to use equal parts of grated and mashed potatoes. Mrs. Cutler uses a bit more than one mashed potato for every two she grates. Next mix the potatoes with flour, about half as much as there is potato, until the whole becomes "nice and dry," then form it into puck-shaped, circular "hurleys," five inches across and one in depth. To cook they need more water than a saucepan will hold, so fill the big black pot, get the water "mad boilin," and slip the hurleys in, remembering to put a plate in first to prevent them from sticking to the bottom. Keep the hurleys moving with a spoon, and in half an hour they will be white clear through and ready for eating. Boxty is eaten "hot out of the pot" with butter and sugar, or the hurleys are split in two or sliced in strips and fried the next day in "drip-pancakes." For them Meta rooney adds water and mashed potato to the "gratins," while Ellen Cutler uses only grated potatoes, but both women add flour, "a lock of salt, and a wee taste of soda" to make a pancake that you butter while hot. "You'd do yourself harm eatin it," Mrs. Cutler said, "it was that good!"

Source: *Passing the Time in Ballymenone* by Henry Glassie. Philadelphia: University of Pennsylvania Press, 1982, p. 492.

Sweden

Second day of Christmas

"The second day of Christmas," or Boxing Day as we call it is specially reserved for family parties. Traditional games and songs break in upon the peace and quiet of the day before. And, if you haven't danced through the house, hand in hand, earlier, you do so now. Aunts and uncles and cousins help swell out the line to imposing proportions. With the well-known words of the old carols on everyone's lips, off you go. In wide circles through the rooms, then round the Christmas tree, up the stairs, down again and into the kitchen this time—where's the leader? Oh, on his way upstairs again. Well, once more:

> "Oh, now it's Christmas-time
> And now it's Christmas-time
> And Christmas last right up to Lent-tide."

Source: *Round the Swedish Year* by Lorna Downman, Paul

Britten Austin, and Anthony Baird. Stockholm: Swedish Institute/Bokförlaget, 1967, p. 101.

December 26
Kwanza

Canada

The Kwanza custom was started in California in 1966 as a distinctly Afro-American celebration. A seven-pronged candle is lit, one candle the first night, two the second, and so forth until the seventh and last day of Kwanza. Each day stands for one of the seven principles of Kwanza: unity, self-determination, working together, sharing, purpose, creativity, and faith.

Source: *Let's Celebrate!* by Caroline Parry. Toronto: Kids Can Press, 1987, p. 49.

For more information on Kwanza see: *The African-American Holiday of Kwanzaa: A Celebration of Family, Country, and Culture* by Maulana Karenga. Los Angeles: Univ. of Sandore Press, 1988; *Kwanza* by Sister Makinya. Berkeley, Calif.: Educational Services, 1971; *The Kwanza Handbook.* Palo Alto, Calif.: Celebrants, 1977; *Kwanzaa* by Cedric McClester. New York: Gumbs & Thomas, 1985.

December 26

St. Stephen's Day

Stephen, the first Christian martyr, was stoned to death after giving an impassioned speech in his own defense before the Jewish Council. He had been appointed by the apostles as one of seven men who would look after the needs of widows and he worked many wonders, but he was accused of planning to destroy the Jewish Temple.

Austria

St. Stephen's Day customs in prewar Austria

When we lived in Austria, the three greatest feasts of the year were distinguished by two church holidays each: Easter Sunday and Easter Monday, Pentecost Sunday and Pentecost Monday, and St. Stephen's Day after Christmas Day. We know that the war did away with these second Church holidays, but they still exist in our memory and we always keep them in our house. In Austria the peasants used to celebrate St. Stephen's Day in a special way, because St. Stephen is the patron saint for horses, watching over their health. After the Solemn High Mass the pastor would come in surplice and stole and wait in front of the church door with holy water and sprinkler. The horses of the village, beautifully decorated with ribbons in their manes and tails, would now parade before him in solemn procession and he would bless every single one of them. He would also bless oats and hay, which each farmer had brought along for that purpose; the horses would be fed with the blessed feed, to protect them against sickness and accidents.

Source: *Around the Year with the Trapp Family* by Maria Augusta Trapp. New York: Pantheon, 1955, p. 64.

Ireland

"Hunting the Wren"

In 1959 "Hunting the Wren" was still taking place in southern Ireland, especially in Cork and Kerry and in Dublin. Young boys with blackened faces, sometimes dressed as girls, roam the streets on St. Stephen's morning. They carry a wren-bush of holly or gorse tied with ribbons and colored papers. It is supposed to carry the body of a dead wren. In Dublin boys hold out a hat asking, "Give us a penny to bury the wren." They sing chants such as

> "The wren, the wren, the king of all birds.
> St. Stephen's Night was caught in the furze.
> Though he is small, his family is great.
> So rise up your honours and give us a treat.
> God bless the mistress of the house,
> A golden chain around her neck,
> And if she is sick, or if she's sore,
> The Lord have mercy on her soul.
> Up with the kettle and down with the pan
> Give us our money and let's be gone!"

They make a din until the householder comes out and pays them. In County Kerry some carry a live wren in a jar as they beg.

In earlier days a dead wren might actually be hung from a pole and carried in procession. Everyone who gave money received a feather from the dead wren as a talisman. The practice was popular at one time in Wales, southeast England, and the Isle of Man, and the hunting of the wren was known in the south of France.

Source: *Lore and Legends of Schoolchildren* by Peter and Iona Opie. Oxford: Oxford Univ. Press, 1959, pp. 288-289.

St. Stephen's Day wren songs

As we continued on our way, prying into bushes, brambles and hedges, I was thinking how strange it was the wren should be so famous.

On Saint Stephen's day, all over Ireland, this tiny bird is honored.

Well do I remember Father giving us pennies to give to the wren boys on that day.

The wren boys went from house to house in pairs, each one carrying a berib-boned furze bush hung with pasteboard images of the wren. They would come to the front door and knock very hard with the knocker to make certain of an audience before singing the wren song which, I am at a loss to explain why, has some very cruel lines, lines that are as untruthful as they are cruel, for no Irish boy would lay finger to a wren. The words of the wren song vary in different parts of Ireland. It is the Waterford version, as sung in front of our house during my boyhood, that I quote here:

> The wren, the wren, the king of all birds,
> On Saint Stephen's day was caught in the furze.
> I up with my wattle and knocked him down,

And brought him into Tramore town.
Now, Mr. Buck is a wealthy man,
So, to his house we brought the wren.
Pockets of money and barrels of beer
We wish you all, a Happy New Year!
Up with the kettle and down with the pan,
Give us some pence and let us be gone!

At the conclusion of the wren song, Bobby and I took great delight in opening the door and distributing our pennies, receiving, in turn for our generosity, God's blessing on ourselves and on our home before the wren boys departed elsewhere.

Source: *When I Was a Boy in Ireland* by Alan M. Buck. New York: Lothrop, Lee & Shepard Co., 1936, pp. 40-41.

Poland

St. Stephen's Day in Poland

On this ''second day of Christmas'' families attend church and visit relatives. Blessings may be exchanged by tossing a handful of rice at each other, recalling the stoning of St. Stephen.

Source: *Joy through the World.* United States Committee for UNICEF. New York: Dodd, Mead & Co., 1985, p. 72.

Sweden

Staffan day in old Sweden

Clearly, what sleep was had was thought to be enough, for next day it was necessary to be up early. Those who arose indecently late were called Staffan or Staffan's fool (In the old almanac the day bore the name of Staffan), and were required to run a ludicrous circuit of the ways between the farms. They were greeted with the words: ''You are a lazy dog and shall be the laziest all they year, you seven-fold sleeper.'' After sufficient raillery the victim was offered a drink—which he put down while in the dunce's corner, one may assume.

As always during Christmas, one ate early in the morning and well. [This Staffan was] not generally indentified with the martyred Stephen, but was commonly thought to be identical with a certain person from Bremen, one of the missionaries sent from there in the middle of the ten hundreds, according to Adam of Bremen, to work in the country of the ''Finnish skaters'', that is to say, northern Norrland. Folk traditions have since coupled him with another Staffan, presumably a monk of the late middle ages, of whom we otherwise know practically nothing, but who is mentioned in certain sources from the fifteen hundreds. Such traditions have combined both these men spiritually into the patron saint of Norrland.

Outside the various farm houses the old Staffan song was sung. The ceremony following this varied greatly, depending upon the degree of generosity which had been shown. If everything went well, the singers were immediately offered a drink, and if they waited too long for the invitation they were likely to improvise songs of more impatient character such as this:

If we sit here long at this wall,
We'll grow ice in our beards in the cold.

If the treat was not offered, or if the gifts were particularly poor, the singers on occasion could behave in a manner about which it is impossible to write.

Source: *Swedish Christmas.* Gottenburg: Tre Tryckare, 1955, pp. 69-70.

December 27

St. John's Day

This is the day of St. John the Divine, the author of the Book of Revelations and the Gospel of St. John.

John was a fisherman, called by Christ along with his brother James to be one of his apostles. According to some legends, he was cast into a vat of boiling oil by Domitan but remained unhurt and was banished to Patmos. This tradition was formerly commemorated in the Western Church on May 6, "Saint John before the Latin Gate."

Austria

St. John's Day toasting in an Austrian family

According to tradition, St. John the Apostle was once presented by his enemies with a cup of poisoned wine intended to kill him. When the Apostle made the sign of the cross over the wine, however, the cup split in half and the poisoned wine was spilled. In memory of this, the Church has a special blessing, the "Benedictio Sancti Johannes." On the 27th, the feast of St. John, the people bring wine along to church and before Holy Mass the priest blesses it. At the main meal at home the wine is poured into as many glasses as there are people. Just before the meal begins, everybody stands up, holding his glass, while the father and mother begin the St. John's Day ceremony: The father touches the mother's glass with his glass, looks her in the eyes and says, "I drink to you the love of St. John." The mother answers, "I thank you for the love of St. John," and they both take a sip. Then the mother turns to the oldest child and repeats, "I drink to you the love of St. John," and the child answers, "I thank you for the love of St. John." Again they take a sip and the child turns to the next oldest, and so it goes around the table until the last one turns to the father and the family circle is closed. Some of the blessed wine is kept for days of sickness or of great celebration. If someone in the family is about to take a journey, a few drops of the blessed wine are added to each wine glass and the whole family again drinks "the love of St. John." Immediately after the wedding ceremony, the newly-wed couple also drink to each other "the love of St. John."

Source: *Around the Year with the Trapp Family* by Maria Augusta Trapp. New York: Pantheon, 1955, pp. 64-66.

Bolivia

San Juan's Day

Uwiha ch'uyay, ceremonial force-feeding of sheep

San Juan celebrations for the sheep begin before daybreak, when the rising Sun, just past the winter solstice, is believed to have special energizing powers. In 1975, as the San Juan sun rose brilliantly and seemed to tremble in the sky. Luis remarked with satisfaction. "*Inti tu-sun.*" ("The Sun dances.") At that moment, he said, the water in the streams momentarily turned to *hampi* (medicine). From sunrise to early afternoon, families sit in their corrals with the sheep, chewing coca from the ritual cloth, drinking *chicha,* and playing "Sargento." The Carnival *ch'uyay* is held at sunset, and the herds are sprinkled with tiny red and yellow flowers called *wakankilla* while the Sun disappears behind the peak of Sawasiray-Pitusiray.

Unlike the llamas, who drink *hampi* and are decorated with tassels, the sheep get daubed with red paint and are made to chew coca. They are stretched out on a poncho facing each other in male-female pairs to "get married." Afterward, the human participants pair themselves to perform the *ch'uyay*. Finally, they drive the confused animals out of the corral, playing "Sargento" on flutes and drums and dancing wildly as the sheep fan out over the hillsides and begin to graze.

"*Urqokuna uwihatan hap'ichishanku*" ("The hills are turning on the sheep"), remarked Gavina a few weeks later as we listened to my tapes of "Sargento."

The verb *hap'ichiy* (to turn on) also refers to lighting candles or to turning on the radio. And while the hills may "turn on" the sheep, they also turn on the people, who play "Sargento" and dance to the point of exhaustion.

Source: *The Hold Life Has: Coca and Cultural Identity in an Andean Community*. Washington and London: Smithsonian Institution Press, 1988, p. 168.

December 28

Holy Innocents' Day

Herod, learning from the Three Magi that they had come to worship a newly born king, ordered every male child in Bethlehem killed. The Magi had been warned in a dream not to reveal the Christ's hiding place to Herod, and Joseph took Mary and the Babe away into Egypt to escape Herod's wrath. This day commemorates that slaughter.

Austria

The boy bishop on Holy Innocents' Day

The day following St. John's Day is a great day for the children. This goes back to a medieval custom in monastery schools. On December 28th, the day dedicated to the Holy Innocents, the boys used to elect one from their midst as bishop—"the Episcopus Puerorum." This boy-bishop would take over the direction of the abbey for this one day. Dressed in pontifical vestments, surrounded by his schoolmates, he would sit in the place of the abbot and the others in the choir stalls of the monks, whereas abbot and monks moved over to the places of the pupils. This custom is still alive in many convents and monasteries, where the young ones in the novitiate have the ruling of the house for this particular day. It also is preserved in many families, where the little ones take the seats of the father and mother and try to play a few little tricks on the grownups as long as they are in authority.

Source: *Around the Year with the Trapp Family* by Maria Augusta Trapp. New York: Pantheon, 1955, p. 66.

Great Britain

Childermas

Childermas prohibitions

CHILDERMAS is the day when Herod ordered the massacring of all the children when Jesus was a baby. There are many strange rites and ceremonies kept on this day and all involve children. Many of them are to remind children of that dreadful happening. In some places they are switched with fir and rosemary twigs. In others children read the prayers in church and in others there are mock ceremonies.

Of all the days in the year, none is so unlucky as Childermas. No work should be begun on it nor the finger nails pared nor any promises made nor undertakings given. In Cornwall they wouldn't even scrub over the kitchen! There is a saying that what is begun on Childermas Day will never be finished. In Ireland they call it "The Cross Day" of the year and believe that anything begun that day will come to a bad ending!

Source: *Happy Holidays* by Eleanor Graham. New York: E.P. Dutton, 1933, p. 247.

Mexico

Los Santos Inocentes

The twenty-eighth of December, the day of Los Santos Inocentes or the Day of the Holy Innocents, is Mexico's April Fools Day. A favorite trick is to ask someone seriously for a loan of some money or some object—and to return immediately a silly toy or a note:

Inocente palomita,	Innocent little dove,
Que te dejaste engañar,	You have let yourself be fooled
Sabiendo que en este día	Knowing that on this day,
Nada se debe prestar.	You should lend nothing.

Sometimes one says the verse without even taking the loan.

Another favorite trick to play on one's friends is to invite them to supper or tea and to serve some pastry filled with cotton, or almond paste filled with flour. This is called making an "innocent" of one.

Source: *A Treasury of Mexican Folkways* by Frances Toor. New York: Crown, 1947, pp. 250-251.

Spain (Catalan)

Town fires and street cleaners

On Holy Innocents' day fires are lit in town gateways, and toll levied on those who enter, a mock mayor is chosen, who forces people to clean up the streets—an admirable idea—and imposes fines which pay for a feast.

Source: *Pyrenean Festivals* by Violet Alford. London: Chatto and Windus, 1937, p. 15.

December 31

New Year's Eve

New Year's Eve is a night of revelry in many cultures as young and old stay up to welcome in the New Year, often with loud noisemaking and toasting.

Armenia

Chimney presents on New Year's Eve

New Year's Eve is the most desirable of evenings, so every Armenian boy will tell you, for it is a day of genuine good time for all the youngsters.

New Year's Eve is not celebrated in Armenia as it is in America. Each Armenian family celebrates New Year's Eve within the home. After supper, the fireplace is used and a fire kept burning until after midnight, so that, light being the sign of life, the family life may be continuous and bright. In the center of the room is put up a large table upon which are set dishes of raisins, nuts, and sweets (*basdegh, rojik*). The boys and girls eat what they can, and fill their pockets with what is left. While the celebration is going on, the neighbors, one at a time, lower through the chimney a basket full of goodies. No one knows who is our Santa Claus. After dividing among us the contents of the basket, it is our turn to do the same thing to our neighbors, so that every family has its Santa Claus every New Year's Eve.

All this struck me very curiously. Many a time have I run to the roof of our house to see who it was that lowered the basket through the chimney; but, unfortunately, each time I was too late, as I found the end of the rope tied to the chimney, and that the person had disappeared. In fact, no one ever did catch our invisible and evasive Santa Claus.

Source: *When I Was a Boy in Armenia* by Manoog Der Alexanian. Boston: Lothrop, Lee & Shepard Co., 1926, pp. 116-117.

Bolivia

New Year soup

The New Year is celebrated with "picana", a soup made with beef, chicken, pork and lamb. It is made with aji and either wine or beer.

Source: *An Insider's Guide to Bolivia* compiled by Peter McFarren. La Paz: Fundacion Cultural Quipus, 1990, p. 264.

Denmark

Protecting the farm from fire

In Zealand there was also the custom that the farmer, while the others still sat at supper, climbed on to the roof-ridge of his house and in a loud voice called the names of the Three Wise Men: Caspar, Balthasar and Melchior. As far as his cry could be heard round about there would be no conflagration that year.

New Year's pranks

The New Year season fell within the Yule Twelve, New Year's Eve signifying a time of unrestrained behaviour, especially on the part of the young. They ran round to the various households in the village, shooting New Year in with guns, beating on the doors with earthenware jars or creating a din with "rumbling pots". Up to our time their fun can go as far as to carry away garden gates, fireladders or tools. It was nothing uncommon for a farmer next day to find his cart dragged up on the roof of his house or his chimney blocked up, so that the kitchen was filled with smoke when the fire was lighted for the morning meal.

Source: *Danish Peasant Culture*. Copenhagen: Danish National Museum, 1955, p. 65.

New Year pot smashing in Ribe, Denmark, c. 1890

The Old Year went out with much such a racket as we make nowadays, but of quite a different kind. We did not blow the New Year in, we "smashed" it in. When it was dark on New Year's Eve, we stole out with all the cracked and damaged crockery of the year that had been hoarded for the purpose and, hieing ourselves to some favorite neighbor's door, broke our pots against it. Then we ran, but not very far or very fast, for it was part of the game that if one was caught at it, he was to be taken in and treated to hot doughnuts. The smashing was a mark of favor, and the citizen who had most pots broken against his door was the most popular man in town.

Source: *The Old Town* by Jacob A. Riis. New York: Macmillan, 1909, p. 100.

A boy's memories, c. 1910

The approach of New Year's Eve . . . meant the display of

much festivity. On New Year's Eve they display immense fireworks all over Denmark, and it is not overdrawn to state that Copenhagen on that night, between ten o'clock and one A.M., resembles the Fourth of July as that day was celebrated in earlier years. From every house are fired Chinese pistols, Skrubtudser (literally ''toads''. . .), sky-rockets, and diverse fireworks. When the clock strikes midnight the noise increases stupendously till it reaches its climax in an ear-splitting, thunderous bombardment. Thus the new year is ''shot in,'' as the Danish saying goes.

When the clocks strike the midnight hour on the last day in December, pandemonium breaks loose. All people go out in the streets, and along the main thoroughfares there is a constant stream of pedestrians bent upon pranks and frolics. Some wear their coats inside out, others are dressed in gay carnival suits, but nearly all discharge fireworks and Chinese pistols. The rougher element is somewhat feared on that night, and hence the greater restaurants have their windows facing the street covered up with a strong framework of boards. I remember having seen some ultra-gay fellows go bathing in the Storke-Springvand, one of the most popular fountains in the city, that boasts so many pretty fountains.

Source: *When I Was a Boy in Denmark* by H. Trolle-Steenstrup. Boston: Lothrop, Lee & Shepard Co., 1923, pp. 205-207.

Germany

Traditional food and drink

New Year's Eve parties are popular, with special foods such as carp or herring salad, hot wine-punch, and traditional New Year doughnuts. A special ''fire tongs punch'' (*Feuerzangenbowle*) may be served. Special cones of sugar are hung over the punch bowl, drenched with liquor, and then set aflame so that the alcoholic sugar drips into the hot wine below.

At midnight the partygoers toast each other with champagne as the church bells ring. ''Prost Neujahr!'' Streamers and crackers are employed and fireworks displays may be seen. New Year's pranks such as chocolates containing mustard, sugar lumps with spiders inside, and firework dogs, which emit a string of black sausage-like material when lit, are popular.

Source: *German Festivals and Customs* by Jennifer M. Russe. London: Oswald Wolff, 1982.

Great Britain

Celebrations c. 1980

Revelers gather at spots such as Edinburgh's Iron Kirk, Glasgow's George Square, and London's Trafalgar Square to make a great racket at the stroke of midnight, link arms and sing ''Auld Lang Syne,'' and hug and kiss all in sight. Church bells toll out the old with muffled bells, then remove the muffles to ring in the New. Bonfires and torchlight processions are held in Scotland and the Borders at certain places.

Source: *The Customs and Ceremonies of Britain* by Charles Kightly. London: Thames and Hudson, 1986, p. 174.

Iceland

New Year's elves

''Because it has been common belief in Iceland that elves move on New Year's Eve, that night was chosen for sitting out on crossroads in order to be in their way. The elves cannot get past the man sitting on the roads and therefore make him all kinds of offers, gold and treasures, choice objects and tasty foods. If the man keeps silent all through it, the treasures and the food will remain with him and they will be his if he endures until daybreak.''

It was an old custom, either in fun or in earnest, to *invite the elves* on New Year's Eve or Christmas Eve, for it was thought that those of them who were moving might want to drop in and rest on their way. So, the lady of the house would sweep out the farm from one end to the other and put lights in every nook and cranny, driving out all shadows. Then she would go out and circle the house three times, saying: ''Come whoever wants to come, stay whoever wants to stay, go whoever wants to go, without harm to me and mine.''

Burning lights were often left in every corner all through the night. And for a long time it was considered a matter of course to leave at least one light burning in the house on the eves of Christmas and New Year.

Pantry drift

The *pantry drift* was a peculiar phenomenon. It was supposed to be the hoarfrost that on New Year's Eve fell through the pantry window, which was left open. Similar to loose snow, it was fine-grained and sweet to the taste, but could neither be seen nor obtained except in the dark, and by New Year's morning it would be gone unless something was done about it. Shrewd house mistresses, therefore, would put a pot on the pantry floor and remain themselves in the pantry all night, while the drift was gathering. When the pot was full, they would put a cross-tree over it; so consecrated, the drift would be unable to get out of the pot. The pantry drift was supposed to bring unique prosperity.

New Year's bonfires

''What has been most characteristic of New Year's celebrations for a long time now are the *New Year's bonfires* and *Elf dances.*''

Toward the end of the 18th century two things happened in Reykjavik: a small urban center was formed, with the school boys as its youthful core, and some burnable refuse began to become available. Still to this day, the New Year's bonfires are a kind of "cleaning out" of trash.

In villages and towns the fires were not usually kindled until after supper, at which time people would get together and dance around the fire, some in the costumes of elves, imps, or trolls, as is commonly done today. But bonfires at individual farms have become much less prevalent, since it is now easy to drive to the next town for a fire."

Source: *Icelandic Feasts and Holidays: Celebrations, Past and Present* by Arni Bjornsson. Translated by May and Hallberg Hallmundson. Reykjavik: Iceland Review History Series, 1980, pp. 98-100.

Ireland

New Year's foods

On New Year's Eve a big supper was eaten as it was believed that the new year would continue as it began, and in Co Clare, bread was left at the door for the poor on New Year's Day to ensure a blessing of plenty for the year which followed.

Source: *Life & Tradition in Rural Ireland* by Timothy P. O'Neill. London: J.M. Dent & Sons Ltd., 1977, p. 64.

Italy (Naples)

Smashing pots at midnight on New Year's Eve

In Naples pots and dishes are thrown out the window at midnight for good luck.

Source: *Festivals and Folkways of Italy* by Frances Toor. New York: Crown, 1953, p. 112.

Japan

The year-end fire watch in a Tokyo neighborhood

The fire watch is conducted only on the last two days of the year and is seen as a customary part of the preparations and events leading up to O-Shōgatsu—the New Year, Japan's most important holiday.

Around eight in the evening of December 30 and December 31, men of the chōkai, mostly younger leaders or would-be leaders, gather at the chōkai hall, which for the occasion has a large sign hanging on the door proclaiming it the Yanagi Miyamotochō Guard Headquarters. Inside they sip tea as they huddle around a gas stove in the otherwise unheated building, waiting for enough members to show up to begin the patrols. When 10 or 12 men have appeared, they divide into two teams and agree on which group will patrol kami and which shimo, the upper and lower halves of the neighborhood. Narita-sensei, the former chōkai president and current leader of the fire-prevention division, stays at the hall to receive any visitors who might drop by to pay their respects, and with him remain a couple of other men who can serve as messengers to contact the two patrols in the unlikely event some emergency arises.

In their groups of five or six, the men set out carrying powerful flashlights and candle-lit paper lanterns. The lanterns do nothing to dispel the gloom, but they are emblematic of official chōkai activity; chōkai leaders carry and display them on this and other official occasions. One member of each group carries a pair of wooden clappers joined by a long cord looped behind his neck. The wooden clappers are a crucial part of the patrol. Every few yards the bearer of the clappers beats out a distinctive and customary rhythm—CLAP! CLAP! clap-clap!—and calls out in a deep, long-drawn-out voice, "*Hi no yōjin,*" "Take care with fire!"

Source: *Neighborhood Tokyo* by Theodore C. Bestor. Stanford, Calif.: Stanford Univ. Press, 1989, pp. 133-134.

Mexico

New Year on the Tehauntepec isthmus, c. 1940

Two or three days before New Year's Day the markets of Tehuantepec and Juchitán blossom forth in great colorful displays of little clay figurines, crudely but expressively modeled and gaily painted, which invade the sidewalks and passages between the stands of the crowded markets. These little figurines, called *tanguyú,* are made by the women and are given to the children as New Year's presents—horses and their riders for boys, statuettes of women with bell-shaped skirts, a baby in arms, and a load of fruit on their heads for little girls, as well as little clay replicas of pots, grinding stones, and painted plates. In Juchitán they are painted white, with crude designs in brilliant blue, red, and yellow; those from Tehuantepec, made in the barrio of Bixhana, are red all over, with daubs of white and gold paint. The *tanguyú* have vigor and humor and are plastically reminiscent of the figurines of ancient Crete in their form and spirit, crude in workmanship, sophisticated in spirit, with neo-classic features, molded perhaps from some European statuette, the molded face stuck on a body modeled by clever hands that have made thousands of *tanguyú.*

The children are passionately fond of their *tanguyú,* even if only for a few hours, as is illustrated by this touching child's song of Juchitán:

tanguyú, tanguyú	my clay doll, my clay doll,
si nudie' nuyà:lu'	what wouldn't I give if you could dance,
si nudie' nuyà:lu'	what wouldn't I give if you could dance,
tanguyú. . . .	my clay doll. . . .

On the night of December 31 the boys of every town on the Isthmus make a dummy of an old man from old clothes stuffed with cornhusks. This they seat on a chair and parade over the town, beating old cans, asking for alms from house to house and at food and coffee stands, wherever people are gathered, singing: "Alms, please, alms for this poor old man who dies tonight, but leaves a son, the New Year." The coins received are deposited in a wooden bank with a slit, hung from the dummy's neck.

Source: *Mexico South: The Isthmus of Tehuantepec* by Miguel Corvarrubias. London: Cassell and Company, n.d., pp. 176-177.

The Netherlands

In Holland c. 1910

On New Year's Eve we again went to church. To the large congregation, the preacher, called "domine" in Dutch, would review the year's events and remember those of the village people who had died during the past twelve months. By nine o'clock we were home and soon after went to bed.

On New Year's Day we arose early. It was great fun for us to hide behind a door and to await the coming of mother and older sisters, and sometimes of neighbors and friends whom we had seen approaching, and surprise them by crying the Frisian equivalent for Happy New Year. The fun came in trying to "beat the other to it." However, one had to be out of bed, though it was not necessary to be all dressed. A little later, there was more excitement. The poorest of the village children would come, in twos, in threes or in fours, knock at the door, open it as far as the brass chain would allow, and cry with loud voice: "Much happiness and many blessings in the New Year." That sounds like a big mouthful, but expressed in Frisian it was rather short. One of us children would sit near the door, with a cup full of pennies, and to each child we gave a couple of them. These poor urchins would go to all the farmers and well-to-do villagers, all before noon, and for the pennies thus gathered, their mothers would buy them a warm cap, a pair of mittens, klompen, or wool mufflers.

At about twelve, we had still greater fun. The postman, overworked man as he was that day, but also much-treated man (many people insisted upon his drinking a glass of gin when delivering the mail that day) brought us a stack of post-cards, some for father and mother, and some for each of us. All our friends, though some lived next door, remembered us with pretty cards, and it was fun to read the little verses underneath the pictures.

And in the afternoon, if the ice was strong, we went skating.

Source: *When I was a Girl in Holland* by Cornelia de Groot. Boston: Lothrop, Lee & Shepard Co., 1910, pp. 76-77.

Nigeria

Celebrations in Calabar

New Year celebrations also demonstrate an observable continuity with traditional rites of ndok. The rite of purification and renewal has been readily adapted to the practice of seeing out the old (calendar) year and welcoming in the new. Rowdy, disorderly behaviour, the breaking of bottles at crossroads (believed to be a meeting-place for spirits) and the use of guns and firecrackers and any noisy object represent an attempt to scare away evil spirits in preparation for the order and harmony of the incoming year. Such behaviour is generally limited to groups of men and young boys, with others preferring to attend New Year's Eve services in their respective churches. The midnight services are very popular and churches are packed as people offer thanks for having survived the year and pray for blessings in the next.

New Year's Day itself, a public holiday, is a time of festivity and rejoicing—traditional masquerades appear on the streets together with a series of improvised masquerades by people dressed in all manner of costumes (crash helmets, raincoats, leaves, painted faces, bowler hats, etc.) The Biblical theme is growing more popular and in 1983 a troupe of dancers and players known as "Religious Group" were witnessed performing on the streets of Calabar.

The ndok ceremony

The *ndok* ceremony which was held biennially in November or December seems to have had some connection with the spirits of the dead. It was essentially a ritual which involved the purging of the town of the spirits of people who had died in the two preceding years. Effigies known as *nabikim* were made and eventually thrown into the river amidst much noise-making and uproar. The fact that the effigies had animal forms suggested some link between these representations and the animal souls of the departed relatives. Later accounts describe the effigies as resembling human beings—"Judases"—and that the whole ceremony had been suppressed by 1913.

Source: *Religion in Calabar: The Religious Life and History of a Nigerian Town* by Rosalind I. J. Hackett. Berlin/New York: Mouton de Gruyter, 1989, p. 275.

Roumania

The Plugusorul (plough) at the turn-of-the-century

Boys announce the new year with the *Plugusorul,* or little plough, on New Year's eve. Standing in the front of windows we recited verses to the accompaniment of cracking and crashing of whips and the sound of large cow bells with which we tried to make as much noise as possible. In times past it was the custom to carry around a toy plough but this has been replaced in later years by the *buhai,* or bull. The *buhai* is made out of the frame of a small wooden cask or barrel. Over the bottom a dried skin is stretched and this is secured on the sides with heavy rope and nails. Through the middle of this cover of hide a cord of horsehair is drawn. Passing the fingers of each hand over the cord of hair a strong though unmusical *bo-o-o* is produced. This is supposed to resemble the bellowing of a bull, hence the name. A strong boy holds the "bull" while the other boys take turns in drawing the cord of horsehair and the recital thus goes on to the accompaniment of the continuous *boo-o-o*.

The bull is supposed to draw a plough through a meadow. The recital, which is long, amounting to several hundred verses, describes the work. It is an agricultural story. The hero of the recital is generally Master Trajan, *Badica Traian,* the Roman emperor.

Each stanza in the long recital begins: "Aho, aho! Plough with ten oxen!" and ends with the refrain: "Now drive on, boys, Hei, Hei!" This is repeated several times, as if we were actually at work drawing a plough and got stuck. We use our lungs as well as we can and try to give the good people an idea of what ploughing with ten oxen really means.

The *Plugusor* is another pagan custom. It is a remnant of the old Roman *Opalia,* festivals in honor of *Ops,* the Goddess of abundance.

Source: *When I Was a Boy in Roumania* by Dr. J. S. Van Teslaar. Boston: Lothrop, Lee & Shepard Co., 1917, pp. 94-96.

Russia

New Year's chasing away of the demons

In Russia there used to be a chasing away of demons and sprites and fairies and other evil beings who bewitch and vex men during the long dark cold winter. A wonderful account of this was written by Mr. F. H. E. Palmer. He was in a thickly wooded part of Russia where there was a great lake. From the ice, which covered it deeply in January, blocks had been hewn to make a cross which stood high up, glittering and sparkling in the winter sunlight. From the village the priest led his flock, old and young, through the dark, snowladen fir trees, with banners flying, over the hard white snow towards the lake. As they came they chanted wild melancholy music. A space was left in the middle of the procession for the spirits when they should no longer be able to withstand the colour and the music. When they reached the lake they formed a circle round the cross while six peasants hewed a hole down through the ice to the cold dark water beneath. When the hole was dug the priest uttered solemn words which, it was believed, sent the gnomes and sprites and all the rest of the imps leaping down into the icy chasm from whence they could not escape.

Source: *Happy Holidays* by Eleanor Graham. New York: E.P. Dutton, 1933, pp. 19-20.

Scotland

"Daft Days" customs

OLD YEAR'S NIGHT. NEW YEAR'S DAY. YES, "the Daft Days," that is what they used to call those two days in Scotland, and you can guess from that what sort of cantrips they used to get up to! They were far madder than people in the South of England have ever been over seeing the old year out and the new year in.

People say that the streets in Edinburgh and Glasgow on Old Year's Night used to be as full of traffic as in the busiest part of a week day. Everyone was out "first footing." At least, someone from every household was out and someone from almost every household was in waiting to receive the visitors. It was a very important business, "first footing." The first person to cross any threshold after midnight was the first foot. He must not enter the door empty handed, so everyone carried round cakes and wine, and whisky, even hot punch in a kettle. Then a man first foot was luckier than a woman. He should be dark haired, not fair, and he must not have *flat feet!* Strictly speaking, he should enter without knocking and go straight in and stir the fire before speaking to anyone.

For many, many years the Scotch people in London have met together in St. Paul's Churchyard to see the New Year in together; to toast each other and listen to familiar accents and to sing together "For Auld Lang Syne."

Source: *Happy Holidays* by Eleanor Graham. New York: E.P. Dutton, 1933, pp. 14-15.

December 31

Hogmanay

Great Britain

The Old Year's Day custom of Hogmanay

''Hogmanay'' is another custom of this season only practised in the north. It was kept on Old Year's Day and children used to go from door to door, holding up their pinafores for gifts of oatcake or bannock or cake. As they went they sang one of the ''Hogmanay'' rhymes.

> ''Hogmanay!
> Trollolay!
> Give us of your white bread
> And none of your grey.''
>
> ''Get up, gude wife, and shake your feathers,
> And do not think that we are beggars.
> For we are bairns come out to play
> Get up and gie's our Hogmanay.''
>
> ''My feet's cauld and me shoon's thin.
> Gie's my cakes and let me rin.''

Source: *Happy Holidays* by Eleanor Graham. New York: E.P. Dutton, 1933, p. 15.

December 31

Sylvester Day

This day is set aside to honor Pope Sylvester. Sylvester was a Roman who was Pope from 314 to 335. As Constantine had granted tolerance to Christianity in the Edict of Milan in 313, Sylvester was able to govern a church free of persecution. He died in 335 and his remains are enshrined at San Silvestro in Capite, Rome. Falling on New Year's Eve, his holiday has acquired general festive celebrations.

Austria

Sylvesterabend

Sylvesterabend punch

Close to eleven o'clock, Agathe and Maria will disappear into the kitchen, soon to return with trays of "Sylvester Punch." In Austria the last day of the year is dedicated to the Holy Pope, St. Sylvester, who baptized Constantine the Great, thereby bringing about the dawning not only of the New Year but of a new era; for this reason, the night before the New Year is called *Sylvesterabend* (Eve of St. Sylvester).

Sylvester Punch

Red burgundy (count one bottle for six people)
Equal amount of hot tea
12 cloves
rind of 1 lemon
2 tbsp. sugar to each bottle of wine
2 cinnamon sticks to each bottle of wine

Pour the liquid into an enamel pot, add the cloves, the thinly pared rind of 1 lemon, the sugar, and the cinnamon. Heat over a low flame but do not allow to boil. At the last moment add the tea. Serve hot.

Source: *Around the Year with the Trapp Family* by Maria Augusta Trapp. New York: Pantheon, 1955, p. 69.

Switzerland

Tardy "Sylvesters"

The last day of the year, Sylvester Day, was observed in both homes and schools. Whoever was last to rise on that day was Sylvester in the home, and whoever came last to school was Sylvester at school. One year I was late in school on that day, and as I walked in, the roar of "SYLVESTER!" was so deafening that my knees caved. I had to catch hold of the door-latch to keep from falling.

Source: *When I Was a Girl in Switzerland* by S. Louise Patteson. Boston: Lothrop, Lee & Shepard Co., 1921, p. 148.

Moon 12, Day 8 (December-January)

Mochi No Matsuri

Special rice cakes are prepared, offered in prayer, and served to guests on this day.

Okinawa

Preparing the mochi

There is a minor public holiday, the rice cake festival (*mochi no matsuri*), said to be native to Okinawa, on the 8th day of the 12th lunar month (January 4, 1952). On the day before, women prepare red and white cylindrical rice cakes, about 4 inches long and one inch in diameter. These are wrapped in the leaf of the *sannin* plant or in the leaves of sugar cane. The glutinous rice cake is made by first soaking rice in water and then mashing it in a hand mill. The rice is put in a cloth bag to allow excess water to drip out. The following morning the rice is boiled and shaped and wrapped in the leaves. The cake is doughy and insipid to taste. On the morning of the 8th, the cakes are placed on the god shelf and after prayers the cakes are removed. They are served during the day to guests. Sometimes children attach strings to these cakes and hang them about the room.

Source: *Studies of Okinawan Village Life* by Clarence J. Glacken. Scientific Investigations in the Ryukyu Islands (SIRI). Report no. 4. Washington, D.C.: Pacific Science Board. National Research Council, 1953, p. 326.

Moon 12, Day 20 (December-January)

Day for Sweeping Floors

The entire household is cleaned in preparation for the New Year.

Hong Kong

Symbolism of the annual cleaning

The twentieth day of the Twelfth Moon is marked on the calendar as the 'day for sweeping the floors'. This means that a complete house cleaning begins in every home. Nothing is left untouched.

Like spring-cleaning in some western countries, the operation is symbolic as well as practical. Removing the old year's dust and dirt stands also for getting rid of its shortcomings and disappointments. Material renovation signifies spiritual and social renewal.

Once the household cleaning is complete, Chinese housewives begin to stock up for the coming holiday period. Shops and markets are at their busiest, hawkers do a roaring trade, and all the streets are full of people. Having bought the ingredients the women must set to and cook them fast. Once the New Year dawns no one may use a knife, or indeed do any work at all for two days, so the days at the end of the month are the busiest of the year in the kitchen.

Source: *Chinese Festivals in Hong Kong* by Joan Law and Barbara E. Ward. Hong Kong: A South China Morning Post Production, 1982, p. 17.

Moon 12, Day 23 or 24 (December-January)

Kitchen God Visits Heaven

Once a year the Kitchen God visits the Jade Emperor in heaven to report on the behavior of the family. His picture is removed from its shrine and burned outside the kitchen to send him on his way. His mouth may be smeared with sweet foods or wine to ensure that he says only sweet things about the family.

China

Sending off the Kitchen God in Wuch'ang, Hupeh province, c. 1920

There was always a big banquet at our house to celebrate the New Year. On the evening of the twenty-third of the month, a sacrifice was made to the Kitchen God. But this was not an occasion for girls, only for boys. Ho had to go into the kitchen after dinner, when the sacrificial table had been prepared before the Kitchen God's altar. He had to burn incense and bow low before the god. There is a place for the Kitchen God in every Chinese kitchen and his name is written on—or his image cut out of—red paper.

On the evening of the twenty-third he climbs up to heaven, to report to the Lord of Heaven on the events of the past year in that particular house—whether remains of rice have been thrown away, or whether there have been unreasonable economies made on food. A horse cut out of paper is burnt so that he can ride to heaven, and sticky sweets are laid on the sacrificial table in the hope of preventing him from saying too much! Then, on New Year's Eve the ceremony is repeated to lead him back home.

Source: *The Lotus Pool* by Chow Chung-cheng. New York: Appleton-Century-Crofts, 1961, p. 45.

Sending the Kitchen God on his way, pre-1949

On this day offerings were placed before the Kitchen God's portrait and inscriptions pasted around it. A horizontal inscription might read, "The Lord Kitchen God." Vertical strips could read, "Speak well of us in Heaven" and "Bring Good Fortune to us on Earth." Males presided at this ceremony and females were excluded in some areas. Light snacks made from malt sugar and glutinous rice flour were offered on this occasion. People in some areas smeared the god's lips with honey so he would say only sweet things in heaven, or opium or rice wine might be used to make him forgetful of unpleasant events. The Kitchen God's shrine was carried into the courtyard; the food, liquor, and tea placed before it; and incense lit. The head of the family offered prayers on the family's behalf. Fireworks were a highlight of the ceremony for the children. Money was burnt for the Kitchen God's expense en route and straw might be burnt for his horse. Sometimes people threw handfuls of beans onto the rooftops to simulate the sound of his ascending hoofbeats. Since this heavenly watcher was now away from the house, people could be a bit lax until his return. Women could comb their hair, wash their hands, sharpen knives in the kitchen, and even spit toward the hearth until his return.

Source: *Chinese Traditional Festivals* by Marie-Luise Latseh. Beijing, China: New World Press, 1984, p. 86-88.

People's Republic of China

The Kitchen God after the cultural revolution

According to what I was told, the Spring Festival was observed very much the same during the "cultural revolution" as before. There were certain differences, however. No pictures of the Kitchen God could be bought, so one painted him oneself and hung up New Year couplets written by oneself. When there were no incense-sticks to be bought, they could be replaced in certain localities with high-quality cigarettes. The persistence of these customs shows that one cannot arbitrarily abolish such festivals. Where a popular basis for the festival exists the people will find a way to realize it.

In 1959 the newspapers carried the official edict that people should no longer honor the Kitchen God, but rather hang up in his stead pictures of workers, peasants, and good harvests. But I was informed in 1980 that incense was still burned and offerings made to the Kitchen God in some villages in the countryside in Shandong Province. Instead of pictures, one saw two scrolls with the couplet "Go up to the sky and then come again bringing good luck." I found no evidence of such practices in Beijing. I think that among the middle-aged and younger generation in the cities, the belief in the old deities has vanished, while the number of country people who still observe the old customs must surely be diminished.

Source: *Chinese Traditional Festivals* by Marie-Luise Latsch. Beijing, China: New World Press, 1984, pp. 32-33.

See also: ''The God That Lived in the Kitchen'' in *Tales of a Chinese Grandmother* by Frances Carpenter. Garden City, N.Y.: Doubleday, 1937, pp. 39-46. (Pre-1949 customs set in a children's story.)

Moon 12, Day 28 (December-January)

Dosmoche (The King's New Year)

This five-day Tibetan New Year's festival occurs usually in early February. A large *dosmo* (propitious pole) is erected and decorated. Numerous other propitious rituals, such as *tsamba* (toasted barley or wheat flour) throwing take place.

Tibet

Dosmoche in Leh

On the morning of the first holiday the lamas and the onpos first of all erect the large dosmo (magical pole) in an open place in the desert outside the town of Leh. The dosmo has already been described earlier. The one used here is distinguished by its height and by the large number of string stars, string crosses and pentagrams that are attached to it. The pole is about eight meters high and everything about it is proportionately larger than other dosmos used on other occasions, such as the dedication of a house, the exorcism of demons of disease, and the like. The lamas and some pious laymen have prepared themselves for the festival by fasting and the reading of sacred books, praying, and pilgrimages. After the large dosmo has been erected the lamas present a food and drink offering (ser-skyems) to the Buddhas and the gods.

On the 29th day of the twelfth month the lamas bring the storma offering (gtor-ma). In so doing the monks and onpos separately read prayers and exorcizing texts in order to drive out the evil spirits of the old year with them. The dances which the magicians perform with hideous demons' masks before their faces and magical daggers and skull drums in their hands, have as their purpose the banishment of those hostile spirits so that they will leave the people unharmed in the new year. This is the "ceremony of the dying/year" (lo si-sku-rim). After the reading of the particular formulas involved, one of the lamas takes up the pyramid-shaped offering cake which has been placed in readiness and carries it out to a crossing in the road in the desert. There he flings this cast offering amonng the rocks, so that it breaks into countless little pieces, and invokes the spirits telling them to refresh themselves with the "precious meal," and in exchange for this to let the people live in peace during the new year, and not to inflict upon them any kind of harm or malicious attacks. Some Tibetans who can afford the expense, have the lama fling their own cast offering (for which they pay him), in order to be perfectly secure against the evil activities of the demons.

Towards evening the great magical pole with all its crosses made of string and its pentagrams, is surrendered to the people, who have been standing around with tense expectation, in order that they may tear the pole down.

Source: *Progpa Namgyal: Ein Tibeterleben (Progpa Namgyal: The Life of a Tibetan)* by Samuel Heinrich Ribbach. München-Planegg: Otto Wilhelm Barth-Verlag GMBH, 1940, pp. 141-142.

New Year's foods in Lhasa, c. 1902

On New Year's morning a piece of fire-colored silk, or handkerchiefs sewn together in the shape of a flag, is put over a heap of baked flour, on which are strewn some dried grapes, dried peaches and small black persimmons. The head of the house first picks up some of the fruits with his right hand, tosses them up three times, and eats them. Then his wife, guests and servants follow his example one after another. Next comes Tibetan tea, with fried cakes of wheat flour for each.

Source: *Three Years in Tibet* by Ekai Kawaguchi. Adyar, Madras: The Theosophist Office, 1909, p. 408.

New Year's tsamba throwing

The chest is now sealed up and the lamas and members of the family all help themselves to a pinch of tsamba from the draba's plate. Then, gathering round a large basin or bag filled with dry tsamba, which stands in the middle of the room, they take out handfuls and throw them at each other, shouting: "Come, luck! Come, luck!" Soon everyone is covered with meal and the floor of the room is white. As red is the auspicious colour in China, so is white in Tibet, and the throwing of the tsamba signifies "A Happy New Year!"—a wish that, in the year just begun, the house and its inmates will always be white, that is, have the best of luck. This ceremony is known as "Yangdrub," the "gathering of luck," and with modifications to suit varying degrees of fortune it is celebrated in every home in Tibet.

Source: *A Tibetan on Tibet* by G.A. Combe. London: T. Fisher Unwin Ltd., 1926, p. 55.

Index

B

G

H

J

K

L

M

O

U

V

W

X

Y

Z